Criminal LAW

ninth edition

Joycelyn M. **Pollock**
Texas State University-San Marcos

John C. Klotter Justice Administration Legal Series

 LexisNexis®

 anderson publishing
A member of the LexisNexis Group

Criminal Law, Ninth Edition

Copyright © 1983, 1986, 1990, 1994, 1998, 2001, 2004, 2006, 2009
Matthew Bender & Company, Inc., a member of the LexisNexis Group

Phone   877-374-2919
Web Site www.lexisnexis.com/anderson/criminaljustice

Library of Congress Cataloging-in-Publication Data

Pollock, Joycelyn M., 1956-
   Criminal law / Joycelyn M. Pollock. -- 9th ed.
      p. cm.
   Rev. ed. of: Criminal law / John C. Klotter, Joycelyn M. Pollock. 8th ed. 2006.
   Includes index.
   ISBN 978-1-59345-504-0 (softbound)
   1. Criminal law--United States. I. Klotter, John C. Criminal law. II. Title.
   KF9219.K56 2009
   345.73--dc22

                       2009010586

Cover design by Tin Box Studio, Inc.

EDITOR Elisabeth Roszmann Ebben
ACQUISITIONS EDITOR Michael C. Braswell

Preface

I was deeply honored to be asked to take over John Klotter's *Criminal Law*. I have used the book in teaching and believe it to be an excellent resource. It combines the best features of a traditional law casebook with those of a textbook, in that it explains the law, but also offers the student a chance to read cases. One of the best features of a casebook is that students learn how to identify the issues and holdings from court decisions. In order to assist in this, we have shaded the issue, holding, and important findings within each of the first cases for each chapter in Part II of the book. Hopefully, this will help students learn how to find these elements themselves.

A change that was made in the last edition was to move the discussion of federal law to Chapters 13, 14, and 15. For students who have trouble grasping the different jurisdictional issues in federal jurisprudence, we hoped that moving all federal cases to their own chapters would make it more clear how federal laws are created and enforced. Instructors who prefer to discuss federal laws within the relevant chapters can easily assign those sections because they are numbered to reflect their association with the preceding state chapters.

In this edition, I have added several new cases to illustrate current issues or to replace the existing cases representing traditional elements. As with the last edition, there has been an effort to use Supreme Court cases in order to simplify the jurisdictional impact of the case. I have also added "news" boxes to show current legal concepts and how they apply to "real life." I expanded some material, such as that of wiretapping and computer crimes, including child pornography. I have shortened or combined some existing sections to accommodate new material. The format remains the same in that, for each crime, there is a presentation of the common law, the Model Penal Code, and then examples of state statutes for each of the crimes discussed.

I want to thank Mickey Braswell, Elisabeth Ebben, and the staff at Lexis/Nexis for giving me the opportunity to make the changes to John Klotter's text that I think will help ensure its continued success. I also appreciate, as always, their incredible assistance in its preparation. Of course, I also thank John Klotter for producing a well-researched, comprehensive, well-written text; it is a pleasure and honor to be associated with it.

As always, I want to thank Eric and Greg for putting up with me.

Joycelyn M. Pollock

Table of Contents

Chapter 14
United States Criminal Code: Offenses Against: Morality
and Decency; Public Peace; Justice Administration   559

Sample Case Citations

Gideon v. Wainwright, 372 U.S. 335 (1963). This case is located in volume 372 of the *United States Reports*, beginning on page 335. It was decided in 1963.

Gideon v. Wainwright, 83 S. Ct. 792 (1963). Gideon v. Wainwright is published in volume 83 of the *Supreme Court Reporter*, beginning on page 792.

Gideon v. Wainwright, 9 L. Ed. 2d 799 (1963). Gideon v. Wainwright is also published in volume 9 of *Supreme Court Reports, Lawyers' Edition*, Second Series, beginning on page 799.

Phillips v. Perry, 106 F.3d 1420 (9th Cir. 1997). This case is located in volume 106 of *Federal Reports*, Third Series, beginning on page 1420. It was decided by the Ninth Circuit Court of Appeals in 1997.

Brockway v. Shepherd, 942 F. Supp. 1012 (M.D. Pa. 1997). This case is located in volume 942 of *Federal Supplement*, beginning on page 1012. It was decided in 1997 by the Federal District Court for the Middle District of Pennsylvania.

Defining Crime   1

Chapter Outline

Cases

Constitutional Challenge (vagueness): *City of Chicago v. Morales,*
    427 U.S. 41 (1999)
Constitutional Challenge (First Amendment): *Texas v. Johnson,*
    491 U.S. 397 (1989)
Burden of Proof: *In re Winship*, 397 U.S. 358 (1970)

§ 1.1 Introduction

Why are some acts defined as crimes and punished? Who has the power to define crime? In this first chapter, we discuss:

- the definition of crime and criminal law,

- the purpose, objective, and sources of criminal law, and

- the limitations placed upon those who make and enforce such laws.

We will also discuss the approach taken in interpreting criminal laws and the **"burden of proof"** (the responsibility of the prosecution to prove the various elements of the crime charged).

§ 1.2 Definitions of Crime and Criminal Law

What is a "crime?" Blackstone, a famous English jurist, defined **crime** as "an act committed or omitted in violation of public law, either forbidding or commanding it."[1] In a broad sense, the word "crime" includes every violation of law, including treason, felonies, and misdemeanors.[2] In its narrow sense, it does not include petty offenses that were triable without a jury at common law.[3] Among the many other definitions are these:

- "A crime may be generally defined as the commission or omission of an act which the law forbids or commands under pain of punishment to be imposed by the state by a proceeding in its own name,"[4]

- "a crime is a violation or a neglect of legal duty, of so much public importance that the law, either common or statute, provides punishment for it."[5]

- "An offense defined by this code [Model Penal Code] or by any other statute of this state, for which a sentence of death or of imprisonment is authorized, constitutes a crime.[6]

Criminal law is the branch or division of law that defines crimes and provides for their punishment.[7] In a criminal case, the sovereign, or state, is the plaintiff, and the purpose of the prosecution is to preserve the public peace, or redress an injury to the public at-large.

Substantive criminal law declares what acts are crimes and prescribes the punishment for committing them. **Procedural criminal law** regulates the steps by which one who commits a crime is to be punished. Substantive criminal law, for instance, is concerned with the definition of homicide and the elements that distinguish homicide from manslaughter. Procedural criminal law is concerned with whether or not the due process steps required during the pretrial period and during trial were followed before a conviction.

Abortion Law: Substantive Challenges

- The act of voluntary abortion has been an extremely controversial issue before and after the landmark case of *Roe v. Wade*, 410 U.S. 113 (1973). Abortion had been illegal in this country until the Supreme Court held that laws criminalizing abortion infringed upon women's privacy rights, at least in the first and second trimesters. Several cases came after *Roe v. Wade* that further refined individual rights and constitutional restrictions in this area. The latest case concerning fetal rights and women's right to choose was *Gonzales v. Carhart*, 550 U.S. 12 (2007). In this case, the Supreme Court upheld the constitutionality of the federal law titled the Partial Birth Abortion Ban Act of 2003. The federal law defined as criminal any and all procedures of abortion that involved inducing a partial birth and destroying the fetus after it had been removed from the womb. This procedure occurred in a very small number of cases during late-term abortions. Currently several states are passing laws that criminalize other forms of abortion, therefore, the challenges to *Roe v. Wade* will continue to be addressed by the Supreme Court.

Specifically, the objectives of criminal law in a free society are to:

- make it possible for individuals to coexist in society,

- define the wrongs that are considered necessary to protect the individuals,

- define the method of determining guilt or innocence, and

- designate the type of punishment or treatment following conviction for violating the laws of society.

§ 1.3   The Purpose of Criminal Law

The purpose of criminal law is to protect society so that members of that society can be reasonably secure in carrying out their constructive activities. Only behaviors that are detrimental to the welfare of society should be made criminal. There is always a balance to be achieved between the rights of the individual and the protection of society. In the **social contract**, a concept originating with Thomas Hobbes and John Locke, individuals give up certain liberties in return for being protected by society. We give up the "right" to steal what we want in return for society's protection against our being victimized by others. We also give up other rights as members of a lawful society, but, in return, that society must impose only laws that have a purpose consistent with protection and that are minimally intrusive on our individual liberties.

There are three forms of harm that criminal law protects against:

- protection from the harm caused by others;

- protection from the harm caused by ourselves; and

- protection of societal morals.

The most obvious protection that the criminal law provides is protection against harm caused by others. Laws against homicide, rape, theft, and arson offer obvious protections. We feel reasonably secure that most people, most of the time, will not harm us in these or other ways, and that if we are harmed, the offender will be caught and punished.

The second form of protection that the law provides is protection against harm caused by ourselves. So-called **paternalistic laws** protect us against ourselves—a seat belt law is one example of a paternalistic law. Although you may prefer to drive your car without such a restraint, you will be punished with a fine if you do so because your duly elected representatives have determined that such behavior is so potentially harmful that it must be criminalized (albeit in a fairly minor manner). Other paternalistic laws include those that punish:

- drivers for not having children restrained in child safety seats,

- drivers for not having chains while going over mountain passes, and

- motorcycle drivers for not wearing a helmet

The third form of protection the law provides is protection of societal morals. This purpose of law is as old as the others and is as legitimate. In fact, we used to have many more laws that protected societal morals. For instance, laws against businesses operating on Sunday, laws against blasphemy, and laws against adultery may all be relics of the past, but the major purpose of some of our current laws (gambling, pornography, prostitution) continues to be enforcing society's morals.

In 1933, authors Michael and Adler listed three factors that should be considered when deciding whether a harmful behavior should be made criminal:

1. the *enforceability* of the law,

2. the *effects* of the law, and

3. the *existence of other means* to protect society against undesirable behavior.[8]

If the law is *unenforceable*, then the act probably should not be criminalized. A lesson learned during the Prohibition Era was that enacting unenforceable laws only breeds contempt for the law. Another example of a law that proved difficult to enforce was the 55 mile-per-hour speed limit.

If the *effects* of the law are more disadvantageous than advantageous, it may not be a good law. For instance, in the mid-1980s at the height of the "crack epidemic," some prosecutors advocated passing laws that made it a crime to ingest drugs while pregnant (in addition to existing drug laws). The purpose of the proposed law was to protect unborn fetuses. Health professionals argued, on the other hand, that when drug-using pregnant women were prosecuted, the effect was that women simply stopped going to doctors for prenatal care in order to avoid detection. Lack of prenatal medical care was an extremely negative effect of the new law (or new use of existing laws). Thus, the effect (worse birth outcomes) may have been just the opposite of what was intended (protection of the unborn).

The final consideration is whether *other means exist* to control or restrict negative behavior. In protecting society and public interests, the criminal law approach is a negative one. Because there are more positive approaches to change behavior, punishment for engaging in certain acts should be a last resort. For example, perhaps better education would limit the need for so many criminal laws. Also, emphasizing ethical and religious codes that distinguish between good and evil conduct might reduce the need for the enactment and enforcement of criminal laws.

Even if the informal social controls of family, church, community, and education have been unsuccessful in controlling behavior, there are still other alternatives that are less stigmatizing than criminal law. Some of the possible alternatives include:

- tort law,
- administrative sanctions, and
- regulations.

§ 1.4 Common Law Crimes

Every civilization has devised a system for protecting the lives and property of their citizens. In so doing, codes, laws, rules, and regulations have been
established.[9] In some instances, criminal laws are interrelated with religious
commandments. In some societies, laws have been established by a monarch
or a dictator, others are the product of legislative bodies. In other instances, the
court or judicial branch of government has established the criminal laws. The
system of laws in the United States is especially complex, in that the criminal
law is derived from English common law, statutory law and our own case law
tradition, split into 50 different state jurisdictions and the federal system.

Most of the present-day crimes in the various states have their origins in
the so-called **"common law"** of England. This was the law that developed
in the early English case decisions. While formal laws were developed in
England as early as the reign of King Aethelbert in the seventh century, William the Conquerer (1066) and his son, Henry I (1100-1135), are generally
accepted as responsible for the development of a national court system that
involved judges who traveled across England and provided guidance to local
magistrates. The effect was a gradual consistency in court decisions that led
to the establishment of common decisions in similar cases—thus, the "common law." By 1400, judges held themselves bound to decide the cases that
came before them according to established principles and, as new combina-
tions of circumstances arose, the principles were more fully developed. Even
though, eventually, legislation supplemented common law, it still continued
as a body of authoritative material. In 1765, William Blackstone published
Commentaries on the Laws of England. This series of reports on the law of
England is still widely cited as a legal source and the most comprehensive
written source of the common law at the time.

This body of English law, except that which was not applicable in the
American colonies because of different circumstances and conditions, was
brought to our shores by colonists when they emigrated from England, and
it became the starting point for American criminal law.[10]

In referring to "common law," some authorities hold that the common law,
strictly speaking, is the case law of England as it existed during the American
colonial period, and does not include changes by the courts of this country.
Other authorities are convinced that the common law includes changes brought
about by early court decisions in the United States.[11] Regardless of which
approach is more persuasive, the study of the common law is still important.
In states that retain the common law, common law definitions are still enforced
until they are supplanted by new statutes. For instance, in *Keeler v. Superior
Court* in 1970, the defendant was prosecuted for intentionally killing his wife's
unborn child by kicking her in the stomach. However, because the California
statute in question defined homicide as the killing of a person, and the common law definition of "person" did not include the unborn, Keeler could not
be prosecuted.[12] This led to California and other states passing statutes that

redefined "person" to include fetuses or creating a new crime of "feticide." Even in states that have replaced the common law crimes with a state penal code (which is an organized set of statutes that fully defines the law for the state), a study of the common law still serves a practical, useful purpose because it illustrates the origin of the modern-day statutes.

§ 1.5 Statutory Crimes

While most of the present-day crimes in the various states have their origin in the common law of England, it can be safely said that most state law is now statutory law rather than common law. Some states have completely replaced the common law with statutory law; for instance, Kentucky's law states: "Common law offenses are abolished and no act or omission shall constitute a criminal offense unless designated a crime or violation under this code or another statute of this state."[13] Where such provisions have been adopted, a person's act or omission may go unpunished, despite the basic seriousness or undesirability of such behavior, unless the legislature has specifically decreed it to be criminal in nature. In the federal system, there are no common law crimes, because the federal government has only the power that is delegated to it by the Constitution.

When a legislative body (federal or state) determines that certain conduct is undesirable and should be forbidden, a bill is prepared describing what conduct should be prohibited. This is introduced in the House of Representatives or the Senate, and is voted upon by the elected members of the legislative body. If both houses of the legislature approve the bill, it then goes to the governor or president for consideration and approval. If the chief executive officer signs the legislation, it then becomes a law to be enforced by those involved in the justice process. Even if the chief executive officer vetoes the bill, the bill may become law if enough members of the legislative body approve it, overriding the veto.

The legislature is permitted to define criminal offenses in any way it chooses, as long as its decision is not arbitrary or violative of the Constitution, and it also is free to define the elements of criminal offenses.[14] Despite this broad authority, statutes are challenged on constitutional grounds. Some of these challenges are discussed in Section 1.6.

A. State Legislation

The primary **police power** lies with the state, i.e., the states have the primary authority to enact and enforce legislation to protect the health, welfare, morals, and safety of the people of the state. This "police power" is inherent in the government of the state and is a power that the state did not surrender by becoming a member of the Union.[15] When the First Congress met, the

Tenth Amendment to the Constitution was added to make clear that the powers not delegated to the United States by the Constitution would remain in the states, respectively, and the people. The Tenth Amendment states:

> The powers not delegated to the United States by the Constitution, nor prohibited by it to the States, are reserved to the States respectively, or to the people.

According to the Supreme Court, the police power of the state is one of the most essential powers and is one that the federal government cannot usurp. Under this power, states have passed laws defining crimes, regulating traffic, and providing for criminal procedural rules.[16] While there is considerable doubt that the intent of the framers of this provision of the Constitution has been carried out, the courts still emphasize that the primary authority to make and enforce laws to protect the health, welfare, and morals of the people resides in the state. Current examples still occur where the federal courts remind the federal government that it is the primary responsibility of the states, and not the federal government, to define and enforce criminal law.[17]

State legislative bodies do have limitations when enacting laws, however. First, the laws must comply with the state constitution. Second, the laws must also comply with the federal Constitution as interpreted by the U.S. Supreme Court. However, the state is still primarily responsible for enacting and enforcing criminal laws to protect the health, welfare, safety, and morals of the people.

B. Federal Legislation

Strictly speaking, the federal government has no inherent police power. However, Congress may exercise a similar power, incident to the powers expressly conferred upon it by the Constitution.[18] The validity of any statute enacted by Congress depends upon whether it directly relates to one of the powers delegated to the federal government by the Constitution. The enumerated powers granted to the federal government to enact and enforce criminal laws are found primarily in Article I, Section 8 of the Constitution. Although these powers are stated specifically and succinctly in these clauses, their interpretation has been a matter of debate for two centuries.

In Article I, Section 8, Congress was delegated 17 specific powers and one power of a general nature.[19] Certain crimes, such as treason, counterfeiting, crimes against the law of nations, and crimes committed on the high seas are specifically enumerated. Other crimes are consistent with other powers. For instance, federal smuggling crimes derive from the power of the federal government to protect the country's borders. These powers have been broadly interpreted and other crimes have been enacted that are not so obviously connected to the powers assigned to the federal government. For example, under the power to regulate interstate and foreign commerce, Congress has created federal crimes such as interstate transporting of stolen vehicles, kidnapping (if the victim is taken across state lines), and drug trafficking. All have been made federal crimes because of some connection to interstate commerce. Similarly, the 1964 Civil Rights Act, which made it illegal to discriminate on the basis of race, religion, ethnicity, or sex, was predicated on the Commerce Clause under the rationale that all businesses participate in interstate commerce. There are limits, however, to how far Congress can take its authority under the Commerce Clause. In *United States v. Lopez*, the Supreme Court held that the Gun-Free School Zones Act passed by Congress under the power of the Commerce Clause was an unconstitutional overreach of federal power.[20] The rationale of the Act was that the presence of guns made it difficult to learn, which affected the economic productivity of the nation. The Supreme Court rejected this line of reasoning and held that the Act was beyond federal powers to enact. Basically, Congress has the power to create a law based on the Commerce Clause when: (a) the activity affects instrumentalities used in interstate commerce (i.e., arson of a railroad); (b) when it affects persons or things involved in interstate commerce (i.e., bank robbery of an FDIC-insured bank), or (c) when it has a substantial effect on interstate commerce (monopolies).

Congress is limited by the provisions of the Constitution and especially by the **Bill of Rights**, the first 10 amendments, which were added specifically to limit the power of Congress. We will discuss some constitutional challenges in Section 1.6.

C. Legislation by Political Subdivision

Legislative bodies of political subdivisions, including cities, counties, townships, and municipal corporations, also have limited authority to make and enforce rules and regulations prohibiting acts or penalizing the failure to act. After the American Revolution, the state legislature became the depository for all legislative power and took over the granting of power to political subdivisions. These units of government have been invested by the state legislature with subordinate legislative powers to administer the government and enact legislation that does not conflict with the Constitution or laws of the state. The state may withhold, grant, or withdraw powers and privileges as it sees fit. However great or small its sphere of action, the political subdivision remains a creature of the state, exercising and holding powers and privileges subject to the sovereign will of the state.[21]

The states have delegated certain authority to political subdivisions, either specifically, or by way of broad general authority, to enact ordinances to protect the safety and welfare of their inhabitants and to preserve good order within their limits. Unlike states, however, the police powers of political subdivisions are not inherent and the police power of the municipality exists solely by virtue of a legislative or constitutional grant of powers.[22] Thus, a city's right to enact ordinances that make it illegal to ride a skateboard on a sidewalk or park by red-painted curbs derives from state "police power" that has been delegated to the municipality.

Municipal ordinances and the laws of other political subdivisions (such as counties) are subject to the same state and federal constitutional limitations and restrictions as state laws. Specifically, the police power of a municipality, broad as it may be, cannot justify the passage of a law or ordinance that runs counter to any of the limitations of state or federal Constitutions.[23]

D. Model Penal Code

Promulgated by the American Law Institute, The Model Penal Code is not the law in any state, but rather serves as a guide to state lawmakers. The American Law Institute is an association of judges, lawyers, and law professors and they created the Model Penal Code in 1962 with revisions and commentary being added through 1985. The MPC is helpful to students as a general outline of modern criminal law because the specific criminal statutes of the 50 states and the federal government are different enough that it is impossible to comprehensively discuss them all. Some provisions of the Code are not followed in some states, and some are not followed in the majority of states; however, no one disputes that the general approach to the construction of law and some substantial changes to the common law have taken place largely through the influence of the MPC. For this reason, we offer the Model Penal Code throughout this book, along with examples of state statutes, to represent the modern criminal law.

§ 1.6 Constitutional Challenges

The federal government does not have the power to pass a law that violates one of the rights granted by the United States Constitution. Specifically, protections are most often found in the first 10 amendments that make up the Bill of Rights. We are protected against laws that are vague, that punish behavior after the fact (**ex post facto laws**), or that infringe upon our freedom of expression, association, or religion. It should be noted that the Bill of Rights protected citizens against laws or actions of the federal government. As written, it did not apply to the states. A summary of the rights granted in the Bill of Rights appears in the display box below.

Bill of Rights

First Amendment—Freedom of religion, expression, association, press

Second Amendment—Right to bear arms as a civilian militia

Third amendment—Right not to have soldiers quartered in peoples' homes

Fourth Amendment—Right to be free in person and home from unreasonable governmental search and seizure (must have probable cause and define item with specificity)

Fifth Amendment—Right to be free from compulsory self-incrimination, federal right to grand jury, protection against double jeopardy, due process

Sixth Amendment—Right to an impartial jury trial that is speedy and public with specified due process elements

Seventh Amendment—Right to trial in suit at common law, jury to be trier of fact

Eighth Amendment—Right against excessive bail, right to be free from cruel and unusual punishment

Ninth Amendment—States "The enumeration in the Constitution, of certain rights, shall not be construed to deny or disparage others retained by the people."

Tenth Amendment—Reserves all other powers not specifically delegated in the Constitution for the states

---

A. Incorporation

While the Bill of Rights protected American citizens against encroachments of the federal government, they had almost no protection from violations of rights by state actors or laws until after the Civil War. The Fourteenth Amendment, ratified in 1868, was passed to detail how representation was to be apportioned among the states, but also to protect newly freed slaves from state laws that withheld the rights to vote, own property, or contract. It reads:

> Section 1. All persons born or naturalized in the United States and subject to the jurisdiction thereof, are citizens of the United States and of the State wherein they reside. No State shall make or enforce any law which shall abridge the privileges or immunities of citizens of the United States; nor shall any State deprive any person of life, liberty, or property, without due process of law; nor deny to any person within its jurisdiction the equal protection of the laws.

The due process clause in the Fourteenth Amendment is virtually the same as that found in the Fifth Amendment but has been more broadly applied in some ways, in that it acts as the vehicle by which some of the rights recognized in the Bill of Rights have been "incorporated" to protect citizens against state actions. Thus, the federal government cannot pass laws or act in ways that violate the rights enumerated in the Bill of Rights, and, if the right has been "incorporated" through a Supreme Court holding, neither can state (or local) governments encroach upon the right. In effect, the Fourteenth Amendment has applied most of the Bill of Rights to you as a state citizen as well as a federal citizen.

B. Due Process and Vagueness Challenges

One element of due process is *notice*. Legislation must not be vague and must not be so uncertain as to leave doubt as to its meaning. For example, the Court of Appeals of New York, in the case of *People v. Munoz*, held that a statute that made it unlawful for any person under 21 to "carry on his person or have in his possession, in any public place, street, or park any knife or sharp-pointed or edged instrument which may be used for cutting or puncturing" was unconstitutional because it was too broad and vague in its definition of cutting instruments.[24] In this case, the proscribed action (carrying any type of cutting instrument) was just as likely to be consistent with harmless behavior as harmful behavior, and thus was overbroad in its scope.

On the other hand, a federal statute that proscribes "mailing pistols, revolvers and other firearms capable of being concealed on the person" was upheld by the U.S. Supreme Court. The court agreed that the law intelligibly forbids a definite course of conduct: the mailing of concealable firearms. It held that the drafting of a law did not have to be foolproof and even if the language could have been more clear, that fact alone does not make a statute unconstitutionally vague.[25]

In 1991, in the case of *Chapman v. United States*, the U.S. Supreme Court considered the "vagueness" rule in determining the validity of a drug possession statute.[26] In this case, the defendant argued that a statute calling for a five-year mandatory minimum sentence for the offense of distributing more than one gram of a "mixture or substance containing a detectable amount of LSD" was unconstitutionally vague. The court held that although there may have been plausible arguments against describing blotter paper impregnated with LSD as a "mixture or substance" containing LSD for purposes of determining the appropriate sentencing, this statute was not unconstitutionally vague, given the fact that any debate would center on the appropriate sentence rather than the conduct's criminality.

Legal News

In 2008, the Supreme Court for the first time recognized that the right to firearms as described in the Second Amendment was an individual right and that the government could not unduly infringe upon that right by onerous handgun control laws. In *District of Columbia et al. v. Heller*, the Supreme Court ruled that the District of Columbia handgun law that required owners of handguns to have their guns totally dysfunctional or have trigger locks installed was an unconstitutional burden on their Second Amendment right to bear arms. Because this was a District of Columbia law, this case was decided under the Supreme Court's direct jurisdiction; however, the majority holding of the Court made it clear that state handgun regulations may also be ruled unconstitutional in future cases.

District of Columbia et al. v. Heller, 534 U.S. __ (2008).

In *City of Chicago v. Morales*, the Supreme Court struck down an anti-gang law that prohibited those believed to be criminal street gang members from loitering in any public place.[27] Some members of the court objected to the vague manner in which loitering and the identity of street gang members was defined, and the majority objected to the fact that it was solely within the police officer's discretion to define when loitering was occurring. The language of the court indicated that there may be anti-gang laws that could pass the vagueness test, but they needed to be written in a way that definitely stated what actions would be defined as criminal.

CASE: *City of Chicago v. Morales*, 427 U.S. 41 (1999)

What was the holding of the Court?

Where does the right to not have vague laws enforced upon individuals come from?

What could the city of Chicago do to prevent gangs from intimidating neighbors and passersby?

Other courts, in explaining the vagueness doctrine, have used these terms:

- The void-for-vagueness doctrine requires that a penal statute define the criminal offense with sufficient definiteness that ordinary people can understand what conduct is prohibited, and in a manner that does not encourage arbitrary and discriminatory endorsement.[28]

- While a state statute need not be so precise as to enable a person in every case to determine in advance what conduct is within reach of the statute, a reasonable degree of certainty is required to avoid unconstitutional vagueness.[29]

Basically, the right to be free from vague and overbroad laws comes from the Fifth and Fourteenth Amendments. Both amendments provide that an individual should receive "due process of law" before being deprived of life, liberty, or property. The Fifth Amendment provision has been interpreted to provide protection from federal actors and the Fourteenth Amendment provision protects us from state governmental actors. **Due process** includes the right to notice (to know what we are being accused of). Obviously, in order to have notice, a law must be certain and not subject to arbitrary definitions.

C. Equal Protection Challenges

Laws that treat "similarly situated" people differently also violate the Fourteenth Amendment's "equal protection" clause. The government must have a very good reason for treating a certain group of people differently under the law. If a law that is neutral on its face differentially affects only one group of people, it would also be scrutinized.

In 1967, the Supreme Court struck down Virginia's miscegenation laws, which made it a crime to marry someone of a different race.[30] The groups at issue were those who wished to marry a person from the same race compared to those who wished to marry someone of a different race. The Court held that the state did not have a reason that was sufficiently important to justify treating these groups differently and the holding invalidated all miscegenation laws in not only Virginia, but also the other states that had them.

In the case of *Craig v. Boren*, the Supreme Court struck down a law that prohibited the sale of beer to girls under the age of 18 and boys under the age of 21 on the grounds that boys and girls were "similarly situated" and there was no reason to treat them differently. On the other hand, in the case of *In re Michael M.*, a California statutory rape law was upheld, even though it treated male and female actors differently by defining a crime with only male perpetrators and female victims.[31] In this case, the Supreme Court upheld the law because the parties were not considered similarly situated in that only female victims could become pregnant and the law's imputed purpose was to prevent teenage pregnancy. Other laws that treated the sexes differently have been struck down because the Court did not see any reason for the different treatment.

D. Ex Post Facto Challenges

The U.S. Constitution and provisions of the constitutions of the various states specifically prohibit ex post facto laws. The two sections of the federal Constitution that relate to ex post facto laws are Article I, Section 9, which provides that "no bill of attainder or ex post facto law shall be passed," and Section 10, which provides that "[n]o state shall . . . pass any ex post facto law."[32]

These provisions were added to the Constitution of the United States and similar provisions have been added to the constitutions of the respective states to prohibit legislative bodies from punishing a person for an act that was neither a crime nor punishable when the act was committed, or from increasing the punishment after the fact. A bill of attainder is a special legislative act that declares a person or group of persons guilty of a crime and subjects them to punishment without trial. An ex post facto law, within the meaning of these constitutional provisions, is "one which, in its operation, makes that criminal which was not so at the time the action was performed, or which increases the punishment, or, in short, which in relation to the offense or its consequences, alters the situation of a party, to his disadvantage."[33]

Two critical elements are necessary to establish an ex post facto claim:

1. The law must be retrospective—that is, it must apply to events occurring before its enactment.

2. It must disadvantage the offender affected by it.[34]

A mere procedural change in the law, not increasing punishment or changing the elements of the offense, does not result in an ex post facto violation. Statutes that delay or postpone the eligibility of an inmate for parole have also generally been upheld and found not to be a violation of the ex post facto provision.[35] However, a statute that created a new term of supervised release was ruled retroactive and, thus, unconstitutional. The imposition of a new term of supervised release increased the punishment and thus violated the ex post facto clause.[36]

It should be noted that the fact that a law is ex post facto as to a person who committed an act before its enactment does not affect its validity generally. A legislative body, after considering all of the consequences, may determine that an act should be made a crime and enact legislation to prohibit such acts in the future. Such legislation would be ex post facto in relation to a person who committed the act prior to the enactment of the legislation, but would not be considered ex post facto when applied to persons who commit the same act after the legislation.

Ex post facto provisions apply if legislation relates to substantive criminal law or the rules of evidence. For example, a change in a rule of evidence that would allow a conviction on less evidence or proof than one previously required is considered ex post facto and unenforceable.[37] Further, where a criminal sentencing statute is amended, acts occurring prior to the effective date of the amendment may be considered to enhance or increase the sentence, as long as the statute provided adequate notice that pre-amendment actions would be taken into consideration.[38]

E. First Amendment Challenges

In drafting criminal legislation, the legislative body is also limited by other constitutional restrictions. A federal or state criminal statute may be clear yet unenforceable if it violates constitutionally protected activities. This is especially true if the First Amendment to the federal Constitution is in question. If the legislation infringes on rights protected by the First Amendment, the legislation is unconstitutional and unenforceable.[39]

As you know, the First Amendment protects our freedom of speech, association, and religion, as well as ensures the freedom of the press. The government has a right to pass laws that do not unduly interfere with these rights. Thus, if our speech creates an imminent danger to others it can be prohibited and punished. For instance, one does not have the right to incite a riot. On the other hand, an ordinance that makes it criminal to simply *verbally* (not physically) object to the arrest of another has been ruled as unconstitutional in that it infringes upon free speech.[40] Generally, "fighting words," "obscenity," and "commercial speech" can be prohibited and punished.

In *Texas v. Johnson,* the Supreme Court ruled that the state could not create a crime that punished flag burning.[41] This controversial issue has been resurrected today and there are a large number of people who believe that such an act should be criminalized. In deciding the way it did, the Supreme Court had to find that the act was protected speech. The response to the Supreme Court's opinion in this case has led to a proposal for a constitutional amendment that would criminalize flag burning. In this issue, there is a fairly even difference of opinion as to whether such a law should exist. In one survey, about 63 percent of the population opposed a flag burning amendment to the Constitution, but evidently the rest were in favor of such an amendment.[42]

> **CASE: *Texas v. Johnson,*
> 491 U.S. 397 (1989)**
>
> What was the holding of the Court?
>
> How can flag burning be considered free speech?
>
> Why wasn't flag burning considered similar to "fighting words," which aren't protected?

Other constitutional challenges may involve the First Amendment's protections of religion, speech, or association. Can one's freedom of religion, for instance, include the freedom to sacrifice children at midnight? (Obviously not.) What about sacrificing goats? (Maybe. According to the Supreme Court in one case, a city could not fashion an ordinance prohibiting animal slaughter in religious ceremonies because it was overly broad in the conduct it prohibited and discriminatory because it targeted one religion.)[43] What if your religion allowed you to have multiple wives, would you still be subject to bigamy laws? (Yes.) If your religion uses peyote, are you exempt from drug laws that criminalize the use and possession of this controlled substance? (Yes. After the Supreme Court upheld the right of states to enforce drug laws against Native Americans using peyote in *Employment Division, Oregon v. Smith* in 1990, Congress passed the American Indian Religious Freedom Act Amendments in 1994 that protects the right of Native Americans to use peyote in religious ceremonies despite federal or state drug laws).[44]

In all cases, federal and state courts must weigh the individual's rights against the need for the law.

F. *Privacy Challenges*

The right to privacy is not identified specifically in the Constitution, but has been recognized by the Supreme Court as existing based on their interpretation of what the framers meant by such rights as those previously discussed. One of the most important cases that established the protected right of privacy against governmental interference was *Griswold v. Connecticut.*[45] In that case, the Supreme Court struck down Connecticut's criminal laws that punished the distribution of information regarding birth control to married couples. According to Justice Douglas, the First, Third, Fourth, Fifth, Ninth, and Fourteenth Amendments can be read to construe a privacy right that restricts the government from interfering with private decisions on procreation by a married couple.

Another right of privacy case was *Stanley v. Georgia* in 1969, in which the Supreme Court held that states could not criminalize the mere possession of obscene materials, although states could prohibit and punish any distribution or sale of such materials (and states could criminalize the mere possession of child pornography).[46] In later chapters, especially Chapter 10, which deals with gambling, some sexual behaviors, drugs, and prostitution, we will see that some laws have been struck down as violative of protected privacy rights, but other laws are upheld as legitimate safeguards of societal morals.

§ 1.7 Construction of Criminal Law Statutes

Criminal law statutes are not always clear to those who interpret them. In fact, many who are charged with criminal violations are released when their attorney convinces the court that the construction given to the statute by the state is inaccurate. As indicated, it is a fundamental principle of criminal law that legislation must not be vague and must not be so uncertain as to leave doubt as to its meaning. If persons of ordinary intelligence must guess at the meaning of a statute, it is unenforceable.

When the meaning of a statute is doubtful, the court may take into consideration the purpose of its enactment when construing it and give effect to the intent of the legislature.[47] However, if the wording is clear and the statute is clear on its face, it is not permissible to add or vary the provisions of the statute to accomplish a supposed legislative purpose.[48]

Finally, in construing a statute, the intent of the legislature is not to be ascertained from any particular expression or section but from the whole act. All of the words used in the act are to be given force and meaning rather than any one section of the statute.[49]

§ 1.8 Classification of Crimes

Crimes may be statutory or common law, but in either case they fall into various categories or grades.

A. Classification According to the Nature of the Crime

Crimes have been divided according to their nature into *mala in se* and *mala prohibita*.

1. *Mala in se*: These are acts that are immoral or wrong in themselves, or acts that are naturally evil. *Mala in se* crimes are considered wrong in any society and include the common law crimes of murder, rape, arson, burglary, and larceny.

2. *Mala prohibita*: These crimes are not naturally evil, but are prohibited by statute because they infringe upon the rights of others. This type of act is not wrong in some societies, but is wrong in other societies. It is wrong because it is prohibited by statute. Generally, *mala in se* crimes involve moral turpitude, while *mala prohibita* crimes do not. Examples would include all traffic offenses, as well as some laws regarding "gray" areas of crime, such as pornography and gambling. Also, regulatory offenses are generally *mala prohibita* crimes.

Some crimes are difficult to classify. Individual or subjective beliefs involving religion, politics, and ethics create diverse views as to whether activities such as gambling and prostitution are *mala in se* or *mala prohibita*. Cultural norms weigh heavily in any attempt to classify sexual offenses.

B. Classification According to Degree

All crimes are classified as felonies, misdemeanors, or treason. These classifications become important not only in determining the degree of punishment, but also when determining the authority of justice personnel to take action. For example, in some states, law enforcement officers may not make misdemeanor arrests unless the offense was committed in their presence (or they have a warrant).

1. Felonies

According to most authorities, crimes punishable by death or imprisonment in a state prison or penitentiary are felonies. A crime may be made a **felony** by reference to the punishment attached or it may be made a felony by a statute that specifically says that it is a felony. When an offense is not designated by statute as either a felony or a misdemeanor, but a specific punishment is prescribed, then the grade, or class, of the offense is determined by the punishment. Generally, felonies are punishable by at least one year in prison, but this is not a requirement if the statute provides that the crime is a felony and sets the punishment at less than one year.

2. Misdemeanors

Crimes or offenses not amounting to felonies are **misdemeanors**. Another definition is that misdemeanors are offenses for which the punishment is other than death or imprisonment in a state prison, or that have not been designated felonies by statute. A person convicted of a misdemeanor will ordinarily be incarcerated in a local jail or be required to pay a fine, but ordinarily will not be sent to a state penitentiary.

Although there is apparent consensus in the technical definitions of felony and misdemeanor, what is regarded as a felony in one state may constitute a misdemeanor in another. Except for the most serious crimes, such as murder, robbery, and rape, generalizations in the area of what crimes are felonies or misdemeanors are unreliable. Therefore, the legislative designations in the particular jurisdiction must be carefully examined.

3. Treason

Treason is the only crime that is described in the Constitution.[50] Because those who commit treason threaten the very existence of the nation, it is given a higher classification than a felony.

Also, the Constitution provides that no person shall be convicted of treason unless on the testimony of two witnesses to the same overt act, or on confession in open court.

C. Classification Based on Punishment

States often choose to distinguish, or classify, their criminal statutes based on the range of possible sentences available upon conviction. For example, in Kentucky, any offense for which the legislature has authorized a sentence of one to five years in prison is classified as a "Class D" felony. Misdemeanors are also often classified by the states into degrees based on their range of punishments.[51]

§ 1.9   Distinction between Crimes and Torts

When one person is wronged by another, he or she may seek a remedy against the wrongdoer by bringing what is known as a civil action. The state may also initiate a criminal action against that person for the same wrongful act. The process by which a person initiates an action against another is known as the law of torts. A function of tort law is to compensate an injured person for the harm he or she has suffered. For example, if Henry is struck by Sophia, causing him bodily injury, Henry may bring an action in court for recovery of expenses and for compensation for losses incurred. The state may also initiate an action against Sophia for assault and battery and prosecute the case in criminal court. The most famous example of this is the successful civil suit against O.J. Simpson for wrongful death after his 1994 acquittal for murder in criminal court. It is entirely possible for a defendant to "win" in one court and "lose" in the other.

Legal News

Recently O.J. Simpson was in criminal court again, and in December 2008 he received a nine- to 33-year prison sentence for his role in a botched robbery and unlawful imprisonment incident. Defense attorneys speculated that the jury in this case was influenced by their belief that he had gotten away with murder in the earlier case. The case is on appeal.

Source: Powers, A., and H. Ryan (2008). "O.J. Simpson Sentenced to Lengthy Prison Term." *Los Angeles Times*; December 6, 2008. Accessed 3/5/2009 from www.latimes.com/news/local/la-na-oj-sentencing6-2008dec06,0,3919620.story.

Civil law resolves the conflicting interests of individuals. Criminal law deals with public wrongs and views a crime as a violation of the public's rights and as an injury to the whole community. In spite of the differences between tort law and criminal law, there are many ideas and concepts common to both areas. For example, some of the defenses that will be discussed in Chapter 3 are available to a defendant in a civil case as well as a defendant in a criminal case. The differences between tort law and criminal law are illustrated in the Table 1.1.

Table 1.1
Distinctions between Torts and Crimes

Torts	Crimes
Private wrong	Public wrong
Action initiated by an individual	Action taken by the state
Private attorney represents plaintiff	Prosecutor represents the state
Action for money damages	Punishment by fine or imprisonment
Unanimous verdict of jury not usually required	Unanimous verdict of jury usually required
Proof by a preponderance of the evidence	Proof beyond a reasonable doubt

§ 1.10 Burden of Proof—Prosecution

In a criminal case, the state has the burden of proving the guilt of the accused beyond a reasonable doubt. That means that the prosecution has the responsibility to prove each element of the crime with which the accused is charged. For example, the common law crime of burglary has six elements:

1. breaking,

2. entering,

3. the dwelling,

4. of another,

5. at night,

6. with intent to commit a felony therein.

These elements must be proved in accordance with the definition of each element as described by the court. If the prosecution fails to prove one element of the crime beyond a reasonable doubt but proves the other elements, the accused may sometimes be found guilty of a lesser crime. But ordinarily, if any element is not proved beyond a reasonable doubt, the person charged cannot be convicted of the crime charged. Failure of those involved in the criminal justice process to gather and introduce sufficient evidence to meet this burden will result in an acquittal or, at least, in the conviction of a less serious crime.

While in a civil case the degree of proof is a "preponderance of the evidence," in a criminal case the degree of proof is "beyond a reasonable doubt." In some states, the exact wording of the charge to the jury dealing with the standard of proof is stated by statute. In other states, there is no such requirement and, in fact, the judge does not have to explain the term at all.[52] When a statute specifically includes the charge that the judge is to read to the jury, it must be read as stated. An example of such a statute is that of California, which provides:

> It (reasonable doubt) is not a mere possible doubt; because everything relating to human affairs is open to some possible or imaginary doubt. It is that state of the case which, after the entire comparison and consideration of all the evidence, leaves the minds of the jurors in that condition that they cannot say that they feel an abiding conviction of the truth of the charge.[53]

The "beyond a reasonable doubt" standard is a constitutional requirement. In 1970, the Supreme Court left no doubt about the requirement in its holding in *In re Winship*:

> Lest there remain any doubt about the constitutional stature of the reasonable-doubt standard, we explicitly hold that the Due Process Clause protects

the accused against conviction except on proof beyond a reasonable doubt of every fact necessary to constitute the crime with which he is charged.[54]

Referring to the *In re Winship* decision and reiterating that the government must prove beyond a reasonable doubt every element of a charged offense, the United States Supreme Court in 1994 acknowledged that this ancient and honored aspect of our criminal justice system defies easy explanation.[55]

CASE: *In re Winship*, 397 U.S. 358 (1970)

What was the holding of the Court?

What is the source for the defendant's right to have every element of the crime proven "beyond a reasonable doubt"?

Why had the burden been different in juvenile court?

§ 1.11   Burden of Proof—Defendant

The previous section makes it clear that the prosecution has the duty to prove the defendant's guilt beyond a reasonable doubt, as well as every element of the crime charged. However, when claiming an affirmative defense such as coercion, self-defense, entrapment, mistake, alibi, or insanity, all of which would absolve the defendant of culpability, the defense has the responsibility of "going forward with the evidence."

To warrant submission of the defense to the jury, the defendant must produce substantial evidence.[56] The burden to prove an affirmative defense such as insanity or self-defense is by a *preponderance of the evidence* and not by evidence beyond a reasonable doubt. Legislative bodies may enact legislation modifying the burden of proof where this does not violate constitutional principles.

An example of laws relating to the burden of proof are those that define the insanity defense. Evidence of the defendant's insanity must be brought forward by the defendant and meet some minimum threshold, but then, the prosecution has the ultimate burden of disproving insanity. The United States Supreme Court, in several instances, has determined that placing the burden on the defendant does not violate the Constitution. In 1984, as part of the Comprehensive Crime Control Act, Congress enacted legislation titled the Insanity Defense Reform Act of 1984. This section of the Code defines the scope of the insanity defense for the federal offenses and shifts the burden of proof to the defendant. The section provides:

a.   Affirmative Defense—It is an affirmative defense to the prosecution under any federal statute that, at the time of the commission of the acts constituting the offense, the defendant, as a result of a severe mental disease or defect, was unable to appreciate the nature and quality of the wrongfulness of his acts. Mental disease or defect does not otherwise constitute a crime.

b.   Burden of Proof—The defendant has the burden of proving the defense of insanity by clear and convincing evidence.[57]

The standard of proof—clear and convincing evidence—is a higher standard than a mere preponderance of the evidence, but is less than beyond a reasonable doubt. The federal courts have been consistent in holding that the provisions of the Insanity Defense Reform Act that shift to the defendant the burden of proving the affirmative defense by clear and convincing evidence do not violate due process.[58]

In other situations in which the defendant claims an affirmative defense, the state may require that the defense be proven by either a preponderance or clear and convincing evidence. The Supreme Court in 1987 upheld an Ohio law that required the defendant to prove self-defense by a preponderance of the evidence.[59] Although the defendant may be required to meet the preponderance or clear and convincing burden to submit the defense to the jury, it is still up to the prosecutor to prove beyond a reasonable doubt that the defendant is guilty of each element. Thus, once a defendant proves by a preponderance of evidence that he is insane, it is the duty of the prosecutor to prove sanity beyond a reasonable doubt. It is always unconstitutional to shift the burden to the defendant to show that he or she is innocent.[60]

§ 1.12   Summary

When someone causes harm to another or to the property of another, not only is the victim harmed, but society and the state also are considered victimized. Criminal law, then, is the branch or division of law that defines crimes, their elements, and provides for their punishment. In a criminal case, the sovereign, or state, is the plaintiff, and the purpose of the prosecution is to preserve the public peace or address an injury to the public-at-large. The protections of law fall into the three areas of:

1. protection from harm from others
2. protection from harm from oneself and
3. protection of society's morals.

Since the beginning of time, various societies have been faced with the problem of determining what standards of conduct must be established. In determining what acts should be made criminal, at least three factors should be given weight:

1. the enforceability of the law,
2. the effects of the law, and
3. the existence of other means to protect society against the undesirable behavior.

Once the legislative or judicial branch of government decides that certain conduct is prohibited or required, criminal justice personnel are charged with enforcing those laws, and have the responsibility to do so until the laws are repealed or declared unconstitutional.

Most of the present-day crimes in the various states had their origins in the common law of England. This was the law developed in the early English court decisions and modified by English legislative bodies. All of this body of English law, except that which was not applicable in the American colonies, was brought by the colonists when they emigrated from England. This became the starting point for our criminal law. While most present-day crimes have their origin in the common law of England, no state currently follows the common law without modification.

Criminal laws (either federal or state) can be created and enforced only if they do not violate the constitutions of the various states and the Constitution of the United States, as interpreted by the courts. Some of the more common constitutional challenges include: vagueness, equal protection, ex post facto, First Amendment, and privacy challenges.

Crimes are classified according to the nature of the crime, such as *mala in se* and *mala prohibita*. Crimes are also classified as felonies, misdemeanors, and treason. According to most authorities, crimes punishable by death or imprisonment in a state prison are felonies, while crimes not amounting to felonies are classified as misdemeanors. What is regarded as a felony in some states may constitute only a misdemeanor in others, although the more serious crimes, such as murder, robbery, and rape, are classified as felonies in all jurisdictions.

When one person is wronged by another, that person may seek a remedy against the wrongdoer by bringing a civil, or tort, action. With torts, the emphasis is on adjusting the conflicting interests of individuals to achieve a desirable social result, while a crime is a public wrong that affects public rights and is an injury to the entire community. When a crime is committed, attorneys and judges look to statutes, codes, constitutions, and case decisions to determine what conduct has been prohibited by law and for procedures to be followed in proving guilt.

In the criminal law system in the United States, the prosecution has the heavier burden of proof. The prosecution has the responsibility to prove each element of the crime with which the accused is charged beyond a reasonable doubt. If one element is not proved beyond a reasonable doubt, the person charged cannot be convicted of that particular crime. Although it is unconstitutional to shift the burden of proof or guilt, or any element of the crime, to the defendant in a criminal case, the defendant may be required to prove an affirmative defense by a preponderance or clear and convincing evidence in order to submit the defense to the jury.

Our legal system protects us by defining harmful behavior and setting punishments. The government is not free to declare any act criminal, however, and the federal and state constitutions protect us from laws that violate our protected liberties. Further, the state must prove each element of the crime beyond a reasonable doubt in order to find us guilty.

Review Questions

1. What is a crime? What is the difference between substantive and procedural law?

2. What are the three forms of harm that criminal law protects against? What are paternalistic laws?

3. What are the three factors that should be considered before making certain acts a crime?

4. What are some alternatives to controlling behavior besides criminal law?

5. What is common law? What is the importance of William Blackstone?

6. What is the difference between statutory law and common law?

7. What is police power? Where does it primarily lie? What does the 10th Amendment to the Constitution say?

8. When can the federal government pass criminal laws? When can political subdivisions pass laws?

9. What is the Model Penal Code?

10. When can a law be challenged?

11. What are the rights guaranteed by the Bill of Rights, and the Fourteenth Amendment?

12. What do we mean when we say most of these rights have been incorporated to your rights as a state citizen?

13. Describe the vagueness challenge.

14. Describe the ex post facto challenge.

15. Describe the equal protection challenge.

16. Describe first amendment challenges.

17. Describe privacy challenges.

18. What are mala in se crimes versus mala prohibita crimes? What are the differences between felonies and misdemeanors?

19. What are the differences between crimes and torts?

20. Who has the burden of proof? When does it shift? What are affirmative defenses?

Notes

[1]   4 BLACKSTONE, COMMENTARIES 15.

[2]   Schick v. United States, 195 U.S. 65, 24 S. Ct. 826, 49 L. Ed. 99 (1904).

[3]   Callan v. Wilson, 127 U.S. 540, 8 S. Ct. 1301, 32 L. Ed. 223 (1888).

[4]   MARSHALL, LAW OF CRIMES § 201 (7th ed. 1967).

[5]   MILLER, CRIMINAL LAW 16 (1934).

[6]   MODEL PENAL CODE § 1.04(1) (Proposed Official Draft 1980).

[7]   22 C.J.S. *Criminal Law* § 2 (1989).

[8]   MICHAEL & ADLER, THE LAW AND SOCIETY 353 (6th ed. 1997).

[9]   *See generally*, KLOTTER AND INGRAM, CRIMINAL EVIDENCE (9th ed. 2007), for a discussion of the methods followed in determining guilt or innocence in various cultures and civilizations.

[10]   Patterson v. Winn, 5 Pet. 233 (1831).

[11]   State v. McElhinney, 80 Ohio App. 431, 100 N.E.2d 273 (1950).

[12]   Keeler v. Superior Court, 470 P.2d 617 (Cal. 1970).

[13]   KY. REV. STAT. § 500.020(1).

[14]   Smith v. State, 968 S.W.2d 490 (Tex. 1998); Smith v. State, 964 P.2d 421 (Wyo. 1998).

[15]   Jacobson v. Massachusetts, 197 U.S. 11, 25 S. Ct. 358, 49 L. Ed. 643 (1904).

[16]   District of Columbia v. Brook, 214 U.S. 138, 29 S. Ct. 560, 53 L. Ed. 941 (1909).

[17]   Ameritech Corp. v. McCann, 176 F. Supp. 2d 870 (E.D. Wis. 2001).

[18]   United States v. DeWitt, 76 U.S. 41, 19 L. Ed. 593 (1869).

[19]   *See generally*, KANOVITZ & KANOVITZ, CONSTITUTIONAL LAW (10th ed. 2006).

[20]   United States v. Lopez, 514 U.S. 549 (1995).

[21]   Bissell v. Jeffersonville, 66 U.S. 287, 16 L. Ed. 664 (1861); City of Owensboro v. Commonwealth, 105 Ky. 344, 49 S.W. 320 (1899).

[22]   Salt Lake City v. Young, 45 Utah 349, 145 P. 1047 (1915); Akron v. McElligott, 166 Iowa 297, 147 N.W. 773 (1914).

[23]   Spann v. Dallas, 111 Tex. 359, 235 S.W. 513 (1921).

[24]   9 N.Y.2d 51, 172 N.E.2d 535 (1961). *See also* State v. Harris, 942 F.2d 1125 (7th Cir. 1991) and State v. Hayes, 408 S.E.2d 614 (W. Va. 1991).

[25]   United States v. Powell, 423 U.S. 87, 96 S. Ct. 316, 46 L. Ed. 2d 228 (1975). *See also* United States v. Petrillo, 332 U.S. 1, 67 S. Ct. 1686, 91 L. Ed. 1877 (1946); Coates v. City of Cincinnati, 402 U.S. 611, 91 S. Ct. 1686, 29 L. Ed. 2d 214 (1971); Gant v. State, 814 S.W.2d 444 (Tex. 1991).

[26]   Chapman v. United States, 500 U.S. 453, 111 S. Ct. 1919, 114 L. Ed. 2d 524 (1991).

[27]   119 S. Ct. 1849 (1999).

[28]   United States v. Sun, 278 F.3d 302 (4th Cir. 2002).

[29]   State v. Ausmus, 37 P.3d 1024 (Or. Ct. App. 2001).

[30]   Loving v. Virginia, 388 U.S. 1 (1967).

[31]   Craig v. Boren, 429, U.S. 190 (1976); In re Michael M., 450 U.S. 464 (1981).

[32]   U.S. CONST. art. I, §§ 9 and 10, cl. 1.

[33]   Duncan v. Missouri, 152 U.S. 377, 14 S. Ct. 570, 38 L. Ed. 485 (1894).

[34]   United States v. Abbington, 144 F.3d 1003 (6th Cir. 1998); Myers v. Ridge, 712 A.2d 791 (Pa. 1998).

[35]   Jones v. Georgia State Board of Pardons and Paroles, 59 F.3d 1145 (11th Cir. 1995); Allison v. Kyle, 66 F.3d 71 (5th Cir. 1995), and Kruger v. Erickson, 875 F. Supp. 583 (D. Minn. 1995). For a thorough discussion of ex post facto law and parole hearings, *see* California Dept. of Corrections v. Morales, 514 U.S. 499, 115 S. Ct. 1597, 131 L. Ed. 2d 588 (1995).

[36]   United States v. Lominac, 144 F.3d 308 (4th Cir. 1998).

[37]   Duncan v. Missouri, 152 U.S. 377, 14 S. Ct. 570, 38 L. Ed. 485 (1894).

[38]   United States v. Cooper, 63 F.3d 761 (8th Cir. 1995).

[39]   Miller v. California, 413 U.S. 15, 93 S. Ct. 2607, 37 L. Ed. 2d 419 (1973).

[40]   City of Houston v. Hill, 482 U.S. 451 (1987).

[41]   491 U.S. 397 (1989).

[42]   C. Lindell, "Speech: Public's View of What's OK Remains in Flux," AUSTIN AMERICAN-STATESMAN, October 5, 2005, at H5.

[43]   Church of Lukami Babalu Aye v. City of Hialeah, 508 U.S. 520 (1993).

[44]   Employment Division, Oregon v. Smith, 494 U.S. 872 (1990).

[45]   381 U.S. 479 (1965).

[46]   394 U.S. 557 (1969).

[47]   United States v. Lacher, 134 U.S. 624, 10 S. Ct. 625, 33 L. Ed. 1080 (1890).

[48]   State v. Meyers, 56 Ohio St. 340, 47 N.E. 138 (1897).

[49]   United States v. Standard Brewing Co., 251 U.S. 210, 40 S. Ct. 139, 64 L. Ed. 229 (1920).

[50]   U.S. CONST. art. III, § 3.

[51]   *See* KY. REV. STAT. § 532.060 (1994) and IND. REV. ST. 35-50-2-4 to 35-50-2-7 (1994).

[52]   MCCORMICK, EVIDENCE 684 (2d ed. 1972).

[53]   CAL. PENAL CODE § 1096 (1995).

[54]   In re Winship, 397 U.S. 358, 90 S. Ct. 1068, 25 L. Ed. 2d 368 (1970).

[55]   Victor v. Nebraska, 311 U.S. 1, 114 S. Ct. 1239, 127 L. Ed. 2d 583 (1994).

[56]   State v. Babers, 514 N.W.2d 79 (Iowa 1994).

[57]   Title 18 U.S.C. § 17.

[58]   United States v. Amos, 803 F.2d 419 (8th Cir. 1986); United States v. Byrd, 834 F.2d 145 (8th Cir. 1987); Patterson v. New York, 432 U.S. 197, 97 S. Ct. 2319, 53 L. Ed. 2d 281 (1977).

[59]   Martin v. Ohio, 480 U.S. 228, 107 S. Ct. 1098, 94 L. Ed. 2d 267 (1987).

[60]   State v. Corley, 587 So. 2d 193 (La. Ct. App. 1991).

Principles of
Criminal Liability

2

Chapter Outline

Cases

Accessory liability: *Sutton v. Commonwealth,* 228 Va. 654, 324 S.E.2d 665 (1985)

Actus reus of crime: *Powell v. Texas,* 392 U.S. 514, 88 S. Ct. 2145, 20 L. Ed. 2d 1254 (1968)

§ 2.1   Introduction

In this chapter, we will discuss some general principles of criminal responsibility and liability. Obviously, those people who actually commit a criminal act are legally culpable; however, others who *encourage, assist,* or *hinder apprehension* may also be liable under the law. The prosecution must prove that there was, in fact, a criminal act (*actus reus*) and that the persons charged committed the act or participated to the extent that they shared culpability with the primary actor. The law specifies the level of participation necessary in order to find criminal culpability. We will discuss these levels of culpability in Section 2.2.

We will also explain the elements of a crime. Before there can be a finding of guilt, the following elements of any crime must be proven:

- parties to crimes (at least one),

- the criminal act or omission (*actus reus*),

- the criminal state of mind (*mens rea*),

- causation, and

- concurrence.

Thus, the general "formula" for criminal liability becomes:

Act/Omission + Requisite State of Mind + Causation
+ Concurrence of Act and State of Mind = Crime

For example, when one or more human beings (parties) take the life of another human being (act) with a plan or design to take that life (intent), absent a break in the chain of events (causation) they will be liable for the crime of murder (assuming there is no justification or excuse). These and other principles are discussed in Sections 2.3 through 2.8.

§ 2.2 Parties to Crimes

When a crime is committed, one or several persons may be involved. For example, if one person pulls the trigger that results in the firing of a handgun and the bullet injures or kills another person, the person who fired the handgun might be the only participant in the felony crime. However, many others could be involved. For example, some may have been involved in planning the crime, the weapon may have been purchased from a person who knew it was going to be used to commit a crime, other people may have been present when the weapon was fired, and still others could have helped the person who fired the weapon to escape justice after the crime was committed.

A. Common Law

According to common law concepts of "parties to crime," it was accepted that one incident could result in four different categories of individuals being found guilty of a crime. They might be, respectively:

1. principals in the first degree,

2. principals in the second degree,

3. accessories before the fact, or

4. accessories after the fact.

1. Principals in the First Degree

One who actually commits the act that causes a crime to occur is a **principal in the first degree.** One who is actually or constructively present during the commission of the crime and participates in a *substantial* way is also a principal in the first degree, provided that the offense is attempted or completed by at least one party.

One may perpetrate a crime, not only with his or her own hands, but through an agency of mechanical or chemical means, as by instruments, poisons, or powder, or by an animal, child, or other innocent agent acting under his or her direction.[1] Therefore, there may be joint principals in the first degree, such as when two or more cause the death of another by beating, stabbing, shooting, or other means, in which both, or all, participate.

2. Principals in the Second Degree

One who *aids* or *abets* a principal in the first degree as he or she commits the criminal act, or *incites* the commission of the crime, and who is actually or constructively present at the time of the commission, is a **principal in the second degree**. A principal in the second degree differs from a principal in the first degree only in that he or she does not commit the offense personally or with an innocent agent, but instead *aids* or *encourages* the principal in the first degree to commit the crime; for example, a person who acts as a lookout or is the driver of the getaway car in a robbery situation is a principal in the second degree.

In order for a person to be a principal in the second degree, he or she must be present at the scene of the crime; however, presence may be either actual or constructive. A person is constructively present when he or she assists the principal in the first degree at the very time the offense is committed, but from such distance that he or she is not actually present.[2]

In a joint trial in Virginia, a man was found guilty of raping his wife's 15-year-old niece, and the wife was found guilty as a principal in the second degree, even though she was not actually present. The Supreme Court of Virginia agreed that the wife was guilty of rape as a principal in the second degree because she *procured*, *encouraged*, *countenanced*, and *approved* the husband's having sexual intercourse by intimidation with the victim against her will.[3]

In a 1986 case, a Maryland court reaffirmed the rule that "a principal in the second degree is one who actually or constructively was present when the felony was committed, and who aids or abets in its commis-

> **CASE:** *Sutton v. Commonwealth of Virginia*, 228 Va. 654, 324 S.E.2d 665 (1985)
>
> What was the holding of the Court?
>
> What evidence went to prove Sutton's participation in the rape?
>
> Why wasn't she guilty merely of accessory before the fact?

sion." In this case, the defendant was convicted as a principal in the second degree even though the defendant did not actively participate in the acts but was present when the acts occurred.[4] The prosecution must prove that that person *aided*, *abetted*, *advised*, *assisted*, or *encouraged* the actual perpetration of the crime. Mere presence would not be sufficient to create criminal culpability; however, the level of participation is not extremely high; for instance, "encourage" may be proven by a simple statement of support for the offender to engage in the criminal act.

Generally, the prosecution must prove that a crime was committed by the principal in the first degree and that the defendant aided and abetted him or her in order to obtain a conviction of that person as a principal in the second degree. It makes no difference, however, if the principal in the first degree is found not guilty by another jury as long as the jury that convicts the principal of the second degree finds, as a matter of fact, that the principal in the first degree is guilty beyond a reasonable doubt.[5]

3. Accessory Before the Fact

Accessories before the fact are persons who *counsel, procure,* or *command* the principal in the first degree to commit a criminal offense, yet who are too far away to have participated in the felonious act. Accessories before the fact are distinguished at common law from principals in the second degree (aiders and abettors) by the fact that the latter must be present during the commission of the offense, but accessories do not need to be present at all.[6]

To be guilty as an accessory before the fact, the defendant must have acted in some manner as a participant in the scheme of events in preparation for, or commission of, the offense. Mere knowledge that a crime is to be committed is insufficient to support a guilty verdict, even though the defendant might later have concealed the crime. It is immaterial that such participation is small, as long as it has the effect of inducing the principal to commit the crime.

In the case of *State v. Walden*, the court noted that at common law one who encouraged or aided another in committing a crime but who was not present at the commission of the crime was classified as an accessory before the fact.[7] Concluding that this test was met in this case, the court indicated that the state had offered substantial evidence of each and every element of, and the judge properly instructed the jury on, accessory before the fact, i.e., that: (a) the defendant *counseled, procured,* or *commanded* the principal to commit the offense; (b) the defendant was not present when the principal committed the offense; and (c) the principal committed the offense. This was sufficient to find the defendant guilty as an accessory before the fact under the common law rule that existed in North Carolina at the time.

4. Accessory After the Fact

An **accessory after the fact** is one who *receives, comforts,* or *assists* another, knowing that the other has committed a felony, in order to hinder the perpetrator's arrest, prosecution, or conviction.[8] In order to convict a party charged as an accessory after the fact, it is essential to prove that:

- a felony was committed,
- the defendant *knew* the felony had been committed, and
- he or she intended to shield the perpetrator from the law.

If an act of assistance is offered to enable a felon to escape justice after the crime has been committed, the assistance is rendered with the knowledge that the act has been committed, and the person assisted did in fact commit the crime, this constitutes the crime of accessory after the fact. The fact that the person who gave the assistance discontinues the assistance at a later date, and notifies the authorities, does not relieve that person of criminal liability for the acts committed before notification.

B. Model Penal Code

Under modern statutes and the Model Penal Code, the trend has been to reduce the number of categories of culpability. The liability of those who participate in any way in the crime is equal to the primary actor under many state statutes today. The Model Penal Code provides that a person is guilty of an offense if it is committed by his or her own conduct or by the conduct of another person for whom he or she is "legally accountable." One is "legally accountable" for the conduct of another if he or she causes an innocent person to engage in conduct constituting a crime or if he or she is an accomplice to the conduct of the other person. An accomplice is one who *solicits* the commission of an offense, *aids* in its commission or, having a legal duty to prevent the commission of the offense, *fails to make proper effort to prevent it*, or his or her conduct is expressly declared by law to establish complicity.

---

§ 2.06 Liability for Conduct of Another; Complicity[9]

(1) A person is guilty of an offense if it is committed by his own conduct or by the conduct of another person for which he is legally accountable, or both.

(2) A person is legally accountable for the conduct of another person when:

  (a) acting with the kind of culpability that is sufficient for the commission of the offense, he causes an innocent or irresponsible person to engage in such conduct; or
  (b) he is made accountable for the conduct of such other person by the Code or by the law defining the offense; or
  (c) he is an accomplice of such other person in the commission of the offense.

(3) A person is an accomplice of another person in the commission of an offense if:

  (a) with the purpose of promoting or facilitating the commission of the offense, he:

    (i)   solicits such other person to commit it; or
    (ii) aids or agrees or attempts to aid such other person in planning or committing it; or
    (iii) having a legal duty to prevent the commission of the offense, fails to make proper effort so to do; or

  (b) his conduct is expressly declared by law to establish his complicity.

The Model Penal Code has done away with the distinctions of second-degree principals and accessories before the fact—these individuals would now be considered and punished as principals. One other important change occurred in the Model Penal Code as compared to common law regarding accomplice liability. Prosecutors must prove that accomplices had the mens rea attached to the crime(s). Under the MPC, accomplices are not liable for natural and forseeable acts of the principal unless they also intended those acts. In cases where the mens rea is reckless, the prosecutor need only show a reckless mens rea on the part of the accomplice.

Accessories after the fact, those who knowingly harbor or help offenders but do not directly assist or encourage the crime, are still distinguished. The Model Penal Code, which has been adopted by some states, is specific in stating that a person commits the offense of accessory after the fact if he or she:

1. harbors or conceals another;

2. provides aid;

3. conceals, destroys, or tampers with evidence;

4. warns of impending discovery or apprehension; or

5. volunteers false information to a law enforcement officer.[10]

C. State Statutes, Codes, and Cases

Most state statutes have simplified the concept of culpability and no longer follow the common law principles. For instance, a fairly dramatic change has been that, unlike common law, an accomplice can now be tried and convicted for their part in an offense even if the principal party was acquitted or even if the principal was never prosecuted at all. The Alabama and California statutes provide:

§ 13A-2-23—Criminal Liability Based Upon Behavior of Another—Complicity. A person is legally accountable for the behavior of another constituting a criminal offense if, with the intent to promote or assist the commission of the offense:

1. He procures, induces or causes such other person to commit the offense; or

2. He aids or abets such other person in committing the offense; or

3. Having a legal duty to prevent the commission of the offense, he fails to make an effort he is legally required to make.[11]

> Cal. Penal Code § 30-33
>
> —32. Who are Principals. All persons concerned in the commission of a crime, whether it be felony or misdemeanor, and whether they directly commit the act constituting the offense, or aid and abet in its commission, or, not being present, have advised and encouraged the commission, and all persons counseling, advising, or encouraging children under the age of fourteen years, or persons who are mentally incapacitated, to commit any crime, or who, by fraud, contrivance, or force, occasion the drunkenness of another for the purpose of causing him to commit any crime, or who, by threats, menaces, command, or coercion, compel another to commit any crime, are principals in any crime so committed.

A Wisconsin court, in determining the application of that state's statute, explained that there are three alternative ways in which a defendant can be found liable for the commission of an offense under the party-to-a-crime theory:

- by aiding and abetting,

- by conspiracy, or

- by direct commission of a crime.[12]

In interpreting the "aids and abets" provision of a similar statute, a Louisiana court held that a person who aids and abets another in a crime is just as liable as the person who directly commits it. Explaining the scope of the term *principal*, a Louisiana court held that this term is broadly defined to include the actual perpetrator of the crime as well as one who assists in the perpetration. The court noted, however, that only those persons who *knowingly* participate in the planning or execution of the crime are principals; mere presence at the scene is not enough to involve an individual in the crime. In addition, the court noted that an individual may only be convicted as a principal for those crimes for which he personally has the requisite mental state.[13] There have

---

Legal News

In San Antonio, Texas, Ansel Abdygapparova was tried for rape and first-degree homicide. The prosecutor sought the death penalty against her even though she did not actively participate in either the rape or the murder of the victim by her boyfriend and another man. Abdygapparova did participate to the extent that she purchased a shovel to bury the body. She argued that she was merely present and anything she did was under duress because her boyfriend physically abused her and she was afraid of him. She was convicted and sentenced to life in prison. The jury found that her actions constituted the necessary *actus reus* to constitute criminal culpability for the crimes.

Source: *San Antonio Express News*, February 13, 2005 at A48; March 3, 2005 at A20.

been some cases in which presence plus "implicit encouragement" have been sufficient to find culpability.[14]

An accessory after the fact is generally treated as a separate offense and is accorded different treatment in modern codes.

To establish the crime of accessory after the fact, the state must establish:

- the completed felony was completed by another party prior to any acts engaged in by the defendant,

- the accessory was not a principal in the commission of the felony,

- the accessory had knowledge of the felony, and

- the accessory acted personally to aid or assist a felon to avoid detection or apprehension for the crime or crimes.[15]

There is disagreement between states as to whether or not to hold parties liable when they knew their actions may assist in a crime, but did not intend the crime to occur. Some states hold such persons liable, others require the prosecutor to prove the accomplice had the same level of mens rea as the primary party. Some states solve the problem by creating a new statute. **Criminal facilitation** statutes impose liability for providing aid to someone, knowing that he or she has committed or is about to commit an offense. Typical of these statutes is that of Kentucky, KRS § 506.080(1), which states:

> A person is guilty of criminal facilitation when, acting with knowledge that another person is committing or intends to commit a crime, he engages in conduct which knowingly provides such person with means or opportunity for the commission of the crime and which in fact aids such person to commit the crime.

The major difference between being charged under a complicity statute or being charged under a facilitation statute is the intent of the actor. If the aid is provided with the intent to commit the same crime as the person being assisted, the offense is charged under the complicity statute and both the "doer" and the one providing assistance are guilty of the substantive crime. However, if aid is offered only "with knowledge" that the recipient is committing a crime, then the aider is guilty of the offense of facilitation, not the substantive offense committed by the one who was assisted. In most jurisdictions, the penalty for facilitation is one level, or class, lower than the substantive offense for which the aid was offered.

D. Summary

In sum, the liability of an actor is categorized according to proximity to the offense and the level of participation. In most modern statutes, the only two types of criminal parties are:

1.   party (includes principals and accomplices), and

2.   accessory after the fact.

However, in some jurisdictions, there is also the lesser crime of:

3.   criminal facilitation.

§ 2.3   Criminal Act Requirements

In order to find someone guilty of a crime, every element of this formula must be proven:

---

*Criminal Act + Requisite State of Mind + Causation +
Concurrence (of Act and State of Mind) = Crime*

If the prosecution is unable to prove all of the elements, there can be no conviction. Before a person may be convicted of a crime, the prosecution must show that the person committed an act prohibited by some law, or failed to act when he or she had a legal obligation to do so. Often this principle is referred to as the ***actus reus***. The law does not punish mere criminal thoughts, nor does it punish a person for his or her status. As a rule, legal liability is typically based upon an affirmative physical act by the person charged, but in some instances liability can rest upon a failure to act, if it is determined that a person had a legal obligation to act under the circumstances. In this section, the *criminal act* requirement is discussed. Omission is analyzed in § 2.4.

The Model Penal Code describes criminal acts and omissions as follows:

---

§ 2.01 Requirement of Voluntary Act; Omission as Basis of Liability; Possession as an Act[16]

(1) A person is not guilty of an offense unless his liability is based on conduct which includes a voluntary act or the omission to perform an act of which he is physically capable.

(2) The following are not voluntary acts within the meaning of this Section:
     (a) a reflex or convulsion;
     (b) a bodily movement during unconsciousness or sleep;
     (c) conduct during hypnosis or resulting from hypnotic suggestion;
     (d) a bodily movement that otherwise is not a product of the effort or determination of the actor, either conscious or habitual.

> (3) Liability for the commission of an offense may not be based on an
>   omission unaccompanied by action unless:
>   (a) the omission is expressly made sufficient by the law defining the
>   offense; or
>   (b) duty to perform the omitted act is otherwise imposed by law.
>
> (4) Possession is an act, within the meaning of this Section, if the possessor
>   knowingly procured or received the thing possessed or was aware of
>   his control thereof for a sufficient period to have been able to terminate
>   his possession.

The authorities are in general agreement that no one should be subjected to criminal punishment except for specifically designated acts or conduct. The act or the conduct may consist of the physical movement of a person, such as pulling the trigger of a gun or breaking into a house to commit theft, or it may consist of verbal acts—for example, making verbal threats that induce fear in a victim. Possession can also form the basis of criminal liability even though it does not seem like an act, as long as the prosecutor can prove that the defendant knowingly possessed the contraband.

A related doctrine states that acts or conduct may not be treated as criminal unless the act or conduct has been so defined by statute or case decision as to make the conduct prohibited reasonably clear. When the prohibited act or conduct is made reasonably clear by lawmakers and a specific person violates such prohibitions, state officials may prosecute.

A. *Voluntary Act*

The act must be voluntary. There have been a few cases in criminal law in which the act was deemed to be not "volitional" or voluntary on the part of the perpetrator. Examples of acts that are not considered voluntary include epileptic seizures or spasms, reflexive actions, or actions taken while sleepwalking or in some other form of "unconscious" state. In cases of sleepwalking, for instance, any acts carried out by the sleepwalker are held to be not voluntary for purposes of criminal liability. Note that this is not a mental illness or capacity defense, nor is it a question of *mens rea*—rather, because the action is not under the volition of the actor, the first element of the crime (a voluntary act) is missing.

One example of this type of situation was the case of a man who killed his mother-in-law while sleepwalking. He drove 14 miles to her home and beat her to death with a tire iron. Medical experts testified that this behavior was indeed possible and, in fact, dozens of cases exist in which sleepwalkers have killed someone. In this case, the man had a very good relationship with his mother-in-law and there was no apparent reason for the killing. The jury acquitted him and the appellate court upheld the acquittal.[17]

Other possible situations that might raise the argument that the defendants' acts are not voluntary might be individuals who suffer epileptic seizures while driving and kill innocent bystanders. In these cases, the question of voluntariness typically turns on whether the individual knew that they were subject to loss of control, and knew that they posed a risk to others. If they had had seizures before and drove anyway, they typically are held liable under some form of gross recklessness or negligence.[18] The act in those cases is not the involuntary seizure that led to the automobile accident, but rather, the act of starting to drive the car in the first place.

What about brainwashing or hypnosis? Is it possible for someone to have no control over their actions because their will has been compromised by some form of mind control? The courts have not been open to such defenses, but there may be situations in which a defendant might successfully argue that they not only did not have *criminal intent,* but also that they did not even perform a *criminal act* because the action was not voluntary.

B. Act versus Status

The criminal law does not punish thoughts, emotions, personality, or character. No legitimate function could be served by subjecting people to criminal liability solely for harboring evil intent. Following this reasoning, the courts have determined that a statute that punishes someone for "who" or "what" they are, rather than "what they've done" violates the Eighth Amendment, which prohibits cruel and unusual punishment. For example, these are examples of statuses—"vagrancy," "being a common drunkard," or "being addicted to the use of narcotics," and, as such, cannot be the basis of criminal culpability because there is no act involved.

In the case of *Robinson v. California,* the Supreme Court of the United States declared that a California law that provided "no person shall use, or be under the influence of, or be addicted to the use of narcotics . . ." was unconstitutional because making the status of being an addict a crime violated the Eighth Amendment as applied to the states by way of the Fourteenth Amendment.[19] The justices made clear, however, that this interpretation did not prohibit punishment for the *use of* narcotics, because use is prohibited conduct. The Court summarized with this paragraph:

> We hold that a state law which imprisons a person thus affected as a criminal, even though he has never touched any narcotic drug within the state or been guilty of any irregular behavior there, inflicts a cruel and unusual punishment in violation of the Fourteenth Amendment.[20]

However, a statute that prohibits being in public while drunk was held to be constitutional. In *Powell v. Texas*, the U.S. Supreme Court distinguished the two cases.[21] They held that California punished someone for the mere *status* of being an addict, but the Texas statute against public drunkenness punished the *act* of being drunk in public, a behavior that may create substantial health and safety hazards. The Supreme Court held that the Texas law was quite different from convicting a person for simply being an addict, a chronic alcoholic, a leper, or someone who is mentally ill.

C. Possession

"Possession" offenses sometimes pose problems because it is claimed that, in some instances, the possession of property often involves no physical action to gain control of the contraband item. Although in some of the early cases the courts held that mere possession was not a crime because no "act" was involved, modern statutes, which make possession of contraband (such as narcotics or stolen goods) a crime, have been upheld. The rationale is that the "act" requirement is complied with because the defendant either actively procured or received the items, or violated the legally imposed duty to divest him- or herself of control as soon as possible upon discovering the illegal nature of the possession.[22] In this sense, possession crimes might be considered crimes of omission because the individual did not divest themselves of contraband once they had knowledge, and this omission created criminal culpability.

D. Summary

In order to be convicted of a crime, the accused must have committed a criminal act (or omission as will be explained in § 2.4). The act may involve an actual physical movement, or it may consist of verbal acts. One cannot be punished for evil intent alone, nor for any status (such as being an addict or an alcoholic). When criminal liability is based upon the defendant's affirmative act, there usually must be a showing that he or she made some conscious movement. However, "possession" crimes have been upheld even if there is no proof of a conscious movement.

§ 2.4 Criminal Omission

Although in the usual case an affirmative act is required for criminal culpability, in some instances, liability can rest on the failure to act. This is referred to as "**criminal omission**," "acts of omission," or in some instances, "failure to act."

There are many statutes that make failure to act a violation of the law; for example, failure to register for the draft or failure to prepare income tax returns. Although the cases concerning failure to act generally arise in homicide cases in which the defendant's conviction is predicated on the theory that the defendant failed to take steps to save the victim's life, the rationale also applies in other cases. The rule is that the defendant's omission will support a finding of criminal liability when it is shown that he or she was under a legal duty to act and that it would have been possible for him or her to act. In the case of *Jones v. United States*, the court held that a person who failed to act may be found guilty of homicide, if there existed a duty, declaring:

> There are at least four situations in which the failure to act may constitute a breach of legal duty. One can be held criminally liable: first, where a statute imposes a duty to care for another; second, where one stands in a certain status relationship to another; third, where one has assumed a contractual duty to care for another; and fourth, where one has voluntarily assumed the care of another, and so secluded the helpless person as to prevent others from rendering aid.[23]

A. Duties

The four types of duty that might create liability if there is an omission or failure to act are: statutory duties, duties derived from relationships; contractual duties; and failure to continue care duties.[24]

1. Statutory Duty

Where a statutory duty is imposed, criminal liability could result if the person charged had the opportunity and ability to perform the act and did not. Examples of statutory duties are, for instance, the duty to file tax returns and the duty (of convicted sex offenders) to register in sex-offender registries. Failure to perform these duties is a crime in itself. Another example of a statutorily created duty is the duty to provide safe working conditions.

Other statutory duties may create the potential for criminal liability if their omission results in a death or injury. For instance, a parent has a duty to provide care to their child; thus, the failure to act when someone else is hurting the child creates criminal liability. Statutory duties may include:

- The duty to stop and render assistance if involved in a traffic accident

- The duty to care for a minor child

- The duty of "mandated reporters" to report child abuse to law enforcement

- The duty to render assistance to someone in danger ("Good Samaritan" statutes)

It should be noted that, although they are fairly common in Europe, most states do not have "**Good Samaritan**" **laws** that create a duty to render assistance when one citizen sees another in distress. Actually, all states have what are called Good Samaritan laws, but they do not create criminal liability. They protect citizens from civil liability if they stop and render assistance to a victim and are sued as a result of their actions. In 1964, when 28-year-old Catherine Genovese was murdered in New York, 37 people who witnessed the attack did not call the police, yet there was no criminal liability on the part of those who refused to help. A newspaper article expressed shock that we, in this country, are not interested enough in our fellow humans to take action under such circumstances.[25] However, as a federal court explained, in the United States, a breach of a legal duty—rather than a mere moral command—is necessary to impose criminal liability for failure to assist one in need.[26] Only a few states have a legal duty to render assistance, including Rhode Island, Wisconsin, Minnesota and Vermont. For instance, Vermont's statute specifies that:

> A person who knows that another is exposed to grave physical harm shall, to the extent that the same can be rendered without danger or peril to himself or without interference with important duties owed to others, give reasonable assistance to the exposed person unless that assistance or care is being provided by others.[27]

Note that the statute creates a duty to act only to the extent that the citizen can do it without danger to self; further, the law would only require intervention to the extent of one's abilities. This means, for instance, that if a passerby could not swim, they would not be obligated to jump in the river to save a drowning person; they would have a duty, however, to alert others or help by throwing in a life ring or do some affirmative act to help the drowning victim.

Slightly different are statutes that require one to report a crime. Fewer than 10 states have such laws. For instance, Massachusetts has a statute that requires someone to report certain enumerated crimes (aggravated assault, rape, murder, manslaughter, and armed robbery) if they are witnessing it and can report it without danger to themselves or others. They must report it as soon as is reasonably practicable. Violation of this law is a misdemeanor.[28] Other states may have statutes against false reports to police, but do not require citizens to report a crime.

2. Relationship Duties

At common law, certain affirmative duties were placed upon persons with designated relationships. For example, a parent has the duty to prevent physical harm to his or her children. Today, there is disagreement in case decisions regarding the duty of a stepparent to stepchildren, but generally, if the adult has been acting in the role of a parent, a duty has been created. On the other hand, there is no such duty (at least recognized in common law) to provide for the care of one's parent. Thus, an adult child may have no duty (depending on the state) to see that the parent is taken care of or even has enough to eat. A duty can be created, however, if the adult child is the legal agent of the parent or there has been a contract formed where the adult child has promised to care for the parent in return for some type of consideration. In about 28 states, **"filial responsibility" laws** exist. These statutes create a duty to financially provide for one's aged and infirm parents if one is able to do so. In some states, a defense can be offered that the parent abandoned the child before the age of majority. Despite the fact that these state statutes exist, they are rarely enforced; in 11 of these states, no one has ever been prosecuted.[29] Consider other relationships that may have inherent duties:

- Does Person A have a duty to warn Person B of the imminent threat made by Person C to Person B? (Generally, there is no duty unless there is a special relationship between A and B.)

- Do psychiatrists have a duty to warn others if there is an imminent and clear threat that a patient is going to harm someone? (Generally, yes, if the threat is specific and the patient has a history of violence).

- Do psychiatrists or psychologists have a duty to protect their patients from themselves (if they say they are going to kill themselves)? (Yes, this is also a contractual duty as we will see below.)

3. Contractual Duties

Where a person has a contractual duty to protect or care for others and fails to carry out that contractual duty, he or she may be criminally liable for not performing that duty. For example, in the case of *People v. Montecino*, a nurse was held liable for failing to care for a patient she had been hired to care for.[30] Another example is the failure of a railroad gateman, who was employed to lower the gates to protect the cars and pedestrians from passing trains, with the resulting death of the driver of a car. The gateman was criminally responsible for failing to carry out his contractual obligation.[31] In an example of a verbal contractual duty, a grandmother who took care of a grandchild violated the duty of reasonable care when she became so intoxicated that she let the child smother. In that case, the court held the grandmother guilty of manslaughter.[32]

Other examples of contractual duties exist between the following actors:

- Lifeguards to swimmers

- Child care provider to those in their care

- Police officer to citizen

- Adult child to parent (if they are a legal agent, i.e. have power of attorney)

- Doctor to patient

In these cases, gross negligence in failing to perform one's duties may give rise to a finding of criminal culpability if there is a death or serious injury. Of course, the omission or failure to act must be the direct cause of the death or serious injury in order for there to be criminal culpability.

4. Failure to Continue Care Duties

If a person who has no statutory, relationship, or contractual obligation to render aid assumes this obligation, that person must not put the helpless person in such a position as to prevent others from rendering aid. For instance, unless a state has a Good Samaritan law, there is no statutory duty to stop and render assistance if one sees a traffic accident. However, if a driver does stop and begins to help, then they must continue until such time as others have arrived. If one sees a person in distress on the street, there is no duty to render aid, however, if a passerby helps the person in distress to a park bench or helps them to a doorway or in any other way moves them away from where they might receive assistance from others, then the duty to continue care has been created. The rationale is that abandoning one's effort would leave the victim in a worse condition than before.

Consider two different scenarios.

Situation 1. Defendant socializes with Victim in bar; Victim is extremely drunk and becomes incoherent; Victim tells Defendant that he has ingested a large amount of drugs as well as alcohol; Defendant leaves Victim in bar and goes home.

Situation 2. Defendant socializes with Victim in bar; Victim is extremely drunk and becomes incoherent; Victim tells Defendant that he has ingested a large amount of drugs as well as alcohol; Defendant assists Victim to his or her house where Victim passes out on floor. Defendant goes to bed. Victim dies from drug overdose or alcohol poisoning.

In Situation 2, the defendant may be charged with involuntary manslaughter because when the defendant moved the victim from a place where others might help, he or she created a continuance of care duty. Therefore, if gross negligence or recklessness was proven (i.e., that the defendant should have known to call for medical assistance), the defendant may be criminally culpable.

B. Knowledge and Impossibility

Before a person can be held responsible for an omission, knowledge of one's duty and an opportunity to perform and failure to perform the act must be shown. The majority view is that, although one may be under a legal duty to act, an omission will not render the defendant criminally liable unless he or she has knowledge of the facts creating the duty. For example, a person charged with "failure to stop" after causing an accident must be aware that the accident had occurred. The responsibility of showing knowledge falls upon the prosecution.[33]

On the other hand, lack of knowledge *of the law* does not provide an excuse. For example, a defendant's claim that he did not know that he had to report an accident as required by law would not be a defense. However, if a statute punished for the *willful* (intentional) failure to return an income tax report, then knowledge of the law must be proved. The reasoning is that there can be no *willful* violation if there is no knowledge.[34]

Also, there can be no criminal prosecution if the failure to act is based upon impossibility. There is no criminal act, or criminal failure to act, when the defendant's omission was due to the fact that he lacked the means or ability to perform. Evidence should be introduced to show that defendant had the ability to take action. However, failure due to impossibility is not a defense if a person could have gotten help, even if that person was not able to perform the duty; for example, failure to seek aid for a person who needs medical care.[35]

C. Summary

In order for an omission to create criminal culpability, there must be a duty. Duties are created through statute, relationship, contract, or through undertaking to care for a person in distress. Simple ignorance of the law defining the duty is not sufficient to relieve one of liability. However, a failure to act cannot create criminal liability unless there is:

- knowledge of facts that give notice to the person that they have a duty to perform, and

- an ability to perform one's duty (i.e., through ignorance or incapacity, the person with the duty is unable to complete the required acts).

§ 2.5 Criminal State of Mind—*Mens Rea*

Recall that in order for there to be a crime, there must be an act (*actus reus*), a criminal state of mind (***mens rea***), causation, and concurrence. We turn now to the requisite mental state in order for a person to be criminally cupable. The criminal state of mind generally must unite with the overt act, or there must be a union or joint operation of the criminal act and intention. The criminal intent need not have existed for any length of time before the act, as long as it existed at the instant of the act.[36]

A. *Common Law*

The common law evolved through the slow accumulation of individual case decisions. The definitions of crimes, therefore, were not conceived in any organized or comprehensive way. Each crime possessed a *mens rea*, but the language used in old English cases and early state statutes and cases in this country was not uniform; thus, for instance, the necessary intent for homicide might have been malicious, premeditated, depraved indifference, depraved heart, wanton disregard, or some other term. Each statute utilized specific language to describe the different levels of *mens rea* for different levels of culpability.

The *mens rea* requirement for crimes traditionally falls into one of three categories: specific intent, general intent, or negligence. In the case of *People v. Hood*, the majority of the Supreme Court of California acknowledged that "Specific and general intent have been notoriously difficult terms to define and apply."[37] However, they are still relevant to the understanding of criminal culpability and serve to distinguish certain crimes.

1. Specific Intent

Specific intent refers to an intention to commit some act to accomplish a result that is known to be illegal. If the statute defining a crime includes specific intent as an ingredient of criminality, such intent must be established as any other element of the crime. One way to think about specific intent is that the offender intended to do the act AND intended the consequence of the act (even if the consequence, apart from the act, was only to break the law).

In the case of *State v. LeBlanc*, the defendant was convicted of second-degree murder and attempted first-degree murder of a police officer. On appeal, the defendant argued that the trial court erred in charging the jury that it could convict the defendant of attempted first-degree murder upon proof that the defendant specifically intended either to kill Detective Mims or inflict great bodily harm upon him. The reviewing court agreed that this instruction was incorrect, as the *gravamen* of attempted murder is a specific attempt to kill, not simply to inflict great bodily harm. Included in the decision is this definition of specific intent:

> Specific intent is that state of mind which exists when the circumstances indicate that the offender actively desires the prescribed consequences to follow from his act or failure to act. . . . Specific intent need not be proven as a fact, but may be inferred from the circumstances of the transaction and the actions of the defendant.[38]

In distinguishing between specific intent and general intent, a Michigan court indicated that specific intent requires a particular criminal intent beyond the act done, while a general intent crime requires merely the intent to perform a proscribed physical act.[39] First-degree or capital murder, for instance, is often defined as a specific intent crime because the prosecutor must prove not only that the offender *intended to do the act* that resulted in a death (i.e., shoot, stab, hit the victim), but that the offender *intended the result* (death). On the other hand, second-degree murder is a general intent crime because the prosecutor must prove only that the defendant intended to do the act that resulted in the death of the victim. Another specific intent crime is burglary (breaking and entering *with intent* to commit a felony inside). If it cannot be proven that the defendant intended to commit a felony after entry, then the crime committed is only breaking and entering or trespassing. Possession of drugs is a general intent crime, but possession *with intent* to distribute is a specific intent crime. All crimes of attempt are specific intent because the prosecutor must show that the acts were committed *with the intent* to achieve the unconsummated substantive crime.

2. General Intent

General intent is present when a person consciously chooses to do a prohibited act. The only state of mind required is the intent to commit the act constituting the crime. The person charged need not have intended to violate the law, nor have been aware that the law made the act criminal. If specific intent is not required as an element of the crime, general intent may be inferred from the fact that the defendant engaged in the prohibited conduct.

Criminal intent may be found by the jury upon consideration of the "words, conduct, demeanor, motive and all other circumstances connected with the act for which the accused is prosecuted."[40] In defining general intent, a New York court stated that in a prosecution for a general intent crime, the government needs to prove only that the defendant intended to do what the law forbids; it is not necessary for the prosecution to prove that the defendant intended the precise result that occurred.[41]

Thus, think of specific intent as premeditated murder and general intent as other "garden variety" murders in which there is no proof that the offender intended the result. It is the difference, for instance, between a murder in which the offender planned the act, made preparations, laid in wait for the victim, and then cold-bloodedly killed the victim, versus a situation in which the offender grabbed a nearby gun and shot the victim during an argument. The offender could say that he never meant to kill the victim; he was only trying to scare or injure him. In most cases, this is a general intent murder and not the lesser crime of manslaughter because a grave injury was almost certain to occur. The prosecutor can prove that the offender meant to do the act (shooting), and we will hold him responsible for the almost certain effect of his act, but his criminal culpability will be limited to a general intent homicide rather than specific intent homicide (first degree). To reiterate: specific intent is when the actor intends the act and intends the consequence; and general intent is when the actor intends the prohibited act.

3. Negligence

In common law, **negligence** is the failure to perform a duty when such conduct is reckless and indifferent to the consequences. It must be more, or of a greater degree, than "ordinary negligence." Criminal negligence is not established simply by the fact that the defendant failed to exercise due care; the negligence must involve a higher probability of harm than is necessary for purposes of imposing civil liability. Because they are so similar, many statutes and cases combine recklessness and negligence as one category of criminal culpability.

B. *Model Penal Code*

The Model Penal Code includes the following section on culpability:

---

§ 2.02 General Requirements of Culpability[42]

(1) Minimum Requirements of Culpability
Except as provided in § 2.05, a person is not guilty of an offense unless he acted purposely, knowingly, recklessly or negligently, as the law may require, with respect to each material element of the offense.

(2) Kinds of Culpability Defined
(a) Purposely
A person acts purposely with respect to a material element of an offense when:
(i) if the element involves the nature of his conduct or a result thereof, it is his conscious object to engage in conduct of that nature or to cause such a result; and
(ii) if the element involves the attendant circumstances, he is aware of the existence of such circumstances or he believes or hopes that they exist.

(b) Knowingly
A person acts knowingly with respect to a material element of an offense when:
(i) if the element involves the nature of his conduct or the attendant circumstances, he is aware that his conduct is of that nature or that such circumstances exist; and
(ii) if the element involves a result of his conduct he is aware that it is practically certain that his conduct will cause such a result.

(c) Recklessly

A person acts recklessly with respect to a material element of an offense when he consciously disregards a substantial and unjustifiable risk that the material element exists or will result from his conduct. The risk must be of such a nature and degree that, considering the nature and purpose of the actor's conduct and the circumstances known to him, its disregard involves a gross deviation from the standard of conduct that a law-abiding person would observe in the actor's situation.

(d) Negligently

A person acts negligently with respect to a material element of an offense when he should be aware of a substantial and unjustifiable risk that the material element exists or will result from his conduct. The risk must be of such a nature and degree that the actor's failure to perceive it, considering the nature and purpose of his conduct and the circumstances known to him, involves a gross deviation from the standard of care that a reasonable person would observe in the actor's situation.

Some argue that one of the greatest contributions of the Model Penal Code is that all the myriad definitions of *mens rea* were condensed into only four enumerated mental states. In all states that have adopted the Model Penal Code, statutes clearly specify that the actor must have acted purposely, knowingly, recklessly, or negligently. Recall that the definitions of these terms are as follows:

- *Purposely:* when the actor intends the act and intends to cause the result

- *Knowingly:* when the actor is aware of the nature of his conduct and is aware of the practical certainty of the result of his conduct

- *Recklessly*: when the actor knows of but consciously disregards an unjustifiable risk (and the action involves a gross deviation from a reasonable standard of conduct)

- *Negligently:* when the actor is unaware of but *should have been* aware of an unjustifiable risk (and the action involves a gross deviation from a reasonable standard of conduct)

In states that do not use the Model Penal Code's structure for defining criminal culpability, different terms may mean the same thing. For instance, "wantonly," as used in the Kentucky Code, is defined as when an individual is aware of and consciously disregards a substantial and unjustifiable risk and that creates a gross deviation from the standard of conduct.[43] This is, of course, very similar to the MPC definition of "reckless," but in the Kentucky code, "reckless" is the term used to refer to failing to perceive a risk. The MPC uses similar terminology to refer to negligence. Furthermore, some states, even if they have adopted the MPC definitions, still refer to specific intent and general intent. We can see from the definitions above that specific intent roughly equates to the *mens rea* of "purposely" and general intent to the *mens rea* of "knowingly."

C. Transferred Intent

One other concept important to criminal *mens rea* is the principle of **transferred intent**. Under the common law and most modern applications of criminal culpability, the offender is culpable to the level of his or her intent, not to the actual target of his actions.[44] This can be remembered as "bad aim" intent because the classic example is that if Defendant intends to kill Victim A, but misses and kills Victim B instead, he will be guilty of first-degree murder (for B's death) and Attempted Murder (for trying to kill A). The intent to kill was transferred to the actual victim. Arson is another crime where one might see the applicability of transferred intent. If Offender Joe intends to burn down his mother-in-law's house but is mistaken as to the address and burns another's house instead, the crime is still arson.

This applies only within the limits of the same crime, however. For example, Defendant's intent to commit arson by burning down Victim A's house would not translate into culpability for murder if B's property was burned by mistake and B was killed during the fire (although the defendant would be guilty of arson and, perhaps, felony murder). While a defendant can be convicted when he or she has both the *mens rea* and commits the *actus reus* required for a given offense, he or she cannot be convicted if the *mens rea* relates to one crime and the *actus reus* to another. The Model Penal Code endorses the principle of transferred intent in Section 2.03(2)(a), which provides when an act purposely causes a particular result, that element is established if the actual result differs only in that a different person or different property is harmed.

The defendant will only be culpable to the extent of his original intent. Thus, for instance, if he drunkenly intends to push (assault) Victim A, but mistakenly pushes Victim B instead and B falls down, hits his head and dies, then the death is still only manslaughter—not homicide. The drafters of the Model Penal Code, in providing for this principle, included a provision that the elements of "purposely" or "knowingly" causing a particular result are not established when the actual result is not within the original purpose or contemplation of the actor.[45]

D. Summary

Mens rea can be defined as criminal state of mind. It is not just intent, although that is one level of *mens rea*. The four different levels of criminal states of mind that are recognized in the Model Penal Code and many state criminal codes are: *purposely, knowingly, recklessly*, and *negligently*. The level of *mens rea* is related to the seriousness of the crime and the degree of punishment. Although we hold negligent offenders responsible for their actions, we do not believe they are as culpable as those who commit their crime with premeditation. Specific intent can be roughly equated to *purposely*, and general intent can be roughly equated to *knowingly*. Transferred intent is a doctrine whereby the offender is charged with the crime that he intended regardless who is actually harmed.

§ 2.6 Causation

Recall the equation that identifies the elements of any crime (*Actus Reus + Mens Rea + Causation + Concurrence = Crime*). We have discussed the criminal act (*actus reus*), and the requisite mental state (*mens rea*). Now we will turn our attention to causation. In order for one who is accused of a crime to be convicted of that crime, the prosecution must show that the act of the defendant constituted a substantial factor in bringing about the result. Those who wrote the Model Penal Code and those who have drafted federal and state legislation have faced a difficult problem of defining causation. The following provision is included in the Model Penal Code.[46]

> § 2.03 Causal Relationship Between Conduct and Result; Divergence Between Result Designed or Contemplated and Actual Result, or Between Probable and Actual Result
>
> (1) Conduct is the cause of a result when:
>   (a) it is an antecedent but for which the result in question would not have occurred; and
>   (b) the relationship between the conduct and result satisfied any additional causal requirements imposed by the Code or by the law defining the offense.

A Proximate Causation

In order for a person to be guilty of a crime, his or her act or omission (performed with the requisite mental state) must have *caused* the result that creates the crime. On the other hand, the law does not hold one liable for everything that happens as a result of one's actions. The concept of "**proximate causation**" is a common sense approach to cut off liability even though one's actions may have actually caused the result or contributed to the result.

A person's action will be defined as the proximate cause of the result when there are no intervening superseding factors that come between the actions and the end result. Intervening and superseding factors are defined as those that are *unforeseeable* or *unnatural*, and will break the causal chain. If the intervening factors are *foreseeable* or *natural*, then the causal chain is not broken.

In most situations, events that can naturally occur as a result of the defendant's actions will not break the causal chain. For example, where the defendant struck the deceased, who was a hemophiliac, once on the jaw with his fist, which resulted in a hemorrhage from which the deceased died 10 days later, the defendant was properly convicted of manslaughter.[47] The court in *State v. Frazier* explained that it is immaterial that the defendant did not know that the deceased was in a feeble condition, or that he did not reasonably anticipate that the result would be death. This conclusion stems from a legal doctrine that the offender "takes his victim as he finds him"—meaning that if the victim is a hemophiliac and bleeds to death from a cut or hit that would not have killed another person it is still a natural result or if the victim has a "glass jaw" and is seriously injured from a blow that would not have harmed another, it is still a natural result of the assault. The defendant is legally culpable even when the victim does not care for himself and may contribute to his own death, for instance, when a victim refuses medical assistance and, because of the refusal, dies.

In the following situations, the defendant's actions were considered to be the proximate cause of the resulting death:

- The defendant struck the victim, knocking him unconscious, and while unconscious, the victim vomited and choked to death.[48]

- The defendant wounded the victim and, after he was taken to the hospital, the victim pulled out supporting tubes while he was in a semiconscious condition.[49]

- The defendant inflicted knife wounds on the victim who ultimately died from a pulmonary embolism.[50]

On the other hand, if there is a **superseding intervening factor**—an independent act or occurrence that supersedes the defendant's act as the legally significant causal factor—the defendant's conduct will not be the legal cause of the result. To constitute a superseding cause, the independent occurrence must be:

- intervening,

- unforeseeable (or unnatural), and

- the sole direct cause of the result.

In general, whether something is considered unforeseeable or unnatural relates to the likelihood of it happening as well as whether it is an intentional or volitional act of another. For instance, consider the following two situations:

- a defendant shoots a victim who is taken to the hospital, contracts an infection during surgery and dies

- a defendant shoots a victim who is taken to the hospital and is killed by a homicidal nurse.

In both situations, one could say that the defendant's actions "caused" the death of the victim because the victim would not have been in the hospital *but for* the acts of the defendant. However, the second situation is an example of when a superseding intervening cause breaks the causal chain for the defendant. The defendant is still guilty of aggravated assault or attempted murder, but not homicide because the homicidal nurse is an unforeseeable, unnatural intervening event. Part of the reason this case is considered one of superseding intervening factors is that the acts of the nurse are the volitional acts of a third party that the defendant in no way controls. Case decisions in this area are not always consistent. What some courts may find to be superseding intervening factors may be considered foreseeable and natural by other courts.

In one case, a victim is taken to a hospital after being injured by the defendant, and the injury would not normally be serious, but the victim contracts scarlet fever from a doctor and dies of the disease.[51] In this case, the court ruled that injury was not the proximate cause of death; however, other courts have held that any fatal infection or disease acquired in a hospital where the victim is taken after an assault will *not* break the causal chain.

In another case, the defendant, who had stolen a car, led the police on a high-speed car chase and two police helicopters collided due to the careless action of one of the pilots.[52] The court ruled that the defendant's actions were the proximate cause of the subsequent deaths of police officers. In this case, even though there was evidence that one of the helicopter pilots operated the helicopter improperly; the court held that the driver's actions contributed more substantially to the end result. In general, offenders who engage in high-speed car chases with police are held criminally culpable for any accidental deaths that occur as a result of the chase.[53]

Case decisions have held that intentional or criminally negligent actions on the part of a third actor *will* break the causal chain. The central question is forseeability. In referring to the intervening cause principle, the court explained:

> An independent intervening variable will not be superseding in three instances: (1) where it is merely a contributing cause to the defendant's direct cause; (2) where the result was intended; or (3) where the resulting harm was reasonably foreseeable when the act was done. . . . As to the third exception, the consequence need not have been a strong probability; a possible consequence which might reasonably have been contemplated is enough. . . . The precise consequence need not have been foreseen; it is enough that the defendant should have foreseen the possibility of some harm of the kind which might result from his act.[54]

B. Summary

The main thing to remember about causation is that the law is only concerned with "proximate causation" or legal causation. This is when there is no break in the causal chain between the offender's action and the result. If there is a superseding intervening factor, then the causal chain is broken and the offender is not responsible for the ultimate result (although he would still be responsible for his action). It helps to think of it as a time line:

Offender's action > events that are foreseeable and/or natural > result
= proximate causation/culpable

Offender's action > events that are unforeseeable and/or unnatural > result
= not proximate/not culpable

---

§ 2.7 Concurrence—Criminal Act and State of Mind

We will now turn to "**concurrence**," the last element in the crime equation. Although this principle is not as well known, and becomes an issue in relatively few cases, it should be mentioned. If the crime is one that requires a particular *mens rea*, such as intent, knowledge, or negligence, in addition to the act or omission, the physical act and the state of mind must occur at the same time. For example, in some states, the crime of first-degree burglary is committed when the person "*knowingly* enters or remains unlawfully in a dwelling *with the intent* to commit a crime." Under the principle of concurrence, the *intent* to steal must be concurrent with the *act* of entry or with unlawfully remaining in the dwelling.[55] If the intent to steal does not exist at the time of the entry, then burglary has not occurred. In criminal law, the intent will not relate to the entry. Of course, the person might be found guilty of breaking and entering if one cannot prove the elements of burglary.

§ 2.8 Attendant Circumstances

Before concluding this discussion of the principles of criminal liability, mention must be made of the fact that, in some crimes, proof must be offered to show that certain circumstances existed at the time of the act in question. For example, the common law crime of burglary requires that the entry be made at night, the crime of receiving stolen property requires that the goods received be stolen goods, and bigamy requires proof of a previous marriage. Also, statutory rape requires that the victim be underage, and perjury requires that the person be sworn. In these cases, evidence must be offered to prove that certain circumstances specified by the criminal statute existed at the time the act occurred. Thus, evidence must be introduced in a statutory rape case to show that the victim was under the statutory age. Further, all states have adopted "threshold" dollar levels in theft statutes delineating the line between felonies and misdemeanors, and these dollar figures must be proven. In many instances, these attendant circumstances are listed as elements of the crime.

§ 2.9 Strict Liability

As indicated in § 2.5, *mens rea* (i.e., purposeful, knowing, reckless, or negligent) is considered an essential element of any crime. However, **strict liability** crimes do not require any level of *mens rea*. The legislature may either forbid or require an act without regard to the mental state of the actor. The following provision describing this type of liability is from the Model Penal Code.[56]

> § 2.05 When Culpability Requirements Are Inapplicable to Violations and to Offenses Defined by Other Statutes; Effect of Absolute Liability in Reducing Grade of Offenses to Violation
>
> (1) The requirements of culpability prescribed by §§ 2.01 and 2.02 do not apply to:
>   (a) offenses which constitute violations, unless the requirement involved is included in the definition of the offense or the Court determines that its application is consistent with effective enforcement of the law defining the offense; or
>   (b) offenses defined by statutes other than the Code, insofar as a legislative purpose to impose absolute liability for such offenses or with respect to any material element thereof plainly appears.
>
> (2) Notwithstanding any other provision of existing law and unless a subsequent statute otherwise provides:
>   (a) when absolute liability is imposed with respect to any material element of an offense defined by a statute other than the Code and a conviction is based upon such liability, the offense constitutes a violation; and
>   (b) although absolute liability is imposed by law with respect to one or more of the material elements of an offense defined by a statute other than the Code, the culpable commission of the offense may be charged and proved, in which event negligence with respect to such elements constitutes sufficient culpability and the classification of the offense and the sentence that may be imposed therefor upon conviction are determined by § 1.04 and Article 6 of the Code.

The rationale for strict liability crimes is that, if the prosecution were required to prove the mental element, convictions would be so difficult to obtain that the existence of the criminal statute would not deter the conduct.

The legislature might reason that it is important to reduce harmful conduct at all costs, even at the risk of convicting innocent-minded persons as a result. The actor may be criminally liable even though he or she does not know the act is criminal or even does not know that the law exists.[57]

Although such liability is usually limited to the so-called "regulatory" or "public welfare offenses" or to violations that carry only a relatively small penalty and do not involve moral stigma, the rationale for not requiring criminal intent has been held to apply in some *mala in se* crimes. The crimes of bigamy and statutory rape are the classic examples of traditional crimes that incorporate an element of strict liability. In some states, a person can be convicted of bigamy even though that person reasonably believed that he or she was unmarried at the time of the second marriage.[58] Also, a man can be convicted of statutory rape even though he reasonably believed the female with whom he had intercourse was above the age of consent.[59]

The courts have been more likely to find strict liability in narcotics cases. For example, in the case of *State v. Hermann*, a Wisconsin court found that the state is not required to prove that the defendant, charged with an illegal drug transaction, knew that he was within 1,000 feet of a school when committing the felony in order for the defendant to be sentenced to the mandatory minimum prison term of at least three years. Referring to the purpose of the statute, the court explained: When the legislature's primary goal is to regulate, to accomplish a social good, or to obtain a high standard of care, proof of a criminal state of mind often is eliminated to achieve the desired result.[60] The court reasoned that, because the statute was designed to deter drug distribution in and around schools, even the potential for a lengthy incarceration does not make a strict liability statute unconstitutional. New Jersey and other states have a statute that holds individuals responsible for deaths that occur when the death is the direct result of ingesting a dangerous controlled substance manufactured or distributed by the defendant.[61] The defendant is strictly liable and does not need any *mens rea* in regard to the death, only the drug crime.

Generally, when an offense is *mala prohibita*, the courts find little problem with enforcing the statute when intent or knowledge are not required. On the other hand, courts have had some difficulty with statutory crimes when the penalty was more severe. For instance, in *Lambert v. California*,[62] the Supreme Court overturned the defendant's conviction under a California statute that required convicted felons to register. As written, the failure to register was a strict liability crime; however, the Supreme Court held that "fair notice" demanded at least a warning to show some level of *mens rea* because the failure to know of the requirement was not unreasonable.

Where the criminal statutes do not specify any level of *mens rea*, the courts have sometimes held that the statute means what it says and impose criminal liability with no proof of any level of *mens rea*. On the other hand, in some instances, the courts have read into the statutes some requirements of *mens rea*. In reaching a compromise on the issue, the Model Penal Code provides that culpability is an element of all offenses, except in specific classes of crimes.[63] Under the Model Code, the maximum penalty for violation of a strict liability crime is a fine. State statutes will designate the requirements for criminal liability. For example, the Ohio Criminal Code provides:

> When the section defining an offense does not specify any degree of culpability, and plainly indicates a purpose to impose strict criminal liability for the conduct described in such sections, then culpability is not required for a person to be guilty of the offense. When the section neither specifies culpability nor plainly indicates a purpose to impose strict liability, recklessness is sufficient culpability to commit the offense.[64]

§ 2.10 Vicarious Liability

In previous sections, it was noted that, in order for a crime to be committed, there must be a concurrence of *actus reus* and *mens rea*. In § 2.9, which discusses the strict liability exception, it was pointed out that, in a few crimes, a person may be held liable without any *mens rea*. There are other crimes that do not require the *actus reus* OR the *mens rea*. **Vicarious liability** is liability for crimes committed by another person, imposed simply because of the relationship between the parties. It is unnecessary to show that the defendant acted in any way or participated in the offense; it need only be established that the crime was committed by another person and that the defendant stood in the required relationship as stated by statute.

In most instances, vicarious liability applies when one conducting a business is made liable without personal fault for the conduct of someone else, generally an employee. For example, some criminal statutes specifically impose criminal liability upon the employer if his or her agent sells articles at short weight. Some statutes provide that persons under the age of 14 shall not be employed at certain jobs.[65] These statutes are generally misdemeanor in character, and are construed to impose vicarious liability upon the employer even though the employer was not aware that his or her agent acted in violation of the statute. Statutes imposing criminal liability upon an innocent employer for the illegal conduct of his or her employee are generally upheld as constitutional.[66] In *United States v. Park*, for example, the president of a corporation was held criminally liable for the actions of his employees, who allowed food to be stored in a warehouse contaminated by rats.[67] That is, the courts have found that this is not a violation of the due process clause. However, if the statute, as interpreted, imposes a jail sentence as well as a fine, there is a good possibility that the courts will find that this violates due process guarantees.[68]

Some cities have passed ordinances and states have statutes that hold parents responsible for the criminal acts of their children. Of course, parents are civilly responsible for their children's torts, but these statutes make them criminally responsible as well. For instance, a Salt Lake city ordinance holds parents responsible for failure to control their children when the child becomes involved in the juvenile system. The parent may be sentenced to counseling or community service.[69] California's statute was passed as an anti-gang statute, and holds parents responsible when they do not "exercise reasonable care, supervision, protection, and control" over their children. Parents can be fined or even jailed for the offense. The statute was upheld by the California Supreme Court against a challenge that it was vague and intruded on family privacy rights.[70] Other laws hold parents responsible when their child uses a gun that they did not secure in a way that made it inaccessible. In general, parental responsibility laws are acceptable as long as the punishment is reasonable and there is evidence of negligent supervision.

§ 2.11   Lesser Included Offenses

All states and the federal courts adhere to the concept that defendants may be convicted of "lesser included offenses." That is, when a defendant has been charged with the crime of "X," consisting of elements A, B, and C, a verdict of guilty may be returned for the crime of "Y" as long as all of the elements of "Y" are included within the original crime charged. In this example, because the crime of "X" consists of the elements of A, B, and C, the defendant could be found guilty of any "lesser included offense" that consisted of any combination of these elements (A and B, A and C, or B and C). Specific examples of lesser included offenses are: (1) manslaughter: a lesser included offense of murder in that all the elements of manslaughter are included within the elements of murder and (2) trespass: a lesser included offense of burglary in that burglary contains all the elements of trespass (plus other elements).[71]

If a defendant is convicted of a crime of a higher degree, that defendant cannot be convicted of a lesser included offense arising from the same act or omission. Applying this principle, a New York court held that where the defendant was convicted of criminal possession of a controlled substance in the third and fourth degrees, his conviction of criminal possession of a controlled substance in the seventh degree, based upon possession of the same cocaine, had to be reversed.[72]

§ 2.12   Summary

At common law, and by statute in some states, participants in crime are either principals or accessories. Principals are further divided into principals in the first degree and principals in the second degree. A principal in the first degree is one who actually commits the act that causes the crime to occur, while a principal in the second degree does not actually commit the crime, but instead aids or encourages the principal party to commit the crime, and is present at the scene.

An accessory also may be guilty of a criminal offense even though he or she did not actually participate in the crime and was not present when the crime occurred. Accessories are categorized as accessories before the fact and accessories after the fact. An accessory before the fact is one who counsels, procures, or commands the principal to commit a criminal act, but who is too far away to aid in the act. An accessory after the fact is one who gives comfort or assists another, after the crime has occurred, knowing that the other has committed a felony, in order to hinder the perpetrator's apprehension, prosecution, or conviction.

Most modern statutes and the Model Penal Code dispense with the distinctions between principals and accessories, and hold persons legally accountable if they commit the act, solicit the commission of offense, aid in commission, or, in some instances, fail to take proper efforts to prevent it. Modern statutes do distinguish the accessory after the fact and treat the crime as a lesser offense.

In order for a person to be convicted of a crime, the prosecution must show that the person charged committed a prohibited act or failed to act when he or she had the legal obligation to do so. This principle, referred to as *actus reus*, may involve an actual physical movement or may consist of verbal acts. However, one cannot be punished for evil intent without an act, nor for a violation of a statute that makes status alone a violation. Although in the usual case an affirmative act is required to support a conviction, in some instances, liability can rest upon the failure to act if there was a legal responsibility to do so.

The second requirement for conviction of a crime is that the act, except as otherwise provided by statute, must be accompanied by a criminal state of mind (i.e., purpose, knowing, reckless, or negligent). This criminal state of mind is referred to as *mens rea*.

The third requirement is that the alleged unlawful act or omission must be so integrated with and related to the ultimate result that it can be said to have proximately caused or contributed to it. In other words, the prosecution must show that the conduct was the proximate cause of the crime. This principle is often referred to as causation. Finally, the physical act and state of mind must be in concurrence. That is, the prosecution must show that the intent or *mens rea* existed at the time the act was perpetrated.

There are a few crimes that do not require all of the elements discussed above. In strict liability crimes, *mens rea* is not required. In "vicarious liability" crimes, there is no requirement for either *mens rea* or *actus reus* because this type of liability occurs through a relationship with others who do prohibited acts. For instance, a business owner may be liable for the conduct of someone else, generally an employee. These statutes have been upheld, because the penalty is a fine rather than a jail sentence.

Review Questions

1. List and define the four different parties to a crime under common law.

2. Explain the two parties recognized by the Model Penal Code.

3. Explain the changes that were made in accomplice liability in the MPC from common law (hint: forseeable acts and convicted principals).

4. Describe criminal facilitation statutes and why they were created.

5. Describe the elements of actus reus (i.e. voluntariness, status).

6. What were the holdings of *Robinson v. California* and *Powell v. Texas*.

7. Explain how words and possession can form the actus reus of a crime.

8. Describe when an omission can form the basis of liability (mention the four types of duty and provide examples).

9. Describe Good Samaritan laws.

10. Describe "filial responsibility" laws.

11. Explain the importance of knowledge and impossibility in relation to liability for an omission.

12. Describe the four levels of mens rea under the Model Penal Code.

13. Distinguish between specific intent and general intent.

14. Explain the doctrine of transferred intent.

15. Describe the concept of proximate causation. When is culpability cut off even though the defendant's act was the "but for" cause of the ultimate result?

16. Explain the concept of concurrence.

17. Define "attendant circumstances" and provide examples.

18. Explain the concept of strict liability.

19. Explain the concept of vicarious liability.

20. List and define all five elements necessary for any crime.

Notes

[1] Agresti v. State, 2 Md. App. 278, 234 A.2d 284 (1967); Beausoliel v. United States, 107 F.2d 292 (D.C. Cir. 1939).

[2] State v. Sauls, 29 N.C. App. 457, 224 S.E.2d 702 (1976); State v. Wade, 11 N.C. App. 169, 180 S.E.2d 328 (1971).

[3] Sutton v. Commonwealth of Virginia, 228 Va. 654, 324 S.E.2d 665 (1985).

[4] Smith v. State, 66 Md. App. 603, 505 A.2d 564 (1986).

[5] Forbes v. State, 513 S.W.2d 72 (Tex. Crim. App. 1974).

[6] State v. Mower, 317 A.2d 807 (Me. 1974); Huff v. State, 23 Md. App. 211, 326 A.2d 198 (1974).

[7] State v. Walden, 330 S.E.2d 271 (N.C. 1985). *See also* Duke v. State, 137 Fla. 513, 188 So. 124 (1939), which held that presence, actual or constructive, is the determining factor in the distinction between a principal in the second degree and an accessory before the fact.

[8] Whorley v. State, 45 Fla. 123, 33 So. 849 (1903).

[9] Model Penal Code § 2.06(1), (2), and (3) (1985).

[10] Model Penal Code § 242.3 (1985).

[11] Ala. Code § 13A-2-23 (1998).

[12] State v. Hamm, 586 N.W.2d 5 (Wis. 1998).

[13] State v. Cayton, 721 So. 2d 542 (La. 1998); State v. Arnold, 801 So. 2d 408 (La. 2001).

[14] State v. Doody, 434 A2d 523 (Me 1981), *but see* State v. Vaillancourt, 453 A2d 1327 (N.H. 1982).

[15] Little v. United States, 709 A.2d 708 (D.C. 1998).

[16] Model Penal Code § 2.01 (1985).

[17] The Queen v. Parks [1992] 2 S.C.R. 871 (Can.); *but see* Sallee v. State, 544 P.2d 902 (Okla. Crim. App. 1975).

[18] People v. Decina, 138 N.E.2d 799 (N.Y. 1956).

[19] Robinson v. California, 370 U.S. 660, 82 S. Ct. 1417, 8 L. Ed. 2d 758 (1962).

[20] *Id.*

[21] Powell v. Texas, 392 U.S. 514, 88 S. Ct. 2145, 20 L. Ed. 2d 1254 (1968).

[22] Model Penal Code § 2.01(4) (1985).

[23] Jones v. United States, 308 F.2d 307 (D.C. Cir. 1962). *See also* Commonwealth v. Kellam, 719 A.2d 792 (Pa. 1998).

[24] Jones v. United States, 308 F.2d 307 (D.C. Cir. 1962).

[25] N.Y. Times, Mar. 28, 1964.

[26] *See generally, Culpable Non-Intervention: Reconsidering the Basis for Party Liability by Omission*, 18 Crim. L.J. 90-107 (1994); The Efficient Duty to Rescue, 15 Inter. Rev. of L. & Econ. 141-150 (1995); *Cal. Penal Code § 654 and the Neal Doctrine*, 26 Univ. of W. L.A. L. Rev. 335-363 (1995); *see also* French Penal Code, Art. 63 and United States v. Bonetti, 277 F.3d 441 (4th Cir. 2002).

[27] Vt. Stat. Ann. Tit. 12, Sec. 519.

[28] Mass. Gen. Code, Ch. 268, § 40.

[29] *See Caring for Our Parents in an Aging World: Sharing Public and Private Responsibility for the Elderly*, 5 N.Y.U.J. Legis. and Pub. Pol'y 563 (2001).

[30] 66 Cal. App. 2d 85, 152 P.2d 5 (1944).

[31] State v. Harrison, 107 N.J. 213, 152 A. 867 (1931).

[32] Cornell v. State, 159 Fla. 687, 32 So. 2d 610 (1947).

[33] People v. Henry, 23 Cal. App. 2d 155, 72 P.2d 915 (1937).

[34] United States v. Murdock, 290 U.S. 389, 54 S. Ct. 223, 78 L. Ed. 381 (1933).

[35] People v. Beardsley, 150 Mich. 206, 113 N.W. 1128 (1907).

[36] United States v. Lester, 363 F.2d 68 (6th Cir. 1967), *cert. denied*, 385 U.S. 1002 (1967); State v. Morgan, 22 Utah 162, 61 P. 527 (1900).

[37] 1 Cal. 3d 444, 462 P.2d 370 (1969).

[38] State v. LeBlanc, 719 So. 2d 592 (La. 1998).

[39] People v. Whitney, 228 Mich. App. 230, 578 N.W.2d 329 (1998).

[40] Miller v. State, 233 Ga. App. 814, 506 S.E.2d 136 (1998).

[41] United States v. Francis, 975 F. Supp. 288 (S.D.N.Y. 1997).

[42] MODEL PENAL CODE § 2.02 (1985).

[43] KY. REV. STAT. §. 501.020 (2002).

[44] People v. Scott, 927 P.2d 238 (1996).

[45] See MODEL PENAL CODE § 2.03 (1985), and the other included exceptions.

[46] MODEL PENAL CODE § 2.03(1) (1985).

[47] State v. Frazier, 339 Mo. 966, 98 S.W.2d 707 (1936).

[48] People v. Geiger, 10 Mich. App. 339, 159 N.W.2d 383 (1968).

[49] United States v. Hamilton, 182 F. Supp. 548 (D.D.C. 1960).

[50] Pittman v. State, 528 N.E.2d 67 (Ind. 1988).

[51] Bush v. Commonwealth, 78 Ky. 268 (1880).

[52] People v. Acosta, 284 Cal. Rptr. 117 (Cal. Ct. App. 1991). *See also* Ewing v. State, 719 N.E.2d 1221 (Ind. 1999).

[53] *See* People v. Harris, 52 Cal. App. 3d 419, 125 Cal. Rptr. 40 (1975), in which the Court of Appeals reversed the dismissal of a vehicular manslaughter prosecution in a case in which a police car pursuing a defendant in a high-speed chase collided with another vehicle, killing one of its passengers. *See also* People v. Pike, 197 Cal. App. 3d 732, 243 Cal. Rptr. 54 (1988), in which the Court of Appeals affirmed a vehicular manslaughter conviction that arose when two police cars pursuing the defendant in a high-speed chase collided, resulting in the death of one of the officers.

[54] People v. Acosta, 284 Cal. Rptr. 117, 137 (Cal. Ct. App. 1991).

[55] Jackson v. State, 102 Ala. 167, 15 So. 344 (1894).

[56] *See generally* MODEL PENAL CODE §§ 2.01, 2.02, 2.05 (1985).

[57] Landen v. United States, 299 F. 75 (6th Cir. 1924); United States v. Park, 499 F.2d 839 (4th Cir. 1974).

[58] People v. Vogel, 46 Cal. 2d 798, 299 P.2d 850 (1956).

[59] State v. Superior Court, 104 Ariz. 440, 454 P.2d 982 (1969).

[60] State v. Hermann, 474 N.W.2d 906 (Wis. 1991).

[61] N.J. GEN. STAT. Ch. 35 § 9.

[62] 355 U.S. 225 (1957).

[63] *See* MODEL PENAL CODE §§ 2.02(1), 2.05 (1985).

[64] OHIO REV. CODE ANN. § 2901.21(B) (Anderson 2002).

[65] KY. REV. STAT. § 339.220 (2001).

[66] In re Marley, 29 Cal. 2d 525, 175 P.2d 832 (Cal. Ct. App. 1946).

[67] United States v. Park, 421 U.S. 658 (1975).

68 Pennsylvania v. Koczwara, 397 Pa. 575, 155 A.2d 825 (1959).

69 Salt Lake City Ordinance 11.60.020-060.

70 *Gang Member's Mother Denies 'Failure' Charge*, L.A. Times, May 20, 1989, at 2. Adam Culbreath, *Parental Liability Law Upheld in California*, Youth Law News, Sept.-Oct. 1993, at 12.

71 For a discussion of the laws regarding lesser included offenses, *see* United States v. Quintero, 21 F.3d 885 (9th Cir. 1994) and United States v. Browner, 889 F.2d 549 (5th Cir. 1989).

72 People v. Jones, 680 N.Y.S.2d 764 (App. Div. 1998).

Capacity and Defenses   3

Chapter Outline

Cases

Test of Insanity: *Clark v. Arizona*, 548 U.S. 735 (2006)
Diminished Capacity: *Montana v. Egelhoff*, 518 U.S. 37 (1996)
Entrapment: *Jacobsen v. United States,* 503 U.S. 540 (1992)

§ 3.1 Introduction

One purpose of criminal law is to establish and define standards of human conduct. A general legal principle is that all persons have the power to choose between right and wrong and to do or refrain from doing that which the law commands. Notwithstanding this general principle, courts in England and other countries recognized early that there are situations in which persons, for one reason or another, do not have the capacity to distinguish between right and wrong, or do not have the capacity to form the mental intent that may be required as an element of some crimes. There are generally "classes" of people who cannot, by definition, form the necessary criminal intent; for instance, infants or the insane. There are others who, while not a member of an "incompetent" class, may experience circumstances, such that they should not be held responsible for their actions.

In this chapter, most of the common defenses claimed by defendants who are accused of crime are considered. They include incapacity to commit crimes due to infancy or mental impairment, duress or compulsion, necessity, defense of self or others, entrapment, alibi, ignorance or mistake, statute of limitation defenses and others.

§ 3.2 Infancy or Immaturity

A crime is not committed if the mind of the person doing the act is incapable of forming a culpable *mens rea*; therefore, an infant is exempt from criminal responsibility for his or her acts if sufficient mental capacity is lacking. **Infancy**, in this case, means only that the child does not have the capacity to determine right and wrong, the age of infancy is set by case law or statute.

A. Common Law

At common law, a child under the age of seven was conclusively presumed to be incapable of having the necessary criminal intent and could not commit a crime. Even if the child confessed to the act, and even if the state introduced evidence to indicate that the child knew the difference between right and wrong, there could be no conviction for that crime. A child between the ages of seven and 14 was *presumed* not to have the capacity to commit the crime; however, the presumption was rebuttable. That is, the prosecution could introduce evidence to show that, in fact, the child did possess the necessary mental capacity to entertain the criminal intent.[1]

The common law definitions and distinctions are still followed in a few states and have had a significant bearing on statutes in other states. Today, most state statutes have specifically defined the jurisdiction of juvenile courts and detailed the procedures necessary to "waive" jurisdiction to adult courts.

B. Model Penal Code

The Model Penal Code establishes the age at which the juvenile court shall have exclusive jurisdiction and briefly states the procedure to be followed in transferring a case from the juvenile court to the criminal court. Section 4.10 of the Model Penal Code provides:

§ 4.10 Immaturity Excluding Criminal Conviction; Transfer of Proceedings to Juvenile Court[2]

(1) A person shall not be tried for or convicted of an offense if:

    (a) at the time of the conduct charged to constitute the offense he was less than sixteen years of age, in which case the juvenile court shall have exclusive jurisdiction; or

> (b) at the time of the conduct charged to constitute the offense he was
>   sixteen or seventeen years of age, unless:
>
>   (i)   the Juvenile Court has no jurisdiction over him or
>   (ii) the Juvenile Court has entered an order waiving jurisdiction
>   and consenting to the institution of criminal proceedings
>   against him.

This section proposes that no one less than 16 years old at the time of the alleged offense may be tried for or convicted of the offense in criminal court. However, if the juvenile was 16 or more years of age, but less than 18 at the time of the offense, the juvenile court, after a hearing, may enter an order waiving jurisdiction and the case will be transferred to adult criminal court.

C. State Statutes, Codes, and Cases

Under the laws that exist in most states today, infancy is a defense. Juveniles may avail themselves of the infancy defense and come under the jurisdiction of the juvenile court in most instances. However, there is no recognized constitutional right to be treated as a juvenile. That right is granted by the legislature, which may restrict or qualify that right as it sees fit, as long as no arbitrary or discriminatory classification is involved.[3]

At present, all states have established juvenile court systems that deal with juveniles who have been charged with criminal violations. However, even in states that have enacted juvenile justice laws, the question of capacity is often raised. For example, in the case of *State v. Q.D.*,[4] the Supreme Court of Washington was called upon to determine whether the state statutory presumption of infant incapacity applied in juvenile proceedings. A Washington statute provides, in part:

Children under the age of 8 are incapable of committing crime. Children of 8 and under 12 years of age are presumed to be incapable of committing crime, but this presumption may be removed by proof that they have sufficient capacity to understand the act or neglect and to know that it was wrong.[5]

In the majority of states, criminal acts committed by juveniles are generally adjudicated in juvenile court. Exceptions, however, are made when certain more serious crimes are committed, in which case the juvenile court may waive jurisdiction. While the juvenile court must afford a hearing before a case can be transferred from juvenile court to criminal court, more juveniles, especially those who have reached the chronological age of 16 or above, are being processed through adult criminal courts.

Legal News

The most recent case of a child committing homicide may have occurred in November 2008 in St. Johns, Arizona, when an eight-year-old boy was charged with two counts of murder for allegedly shooting his father and a male roommate. At the time this book went to press, no motive for the murders was revealed. Because of the severity of the crimes, it is possible that this eight-year-old may be prosecuted as an adult.

Source: abcnews.go.com/GMA/story?id=6320539&page=1.

D. Summary

Under the common law and under state statutes in all 50 states, infancy may be a defense to criminal culpability. In common law and in most states today, there is an age under which a child is believed to be incapable of forming criminal intent, which is usually around age 7 or 8. There is also an age range where the presumption of incompetence is rebuttable; that is, the state may show (by clear and convincing evidence) that the child knows right from wrong and can understand the proceedings. In these cases, the child may be held responsible for their actions. Juvenile court may adjudicate proceedings against children who are found competent; or the case may be transferred to adult court, depending on the statutory authority of the state.

§ 3.3   Mental Impairment or Insanity

In some criminal cases, the defendant claims that he is entitled to an acquittal because at the time of the crime he was so impaired by mental illness as to be "insane" within the meaning of the criminal law definition. **Insanity** is a legal term, not a medical term. It refers to any mental illness that meets the legal threshold for incapacity. Mental incapacity or insanity may be used by one accused of crimes at several points in the criminal process. The following describe the various ways mental incapacity may become an issue in a criminal proceeding.

- "Competency": Mental incapacity may be used to argue **incompetency** to stand trial; specifically, that the defendant's mental state is such that he is unable to understand the proceedings against him or help in his own defense.

- "Insanity": Insanity is a type of mental incapacity; specifically, that the defendant's mental state was such at the time of the crime, that he should not be held responsible for his crime. Insanity and incompetency to stand trial are different findings and the standards for determining each are different.[6]

- "Diminished capacity/responsibility": The defendant's mental state at the time of the crime (or at the time of sentencing) may be taken into consideration even though the legal standard of insanity was not reached.

A. Common Law

The practice of recognizing the defense of mental impairment is long-standing and was present in common law rulings. Basically, courts held that if the defendant had no understanding or memory to know what he was doing was wrong, he was like an infant or wild beast and, therefore, not culpable. Most authorities indicate that the modern insanity defense began with the *M'Naghten* case.[7] In this case, Daniel M'Naghten was charged with murder. The facts indicate that M'Naghten suffered delusions that he was being persecuted by the Prime Minister of Great Britain, Sir Robert Peel. On January 20, 1843, M'Naghten shot and killed Peel's assistant, Edward Drummond, believing him to be Peel. At the trial, the medical evidence showed that M'Naghten was in a seriously disordered medical condition at the time of the incident. The jury returned a verdict of not guilty after being instructed to convict if the defendant was in a sound state of mind at the time, but that he would be entitled to a verdict in his favor if he "had not the use of his understanding so as to know he was doing a wrong or wicked act." The resulting uproar led the House of Lords to inquire of the 15 judges of the Queen's Bench as to the proper test to be applied in such cases.[8]

The doctrine announced by Lord Chief Justice Tindal of the Common Pleas Court had three important aspects and thus the court's declaration is properly labeled *M'Naghten's Rules*. First, and most importantly, the general rule was set down that a jury should acquit a defendant if it found that the accused "was laboring under such a defect of reason, from disease of the mind, as not to know the nature and quality of the act he was doing, or, if he did know it, that he did not know he was doing what was wrong." Second, the judges also addressed the issue of partial insanity, the situation in which a person, otherwise sane, is laboring under some insane delusion involving the situation in question. In such a case of "partial delusion," the judges declared, acquittal would depend upon whether the act would have been right if the situation had actually been as the person believed it to be. Third, the judges opined that a "medical man" might, in some cases, give his opinion to the jury as to the state of the accused's mind at the time of the offense.

M'Naghten's Rules were quickly adopted throughout Anglo-American jurisdictions, and the so-called "right and wrong test" became the bedrock of the insanity defense. This test has been and still is followed in many jurisdictions. Briefly stated, the test asks "Was the defendant, at the time of committing the act, laboring under such a defect of reason, from disease of the mind, as not to know the nature and quality of the act he was doing; or, if he did know it, he did not know what he was doing was wrong?"

B. Model Penal Code

The drafters of the Model Penal Code prepared this provision:

Model Penal Code § 4.01[9]

1. A person is not responsible for criminal conduct if at the time of such conduct as a result of mental disease or defect he lacks substantial capacity either to appreciate the criminality of his conduct or to conform his conduct to the requirements of the law.

2. The terms "mental disease or defect" do not include an abnormality manifested only by repeated criminal or otherwise antisocial conduct.

   Under the provisions of the Model Code, a defendant is entitled to acquittal by reason of insanity if the evidence shows that, because of a mental disease or defect, he:

   a. lacked substantial capacity to appreciate the criminality of his conduct; or
   b. lacked substantial capacity to conform his conduct to the requirements of the law.

The Model Penal Code has attempted to incorporate the various tests used by state statutes to determine whether insanity should excuse criminal conduct. Although the Model Code approach has been looked upon favorably by many jurisdictions, most states have not adopted the formula.

C. State Statutes, Codes, and Cases

Insanity is an "**affirmative defense**." In order to raise the issue, a defendant need only present evidence that is sufficient to raise a reasonable doubt as to his or her sanity before the burden of proof shifts to the state. The level of proof necessary is usually a preponderance, but some jurisdictions have raised the defendant's burden of proof to clear and convincing. If the defendant meets this burden of proof, then the burden shifts to the state and the prosecution must introduce evidence to prove sanity beyond a reasonable doubt. In the case of *State v. Doyle*, for instance, the reviewing court indicated that because the state introduced no evidence at all on the issue of sanity, it failed to meet this burden.[10]

1. Tests of Insanity

What is the modern test for "insanity"? There is considerable disagreement among the states as to what standard should be used to determine whether a mental disorder or impairment is sufficient to render the defendant legally not guilty because of insanity. States have widely varying statutes and some states have abolished the insanity defense, except as it is relevant to *mens rea*. The more common tests are discussed here.

a. M'Naghten's Rule (Right/Wrong Test)

This test, as described above, is often referred to as the right-wrong test and is still used in the majority of jurisdictions. To establish criminal incapacity under this test, a defendant must introduce at least some evidence to show that, as a result of his mental condition, he (a) did not know the nature and quality of his act; OR (b) did not know that the act was wrong.

The more than 100-year-old *M'Naghten* Rule (referring to the first of the *M'Naghten* Rules described earlier) is criticized in modern times because psychiatrists and psychologists arguably have more to say about the defendant's mental state than can be succinctly explained by simple "yes" or "no" answers to the questions of the rule. In Minnesota, for instance, where the *M'Naghten* Rule is followed, the court held that the *M'Naghten* insanity defense did not require consideration of the defendant's volition and capacity to control behavior.[11] Because of the difficulty in applying the *M'Naghten* Rule, other rules have developed in the United States.

b. Irresistible Impulse Rule

The **irresistible impulse rule** was added to the right-wrong test in some states, but has been rejected in most states and in England and Canada. In states where this rule is followed, it is added to the basic *M'Naghten* test. The theory is that if a person acts under an irresistible impulse, from disease of the mind, he is incapable of restraining himself, though he may know that he is doing wrong.[12] To state this differently, a person may know, at the time the act was committed, the nature and quality of the act he was doing, and (or) that what he was doing was wrong, but because of a mental disease, he may have lost power to choose between right and wrong and to avoid doing the act, his free agency being at the time destroyed.[13] In another case, the court made this point about the irresistible impulse rule:

> The jury must be satisfied that at the time of committing the act, the accused, as a result of disease of the mind:
>
> (a) did not know the nature and quality of the act or
> (b) did not know that it was wrong or
> (c) was incapable of preventing himself from doing it.[14]

However, the irresistible impulse test was never adopted by a majority of states and has been rejected even by some states that had previously utilized it. One major criticism of the test is that it is hard to know whether or not the impulse was irresistible—the only thing that is known for sure is that the defendant did not resist it.

c. Durham Rule

In 1954, a District of Columbia court concluded that the proper solution was to discard all tests of insanity and have the jury determine: (a) whether the defendant had a mental disease or defect at the time of the alleged crime and, if so, (b) whether the harmful act was the *product* of his insanity.[15] This is known as the **Durham Rule**. Apparently the court took the position that the right-wrong test and the irresistible impulse test had not been displaced but were merely supplemented by the "product" test, and that it was proper for the jury to be instructed as to all three.[16]

The objective of the court was to simplify the test and to make it possible to use more modern methods of determining mental impairment or disease. This rule has been criticized because it provides no criteria to guide the jury, but hands the case to them for a verdict to be returned on the basis of intuition or conjecture, rather than law.[17] Many of the critics also believe that the test is too broad and leaves too much to the jury with inadequate guidance. Today the rule has only a limited following and has in fact been abandoned by the District of Columbia.[18]

d. A.L.I. Test (Model Penal Code)

Described earlier, this test expands the definition by allowing more testimony other than whether or not the defendant knew what he was doing or what he was doing was wrong. The test determines whether the defendant lacked "substantial capacity" to conform his behavior to the law. It allows the expert witness to discuss how the act was a product of the mental illness, and also allows for the defense of irresistible impulse. However, as stated above, it has not been adopted in the majority of jurisdictions.

2. Recent Issues and Applications

Andrea Yates drowned her five children in 2001 and was convicted of second-degree murder. She pled insanity and there was ample evidence that she was mentally ill: she had been under psychiatric care and had taken anti-psychotic medications in the past, her doctor testified she suffered from extreme postpartum depression and delusions. Five different mental health experts testified she did not know right from wrong or that she thought she was doing right by sending the children to God before she ruined their chances of getting into heaven. The state's psychiatrist, however, provided testimony that she met the legal definition of sanity. Texas, like many states, has a version of the *M'Naghten* rule. Defense attorneys agreed that she knew what she was doing when she drowned her children; however, they argued she did not know that it was wrong because she was under the delusion that she was protecting them. However, the state argued that she knew it was wrong because she called the police afterwards. Yates thought she was saving her children, but because she demonstrated knowledge of the wrongfulness of her action (by calling police), she was found sane.

Does the wrongfulness of the act refer to rational, legal knowledge, or "moral" knowledge? If someone in a delusional state thought they were saving the world by killing someone, but they knew that killing was against the law, they could be found sane, not insane, because most jurisdictions instruct the jury that the knowledge requirement relates to *legal or societal* definitions, not *moral* definitions. There have been some jurisdictions that allowed for an exception to this general rule when the defendant believed they were following a rule of God. The exception is consistent with the concept that the wrongfulness must be based on societal definitions arguably because the defendant would believe that God's commands would be supported by society.[19]

While most states follow, or have adapted, the *M'Naghten* rules or the Model Penal Code, some states and the federal government have formulated alternatives. After John Hinckley attempted to assassinate Ronald Reagan in 1981 and won an acquittal by reason of insanity, Congress passed the Insanity Defense Reform Act,[20] which abolished the irresistible impulse test and increased the burden of proof on the defendant to prove insanity to "clear and convincing" evidence rather than by a preponderance of the evidence. About 13 states now have adopted the "guilty but mentally ill" concept, which preserves the traditional insanity defense but provides an alternative to it. A jury can choose between a verdict of "not guilty by reason of insanity," which results in acquittal, or a verdict of "guilty but mentally ill," which will result in a sentence for the same term provided for a regular guilty verdict. The sentence, however, would be served in a state mental hospital.[21] Between 1979 and 1983 three states—Idaho, Montana, and Utah—passed legislation that restricted the admission of psychiatric evidence to the issue of *mens rea*, abolishing insanity as a separate affirmative defense.[22] What this means is that if the defendant knows what he is doing, whether or not they know it is wrong is irrelevant to the finding of guilt. Thus, someone who is in an active psychotic state and literally does not know that he is killing someone lacks any level of *mens rea* (purposeful, knowing, reckless or negligent), but the defendant who kills because voices tell him to do so or a woman who kills her child because she is "saving" the infant from the Devil, will be found guilty.[23]

Legal News

Andrea Yates was retried in Houston in June of 2006. Her conviction was overturned on appeal because of the testimony of a state psychiatrist-witness that there was a *Law and Order* television program episode about a woman who drowned her baby and was acquitted. The implication of the testimony was that Yates mimicked the crime in hopes that she would be acquitted. However, there was no such television show and the psychiatrist was either mistaken or intentionally misled the jury. Without the testimony, the new jury still was faced with the difficult question of whether she was insane. They decided she was. She was sent to a mental hospital after acquittal.

> **CASE:** *Clark v. Arizona,*
> **548 U.S. 735 (2006)**
>
> What were the issues in this case?
>
> What level of proof is necessary for the defendant to utilize the defense of insanity under Arizona's law?
>
> What was the Supreme Court holding?

In general, these changes in statutes have been upheld against constitutional challenges. For instance, an Indiana court upheld the state statute that permits the jury to find the defendant guilty but mentally ill, agreeing that the statute did not violate the equal protection clause and the statute had a rational relationship to a legitimate state interest in securing convictions and obtaining treatment for defendants who suffer from mental illness.[24] In *Ake v. Oklahoma*, the Supreme Court held that it was "highly doubtful" that due process required a state to have the insanity defense available to criminal defendants.[25] In the case of *State v. Searcy*, the Idaho Supreme Court upheld the constitutionality of the state statute that had abolished insanity as an affirmative defense. The court noted that previous U.S. Supreme Court cases have given the states broad discretion to determine the burden of proof to impose on the defendants raising the insanity defense.[26]

Today, very few states (Idaho, Kansas, Montana, and Utah) have completely discarded the traditional insanity defense. Even in those states, evidence of mental illness might be used to rebut the state's evidence of *mens rea* because mental illness may preclude a finding that the defendant was capable of the requisite premeditation or intent. There is considerable debate that continues over this difficult legal issue. The basic question is to what extent do we hold people responsible for their actions when it is clear that they suffer from mental disease or defect.

Legal News

In *Clark v. Arizona* (2006), a teenager who killed a police officer, believing that he was an alien, appealed his conviction for murder. According to Arizona law, evidence of mental illness could be used to attempt to show insanity, but not to show lack of *mens rea*. Even if he had been found insane, the verdict under Arizona law would have been "guilty but insane," and he would have been committed to a mental hospital. The Supreme Court ruled that Arizona's law regarding the insanity plea did not violate due process.

3. Incompetency to Stand Trial

The issue of mental impairment may first arise when determining whether the defendant is capable of making a proper defense, aiding his or her attorney, or securing evidence at the time of the trial. The test for incompetency was set forth in the case of *Dusky v. United States*, as follows:

> Whether he (accused) has sufficient present ability to consult with his lawyer with a reasonable degree of rational understanding and whether he has a rational as well as factual understanding of the proceedings against him.[27]

In the case of *Dunn v. Commonwealth*, a Kentucky court approved the test as follows:

> The test is whether he has substantial capacity to comprehend the nature and consequences of the proceeding pending against him and to participate rationally in his defense. It is not necessary that this determination be made by a jury.[28]

Although these standards are worded differently, most state requirements are basically the same—if an individual cannot help in his or her own defense, they cannot be forced to stand trial.[29] The typical result is that they are held in a mental facility until such time that they are proven competent. Case decisions have indicated that the Supreme Court continues to uphold the idea that a trial cannot proceed if the defendant is unable to understand the proceedings against him or her.[30] It is possible, however, that the defendant may be found competent to stand trial, and then, at trial, be found legally insane.

It should also be noted that there may be other reasons why a defendant is found incompetent to stand trial. The defendant may be mentally handicapped and not have sufficient cognitive abilities to understand the consequences of criminal prosecution. The defendant may have amnesia and may not be able to help in his or her own defense. It is also possible that the defendant is either injured or ill to the extent that they are unable to assist in their defense. In these cases, the prosecution cannot go forward.

D. Diminished Capacity

When someone does not meet the test for legal insanity, it is possible that their mental state affects the level of their *mens rea*. In this case, their culpability (and capacity) is not absent, but merely diminished. Thus, it may be found that they were unable to form the intent required for specific intent crimes, or that they could not form the *mens rea* required for murder, and thus manslaughter would be the appropriate finding. Diminished capacity is not a clear concept and states have different approaches as to how it can be brought in, as well as what types of evidence can be used for proof. As you read in *Clark v. Arizona*, the state of Arizona does not allow evidence of mental illness to be used to reduce the *mens rea* of homicide from specific intent to manslaughter. Some states allow such evidence only in homicide cases, others allow it only for specific intent crimes, while other states do not allow the defense at all (i.e., Arizona, Florida, D.C.). The so-called "Twinkie Defense" was coined in the 1979 trial of Dan White, a former San Francisco county supervisor who killed Mayor George Moscone and Supervisor Harvey Milk. Some aspects of this case were shown in the 2008 movie *Milk*, which focused on one of the victims, known today for being one of the first openly gay politicians. Defense attorneys presented evidence that White lived on a diet of soda, candy bars and Twinkies, and the diet created biochemical changes in his brain that reduced his ability to reason and control his behavior. There was also evidence that he suffered from manic depression. None of the evidence was sufficient to prove insanity; however, his defense was successful in reducing his culpability from first degree murder to voluntary manslaughter. The following presents a sampling of some of the types of diminished capacity defenses. Some of the "syndromes" below are not recognized in some states.

1. Premenstrual Syndrome (PMS) and Post Partum Depression Syndrome (PPD)

Premenstrual Syndrome (PMS) affects a small percentage of the population, but in its most extreme forms, has been associated with a form of psychosis. In England, it has been used successfully to acquit a defendant who killed her husband. It has had less success in this country as an accepted defense.[31]

Another syndrome that affects only women is Post Partum Depression (PPD) Syndrome. As discussed earlier, Andrea Yates suffered from this hormonal imbalance that, in its most severe form, can cause psychosis.

2. Intoxication

About one-third of states have statutorily barred the use of voluntary intoxication as a defense to any crime, and the Supreme Court, in *Montana v. Egelhoff*,[32] upheld these statutes. However, other states do allow evidence to be used to rebut the state's evidence that the defendant had the *mens rea* to commit the crime. Generally, such a defense only reduces culpability by reducing the level of *mens rea* from intentional to reckless or negligent. For instance, it may be possible to show extreme intoxication negated the ability to form intent for first degree murder, burglary, or robbery. This means, for instance, that the defendant might prove that he was extremely intoxicated, and therefore could not have formed the intent to murder.

> **CASE: *Montana v. Egelhoff*, 518 U.S. 37 (1996)**
>
> What was the holding of the case?
>
> What was evidence of intoxication used for?
>
> Why did the Supreme Court agree that the state of Montana could ignore such evidence?

Even in states that bar voluntary intoxication evidence, if the defendant can show that his intoxication was not voluntary, i.e., that he unknowingly ingested alcohol, then such evidence could be presented to show that he was incapable of forming the *mens rea* required for the crime.

3. Post-Traumatic Stress Syndrome

This phrase was first created in association with Vietnam veterans; however, the condition had different names in earlier wars (such as "shell-shocked" from World War II). Generally, the diagnosis is used for individuals who suffer from traumatic incidents or long periods of severe stress. Their symptoms may include flashbacks, dreams, sensory hallucinations and, in some cases, their delusions may cause them to commit crimes. Today, the diagnosis is used not just for returning soldiers, but for anyone who has experienced trauma and is experiencing some or all of the symptoms described above.

4. Battered Woman Syndrome

The Battered Woman Syndrome has been described as a type of post-traumatic stress syndrome because the victim has been subjected to a long period of severe stress that causes her, in some cases, to do extreme acts. However, it has also been described as a type of duress, as a type of self-defense, and as a type of temporary insanity. We describe the syndrome more fully in the section on duress.

E. Summary

From the foregoing, it is obvious that the questions relating to mental impairment as a defense to crime have not been resolved. At present it is safe to say that the majority of the states still follow the *M'Naghten* Rule with possibly some modifications. The other tests that are not used by a majority of the states are the Irresistible Impulse Test, the *Durham* Rule, and the Model Penal Code (A.L.I.) Rule. The three situations in which mental impairment is considered during adjudication are: a plea of incompetency at time of trial (whether the individual can be tried at all); an affirmative defense of insanity (usually with the *M'Naghten* Rule applied to determine whether insanity was present at the time of the offense); and at sentencing (as a mitigating factor). Diminished capacity defenses are used when the defendant is not legally insane, but his or her mental condition does call into question whether the required *mens rea* for the crime could be formed.

§ 3.4 Duress or Compulsion

What would ordinarily be a criminal act may be excused at law if the act is committed under **duress** or compulsion. Except in the case of homicide, an act that would otherwise constitute a crime may be excused when committed under duress or compulsion that is imminent, and produces a well-grounded apprehension of death or serious bodily harm.[33]

There are conditions to the application of this defense in criminal cases. The coercion must be of such a nature as to induce a well-grounded apprehension of death or serious bodily harm and there must be no reasonable escape without committing the crime.[34] Also, a threat of future injury is not enough to justify committing a crime. If there is a possibility of seeking help and avoiding the necessity of taking action, this avenue must be pursued. However, the theory that there must be a "gun to the head" is not a required condition to the application of this defense, as long as a threat is real.[35]

A. Common Law

The common law recognized duress or compulsion as a defense for some crimes, but not all. It did not recognize any compulsion, even the threat of instant death, as sufficient to excuse the intentional killing of an innocent person.[36] The common law rule is still recognized and has been incorporated in some of the statutes. For example, the common law rule was applied in the case of *Harris v. State* in 1977.[37] In this case, the court refused an instruction submitted by the defense that "if defendant was not intending any wrong, was swept along by a party of persons whom he did not resist, he would not be responsible for any wrong done if he was compelled to do the said wrong." The reviewing court stated that the instruction was properly refused when the defendant was indicted for murdering a prison guard during a riot. The court explained that the instruction was an incorrect statement of law for two reasons: First, the common law never allowed the compulsion defense for the taking of the life of an innocent person; and second, the defendant knew that the riot was about to occur and could have escaped from the cell block before it took place.

B. Model Penal Code

According to the comments following the Model Penal Code, at the time the Model Code was considered, 20 states had legislation dealing with the defense of duress in criminal cases. The Model Code recognizes some of the provisions of the state statutes in existence and also some of the common law exceptions.

---

§ 2.09 Duress[38]

(1) It is an affirmative defense that the actor engaged in the conduct charged to constitute an offense because he was coerced to do so by the use of, or a threat to use, unlawful force against his person or the person of another, that a person of reasonable firmness in his situation would have been unable to resist.

(2) The defense provided by this Section is unavailable if the actor recklessly placed himself in a situation in which it was probable that he would be subjected to duress. The defense is also unavailable if he was negligent in placing himself in such a situation whenever negligence suffices to establish culpability for the offense charged.

> (3) It is not a defense that a woman acted on the command of her husband, unless she acted under such coercion as would establish a defense under this Section. (The presumption that a woman acting in the presence of her husband is coerced is abolished.)
>
> (4) When the conduct of the actor would otherwise be justifiable under § 3.02, this Section does not preclude such defense.

Under the Model Code, the defense of duress is not established simply by the fact that the defendant was coerced; he must have been coerced in circumstances under which a person of reasonable firmness in his situation would likewise have been unable to resist. Subsection (2) of the Model Code deprives the actor of the duress defense if he recklessly places himself in a situation in which it was probable that he would be subject to duress.

C. State Statutes, Codes, and Cases

As stated before, duress is not available as a defense to murder.[39] In order for duress or compulsion to be recognized as a defense to criminal charges, the compulsion must come from an outside source and be of such a degree as to overcome the will of the actor. Applying this rationale, a North Dakota court affirmed a lower court's decision that the defendant's claim that he was compelled to commit robberies in order to provide money for his family for food and shelter did not constitute "duress" as a defense to robbery charges.[40]

Some state statutes deny the defense of duress to an individual who intentionally or wantonly places himself in a situation in which coercion is likely to be applied. For example, if a person joins criminal activity voluntarily and seeks exoneration for some act committed by him or her in the course of the activity by asserting that a companion threatened him or her with death, the defense of duress is not available.

In a Connecticut case, the court concluded that the defense of duress does not justify carrying a pistol without a permit.[41] A Missouri appeals court refused to allow the defense of duress alleged by a prisoner who claimed that his acts were forced by other prisoners. The court declared that the defense of duress is not available to a prisoner who could, but did not, seek the alternative of protective custody.[42]

Duress excuses criminal behavior where the defendant shows that the acts were the product of threats inducing a reasonable fear of immediate death or serious bodily injury. Where it is properly shown, duress is a complete defense to a crime.[43] The defense of duress requires that the perceived threat or use of unlawful force be against the actor or another person; it does not encompass threats made to or force used against a third party of which the actor was unaware.[44]

The threat must be imminent. In *State v. Rosillo*,[45] the defendant committed perjury because of threats to his and his family's life, but the threats were determined not to constitute an imminent threat, and, therefore, the defense of duress was rejected in his prosecution for perjury. In its application to the affirmative defense of duress, an "imminent threat" has two components of immediacy: first, the person making the threat must intend and be prepared to carry out the threat immediately, and second, carrying out the threat must be predicated on the threatened person's failure to commit the charged offense immediately.[46] Applying this standard, a court held that the alleged threat that the defendant and his family would be killed if the defendant did not rob a bank, made four days before the robbery, did not qualify as an "imminent threat" required for the affirmative defense of duress, even if the defendant believed no law enforcement agency could protect him, absent any showing that persons who made the threat intended or were prepared to carry it out immediately, or that they even gave the defendant any time frame for committing the robbery.

1. Battered Spouse/Woman Syndrome

Beginning in the late 1980s, the **"battered woman defense"** was developed as a type of duress defense. If an individual is defending oneself, the traditional affirmative defense/justification of "self-defense" can be used. However, in some cases of domestic violence, the victim does not use violence against the abuser during a violent episode, but rather during a time when the batterer is either asleep or otherwise incapacitated (i.e., intoxicated). By doing so, the victim/attacker precludes the use of self-defense because one element of the justification is that the threat be "imminent." *The Burning Bed* was a movie that presented the case of Francine Hughes, a woman who set her husband on fire while he was sleeping. In subsequent cases, women killed their abusers in similar situations; however, it is a myth that most battered women kill their abusers during times when the abuser is asleep or unable to defend himself. In fact, one study indicated that 75 percent of all cases in the sample involved killings during active confrontations.[47]

The battered woman syndrome/defense, as created and championed by Lenore Walker, a clinical social worker, argues that the victim in a consistent, serious pattern of abuse becomes "helpless" to escape, similar to victims of concentration camps. The victims attempt to escape the abuse, only to have their abuser threaten their children or their parents. Law enforcement seems unable to help and, therefore, the victim comes to feel there is no escape. At some point, some victims "snap" and, believing there is no way out of their abuse, kill the abuser. They may do so during a time when he is incapacitated because they are simply too frightened of him to fight back when he is threatening them.[48]

In the 1990s, in response to the increasing number of cases involving this issue, and in deference to the public's demand that these defendant-victims be accorded some relief, many legislative bodies codified new defenses, or amended existing ones, to permit defendant-victims to introduce evidence of their abuse as part of their defense. The new statutes came to be known in some jurisdictions as the "Battered Spouse Syndrome" defense and in other jurisdictions as the "Battered Woman Syndrome" defense.[49] Regardless of the name, defendant-victims were now, statutorily, permitted some leeway in linking their abusive past to a defense in a criminal trial.

In the majority of jurisdictions, the statutes did not create a new statutory defense, but rather permitted the introduction of evidence that the defendant-victim suffered from the syndrome in cases in which the defendant-victim was relying on the traditional and long-recognized defenses of self-defense, duress, necessity, or defense of others.[50] Most statutes permitted such evidence to be introduced through the expert testimony of a psychologist or psychiatrist.

As one court noted in describing the nature of the Ohio statute:

> A woman's status as a battered woman does not alter the evidentiary burden in establishing a self-defense claim in a homicide prosecution; but evidence of that status may be offered to assist the jury in determining whether the defendant acted out of a reasonable belief that she was in imminent danger of death or great bodily harm and that the use of force was the only means of escaping that danger.[51]

Generally, the defense is unavailable when a woman hires a third party to kill her abuser.[52]

A very different situation is when the battered woman uses duress as a defense to crimes other than assaulting or killing her abuser. In these cases, the defendant argues that her fear of the batterer compelled her to commit crimes. These are more similar to standard duress claims and, thus, the same elements, apply. Battered woman syndrome testimony may be allowed to show the reasonableness of her belief of imminent harm, a necessary component of a duress defense.[53] In *People v. Romero*, a California court overturned a robbery conviction and remanded for a new trial, ordering the court to consider evidence that the defendant was a battered spouse of her co-defendant and helped him commit the robberies under duress.[54]

D. Summary

The defense of duress has been an accepted defense since the common law, but it is very limited in its application. The defendant must be in imminent fear of bodily harm by another with no escape, the crime cannot be homicide (or probably any serious personal violent crime), and the defendant must not have been reckless in putting themselves in harm's way. The Battered Woman's defense is a special type of duress defense but is not universally recognized.

§ 3.5 Necessity (Choice of Evils)

Duress and **necessity** are somewhat similar defenses; however, while duress always involves fear of harm or intimidation, necessity is a broader defense that justifies criminal actions if the harm that will result from compliance with the law is greater than that which will result from violation of it. The traditional view is that the pressure or the factors that made the violation necessary must come from the physical forces of nature rather than from human beings. For instance, if one is trapped in a snowstorm on a mountaintop and the choice is to freeze to death or break into someone's cabin, the law allows the person to choose the criminal action (as long as there is compensation to the victim). However, the necessity defense, as is true with duress, will not allow one to sacrifice an innocent to save oneself or one's property. The classic necessity case is *Regina v. Dudley and Stephens*.[55] In this case, Dudley and Stephens were tried for the murder of another sailor. All three had been adrift in an open boat for 20 days and were starving. They killed and ate the victim because he was the youngest and the weakest and were rescued four days later. The court found that they would have most probably died if they had not committed the act and that the boy would have died before them; however, they were convicted because necessity was not recognized as a defense to murder. They were sentenced to death but the Crown commuted their sentence to six months' imprisonment.[56] A similar early case in the United States involved ship crewmen who threw 14 male passengers out of a lifeboat when it began taking on water to save other passengers and themselves. The court held that the defense of necessity was not applicable to their actions and their convictions of manslaughter were upheld.[57]

A. Common Law

The defense of necessity should be and has been very strictly applied. Under the common law, one may be justified by necessity in violating the law and causing harm in order to avoid a greater harm caused by complying with the law. However, this defense was not recognized unless the defendant acted with the intention of avoiding the greater harm, and it was for the court, not the defendant, to weigh the relative harmfulness of the two alternatives.

B. Model Penal Code

Section 3.02 of the Model Penal Code includes the recommended model statute relating to necessity under the title "Choice of Evils."

---

§ 3.02 Choice of Evils[58]

(1) Conduct that the actor believes to be necessary to avoid a harm or evil to himself or to another is justified, provided that:

   (a) the harm or evil sought to be avoided by such conduct is greater than that sought to be prevented by the law defining the offense charged; and

   (b) neither the Code nor other law defining the offense provides exceptions or defenses dealing with specific situations involved; and

   (c) a legislative purpose to exclude the justification claim does not otherwise plainly appear.

Under this provision of the Model Code, as in the common law and other statutes, the evil sought to be avoided must be greater than that sought to be prevented by the law defining the offense. Also, the legislature must not have previously foreclosed the choice that was made by resolving the conflict of values at stake. It is broader than the common law necessity defense in that it does not demand an immediate harm, nor is the emergency limited to natural forces or physical harm. Some examples in the commentary include property may be destroyed to prevent the threat of fire, a speed limit may be violated in pursuing a suspected criminal, and an ambulance may pass a traffic light.[59] The Model Penal Code expands the common law parameters of the necessity defense, but it is not universally accepted by the states.

C. State Statutes, Codes, and Cases

Some states apply the common law rule in dealing with the necessity defense issue. In about half of the states, statutes have been enacted to more specifically define the necessity defense. In Virginia[60] the court explained that the essential elements of the common law necessity defense include a reasonable belief that the action was necessary to avoid imminent threatened harm, lack of adequate means to avoid the threatened harm, and a direct causal relationship that may be reasonably anticipated between the action taken and avoidance of harm.

In Indiana, the court explained the elements of the necessity defense.[61] In order to prevail on a claim of necessity, the defendant must show:

- The act charged as criminal must have been done to prevent a significant evil.

- There must have been no adequate alternative to the commission of the act.

- The harm caused by the act must not be disproportionate to the harm avoided.

- The accused must entertain a good faith belief that this act was necessary to prevent greater harm.

- Such belief must be objectively reasonable under all the circumstances.

- The accused must not have substantially contributed to the creation of the emergency.

After stating these requirements, the court opined that reasonable options other than carrying a handgun to school were available to a juvenile, who claimed he did so in order to protect himself from threatened retaliation by members of his former gang.

In an Illinois case, the court comprehensively explained the conception of legal necessity. The defense of necessity does not negate any element of the crime, but represents the public policy decision not to punish someone, despite proof of the crime.[62] The court continued by stating that to invoke the defense of necessity, the defendant must show the immediacy of peril and that violating the law was the only reasonable action available to him under the circumstances; the situation must have been an emergency, must have threatened physical harm, and must have left the defendant with no legal alternative.

Examples of successful and unsuccessful uses of the necessity defense include:

- a convicted felon who is barred from possession of firearms grabs a gun from an aggressor to prevent him from using it (successful)[63]

- someone who steals food out of economic necessity (unsuccessful)[64]

- a defendant who kidnaps another to save them from a religious cult (unsuccessful)[65]

- defendants who leave their children in the car while they work when it is below freezing weather because they don't have a babysitter (unsuccessful)[66]

Recently there have been new and intriguing applications of the necessity defense, most of which have been met with little success in the courts.

1. Marijuana as a Medical Necessity

A growing number of people argue that marijuana is the only effective treatment for symptoms of medical conditions such as glaucoma, cancer (nausea), multiple sclerosis (pain), and AIDS (pain). In medical necessity cases, the defendants argue that medical necessity overcomes criminal drug laws and provides a defense to conviction for possession (if not distribution).[67] Although many states have statutes recognizing medical necessity, the Supreme Court has not recognized a medical necessity defense that overcomes the 1970 Controlled Substances Act; therefore a person may conform to state law but still be in violation of federal drug laws.[68] Proponents argue that the sole Supreme Court case involved distribution, not possession, and that it is possible the Court would be more sympathetic to a case of a seriously ill individual who possessed marijuana for their medical needs. More than a dozen states have legalized the medical use of marijuana; therefore, this issue will continue to be contentious.[69]

2. Escape from Prison to Avoid Injury

In a few cases, inmates have used duress or necessity as a defense to prison escape. In *People v. Lovercamp*,[70] the inmate successfully argued that his escape was to avoid an immediate rape, but the court offered a very narrow holding that required the threat to be imminent, that there be no alternatives, and that the inmate immediately turn himself in. A subsequent court refused to allow the defense in another case because the inmate did not immediately turn himself in to authorities.[71] Courts seem to disagree on whether the proper defense to escape prison conditions is necessity or duress; however, it is clear that whatever form the defense takes, it is limited to rare circumstances.[72]

3. Civil Disobedience to Prevent Government Wrongs

Can a protestor argue necessity when they violate a crime or a city ordinance in their opposition to government policy? They can, but they are rarely successful, because there are, arguably, other alternatives to committing a crime for one who is attempting to stop some governmental action.[73] In cases of direct acts of civil disobedience, the defendant violates a law that they believe to be unconstitutional (such as civil rights demonstrators who broke Jim Crow laws in the south). In cases of indirect civil disobedience, the demonstrator breaks some unrelated law (typically trespass, obstruction of justice, or failure to disperse), in the course of protesting a government action. In no case has indirect civil disobedience been successfully defended with the necessity defense.

D. Summary

In distinguishing between the defenses of compulsion or duress and necessity, an Illinois court advised that compulsion is a defense distinct from necessity; compulsion implies a complete deprivation of free will and absence of choice, while necessity involves choice between two or more admitted evils.[74] Both tend to be limited to property offenses and cannot be used to justify harming an innocent victim.

§ 3.6 Self-Defense

An act that might otherwise be a crime is not punishable if the act was committed in **self-defense**. The general rule is that a person is privileged to use force as reasonably appears necessary to defend himself or herself against an apparent threat of unlawful and immediate violence from another.

A. Common Law

The right to protect oneself, one's family, and one's "castle" is a time-honored right that existed before the common law and was recognized by it. The right to defend oneself in places other than one's home is a natural outgrowth of the "castle" defense. Availability of this privilege as a defense to a criminal charge depended, under common law, upon a showing that:

- the defendant believed physical force to be necessary for self-protection, or protection of another;

- his or her belief was based upon reasonable grounds;

- the threat of danger was imminent;

- the force used was not in excess of that believed necessary to repel the unlawful attack.

B. Model Penal Code

The Model Penal Code includes a comprehensive section relating to the use of force and self-protection.

> § 3.04 Use of Force in Self-Protection[75]
>
> (1) Use of Force Justifiable for Protection of the Person. Subject to the provisions of this Section and of Section 3.09, the use of force upon or toward another person is justifiable when the actor believes that such force is immediately necessary for the purpose of protecting himself against the use of unlawful force by such other person on the present occasion.

Under this section, the use of force upon or toward another person is justifiable when the actor believes that such force is immediately necessary for the purpose of protecting himself against the use of unlawful force by such other person on the present occasion. The actor's actual belief is sufficient to support the defense. The use of force is not justified to resist an arrest that the actor knows is being made by a police officer although the arrest is unlawful. Also, the use of deadly force is not justified if the actor can avoid the necessity of using such force with complete safety by taking certain alternative steps such as retreating, surrendering possession of the thing to a person asserting the claim of a right thereto, or complying with the demand that he abstain from action that he has no duty to take.

C. *State Statutes, Codes, and Cases*

The elements relating to self-defense are somewhat different from state to state. It is important to be familiar with the case decisions in any particular jurisdiction that refine the basic elements of self-defense.

1. Fear of Physical Harm to Self or Another

Self-defense is most often claimed as a defense in homicide or assault cases. To establish self-defense, a defendant must show some evidence that unlawful force was threatened against him, the danger of serious harm was imminent, he was not the aggressor, he fully believed that danger existed, force was necessary to avert the danger, and the type and amount of force used was necessary.

2. Reasonableness of Fear

The jury is required to determine whether the defendant's perception of the need for self-defense, or the degree of force that was used, was reasonable.[76] For example, in an aggravated assault case, the court found that it was reversible error to refuse to allow the defendant to show that there had been a long-standing dispute with the victim and the victim's brother over a $400 debt.[77] In this case, the victim was outside in a car while his brother went to the defendant's door to collect a debt. The defendant came outside and fired three shots at the victim. Days before the incident, the victim had broken the defendant's nose. The trial court had refused to admit evidence that the victim's brother had waved a gun at the defendant and threatened to shoot him nine months before the incident. This refusal, according to the court, was error and the conviction was reversed. The court pointed out that the testimony bore on the issue of self-defense; and although the victim himself had not communicated the threat, it was relevant to prove the hostility of both the brothers.

On the one hand, if the test applied is an objective "reasonable man" test, the jury must find that a reasonable person, placed in the defendant's situation, would have experienced fear. On the other hand, a subjective test allows the jury to determine whether the defendant experienced fear, whether or not such fear was reasonable. Even in states that use an objective reasonableness standard, there is some opinion that there should be a "reasonable woman" standard that is different from a reasonable man standard allowing for differences in size and strength between the sexes.[78]

A Connecticut court, in a comprehensive statement, held that subjective-objective inquiry into the defendant's belief regarding the necessary degree of force to repel the victim's alleged attack requires the jury to make two separate affirmative determinations for the defendant's claim of self-defense to succeed: (1) the jury must determine whether, on the basis of all evidence presented, the defendant in fact believed that he needed to use deadly physical force, as opposed to some lesser degree of force, to repel the victim's alleged attack; and (2) if the jury determines that the defendant in fact believed that the use of deadly force was necessary, the jury must make a further determination as to whether that belief was reasonable, from the perspective of a reasonable person in the defendant's circumstances.[79]

If the defendant's fear was unreasonable but honest, he is not entitled to the absolute defense of self-defense; however, some states may allow a finding that his culpability is reduced from homicide to manslaughter.[80] This finding is not a recognition of self defense per se, but rather a finding that the *mens rea* elements of murder are missing.

3. Imminence of Danger

Under the statutes and case law, the person claiming self-defense must show evidence that he or she reasonably perceived an "imminent" danger. If the danger is to take place some time in the future and can be avoided, then the defense will not prevail.

The most famous self-defense case is *People v. Goetz*.[81] In that case, Goetz shot and wounded four African-American teenagers in a subway car in New York due to a fear that they were about to rob him. The only words that passed between him and his victims were when they asked him for money. He perceived the request as a precursor to a robbery; they testified that they were not planning to rob anyone, although two were carrying screwdrivers, which they admitted they used to break into coin boxes. He was indicted, appealed his indictment, and the Court of Appeals of New York upheld the indictment, but a jury acquitted him of aggravated assault and attempted murder, although he was convicted for unlawful possession of a weapon. In 1996, Goetz lost a civil suit against him by one of the youths who was paralyzed by the shooting.

4. Proportionality of Force Used

The amount of force that may be justifiable must be reasonably related to the threatened harm that the user seeks to avoid. One may justifiably use deadly force against another in self-defense only if the person using the force reasonably believes that the other is about to inflict unlawful death or serious bodily harm, and that it is necessary to use the deadly force to prevent it.[82]

5. "Clean Hands"

Another element of self defense that is fairly consistent throughout the states is that the defendant is barred from using self-defense if he started the incident that led to the imminent danger. Generally, those who start a "bar room brawl" will not be able to use self-defense to excuse their culpability unless they can show that they made a substantial effort to get away or stop the fracas. This is known as the "clean hands" doctrine.

In a 1997 case, a South Carolina court interpreted the requirements by stating that to establish self-defense, the defendant must prove: (1) he was without fault in bringing on the difficulty; (2) he actually believed he was in imminent danger of losing his life or sustaining serious bodily injury; (3) a reasonably prudent person of ordinary firmness and courage would have entertained the same belief; and (4) he had no other probable means of avoiding the danger.[83]

6. Duty to Retreat

State courts have disagreed on the obligation to attempt to retreat before responding with force or deadly physical force to repel the attack. In an early case, Justice John M. Harlan is quoted as stating that "he was not obligated to retreat, nor to consider whether he could safely retreat, but was entitled to stand his ground and meet attack upon him with a deadly weapon."[84] And in a Kentucky case, the court held that, "it is the tradition that a Kentuckian never runs. He does not have to."[85] A South Carolina court noted that a person attacked on his own premises, without fault, has the right to claim immunity from the law of retreat.[86]

On the other hand, some courts look upon the duty to retreat with more favor. A Louisiana court, in discussing the duty to retreat, stated that while there is no unqualified duty to retreat from an altercation, the possibility of escape is a recognized factor in determining whether a defendant had a reasonable belief whether deadly force was necessary to avoid the danger, to support a claim of self-defense on a homicide charge.[87]

Some courts have made it quite clear that there is a duty to retreat before using deadly force in self-defense. A Florida court explained that a person may use deadly force in self-defense if he or she reasonably believes that deadly force is necessary to prevent imminent death or great bodily harm; however, even under those circumstances, a person may not resort to deadly force without first using every reasonable means within his or her power to avoid the danger, including retreat. The court noted in this case that the duty to retreat before using self-defense emanates from common law, rather than from statute.[88] An earlier Florida court had held that before taking a life, the combatant must retreat to the wall using all means in his or her power to avoid that need.[89]

Even in states that recognize a duty to retreat, the "castle exception" indicates that one is not obligated to retreat if the threat occurs within the parameters of one's own home. Thus, an intruder who poses an imminent threat of bodily harm may be met with force without having to retreat out of the home or within the home to a different room.[90]

7. "Make-My-Day" Laws and Defense of Property

Named after Clint Eastwood's famous quote in the "Dirty Harry" movie, these laws allow the use of deadly force to protect one's home. Recall that, under common law, individuals had a right to use deadly force to prevent entry. Generally, statutory definitions of the right of self-defense restricted its use to fear of grievous bodily harm. The Model Penal Code allowed the use of deadly force in order to prevent serious crimes (such as arson, burglary, robbery or theft) if the force was immediately necessary and the other person had previously used deadly force against the defendant or another person or there was substantial risk of injury. Make-my-day statutes expand self-defense in that an individual is privileged to use deadly force against a home intruder in situations where the user of lethal force does not feel an immediate threat from the person who made the unlawful entry, as long as there is a reasonable belief that a crime is intended. Colorado's law, for instance, states that:

> . . . any occupant of a dwelling is justified in using any degree of physical force, including deadly physical force, against another person when that person has made an unlawful entry into the dwelling, and when the occupant has a reasonable belief that such other person has committed a crime in the dwelling in addition to the uninvited entry, or is committing or intends to commit a crime against a person or property in addition to the uninvited entry, and when the occupant reasonably believes that such other person might use any physical force, no matter how slight, against any occupant . . .[91]

Case law has generally prohibited the use of spring guns or devices that would harm someone attempting an illegal entry because they are not capable of distinguishing a burglar from a fire fighter or other person who may have a justification for entry. Another reason such devices are illegal is that the homeowner is only privileged to use deadly force in cases where there is a serious risk to self; in some cases of children breaking in with no weapons, no such risk presents itself and, therefore, the use of lethal force is unwarranted. Recently, however, more than a dozen states have passed "stand my ground" laws that allow the use of lethal force to protect against all felonies that involve one's home or automobile, including property crimes.

Legal News

In a 2008 case, a south Texas man was prosecuted for murder after he caught four boys ranging in age from 11 to 15 burglarizing a mobile home on his property. A victim of several burglaries, the homeowner had a shotgun and ordered the boys to their knees. He then shot one of the boys in the back and ordered the others to take the body outside. The homeowner said the boy was lunging at him; the boys said that he shot the victim and then kicked him. The murder trial of the homeowner resulted in an acquittal, largely because Texas has a "defense of property statute" that allows a homeowner to use deadly force to protect his or her property. A similar case in Houston, where a man shot and killed two burglars outside his neighbor's house despite the order of a police dispatcher to stay inside his house, resulted in an aquittal as well.

Source: "Verdict: Prosecutor Said Case About When Deadly Force is Justified." *Austin American-Statesman*, September 28, 2008: B1, B6.

---

8. Right to Resist Unlawful Force by Police

Self-defense is often claimed by a defendant who is charged with assaulting a law enforcement officer. In a Rhode Island case, the court held that a defendant has a right to defend himself when police use excessive force against him in placing him under arrest.[92] Whether the defendant has a right of self-defense against the police naturally depends upon whether there was excessive force in effecting the arrest. If the arresting officer uses reasonable force, the privilege of self-defense is inapplicable. However, some states and the federal statutes provide that an arrestee does not have the right to defend himself even when the police use excessive force.[93]

The reverse situation is what level of force police officers are privileged to use in effecting an arrest. Generally, police officers are justified in using deadly force for the same reason civilians are—for self-defense. Under common law, officers had the right to use deadly force against "fleeing felons," but that right has been rejected under modern law. In *Tennessee v. Garner*, the Supreme Court held that officers could not use deadly force to capture fleeing felons who did not pose a risk to the officers or others.[94]

D. Summary

Self-defense has been recognized since common law. Generally, people have the legal right to defend themselves or others against an imminent danger. The general elements of self-defense are that the fear must be: of bodily harm, reasonable, and the danger must be imminent. Also, the defendant cannot have instigated the danger, and in some states, there is a duty to retreat before resorting to force.

§ 3.7 Entrapment

In the early 1980s, members of Congress caught in the ABSCAM scandal claimed that the government had *created* rather than *uncovered* criminal conduct. Seven defendants, including four former members of the House of Representatives, failed to convince the court that they were victims of entrapment or that the agents responsible for ABSCAM acted "outrageously." The U.S. Court of Appeals for the Third Circuit agreed that the action by the U.S. government agents did not amount to **entrapment.** In the case before that court, the facts were as follows. The investigators, posing as representatives of an Arab sheik, told the defendants that the sheik was interested in building a hotel in Philadelphia, but that he wanted to make sure of having friends in high places to take care of any problems that might develop. A defendant, Schwartz, accepted a $30,000 payment from the agents and Congressman Jannotti received $10,000. The court found that the evidence presented at the trial, particularly the videotapes showing the defendant taking the payments, supported a jury's finding of predisposition.[95]

In subsequent years, governmental actions in undercover drug operations and in investigating and apprehending purveyors of obscenity have come under scrutiny most often. The entrapment defense argues that even if the defendant *committed* the crime, he or she should not be punished because government agents *created* the crime.

Legal News

Congressman William Jefferson (D-LA) may use the defense of entrapment in his bribery trial, due to begin in 2009. In an FBI sting, he was found to have received money from a start-up company, allegedly for his influence in helping them get business. A search of his home uncovered $90,000 in cash in his freezer. He lost his bid for reelection in November of 2008 by a slim margin.

Source: www.nola.com/news/index.ssf/2009/01/william_jefferson_bribery_tri.html

A. Common Law

Entrapment, as a defense to criminal culpability, is not a legacy of the common law. The defense of entrapment was first recognized by the U.S. Supreme Court in *Sorrells v. United States* in 1932. In the *Sorrells* case, Chief

Justice Hughes noted that merely to afford an opportunity or facilities for the commission of the offense does not defeat the prosecution. The majority continued with this:

> However, a different question is presented when the criminal design originates with the officials of the government and they implant in the mind of an innocent person the disposition to commit the alleged offense and induce its commission in order that they may prosecute.[96]

The views of the U.S. Supreme Court were solidified in *Sherman v. United States* in 1958.[97] *Sorrels* and *Sherman,* taken together, were said to create an entrapment "test" that looked to government action to determine whether entrapment occurred. If government agents played too large a role, for instance, by providing essential ingredients or creating the idea of the crime and providing all the materials for it, then they have "entrapped" the defendant and the defendant carries less culpability than the government agents for the crime.

This so-called objective test was supplanted by the "subjective test" in *United States v. Russell.*[98] In *Russell*, the Supreme Court changed the focus of the test from government actions to the "predisposition" of the offender. If the offender was predisposed to commit the crime, then it did not matter what the government did. Only when the offender was a true innocent who had no predisposition could entrapment serve as a defense under this new test of entrapment.

B. Model Penal Code

The Model Penal Code utilized elements of both the objective and subjective entrapment tests. It designates two ways in which a public law enforcement official or person acting in cooperation with such an official can perpetrate an entrapment. The first is by making representations known to be false for the purpose of inducing a belief that the conduct is not prohibited by law (this would be a type of objective test but one that is very specific). The second is by employing methods of persuasion that create a substantial risk that such offense would be committed by persons other than those who are ready to commit it (this is a predisposition test). However, the Model Penal Code has an exception that denies the defense in situations in which the defendant causes or threatens bodily injury to someone other than the person perpetrating the entrapment.

> § 2.13 Entrapment[99]
>
> (1) A public law enforcement official or a person acting in cooperation with such an official perpetrates an entrapment if for the purpose of obtaining evidence of the commission of an offense, he induces or encourages another person to engage in conduct constituting such offense by either:

(a) making knowingly false representations designed to induce the belief that such conduct is not prohibited; or

(b) employing methods of persuasion or inducement that create a substantial risk that such an offense will be committed by persons other than those who are ready to commit it.

(2) Except as provided in Subsection (3) of this Section, a person prosecuted for an offense shall be acquitted if he proves by the preponderance of evidence that his conduct occurred in response to an entrapment. The issue of entrapment shall be tried by the Court in the absence of the jury.

(3) The defense afforded by this Section is unavailable when causing or threatening bodily injury is an element of the offense charged and the prosecution is based on conduct causing or threatening such injury to a person other than the person perpetrating the entrapment.

C. State Statutes, Codes, and Cases

While many states choose to rely upon the entrapment defense as defined by state and federal appellate courts, some states have enacted statutes that codify the defense. One such statute is that of Colorado.

COLO. REV. STAT. § 18-1-709[100]

The commission of acts which would otherwise constitute an offense is not criminal if the defendant engaged in the proscribed conduct because he was induced to do so by a law enforcement official or other person acting under his direction, seeking to obtain that evidence for the purpose of prosecution, and the methods used to obtain that evidence were such as to create a substantial risk that the acts would be committed by a person who, but for such inducement, would not have conceived or engaged in conduct of the sort induced. Merely affording a person an opportunity to commit an offense is not entrapment even though representations or inducements calculated to overcome the offender's fear of detection are used.

This statute and other state statutes make it clear that merely affording the person an opportunity to commit an offense is not entrapment.[101] The line between police conduct that amounts to entrapment and merely affording an opportunity for the defendant to commit the offense is often a fine one. In showing the willingness of the defendant to engage in criminal conduct, especially in conduct involving illegal drugs, the question arises as to whether evidence of prior use of illegal drugs is admissible. The general rule is that a defendant's previous unlawful involvement with a controlled substance can be given consideration when evaluating his predisposition to commit other narcotics offenses. In *State v. Eib*, evidence was introduced to show that the appellant sold cocaine on two different occasions to a Kansas City police officer, after the transactions were negotiated by a police informant. After arrangements were made by the informant, the appellant handed the officer cocaine, which was contained in clear plastic bags, and received $300 for the cocaine. On appeal, the defendant claimed that the sale was the result of entrapment by the officer and the informant. The reviewing court, however, noted that "to show entrapment, the defendant must show both unlawful mental inducement to engage in unlawful conduct and his lack of predisposition." The reviewing court, in determining what evidence is admissible to show predisposition, held that a "defendant's unlawful involvement with a controlled substance can be given consideration when evaluating his previous position to commit other narcotics offenses." The court continued by stating that "more specifically the defendant's prior use of other illegal drugs constitutes substantial evidence of predisposition in cases involving the sale of narcotics."[102]

It has been argued that the predisposition test bars a defendant from ever utilizing the entrapment defense if they have prior convictions. For instance, if a former drug addict is enticed to sell drugs to an undercover officer, can he ever argue that he was not predisposed to drug use and sales? The distinction between what is or is not entrapment has been articulated in many cases:

- To rely upon the entrapment defense, the defendant must, as a threshold matter, present evidence that the government conduct created a substantial risk that the offense would be committed by a person other than one ready to commit it, and if the defendant succeeds in meeting this burden, the government must prove beyond a reasonable doubt that the defendant was predisposed to commit the offense.[103]

- The essence of the offense of entrapment occurs where the evil intent and the criminal design of the offense originate in the mind of the government agent, and the defendant would not have committed an offense of that character except for the urging of the agent.[104]

- Entrapment may be found on the basis of reprehensible police conduct if the furnishing of the opportunity for a target to commit an offense requires the police to commit certain criminal, dangerous, or immoral acts.[105]

Entrapment is an affirmative defense, which means that the defendant must affirmatively raise the defense and offer some level of proof before the state is required to offer evidence or rebut the alleged entrapment.[106]

The federal government and most states follow some version of the subjective predisposition test. However, a minority of states continue to apply the objective test and a few combine the tests and require that the defendant prove both elements (government activity and lack of predisposition) and at least one state (New Mexico) requires the defendant to prove either one or the other.[107]

CASE: *Jacobson v. United States,* **503 U.S. 540 (1992)**

What was the holding of the case?

What did the federal agents do to entrap Jacobsen?

What was the evidence that indicated he did not have a predisposition?

D. Summary

Entrapment is an affirmative defense. Once the defendant has made out a *prima facie* case to raise the issue of entrapment, the government bears the burden of proving beyond a reasonable doubt that the defendant was not entrapped. In most states, once the defendant offers some proof of entrapment, the government must establish that the defendant had a predisposition, independent of government action, to commit the crime.

§ 3.8 Ignorance or Mistake

There are two types of mistakes—mistake about the legality of an action ("I didn't know it was against the law") and mistake about an essential fact ("I didn't know the goods were stolen"). Mistake of law is rarely successful as a defense; mistake of fact (if honest and reasonable) is likely to excuse criminal culpability if it negates an element of the offense.

A. Common Law

Generally ignorance of the law or *mistake of the law* is no excuse for violating it. Mistake about the law is disallowed as a defense because of practical considerations. It would be very difficult to prove, in every situation, that the person charged with a violation of the law knew the law.

Under common law, if there is an honest and reasonable *mistake of fact*, such ignorance or mistake of fact may exempt a person from criminal liability, unless the mistake arose from want of proper care on the part of the accused. The question as to whether a person acts in good faith, honestly, and without fault or negligence is determined by the circumstances as they appear to the person when the mistake is made and the effect that the surrounding circumstances might reasonably be expected to have on his or her mind in forming the intent, criminal or otherwise, upon which he or she acted.[108] The mistake-of-fact defense requires a showing that the mistaken belief is not the result of negligence or fault of the defendant.[109]

If there is a mistake of fact, a person will be relieved of criminal liability only if his or her belief is of such a nature that the conduct would have been lawful had the facts been as he or she reasonably supposed them to be. The classic example of a mistake of fact defense is when someone mistakenly takes another's coat from a restaurant. Taking possession of the property of another is ordinarily theft, but since the *mens rea* of theft is *intentionally* taking the property of another, the mistake negates the *mens rea* requirement.

B. Model Penal Code

The Model Penal Code views mistakes of fact as relevant to a finding of *mens rea*.

Section 2.04. Ignorance or Mistake[110]

(1) Ignorance or mistake as to a matter of fact or law is a defense if:

    (a) the ignorance or mistake negatives the purpose, knowledge, belief, recklessness or negligence required to establish a material element of the offense; or

    (b) the law provides that the state of mind established by such ignorance or mistake constitutes a defense.

(2) Although ignorance or mistake would otherwise afford a defense to the offense charged, the defense is not available if the defendant would be guilty of another offense had the situation been as he supposed. In such case, however, the ignorance or mistake of the defendant shall reduce the grade and degree of the offense of which he may be convicted to those of the offense of which he would be guilty had the situation been as he supposed.

(3) A belief that conduct does not legally constitute an offense is a defense to a prosecution for that offense based upon such conduct when:

    (a) the statute or other enactment defining the offense is not known to the actor and has not been published or otherwise reasonably made available prior to the conduct alleged; or

    (b) he acts in reasonable reliance upon an official statement of the law, afterward determined to be invalid or erroneous, contained in (i) a statute or other enactment; (ii) a judicial decision, opinion or judgment; (iii) an administrative order or grant of permission; or (iv) an official interpretation of the public officer or body charged by law with responsibility for the interpretation, administration or enforcement of the law defining the offense.

(4) The defendant must prove a defense arising under Subsection (3) of this Section by a preponderance of evidence.

Because the Model Penal Code is much more specific in the *mens rea* required for each crime, mistakes are easier to deal with. If the defendant's honest mistake negates the required *mens rea*, then it is a defense. If a defendant is mistaken, for instance, in a victim's consent to sexual intercourse, but he is reckless in his belief that she consents, then he is still guilty if the requisite *mens rea* is purposeful, knowing, or reckless. If the defendant is mistaken in her honest belief that the property she acquires is not stolen, then she cannot be guilty of receipt of stolen property because the requisite *mens rea* is knowing.

The Model Penal Code also covers the situation of undercover operations and drug dealers or smugglers who are mistaken in their belief about the substance they are dealing with. If a drug dealer purchases or sells to anyone a substance that he believes to be a drug, or smuggles in a substance he believes to be a drug, but the substance is really powdered sugar, sheetrock or some other non-contraband, then Subsection 2 applies because the defendant would have been committing a crime if the circumstances had been as he thought they were.

C. State Statutes, Codes, and Cases

1. Mistake of Law

In general, state statutes have followed common law in that ignorance of the law is no excuse. However, when specific intent (instead of general intent) is the *mens rea* of the crime charged, then ignorance of the law negates the existence of such intent.[111] For instance, for laws that make it a crime to intentionally violate an open meetings law, then the general intent to meet is not sufficient, and there must be evidence that the defendant knew of the law and intended to violate it.

There also is a small exception to this general rule when the law in question is so obscure that a "reasonable person" would not be expected to know of it. The Supreme Court has held that if the law is so technical or obscure that it threatens to ensnare innocent people, then it violates due process protections.[112] Examples of mistake of law defenses would be:

- defendant erroneously believes a type of gambling is not prohibited by a state's gambling laws (unsuccessful defense)

- defendant erroneously believes that seatbelts are not required for passengers (unsuccessful defense)

- defendant depended on Attorney General's written opinion that his actions were not in violation of the law (successful defense).

2. Mistake of Fact

Some states have codified the mistake-of-fact defense. For example, the Georgia statute provides:

> A person shall not be found guilty of a crime if the act or omission to an act constituting the crime was induced by misapprehension of fact which, if true, would have justified the act or omission.[113]

In interpreting this statute, the Court of Appeals of Georgia decided that the defendant's testimony that he knew the arresting officers were police officers, but he did not believe that they had a warrant for his arrest, did not constitute a valid "mistake of fact" defense to the charge of obstruction of an officer.[114] The court said that this was a misapprehension of law rather than fact. Examples of mistake of fact are:

- defendant erroneously believed that the horse he took from the field was his (successful)

- defendant erroneously believed that the woman he was having sex with had consented (perhaps successful if belief is reasonable)

- defendant erroneously believed that house he was burning down belonged to his mother-in-law (unsuccessful because it does not negate any element of the *mens rea* of arson)

D. Summary

In general, mistakes of law are generally not a defense unless the crime requires specific intent. Mistakes of fact may be a defense if they negate an element of the crime.

§ 3.9   Alibi

It has been argued that **alibi** is not really an excuse or justification as are all the other defenses described in this chapter since in these cases, the defendant admits he committed the crime but that he had a reason (or excuse). In alibi defenses, on the other hand, the defendant argues that he did not commit the offense.

A. Common Law

Because in the defense of alibi the defendant is arguing that he was at another place at the time of the crime, the defense has been recognized from the time of common law. The argument that still continues is whether it is an affirmative defense (which involves shifting burdens of proof on the part of the prosecutor and defendant), or is simply a negation of an element of the crime.

B. Model Penal Code

The Model Penal Code does not include any provisions for alibi defenses under either Section 2 (General Principles of Liability) or Section 3 (General Principles of Justification).

C. State Statutes, Codes, and Cases

The defense of alibi is universally recognized, but safeguards have been established to avoid the abuse of this defense. For example, it is not enough for the accused to say that he was not at the scene of the crime; he must show that he was at another specified place at the time the crime was committed.[115]

The Latin term *alibi* means "elsewhere." It is a defense that places the defendant, at the relevant time, in a different place from the location involved in the crime as to render it impossible for the defendant to be the guilty party. In the context of a criminal prosecution, *alibi* denotes an attempt by the defendant to demonstrate that he or she did not commit the crime because, at the time, he or she was in another place or so far away or in a situation preventing the defendant from doing the act charged against him or her.[116]

Although the state retains the burden to prove each element of the crime charged, it need not offer evidence directly showing that the alibi was fabricated; it is sufficient if, by the introduction of evidence inconsistent with the proffered alibi, the prosecution is able to establish the factual predicates necessary to support a conviction.[117]

While some courts indicate that alibi is an affirmative defense that attempts to negate elements of the crime charged, others insist that alibi is not an affirmative defense, but that the fact of the defendant's presence elsewhere is an affirmative fact logically operative to negate his presence at the time and place of the crime.[118]

In explaining the alibi defense, one court, quoting other cases, commented:

> In the context of a criminal prosecution, "alibi" denotes an attempt by the defendant to demonstrate he "did not commit the crime because at the time he was in another place so far away, or in a situation preventing his doing the thing charged against him . . . Strictly speaking, *alibi evidence* is merely rebuttal evidence directed to that part of the state's evidence which tends to identify the defendant as the person who committed the alleged crime."

In acknowledging that the alibi defense is not truly an independent affirmative defense, the court noted that it is simply evidence in support of the defendant's plea of not guilty and should not be treated merely as evidence tending to disprove one of the essential factors in the case of the prosecution.[119]

If the defendant is successful in convincing the judge or jury that he or she was at another place and that he or she therefore could not have committed the crime, the "alibi" defense is a complete defense and precludes the possibility of guilt. However, there is no obligation on the part of the trial court to believe the alibi testimony over positive identification of the accused, even though the alibi testimony may be given by a greater number of witnesses.[120]

The defendant may claim the defense of alibi at the trial even though he or she did not tell the police or district attorney that he or she had an alibi defense. In one case, the defendant was convicted of robbery, attempted robbery, assault, and criminal possession of a weapon. At the trial, the defendant presented an alibi defense. The district attorney encouraged the jury to infer that the alibi defense was a recent fabrication because the defendant was silent about the alibi from the time of his arrest until trial. The appellate division reversed the defendant's conviction, pointing out that a defendant has no obligation, when in custody, to tell either the police or the district attorney that he has an alibi defense.[121]

D. Summary

The only real issue in the defense of alibi is whether it is a true affirmative defense or simply an argument as to the lack of one of the elements of the crime. All states recognize the defense of alibi but the defendant must, in order to present a prima facie case of alibi, cover the time of the crime exactly. Further, the jury or judge is free to weigh the credibility of the alibi evidence against other evidence, as is true in all aspects of trial evidence. This is the only defense where the defendant's position is one of actual innocence.

§ 3.10 Time Limitations (Statute of Limitations)

A defendant charged with a crime may claim that he should not be tried for that offense because the time limitation for prosecution has expired. This is often referred to as the **statute of limitations** defense. The rationale for the time limitations is that the defendant should have some substantial safeguards against an erroneous conviction because of the staleness of the evidence and because the defendant is entitled to a speedy trial. Therefore, when the defendant claims that the statutory period has expired, the guilt or innocence of the defendant is not an issue. If the statutory period has expired, the defendant is entitled to an acquittal as a matter of right.

Generally speaking, a statute of limitations begins to run as soon as the offense is completed. While determining the date of the crime ordinarily is not difficult, in some instances this can cause a problem, especially in drug-related cases in which several offenses are committed over a period of time.

As a general rule, the time begins to run when the crime is committed and runs until the prosecution is commenced. Depending upon the provisions of the statute, the running of the time is stopped by the filing of an indictment or information or at the time a complaint is laid before a magistrate and a warrant of arrest is issued.[122]

It is obvious that justice would not be served if the defendant conceals himself or otherwise makes it impossible for an investigation to take place or for the prosecution to commence. To overcome this possibility, statutes have been enacted that provide that if the person who has committed the offense is absent from the state, or so conceals himself that process cannot be served upon him, or conceals the fact of the crime, the time of the absence or concealment is not to be included in computing the period of limitations. This is often referred to as tolling the statute of limitations.

A. *Common Law*

Since statutes of limitation are identified by statute, common law is not relevant to the defense.

B. *Model Penal Code*

The Model Penal Code includes a time limitation for all offenses, including felonies and misdemeanors, with the exception of murder. In the case of murder, the prosecution may be commenced at any time. This recommended statute specifies four periods of limitation:

- six years for felonies of the first degree
- three years for less serious felonies
- two years for misdemeanors
- six months for petty misdemeanors and violations.

The Model Penal Code also includes a subsection that defines when an offense is commenced for statute of limitations purposes and indicates specifically when the statute of limitations does not run.[123]

C. *State Statutes, Codes, and Cases*

Most jurisdictions have enacted statutes to limit the time for the commencement of some criminal proceedings. These statutes vary in their terms and almost always provide that a prosecution for murder may be commenced at any time. Some statutes provide that the prosecution for *any* felony is not subject to a period of limitations and may be commenced at any time. An example of the latter provision is that of Kentucky. The Kentucky statute provides:

K.R.S. 500.050 Time Limitations[124]

(1) Except as otherwise expressly provided, the prosecution of a felony is not subject to a period of limitation and may be commenced at any time.

(2) Except as otherwise expressly provided, the prosecution of an offense other than a felony must be commenced within one year after it is committed.

(3) For the purpose of this Section, an offense is committed either when every element occurs, or if a legislative purpose to prohibit a continuing course of conduct plainly appears, at the time in the course of conduct of the defendant's complicity therein is terminated.

The statute of limitations exists primarily to ensure against the inevitable prejudice and injustice to a defendant occasioned by delay in prosecution. The statute of limitations strikes a balance between an individual's interest in being placed on notice to formulate a defense for a crime charged, and the state's interest in having sufficient time to investigate and develop its case. One court noted that any exceptions to the limitation period must be construed narrowly and in a light most favorable to the accused.[125] The state bears the burden of showing that there has been a just and legal cause for the interruption of the "tolling" of the time period, for instance, by the defendant's flight and/or concealment from the jurisdiction.[126] In these cases, the government must prove, by a preponderance of the evidence, that the accused acted with the intent to avoid arrest or prosecution.[127]

§ 3.11   Other Defenses

1. Acting under the Authority or Direction of Others

Those who are charged with crimes often seek to justify their actions by explaining that they acted because they were ordered to do so. This defense is very difficult to demonstrate, especially when one acts under the authority of a military or quasi-military commanding officer. However, the general law is that, except insofar as the element of duress or compulsion may be present, the fact that one undertakes a crime or performs a criminal act under the authority or direction of a supervisor, one nevertheless is responsible for that act.[128]

An exception to the general law is recognized where a statute provides that a layperson acting on the orders of a peace officer is immune from prosecution for violations so committed. This defense applies only if the person accused is acting directly under the order of the police officer who is at that time carrying out his or her assigned responsibilities.[129]

2. Immunity

At least in some states, a witness who is granted immunity by the prosecutor may claim this as a defense if charged with a crime for which the immunity was granted. For example, if the prosecutor agrees not to prosecute the defendant if he or she cooperates with the police, despite the prosecutor's knowledge that the defendant was apparently involved in a bank robbery as the driver of the getaway car, this agreement established an enforceable agreement not to prosecute. Defendants who are granted immunity are entitled to use this as a defense to any subsequent prosecutions.[130]

3. Constitutional Challenges

As discussed in Chapter Two, defendants may seek to avoid conviction by claiming that statutes were unconstitutional as being vague or overbroad, or that evidence is inadmissible due to an illegal search or seizure, improper techniques in obtaining a confession, or violation of the right to counsel.[131] Double jeopardy is also prohibited by the Constitution. This is a defense that the criminal act has already been prosecuted and the state or federal government is barred from further prosecution. However, double jeopardy bars prosecution for the same offense and lesser included offenses, but not a different but related offense; thus, a defendant who is acquitted for murder might be retried for kidnapping because kidnapping is not a lesser included offense of murder. Furthermore, double jeopardy does not bar prosecutions by different jurisdictions; therefore, for instance, defendants who were acquitted of racial murders during the Civil Rights era were retried for the same deaths by federal courts for federal crimes.

4. Outrageous Government Conduct

One particular constitutional challenge falls under due process protections. A defense claim that has received more attention in recent years has been labeled "outrageous government conduct" or "egregious law enforcement conduct." The argument made is that the indictment should be dismissed on the grounds that the government's outrageous conduct violated the due process clause of the Constitution. The courts have hesitated to recognize this doctrine. In *State v. Romero*, the court cautioned that the doctrine of outrageous government conduct is a most narrow defense, and thus protection afforded by the due process clause of the Fifth Amendment applies only when the government activity in question violates some protected right of the defendant.[132]

To support dismissal of an indictment on grounds of outrageous government conduct, the defendant must prove that the government's conduct was so excessive, flagrant, scandalous, intolerable, and offensive as to violate due process.[133] Applying the "outrageous conduct" defense claim, a federal appeals court held that the government did not engage in outrageous conduct as would violate due process, even if the government induced the defendants to attempt to rob an armored car and allowed the informant to let the defendants use his apartment to store guns and ammunition, to organize a time to unload the fire-arms, to supply ammunition, and to drive the defendants to the robbery scene, and even if the government put lives at risk by allowing an informant to store automatic weapons in his home and to give the defendants access to them.[134]

5. Vindictive Prosecution

Another defense that has received attention is the defense of "vindictive prosecution." Prosecutorial vindictiveness requires objective evidence that a prosecutor's actions were designed to punish a defendant for asserting his legal rights.[135] A showing of actual prosecutorial vindictiveness is exceedingly dif-ficult to make; however, a presumption of vindictiveness may be established in cases in which a reasonable likelihood of vindictiveness exists. When con-sidering the vindictive prosecution defense, a federal court decided that the prosecution of an attempted reentry case was not vindictive even when the prosecutor did not seek to add charges until after the alien made it clear that he was going to trial rather than pleading guilty; the prosecutor's office had a system of expediting such cases by initially charging only reentry offenses, with additional charges being sought after the file was scrutinized more closely.[136]

§ 3.12 Summary

The courts have recognized that there are situations in which persons who commit acts that would ordinarily be crimes may introduce evidence to show they do not have the capacity to form the criminal intent that is required as an element of some crimes, or to demonstrate other legitimate defenses.

An infant is exempt from criminal responsibility for his or her act if he or she lacks sufficient mental capacity to entertain the criminal act. Also, most states provide a method of treating juvenile offenders that is distinct from that of treating adult offenders.

Under the common law, and by statutes and court decisions in all states, mental incapacity or insanity may be alleged by one accused of crimes at several points in criminal procedure. Several tests have been used by the courts over the years to determine whether the mental disorder or impairment is sufficient to eliminate the ability of the defendant to form any level of *mens rea* that would create criminal culpability. These include the:

- *M'Naghten* Rules
- Irresistible Impulse rule
- *Durham* Rule
- Model Penal Code (A.L.I.) test

The law in this area continues to evolve and several states have changed their statutes to restrict the use of this defense. The issue of insanity or mental impairment may also arise when determining whether the defendant is competent to stand trial. The elements for this determination are whether the defendant is capable of making a proper defense, aiding his attorney, or securing evidence at the time of the trial.

What would ordinarily be a criminal act may be excused at law if the act is committed under duress or compulsion. In order to excuse an act that would ordinarily be a crime, the compulsion or coercion must be present, imminent, or impending. Closely related to duress and compulsion is the defense of necessity. The general rule is that "a criminal offense may be justified or excused if done under necessity." Neither of these defenses will excuse harming an innocent victim.

Self-defense requires the force used by the defendant to be reasonable to defend against an apparent threat of unlawful and immediate violence from another. In order to successfully claim this defense, the defendant must show that:

- he believed physical force to be necessary for self-protection against an unlawful attack,

- his belief was based upon reasonable grounds,

- the force used was believed necessary to avoid imminent danger, and

- the force used was not in excess of that believed necessary to repel the unlawful attack.

The statutes and cases differ as to what force is justified, and under what circumstances.

Entrapment is a defense in a criminal case. If the criminal design originates in the mind of the police and not with the accused, entrapment is a proper defense. The rationale for the entrapment defense is that no person should be convicted of a crime that he or she was induced to commit by the very government that is prosecuting him or her for committing the crime.

Although ignorance or mistake of the law is no excuse, an honest and reasonable mistake of fact that negates one element of the crime may result in no criminal culpability unless the mistake arises from a want of proper care on the part of the accused.

Other defenses include: alibi, statute of limitations, authorization by an authority, constitutional challenges that the law itself was unconstitutional (as overbroad or vague) or procedural due process challenges (procedural violations, outrageous government conduct, and vindictive prosecution).

Review Questions

1. What was the age at which a child could not be held culpable for their acts under common law? What were the ages where the presumption of incompetence was rebuttable? What about the Model Penal Code?

2. What are the three ways (or times in the process) in which one's mental capacity are considered during criminal adjudication and punishment?

3. Describe the four tests of insanity. Which is the most frequently used?

4. Explain changes in some state laws regarding the defense of insanity. What is the verdict of Guilty but Insane?

5. Describe the test for incompetency.

6. Explain the diminished capacity defense. Describe some examples.

7. Explain how intoxication might be used as a diminished capacity defense. Describe whether such a defense is successful in all states.

8. Describe the elements to the defense of duress.

9. Describe the battered woman's defense.

10. Describe the elements of the defense of necessity. Provide examples of successful and unsuccessful uses.

11. Describe the six elements of self defense.

12. What are "Make my Day" laws and how are they different from traditional self defense.

13. Did the entrapment defense exist under common law? Describe the objective versus subjective tests of entrapment.

14. Explain the mistake of law and mistake of fact defense. Which is almost never a defense to criminal culpability?

15. Describe the defense of alibi.

16. Describe the defense of statute of limitations.

17. Describe the defense of "acting under the authority of others."

18. Describe the defense of immunity.

19. Describe some constitutional challenges that may be used as defenses.

20. Describe the defenses of outrageous governmental conduct and vindictive prosecution.

Notes

1   Angelo v. People, 96 Ill. 209 (1880).

2   MODEL PENAL CODE § 4.10 (1985).

3   Miles v. State, 594 A.2d 1208 (Md. Ct. App. 1991).

4   State v. Q.D., 685 P.2d 557 (Wash. 1984).

5   REV. CODE WASH. § 9A.04.050.

6   United States v. Santos, 131 F.3d 16 (1st Cir. 1997), which held that the standards of competency
     and insanity are different and the finding of competency to stand trial is not prejudicial to an insanity
     defense or admissible at the trial.

7   Smith, *Insanity Plea in Mississippi*, 10 MISS. C. L. REV. 147 (1990).

8   M'Naghten's Case, 8 Eng. Rep. 718 (1843), discussed in Leland v. Oregon, 343 U.S. 790, 725 S. Ct.
     1002, 966 L. Ed. 1302 (1952).

9   MODEL PENAL CODE § 4.01 (1985).

10   State v. Doyle, 117 Ariz. 349, 572 P.2d 1187 (1977).

11   State v. Schreiber, 558 N.W.2d 474 (Minn. 1997).

12   People v. Lowhone, 292 Ill. 32, 126 N.E. 620 (1920).

13   Parsons v. State, 81 Ala. 577, 2 So. 854 (1887).

14   State v. White, 58 N.M. 324, 270 P.2d 727 (1954).

15   Durham v. United States, 214 F.2d 862 (D.C. Cir. 1954).

16   Douglas v. United States, 239 F.2d 52 (D.C. Cir. 1956).

17   United States v. Smith, 5 C.M.A. 314, 17 C.M.R. 3 (1954).

18   United States v. Brawner, 471 F.2d 969 (D.C. Cir. 1972).

19   State v. Crenshaw, 659 P.2d 488 (Wash. 1983).

20   18 U.S.C.A. §17 (1988). *See* Chapter 13.

21   730 ILL. COMP. STAT. § 515-2 (1999); MICH. COMP. LAWS § 768.36 (1999).

22   IDAHO CODE § 18-207 (1990); MONT. CODE ANN. § 46-14-102 (1989); UTAH CODE ANN. § 76-2-305
     (1990).

23   *See*, for instance, State v. Herrera, 895 P.2d 359 (Utah 1995).

24   Gambill v. State, 675 N.E.2d 668 (Ind. 1997).

25   470 U.S. 68, 105 S.Ct. 1087, 84 L.Ed. 2d 53 (1985).

26   State v. Searcy, 789 P.2d 914 (Idaho 1990).

27   Dusky v. United States, 362 U.S. 402, 80 S. Ct. 788, 4 L. Ed. 2d 824 (1960).

28   Dunn v. Commonwealth, 573 S.W.2d 651 (Ky. 1978).

29   Cooper v. Oklahoma, 515 U.S. 348 (1996).

30   *Id.*

31   *Premenstrual Syndrome: A Criminal Defense*, 59 NOTRE DAME L. REV. 263 (1983).

32   Montana v. Egelhoff, 518 U.S. 37 (1996).

[33]   United States v. Anthony, 145 F. Supp. 323 (M.D. Pa. 1956); Jackson v. State, 558 S.W.2d 816 (Mo. Ct. App. 1977).

[34]   State v. St. Clair, 262 S.W.2d 25 (Mo. 1953); Jackson v. State, 504 S.W.2d 488 (Tex. Crim. App. 1974).

[35]   People v. Unger, 33 Ill. App. 3d 770, 338 N.E.2d 442 (Ill. Ct. App. 1975).

[36]   Arp v. State, 97 Ala. 5, 12 So. 301 (1893).

[37]   352 So. 2d 460 (Ala. Crim. App. 1977).

[38]   MODEL PENAL CODE § 2.09 (1985).

[39]   Wright v. State, 402 So.2d 493 (Fla. Dist. Ct. App. 1981).

[40]   State v. Gann, 244 N.W.2d 746 (N.D. 1976).

[41]   State v. Hopes, 602 A.2d 23 (Conn. 1992).

[42]   State v. Hope, 935 S.W.2d 85 (Mo. 1996).

[43]   Arnold v. Commonwealth, 560 S.E.2d 915 (Va. 2002).

[44]   Pujh v. State, 89 S.W.3d 909 (Ark. 2002).

[45]   282 N.W.2d 872 (Minn.1979).

[46]   Anguish v. State, 991 S.W.2d 883 (Tex. 1999).

[47]   Holly Maguigan, *Battered Women and Self Defense: Myths and Misconceptions in Current Reform Proposals*, 14 U. PA. L. REV. 379 (1992).

[48]   LENORE WALKER, THE BATTERED WOMAN. New York: Harper Collins, 1979.

[49]   *See*, for instance, MO. REV. STAT. § 563.033 (1996); OHIO REV. CODE ANN. § 2901.06 (Anderson 1994).

[50]   State v. Riker, 123 Wash. 2d 351, 869 P.2d 43 (1994).

[51]   State v. Daws, 104 Ohio App. 3d 448, 662 N.E.2d 805 (1994), *appeal allowed*, 71 Ohio St. 3d 1406, 641 N.E.2d 203 (1995), appeal dismissed as improvidently allowed, 74 Ohio St. 3d 1284, 659 N.E.2d 1282 (1996). For a superb discussion of the law regarding this issue, see Laurie Kratky Dore, *Downward Adjustment and the Slippery Slope: The Use of Duress in Defense of Battered Offenders*, 56 OHIO STATE L.J. 665-766 (1995). This article has an excellent appendix containing a summary of the duress laws of all 50 states.

[52]   People v. Yaklich, 833 P.2d 758, 762 (Col. Ct. App. 1991).

[53]   United States v. Willis, 38 F.3d 170 (5th Cir. 1994); United States v. Marenghi, 893 F. Supp. 85 (D. Me. 1995). United States v. Willis, 38 F.3d 170 (5th Cir. 1994).

[54]   People v. Romero, 15 Cal. App. 4th 1519 (1992).

[55]   14 Q.B.D. 273 (1884).

[56]   A similar American case was United States v. Holmes, 26 F. Cas. 360 (C.C.E.D. Pa. 1842).

[57]   United States v. Holmes, 26 F. Cas. 360 (C.C.E.D. Pa. 1842).

[58]   MODEL PENAL CODE § 3.02 (1985).

[59]   *See* the Model Penal Code for a discussion of the rationale for this defense and a list of the states that have adopted all or part of the Model Penal Code.

[60]   Long v. Commonwealth, 478 S.E.2d 424 (Va. Ct. App. 1996).

[61]   Dozier v. State, 709 N.E.2d 27 (Ind. 1999).

[62]   People v. Galambos, 128 Cal. Rptr. 844 (2002).

63   United States v. Paolello, 951 F.2d 537 (3d Cir. 1991).

64   State v. Moe, 24 P.2d 638 (Wash. 1933).

65   People v. Brandyberry, 812 P.2d 674 (Colo. Ct. App. 1991).

66   People v. Turner, 619 N.E.2d 781 (1993).

67   Jenks v. State, 582 So.2d 676 (Fla. Dist. Ct. App. 1991); State v. Hanson, 468 N.W.2d 77 (Minn. Ct.
      App. 1991), State v. Ownbey, 996 P.2d 510 (Ore. App. 2000), State v. Poling, 531 S.E.2d 678 (W.
      Va. 2000), United States v. Randall, 104 Daily Wash. L. Rptr. 2249 (D.C. Super. Ct. 1976).

68   United States v. Oakland Cannabis Buyer's Cooperative, 532 U.S. 483 (2001).

69   The following states had statutes that recognized medical exceptions to legal prohibitions against
      marijuana possession or use: AK; CA; CO; HA; MD; ME; MT; NV; OR; VT; WA.

70   43 Cal. App. 3d 823 (1974).

71   State v. Reese, 272 N.W.2d 863 (1978).

72   See, in addition to already cited cases, People v. Unger, 362 N.E.2d 319 (1977); Spakes v. State, 913
      S.W.2d 597 (Tex. Crim. App. 1996); People v. Harmon, 220 N.W.2d 212 (Mich. Ct. App. 1974);
      State v. Kinslow, 799 P.2d 844 (Ariz. 1990)k.

73   United States v. Schoon, 971 F.2d 193 (9th Cir. 1992).

74   People v. Roberson, 780 N.E.2d 1144 (Ill. 2002).

75   MODEL PENAL CODE § 3.04 (1985).

76   People v. Brown, 578 N.E.2d 1168 (Ill. 1991); People v. Willis, 577 N.E.2d 1215 (Ill. 1991); Holbrook
      v. Commonwealth, 813 S.W.2d 811 (Ky. 1991).

77   Manofsky v. State, 354 So. 2d 1249 (Fla. Dist. Ct. App. 1978).

78   State v. Wanrow, 559 P.2d 548 (Wash. 1977).

79   State v. Adams, 52 Conn. App. 643, 727 A.2d 780 (1999).

80   In re Christian S., 872 P.2d 574 (1994); Swann v. United States, 648 A.2d 928 (1994); State v. Cam-
      pos, 921 P.2d 1266 (N.M. 1996).

81   497 N.E.2d 41 (N.Y. 1986).

82   State v. Philbrick, 402 A.2d 59 (Me. 1979).

83   State v. Long, 480 S.E.2d 62 (S.C. 1997).

84   Beard v. United States, 158 U.S. 550 (1895).

85   Gibson v. Commonwealth, 34 S.W.2d 936 (Ky. 1931).

86   State v. Long, 480 S.E.2d 62 (S.C. 1997).

87   State v. Barnes, 729 So. 2d 44 (La. 1999).

88   Weland v. State, 732 So. 2d 1044 (Fla. 1999).

89   Hunter v. State, 687 So. 2d 277 (Fla. Dist. Ct. App. 1997).

90   State v. Marsh, 593 N.E.2d 35 (Ohio Ct. App. 1990); Gainer v. State, 391 A.2d 856 (Md. Ct. Spec.
      App. 1978); State v. Thomas, 673 N.E.2d 1339 (Ohio 1997).

91   COLO. REV. STAT. §18-1-704.

92   State v. Hurteau, 810 A.2d 222 (R.I. 2002).

93   Title 18 § 111. See United States v. Lopez, 710 F.2d 1071 (5th Cir. 1983).

94   471 U.S. 1 (1985).

[95]   United States v. Jannotti, 673 F.2d 578 (3d Cir. 1982).

[96]   287 U.S. 435, 53 S. Ct. 210, 77 L. Ed. 413 (1932).

[97]   356 U.S. 369, 78 S. Ct. 819, 2 L. Ed. 2d 848 (1958).

[98]   411 U.S. 423 (1973).

[99]   MODEL PENAL CODE § 2.13 (1985).

[100]   COLO. REV. STAT. § 18-1-709 (2002). *See also* § 18-1-710, which provides that entrapment is an affirmative defense.

[101]   Bailey v. People, 630 P.2d 1062 (Colo. 1987); Sayre v. State, 533 So. 2d 464 (Miss. 1988).

[102]   State v. Eib, 716 S.W.2d 304 (Mo. 1986).

[103]   United States v. Purneda-Gonzalez, 953 F.2d 190 (5th Cir. 1992).

[104]   State v. Schuman, 226 Wis. 2d 398, 595 N.W.2d 86 (1999).

[105]   People v. Connolly, 232 Mich. App. 425, 591 N.W.2d 340 (1998).

[106]   McGowan v. State, 671 N.E.2d 872 (Ind. 1996).

[107]   *See* State v. Little, 435 A.2d 517 (N.H. 1981); England v. State, 887 S.W.2d 902 (Tex. Crim. App. 1994); State v. Vallegjos, 945 P.2d 957 (N.M. 1997).

[108]   United States v. Squires, 440 F.2d 859 (2d Cir. 1971); United States v. Jewell, 532 F.2d 697 (9th Cir.), *cert. denied*, 426 U.S. 951, 96 S. Ct. 3173, 49 L. Ed. 2d 1188 (1976); Jones v. State, 439 S.E.2d 645 (Ga. 1994).

[109]   Johnson v. State, 831 So. 2d 1171 (Miss. 2002).

[110]   MODEL PENAL CODE §2.04, Ignorance or Mistake.

[111]   United States v. Ehrlichman, 376 F. Supp. 29 (D.D.C. 1974). *See also* D.F. v. State, 682 So. 2d 149 (Fla. 1996).

[112]   Bryan v. United States, 524 U.S. 184, 118 S. Ct. 1939, 141 L. Ed. 2d 197 (1998).

[113]   GA. CODE ANN. § 16-3-5 (1996).

[114]   Woolfolk v. State, 413 S.E.2d 242 (Ga. 1991). See also State v. Brumback, 671 N.E.2d 1064 (Ohio Ct. App. 1996).

[115]   Commonwealth v. McQueen, 178 Pa. Super. 38, 112 A.2d 820 (1955).

[116]   Commonwealth v. Warrington, 326 A.2d 427 (Pa. 1974). State v. El-Tabech, 405 N.W.2d 585 (Neb. 1987). *See also* Commonwealth v. Mikell, 729 A.2d 566 (Pa. 1999).

[117]   State v. Watkins, 806 A.2d 1072 (Conn. 2002).

[118]   State v. Armstad, 283 S.W.2d 577 (Mo. 1955).

[119]   Villarreal v. State, 821 S.W.2d 682 (Tex. Ct. App. 1991).

[120]   People v. Woodson, 41 Cal. Rptr. 487 (1964); State v. Martin, 2 Ariz. App. 510, 410 P.2d 132 (1966). People v. Smallwood, 166 Ill. Dec. 978, 586 N.E.2d 636 (1991).

[121]   People v. Smoot, 59 A.D.2d 898, 399 N.Y.S.2d 133 (N.Y.A.D. 1977).

[122]   Jarrett v. State, 49 Okla. Crim. 162, 292 P. 888 (1930).

[123]   MODEL PENAL CODE § 1.06 (1985).

[124]   KY. REV. STAT. § 500.050 (Baldwin 2002).

[125]   Roberts v. State, 712 N.E.2d 23 (Ind. 1999).

[126]   State v. McCord, 727 So. 2d 1262 (La. 1999).

[127] Ross v. United States Marshal for the Eastern District of Oklahoma, 168 F.3d 1190 (10th Cir. 1999).

[128] Canales v. State, 496 S.W.2d 614 (Tex. Crim. App. 1973).

[129] People v. Benford, 53 Cal. 2d 1, 345 P.2d 928 (1959).

[130] People v. Jackson, 480 N.W.2d 283 (Mich. 1991). *See also* United States v. Barone, 781 F. Supp. 1072 (E.D. Pa. 1991); United States v. Van Trourout, 100 F.3d 590 (1996).

[131] *See* KANOVITZ & KANOVITZ, CONSTITUTIONAL LAW (10th ed. 2006) and KLOTTER, WALKER, AND HEMMENS, LEGAL GUIDE FOR POLICE (7th ed. 2005).

[132] State v. Romero, 926 P.2d 717 (Mont. 1996).

[133] United States v. Edmonds, 103 F.3d 822 (9th Cir. 1996).

[134] United States v. Rodriquez, 54 F.3d 739 (3d Cir. 2002), *cert. denied*, 537 U.S1179, 123 S. Ct. 1010, 154 L. Ed. 3d 926 (2002).

[135] State v. Tilson, 794 A.2d 465 (R.I. 2002).

[136] United States v. Gonzales, 52 F.3d 330 (9th Cir. 2002).

Preparatory
Activity Offenses

4

Chapter Outline

Cases

Attempt: *Commonwealth of Pennsylvania v. Henley*, 504 Pa. 408 (1984)
Conspiracy: *Bolden v. Nevada*, 124 P.3d 191, 121 Nev. Adv. Rptr 86
    (2005).

§ 4.1 Introduction

The most common preparatory activity crimes are "attempt," "conspiracy," and "solicitation." Legislative bodies have provided penalties for these preparatory acts to reach those who have not actually perpetrated a substantive crime, but have been involved in preparing to commit a crime.

In this chapter, the three most often charged preparatory activity crimes (attempt, solicitation, and conspiracy) are defined and explained.

§ 4.2 Attempt

An **attempt** to commit a crime has been defined as an act done with intent to commit a crime, beyond mere preparation, but falling short of its actual commission.[1] It is also defined as "any overt act done with intent to commit the crime which and except for the interference of some cause preventing the carrying out of the intent, would have resulted in the commission of the crime."[2]

The distinction between "intent" and an "attempt" to do a thing is that the former implies the purpose only, while the latter implies both the purpose and an actual effort to carry that purpose into execution. Because the purpose of the law concerning criminal intent is to permit the courts to adjudge a penalty in cases in which conduct falls short of a completed substantive crime, an attempt to commit a crime is, as a general rule, an indictable offense that is separate and distinct from the substantive crime.[3]

A. Common Law

In early days, no crime was committed until the defendant carried out the *actus reus* of a substantive crime. Later, common law decisions and early court cases recognized attempts as crimes separate from the substantive crime, but considered them misdemeanors. Eventually, statutes were created that ascribed the same level of seriousness to the attempt as the crime attempted.

Because the elements of the offense of attempt are often unclear and difficult to prove, many courts have framed their own definitions. These indicate the requirements that are necessary to prove this offense. One court coined a short definition: "An 'attempt' to commit a crime is an act done with intent to commit that crime, carried beyond mere preparation to commit it, but falling short of its actual commission.[4]

The criminal law is not designed to impose liability for bad thoughts alone. While one might consider committing a specific crime, such thoughts do not create criminal culpability unless there is an overt act to go along with the intent. The overt act must also be sufficiently proximate to the intended crime. While mere preparation to commit an offense does not constitute an attempt, preparation plus an overt act going beyond mere preparation, toward commission of the crime, does constitute the offense.[5] Unless the statutory elements are different, the traditional elements of an "attempt" to commit a crime generally are:

1. a specific intent to commit a crime,

2. an overt act toward its commission,

3. the apparent possibility of commission, and

4. failure of consummation.

1. Specific Intent

Although there seems to be a minority opinion that only general intent is necessary for the crime of attempt[6]; the better approach is that because the substantive crime has not been consummated, it is incumbent on the prosecutor to show the higher level of intent. Generally, prosecutors must show **specific intent**; that is, proof must be offered that the offender intended to do the act (the overt act that was in furtherance of the crime); and intended the outcome (that is, the ultimate crime). However, specific intent can be inferred from circumstantial evidence.

2. Tests for Overt Act

Different courts have used different tests to decide whether an act has been committed that is sufficiently beyond preparation to constitute the **overt act** requirement. The tests can be remembered as:

- "Any" Act
- Substantial Step
- Act Beyond Mere Preparation
- All but the Last Step

The "any act" test would be the easiest for the prosecutor to prove and the "all but the last step" test would be the hardest. The **"substantial step"** test is the most common language employed. Courts note that an overt act to prove attempt requires conduct that is strongly corroborative of the actor's criminal purpose. The overt act consists of conduct constituting a "substantial step" toward commission of the crime and consists of conduct that is strongly corroborative of the firmness of the defendant's criminal intent. Mere preparation does not constitute a "substantial step."[7]

3. Apparent Ability: Impossibility as a Defense

Because one of the elements of attempt is the apparent ability to complete the substantive crime, can a person be guilty of attempt if it is impossible to succeed in the commission of the crime? For example, can a man be guilty of attempted murder when, with intent to commit murder, he shoots a body, but unbeknownst to the offender, the person was already dead?

The courts have differed in their response to situations in which the defendant could not have succeeded in the attempt to commit a crime. There is agreement that its consummation must be *apparently possible* and there must be at least an *apparent ability* to commit it. Further, the act itself, if consummated, must be a crime. The general rule is that **factual impossibility** does not constitute a defense. For example, when a defendant attempted to steal money from the victim's pocket and did everything he could to commit theft, but the crime failed only because the pocket was empty, impossibility was not a defense.[8]

The courts have held that it is not necessary that there be a actual ability to complete the crime—only an apparent ability. Therefore:

> if there is an apparent ability to commit the crime in the way attempted, the attempt is indictable, although, unknown to the person making the attempt, the crime cannot be committed, because the means employed are in fact unsuitable, or because of extrinsic facts, such as the non-existence of some essential object or an obstruction by the intended victim or by a third person.[9]

Think of it this way: if the offender had been successful in achieving what he attempted to do and the result would have been a crime, then the existence of factual impossibility will not excuse the attempt. Some situations will illustrate factual impossibilities that do not create a defense for the offender. In these cases, the offender would still be guilty of the attempted crime.

- Attempt to shoot someone but the gun was unloaded or inoperable (unknown to the offender)

- Attempt to solicit murder but asks an undercover police officer

- Attempt to commit rape but intended victim is not in bed

- Attempt to kill someone but victim was already dead

- Attempt to commit theft but safe is empty

- Attempt to rob bank but bank is closed and offender cannot get in the door

- Attempt to solicit sex from a minor in an Internet chat room, but "minor" is really police officer.

However, **legal impossibility** may be a defense. If it is not a crime to do what the person is attempting to do, then the attempt is not indictable. For example, if the defendant thought that bringing dried fruit rolls into the country violated customs laws and hid them in her luggage, she has not attempted smuggling because what she thought she was doing is not a crime. Even if she was caught with dried fruit rolls, she would not be guilty of attempted smuggling even though she thought she was breaking a law. Other examples of pure legal impossibility are:

- Attempting to commit patronizing prostitutes but doing so in a Nevada county where prostitution is legal

- Attempting to break speeding law by going 65 but not aware that the speed limit was 65

- Attempting to commit gambling violation but gamble in a way that is legal in that state

Contrast this situation with a person who thinks they are smuggling cocaine (but it turns out to be baking powder). The defendant is correct in the belief that smuggling cocaine is illegal, but is incorrect that what they are hiding is cocaine. While some would define this as another example of factual impossibility and others incorrectly define it as legal impossibility because smuggling baking powder is not criminal; the more accurate characterization is to define it as "hybrid legal impossibility." Other examples of hybrid legal impossibility include a case in which the defendant attempted to bribe someone he mistakenly believed to be a juror but the person was not a juror. The court held that no attempt had been committed because even if the person had accepted the money, the elements of bribery were not be present.[10] Other instances of this type of hybrid legal impossibility follow (along with the court opinions where they were considered):

- Not attempted poaching by shooting a stuffed deer (because if the offender was successful it would still be shooting a stuffed deer)[11]

- Not attempted possession of marijuana by smoking substance that is not illegal (because no matter what the offender thought he was doing, it was not an illegal substance)

- Not attempted receipt of stolen goods when goods were not stolen (because it was not illegal to receive and could not be made so by offender's mistaken belief)[12]

- Not attempted subornation of perjury when issue was not material to case (because even if offender thought he was committing crime, the immateriality of the issue meant it could never be a crime)[13]

The distinction between true legal impossibility and hybrid legal impossibility is this: in true legal impossibility the person believes some act is against the law but it is not. Examples might be the fruit roll smuggler above, or other situations in which a person believes there is a law against their behavior, but there is not. In hybrid legal impossibility, the defendant is *correct* in their belief that the act is against the law, but *incorrect* as to an essential element of the law. An essential element of bribing jurors, for instance, is that it is a juror who is offered the bribe. The difference between factual and hybrid legal impossibility is that in factual impossibility, the mistake is not concerning an element of the crime. An attempted murder when the gun has no bullets is factual impossibility because the mistake is not an element of the crime, but attempted poaching by shooting a stuffed deer is hybrid legal impossibility because the poaching laws specify deer, not deer facsimiles. Finally, a mistake in thinking that there is a law regarding hunting in a certain area when the law does not exist at all is an example of legal impossibility.

1. Mistaken belief	not related to element of crime	of a true crime =	factual impossibility.
2. Mistaken belief	that action is a crime	but there is no crime =	legal impossibility.
3. Mistaken belief	related to element of a	true crime =	legal hybrid impossibility.

1. D shoots and hits V (with intent to kill V); but V is already dead; if D had been successful, it would have been murder = factual (no defense to attempt charge).

2. D buys lottery ticket (with intent to commit a gambling crime); but lottery is legal (no crime); if D had been successful in buying the ticket, he would have bought a legal lottery ticket = legal (no criminal attempt).

3. D shoots at deer (with intent to hunt out of season); but deer is fake; if D had been successful in shooting at what he thought was a deer, he would have been guilty of a crime = legal hybrid (no defense to attempted illegal hunting now in most jurisdictions)

These distinctions are difficult to make, and a review of court cases would support the contention that sometimes even judges and juries are confused about the difference between the two. It is also the case that the current trend is to disallow the defense of hybrid legal impossibility; therefore, the cases discussed earlier may be decided differently by today's courts. No doubt partially due to the difficulties in distinguishing the forms of impossibility, the Model Penal Code has chosen to eliminate the defense of legal impossibility entirely.

4. Failure of Consummation: Abandonment as a Defense

Obviously, if the crime is completed, the defendant would be prosecuted for the substantive crime; thus, attempts are those situations in which, for whatever reason, the crime was not completed. **Abandonment** or withdrawal is a defense if the attempt to commit a crime is freely and voluntarily abandoned before the final execution of the crime, and if there is no outside cause prompting the abandonment. To state this differently, if a person voluntarily abandoned his or her proposed plan of crime before actual commission of the crime, and he or she does so voluntarily, he or she cannot be held guilty of an attempt.[14]

Abandonment is no defense if failure to complete the crime is due to **extraneous intervening circumstances**. For example, failure to complete the crime because of a threatened arrest or appearance of the police is not the free and voluntary abandonment necessary to constitute the defense.[15] Abandonment is not a defense when it is due to factual impossibility; for instance, if a person attempted to rob a bank but arrived as the door was locked. Even if the offender walked away, he might still be indicted for attempt because his abandonment was due to the extrinsic factor of the locked door. Only if the abandonment is a voluntary decision on the part of the offender, and not due to external reasons, will it serve as a defense.

B. Model Penal Code

The Model Penal Code uses the "substantial step" test to determine whether an overt act has been committed sufficient to create criminal culpability. There are also specific examples of what constitutes a substantial step. The Code deviates from the traditional approach because it does not recognize the defense of legal impossibility. Attempt is defined in terms of conduct that would constitute the crime if circumstances were as the defendant believed them to be. This opens the door to attempted smuggling when the smuggler is carrying non-drugs; attempted receipt of stolen property when the property is really recovered property in an undercover sting operation; and attempted murder when the hired hit man is really a police officer. The Code does, however, follow traditional statutes in that abandonment is recognized as a defense only if it is free, voluntary, and unrelated to extrinsic circumstances.

§ 5.01 Criminal Attempt[16]

(1) Definition of Attempt. A person is guilty of an attempt to commit a crime if, acting with the kind of culpability otherwise required for commission of the crime, he:

   (a) purposely engages in conduct which would constitute the crime if the attendant circumstances were as he believes them to be; or

   (b) when causing a particular result is an element of the crime, does or omits to do anything with the purpose of causing or with the belief that it will cause such result without further conduct on his part; or

   (c) purposely does or omits to do anything which, under the circumstances as he believes them to be, is an act or omission constituting a substantial step in a course of conduct planned to culminate in his commission of the crime.

(2) Conduct Which May Be Held Substantial Step Under Subsection (1)(c). Conduct shall not be held to constitute a substantial step under Subsection (1)(c) of this Section unless it is strongly corroborative of the actor's criminal purpose. Without negating the sufficiency of other conduct, the following, if strongly corroborative of the actor's criminal purpose, shall not be held insufficient as a matter of law:

   (a) lying in wait, searching for or following the contemplated victim of the crime;

   (b) enticing or seeking to entice the contemplated victim of the crime to go to the place contemplated for its commission;

   (c) reconnoitering the place contemplated for the commission of the crime;

   (d) unlawful entry of a structure, vehicle or enclosure in which it is contemplated that the crime will be committed;

   (e) possession of materials to be employed in the commission of the crime, which are specially designed for such unlawful use or which can serve no lawful purpose of the actor under the circumstances;

   (f) possession, collection or fabrication of materials to be employed in the commission of the crime, at or near the place contemplated for its commission, where such possession, collection or fabrication serves no lawful purpose of the actor under the circumstances;

   (g) soliciting an innocent agent to engage in conduct constituting an element of the crime.

(3) Conduct Designed to Aid Another in Commission of a Crime. A person who engages in conduct designed to aid another to commit a crime which would establish his complicity under § 2.06 if the crime were committed by such other person, is guilty of an attempt to commit the crime, although the crime is not committed or attempted by such other person.

(4) Renunciation of Criminal Purpose. When the actor's conduct would otherwise constitute an attempt under Subsection (1)(b) or (1)(c) of this Section, it is an affirmative defense that he abandoned his effort to commit the crime or otherwise prevented its commission, under circumstances manifesting a complete and voluntary renunciation of his criminal purpose. The establishment of such defense does not, however, affect the liability of an accomplice who did not join in such abandonment or prevention.

Within the meaning of this Article, renunciation of criminal purpose is not voluntary if it is motivated, in whole or in part, by circumstances, not present or apparent at the inception of the actor's course of conduct, which increase the probability of detection or apprehension or which make more difficult the accomplishment of the criminal purpose. Renunciation is not complete if it is motivated by a decision to postpone the criminal conduct until a more advantageous time or to transfer the criminal effort to another but similar objective or victim.

C. State Statutes, Codes, and Cases

Many states have created general attempt offenses that replace scores of statutes creating special attempt crimes. Some state statutes still include separate provisions for punishment for "attempted rape," "attempted arson," and "attempted burglary," but the more recent approach is to consolidate all of the statutes into a single attempt provision uniformly relating the penalty for criminal attempt to the penalty for the crime attempted. An example of such a statute is that of Kentucky, which provides:

§ 506.010—Criminal attempt[17]

(1) A person is guilty of criminal attempt to commit a crime when, acting with the kind of culpability otherwise required for commission of the crime, he:
   (a) Intentionally engages in conduct which would constitute the crime if the attendant circumstances were as he believes them to be; or
   (b) Intentionally does or omits to do anything which, under the circumstances as he believes them to be, is a substantial step in a course of conduct planned to culminate in his commission of the crime.

(2) Conduct shall not be held to constitute a substantial step under Subsection (1)(b) unless it is an act or omission which leaves no reasonable doubt as to the defendant's intention to commit the crime which he is charged with attempting.

(3) A person is guilty of criminal attempt to commit a crime when he engages in conduct intended to aid another person to commit that crime, although the crime is not committed or attempted by the other person, provided that his conduct would establish complicity under KRS 502.020 if the crime were committed by the other person.

(4) A criminal attempt is a:
   (a) Class C felony when the crime attempted is a violation of KRS 521.020 or 521.050;
   (b) Class B felony when the crime attempted is a Class A felony or capital offense;
   (c) Class C felony when the crime attempted is a Class B felony;
   (d) Class A misdemeanor when the crime attempted is a Class C or D felony;
   (e) Class B misdemeanor when the crime attempted is a misdemeanor.

Section 506.020 of the Kentucky Penal Code offers the defense of renunciation. As with most modern codes, this makes voluntary renunciation a defense to criminal attempt. It provides that renunciation is not voluntary within the meaning of this provision if motivated by a "belief that circumstances exist that pose a particular threat of apprehension or detection." This is interpreted to mean that if an offense is not completed due to the interference of a police officer, the defense of renunciation would not be available.[18]

In an attempt case, one can expect the defense to emphasize that: (1) the intent element has not been proved; (2) there was no overt act; and (in some cases); (3) the defendant voluntarily "abandoned the intent prior to committing an overt act in furtherance of the plan."

In the case of *State v. Miller*, the defendant shot a victim during a robbery attempt and then ran away without taking the victim's money. He was convicted of murder and attempted armed robbery. The attempted robbery was appealed, arguing that there was insufficient evidence of attempted armed robbery, either because there was no action beyond preparation and, even if there was, the defendant abandoned the attempt, which negated his culpability.[19] The appeals court first pointed out that the elements of attempt to commit any crime are: (1) intent to commit the substantive offense; and (2) an overt act done for a purpose that goes beyond mere preparation; but (3) falls short of a completed offense. The court held that prior statements the defendant made indicating his desire to rob the victim, in addition to his actions, which entailed sneaking up on the victim and firing his gun into the victim's head, were sufficient to prove specific intent and an overt act. He was not entitled to an abandonment defense because, under North Carolina law, once an overt act is committed, even a defendant who voluntarily abandons the effort with no outside interference is guilty of attempt (this is different from many other states that do recognize the defense of abandonment in these circumstances).

To prove the "intent" element, the prosecution must offer evidence to show a specific intent to commit a specific offense. In *People v. Ritson*, the defendant was convicted of attempted kidnapping, among other charges. He sexually solicited two young boys in a park and when they refused, he drove to a shopping center and stopped next to a 12-year-old boy who was alone, opened the car door, and told him to "get the hell in the car." The boy ran to his mother and Ritson was eventually arrested and charged. He challenged the conviction, arguing that there was insufficient evidence of attempted kidnapping. The appellate court found the facts, taken together with the prior incident, indicated an attempt to complete the elements of kidnapping which included taking, holding, or detaining someone by instilling fear.[20]

Even when the defendant's intent is clear, his or her actions, in order to support an attempt conviction, must cross the line between mere preparation and an unequivocal demonstration that the crime will take place unless interrupted by independent circumstances. That is, there must be an overt act. In *State v. Green*, the defendant picked out a woman, seemingly at random, and decided to kill her. When she parked her van in a store parking lot and went in, he hid inside her van and planned to stab her and "drink her blood." When she came back, she surprised the defendant by pulling open the sliding door of the van instead of getting in the driver's seat. When she angrily demanded he get out, he did so docilely and made up a story as to why he had climbed inside. Passersby restrained him and he was subsequently convicted of attempted aggravated murder. The defendant argued that he had not completed a substantial step toward the completion of the crime but the appellate court disagreed and upheld the conviction.[21]

In *People v. Sabo*, the defendant hired "John Doe" to kill the victim, but instead Doe went to the police. They arranged for him to accept the assignment and Sabo gave him a plan to carry to out the murder, a photograph of the intended victim, and a down payment of $10,000 with a promise of $15,000 more once the deed was done. Conversations regarding the murder were recorded and the police even created a photograph that showed what appeared to be the dead victim. Sabo did not accept the photograph as proof and demanded that the body be found in a public place and the victim's family hold a funeral for the intended victim before he would pay the remaining money. He was arrested shortly after and indicted for attempted murder, criminal solicitation, and criminal conspiracy. Sabo challenged his indictment by arguing that attempt is defined by New York law as coming "dangerously close" to the completion of the crime. Since the apparent "hit man" was actually working with police, there was no way that the crime would have ever been committed. (Was this a defense of factual or legal impossibility?) However, New York law did not recognize either factual or legal impossibility as a defense, and therefore the indictment was not quashed. The court noted that in this case, the acts Sabo took did come "dangerously close" to completion because the crime itself would have been committed but for timely interference.[22] In *Pennsylvania v. Henley*, the court also ruled on a case of legal or factual impossibility.

> **CASE:** *Commonwealth of Pennsylvania v. Henley, 504 PA 408 (1984)*
>
> What was the issue?
>
> What is the Pennsylvania's court holding in regard to the defense of "legal impossibility"?
>
> Was this a case of factual, legal or hybrid legal impossibility?

D. Summary

The offense of criminal attempt is especially important to enforcement officials. It is often overlooked and no action is taken when the intended offense is not consummated. However, legislatures in all jurisdictions have recognized that a person who goes as far as possible in implementing a criminal purpose manifests dangerousness sufficient to warrant some sanctions. The rationale for including attempt as an offense is that other crimes might be prevented by taking action against the person who has indicated this criminal purpose.

Attempt	
A/R	an overt act toward the completion of a crime (beyond mere preparation; usually the test is "substantial step"); apparent ability; non-completion of the crime
M/R	specific intent (to do the intended crime)

§ 4.3 Criminal Solicitation

A. Common Law

The common law crime of **solicitation** is defined as "to solicit another to commit a felony." The rationale for making solicitation of another a separate offense is similar to the rationale for making attempt a crime: the criminal culpability of the solicitor is as great as it would be if the proposal were accepted and the underlying offense completed. The offense of solicitation was punishable at common law without regard for the nature of the substantive crime solicited; that is, criminal solicitation of murder had the same potential sanction as criminal solicitation of larceny.[23]

Commenting on the common law, an Oregon court stated that at common law, a person was guilty of solicitation if that person requested, commanded, or importuned another to commit a felony or serious misdemeanor. If the solicited person agreed to commit the crime, each party was guilty of conspiracy. The court pointed out that solicitation was a well-established crime when the first American guarantees of free expression were adopted.[24] The offense is complete even though the person solicited refuses to commit the crime.[25] The elements of solicitation are:

1. An intent to promote or facilitate the commission of a particular criminal offense.

2. Some overt act, such as the initiatory act of solicitation, request, command, or encouragement.

B. Model Penal Code

Under the Model Penal Code, it is necessary to show "intent" (the mental element) plus asking another to engage in specific conduct. The Model Code includes a specific defense of **renunciation**, provided the renunciation is complete and voluntary. "Solicitation" is defined as an offer or invitation to another to commit a crime; it does not, by itself, constitute an attempt, but may escalate into an attempt to commit a crime after the offeror commits a direct, unequivocal act toward committing the crime.

---

§ 5.02 Criminal Solicitation[26]

(1) Definition of Solicitation. A person is guilty of solicitation to commit a crime if with purpose of promoting or facilitating its commission he commands, encourages or requests another person to engage in specific conduct which would constitute such crime or an attempt to commit such crime or which would establish his complicity in its commission or attempted commission.

(2) Uncommunicated Solicitation. It is immaterial under Subsection (1) of this Section that the actor fails to communicate with the person he solicits to commit a crime if his conduct was designed to effect such communication.

(3) Renunciation of Criminal Purpose. It is an affirmative defense that the actor, after soliciting another person to commit a crime, persuaded him not to do so or otherwise prevented the commission of the crime, under circumstances manifesting a complete and voluntary renunciation of his criminal purpose.

C. State Statutes, Codes, and Cases

Although solicitation was recognized as an offense at common law, it was not made a statutory offense in all states. The offense of solicitation was punishable at common law as a misdemeanor without regard to the nature of the substantive crime solicited; however, recently enacted statutes provide a penalty structure that gears the penalty to the crime solicited.

In some states, there are specific solicitation statutes attached to certain crimes, such as murder. In Illinois, the statute provides: "A person commits solicitation when, with intent that an offense be committed, other than first-degree murder, he commands, encourages or requests another to commit that offense."[27] Under the Illinois Code, specific intent is required for a conviction of the crime of solicitation, but the intent may be inferred from surrounding circumstances and acts of the defendant.[28] In addition to the element of specific intent, the prosecution must show that the defendant commanded, encouraged, or asked another to commit a specific crime. The offense is complete when the principal offense is commanded, requested, or encouraged with the specific intent that the principal offense be committed.[29]

The Nevada statute provides:

> (1) Every person who counsels, hires, commands or otherwise solicits another to commit kidnapping or arson is guilty of a gross misdemeanor if no criminal act is committed as a result of that solicitation.

> (2) Every person who counsels, hires, commands or otherwise solicits another to commit murder, if no criminal act is committed as a result of the solicitation, shall be punished by imprisonment in the state prison for not less than one year nor more than ten years, and may be further punished by a fine of not more than $10,000.00.[30]

In *Moran v. Schwarz*, the defendant was charged with a violation of this statute. The defendant was accused of having solicited two men to kill a man named Thomas Susman in exchange for money and jewelry, and having provided them with information about Susman so they could carry out the murder.[31] The defendant appealed his conviction, arguing that he changed his mind about the murder and abandoned his plan. The Nevada appellate court rejected this defense, stating that, in Nevada, the harm was "in the asking," and the crime of solicitation was complete at that point.

Similarly, a Virginia court held that criminal solicitation involves an attempt of the accused to incite another to commit a criminal offense; it is immaterial whether the solicitation is of any effect and whether the crime solicited is in fact committed, because the *actus reus* of the offense is the incitement.[32]

Other states have more general solicitation statutes. For instance, Florida's statute states:

> 777.04 Attempts, solicitation, and conspiracy.—

> (1) A person who attempts to commit an offense prohibited by law and in such attempt does any act toward the commission of such offense, but fails in the perpetration or is intercepted or prevented in the execution thereof, commits the offense of criminal attempt, ranked for purposes of sentencing as provided in subsection (4). Criminal attempt includes

> the act of an adult who, with intent to commit an offense prohibited by law, allures, seduces, coaxes, or induces a child under the age of 12 to engage in an offense prohibited by law.
>
> (2) A person who solicits another to commit an offense prohibited by law and in the course of such solicitation commands, encourages, hires, or requests another person to engage in specific conduct which would constitute such offense or an attempt to commit such offense commits the offense of criminal solicitation, ranked for purposes of sentencing as provided in subsection (4).
>
> (3) A person who agrees, conspires, combines, or confederates with another person or persons to commit any offense commits the offense of criminal conspiracy, ranked for purposes of sentencing as provided in subsection (4).
>
> (4)(a) Except as otherwise provided in . . . , the offense of criminal attempt, criminal solicitation, or criminal conspiracy is ranked for purposes of sentencing under chapter 921 and determining incentive gain-time eligibility under chapter 944 one level below the ranking under . . . the offense attempted, solicited, or conspired to. If the criminal attempt, criminal solicitation, or criminal conspiracy is of an offense ranked in level 1 or level 2 under . . . such offense is a misdemeanor of the first degree, . . . (b) If the offense attempted, solicited, or conspired to is a capital felony, the offense of criminal attempt, criminal solicitation, or criminal conspiracy is a felony of the first degree, . . . if the offense attempted, solicited, or conspired to is a life felony or a felony of the first degree, the offense of criminal attempt, criminal solicitation, or criminal conspiracy is a felony of the second degree, . . .

Many of the recently enacted statutes include specific provisions regarding the defense of renunciation or incapacity. The wording of the renunciation provision is usually similar to the wording of § 5.02(3) of the Model Penal Code. Generally, the incapacity provision of the statutes provides for a defense if the accused would not be guilty of the principal offense committed because of some individual incapacity the accused might have, such as being underage; but it would not be a defense for the accused that the person solicited would not be guilty of the principal offense, because of some legal incapacity or immunity.

D. Summary

The crime of solicitation under common law was a misdemeanor and carried the same punishment regardless of the seriousness of the crime solicited. Today, states often tie solicitation to the specific crime, or they have gradations of solicitation depending on the seriousness of the crime. While some states offer the defense of renunciation; others do not, holding the position that the crime "is in the asking."

Solicitation

A/R   Request, solicit, encourage, incite another to commit a specified crime

M/R   Specific Intent

---

§ 4.4 Conspiracy

Conspiracy is basically an agreement between individuals to commit a crime. The rationale for making conspiracy a crime is that society, having the power to punish for dangerous behavior, cannot be powerless against those who work to bring about that behavior.[33] As one court indicated, the law punishes for conspiracy because it does not deem it prudent to wait until the criminal plan has reached fruition.[34]

A. Common Law

Conspiracy was an offense at English common law and is an offense under all state statutes. Conspiracy has been defined as an agreement between two or more persons to accomplish a criminal or unlawful purpose, or some purpose, not in itself criminal or unlawful, by criminal or unlawful means. However, there must be some act in addition to the conspiring. It has also been defined as "an agreement among conspirators, an act of conspiring together; and it necessarily implies acting in concert, undertaking some joint action."[35] A conspiracy to commit an offense and the actual commission of the offense are separate crimes and may be punished separately.[36]

1. An Intentional Agreement

One court defined conspiracy as:

> "Conspiracy" consists in a corrupt agreement between two or more persons to do an unlawful act, existence of which agreement may be established by direct proof, or by inference, as deduction from acts and conduct, which discloses the common design on their part to act together for accomplishment of an unlawful purpose.[37]

2. Between Two or More

There must be at least two persons agreeing to do an act; that is, the conspiracy is a joint undertaking or a combination, agreement or understanding, tacit or otherwise, between two or more persons for the purpose of committing the unlawful act. Under the **Wharton Rule**, in crimes that require at least two people (bigamy, adultery, incest), a conspiracy charge cannot be based solely on the agreement of only the two people necessarily involved in the crime. The Wharton rule has been rejected in some states.

3. To Commit Criminal Act or Commit Lawful Act in an Unlawful Manner

Because the essence of the crime of "conspiracy" is the agreement rather than the commission of the objective substantive crime, conspiring to commit a crime is an offense separate and distinct from the crime, which may be the objective of the conspiracy.[38] It is not double jeopardy to bring criminal actions against a defendant under the conspiracy statute as well as the substantive crime statute.

4. Some Overt Act by One of the Parties

As in the crime of attempt, it must be shown that one of the conspirators committed an overt act in furtherance of the conspiracy. The overt act must at least start to carry the conspiracy into effect or reach far enough toward the accomplishment of the desired result to amount to the commencement of the consummation.[39] The **Pinkerton rule**, from an early federal criminal case, states that any co-conspirator is culpable for all natural and foreseeable acts committed by co-conspirators within the scope of the conspiracy. This rule has been rejected by states and the Model Penal Code. The more general rule is that co-conspirators are culpable for all crimes that are part of the criminal enterprise agreed upon.

5. Withdrawal as a Defense

Traditionally, withdrawal from the criminal conspiracy did not constitute a defense to the crime, but most courts now recognize that if a defendant effectively withdraws from the criminal conspiracy, it is a defense.[40] The majority of federal courts confronted with the issue have held that it is the defendant who bears the burden of proving withdrawal. However, in a 1981 case, the U.S. Court of Appeals for the Seventh Circuit concluded that due process requires the government to disprove withdrawal beyond a reasonable doubt once the defendant has met the burden of going forward with evidence of withdrawal.[41] In order to prove withdrawal, evidence must be introduced to show that the defendant disavowed or defeated the purpose of the conspiracy.

B. Model Penal Code

Under the Model Penal Code, the offense is committed if there is an agreement with another person or persons to engage in such conduct that constitutes a crime or an attempt or solicitation to commit such crime; or where the agreement is to aid such other person or persons in the planning or commission of such crime or of an attempt or solicitation to commit such crime.

§ 5.03 Criminal Conspiracy[42]

(1) **Definition of Conspiracy.** A person is guilty of conspiracy with another person or persons to commit a crime if with the purpose of promoting or facilitating its commission he:

    (a) agrees with such other person or persons that they or one or more of them will engage in conduct which constitutes such crime or an attempt or solicitation to commit such crime; or

    (b) agrees to aid such other person or persons in the planning or commission of such crime or of an attempt of solicitation to commit such crime.

(2) **Scope of Conspiratorial Relationship.** If a person guilty of conspiracy, as defined by Subsection (1) of this Section, knows that a person with whom he conspires to commit a crime has conspired with another person or persons to commit the same crime, he is guilty of conspiring with such other person or persons, whether or not he knows their identity, to commit such crime.

(3) **Conspiracy With Multiple Criminal Objectives.** If a person conspires to commit a number of crimes, he is guilty of only one conspiracy so long as such multiple crimes are the object of the same agreement or continuous conspiratorial relationship.

(4) **Joinder and Venue in Conspiracy Prosecutions.**

    (a) Subject to the provisions of paragraph (b) of this Subsection, two or more persons charged with criminal conspiracy may be prosecuted jointly if:

        (i) they are charged with conspiring with one another; or

        (ii) the conspiracies alleged, whether they have the same or different parties, are so related that they constitute different aspects of a scheme of organized criminal conduct.

    (b) In any joint prosecution under paragraph (a) of this Subsection:

        (i) no defendant shall be charged with a conspiracy in any county [parish or district] other than one in which he entered into such conspiracy or in which an overt act pursuant to such conspiracy was done by him or by a person with whom he conspired; and

        (ii) neither the liability of any defendant nor the admissibility against him of evidence of acts or declarations of another shall be enlarged by such joinder; and

        (iii) the Court shall order a severance or take a special verdict as to any defendant who so requests, if it deems it necessary or appropriate to promote the fair determination of his guilt or innocence and shall take any other proper measures to protect the fairness of the trial.

(5) Overt Act. No person may be convicted of conspiracy to commit a crime, other than a felony of the first or second degree, unless an overt act in pursuance of such conspiracy is alleged and proved to have been done by him or by a person with whom he conspired.

(6) Renunciation of Criminal Purpose. It is an affirmative defense that the actor, after conspiring to commit a crime, thwarted the success of the conspiracy, under circumstances manifesting a complete and voluntary renunciation of his criminal purpose.

(7) Duration of Conspiracy. For purposes of § 1.04(4):
  (a) conspiracy is a continuing course of conduct which terminates when the crime or crimes which are its object are committed or the agreement that they be committed is abandoned by the defendant and by those with whom he conspired; and
  (b) such abandonment is presumed if neither the defendant nor anyone with whom he conspired does any overt act in pursuance of the conspiracy during the applicable period of limitation; and
  (c) if an individual abandons the agreement, the conspiracy is terminated as to him only if and when he advises those with whom he conspired of his abandonment or he informs the law enforcement authorities of the existence of the conspiracy and of his participation therein.

The Model Code handles the overt act element by providing that an overt act is a requirement in cases other than a felony of the first or second degree. It is an affirmative defense that the actor, after conspiring to commit a crime, thwarted the success of the conspiracy, under circumstances manifesting a complete and voluntary renunciation of criminal purpose. It is interesting to note that the Model Penal Code also only requires an agreement "by" the defendant rather than between the parties. This makes it possible to convict a person of conspiracy with a person who has been acquitted or a police officer who has pretended to be a conspirator.

C. State Statutes, Codes, and Cases

Many of the more recently revised codes follow the Model Penal Code at least in part. An example of a state statute that takes a somewhat different approach is that of Indiana.

§ 35-41-5-2. Conspiracy.[43]

(a) A person conspires to commit a felony when, with intent to commit the felony, he agrees with another person to commit the felony. However, a conspiracy to commit murder is a Class A felony.

(b) The state must allege and prove that either the person or the person with whom he agreed performed an overt act in furtherance of the agreement.

(c) It is no defense that the person with whom the accused person is alleged to have conspired:
  (1) Has not been prosecuted;
  (2) Has not been convicted;
  (3) Has been acquitted;
  (4) Has been convicted of a different crime;
  (5) Cannot be prosecuted for any reason; or
  (6) Lacked the capacity to commit the crime.

The Indiana statute specifically provides that the prosecution must present evidence to prove an overt act in furtherance of the agreement and states that it shall be no defense that the person who performed the act has not been prosecuted, has not been convicted, has not been acquitted, has been convicted of a different crime, or cannot be prosecuted for any reason or lacked the capacity to commit the crime. This takes away some of the indefiniteness that sometimes makes it difficult to prosecute for a conspiracy. Because of the wording of the statute, the Indiana courts have found that it is no defense to a charge of conspiracy that one of the conspirators was an undercover police agent. The Indiana Court of Appeals also made it clear that in proving a conspiracy, it is not necessary to prove that the object of the conspiracy has been carried out.[44]

In *Sawyer v. State*, a conspiracy conviction that resulted from a sting operation was appealed. In the sting operation, an employee of the prosecutor's office and an FBI agent met with the defendant and expressed an interest in buying a tavern. During this meeting, the FBI agent, using an assumed name, told the defendant that he would buy the tavern, but only if he had a guarantee that there would be no zoning problems. The defendant then suggested that he knew of a person who could be very valuable in obtaining the zoning variance that had been requested and denied. At a later meeting, the defendant accepted $1,000.00 for his part in this deal. He was charged with conspiracy to commit bribery and bribery. The defendant was acquitted of the bribery charge because the person who was to have obtained the zoning variance was not a public servant. However, he was convicted of conspiring to commit bribery.

The appellate court confirmed the conspiracy conviction, holding that: "Although it may have been impossible for Sawyer to have committed bribery, impossibility generally is not a defense to a charge of conspiracy." The court continued by explaining that the crime of conspiracy focuses on the intent with which the defendant agrees with another person. It is irrelevant that the defendant's conduct could not constitute bribery; what is relevant is the intent and belief Sawyer had when he agreed with the others to "confer, offer or agree to confer" money to another in exchange for the other party's influence in resolving the zoning matter. The evidence was sufficient to support the conspiracy conviction.[45] A case involving conspiracy to receive stolen property with property that turned out not to be stolen ended in a similar holding.[46]

In 2003, the United States Supreme Court considered a conspiracy appeal. The defendant argued that he could not be guilty of conspiracy because under-cover agents were running the alleged drug operation at the time that he agreed to participate. The Court opined that conspiracy poses a threat to the public over and above the threat of the commission of the relevant substantive crime, both because the partnership in crime makes more likely the commission of other crimes and because it decreases the probability that the individuals involved will depart from the path of criminality. After stating that the essence of a conspiracy is an agreement to commit an unlawful act, the Court continued by explaining that the agreement to commit an unlawful act, which constitutes the essence of a conspiracy, is a distinct evil that may exist and may be punished whether or not the substantive crime ensues. They also held that the government's involvement that acted to defeat the conspiracy does not automatically end the potential culpability of subsequent conspirators.[47]

Generally, state statutes require that the state prove intent and an overt act. A California court opined that a conviction of conspiracy requires proof that the defendant and another person had the specific intent to agree or conspire to commit an offense, as well as a specific intent to commit the elements of that offense, together with proof of the commission of an overt act by one or more of the parties to such agreement in furtherance of the conspiracy.[48]

CASE: *Bolden v. Nevada*, 124 P.d 191 (2005)

Bolden was charged and convicted of a list of crimes; what were those crimes and which were the object of the appeal?

What was the specific issue the court addressed in this part of the holding?

What was the court's opinion regarding the Pinkerton rule?

Why were the crimes of burglary and kidnapping distinguished from the crime of robbery?

Intent is generally proven in a conspiracy prosecution by circumstantial evidence because direct evidence of the accused's state of mind is rarely available.[49] Commenting on the proof necessary to convict in a conspiracy case, a Pennsylvania court included a statement that conspiracy can be proven by the relation, conduct, or circumstances of the parties.[50]

In a Nevada case, the court warned that mere knowledge or approval of, or acquiescence in, the object and purpose of the conspiracy *without agreement* to cooperate in achieving the object or purpose does not make one a party to the conspiracy.[51] Any one of the conspirators may commit the overt act toward achievement of the goal; it does not have to be performed by the defendant.[52] In a more recent case, a Nevada court dealt with the Pinkerton Rule that held each co-conspirator culpable for all the natural and foreseeable acts of each co-conspirator. Nevada, along with many other states, has rejected this approach.[53]

In some states, the statute includes a provision regarding the defense of renunciation.[54] Under these statutes, it is a defense if the facts manifest a voluntary and complete renunciation of the criminal purpose and the defendant prevented the commission of the crime. However, renunciation is not voluntary if motivated by the belief that circumstances exist that pose a particular threat of apprehension or detection.

D. Summary

Conspiracy was a crime at common law and is a crime in all states. While it is not a crime to think about committing a crime; and it is not a crime to discuss committing a crime, once that discussion changes to an agreement among the parties and at least one party commits at least one overt act, the crime of conspiracy has occurred.

Conspiracy	
A/R	Agreement by one party with another, to commit a criminal act or a lawful act in a criminal manner, and an overt act by at least one of the parties
M/R	Specific intent

§ 4.5 Summary

Persons may be guilty of an offense if their acts or conduct are part of the preparation for the commission of substantive crimes even though those crimes are not consummated. The rationale of the lawmakers is that conduct that clearly indicates the dangerousness of a defendant or a predisposition toward criminality should not go unpunished even though the intended criminal act is not completed. These preparatory activity crimes usually consist of "attempt," "solicitation," and "conspiracy."

One may be punished for attempt if the prosecution can show intent to commit a crime plus performance of some overt act toward the commission of the crime. To constitute attempt, the defendant's conduct must be more than merely preparatory, but it is not necessary to show that the ultimate step toward commission of the substantive crime occurred. The fact that it is impossible to commit the crime is not necessarily a defense; however, its consummation must be at least apparently possible. Also, abandonment or withdrawal is a defense if the intent to commit the crime is freely and voluntarily abandoned before the act was put in progress for final execution and if no outside cause prompted the abandonment.

The crime of solicitation consists of: an intent to promote or facilitate the commission of a particular criminal offense and some overt act, such as the initiatory act of solicitation, request, command, or encouragement. At common law, the offense of solicitation was punishable as a misdemeanor without regard to the nature of the substantive crime solicited. However, some recently enacted statutes provide a penalty structure that is geared toward the penalty for the crime solicited.

The crime of conspiracy was an offense under the English common law and is an offense in all states. The rationale for making conspiracy a crime is that society, having the power to punish for dangerous behavior, cannot be powerless against those who work to bring about that behavior.

Conspiracy has been defined as an agreement or combination of two or more persons to do a criminal or unlawful act or to accomplish a criminal or unlawful purpose, followed by an overt act. Withdrawal from a conspiracy may be a defense—that is, the defendant may introduce evidence to show that he disavowed or defeated the purpose of the conspiracy before the agreement was carried out. The majority rule seems to be that the defendant bears the burden of proving withdrawal from a conspiracy.

Review Questions

1. What were the three preparatory offenses discussed in this chapter.

2. Under common law was attempt a felony or a misdemeanor?

3. What does it mean to say that attempt is a specific intent crime?

4. What are the four traditional elements of attempt?

5. What are the four tests to prove the "overt act" element?

6. Distinguish between factual and legal impossibility.

7. Explain hybrid legal impossibility and whether or not the majority of states allow this as a defense to culpability in attempt cases.

8. Explain when abandonment might be used as a defense to a charge of attempt.

9. What test does the MPC use to prove "overt act"? Does the MPC recognize legal impossibility as a defense? Does the MPC allow abandonment (or renunciation) as a defense?

10. Under common law was solicitation to murder a more serious crime than solicitation to commit forgery?

11. What are the traditional elements of solicitation? Is it a specific intent crime?

12. Can one renunciate a solicitation as a defense?

13. What are the traditional elements of the crime of conspiracy?

14. Is it a defense to a charge of conspiracy that the defendant is really in league with government informants who have no intention of carrying out the crime?

15. Describe the Wharton Rule.

16. Describe the Pinkerton Rule. Is it still the law in most states?

17. Is there available a defense of abandonment for the charge of conspiracy?

18. The MPC requires an overt act in only some types of conspiracies - which are they?

19. Is conspiracy a specific intent crime?

20. Can someone be convicted of conspiracy if other conspirators are never charged with a crime?

Notes

[1]   State v. Reis, 230 N.C. 272, 52 S.E.2d 880 (1949).

[2]   State v. Leach, 36 Wash. 2d 641, 219 P.2d 972 (1950).

[3]   People v. Crane, 302 Ill. 217, 134 N.E. 99 (1922).

[4]   State v. Goodman, 322 S.E.2d 408 (N.C. 1984).

[5]   Fleming v. State, 374 So. 2d 954 (Fla. 1979); Gilley v. Commonwealth, 280 Ky. 306, 133 S.W.2d 67 (1939).

[6]   *See*, however, Smith v. United States, 813 A.2d 216 (D.C. 2002), in which the court held that the only intent required to commit the crime of "attempt" is an intent to commit the offense allegedly attempted.

[7]   State v. Group, 781 N.E.2d 980 (Ohio 2002); United States v. Buffington, 815 F.2d 292 (9th Cir. 1987).

[8]   People v. Fiegelman, 33 Cal. App. 2d 100, 91 P.2d 156 (1933).

[9]   22 C.J.S. *Criminal Law* § 123 (1989).

[10]   State v. Taylor, 345 Mo. 325, 133 S.W.2d 336 (1939).

[11]   State v. Guffey, 262 S.W.2d 152 (Mo. Ct. App. 1953).

[12]   People v. Jaffe, 185 N.Y. 497, 78 N.E. 169 (N.Y. 1906). See also United States v. Monasterski, 567 F.2d 677 (E.D. Mich. 1987).

[13]   People v. Teal, 196 N.Y. 372, 89 N.E. 1086 (1909).

[14]   People v. Montgomery, 47 Cal. App. 2d 1, 117 P.2d 437 (1941).

[15]   People v. Walker, 33 Cal. 2d 250, 201 P.2d 6 (1948), *cert. denied*, 336 U.S. 940, 69 S. Ct. 744, 93 L. Ed. 1098 (1949).

[16]   Model Penal Code § 5.01 (1985).

[17]   Ky. Rev. Stat. § 506.010 (Baldwin 2002).

[18]   Luttrell v. Commonwealth, 554 S.W.2d 75 (Ky. 1977)

[19]   State v. Miller, 477 S.E.2d 915 (N.C. 1996). *See also* State v. Williams-Rusch, 928 P.2d 169 (Mont. 1996).

[20]   People v. Ritson, 74 Cal. Rptr. 2d 698 (1998). *See also* People v. Saous, 661 N.Y.2d 488 (1997).

[21]   State v. Green, 122 Ohio App. 3d 566, 702 N.E.2d 462 (1997).

[22]   People v. Sabo, 687 N.Y.S.2d 513 (1998).

23   Commonwealth v. Randolph, 146 Pa. 83, 23 A. 388 (1882).

24   State v. Grimes, 735 P.2d 1277 (Or. 1987).

25   People v. Burt, 45 Cal. 2d 311, 288 P.2d 503 (1955).

26   MODEL PENAL CODE § 5.02 (1985).

27   720 ILL. COMP. STAT. 5/8-1 (2003).

28   People v. Lewis, 84 Ill. App. 3d 556, 406 N.E.2d 11 (1980).

29   People v. McCommon, 79 Ill. App. 3d, 399 N.E.2d 224 (1979).

30   NEV. REV. STAT. § 199.500 (1995).

31   Moran v. Schwarz, 826 P.2d 952 (Nev. 1992).

32   Branche v. Commonwealth, 25 Va. App. 480, 489 S.E.2d 692 (1997).

33   Scales v. United States, 367 U.S. 203, 81 S. Ct. 1469, 6 L. Ed. 2d 782 (1961).

34   United States v. Cryan, 490 F. Supp. 1234 (D.N.J. 1980).

35   Miller v. United States, 382 F.2d 583 (9th Cir. 1967); United States v. Heck, 449 F.2d 778 (9th Cir. 1974).

36   United States v. Jenkins, 313 F.3d 549 (10th Cir. 2002)

37   Kennemore v. State, 149 S.E.2d 791 (Ga. 1966).

38   United States v. Cantu, 557 F.2d 1173 (5th Cir. 1977).

39   Hall v. United States, 109 F.2d 976 (10th Cir. 1940); State v. Porro, 377 A.2d 909 (N.J. 1977).

40   Orear v. United States, 261 F. 257 (5th Cir. 1919).

41   United States v. Bradsby, 628 F.2d 901 (5th Cir. 1980); Krasn v. United States, 614 F.2d 1229 (9th Cir. 1980); United States v. Read, 658 F.2d 1225 (7th Cir. 1981).

42   MODEL PENAL CODE § 5.03 (1985).

43   IND. CODE ANN. § 35-41-5-2 (Burns 2002).

44   Williams v. State, 274 Ind. 578, 412 N.E.2d 1211 (1980); Lee v. State, 397 N.E.2d 1047 (Ind. Ct. App. 1979), *cert. denied*, 449 U.S. 983, 101 S. Ct. 399, 66 L. Ed. 2d 245 (1980). *See also* State v. Nichols, 481 S.E.2d 118 (S.C. 1997) and Buell v. State, 668 N.E.2d 251 (Ind. 1996).

45   Sawyer v. State, 583 N.E.2d 795 (Ind. Ct. App. 1991).

46   United States v. Bobo, 586 F.2d 355 (5th Cir. 1978).

47   United States v. Jimenez Recio, 537 U.S. 270, 123 S. Ct. 819, 154 L. Ed. 2d 744 (2003).

48   People v. Athar, 129 Cal. Rptr. 2d 351 (2002).

49   United States v. Oberdick, 810 A.2d 296 (Conn. 2002).

50   Commonwealth v. Baskerville, 681 A.2d 195 (Pa. 1996).

51   Doyle v. State, 921 P.2d 901 (Nev. 1996).

52   Bolden v. Nevada, 124 P.3d 191 (2005)

53   *See*, for instance, KY. REV. STAT. § 506.060 (Baldwin 2002); or KY. REV. STAT. 161.430 (Baldwin 1995); TEX PENAL CODE § 15.04 (2002).

Offenses Against Persons— Excluding Sex Offenses

Chapter Outline

Cases

Voluntary Manslaughter: *State v. Thornton*, 730 S.W.2d 309 (Tenn. 1987)
Hate Crimes: *Wisconsin v. Mitchell*, 508 U.S. 476 (1993)

Key Terms and Concepts

assault	justifiable homicide
asportation	kidnapping
assisted suicide	malice aforethought
battery	mayhem
depraved heart murder	murder
excusable homicide	negligent homicide
felony-murder doctrine	premeditation
feticide	provocation
hate crime	transferred intent
homicide	unlawful imprisonment
involuntary manslaughter	voluntary manslaughter
	year-and-a-day rule

§ 5.1 Introduction

Crimes are usually classified according to the social harm they cause. In Chapters 5 through 12, crimes are placed in categories that roughly approximate most state penal codes. The United States Code, which defines federal crimes, will be reviewed in Chapters 13 through 15.

Although the terminology is often "offenses against the person" and "offenses against the habitation," what is really meant is "an offense against the state in the form of harm to the person" as well as "an offense against the state in the form of harm to the habitation." When charged with an "offense against property," the defendant is prosecuted in the interest of the state, and not in the interest of the individual whose property was involved, although, of course, the individual who owns the property is concerned. In this book, the discussion regarding state crimes is divided into these segments:

1. offenses against persons, excluding sex crimes (Chapter 5);

2. offenses against the person, sex crimes (Chapter 6);

3. offenses against property—destruction and intrusion offenses (Chapter 7);

4.   offenses against property involving theft (Chapter 8);

5.   offenses involving forgery, counterfeiting, and other fraudulent practices (Chapter 9);

6.   offenses against the public health and morals (Chapter 10);

7.   offenses against the public peace, including drugs (Chapter 11);

8.   offenses against justice administration (Chapter 12).

In this chapter (after first defining and explaining homicide in general), the specific crimes of murder, manslaughter, suicide, assault and battery, kidnapping and related offenses, and other crimes against the person are explained. The discussion for every crime will follow the same organization:

■   a discussion of common law;

■   the presentation of the Model Penal Code;

■   a discussion of current state statutes and any special issues or circumstances.

§ 5.2   Homicide

Not all deaths are homicides. The elements of homicide come to us from the common law.

A.   Common Law

In early common law, any intentional killing was homicide, even if it was suicide. However, in later years, **homicide** was generally defined as the unlawful killing of a human being *by another* human being. Homicide has also been defined as: "the unlawful killing of a human being under any circumstances, by the act, agency, or omission of another."[1] The use of "another" was added to separate homicide from suicide, although suicide or attempted suicide was still an ecclesiastical offense.

According to the most modern definitions, suicide is not a homicide, and may or may not be a crime, depending on the statutory provisions of the jurisdiction. Applying this definition, it is not homicide for a man to kill an animal or for an animal to kill a man.[2] It is a homicide if an animal is used as a means of killing another person. In such a case, the law attributes the killing of the human to the person who set in motion the means of causing death.

1.   Year-and-a-Day Rule

Under common law, death was defined as the cessation of cardiac and respiratory functions. One causation issue occurred when the death resulted long after the injury. The law developed a rule to resolve the issue called the "**year-and-a-day rule**." At common law, as early as 1763, the courts recognized the "year-and-a-day" rule.[3] This rule, as stated, for instance, in *State v. Orrell* (1826), was:

> If death did not take place within a year and a day of the time of receiving the wound, the law draws the conclusion that it was not the cause of death; and neither the court nor jury can draw a contrary one.[4]

The reason for applying the rule in murder prosecutions was the uncertainty of medical science in determining the cause of death, and that when a defendant's life was at stake, the rule of law ought to be certain. Of course, the offender could be prosecuted and tried for other offenses, such as assault or attempted murder.

2. Mens Rea

The common law recognized that, in order to be murder, the killing had to be done with **malice aforethought**; however, the *mens rea* that distinguished first-degree from second-degree murder, or murder from manslaughter, was not consistent across jurisdictions. The Model Penal Code addressed this issue.

B. Model Penal Code

The Model Penal Code's greatest contribution to jurisprudence is that it specifically defined the levels of *mens rea* that relate to the different degrees of homicide. The level of *mens rea* determines the type of homicide: murder, manslaughter, or negligent homicide. The basic elements of homicide are the same as in common law.

---

§ 210.1 Criminal Homicide[5]

(1) A person is guilty of criminal homicide if he purposely, knowingly, recklessly or negligently causes the death of another human being.

(2) Criminal homicide is murder, manslaughter or negligent homicide.

C. State Statutes, Codes, and Cases

Some states have adopted much of the wording of the Model Penal Code, but have retained the distinction between first and second degrees of murder.[6] Other states have divided manslaughter into degrees.[7] The *actus reus* of homicide is always an act that results in the death of another. The *mens rea* determines the type of homicide.

1. *Actus Reus*: (Causation: Year-and-a-Day Rule)

Advancements in medical science have necessitated modifications of the common law "year-and-a-day" rule, although some state courts have concluded that it is up to the legislature to change the rule.[8] In the case of *State v. Hefler*, the Supreme Court of North Carolina took judicial notice of the rapid development and proliferation of the arts and sciences of medicine and crime detection, and concluded that the law was an anachronism.[9]

In *Rogers v Tennessee*, a defendant appealed his conviction of second degree murder. His victim died of a kidney infection 15 months after the defendant stabbed the man in the heart. The defendant/appellant argued that the year and a day rule was part of the law of Tennessee, having been carried over to statutory law from the common law; he argued that not applying it to him would be a violation of due process and an unconstitutional ex post facto application of law. The Supreme Court upheld the Tennessee court decision that affirmed his conviction and held that it was not a violation of due process because it was not unexpected (and therefore there was notice) that the rule would be abandoned. Justice O'Connor, writing for the majority, said:

> The year and a day rule is widely viewed as an outdated relic of the common law. Petitioner does not even so much as hint that good reasons exist for retaining the rule, and so we need not delve too deeply into the rule and its history here. . . . For this reason, the year and a day rule has been legislatively or judicially abolished in the vast majority of jurisdictions recently to have addressed the issue . . . the fact that a vast number of jurisdictions have abolished a rule that has so clearly outlived its purpose is surely relevant to whether the abolition of the rule in a particular case can be said to be unexpected and indefensible by reference to the law as it then existed.

Finally, and perhaps most importantly, at the time of petitioner's crime the year and a day rule had only the most tenuous foothold as part of the criminal law of the State of Tennessee. The rule did not exist as part of Tennessee's statutory criminal code. And while the Supreme Court of Tennessee concluded that the rule persisted at common law, it also pointedly observed that the rule had never once served as a ground of decision in any prosecution for murder in the State. Indeed, in all the reported Tennessee cases, the rule has been mentioned only three times, and each time in dicta.[10]

2. *Actus Reus*: Defining Death

Under common law, death was defined as the cessation of respiratory functions. As medical science is now able to maintain cardiorespiratory systems even after the brain stops functioning, brain-death statutes have been substituted for the common law in determining when a person is dead.[11]

According to the National Conference of Commissioners on Uniform State Laws and the American Law Institute, the Uniform Determination of

Death Act (1980) codifies the existing common law basis of determining death—total failure of the cardiorespiratory system—and extends the common law determination of death to include irreversible loss of all brain function. The entire brain must cease to function, irreversibly. The "entire brain" includes the brain stem, as well as the neocortex. The concept of "entire brain" distinguishes determination of death under this Act from "neocortical death" or "persistent vegetative state."

In deciding who makes the determination of death, a Washington court held that it is for the law, rather than medicine, to define the standard of death, and although the law adopts the brain death standard, it is for the medical profession to determine the applicable criteria, in accordance with accepted medical standards, for deciding whether brain death has occurred. In *In re Welfare of Bowman*, the court reiterated that an individual who has sustained either: (1) irreversible cessation of circulation and respiratory functions, or (2) irreversible cessation of all functions of the entire brain, including the brain stem, is "dead."[12]

The Terry Schiavo case was a sad example of the difficulties of determining death and the problems that arise when someone is in a permanent vegetative state with minimal brain functioning. In this case, Schiavo was diagnosed as being in a permanent vegetative state and had been for 15 years. However, she was not "brain dead" according to the definitions above. According to Florida law, her husband and her doctors had the legal authority to remove her feeding tubes, thus allowing her to die. The legal wrangling that resulted occurred because her parents did not want that to happen. Some of the legal questions that were litigated were: Who had legal authority to decide whether to remove the feeding tubes? And in what circumstances must medical authorities prolong life despite lack of neo-cortical functioning? The fact is that medical science can keep a person's body "alive" long after the body would die naturally. States have had to deal with this fact by statutorily defining death and defining the authority to stop life-prolonging procedures. Without statutory authority, removing feeding tubes from someone in a vegetative state may be murder.

3. Exception to Double Jeopardy

What happens if a victim dies as a result of an assault after the perpetrator has already been charged and convicted of a lesser crime (assault or attempted murder)? One would assume that the prohibition of double jeopardy would prevent such a prosecution but that is not necessarily the case. In an exception to double jeopardy recognized by some state statutes, a second prosecution may commence because of a finding that the more serious crime of homicide includes additional elements to the lesser crime of assault. In *New York v. Latham*, the defendant had pled guilty to attempted murder in the second degree after he stabbed his ex-fiancee. She was, at the time, completely paralyzed after having suffered a stroke as a result of the stabbing. Seven weeks after he was sentenced, she died and an indictment for depraved indifference murder was returned. The state statute authorized a "delayed death" exception to the double jeopardy protections in federal and state constitutions. The court held that double jeopardy is not violated by a second prosecution because the attempted homicide charge does not contain the *actus reus* of causing the death of another, while a homicide charge does require a death. Therefore, the two prosecutions are not based on the same offense and are not violative of double jeopardy.[13] Note that if the state has abolished the year-and-a-day rule, the second prosecution may come long after the first conviction.

4. Summary

Although the law of homicide has been changed greatly by statute, one can get an overall concept of the common law relating to homicide if the elements of the various crimes are summarized and distinguished.

Murder—first degree (aggravated or premeditated)
1. Unlawful killing
2. One person by another
3. With malice aforethought
4. With deliberation, purpose, design, or premeditation

Murder
1. Unlawful killing
2. One person by another
3. With malice aforethought

Felony Murder
1. Unlawful killing
2. One person by any other or foreseeable cause
3. During an inherently dangerous felony

Voluntary manslaughter
1. Unlawful killing
2. One person by another
3. Intentional killing but with adequate provocation and committed in the heat of passion

Involuntary manslaughter
1. Unlawful killing
2. One person by another
3. During unlawful act or lawful act done in a criminally negligent manner

Misdemeanor Manslaughter
1. Unlawful killing
2. One person by any other or foreseeable cause
3. During the commission of a misdemeanor

---

§ 5.3   Murder

A. *Common Law*

At common law, and traditionally in the United States, **murder** is defined as a homicide committed with malice aforethought. Because the prosecutor is required to introduce evidence to prove each of the specific elements, each element is discussed here.

1. Unlawful Killing

In homicide, a killing is unlawful unless it comes under the **justifiable homicide** or excusable category. Homicide is justifiable if it is either commanded or authorized by law; for example, the killing of an enemy on the field of battle as an act of war and within the rules of war. Another example is the execution of a sentence of death pronounced by a competent tribunal. **Excusable homicide** is committed by one doing a lawful act without intention to hurt, or in self-defense. If death occurs by accident while the person causing the death is engaged in a lawful act and performing it with due care, the homicide is excusable.[14]

The distinction between justifiable and excusable homicide was important at early common law, because excusable homicide resulted in forfeiture of goods. However, the distinction is less important today, because neither entails any criminal responsibility. Today, the two terms are often used synonymously.

2. A Human Being

In the absence of a statute, a person cannot be convicted of murder unless the person whose death occurred was born alive. This means that under common law if a defendant beat a pregnant woman with the express purpose of killing her fetus, the crime was assault, not murder (if the fetus was killed) or attempted murder. As one court stated, "there is no murder without homicide, and no homicide without birth alive."[15] However, almost half of the states have amended their statutes to define murder as the "unlawful killing of a human being, or a fetus . . ."[16] or created a new "**feticide**" statute to cover the killing of an unborn.[17] In crafting new laws or applying old ones, care must be taken to avoid coming into conflict with Supreme Court decisions that prohibit laws that "unreasonably intrude" upon a woman's right to choose an abortion. Laws typically distinguish by stage of pregnancy and/or intent and mindset of the woman. In many states, the right to an abortion is narrowly defined, and anything that falls outside of the statutory limits could be charged as a homicide.

Legal News

A Texas law prohibits abortions during the third trimester or without parental approval. Because of the state's fetal protection law, it is possible, according to some legal groups in Texas, that doctors could face the death penalty for performing such abortions. The fetal protection law is one of the nation's strongest and has enumerated exceptions to culpability, such as when a fetus dies through legal drug use, action taken by the mother, or a lawful medical procedure. Because abortions, other than those described above, would not be lawful, the death would be ruled a homicide and, because the death of a child under age six is a capital crime in Texas, the doctor could face the death penalty—although legislators have stated that this result was not their intent in passing the law.[18]

In an interesting application of the fetal protection law, a teenage boy in south Texas was convicted of murder for hitting his girlfriend and stepping on her stomach to cause a miscarriage. The defense argued that the girl asked him to do it and equal protection was violated because he could be prosecuted for murder, but no criminal charges could be leveled against the girl because the statute specifically excluded the pregnant woman from culpability. Facts were disputed and the prosecutor argued that the girl was coerced to say that she agreed to the beating and wanted the miscarriage.[19] An appeal of the conviction was unsuccessful.

Source: Cook, A. (2007). "Ninth Circuit Court of Appeals Denies Man's Claims." *Lufkin Daily News*, January 26, 2007:A1.

3. By Another Human Being

Proof that the killing was committed by another human being requires that evidence be produced to show that the person accused committed the act or put into motion the means that resulted in the death. In modern law, suicide is not homicide, but attempted suicide might be. We will discuss these concepts in a later section.

4. With Malice Aforethought

Early common law required at least an attempt to kill, plus an element of hatred, spite, or ill-will, in order to bring the killing within the malice definition. Also, at first, judges required that the prosecution prove that the defendant actually had a previously thought-out intent to kill, though spite probably was never actually necessary.[20] Gradually, judges in England came to recognize that a murder may be committed even though there was no premeditated intent to kill. The older authorities resorted to an "implied intent" rationale in which no intent, in fact, existed. Later the courts spoke more factually and frankly, agreeing that murder may be committed under some circumstances without the intent to kill.[21] In fact, even though early statutes required "malice aforethought," the defendant did not need to have ill will toward the victim, nor was there a necessity that the intent to kill was anything more than a split-second before the act as long as there is a showing of intent to kill. "Malice" may be found even though the killing is a "mercy killing."[22] In this case, there may be no malicious intent as originally defined, but the intent to kill is there and that is sufficient to support a murder conviction.

5. Felony-Murder

In England, a doctrine gradually developed that came to be known as the **felony-murder doctrine**. Under early English law, one who, in the commission or attempted commission of any felony, caused another's death, could be found guilty of murder. Blackstone's view was that: "If one intends to do another a felony, and undesignedly kills a man, this is also murder."[23]

The justification for this rule is that it places upon the person committing or attempting a felony the hazard of possible guilt of murder if he or she creates a substantial risk that could result in the loss of life. According to this reasoning, common experience points to the presence of a substantial human risk from the perpetration of some felonies.

When the felony-murder doctrine was originated, it was included to protect human life, but at that time there were few felonies. Later, as the number of felonies multiplied to include a great number of relatively minor offenses, many of which involved no great danger to life or limb, it became necessary, in order to alleviate the harshness of the rule, to limit it to designated felonies. Thus, case decisions and early statutes identified "inherently dangerous" felonies (typically attempted murder, robbery, arson, escape, and a few others) where unintentional deaths may result in felony-murder prosecutions. The Model Penal Code has continued this limitation.

B. Model Penal Code

The Model Penal Code has had great influence on the revision of the state laws. In the Model Penal Code, murder is not differentiated into first and second degree as it is in many state codes.

---

§ 210.2 Murder[24]

(1) Except as provided in § 210.3(1)(b), criminal homicide constitutes murder when:

    (a) it is committed purposely or knowingly; or

    (b) it is committed recklessly under circumstances manifesting extreme indifference to the value of human life. Such recklessness and indifference are presumed if the actor is engaged or is an accomplice in the commission of, or an attempt to commit, or flight after committing or attempting to commit robbery, rape or deviate sexual intercourse by force or threat of force, arson, burglary, kidnapping or felonious escape.

(2) Murder is a felony of the first degree [but a person convicted of murder may be sentenced to death, as provided in § 210.6].

The Model Penal Code makes no reference to such terms as "malice afore-thought" and "premeditation," but instead substitutes a different grading structure. Under § 210.2(1)(a), a person may be found guilty of murder if the killing was done purposely or knowingly. Purposeful murders are those that are premeditated and with specific intent. Knowing murders are those where the person may not have specifically intended to murder, but their actions were such that a death was almost certain to result; for instance, shooting a gun at someone to "only injure" them or scare them would be an example of this type of murder.[25]

Under Subsection (b), criminal homicide also constitutes murder when it is "committed recklessly under circumstances manifesting extreme indifference to the value of human life." The idea is that the action is so egregious that the person must have intended the result or, when undertaking an act of gross recklessness, simply did not care if someone would be killed. It is sometimes referred to as "wanton disregard" or depraved heart murder. Playing Russian Roulette would be an example of this type of murder.[26] There is such a high probability of someone being killed or injured by this activity that the law holds the surviving player responsible for a type of murder.

The recklessness displayed in this type of murder is different from the *mens rea* of recklessness found in other crimes. Consider the difference: speeding or drinking and driving may be considered reckless (you knew of the risk and did it anyway), and if a death results, you would no doubt be charged with some form of vehicular or involuntary manslaughter. However, it is quite another thing to drive a car up onto a sidewalk through a crowd of people, or shoot a gun into a crowded bar. Even though you may not have intended to kill someone, you would probably be charged with murder rather than manslaughter because of your "wanton disregard," "extreme indifference," or "depraved indifference" to human life. In effect, the law will hold you to the natural and foreseeable consequences of your act and because it is extremely probable that someone will be killed, the law will hold you to the same degree of culpability as if you intended someone to die.

The different levels of *mens rea* offered by the Model Penal Code were defined and described in the last chapter. Purposeful is when the actor has a conscious objective to conduct the act and cause the result and is aware of the existence of any attendant circumstances of the crime. Knowing is when the actor is aware of any material element of the crime and/or that his conduct is of the nature prohibited. Recklessness is when the actor is aware of a substantial and unjustifiable risk and engages in an action despite that knowledge. Negligence is when the actor engages in action while unaware of a substantial and unjustifiable risk, but should have known of the risk.

The Model Penal Code does not distinguish between first-degree and second-degree murder, and provides that murder is a felony of the first degree. The Model Penal Code does not use the term "felony-murder," but provides that murder committed in the perpetration, or an attempt to perpetrate, other crimes will be murder in the first degree. It does, however, limit the culpability only to certain designated crimes (those that have been determined to be "inherently dangerous").

C. State Statutes, Codes, and Cases

Some states have modified the common law relating to murder, others have adopted the Model Penal Code in substance, while still others have taken parts of the Model Penal Code and retained parts of their previously written statutes. Some states include provisions that retain the felony-murder doctrine.

New Mexico's revised statute deviates from the common law, but uses different language from the Model Penal Code. This statute provides:

> § 30-2-1 Murder.
>
> A. Murder in the first degree is the killing of one human being by another without lawful justification or excuse, by any of the means with which death may be caused:
> (1) by any kind of willful, deliberate and premeditated killing;
> (2) in the commission of or attempt to commit any felony; or
> (3) by any act greatly dangerous to the lives of others, indicating a depraved mind regardless of human life.
>
> Whoever commits murder in the first degree is guilty of a capital felony.
>
> B. Unless he is acting upon sufficient provocation, upon a sudden quarrel or in the heat of passion, a person who kills another human being without lawful justification or excuse commits murder in the second degree if in performing the acts which cause the death he knows that such acts create a strong probability of death or great bodily harm to that individual or another.
>
> Murder in the second degree is a lesser included offense of the crime of murder in the first degree.
>
> Whoever commits murder in the second degree is guilty of a second degree felony . . .[27]

1. First-Degree Murder

In most states, legislatures decided very early that the crime of murder should be divided into two categories for the purpose of fixing the penalty. First-degree murder encompasses the intent to commit murder, accompanied by premeditation and deliberation. In some states, the first-degree category of murder includes murder by lying in wait, by poison, or by torture. The distinguishing factors in first-degree murder are premeditation and deliberation. When these terms are used, the prosecution must show not only that there was malice, but also must prove **premeditation** or deliberation. Premeditation means that one in fact did reflect, at least for a short period, before the act of killing.[28]

In most states that require proof of deliberation and premeditation to sustain a finding of first-degree murder, the evidence must establish that a human being was unlawfully killed, that the defendant did the killing, and that the killing was done in an intentional, deliberate, and premeditated way. In defining premeditation, a Florida court noted that premeditation, as an element of first-degree murder, is a fully formed conscious purpose to kill, which exists in the mind of the perpetrator for a sufficient length of time to permit reflection, and in pursuance of which an act of killing ensues. Premeditation does not have to be contemplated for any particular period before the act, and may occur in moments before the act.[29] In some states, other forms of murder are also designated by statute as first degree. An example would be the killing of a peace officer.

2. Second-Degree Murder

If premeditation or intent cannot be proven (or the particular *mens rea* requirements specified by statute), then the murder would be prosecuted as second degree. Recall the concepts of specific intent and general intent. First-degree murder is a specific intent crime (one intends the act and intends the consequence), and second-degree murder is a general intent crime (one intends the act but not necessarily the consequence). In other words, the prosecutor does not have to prove that the defendant intended that his act would result in the death of the victim. An individual who beats a victim, shoots at a victim, pushes a victim out of a boat and the victim drowns, or in any other way commits dangerous acts that put the victim in peril, may argue that he or she never intended for the victim to die; however, if death or grievous bodily harm is the natural and foreseeable consequence of the defendant's actions and the defendant intended to do the actions, then a second degree murder conviction can be sustained.

3. Depraved Indifference Murder

Under common law and the Model Penal Code, when an offender does an act that shows a complete disregard (or depraved indifference) for human life and there is a probable certainty of injury, that offender may be found guilty of **depraved heart murder** even if they had no intent to kill. One example is a person shooting into a crowded bar but not aiming at anyone or intending anyone to die.

In a federal case in 1983, the court explained that the malice required for a conviction of first- or second-degree murder does not require subjective intent to kill, but may be established by evidence of conduct that is reckless, wanton, and a gross deviation from reasonable standards of care, of such a nature that the jury is warranted in inferring that the defendant was aware of a serious risk of death or serious bodily harm.[30]

In some cases, homicides resulting from drunk driving may be prosecuted as depraved indifference murders rather than involuntary homicides. The degree of drunkenness and extent of prior offenses are factors that go into a prosecutor's decision to charge.[31]

4. Transferred Intent

The doctrine of **transferred intent** holds an offender responsible even when the end result is not what was intended. If there is an *actus reus* and a *mens rea*, then the *mens rea* need not be directed toward the person killed. For example, if one intends to kill one person or group of persons, but instead kills someone else, this is sufficient to bring the crime within the category of murder.[32]

5. Felony-Murder

Under the common law, any killing that occurred during the course of a felony could be a "felony-murder," which was the same degree of seriousness as murder with "malice aforethought." The Model Penal Code continued the felony-murder doctrine, but limited it to specific felonies that were "inherently dangerous." Most state statutes also restrict felony-murder culpability to only certain felonies; however the felony-murder doctrine may include victims that range from the target of the underlying felony, to passersby, onlookers, public safety officials responding to the felony, and even co-defendants killed by police officers. Some state courts, however, evidently would prefer to abolish the doctrine.

In discussing the constitutionality of the felony-murder rule, the Supreme Court of New Mexico discerned that "[f]ew legal doctrines have been as maligned and yet have shown as great a resiliency as the felony-murder rule."[33] The court pointed out that this rule has been described as "astonishing," "monstrous," and an insupportable "legal fiction." The court quoted from another case in holding that there is "no logical or practical basis for its existence in modern law." While not declaring the felony-murder statute to be invalid, the Supreme Court of New Mexico first imposed the requirement that, in order to charge a felony-murder for a killing in the commission or attempted commission of a felony, the felony must be either a first-degree felony or the lesser-degree felony must be inherently dangerous or committed under circumstances that are inherently dangerous. In addition, to prove that the defendant caused the killing, "there must be proof that the defendant intended to kill (or was knowingly heedless that death might result from his conduct)."[34]

An example of a statute that uses some of the terminology of the Model Penal Code but also contains provisions concerning felony-murder is that of Indiana.[35] Note that the Indiana statute has added provisions concerning the killing of a human being while committing crimes related to drugs and carjacking. It provides:

35-43-1-1. Murder—a person who:

(1) Knowingly or intentionally kills another human being;
(2) Kills another human being while committing or attempting to commit arson, burglary, child molesting, consumer product tampering, criminal deviate conduct, kidnapping, rape, robbery, or carjacking;
(3) Kills another human being while committing or attempting to commit:
     (A) Dealing in or manufacturing cocaine, a narcotic drug, or methamphetamine [IC 35-48-4-1];
     (B) Dealing in a schedule I, II, or III controlled substance [IC 35-48-4-2];
     (C) Dealing in a schedule IV controlled substance [IC 35-48-4-3]; or
     (D) Dealing in a schedule V controlled substance; or
(4) Knowingly or intentionally kills a fetus that has attained viability (as defined in IC 16-18-2-365);

Commits murder, a felony.

The courts have found several ways of justifying the felony-murder rule. For example, one court indicated that the general rationale behind the felony-murder rule is that the intent to commit the felony substitutes for the malice aforethought.[36] The felony-murder statutes have been held valid as a proper exercise of the legislature's authority to prescribe serious punishment for killings committed with the requisite criminal intent. If the killing occurred during the commission or the attempted commission of inherently dangerous felonies as described in the respective codes, the statutes are constitutional and enforceable.

The felony-murder rule can produce harsh results. For example, a defendant left a loaded gun on a table and, unaware that his friend had turned the firing chamber, fired at and killed his friend. His lack of intent would negate any intentional murder charge; however, instead of involuntary manslaughter, he was successfully charged with felony-murder based on the felonies of aggravated assault and possession of a firearm during the commission of a felony.[37]

Offenders may be held responsible for accidental deaths that occur during the course of a felony—the decedent might be the targeted victim, a bystander, crime partner, or even a police officer or public safety official. For instance, an arsonist would very likely be charged with felony murder if a firefighter died in the fire. In *People v. Stamp*, a robbery victim died of a heart attack during the robbery. The conviction was upheld even though there was evidence that with the victim's heart problems, he might have died soon anyway.[38] In another case, the victim died of cardiac arrest while pursuing a purse snatcher.[39] The purse snatcher was convicted of felony-murder and sentenced to 30 years imprisonment.

A felony that results in a death may be charged as felony-murder; while a misdemeanor that results in a death may be charged as misdemeanor manslaughter. Generally, deaths that result from drunk driving are charged as involuntary manslaughter, vehicular manslaughter, negligent manslaughter or misdemeanor manslaughter. If state statutes define a DWI as a felony (in many states the second or third offense does increase the charge to a felony), and allows for that type of felony to be used as the underlying felony for felony-murder, then a death that occurs because of a DWI may be charged as felony-murder (which is first degree and carries the heaviest sanctions).

During the 1980s, the U.S. Supreme Court considered the constitutionality of felony-murder convictions in state courts when they resulted in death sentences. In *Enmund v. Florida*, the defendant was convicted, along with his co-defendant, of first-degree robbery and the murder of two elderly people in their farmhouse. Both were sentenced to death.[40] The defendant claimed that, because he was not present at the killings, and he was only the driver of the car parked at the side of the road near the farmhouse at the time of the killings, the imposition of the death sentence was inconsistent with the Eighth and Fourteenth Amendments. The Supreme Court of the United States agreed. The majority pointed out that only a small minority of states (nine) allowed the death penalty to be imposed solely because the defendant somehow participated in the robbery in the course of which a murder was committed, but did not take or intend to take life, or intend that lethal force be employed. The Court also indicated that, while robbery is a serious crime deserving serious punishment, it is not a crime that is so grievous an affront to humanity that the only adequate response may be the penalty of death. The court concluded that putting the defendant to death to avenge two killings that he did not commit or intend to commit or cause would not measurably contribute to the retribution end of ensuring that the criminal gets his or her just deserts.

However, in the case of *Tison v. Arizona* in 1987, the U.S. Supreme Court affirmed the defendant's conviction of capital murder under Arizona's felony-murder and accomplice-liability statutes.[41] The defendants had challenged their death sentence in a state post-conviction proceeding, alleging that the *Enmund v. Florida* case discussed above required a finding of "intent to kill." They argued that the finding in the *Enmund* case included situations in which the defendant intended, contemplated, or anticipated that lethal force would or might be used, or that life would or might be taken in accomplishing the underlying felony.

The majority of the U.S. Supreme Court agreed that the Eighth Amendment does not prohibit the death penalty as disproportionate in the case of a defendant whose participation in a felony that results in murder is major and whose mental state is one of reckless indifference. In explaining their decision, the majority referred to a survey of state felony-murder laws and judicial decisions after *Enmund*, which indicated a societal consensus that a combination of factors may justify the death penalty, even without a specific "intent to kill." However, as the Arizona Supreme Court had affirmed the death sentences upon a finding that the defendants had "intended, contemplated, or anticipated that lethal force would or might be used or that life might be taken," the case was remanded, which means it was sent back to the state court for a rehearing to determine whether the brothers had acted with "reckless indifference" to human life. Upon retrial, the Tison brothers were again convicted and sentenced to death.

Legal News

Lillo Brancato Jr., an actor in the popular Sopranos drama series about organized crime, was acquitted of felony-murder in December 2008. The trial stemmed from his participation in a 2005 attempted burglary during which a police officer was shot by his crime partner. The jury declined to convict him on the more serious felony-murder charge, arguably because they believed him when he argued that he did not know that his crime partner had a gun, nor could he have reasonably foreseen that there would be a killing during the burglary attempt.

Source: Source: Fahim, K. (2008). "Weighing Guilt When the Man on Trial Did No Killing." New York Times, December 24, 2008:B1.

Note that an alternative theory to culpability is the law of parties. Recall that under many states' laws today, anyone who participates as an accessory to a crime is as guilty as every other party, so if the murder is part of the criminal transaction, then every co-defendant is equally responsible, regardless of who pulled the trigger. However, this theory of culpabilty is more restricted than felony-murder and would not include culpability for inadvertent deaths. In summary, while the felony-murder rule has some restrictions in application, a defendant may be found guilty of murder even if he or she does not "intend to kill" or participate in the act that results in the killing. Defendants may be found guilty and may even receive the death penalty if the court finds a reckless disregard for human life in combination with major participation in the felony resulting in the death.

D. Summary

Murder is often divided into first- and second-degree in modern statutes. The difference between the two levels of murder is based on the *mens rea.* The degree of the murder will affect the level of punishment. The *actus reus* and *mens rea* of murder are summarized below:

First Degree

(A/R)   unlawful killing of one by another human

(M/R)   intentional, premeditated

Second Degree

(A/R) unlawful killing of one by another human

(M/R) "without premeditation" or "with callous disregard" or "wanton disregard" or "depraved indifference"

Felony Murder

(A/R) unlawful killing or foreseeable death + A/R of underlying felony

(M/R) intentional (of the underlying felony) + (in some states) callous disregard

---

§ 5.4 Voluntary Manslaughter

A. Common Law

Voluntary manslaughter is the intentional killing of one human being by another without justification or excuse, but committed under the influence of passion induced by great provocation. In most societies, the law does not condone killing, even though there is provocation or passion; however, the law does not ignore the weaknesses of human nature. Therefore, if there is absence of malice and the killing is due to the influence of sudden passion, the crime is reduced from murder to manslaughter.

In order for a killing that otherwise would be murder to be considered manslaughter, the following conditions must exist:

1. there must have been adequate provocation,

2. the killing must have been in the heat of passion,

3. it must have been a sudden passion, i.e., the killing must have followed the provocation before there has been a reasonable opportunity for the passion to cool, and

4. there must have been a causal connection between the provocation, the passion, and the fatal act.

B. Model Penal Code

The Model Penal Code, unlike the common law, does not distinguish between voluntary and involuntary manslaughter, but it retains the concept that reducing the crime from murder to manslaughter is justified when there is sufficient mental or emotional disturbance.

---

§ 210.3[42]

(1) Criminal homicide constitutes manslaughter when
    (a) it is committed recklessly; or
    (b) a homicide which would otherwise be murder is committed under the influence of extreme mental or emotional influence for which there is reasonable explanation or excuse. The reasonableness of such explanation or excuse shall be determined from the viewpoint of the person in the actor's situation under the circumstances as he believes them to be.
(2) Manslaughter is a felony of the second degree.

C. State Statutes, Codes, and Cases

Some states have adopted Model Penal Code concepts. Some retain part of the common law distinctions, and some have elements of both. Two of the elements of manslaughter are exactly the same as those of murder:

1. an unlawful killing,

2. one person by another.

The most distinguishable element of voluntary manslaughter is the sudden passion aroused by extreme provocation. It is this element that separates these killings from second-degree murders. Other definitions of voluntary manslaughter from cases include:

- "manslaughter is the unlawful killing of a human being without malice aforethought, either express or implied."[43]

- "manslaughter is the unlawful killing of a human being without malice and without premeditation and deliberation."[44]

- [manslaughter includes an] "absence of malice; that while the killing may be with the design to effect death, the offense is reduced to manslaughter by circumstances of great and sudden provocation."[45]

An example of a statute that generally follows the Model Penal Code, but has a different provision concerning voluntary manslaughter, is that of Ohio, which provides:

No person while under the influence of sudden passion or in a sudden fit of rage, either of which is brought on by serious provocation occasioned by the victim that is reasonably sufficient to incite him into using deadly force, shall knowingly cause the death of another.[46]

The Indiana statute defining voluntary manslaughter includes the terms *knowingly* and *intentionally*, but also reduces the crime from murder to voluntary manslaughter if the killing of another person occurs while acting under "sudden heat." That statute provides:

> Voluntary manslaughter. (a) A person who knowingly or intentionally kills another human being while acting under sudden heat commits voluntary manslaughter, a Class B felony. However, the offense is a Class A felony if it is committed by means of a deadly weapon. (b) The existence of sudden heat is a mitigating factor that reduces what otherwise would be murder under section 1(1) of this chapter to voluntary manslaughter.[47]

The Indiana statute makes it clear that voluntary manslaughter is a knowing or intentional killing committed while acting under "sudden heat."

1. Provocation

Provocation necessary to reduce the crime from murder to manslaughter must be of such a nature as to be recognized at law as adequate for that purpose. Provocation must be of a nature calculated to inflame the passions of an ordinary reasonable person under the circumstances. Under common law, words alone could never be provocation enough to justify a voluntary homicide finding. Consider the following cases in which the court decided whether the provocation was sufficient to induce passion:

- a bare claim of "fear" (no)[48]
- staggering blows to the face of the person (yes)[49]
- the infliction of pain and bloodshed (yes)[50]
- the killing or assaulting of a relative (yes)[51]
- finding one's spouse engaged in sexual relations (yes)[52]

The latter situation is the most commonly described example of voluntary homicide; so much so that it has sometimes been called the "paramour defense." However, case law indicates that it was a defense more successfully used by men than women.

The court holdings are not consistent in their finding that discovering one's spouse *in flagrante delicto* is sufficient provocation to inflame the passion of a reasonable person. Generally, the slayer must discover the deceased in the very act of intercourse or immediately before or after intercourse, and the killing must have followed immediately on detection and must have been committed under the influence of passion engendered by the discovery.[53]

While the common law rule was that words alone are insufficient provocation, there are some exceptions in state cases. If the words are informational, i.e., they convey a fact that constitutes reasonable provocation rather than morally insulting or abusive words, this could be sufficient provocation. For instance, if the victim taunts the killer with the fact that they just murdered his or her child, it may be sufficient provocation to reduce a murder conviction to manslaughter. It has been held by some courts that a husband who kills his wife's lover immediately after she confesses adultery, and before the lapse of reasonable cooling-off time, is guilty of manslaughter only.[54]

2. Heat of Passion

Not only must there be provocation, but the provocation must have led to "heat of passion" or "hot blood." That is, the emotional state must have dominated the slayer at the time of the homicidal act, and it must have been entertained toward the person slain, and not to another person. It is difficult to separate the provocation from the resulting heat and passion. In determining whether the act that caused the death was impelled by heat of passion, all of the surrounding circumstances and conditions are to be taken into consideration. In order to reduce the crime to manslaughter, the provocation must be such as would naturally and reasonably arouse the passions of an ordinary person beyond his or her power of control.

One court indicated that the passion of the killer must have been such as to negate deliberation. That is, the degree of mental disturbance must have been such as to deprive the killer of the power to form a design to kill with a deliberate mind. Another court noted that the passion of the killer must have been such as to render his or her mind incapable of cool reflection and to overcome and dominate or suspend the exercise of judgment and self-control.[55]

Legal News

In 2002, Clara Harris, a Houston woman, confronted her husband and his lover in a hotel lobby. She screamed at and assaulted the woman and was pulled away and ejected from the hotel by employees. Immediately afterward, she killed her husband by running over him three times in the parking lot. In a strange coincidence, the private investigator she hired happened to videotape the incident because they had been following her husband. The jury decided that she did commit the act in sudden passion, but under Texas law, that only reduced first-degree murder to second-degree murder. She was sentenced to 20 years in prison. The case became the basis for a 2004 television movie called *Suburban Madness*. She lost her appeal.

Source: http://topics.nytimes.com/top/reference/timestopics/people/h/clara_harris/index.html.

Manslaughter may also occur when a person kills another in the heat of sudden combat, if upon reasonable provocation. Reasonable provocation is the provocation that would inflame a reasonable and law-abiding person to the point at which he or she would be capable of killing another. Even with these general definitions, it is difficult to define the point at which the degree of passion is sufficient to reduce the crime from murder to manslaughter. In order to meet the heat of passion test, "the defendant must have in fact been deprived of his self-control under the stress of such provocation and must have committed the crime while so deprived."[56]

3. No "Cooling-Off"

Even if there was sufficient provocation to reduce the crime from murder to manslaughter, and there were sufficient facts to constitute passion or "hot blood," a manslaughter instruction is not justified if the passion cooled before the commission of the homicidal act. If it appears that the defendant reflected, deliberated, or cooled off for any period before the fatal act, the killing is murder, being attributable to malice or revenge and not to mental disturbance.

What constitutes "cooling-off time" depends upon the nature and circumstances of provocation, the extent to which the passion has been aroused, and the nature of the act causing the provocation. Therefore, no precise time can be laid down as a rule within which the passions must be held to have subsided and reason to have resumed its control. In some instances, the court is authorized to say, as a *matter of law*, that the cooling-off time is sufficient if an unreasonable period has elapsed between the provocation and the killing, while in other situations this determination becomes a difficult problem and is one that must be decided by the jury.[57]

In an early case, a defendant contended that information given him by his wife as to rape and incest committed upon her by the deceased so aroused his passions and deprived him of self-control that voluntary manslaughter rather than murder should be the conviction. The state contended that because at least one day, and probably longer, had elapsed after the defendant had been informed of the acts of the deceased, his blood had cooled and he was no longer

> **CASE:** *State v. Thornton,*
> **730 S.W.2d 309 (Tenn. 1987)**
>
> What was the holding of the case?
>
> Exactly when did the defendant feel a "sudden passion"?
>
> Was there time to "cool off"?
>
> What was the state's argument as to why this was first degree murder, not voluntary manslaughter?
>
> How do you distinguish this case from the Clara Harris case?

"in the heat of passion" necessary to sustain a voluntary homicide finding. However, the court agreed with the defendant's contention and explained that the crime of the deceased, if true, was most heinous and was calculated to create a most violent passion in the mind of the defendant, and it hardly can be expected that it would, as a matter of law, subside within so short a time.[58]

On the other hand, in the case of *Weaver v. State*, the court found that one day was a sufficient cooling-off period. The defendant had killed the victim one day after becoming angry while overhearing the victim planning to kill the defendant's brother. The defendant invited the victim to his place to get money from his safe, and shot him in the head while the victim was reaching into the safe. The evidence also indicated that the defendant took great pains to clean up the area afterward. The court decided that the defendant had not displayed the "sudden heat" necessary to reduce the charge from murder to voluntary manslaughter.[59]

Thus, there is no definite time for the cooling-off period that would negate the passion required before a defendant can have a murder charge reduced to voluntary manslaughter. Many courts submit this question to the jury under proper instructions.

4. A Causal Connection

In order for a homicide to be reduced from murder to manslaughter, the defendant must show that the heat of passion resulted from justifiable provocation and that the heat of passion caused the act that resulted in death. If the heat of passion element existed prior to the provocation, there is no justification for reducing the crime to manslaughter. If there was adequate provocation, but the order of provocation and the heat of passion are reversed, i.e., the provocation was not the cause of the heat of passion, there can be no reduction.[60]

There must be a causal link between the provocation, the passion, and the act. For example, if one has, for some time, intended to kill the victim to get even for mistreatment over a period of years, but immediately before he is about to carry out his intent to kill the victim, he finds the victim in bed with his daughter, it would be difficult to justify a reduction from murder to manslaughter.

5. Burden of Proof

Note that, in general, the provocation and passion elements are mitigating factors to a murder charge rather than elements to a crime. That is, prosecutors will typically charge a defendant with second-degree murder and it is up to the defendant to make some showing of provocation and passion in order to reduce a murder conviction to one of voluntary manslaughter. Once a defendant places provocation and passion in issue, the state then bears the burden of negating the presence of sudden heat beyond a reasonable doubt.[61] Determining whether provocation of the defendant is sufficient to excite a sudden, violent, and irresistible passion in a reasonable person, thereby reducing the offense from murder to manslaughter, is a question for the jury.[62]

D. Summary

Voluntary manslaughter shares the same elements as murder but has special circumstances.

Voluntary Manslaughter

(A/R) unlawful killing of one by another human

(M/R) intentionally, knowingly but without "malice"—may be defined as "without premeditation"

(Attendant circumstances)—provocation sufficient to incite a reasonable person to passion that undermines reason with no cooling-off period, and death was the direct cause of the provocation

---

§ 5.5 Involuntary Manslaughter

A. *Common Law*

The distinguishing factor of **involuntary manslaughter** is that it is unintentional. If the act was intended, then it could not come within the involuntary manslaughter category. There are two kinds of involuntary manslaughter:

1. the killing occurs in the course of committing an unlawful act, or

2. death occurs during the negligent commission or omission of an otherwise lawful act.

The elements of involuntary manslaughter are:

1. an unlawful killing of one person by another,

2. unintentional *but*:

 a. during commission of a lawful act performed with gross negligence or

 b. failure to perform a duty or

 c. during the commission of a crime not a felony (misdemeanor manslaughter).

A killing may be unlawful if death results from gross, wanton, or culpable negligence. A distinction is made between simple or ordinary negligence and criminally culpable negligence or recklessness.[63] For instance, if a doctor is negligent, he or she may be sued in the civil court system for medical malpractice. However, the degree of negligence required to prove involuntary manslaughter is much higher than simple negligence and goes up to the level of recklessness. The mistake must be egregious, not merely careless. Examples of recklessness that may result in charges of involuntary homicide are: bar owners who lock the fire doors and patrons subsequently die in fires, target shooting when there is awareness that other people are about, and driving in an extremely reckless manner.

The second situation is when a killing occurs because of a failure to perform a legal duty. If a person is required by law to do an act but, in disregarding that duty, causes the death of another, he or she can be guilty of involuntary manslaughter.[64] For instance, when a childcare provider sees a child seriously injured by another child and does nothing about it, tells no one and covers up the incident; if the child dies from an untreated head injury, the provider could be found guilty of involuntary manslaughter.

The third situation is when the defendant has committed a crime, but not an inherently dangerous felony, and a death results. Recall that if a death occurs while a person is engaged in certain felonies, the crime could be murder under the felony-murder doctrine. However, if death occurs during a felony that is not inherently dangerous or during a misdemeanor, the crime is involuntary manslaughter.[65] To constitute involuntary manslaughter, the prosecution must show that there is a causal connection between the unlawful act and the death; that is, the unlawful act was the cause of the death. For instance, in *People v. Crucoani*, the defendant assisted a person who was injecting heroin into his arm. The defendant was charged with involuntary manslaughter for his acts when the victim died of a drug overdose.[66]

The difference between second-degree "depraved indifference" murder and involuntary manslaughter is the degree or egregiousness of the recklessness. For instance, driving while drunk and killing someone may be charged as involuntary homicide, but driving with an extremely high intoxication level, after having successive arrests for DWI, and driving up onto a sidewalk in a school zone, killing several children, may be charged as second-degree (depraved indifference) murder. Doing target practice in your backyard in a rural area and accidentally killing a neighbor would probably be charged as involuntary manslaughter, but shooting into a crowded bar could be charged as depraved indifference murder. The difference is that in second-degree depraved indifference murder, there is a virtual certainty of the action resulting in a death or serious injury.

B. Model Penal Code

The Model Penal Code has no section on involuntary manslaughter. It has a provision regarding **negligent homicide** that is similar to some of the existing statutes and addresses homicide caused by negligence, which was the *mens rea* for common law involuntary manslaughter. This provision is as follows:

§ 210.4 Negligent Homicide[67]

(1) Criminal homicide constitutes negligent homicide when it is committed negligently.

(2) Negligent homicide is a felony of the third degree.

The standard of negligence required for violations of § 210.4 requires proof of substantial fault and limits penal sanctions to cases in which there are gross deviations from ordinary standards of conduct. Note that negligent manslaughter defines an even lower level of *mens rea* than required for involuntary manslaughter. Consider the following levels of less-than-intentional *mens rea*:

depraved indifference - second degree murder

recklessness, gross negligence - involuntary manslaughter

criminal negligence - negligent homicide

negligence - civil negligence (no criminal culpability)

The lines between each of these levels of culpability are fluid and court cases among the states vary in what level of culpability would attach to any specific type of behavior.

C. State Statutes, Codes, and Cases

Some states follow the Model Penal Code and use the negligent homicide definition. Other jurisdictions retain the common law involuntary manslaughter rule, at least in part.[68] Still others have added special statutes to meet the needs of a society in which many homicides involve automobiles. For example, the Ohio Criminal Code includes the crimes of negligent homicide, aggravated vehicular homicide, and vehicular homicide. These are in addition to the crimes of aggravated murder, murder, voluntary manslaughter, and involuntary manslaughter. The Ohio Criminal Code provides:

§ 2903.05 Negligent homicide[69]

(A) No person shall negligently cause the death of another or the unlawful termination of another's pregnancy by means of a deadly weapon or dangerous ordinance as defined in section 2923.11 of the Revised Code.

§ 2903.06 Aggravated vehicular homicide; vehicular homicide; vehicular manslaughter

(A) No person, while operating or participating in the operation of a motor vehicle, motorcycle, snowmobile, locomotive, watercraft, or aircraft, shall cause the death of another or the unlawful termination of another's pregnancy in any of the following ways:

(1) As the proximate result of committing a violation of division (A) of section 4511.19 of the Revised Code or of a substantially equivalent municipal ordinance;
(2) Recklessly;
(3) Negligently;

> (4) As the proximate result of committing a violation of any provision of any section contained in Title 45 of the Revised Code that is a minor misdemeanor or of a municipal ordinance that, regardless of the penalty set by ordinance for the violation, is substantially equivalent to any provision of any section contained in Title 45 of the Revised Code that is a minor misdemeanor.
>
> (B) (1) Whoever violates division (A)(1) or (2) of this section is guilty of aggravated vehicular homicide . . .
> (2) Whoever violates division (A)(3) of this section is guilty of vehicular homicide . . .
> (3) Whoever violates division (A)(4) of this section is guilty of vehicular manslaughter . . .

Note that the difference between "aggravated vehicular homicide" and "vehicular homicide" is that "recklessly" is used in the former and "negligently" in the latter.

Involuntary manslaughter in North Carolina is defined as: (1) an unlawful act not amounting to a felony nor naturally dangerous to human life; or (2) a culpably negligent act or omission.[70] An Illinois court commented that, in general, a defendant acts recklessly for purposes of the offense of involuntary manslaughter when he or she is aware that his or her conduct might result in death or great bodily harm, although that result is not substantially certain to occur.[71]

Involuntary manslaughter, or second-degree manslaughter, is often referred to as the "catch-all" in the law of homicide. It includes all unlawful homicides that are not covered under one of the other categories.

- Manslaughter in the second degree or "involuntary manslaughter" is the unlawful killing of a human being without malice, either express or implied, and without intent to kill or inflict injury causing death, committed accidentally in the commission of some unlawful act not felonious, or in the improper or negligent performance of an act lawful in itself.[72]

- "Manslaughter in the second degree" occurs where it plainly appears that neither death nor great bodily harm was intended but death was accidentally caused by some unlawful act or act strictly lawful in itself but done in an unlawful manner and without due caution.[73]

- involuntary manslaughter [occurs] if he or she recklessly causes the death of another and reckless is when one "consciously disregards a substantial and unjustifiable risk that circumstances exist or that a result will follow, and such disregard constitutes a gross deviation from the standard of care that a reasonable person would exercise in this situation"[74]

In *Commonwealth v. Welansky*, the defendant was convicted of involuntary manslaughter when the night club he owned caught fire and several people were killed. His culpability stemmed from findings that he provided inadequate exits.[75] A somewhat similar fact situation occurred in a more recent case when a band manager pled guilty in 2006 to 100 counts of involuntary manslaughter after the pyrotechnics used in the band's performance caused a tragic fire in a Rhode Island nightclub in 2003.[76]

1. Burden of Proof and Instructions to Jury

Frequently, a person charged with murder requests an instruction on the lesser included offense of involuntary manslaughter. If there is any evidence, however slight, as to whether the offense is murder or involuntary manslaughter, an instruction as to the law of both offenses should be given. However, if there is no evidence whatsoever to indicate negligence rather than intent, then an instruction on involuntary manslaughter is not required.[77]

D. *Summary*

The major concept to remember about involuntary manslaughter is that the level of *mens rea* is either recklessness or negligence.

Involuntary Manslaughter

(A/R) killing of one by another human while doing an unlawful act or a lawful act in a criminally negligent or reckless manner

(M/R) reckless, negligent

Misdemeanor Manslaughter

(A/R) killing during the commission of a non-inherently dangerous felony or misdemeanor

(M/R) the *mens rea* required for the underlying crime

Negligent Homicide (MPC)

(A/R) unlawful killing of one by another human being while doing an act in a criminally negligent manner

(M/R) criminal negligence

---

§ 5.6 Suicide and Assisted Suicide

A. *Common Law*

Suicide is defined as intentional self-destruction. Although suicide is not strictly a homicide, because there is no killing of one person by another person, it is often considered in relation to the law of homicide. At common law suicide was a felony and was known as *felo de se* or felon of oneself—unless the person was a minor.[78] At early common law, suicide was punished by an ignominious burial and the forfeiture of goods and chattels to the king. If two persons mutually agreed to commit suicide, and the means employed to produce death was effective only as to one, the survivor was guilty of the murder of the one who died.[79]

B. Model Penal Code

The Model Penal Code does not define suicide as a crime; however, there is the crime of solicited or **assisted suicide**.

---

§ 210.5 Causing or Aiding Suicide[80]

(1) Causing Suicide as Criminal Homicide. A person may be convicted of criminal homicide for causing another to commit suicide only if he purposely causes such suicide by force, duress or deception.

(2) Aiding or Soliciting Suicide as an Independent Offense. A person who purposely aids or solicits another to commit suicide is guilty of a felony of the second degree if his conduct causes such suicide or an attempted suicide, and otherwise of a misdemeanor.

Section 210.5 provides that a person is guilty of criminal homicide if, with the requisite culpability, he or she causes the death of another by "causing another to commit suicide." Only when the person actively participates in inducing the suicide will criminal penalties result. The second subsection of § 210.5 more closely defines an act that was a crime under the common law. This section creates a separate offense of aiding or soliciting suicide, even though suicide itself is not a crime. To prove a violation in this case, the prosecutor must introduce evidence to show that the accused "purposely" aided or solicited another to commit suicide. Thus, conduct not seriously intended to aid or persuade another to take his own life may not be punishable under this section.

C. State Statutes, Codes, and Cases

Even though the early common law took the position that suicide was a crime, the great majority of states today do not criminalize suicide. However, in most states it is a crime to help another to commit or attempt suicide.[81] The laws making it a crime to aid, advise, or encourage another to commit suicide have taken several forms. California law provides: "Every person who deliberately aids, or advises, or encourages another to commit suicide is guilty of a felony."[82] The New York law includes the offense as part of the manslaughter statutes. This law provides that: "A person is guilty of manslaughter in the second degree when . . . (3) he intentionally causes or aids another to commit suicide."[83] The most famous opponent to assisted suicide laws is Dr. Jack Kevorkian. He flagrantly violated Michigan's assisted suicide law until he was convicted and sentenced to prison in the early 1990s.[84]

The state statutes have been challenged on constitutional grounds. Several of these cases have reached the United States Supreme Court. In the case of *Washington v. Glucksberg,*[85] three terminally ill patients, four physicians, and non-profit organizations brought an action against the state of Washington for a declaratory judgment that the statute banning assisted suicide violated the due process clause of the United States Constitution. In holding that the Washington prohibition against causing or aiding a suicide does not violate the due process clause, the Supreme Court explained that an examination of our nation's history, legal traditions, and practices demonstrates that Anglo-American common law has punished or otherwise disapproved of assisted suicide for more than 700 years. The court continued by indicating that the asserted right to assistance in committing suicide is not a fundamental liberty interest protected by the due process clause and that the history of the law's treatment of assisted suicide has been and continues to be rejection of nearly all efforts to permit it.

In the case of *Vacco v. Quill,*[86] physicians brought an action challenging the constitutionality of the New York statute that made it a crime to aid a person in committing suicide or attempting to commit suicide. In this case, the New York statute outlawing assisted suicide was challenged as a violation of the equal protection clause of the United States Constitution. The argument is that, because New York law treats competent, terminally ill persons who wish to hasten their deaths by self-administering prescribed drugs differently from those who wish to do so by directing the removal of life-support systems, this violates the equal protection clause. The United States Supreme Court disagreed with this argument, concluding that the two groups were not similarly situated. The United States Supreme Court found that the overwhelming majority of state legislatures have drawn a clear line between assisting suicide and withdrawal or permitting the refusal of unwanted life-saving medical treatment by prohibiting the former and permitting the latter. The case includes citations from many state courts.

On the other hand, the most recent Supreme Court decision regarding assisted suicide involved Oregon's "Death with Dignity" statute,[87] which allows physicians, in certain limited situations, to assist a patient by prescribing controlled substances in order to end their life.[88] Because this case deals with federal drug laws it will be discussed and offered as a case reading in Chapter 13. In 2005, in *Gonzales v. Oregon,* the federal government sought a ruling that the physician's prescription of drugs to end one's life was not a legitimate medical use and, therefore, doctors could be guilty under the Controlled Substances Act of 1970. The Supreme Court did not rule directly on Oregon's Death with Dignity Act, but did hold that it exceeded the authority of the Attorney General to determine what was a legitimate medical purpose. At this point, the Oregon law has not been overturned and is still good law.

It should be noted that doctors can only prescribe fatal drugs for a strictly limited group of people. If anyone administers the drugs to the individual, they may still be guilty of some form of homicide.

Legal News

Washington state has now joined Oregon in its passage of a "right-to-die" statute. In November 2008, 59 percent of Washington voters passed a statute allowing physician-assisted suicide. The statute, known as the Death with Dignity Act, will go into effect in March 2009. Patients who are over 18, mentally competent, and with less than six months to live can now ask their doctors for a prescription for lethal medicine that they then can self-administer. Doctors and pharmacists opposed to the practice are not obligated to participate.

Source: Kapralos, K. (2008). "Physician-assisted Suicide Law Goes into Effect in March." Everett Herald, November 10, 2008:A1.

D. Summary

Although there are no current statutes or case law that criminalize suicide, most states do have laws that prohibit one party from assisting another in committing suicide and the Supreme Court has upheld such laws, finding that there is no constitutional right to die. Since *Gonzales v. Oregon*, however, the door is open for states to pass their own laws that allow for assisted suicide by physicians in certain limited circumstances when a patient is terminally ill.

Assisting Suicide (or other statutes)

(A/R) Cause (through duress or force), solicit, assist, aid, advise suicide of another

(M/R) Purposeful

---

§ 5.7 Assault and Battery

A. Common Law

At common law, assault and battery were two separate crimes. In many jurisdictions and in the Model Penal Code, the crimes are classified under the designation of "assault" without use of the word "battery." However, under common law they were distinguished in the following manner.

1. Assault

An "**assault**" was any unlawful offer or attempt to injure another, with an apparent present ability to effectuate the attempt under circumstances creating a fear of imminent peril. To constitute an assault, no touching was necessary, but there must have been an unlawful threat to do bodily harm to another with the apparent present ability to accomplish the deed if not prevented. An example would be a person who points a loaded firearm at another to cause injury or induce fear.[89] Note that the intent to cause injury or fear can be proven by circumstantial evidence, but assault was a specific intent crime, meaning that the defendant must have intent to make the threat and have the intent that his or her action would cause fear or apprehension.

2. Battery

Under common law, **battery** was the unlawful touching of the person of another by the aggressor or by some substance put in motion by him. A battery has been defined as the "consummation of the assault," and the "unlawful application of force to the person of another."[90] "Battery" is the actual use of force and occurs when the violence is accomplished.[91] Unlike assault, battery is a general intent crime because all that is necessary is the intent to perform the unlawful touching.

B. Model Penal Code

The Model Penal Code eliminates the common law categories of assault and battery. It merges several kinds of misconduct under the generic offense of assault. Offenses are graded according to the gravity of harm intended or caused and the dangerousness of the means used. Under the Model Penal Code, assault is limited to cases involving either the *fact* or *prospect* of physical injury.

---

§ 211.1 Assault[92]

(1) Simple Assault. A person is guilty of assault if he:
  (a) attempts to cause or purposely, knowingly or recklessly causes bodily injury to another; or
  (b) negligently causes bodily injury to another with a deadly weapon; or
  (c) attempts by physical menace to put another in fear of imminent serious bodily harm.

Simple assault is a misdemeanor unless committed in a fight or scuffle entered into by mutual consent, in which case it is a petty misdemeanor.

(2) Aggravated Assault. A person is guilty of aggravated assault if he:
  (a) attempts to cause serious bodily injury to another, or causes such injury purposely, knowingly or recklessly under circumstances manifesting extreme indifference to the value of human life; or
  (b) attempts to cause or purposely or knowingly causes bodily injury to another with a deadly weapon.

Aggravated assault under paragraph (a) is a felony of the second degree; aggravated assault under paragraph (b) is a felony of the third degree.

C. State Statutes, Codes, and Cases

Some states have followed the reasoning of the drafters of the Model Penal Code. Others have separate provisions relating to assaults on police officers and other designated categories of persons.[93] Still others take a different approach and define degrees of assault, or provide more or less serious penalties according to the offender's degree of guilty mind, the means used to commit the offense, and the actual harm to persons involved. An example of the latter is Ohio, where six categories of assault and menacing deal with offenses formerly characterized as different kinds of assault, battery, and menacing threats. The six categories are: felonious assault, aggravated assault, assault, negligent assault, aggravated menacing, and menacing.[94]

1. Elements of Assault

Most states have now combined assault and battery under one statute. In those states that have combined assault and battery, to constitute an actionable assault, the following elements must be proved beyond a reasonable doubt: an attempt or offer; with force and violence; to do some immediate physical injury to the person of another; and with the apparent present or immediate ability *or* any unlawful touching.

1. *Attempt or offer*. The force intended to be applied must be put into motion. Mere preparation does not amount to an assault; there must be some act that could apparently produce injury.

2. The *force or violence* offered must be unlawful, but it may be in any degree. For example, when a defendant attempted to apply force to the victim's person and grab money held fast in the victim's hand, this action constituted the necessary force to constitute assault.[95]

3. The attempt or offer must be *directed toward another person*. There need not be any touching or striking of the person; but there must be an offer to use force to injure another.[96] The prosecution must show that the person is placed in reasonable apprehension of receiving an immediate battery; there must be a showing of force or menace of violence that would be sufficient to put a person of reasonable firmness in fear of immediate bodily harm.[97]

4. It is necessary is to show "*apparent present ability*" to effectuate the harm. Assault does not occur unless the individual is placed in reasonable fear of *imminent* bodily harm, but if the victim is placed in reasonable fear of bodily harm, by conduct of the defendant, and the defendant had the apparent ability to carry out the threatening nature of his act, it is not necessary that the prosecution show that the defendant had the *actual* ability to carry out the act. For example, one may be found guilty of assault by pointing an unloaded firearm at another when the person threatened does not know that the gun is not loaded.[98]

5. *(Or) An unlawful; application of force; to the person of another.* The application of force must be unlawful (i.e., a police officer has the right to use force to subdue an arrestee).[99] The force may be direct or indirect, as by exposing a helpless person to the inclemency of the weather.[100] Any touching, if it is unlawful, may constitute the force necessary for a battery.[101] The force must be to the person of another and be unpermitted; for example, the defendant putting his hand into the victim's pants and upon the victim's penis.[102] But it is unnecessary that the victim's body or even his or her clothing be touched, because touching anything connected with his or her person is sufficient. For example, the intentional snatching of a patron's dinner plate from him by the manager of the hotel's club in a loud and offensive manner was sufficient to constitute battery.[103]

While touching with one's hands may constitute application of force to another person, not every touch is a criminal battery. Generally, the courts have required that the act be done in a wrongful or intentionally angry, resentful, rude, or insolent manner to make the act a battery. If the touching is the result of an unavoidable accident in the pursuit of a lawful act, this is a valid defense to a charge of battery.[104]

3. Issues of Actus Reus and Mens Rea

As discussed above, typically statutes now use one word—assault—for what was assault and battery. Many state statutes divide the crime of assault into simple and aggravated assault. The difference between the two can be either the degree of harm and/or the status of the victim. For instance, statutes have designated as aggravated assault those that were performed with a weapon, assaults against peace officers or children, and those that were conducted with extreme indifference to human life. The application of these statutes may create issues in the definition of *actus reus* or *mens rea*. For instance, in statutes that make the assault of a "peace officer" a more serious crime (aggravated assault), consider the following questions:

- Who is considered a peace officer to constitute the *actus reus*? (A juvenile probation officer was included in the definition)[105]

- What is the *mens rea* required in regard to the knowledge that the victim is a police or peace officer? (if the defendant *should have known*, that is sufficient *mens rea*)[106]

To provide more serious penalties for assaults that are considered especially troublesome, legislation designates specific types of assaults. Consider some of the following specific types of assault, which can be found in state statutes:

- assault with a deadly weapon[107]

- assault with a caustic or flammable chemical[108]

- assaults with tasers or stun guns[109]

- assaults on an unborn child[110]

It should be noted that assault crimes may not only serve as original charges, but also they may be used as a lesser included offense of murder or attempted murder. If, for example, the evidence against a murder defendant leaves room for doubt as to whether his or her act was the cause of death, an assault instruction is appropriate when all of the elements of assault are present.

4. Assault via HIV/AIDS

With the number of HIV/AIDS cases growing steadily, it was inevitable that criminal courts would be asked to resolve issues involving defendants who knew they were HIV positive. In *Smallwood v. State*,[111] the court upheld a defendant's conviction for assault with intent to commit murder where the defendant, who knew he was HIV positive, attempted to rape the victim without wearing a condom. Other courts reviewing HIV/AIDS as an aggravated condition or factor have reached similar conclusions.[112]

In a Michigan case, a statute making it a crime for one who is aware that he or she has Acquired Immune Deficiency Syndrome (AIDS), or has tested positive for HIV, to fail to inform a sexual partner that he or she is infected was challenged on the grounds that it violated the First Amendment to the Constitution. The court upheld the conviction under the statute, finding that the statute did not violate the First Amendment right against compelled expression, because the state had an overwhelming interest in compelling the disclosure in order to stop the spread of AIDS and HIV.[113]

5. Definition of Weapon (in Aggravated Assault)

Where the state statute includes the crime of assault with a dangerous weapon, the prosecution must show that a dangerous weapon was, in fact, involved. In a Michigan case, the defendant was charged with and convicted of felonious assault against two small girls. He had no weapon, but used his hands to hold both victims, with one hand being placed over the lower face of one victim to quiet her as well as to restrain her. On appeal, the defendant contended that he could not be convicted of felonious assault, because he had no dangerous weapon. The state claimed that the pair of hands should be considered dangerous weapons. The reviewing court held that the statute is not limited to the dangerous weapons specifically listed, but bare hands cannot be considered weapons. The court based its decision to some extent on the fact that another statute defined assault not involving dangerous weapons, reasoning that if bare hands were construed as "dangerous weapons," the distinction between categories of assault would be meaningless.[114]

While a person's hand is not generally considered a dangerous weapon under a statute that prohibits assault with a deadly instrument, the courts have found that other instruments can be considered dangerous weapons under certain circumstances. For example, an Alabama court found that intentionally putting an automobile in motion and violently and intentionally driving it against a police officer is "an assault with a deadly instrument," in violation of the statute.[115]

In the case of *State v. Torres*, the court of appeals of North Carolina agreed with the lower court that four large metal rings worn by the defendant were properly the basis for a conviction on a charge of assault with a deadly weapon.[116] In this case, the defendant was involved in a fistfight in the parking lot of a Durham County high school. The defendant was wearing four large silver rings ornamented with a skull or pirate head. The victim suffered a broken jaw, and the rings on the hand of the defendant were found to be covered with blood at the time of the arrest. The defendant was charged with using metal, raised-design rings on his fingers as deadly weapons to assault and inflict serious injury. The reviewing court refused to find error on the part of the trial court in allowing this as evidence of a deadly weapon under the North Carolina statute. Other courts have defined dangerous weapons to include:

- sulphuric acid[117]
- automobile[118]
- imitation or "blank" pistol[119]

6. Sporting Events

Why aren't boxers arrested for assault? The answer lies in the concept of consent. Recall that one of the elements of common law battery was *unpermitted* touching. Consent is recognized as a defense when one of the elements of a crime is "against the will" of the victim. This is obvious in sexual assault, and is applicable, to some degree, in assault as well. As case law has developed, the rule is that sporting events give individuals the right to engage in a certain amount of sanctioned force against other players. However, if players violate the rules and normal practices of the game, then they can be charged with assault and battery. For instance, boxing necessarily involves hitting each other (which would otherwise be assault), but it does not allow biting; thus, when Mike Tyson bit off a part of his opponent's ear, that act was not consented to and could be defined as assault. If baseball players intentionally throw a bat at someone, that could be assault; and if football players intentionally injure another player in a "late hit," that could be charged as assault.

While sports events are a type of consent to simple assault, there is no general right to consent to aggravated assault (injury). That is, victims cannot agree to be killed (recall the assisted suicide section above), or even whipped or otherwise injured.[120] While case law is mixed in this area, generally courts have held that, for public policy reasons, a defendant cannot use the defense that the victim asked to be hurt.

7. Mayhem

Under common law, there was a specific type of battery called "**mayhem**." This was described as maliciously depriving another of the use of his limbs so as to make him unable to defend himself against adversaries. Later, it included other forms of injury that included any kind of dismemberment or disfigurement. There was no specific provision for mayhem under the Model Penal Code, although a few current state statutes still distinguish this crime. For instance, Idaho's statute specifies that a person guilty of mayhem "maliciously deprives a human being of a member of his body, or disables, disfigures or renders it useless, or cuts or disables the tongue, puts out an eye, slits the nose, ear or lips, . . ."[121]

Legal News

The most famous mayhem case in the United States is probably that of Lorena Bobbitt, who cut off her husband's penis when he was sleeping. Her defense was that her husband had raped her and she was a victim of domestic violence. She claimed temporary insanity and was committed to a mental health facility for 45 days for observation.

Source: http://www.cbsnews.com/stories/2008/06/25/earlyshow/leisure/celebspot/main4207517.shtml.

D. Summary

There is a wide variety of statutes in the assault and battery area; however, the general elements are fairly standard and merely combine the common law crimes of assault and battery as indicated below.

Assault

(A/R) Attempt, threaten or offer, with unlawful force, to inflict immediate bodily injury accompanied with apparent present ability *or* offensive touching upon another

(M/R) Purposely, Knowingly, Recklessly, or Negligently (depending on level or particular type of assault)

---

§ 5.8 Kidnapping and Related Offenses

A. Common Law

At common law, "**kidnapping**" was defined as the forcible abduction and carrying away of a man, woman, or child from his or her own country into another.[122] Other older definitions of kidnapping include:

- willfully seizing, confining, or luring another, with the intent to cause him or her, without authority of law, to be secretly confined or imprisoned within the state; to be sent out of the state; to be sold as a slave or to be in any way held to service; or to be kept or detained against his or her will.[123]

- forcibly detaining another against his will to unlawfully obtain ransom, or unlawfully restraining another and forcibly moving the person imprisoned to another place.[124]

The essence of kidnapping is the intentional taking of a person and detaining that person against his or her will. The traditional elements of kidnapping are:

1. unlawful imprisonment

    a.   detaining another,

    b.   by force or fraud,

    c.   without his or her consent,

    d.   without legal cause

2. moving him or her to another place (asportation)

3. to unlawfully obtain ransom.

1. Unlawful Imprisonment

One of the elements of kidnapping under the common law and under some statutes is **unlawful imprisonment**, which means unlawfully restraining, unlawfully removing, or unlawfully confining a person against their will. For instance, a court held the act of holding the person for a proscribed purpose necessarily implies an unlawful physical and mental restraint where the detention is for an appreciable period, is against the person's will, and is done with a willful intent to confine the victim.[125]

If all of the elements for the crime of kidnapping are not present (such as the demand for ransom or asportation), a person may be guilty of unlawful imprisonment. For example, a person is guilty of unlawful imprisonment under some statutes when he or she knowingly and unlawfully restrains another under circumstances that expose that person to a risk of serious physical injury. The elements of unlawful imprisonment under this statute are:

1. knowingly;

2. unlawfully;

3. restraining another; and

4. under circumstances that expose the victim to a risk of physical injury.

B. Model Penal Code

Under the Model Penal Code, kidnapping is a felony of the first degree unless the actor voluntarily releases the victim alive and in a safe place, in which case it is a felony of the second degree. Removal or confinement of a person is unlawful within the meaning of this section if it is accomplished by force, threat, or deception, or, in the case of a person who is under the age of 14 or incompetent, if it is accomplished without the consent of a parent, guardian, or other person responsible for his or her general supervision. The penalty for kidnapping under the Model Penal Code is determined by the treatment of the victim and the circumstances surrounding the kidnapping.

§ 212.1 Kidnapping[126]

A person is guilty of kidnapping if he unlawfully removes another from his place of residence or business, or a substantial distance from the vicinity where he is found, or if he unlawfully confines another for a substantial period in a place of isolation, with any of the following purposes:

(a) to hold for ransom or reward, or as a shield or hostage; or
(b) to facilitate commission of any felony or flight thereafter; or
(c) to inflict bodily injury on or to terrorize the victim or another; or
(d) to interfere with the performance of any governmental or political function.

The wording of the Model Penal Code is cast in terms of removal of the victim "from" a location, rather than transporting him "to" another place as was used in some pre-Model Code statutes. To avoid confusion and technical interpretations, the word "vicinity" is used, rather than "place." Also, "substantial" removal is required to preclude kidnapping convictions based on trivial changes of location having no bearing on the evil at hand. The Model Penal Code definition includes unlawful confinement of another "for a substantial period in a place of isolation." This eliminates the "asportation" element that was included in the common law definitions, but still leaves questions as to what is "substantial" and what amounts to "a place of isolation."

The Model Penal Code includes the offenses of Felonious Restraint, False Imprisonment, Interference with Custody, and Criminal Coercion as offenses related to kidnapping.[127] These and other specifically defined offenses were added in many states to make it possible for the state to take action when a wrongful act is committed, but the wrong is not serious enough to come within the technical definition of kidnapping. Generally, these less serious offenses, as defined by statute, have a penalty attached that is of a lower degree than the penalty for kidnapping.

C. State Statutes, Codes, and Cases

All states have modified the common law. Statutory provisions greatly enlarge the scope of kidnapping and, in some instances, add other offenses that directly relate to kidnapping, but do not require that all elements be proved. As the following definitions indicate, the terms used in defining kidnapping vary from jurisdiction to jurisdiction.

- " . . . [falsely imprisoning a] victim by acquiring complete dominion and control over him for some appreciable period of time and must have carried him beyond the immediate vicinity of the place of such false imprisonment."[128]

- "Kidnapping" constitutes carrying away of the person for a purpose such as ransom or committing bodily felony; elements of kidnapping are taking or seizure of a human being, asportation or movement of the seized individual, by means of unlawful force or fraud, and for the purpose of ransom, reward or committing a felony.[129]

- to take and carry away any person by unlawful force or fraud and against his will.[130]

The elements of the crime of kidnapping depend upon the wording of the respective statutes. In general, most of the elements of common law kidnapping can be found in most state statutes so we will discuss the traditional elements.

1. Detaining Another

Some states require that the victim's confinement be substantial. In the case of *State v. Denmon*, a New Jersey court held that the determination of whether a victim's confinement is substantial, and thus supports a kidnapping charge, is not determined by its duration; rather, the jury should look at the enhanced risk of harm resulting from the confinement and isolation of the victim.[131]

2. By Force or Fraud

The "force" element of kidnapping may be accomplished either by actual physical coercion or force to the body of such a person, or by coercion of the will of the person by threats, fear, intimidation, deception, or other inducement that deprives the victim of the will to resist.[132]

3. Without Consent

A defendant cannot be convicted of kidnapping if the alleged victim consented to the restraint or consented to go with the defendant. However, the initial consent is converted into an unlawful detention if the defendant refuses to allow the person to leave. For example, when hitchhikers consented to be given a ride to their home, but instead, over their objection and under threats of death, they were driven to a far distant place where one of them was raped, the court found that, even if the original taking was not forcible or fraudulent, the unlawful detention commenced when the defendant refused to drive the hitchhikers home and drove away from the area.[133] In addition, minors generally cannot give consent so even if they go willingly, it would still be considered kidnapping. Finally, if someone is misled as to the true nature of the situation (i.e., the kidnapper tells the victim that their child is injured and they will take them to the injured child), under the law they have not given consent because consent requires that one knowingly and voluntarily offered their assent; in the case of deception there can be no consent.

4. Without Legal Cause

A police officer who restrains another is not guilty of kidnapping when, acting in his or her official capacity, he or she detains a person pursuant to a warrant issued by a court, or is otherwise carrying out his or her official duties. But if the officer does not act in good faith and the entire transaction indicates an unlawful purpose, the officer technically could be held for kidnapping.[134] This is especially true when a peace officer goes into another state and, without authority, apprehends a person and returns him or her to the state where the officer has jurisdiction.

5. Asportation

Under the common law, and under some statutes, an element of kidnapping is **asportation**: this is the taking, leading, carrying away, or transportation of the victim. The degree of movement from one place to another depends upon the wording of the statute. If, for example, the statute requires that the person be removed from the state, then the prosecution must show that the person was, in fact, moved from the state. However, if the statute provides that "a person is guilty if he unlawfully removes one from his place of residence or business, or a substantial distance from the vicinity where he is found," then all that is necessary is to show that the unlawful removal took place. In this regard, one court upheld a kidnapping conviction when the accused, under the pretense of being a good faith passenger, forced a taxi driver at gunpoint to drive him to another destination. The appellant had argued that the taxicab driver was not carried from any "place" because the moving vehicle was not a place.[135]

In the case of *State v. Morris*, a Minnesota court determined that the removal of a victim the distance of only 150 feet, and detention for five minutes in the process of committing indecent assault, constituted "kidnapping" and it was proper to charge kidnapping as a separate offense.[136] In another case, the court determined that the word "kidnapping," as used in the statute of that state, means the unlawful taking and carrying away of a person by force and against his or her will. That court agreed that it is the fact, not the distance, of forcible removal of the victim that constitutes the kidnapping; any carrying away is sufficient and the distance is immaterial.[137]

In interpreting the North Carolina statute that requires the victim to be "removed," the state court determined that the "removal" of the victims from the main room of stores was independent of the robberies committed, and therefore the defendant could be convicted of kidnapping in addition to robbery. In this case, the victims were moved from the main area of stores into bathrooms or offices, and rooms to which victims were ordered to go did not contain safes, cash registers, or locked boxes that held the property that was taken.[138]

In interpreting the "removal" provision of the state's statutes, a Georgia court concluded that the offense of kidnapping does not require a showing that the movement of the victim was made in a clandestine or surreptitious manner and that the slightest movement of a victim will establish the asportation requirement for kidnapping.[139]

In a case decided by the District of Columbia Court of Appeals, it was held that under the District of Columbia statute there is no requirement that the victim be removed any particular distance or held for any particular length of time; all that is required is "seizing," "confining," or the like, and holding or detaining for ransom or reward "or otherwise."[140]

6. For Ransom or Other Unlawful Purpose

Under common law and the Model Penal Code, the purpose for the detainment had to be unlawful, i.e., for ransom or other nefarious purpose. Some states have eliminated this requirement or, through case law, defined any reason as unlawful, i.e., to get an ex-girlfriend to agree to marry; to induce action on the part of the victim; or to frighten a parent by taking their child.

7. Example of State Statute

An example of a state statute that differs from the Model Penal Code in various ways is that of New York. In addition to the offenses of "unlawful imprisonment" in the first and second degree, the New York law provides heavier penalties for the offenses of kidnapping in the second degree and kidnapping in the first degree.[141]

> § 135.05 Unlawful imprisonment in the second degree
>
> A person is guilty of unlawful imprisonment in the second degree when he restrains another person.
>
> Unlawful imprisonment in the second degree is a Class A misdemeanor.

§ 135.10 Unlawful imprisonment in the first degree

A person is guilty of unlawful imprisonment in the first degree when he restrains another person under circumstances which expose the latter to a risk of serious physical injury.

Unlawful imprisonment in the first degree is a Class E felony.

§ 135.20 Kidnapping in the second degree

A person is guilty of kidnapping in the second degree when he abducts another person.

Kidnapping in the second degree is a Class B felony.

§ 135.25 Kidnapping in the first degree

A person is guilty of kidnapping in the first degree when he abducts another person and when:
1. His intent is to compel a third person to pay or deliver money or property as ransom, or to engage in other particular conduct, or to refrain from engaging in particular conduct; or
2. He restrains the person abducted for a period of more than twelve hours with intent to:
   (a) Inflict physical injury upon him or violate or abuse him sexually;
   (b) Accomplish or advance the commission of a felony; or
   (c) Terrorize him or a third person; or
   (d) Interfere with the performance of a governmental or political function; or
3. The person abducted dies during the abduction or before he is able to return or to be returned to safety. Such death shall be presumed, in a case where such person was less than sixteen years old or an incompetent person at the time of the abduction, from evidence that his parents, guardians or other lawful custodians did not see or hear from him following the termination of the abduction and prior to trial and received no reliable information during such period persuasively indicating that he was alive. In all other cases, such death shall be presumed from evidence that a person whom the person abducted would have been extremely likely to visit or communicate with during the specific period were he alive and free to do so did not see or hear from him during such period and received no reliable information during such period persuasively indicating that he was alive.

Kidnapping in the first degree is a Class A-I felony.

§ 135.30 Kidnapping; defense

In any prosecution for kidnapping, it is an affirmative defense that:
(a) the defendant was a relative of the person abducted, and
(b) his sole purpose was to assume control of such person.

8. Parental Kidnapping

In more recent times, the courts have had to deal with the issue of parental kidnappings that occur when a parent who does not have legal custody of a child refuses to return the child to the custodial parent, and/or abducts the child. Because of the difficulties of applying traditional kidnapping statutes to such behavior, and the reluctance of juries to find guilt when the kidnapper is a parent, many states have created new statutes that define the behavior as a crime separate from kidnapping. One such statute is Oregon's "Custodial Interference" statute.

> Oregon Revised Statute 163.245-Custodial Interference in the Second Degree
>
> A person commits the crime of custodial interference in the second degree if, knowing or having reason to know that the person has no legal right to do so, the person takes, entices or keeps another person from the other person's lawful custodian or in violation of a valid joint custody order with intent to hold the other person permanently or for a protracted period.
>
> Oregon Revised Statues 163.257-Custodial Interference in the First Degree
>
> A person commits the crime of custodial interference in the first degree if the person violates ORS 163.245 and:
> (a) Causes the person taken, enticed or kept from the lawful custodian or in violation of a valid joint custody order to be removed from the state; or
> (b) Exposes that person to a substantial risk of illness or physical injury.

An Ohio statute designed to prevent child stealing and enticing a child away is titled "Interference with Custody." It provides:

> (A) No person, knowing he is without privilege to do so or being reckless in that regard, shall entice, take, keep, or harbor a person identified in Division (A)(1), (2), or (3) of this section from his parent, guardian, or custodian:
>
>   (1) A child under the age of eighteen, or a mentally or physically handicapped child under the age of twenty-one;
>   (2) A person committed by law to an institution for delinquent, unruly, neglected, abused, or dependent children;
>   (3) A person committed by law to an institution for the mentally ill or mentally retarded.[142]

The Ohio statute provides a defense for enticing a child away if there is a reasonable belief that it is necessary for the child's protection, and also provides a defense to harboring a child if the actor notifies the authorities of the child's whereabouts in a timely fashion.

D. Summary

Kidnapping has maintained the elements of common law for the most part; however, case law has greatly reduced the asportation requirement. The common law requirement that the reason for the kidnapping be for ransom or another unlawful purpose has also been expanded, either by case law or statute. The most recent issue concerning the law of kidnapping is how to deal with parental kidnappings, especially those in which the parent has at least some arguably noble purpose in protecting their child from an abusive custodial parent. States must honor the custodial orders of other states and, therefore, parents must be deterred from taking the law into their own hands by seizing the child. Everyone can agree, however, that these cases are different from kidnappings for ransom.

Kidnapping

(A/R) Detaining another, with force or fraud, without consent, asportation, for ransom or other unlawful purpose

(M/R) Purposefully, Knowingly

---

§ 5.9 Hate Crimes (Bias Crimes)

A. Common Law

There was no such crime under common law. The concept of hate crimes is purely statutory.

B. Model Penal Code

The impetus for and creation of the first hate crime statutes occurred well after the development and dissemination of the Model Penal Code.

C. State Statutes, Codes, and Cases

Several well-publicized incidents involving victims who were targeted because they were African-American, Jewish, or homosexual in the late 1980s and early 1990s resulted in the creation of criminal statutes that came to be known as "hate crime" statutes. **Hate crime** statutes are similar to traditional criminal statutes prohibiting acts such as assault, battery, or vandalism; however, the hate crime statutes require an additional element—that the victim (or property) was selected as a target because of the victim's membership in a protected group. One author described these crimes as crimes that have been "committed not out of animosity toward the victim as an individual, but out of hostility toward the group to which the victim belongs."[143]

1. Construction

Hate crime statutes generally have two components: prohibited acts and protected groups. The prohibited acts addressed by a hate crime statute may either be listed by name (assault, battery, aggravated assault, misdemeanor theft, criminal trespass to residence, misdemeanor criminal damage to property, criminal trespass to vehicle, criminal trespass to real property, or mob action) or the statute may simply refer to particular crimes by category or statute number.[144]

Specific groups that are protected by hate crime statutes vary from jurisdiction to jurisdiction. Generally, however, most statutes include the following categories: age, race, color, creed, religion, ancestry, gender, sexual orientation, physical or mental disability, or national origin.

Hate crimes also vary by the nature of the penalty. In some jurisdictions, the determination that a particular crime qualifies as a hate crime serves to enhance, or increase, the sentence of the underlying criminal offense,[145] while in other jurisdictions a hate crime is a separate and distinct criminal offense carrying a separate penalty.[146]

California's statute is as follows:

> 422.6 (a)[147]
>
> No person, whether or not acting under color of law, shall by force or threat of force, willfully injure, intimidate, interfere with, oppress, or threaten any other person in the free exercise or enjoyment of any right or privilege secured to him or her by the Constitution or laws of this state or by the Constitution or laws of the United States because of the other person's race, color, religion, ancestry, national origin, disability, gender, or sexual orientation, or because he or she perceives that the other person has one or more of those characteristics.

Forty-nine states have adopted some form of hate crime legislation.[148] Further, at the federal level, legislation has been enacted that requires states to keep track of hate crime statistics.[149] Bias crime statutes are almost as varied in their scope, linguistic particulars, and the circumstances of creation as the jurisdictions that have enacted them. There is no formal or historic feature that a law must have in order to be properly called a "hate crime statute."

Legal News

In 2008, the federal government released figures that indicated that the number of hate crimes involving race and religion had declined in recent years, but crimes based on sexual orientation and ethnicity showed increases. Hate crimes ranged from murders to rapes, assaults, and intimidation. Hate crime statistics are based on state reports, and only the state of Mississippi reported that there were no hate crimes in the previous year.

Source: Branigan, W. (2008). "Hate Crimes Register Slight Decline Overall." *Washington Post*, October 28, 2008:A 15.

2. Judicial Review of Hate Crimes

Care must be taken when drafting hate crime legislation to not criminalize speech (or symbolic speech) that is constitutionally protected. Two recent decisions by the U.S. Supreme Court have clarified the relationship between actions that can constitutionally be criminalized by a hate crime statute and actions that must be tolerated as protected free speech.[150]

In *R.A.V. v. St. Paul*, juveniles burned a cross on the lawn of an African-American family. They were convicted of violating a city ordinance that prohibited actions based on "bias-motivated hatred." In striking down that particular hate crime ordinance, the Supreme Court noted that the ordinance was "content-based" toward particular forms of speech rather than facially neutral, prohibiting all speech or actions likely to provoke a fight. In other words, rather than criminalizing all actions or words likely to invoke a violent response ("fighting words"), the St. Paul ordinance singled out, by content, specific activities to criminalize:

> Whoever places on public or private property, a symbol, object, appellation, characterization or graffiti, including, but not limited to, a burning cross or Nazi swastika, which one knows or has reasonable grounds to know arouses anger, alarm or resentment in others on the basis of race, color, creed, religion or gender commits disorderly conduct and shall be guilty of a misdemeanor.

In *Wisconsin v. Mitchell*, the defendant, who was black, specifically selected a white victim to assault. The defendant was convicted under the Wisconsin statute that mandated an enhanced sentence when a defendant "[i]ntentionally selects the person against whom the crime . . . is committed . . . because of the [victim's] race. . . ." In upholding the validity of the Wisconsin statute, the Court distinguished *R.A.V. v. St. Paul* because the Wisconsin statute was "content-neutral" in that ". . . the statute . . . is aimed at conduct unprotected by the First Amendment."

> **CASE: *Wisconsin v. Mitchell*,**
> **508 U.S. 476, 113 S. Ct. 2194,**
> **124 L. Ed. 2d 436 (1993)**
>
> What was the holding of the case?
>
> How was Wisconsin's law distinguished from Minnesota's?

The Court's rulings in these two cases indicate that hate crime legislation will be upheld as being valid as long as the statute or ordinance criminalizes traditionally prohibited acts ("fighting words") and such legislation does not single out specific actions based on the speech-related content.

In a challenge to the Illinois hate crime statute, a defendant sought to overturn his conviction, alleging that the statute was unconstitutional because it violated the free speech, due process, and equal protection provisions of the U.S. Constitution. The Illinois appellate court upheld the statute, noting that the Illinois statute was more like the content-neutral statute upheld in *Wisconsin v. Mitchell* than the content-based ordinance struck down in *R.A.V. v. St. Paul*. The court went on to note that the due process claim must also fail because the statute was not constitutionally vague regarding what actions were prohibited. Finally, the court dismissed the defendant's equal protection claim, noting that "[i]n light of the greater degree of harm suffered by minority groups that have been systematically victimized, the majority of courts across the country have agreed that they deserve special attention."[151] Several state courts have come to similar conclusions in upholding the validity of their hate crime statutes.[152]

D. Summary

Hate or bias crimes are recent additions to the law. They add specific penalties or enhanced penalties when crimes are perpetrated against members of protected groups.

Hate or Bias Crimes

(A/R)   certain specified (illegal) acts, i.e., murder, assault, vandalism, kidnapping; against specific victims (members of protected groups)

(M/R)   intentional

---

§ 5.10 Summary

Crimes that are considered under the heading "Offenses Against Persons" are homicide, suicide, assault and battery, kidnapping and related offenses, mayhem, hate crimes, and "other crimes against the person." The most serious of these are in the homicide category. Homicide is defined as the killing of a human being by another human being. Not all homicides are illegal. At the top of the scale of crimes relating to homicide is murder in the first degree. At the other end of the scale are excusable and justifiable homicides, which are not subject to punishment under the law.

The common law crime of murder is defined as "the unlawful killing of a human being by another human being with malice aforethought." At common law, and in some states, there are no degrees of murder. However, in most states, the crime of murder is divided into two categories: first degree and second degree. The distinguishing factors of first degree murder are premeditation and deliberation.

Manslaughter is defined as the unlawful killing of a human being, done without malice, express or implied, either in a sudden quarrel or unintentionally while in the commission of an unlawful act. Manslaughter is usually divided into two categories: voluntary, when the homicidal act is intentional but passion-produced and occasioned by some provocation; and involuntary, when it results from the commission of certain unlawful acts not accompanied by any intention to take life.

Suicide is not a homicide, because there is no killing of one person by another person. While some of the early courts took the position that suicide was a crime, even if no punishment could be inflicted, today suicide is not considered a crime. However, a person may be guilty of criminal homicide if, with the requisite culpability, he or she causes the death of another by causing that person to commit suicide. Also, under some statutes, a person may be guilty of a separate offense of aiding or soliciting suicide even when suicide itself is not a crime.

Although assault and battery were two separate common law crimes, under the modern statutes, they are usually combined into one crime of assault. The common definition of assault is "an unlawful offer or attempt to injure another, with apparent present ability to effectuate the attempt under circumstances creating a fear of imminent peril"(or) "the unlawful touching of the person of another by the aggressor or by some substance put in motion by him," which was the common law definition of battery.

Kidnapping is "the forcible detaining of another against his will to unlawfully obtain ransom, or unlawfully restraining another and forcibly moving the person imprisoned to another place." The essence of kidnapping is the intentional taking of a person and compelling him or her to be detained against his or her will. Kidnapping is considered a very serious crime and under the Model Penal Code is designated a felony in the first degree, unless the actor voluntarily releases the person alive and in a safe place, in which case it is a felony in the second degree. Parental kidnapping laws are a recent addition to penal codes.

Recently, hate crime laws have been added to the group of laws under the category of "Crimes Against a Person." Hate or bias crimes have been defined as crimes that have been committed not out of animosity toward the victim as an individual, but out of hostility toward the group to which the victim belongs. Specific groups that are protected by hate crime statutes vary from jurisdiction to jurisdiction. Generally, however, most statutes include the following categories: age, race, color, creed, religion, ancestry, gender, sexual orientation, physical or mental disability, or national origin. They have been upheld as long as they do not infringe on constitutional rights of free speech.

Review Questions

1. What are the different types of homicide and what are the elements of each?

2. Distinguish first degree from second degree murder and voluntary from involuntary manslaughter.

3. What are assisted suicide laws? How many states have them?

4. What is the "year and a day rule"?

5. What are the three types of homicide defined in the Model Penal Code?

6. How does current law define death? How does current law define a person?

7. Distinguish justifiable and excusable homicide.

8. Discuss the concepts of "delayed death exceptions" to double jeopardy.

9. Describe transferred intent.

10. Describe the felony murder doctrine. Explain what type of deaths could be attributable to defendant in felony murder cases.

11. Describe depraved heart or depraved indifference murder and distinguish it from involuntary manslaughter..

12. Describe the types of provocation necessary to prove voluntary manslaughter and those that would not provide a defense. What are the other elements of voluntary manslaughter?

13. Distinguish between depraved heart (or depraved indifference) murder, involuntary manslaughter, and negligent homicide.

14. What are the elements of assisted suicide. How many states have laws allowing assisted suicide?

15. Distingish assault and battery under the common law. How does the MPC change these traditional definitions? Provide the elements of assault.

16. When can consent be used as a defense to assault?

17. What is the crime of mayhem?

18. Distinguish between unlawful imprisonment and kidnapping. What are the elements of each.

19. What are the elements and defenses to parental kidnapping statutes?

20. Describe hate crime statutes. Describe when such statutes would be ruled unconstitutional and when they would be ruled constitutional.

Notes

[1] Kinsey v. State, 49 Ariz. 201, 65 P.2d 1141 (1937). *See* WHARTON, HOMICIDE § 1 (3d ed.).

[2] Kinsey v. State, 49 Ariz. 201, 65 P.2d 1141 (1937).

[3] STATUTES OF GLOUCESTER, EDW. I., c IX (1763).

[4] State v. Orrell, 12 N.C. 139 (1826).

[5] MODEL PENAL CODE § 210.1 (1985).

[6] Examples are Ariz., Ark., Conn., Fla., Ind., Mont., N.H., N.M., N.Y., Pa., Tex., Utah, and Wash.

[7] Examples are Conn., Ga., Ill., Ind., Iowa, Kan., Ky., Minn., N.M., N.Y., Or., S.D., Tex, and Wash.

8   State v. Young, 390 A.2d 556 (N.J. 1978), State v. Gabehart, 836 P.2d 102 (N.M. Ct. of App. 1992).

9   State v. Hefler, 310 S.E.2d 310 (N.C. 1984).

10   Rogers v. Tennessee, 532 U.S. 451, 453 (2001).

11   UNIFORM DETERMINATION OF DEATH ACT, 120 U.L.A., 1987 Pocket Part 287.

12   In re Welfare of Bowman, 94 Wash. 2d 407, 617 P. 2d 731 (1980). *See also* People v. Eulo, 482 N.Y.S. 436 (1984).

13   New York v. Latham, 83 N.Y.2d 233, 631 N.E.2d 83 (1994)

14   United States v. Meacher, 37 F. 875 (1888); People v. Lyons, 110 N.Y. 618, 17 N.E. 391 (1888).

15   Keeler v. Superior Court, 80 Cal. Rptr. 865 (Cal. Ct. App. 1969).

16   CAL. PENAL CODE § 187 (2002).

17   State v. Beale, 376 S.E.2d 1 (N.C. 1989).

18   Kelley Shannon, *Execute Doctors for Abortions?* AUSTIN AMERICAN-STATESMAN, August 30, 2005 at B3.

19   Pam Easton, *Man Convicted for Causing Miscarriage Taunted Girlfriend.* FORT WORTH STAR TELE-GRAM, June 18, 2005 at A1.

20   *See generally*, MORELAND, THE LAW OF HOMICIDE (1952); Perkins, *The Law of Homicide*, 36 J. CRIM. L. & CRIMINOLOGY 391 (1946).

21   People v. Hartwell, 341 Ill. 155, 173 N.E. 112 (1930). *See also* State v. Russell, 106 Utah 116, 145 P.2d 1003 (1944).

22   Commonwealth v. Noxon, 319 Mass. 495, 66 N.E.2d 814 (1946).

23   Regina v. Serne, 16 (Cox) CC 311 (1887).

24   MODEL PENAL CODE § 210.2 (1985).

25   Myrick v. State, 199 Ga. 244, 34 S.E.2d 36 (1945).

26   Commonwealth v. Malone, 354 PA 180, 47 A.2d 445 (1946).

27   N.M. STAT. ANN. § 30-2-1 (Michie 2002).

28   State v. Bowser, 214 N.C. 249, 199 S.E. 31 (1938). *See also* State v. Hutchins, 303 N.C. 321, 279 S.E.2d 788 (1981). In State v. Hutchins, the North Carolina Supreme Court reaffirmed that premedita-tion and deliberation may be inferred from circumstantial evidence. The court also determined that no fixed period is required for these mental processes to occur.

29   Loehrke v. State, 722 So. 2d 867 (Fla. 1998).

30   United States v. Shaw, 701 F.2d 367 (5th Cir.), *reh'g denied*, 714 F.2d 544 (5th Cir.), *cert. denied*, 104 S. Ct. 1419 (1983).

31   Pears v. State, 672 P.2d 903 (Alaska App. 1983).

32   Banks v. State, 85 Tex. Crim. 165, 211 S.W. 217 (1919).

33   State v. Harrison, 90 N.M. 439, 564 P.2d 1321 (1977).

34   State v. Ortega, 112 N.M. 554, 817 P.2d 1196 (1991).

35   IND. CODE ANN. § 35-42-1-1 (Burns 2002).

36   State v. Cheatham, 134 Idaho 565, 6 Pa.3d 815 (2000).

37   Dunagan v. State, 269 Ga. 590, 502 S.E.2d 726 (1998).

38   People v. Stamp, 82 Cal. Rptr. 598 (Ct. App. 1969).

39   State v. McClain, 623 A.2d 280 (N.J. Super. Ct. App. Div. 1993).

40   Enmund v. Florida, 458 U.S. 782, 102 S. Ct. 3368, 73 L. Ed. 2d 1140 (1982).

41   Tison v. Arizona, 481 U.S. 137, 107 S. Ct. 1676, 95 L. Ed. 2d 127 (1987).

42   MODEL PENAL CODE § 210.3 (1985).

43   State v. Lillibridge, 454 A.2d 237 (R.I. 1982).

44   State v. Cousins, 223 S.E.2d 338 (N.C. 1976).

45   State v. Nelson, 103 N.H. 478, 175 A.2d 814 (1961).

46   OHIO REV. CODE ANN. § 2903.03(A) (Anderson 1999).

47   IND. STAT. ANN. § 35-42-1-3 (Burns 2002).

48   Moore v. State, 694 S.W.2d 529 (Tex. Crim. Ct. App. 1985).

49   Stewart v. State, 75 Ala. 436 (1885).

50   State v. Michael, 74 W. Va. 613, 82 S.E. 611 (1914).

51   Commonwealth v. Paese, 220 Pa. 371, 69 A. 891 (1908).

52   State v. Thornton, 730 S.W.2d 309 (Tenn. 1987).

53   State v. Young, 52 Or. 227, 96 P. 1067 (1908).

54   Haley v. State, 123 Miss. 87, 85 So. 129 (1920).

55   White v. State, 44 Tex. Crim. 346, 72 S.W. 173 (1902). State v. McLawhorn, 270 N.C. 622, 155 S.E.2d 198 (1967); State v. Coop, 223 Kan. 302, 573 P.2d 1017 (1978).

56   State v. King, 37 N.J. 285, 181 A.2d 158 (1962).

57   State v. Flory, 40 Wyo. 184, 276 P. 458 (1929).

58   Id.

59   Weaver v. State, 583 N.E.2d 136 (Ind. 1991). See also People v. Spurlin, 156 Cal. App. 3d 199 (1984) and State v. Landry, 449 So. 2d 1320 (La. Ct. App. 1986).

60   Rex v. Thomas, 7 Car. P. 817, 173 Eng. Rep. 356 (1837); State v. Speors, 76 Wyo. 82, 300 P.2d 555 (1956).

61   Evans v. State, 727 N.E.2d 1072 (Ind. 2000).

62   Moses v. State, 270 Ga. 127, 508 S.E.2d 661 (1998); Carsner v. State, 970 P.2d 28 (Idaho 1998).

63   Maryland v. Chapman, 101 F. Supp. 335 (D. Md. 1951).

64   Jones v. United States, 308 F.2d 307 (D.C. Cir. 1962).

65   People v. Penny, 44 Cal. 2d 861, 285 P.2d 926 (1955).

66   People v. Crucoani, 70 Misc. 2d 528, 334 N.Y.2d 515 (1972)]

67   MODEL PENAL CODE § 210.4.

68   Statutory schemes may be found in: ALASKA STAT. § 11.41.120 (1995); CAL. PENAL CODE § 192 (West 1996); D.C. CODE ANN. § 22-2405 (1995); MD. CODE ANN., Crim. Law § 387, 388, 388A (1992); MASS. GEN. LAWS ANN. ch. 265, § 13 (West 1995); MICH. COMP. LAWS § 750.321 (1995).

69   OHIO REV. CODE ANN. § 2903 et seq. (Anderson 1999).

70   Keel v. French, 162 F.3d 263 (4th Cir. 1998).

71   People v. Kolzow, 703 N.E.2d 424 (Ill. 1998).

72   Callahan v. State, 343 So. 2d 551 (Ala. Ct. App. 1977).

73   Pitts v. State, 122 So. 2d 542 (Ala. Ct. App. 1960).

74   State v. Miller, 981 S.W.2d 623 (Mo. 1998).

75   Commonwealth v. Welansky, 55 N.E.2d 402 (Mass. 1944).

[76] Eric Tucker, *Band Manager to Plead Guilty in R.I. Nightclub Fire*. BOSTON.COM NEWS. Retrieved June 29, 2006 from http://www.boston.com/news/local/rhode_island/articles/2006/01/31/band_man-ager_reach_plea_agreement_in_nightculb_fire_case/

[77] Boone v. State, 234 Ga. App. 373, 506 S.E.2d 884 (1998); Commonwealth v. Souza, 429 Mass. 478, 702 N.E.2d 1167 (1998).

[78] Commonwealth v. Mink, 123 Mass. 422 (1877).Grace v. State, 44 Tex. Crim. 193, 69 S.W. 529 (1902).

[79] Burnett v. People, 204 Ill. 208, 68 N.E. 505 (1903).

[80] MODEL PENAL CODE § 210.5 (1985).

[81] Vacco v. Quill, 521 U.S. 793, 117 S. Ct. 2293, 139 L. Ed. 2d 834 (1997). (See this case for a list of states that prohibit assisted suicide.) *See also* Kevorkian v. Arnett, 939 F. Supp. 725 (C.D. Cal. 1996).

[82] CAL. PENAL CODE § 401 (1999).

[83] N.Y. PENAL LAW § 125.15 (McKinney 1997).

[84] People v. Kevorkian, 527 N.W.2d 714 (Mich. 1994).

[85] Washington v. Glucksberg, 521 U.S. 702, 117 S. Ct. 2258, 138 L. Ed. 2d 792 (1997).

[86] Vacco v. Quill, 521 U.S. 793, 117 S. Ct. 2293, 139 L. Ed. 2d 834 (1997).

[87] OR. REV. STAT. § 127.880 *et seq.*

[88] Gonzales v. Oregon, 126 S.Ct. 904, 163 L.Ed.2d 748 (2006).

[89] State v. Heitman, 618 S.W.2d 902 (Mo. Ct. App. 1981).

[90] State v. Hefner, 199 N.C. 778, 155 S.E. 879 (1930).

[91] Commonwealth v. Hill, 237 Pa. Super. 543, 353 A.2d 870 (1975).

[92] MODEL PENAL CODE § 211.1 (1985).

[93] N.H. REV. STAT. ANN. § 632-A:2 (1994); N.J. REV. STAT. § 2C:12-1 (1995); PA. CONS. STAT. 18 § 2701(b)(2) (1995).

[94] OHIO REV. CODE ANN. §§ 2903.11, 2903.12, 2903.13, 2903.14, 2903.21, 2903.22 (Anderson 1999).

[95] People v. LeFlore, 96 Mich. App. 557, 293 N.W.2d 628 (1980).

[96] Albright v. State, 214 So. 2d 887 (Fla. Dist. Ct. App. 1968).

[97] State v. Harding, 22 N.C. App. 66, 205 S.E.2d 544 (1974).

[98] Allen v. Hannaford, 138 Wash. 223, 244 P. 700 (1926).

[99] Trougn v. Fruchtman, 58 Wis. 2d 569, 207 N.W.2d 297 (1973).

[100] Pallis v. State, 123 Ala. 12, 26 So. 339 (1899).

[101] Scruggs v. State, 161 Ind. App. 666, 317 N.E.2d 807 (1974).

[102] Brenneman v. State, 458 S.W.2d 677 (Tex. Crim. App. 1970).

[103] Fisher v. Carrousel Motor Hotel, 424 S.W.2d 627 (Tex. 1967).

[104] Crabtree v. Dawson, 83 S.W. 557 (Ky. 1904).

[105] In re David H., 967 P.2d 134 (Ariz. 1998).

[106] Dawsey v. State, 234 Ga. App. 540, 507 S.E.2d 786 (1998); *see also* State v. Chang, 587 N.W.2d 459 (Iowa 1998).

[107] S.D. CODIFIED LAWS ANN. § 22-18-11 (Michie 1995).

[108] CAL. PENAL CODE § 244 (West 1995).

[109] CAL. PENAL CODE § 244.5 (West 1995).

[110] S.D. CODIFIED LAWS ANN. 22-18-1.3 (Michie 1995).

[111] Smallwood v. State, 661 A.2d 747 (Md. Ct. App. 1995).

[112] Scroggins v. State, 198 Ga. App. 29, 401 S.E.2d 13 (1990). Condition was a "deadly weapon"; State v. Deal, 459 S.E.2d 93 (S.C. 1995), HIV status was "aggravating circumstance"; State v. Smith, 262 N.J. Super. 487, 621 A.2d 493 (App. Div. 1993), "aggravated assault"; Commonwealth v. Brown, 413 Pa. Super. 421, 605 A.2d 429 (1992), "serious bodily injury" was upheld. *See also* State v. Bird, 81 Ohio St. 3d 582, 692 N.E.2d 1013 (1998), in which the court upheld the conviction of an HIV-infected defendant for felonious assault when the defendant spit in a police officer's face.

[113] People v. Jensen, 231 Mich. App. 439, 586 N.W.2d 748 (1998).

[114] People v. Van Diver, 80 Mich. App. 352, 263 N.W.2d 370 (Mich. Ct. App. 1978). *See also* People v. Nealy, 681 N.Y.S.2d 29 (1998).

[115] Kelly v. State, 362 So. 2d 1292 (1978).

[116] State v. Torres, 335 S.E.2d 34 (N.C. Ct. App. 1985).

[117] Bishop v. United States, 349 F.2d 220 (D.C. Cir. 1965).

[118] Powell v. United States, 485 A.2d 596 (D.C. Ct. App. 1984), *cert. denied*, 474 U.S. 981, 106 S. Ct. 420, 88 L. Ed. 2d 339 (1985).

[119] Harris v. United States, 333 A.2d 397 (D.C. Ct. App. 1975).

[120] State v. Fransua, 510 P.2d 106 (1973).

[121] IDAHO CODE § 18-5001 (1995).

[122] Tate v. State, 32 Md. App. 613, 363 A.2d 622 (1976).

[123] State v. Croatt, 227 Minn. 185, 34 N.W.2d 716 (1948).

[124] Gwooch v. United States, 82 F.2d 534 (10th Cir. 1936).

[125] Chatwin v. United States, 326 U.S. 455, 66 S. Ct. 233, 90 L. Ed. 198 (1946).

[126] MODEL PENAL CODE § 212.1 (1985).

[127] MODEL PENAL CODE §§ 212.2-212.5 (1985).

[128] State v. Roberts, 286 N.C. 265, 210 S.E.2d 396 (1974).

[129] Lovell v. State, 92 Nev. 128, 546 P.2d 1301 (1976).

[130] State v. Ayers, 198 Kan. 467, 426 P.2d 21 (1967).

[131] State v. Denmon, 347 N.J. Super. 457, 790 A.2d 921 (2002).

[132] State v. Brown, 181 Kan. 375, 312 P.2d 832 (1957).

[133] Matter of Appeal in Maricopa County Juvenile Action, 25 Ariz. App. 377, 543 P.2d 806 (1975).

[134] People v. Fick, 89 Cal. 144, 26 P. 759 (1891).

[135] Epperson v. State, 211 Ind. 237, 6 N.E.2d 538 (1937).

[136] State v. Morris, 281 Minn. 119, 160 N.W.2d 715 (1968).

[137] State v. Dix, 14 N.C. App. 328, 188 S.E.2d 737 (1972).

[138] State v. Joyce, 410 S.E.2d 516 (N.C. 1991). *See also* Elozar v. State, 825 So.2d 490 (2002).

[139] Cosby v. State, 234 Ga. App. 723, 507 S.E.2d 551 (1998). *See also* Duncan v. State, 253 Ga. App. 239, 558 S.E.2d 783 (2002), which held that any unlawful asportation, however slight, will support a kidnapping conviction.

[140] West v. United States, 599 A.2d 788 (D.C. Ct. App. 1991).

[141] N.Y. PENAL LAW §§ 135.05-135.30 (McKinney 1999).

[142] OHIO REV. CODE ANN. § 2919.23 (Anderson 2002).

[143] Elizabeth A. Pendo, *Recognizing Violence Against Women: Gender and Hate Crime Statistics*, 17 HARV. WOMEN'S L.J. 157 (1994).

[144] Illinois, 720 ILL. COMP. STAT. § 5/12-7.1 (West 1994); WIS. STAT. § 939.645(1)(b).

[145] Wisconsin.

[146] Illinois.

[147] CAL. PENAL CODE 422(a).

[148] Marlene Z. Stanger, *Hate Crime Legislation: Panacea or Protractor of Societal Ills?* 3 SAN DIEGO JUST. J. 419 (1995).

[149] FEDERAL HATE CRIMES STATISTICS ACT OF 1990, 28 U.S.C. § 534(b)(1).

[150] R.A.V. v. St. Paul, 505 U.S. 377, 112 S. Ct. 2538, 120 L. Ed. 2d 305 (1992); Wisconsin v. Mitchell, 508 U.S. 476, 113 S. Ct. 2194, 124 L. Ed. 2d. 436 (1993).

[151] In re Vladimir P., 670 N.E. 2d 839 (Ill. Ct. App. 1996).

[152] The court specifically referenced the findings in *Crimes Motivated By Hatred: The Constitutionality and Impact of Hate Crime Legislation in the United States*, 1 SYRACUSE J. LEGIS. & POL'Y 29 (1995). See also Anthony M. Dillof, *Punishing Bias: An Examination of the Theoretical Foundation of Bias Crime Statutes*, 91 NW. U. L. REV., Spring 1997. See also Steven G. Gey, *What if Wisconsin v. Mitchell had involved Martin Luther King, Jr.? The Constitutional Flaws of Hate Crime Enhancement Statutes.* 65 GEO. WASH. L. REV., August 1997. Frederick M. Lawrence, *Federal Bias Crime Law Symposium*, B.U. L. REV., Vol. 80, pg. 1185 (2000). This article is followed by other articles that consider the pros and cons of federalizing hate crimes. Christopher Chorba, *The Danger of Federalizing Hate Crimes*, VA. L. REV., Vol. 87, 319-379, 2001.

Offenses Against Persons—Sex Related

6

Chapter Outline

Cases

Marital Exemption: *People v. Liberta,* 474 N.E.2d 567 (N.Y. 1984)
Sodomy: *Lawrence et al. v. Texas,* 539 U.S. 558 (2003)

§ 6.1 Introduction

Although some sex-related offenses are also offenses against the person, they are considered separately for several reasons. Some sexual acts were considered serious offenses in the past, but not today. For example, adultery and fornication were classified as felonies at common law and by some early statutes. Today they are minor misdemeanors if they are crimes at all.[1] On the other hand, some acts that were not considered serious crimes in the past or were neglected by the law now receive greater attention; for instance, acquaintance rape, sexual harassment, and HIV/AIDS transmission. Some sex-related crimes are consensual and, therefore, are not "offenses against the person." In this chapter, non-consensual sex crimes are considered and in Chapter 10 other sex-related crimes, such as adultery, prostitution, incest, and obscenity offenses are discussed.

The specific offenses defined and explained in this chapter are rape; sodomy and related crimes; sexual abuse (sexual assault); lewdness (indecent exposure); and other crimes such as seduction, importuning, voyeurism, sexual misconduct, and intercourse with a person in custody.

---

§ 6.2 Rape

A. Common Law

The common law definition of **rape** is "the act of having unlawful carnal knowledge by a man of a woman, forcibly and against her will."[2] In reflecting on the common law, as compared to statutory law, one court indicated that common law rape is the act of a man having unlawful carnal knowledge of a female over the age of 10 years by force without the consent and against the will of the victim.[3]

Thus, the common law elements of rape are: unlawful; carnal knowledge (sexual intercourse); by force or fear; without consent or against the will; of a woman.

1. Unlawful

Unlawful, as used in this context, is defined as "not authorized by law," and interpreted to be intercourse between those who are not husband and wife.[4] Under the common law, and as defined by most early statutes, rape was an act of sexual intercourse with a female, not the wife of the perpetrator.[5]

The rationale for the concept that intercourse between husband and wife was lawful was that the matrimonial consent that the wife gave when she assumed the marital relationship could not be revoked. A seventeenth-century jurist, Matthew Hale, formulated the concept that by "their mutual matrimonial consent and contract the wife hath given of herself in this kind unto her husband, which she cannot retract."[6]

The first American case to recognize the **marital exemption** was decided in 1857 by the Supreme Judicial Court of Massachusetts, which included a comment that "it would always be a defense to rape to show marriage to the victim."[7] Decisions to the same effect by other courts followed, usually with no rationale or authority cited, other than Hale's implied consent view. In New York, a 1922 decision noted the marital exemption in the penal laws, and stated that it existed "on account of the matrimonial consent which the wife has given, and which she cannot retract."[8]

2. Carnal Knowledge (or Sexual Intercourse)

Carnal knowledge is synonymous with sexual intercourse. Regardless of the definition used, according to all early authorities, to complete the crime of rape there must be some penetration, although the least penetration is sufficient. According to one court, the slightest penetration of the vulva is sufficient to constitute rape and emission is not necessary.[9] However, the prosecution must prove beyond a reasonable doubt that penetration in fact occurred.[10]

3. Force or Fear

The force that is a necessary element in the commission of the common law crime of rape includes actual physical force in compelling submission of the female and also includes threatened force or violence for the purpose of preventing resistance. This element may be met by showing that there was actual force or that the force was constructive. *Forcibly* does not necessarily mean *violently*. In one case, the court determined that:

> . . . the force must be such as may reasonably be supposed adequate to overcome physical resistance of the woman upon whom rape is charged to have been committed, taking into consideration the relative strength of the parties and other circumstances of the case, such as outcries and giving alarm.[11]

The offense is complete even if no actual force is used, if it can be shown by the evidence that the woman is made to yield through fear and does not consent voluntarily to the act of sexual intercourse.[12]

The force necessary to constitute rape may also be constructive. For example, if the female is mentally unconscious from drink or is asleep, or from other causes is in a state of insensibility, so that the act of unlawful carnal knowledge on the part of the man is committed without conscious and voluntary permission, force is necessarily involved in the wrongful act itself. The unlawful imposition constitutes the necessary force if the man knows that the woman is in a state of unconsciousness.[13] Note that such a condition also negates the ability to give consent, another element of the crime.

Without force, actual or constructive, there can be no rape. If the prosecution can show that actual force was used, or he can show that the victim submitted as a result of terror or fear caused by threats or intimidation, or if the force is constructive in that the woman is unconscious, this is sufficient to meet the "force" requirement in proving the crime of rape.

4. Without Consent or against the Will

This element, which is sometimes stated in terms such as "without her consent," has been interpreted to mean that the sexual act must be committed against the will of the woman without her voluntary consent. Intercourse accomplished by force is without consent; however, voluntary consent given at any time prior to the penetration deprives the subsequent intercourse of its criminal character, regardless of how reluctantly it may have been given or how much force theretofore had been employed.[14] Whether the consent was voluntary depends upon the facts of each particular case and if the jury, after hearing all of the evidence, finds that there was consent at the time of the intercourse even though there was some persuasion in the initial contact, the court will be hesitant to find this element of the crime.

It is not necessary that the victim resist physically if the evidence indicates that she physically feared the defendant and expressed her unwillingness to engage in intercourse. When the victim is prevented from resisting by the threats of creating bodily harm, accompanied by apparent power of execution, this element of the crime of rape is present. On the other hand, early cases also sometimes discussed the "**utmost resistance standard**." This was the idea that a woman should want to resist at all costs any attempt of rape. If she did not appear to have suffered any injury, there was an inclination to use that as evidence that consent was granted. Some cases have led to seemingly unfair findings, such as a case in which a woman had been in a physically abusive relationship with the assailant but had left him. He threatened her and her mother if she did not accompany him and then took her to a house and told her she was going to have sex with him. Even though she told him she did not want to, she did not physically resist, arguably because she was afraid of him. The appellate court overturned the conviction because although the victim had not consented, there was no showing of force or threats to overcome the resistance of the victim.[15] It is this narrow and tortured reading of the difference between consent and force that has spurred a re-examination of the definitions of traditional elements of rape.

There can be no consent if the woman is wholly insensible so as to be incapable of consenting.[16] Therefore, unlawful intercourse with a woman who had fainted was held to be rape in a Georgia case.[17] When a man has reduced a woman to a state of insensibility through alcohol, she is unable to give consent; however, cases have held that inducing a woman to drink intoxicating beverages or to use drugs to excite her passions, leaving her at the same time capable of comprehending the nature of the act, does not amount to rape, because there has been consent.[18]

Also, where consent is obtained by fraud, there is no legal consent. For example, where a doctor had sexual intercourse with a woman under the fraudulent pretense of medical treatment, this was rape because there was no voluntary consent.[19] However, there is some legal authority to the premise that the victim's misapprehension due to deception must be in regard to the sexual intercourse, not some other fact. In other words, if a doctor convinces a patient that what is happening is not sexual intercourse, but is a medical treatment instead, it is rape; but if a doctor lies to a patient and says that sexual intercourse is necessary to make her healthy and she consents, it is not rape.[20]

5. Of a Female

Under common law, only women could be raped, and only men could rape (although a male victim would be protected under the laws of assault and battery). The history of this crime originates in the man's dominion over his female relatives (both spouse and child). The rape was seen as an offense against her, but also against him. It was, in a sense, an affront to his property rights because any resulting pregnancy might be the seed of the rapist instead of his, confusing the rightful lines of inheritance.

6. Mens Rea

The *mens rea* of common law rape was intentional. The perpetrator also has to know that the victim is not consenting to sexual intercourse.

7. Common Law-Statutory Rape

Under the early English cases, it was not rape to have sexual intercourse with a female child if she consented.[21] However, later English statutes included sections that provided that females under 12 years of age were incapable of consent, and to have sexual intercourse with a female child under this age was considered rape, even though there was consent.[22] This has come to be known as **statutory rape**. In the United States, the age of consent was fixed by statute in practically all states; some states set the age at 14, some at 16, and some at 18.

B. Model Penal Code

The Model Penal Code clarified the required elements of the crime of rape, and graded different types of sex offenses.

---

§ 213.1 Rape and Related Offenses[23]

(1) Rape. A man who has sexual intercourse with a female not his wife is guilty of rape if:
   (a) he compels her to submit by force or by threat of imminent death, serious bodily injury, extreme pain or kidnapping, to be inflicted on anyone; or
   (b) he has substantially impaired her power to appraise or control her conduct by administering or employing without her knowledge drugs, intoxicants or other means for the purpose of preventing resistance; or
   (c) the female is unconscious; or
   (d) the female is less than 10 years old.

Rape is a felony of the second degree unless:
   (i) in the course thereof the actor inflicts serious bodily injury upon anyone, or
   (ii) the victim was not a voluntary social companion of the actor upon the occasion of the crime and had not previously permitted him sexual liberties, in which case the offense is a felony of the first degree.

(2) Gross Sexual Imposition. A male who has sexual intercourse with a female not his wife commits a felony of the third degree if:
   (a) he compels her to submit by any threat that would prevent resistance by a woman of ordinary resolution; or

---

> (b) he knows that she suffers from a mental disease or defect which renders her incapable of appraising the nature of her conduct; or
> (c) he knows that she is unaware that a sexual act is being committed upon her or that she submits because she mistakenly supposes that he is her husband.

These provisions encompass many of the acts that were made illegal under the common law and various state statutes, and bring them together in a more uniform way. Similar to common law, the MPC defines rape in such a way that only men can rape and only women (and not the wife of the rapist) can be raped. Also, penetration is required.

C. State Statutes, Codes, and Cases

State statutes follow the MPC in grading different degrees of rape based on characteristics of the victim and/or the violation. The specific elements within each grading system vary from state to state. Parts of the Kentucky Code are included here.

> § 510.040—Rape in the first degree.
>
> (1) A person is guilty of rape in the first degree when:
>
> (a) he engages in sexual intercourse with another person by forcible compulsion; or
> (b) he engages in sexual intercourse with another person who is incapable of consent because he:
>   (1) is physically helpless; or
>   (2) is less than twelve (12) years old.
>
> (2) Rape in the first degree is a Class B felony unless the victim is under twelve (12) years old or receives a serious physical injury in which case it is a Class A felony. (Enact. Acts 1974, Ch. 406, § 84)
>
> § 510.050—Rape in the second degree.
>
> (1) A person is guilty of rape in the second degree when, being eighteen (18) years old or more, he engages in sexual intercourse with another person less than fourteen (14) years old.
> (2) Rape in the second degree is a Class C felony. (Enact. Acts 1974, Ch. 406, § 85)
>
> § 510.060—Rape in the third degree.
>
> (1) A person is guilty of rape in the third degree when:

> (a) he engages in sexual intercourse with another person who is incapable of consent because he is mentally retarded or mentally incapacitated; or
> (b) being twenty-one (21) years old or more, he engages in sexual intercourse with another person less than sixteen (16) years old.
>
> (2) Rape in the third degree is a Class D felony.

As state statutes are different, we will use the traditional elements of rape from the common law to illustrate the changes that have taken place in the definition and prosecution of rape.

1. Unlawful

Recall that under the common law, it was legally impossible to rape one's wife. This was called the marital exemption or marital immunity. Even as recently as 1984, the Model Penal Code and about 40 states retained some form of marital exemption for rape. However, since then there has been a rapid movement to remove this exclusion, either by statute or court decision.[24] Today some state courts have judicially determined that a man can be convicted of rape of his wife if other factors are proved[25] and some states have changed their statutes and omitted the words "not his wife" from the statutory definition of rape.[26]

In a 1981 New Jersey case, the husband of the victim broke into his wife's apartment and forced her to have sexual intercourse. The trial court granted a motion to dismiss the rape charges because the couple was married and the rape took place before the statute was passed by the New Jersey legislature. However, the couple were separated at the time of the rape and had been living apart for more than a year. In addition to the rape, the victim was choked, beaten, and held against her will for several hours. The New Jersey Supreme Court, after discussing the changes in the divorce laws and other legal developments, reasoned that the corollary of a spouse's right to make a unilateral decision to end the marriage is "a wife can refuse sexual intercourse with her husband during the period of separation prior to divorce." The court continued, stating:

> If a wife has a right to refuse intercourse, or deny consent, then a husband's forceful carnal knowledge of his wife clearly includes all three elements of the crime of rape. He cannot defend by asserting that there was no lack of consent because he was still legally married to the victim.[27]

Thus, the holding was that even though new laws cannot be applied retroactively, due process and equal protection required that at least in cases in which the couple were separated and no longer shared the "marital bed," the marital exemption did not apply to excuse criminal culpability when sexual intercourse was achieved through force and without a wife's consent.

In the case of *People v. Liberta*, the Court of Appeals of New York, after carefully considering the "marital exemption rule," declared the rule to be unconstitutional. The court declared that there is no rational basis for distinguishing marital rape and nonmarital rape. The court reasoned that:

> [t]he various rationales which have been asserted in defense of the exemption are either based upon archaic notions about the consent and property rights incident to marriage or are simply unable to withstand even the slightest scrutiny. We, therefore, declare the marital exemption for rape in the New York statute to be unconstitutional.[28]

CASE: *People v. Liberta*, 474 N.E.2d 567 (N.Y. 1984)
What was the holding of the case?
What was the appellant's argument?
Did the appellant win or lose?

More recently, in the case of *People v. M.D.*, the Illinois Supreme Court, citing *Liberta* and other cases, also declared the Illinois marital exemption statute (completely prohibiting prosecution for sexual abuse and permitting only very limited prosecution for sexual assault) unconstitutional in that it violated public policy, equal protection, and due process.[29]

Statutes regarding the marital exemption are varied:

- some totally abolish the marital rape exemption for any kind of sexual contact or persuasion,

- some abolish the exemption for forcible rape but not for lesser sexual assault crimes,

- some premise the exemption on a continuing marital relation,

- some expand the exemption to persons within a marriage-like relationship even though not married.

While some state courts have determined that the marital rape exemption is unconstitutional, the U.S. Supreme Court has not made such a determination. Therefore, it is necessary to consult state statutes and state court decisions to determine the applicable law. Nevertheless, it is safe to conclude that the rationale for the exclusion has been dissipating rapidly and that the trend is to abolish the marital exemption either by statute or court decision.[30]

2. Carnal Knowledge (or Sexual Intercourse)

Most states still have some requirement of penetration; however, the penetration may be by an object rather than a penis, and the slightest penetration will suffice.[31] Some state criminal statutes define the term "sexual intercourse" to include penetration of the sex organs, or in some cases the anus, by foreign objects manipulated by third parties.[32] A majority of the states have specifically eliminated the requirement of "emission"(or "ejaculation") by statute.[33] However, where an assailant experiences an emission or ejaculation, absent evidence of some penetration, the crime of rape is not complete, although the offense of attempted rape will most likely be found.[34] The slightest penetration can constitute rape; however, repeated penetrations during the act, which, if a continuous process, constitute but one crime.[35]

Some courts have judicially created a broad definition of the term "sexual intercourse" to include homosexual acts as well as heterosexual acts.[36] The federal statutes employ the term "sexual act" rather than "sexual intercourse" and define the term to include biological sexual intercourse, oral sex (cunnilingus and fellatio), and penetration by hands, fingers, and objects.[37]

The crime of rape requires sexual intercourse with a living victim. However, if a criminal statute prohibits "deviate sexual intercourse" and if the statute further defines the term to include sexual intercourse with a corpse, an assailant will be guilty of that substantive offense, in addition to attempted rape. A New Jersey court held that because the victim was alive when the defendant was choking her and when the co-defendant began removing her clothing, the defendant could be convicted of sexual assault, even if the victim was dead by the time the sexual penetration actually occurred.[38]

3. Force or Fear

In the case of *People v. Taylor*, the Supreme Court of Illinois explained the "force" requirement:

> . . . Proof of physical force is unnecessary if the prosecuting witness was paralyzed by fear or overcome by the superior strength of her attacker; that it is, however, fundamental that in order to prove the charge of forcible rape there must be evidence to show that the act was committed by force and against the will of the female and if she has the use of her faculties and physical powers, the evidence must show such resistance as will demonstrate that the act was against her will.[39]

Modern statutes, as did the common law, overlap the concepts of force and consent. When the term "compulsion" is used, the term is defined as physical force that overcomes earnest resistance, or any threat, express or implied, that overcomes earnest resistance by placing a person in fear of immediate death or physical injury to self or fear that another person will be harmed.

In determining the presence or absence of forcible compulsion for purposes of the offense of rape, the issue is whether the victim perceived the aggressor's force or imminent threat of force as compelling her compliance. In the case cited, the court pointed out that it is the victim's perspective, not the assailant's, from which the presence or absence of forcible compulsion is to be determined. This is a subjective test that looks to the victim's perception of the circumstances surrounding the incident in question.[40]

4. Without Consent or against the Will

Recall that, under common law, if the woman consented (even if duress preceded the consent), then no rape was said to have occurred. A woman's

consent to sexual intercourse is void if it is given in fear of personal violence.[41] However, the line between force, duress, and persuasion is sometimes
not an easy one to make. The victim of a sexual assault is not required to
physically resist the assault and the courts agree that "no means no;" however, it is incumbent on the victim to make it clear to the attacker that she is
unwilling.[42] Courts allow an inference from "torn clothing, bruises, and body
position" to overcome the claim of the defendant that it was consensual.[43]

Modern courts continue to struggle with the concept of consent. The
general rule is that if the victim consents to sexual intercourse prior to penetration and withdraws consent following penetration, there is no rape.[44]
However, this does not preclude the perpetrator from being found guilty of
another crime, such as assault, if warranted by the evidence.

The biggest change in the prosecution of rape has not been in the
definitions or elements, but rather in the application or interpretation of the
definitions to cases. The "utmost resistance" standard, for instance, has been
discounted and abolished. A New York court refused to give an instruction that "to be guilty of rape in the first degree the victim must oppose the
perpetrator to the utmost limit of her power by genuine active resistance."
The trial judge instead explained that "the degree of force required to place
somebody in fear will vary with the person involved."[45]

The idea that a woman can withhold consent even in circumstances
of "date-rape" is more accepted. Some case decisions today would have
probably been decided differently 50 years ago. For instance, in *People
v. Reed*, the defendant was convicted of rape and three counts of deviate
sexual assault.[46] On appeal, he claimed that the complainant consented to the
sexual activities and explained that she had consented to a nude massage in
order to relieve muscle tension and, by her actions, consented to the sexual
intercourse. The reviewing court reasoned that, although the complainant's
consent to a nude massage with no apprehension of sexual involvement was
naïve, it might reasonably be explained by the fact that defendant, who was
30 years older than she, introduced himself as an acquaintance of her best
friend, and indicated that he was a doctor and psychologist. The court found
that this was rape and there was no consent to the sexual intercourse.

A variety of opinions relate to the use of liquor or drugs in obtaining
consent. There is no doubt that unlawful sexual intercourse by a man with a
woman whom he has reduced to a state of insensibility by intoxicating liquor
or drugs is rape.[47] However, anything less than insensibility on the victim's
part would still render her capable of consent. The statutory definition that
includes any type of insensibility addresses situations such as occurred in a
New York case in which the victim was undergoing nitrous oxide treatment
at her dentist's office and was mentally alert, but physically unable to resist
sexual intercourse by the dentist.[48] In a Kansas case, the court held that the
victim did not consent where the evidence supported that the victim was
both psychologically and physiologically impaired due to the effects of her
medical condition and medications.[49]

In one case that illustrates the difficulty the law has with the concept of consent, the rape victim requested that her assailant wear a condom before engaging in sexual intercourse. The victim had obtained the condom from a package of condoms she kept in the trunk of her vehicle. At trial, the assailant raised the defense of consent, based on the actions of the victim in keeping condoms in her vehicle and her request that one be used during intercourse; however, the assailant did not prevail on his claim.[50] In another case, a rape victim, in the presence of her assailant, shoplifted a pack of condoms. Although convicted, the defendant successfully convinced the trial court to allow evidence about the victim's actions in obtaining the condoms, as relevant evidence of her intent to consent to sexual intercourse.[51]

Legal News

Another "condom rape case" was that of Xan Wilson in Austin, Texas. She was assaulted by the defendant, who broke into her home. Faced with an inevitable rape, she pleaded with her attacker to wear a condom because she was afraid she would be infected with HIV/AIDS. Because of her request that he wear a condom, the grand jury declined to indict him under the belief that she consented. After a firestorm of publicity, he was subsequently indicted by a different grand jury, prosecuted, convicted, and sentenced to 40 years' imprisonment.

Source: *Austin American-Statesman*, June 10, 1993 at B1.

---

5. Of a Female

States have made rape statutes gender-neutral, using terms such as "person" or "actor," so as to make it possible to convict a person of a sex crime regardless of whether that person is male or female.[52] Under the Michigan statute, for instance, a person is guilty of criminal sexual conduct in the first degree if she or he engages in sexual penetration with another person and if other circumstances exist. The terms "male" and "female" are not used and either may be guilty of criminal sexual conduct. Today, virtually all rape statutes, both forcible and statutory, are gender-neutral and use the term "person" when referring to the assailant. Thus, both males and females may be found guilty of rape.[53]

6. *Mens Rea*

There must be intent to force sexual intercourse on an unwilling victim (and one must know that the victim is unwilling). It is a general intent crime.

7. Statutory Rape

The act of having intercourse with a female under the age of consent became commonly known as "statutory rape." Where the female is under the age of statutory consent, as stated by the respective statutes, it makes no difference whether the act was accomplished against her will, or without her consent, or even with her consent.[54] Also, the chastity of the female before the age of consent is immaterial.[55]

The state is not required to show evidence that the act was accomplished against the will of the minor, or without her consent or by force. However, failure to introduce evidence to establish that the victim was under the age specified by the statute when the offense occurred will require reversal of the conviction. In *State v. Dixon*, the court held that an element of the offense is the establishment of the victim's age, and failure to introduce testimony establishing the victim's age requires reversal.[56]

Unless statutes specifically provide for the defense of mistake, a defendant will not be permitted to argue that he or she thought the victim was of the age permitted by the statutes. However, some states have enacted statutory provisions that permit the defense of mistake regarding the age of the victim if evidence establishes that "at the time he engaged in the conduct constituting the offense he did not know of the facts or conditions."[57] Other states require a defendant to base the mistake specifically on the statements of the victim and, absent such explicit statements, will not permit a defense of mistake based on the victim's appearance.[58] Another form of statutory relief involves statutes that declare that no offense is committed when the underage victim and the defendant were legally married at the time of the sexual intercourse.[59]

In the case of *Owens v. State*, the reviewing court determined that the defendant's rights to due process under the state and federal constitutions were not violated, when, upon being charged with statutory rape, the trial court prevented the defendant from presenting his defense that he reasonably believed the victim was more than 13 years of age. The defendant's assertion that he had made a reasonable mistake regarding the victim's age was best considered as mitigating circumstances at his sentencing for statutory rape, but the defendant could not assert the mistake-of-age defense.[60]

Some states have mitigated the severity of statutory rape by making exceptions to strict liability or making exceptions for when the age difference between the two parties is not large. For instance, the Texas Criminal Code has a statute called "Indecency with a Child" that prohibits sex acts with a child younger than 17 that is not the defendant's spouse. However, the statute also provides that:

> It is an affirmative defense to prosecution for this crime that the actor: (1) was not more than three years older than the victim and of the opposite sex; and (2) did not use duress, force, or a threat against the victim at the time of the offense.[61]

However, even in these states, victims below a certain age will maintain the mantle of protection of strict liability with no defense of mistake or age. For instance, in Pennsylvania, a defendant may use mistake of age as a defense when he or she is within four years of the age of the victim; however, sex with a victim under the age of 13 is a strict liability crime.[62]

When both parties are under the age of majority (21 or 18), typically the crime is graded as less serious. Statutes covering this behavior, such as Kentucky's Sexual Misconduct statute, are described later in this chapter. In general, today's statutory rape statutes are gender-neutral. Historically, statutory rape was reserved for the protection of girls. The reason for the law was to protect of the virginity of young women. Even fairly recently, the Supreme Court has held that it is a legitimate state purpose to protect against pregnancies of young girls and that is sufficient to distinguish young men and young women in order to justify different treatment.[63] However, many states use the term "person" or "someone" in their statutory rape laws and, thus, women can be guilty of statutory rape as well.

Legal News

Mary Kay Letourneau in Washington State became a tabloid celebrity when she was convicted of statutory rape for having sex with a sixth grade student when he was 12 and she was 34. The affair was exposed when she became pregnant with his child. She went to prison and, after an early release, became pregnant again with the young man's child, despite a no-contact condition on her parole. She was sent back to prison and ultimately served $6^1/_2$ years. Once released, the couple reunited and have since married. Washington's laws were gender-neutral.

---

8. Rape Shield Statutes and Decisions

Traditionally, defense attorneys would attempt to impugn the chastity and veracity of the rape victim in order to create reasonable doubt that the sexual intercourse was without consent. Many states, after carefully considering the desirability of protecting the rape victim, enacted legislation that became known as "**rape shield laws**." The rationale behind such statutes is that evidence of a rape victim's prior sexual activity is of dubious probative value and relevance, and is highly embarrassing and prejudicial. Those who argued for such statutes assert that the protection offered by the statutes would encourage victims of sexual assault to report the crimes without fear of having their sexual history exposed to the public.[64]

Today, most state statutes and the federal code include provisions restricting testimony on the victim's prior sexual behavior to that genuinely relevant to the defense.[65] In October 1978, President Jimmy Carter signed H.R. 4727 into law, creating Federal Rule of Evidence 412, the Rape Shield Statute. Rule 412 prohibits the introduction at trial of reputation or opinion evidence of a rape victim's sexual history. The rule also prohibits introduction of sexual history evidence not in reputation or opinion form, subject to three exceptions:

1. The first exception concerns evidence that a rape defendant has a constitutional right to have introduced.

2. The second exception is for evidence of the victim's behavior with persons other than the defendant that the defendant offers to show that he was not the source of semen or injury.

3. The third exception is for the past sexual behavior of the victim with the defendant himself, which the defendant offers to show consent.

Even if the evidence fits into one of the latter two categories, it is admissible only if the trial judge finds, after an *in camera* (in chambers) hearing, that it is both relevant and more probative than prejudicial.[66]

Most states follow the basic contours of Federal Rule of Evidence 412. Many states, however, do not expressly provide an exception for constitutionally required evidence. Other states ban sexual history evidence subject to an exception only for specific instances of conduct with the defendant.

Although the rape shield statutes generally serve the two basic purposes of protecting the privacy of the rape victims and encouraging rape victims to come forward, the courts have also given consideration to the rights of the defendant. For example, in a 1986 case, the defendant, appealing a rape conviction, argued that the lower court erred in refusing to allow him to introduce evidence that he had a previous sexual relationship with the victim. The single issue was whether the trial court erred, as a matter of law, in ruling that any evidence of a prior sexual relationship between the defendant and the victim was inadmissible. The issue related not only to the question of consent on the part of the victim, but to the whole question of her credibility as a witness. At trial the victim had said that she had never had intercourse with the defendant, and the defendant offered to introduce evidence to prove that she had had a previous sexual relationship with the defendant. The reviewing court agreed with the defendant that, under these circumstances, evidence should have been admitted. The court determined that the evidence should be admissible if its probative value outweighs its inflammatory or prejudicial nature, and it is material to an issue of fact. In reversing the decision of the lower court, the reviewing court agreed that "clearly, the testimony was material and relevant to the question of consent; and this court finds its probative value outweighed any resulting prejudice."[67]

A different court ruled that a rape defendant was not entitled to present evidence regarding the victim's alleged sexual relations with another party on the date of the alleged rape, in an effort to establish that he was not the perpetrator of the rape. The court ruled that evidence of the victim's past sexual behavior is admissible only to establish a source of semen, pregnancy, disease, or injury.[68]

The "interests of justice" exception to the rape shield law has been offered as a defense in numerous federal and state courts. In a Minnesota case, the court precisely stated that the rape shield statute serves to emphasize the general irrelevance of a victim's sexual history, not to remove relevant evidence from the jury's consideration. The court continued by stating that the rape shield law is a legislative limitation on a citizen's Sixth Amendment right to

confront and cross-examine opposing witnesses and the law must be scrutinized to determine whether it provides or prevents a fair and orderly trial.[69]

An Alabama court held that the rape shield law does not require an absolute exclusion of all evidence of past sexual activity between the victim and
third persons. That court held that, notwithstanding the rape shield law, a rape
victim's testimony that she had never had any kind of sexual relations with
anyone other than the defendant opened the door to introduction of impeach-
ment evidence supporting inferences that the victim had, in fact, experienced
sexual intercourse with others than the defendant.[70]

In a case that considered the application of the rape shield statute where
the female was under the age of consent, a Wisconsin court established some
specific guidelines. In that case, the court held that to admit evidence of a
child complainant's past sexual misbehavior under the judicial exception
to the rape shield law, the defendant must show that the proffered evidence
meets the following five criteria and then balance the parties' interests to
determine whether the evidence is admissible:

1. the prior acts must have clearly occurred;

2. the prior acts must closely resemble those of the present case;

3. the prior acts must be clearly relevant to a material issue;

4. the evidence must be necessary to a defendant's case; and

5. the probative value of the evidence must outweigh its prejudicial effect.[71]

Rape shield laws have been challenged as being unconstitutional because
they violate the defendant's right of confrontation. In a Texas case, the defendant appealed his conviction of aggravated rape, claiming that the rape shield
law in that state violated his right of confrontation and his due process rights.
The rape shield law in Texas provided, in part, that:

> Evidence of specific instances of a victim's sexual conduct, opinion evidence
> of the victim's sexual conduct, and reputation evidence of the victim's sexual
> conduct may be admitted . . . only if, and only to the extent that, the judge
> finds that the evidence is material to a fact at issue in the case and that its
> inflammatory or prejudicial nature does not outweigh its probative value.

The Texas statute establishes procedures for introduction of evidence,
provides for an *in camera* hearing, and requires that the record be sealed.
The reviewing court, in upholding the constitutionality of the rape shield law,
reasoned that the right to confront and cross-examine is not absolute and may,
in appropriate cases, bow to accommodate other legitimate interests in the
criminal law process. In applying that reasoning to the rape shield law, the
court indicated that, although statutory, the rape victim shield law is analogous
to judge-made rules of evidence that prevent the admissibility of opinion evidence, hearsay testimony, and convictions of very old standing, if the probative
value of the evidence is outweighed by the possibility of jury prejudice.[72]

D. Summary

Because there have been several changes from common law definitions of rape, and because state statutes vary so widely in their definitions and interpretations of the elements of rape, the summary provided here should be viewed as a rough generalization of what might be the case in any particular state. The most dramatic changes have been:

- the elimination of marital exemption or immunities,
- the development of rape victim shield laws
- the expansion of sexual assault to cover sex acts in addition to penetration
- the definition of rape as a gender-neutral crime.

Statutory rape is also quite different from state to state and some states allow for the mistake of age defense.

Rape

(A/R) Unlawful sexual intercourse, with force or threat of force, without consent

(M/R) Intentional

Statutory Rape

(A/R) Unlawful sexual intercourse with a minor (statutorily defined) by someone over 18 (or an age that is statutorily defined)

(M/R) Strict liability (except in those states that allow for mistake of age defense in which case it would be knowing or reckless)

---

§ 6.3 Sodomy and Related Crimes

A. Common Law

In England, **sodomy** at first was subject only to punishment by the ecclesiastical authorities. However, early English statutes made sodomy a criminal offense, and it was this offense under the common law that was used as a basis for the laws in the United States.[73] While the original English enactments proscribed only anal intercourse between males, the coverage was extended so as to punish fellatio and cunnilingus, as well as anal intercourse and bestiality. In some states, the crime was designated by statute as "crime against nature."[74]

The term "sodomy" has been defined in many ways by many jurisdictions. In its broadest terms, sodomy is the "carnal copulation by human beings with each other against nature, or with a beast." The broad definition includes bestiality, buggery, cunnilingus, and fellatio.[75] A definition, included in an early case, is:

> A person who carnally knows in any manner any animal or bird, or carnally knows any male or female person by the anus, or with the mouth, or voluntarily submits to such carnal knowledge, or attempts sexual intercourse with a dead body, is guilty of sodomy.[76]

From the foregoing, it becomes clear that some sodomy crimes are consensual. These offenses are considered in this chapter because the trend in modern statutes has been to require the presence of force or imposition.

B. Model Penal Code

Rather than using the term "sodomy," the drafters of the Model Penal Code took a different approach, defining the offense as "deviate sexual intercourse by force or imposition." It is immediately apparent that the words "by force or imposition" change the common law concept and make this a crime against another person. The Model Penal Code exempts from criminal sanction deviate sexual intercourse between consenting adults. Under the Model Code, **deviate sexual intercourse** is not criminal if both participants consent and each is of sufficient age and mental capacity to give consent and they conduct their relations in private and create no public nuisance. Also, it should be noted that, under the Model Code, homosexual relations between consenting parties is not a violation of the law.

---

§ 213.2 Deviate Sexual Intercourse by Force or Imposition[77]

(1) By Force or Its Equivalent. A person who engages in deviate sexual intercourse with another person, or who causes another to engage in deviate sexual intercourse, commits a felony of the second degree if:

(a) he compels the other person to participate by force or by threat of imminent death, serious bodily injury, extreme pain or kidnapping, to be inflicted on anyone; or

(b) he has substantially impaired the other person's power to appraise or control his conduct, by administering or employing without the knowledge of the other person drugs, intoxicants or other means for the purpose of preventing resistance; or

(c) the person is unconscious; or

(d) the other person is less than 10 years old.

(2) By Other Imposition. A person who engages in deviate sexual intercourse with another person, or who causes another to engage in sexual intercourse, commits a felony of the third degree if:

(a) he compels the other person to participate by any threat that would prevent resistance by a person of ordinary resolution; or

---

> (b) he knows that the other person suffers from a mental disease or defect which renders him incapable of appraising the nature of his conduct; or
>
> (c) he knows that the other person submits because he is unaware that a sexual act is being committed upon him.

C. State Statutes, Codes, and Cases

Because there are many statutory crimes in the general sodomy category, it is difficult to enumerate elements. A few early statutes included these definitions:

- Sodomy is carnal copulation with members of the same sex or with an animal or unnatural carnal copulation with a member of the opposite sex.[78]

- [sodomy] is a carnal copulation between two human beings per anus or by a human being in any manner with a beast.[79]

When the statute uses the term "carnal copulation," the prosecution must show that some sexual intercourse took place, including intercourse by way of the mouth.[80] Under many statutes, and at common law, penetration was an essential element of the crime of sodomy. Where penetration is an element, any penetration, however slight, is sufficient to constitute the element. For example, in the case of *People v. Hickock*, the complaining witness had been hypnotized to a point at which she was unable to move, but retained consciousness and had her teeth tightly clenched when the accused placed his penis inside her lips. In this case, the court said that this was a penetration sufficient to allow conviction under the statute providing that "any person participating in the act of copulating the mouth of one person with the sexual organ of another is punishable by imprisonment not exceeding fifteen years."[81] Although there has been some conflict in interpretation, the general rule is that emission is not required as an element of the offense. This was made clear by some statutes that specifically provide that emission is not essential and that penetration is sufficient to constitute the crime.[82] A Texas statute, for instance, defined "Deviate Sexual Intercourse" as any contact between any part of the genitals of one person and the mouth or anus of another person. The Texas Court of Appeals interpreted this statute to require only "any contact," not penetration.[83]

All statutes similar to the Model Penal Code provide sanctions where the person engages in deviate intercourse with another person where the deviate sexual intercourse results *from force or imposition*. Some state statutes, however, provided that a person was guilty of sodomy when he or she engaged in deviate sexual intercourse with another person of the same sex *even if no force or imposition was involved*. These statutes have been challenged as violating the constitutional right to privacy.

In the 1986 case of *Bowers v. Hardwick*, the United States Supreme Court, by a five-to-four majority, upheld the constitutionality of the Georgia sodomy law, agreeing with the Georgia court that the United States Constitution does not confer a fundamental right upon homosexuals to engage in homosexual sodomy.[84] However, by 2001, only 18 states still retained sodomy laws that criminalized same-sex consensual activity.[85]

In 2003, the Supreme Court overturned the *Bowers* decision in *Lawrence et al. v. Texas*.[86] In this case, Houston police entered Lawrence's apartment while responding to a reported weapons disturbance and saw him and another adult man engaging in a private consensual act. The men were arrested and convicted of deviate sexual intercourse in violation of the Texas sodomy statute. The majority held that the Texas statute violated the due process clause of the Fourteenth Amendment.

Statutes that prohibit such activity through the use of force or imposition, against children, or against animals are not affected by the *Lawrence* decision.

> **CASE: *Lawrence et al. v. Texas*, 539 U.S 558, 123 S. Ct. 2472, 156 L. Ed. 2d 508 (2003)**
>
> What was the holding of this case?
>
> What constitutional right was said to have been violated?
>
> What is the state's interest in maintaining laws regarding private sexual activity between consenting adults?

D. Summary

Historically, sodomy laws covered all forms of "deviate" sexual activity which, in the broadest definition, was any form of sexual activity that was not sexual intercourse between a man and a woman that could lead to procreation. Sodomy laws were gradually restricted so that such forms of sexual activity between men and women were decriminalized, and with the decision of *Lawrence v. Texas,* consensual sex between same-sex adults has been decriminalized. However, states still have the power to criminalize such activity when it is accompanied by force or imposition (so that, for instance, in some states, a rapist may be charged with both rape and sodomy). Further, sex between humans and animals is still illegal in most states although it may be defined under other statutes. Our general summary of elements below may or may not represent your state's sodomy law.

Sodomy

(A/R)   Deviate sexual activity (defined as when the sexual organ of one person comes into contact with, or penetrates, the mouth or anus of another person); by force; or without consent

(M/R)   Intentional, Knowing

---

§ 6.4 Sexual Abuse (Sexual Assault)

A. Common Law

Under common law, rape required penetration; therefore, anything short of penetration was generally dealt with under battery prosecutions. Today, such conduct is covered under more general sexual assault statutes.

B. Model Penal Code

In the Model Penal Code, forms of sexual touching that do not include penetration are called "**sexual assault**." This crime is treated as a sexual offense rather than included under the crime of assault.

---

§ 213.4 Sexual Assault[87]

A person who has sexual contact with another not his spouse, or causes such other to have sexual conduct with him, is guilty of sexual assault, a misdemeanor, if:

(1) he knows that the contact is offensive to the other person; or
(2) he knows that the other person suffers from a mental disease or defect which renders him or her incapable of appraising the nature of his or her conduct; or
(3) he knows that the other person is unaware that a sexual act is being committed; or
(4) the other person is less than 10 years old; or
(5) he has substantially impaired the other person's power to appraise or control his or her conduct, by administering or employing without the other's knowledge drugs, intoxicants or other means for the purpose of preventing resistance; or
(6) the other person is less than [16] years old and the actor is at least [four] years older than the other person; or
(7) the other person is less than 21 years old and the actor is his guardian or otherwise responsible for general supervision of his welfare; or
(8) the other person is in custody of law or detained in a hospital or other institution and the actor has supervisory or disciplinary authority over him.

"**Sexual contact**" as used in the Model Code is defined to include "any touching of the sexual or other intimate parts of the person for the purpose of arousing or gratifying sexual desire." The prosecution must show that the "purpose" of the touching was to arouse or gratify sexual desire. Also, the prosecution must prove the touching of the sexual or other intimate parts of the person.

C. State Statutes, Codes, and Cases

State statutes have also provided sanctions for offensive sexual contact that is not protected by rape laws. Various statutes were given titles such as "indecent or immoral practices with another," "**sexual abuse**,"[88] or "sexual imposition."[89] Other states have provided punishment under the general laws relating to assault and battery.[90]

States provide special coverage for taking indecent liberties with children.[91] Sometimes called child molestation, state statutes criminalize touching of children for sexual gratification. Consent of the child is never a defense. An example of this is a Kentucky statute passed in 1962, which provided:

> Any person of the age of seventeen years or over who carnally abuses the body, or indulges in any indecent or immoral practices with the body or organs of any child under the age of 15 years, or who induces, procures or permits a child under the age of 15 years to indulge in immoral, sexual or indecent practices with himself or any person shall be guilty of a felony, punishable on conviction thereof by imprisonment in the penitentiary for not less than one year nor more than ten years.[92]

Some states have followed the Model Code in establishing only one degree of sexual abuse, but grade the offense as a lesser felony.[93] However, in some statutes, the offenses of sexual assault or sexual abuse are graded according to the degree of force and the age or mental condition of the victim.[94] An example of a statute that graduates the penalty based upon age is that of New York.[95]

> § 130.55 Sexual abuse in the third degree
>
> A person is guilty of sexual abuse in the third degree when he or she subjects another person to sexual contact without the latter's consent; except that in any prosecution under this Section, it is an affirmative defense that (a) such other person's lack of consent was due solely to incapacity to consent by reason of being less than seventeen years old, and (b) such other person was more than fourteen years old, and (c) the defendant was less than five years older than such other person.
>
> Sexual abuse in the third degree is a Class B misdemeanor.
>
> § 130.60 Sexual abuse in the second degree
>
> A person is guilty of sexual abuse in the second degree when he or she subjects another person to sexual contact and when such other person is:
>
> (1) incapable of consent by reason of some factor other than being less than seventeen years old; or
> (2) less than fourteen years old.
>
> Sexual abuse in the second degree is a Class A misdemeanor.

"Sexual contact" as used in this Section means "any touching of the sexual or other intimate parts of a person for the purpose of arousing or gratifying sexual desire." In interpreting the term "sexual contact," as used in New York statute, the New York courts decided that kissing the victim against her will and inserting the tongue into her mouth was "sexual contact" within the meaning of the sexual abuse statute, because the mouth is an intimate part of the body.[96] Another New York court found that allegations that the defendant "fondled" the 16-year-old complainant's leg and upper thigh were sufficient to allege that the defendant fondled "intimate parts" of the complainant, necessary to the charge of third degree sexual abuse.[97]

A New York court held that, to establish the crime of third-degree sexual abuse, the statute does not require that actual gratification occur, but only that the touching be for that purpose. Therefore, the intentional and sexually motivated touching of a person's covered buttocks, whether by a co-worker, social acquaintance, or other, unquestionably qualifies as "sexual contact" under sexual abuse in the third degree statute, and is properly punishable by criminal sanction.[98]

In interpreting the Indiana statute titled "sexual battery," the court held that to convict a defendant of sexual battery, the state was required to prove that the defendant:

1.   with intent to arouse or satisfy his own sexual desires;

2.   touched the victim;

3.   when the victim was compelled to submit to touching by force or threat of force.

The court explained that the force used to compel the victim to submit to touching, as an element of the crime of sexual battery, need not be physical or violent, but may be implied from the circumstances. The court further noted that courts considered the victim's perspective, not the assailant's, when determining whether the presence or absence of forceful compulsion necessary to a conviction for sexual battery existed.[99] Because the state statutes differ and state court interpretations of statutes differ, it is essential that both the statute and case decisions be studied to determine whether a crime has been committed.

D. Summary

Sexual assault, sexual contact, or sexual lewdness laws did not exist under common law. They have been created to protect victims against offensive sexual contact that does not reach the definition of rape.

Sexual Assault

(A/R)   Any touching; of the sexual or other intimate parts of a person; for the purpose of arousing or gratifying sexual desire; without consent; or toward a person of a particular age (defined by statute); or a person unable to give consent (i.e., unconscious or incompetent)

(M/R)   Intentional and knowing

---

§ 6.5   Lewdness (Indecent Exposure)

A. Common Law

At common law, particular acts and forms of lewdness constituted criminal offenses. The word "**lewdness**" means open and public indecency. Usually in order to amount to an indictable crime, the offense must have been committed in a public place and seen by persons lawfully in that place. However, the early statutes provided a broader interpretation. Under these statutes, it was not necessary to allege or prove that such act was committed in a public place or in the presence of many people.

In the 1845 case of *State v. Willard*, the statute prohibited "open and gross lewdness:"

> If any man or woman, married or unmarried, shall be guilty of open and gross lewdness or lascivious behavior, he shall be imprisoned in the common jail not more than two years, or fined not exceeding $300.[100]

However, the court could find no particular definition in the statute as to what constituted lewdness, saying that "the indelicacy of the subject forbids it, and does not require of the court to state what particular conduct will constitute the offense." In this case, the respondent entered the house of a woman and "exposed his private parts and persistently urged her to have sexual intercourse with him." The court said there was no question that this was "lewdness" within the meaning of the statute and was "open within the meaning of the statute," defining openness to mean "undisguised, not concealed, and opposite to private, concealed, and unseen." Interestingly, in another early case, disrobing in a "house of ill fame" and intercourse therein did not warrant conviction for lewdness.[101]

Under the common law and early statutes, the elements that were required to convict a person of lewdness were: intentionally; indecently and offensively exposing the sex organs; in the presence of another; in an offensive manner.[102]

B. Model Penal Code

Prior to the drafting of the Model Penal Code, indecent exposure and related crimes were covered under a multitude of statutes and given such titles as "Lewd and Lascivious Behavior," "Public Lewdness," and even "Appearing on the Highway in Bathing Garb."[103] To make the offense more definite and the terms less likely to be misinterpreted, the Model Penal Code defines **indecent exposure** more narrowly.

> § 213.5 Indecent Exposure[104]
>
> A person commits a misdemeanor if, for the purpose of arousing or gratifying sexual desire of himself or of any person other than his spouse, he exposes his genitals under circumstances in which he knows his conduct is likely to cause affront or alarm.

It requires, specifically, the exhibition of the genitals (a display of the buttocks or breasts is not prohibited under this statute). Second, the Model Code requires that the actor have a purpose to arouse or gratify the sexual desire of himself or another not his spouse. Third, the offense requires the actor to know that his conduct is likely to affront or alarm another. This would exclude from the scope of the crime the member of a nudist colony and even the bottomless dancer who performs only for those desiring such entertainment.[105]

Legal News

The Moscow, Idaho, city council was prompted to pass an ordinance that prohibited women from showing their breasts in public when a group of women decided to open a topless car wash. The old indecency ordinance had recently been voided by the state supreme court as unconstitutionally vague and the state indecency law does not include the exposure of breasts as unlawful. The city attorney argued that the topless car washers could not be guilty of public nuisance laws because they were not creating a nuisance, although zoning laws may have been relevant. The city council vowed to resolve the problem by passing an ordinance requiring women to wear at least bikini tops while in public.

Source: Associated Press (2002). "Topless Car Wash Raises Ire of City Council." Seattle Post-Intelligencer, June 29, 2002:B1.

C. State Statutes, Codes, and Cases

Some statutes retain the terminology used before the Model Penal Code was written, and prohibit essentially the same conduct. Some use the terminology of the Model Code, but prohibit display of "sex organs" or other specifically named areas of the body, such as breasts.[106] Where a statute contains language such as "in a vulgar or indecent manner," or "with an immoral purpose," or "indecently," the prosecution must offer evidence to prove these elements as defined by the statute or by cases interpreting the statute.[107]

An example of an indecent exposure statute is the Texas statute,[108] which provides:

> **Indecent Exposure**
>
> (a) A person commits an offense if he exposes his anus or any part of his genitals with intent to arouse or gratify the sexual desire of any person, and he is reckless about whether another is present who will be offended or alarmed by the act.
> (b) An offense under this class is a Class B misdemeanor.

The Texas statute does not proscribe exposure of the buttocks or the female breasts as these two areas of the anatomy are not traditionally included within the term "genitals." The intent must be to arouse or gratify the sexual desire of any person. The court has upheld the statute against a challenge of being impermissibly vague.[109] Also, the Texas statute reduces *mens rea* from knowing to reckless in the actor's belief that anyone present would be offended or alarmed. The standard for determining offensiveness is objective; that is, it is not whether the defendant knows others would be offended or whether those present were actually offended, but rather, whether it would offend an ordinary person. Applying this standard, the court held that it was irrelevant whether the officer to whom the defendant exposed his penis was offended; the issue was whether the defendant was reckless about whether another was present who would be offended.[110]

Legal News

Breastfeeding in public has been a perennial point of contention between those who argue it is natural and should be considered acceptable anywhere, even if the breast is fully exposed, and those who argue that exposing the breast, if not illegal, is unacceptable in public. In December 2008, the popular computer social networking site, Facebook, was the target of a mass protest for their policy of removing pictures of breastfeeding when too much of the breast was exposed. The issue has prompted at least nine states to pass a law specifically protecting the act in public. Montana, for instance, has a statute that says:

> The Montana Legislature finds that breastfeeding a baby is an important and basic art of nurturing that must be protected in the interests of maternal and child health and family values. A mother has a right to breastfeed the mother's child in any location, public or private, where the mother and child are otherwise authorized to be present, irrespective of whether or not the mother's breast is covered during or incidental to the breastfeeding. The act of breastfeeding may not be considered a nuisance, indecent exposure, sexual conduct or obscenity (Montana Code Annotated: 50-19-501)

Source: Devlin, V. (2009). "Complaints on Breastfeeding Lead to Lesson on Breastfeeding Law." Missoulian.com. Accessed 1/2/2009 from www.missoulian.com/articles/2009/01/02/news/local/znews06.txt.

A Michigan statute addressing the problem of indecency in public places was reviewed and interpreted by the courts of that state. The court held that an act of masturbation in a public restroom between adult males was "grossly indecent" within the meaning of the statute. In the Michigan statute, the crime is a felony.[111]

Legal News

Senator Larry Craig (R-Idaho) was arrested in a Minneapolis airport restroom in June 2007 after his actions were determined to be a sexual solicitation by an undercover officer. He was originally charged with public lewdness but pled guilty to disorderly conduct. Some argued that the specific actions performed should not have been the basis for a criminal charge. The officer said that while both were in bathroom stalls, Craig's foot slid over and touched the officer's foot and he passed his hand under the partition several times. The officer's offense report stated that these were well-known sexual solicitation cues. The ensuing scandal created pressure for him to resign, but he held on to his seat until the end of his term. He did not run for re-election and ended his career in Congress in January 2009.

Source: http://blogs.usatoday.com/ondeadline/2007/08/sen-craig-arres.html.

D. Summary

Under common law, the elements of lewdness were: intentionally; indecently and offensively exposing the sex organs; in the presence of another; in an offensive manner. The Model Penal Code added that the exposure should be for the purpose of sexual arousal. Some statues reduce the *mens rea* to reckless in the actor's belief whether others would be offended and employ an objective standard as to offensiveness. In general, exposure of breasts or buttocks are not considered genitals but may be specifically added to the definition in the statute. The most common elements of this crime include the following elements.

Public Lewdness (Indecent Exposure)

(A/R) Exposure of genitals; in a public place; for the purpose of sexual arousal; in a manner that is offensive

(M/R) Reckless

---

§ 6.6 Other Sex-Related Offenses Against the Person

There are other statutes in various states that relate to sex offenses. Some of these are discussed briefly here.

A. Seduction

The crime of **seduction** is "the act of a man inducing a woman to commit unlawful sexual intercourse with him by means of enticement, persuasion, solicitations, promises, bribes or other means without the employment of force, therefore overcoming her reluctance and her scruples."[112] Under the provisions of some early statutes, as interpreted, consent of the woman seduced to the intercourse was no defense and, in some jurisdictions, unless so provided by statute, marriage to the accused after the seduction was no defense.[113] Generally, the woman who was seduced had to be both unmarried and chaste at the time.[114] Under common law, the elements of seduction were: inducement that overcomes the female's reluctance and scruples; unlawful sexual intercourse; by means of arts, persuasion, solicitations, promises, or bribes. Also, generally, the woman had to be unmarried and chaste.

The Model Penal Code restricts the coverage of seduction when compared to common law and earlier statutes. It applies to a male who induces a female to participate in intercourse "by a promise of marriage which the actor does not mean to perform." It does not cover other types of deception that might give rise to liability.

Although most states have modified older statutes to limit the scope of the crime, some type of seduction offenses still exist in some states, as well as the opportunity to seek civil damages. Generally, the definition of seduction is the same in civil and criminal matters. Some states have statutes modeled after the Model Penal Code.[115]

B. Importuning/Sexual Solicitation of a Minor

In most states, there are statutes prohibiting solicitation of sexual activity to minors. This is sometimes called **importuning**. For example, the Ohio Revised Code[116] provides:

> (a) No person shall solicit a person under thirteen years of age to engage in sexual activity with the offender, whether or not the offender knows the age of such person.
>
> (b) No person shall solicit a person of the same sex to engage in sexual activity with the offender, when the offender knows such solicitation is offensive to the other person, or is reckless in that regard.
>
> (c) No person shall solicit another, not the spouse of the offender, to engage in sexual conduct with the offender, when the offender is eighteen years of age or older and four or more years older than the other person, and the other person is over twelve but not over fifteen years of age, whether or not the offender knows the age of the other person.

This and similar statutes are designed to prohibit soliciting a person under age 13 to engage in sexual activity, or soliciting a person age 13 to 15 to

Legal News

Recently, Internet chat rooms have been the focus of both sexual predators of children and police officers who seek to catch them before any children are harmed. Police officers pretend to be children and engage in cyber-conversations with individuals who show a sexual interest. When the defendant solicits the "child" and sets up a meeting, he is arrested. There is even a reality television show (To Catch a Predator) that sets up the same situation and films the unsuspecting man as he meets a young girl and his surprise when the camera crew and producers reveal themselves. The defense of those caught is typically that they didn't believe the "child" was truly underage, or that they did not plan to have sex with the child. Generally, the fact that the "child" was a police officer is a case of factual impossibility and the charges are both sexual solicitation (the asking), and attempted sexual contact.

A Texas statute has been created to specifically address this activity and eliminate the typical defenses of the perpetrators.

Sec. 33.021. ONLINE SOLICITATION OF A MINOR.

(a) In this section:

(1) "Minor" means:
   (A) an individual who represents himself or herself to be younger than 17 years of age; or
   (B) an individual whom the actor believes to be younger than 17 years of age.
      (2) "Sexual contact," "sexual intercourse," and "deviate sexual intercourse" have the meanings assigned by Section 21.01.
      (3) "Sexually explicit" means any communication, language, or material, including a photographic or video image, that relates to or describes sexual conduct, as defined by Section 43.25.

(b) A person who is 17 years of age or older commits an offense if, with the intent to arouse or gratify the sexual desire of any person, the person, over the Internet, by electronic mail or text message or other electronic message service or system, or through a commercial online service, intentionally:
   (1) communicates in a sexually explicit manner with a minor; or
   (2) distributes sexually explicit material to a minor.

(c) A person commits an offense if the person, over the Internet, by electronic mail or text message or other electronic message service or system, or through a commercial online service, knowingly solicits a minor to meet another person, including the actor, with the intent that the minor will engage in sexual contact, sexual intercourse, or deviate sexual intercourse with the actor or another person.

(d) It is not a defense to prosecution under Subsection (c) that:
   (1) the meeting did not occur;
   (2) the actor did not intend for the meeting to occur; or
   (3) the actor was engaged in a fantasy at the time of commission of the offense.

(e) It is a defense to prosecution under this section that at the time conduct described by Subsection (b) or (c) was committed:
 (1) the actor was married to the minor; or
 (2) the actor was not more than three years older than the minor and the minor consented to the conduct.

(f) An offense under Subsection (b) is a felony of the third degree, except that the offense is a felony of the second degree if the minor is younger than 14 years of age or is an individual whom the actor believes to be younger than 14 years of age at the time of the commission of the offense. An offense under Subsection (c) is a felony of the second degree.

(g) If conduct that constitutes an offense under this section also constitutes an offense under any other law, the actor may be prosecuted under this section, the other law, or both.

Added by Acts 2005, 79th Leg., Ch. HYPERLINK "http://www.legis.state.tx.us/tlodocs/79R/billtext/html/ HB02228F.HTM" \t "new" 1273, Sec. 1, eff. June 18, 2005.
Amended by: Acts 2007, 80th Leg., R.S., Ch. HYPERLINK "http://www.legis.state.tx.us/tlodocs/80R/ billtext/html/HB00401F.HTM" \t "new" 610, Sec. 2, eff. September 1, 2007.
Acts 2007, 80th Leg., R.S., Ch. HYPERLINK "http://www.legis.state.tx.us/tlodocs/80R/billtext/html/ SB00006F.HTM" \t "new" 1291, Sec. 7, eff. September 1, 2007.

engage in sexual conduct, when the solicitor is 18 years or older and four or more years older than the person solicited. The solicitation of homosexual or lesbian activity is also prohibited when the solicitor knows or has reasonable cause to believe that the solicitation is offensive to the person solicited.

C. Voyeurism

Traditionally, "peeping toms" were those who, for sexual gratification, peered in windows at unsuspecting victims, watching while homeowners undressed or engaged in private behavior. Today's technology greatly expands the opportunities for voyeurs who may now use camera phones, "spy cameras," and small video recorders to secretly invade the privacy of individuals in stores, locker rooms, bathrooms, and a range of other places. Many state statutes are written generally enough that they cover newer forms of **voyeurism**. The Ohio Revised Code[117] includes a section providing:

(A) No person, for the purpose of sexually arousing or gratifying himself or herself, shall commit trespass or otherwise surreptitiously invade the privacy of another, to spy or eavesdrop upon another.
(B) Whoever violates this Section is guilty of voyeurism, a misdemeanor of the third degree.

This section prohibits not only trespassing, but any invasion of privacy, to eavesdrop or spy on another for the purpose of obtaining a vicarious sexual thrill. Other states have passed related laws, such as a Florida statute which is directed specifically at merchants and does not mention sexual gratification.

877.26 Direct observation, videotaping, or visual surveillance of customers in merchant's dressing room, etc., prohibited; penalties.—

(1) It is unlawful for any merchant to directly observe or make use of video cameras or other visual surveillance devices to observe or record customers in the merchant's dressing room, fitting room, changing room, or restroom when such room provides a reasonable expectation of privacy. However, a merchant may directly observe a customer from outside such room if the observation is within the scope of the merchant's duties and the observation does not otherwise violate 810.14 or 810.145 or if the customer invites or consents to the presence of the merchant in the room . . .

D. Sexual Misconduct

While statutory rape laws are directed to perpetrators over the age of consent and underage victims, states also have laws covering sexual conduct between minors, calling it **sexual misconduct**. Some statutes have been challenged when they provide too harsh a penalty for minors engaged in consensual sex. For instance, the Florida Supreme Court overturned the conviction of a 16-year-old who had consensual sex with another 16-year-old. The Florida statute that was voided specified that "any person" who had sexual contact with a minor was guilty of the offense.[118] Today, the statute requires the person be 24 years of age or older.

Legal News

Genarlow Wilson spent two years in a Georgia prison after he was convicted of a sexual crime for having consensual oral sex with a 15-year-old even though he was only 17 years old at the time. His 2003 conviction earned him a mandatory 10-year sentence and the ensuing scandal prompted the Georgia legislature to revise the law so that consensual sex by underage participants became only a misdemeanor, but they did not make the law retroactive. Upon appeal, the Georgia Supreme Court ruled that Wilson's 10-year sentence was cruel and unusual and ordered an immediate release on October 26, 2007. He had already served two years of his 10-year sentence by the time of his release.

Source: WSB Atlanta (2007). "Genarlow Wilson Speaks at Ebeneezer Baptist Church." Retrieved online from http://www.wsbtv.com/news/14429689/detail.html on 12/28/2008.

E. Intercourse with a Person in Custody

The Model Penal Code includes a provision that provides a penalty when a person engages in sexual intercourse or deviate sexual relations, or causes another to engage in such relationship, if the person with whom he has sexual intercourse or causes another to have sexual intercourse with is in custody of law enforcement officials or detained in a hospital or other institution and the actor has supervisory or disciplinary authority over him. This provides a penalty for one who engages in intercourse with a person under his supervisory or disciplinary authority, and is designed to deter abuse of custodial authority.[119]

All states except Vermont now have laws criminalizing sex, even consensual sex, between prisoners and correctional officials or civilian employees of the corrections system. The legal premise of such laws is that persons under confinement are not in a position to give free and knowing consent to someone who holds power over them. Congress passed the Prison Rape Elimination Act in 2003, which mandated the Federal Bureau of Statistics to collect the numbers of rapes that occur in prison. Unfortunately, one of the findings that has emerged is that a substantial percentage of sexual assaults in prison, especially in prisons for women, are perpetrated by correctional personnel.[120]

F. Sex Offenses Involving Human Immunodeficiency Virus (HIV) and Acquired Immune Deficiency Syndrome (AIDS)

In addition to civil statutes and administrative regulations, which authorize tort liability for transmission of HIV, a number of states have enacted substantive HIV/AIDS-specific statutes. An example is that of Illinois:

§ 12-16.2 Criminal Transmission of HIV[121]

(a) A person commits criminal transmission of HIV when he or she, knowing that he or she is infected with HIV:
  (1) engages in intimate contact with another;
  (2) transfers, donates, or provides his or her blood, tissue, semen, organs, or other potentially infectious body fluids for transfusion, transplantation, insemination, or other administration to another; or
  (3) dispenses, delivers, exchanges, sells, or in any other way transfers to another any nonsterile intravenous or intramuscular drug paraphernalia.

Under this statute, the defendant does not have to have sexual intercourse; "intimate sexual contact" is defined as exposing the body of the victim to bodily fluid in a manner that could result in the transmission of HIV. The victim does not have to acquire HIV in order for the defendant to be convicted.

It is an affirmative defense that the person exposed knew that the infected person was infected with HIV, knew that the action could result in infection with HIV, and consented to the action with the knowledge.

Both the Illinois statute and a similar Michigan statute were challenged as being unconstitutional, but the court determined that the statute was not unconstitutionally overbroad or vague and did not violate the First Amendment.[122]

A Florida appeals court held that a defendant who had been charged with sexual offenses involving transmission of body fluids could be required to submit to HIV testing upon the request of the victim or the victim's parent.[123]

In jurisdictions where specific HIV/AIDS-related criminal statutes have not been enacted, individuals transferring, or attempting to transfer, body fluids, knowing they are HIV-positive or infected with AIDS, have been convicted of battery, aggravated assault, and even attempted murder under existing criminal statutes.[124]

G. Sexual Predator Laws

Unlike the other statutes described in this chapter, **sexual predator laws** do not identify a particular behavior as criminal. Rather, they identify the types of crimes that lead to a sexual predator designation, and then may specify certain enhanced punishments, treatment, or, more controversially, sexual predator registration. Kansas, for instance, requires those who are prosecuted as "sexually violent predators" and have a mental abnormality or personality disorder be committed to a mental hospital for treatment.[125]

Megan's Law emerged because of the tragic rape and murder of seven-year-old Megan Kanka by a sex offender who lived in her neighborhood. President Clinton signed Megan's Law on May 17, 1996, which required states to set up sex offender registries and provide information to community members regarding whether sex offenders were living in the community if they wanted access to federal funding. Typically it is a violation of parole or probation and/or a new crime if a sex offender does not register. Public dissemination of sex offender registries allows anyone to see who has a sex offender label. Critics argue that the punishment is especially harsh when states include all sex offenses as those requiring registration. In several cases thus far, the Supreme Court has upheld registry laws.

§ 6.7 Summary

In this chapter, nonconsensual sex crimes were considered and the elements of the crimes were discussed. The most serious sex crime is rape. Rape is defined as the act of unlawful carnal knowledge by a man of a woman, forcibly and against her will. While some courts in the past have admitted evidence concerning the complainant's past sexual activities on the issue of whether the carnal knowledge was against the will of the female, the modern trend is to limit the use of evidence relating to such sexual activities.

The Model Penal Code defines the crime of rape in different terms than were used in the common law offenses. The differences include grading the crime by degree of seriousness determined by the dangerousness manifested by the actor and the degree of harm inflicted upon the victim. In general, modern rape statutes may be characterized as either "forcible rape" (sexual intercourse by force or threat of force), or "statutory rape" (sexual intercourse with victims incapable of giving consent because of age or mental incapacity). Within the latter category, most states have adopted statutes that increase punishment according to the age of the victim, with younger victims (typically under the age of 12) receiving the greatest protection.

A second sex crime in the category of offenses against the person is sodomy. Sodomy has been defined as "carnal copulation by human beings with each other against nature or with a beast." Rather than using the term *sodomy*, the drafters of the Model Penal Code took a different approach, defining the offense as "deviate sexual intercourse by force or imposition." The Model Code never did and modern statutes cannot prohibit such sexual intercourse between consenting adults. The Supreme Court ruled it an unconstitutional invasion of privacy, as long as both have the age and mental capacity to render consent and if they conduct their relations in private and create no public nuisance.

The third sex crime considered is sexual abuse (or assault). Under various titles, states provided penalties for unlawfully subjecting another person to sexual contact without the other's consent. The crime is covered in the Model Penal Code under the term "sexual assault." The MPC only established one degree of sexual abuse, grading it a lesser felony. In other states, the offenses of "sexual assault" or "sexual abuse" are graded according to the degree of force and the age or mental condition of the victim.

At common law, particular acts and forms of lewdness constituted a criminal offense. The word "lewdness" means open and public indecency. Under the Model Penal Code, a person commits the crime of indecent exposure if, for the purpose of arousing or gratifying the sexual desire of himself or any other person other than his spouse, he exposes his genitals under circumstances in which he knows his conduct is likely to cause affront or alarm. Some of the more recently revised statutes use the terms in the Model Penal Code, but extend the coverage to exposure of other specifically named areas of the body.

Other acts subject to penalty are:

- Seduction: the act of a man inducing a woman to commit unlawful sexual intercourse with him by means of enticement, persuasions, solicitations, promises, bribes, or other means without the employment of force, thereby overcoming her reluctance and her scruples.

- Importuning or Sexual Solicitation of a Minor: solicitation of sexual activity from an underage person

- Voyeurism: trespass or invasion of privacy of another to spy or eavesdrop for the purpose of sexual gratification

- Sexual misconduct: Sexual intercourse between a defendant under 18 and a victim under 16 (in some states) who is incapable of giving consent because of age

- Intercourse with a person in custody: any correctional official who has sexual intercourse with a person in custody whether or not such intercourse was consensual

- Transmission of HIV and AIDS: Intentional sexual contact with knowledge of the possibility of transmitting the HIV virus.

- Sexual registry laws: the requirement that sexual offenders, as specified by statute, register as a sex offender.

Criminal law mirrors science and politics in that many states recently enacted criminal statutes addressing the transmission of HIV/AIDS. Even where criminal legislation has not been enacted, the courts are being asked to address HIV/AIDS issues as they relate to existing criminal law.

As statutes relating to sexual offenses against the person now vary from state to state, these statutes must be consulted to determine the particular statute applicable.

Review Questions

1. What are the six elements of common law rape? Is rape a specific intent or general intent crime?

2. What was the utmost resistance standard?

3. Define statutory rape.

4. What was the common law marital exemption for rape? Does it still exist?

5. What are the categories of victims who cannot give consent and, therefore, any sexual intercourse is considered rape?

6. What are the current changes to the traditional mens rea of statutory rape?

7. What are rape shield laws? What are the exceptions?

8. What are the four major changes in rape/sexual assault laws from the common law?

9. Define common law sodomy and how current laws are different from common law sodomy.

10. Describe the case holding that ruled that laws against consensual sodomy violated the right to privacy.

11. What is sexual assault or sexual abuse (as distinguished from rape?)

12. Define child molestation.

13. What is the actus reus and mens rea for lewdness (indecent exposure)?

14. Define the crime of sexual solicitation of a minor.

15. Define the crime of seduction.

16. Define the crime of voyeurism.

17. Define the crime of sexual misconduct.

18. Define the crime of intercourse with a person in custody.

19. Define the crime of intentional transmission of HIV/AIDS.

20. Define sexual predator laws and Megan's laws.

Notes

[1]   State v. Young, 52 Or. 227, 96 P. 1067 (1908).

[2]   State v. Tuttle, 67 Ohio St. 440, 66 N.E. 524 (1903).

[3]   Hazel v. State, 221 Md. 464, 157 A.2d 922 (1960).

[4]   Frazier v. State, 48 Tex. Crim. 142, 86 S.W. 754 (1905).

[5]   Adams v. State, 5 Okla. Crim. 347, 114 P. 347 (1911).

[6]   1 Hale, History of the Pleas of the Crown 619 (1800).

[7]   Commonwealth v. Fogerty, 74 Mass. 489 (1857).

[8]   People v. Meli, 193 N.Y.S. 365 (1922).

[9]   State v. Pollock, 57 Ariz. 414, 114 P.2d 249 (1941).

[10]   Davis v. State, 43 Tex. 189 (1875).

[11]   Powell v. Commonwealth, 179 Va. 703, 20 S.E.2d 536 (1942).

[12]   Turner v. State, 32 Ala. App. 465, 27 So. 2d 239 (1946).

[13]   Commonwealth v. Stephens, 143 Pa. Super. 394, 17 A.2d 919 (1941).

[14]   Reynolds v. State, 27 Neb. 90, 42 N.W. 903 (1889); Whittaker v. State, 50 Wis. 518, 7 N.W. 431 (1880).

[15]   State v. Alston, 312 S.E.2d 470 (N.C. 1984).

[16]   Commonwealth v. Burke, 105 Mass. 376, 7 Am. Rep. 531 (1870).

[17]   Lancaster v. State, 168 Gu. 470, 148 S.E. 139 (1929).

[18]   State v. Lung, 21 Nev. 209, 28 P. 235 (1891).

[19]   State v. Ely, 114 Wash. 185, 194 N.W. 988 (1921).

[20]   Boro v. Superior Court, 210 Cal. Rptr. 122 (Ct. App. 1985)

[21]   Wilson v. Commonwealth, 290 Ky. 223, 160 S.W.2d 649 (1942).

[22]   State v. Westminster I, 3, Edward I, chapter 13; 75 C.J.S. *Rape* § 13 (1952).

[23]   Model Penal Code § 213.1 (1985).

[24]   See cases cited in People v. Liberta, 474 N.E.2d 567 (N.Y. 1984). For a discussion of the various statutory and judicial variations of the marital exemption, *see Old Wine in New Bottles: The "Marital" Rape Allowance*, 72 N.C. L. REV. 261 (1993) and *Legal Rape: The Marital Exemption*, 24 J. MARSHALL L. REV. 393 (1991).

[25]   For example, People v. Liberta, 474 N.E.2d 567 (N.Y. 1984).

[26]   For example, *see* TEX. PENAL CODE ANN. § 22.011(c)(2) (West 1994).

[27]   State v. Smith, 85 N.J. 193, 426 A.2d 38 (1981).

[28]   People v. Liberta, 474 N.E.2d 567 (N.Y. 1984).

[29]   595 N.E.2d 702 (Ill. 1992).

[30]   For discussion of the marital exemption and arguments for abolishing the marital exemption, *see Abolishing the Marital Exemption for Rape: A Statutory Proposal*, 77 U. ILL. L. REV. 201 (1983), and *The Marital Rape Exemption*, 52 N.Y.U. L. REV. 306 (1977). For a list of the states that have abolished the marital exemption or have modified the law relating to rape, see 35 WAYNE L. REV. 1219 (1989).

[31]   Rhodes v. State, 462 P.2d 722 (Wyo. 1969).

[32]   KY. REV. STAT. § 510.010(8) (1994).

[33]   DEL. CODE ANN., tit. 11 § 761 (1994). *See* ALA. CODE 13A-6-20 (1994); MICH. COMP. LAWS § 750.520(1); TENN. CODE ANN. § 39-13-501 (1986); and others.

[34]   Miller v. State, 82 P.2d 317 (Okla. 1938); Smith v. State, 601 So. 2d 201 (Ala. 1992).

[35]   Beasley v. State, 94 Okla. Crim. 353, 236 P.2d 263 (1952).

[36]   Owens v. Owens, 274 S.E.2d 484 (Ga. 1981), adultery; Allen v. State, 316 S.E.2d 500 (Ga. 1984), prostitution.

[37]   18 U.S.C. § 2245.

[38]   State v. Jones, 705 A.2d 805 (N.J. 1998). *See also* People v. Rowland, 841 P.2d 897 (Cal. 1992); People v. Kelly, 822 P.2d 385 (Cal. 1992). *See* N.D. CENT. CODE § 12.1-20-02(1) (1989).

[39]   People v. Taylor, 48 Ill. 2d 91, 268 N.E.2d 865 (1971).

[40]   Ruth v. State, 706 N.E.2d 257 (Ind. 1999).

[41]   State v. Schuster, 282 S.W.2d 553 (Mo. 1955); Spaulding v. State, 373 N.E.2d 165 (Ill. 1978).

[42]   State v. O'Bryan, 572 N.W.2d 870 (Wis. 1997).

[43]   People v. Miller, 620 N.Y.S.2d 179 (1994).

[44]   People v. Burroughs, 19 Cal. Rptr. 344, 200 Cal. App. 2d 629 (1962); People v. Vela, 218 Cal. Rptr. 161, 172 Cal. App. 3d 237 (1985).

[45]   People v. Yanik, 400 N.Y.S.2d 778, 371 N.E.2d 497 (1977), *on remand*, 404 N.Y.S.2d 633, 63 App. Div. 574 (1978); *see also* State v. Ricks, 34 N.C. App. 734, 239 S.E.2d 602 (1977).

[46]   373 N.E.2d 538 (Ill. 1978).

[47]   Milton v. State, 160 Tenn. 273, 23 S.W.2d 662 (1930).

[48]   People v. Wankowitz, 564 N.Y.S.2d 488 (1991).

[49]   State v. Requena, 41 P.3d 862 (Kan. 2001).

[50]   State v. Davis, 824 S.W.2d 936 (Mo. 1992).

[51]   State v. Woodfork, 454 N.W.2d 332 (S.D. 1990); for a complete discussion of the issue, *see Condom or Not, Rape is Rape: Rape Law in the Era of AIDS—Does Condom Use Constitute Consent?* 19 DAYTON L. REV. 227 (1993).

[52]   MICH. COMP. LAWS §§ 750.520(a)-750.520(c) (2002). *See* Michael v. Superior Court of Sonoma Co., 450 U.S. 464, 101 S. Ct. 1200, 67 L. Ed. 2d 437 (1981). TEX. PENAL CODE ANN. § 22.011 (West 1999).

[53]   State v. Stevens, 510 A.2d 1070 (Me. 1986).

[54]   Fields v. State, 203 Ark. 1046, 159 S.W.2d 745 (1942).

[55]   State v. Porter, 188 N.C. 804, 125 S.E. 615 (1924).

[56]   State v. Dixon, 70 S.W.3d 540 (Mo. 2002).

[57]   KY. REV. STAT. § 510.030 (2002); *see also* ALASKA STAT. § 11.41.445 (1994) and State v. Guest, 583 P.2d 836 (Alaska 1978).

[58]   State v. Bennett, 672 P.2d 772 (Wash. 1983).

[59]   KY. REV. STAT. § 510.035 (Baldwin 2002).

[60]   Owens v. State, 724 A.2d 43 (Md. 1999).

[61]   TPC 21.11.

[62]   Commonwealth v. Dennis, 784 A.2d 179 (Pa. 2001).

[63]   Michael M. v. Superior Court of Sonoma County, 450 U.S. 464; 101 S. Ct. 1200; 67 L. Ed. 2d 437 (1981).

[64]   *See* Berger, *Man's Trial, Woman's Tribulations: Rape Cases in the Court Room*, 77 COLUM. L. REV. 1 (1977); *The Road to Reform*, 4 AM. J. CRIM. L. 1 (1975). Bell v. Harrison, 670 F.2d 656 (6th Cir. 1982). *See also* Hook v. State, 705 N.E.2d 219 (Ind. 1999), in which the court stated that the purpose of the rape shield statute is to encourage the reporting of sexual assaults and to prevent victims from feeling as though they are on trial for their sexual histories.

[65]   For a list of the states that have rape shield statutes and a discussion of the similarities and differences in the statues, *see* Sakthi Murphy, 79 CAL. L. REV. 541 (1991); and *Pattern of Sexual Conduct Evidence and Present Consent: Limiting the Admissibility of Sexual History Evidence in Rape Prosecutions*, 14 WOMEN'S RTS. L. REP. 79 (1992).

[66]   Sakthi Murphy, *Unreasonable Sexual Expectation*, 79 CAL. L. REV. 541 (1991).

[67]   Bixler v. Commonwealth, 712 S.W.2d 366 (Ky. 1986).

[68]   Levy v. State, 724 So. 2d 405 (Miss. Ct. App. 1998).

[69]   State v. Carroll, 639 N.W.2d 623 (Minn. 2002).

[70]   Ex parte D.L.H., 806 So. 2d 1190 (Ala. 2001). *See also* State v. Pugh, 640 N.W.2d 79 (S.D. 2002), which held that evidence of a rape victim's prior sexual encounters may be admitted if the trial court finds that it is relevant and material to a fact at issue in the case.

[71]   State v. Dunlap, 250 Wis. 2d 466, 640 N.W.2d 112 (2002).

[72]   Allen v. State, 700 S.W.2d 924 (Tex. Crim. App. 1985).

[73]   Johnsen, *Sodomy Statutes—A Need for Change*, 13 S.D. L. REV. 384 (1968).

[74]   Fellatio is defined as oral stimulation of the penis; cunnilingus is oral stimulation of the vulva or clitoris, and bestiality is copulation between human and animal. MASS. ANN. LAWS ch. 272, § 34 (Law. Co-op. 1980).

[75]   81 C.J.S. *Sodomy* § 1 (1985).

[76]   State v. Schwartz, 215 Minn. 476, 10 N.W.2d 370 (1943).

[77]   MODEL PENAL CODE § 213.2 (1985).

[78]   People v. Durham, 74 Cal. Rptr. 262, 449 P.2d 198 (1969).

[79]   Pruitt v. State, 463 S.W.2d 191 (Tex. Crim. App. 1971).

[80]   Furstonburg v. State, 148 Tex. Crim. 638, 190 S.W.2d 362 (1945).

[81]   96 Cal. App. 2d 621, 216 P.2d 140 (1950).

[82]   State v. Massey, 58 N.M. 115, 266 P.2d 359 (1954).

[83]   Donoho v. State, 628 S.W.2d 485 (Tex. 1982).

84   Bowers v. Hardwick, 478 U.S. 186, 106 S. Ct. 2841, 92 L. Ed. 2d 140 (1986).

85   Marc S. Spindelman, *Reorienting Bowers v. Hardwick*, 79 N.C. L. REV. 359 (2001).

86   Lawrence et al. v. Texas, 539 U.S 558, 123 S. Ct. 2472, 156 L. Ed. 2d 508 (2003).

87   MODEL PENAL CODE § 213.4 (1985).

88   N.Y. PENAL LAW §§ 130.55-130.60 (McKinney 1994); KY. REV. STAT. §§ 510.110-510.130 (2001).

89   OHIO REV. CODE ANN. § 2907.06 (Anderson 2002).

90   MASS. ANN. LAWS ch. 265 (Law. Co-op. 1992).

91   ALASKA STAT. § 11.41.434-440 (1994); IDAHO CODE § 18-6607 (1993).

92   KY. REV. STAT. § 435.105 (1975).

93   ARIZ. REV. STAT. ANN. § 13-1404 (2001); ME. REV. STAT. ANN. tit. 17A § 255 (1991).

94   COLO. REV. STAT. § 18-3-404 (1994); MONT. CODE ANN. § 45-5-502 (1995); N.H. REV. STAT. ANN. § 632-A:3-4 (1995).

95   N.Y. PENAL LAWS § 130.55 (McKinney 2002), and following commentaries.

96   People v. Rivera, 525 N.Y.S.2d 118 (1988). *See also* People v. Brown, 674 N.Y.S.2d 149 (1998).

97   People v. Morvelli, 544 N.Y.S.2d 442 (1989).

98   People v. Sumpter, 737 N.Y.S.2d 219 (2001).

99   Bailey v. State, 764 N.E.2d 728 (Ind. 2002).

100   State v. Willard, 18 Vt. 574, 46 Am. Dec. 170 (1845); the statute is quoted in the case.

101   State v. Gardner, 174 Iowa 748, 156 N.W. 747 (1916).

102   *See* Commonwealth v. Wardell, 128 Mass. 52, 35 Am. Rep. 357 (1880), for a more comprehensive discussion of the requirements.

103   KY. REV. STAT. § 436.140 (1975).

104   MODEL PENAL CODE § 213.5 (1985).

105   People v. Conrad, 334 N.Y.2d 180, 70 Misc. 2d 408 (1972).

106   For example, ARIZ. REV. STAT. ANN. § 13-1402 (1994), prohibits exposure of genitals, anus, and the areola or nipple of a female breast.

107   FLA. STAT. § 800.03 (1992). *See* State v. Coyle, 718 S.E.2d 218 (Fla. 1998). S.D. CODIFIED LAWS § 22-24-1 (Michie 1995). WIS. STAT. § 944.20 (1994).

108   TEX. PENAL CODE § 21.08 (Vernon 1999).

109   Kew v. Senter, 416 F. Supp. 1101 (N.D. Tex. 1976).

110   Hefner v. State, 934 S.W.2d 855 (Tex. 1996); *see also* Young v. State, 976 S.W.2d 771 (Tex. 1998).

111   People v. Bono, 641 N.W.2d 278 (Mich. 2002).

112   Mackey v. Commonwealth, 255 Ky. 466, 74 S.W.2d 915 (1934); Spangler v. Commonwealth, 188 Va. 436, 50 S.E.2d 265 (1948).

113   Blount v. State, 102 Fla. 1100, 138 So. 2 (1931).

114   Smith v. State, 13 Ala. App. 388, 69 So. 402 (1915). State v. Dacke, 59 Wash. 238, 109 P. 1050 (1910).

115   S.C. CODE ANN. § 16-15-50 (1995).

116   OHIO REV. CODE ANN. § 2907.07 (Anderson 1999).

117   OHIO REV. CODE ANN. § 2907.08 (Anderson 2002).

118   B.B. v. Florida, 659 So. 2d 256 (1995).

[119] Model Penal Code § 213.3 (1985).

[120] Beck, A. and Harrison, P. (2007). *Sexual Victimization Reported in State and Federal Prisons, Reported by Inmates, 2007*. Washington, DC: B.J.S., U.S. Dept. of Justice.

[121] 720 Ill. Comp. Stat. 5/12-16.2 (2002). *See also* N.D. Cent. Code § 12.1-20-17(2) (1989).

[122] People v. Russell, 630 N.E.2d 794 (Ill. 1994); People v. Jensen, 231 Mich. App. 439, 586 N.W.2d 748 (1998).

[123] Isom v. State, 722 So. 2d 237 (Fla. 1998).

[124] See the discussion of HIV/AIDS cases in Chapter 3; *see also* Smallwood v. State, 680 A.2d 512 (Md. 1995).

[125] Kan. Stat. Ann. §59-29a01 (1994).

Offenses Against Property—Destruction and Intrusion Offenses 7

Chapter Outline

Cases

Arson: *Michigan v. Reeves et al.,* 528 N.W.2d 160 (1995)
Burglary: *People v. Ramos*, 52 Cal. App. 4th 300, 60 Cal. Rptr. 523 (1997)

§ 7.1   Introduction

In studying the history of criminal law and procedure, one recognizes that, in most societies, offenses that interfere with the sanctity of a person's home are considered more serious than other property offenses, and are treated accordingly. This is especially true in countries that have followed traditional English law, in which the concept that a person's home is his "castle" was recognized very early, and honored throughout many generations. Therefore, although certain crimes, such as arson and burglary, are essentially offenses against property, they are considered two of the most serious crimes. In addition, malicious mischief and trespass are included in this chapter. These two offenses are not normally as serious as arson and burglary, but share the characteristics of destruction and intrusion.

The process followed in discussing these and other property destruction and intrusion crimes is first to define the common law crime, and the Model Penal Code, and then discuss the statutory and code changes that have taken effect in most states.

§ 7.2   Arson

A.   Common Law

Because of the great danger to human life resulting from the burning of a dwelling house, **arson** at common law was considered to be a heinous felony punishable by death.[1] The primary purpose of the laws relating to arson was to preserve the security of the habitation, to protect dwellers within the building from injury or death by fire, and to protect the possessory interest in the house. It was considered one of the most serious common law felonies and, according to Sir William Blackstone, was frequently more destructive than murder itself because of the inability to control fire.[2]

At common law, arson was defined in the following ways:

- the willful and malicious burning of another's dwelling house or of an outbuilding within its curtilage.[3]

- the willful and malicious burning of a dwelling house of another person.[4]

Common law arson has the following four elements: burning; a dwelling house (or any building within the curtilage); of another person; maliciously.

1. Burning

In order to constitute the traditional crime of arson, there must be a **burning**—i.e., there must have been some consuming of the material with which the house is built. It was sufficient for common law arson if any part of the dwelling house itself was burned, no matter how small, and no matter how insignificant to the structural integrity of the building. For example, a spot on the floor that was charred was held sufficient to constitute this element of the crime of arson. There need not be a blaze and it is immaterial how soon the fire was extinguished or whether it was put out or went out by itself. While it was necessary that there be some "combustion," "ignition," or "charring" to constitute burning, this element was not present if there was only damage caused by smoke.[5]

2. Dwelling House or Outbuilding Used in Connection Therewith

Because the essence of the offense at common law was the danger to the lives of persons who dwelt in or occupied the house, or the buildings used in connection therewith, it was necessary that the dwelling be occupied. However, it is not necessary that the house be actually inhabited at the time of the burning, provided that it was usually inhabited and the owner only temporarily absent.[6]

At least under some interpretations, a building that was not itself a dwelling house could be the subject of arson if it were within the **curtilage** of a dwelling house. This was defined as the space adjoining a dwelling and habitually used for family purposes.[7] Some examples of buildings that were considered under the definition of "dwellings" under the common law arson were a barn, a stable, a cow-house, a sheep-house, a dairy-house, and a milk-house, all of which were located within the curtilage of a dwelling house.[8]

3. The House Must Belong to or Be Occupied by Another

The common law definition requires that the house burned be possessed by another. Accordingly, it was arson for the legal owner of the house to burn his own house, which was in the possession of another. Conversely, it was not arson at common law for a person to burn his own dwelling, which was occupied by him. While the person could not be found guilty under the common law for burning his own dwelling house occupied by him, it was arson if one tenant in an apartment house burned his own apartment even if the fire was totally contained within that single apartment unit.[9]

As insurance on the dwelling became common and houses sometimes were burned in order to collect insurance, additional statutes were enacted to supplement the common law crime of arson. Under these statutes, it is unlawful to burn insured property with the specific intent to injure, prejudice, or defraud the insurer.[10]

4. The Burning Must Be Done Maliciously

Perhaps the most difficult task of a prosecutor in proving the common law crime of arson is to show that the burning was willful or malicious. Mere accident, carelessness, or simple negligence is not enough to constitute the common law crime of arson. If the prosecutor introduces evidence to show that the person intentionally started the fire that resulted in the burning, this is a clear-cut case. However, it is more difficult to prove malice when the acts amounted to a wanton burning without justification or excuse. In the latter situation, the requirements of arson could be met if evidence indicated that the actor performed an intentional act that created a very high risk of the burning of a dwelling house. Also, there is sufficient intent or malice to constitute the crime of arson if there exists general malice or an intent to burn a structure; a particular intent or malice against a particular person or thing is not required.[11]

B. Model Penal Code

Under the Model Penal Code, arson is enlarged to include exploding as well as burning and buildings other than dwellings. The crime of arson is graded partly according to the kind of property destroyed or imperiled and partly according to the danger to persons. The most serious type of arson is a felony in the second degree and is most similar to common law arson. Under this definition, arson occurs when a person starts a fire or causes an explosion, either to destroy a building or occupied structure of another, or his or her own or another's property to collect insurance for such loss.

§ 220.1 Arson and Related Offenses[12]

(1) Arson. A person is guilty of arson, a felony of the second degree, if he starts a fire or causes an explosion with the purpose of:

  (a) destroying a building or occupied structure of another; or
  (b) destroying or damaging any property, whether his own or another's, to collect insurance for such loss. It shall be an affirmative defense to prosecution under this paragraph that the actor's conduct did not recklessly endanger any building or occupied structure of another or place any other person in danger of death or bodily injury.

(2) Reckless Burning or Exploding. A person commits a felony of the third degree if he purposely starts a fire or causes an explosion, whether on his own property or another's, and thereby recklessly:

  (a) places another person in danger of death or bodily injury; or
  (b) places a building or occupied structure of another in danger of damage or destruction.

(3) Failure to Control or Report Dangerous Fire. A person who knows that a fire is endangering life or a substantial amount of property of another and fails to take reasonable measures to put out or control the fire, when he can do so without substantial risk to himself, or to give a prompt fire alarm, commits a misdemeanor if:

  (a) he knows that he is under an official, contractual, or other legal duty to prevent or combat the fire; or
  (b) the fire was started, albeit lawfully, by him or with his assent, or on property in his custody or control.

The other two crimes defined in the Model Penal Code are "Reckless Burning or Exploding" and "Failure to Control or Report a Dangerous Fire." These obviously have been added to provide a penalty for an act that results in a burning or explosion when some of the technical requirements of the crime of arson are missing.

C. State Statutes, Codes, and Cases

Similarly to the Model Penal Code, most state statutes protect property other than dwellings and provide a penalty for burning of property that was not within the common law *mens rea* requirements. Further, all states except Maine now grade arson by severity.[13] These statutes establish degrees of arson determined by:

1. the value of the property,

2. the use of property, such as a dwelling house, and

3. whether the place is inhabited

4. level of *mens rea*

Also, statutes have been enacted to punish those who *attempt* to commit the crime of arson. The modern state statutes have expanded not only the coverage of arson and related laws, but have simplified the wording so as to make definition easier. As the state statutes differ in some respects, it is essential that the statutes be checked to determine the exact elements of arson and related crimes.

An example of a statute that takes into consideration the type of property as well as the injury inflicted is that of California.[14]

> Arson of structure, forest land or property; great bodily injury; inhabited structure or property; owned property; punishment
>
> A person is guilty of arson when he or she willfully and maliciously sets fire to or burns or causes to be burned or who aids, counsels, or procures the burning of, any structure, forest land, or property.
>
> (a) Arson that causes bodily injury is a felony punishable by imprisonment in the state prison for five, seven, or nine years.
> (b) Arson that causes an inhabited structure or inhabited property to burn is a felony punishable by imprisonment in the state prison for three, five, or eight years.
> (c) Arson of a structure or forest land is a felony punishable by imprisonment in the state prison for two, four, or six years.
> (d) Arson of property is a felony punishable by imprisonment in the state prison for 16 months, two, or three years. For purposes of this paragraph, arson of property does not include one burning or causing to be burned his or her own personal property unless there is an intent to defraud or there is injury to another person or another person's structure, forest land, or property.

Vermont also distinguishes types of arson. First degree arson covers dwelling houses (occupied or vacant), and any adjoining buildings. Second degree arson covers any other buildings or property. Third degree arson covers personal property. Fourth degree arson is when the offender attempts to burn a structure but is unsuccessful.[15] In many states, the courts refer to the common law in determining definitions and elements; thus, we will revisit the common law elements.

1. Burning

Modern definitions of burning are consistent with case decisions under the common law in that any type of burning is sufficient to prove this element of the crime. For example, the "burning" element was satisfied when the court found evidence that indicated the building suffered blistering from the fire.[16]

2. Dwelling House (or Outbuilding within the Curtilage)

Recall that one of the issues under the common law was what type of building met the definition of **dwelling**. In general, the building had to be a dwelling house, but it need not have someone living in it at the time. In the 1993 case of *Barnes v. State*, a Wyoming court explained that an occupied structure within the meaning of the arson statute meant one that was intended to be occupied and usually was occupied.[17] However, a 1995 Michigan court held that when the house was unoccupied and dilapidated to the extent that it was deemed abandoned, it was no longer considered a dwelling house.[18]

Some court decisions have refined and restricted the meaning of dwelling to include only those dwellings currently inhabited. In interpreting the term "inhabited structure" as used in the California statute, a California court declared that the offense of setting a fire to an inhabited structure requires someone to be using the structure as a dwelling at the time of the fire and not merely that the structure's purpose is to serve as a dwelling.[19] A North Carolina court reiterated that, "it is an essential element of the crime of arson that the burned house be inhabited.[20] Of course, in these states, burning other types of buildings would be prosecuted as a less serious type of arson.

3. Of Another

Generally, setting fire to your own dwelling is not considered arson; however, statutes may include it as such when the purpose is for insurance proceeds. Case law in this area typically deals with the definition of ownership. Even if the burning does not come into the definition of arson, there may be other laws broken, especially if such conduct is defined as reckless or negligent.

4. Malicious Intent

Under common law, the act of burning had to be "malicious," meaning intentional. In referring to the malice element, a Mississippi court held that where statutes make malice and willfulness an ingredient of the crime of arson, a particular intent or malice against a person or thing is not essential; it is sufficient to show that the accused acted on a malicious motive and that he set the fire willfully rather than negligently or accidentally.[21] In other words, if an offender intended to burn down his mother-in-law's house but mistakenly burned down her neighbor's house instead, it would still be first degree arson.

In order to obtain a conviction for intentional arson, the prosecutor must show both the act (*actus reus*) and the intent (*mens rea*) to set fire to a structure (this is the concept of concurrence). If the actor intended to set fire to a dwelling but only managed to set fire to property, then that is attempted arson and perhaps some lesser form of unlawful fire covered in the statute, but not typically first-degree arson. Likewise, if the actor intended to set fire to property and accidentally caused a dwelling to burn, then the *mens rea* is missing. In a California case, the defendant was convicted of arson. The reviewing court held that the court should have instructed on the lesser included offense of unlawfully causing a fire to a structure, where the evidence developed by the prosecution and reasonable inferences drawn therefrom supported the conclusion that the defendant only intended to set fire to cars in a service garage and not to the garage itself.[22]

Recall that some states grade the offense of arson depending on whether the building was inhabited. An intent to set fire to a home when people are inside is the most serious grade of arson; however, some states also include a type of "wanton disregard" as equivalent to intentional. For instance, in Missouri, if the actor sets fire to a dwelling in "conscious disregard of the substantial risk" that a person might be inside the building or in proximity thereto, that is also considered the highest level of *mens rea*.[23]

Some states have expanded the definition of arson to include lesser levels of *mens rea* and then graded the offense based on the level. Obviously, purposefully or intentionally is the highest level of *mens rea*. Statutes also, however, have lower grades of arson that include reckless and negligent fires. An example of a statute that punishes for *negligent* burning is that of Alaska. There, the law provides that a person commits the crime of criminal negligent burning if, with criminal negligence, he or she damages the property of another by fire or explosion.[24]

5. Burning of Personal Property

While common law arson was only defined as setting fire to dwellings, modern law covers all types of property, albeit in an inconsistent fashion from state to state. The Model Penal Code categorized the burning of personal property valued at less than $5,000.00 as a misdemeanor. Most state statutes, however, define any burning of personal property valued at more than $250 as a felony. Also, 29 states allow for imprisonment of more than one year for setting fire to personal property valued at more than $2,000. Further, Massachusetts and Hawaii, do not even define burning of personal property as a lesser crime, but include it under their arson statute.[25]

Thus, modern statutes may be different from the common law, but they are based on common law definitions, as *Michigan v. Reeves*, the example case, indicates.

> **CASE: *Michigan v. Reeves et al.***
>
> What was the holding of the court?
>
> What was the definition of arson and how was it different from the statutory definition?
>
> Why was the definition of arson important?

D. Summary

First degree arson is considered a very serious crime because it threatens human life. The highest level of *mens rea* (intent), and the greatest likelihood that someone will be harmed (occupied dwelling house) are elements of first degree arson. Other forms of arson include other types of buildings and lower levels of *mens rea* (recklessness). We will conclude this section by using the common law elements of arson with the understanding that these elements are most similar to first degree arson. Any particular state, however, may include other forms of structures (other than dwellings) and/or other forms of *mens rea* (other than malicious).

Arson

(A/R)   Setting fire to; dwelling; of another

(M/R)   Malicious (Intentional)

---

§ 7.3 Malicious Mischief (*Criminal Mischief*)

A. Common Law

Although there is some doubt concerning whether **malicious mischief** was a crime at common law in England, a number of very early cases enforced it as a common law crime.[26] The crime commonly known as malicious mischief is difficult to define, because the name is applied to acts varying widely as to terms, phraseology, and purpose. Generally, it has been defined as the willful and unlawful injury to or destruction of the property of another with the malicious intent to injure the owner.

Malicious mischief is distinguished from larceny in that, in larceny, goods are fraudulently taken against the owner's will with the intention of converting the goods to the taker's use, whereas in malicious mischief, the property is maliciously injured without being taken and converted to another's use.[27] It is distinguished from arson in that forms of destruction other than fire are included and statutes cover personal property as well as dwellings. The elements of the crime of malicious mischief vary, but the common elements are described below. Failure to prove every element constitutes a complete defense.[28]

1. Malice

Malice is generally held to be an essential ingredient of the offense of malicious mischief.[29] The name itself implies that malice must be proved. Malice can be thought of as *intent to do harm.*

2. Injury or Destruction

At common law, either an injury to or destruction of property suffices as the *actus reus* of the offense.[30] Modern statutes require that the damage be measured by monetary damages and reach some minimum level.

3. Property of Another

While in some jurisdictions malicious mischief may be committed as to personal property only, in others, real property as well as personal property can be the subject of the offense. In any event, it is necessary to prove that the property belonged to another person.

B. Model Penal Code

The Model Penal Code section is titled "Criminal Mischief" rather than "Malicious Mischief." The Model Code takes the approach of consolidating the form of malicious mischief provisions of various statutes and even the common law into a single comprehensive offense.

§ 220.3 Criminal Mischief[31]

(1) Offense Defined. A person is guilty of criminal mischief if he:
  (a) damages tangible property of another purposely, recklessly, or by negligence in the employment of fire, explosives, or other dangerous means listed in § 220.2(1); or
  (b) purposely or recklessly tampers with tangible property of another so as to endanger person or property; or
  (c) purposely or recklessly causes another to suffer pecuniary loss by deception or threat.

(2) Grading. Criminal mischief is a felony of the third degree if the actor purposely causes pecuniary loss in excess of $5,000, or a substantial interruption or impairment of public communication, transportation, supply of water, gas or power, or other public service. It is a misdemeanor if the actor purposely causes pecuniary loss in excess of $100, or a petty misdemeanor if he purposely or recklessly causes pecuniary loss in excess of $25. Otherwise criminal mischief is a violation.

Section (1)(a) reaches purposeful or reckless damage to the tangible property of another, as well as negligent damage caused by dangerous instrumentalities. Section (1)(b) expands the traditional offense to include tampering with another's property so as to endanger the person or property, and § (1)(c) adds a penalty for purposely or recklessly damaging personal property and causing another to suffer pecuniary loss by deception or threat.

As in the traditional offense of malicious mischief, the Model Code offense differs from the theft, forgery, and fraud provisions in that the focus is not upon the misappropriation of property, but rather upon its destruction.

C. State Statutes, Codes, and Cases

Legislation in many states expands upon the common law crime of malicious mischief in defining particular types of malicious mischief. While the original crime related only to *personal* property, some legislation enlarged the definition to include malicious injury or destruction of *real* property (real estate), including trees, mines, coal, and even tobacco plants. The legislatures apparently responded to needs as they arose in particular jurisdictions. The grade of the offense of malicious mischief and the amount of punishment are ordinarily prescribed by the statute. These are usually determined on the basis of the amount of injury or damage inflicted, or by the value of the property injured or destroyed.

Some of the recently drafted codes have followed the Model Penal Code approach of consolidating the former malicious mischief provisions into a single comprehensive offense or an integrated series of related offenses.[32] Other codes integrate a series of related offenses into a single crime.[33] Still others retain parts of the old approach to criminal mischief.[34]

An example of a statute that consolidates former malicious mischief and similar crimes into two sections is that of Missouri.

§ 569.100 Property damage in the first degree[35]

(1) A person commits the crime of property damage in the first degree if:
   (a) He knowingly damages property of another to an extent exceeding seven hundred and fifty dollars; or
   (b) He damages property to an extent exceeding one thousand dollars for the purpose of defrauding an insurer.

(2) Property damage in the first degree is a Class D felony.

§ 569.120 Property damage in the second degree

(1) A person commits the crime of property damage in the second degree if:
   (a) He knowingly damages property of another; or
   (b) He damages property for the purpose of defrauding an insurer.

(2) Property damage in the second degree is a Class B misdemeanor.

As with the common law and the Model Penal Code, the Missouri statute requires property to be damaged. The *mens rea* is *knowing* (which can be thought of as general intent—the prosecutor must prove the actor knew he was doing an act that would cause the damage). In the Missouri statute, a person may be convicted of the offense even if they damage their own property if it is for the purpose of defrauding an insurer (but the required cost of damage is higher). In interpreting § 569.100 of the Missouri statutes, the Missouri courts agreed that although there must be some evidence of injury to property to sustain a conviction for property damage, the damage need only be slight. The damage can be to an automobile.[36]

1. Malice

In general, the *mens rea* for malicious mischief is "malicious," which can be equated to general intent. As we saw above, Missouri defined the *mens rea* requirement as *knowing* rather than *intentional.* On the other hand, Massachusetts requires that the defendants' conduct be motivated by cruelty, hostility, or revenge.[37] Each state's statute and case law must be examined to determine the level of *mens rea* required for conviction. Reckless or criminally negligent actions that result in the destruction of personal or real property of another are covered in state statutes as less serious forms of criminal mischief or by other statutes.

2. Injury or Destruction

In a Montana case, the defendant was found guilty of violating the criminal mischief statute after a police car was blown up by explosives. Evidence that a particular brand of safety fuse and dynamite had been used, that the defendant had access to such safety fuses and dynamite through his employer, that the employer was missing large amounts of blasting caps and fuses, and that the defendant confided to a friend that he had blown up the police car was sufficient to justify conviction.[38]

The amount of damage determines the degree, or the class, of the crime. If the amount of damage is an element of the crime, then evidence must be introduced to indicate that the damage resulted from the acts of the defendant. This may be shown by cost of repair, by diminution in value, or by replacement costs.

3. Property of Another

One of the continuing issues in the prosecution of malicious mischief is when property is shared. In this case, typically the actor who damages shared property will be guilty of a crime. For instance, evidence was sufficient to support a conviction for second-degree malicious mischief when a police officer testified that the defendant's wife reported that the defendant broke a mirror, a birdcage, and other household items after an argument, and that she estimated the total amount of damage to be $620.66.[39]

4. Related Statutes

Vandalism and **criminal mischief** cover similar types of behaviors. The Model Penal Code does not have a separate crime of vandalism, nor was there such a crime under common law. An example of a vandalism statute is that of Ohio, which provides:

§ 2909.05 Vandalism.

(A)   No person shall knowingly cause serious physical harm to an occupied structure or any of its contents.

(B)(1)   No person shall knowingly cause serious physical harm to property that is owned or possessed by another, when either of the following applies:

(a) The property is used by its owner or possessor in his profession, business, trade, or occupation, and the value of the property or the amount of physical harm involved is five hundred dollars or more;

(b) Regardless of the value of the property or the amount of damage done, the property or its equivalent is necessary in order for its owner or possessor to engage in the owner's or possessor's profession, business, trade, or occupation.[40]

This section of the Ohio statute contains the usual provisions prohibiting vandalism. This would be the crime charged for breaking windows in a home, destroying furniture, or causing other damage, making it temporarily unusable or requiring a substantial amount of time, effort, or money to repair the damage. This section also embraces a relatively new concept: that of knowingly causing serious harm to property used in or necessary to the occupation of its owner or possessor. Examples of this type of violation include rifling and scattering case files of an attorney, damaging the samples of a traveling salesperson, or destroying a plumber's tools.[41] Other states have vandalism statutes that cover public buildings and/or churches.[42]

D. Summary

Although the elements of malicious mischief are fairly simple, the specific definition and interpretation of them may vary widely from state to state.

Malicious Mischief (Criminal Mischief)

(A/R)   Injury or destruction; of property; of another

(M/R)   Malicious (knowing)

§ 7.4 Trespass (Criminal Trespass)

The next three sections deal with three sequentially more serious crimes: trespass, breaking and entering, and burglary. It is helpful to think of these crimes as building blocks with elements added to the *actus reus* and *mens rea* for each successively more serious crime.

A. Common Law

At common law, **trespass** had a much different meaning than the generally used definition today. In its broadest sense, it encompassed any misfeasance, transgression, or offense that damaged another's person, health, reputation, or property.[43] However, at common law, trespass referred to the remedy, not the offense. An *action of trespass* was the proper remedy to recover damages when the injury consisted of damage to personal property or real property. Where the trespass was an intrusion upon the real property of another, the writ was known as "*trespass quare clausum fregit.*"[44] Generally, the *action in trespass* was a civil action to recover damages.

At common law, every man's land was deemed to be enclosed, so that every unwarrantable entry on such land necessarily carried with it some damages for which the trespasser was civilly liable.[45] Civil action in trespass is for money damages, and because every unauthorized entry onto the land of another infers some damages, nominal damages were recoverable even though there was no substantial damage to the property. When there was actual damage to realty from the trespass, damages were awarded in an amount that would constitute just compensation for the injury done.[46]

While at common law most of the trespass actions were civil actions, certain acts of trespass that were accompanied by a breach of the peace were regarded as crimes. However, it seems clear from a study of the cases that every trespass that was the subject of a civil action was not an indictable offense. Where criminal trespass actions were authorized at common law, the definition of trespass was more precise, and the mere invasion of private property without a disturbance of the peace was not considered a crime.[47]

B. Model Penal Code

The Model Penal Code represents the modern view that entry onto another's property with notice that was one is not invited or permitted is a crime.

§ 221.2 Criminal Trespass[48]

(1) Buildings and Occupied Structures. A person commits an offense if, knowing that he is not licensed or privileged to do so, he enters or surreptitiously remains in any building or occupied structure, or separately secured or occupied portion thereof. An offense under this Subsection is a misdemeanor if it is committed in a dwelling at night. Otherwise it is a petty misdemeanor.

(2) Defiant Trespasser. A person commits an offense if, knowing that he is not licensed or privileged to do so, he enters or remains in any place as to which notice against trespass is given by:

(a) actual communication to the actor; or
(b) posting in a manner prescribed by law or reasonably likely to come to the attention of intruders; or
(c) fencing or other enclosure manifestly designed to exclude intruders.

An offense under this subsection constitutes a petty misdemeanor if the offender defies an order to leave that is personally communicated to him or her by the owner of the premises or another authorized person. Otherwise it is a violation.

(3) Defenses. It is an affirmative defense to prosecution under this Section that:

(a) a building or occupied structure involved in an offense under Subsection (1) was abandoned; or
(b) the premises were at the time open to members of the public and the actor complied with all lawful conditions imposed on access to or remaining in the premises; or
(c) the actor reasonably believed that the owner of the premises, or other person empowered to license access thereto, would have licensed him to enter or remain.

Under the provisions of the Model Penal Code, the prosecution must first show that the actor knowingly intruded into a place where he knew he was not licensed or privileged to be. As indicated in subsection (1), the trespass is aggravated if committed at night. If at night, it is a misdemeanor, while at any other time it is a petty misdemeanor. Subsection (2) deals with the person who enters or remains on property after some form of notice has been communicated. Communication may be actual or by posting or fencing. This provision carries over some of the provisions of previous statutes.

It is noted also that the grading of the offense is determined partly by whether the surreptitious entry is into an occupied building or "any place as to which notice against trespass is given." Model Code § 221.2 also lists affirmative defenses.

C. State Statutes, Codes, and Cases

Using the common law concept of criminal trespass as a basis, many statutes were passed, making certain acts of trespass punishable as crimes. For example, some statutes make it an offense to trespass willfully on the premises of another after being ordered not to do so.[49]

Criminal trespass statutes, being penal in nature, have been construed somewhat strictly. For example, where a statute states that the charge will be valid only after a person has been ordered to depart, the prosecution must introduce evidence to show that there was such an order. Criminal trespass, as it has developed, usually covers only impermissible entries into a structure or "premises"; however, the definitions are very broad and have been interpreted to include warehouses, docks, wharfs and the curtilage of structures.

During the 1960s and early 1970s, many trespassing statutes were found to be unconstitutional as conflicting with the First Amendment when they were applied to public buildings.[50] However, in the case of *Hudgens v. National Labor Relations Board*, handed down in 1976, the Supreme Court decided that shopping center owners are not constitutionally compelled to allow the use of property for demonstrations by members of the public.[51] Also, the courts now agree that private property is not constitutionally available for picketing, handbilling, marching, and other such activities unless the owner is willing to voluntarily submit to this use.

While some of the more recent statutes and codes follow the Model Penal Code substantially, others are worded differently. For example, the Texas Penal Code provides:

§ 30.05 Criminal Trespass[52]

(a) A person commits an offense if he enters or remains on property or in a building of another without effective consent and he:
    (1) had notice that the entry was forbidden; or
    (2) received notice to depart but failed to do so.

(b) For purposes of this Section:
    (1) "Entry" means the intrusion of the entire body.
    (2) "Notice" means:
        (A) oral or written communication by the owner or someone with apparent authority to act for the owner;
        (B) fencing or other enclosure obviously designed to exclude intruders or to contain livestock;
        (C) a sign or signs posted on the property or at the entrance to the building, reasonably likely to come to the attention of intruders, indicating that entry is forbidden;
        (D) the placement of identifying purple paint marks on trees or posts on the property, provided that the marks are:

> (i)   vertical lines of not less than eight inches in length and not less than one inch in width;
>
> (ii) placed so that the bottom of the mark is not less than three feet from the ground or more than five feet from the ground; and
>
> (iii) placed at locations that are readily visible to any person approaching the property and no more than:
>
>> (a) 100 feet apart on forest land; or
>>
>> (b) 1,000 feet apart on land other than forest land; or
>
> (E) the visible presence on the property of a crop grown for human consumption that is under cultivation, in the process of being harvested, or marketable if harvested at the time of entry.
>
> (3) "Shelter center" has the meaning assigned by Section 51.002(1), Human Resources Code.
>
> (c) It is a defense to prosecution under this Section that the actor at the time of the offense was a fire fighter or emergency medical services personnel, as that term is defined by Section 773.003, Health and Safety Code, acting in the lawful discharge of an official duty under exigent circumstances.
>
> (d) An offense under this section is a Class B misdemeanor unless it is committed in a habitation or a shelter center or unless the actor carries a deadly weapon on or about his person during the commission of the offense, in which event it is a Class A misdemeanor.

Under Texas law, the elements of the offense of criminal trespass are: (1) a person; (2) without effective consent; (3) enters or remains on property or in the building of another; (4) knowingly, intentionally, or recklessly; (5) when he or she had notice that entry was forbidden or received notice to depart but failed to do so. A Texas court explained that "a person commits the offense of trespass if he enters the property of another without effective consent, and he has notice that the entry is forbidden."[53] Where the trespass is on land or into a building, there is no violation unless notice was given that the entry was forbidden and the actor entered without "effective consent." Subsection (b)(2) establishes five methods of giving notice.

The Texas Code has been challenged on two constitutional grounds: the First Amendment to the Constitution and the "void for vagueness" issue. One Texas court found that the statute, as enforced, did not violate the First Amendment to the Constitution, when the defendant was charged with trespassing after distributing anti-abortion booklets to high school students while he was standing on the sidewalk inside the school campus.[54]

A second Texas appeals court held that the use of the undefined term "remain," in this section, which defines the crime as entering or remaining on property of another without effective consent, does not render the section vague, because the term "remain" can be construed according to its ordinary usage, as meaning to "stay," and thus a stay of any length of time after entry satisfies the "remain" requirement.[55]

The statutes in some states have strict requirements that must be met before a criminal action can be brought against a person for trespass. California prohibits "entering upon uncultivated or unenclosed lands where signs forbidding trespass are displayed" at intervals not less than three to the mile along all exterior boundaries and at all trails and roads entering the land.[56]

In an Illinois case in which the purpose and scope of the trespass law was considered, the court commented that in committing criminal trespass to property, the fundamental criminal act is the actual unlawful entry on the property of another, which requires notice of the owner's lack of consent.[57]

There is no trespass when the possessor has consented to the entry.[58] But for the purposes of criminal trespass, a parent-owner of premises has a superior interest in the home to that of an unemancipated minor residing there and the parent's withdrawal of authority to enter the home supersedes any authority a minor may have to invite others to enter the home.[59] Actual notice generally is not required when an enclosure manifestly is designed to exclude intruders such as, for example, a home. In addition, a few states add a fourth element: a specific intent to enter for some unlawful purpose, which makes trespass much more similar to burglary.[60]

D. Summary

The common law definition of trespass was more often related to a civil action taken to recover damages for unwarranted entry onto one's property. However, there were occasions when the trespass could be a crime. The modern crime of trespass generally include the elements listed below; however, many statutes require notice (posted signs) to prove the "without consent" element. Further, Supreme Court cases have restricted the ability to define and prosecute trespass when the entry is to a "public" place.

Trespass

(A/R)   Entry onto property (land or building); owned by another; without consent

(M/R)   Knowing

---

§ 7.5   Breaking and Entering

A. Common Law

There was no separate crime of **breaking and entering** under common law, although these elements were part of the *actus reus* of burglary, or the act might have been punished under trespass.

B. Model Penal Code

The Model Penal Code does not have a separate crime defined as breaking and entering; however, trespass covers the circumstances in which an offender enters the home or building of another, knowing they do not have permission to do so. This comprises the "entry" element of breaking and entering, but some states are more specific in their distinction between trespass and breaking and entering.

C. State Statutes, Codes, and Cases

All of the states have enacted legislation to provide punishment for offenses that do not meet the definition of common law burglary. Some statutes provide a penalty for breaking and entering, which is considered more serious than simple trespass but less serious than burglary.

> § 2911.13 Breaking and Entering.[61]
>
> (A) No person by force, stealth, or deception, shall trespass in an unoccupied structure, with purpose to commit therein any theft offense as defined in § 2913.01 of the Revised Code, or any felony.
> (B) No person shall trespass on the land or premises of another, with purpose to commit a felony.
> (C) Whoever violates this Section is guilty of breaking and entering, a felony of the fifth degree.

The purpose of this Ohio statute is to establish a violation when all of the elements of burglary are not present. An offense similar to burglary is defined, except that the structure involved is unoccupied rather than occupied. This is classified as a felony of the fourth degree, the rationale being that there is comparatively less risk of personal harm.

Other state statutes add additional aggravating factors. For example, in Oregon, being armed with a burglar's tool is an aggravating factor.[62] In Puerto Rico, a higher penalty is available when force is used to enter.[63]

The rationale of having a breaking and entering crime separate from burglary and separate from trespass is that trespass is often a misdemeanor and covers entry onto land (not homes), and entry or remaining in a building without any degree of force required to enter (i.e., through an open door or remaining in a place beyond the parameters of one's permission to do so). Breaking and entering implies a greater property intrusion. It covers situations in which the offender took steps to actually break through the property's boundary protections (i.e., by getting through a window or door). The only thing, in fact, that is different between breaking and entering and burglary is the inability to prove the specific intent to commit a crime inside the dwelling.

D. Summary

Breaking and entering did not exist under common law and is not a separate crime under the Model Code; however, some states have chosen to distinguish breaking and entering from simple trespass to cover situations that are more serious than trespass, but do not meet the technical definition of burglary. While many states utilize the elements of breaking and entering as a more serious grade of trespass, the general elements are as follows.

Breaking and Entering

(A/R)   breaking and entering; of a building; of another

(M/R)   general intent

---

§ 7.6 Burglary

A. Common Law

One of the most serious crimes in practically every society is the crime of **burglary**. Burglary is considered more serious than crimes such as larceny, due to the possible injuries to people within the dwelling and the fact that the courts and legislative bodies have long looked upon the home as deserving special protection. According to one court, the crime is against possession and is primarily intended to protect the sanctity of one's home, especially at night when peace, solitude, and safety are most desired and expected. From early times, burglary was considered a felony and at one time was punishable by death.[64]

The term *burglary* is a combination of the Saxon term "burg," meaning *house*, and "laron," meaning *theft*.[65] Burglary was defined in one early case in the following way:

> "Burglary" is the breaking into a house in the night season with intent to commit a felony, and if a house is so entered, it is burglary, whether the felony be executed or not, and regardless of the kind of felony intended or the manner in which the felony may be frustrated, or the value of the property taken, or any other circumstance which is not intrinsic.[66]

The common law crime of "burglary" was an offense against the habitation, and the essential elements were: a breaking; and entry; of a dwelling house; of another; in the nighttime; with intent to commit a felony therein.[67]

1. Breaking

In order to meet this element, the prosecution must prove that some *breaking [in]* of the structure, either actual or constructive, occurred. Breaking consists of putting aside a part of the house that obstructs the entrance and is closed, or in penetrating an opening that is as much closed as the nature of the case admits. The law puts a premium upon a reasonable degree of care in acting to prevent burglaries by closing doors, windows, and other openings. Therefore, under the common law, an entry through an open door or window would not complete this element, even if there was intent to commit a felony.[68]

The early courts did, however, recognize "constructive breaking." To constitute this element, the breaking could be by an entry effected through fraud, or by threat or intimidation. An example is where the defendant pretended that he had business with the owner of the house and gained entry.[69]

2. Entry

An entry is also necessary to constitute the crime of burglary. A breaking without entry is not burglary, but an entry, however slight after breaking, is sufficient; for example, where a head, a hand, an arm, a foot, or even a finger is thrust within the house.[70] In the case of *People v. Peddinger*, the breaking of the window of a service station by the defendant and insertion of an arm into the building was sufficient "entry" in a burglary prosecution.[71] And in the case of *People v. Davis*, the court held that it is not the size of the hole that determines whether an entry was made, but whether a hand or instrument was actually inserted into the hole for the purpose of committing the felony.[72]

3. Dwelling House

At common law, and under many statutes, breaking and entering, to constitute burglary, must be of a dwelling house. The dwelling house has been defined as any kind of structure used as a place of habitation and occupied by persons other than the defendant. Temporary absence of the occupant will not deprive the dwelling house of its character as such. It is not necessary to prove that the owner or occupant or some member of the family was in the house at the time of the burglary, but the house, although furnished as a dwelling house, loses its character as such for purposes of burglary if the occupant leaves it without the intention to return.[73] The house must be occupied as a dwelling and not merely be suitable or intended for such purpose.[74]

Under the common law, shops, stores, and warehouses, unless they were occupied in part as a dwelling, were not covered under the law against burglary. On the other hand, stables, smokehouses, kitchens, shops, offices, or other outbuildings, if they are within the curtilage of a dwelling house, were regarded as parts of the dwelling so that it was burglary to break and enter them with felonious intent, although there may be no entry into the dwelling house itself.[75]

4. Of Another

Recall that in the case of arson, the law prohibited setting fire to the house of another, but the definition was primarily if it was *occupied* by another, not necessarily *owned* by another. So, for instance, if a landlord set fire to his own home, but others lived in it, it could be charged as arson. The definition of ownership is the same in common law burglary. The law is concerned with the protection of habitation rather than the title to property, consequently with occupancy rather than ownership. Therefore, it is not a question of whether a person actually owns the house that is broken into; possession (who is living in the house) constitutes sufficient ownership in burglary cases.[76]

5. In the Nighttime

At common law, breaking and entering a dwelling house in the daytime was not burglary. According to some decisions, nighttime begins when daylight ends, or when the countenance ceases to be reasonably discernible by the light of the sun, and ends at dawn, or as soon as the countenance becomes discernible.[77]

6. With Intent to Commit a Felony Inside

Burglary is a "specific intent" crime. Breaking and entering of a dwelling of another is not enough to define the act as burglary under common law or modern statutes. The intent to break and enter is not sufficient—there must also be proof that the defendant intended to break and enter with the intent to commit a felony inside. Specific intent may be inferred from the facts.[78] The prosecution must prove that the intent to commit a felony inside existed in the mind of the perpetrator at the moment of entry.[79] The intent must be concurrent with the breaking and entering but may be formed at the moment the breaking occurs. The early courts determined that if the intent does not exist until after the house was entered, there could be no burglary under the common law definition.[80]

Burglary is generally committed with the intent to steal, which is a felony, but the indictment may allege breaking and entering with intent to commit other felonies, such as murder or rape. In any event, the prosecution must introduce evidence to show specific intent on the part of the perpetrator to commit a specific felony.[81] If there was intent to commit a felony inside, and a breaking and entry occurs, then even if the actor abandons the effort once inside, the crime of burglary is complete.[82]

B. Model Penal Code

The Model Penal Code retains much of the common law concept of burglary but simplifies the definition. Instead of a dwelling house, any building can be burglarized. Also, the strict definitions of breaking and entering have been reduced to entry with the intent to commit a crime inside.

---

§ 221.1 Burglary[83]

(1) Burglary Defined. A person is guilty of burglary if he enters a building or occupied structure, or separately secured or occupied portion thereof, with purpose to commit a crime therein, unless the premises are at the time open to the public or the actor is licensed or privileged to enter. It is an affirmative defense to prosecution for burglary that the building or structure was abandoned.

(2) Grading. Burglary is a felony of the second degree if it is perpetrated in the dwelling of another at night, or if, in the course of committing the offense, the actor:
 (a) purposely, knowingly or recklessly inflicts or attempts to inflict bodily injury on anyone; or
 (b) is armed with explosives or a deadly weapon.

Otherwise, burglary is a felony of the third degree. An act shall be deemed "in the course of committing" an offense if it occurs in an attempt to commit the offense or in flight after the attempt or commission.

(3) Multiple Convictions. A person may not be convicted both for burglary and for the offense which it was his purpose to commit after the burglarious entry or for an attempt to commit that offense, unless the additional offense constitutes a felony of the first or second degree.

In subsection (2), the factors that accompany the entry and determine the grade of the offense are considered. The common law reasoning that entry at night is more serious than entry in the daytime is carried over into the Model Code. The Model Code does not provide an offense for one who surreptitiously remains on the premises, and apparently the common law definition as to what amounts to entry still prevails.

Under the Model Code, an "occupied structure" is any structure, vehicle, or place adapted for overnight accommodation of persons, or for carrying on business therein, whether or not a person is actually present. Therefore, it is not necessary to allege that the building was occupied. However, the final sentence of subsection (1) provides a defense that would bar prosecution for burglary of abandoned or derelict buildings unsuited and, in fact, unused for human occupancy.

The phrase "purpose to commit a crime therein" differs from that used in common law definitions in that "purpose" is substituted for "intent" and "crime" is substituted for "felony." The word *crime* is defined as "an offense for which a sentence of imprisonment is authorized."

Apparently to forestall any arguments concerning the possibility of double jeopardy, subsection (3) of the Model Code precludes accumulation of penalties for burglary and for the intended offense in all circumstances, except where the offense is itself a felony of the first or second degree. For example, consecutive sentences may be given when a person is convicted of burglary and the purpose was to commit rape, and the elements of rape are also proved by the prosecution. "At night" is defined in the Model Penal Code as "the period thirty minutes past sunset and thirty minutes before sunrise."[84]

C. State Statutes, Codes, and Cases

Generally, state statutes follow the Model Penal Code and are not too different from the common law except that they are more inclusive of the types of offenses that could be covered under a burglary definition. The state of Ohio provides for three related statutes: breaking and entering (which we discussed in the previous section) burglary; and aggravated burglary.

§ 2911.12   Burglary[85]

(A) No person, by force, stealth or deception, shall do any of the following:

 (1) Trespass in an occupied structure or in a separately secured or separately occupied portion of an occupied structure, when another person other than an accomplice of the offender is present, with purpose to commit in the structure or in the separately secured or separately occupied portion of the structure any criminal offense.

 (2) Trespass in an occupied structure or in a separately secured or separately occupied portion of an occupied structure that is a permanent or temporary habitation of any person when any person other than an accomplice of the offender is present or likely to be present with purpose to commit in the habitation any criminal offense.

 (3) Trespass in an occupied structure or in a separately secured or separately occupied portion of an occupied structure, with purpose to commit in the structure or separately secured or separately occupied portion of the structure any criminal offense.

 (4) Trespass in a permanent or temporary habitation of any person when any person other than an accomplice of the offender is present or likely to be present.

(B) As used in this section, "occupied structure" has the same meaning as in § 2909.01 of the Revised Code.

(C) Whoever violates this section is guilty of burglary. A violation of division (A)(1) or (2) of this section is a felony of the second degree. A violation of division (A)(3) of this section is a felony of the third degree. A violation of division (A)(4) of this section is a felony of the fourth degree.

Note that instead of the nighttime element of common law, the Ohio statute defines burglary and entry when someone else is likely to be present. In interpreting the "likely to be present" provision, the court held that there is no evidence that a person is "likely to be present," for purposes of the statute proscribing burglary, where a burglary occurs during the regular working hours of the homeowner and there is no evidence that the homeowner was in or out or that he or she was likely to return at varying times.[86] The more serious grade of burglary is "aggravated burglary."

§ 2911.11 Aggravated Burglary.[87]

(A) No person, by force, stealth, or deception, shall trespass in an occupied structure as defined in § 2909.01 of the Revised Code, or in a separately secured or separately occupied portion thereof, with purpose to commit therein any theft offense as defined in § 2913.01 of the Revised Code, or any felony, when any of the following apply:

(1) The offender inflicts, or attempts or threatens to inflict physical harm on another;

(2) The offender has a deadly weapon or dangerous ordnance as defined in § 2923.11 of the Revised Code on or about his person or under his control;

(B) Whoever violates this Section is guilty of aggravated burglary, a felony of the first degree.

Other state statutory definitions of burglary include:

- A person commits the crime of burglary if he knowingly enters or remains unlawfully in a building with the intent to commit a felony therein.[88]

- In order to commit the felony of burglary, a suspect must enter a conveyance or structure without consent and with intent to commit an offense inside.[89]

- To convict a person of the crime of burglary, the state must prove two elements: (1) unlawful breaking and entering; and (2) intent to commit some crime once entry has been gained.[90]

Statutes generally criminalize some of the activities that were not covered under common law burglary. We will consider some of these changes below.

1. Breaking

In a number of states, the necessity for "breaking" was omitted and entry alone was sufficient if the required intent was also present.

2. Entry

In New York and other states, the statute also provides a penalty for one who remains unlawfully on the premises as well as for one who enters unlawfully.[91] For instance, in one case a police officer was convicted of burglary because he stole several items when investigating a warehouse theft. His presence in the warehouse was defined as unlawfully remaining in the building after his official duties were completed.[92] Similarly to common law, any part of the body is sufficient to be defined as entry. A court in a New York case agreed that testimony that the defendant reached a gloved hand through a broken window to reach an inside doorknob was sufficient to establish an entry in a prosecution for violating a burglary statute.[93] A California court agreed that for purposes of the burglary statute, entry that is just barely inside the premises, even if the area penetrated is small, is sufficient.[94]

3. Dwelling House

Statutes enlarged the scope of the dwelling requirement to include businesses and other buildings, warehouses, shops, offices, barns, and stables. In some states, even if the statute specifies dwelling, it need not be occupied. In one case, the court decided that if the structure initially qualifies under the statutory definition of a dwelling, and its character is not substantially changed to the extent that it becomes unsuitable for lodging by people, it remains a dwelling irrespective of actual occupancy.[95] In Florida, houses under construction are "dwellings" within the meaning of the burglary statute, which define the dwelling as a building of any kind that has a roof over it and was designed to be occupied by people lodging therein at night.[96] In Mississippi, a house was a "dwelling" for purposes of the burglary statute, even though the owner lived there only four months out of the year, because the owner received her mail there and kept her personal property there, indicating her clear intent to return to the house.[97] On the other hand, in California, evidently a house loses its character as a dwelling immediately upon the death of the occupant. As we see in *People v. Ramos*, a burglar can then be charged only with a less serious degree of burglary.

> **CASE: *People v. Ramos***
> **52 Cal. App.4th 300,**
> **60 Cal. Rptr. 2d 523 (1997)**
>
> What were the issue and holding of the case?
>
> Define "dwelling" according to the California statute.
>
> What could he be charged and convicted of?

4. Of Another

Generally, modern statutes are interpreted in the same way as the common law. Possession is more important than title. An Ohio court, for instance, concluded that when the defendant took a child from its mother's home after the defendant moved out, he could be convicted of burglary.[98] In this definition of ownership, a landlord could burglarize his own house if he had rented it to someone else, and a man could burglarize his own house if he was legally separated from his spouse and the court had awarded her the use of the family home, or even if she had been exercising custody or control of that dwelling.[99]

5. In the Nighttime

In almost all states, statutes have been enacted to punish those who commit the act in the daytime, as well as at night. In statutes that retain the requirement of nighttime (perhaps, for instance, to define an aggravating factor), they have generally defined nighttime as the period between sunset and sunrise.[100]

6. With Intent to Commit Felony (or Crime) Inside

State statutes differ in regard to the intent to commit a crime element. In some states, the intent to commit a felony is not required, and the intent to commit a misdemeanor is sufficient. The Texas statute requires "an attempt to commit any felony or theft."[101] To obtain a burglary conviction, a state must prove that the defendant intended to commit an independent crime other than trespass after an illegal entry into a building.[102] However, it is not an element of burglary that the victim's property be taken. For example, a New York court held that burglary requires only the intent to commit a crime inside the dwelling.[103] Intent to commit a crime in the building can be inferred from circumstances of the breaking and entering.[104] In the case described in the Legal News box below, the circumstances generally support a burglary charge, but if the intent was to commit theft, why did he curl up for a nap under a desk?

Legal News

On June 16, 2006 it was reported that Michael Pickens, the son of billionaire T. Boone Pickens, was found sleeping under a desk of a fly-fishing shop by the owner who had just discovered that the shop had been broken into and that $3,000 worth of merchandise had been placed in a cooler. He was under indictment for securities fraud violations at the time of the incident. The police charged him with burglary.

Source: Retrieved on June 29, 2006 from http://www.msnbc.msn.com/id/13368639/

---

7. Other Issues

In some states, the defendant may be charged with and convicted of a higher degree of burglary, such as aggravated burglary, if the entrance was by force; if the defendant purposely, knowingly, or recklessly inflicted or attempted to inflict bodily injury; or if the person entering the premises was armed.

D. Summary

Although there are differences in wording and interpretation of the elements of burglary among the states, in general, the elements are the same as the common law except that in the majority of states: (a) a dwelling has been generously defined and can include businesses or other buildings; and (b) burglary can occur during the daytime.

Burglary

(A/R) Breaking and entering (or remaining in; and sometimes no breaking); of a dwelling or building; of another; with intent to commit a felony (or crime) inside

(M/R) Specific intent

---

§ 7.7 Causing or Risking Catastrophe

A. *Common Law*

This crime did not exist under the common law.

B. *Model Penal Code*

The Model Penal Code defines as criminal behavior that which causes or has a high likelihood of causing a "catastrophe" (which is also defined in the statute).

---

§ 220.2 Causing or Risking Catastrophe[105]

(1) Causing Catastrophe
A person who causes a catastrophe by explosion, fire, flood, avalanche, collapse of a building, release of poisonous gas, radioactive material, or other harmful force or substance, or by any other means of causing potentially widespread injury or damage, commits a felony of the second degree if he does so purposely or knowingly, or a felony of the third degree if he does so recklessly.

(2) Risking Catastrophe
A person is guilty of a misdemeanor if he recklessly creates a risk of catastrophe in the employment of fire, explosives or other dangerous means listed in Subsection (1).

Under the provisions of subsection (1), if a person purposely or knowingly causes a catastrophe by one of the specified means or by any other means of causing potentially widespread injury or damage, the offense is a second degree felony. However, if the action is reckless rather than purposeful or knowing, the offense is a third degree felony.

The crime is divided into two sections; the first covering situations in which a catastrophe did occur; and the second covers situations in which the offender risked a catastrophe by his behavior, but it did not occur. The *mens rea* is either intentional, knowing, or reckless.

C. State Statutes, Codes and Cases

Several states have statutes similar to the Model Penal Code that provide a penalty for the specific wrong of causing or risking a catastrophe.[106] The purpose of such statutes is to punish those who purposely, knowingly, or recklessly bring about a catastrophe.

D. Summary

The elements of the crime have been suggested by the Model Penal Code, and thus we will use it to specify the elements.

Causing or Risking Catastrophe

(A/R)   Cause or risk catastrophe by explosion, fire, flood, avalanche, collapse of a building, release of poisonous gas, radioactive material, or other harmful force or substance

(M/R)   Purposely, knowingly, recklessly

---

§ 7.8 Summary

Under common law, offenses against the home were considered extremely serious offenses. Arson and burglary are two examples of common law crimes that received the death penalty in early England and the colonies. Common law arson was defined as the willful and malicious burning of the dwelling house of another. Modern statutes, however, provide punishment for burning structures other than dwellings and provide a penalty when a person burns his or her own house or property in order to defraud an insurer.

Another property destruction crime is malicious mischief, sometimes designated "criminal mischief." It is generally defined as the willful and unlawful injury to or destruction of the property of another with malicious intent to injure the owner. The more recent codes consolidate many of the former malicious mischief provisions that were enacted to meet the needs of society at the time into a single comprehensive offense or an integrated series of related offenses. Vandalism is a similar crime and may be used in addition to or instead of criminal mischief in a state's penal code.

At common law, trespass was the civil remedy to recover damages when the injury consisted of damage to personal property or real property. However, in addition, certain acts of trespass were considered crimes. Trespass can be defined as an unlawful intrusion upon the real property of another without the other's consent. Many states have enacted specific trespass statutes to prohibit willful and unlawful entry upon the premises of another for certain purposes. All states currently have provisions prohibiting entering or remaining on property without the consent of the owner. Some require that notice be given that entry is forbidden, and some require that a specific intent to enter for some unlawful purpose be proved. In some statutes, one requirement is that a fence be constructed or that the trespasser be ordered off the property before any action can be taken.

Another crime that was and is considered very serious is burglary. At common law, the crime consisted of breaking and entering into the dwelling house of another in the night with the intent to commit a felony therein. Most states today have enlarged the definition to include other types of buildings and to include the intent to commit a misdemeanor therein. Also, many statutes do not require the breaking and entering to occur at night. The grade of the crime is determined by such factors as the time the crime was perpetrated (day or night), whether bodily injury was inflicted or attempted purposely or knowingly, and whether the person was armed or unarmed. Most states today provide a penalty for breaking and entering structures, including homes and other buildings, when the intent to commit a crime inside cannot be proven.

While there are still some wrongs that probably are not covered by statute, in most instances a statute or code can be found to make it possible to take action against persons who wrongfully destroy or intrude upon the property of another. Other state statutes provide penalties for offenses of which property damage is the main thrust. For instance, the Model Penal Code suggested the crime of "Causing or Risking a Catastrophe." Other examples are damaging public utilities property.[107] If one studies the state statutes carefully, most likely a statute will be located that makes it possible to arrest and prosecute persons who have wrongfully destroyed or intruded upon the property of another.

Review Questions

1. What are the four elements of the common law crime of arson?

2. Define *dwelling*. Is an abandoned house a dwelling? What is meant by *curtilage*? Define *burning*.

3. When can one be convicted of arson for burning one's own house down?

4. How did the MPC change the common law definitions of arson?

5. In modern statutes, is it a crime to burn down structures other than dwellings? What factors affect the seriousness of various types of burning?

6. Define *malicious mischief* (provide the mens rea as well) and distinguish it from larceny and arson. Give some examples of criminal mischief.

7. Describe the crime of vandalism.

8. Would destroying shared property (i.e., a husband or wife destroys marital property) support a charge of criminal mischief or vandalism?

9. The crime of burglary can be thought of as the most serious of a sequence of property intrusions—what is the sequence?

10. Explain *"trespass quare clausum fregit."*

11. What are the elements of modern criminal trespass? What is the mens rea required by most trespass statutes?

12. In the 1976 case of *Hudgens v. National Labor Relations Board*, the Supreme Court of the United States was asked to determine the constitutionality of a trespass statute protecting a shopping center (which arguably is also a type of public place). What was the decision of the Court in regard to the constitutionality of such a statute?

13. The modern crime of breaking and entering is often available when which element of burglary cannot be proven?

14. The common law crime of burglary was very technical. In order to find a person guilty of burglary, it was necessary to prove many elements. What are the elements of the common law crime of burglary?

15. Under the common law, only one type of building was protected under burglary statutes—what was it? How is it defined?

16. What constitutes *breaking* under common law burglary definitions?

17. What constitutes *entry* under most burglary statutes? Is reaching into a building through an open window considered *breaking*?

18. Under the common law, an indictment for burglary must allege a specific intent to commit a particular felony. What is meant by specific intent, as used in burglary cases?

19. The Model Penal Code, in defining the offense of burglary, carries over some of the concepts of the common law. However, the grade of the crime of burglary is determined by several factors. What are those factors? At what point must the intent exist?

20. Define the crime of "causing or risking a catastrophe."

Notes

[1]   Williams v. State, 100 Fla. 1054, 132 So. 186 (1930).

[2]   1 BLACKSTONE, COMMENTARIES 220-228.

[3]   Fox v. State, 179 Ind. App. 267, 384 N.E.2d 1159 (1979).

4   State v. White, 291 N.C. 118, 229 S.E.2d 152 (1976)

5   Commonwealth v. Van Schaack, 16 Mass. 104 (1819); State v. Braathen, 77 N.D. 309, 43 N.W.2d 202 (1950); State v. Wyatt, 48 N.C. App. 709, 269 S.E.2d 717 (1980); State v. Hall, 93 N.C. 571 (1885); Honey v. State, 112 Tex. Crim. 439, 17 S.W.2d 50 (1929).

6   State v. Wyatt, 48 N.C. App. 709, 269 S.E.2d 717 (1980).

7   United States v. Potts, 297 F.2d 68 (6th Cir. 1961).

8   1 HAWKINS, PLEAS OF THE CROWN, 105-106 (1716).

9   State v. Tennery, 9 Iowa 436 (1859); State v. Keena, 63 Conn. 329, 28 A. 522 (1893). *See also* In re Gabriel M., 132 N.M.124, 45 P.2d 64 (2002), which held that at common law, arson is the willful and malicious burning of the dwelling house of another; it is an offense against the security of habitation or occupancy, rather than against ownership or property; State v. Jones, 296 N.C. 75, 248 S.E.2d 858 (1978).

10   Edwards v. Commonwealth, 204 Ky. 515, 264 S.W. 1083 (1924).

11   Colbert v. State, 125 Wis. 423, 104 N.W. 61 (1905); Hough v. State, 929 S.W.2d 484 (Tex. 1996).

12   MODEL PENAL CODE § 220.1 (1985).

13   Poulos, *The Metamorphosis of the Law of Arson*, 51 MO. L. REV. 295 (1986).

14   CAL. PENAL CODE § 451 (2002). See also CAL. PENAL CODE § 451.1 (2002).

15   13 VT. CODE R. § 502-05 (West 2007).

16   People v. Calderon, 682 N.Y.S.2d 38 (App. Div. 1998).

17   Barnes v. State, 858 P.2d 522 (Wyo. 1993).

18   People v. Reeves, 528 N.W.2d 160 (Mich. 1995).

19   People v. Jones, 245 Cal. Rptr. 85 (1988) The fact that some furniture was left in the house after the tenants were evicted was not determinative.

20   State v. Britt, 510 S.E.2d 683 (N.C. 1999).

21   Barnes v. State, 721 So. 2d 1130 (Miss. 1998).

22   People v. Schwartz, 3 Cal. Rptr. 2d 816 (1992).

23   MO. REV. STAT. § 569.040 (2002).

24   ALASKA STAT. § 11-46-430 (1995).

25   Statistics cited in United States v. Hathaway, 757 F. Supp. 324 (D. Vt. 1991).

26   State v. Watts, 48 Ark. 56, 2 S.W. 342 (1886); State v. Manuel, 72 N.C. 201, 21 Am. Rep. 455 (1875).

27   State v. Hawkins, 8 Port. 461, 33 Am. Dec. 294 (Ala. 1839).

28   State v. Minor, 17 N.D. 454, 117 N.W. 528 (1908).

29   State v. Ward, 127 Minn. 510, 150 N.W. 209 (1914).

30   State v. Watts, 48 Ark. 56, 2 S.W. 342 (1886).

31   MODEL PENAL CODE § 220.3 (1985).

32   Ala., Del., Fla., Ind., Minn., Mont., Neb., N.H., N.D., Pa., Tex., Utah, and Wis.

33   Ala., Conn., Haw., Iowa, Me., Mo., Or., and Wash.

34   Ark., Colo., Ga., Ill., Kan., Ky., La., N.M., N.Y., Ohio, and S.D.

35   MO. REV. STAT. § 569.100 (2002).

36   In the Interest of V.H., 655 S.W.2d 833 (Mo. 1983); State v. Walker, 755 S.W.2d 404 (Mo. 1988).

37   Commonwealth v. Lauzier, 760 N.E.2d 1256 (Mass. 2002).

[38] State v. Wolfe, 821 P.2d 339 (Mont. 1991).

[39] State v. Coria, 48 P.3d 980 (Wash. 2002).

[40] OHIO REV. CODE ANN. § 2909.05 (Anderson 2002).

[41] See commentary, OHIO REV. CODE ANN. § 2909.05 (Anderson 2002).

[42] 18 PA. CONS. STAT. ANN. 3307(a) 2001.

[43] Cox v. Strickland, 120 Ga. 104, 47 S.E. 912 (1904).

[44] 3 STREET, FOUNDATIONS OF LEGAL LIABILITY 229 *et seq.* (1980).

[45] Bailey v. People, 54 Colo. 337, 130 P. 832 (1913); Malerba v. Warren, 438 N.Y.S.2d 936 (1981).

[46] Irvin v. Nolde, 176 Pa. 594, 35 A. 217 (1896).

[47] State v. Wheeler, 3 Vt. 344, 23 Am. Dec. 212 (1830).

[48] MODEL PENAL CODE § 221.2 (1985).

[49] Commonwealth v. Richardson, 313 Mass. 632, 48 N.E.2d 678 (1943).

[50] *See* KANOVITZ & KANOVITZ, CONSTITUTIONAL LAW (10th ed. 2006).

[51] 424 U.S. 507, 96 S. Ct. 1029, 47 L. Ed. 2d 196 (1976).

[52] The Texas statute on criminal trespass was amended to provide that a person commits an offense if he or she enters or remains on property, including the aircraft of another, without effective consent. TEX. PENAL CODE ANN. § 30.05 (Vernon 2002); Daniels v. State, 633 S.W.2d 899 (Tex. 1982).

[53] Young v. State, 976 S.W.2d 771 (Tex. 1998).

[54] Reed v. State, 762 S.W.2d 640 (Tex. 1988).

[55] Hernandez v. State, 783 S.W.2d 764 (Tex. 1990).

[56] CAL. PENAL CODE ch. 720. § 5/21-3 (2002).

[57] People v. Likar, 768 N.E.2d 150 (Ill. Ct. App. 2002).

[58] Harris v. Carbonneau, 685 A.2d 296 (Vt. 1996).

[59] People v. Long, 669 N.E.2d 1237 (Ill. 1996).

[60] GA. CODE ANN. § 16-7-21(b) (2002).

[61] OHIO REV. CODE ANN. §§ 2911.11 (Anderson 1999).

[62] OR. REV. STAT. § 164.225 (1999).

[63] P.R. LAWS ANN. tit. 33 § 4277 (1992).

[64] State v. Brooks, 277 S.C. 111, 283 S.E.2d 830 (1981); State v. Allison, 169 N.C. 375, 85 S.E. 129 (1915).

[65] Anderson v. State, 48 Ala. 665, 17 Am. Rep. 36 (1872).

[66] Conrad v. State, 75 Ohio St. 52, 78 N.E. 957 (1906).

[67] Stowell v. People, 521 Colo. 255, 90 P.2d 520 (1939).

[68] Adair v. State, 19 Ala. App. 174, 95 So. 827 (1923); State v. Petit, 32 Wash. 129, 72 P. 1021 (1903); People v. Webber, 138 Cal. 145, 70 P. 1089 (1902).

[69] Davis v. Commonwealth, 132 Va. 521, 110 S.E. 356 (1922); Johnson v. Commonwealth, 85 Pa. 54, 27 Am. Rep. 622 (1877); Nichols v. State, 68 Wis. 416, 32 N.W. 543 (1887).

[70] Penman v. State, 163 Ind. App. 583, 325 N.E.2d 478 (1975).

[71] 94 Cal. App. 297, 271 P. 132 (1928); *see also* Commonwealth v. Myers, 223 Pa. Super. 75, 297 A.2d 151 (1972).

[72] People v. Davis, 3 Ill. App. 3d 738, 279 N.E.2d 179 (1972).

[73]   Smith v. State, 80 Fla. 315, 85 So. 911 (1920); Henderson v. State, 80 Fla. 491, 86 So. 439 (1920).

[74]   Carrier v. State, 227 Ind. 726, 89 N.E.2d 74 (1949).

[75]   Henderson v. United States, 172 F.2d 289 (D.C. Cir. 1949); State v. Gatewood, 169 Kan. 679, 221 P.2d 392 (1950).

[76]   Wilson v. State, 247 Ala. 84, 22 So. 2d 601 (1945).

[77]   Ashford v. State, 36 Neb. 38, 53 N.W. 1036 (1893).

[78]   State v. Fox, 80 Iowa 312, 45 N.W. 874 (1890).

[79]   People v. Markus, 147 Cal. Rptr. 151, 82 Cal. App. 3d 477 (1978).

[80]   Jackson v. State, 102 Ala. 167, 15 So. 344 (1894).

[81]   State v. Robinson, 441 So. 2d 364 (La. Ct. App. 1983).

[82]   Schwartz v. State, 114 S.W. 809, 55 Tex. Crim. 36 (1909).

[83]   MODEL PENAL CODE § 221.1 (1985).

[84]   MODEL PENAL CODE § 221.0 (1985). This is the same definition that appeared in the Texas Penal Code and was quoted in Weathered v. State, 101 Tex. Crim. 520, 276 S.W. 436 (1925).

[85]   OHIO REV. CODE ANN. §§ 2911.12 (Anderson 1999).

[86]   State v. Cantin, 726 N.E.2d 565 (Ohio 1999).

[87]   OHIO REV. CODE ANN. §§ 2911.13 (Anderson 1999).

[88]   Dyson v. State, 722 So. 2d 782 (Ala. 1997).

[89]   Nickell v. State, 722 So. 2d 924 (Fla. 1998).

[90]   Harrison v. State, 722 So. 2d 681 (Miss. 1998).

[91]   N.Y. PENAL LAWS §§ 140.20-140.30 (McKinney 1999).

[92]   People v. Czerminski, 464 N.Y.S.2d 83 (App. Div. 1983).

[93]   People v. Clark, 649 N.Y.S.2d 568 (1996).

[94]   People v. Valencia, 120 Cal. Rptr. 2d 131, 46 P.3d 970 (2002).

[95]   Perkins v. State, 672 N.E.2d 417 (Ind. 1996).

[96]   Gonzalez v. State, 724 So. 2d 126 (Fla. 1998).

[97]   Wilkerson v. State, 724 So. 2d 1089 (Miss. 1998).

[98]   State v. Hill, 75 Ohio St. 3d 195, 661 N.E.2d 1068 (1996).

[99]   State v. Lilly, 717 N.E.2d 322 (Ohio 1999).

[100]   State v. Richards, 29 Utah 310, 81 P. 142 (1905).

[101]   TEX. PENAL CODE ANN. § 30.02 (1999); White v. State, 630 S.W.2d 340 (Tex. 1982).

[102]   State v. Ring, 554 N.W.2d 758 (Minn. 1996).

[103]   Briecke v. New York, 936 F. Supp. 78 (E.D.N.Y. 1996).

[104]   People v. Clark, 649 N.Y.S.2d 568 (1996). *See also* State v. Martin, 587 N.W.2d 606 (Iowa 1998).

[105]   MODEL PENAL CODE § 220.2.

[106]   Among the states having statutes of this type are Alaska, Ark., Me., Mo., N.J., N.D., Pa., Utah, Vt., and W. Va.

[107]   OHIO REV. CODE ANN. § 2909.04 (Anderson 1999).

Offenses Involving Theft   8

Chapter Outline

Cases

Robbery: *Lattimore v. United States*, 684 A.2d 357 (D.C. App. 1996).
Extortion: *Ohio v. Cunningham*, No. 08-CA-09 (Ohio App., October 3, 2008)

§ 8.1   Introduction

All societies have laws or rules that are designed to protect property against theft. In the United States, theft offenses make up the great majority of crimes, and criminal justice personnel spend much of their time investigating crimes that relate to theft. Although statutes have changed the common law, it is essential that the history of theft crimes be studied in order to understand the terminology and the elements that make up the various crimes relating to theft.

At early common law in England, larceny was the only form of theft that was criminally punishable. Because the offense became more and more narrowly construed, many forms of deception were not commonly regarded as criminal. Citizens relied upon civil law to correct wrongs that did not come within the technical definition of larceny. However, as commerce increased, the criminal law was expanded to punish other forms of theft, such as embezzlement, theft by false pretenses, and extortion.

Even after adding the new crimes, the technicalities made application of the laws involving theft very difficult. In recent years, efforts have been made to simplify the laws. Some states have abolished the separate offenses of larceny, embezzlement, and related theft crimes, and combined them into new, comprehensive theft statutes. It is important to recognize that theft offenses are not the same in all jurisdictions.

§ 8.2 Larceny

A. Common Law

Larceny was defined at common law as the felonious taking, by trespass and carrying away by any person, of the personal goods or things of another from any place, without the owner's consent and with the felonious intent to permanently deprive the owner of his or her property and to convert it to the taker's own use or to the use of some person other than the owner.[1]

To constitute the common law crime of larceny, the property taken must be personal property, as distinguished from **real property** (real estate and what is part of the realty), and the property must belong to another. It must be taken by trespass from the possession of another and carried away from the place it occupies. In addition, the taking and removal must be accompanied by the intent to deprive the owner of the property. The following elements constitute the common law crime of theft or larceny.

1. Trespass (Unlawful)

To constitute larceny, there must be a taking of the property against the will of one who has actual or constructive possession of it. This intrusion upon the personalty of another is referred to as "**trespass**." Obviously the use of the term is not the same as the modern-day crime of trespass, nor is it the same as the crime of trespass of premises. It is related to the writ of *trespass de bonis asportatis* (trespass for goods carried away) which was the civil law approach to retrieving stolen goods.

As one court stated, larceny, as it developed at common law, is best defined as the taking and removal, by trespass, of personal property, which the trespasser knows to belong to another, with the felonious intent to deprive him of his ownership therein.[2] In larceny, it is not necessary that the trespass be accompanied by violence if the taker secures physical custody of the property and has it in his power to take it away and appropriate it.

2. Taking (Caption)

A taking occurs when the offender secures dominion over the property. There can be no taking (**caption**) or dominion if the defendant, in an attempt to steal another's property, fails to gain possession of it. In a 1978 case, the North Carolina Supreme Court determined that, in order to satisfy the taking element in larceny, the accused must have the goods in his or her possession and under his or her control, even if only for an instant.[3] Stated in different terms, to constitute larceny, there must be a severance of the possession of the owner and an actual possession by the wrongdoer.[4]

3. Carrying Away (Asportation)

To constitute carrying away or **asportation**, the property must be moved from the place where it was. The distance moved may be very minor. In the North Carolina case cited earlier, the defendant had moved an air conditioner in a motel room approximately four inches from its base and toward the door. The reviewing court agreed that this movement was sufficient to establish asportation. If there is a complete severance of the chattel from the possession of the person from whom it was taken, and the goods are actually carried away at least a short distance, this is sufficient to constitute taking and asportation, even if possession of the taker is immediately interrupted.[5]

4. Personal Property

At common law, and in some states today, larceny is limited to theft of goods and chattels. Under this definition, it is not larceny to carry away real property such as trees, crops, minerals, and fixtures that are part of realty. According to the definition of larceny, unless a statute modifies the common law, one cannot be found guilty of larceny if items such as stocks, bonds, checks, and promissory notes were the subject of the taking. The statutes in most states today have expanded the scope of larceny by modifying the definition of property, or by including additional offenses that prohibit the taking of specific items of real property as well as intangibles and negotiable instruments.

5. Of Another

To constitute larceny, the property taken must be property of another person. That is, it must be owned by or in the possession of someone other than the thief. It is not essential that the thief know who the owner is; it is sufficient if he knows that the property is not his own and takes it in order to deprive the true owner of the property. As one court indicated, it is not that the property belongs to or is owned by a specific person or entity, but rather that it is the property of someone other than the thief.[6] Also, it makes no difference that the property stolen belongs to one person or several persons jointly or to several persons each owning separate parts thereof.[7] All that is necessary is that the prosecution include a description of the property for purposes of identification and to show ownership in a person or persons other than the accused.

6. With Intent to Steal

The *mens rea* for larceny is intent to permanently deprive the owner of his or her property. This element may be difficult to prove. If the defense introduces evidence to show that the property was taken for temporary use only, the jury could find that the suspect lacked the intent to steal as required for the crime of larceny. One court explained that it is the *intent* to return the property, but not its *actual return*, that constitutes a defense in larceny.[8] Further, to constitute larceny, the intent to steal must exist at the time of the taking; that is, the taker must have a conscious purpose to steal that which did not belong to him at the time he took the property and carried it away.[9]

B. Model Penal Code

In the Model Penal Code, all theft offenses are consolidated into a single offense. Traditional offenses designated as larceny, embezzlement, obtaining property by false pretenses, cheating, blackmail, extortion, fraudulent conversion, receiving stolen property, and others are not separated into individual statutory offenses.

After first explaining that the theft offenses are consolidated, the grading of theft offenses is detailed, affirmative defenses are enumerated, and for a purpose that is not sufficiently explained, reference is made to the fact that interspousal immunity is abolished except in narrowly specified circumstances.

> § 223.1 Consolidation of Theft Offenses; Grading; Provisions Applicable to Theft Generally[10]
>
> (1) Consolidation of Theft Offenses. Conduct denominated theft in this Article constitutes a single offense. An accusation of theft may be supported by evidence that it was committed in any manner that would be theft under this Article, notwithstanding the specification of a different manner in the indictment or information, subject only to the power of the Court to ensure fair trial by granting a continuance of other appropriate relief where the conduct of the defense would be prejudiced by lack of fair notice or by surprise.
>
> (2) Grading of Theft Offenses.
>   (a) Theft constitutes a felony of the third degree if the amount involved exceeds $500, or if the property stolen is a firearm, automobile, airplane, motorcycle, motorboat, or other motor-propelled vehicle, or in the case of theft by receiving stolen property, if the receiver is in the business of buying or selling stolen property.
>   (b) Theft not within the preceding paragraph constitutes a misdemeanor, except that if the property was not taken from the person or by threat, or in breach of a fiduciary obligation, and the actor proves by a preponderance of the evidence that the amount involved was less than $50, the offense constitutes a petty misdemeanor.
>   (c) The amount involved in a theft shall be deemed to be the highest value, by any reasonable standard, of the property or services which the actor stole or attempted to steal. Amounts involved in thefts committed pursuant to one scheme or course of conduct, whether from the same person or several persons, may be aggregated in determining the grade of the offense.

(3) Claim of Right. It is an affirmative defense to prosecution for theft that the actor:
    (a) was unaware that the property was that of another; or
    (b) acted under an honest claim of right to the property or service involved or that he had a right to acquire or dispose of it as he did; or
    (c) took property exposed for sale, intending to purchase and pay for it promptly, or reasonably believing that the owner, if present, would have consented.

(4) Theft from Spouse. It is no defense that theft was from the actor's spouse, except that misappropriation of household and personal effects, or other property normally accessible to both spouses, is theft only if it occurs after the parties have ceased living together.

§ 223.2 Theft by Unlawful Taking or Disposition

(1) Movable Property. A person is guilty of theft if he unlawfully takes, or exercises unlawful control over, movable property of another with purpose to deprive him thereof.

(2) Immovable Property. A person is guilty of theft if he unlawfully transfers immovable property of another or any interest therein with purpose to benefit himself or another not entitled thereto.

Section 223.2 of the Model Code does not use the term larceny, but has the same elements as common law larceny (as indicated in the parentheses). The elements of theft under the Model Penal Code are:

- unlawful (*the idea of trespass*)

- taking, or unlawfully exercising control over (*caption and asportation*)

- movable property (*expanded definition of property*)

- of another

- with the purpose to deprive him thereof (*intent to permanently deprive*)

As mentioned above, the concept of property has been expanded under the Model Penal Code. "Movable property" is defined in § 223.0 as "property, the location of which can be changed, including things growing on, affixed to, or found in land, and documents, although the rights represented thereby have no physical location." "Property of another" includes property in which any person other than the actor has an interest that the actor is not privileged to infringe, regardless of the fact that the actor also has an interest in the property, and regardless of the fact that the other person might be precluded from civil recovery because the property was used in an unlawful transaction or was subject to forfeiture as contraband.

The Model Penal Code also provides a definition of "deprive":

> (a) to withhold property of another permanently or for so extended a period as to appropriate a major portion of its economic value, or with intent to restore only upon payment of reward or other compensation, or
> (b) to dispose of the property so as to make it unlikely that the owner will recover it.[11]

With these definitions, it is readily apparent that the coverage of this statute is more comprehensive than the coverage of traditional larceny statute. For example, while the traditional statute applied only to personal property, this section includes a penalty for taking either personal or real property, including intangible property.

C. State Statutes, Codes, and Cases

Definitions by state courts differ, but the general elements are fairly consistent. Some examples will point out the differences and similarities:

- To constitute "larceny," there must be an unlawful acquisition of property with intention to convert it to the taker's use and an appropriation by one who took it.[12]

- "Larceny" is the wrongful taking and carrying away of personal property of another from any place, with a felonious intent to convert it to the taker's own use without consent of the owner.[13]

- Generally, "larceny" is the felonious taking and carrying away of personal property of another with intent on the part of the taker to convert it to his own use or to deprive the owner thereof.[14]

Many states have followed the Model Penal Code and consolidated most of the theft offenses into one statute. That is, what formerly was larceny, embezzlement, false pretenses and, in some instances, other statutory crimes are consolidated into one comprehensive provision. An example of a statute that consolidates many theft crimes is that of Kentucky.

> § 514.030—Theft by unlawful taking or disposition; penalties
>
> (1) Except as otherwise provided in KRS217.181 or 218A.1418, a person is guilty of theft by unlawful taking or disposition when he unlawfully:
>   (a) Takes or exercises control over movable property of another with intent to deprive him thereof; or
>   (b) Obtains immovable property of another or any interest therein with intent to benefit himself or another not entitled thereto.

(2) Theft by unlawful taking or disposition is a Class A misdemeanor unless the value of the property is three hundred dollars ($300) or more, in which case it is a Class D felony; or unless:
   (a) The property is a firearm (regardless of the value of the firearm), in which case it is a Class D felony; or
   (b) The property is anhydrous ammonia (regardless of the value of the ammonia), in which case it is a Class D felony unless it is proven that the person violated this section with the intent to manufacture methamphetamine in violation of KRS218A.1432, in which case it is a Class B felony for the first offense and a Class A felony for each subsequent offense.[15]

Under the provisions of this statute and other similar statutes and codes, the elements are: taking or exercising control, movable property of another, with intent to deprive; or obtaining immovable property of another or any interest therein or with intent to benefit him or to benefit another not entitled to the property. "Deprive," as used in this statute, is similar to the Model Penal Code's definition: it means to "withhold property of another permanently, or for so extended a period as to appropriate a major portion of its economic value or with intent to restore only upon payment of reward or other compensation, or to dispose of the property so as to make it unlikely that the owner will recover it."[16]

Some state statutes enumerate the types of personal property that are subject to larceny. For instance, part of the Michigan statute provides:

750.356. Larceny

Sec. 356. (1) A person who commits larceny . . . by stealing any of the following property of another person is guilty of a crime as provided in this section:
   (a) Money, goods, or chattels.
   (b) A bank note, bank bill, bond, promissory note, due bill, bill of exchange or other bill, draft, order, or certificate.
   (c) A book of accounts for or concerning money or goods due, to become due, . . . or to be delivered.
   (d) A deed or writing containing a conveyance of land or other valuable contract in force.
   (e) A receipt, release, or defeasance.
   (f) A writ, process, or public record.[17]

Unlike Kentucky, which has a consolidated theft statute, Michigan covers theft in several larceny-related statutes, including: "larceny from motor vehicles or trailers; stealing firearms of another; theft of motor vehicle fuel; and larceny of a rented motor vehicle, trailer or other tangible property."[18]

States have had to expand the definition of property either by statute, as in the Michigan example, or by case law, because the types of valuable items today could hardly have been imagined by those who developed the common law. For instance, consider the following: a password to a bank account, electric power, cable service, food stamps, an algorithm, a telephone authorization code. Are these property and can their theft give rise to a conviction for larceny? State case law varies in the application of property to these and other items.[19]

The degree of punishment is determined by the *value* of the property as well as the *number* of previous theft convictions. As a general rule, the value of property is determined by applying the fair market value. Even if there is no legal market value for the personal property, value may be determined by other methods. For example, a Michigan case held that in a prosecution for larceny of more than $100 arising out of the defendant's theft of a deer carcass from a third person, expert testimony was properly allowed to establish the value of the carcass, even though no legal market existed for deer carcasses.[20]

Legal News

A Texas news item from the Palestine Herald Press indicates that cattle rustling is still a problem for ranchers. In this news story, a livestock broker received a telephone call offering the sale of a pen of cattle. The representative of the company met a couple at a cattle pen in rural Texas and instructed the company's agent where to mail the payment for the cattle. The driver became suspicious and located the true owner of the cattle who didn't know the purported "sellers" and didn't plan on selling his cattle. Today, instead of being "strung up" from the nearest tree, rustlers are arrested and charged with theft. In this case, if successful, the offenders would have committed theft (from the rancher) and theft by false pretenses (from the livestock broker).

Source: Retrieved on 1/30/2006 from http://www.palestineherald.com/local/local_story_028223002.html/resources_printstory.

D. Summary

The Model Penal Code and many states have consolidated theft statutes into one crime; however, even these statutes require proof of specific elements for each individual crime whether it is larceny, embezzlement, or theft by false pretenses. The general elements for larceny are indicated below.

Larceny

(A/R): Unlawful; taking; of property; of another; without permission

(M/R): Intent to permanently deprive (specific intent)

---

§ 8.3   Robbery

A. *Common Law*

Larceny is a lesser included crime of **robbery**. All the elements of larceny exist, with a couple added elements. The elements that distinguish robbery from larceny are:

1. the taking of property *from the person or presence* of the victim, and

2. the taking is accompanied by means of *force or threat of force.*

Robbery is a crime against property and an aggravated form of larceny, but it is also a crime against the person. There are valid arguments for treating the crime of robbery as an offense against the person; however, there are also arguments for considering it in the category of "offenses involving theft," because, most often, the primary objective of the actor is to take the personal property of another.

Legal News

O.J. Simpson was convicted of robbery and kidnapping in October 2008 for his role in a botched attempt to retrieve sports memorabilia. He and five other men, one of whom used a weapon, held the victims in a room and demanded the return of items that Simpson argued were his. The jury found that the state had proven all the elements of not only robbery, but also kidnapping. O.J. supporters argued that the jury was influenced by his acquittal almost 15 years ago in the death of his wife and Ronald Goldman.

Source: Friess, S. (2008). "Simpson's Path: Celebrity to Pariah to Afterthought." *Austin American-Statesman*, October 5, 2008:A1, A12.

Where the common law offense of robbery still exists, and in states where the term is not defined by statute, robbery consists of eight elements: the six elements of larceny plus two additional elements that are unique to robbery. These eight elements are listed and briefly described (or reviewed) here.

1. Trespass (From Possession and Against the Will)

Historically, one of the elements of robbery and larceny was that the thief took the property out of another's possession and against the will of one who had actual or constructive possession of it. However, it is not necessary that the victim of a robbery also be the owner of the goods taken, because robbery is an offense against the person who has either actual or constructive possession of the goods.[21]

2. Taking (Caption)

Taking is defined as securing dominion or absolute control over the property. At common law, this was called "caption." Before the crime of robbery or larceny is complete, the prosecution must offer evidence to show that the actor had actual physical caption; that is, he or she had dominion over the property and left no control in the owner or possessor. If the accused has not gained complete control of the property, there can be no caption or taking, even if he thinks he has the property in his possession.[22] In this case, the correct charge would be attempted robbery.

3. Carrying Away (Asportation)

The offense of robbery is not necessarily complete at the moment the stolen property is in the robber's possession, because robbery also includes the element of asportation. There must be such a carrying away or asportation as to supersede the possession of the owner for an appreciable time. If the prosecution can show that the person charged with robbery removed the property from the place it originally occupied, even for an instant and even to a small degree, this is sufficient asportation to constitute the offense.[23]

4. Personal Property

In proving this element, all that is necessary is that it is shown that the property is personal, as compared to real property. Generally, the type and value of the property taken are immaterial insofar as the offense of robbery is concerned. While the property must have some value, proof of a specific monetary value is not required.[24]

5. Of Another

To constitute robbery, evidence must be introduced to show that the ownership or right of possession of the property taken is vested in a person other than the taker. It is not necessary that the ownership of the property taken be in the person who was robbed; it is sufficient if he or she had exclusive possession of it at the time. For example, robbery was a proper charge when the defendant took money from the person of a filling station attendant, even though he was not the actual owner of the stolen property. This element is present, therefore, if the property is taken from a bailee, an agent, an employee, or other representative of the owner.[25]

6. With Intent to Steal

One of the most difficult elements to prove in the crimes of robbery and larceny is intent (*animus furandi*). Unless a statute changes the definition of the offense, robbery and larceny require specific intent. That is, evidence must be introduced to prove, beyond a reasonable doubt, that the accused intended to appropriate the property to a use inconsistent with the rights of the person from whom it was taken. Therefore, when the taking is under an honest, though mistaken, claim of ownership, or claim of a lawful right to possess the property, the crime is not robbery or larceny.[26]

The definition of robbery requires that there be intent to steal the personal property of another. This intent must be to deprive the owner, wholly and permanently, of his or her property. This element has resulted in some very technical distinctions. For example, in Arizona, a charge of robbery failed when the attempt was to collect a bona fide debt.[27] However, this defense is not available to a defendant when the amount he or she claims is uncertain. Therefore, in another case, the conviction for robbery was upheld even though the defendant claimed that he was seeking return of monies lost in an illegal card game. In this case, the appellate court held that the jury could have drawn an inference from the evidence that the defendant did not, in good faith, intend to take only money that he had lost, but additional money.[28] In discussing specific intent, a distinction has been made between reclaiming specific personal property and taking money claimed to be owed. Referring to a previous case, one court used the example that although a debtor may owe $100, and $100 is in the debtor's pocket, it is not the same $100 that belongs to the creditor, and the creditor may not take the money even if he or she intends to apply it to the debt.[29]

7. From the Person or Presence of Another

One of the elements that distinguishes robbery from larceny and justifies a more severe penalty is the aggravating element of taking from the person. Robbery requires more than a simple trespassory taking. The taking must be from the person or presence of the victim, as well as from his or her possession. Property is taken from the person if it is taken from his or her hand, pocket, clothing, or from a package in his or her hand. However, it is not required that the property be taken directly from the person. This element is complete if the property is taken from his or her presence, which includes the area under the victim's immediate control. "Presence" is not so much a matter of being within the view of the victim as it is a matter of proximity and control. The test is that the property taken in the robbery must be close enough to the victim and sufficiently under his control that, had the latter not been subjected to violence or intimidation by the robber, he or she could have prevented the taking.[30]

8. By Violence or Intimidation

The second additional element that distinguishes robbery from larceny is that the taking must involve some violence or intimidation. This has been explained in several ways. For example, one court indicated that "the taking must be against the will of the possessor accompanied by means of force or fear."[31] The particular means of force, or manner in which fear is imparted, is immaterial in determining this element of robbery.[32]

Violence is present, even if the force is very slight, if it is sufficient to achieve the purpose of the accused. The following may be sufficient to prove force was used:

- struggling with the victim;
- use of an intoxicant or drugs to make the victim compliant;
- intimidating/threatening the victim with or without a weapon.[33]

B. Model Penal Code

In the Model Code, robbery is considered under a separate heading from the consolidated theft statute because of the special elements of danger commonly associated with forcible theft from the person. Although only one robbery offense is defined, it includes aggravated behavior occurring in the course of committing a theft. For purposes of punishment, a grading scheme is included in the Model Penal Code. Robbery is a felony of the second degree, except that it is a felony of the first degree if, in the course of committing the theft, the actor attempts to kill anyone, or purposely inflicts, or attempts to inflict, serious bodily injury.

---

§ 222.1 Robbery[34]

(1) Robbery Defined. A person is guilty of robbery if, in the course of committing a theft, he:
  (a) inflicts serious bodily injury upon another; or
  (b) threatens another with or purposely puts him in fear of immediate serious bodily injury; or
  (c) commits or threatens immediately to commit any felony of the first or second degree.

An attempt shall be deemed "in the course of committing a theft" if it occurs in an attempt to commit theft, or in flight, after the attempt or commission.

(2) Grading. Robbery is a felony of the second degree, except that it is a felony of the first degree if in the course of committing the theft the actor attempts to kill anyone, or purposely inflicts or attempts to inflict serious bodily injury.

"In the course of committing a theft" includes an attempt to commit theft or flight after the attempt or commission. In addition to the infliction or threatened infliction of serious bodily harm, which is the usual statutory provision, the Model Code provides an alternative. Even if there is no actual threat against the personal safety of the victim, the offender can be found guilty of robbery if, in the course of committing the theft, he commits or threatens to commit any other felony of the first or second degree.

The traditional requirement of "taking from the person" has not been included in Model Penal Code §222.1. Also, the Model Code, following the lead of some of the pre-Model Code statutory provisions of the various states, has eliminated the "intent to permanently deprive" requirement.

C. State Statutes, Codes, and Cases

Some of the contemporary statutes are the same as the Model Penal Code, and some have used parts of the wording of the Model Code. As a result of the technical requirements of robbery under the common law, state statutes have modified the elements. These changes make it possible to prosecute persons for crimes in which the technical elements, such as asportation, may not be present.

1. Taking and Asportation

The taking requirement is obviously still very much an element of modern statutes and case law concerning robbery. Taking requires custody and control, but not necessarily physical possession. For instance, if the robber obtains keys to a car through the threat of force, he, not the victim, has constructive control over the car and the robbery would be complete. Some state statutes still include the common law element of asportation; however, case law has virtually eliminated the requirement of proof because any distance, however, slight, will be defined as asportation.

> **CASE:** *Lattimore v. United States,* 684 A.2d 357 (D.C. App. 1996)
>
> What was the issue in this case?
>
> Did the court require asportation?
>
> What distance meets the definition of asportation?

2. Personal Property of Another

As with larceny, the definition of property has been expanded from the common law definition to include intangibles, negotiable instruments, and other items of value.

3. With Intent to Permanently Deprive

Recall that, under common law, in order to be convicted of robbery, specific intent must be proven. That is, it must be proven that the defendant intended the actions (i.e., putting the victim in fear) and intended the conse-quence (to acquire the personal property and to permanently deprive the victim of their property). Because the intent element has been difficult to prove, resulting in the miscarriage of justice, states have modified this element in their statutes. For example, in Florida, the legislature expanded the scope of robbery by eliminating the requirement of specific intent. The supreme court of that state upheld a conviction of robbery under the statute that defines robbery as the "taking of money or other property from the person or custody of another by force."[35] This means that there is no need to prove that the defendant meant to permanently deprive the victim, only that there was a taking.

4. Using Force or Threat of Force from their Person or in their Presence

Although it is not necessary to prove *both* force and intimidation, both *may* be used together to constitute robbery, if acted upon by the victim and the property is given to the defendant. Both state and federal courts have been called upon to decide whether "pocket picking," without the knowledge of the victim, is robbery. Generally speaking, pocket picking is not robbery, because the element of violence or intimidation is not present. However, if there is a struggle by the owner to maintain possession, this element will be present and the actions could amount to robbery. For example, in a 1978 case, a defendant, attempting to snatch the pocketbook of a woman standing on a subway platform, was met with resistance, and the ensuing struggle resulted in the woman being hit by the train. The court reasoned that, while purse-snatching, when unaccompanied by resistance on the part of the victim, generally is not sufficient to constitute robbery, there was, in this case, sufficient evidence to support a jury finding that the victim resisted by clinging to her purse, and that the overcoming of this resistance through the use of overwhelming momentum of the train, constituted attempted robbery.[36]

In other cases, juries and courts are called upon to determine whether there has been sufficient intimidation or threat of force to constitute robbery. For instance, in a Texas case, the defendant/appellant entered a convenience store, selected a piece of bubble gum, and placed the gum and a dime on the front counter. When the clerk, who was the only person in the store, opened the register to ring up the sale, the appellant placed his hands inside the register drawer. The clerk grabbed the appellant's wrist and said, "what are you doing?" The frightened clerk released her grip on the appellant, who quickly grabbed two $10 bills and a $20 bill and then ran out of the store. The defendant was convicted of robbery and appealed, claiming that the evidence was insufficient to prove the complaining witness was put in fear of imminent bodily injury or death.

The reviewing court, citing previous cases, held that "fear must arise from the conduct of the accused rather than the mere temperamental timidity of the victim," and "in order to prove the offense of robbery, there must have been actual or threatened violence to the person, or intimidation of such a nature that the threatened or injured party was put in fear." The court then noted that the jury believed that the appellant's actions were calculated to and did invoke the requisite fear. While admitting that the question was a close one, the court found that the appellant's "menacing glance" and "clenched fists" constituted intentionally threatening conduct sufficient to cause fear of imminent bodily injury sufficient to part with property. In making the decision, the court took into consideration the fact that the defendant was five feet ten inches tall and was "huskily built," while the clerk was a "not very tall" woman in her late thirties.[37]

Another issue in determining whether robbery has occurred is when the force was applied. Some states require that the force occur before or at the same time as the taking of property; otherwise, it is not robbery. For instance, if a shoplifter takes property from a store, runs out of the store and struggles with a security guard, knocking the guard to the ground; in some states, this would be prosecuted as larceny and assault because the robbery statute requires the force be used to obtain the property. Other states, however, have statutes that describe the use of force as occurring at any time during the taking and, in these states, force used in escape would meet the definition of robbery.

5. Examples of Statutes

Many states, including Texas, differentiate degrees of robbery based upon the seriousness of the injury that has been caused. Aggravated robbery is a more serious crime with more serious punishment. If the bodily injury is "serious," or if a deadly weapon is used, then the offense is aggravated robbery and is graded as a felony in the first degree.

§ 29.02 Robbery[38]

(a) A person commits an offense if, in the course of committing theft as defined in Chapter 31 of this Code and with intent to obtain or maintain control of the property, he:
   (1) intentionally, knowingly, or recklessly causes bodily injury to another; or
   (2) intentionally or knowingly threatens or places another in fear of imminent bodily injury or death.

(b) An offense under this Section is a felony of the second degree.

§ 29.03 Aggravated Robbery

(a) A person commits an offense if he commits robbery as defined in § 29.02 of this code, and he:
   (1) causes serious bodily injury to another;
   (2) uses or exhibits a deadly weapon; or
   (3) causes bodily injury to another person or threatens or places another person in fear of imminent bodily harm or death, if the other person is:

(A) 65 years of age or older; or

(B) a disabled person

(b) An offense under this section is a felony of the first degree.

(c) In this section, "disabled person" means an individual with a mental, physical, or developmental disability who is substantially unable to protect himself from harm.

In states that have provisions that increase the penalty if an aggravating factor is the use of a "deadly weapon," case law must be examined to determine how that phrase is defined. The Texas court, in making this determination, found that a weapon is "deadly" if it is capable of causing serious bodily injury in the manner of its use, without regard to whether the actual result is infliction of serious bodily injury.[39] One would assume that a gun or a knife would always be a dangerous weapon but that is not the case. In one Texas case, the court distinguished a firearm and a gun; holding that a "gun" is a much broader term than "firearm" and may include such non-lethal instruments as BB guns, blowguns, popguns, and grease guns. Thus, because the statute's definition of a dangerous weapon specified a firearm, it was necessary to prove that the defendant used a firearm, not simply a gun.[40] Another Texas court found that, while a knife could be a deadly weapon, a pocketknife with a two-inch blade was not a deadly weapon and thus the defendant could not be convicted of aggravated robbery.[41]

In Illinois, the statute includes the term "armed robbery" to designate the more serious crime, providing that a person commits armed robbery if the robbery is committed while the person is armed with a dangerous weapon. Armed robbery in Illinois is a Class A felony for which the offender may be sentenced to death.[42] In determining what is a dangerous weapon, an Illinois court decided that a utility knife used in an armed robbery was a "dangerous weapon" when it had a six-inch grip with a one-inch, heavy-duty, single-edge, sharp blade, and where the blade was in a fully exposed position when used. However, a sharp fingernail is not a dangerous weapon as used in this statute, because no portion of the human anatomy is legally a dangerous weapon. Pepper spray that the defendant sprayed on the victims during a bank robbery was a "dangerous weapon," so as to sustain an armed robbery conviction, where the spray temporarily incapacitated the victims and the effects did not wear off completely until several hours after the robbery.[43]

State courts have also dealt with the issue of the use of toy guns. Note that it is a different question as to whether a toy gun constitutes the force or threat of force necessary as an element of the crime of robbery (it does because the threat is from the viewpoint of the victim), and whether a toy gun is a "dangerous weapon" that would increase the severity of the offense to an aggravating category (case decisions are mixed). While a toy gun may not constitute aggravated robbery, an unloaded gun[44] has been defined as a dangerous weapon because, according to the court, it can be used to bludgeon the victim.[45]

Recall that, under party liability principles, those who participate in the offense of armed robbery or aggravated robbery may be convicted even if they were not present when the robbery took place. For instance, in one case, the defendant was convicted of armed robbery because he drove two men to the victim's home, dropped them off, waited nearby, and picked them up as they fled the victim's home after robbing and shooting him.[46] In another case, a federal court agreed with the lower court that evidence was sufficient to support the defendant's conviction for aiding and abetting an armed bank robbery although the defendant was not in the bank at the time the robberies occurred, as the defendant drove the vehicle for the co-defendants, and there was evidence that the use of firearms was discussed during the planning stage of the crime and the defendant was in a position to observe the actual use of firearms in at least some of the robberies.[47]

Legal News

Crimes seem to occur (or at least be reported to occur) in waves and two examples of this seem to be "home invasions" and "carjackings." Both of these crimes are a type of robbery, although home invasions are sometimes mistakenly categorized as burglaries and **carjackings** are mistakenly categorized as auto theft. The intentional use of force or threat of force to accomplish the theft is what sets these crimes apart and, arguably, makes the crimes much more serious than the theft alternatives. Some states have addressed carjackings and home invasions by special statutes, such as Florida's home-invasion robbery statute (Florida Statute § 775.021).

D. Summary

Remember that robbery is larceny with the addition of two elements: the taking must be from the person or the presence of the victim, and there is a use of force or threat of force. The major changes between the common law and modern statutes are that it is not necessary to prove specific intent to permanently deprive, nor is it necessary in most states to show that the property was moved any appreciable distance. In general, the crime of robbery is more straightforward today, with fewer technical problems in prosecuting it. Many states have identified a more serious form of robbery when the victim is injured, when deadly weapons are used, or other elements are present.

Robbery

(A/R) Taking, property, of another, without permission, in presence or from person, with force or threat of force

(M/R) Intentional (specific intent)

§ 8.4   Embezzlement

At common law, if there was no "trespass," because the property came into the possession of the taker lawfully even though he later appropriated the property against the owner's desire, then the person who committed the wrong would often go unpunished. To fill this void, the English Parliament in 1799 and later, states, by legislative action, enacted laws creating the crime of embezzlement. In **embezzlement**, the perpetrator acquires possession of the property lawfully, but converts it to his or her own use. As the chief distinction between larceny and embezzlement lies in the manner of acquiring possession of the property, emphasis is on this distinction. To reiterate, in embezzlement, the property comes lawfully into the possession of the taker but is later fraudulently or unlawfully appropriated by him.

A. *Common Law*

As stated above, there was no crime of embezzlement under the common law. Early as well as recent decisions agree that the offense of embezzlement did not exist at common law and is purely a statutory offense.[48]

B. *Model Penal Code*

Recall that the Model Penal Code consolidated all theft offenses; therefore, embezzlement is one type of theft as described. In addition, Section 223.8 of the Model Penal Code provides for a specific type of embezzlement:

---

§ 223.8 Theft by Failure to Make Required Disposition of Funds Received

A person who purposely obtains property upon agreement, or subject to a known legal obligation, to make specified payment or other disposition, whether from such property or its proceeds or from his own property to be reserved in equivalent amount, is guilty of theft if he deals with the property obtained as his own and fails to make the required payment or disposition. The foregoing applies notwithstanding that it may be impossible to identify particular property as belonging to the victim at the time of the actor's failure to make the required payment or disposition. An officer or employee of the government or of a financial institution is presumed:

(i) to know any legal obligation relevant to his criminal liability under this Section, and

(ii) to have dealt with the property as his own if he fails to pay or account upon lawful demand, or if an audit reveals a shortage or falsification of accounts.

Under the Model Code, the conduct proscribed consists essentially of two elements: (1) obtaining property upon an agreement and/or subject to a known legal obligation to make a specified payment or other disposition; and (2) dealing with the property as one's own and failing to make the required payment or disposition.

C. State Statutes, Codes, and Cases

Although there is a considerable difference in the scope and wording of the statutes of various states defining embezzlement, both regarding the person liable and the kind of property protected, all statutes, as well as the courts, include *wrongful appropriation* or **conversion** as a common element. Some definitions by various courts will help in developing a definition of the offense of embezzlement.

- The crime of "embezzlement" builds on the concept of conversion, but adds two further elements; first, embezzled property must have been in lawful possession of the defendant at the time of its appropriation, and second, "embezzlement" requires knowledge that the appropriation is contrary to the wishes of the owner of the property.[49]

- "Embezzlement" is the wrongful appropriation or conversion of property where the original taking was lawful or with consent of the owner.[50]

To sustain a conviction of "embezzlement," it must be shown that the accused was the "agent" or "bailee" of the victim and had, at one time, lawfully possessed the victim's property but then intentionally converted the victim's property to his own use. The four elements of embezzlement are as follows:

1. Fraudulent Intent

There must be intent on the part of the defendant to unlawfully convert the property. Generally, the fraudulent intent required as an element may be found from the acts of the defendant in using or disposing of the property. As an example, when an official of a union had control of union property, directed the sale of the property, and appropriated part of the proceeds to his own use, he was guilty of embezzlement, because the intent was clear from the actions of the official.[51] Some state statutes require evidence of an intent to "permanently" deprive the owner of the property.[52]

In a Michigan case, the court considered the element of "intent" as used in the Michigan statute.[53] The court explained that proving fraudulent intent by showing lack of consent of the owner is necessary only when the perpetrator hides the property but has not yet converted it. In all other cases, conversion will go to prove lack of consent of the true owner.

2. Appropriation or Conversion

The essence of the crime of embezzlement is that the wrongdoer has the money or other property of another person that comes into his hands legally but is not used as intended by the owner. To constitute wrongful appropriation or conversion, there must be a serious act of interference with the owner's rights. While damage to the property does not amount to conversion or appropriation, selling it, pledging it, giving it away, delivering it to one not entitled to it, claiming it against the owner, unreasonably withholding possession of it from the owner, or spending it (in the case of money) is conversion. To prove this element, the prosecution must establish that the accused converted funds to his own use or to the benefit of another; mere receipt of funds and failure to account for them is not enough.[54]

3. By One in Lawful Possession

To constitute embezzlement, there must be an actual and lawful possession or custody of property of another by virtue of some trust, duty, agency, or employment of the accused, otherwise it is larceny.[55] The very essence of the crime of embezzlement is that the property was converted by one who was entrusted with the property or into whose hands it lawfully came. A common example is conversion by a bank employee who embezzles, purloins, or willfully misapplies bank funds that have come into his or her possession through his or her employment. However, agents, executors, and administrators may also be charged with violating embezzlement statutes.

Even an attorney may be guilty of embezzling the money of his or her client that comes into his or her possession during the course of business.[56] For instance, in the case of *Commonwealth v. Turrell*, an attorney was charged with violation of the Pennsylvania embezzlement statute, which contains almost exactly the same wording as the Model Penal Code. The attorney had accepted funds to hold "for his client" but commingled those funds with his own. The court held that the attorney's commingling of the client's funds transmitted to the attorney for payment to a designated third party in itself does not constitute a crime. However, when the payment was due and the attorney failed to transmit the funds in his possession, the attorney evinced an intent not to make the required payment, thereby meeting the definition of embezzlement.[57]

4. Property of Another

In some statutes, the property that is the subject of theft (and embezzlement) is limited to personal property. In others, "property" includes both real and personal property. And in still others, "property" is defined as personal property and real property that has been "severed." In general, recall that modern statutes have expanded the restrictive common law definition of property in theft statutes.

As in the case of larceny, to constitute embezzlement, the property must be "property of another." In order to prove a violation of an embezzlement statute, the prosecution must prove that the property was that of a person other than the accused. The traditional rule is that a person cannot be guilty of converting his or her own property. Therefore, if both possession and title of the property have been passed to the defendant prior to the alleged conversion, the defendant cannot properly be convicted of embezzlement. Further, the defendant must know that the property is owned by another because the *mens rea* is to intentionally convert another's property.[58]

5. Examples of Statutes

Some states still have not consolidated the crimes of embezzlement and larceny. An example of such a statute is that of Michigan, which provides:

> 750.174. Embezzlement[59]
>
> Sec. 174. (1) A person who as the agent, servant, or employee of another person, governmental entity within this state, or other legal entity or who as the trustee, bailee, or custodian of the property of another person, governmental entity within this state, or other legal entity fraudulently disposes of or converts to his or her own use, or takes or secretes with the intent to convert to his or her own use without the consent of his or her principal, any money or other personal property of his or her principal that has come to that person's possession or that is under his or her charge or control by virtue of his or her being an agent, servant, employee, trustee, bailee, or custodian, is guilty of embezzlement.

The Michigan statute includes an elaborate penalty section based on the value of the property stolen and the number of prior convictions. In addition to this general embezzlement statute, Michigan law includes other embezzlement statutes that provide penalties for embezzlement of specific types of property.[60]

D. *Summary*

Embezzlement is a crime that did not exist under the common law. Embezzlement was created to cover situations in which the defendant was entrusted with the property of another but converted it to his own use. Many states followed the Model Penal Code and incorporated embezzlement into a general theft statute; however, embezzlement still exists as a separate statute in other states. The separate elements of embezzlement are noted below.

Embezzlement	
A/R	Conversion or appropriation, of property of another, lawfully obtained
M/R	Intent to deprive lawful owner (specific intent)

§ 8.5 Obtaining Property by False Pretenses

A. Common Law

Recall that the crime of embezzlement did not exist under the common law. The same is true for obtaining property by **false pretenses**. Common law larceny covered only situations in which the defendant intruded upon the personalty of the rightful owner by a "taking." Common law did not define as crimes situations in which the perpetrator obtains title and possession of the property by means of deception.

In 1757, the British Parliament created the crime of false pretenses to protect victims of unscrupulous criminals who used deception to obtain property. It defined as criminal the person who obtains property of another "knowingly and designedly, by false pretense or pretenses, with intent to cheat or defraud any person or persons of the same."[61] The essence of the crime of obtaining money or property by false pretenses is that the victim transfers the title to the property to the wrongdoer under the influence of false pretenses.[62]

B. Model Penal Code

The Model Penal Code designates the crime we have been calling "false pretenses" as "**theft by deception**." Even though the words are different, many of the elements that existed under the traditional statutes continue as requirements in the Model Code. For example, under the Model Code, the actor must purposely obtain the property of another and must purposely deceive. These are substitutes for "knowledge" and "intent" as used in some pre-Model Code statutes.

§ 223.3 Theft by Deception[63]

A person is guilty of theft if he purposely obtains property of another by deception. A person deceives if he purposely:

(1) creates or reinforces a false impression, including false impressions as to law, value, intention or other state of mind; but deception as to a person's intention to perform a promise shall not be inferred from the fact alone that he did not subsequently perform the promise; or

(2) prevents another from acquiring information which would affect his judgment of a transaction; or

> (3) fails to correct a false impression which the deceiver previously created or reinforced, or which the deceiver knows to be influencing another to whom he stands in a fiduciary or confidential relationship; or
>
> (4) fails to disclose a known lien, adverse claim or other legal impediment to the enjoyment of property which he transfers or encumbers in consideration for the property obtained, whether such impediment is or is not valid, or is or is not a matter of official record.

The Model Penal Code clarifies some of the questions that existed prior to the time that it was adopted. For example, "deception," as used in the Model Code, includes not only creating a false impression, but reinforcing a false impression that the victim may have entertained prior to the intervention by the actor. The term "deceive" does not, however, include falsity as to matters having no pecuniary significance. The crime also does not criminalize what is known as "**puffery**," which refers to exaggerations or statements unlikely to deceive ordinary persons in the group addressed. Many salespeople, for instance, may make exaggerated claims of the product's effects (i.e., perfumes or aftershaves that will make one irresistible to the opposite sex). If one buys the product based on such claims, it does not mean that the salesperson is guilty of theft by deception because a "reasonable" person would not believe the exaggerations.

It is not necessary to show that there was a pecuniary loss by the victim. In interpreting § 405(2) of the Utah statute, which was modeled after this section of the Model Penal Code, a Utah court found that this subsection does not support the contention that pecuniary loss must be an element of the crime of theft by deception. In this case, the Supreme Court of Utah upheld a conviction of theft by deception where the defendant made false representations that he would invest the victim's money in gold and would clear the title to the land used to secure the transaction.[64]

C. State Statutes, Codes, and Cases

While the courts, prior to the Model Penal Code, reached some consensus in defining the offense of false pretenses, the wording of the definitions differed. Some examples will point out these differences and similarities.

- A "false pretense" may consist of any act, word, symbol, or token calculated and intended to deceive, and it may be made either expressly or by implication.[65]

- A "false pretense" may be defined as the false representation of a subsisting fact, whether by oral or written words or conduct, that is calculated to deceive, intended to deceive, and that does, in fact, deceive, and by means of which one person obtains value from another without compensation.[66]

While some recently revised state codes contain most of the provisions of the Model Penal Code, some others contain only parts of these provisions and some states still use the traditional terminology and definitions. The elements of the crime of obtaining money or property under false pretenses (or simply "false pretenses") are, generally, as follows:

1. Obtaining Money, Goods, or Things of Value of Another

Generally, this element is defined in broad terms either by statute or case decisions. In some states, specific articles were enumerated in the statute, while others used such terms as "valuable thing" or "other property." One approach is to consider property that can be obtained by false pretenses in the same class of property that is the subject of larceny. However, some statutes broadened this to include such things as promissory notes, bills of exchange, checks, and other securities.[67] After discussing the definition of "things of value," one court noted that the crime of false pretenses is committed when a chattel, money, or a valuable security is obtained from another by making a false representation with intent to defraud and with knowledge of its falsity.[68]

2. By False Representation

The general rule is that the representation must be false as to facts, past or present. In many early statutes, a statement that something would happen in the future or a mere promise to do something was not considered sufficient. However, a number of states and the general modern trend indicate that "false promises" could equate to false pretenses.[69]

The crime also does not cover other misdeeds where no false misrepresentations have been made. Where a defendant received $600 from a homeowner for work that could have been done for $25, this was not false pretenses, even though ethically indefensible.[70] The court advised that an essential element of the crime is a fraudulent misrepresentation and, in this case, there was no evidence of any misrepresentation. Obviously, the defendant needs to know that he is misrepresenting a fact. If he believes what he is saying, there is no misrepresentation, even if it is untrue.

3. With Intent to Defraud the Owner

The mental element of the crime of false pretenses has two essential phases:

- that the defendant knew the representations which he made to be untrue, and

- that he made them with intent to defraud.

The prosecution has the responsibility to prove *knowledge of the falsity of the statements* on the part of the defendant.[71]

The prosecution must introduce evidence to show that the defendant knew that his or her representation was untrue *and* he or she made it with the intent to defraud.[72] A Texas court explained that there must be *intent* to cheat or defraud, but that this may be inferred from false representations.[73] However, it is not necessary to prove an intent to permanently deprive in many state statutes.[74]

4. Examples of State Statutes

In some states, the traditional crime of false pretenses is incorporated into the theft statute. For example, in the state of Ohio, theft by deception is a part of § 2913.02. This section provides:

(A) No person, with purpose to deprive the owner of property or services, shall knowingly obtain or exert control over either the property or the services in any of the following ways:
  (1) Without the consent of the owner or the person authorized to give consent;
  (2) Beyond the scope of the express or implied consent of the owner or person authorized to give consent;
  (3) By deception;
  (4) By threat.[75]

Under the provisions of this statute, the elements of the crime are similar to traditional larceny elements, except that control over the property is obtained by deception rather than by taking.[76]

Another approach was taken when the Kentucky General Assembly drafted a similar provision. This section provides:

§ 514.040—Theft by deception.[77]

(1) A person is guilty of theft by deception when he obtains property or services of another by deception with intent to deprive him thereof. A person deceives when he intentionally:

  (a) creates or reinforces a false impression, including false impressions as to law, value, intention or other state of mind; or
  (b) prevents another from acquiring information which would affect his judgment of a transaction; or
  (c) fails to correct a false impression which the deceiver previously created or reinforced or which the deceiver knows to be influencing another with whom he stands in a fiduciary or confidential relationship; or
  (d) fails to disclose a known lien, adverse claim or other legal impediment to the enjoyment of property which he transfers or encumbers in consideration for the property obtained, whether such impediment is or is not valid or is or is not a matter of official record; or
  (e) issues or passes a check or similar sight order for the payment of money, knowing that it will not be honored by the drawee.

The key word that distinguishes this crime from others is "deception." Deception, as used in the statute, is broadly defined and specifically includes creating or reinforcing a false impression, preventing another from acquiring information that would affect his judgment of a transaction, failing to correct a false impression, failing to disclose a known lien or other adverse claim and, finally, issuing or passing a check or other order for the payment of money, knowing that it will not be honored by the drawee.

In an interesting Georgia case, a police officer-defendant was charged with eight counts of misdemeanor theft by deception based on allegations that he had obtained wages from two employers (one being the city police department) through the creation of a false impression of fact by working for both of them during the same period. A Georgia appellate court overturned his conviction, stating that if he did not have a contract that specifically said that he could not work for another party during his employment hours, then it was not larceny by deception.[78]

The Georgia Court of Appeals stated that the offense of theft by deception is defined in O.C.G.A. § 16-8-3 as follows:

(a) A person commits the offense of theft by deception when he obtains property by any deceitful means or artful practice with the intention of depriving the owner of the property.
(b) A person deceives if he intentionally: (1) Creates or confirms another's impression of an existing fact or past event which is false and which the accused knows or believes to be false; . . .
(c) "Deceitful means" and "artful practice" do not, however, include falsity as to matters having no pecuniary significance.

The charge of theft of property by deception is appropriate if a contractor fails to perform promised work where the evidence indicates that the promise was made *with the intention* not to perform. In the case of *Baker v. State*, the defendant failed to perform his contractual promise to remodel a person's home. The court found that this was a violation of the statute and that the jury could infer the necessary intent to defraud from the defendant's evasive conduct, delaying tactics, admission that he had spent the victim's money without purchasing materials, and repeated requests for additional money.[79]

Legal News

A news item in 2004 described a teenager who received more than $4,500 from ebay purchasers who thought they were buying a video card from him. Twenty victims paid their money and received nothing. This case is representative of the growth of Internet purchasing and Internet crime. It is high-tech larceny by trick or false pretenses. The 19-year-old faces 40 years in prison and $20,000 in fines.

(Source: Retrieved on 6/29/06 from www.usatoday.com/tech/news/2004-03-12-teen-ebay-scamx._htm.)

D. Summary

False pretenses differs from larceny and embezzlement in that the rightful owner of the property freely hands over title (or money) to the offender, but the transfer occurs because of the deceptive statements of the offender. While not a crime at common law, the offense was defined early as the type of dishonest act that needed to be punished by criminal law. However, it should be clear that "false pretenses" or "theft by deception" does not cover merely unethical business practices, i.e., charging more than the average cost for a product or service to a naïve customer; making vague or ridiculous promises of what might happen when one buys a product, and so on. The general elements of the crime are indicated below.

Obtaining Property by False Pretenses

A/R   Obtaining money, goods, or things of value of another; by false representation; knowing the same to be false

M/R   Intent to defraud (specific intent)

---

§ 8.6   Extortion

A. Common Law

The traditional definition of **extortion** was obtaining money or other things of value by the misuse of official power or position.[80] Extortion was a misdemeanor and could only be committed by officials when they misused their position. The elements of extortion were expanded by early statutes to include what we now think of as blackmail. While robbery is defined as obtaining property through force or threats of force; the common law was silent in situations where threats were other than physical injury, such as threats to one's reputation. Further, robbery requires a present or immediate threat of force, not some future injury. Therefore, early statutes expanded common law to include these traditional elements:

- Obtaining money or property. As in theft, usually the property must be personal property;

- By threats or coercion. The threat may be either oral or written, and may even be by innuendo or suggestions, but it must be such as would ordinarily create alarm;

- To perform certain enumerated acts. Specific acts that must be threatened by the perpetrator are often enumerated. One that was common to most statutes is "to injure the person or property of the individual threatened."

B. Model Penal Code

Recall that the Model Penal Code consolidated all theft statutes. Extortion is considered a type of theft. The Model Penal Code provides that a person is guilty of theft if he purposely obtains property of another by threatening to do one of the seven specific acts enumerated. The list of acts in the Model Code is similar to some used in states prior to the time the Model Code was written. The Model Code does contain a residual provision (Subsection 7) that was not included in most state legislation and makes the Model Code more comprehensive in its application.

---

§ 223.4 Theft by Extortion[81]

A person is guilty of theft if he purposely obtains property of another by threatening to:

(1) inflict bodily injury on anyone or commit any other criminal offense; or
(2) accuse anyone of a criminal offense; or
(3) expose any secret tending to subject any person to hatred, contempt or ridicule, or to impair his credit or business repute; or
(4) take or withhold action as an official, or cause an official to take or withhold action; or
(5) bring about or continue a strike, boycott or other collective unofficial action, if the property is not demanded or received for the benefit of the group in whose interest the actor purports to act; or
(6) testify or provide information or withhold testimony or information with respect to another's legal claim or defense; or
(7) inflict any other harm which would not benefit the actor.

It is an affirmative defense to prosecution based on paragraphs (2), (3) or (4) that the property obtained by threat of accusation, exposure, lawsuit or other invocation of official action was honestly claimed as restitution or indemnification for harm done in the circumstances to which such accusation, exposure, lawsuit or other official action relates, or as compensation for property or lawful services. This means that a person does not commit extortion if they threaten legal action unless the opposing party pays some rightful claim (i.e., for property damage); however, it would be extortion if a person threatened to either offer or withhold testimony in a legal action unless an amount of money was paid.

C. State Statutes, Codes, and Cases

Modern statutes have expanded the crime of extortion to include what is generally called "blackmail." Extortion was originally limited to obtaining money or things of value through misuse of official power, while blackmail referred to obtaining money or property by a private individual. However, as more comprehensive statutes were written, the term blackmail became equivalent to and synonymous with extortion within the non-technical meaning of the term.[82] The crime of extortion under these statutes may be committed by a public officer under color of his or her office, or by a private individual. Generally, a person is guilty of extortion (or blackmail) if he or she obtains the property of another by threats or coercion. The elements are further discussed below:

1. Obtaining Money or Property of Another

As in theft, the definition of property has been expanded in modern statutes, but usually involves money or something of value.

2. By Threats or Coercion

The threat may be either oral or written, and may even be by innuendo or suggestions, but it must be such as would ordinarily create alarm. Obviously, it must be communicated to the victim in order to constitute extortion.

3. To Perform Certain Enumerated Acts (Or Not to Perform Duties Required by One's Office)

Specific acts that must be threatened by the perpetrator are often defined under the law. The statutes vary as to the type of threats that will suffice for the crime. Some examples of the types of threats that have been held to be actionable are threats to:

- unlawfully injure the person or property of the individual threatened or someone else,

- accuse the individual threatened or someone else of a crime, or

- expose any secret affecting the individual threatened or some other person.

4. The Threat Causes Victim to Surrender Property

To constitute extortion, there must be a causal connection between the threats and the victim surrendering the property. That is, it must be shown that the threat was the controlling factor in the victim's decision to part with the property.[83] However, case law also indicates that the extorter may be seeking a "benefit" that is intangible. Note that the example case concerns a threat in order to get the child-victim to recant her testimony of a sexual offense.

> **CASE: *Ohio v. Cunningham*,**
> **No. 08-CA-09 (Ohio App.,**
> **October 3, 2008)**
>
> What was the issue and holding of the case?
>
> What was the specific threat?
>
> What is the meaning of the term benefit?

5. Examples of State Statutes

Missouri's statute is an example of how extortion is dealt with in a consolidated theft statute.

§ 570.030 Stealing[84]

1. A person commits the crime of stealing if he or she appropriates property or services of another with the purpose to deprive him thereof, either without his or her consent or by means of deceit or coercion . . .

"Coercion" is defined under the Missouri statute as:

(3) "Coercion" means a threat, however communicated:

   (a) To commit any crime; or
   (b) To inflict physical injury in the future on the person threatened or another; or
   (c) To accuse any person of any crime; or
   (d) To expose any person to hatred, contempt or ridicule; or
   (e) To harm the credit or business repute of any person; or
   (f) To take or withhold action as a public servant, or to cause a public servant to take or withhold action; or
   (g) To inflict any other harm which would not benefit the actor.

A threat of accusation, lawsuit, or other invocation of official action is not coercion if the property sought to be obtained by virtue of such threat was honestly claimed as restitution or indemnification for harm done in the circumstances to which the accusation, exposure, lawsuit, or other official action relates, or as compensation for property or lawful service. The defendant shall have the burden of injecting the issue of justification as to any threat.[85]

In New York, the crime of extortion is also a part of the larceny statute. The part relating to extortion provides:

§ 155.05 Larceny; defined[86]

1. A person steals property and commits larceny when, with intent to deprive another of property or to appropriate the same to himself or to a third person, he wrongfully takes, obtains or withholds such property from an owner thereof.
2. Larceny includes a wrongful taking, obtaining or withholding of another's property, with the intent prescribed in subdivision (1) of this Section, committed in any of the following ways: . . .

   (e) By extortion.
   A person obtains property by extortion when he compels or induces another person to deliver such property to himself or to a third person by means of instilling in him a fear that, if the property is not so delivered, the actor or another will:

(i)　Cause physical injury to some person in the future; or

(ii)　Cause damage to property; or

(iii)　Engage in other conduct constituting a crime; or

(iv)　Accuse some person of a crime or cause criminal charges to be instituted against him; or

(v)　Expose a secret or publicize an asserted fact, whether true or false, tending to subject some person to hatred, contempt or ridicule; or

(vi)　Cause a strike, boycott or other collective labor group action injurious to some person's business; except that such a threat shall not be deemed extortion when the property is demanded or received for the benefit of the group in whose interest the actor purports to act; or

(vii)　Testify or provide information or withhold testimony or information with respect to another's legal claim or defense; or

(viii)　Use or abuse his position as a public servant by performing some act within or related to his official duties, or by failing or refusing to perform an official duty, in such manner as to affect some person adversely; or

(ix)　Perform any other act which would not in itself materially benefit the actor but which is calculated to harm another person materially with respect to his health, safety, business, calling, career, financial condition, reputation or personal relationships.

According to the provisions of this part of the statute, in addition to the intent element, the prosecution must show that the wrongful taking was by compelling or inducing another to deliver property to the person making the threat or to a third person by means of instilling fear. This last element (instilling fear) limits the application of the statute.

An issue that arises is how to distinguish extortion from expressing a legal right to demand compensation or seek redress for a wrong. It is not extortion when an aggrieved party threatens to sue; however, it is extortion when someone threatens to come forward with damaging information unless money is paid. The difference is in criminal intent. This issue was present when a young woman threatened to expose actor and comedian Bill Cosby as her biological father unless he paid her a large sum of money. He reported the threat to the authorities and Autumn Jackson was convicted of the federal extortion statute (we will read this case in Chapter 13, which covers federal crimes).

The court commented that the New York and federal extortion statutes applied to the defendant's conduct of sending an unsigned contract to the publisher to print the defendant's claim that she was the victim's child born out of wedlock, along with a demand for $40 million dollars from the victim, whose reputation was threatened, and that this was the precise kind of private transaction, motivated purely by selfish desire for gain, that the extortion statutes validly punish. Subsequently, the case was brought to trial and Jackson was convicted. Upon appeal, the circuit court agreed that the jury instructions should have included the definitional element of "wrongfulness" as a part of the definition of extortion; however, because it was ruled as harmless error, the conviction was ultimately upheld.[87]

Other courts have rendered decisions that explain or limit the scope of the extortion statutes. In Michigan, a conviction may be secured upon presentation of proof of a threat of immediate, continuing, or future harm.[88] In a North Carolina case, the court agreed that "a threat made in such a manner and with such circumstances that a reasonable person would believe the threat would be carried out" was the proper instruction.[89] And a Virginia case held that the defendant's assertion that he had a bona fide claim of right to money he was seeking to collect from the victim was not a defense to charges of attempted extortion.[90]

D. Summary

In modern statutes extortion can be committed either by a public official or a private citizen. Extortion occurs when a threat is made to perform an act (or not perform an act) that is made in order to obtain property from the victim unlawfully. If the perpetrator is an official, it is usually in relation to their duties or discretionary power; for instance, an officer of the court will threaten that prosecution will occur if money is not paid. If the perpetrator is an individual it usually involves a threat of injury—either physical or to the victim's reputation. Extortion does not occur when an individual has a legal right to demand just compensation and threatens legal action if compensation is not paid.

Extortion	
A/R	Obtain money or thing of value; by threats or coercion to perform or not perform enumerated acts; and property is given in response to threat
M/R	Intent (specific intent)

§ 8.7 Receiving Stolen Property

A. Common Law

Apparently, under the early English laws, there was no separate and distinct offense of **receipt of stolen property**, but the receiver was subject to indictment and punishment as an accessory to the theft itself. However, the English courts and legislative bodies soon recognized the necessity of creating a substantive crime that was indictable and punishable as an offense separate and distinct from the larceny.[91]

In an effort to reduce the theft of property by punishing those who received the stolen property, the drafters of legislation in this country enacted statutes very early that provided for the prosecution and punishment of those who knowingly aided the takers of property by purchasing the fruits of the crime. Some of the earlier offenses designated the crime of receiving stolen property a misdemeanor, but it was soon recognized that a light penalty was not enough to deter the "fence" (receiver of stolen property). Later statutes made the crime a felony.[92]

Although the terms of the early statutes varied, they generally included the elements of:

- receiving stolen property,

- knowing it to have been stolen,

- with the intent to deprive the owner of it.

The gravamen of the offense is the felonious receiving of stolen property belonging to another knowing that it has been stolen.[93]

B. Model Penal Code

The Model Penal Code retains the general provisions of the pre-Model Code statutes, with some exceptions that were the result of case decisions under the previous statutes. For example, the MPC recognized a defense that the property was ". . . received, retained, or disposed of with purpose to restore it to the owner." The Model Code also uses the words "retains," or "disposes" rather than the single word "receives," as used in previous statutes.

> § 223.6 Receiving Stolen Property[94]
>
> (1) Receiving. A person is guilty of theft if he purposely receives, retains, or disposes of movable property of another knowing that it has been stolen, or believing that it has probably been stolen, unless the property is received, retained, or disposed of with purpose to restore it to the owner. "Receiving" means acquiring possession, control of title, or lending on the security of the property.
> (2) Presumption of Knowledge. The requisite knowledge or belief is presumed in the case of a dealer who:
>
>   (a) is found in possession or control of property stolen from two or more persons on separate occasions; or
>   (b) has received stolen property in another transaction within the year preceding the transaction charged; or
>   (c) being a dealer in property of the sort received, acquires it for a consideration which he knows is far below its reasonable value.

In the Model Penal Code, the property that may be received, retained, or disposed of is limited to "movable property." Movable property is defined as "property, the location of which can be changed, including things growing on, affixed to, or found in land, and documents, although the rights represented thereof have no physical location."[95] Subsection (2) of the Model Code differs from some older statutes in that it details instances in which the requisite knowledge or belief is presumed to exist. This makes it easier to prove the elements of the crime and is apparently aimed also at making it less difficult to prosecute a fence who receives stolen property.

C. State Statutes, Codes, and Cases

Although all states have statutory provisions that prohibit receiving stolen property and provide a penalty for those who violate the statute, there are differences in the wording of the various statutes. Some, for example, use the word "receiving," which is the traditional term, while others define the prohibited conduct as "obtaining control over stolen property" or "criminal possession of stolen property." In fact, New York has five degrees of receiving stolen property.[96] As to culpability, some states require that the receiver "know that the property is stolen;" some provide that the receiver must "know or believe that the property has probably been stolen;" and others use the phrase "reasonable grounds for believing the property is stolen." As in other criminal cases, to prove the crime of receiving stolen property, the state must prove each element beyond a reasonable doubt to the exclusion of every reasonable hypothesis of innocence.[97] The elements of the crime differ to some extent from state to state, but some elements are common to most state statutes; these elements are:

- receipt of property;
- the property was actually stolen;
- the receiver knew at the time that such property had been stolen; and
- felonious intent on the part of the receiver.

1. Receipt of the Property

This has been interpreted to mean that the person has control over the property—not necessarily physical possession. Taking the property into constructive possession is sufficient; for example, where it was agreed that the property would be put in a place where the receiver would have access to it. Nor is it necessary that the receiver receive the stolen property directly from the thief. If he receives it from an innocent agent of the thief, it is the same as a direct conveyance, and if he knows the goods are stolen, he is guilty of receiving.[98] If the statute requires the state to prove that the object received had value, evidence to that effect must be introduced.

2. The Property Must Have Been Stolen

To constitute the crime, the goods must have been stolen and the character of the goods, as stolen goods, must exist at the time they are received. This element is not present if they are, in fact, not stolen goods, even though the receiver may have believed them to be stolen. The state must also show that the property had been the subject of a robbery or theft by another person. Failure of the state to introduce evidence to show that some other person stole the personal property requires reversal of the conviction.[99]

What happens when the receiver is the target of a sting operation and it is really an undercover police officer who is delivering or selling the property to the receiver? In this case, the property is not stolen because it is in police custody. Even if it had been stolen, once recovered by police, it is arguably not stolen property any longer, but rather recovered property. Some courts have held that the defendant cannot be convicted of receipt of stolen property in these circumstances (although, arguably, they may be guilty of attempt).[100] This is a case of either factual or hybrid legal impossibility. It is possible that some courts may not even allow for a conviction of attempted stolen property if they interpret it as a type of legal impossibility (the property's character will make it such that it could never be a crime to receive it). On the other hand, the majority opinion is that it is either an attempted receipt, or statutes can be rewritten to revise the nature of the property to include "apparently stolen" property.

3. The Recipient Must Know That It Was Stolen

One of the most difficult elements to prove is the knowledge of the stolen character of the goods. Knowledge at the time the goods were received, that they have been stolen, is absolutely essential. In proving this element, the jury may infer knowledge from the circumstances.[101] For example, evidence that the defendant had in his possession a wallet containing six stolen credit cards and the complainant's checkbook was legally sufficient to support this element.[102] Guilty knowledge can be established from circumstantial evidence that would, in the opinion of the fact finder, lead a reasonable person to believe the property was stolen.[103] But mere possession of a stolen thing does not rise to a presumption that the possessor knew it was stolen.[104]

One court explained that guilty knowledge that property is stolen, as required to support a conviction for receiving stolen property, may be proved by direct evidence or by any surrounding facts or circumstances from which such knowledge may be inferred. The court continued by stating that evidence of the unexplained possession of recently stolen goods by one charged with unlawfully receiving them is a strong circumstance to be considered with all the evidence on the question of guilty knowledge, and may be sufficient to warrant conviction when it is coupled with attempts at concealment.[105]

4. The Recipient Must Have Felonious Intent

In order to be criminally liable, the prosecution must prove felonious intent. For example, one who receives goods, knowing them to have been stolen, is not guilty if his purpose is to return them to their owner or merely to detect the thief.[106]

5. Examples of State Statutes

A Louisiana court designated the elements that must be proved, stating that in order to convict the defendant of illegal possession of stolen goods valued at more than $500, the state must prove beyond a reasonable doubt that the defendant: (1) intentionally possessed, procured, received, or concealed; (2) anything of value; (3) that has been the subject of any robbery or theft; (4) where circumstances indicate that the offender knew or had good reason to believe that the thing was the subject of one of these offenses; and that (5) the value of the stolen items exceeds $500.[107]

A Virginia appeals court enumerated the elements of the offense of receiving stolen property with this summary:

> Conviction of the defendant for receiving property required proof that the automobile was: (1) previously stolen by another; (2) received by the defendant; (3) with knowledge of the theft; and (4) a dishonest intent.[108]

6. Dealing in Stolen Property

Some states have chosen to utilize separate statutes for those individuals who traffick in stolen goods. Florida's statute, for instance, targets those who "traffics in, or endeavors to traffic in, property that he knows or should know was stolen . . ." and includes those who organize, plan, finance, direct, manage or supervise the theft of property.[109]

D. Summary

The crime of receiving stolen property did not exist under the common law; instead, the perpetrator was charged as an accessory to the theft. However, statutes were created as early as the 1800s that made the crime of receiving stolen property a separate and distinct crime. These statutes are directed toward the "fence"—the individual who makes it more convenient for the thief to receive money for the property he steals. Today, there are strict controls on businesses such as pawnshops and flea market vendors to attempt to regulate the sale of stolen merchandise. These businesses are required to keep invoices and other paperwork and allow police access to inspect these records. When stolen goods are identified, failure to keep these records may go to prove knowledge that the goods were stolen.

Receipt of Stolen Goods

A/R   Receipt (possession or constructive possession) of stolen goods

M/R   Knowledge (that goods are stolen); intent (felonious, i.e., no intent to return goods to owner)

---

§ 8.8 Other Crimes Involving Theft

Although contemporary statutes in the various states are more uniform than they were 15 or 20 years ago, there are still specific acts that are offenses in some states but not in others. In this section, some of the statutes that have not been discussed previously are included as examples of statutes that may or may not be found in the states.

A. Operating a Motor Vehicle without the Owner's Consent

After the use of the automobile became common, there was a problem with the laws of theft when the individual did not keep the automobile but merely "borrowed" it and left it somewhere for the owner to find. Because one of the elements of larceny is "intent to permanently deprive the owner," **"joyriding"** could not be defined as larceny.

The Model Penal Code addresses the unauthorized use of vehicles and is broad enough to include any motor-driven vehicle. The MPC recognizes an affirmative defense that the actor *reasonably* believes that the owner would have consented to the operation had he or she known of it.

> § 223.9 Unauthorized Use of Automobiles and Other Vehicles[110]
>
> A person commits a misdemeanor if he operates another's automobile, airplane, motorcycle, motorboat, or other motor-propelled vehicle without consent of the owner. It is an affirmative defense to prosecution under this Section that the actor reasonably believed that the owner would have consented to the operation had he known of it.

In some states, the larceny statutes were modified to include unlawfully taking, driving, or operating a motor vehicle without the knowledge and consent of the owner, with the punishment being the same as for larceny. Other specific statutes were designed to punish a person who temporarily took possession of automobiles and other motor vehicles for the purpose of temporarily depriving the owner of the use of the vehicle.

While each state has a statute or code dealing with theft of vehicles, they differ in scope and even the penalty attached. Some include any vehicle, while others restrict the coverage to propelled vehicles. Some require that the person charged know that he does not have the consent of the owner,[111] while in other states it is an affirmative defense if the defendant reasonably believes that the owner would have consented.[112]

An example of a state statute that is broad enough in scope to include the unauthorized use of any vehicle and also requires that the prosecution show that the person operating the vehicle knew that he did not have consent is that of New York. The statute provides:

§ 165.05 Unauthorized use of a vehicle in the third degree[113]

A person is guilty of unauthorized use of a vehicle in the third degree when:

1. Knowing that he does not have the consent of the owner, he takes, operates, exercises control over, rides in or otherwise uses a vehicle. A person who engages in any such conduct without the consent of the owner is presumed to know that he does not have such consent; or
2. Having custody of a vehicle pursuant to an agreement between himself or another and the owner thereof whereby he or another is to perform for compensation a specific service for the owner involving the maintenance, repair or use of such vehicle, he intentionally uses or operates the same, without the consent of the owner, for his own purposes in a manner constituting a gross deviation from the agreed purpose; or
3. Having custody of a vehicle pursuant to an agreement with the owner thereof whereby such vehicle is to be returned to the owner at a specified time, he intentionally retains or withholds possession thereof, without the consent of the owner, for so lengthy a period beyond the specified time as to render such retention or possession a gross deviation from the agreement.

For purposes of this Section, "a gross deviation from the agreement" shall consist of, but not be limited to, circumstances wherein a person who, having had custody of a vehicle for a period of fifteen days or less pursuant to a written agreement, retains possession of such vehicle for at least seven days beyond the period specified in the agreement and continues such possession for a period of more than two days after service or refusal of attempted service of a notice in person or by certified mail at an address indicated in the agreement, stating:

(i)   the date and time at which the vehicle was to have been returned under the agreement;
(ii) that the owner does not consent to the continued withholding or retaining of such vehicle and demands its return; and that continued withholding or retaining of the vehicle may constitute a class A misdemeanor punishable by a fine of up to one thousand dollars or by a sentence to a term of imprisonment for a period of up to one year or by both such fine and imprisonment.

In addition to providing a penalty where a person knowingly takes or operates a vehicle without the consent of the owner, the New York statute includes a provision that subjects short-term car renters to criminal liability for failure to return a rental car on time. The elements of unauthorized use of a vehicle under paragraph (1) of the New York statute are: taking, operating, exercising control over, or riding in or otherwise using a vehicle, without the consent of the owner, or knowledge that the owner has not consented.

In interpreting the phrase "exercises control over," one court reasoned that a juvenile's momentary presence in a stripped car did not constitute exercise of dominion over the vehicle and did not constitute "unauthorized use of a vehicle" as used in the statute. In this case, the police officer had indicated that he saw the juvenile exiting the passenger side of the car; the juvenile claimed that he had merely reached into the car to pick up some change. There was no evidence that the car was operable.[114]

Do "taking and using without consent of the owner" statutes apply to the passengers in a car as well as the driver? One must look to the wording of the statute and to the cases interpreting the statute to make this determination. A Washington court determined that finding that the defendant rode in a vehicle knowing that it had been taken without its owner's consent was sufficiently supported by the evidence to show guilty knowledge as required to support the conviction.[115] A Maryland court also held that evidence that the person was a willing passenger in a car that he knew was stolen is sufficient evidence of criminal intent to sustain a conviction for the unauthorized use of a motor vehicle.[116]

The crime of "joyriding" or taking a car without the owner's permission was created because traditional larceny statutes require the prosecutor to prove intent to permanently deprive the owner of the property. All states have some provision to deal with cases in which such intent cannot be proven. The elements are:

- possession and control of auto (sometimes mere passenger)

- without owner's permission

- knowledge of owner's lack of consent (general intent)

B. Theft of Services

Many states have provisions relating to the theft of designated services, such as telephone service, while others have general statutes relating to the **theft of services**. An example is that of Texas, which provides:

§ 31.04 Theft of Service[117]

(a) A person commits theft of service if, with intent to avoid payment for service that he knows is provided only for compensation:

    (1) he intentionally or knowingly secures performance of the service by deception, threat, or false token;

    (2) having control over the disposition of services of another to which he is not entitled, he intentionally or knowingly diverts the other's services to his own benefit or to the benefit of another not entitled to them;

(3) having control of personal property under a written rental agreement, he holds the property beyond the expiration of the rental period without the effective consent of the owner of the property, thereby depriving the owner of the property of its use in further rentals; or

(4) he intentionally or knowingly secures the performance of the service by agreeing to provide compensation and, after the service is rendered, fails to make payment after receiving notice demanding payment.

(b) For purposes of this Section, intent to avoid payment is presumed if:

(1) the actor absconded without paying for the service or expressly refused to pay for the service in circumstances where payment is ordinarily made immediately upon rendering of the service, as in hotels, campgrounds, recreational vehicle parks, restaurants, and comparable establishments;

(2) the actor failed to return the property held under a rental agreement or failed to make payment under a service agreement within 10 days after receiving notice demanding return; or

(3) the actor returns property held under a rental agreement after the expiration of the rental agreement and fails to pay the applicable rental charge for the property within 10 days after the date on which the actor received notice demanding payment.

(c) For purposes of Subsections (a)(4) and (b)(2), notice shall be notice in writing, sent by registered or certified mail with return receipt requested or by telegram with report of delivery requested, and addressed to the actor at his address shown on the rental agreement or service agreement.

(d) If written notice is given in accordance with Subsection (c) of this Section, it is presumed that the notice was received no later than five days after it was sent.

(e) An offense under this Section is:

(1) a Class C misdemeanor if the value of the service stolen is less than $20;

(2) a Class B misdemeanor if the value of the service stolen is $20 or more but less than $500;

(3) a Class A misdemeanor if the value of the service stolen is $500 or more but less than $1,500;

(4) a state jail felony if the value of the service stolen is $1,500 or more but less than $20,000;

(5) a felony of the third degree if the value of the service stolen is $20,000 or more but less than $100,000;

(6) a felony of the second degree if the value of the service stolen is more than $100,000 but less than $200,000;

(7) a felony of the first degree if the value of the service stolen is $200,000 or more.

Under the provisions of this statute and similar statutes, the elements are:

- receipt of services,

- intent to avoid payment,

- knowledge that services are provided only for compensation,

- by one of the three methods indicated.[118]

C. *Theft of Property Lost, Mislaid, or Delivered by Mistake*

One might argue that keeping property that is found, or that was delivered by mistake, should not be a crime. However, in most jurisdictions, the lawmakers have determined that failure to take reasonable measures to restore lost, mislaid, or misdelivered property to the owner with the intent to deprive the owner of the property should be a crime, even though this was not a crime at common law. An example of a statute that punishes for theft of property lost, mislaid, or delivered by mistake is that of Kentucky. It provides:

§ 514.050. Theft of Property Lost, Mislaid, or Delivered by Mistake[119]

(1) Except as provided in KRS 365.710, a person is guilty of theft of property lost, mislaid, or delivered by mistake when:

    (a) he comes into control of the property of another that he knows to have been lost, mislaid, or delivered under a mistake as to the nature or amount of the property or the identity of the recipient; and

    (b) with intent to deprive the owner thereof, he fails to take reasonable measures to restore the property to a person entitled to have it.

(2) Theft of property lost, mislaid, or delivered by mistake is a Class A misdemeanor unless the value of the property is $300, in which case it is a Class D felony.

Under the Kentucky statute and like statutes, the elements of the offense are:

1. control of property by suspect,

2. property of another,

3. knowledge that property had been lost, mislaid, or mistakenly delivered,

4. intent to deprive the owner of the property and

5. failure to take reasonable measures to restore the property to the person entitled to it.

This list of crimes involving theft is not intended to be exhaustive. There are many other crimes involving theft that are included in various federal, state, and local laws.

§ 8.9   Summary

In the United States, most crimes are crimes against property, and the majority of the crimes against property involve theft in one way or another. Criminal justice personnel devote a great deal of their time to the prevention and investigation of crimes that involve theft. Although in many states today, the specific theft crimes of larceny, embezzlement, extortion, and others are combined in a single statute, these and other common law and statutory crimes are important, because many states retain statutes that deal with each of these crimes separately.

At common law, larceny was the only form of nonaggravated theft that was criminally punishable. One definition of larceny is the felonious taking of the property of another without his or her consent and against his or her will, with the intent to convert it to the use of the taker or another. In addition to the element of trespass, other technical elements are taking and carrying away of the personal property of another with intent to steal. If any of these elements is not present, there can be no larceny.

Robbery is often placed in the category of offenses against the person; however, it is covered in this chapter because it is closely related to other theft crimes. Robbery is defined as the felonious taking of money or goods of value from the person of another or in his presence against his will, by force or putting him in fear. It was a felony at common law and is a felony today in all states. The elements that distinguish it from larceny and other theft crimes are "taking from the person or presence of another," and "the taking is accompanied by means of force or putting in fear." Because of these aggravating elements, the penalty for the crime of robbery is more severe than for other theft crimes.

Although embezzlement was not a crime under early English common law, the English legislative body created a new crime to fill the gaps resulting from the technical definition of the elements of larceny. The chief distinction between larceny and embezzlement lies in the manner of acquiring possession of the property. In embezzlement, the property comes lawfully into the possession of the taker but is fraudulently or unlawfully appropriated by him or her, while in larceny there is a trespass in the unlawful taking of the property.

Another crime that was created by statute is that of obtaining property by false pretenses. This is distinguished from larceny in that the property comes into the possession of the taker not by a trespass or taking, but as a result of false pretenses with intent to defraud. It differs from embezzlement in that, in embezzlement, the property comes lawfully into the possession of the taker but he does not obtain title. In false pretenses crimes, the perpetrator obtains title and possession of the property by means of deception. The key element that distinguishes this crime from others is "deception."

If one obtains the property of another by means of threat or coercion and other elements are present, then the crime is extortion. Extortion was originally limited to obtaining money or things of value through the misuse of official power; however, in most states, a private individual, as well as a public official, may be found guilty of this crime.

In an effort to reduce the theft of property by punishing those who receive the property, most states have statutes relating to "receiving stolen property." The general definition is "receiving stolen property knowing it to have been stolen with the intent to deprive the owner of it."

To protect the public against those who would deprive persons of their property, states have enacted other theft statutes. Among these are "unauthorized use of motor vehicle (joyriding)," "theft of services," and "theft of property lost, mislaid, or delivered by mistake." Sometimes the differences between the different types of theft are slight. For instance, consider someone entering a used car lot. If the person saw a car with the keys in the ignition, jumped in and sped away with the car, this would be larceny. If he obtained permission from the clerk to test-drive the car, promising to but with no intent to return it, this would be larceny by deception. If the clerk ran after him and struggled with him through the open window, this would be robbery. If he told the clerk to let go or he would go find and kill his family, this would be extortion. If he was employed by the car dealership and was asked to move the car, but instead took it to his house with the intent to keep it, this would be embezzlement. Various federal, state, and local statutes include other theft crimes designed to protect the public against those who would, by some means, deprive owners of their property.

Review Questions

1. What are the six elements of common law larceny? What changes have occurred in modern statutes?

2. What type of property can be the object of larceny?

3. Define *robbery*. What are the eight elements of the common law offense?

4. What is caption? What is asportation? What evidence is necessary to show asportation?

5. What is trespass (as an element of both theft and robbery)?

6. An element of robbery is that the taking of the personal property be by force or by putting in fear. Is the state required to show that actual force was used? Explain.

7. One of the most difficult elements to prove in a theft or robbery case is "intent to steal." What evidence must be introduced to prove this element? What is the standard of proof?

8. What two elements are required to prove the offense of robbery that are not required when proving the crime of larceny?

9. Define *deadly weapon* and *dangerous weapon* as used in the aggravated robbery statutes. Is the fact that the gun was unloaded a defense? What if the gun was a toy gun--would it still be a deadly weapon?

10. Explain the elements that go into grading different levels of seriousness of robbery.

11. Is it always necessary that the force occurred before or during the taking of property? What about when force is used in the escape after a theft has already occurred?

12. What are the essential elements of the offense of embezzlement? How does embezzlement differ from larceny?

13. One element of the offense of embezzlement is "appropriation or conversion." What are some of the acts recognized by the courts as constituting wrongful appropriation or conversion?

14. Were embezzlement and theft by false pretenses crimes under the common law?

15. What are the elements of "obtaining property by false pretenses"? How do these differ from the elements of larceny and embezzlement? Give some examples.

16. Obtaining property by false pretenses (or larceny by trick) has the *mens rea* of knowing and intent. Explain what *knowing* is relevant to, and what *intent* is necessary to prove guilt.

17. What are the elements of common law extortion? How are they different today?

18. Is it extortion to threaten legal action against someone? Explain why or why not. What types of threats can be used to support a charge of extortion?

19. Define the elements of the crime of "receiving stolen property." How were those who received stolen property dealt with under the common law?

20. Describe the four other crimes involving theft that are described in this chapter.

Notes

[1] Fitch v. State, 135 Fla. 361, 185 So. 435 (1938).

[2] State v. Grant, 135 Vt. 222, 373 A.2d 847 (1977).

[3] State v. Carswell, 296 N.C. 101, 249 S.E.2d 427 (1978).

[4] Mouldin v. State, 376 So. 2d 788 (Ala. Ct. App. 1979).

[5] Hutchinson v. State, 427 P.2d 112 (Okla. Crim. App. 1967).

[6]   State v. Leicht, 124 N.J. Super. 127, 305 A.2d 78 (1973).

[7]   Gaynor v. State, 196 So. 2d 19 (Fla. Dist. Ct. App. 1967)

[8]   Stanley v. State, 61 Okla. Crim. App. 382, 69 P.2d 398 (1937).

[9]   Reid v. Florida Real Estate Comm'n, 188 So. 2d 846 (Fla. Dist. Ct. App. 1966).

[10]   MODEL PENAL CODE (1985).

[11]   MODEL PENAL CODE § 223.0(1) (1985).

[12]   State v. Smith, 2 Wash. 2d 118, 98 P.2d 647 (1939).

[13]   State v. Jackson, 251 Iowa 537, 101 N.W.2d 731 (1960).

[14]   Webb v. State, 55 Ala. App. 195, 314 So. 2d 114 (1975).

[15]   KY. REV. STAT. § 514.030 (2001).

[16]   KY. REV. STAT. § 514.010 (2001).

[17]   MICH. COMP. LAWS § 750.356 (2002).

[18]   MICH. COMP. LAWS §§ 750.356a, 750.357b, 750.362a, 750.367c (2002).

[19]   People v. Tansey, 593 N.Y.S.2d 426 (N.Y. Sup. Ct. 1992).

[20]   People v. Brown, 445 N.W.2d 801 (Mich. 1989).

[21]   People v. Estes, 147 Cal. App. 3d 23, 194 Cal. Rptr. 909 (1983).

[22]   People v. Maier, 75 Cal. 383, 17 P. 431 (1888).

[23]   People v. Melendez, 25 Cal. App. 2d 490, 77 P.2d 870 (1938); Neal v. State, 214 Ind. 328, 14 N.E.2d 590 (1938).

[24]   People v. Nolan, 250 Ill. 351, 95 N.E. 140 (1911).

[25]   Lanahan v. State, 176 Ark. 104, 2 S.W.2d 55 (1928); People v. Cabassa, 249 Mich. 543, 229 N.W. 442 (1930).

[26]   Moyers v. State, 185 Ga. 446, 197 S.E. 846 (1938).

[27]   State v. Lewis, 121 Ariz. 155, 589 P.2d 29 (1978).

[28]   People v. Lain, 57 Cal. App. 2d 123, 134 P.2d 284 (1943).

[29]   Edwards v. State, 49 Wis. 2d 105, 181 N.W.2d 383 (1970).

[30]   People v. Braverman, 340 Ill. 525, 173 N.E. 55 (1930).

[31]   In re Massie, 283 P.2d 573 (Okla. Crim. App. 1955).

[32]   People v. Cortez, 163 Cal. Rptr. 1 (1980).

[33]   State v. Snyder, 41 Nev. 453, 172 P. 364 (1918); *see also* Commonwealth v. Lashway, 634 N.E.2d 930 (Mass. 1994). Tones v. State, 48 Tex. Crim. 63, 88 S.W. 217 (1905).

[34]   MODEL PENAL CODE § 222.1 (1985).

[35]   Bell v. State, 354 So. 2d 1266 (Fla. Dist. Ct. App. 1978).

[36]   People v. Santiago, 62 App. Div. 2d 572, 405 N.Y.S.2d 752 (1978).

[37]   Wilmeth v. State, 808 S.W.2d 703 (Tex. 1991). *See also* Commonwealth v. Lashway, 634 N.E.2d 930 (Mass. 1994).

[38]   TEX. PENAL CODE ANN. § 29.02-29.03 (Vernon 2002).

[39]   Bosier v. State, 771 S.W.2d 221 (Tex. 1989). *See also* People v. Holder, 577 N.Y.S.2d 1022 (1991), which held that a knife brandished by the defendant's accomplice was a "dangerous instrument" supporting a first degree robbery conviction in New York.

[40]   Arthur v. State, 11 S.W.3d 386 (Tex. 2000).

[41] Birl v. State, 763 S.W.2d 860 (Tex. 1988).

[42] ILL. ANN. STAT. ch. 720 § 5/18-2 (Smith-Hurd 1999).

[43] People v. Westefer, 522 N.E.2d 1381 (Ill. 1988); People v. Bias, 475 N.E.2d 253 (Ill. 1985); People v. Ellis, 419 N.E.2d 727 (Ill. 1981). People v. Elliott, 299 Ill. App. 3d 766, 702 N.E.2d 643 (1998).

[44] State v. Felix, 153 Ariz. App. 417, 737 P.2d 393 (1986).

[45] McLaughlin v. United States, 476 U.S. 16 (1986).

[46] State v. Martinez, 47 P.3d 115 (Utah 2002).

[47] United States v. Gordon, 290 F.3d 539 (3d Cir. 2002).

[48] Fortney v. Commonwealth, 162 S.W.2d 193 (Ky. 1942).

[49] United States v. Stockton, 788 F.2d 210 (4th Cir. 1986).

[50] Jones v. State, 79 So. 2d 273 (Miss. 1955).

[51] People v. Swanson, 174 Cal. App. 2d 453, 344 P.2d 832 (1959).

[52] TEX. PENAL CODE ANN. § 31.01(2) (Vernon 1999); MO. ANN. STAT. § 570.010(7)(a) (Vernon 1999); ILL. ANN. STAT. 720 ILCS 5/15-3 (Smith-Hurd 1999); KAN. STAT. ANN. § 21-3705 (1996); WIS. STAT. ANN. § 943-20(1)(a) (West 1998).

[53] People v. Wood, 451 N.W.2d 563 (Mich. 1990).

[54] State v. Randecker, 1 Wash. App. 834, 464 P.2d 447 (1970).

[55] Hart v. State, 41 Ala. App. 221, 127 So. 2d 390 (1961).

[56] People v. Converse, 74 Mich. 478, 42 N.W. 70 (1889).

[57] Commonwealth v. Turrell, 584 A.2d 882 (Pa. 1990).

[58] Commonwealth v. Austin, 393 A.2d 36 (Pa. 1978).

[59] MICH. COMP. LAWS § 750.174 (2002).

[60] § 750.177-182.

[61] W. LAFAVE AND A. SCOTT, CRIMINAL LAW (1986), p. 739.

[62] People v. Cravens, 79 Cal. App. 2d 658, 180 P.2d 453 (1947); Courtney v. State, 174 Miss. 147, 164 So. 227 (1935); State v. Serkau, 128 Conn. 153, 20 A.2d 725 (1941).

[63] MODEL PENAL CODE § 223.3 (1985).

[64] State v. Roberts, 711 P.2d 235 (Utah 1985). The case lists 12 states that have adopted the language of § 223.3 of the Model Penal Code.

[65] Fuller v. State, 221 Miss. 227, 72 So. 2d 454 (1954).

[66] State v. Carlson, 171 N.C. 818, 89 S.E. 30 (1916).

[67] People v. Bertsche, 265 Ill. 272, 106 N.E. 828 (1914).

[68] Baumgartner v. State, 319 A.2d 592 (Md. 1974).

[69] ILL. ANN. STAT. 720 § 5/15-4(e) (Smith-Hurd 1995).

[70] People v. Marks, 163 N.W.2d 506 (Mich. Ct. App. 1968).

[71] Horton v. State, 85 Ohio St. 13, 96 N.E. 797 (1911).

[72] State v. Neimeier, 66 Iowa 634, 24 N.W. 247 (1885); State v. Armstead, 562 S.E.2d 450 (N.C. 2002).

[73] Cowan v. State, 41 Tex. Crim. 617, 56 S.W. 751 (1900).

[74] State v. Grimes, 46 P.3d 801 (Wash. 2002).

[75] OHIO REV. CODE ANN. § 2913.02 (Anderson 2002).

[76]   State v. Brumback, 671 N.E.2d 1064 (Ohio Ct. App. 1996).

[77]   KY. REV. STAT. § 514.040 (2001).

[78]   Wilburn v. State, 410 S.E.2d 321 (Ga. Ct. App. 1991); Jordan v. State, 220 Ga. App. 627, 470 S.E.2d 242 (1996).

[79]   Baker v. State, 588 So. 2d 945 (Ala. Crim. App. 1991); People v. Wooten, 52 Cal. Rptr. 2d 765 (1996).

[80]   Kirby v. State, 57 N.J.L. 320, 31 A. 213 (1894).

[81]   MODEL PENAL CODE § 223.4 (1985).

[82]   Hess v. Sparks, 44 Kan. 465, 24 P. 979 (1890).

[83]   People v. Williams, 127 Cal. 212, 59 P. 581 (1899).

[84]   MO. ANN. STAT. § 570.030 (Vernon 2002).

[85]   MO. ANN. STAT. § 570.010(3) (Vernon 2002).

[86]   N.Y. PENAL LAW § 155.05 (McKinney 1995).

[87]   United States v. Jackson, 180 F.3d 55 (2d Cir. 1999); United States v. Jackson, 196 F.3d 383 (2d Cir. 1999).

[88]   People v. Hubbard, 552 N.W.2d 493 (Mich. Ct. App. 1996).

[89]   State v. Cunningham, 474 S.E.2d 772 (N.C. 1996).

[90]   Strohecker v. Commonwealth, 475 S.E.2d 844 (Va. Ct. App. 1996).

[91]   Kirby v. United States, 174 U.S. 47, 19 S. Ct. 574, 43 L. Ed. 890 (1894).

[92]   4 BLACKSTONE, COMMENTARIES 38.

[93]   Curl v. People, 53 Colo. 578, 127 P. 751 (1912); Yeargain v. State, 57 Okla. Crim. 136, 45 P.2d 1113 (1935).

[94]   MODEL PENAL CODE § 223.6 (1985).

[95]   MODEL PENAL CODE § 223.0(4) (1985).

[96]   N.Y. PENAL LAW §§ 165.40-165.55 (McKinney 2002). *See* People v. Chapman, 682 N.Y.S.2d 5 (1998).

[97]   Washington v. State, 726 So. 2d 209 (Miss. 1998).

[98]   Sanderson v. Commonwealth, 12 S.W. 136 (Ky. 1889); Commonwealth v. White, 123 Mass. 430, 25 Am. Rep. 116 (1877).

[99]   State v. Price, 980 S.W.2d 143 (Mo. 1998).

[100] United States v. Monasterski, 567 F.2d. 677 (1987).

[101] Tolliver v. State, 25 Tex. Crim. 600, 8 S.W. 806 (1888).

[102] People v. Chapman, 682 N.Y.S.2d 5 (1998). *See also* People v. Pharr, 733 N.Y.S.2d 96 (2001), which held that knowledge of stolen property can be established through circumstantial evidence but that flight alone is insufficient proof of the defendant's knowledge of stolen property.

[103] Cunningham v. State, 475 S.E.2d 924 (Ga. 1996).

[104] State v. R.W., 721 So. 2d 743 (La. 1998). *See also* Avett v. State, 928 S.W.2d 326 (Ark. 1996).

[105] Washington v. State, 726 So. 2d 209 (Miss. 1998).

[106] Arcia v. State, 26 Tex. Crim. 193, 9 S.W. 685 (1888).

[107] State v. Alexander, 720 So. 2d 82 (La. 1998).

[108] Bynum v. Commonwealth, 477 S.E.2d 750 (Va. 1996).

[109] FLA. STAT. ANN. § 812.019 (West 1999).

[110] MODEL PENAL CODE § 223.9 (1985).

[111] KY. REV. STAT. § 514.100 (2001).

[112] Mass., N.J., Pa., W. Va.

[113] N.Y. PENAL LAW § 165.05 (McKinney 2002).

[114] Matter of Ruven P., 542 N.Y.S. 272 (1989). *See also* People v. Gray, 546 N.Y.S.2d 387 (1989).

[115] State v. Womble, 969 P.2d 1097 (Wash. 1999).

[116] In re Levon A., 720 A.2d 1232 (Md. 1998).

[117] TEX. PENAL CODE ANN. § 31.04 (Vernon 2002).

[118] MODEL PENAL CODE § 223.7 (1985). *See* comments for states that have statutes relating to theft of services.

[119] KY. REV. STAT. § 514.050 (2001). See MODEL PENAL CODE § 223.5 (1985) for states that have adopted similar statutes

Forgery and Other
Fraud Offenses

9

Chapter Outline

Cases

Forgery: *New Mexico v. Wasson*, 964 P.2d 820 (N.M. App. 1998)
Identity Theft: *Washington v. Leyda*, 138 P.3d 610 (Wash. 2006)

§ 9.1 Introduction

For centuries, legislative bodies and courts have attempted to determine what acts relating to cheating should be made criminal. In England, various types of cheating were made crimes under the early common law. For example, in 1511, it was a crime to add oil or water to woolcloth or to over-stretch cloth. In 1541, a statute was enacted in England that made it a crime to counterfeit letters or privy tokens or to receive money or goods in other men's names. One who violated this statute was subject to

> such correction and punishment, by imprisonment of his body, setting upon the pillory, or otherwise any corporal pain as shall be upon him or them limited, adjudged or appointed by the person or persons before whom he shall be so convicted of said offenses, or any of them.[1]

On the other hand, early courts and legislatures hesitated to make simple dishonesty in business a crime, reasoning that a certain amount of dishonesty in business was expected.

As the law developed in England and in the United States, criminal statutes were enacted to make it a crime to commit various types of cheating and fraud. The extensive use of checks and other commercial paper made it necessary that specific statutes be developed to punish the making of false documents or altering documents with the intent to defraud.

In this chapter, the most common forgery and other fraud offenses are discussed in detail, with other, less common crimes defined in less detail. The crime that is best known is forgery. Closely related to forgery is uttering a forged instrument. In addition to these and other related offenses, false advertising, commercial bribery, computer fraud, and other business and commercial fraud crimes are described and distinguished.

§ 9.2 Forgery

One of the most common crimes in our society today is **forgery**. After some hesitation to enact fraud statutes, lawmakers and merchants recognized that there is a strong social interest in maintaining trust in the genuineness of checks and other commercial paper. If false instruments are prevalent in a community or society, commerce is affected because people will have less trust that these documents are genuine.

A. Common Law

At early common law, forgery belonged to the class of misdemeanors called **"cheats,"** and was regarded as a misdemeanor, not a felony.[2] Later, it was designated a felony in both English and American statutes. One early definition of forgery is the "fraudulent making or alteration of a writing to the prejudice of another man's right."[3] Blackstone's definition included the elements currently recognized: "the false making or materially altering, with intent to defraud, of any writing which, if genuine, might apparently be of legal efficacy or the foundation of a legal liability."[4]

Early statutes in all states had provisions relating to forgery. These statutes, for the most part, included coverage of the common law, but sometimes extended the law to include crimes not within the scope of the common law offense, and often increased the severity of punishment. Definitions of the term "forgery" before the Model Penal Code included:

- "Forgery" is the false making of an instrument, which purports on the face of it to be good and valid for purposes for which it was created, with a design to defraud any person or persons.[5]

- "Forgery" requires the making of a writing which falsely purports to be the writing of another, with intent to defraud, and the crime may exist even though the name is fictitious when the fictitious name is shown to have been used with intent to defraud.[6]

B. Model Penal Code

The Model Code uses the term "writing" and defines writing very comprehensively. Also, the Model Code provision includes what was defined under previous provisions as "uttering a forged instrument." Instead of the term "intent to defraud," the Model Code uses "with purpose to defraud or injure anyone." Subsection (1) provides that forgery is committed if the defendant acts "with knowledge that he is facilitating a fraud or injury to be perpetrated by anyone." This makes it clear that a forger commits an offense even though he does not defraud the person to whom he sells or passes a forged writing.

§ 224.1 Forgery[7]

(1) Definition. A person is guilty of forgery if, with purpose to defraud or injure anyone, or with knowledge that he is facilitating a fraud or injury to be perpetrated by anyone, the actor:

   (a) alters any writing of another without his authority; or

   (b) makes, completes, executes, authenticates, issues or transfers any writing so that it purports to be the act of another who did not authorize that act, or to have been executed at a time or place or in a numbered sequence other than was in fact the case, or to be a copy of an original when no such original existed; or

   (c) utters any writing which he knows to be forged in a manner specified in paragraphs (a) or (b).

"Writing" includes printing or any other method of recording information, money, coins, tokens, stamps, seals, credit cards, badges, trademarks and other symbols of value, right, privilege or identification.

(2) Grading. Forgery is a felony of the second degree if the writing is or purports to be part of an issue of money, securities, postage, or revenue stamps, or other instruments issued by the government, or part of an issue of stock, bonds, or other instruments representing interests in or claims against any property or enterprise. Forgery is a felony of the third degree if the writing is or purports to be a will, deed, contract, release, commercial instrument, or other document evidencing, creating, transferring, altering, terminating, or otherwise affecting legal relations. Otherwise forgery is a misdemeanor.

C. State Statutes, Codes, and Cases

Modern statutes have expanded the types of documents that can be forged and have increased the penalty of the crime. The essential elements of forgery remain unchanged from the earliest cases.

1. Fraudulent or False Writing or Alteration

It is an indispensable requirement of forgery that the writing be false. It may have been false in its inception or may have been made so by subsequent tampering with what was originally genuine.[8]

2. Writing or Document

The subject of forgery may be a deed, a mortgage, a check, bill of exchange, order for goods or money, receipt, or even a diploma.[9] Most forgery cases that reached the courts concerned the forgery of checks or money orders. However,

> **CASE: *State v. Wasson*, 964 P.2d 820 (N.M. App. 1998)**
>
> What was the holding in this case?
>
> Does forgery apply to a traffic ticket?
>
> What does it mean for a document to have "legal efficacy"?

any writing or document may be forged and the forger prosecuted if the document is believed to have "**legal efficacy**." What this means, in general, is a document that creates legal rights or obligations for any party. For instance, a New York court affirmed that a federally issued Resident Alien Card, or "green card," was covered by the state forgery law such that a defendant in possession of an allegedly forged green card could be prosecuted for criminal possession of a forged instrument.[10] In the case of *State v. Wasson*, the issue was whether a traffic ticket was a writing of legal efficacy.

3. Intent to Defraud

Unless there is the intent to prejudice another's right, there is no crime of forgery. As one court explained, the intent is the very essence of forgery. However, it is immaterial whether anyone is actually defrauded.[11] While some courts describe the *mens rea* as specific intent and other call it general intent, basically what is necessary is proof that the offender meant to defraud another by the use of the material alteration or created document.[12]

4. Forgery or Alteration Is Material

While this is not spelled out in the definition itself, the courts have insisted that the forgery or the alteration be material; that is, it must have prejudicial effect. However, even a slight change in the legal meaning will be considered material and thus an alteration. In one case, the court agreed that it was not forgery to change the figures on a check to correspond with the sum recited in words (a statute provided that where there is a discrepancy, the sum expressed by the words is the sum that is payable), because the alteration did not change the legal effect of the instrument.[13] However, this action could be prosecuted as attempted forgery if the other elements of the crime were present.

5. Examples of State Statutes

Some states use the wording of the Model Penal Code; others state the violation and also define the terms used in the statute. For example, the Louisiana statute as rewritten in 2001 provides:

§ 72. Forgery[14]

A. It shall be unlawful to forge, with intent to defraud, any signature to, or any part of any writing purporting to have legal efficacy.

B. Issuing, transferring, or possessing with intent to defraud, a forged writing, known by the offender to be a forged writing, shall also constitute a violation of the provisions of this Section.

C. For purposes of this Section:

(1) "Forge" means the following:

  (a) To alter, make, complete, execute, or authenticate any writing so that it purports:

    (i) To be the act of another who did not authorize that act;

    (ii) To have been executed at a time or place or in a numbered sequence other than was in fact the case; or

    (iii) To be a copy of an original when no such original existed.

  (b) To issue, transfer, register the transfer of, pass, publish, or otherwise utter a writing that is forged in accordance with the meaning of Subparagraph (1)(a).

  (c) To possess a writing that is forged within the meaning of Subparagraph (1)(a).

(2) "Writing" means the following:

  (a) Printing or any other method of recording information;

  (b) Money, coins, tokens, stamps, seals, credit cards, badges, and trademarks; and

  (c) Symbols of value, right, privilege, or identification.

D. Whoever commits the crime of forgery shall be fined not more than five thousand dollars, or imprisoned, with or without hard labor, for not more than ten years, or both.

Most forgery cases involve the forgery of checks. To close loopholes, states have attempted to draft statutes that are more comprehensive and all-inclusive. For example, the Missouri forgery statute provides that a person commits the crime of forgery if, with the purpose to defraud, that person:

(1) Makes, completes, alters or authenticates any writing so that it purports to have been made by another or at another time or place in a numbered sequence other than was in fact the case or with different terms or by authority of one who did not give such authority; or

(2) Erases, obliterates or destroys any writing; or

(3) Makes or alters anything other than a writing, so that it purports to have a genuineness, antiquity, rarity, ownership or authorship which it does not possess; or

(4) Uses as genuine, or possesses for the purpose of using as genuine, or transfers with knowledge or belief that it will be used as genuine, any writing or other thing which the actor knows has been made or altered in the manner described in this section.[15]

Even with such a comprehensive statute, cases still reach the reviewing courts for interpretation. In the case of *State v. Conaway*, the defendant was convicted of eight counts of forgery and was sentenced to a total term of 25 years' imprisonment. The defendant argued, among other things, on appeal that a false "endorsement" cannot be considered a fraudulent authentication as used in the statute. In this case, the endorsements on the checks had been altered by the obliteration of part of the name, with the result that the endorsement attested to the fact that the defendant was the named payee and that he was entitled to payment. In upholding the conviction, the court advised that a false endorsement of a check can be considered a fraudulent authentication for the purposes of the forgery statute. The court concluded that because the defendant had no authority from the legitimate payee to endorse or deposit the checks, and that because he was identified as the depositor of these checks, this was sufficient to constitute a violation.[16] The Missouri court held that intent to defraud, as an element of forgery, is a general intent and can be inferred from the act of the forgery itself, if shown.

Some state statutes have only one degree of forgery. In Ohio, the statute reads:

§ 2913.31 Forgery.[17]

(A) No person, with purpose to defraud, or knowing that the person is facilitating a fraud, shall do any of the following:
(1) Forge any writing of another without the person's authority;
(2) Forge any writing so that it purports to be genuine when it is actually spurious, or to be the act of another who did not authorize that act, or to have been executed at a time or place or with terms different from what was in fact the case, or to be a copy of an original when no such original existed;
(3) Utter, or possess with purpose to utter, any writing which he knows to have been forged.

The definition of "writing," as used in the Ohio Code, includes not only legal and commercial documents traditionally covered by forgery, but also private, noncommercial documents not formerly covered. The subject of forgery under this section may also include any symbol of value, right, privilege, or identification, such as credit cards, I.D. cards, trademarks, and others. The definition of "forge" includes all forms of falsification purporting to authenticate a writing.

In other case decisions, courts have defined the elements of forgery:

- (Pennsylvania) "In order to obtain a forgery conviction, the Commonwealth must prove that this was a false writing, that the instrument was capable of deceiving, and that the defendant intended to defraud."[18]

- (New Mexico) "The elements of forgery include falsely making or altering a writing which purports to have legal efficacy, or knowingly issuing or transferring a forged writing."[19]

- (Georgia) "(1) knowingly making, altering or possessing any writing, (2) in such a manner that the writing as made or altered purports to have been made by authority of one who did not have such authority, and (3) uttering or delivering such writing, (4) with intent to defraud."[20]

- (Massachusetts) ". . . only when the false making is done with specific intent to defraud is the crime of forgery established."[21]

D. Summary

Forgery has been expanded from common law to include almost any document that has "legal efficacy." It also includes the creation or alteration of documents. Some statutes have greatly enlarged the coverage of forgery to include other items in addition to documents of legal efficacy; however, in other states, these items are covered in a separate statute (see Criminal Simulation, below). In general, the elements of forgery are very similar to what they were under the common law.

Forgery

(A/R)   Creation of false document or material alteration of genuine document of legal efficacy

(M/R)   Intent to defraud (general intent)

---

§ 9.3   Uttering a Forged Instrument

A. Common Law

Forging a document and "**uttering**" are two different crimes under the common law and in some states today. To utter a forged instrument is to offer it, directly or indirectly, by words or actions, as good. This, if done with intent to defraud, and with knowledge of the falsity of the instrument, was a violation at common law, and today is a crime in all states. Uttering a forged instrument is offering, as genuine, an instrument known to be false, with intent to defraud.[22]

B. Model Penal Code

The traditional crime of uttering a forged instrument is included in § 224.1 of the Model Penal Code relating to forgery. The specific provision of the code that applies to uttering a forged instrument is:

> (1) Definition. A person is guilty of forgery if, with purpose to defraud or injure anyone, or with knowledge that he is facilitating a fraud or injury to be perpetrated by anyone, the actor: . . .
>
>   (c) utters any writing which he knows to be forged in a manner specified in paragraphs (a) or (b).[23]

The penalty for uttering a forged instrument is the same as that provided for forgery.

C. State Statutes, Codes, and Cases

Uttering is a distinct offense and is not the same as forgery, although in some statutes the two are combined in one section.[24] The elements of uttering a forged instrument include the following.

1. Uttering—Publishing or Offering

The forged instrument is "uttered" when there is an attempt to make use of it. It is not necessary that there be anything more than a declaration that the instrument is good. Further, it need not be actually passed and accepted.[25]

2. A Forged Instrument

One of the elements of uttering a forged instrument is that the instrument was, in fact, forged. For instance, this element is present when it is demonstrated that the person who signed another's name did so without authority.[26] On the other hand, the person who "utters" the forgery does not, necessarily, have to be the same person who forged the document. Thus, someone can be guilty of forgery (but not uttering), uttering (but not forgery), or both.

3. Offering or Publishing as True or Genuine

One of the essential elements of uttering is the presentation of the document *as a true and genuine* document of legal efficacy. This is related to the intent requirement explained below. If someone shows an item and promotes it as a fake or altered document or counterfeit, then this element is not present, nor is there intent to defraud. The important thing to remember is that the person who utters a forged instrument is defrauding the recipient because of the statement, innuendo, or action that infers or states that the document is genuine.

4. Knowledge on the Part of the Offeror that the Instrument Is False

Knowledge on the part of the offender is an essential requirement. However, such knowledge may be established by circumstantial evidence. For example, flight by the defendant, when he saw the one to whom the check was offered go to the telephone, was a strong circumstance indicating guilty knowledge.[27] In a Virginia case, the court found that the required knowledge element was proved when the evidence indicated that the suspect drove away from a bank window after a bank teller attempted to stall the defendant as another teller telephoned the police. This conduct, according to the court, was sufficient evidence of knowledge and intent.[28]

5. Intent to Defraud

Generally, intent to defraud may be proven by the other elements of the crime. If the defendant utters a forged check, for instance, the intent to defraud is proven by the proceeds of the check when cashed. However, it is important to realize that this element must be proven along with the *actus reus*. There may be some instances in which there is no intent, i.e., an individual who gives a forged check to a bank or some other party and explains how it is a forgery has no intent to defraud and would not be guilty of uttering.

6. Examples of State Statutes

Some states consolidate forgery and uttering a forged instrument, as does the Model Penal Code, but use different terminology. For example, in Nebraska, a person is guilty of forgery if the state proves issuing, authenticating, transferring, selling, transmitting, using, presenting, passing, delivering, or causing such uttering.[29]

In other states, the crime of uttering a forged instrument is a separate statute and, in some instances, there are separate degrees of the offense. In Michigan, which has a separate statute on uttering, to prove the elements of uttering and publishing, the prosecution introduces evidence to show that the defendant knew the instrument was false, that he or she had intent to defraud, and that he or she presented the forged instrument for payment. The elements of uttering and publishing in Michigan are: (1) knowledge on the defendant's part that the instrument is false, (2) intent to defraud, and (3) presentation of the forged instruments for payment.[30]

D. Summary

Uttering may be a separate crime from forgery, although many state statutes include uttering in the forgery statute. In these states, uttering may be one of the alternative acts that can constitute a forgery charge. In this case, it is not considered a separate crime; however, it is not a lesser included crime in any case. The most important element of the crime of uttering is that the offender have knowledge of the forgery and intent to defraud.

Uttering a Forged Document

(A/R)　Presenting, publishing or offering, a forged document as genuine, knowing it to be false

(M/R)　Intent to defraud (general intent)

---

§ 9.4   Miscellaneous Forgery-Related Offenses/Identity Theft

The drafters of legislation in the various states have determined that the forgery statutes, as written, are not broad enough to cover some acts that should be criminal offenses. Some of those are briefly discussed here. It should be noted, however, that this is not meant to be exhaustive, because there are other designations and descriptions of offenses not included here.

A. *Criminal Simulation*

Criminal simulation statutes are designed to prohibit forgery when the subject of the offense is not a writing but an object. For example, the Ohio statute provides:

(A) No person, with purpose to defraud, or knowing that the person is facilitating a fraud, shall do any of the following:

   (1) Make or alter any object so that it appears to have value because of antiquity, rarity, curiosity, source, or authorship, which it does not in fact possess;

   (2) Practice deception in making, retouching, editing, or reproducing any photograph, movie film, videotape, phonograph record, or recording tape;

   (3) Falsely or fraudulently make, simulate, forge, alter, or counterfeit any wrapper, label, stamp, cork, or cap prescribed by the Liquor Control Commission under Chapters 4301. and 4303. of the Revised Code, falsely or fraudulently cause to be made, simulated, forged, altered, or counterfeited any wrapper, label, stamp, cork, or cap prescribed by the Liquor Control Commission under Chapters 4301. and 4303. of the Revised Code, or use more than once any wrapper, label, stamp, cork, or cap prescribed by the Liquor Control Commission under Chapters 4301. and 4303. of the Revised Code;

   (4) Utter, or possess with purpose to utter, any object that the person knows to have been simulated as provided in Division (A)(1), (2), or (3) of this section.[31]

Legal News

In 2007, the state of Texas announced its imminent purchase (for close to $500,000) of a letter purported to have been written by Davy Crockett shortly before he was killed at the Alamo. Upon the announcement, several experts hotly contested the authenticity of the letter, offered by Simpson Galleries in Houston, and the state backed out of the purchase when no independent expert would authenticate the letter. Experts argued that, although the letter was written on old paper and probably had been written in roughly the same period, it was not Crockett's handwriting and it contained far fewer grammatical and spelling errors than was his pattern. Some argued that it may have been a copy of a true letter by a family member for the purpose of records. In any event, the state did not purchase the letter. Even though this is a writing, it is more similar to criminal simulation than forgery because the letter has no legal efficacy (it does not create any legal obligations). Only if the seller knew the letter was not genuine and offered it with the intent to defraud would a crime be committed.

Source: Associated Press (2007). "Experts to Authenticate Purported Crockett Letter." Accessed 12/30/2008 from http://www.news8austin.com/shared/print/default.asp?ArID=191812. Also, "Texas Pays $490,000 for Fake Davy Crockett Letter?" MyFineBooks blog, Accessed 3/18/2008 from http://blog.myfinebooks.com/2007/09/texas-pays-4900.html.

B. Misuse of Credit Cards

As the use of credit cards became common, states were forced to enact statutes that covered offenses involving the improper use of such cards. An example is that of Ohio, which provides:

(A) No person shall do any of the following:

    (1) Practice deception for the purpose of procuring the issuance of a credit card, when a credit card is issued in actual reliance thereon;

    (2) Knowingly buy or sell a credit card from or to a person other than the issuer.

(B) No person, with purpose to defraud, shall do any of the following:

    (1) Obtain control over a credit card as security for a debt;

    (2) Obtain property or services by the use of a credit card, in one or more transactions, knowing or having reasonable cause to believe that such card has expired or been revoked, or was obtained, is retained, or is being used in violation of law;

    (3) Furnish property or services upon presentation of a credit card, knowing that such card is being used in violation of law;

    (4) Represent or cause to be represented to the issuer of a credit card that property or services have been furnished, knowing that the representation is false.

(C) No person, with purpose to violate this section, shall receive, possess, control, or dispose of a credit card.[32]

Among other things, this statute prohibits the use of deception in obtaining a credit card in the first instance, buying or selling a credit card, obtaining property or services with a credit card with knowledge that the credit card has expired or has been revoked. It also provides a penalty for the business operator who furnishes property or services and charges it to a credit card knowing that such a card is being used in violation of the law. In other states, the wording is different from that of Ohio. Some provisions require an intent to defraud; others omit any intent requirements.[33] Florida has a comprehensive credit card chapter in its criminal code. Sections include:

- False statement as to financial condition or identity.
- Theft; obtaining credit card through fraudulent means.
- Fraudulent use of credit cards.
- Traffic in counterfeit credit cards.
- Expired or revoked credit cards.
- Fraud by person authorized to provide goods or services.
- Use of scanning device or reencoder to defraud; penalties.
- Possession and transfer of credit-card-making equipment.
- Receipt of money, etc., obtained by fraudulent use of credit cards.
- Alteration of credit card invoice; penalties.[34]

C. Possession of a Forgery Device

Because some forgery statutes do not cover the possession of a forgery device, some states have enacted special legislation to cover this situation. An example is that of Kentucky, which provides:

(1) A person is guilty of possession of a forgery device when he:

(a) Makes or possesses with knowledge of its character any plate, die or other device, apparatus, equipment or article specifically designed or adapted for use in forging written instruments; or

(b) Makes or possesses with knowledge of its character any device, apparatus, equipment or article capable of or adaptable to use in forging written instruments with the intent to use it himself or to aid or permit another to use it for purposes of forgery.[35]

As used in this statute, a "forgery device" means "a plate for counterfeiting, to reproduce tax stamps, or trading stamps, a hard printing set, or rubber stamp equipment."[36] One of the elements of this crime is knowledge; therefore, it is incumbent upon the state to prove the required knowledge element.

D. Other Forgery-Related Offenses

Other offenses that are related to forgery are using slugs (coin replicas), fraudulent destruction, removal, or concealment of recordable instruments, and tampering with records.[37] Most states have some type of statute that prohibits knowingly tampering with records with the purpose to defraud. These statutes have different titles, but the purpose generally is the same. One example is that of Nebraska, which is titled "False Statement or Book Entry; Destruction or Secretion of Records; Penalty, Organization, Defined." A person commits a Class 5 misdemeanor if he or she:

(a) willfully and knowingly subscribes to, makes or causes to be made any false statement or entry into the books of an organization; or

(b) knowingly subscribes to or exhibits false papers with intent to deceive any person or persons authorized to examine into the affairs of any such organization; or

(c) makes, states, or publishes any false statement of the amount of assets or liabilities of any such organization; or

(d) fails to make true and correct entry in the books and records of such organization of its business and transactions in the manner and form prescribed by the Department of Banking and Finances; or

(e) mutilates, alters, destroys, secretes, or removes any of the books or records of such organization, without the consent of the Director of Banking and Finance.[38]

In Ohio, the crime is called "Tampering with Records." This section prohibits tampering with all private, as well as public, records for fraudulent purposes. The rationale is that the substantial harm can, in a given case, result from tampering with a personal letter file, bank statement, or other private document, as well as from tampering with the correspondence files or records in a public office.[39]

E. Identity Theft

Identity theft is reported to be one of the fastest-growing crimes in the United States. It has been reported that 9.9 million Americans had their identities stolen in 2003 and that each year the number grows. Businesses report an average loss $10,200 per instance and individuals report an average loss of $1,180. Beyond dollar amounts, victims experience distress, harassment from creditors, loss of credit ratings, and may even be arrested because of the actions of the thief.[40] Identity theft may be related to computer crimes, discussed in a later section, but it need not be. For instance, one's name, address, and credit card number may be stolen from a company's databank through the computer, but it just as easily might be retrieved from your garbage can if you don't shred your monthly bills.

Legal News

A Department of Justice website warns consumers of identity theft: Many people do not realize how easily criminals can obtain our personal data without having to break into our homes. In public places, for example, criminals may engage in "shoulder surfing"--watching you from a nearby location as you punch in your telephone calling card number or credit card number, or listening in on your conversation if you give your credit card number over the telephone to a hotel or rental car company.

Even the area near your home or office may not be secure. Some criminals engage in "dumpster diving" going through your garbage cans or a communal dumpster or trash bin--to obtain copies of your checks, credit card or bank statements, or other records that typically bear your name, address, and even your telephone number. These types of records make it easier for criminals to get control over accounts in your name and assume your identity.

If you receive applications for "preapproved" credit cards in the mail, but discard them without tearing up the enclosed materials, criminals may retrieve them and try to activate the cards for their use without your knowledge. (Some credit card companies, when sending credit cards, have adopted security measures that allow a card recipient to activate the card only from his or her home telephone number, but this is not yet a universal practice.) Also, if your mail is delivered to a place where others have ready access to it, criminals may simply intercept and redirect your mail to another location.

In recent years, the Internet has become an appealing place for criminals to obtain identifying data, such as passwords or even banking information. In their haste to explore the exciting features of the Internet, many people respond to "spam"--unsolicited e-mail that promises them some benefit but requests identifying data, without realizing that in many cases, the requester has no intention of keeping his promise. In some cases, criminals reportedly have used computer technology to obtain large amounts of personal data.

With enough identifying information about an individual, a criminal can take over that individual's identity to commit a wide range of crimes: for example, false applications for loans and credit cards, fraudulent withdrawals from bank accounts, fraudulent use of telephone calling cards, or obtaining other goods or privileges that the criminal might be denied if he were to use his real name. If the criminal takes steps to ensure that bills for the falsely obtained credit cards, or bank statements showing the unauthorized withdrawals, are sent to an address other than the victim's, the victim may not become aware of what is happening until the criminal has already inflicted substantial damage on the victim's assets, credit, and reputation.

Source: U.S Department of Justice (2008). Accessed 12/31/08 from http://www.usdoj.gov/criminal/fraud/websites/idtheft.html#whatcommonways.

Note that what is commonly referred to as identity theft is often a combination of several crimes. First, there is a theft (offenders typically steal bank statements, credit card information or the cards themselves, or other identity information from the consumer or a business that has such information from multiple consumers), there may be a computer crime involved (if the information was obtained through "**phishing**" (which is appearing to be a legitimate company in order to get a victim to provide personal information) or "hacking" into some person's or organization's computer data systems), then there are usually multiple crimes using the identity that might be charged as forgeries, credit card abuse, or some other theft statute depending on the state penal code. Some states have passed identity theft statutes that encompass the theft of the identity by whatever means, the possession of identity information, and the use of such for fraudulent purposes. Federal laws are also at issue and this discussion will continue in Chapter 15.

> **CASE:** *Washington v. Leyda,*
> **138 P.3d 610 (2006)**
>
> What were the issue and holding of this case?
>
> Where does the protection against double jeopardy come from?
>
> If someone has your credit cards and uses each of the four cards twice, how many crimes have they committed?

F. Summary

While some statutes have a general forgery statute that covers a wide list of behaviors, other states have more specific statutes and in this section, some of the specific crimes detailed in these separate statutes have been illustrated. States that only include documents or "writings" in their forgery statute often have a statute called "Criminal Simulation" or some other name that covers any alteration or creation of a false object. Possessing forgery instruments is a separate crime from using them in some states. Credit cards and their abuse have spawned a wide range of crimes, including fraudulent obtaining and use. These statutes cover dishonest users of credit cards as well as merchants. Tampering with records is often a separate crime and deals with the making of false records or dishonest bookkeeping practices. Identity theft is a growing problem and one that usually includes other crimes in addition to forgery. In general, the movement has been to criminalize a wide range of behaviors that are in the category of dishonesty in the marketplace.

§ 9.5   False Advertising

A. Common Law

False advertising, as such, was not a crime at common law. The phrase *caveat emptor* (let the buyer beware) described the situation between the consumer and merchant. In general, the consumer was expected to know that advertisers may exaggerate or even lie about their product. However, making untrue and fraudulent statements about products became so extensive that both state and municipal governments deemed it necessary for the protection of the public to prohibit the practice. As a consequence, even in the early 1900s, numerous statutes and ordinances were enacted, prohibiting false or fraudulent statements in advertising. The crime of false advertising consisted primarily of the publication and circulation of deceptive matter, and the offense was complete without regard to whether anyone was deceived or damaged.[41]

B. Model Penal Code

The drafters of the Model Code consolidated several older crimes relating to cheating and deceptive practices into one comprehensive statute. Paragraphs (5), (6), and (7) deal with situations in which false or misleading statements are made for specific purposes. Under this provision, the criminality of the conduct is making "misleading" statements. The last paragraphs of the Model Code provide an affirmative defense if the defendant proves, by a preponderance of the evidence, that his or her conduct was not knowingly or recklessly deceptive.

---

§ 224.7 Deceptive Business Practices[42]

A person commits a misdemeanor if, in the course of business, he:

(1) uses or possesses for use a false weight or measure, or any other device for falsely determining or recording any quality or quantity; or

(2) sells, offers or exposes for sale, or delivers less than the represented quantity of any commodity or service; or

(3) takes or attempts to take more than the represented quantity of any commodity or service when as buyer he furnishes the weight or measure; or

(4) sells, offers or exposes for sale adulterated or mislabeled commodities. "Adulterated" means varying from the standard of composition or quality prescribed by or pursuant to any statute providing criminal penalties for such variance, or set by established commercial usage. "Mislabeled" means varying from the standard of truth or disclosure in labeling prescribed by or pursuant to any statute providing criminal penalties for such variance, or set by established commercial usage; or

(5) makes a false or misleading statement in any advertisement addressed to the public or to a substantial segment thereof for the purpose of promoting the purchase or sale of property or services; or

(6) makes a false or misleading written statement for the purpose of obtaining property or credit; or

(7) makes a false or misleading written statement for the purpose of promoting the sale of securities, or omits information required by law to be disclosed in written documents relating to securities.

It is an affirmative defense to prosecution under this section if the defendant proves, by a preponderance of the evidence, that his or her conduct was not knowingly or recklessly deceptive.

C. State Statutes, Codes, and Cases

In today's society, advertising has become a way of life with radio, television, and other means of conveying messages to the public. The dangers of false advertising have become more and more apparent. Generally, the contemporary statutes and codes are more comprehensive than the traditional statutes and have tended to fix responsibility on those who are in a position to know that the advertising is false or misleading. Legislatures of some states enacted comprehensive statutes. The elements of the crime, as stated in most statutes and ordinances, are:

1. Publication

Publication may be by advertisement or by verbal promise or statement to the intended target. It must be made in such a way as to reach the consumer or intended target.

2. False or Misleading Statement or Representation

The crime of false advertising prohibits false or misleading statements made to induce consumers to buy a product; however, the law was not intended to punish "mere puffery," which is the natural and expected exaggeration of merchants regarding their products or services. Further, the statutes do not prohibit ridiculous claims of a product's qualities. For instance, television advertisements routinely show perfumes that attract suitors or trucks that climb up sheer mountain sides, but the consumer is expected to know that this is mere exaggeration and "puffery." The law is intended to punish merchants who make serious statements that purport to be facts about the product or service, intentionally misleading the public.

3. Concerning Merchandise or Anything of Value

In general, false advertising is related to the sale of products, but it could be services or anything of value. For instance, timeshares, vacation memberships, real estate purchases, investments, and other things may be the subject of the false advertising. Even pharmaceutical companies must be careful concerning the claims made on television and other advertising regarding their product (which accounts for the extensive litany of side effects reported and frequent use of qualifying terminology in the ads).

4. For Purpose of Sale, Barter, or Exchange

The false statements or misrepresentations have to be made for the purpose of encouraging or enticing the consumer to buy the product or engage in the transaction.

5. Intent to Deceive or Mislead any Other Person

The person making the false statement must know that it is false and make the statements with intent to deceive the other party.

6. Example of State Statutes

Some states retain separate criminal provisions concerning false advertising. Consumers also have tort remedies. An example is that of Kentucky. It states:

> A person is guilty of false advertising when, in connection with the promotion or the sale of or to increase the consumption of property or services, he knowingly makes or causes to be made a false or misleading statement in any advertisement addressed to the public or to a substantial number of persons.[43]

Under the provisions of Kentucky's statute, the elements of false advertising are: (1) knowingly making or causing to be made a false or misleading statement, (2) for the promotion of the sale or to increase the consumption of property, and (3) the advertisement is addressed to the public.

In addition to false advertising statutes, Kentucky also has a statute that explicitly deals with "bait advertising." The statute provides:

> A person is guilty of bait advertising when in any manner, including advertising or other means of communication, he offers to the public or a substantial number of persons property or service as part of a scheme or plan with the intent not to sell or provide the advertised property or services:
>
> (a) At the price which he offered them; or
> (b) In a quantity sufficient to meet the reasonable expected public demand, unless the quantity is specifically stated in the advertisement; or
> (c) At all.[44]

Florida also has a specific statute directed to false advertising:

> 817.06 Misleading advertisements prohibited; penalty.—
>
> (1) No person, persons, association, copartnership, or institution shall, with intent to offer or sell or in anywise dispose of merchandise, securities, certificates, diplomas, documents, or other credentials purporting to reflect proficiency in any trade, skill, profession, credits for academic achievement, service or anything offered by such person, persons, association, copartnership, corporation, or institution directly or indirectly, to the public, for sale or distribution or issuance, or with intent to increase the consumption or use thereof, or with intent to induce the public in any manner to enter into any obligation relating thereto, or to acquire title thereto, or any interest therein, or ownership thereof, knowingly or intentionally make, publish, disseminate, circulate or place before the public, or cause, directly or indirectly, to be made, published, disseminated or circulated or placed before the public in this state in a newspaper or other publication or in the form of a book, notice, handbill, poster, bill, circular, pamphlet or letter or in any other way, an advertisement of any sort regarding such certificate, diploma, document, credential, academic credits, merchandise, security, service or anything so offered

> to the public, which advertisement contains any assertion, representation or statement which is untrue, deceptive, or misleading.
>
> (2) Any person, persons, association, copartnership, corporation, or institution found guilty of a violation of subsection (1) shall be guilty of a misdemeanor of the second degree, punishable as provided in 775.082 or 775.083.[45]

D. Summary

The crime of false advertising is very similar to false pretenses, described in the last chapter. In each of these crimes, there is an intent to defraud the victim through the use of false statements. The difference is that in false advertising, the attempt is usually to deceive many consumers at once through a public advertisement, while in false pretenses, one or a few victims are targeted. False advertising did not exist under the common law, which upheld the *caveat emptor* principle that the consumer needed to be cautious and protect himself against the natural dishonesty of merchants.

False Advertising

(A/R) Publish, false or misleading statements, about a product or service, to encourage the sale of the product

(M/R) Knowledge that the statement is false; intent to defraud

---

§ 9.6 Commercial Bribery

A. Common Law

At common law, bribery was a crime but was limited to the offering, giving, receiving, or soliciting anything of value with intent to influence the recipient's action *as a public official*. (Bribery of or by public officials will be discussed in Chapter 11). Very early, it was recognized that **commercial bribery** should be a matter of concern in the criminal law as well as under tort law, and early statutes were enacted to control commercial bribery. The purpose of the statutes regarding commercial bribery was to outlaw collusion and kickbacks in commercial and business affairs.[46]

B. Model Penal Code

The Model Penal Code provision is more comprehensive than the traditional statutes relating to commercial bribery. Under the provisions of the Model Code, a person who solicits, accepts, or agrees to accept a consideration must do so "knowingly violating or agreeing to violate a duty of fidelity" in certain specified relationships. In states that have used this terminology, the prosecution must introduce evidence to prove the "knowingly" mental element. Also, the prosecution must prove that the relationship, such as partner, agent, or employee, as specified in the Model Code, existed at the time of the transaction.

---

§ 224.8 Commercial Bribery and Breach of Duty to Act Disinterestedly[47]

(1) A person commits a misdemeanor if he solicits, accepts or agrees to accept any benefit as consideration for knowingly violating or agreeing to violate a duty of fidelity to which he is subject as:
   (a) partner, agent, or employee of another;
   (b) trustee, guardian, or other fiduciary;
   (c) lawyer, physician, accountant, appraiser, or other professional adviser or informant;
   (d) officer, director, manager or other participant in the direction of the affairs of an incorporated or unincorporated association; or
   (e) arbitrator or other purportedly disinterested adjudicator or referee.

(2) A person who holds himself out to the public as being engaged in the business of making disinterested selection, appraisal, or criticism of commodities or services commits a misdemeanor if he solicits, accepts or agrees to accept any benefit to influence his selection, appraisal or criticism.

(3) A person commits a misdemeanor if he confers, or offers or agrees to confer, any benefit the acceptance of which would be criminal under this Section.

C. State Statutes, Codes, and Cases

Very early, the courts upheld commercial bribery statutes against the challenge that they were unconstitutional. In the case of *People v. Davis*, a purchasing agent, R.H. Masey, was indicted for accepting $10 in connection with the purchase of sponges.[48] The defendant attacked the statute as unconstitutional on the ground that it violated equal protection and freedom of contract, and that the state did not have police power to enact such statutes. The court upheld the statute, finding that the state, under its police power, did have the authority to enact such statutes for "without such a statute under the fierce competition of modern life, purchasing agents . . . can be lured all too readily into service of hopelessly conflicting interests." The court also agreed that the statute did not violate the equal protection clause of the U.S. Constitution and did not conflict with the agent's freedom of contract.

The elements of commercial bribery are basically the same as common law bribery of a public official; the difference is that the person who receives the benefit is a private party but is in a **fiduciary relationship** with an innocent victim. A fiduciary relationship means one in which the party owes the other a duty to put their interest above all others, even oneself. This could be exemplified by a CEO or CFO to his or her shareholders, a buying agent to his employer, and so on. The elements of commercial bribery are described below.

1. Giving or Offering to Give Anything of Value

As with other forms of bribery, both the person who offers and the person who accepts the offer are guilty of bribery. It is a crime to solicit bribery as well.

2. To a Private Agent, Employee, or Fiduciary

Recall that common law bribery related only to public officials. This meant that commercial bribery is a statutory crime, created to cover those circumstances in which the bribe is to a private individual in return for something he or she is expected to do in the course of their job. Bribery involving government officials or their agents will be covered in a later chapter.

3. With Intent to Influence the Fiduciary's Action in Relation to the Principal's or Employer's Affairs

Examples of influence would be, for instance, to offer (or receive) a kickback in return for a decision to purchase goods from an individual. Another example might be if a board member of a company was offered a bribe to vote in a particular way. Another example could be to offer a bribe to a real estate appraiser to make his or her appraisal either falsely high or low.

4. Examples of State Statutes

Some states use terminology similar to that of the Model Penal Code, but add to the list of categories of persons subject to prosecution for accepting a bribe. For example, the Nebraska statute adds: "Duly elected or appointed representative or trustee of a labor organization or employee of a welfare trust fund."[49]

Other statutes take a different approach. The Louisiana statute includes this section:

§ 73. Commercial bribery[50]

Commercial bribery is the giving or offering to give, directly or indirectly, anything of apparent present or prospective value to any private agent, employee, or fiduciary, without the knowledge and consent of the principal or employer, with the intent to influence such agent's, employee's, or fiduciary's action in relation to the principal's or employer's affairs.

> The agent's, employee's or fiduciary's acceptance of or offer to accept, directly or indirectly, anything of apparent present or prospective value under such circumstances shall also constitute commercial bribery.
>
> The offender under this article who states the facts, under oath, to the district attorney charged with prosecution of the offense, and who gives evidence tending to convict any other offender under this article, may, in the discretion of the district attorney, be granted full immunity from prosecution for commercial bribery, in respect to the particular offense reported.
>
> Whoever commits the crime of commercial bribery shall be fined not more than five hundred dollars, or imprisoned for not more than six months, or both.

The statute was challenged as being unconstitutionally vague. However, reviewing courts indicated that, because it prohibits behavior about which persons of common intelligence need not guess, it is not unconstitutionally vague.[51]

Some state statutes contain different wording and use other terms to identify the crime. Some state statutes focus on the actions of the recipient of the bribe, rather than on the actions of the person offering the bribe. For example, the California statute states "Any employee who solicits, accepts, or agrees to accept . . ." Further, the California statute does not apply where the value of the item offered is less than $100.[52]

D. Summary

Commercial bribery was created to cover those circumstances in which it is a private person, rather than a public official, who is offered or solicits or accepts a bribe. The types of individuals that are covered by statutes are generally listed or broad categories are given and, in general, the individuals are those who stand in a fiduciary responsibility to an innocent party—either their employer or client.

Commercial Bribery

(A/R) Giving or offering to give (or taking) anything of value, to (or received by) a private agent, employee, or fiduciary

(M/R) Intent to influence the fiduciary's actions; intent to receive in return for being influenced

---

§ 9.7 Miscellaneous Business and Commercial Frauds

When it was determined that specific activities, although fraudulent, were not covered by statutes already in existence, other statutes relating to business and commercial frauds were enacted. For example, a New York court held that a basketball referee was outside the reach of the commercial bribery statute because basketball is not a business or trade.[53] Thereafter, a statute was enacted to cover this activity. Some of the miscellaneous statutes that have been enacted by various states relating to commercial and business-type frauds are included here as examples.

A. Offering or Accepting Bribes in Athletic Contests and Sporting Events

Most states have a statute that covers corruption related to sporting events, athletic contests, or other publicly exhibited contests. An example is that of Massachusetts, which provides punishment by a fine of not more than $1,000 or by imprisonment for not more than two years, or both, if a person gives, promises, or offers anything of value to a professional or amateur athlete with the intent to influence him or her to lose or try to lose or cause to be lost, etc., a sport or game. This also provides penalties for fraudulent activities relating to horse racing, and specifically mentions various sports and sporting activities.[54]

In a Nebraska statute, the terminology designating this offense is "Tampering with Publicly-Exhibited Contests." The statute is broader than most in its application. It provides a penalty where a person tampers with a publicly exhibited contest as a participant or an official as well as one who offers a benefit.[55]

In Kentucky, the crime is limited to "sporting events." Here, the crime of "sports bribery" is a Class D felony, which carries a penalty of one to five years and occurs when someone:

(a) offers, confers, or agrees to confer any benefit upon a sports participant with intent to influence him not to give his best efforts in a sports
contest; or

(b) offers, confers or agrees to confer any benefit upon a sports official
with intent to influence him to perform his duties improperly.[56]

B. Defrauding Creditors

In order to protect those who are involved in business activities, most states have specific statutes dealing with activities that are designed to defraud creditors. These differ from state to state and must be thoroughly studied to determine the elements of the offenses. One example is that of Ohio, which provides that:

(A) No person, with purpose to defraud one or more of the person's creditors, shall do any of the following:

    (1) Remove, conceal, destroy, encumber, convey, or otherwise deal with any of his property;

    (2) Misrepresent or refuse to disclose to a fiduciary appointed to administer or manage the person's affairs or estate, the existence, amount, or location of any of the person's property, or any other information regarding such property which the person is legally required to furnish to the fiduciary.[57]

Under this section, it is an offense if a debtor, in any way, defrauds one or more of his or her creditors by hiding property, or if with the same purpose he or she fails to be truthful with a fiduciary appointed to manage his or her affairs or property, concerning the nature, extent, or whereabouts of his or her property.

C. Other Statutes Relating to Business and Commercial Fraud

In addition to those that have been enumerated and discussed, various states have other statutes that are designed to protect an individual doing business with another individual or an organization. Examples are "Fraud in Insolvency," which provides a penalty for destroying, removing, or otherwise obstructing the claims of a creditor, knowing that proceedings are to be instituted to appoint a receiver, or knowingly falsifying any writing or record, or knowingly misrepresenting or refusing to disclose the existence and identification of property subject to the proceedings.[58] Another example of this type of statute is that relating to "Receiving Deposits in a Failing Financial Institution."[59] The purpose of this type of statute is to protect those who might unknowingly make deposits in a failing financial institution.

It bears repeating that the offenses discussed here are not the only offenses that are designed to protect persons against fraud. Not only are there already statutes on the books to protect against special frauds, but other statutes will also be enacted as enterprising persons find other ways to defraud the public.

§ 9.8 Computer Crimes

The amazing evolution and advances in computer technology in the past three decades have necessitated that society adapt to the social, legal, and ethical consequences. As changes and advances in computer technology have developed, criminals have found new and innovative ways to use computers to assist them in committing crimes. To meet this evolving class of crimes, legislators have experimented with new laws to confront the computer criminals.

The Department of Justice categorized **computer-related crimes** into three categories, according to the computer's role in the particular crime.

- The "object" of a crime. This category primarily refers to the theft of computer hardware or software.

- The "subject" of a crime. The computer is a subject of the attack and the site of the damage caused. Many offenders in this category are motivated by malice or mischief rather than financial gain.

- The "instrument" used to commit the traditional crimes in a more complex manner. These traditional crimes include identity theft, child pornography, copyright infringement, and mail and wire fraud.[60]

A. Common Law

When computer-specific crime legislation was first being considered, arguments were advanced that the acts that constituted computer crimes were all common law crimes or could be prosecuted under existing statutes. It was pointed out that the state laws that can be used to attack computer-assisted crimes include arson, burglary, embezzlement, larceny, criminal mischief, extortion, forgery, theft, receiving stolen property, theft of services or labor under false pretenses, and the theft of trade secrets. Although these arguments had some merit, it was soon determined that it was difficult to apply traditional laws that were developed before the computer age to computer crimes. As the number of computer-assisted crimes proliferated and as studies indicated that few of these crimes were being prosecuted, it became apparent that legislation was needed.

B. Model Penal Code

The Model Penal Code has no provisions identifying computer crimes directly.

C. State Statutes, Codes, and Cases

In 1978, state legislatures began enacting computer crime statutes, beginning with Arizona and Florida. Since then, every state has enacted some form of computer-specific legislation. Approximately one-half of the states modeled their statutes primarily on the 1977 or 1979 version of the proposed "Federal-Computer-Systems Protection Act," while the remainder enacted comprehensive computer-assisted crime statutes less closely related to the proposed federal legislation. Members of state legislative bodies were advised during the consideration of computer crimes that computer crime differs from traditional theft offenses in several respects. First, computer crime is a non-confrontational crime, unlike stealing a purse or robbing a bank. Also, computer crime is more difficult to detect than traditional crime, because the perpetrator can act with ease and speed without fear of being recognized. In response to these distinctive aspects of computer-related crime, 48 states had enacted specific computer crime statutes by 1986.[61]

Some of the state statutes are comprehensive and detailed, while others are more general. An example of a comprehensive statute is that of California.

> § 502. Unauthorized access to computers, computer systems and computer data[62]
>
> (c) Except as provided in subdivision (h), any person who commits any of the following acts is guilty of a public offense:
>
>   (1) Knowingly accesses and without permission alters, damages, deletes, destroys, or otherwise uses any data, computer, computer system, or computer network in order to either (A) devise or execute any scheme or artifice to defraud, deceive, or extort, or (B) wrongfully control or obtain money, property, or data.
>
>   (2) Knowingly accesses and without permission takes, copies, or makes use of any data from a computer, computer system, or computer network, or takes or copies any supporting documentation, whether existing or residing internal or external to a computer, computer system, or computer network.
>
>   (3) Knowingly and without permission uses or causes to be used computer services.
>
>   (4) Knowingly accesses and without permission adds, alters, damages, deletes, or destroys any data computer software, or computer programs which reside or exist internal or external to a computer, computer system, or computer network.
>
>   (5) Knowingly and without permission disrupts or causes the disruption of computer services or denies or causes the denial of computer services to an authorized user of a computer, computer system, or computer network.
>
>   (6) Knowingly and without permission provides or assists in providing a means of accessing a computer, computer system, or computer network in violation of this section.
>
>   (7) Knowingly and without permission accesses or causes to be accessed any computer, computer system, or computer network.
>
>   (8) Knowingly introduces any computer contaminant into any computer, computer system, or computer network.
>
>   (9) Knowingly and without permission uses the Internet domain name of another individual, corporation, or entity in connection with the sending of one or more electronic mail messages, and thereby damages or causes damage to a computer, computer system, or computer network.

In addition to defining terms used in specifically listing the acts prohibited, the California Code provides a graduated system of criminal penalties, authorizes civil action, authorizes the court to award punitive or exemplary damages, and provides for a forfeiture of the computer systems that have been used during the commission of the public offenses described.

In the case of *People v. Hawkins*, the defendant was convicted of a violation of California Penal Code § 502(c)(2): knowingly accessing and taking data from the computer system. The court held that the statute stated that an individual who "knowingly accesses and without permission takes, copies, or makes use of any data from a computer, computer system or computer network" commits a public offense knowingly, and thus could be punished as a felon.[63]

The Louisiana statute has a comprehensive list of definitions of the terms "access," "computer," "computer network," and "computer program," but is less comprehensive than the California Code.[64] The Michigan Code prohibits a person from doing any of the following:

- intentionally and without authorization access or cause access to be made to a computer to acquire, alter, damage, delete, or destroy property or otherwise use the service of a computer program,

- insert or attach or knowingly create the opportunity for an unknowing and unwanted insertion or attachment of a set of instructions or a computer program into a computer,

- intentionally access or cause to access to a computer to devise or execute a scheme or artifice with intent to defraud or obtain money, property, or a service by false or fraudulent pretense, representation, or promise, or

- utilize a computer to commit a crime.[65]

Because computer crimes often have jurisdictional complexities and an offender may victimize individuals in many states, federal laws are more suited to combat this type of crime. We will revisit laws designed to thwart computer crime in Chapter 15.

D. Summary

State and federal statutes have defined computer crimes and apply traditional crime definitions to prosecute wrongdoing that utilizes computer technology. However, there is little doubt that ingenious violators will invent new ways of committing cyber-crime offenses and that new laws will become necessary.

§ 9.9 Summary

While various types of cheating were made crimes under the early English common law, many of the specific laws relating to forgery and commercial fraud did not develop until later. The early approach of *caveat emptor* (let the buyer beware) gave way to greater protections for the consumer and merchant from dishonest dealings. The widespread use of checks and other commercial paper, pervasive advertising, and other modern elements of commerce has led to a proliferation of statutes that criminalize dishonest practices in the marketplace.

One of the most common crimes in our society is forgery. Forgery is defined as the false making or material altering, with intent to defraud, of any writing, which, if genuine, might apparently be of legal efficacy or the foundation of a legal liability. In an effort to more accurately define what wrongs are prohibited, some modern statutes use different terminology and specifically enumerate what instruments are subject to forgery and what conduct is prohibited.

Many modern statutes include the crime of uttering a forged instrument within the statute defining forgery. Others make this a separate offense. To utter a forged instrument is to offer it, directly or indirectly, by words or actions as good. This, if done with intent to defraud and with knowledge of the falsity of the instrument, is a violation of the law in some form in all states.

Finding that some forgery statutes were not comprehensive enough to cover acts that should be made criminal, legislative bodies have enacted legislation to make other acts criminal. Some examples are criminal simulation, where the subject of the offense is not a writing but an object, misuse of credit cards, possession of forged devices, fraudulent destruction, removal, or concealment of recordable instruments, and tampering with records. Identity theft is considered one of the fastest-growing crime problems in the United States. It usually is a combination of crimes, including forgery and credit card abuse.

Numerous statutes and ordinances have been enacted that prohibit false or fraudulent statements in advertising. The crime of false advertising consists primarily in the publication and circulation of deceptive matter and the offense is complete without regard to whether anyone is deceived or damaged. In the Model Penal Code, this is included in the section titled "Deceptive Business Practices," which covers several offenses relating to cheating and deceptive practices.

Common law bribery only concerned *public officials*, not private citizens. However, statutes have been enacted to control commercial bribery. Modern statutes encompass the bribery of general agents and employees of commercial concerns, as well as the bribery of public employees. When the courts determined that specific activities, although fraudulent, were not covered by the statutes in existence, other statutes relating to commercial and business frauds were enacted. Some examples are offering or accepting bribes in athletic contests and sporting events, defrauding creditors, and receiving deposits in failing financial institutions.

One of the newest areas of law is addressing the misuse of computers. Computers can be the target or the instrument of crime. States took the lead in creating legislation prohibiting unauthorized access to computers and the federal government followed. Today, many states have comprehensive computer crime statutes.

The fraud-related statutes are numerous and varied. They have been enacted to protect the public against special frauds. Additional statutes will be enacted as state legislatures determine that other laws are necessary to protect the public against fraudulent acts.

Review Questions

1. Briefly trace the history of fraud offenses in England and the United States.

2. What are the elements of the traditional offense of forgery? Describe each.

3. How do modern statutes differ from the common law?

4. What is a "writing" under most forgery statutes? What does *legal efficacy* mean? Give examples.

5. What is the difference between the offense of forgery and uttering a forged instrument? What are the elements of uttering a forged instrument? Does the instrument have to be accepted before a crime occurs?

6. What does it mean under an uttering statute to "publish or offer" the forged instrument?

7. What is the *mens rea* for uttering? Must the individual know that the instrument is forged? Must the defendant be the one to have forged the instrument? Must the offering be for the intent to defraud?

8. How does the offense of criminal simulation, included in the Ohio statute, differ from forgery?

9. What acts are typically included in credit card abuse statutes?

10. What acts are prohibited by false advertising statutes? What are the usual elements of the offense of false advertising?

11. What is identity theft? How much of a problem is it in the United States? What are the ways in which thieves acquire identity information?

12. What is *phishing*?

13. What is the difference between false advertising and obtaining property through false pretenses? Must the defendant know that the misrepresentation is a lie?

14. What is the purpose of the statutes regarding commercial bribery? Elaborate on the elements of this offense. How are these statutes different from common law bribery?

15. What is a fiduciary? Give some examples of fiduciary relationships.

16. What is the crime directed to sports officials who might solicit bribes?

17. Is it a crime to hide property from a creditor? Explain.

18. What are the various types of computer crimes?

19. What are the types of common law crimes that might be utilized if a state does not have a specific computer crime related to the offense?

20. Is it usually a crime to merely access a company's data without permission with no intent to damage or to obtain money or other benefit from such "hacking"?

Notes

[1]   33 Hen. 8, c. 1 (1541). *See also* L. SALZMAN, ENGLISH LIFE IN THE MIDDLE AGES (1926).

[2]   State v. Murphy, 17 R.I. 698, 24 A. 473 (1892).

[3]   Ratliff v. State, 175 Tenn. 172, 133 S.W.2d 470 (1939).

[4]   4 BLACKSTONE, COMMENTARIES 247 (1765-1869), 2 BISH. CR. LAW, § 523.

[5]   State v. Goranson, 408 P.2d 7 (Wash. 1965).

[6]   State v. Charles, 341 So. 2d 539 (Fla. 1977).

[7]   MODEL PENAL CODE § 224.1 (1985).

[8]   State v. Young, 46 N.H. 266 (1865).

[9]   Hicks v. State, 176 Ga. 727, 168 S.E. 899 (1933); Saucier v. State, 102 Miss. 647, 59 So. 858 (1912).

[10]   People v. Dorneval, 684 N.Y.S.2d 434 (1998).

[11]   Ratliff v. State, 175 Tenn. 172, 133 S.E.2d 470 (1939); People v. Henderson, 373 N.E.2d 1338 (Ill. 1978).

[12]   *See* Footnotes 16 and 21.

[13]   People v. Lewinger, 25 Ill. 332, 96 N.E. 837 (1911).

[14]   LA. REV. STAT. § 14:72 (2001).

[15]   MO. REV. STAT.§ 570.090 (2002).

[16]   State v. Conaway, 824 S.W.2d 50 (Mo. Ct. App. 1991). *See also* State ex rel. Nicholas v. State, 520 So. 2d 377 (La. 1988), which held that where the defendant merely affixes his own signature as his endorsement on an instrument, this evidence was constitutionally insufficient to support a conviction of forgery by false making, absent evidence that the defendant falsely made or altered any signature or part of the check in question.

[17]   OHIO REV. CODE ANN. § 2913.31 (Anderson 1999).

[18]   Commonwealth v. Fisher, 682 A.2d 811 (Pa. 1996).

[19]   State v. Wasson, 125 N.M. 656, 964 P.2d 820 (1998).

[20]   McClure v. State, 234 Ga. App. 304, 506 S.E.2d 667 (1998).

[21]   Commonwealth v. O'Connell, 769 N.E.2d 331 (Mass. 2002). *See also* State v. Johnson, 817 So. 2d 283 (La. 2002), which held that an essential ingredient of the crime of forgery is a specific intent to defraud.

[22]   Maloney v. State, 91 Ark. 485, 121 S.W. 728 (1909).

[23]   MODEL PENAL CODE § 224.1(1)(c) (1985).

[24]   State v. Williams, 152 Mo. 115, 53 S.W. 424 (1899); People v. Brown, 397 Ill. 92, 72 N.E.2d 859 (1947).

[25]   State v. Meeks, 245 Iowa 1231, 65 N.W.2d 76 (1954); Finley v. Commonwealth, 259 S.W.2d 32 (Ky. 1953).

[26]   State v. Phillips, 256 N.C. 445, 124 S.E.2d 146 (1962).

[27]   Smith v. State, 291 P.2d 378 (Okla. 1955).

[28]   Ramsey v. Commonwealth, 343 S.E.2d 465 (Va. Ct. App. 1986). *See also* State v. Brown, 108 Ohio App. 3d 489, 664 N.E.2d 536 (1996).

[29]   NEB. REV. STAT. § 28-602 (2002).

[30]   People v. Dukes, 471 N.W.2d 651 (Mich. Ct. App. 1991); People v. Shively, 584 N.W.2d 740 (Mich. Ct. App. 1998).

[31]   OHIO REV. CODE ANN. § 2913.32 (Anderson 2002). *See also* KY. REV. STAT. § 516.110 (2001) and MODEL PENAL CODE § 224.2 (1985), which includes comments relating to states having similar statutes.

[32]   OHIO REV. CODE ANN. § 2913.21 (Anderson 2002).

[33]   MODEL PENAL CODE § 224.6 (1985).

[34]   Florida Statutes, 2008. Title XLVI. Ch. 817. Credit Card Crimes.

[35]   KY. REV. STAT. § 516.090 (2001).

[36]   Kentucky Penal Code Notebook, Kentucky Dept. of Justice § 7.1 (1975). KY. REV. STAT. §§ 516.120-516.130 (1999).

[37]   MODEL PENAL CODE § 224.3-4 (1985).

[38]   NEB. REV. STAT. § 28-612 (2002). *See also* OHIO REV. CODE ANN. § 2913.42 (Anderson 2002).

[39]   OHIO REV. CODE ANN. § 2913.45 (Anderson 2002).

[40]   Jennifer Lynch, *Law and Technology: II. Cyberlaw: Identity Theft in Cyberspace*. 20 BERKELEY TECH. L. J. 259 (2005).

[41]   *Annotation*, 89 A.L.R. 1005 (1919).

[42]   MODEL PENAL CODE § 224.7 (1985).

[43]   KY. REV. STAT. § 517.030 (2001).

[44]   KY. REV. STAT. § 517.040 (2001).

[45]   FLORIDA STATUTES 2008, Title XLVI, Chapter 817.06 Misleading Advertisements Prohibited.

[46]   *See Control of Nongovernmental Corruption by Criminal Legislation*, 108 U. PA. L. REV. 848 (1960), for an analysis and chart, p. 864, listing states that had enacted legislation relating to commercial bribery at that time.

[47]   MODEL PENAL CODE § 224.8 (1985).

[48]   People v. Davis, 33 N.Y. Crim. 460, 160 N.Y.S. 769 (1915).

[49]   NEB. REV. STAT. § 28-613(1)(c) (2002).

[50]   LA. REV. STAT. ANN. § 14:73 (2002).

[51]   United States v. Perrin, 580 F.2d 730 (5th Cir. 1978).

[52]   CAL. PENAL CODE § 641.3(a)(b) (1999).

53   People v. Levy, 283 App. Div. 383, 128 N.Y.S.2d 275 (1954).

54   MASS. GEN. LAWS ANN. ch. 271 § 39A (West 2002).

55   NEB. REV. STAT. § 28-614 (2002).

56   KY. REV. STAT. § 518.040 (1995). *See also* KY. REV. STAT. § 518.050 (2001), Receiving Sports Bribe; KY. REV. STAT. § 518.060 (1999), Tampering with or Rigging Sports Contests; and KY. REV. STAT. § 518.070 (2001), Ticket Scalping.

57   OHIO REV. CODE ANN. § 2913.45 (Anderson 2002).

58   ME. REV. STAT. ANN. tit. 17-A, § 902 (1995); N.H. REV. STAT. ANN. § 638.9 (2001); UTAH CODE ANN. § 76-6-512 (2002).

59   MODEL PENAL CODE § 224.12 (1985).

60   Heather Jacobson and Rebecca Green, *Computer Crimes*, 39 AMER. CRIM. L. REV. 273 (2002).

61   *Id.* at 315 (2002).

62   CAL. PENAL CODE §502 (2002).

63   People v. Hawkins, 121 Cal. Rptr. 2d 627 (2002).

64   LA. STAT. ANN. §§ 73.1, 73.2, 73.3, 73.4, and 73.5 (West 2002).

65   MICH. COMP. LAWS ANN. §752.795 (West Supp. 2000). *See* Patrick Corbett, *State and Federal Criminal Cyberlaw and Legislation Survey*, 18 T.M. COOLEY L. REV. 7 (2001).

Offenses Involving
Morality and Decency   10

Chapter Outline

Cases

Obscenity: *Miller v. California*, 413 U.S. 15 (1983)
Partial Birth Abortion: *Gonzales v. Carhart*, 550 U.S. 124 (2007)

§ 10.1   Introduction

Some acts, such as murder, burglary, arson, and theft, are so obviously wrong that everyone, or almost everyone, can agree that punishment is necessary. Other acts may be undesirable to many members of society or even "sinful," but are not always designated as crimes. Remaining are those that are so near the borderline that they are considered crimes in some jurisdictions and not in other jurisdictions, or their definition as crimes changes over time. In this chapter, titled "Offenses Involving Morality and Decency," the most well-known offenses in this category are discussed. These include consensual sexual acts, including adultery, fornication, prostitution and related offenses, offenses related to obscenity, offenses that take place within the family setting, including bigamy, polygamy, incest, and abortion. Drug offenses, gambling, and other types of offenses will be covered in the next chapter.

§ 10.2   Adultery and Fornication

A.   Common Law

Sexual intercourse out of wedlock was punished by the church as an ecclesiastical offense at early common law. In England, the common law meaning of the word "**adultery**" was sexual intercourse with another's wife. In 1650 adultery was made a capital crime in England, but the statute was repealed after the Restoration.[1] In this country, the offense was punishable in the common law courts when so provided by statute.[2]

363

Although early definitions of adultery varied, at least one of the parties had to be lawfully married to another and such marriage had to be proven.[3] Under the old Roman law, it was essential to the crime of adultery that the woman be married to another. The crime was not committed where a married man had sexual intercourse with a single woman, the gist of the offense being the danger of putting spurious offspring upon a man.[4] Until recently the majority of jurisdictions held that an unmarried woman who had intercourse with a married man did not commit adultery.[5] While the elements of adultery varied in early state statutes, they typically involved the following elements: voluntary sexual intercourse, between persons unmarried to each other; with one of the parties (under older laws this was the woman) being married to another.

Fornication is voluntary unlawful sexual intercourse, under circumstances not constituting adultery. While fornication was not a crime at common law, it was made a crime by early statutes in many of the states.

B. Model Penal Code

Recognizing that many of the penal statutes against fornication and adultery are unenforced; the Model Penal Code omitted any provisions relating to these offenses. A note on adultery and fornication following the discussion of § 213.6 of the Model Penal Code explains the rationale for not including the common law crimes relating to sexual intercourse with a person of the opposite sex where the persons are unmarried.[6]

C. State Statutes, Codes and Cases

State statutes vary concerning the definition of adultery. One element is consistent: at least one of the parties must be lawfully married to another person. The three common definitions are:

- Voluntary sexual intercourse between persons, one of whom is lawfully married to another, both parties being guilty.

- Intercourse by a married person with one who is not his or her wife or husband, the married person only being guilty of adultery.

- Intercourse with a married woman by one not her husband, both parties being guilty.

While many states have repealed statutes relating to fornication and adultery, or have omitted this offense from the revised drafts of their statutes, others still contain provisions that make it a crime to participate in sexual intercourse out of wedlock. In some of these states, simple adultery—that is, one act of adultery—constitutes a criminal offense, while in others, a relationship that is continuous or "open and notorious" is required. In these states, adultery and fornication are not crimes unless the behavior is "open and notorious" and a single act would not constitute the crime.[7] An example of this type of statute is that of Mississippi.

> § 97-29-1. Adultery and Fornication—Unlawful Cohabitation[8]
>
> If any man and woman shall unlawfully cohabit, whether in adultery or fornication, they shall be fined in any sum not more than five hundred dollars each, and imprisoned in the county jail not more than six months; and it shall not be necessary, to constitute the offense, that the parties shall dwell together publicly as husband and wife, but it may be proved by circumstances which show habitual sexual intercourse.

The Mississippi Supreme Court has held that a few acts of intercourse without showing unlawful cohabitation would not constitute a violation of this statute.[9] While many states have discarded their adultery and fornication statutes; in those that still exist, the punishment for adultery can be more severe than the punishment for fornication. For example, the Massachusetts statute provides a penalty of up to three years for adultery and a maximum of three months for fornication.[10]

The historical justifications for criminalization of adultery are: (1) protection of innocent spouses from potential harm, and (2) protection of public morals.[11] However, it is clear that constitutional rights of privacy call into question the legality of any remaining statutes criminalizing adultery and/or fornication. Since *Lawrence v. Texas*,[12] the Supreme Court case that struck down the Texas statute prohibiting same-sex intercourse, it is doubtful that any of the statutes outlawing private decisions regarding voluntary adult sexual partners would withstand constitutional scrutiny if challenged.

Legal News

One would think that laws against adultery are part of the past, along with "scarlet letters;" however, John Bushey, the city attorney for Luray, Virginia, would beg to differ. He pled guilty to adultery in 2004 for an affair with the city clerk. When he ended the affair, she reported him to the authorities and he was charged with the misdemeanor of adultery. She was not charged because she was unmarried. Despite a likely win at the appellate level, Mr. Bushey pled guilty and accepted 20 hours of community service as punishment.

Source: Retrieved on 3/22/2006 from www.washingtonpost.com/ac2/wp-dyn/A62581-2004Sep4?language=printer.

D. Related Crimes: Sale of Vibrators and Sex Aids

It seems anachronistic, but Alabama, Virginia, Mississippi, and Texas still have laws regulating and restricting the sale of vibrators and other sex aids. Alabama, for instance, has a law that banned the sale of vibrators. Upon challenge, the Eleventh Circuit ruled that Alabama had a legitimate interest in "discouraging prurient interests in autonomous sex . . ." and held that the state could prohibit the commercial sale of such devices (but not the possession or use of them). It interpreted *Lawrence v. Texas* to allow the use of a rational relationship test that allowed the state to control private behavior if they could prove a legitimate state interest.[13] Texas also has a law that prohibited the commercial sale or purchase of vibrators or sex aids. "Passion parties" are the sex-aid equivalent of Tupperware parties where merchandise is offered at an event in one person's home. Undercover detectives in Austin and Fort Worth posed as married couples, purchased vibrators at one of the parties, and then arrested the organizers.[14]

The parent company sued to have the Texas law ruled unconstitutional and, in February 2008, the Fifth Circuit did so, citing *Lawrence v. Texas*. The state defended the law arguing that even if individuals had a privacy right that covered their right to use such devices, vendors had no right to sell them. The Fifth Circuit disagreed, stating that punishing vendors would present an undue burden on individuals' rights. The state also argued that *Lawrence* was based on an equal protection challenge, not substantive due process and privacy. The Fifth Circuit disagreed with this argument as well, stating that the *Lawrence* decision was clearly based on substantive due process and precedents, including *Griswold v. Connecticut*.[15] They concluded:

> Because of *Lawrence*, the issue before us is whether the Texas statute impermissibly burdens the individual's substantive due process right to engage in private intimate conduct of his or her choosing. Contrary to the district court's conclusion, we hold that the Texas law burdens this constitutional right.

> An individual who wants to legally use a safe sexual device during private intimate moments alone or with another is unable to legally purchase a device in Texas, which heavily burdens a constitutional right. This conclusion is consistent with the decisions in *Carey* and *Griswold*, where the Court held that restricting commercial transactions unconstitutionally burdened the exercise of individual rights. Indeed, under this statute it is even illegal to "lend" or "give" a sexual device to another person. This further restricts the exercise of the constitutional right to engage in private intimate conduct in the home free from government intrusion. It also undercuts any argument that the statute only affects public conduct.

> The dissent relegates the burden on this right to rational basis review. The State says we have two alternatives: (1) strict scrutiny if *Lawrence* established this right as a fundamental right or (2) rational basis review if *Lawrence* did not. There has been debate about this and the Eleventh Circuit concluded that *Lawrence* did not establish a fundamental right.

The Supreme Court did not address the classification, nor do we need to do so, because the Court expressly held that "individual decisions by married persons, concerning the intimacies of their physical relationship, even when not intended to produce offspring, are a form of 'liberty' protected by the Due Process Clause of the Fourteenth Amendment. Moreover, this protection extends to intimate choices by unmarried as well as married persons." The Court also carefully delineated the types of governmental interests that are constitutionally insufficient to sustain a law that infringes on this substantive due process right. Therefore, our responsibility as an inferior federal court is mandatory and straightforward. We must apply *Lawrence* to the Texas statute.

Because of the disagreement between the Eleventh and Fifth Circuits, the Supreme Court may have to resolve the dispute as to whether states should be able to prohibit the sale of sex aids.

E. Summary

While many states have discarded adultery laws, they do still exist. There are variations of the definitions of adultery, however. The most common elements are described below. Fornication was the crime when neither party was married, or the crime assigned to the unmarried party in an adulterous relationship. It seems clear that *Lawrence v. Texas* will be the tool used to dismantle any remaining state statutes that seek to control individual decisions regarding sexual practices that are consensual and protected by the right of privacy.

Adultery

(A/R) Voluntary sexual intercourse; between two persons unmarried to each other; with at least one of the parties being married to another

(M/R) Intent to have intercourse; knowing of the marriage to another

Fornication

(A/R) Voluntary sexual intercourse; between two adults who are not married to each other

(M/R) Intentional

---

§ 10.3 Prostitution-Related Offenses

A. Common Law

At the outset, it should be noted that the term **"prostitution"** is not synonymous with the offense of prostitution. The term "prostitution" is defined as the practice of a female offering her body for intercourse with a man, for hire. Prostitution was not a crime at common law and is not a crime in all jurisdictions. It is more appropriate to discuss this matter in terms of "crimes relating to prostitution" rather than using prostitution, the offense, interchangeably with prostitution, the practice.

While the act or practice was not a crime at common law, the courts have recognized that states exercising reasonable police powers may enact restrictive legislation pertaining to prostitution and offenses related to prostitution.[16] As a result, there were very early statutes relating to prostitution. These included: soliciting prostitution, aiding and abetting prostitution, associating with prostitutes, keeping and operating a place or conveyance for the purpose of prostitution, receiving or offering to receive any person into any place for the purpose of prostitution, and so on.

An early court included this definition of prostitution: "performance of indiscriminate sexual acts for hire and indiscriminate solicitation or agreement to perform sex acts for hire; an essential element of proof common to both grounds is the commercial nature of the sexual transaction."[17] Although the early statutes differed as to the required elements, some elements were common to most statutes.

1. Female

Generally, early statutes were sex-specific in that the terminology used indicated that only women could commit prostitution.[18]

2. Offering of One's Self or One's Body

Generally there needed to be a direct or indirect offer of intercourse.

3. For Hire or for Money

Pecuniary gain has been made an element of the crime by statute in most jurisdictions. To constitute the crime of engaging in prostitution, there must be a showing of an offer for money or some profit.[19] In one case, the court held that where the prostitution was defined by statutes as the offering, giving, or using of the body for sexual intercourse *for hire*, the term did not necessarily involve indiscriminate intercourse with more than one man.[20]

B. *Model Penal Code*

The Model Penal Code includes a fairly comprehensive section devoted to prostitution-related offenses. Note that the language, as with most modern statutes, applies to both men and women. The Model Code emphasizes the repression of commercialized sexual activity including "deviate sexual relations" as well as "sexual intercourse." It also deals with procuring, pandering, transportation, and other activities ancillary to the business of prostitution.

§ 251.2 Prostitution and Related Offenses[21]

(1) Prostitution. A person is guilty of prostitution, a petty misdemeanor, if he or she:

    (a) is an inmate of a house of prostitution or otherwise engages in sexual activity as a business; or

    (b) loiters in or within view of any public place for the purpose of being hired to engage in sexual activity.

"Sexual activity" includes homosexual and other deviate sexual relations. A "house of prostitution" is a place where prostitution or promotion of prostitution is regularly carried on by one person under the control, management or supervision of another. An "inmate" is a person who engages in prostitution in or through the agency of a house of prostitution. "Public place" means any place to which the public or any substantial group thereof has access.

(2) Promoting Prostitution. A person who knowingly promotes prostitution of another commits a misdemeanor or felony as provided in Subsection (3). The following acts shall, without limitation of the foregoing, constitute promoting prostitution:

    (a) owning, controlling, managing, supervising or otherwise keeping, alone or in association with others, a house of prostitution or a prostitution business; or

    (b) procuring an inmate for a house of prostitution or a place in a house of prostitution for one who would be an inmate; or

    (c) encouraging, inducing, or otherwise purposely causing another to become or remain a prostitute; or

    (d) soliciting a person to patronize a prostitute; or

    (e) procuring a prostitute for a patron; or

    (f) transporting a person into or within this state with purpose to promote that person's engaging in prostitution, or procuring or paying for transportation with that purpose; or

    (g) leasing or otherwise permitting a place controlled by the actor, alone or in association with others, to be regularly used for prostitution or the promotion of prostitution, or failure to make reasonable effort to abate such use by ejecting the tenant, notifying law enforcement authorities, or other legally available means; or

    (h) soliciting, receiving, or agreeing to receive any benefit for doing or agreeing to do anything forbidden by this Subsection.

(3) Grading of Offenses Under Subsection (2). An offense under Subsection (2) constitutes a felony of the third degree if:

    (a) the offense falls within paragraph (a), (b) or (c) of Subsection (2); or

    (b) the actor compels another to engage in or promote prostitution; or

    (c) the actor promotes prostitution of a child under 16, whether or not he is aware of the child's age; or

    (d) the actor promotes prostitution of his wife, child, ward or any person for whose care, protection or support he is responsible.

Otherwise the offense is a misdemeanor.

(4) Presumption from Living Off Prostitutes. A person, other than the prostitute or the prostitute's minor child or other legal dependent incapable of self-support, who is supported in whole or substantial part by the proceeds of prostitution is presumed to be knowingly promoting prostitution in violation of Subsection (2).

(5) Patronizing Prostitutes. A person commits a violation if he hires a prostitute to engage in sexual activity with him, or if he enters or remains in a house of prostitution for the purpose of engaging in sexual activity. . . .

    (b) Evidence. On the issue whether a place is a house of prostitution the following shall be admissible evidence: its general repute; the repute of the persons who reside in or frequent the place; the frequency, timing and duration of visits by non-residents. Testimony of a person against his spouse shall be admissible to prove offenses under this Section.

The Model Code includes sections relating to "living off" of prostitutes and patronizing prostitutes. This makes it easier to prosecute the customers of prostitutes, who were rarely punished under previous statutes. It is interesting to note that the offense of prostitution, under the Model Code, is a petty misdemeanor, while in some instances, promoting prostitution is a felony of the third degree.

Legal News

In March 2008 the governor of New York, Elliot Spitzer, resigned in a prostitution-related scandal. Spitzer was caught making dates with a Washington, D.C. call girl on a wiretap by the FBI investigating the operation. He also attracted the attention of investigators when he withdrew large sums of money to pay the call girl. By some estimates, he paid more than $80,000 to the call girl operation for the services of one call girl. The irony of the situation was that Spitzer ran for governor on a "tough-on-crime" platform and, as a prosecutor and state attorney general, was known as a zealous opponent of prostitution. Neither state nor federal charges have been filed against him.

Source: Gross, S. and D. Barrett (2008). "Spitzer Tripped Up on Laws He Enforced." www.foxnews.com. March 12, 2008. Accessed 1/2/2009 from http://www.foxnews.com/printer_friendly_wires/2008Mar12/0,0465,SpitzerTheMoneyTrail,00.html.

C. State Statutes, Codes, and Cases

Every state, except Nevada, has a statute outlawing solicitation and other crimes related to prostitution. In Nevada, prostitution is legal but strictly regulated in 10 counties. Prostitutes may only operate out of brothels and must have periodic health inspections. Recently revised codes and statutes make prostitution a gender-neutral crime and include same-sex prostitution as well as heterosexual prostitution. Modern statutes include penalties not only for soliciting sexual activity for a fee, but related offenses. There is a trend to reduce the grade of the offense of soliciting prostitution for a fee and emphasizing the prosecution of those who promote prostitution.

An example of a statute that probably represents the approach taken in the majority of the states is that of Connecticut. This code provides punishment for prostitution, patronizing a prostitute, promoting prostitution in the first degree, promoting prostitution in the second degree, promoting prostitution in the third degree, and permitting prostitution.

§ 53a-82. Prostitution: Class A misdemeanor[22]

(a) A person is guilty of prostitution when such person engages or agrees or offers to engage in sexual conduct with another person in return for a fee.

(b) Prostitution is a Class A misdemeanor.

§ 53a-83. Patronizing a prostitute: Class A misdemeanor

(a) A person is guilty of patronizing a prostitute when:
    (1) pursuant to a prior understanding, he pays a fee to another person as compensation for such person or a third person having engaged in sexual conduct with him; or
    (2) he pays or agrees to pay a fee to another person pursuant to an understanding that in return therefor such person or a third person will engage in sexual conduct with him; or
    (3) he solicits or requests another person to engage in sexual conduct with him in return for a fee.

(b) Patronizing a prostitute is a Class A misdemeanor.

§ 53a–83a. Patronizing a prostitute from a motor vehicle: Class A misdemeanor

(a) A person is guilty of patronizing from a motor vehicle when he, while occupying a motor vehicle: (1) pursuant to a prior understanding, pays a fee to another person as compensation for such person or a third person having engaged in sexual conduct with him; or (2) pays or agrees to pay a fee to another person pursuant to an understanding that in return therefor such person or a third person will engage in sexual conduct with him; or (3) solicits or requests another person to engage in sexual conduct with him in return for a fee; or (4) engages in sexual conduct for which a fee was paid or agreed to be paid.

(b) Patronizing a prostitute from a motor vehicle is a class A misdemeanor.

§ 53a-86. Promoting prostitution in the first degree: Class B felony

(a) A person is guilty of promoting prostitution in the first degree when he knowingly:

(1) advances prostitution by compelling a person by force or intimidation to engage in prostitution, or profits from coercive conduct by another; or

(2) advances or profits from prostitution of a person less than sixteen years old.

(b) Promoting prostitution in the first degree is a Class B felony.

§ 53a-87. Promoting prostitution in the second degree

(a) A person is guilty of promoting prostitution in the second degree when he knowingly:

(1) advances or profits from prostitution by managing, supervising, controlling or owning, either alone or in association with others, a house of prostitution or a prostitution business or enterprise involving prostitution activity by two or more prostitutes; or

(2) advances or profits from prostitution of a person less than eighteen years old.

(b) Promoting prostitution in the second degree is a Class C felony.

§ 53a-88. Promoting prostitution in the third degree

(a) A person is guilty of promoting prostitution in the third degree when he knowingly advances or profits from prostitution.

(b) Promoting prostitution in the third degree is a Class D felony.

§ 53a-89. Permitting prostitution: Class A misdemeanor

(a) A person is guilty of permitting prostitution when, having possession or control of premises which he knows are being used for prostitution purposes, he fails to make reasonable effort to halt or abate such use.

(b) Permitting prostitution is a Class A misdemeanor.

These sections of the Connecticut code make clear that homosexual as well as heterosexual prostitution is prohibited. A distinction is drawn between the various kinds of prostitution-related activities, and the penalties are graded accordingly. The elements of the various crimes are fairly clear. To prove solicitation or patronizing a prostitute, evidence must be introduced to show:

1. Intentionally Engaging, Agreeing or Offering to Engage

When discussing the intent element, a Texas court left no doubt that intent could be inferred by the defendant's acts, conduct, and words.[23] The court indicated that the offense could have been inferred by the jury when the facts showed that a fee had been paid, that sexual contact occurred, and that other fees were paid with the understanding, explicitly or implicitly, that similar acts, contacts, and performances would follow the continued flow of money. It should also be noted that the element of intent is not required in all states.

2. In Sexual Conduct with Another

In a New York case, the court was asked to determine whether the prostitution statutes encompassed acts between two males.[24] After reiterating that the purpose of the misdemeanor prostitution statute is to prohibit the commercial exploitation of sexual gratification or public solicitation of a sex act for a fee, the court agreed that the statute included gender-neutral language. The allegation that a male defendant agreed to engage in sexual intercourse with another male for $100 was factually and legally sufficient to support the charge of prostitution.

3. In Return for a Fee

In the case of *State v. Allen*, the Connecticut statute was challenged as being unconstitutionally vague and infringing upon the fundamental right of privacy.[25] In *Allen*, the defendant approached an undercover officer's car, opened the passenger door, and inquired if the officer had $20. Upon hearing an affirmative response, the defendant got into the car. A conversation ensued in which the defendant offered to have sex for $20. The officer then drove to a prearranged location near a school where the defendant was arrested by other officers. No sexual activity was ever engaged in nor was there any transfer of money. The defendant contended that the statutory terms "sexual conduct" and "fee" were so uncertain in their meanings that they failed to apprise her that her conduct was proscribed. She claimed that the statute was unconstitutionally vague, and that her conviction thereunder violated her rights to due process of law under the Fifth and Fourteenth Amendments to the U.S. Constitution. While agreeing that the laws must give a person of ordinary intelligence a reasonable opportunity to know what is prohibited so that he or she may act accordingly, the court found no difficulty with the definition of "sexual conduct" and "fee" as appearing in the statute prohibiting prostitution. It was noted that while certain words may appear unconstitutionally vague when viewed in a vacuum, when viewed in the context of a statute they can provide fair notice of the conduct to be prohibited. In explaining that the term "sexual conduct" is sufficiently explicit, the court referred to the definition of prostitution as "normally suggesting sexual relations for hire." As to the term "sexual conduct," the opinion was that the language of § 53a-82 was sufficiently precise to give the defendant fair notice that her conduct was prohibited. The court also explained that the term "fee" was not so vague as to make persons of common intelligence guess at its meaning.

Vagueness was also the challenge to the Illinois prostitution statute. There the court held that the statute criminalizing "any" touching or fondling of sexual organs for purposes of arousal and in exchange for money was not unconstitutionally vague for failure to specify whether it also prohibited touching or fondling through the clothing, as applied to a dancer who rubbed an undercover police officer's penis through his pants during a lap dance.[26]

The crime of solicitation of prostitution may not always occur as the classic case of a prostitute soliciting customers from the street. Anytime someone offers money for sexual services, a charge of prostitution might arise. In *State v. Kittilstad*, a landlord offered to waive rent if the young men who were living with him would bring women back to the residence and have sex with them while the landlord watched. Kittilstad's convictions for soliciting prostitution were upheld, with the court defining prostitution as soliciting sex between two parties, not necessarily between the solicitor and another party.[27]

D. Summary

Almost all states have statutes relating to prostitution—"**solicitation**" is the most common charge and applies to the act of offering to engage in sexual conduct for a fee. In general, modern statutes have changed from early statutes in that prostitution now is gender-neutral, covers homosexual prostitution as well as heterosexual, expands the definition from sexual intercourse to sexual conduct, and tends to direct harsher punishments to promotion or to the purveyors of prostitution rather than the individual offenders.

Solicitation of Prostitution

(A/R) Offering to, engaging in, or asking others to engage in sexual conduct, for a fee (or pecuniary gain)

(M/R) Intentional

---

§ 10.4 Offenses Related to Obscenity

A. Common Law

Under the early English system, matters relating to lewd or immodest acts, conduct, and language were handled by the ecclesiastical authorities. Gradually, the courts and legislative bodies assumed the responsibility for setting standards with regard to specific modes of conduct, pictorial representations of conduct, or written and oral descriptions of conduct. In attempting to define conduct that should be prohibited, the courts have, from the beginning, faced a very difficult task. There is no consensus on what should be criminalized and any such statutes must be weighed against the protections offered under the First Amendment to the Constitution (freedom of expression; freedom of press).

First, it is important to note that pornography and obscenity are not synonymous terms. While one might define pornography as depictions of sexual acts; **obscenity** refers to the depictions of sexual acts that are defined as legally impermissible. Statutes outlaw obscenity, not pornography; but that begs the question as to what constitutes obscenity. Since 1957, it has been established that obscenity is not within the ambit of constitutionally protected free speech. However, the U.S. Supreme Court spent more than a decade attempting to determine a legal test for what constitutes obscenity.[28] We will discuss the current standard in the section below.

B. Model Penal Code

Attempting to come to grips with this difficult subject, the Model Code relies to a great extent upon the definition used in cases decided by the U.S. Supreme Court. According to the definition, the material is obscene only if its predominant appeal is to the prurient interest and it goes substantially beyond customary limits of candor in describing or representing such matters.

§ 251.4 Obscenity[29]

(1) Obscene Defined. Material is obscene, if considered as a whole, its predominant appeal is to prurient interest, that is, a shameful or morbid interest, in nudity, sex or excretion, and if in addition it goes substantially beyond customary limits of candor in describing or representing such matters. Predominant appeal shall be judged with reference to ordinary adults unless it appears from the character of the material or the circumstances of its dissemination to be designed for children or other specially susceptible audience. Undeveloped photographs, molds, printing plates and the like, shall be deemed obscene notwithstanding that processing or other acts may be required to make the obscenity patent or to disseminate it.

(2) Offenses. Subject to the affirmative defense provided in Subsection (3), a person commits a misdemeanor if he knowingly or recklessly:
  (a) sells, delivers or provides, or offers or agrees to sell, deliver or provide, any obscene writing, picture, record or other representation or embodiment of the obscene; or
  (b) presents or directs an obscene play, dance or performance, or participates in that portion thereof which makes it obscene; or
  (c) publishes, exhibits or otherwise makes available any obscene material; or
  (d) possesses any obscene material for purposes of sale or other commercial dissemination; or
  (e) sells, advertises or otherwise commercially disseminates material, whether or not obscene, by representing or suggesting that it is obscene.

A person who disseminates or possesses obscene material in the course of his business is presumed to do so knowingly or recklessly.

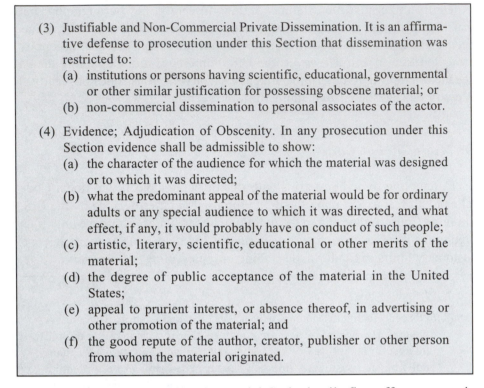

(3) Justifiable and Non-Commercial Private Dissemination. It is an affirmative defense to prosecution under this Section that dissemination was restricted to:
   (a) institutions or persons having scientific, educational, governmental or other similar justification for possessing obscene material; or
   (b) non-commercial dissemination to personal associates of the actor.

(4) Evidence; Adjudication of Obscenity. In any prosecution under this Section evidence shall be admissible to show:
   (a) the character of the audience for which the material was designed or to which it was directed;
   (b) what the predominant appeal of the material would be for ordinary adults or any special audience to which it was directed, and what effect, if any, it would probably have on conduct of such people;
   (c) artistic, literary, scientific, educational or other merits of the material;
   (d) the degree of public acceptance of the material in the United States;
   (e) appeal to prurient interest, or absence thereof, in advertising or other promotion of the material; and
   (f) the good repute of the author, creator, publisher or other person from whom the material originated.

After defining obscenity, the Model Code details five offenses associated with obscenity. The provision requires that the prosecution show that the defendant acted purposely, knowingly, or recklessly. However, there is a presumption that one who disseminates or possesses obscene material in the course of his or her business does so knowingly or recklessly. Subsection (3) of § 251.4 provides an affirmative defense when material is for a scientific or educational purpose or dissemination is non-commercial and only to personal associates. The Model Penal Code also specifies the evidence that is to be admissible in obscenity situations. It concludes with "the Court shall dismiss a prosecution for obscenity if it is satisfied that the material is not obscene."[30]

C. State Statutes, Codes, and Cases

In the case of *Miller v. California*, the United States Supreme Court announced a broad test that defined obscenity. This so-called *Miller* **test** has been followed by both federal and state courts.[31] The Court stated that three questions must be asked before a literary work could be considered obscene and, thus, undeserving of First Amendment protections. These are: (1) Does the material appeal to prurient interests? (2) Does it depict "hard-core" sexual acts previously defined by state law in a patently offensive way? and (3) Does it lack serious literary, artistic, political, scientific, or other value?

1. The *Miller* Test

The three questions that comprise the *Miller* test are designed to separate what is considered so contrary to public morals that it should be criminalized. In this test, the Supreme Court took into consideration that the definition of obscenity may vary from jurisdiction to jurisdiction.

> **CASE:** *Miller v. California,*
> 413 U.S. 15 (1983)
>
> What was the holding of the case?
>
> What is the harm that justifies a law against possession of obscene materials?
>
> How does one know what "community standards" are?

*"Appeals to **Prurient Interests**"* means something more than the tendency to arouse normal, healthy sexual desire.[32] Works that do no more than arouse a normal, healthy interest in sex are not obscene. A work must cater to a morbid, abnormal, or disgusting interest in sex in order to satisfy the first prong of the *Miller* test. In applying the first prong of the *Miller* test, a Nebraska court held:

> "Nudity" and "obscenity" are not synonymous and a nude performance does not become an obscene one, unless, taken as a whole, it appeals predominantly to the prurient interest, a shameful interest in nudity or sex beyond customary limits, it describes any patently offensive way of sexual way of sexual conduct specifically proscribed by state law, and, taken as a whole, it lacks serious or artistic value as determined by the average person applying contemporary community standards.[33]

Depicts "Hard-Core" Sexual Acts Previously Defined by State Law in a Patently Offensive Way. To meet the second test, evidence must be introduced to show that the work depicts patently offensive hard-core sexual acts set forth in the state obscenity laws. State obscenity laws are allowed to list the following acts: patently offensive verbal or visual depictions of ultimate sexual acts (normal or perverted, real or simulated); masturbation; lewd exhibition of the genitals; sadomasochistic sexual behavior; violent sex; bestiality; and sexual perversions.[34]

Lacks Serious Literary, Artistic, Political, Scientific, or Other Value. In addition, the fact finder must determine that the work lacks serious literary, political, scientific, artistic, or other value. The *Miller* test requires the work to be considered as a whole. Works that have serious literary or other value may not be suppressed under the obscenity laws simply because they contain isolated objectionable pictures or passages.

2. Examples of State Statutes

The offense of obscenity, as stated and defined in the various statutes, is a distinct crime involving elements different from those of other crimes. While a state may not define obscenity in such a way that it incorporates material that does not meet the *Miller* test, it can have a more restrictive definition of obscenity so that fewer types of depictions are prohibited.[35] If statutes require other elements to constitute illegal possession or distribution of obscene materials, such as age of purchaser, time and place, motivation, or intent, these elements must be proved by the state in the prosecution.[36]

State statutes vary in wording and in the penalties provided. Many recently revised statutes follow the Model Penal Code position,[37] but the penalties vary. Also, elements such as "the work taken as a whole appeals to the prurient interest" vary from state to state. Some states refer to "contemporary community standards," while others refer to "state standards" as the appropriate reference point in determining whether the predominant appeal is to the prurient interest.

The Illinois statute is similar to the Model Penal Code. It provides in part:

§ 11-20. Obscenity[38]

(a) Elements of the Offense.
   A person commits obscenity when, with knowledge of the nature or content thereof, or recklessly failing to exercise reasonable inspection which would have disclosed the nature or content thereof, he:

   (1) sells, delivers or provides, or offers or agrees to sell, deliver or provide any obscene writing, picture, record or other representation or embodiment of the obscene; or

   (2) presents or directs an obscene play, dance or other performance or participates directly in that portion thereof which makes it obscene; or

   (3) publishes, exhibits or otherwise makes available anything obscene; or

   (4) performs an obscene act or otherwise presents an obscene exhibition of his body for gain; or

   (5) creates, buys, procures or possesses obscene matter or material with intent to disseminate it in violation of this Section, or of the penal laws or regulations of any other jurisdiction; or

   (6) advertises or otherwise promotes the sale of material represented or held out by him to be obscene, whether or not it is obscene.

(b) Obscene Defined.
   Any material or performance is obscene if: (1) the average person, applying contemporary adult community standards, would find that, taken as a whole, it appeals to the prurient interest; and (2) the average person, applying contemporary adult community standards, would find that it depicts or describes, in a patently offensive way, ultimate sexual acts or sadomasochistic sexual acts, whether normal or perverted, actual or simulated, or masturbation, excretory functions or lewd exhibition of the genitals; and (3) taken as a whole, it lacks serious literary, artistic, political or scientific value.

(c) Interpretation of Evidence.
   Obscenity shall be judged with reference to ordinary adults, except that it shall be judged with reference to children or other specially

susceptible audiences if it appears from the character of the material
or the circumstances of its dissemination to be specially designed for
or directed to such an audience.

Where circumstances of production, presentation, sale, dissemination,
distribution, or publicity indicate that material is being commercially
exploited for the sake of its prurient appeal, such evidence is probative
with respect to the nature of the matter and can justify the conclusion
that the matter is utterly without redeeming social importance.

In any prosecution for an offense under this Section evidence shall be
admissible to show:
(1) the character of the audience for which the material was designed
     or to which it was directed;
(2) what the predominant appeal of the material would be for ordinary
     adults or a special audience, and what effect, if any, it would prob-
     ably have on the behavior of such people;
(3) the artistic, literary, scientific, educational or other merits of the
     material, or absence thereof;
(4) the degree, if any, of public acceptance of the material in this State;
(5) appeal to prurient interest, or absence thereof, in advertising or
     other promotion of the material;
(6) purpose of the author, creator, publisher or disseminator.

(d) Sentence.
     Obscenity is a Class A misdemeanor. A second or subsequent offense
     is a Class 4 felony.

In a challenge to the Illinois statute as applied to the sale of adult books,
a reviewing court established some guidelines. The court held that including
children in the instruction on community standards was error. However, it
was not error to refuse to allow testimony that various adult bookstores and
neighborhood video stores sold similar videos and magazines as evidence of
acceptability of those materials by the community.[39]

Another Illinois court agreed that it is difficult to define the term
"obscenity." However, the court found that the following magazine depictions were obscene:

- pictures of naked or nearly naked men, women, and transsexuals engaging in actual or imminent sexual acts, and

- pictures focused almost exclusively on the genitals of models with a
  sparse text describing the events taking place in the pictures.

In this case, the court held that the magazines sold from the defendant's
shop to a police officer lacked any literary, artistic, political, or scientific
value, and thus the trial court's erroneous use of contemporary community
standards in the defendant's obscenity trial was harmless.[40]

Some states use different terminology from the Model Penal Code. An example of a statute that uses terminology different from the Model Penal Code is that of California. Part of the California Code provides:

> (a) every person who knowingly sends or causes to be sent, or brings, or causes to be brought, into this state for sale or distribution, or in this state possesses, prepares, publishes, produces or prints, with intent to distribute or to exhibit to others or who offers to distribute, distributes, or exhibits to others any obscene matter is for a first offense guilty of a misdemeanor.[41]

In the California statute, obscene matter is defined as: "matter taken as a whole, that to the average person, applying contemporary statewide standards, appeals to the prurient interest, that, taken as a whole, depicts or describes sexual conduct in a patently offensive way, and that, taken as a whole, lacks serious literary, artistic, political, or scientific value."[42]

This section of the statute was challenged as being unconstitutionally vague, but the California Court of Appeals determined that the section defining the crime of possessing obscene material with intent to distribute it to others was not unconstitutional; it was not unconstitutionally vague, nor did it violate First Amendment protections.[43]

The state may satisfy its burden by proving, in an obscenity case, that the defendant knew the character and content of the material in question with either direct or circumstantial evidence.[44] Determining whether material is obscene is a question for the jury in an obscenity trial.[45]

Note that the state statutes discussed define as criminal acts those that distribute or display publicly obscene materials. Mere possession is not a crime, although possession with intent to distribute or sell is. The Supreme Court has ruled that one's private possession of obscene materials is within one's privacy rights;[46] however, taking such material across state lines can be a crime.[47] States and the federal government also can and have made the mere possession of child pornography a crime.[48]

During the past decade, legislatures and courts have wrestled with this problem, but now that most are following the guidelines established by the U.S. Supreme Court, it appears that the decisions are reasonably consistent in holding that obscenity can be defined so as to meet the constitutional requirements and that obscenity laws, when carefully drafted, can comply with the standards required by the Constitution.

3. Child Pornography

As mentioned above, even mere possession of child pornography is a crime. Virtually any display of prurient nudity, sexual activity, or presence of a child in relation to sexual activity will fall within the definition of child pornography. For instance, California's statute states:

311.1. (a) Every person who knowingly sends or causes to be sent, or brings or causes to be brought, into this state for sale or distribution, or in this state possesses, prepares, publishes, produces, develops, duplicates, or prints any representation of information, data, or image, including, but not limited to, any film, filmstrip, photograph, negative, slide, photocopy, videotape, video laser disc, computer hardware, computer software, computer floppy disc, data storage media, CD-ROM, or computer-generated equipment or any other computer-generated image that contains or incorporates in any manner, any film or filmstrip, with intent to distribute or to exhibit to, or to exchange with, others, or who offers to distribute, distributes, or exhibits to, or exchanges with, others, any obscene matter, knowing that the matter depicts a person under the age of 18 years personally engaging in or personally simulating sexual conduct, as defined in Section 311.4, shall be punished either by imprisonment in the county jail for up to one year, by a fine not to exceed one thousand dollars ($1,000), or by both the fine and imprisonment, or by imprisonment in the state prison, by a fine not to exceed ten thousand dollars ($10,000), or by the fine and imprisonment. (b) This section does not apply to the activities of law enforcement and prosecuting agencies in the investigation and prosecution of criminal offenses or to legitimate medical, scientific, or educational activities, or to lawful conduct between spouses. (c) This section does not apply to matter which depicts a child under the age of 18, which child is legally emancipated, including lawful conduct between spouses when one or both are under the age of 18. (d) It does not constitute a violation of this section for a telephone corporation, as defined by Section 234 of the Public Utilities Code, to carry or transmit messages described in this chapter or perform related activities in providing telephone services.

The Texas Penal Code is similar in how it defines the crime of possessing or distributing child pornography.

Sec. 43.26. POSSESSION OR PROMOTION OF CHILD PORNOGRAPHY.

(a) A person commits an offense if:

    (1) the person knowingly or intentionally possesses visual material that visually depicts a child younger than 18 years of age at the time the image of the child was made who is engaging in sexual conduct; and

    (2) the person knows that the material depicts the child as described by Subdivision (1).

(b) In this section:

    (1) "Promote" has the meaning assigned by Section 43.25.

    (2) "Sexual conduct" has the meaning assigned by Section 43.25.

    (3) "Visual material" means:

        (A) any film, photograph, videotape, negative, or slide or any photographic reproduction that contains or incorporates in any manner any film, photograph, videotape, negative, or slide; or

> (B) any disk, diskette, or other physical medium that allows an image to be displayed on a computer or other video screen and any image transmitted to a computer or other video screen by telephone line, cable, satellite transmission, or other method.
>
> (c) The affirmative defenses provided by Section 43.25(f) also apply to a prosecution under this section.
> (d) An offense under Subsection (a) is a felony of the third degree.
> (e) A person commits an offense if:
>
> > (1) the person knowingly or intentionally promotes or possesses with intent to promote material described by Subsection (a)(1); and
> > (2) the person knows that the material depicts the child as described by Subsection (a)(1).
>
> (f) A person who possesses visual material that contains six or more identical visual depictions of a child as described by Subsection (a)(1) is presumed to possess the material with the intent to promote the material.
> (g) An offense under Subsection (e) is a felony of the second degree.

In both of these statutes, the individual must know that the performer is a child, but the jury may use circumstantial evidence to find knowledge. Another issue is whether a computer's automatic saving of images in a cache is "possession." While some courts have found that someone who looks at child pornography via the Internet but doesn't intentionally download it is still guilty of possession unless they take steps to remove it from the computer's data storage, other courts have found that only sophisticated computer users understand the cache system and, therefore, possession only occurs if the offender intentionally downloads child pornography.[49]

One of the interesting issues that has emerged in this area is whether "virtual" depictions of obscenity are the same as when real people are used. Computer imagery can be created to represent sexual acts and, thus, what one sees in no way represents an actual person or child (in child pornography). This issue is discussed more fully in Chapter 14 because most crimes that involve computer pornography are prosecuted using federal laws. Recently, the Supreme Court has held that computer-generated images of children engaged in acts that otherwise would be defined as child pornography do not meet the definition of obscenity and cannot be prosecuted if they do not involve real children.[50] This case is presented in the cases attached to Chapter 14.

§ 10.5 Bigamy, Polygamy, and Incest

A. Common Law

Bigamy was not a crime at common law, but was considered an offense of ecclesiastical law with punishment in the hands of the ecclesiastical tribunals rather than the common law courts. During the reign of James I, bigamy was made a felony punishable in the civil courts. The crime of bigamy was included in an early Virginia statute and there has never been a time in any state when polygamy has not been an offense against society punishable in the criminal courts.[51]

The commonly understood meaning of the term *bigamy* is having two wives or husbands at the same time. **Polygamy** has been defined as the offense of having a plurality of husbands or wives. The traditional legal definition of bigamy is willfully and knowingly contracting a second marriage where the contracting party knows that the first marriage still exists. In some states, the traditional crime was designated as either bigamy or polygamy. The definitions are very similar.[52] For practical purposes, it makes no difference whether the crime is called bigamy or polygamy. In this country, if a person who is married contracts a second marriage, that person is violating the law and is subject to a criminal penalty.

Incest was also not a crime at common law, but it was punishable as an offense in the ecclesiastical courts in England. In the United States, incest is a statutory crime, the object of which is to prohibit sexual intercourse between those within certain degrees of relationships.[53] Rape and incest are entirely different crimes. Incest is not a lesser included offense of rape. In most jurisdictions consent is irrelevant in the commission of the crime of incest.

Incest is defined as the intermarriage, or sexual relations without marriage, between a man and woman related to each other in any of the degrees of consanguinity or affinity within which marriage is prohibited. Consanguinity is defined as a blood relationship or relation of persons descended from the same stock or common ancestry. Affinity is the connection existing through marriage, between each of the married persons and the kindred of the other.

B. Model Penal Code

The Model Penal Code defines three offenses and distinguishes between bigamy and polygamy. Although ordinary adultery is not a crime under the Code, bigamous adultery is a crime. The rationale is that bigamous cohabitation amounts to a public affront, and society demands that this act be punished.

The Model Code departs, to some extent, from prior law by creating a separate offense of polygamy with felony sanctions. Such sanctions are provided for those who make a formal commitment to plural marriage.

§ 230.1 Bigamy and Polygamy[54]

(1) Bigamy. A married person is guilty of bigamy, a misdemeanor, if he contracts or purports to contract another marriage, unless at the time of the subsequent marriage:

  (a) the actor believes that the prior spouse is dead; or

(b) the actor and the prior spouse have been living apart for five con-
     secutive years throughout which the prior spouse was not known
     by the actor to be alive; or

(c) a court has entered a judgment purporting to terminate or annul
     any prior disqualifying marriage, and the actor does not know that
     judgment to be invalid; or

(d) the actor reasonably believes that he is legally eligible to remarry.

(2) Polygamy. A person is guilty of polygamy, a felony of the third
     degree, if he marries or cohabits with more than one spouse at a time
     in purported exercise of the right of plural marriage. The offense is a
     continuing one until all cohabitation and claim of marriage with more
     than one spouse terminates. This Section does not apply to parties to a
     polygamous marriage, lawful in the country of which they are residents
     or nationals, while they are in transit through or temporarily visiting
     this State.

(3) Other Party to Bigamous or Polygamous Marriage. A person is guilty
     of bigamy or polygamy, as the case may be, if he contracts or purports
     to contract marriage with another knowing that the other is thereby
     committing bigamy or polygamy.

The Model Code also makes it clear that the partner of the married person
is also guilty of bigamy or polygamy *if* he or she has knowledge that the other
party was married. Unlike some of the statutes in existence at the time the
Model Penal Code was prepared, the Model Code provides specific defenses
to the crime. Most of these defenses go toward the *mens rea* of the crime in
that if a person has reasonable cause to believe that the first spouse is dead,
then that belief becomes an affirmative defense.

The Model Penal Code defines the crime of incest as limited to blood
relatives plus the relationship of parent and child by adoption, thus a relationship between a stepchild and stepparent may not be defined as incest unless
there is a legal adoption.

§ 230.2 Incest[55]

A person is guilty of incest, a felony of the third degree, if he knowingly
marries or cohabits or has sexual intercourse with an ancestor or descendant,
or brother or sister of the whole or half blood [or an uncle, aunt, nephew
or niece of the whole blood]. "Cohabit" means to live together under the
representation or appearance of being married. The relationships referred
to herein include blood relationships without regard to legitimacy, and
relationship of parent and child by adoption.

C. State Statutes, Codes, and Cases

There are two essential elements of the crime of bigamy: a prior marriage, and a second marriage before the first marriage is dissolved. The *mens rea* varies and in some cases, criminal intent is not essential to bigamy, nor is good faith a defense; however, in other states, a reasonable belief that the first marriage was dissolved can be an affirmative defense.

1. Prior Marriage Element

In order for a person to be convicted of the crime of bigamy, the state must prove a valid marriage entered into by the accused before the alleged bigamous marriage. If the defense can show that the prior marriage was invalid for one reason or another, there can be no conviction. However, a false assumption of the invalidity of a former marriage will not serve as a defense.[56] Obviously, if the prior marriage was dissolved by death, divorce, or annulment before the second took place, there is no bigamy. But a divorce obtained by fraud or one that for some reason is ineffectual is not a defense.

2. Subsequent Marriage

Before one can be convicted of the offense of bigamy, proof must be offered to show that the person went through the form of a subsequent marriage. Such a marriage, of course, is void; nevertheless, evidence must be introduced to show that the marriage ceremony was performed.[57]

A person accused of bigamy may defend by showing the absence of one or more of the elements constituting the offense. In some recent cases, those practicing polygamy avoid legal problems by having only one legal marriage and subsequent "spiritual" marriages. Such relationships do not meet the legal tests of polygamy or bigamy because the subsequent unions do not have legal effect.

3. While First Marriage Is Still Legally Binding

Most state statutes provide that if a person is absent and not heard from for a certain number of years he or she is presumed to be dead. In some instances, the period is designated as seven years.

By some authorities, an honest belief, reasonably entertained in the exercise of care that a divorce has been granted, is a defense to a prosecution for bigamy.[58] The reasoning is that a person should not be held criminally liable when he has been misled without his own fault or carelessness concerning the facts. But even here it is not sufficient that the second marriage was contracted on the strength of a mere rumor of a divorce. A *bona fide* effort to ascertain the

Legal News

In April 2008, the state of Texas removed more than 400 children and more than 100 women from a religious compound in Eldorado, Texas, after a telephone call was received by local law enforcement that young girls were being sexually abused. The Eldorado compound is part of the FLDS, a breakaway sect that separated from the Mormon church when the church disavowed polygamy. The leader of the sect, Warren Jeffs, is currently in prison after being convicted of accessory to rape for his role in commanding the marriage of a 14-year-old girl. In the Texas case, after months of investigation, most of the children were returned to their parents, although the state did find evidence that seven teenage girls were "spiritually" married to adult men and had one or more children by those men. The state is continuing to investigate whether charges of neglect can be brought against parents who allowed children to be present in a situation where they knew sexual abuse was occurring.

In November 2008, a Texas grand jury indicted several members of the Fundamentalist Church of Jesus Christ of Latter Day Saints for bigamy. The defense to such a charge will be that the second marriages for these men were "spiritual" rather than civil. Although Texas law recognizes common law marriages of those who "purport" to be married, attorneys argued that it would be an unconstitutional violation of equal protection to enforce the law against those couples versus those who cohabit but do not purport marriage.

Source: Associated Press (2008). "Polygamist Sect Calls Texas Report Fraudulent." MSNBC.com. December 28, 2008. Accessed 1/2/2009 from http://www.msnbc.msn.com/id/28408721 and Associated Press (2008). "Eight New Indictments Issued in Texas Polygamist Case." Washingtonpost.com, November 12, 2008. Accessed 11/21/2008 from http://www.washingtonpost.co/wp-dyn/content/article/2008/11/12/AR2008111202390.html.

truth of the rumor is essential.[59]A person who is contemplating a subsequent marriage may not be able to rely upon the advice of his attorney. One court held that the advice of counsel that there was no impediment to a second marriage was no defense to prosecution for bigamy.[60]

4. Examples of State Statutes

Many recently enacted statutes follow the wording of the Model Penal Code. Note that some are strict liability offenses and some require knowledge of the ineligibility to contract the second marriage. The Alabama statute is an example of a statute that requires at least a *mens rea* of knowing.[61]

> (a) A person commits bigamy when he intentionally contracts or purports to contract a marriage with another person when he has a living spouse. A person who contracts a marriage outside this state, which would be bigamous if contracted in this state, commits bigamy by cohabiting in the state with the other party to such a marriage.

(b) A person does not commit an offense under this section if:

    (1) He reasonably believes that his previous marriage is void or was dissolved by death, divorce or annulment; or

    (2) He and the prior spouse have been living apart for five consecutive years prior to the subsequent marriage, during which time the prior spouse was not known by him to be alive.

    (3) The burden of injecting the issues under this subsection is on the defendant, but this does not shift the burden of proof.

(c) Bigamy is a Class C felony.

The Georgia Code is somewhat different. It also requires a *mens rea* of knowing. This code specifically targets the partner of the married person.[62] The Georgia Code provides for an affirmative defense if the spouse has been absent for a certain period, but in this statute the period is seven years rather than five, as used in some statutes. If the defendant honestly believes that he has a right to make the second marriage, and it appears that this honest belief is the result of reasonable diligence to ascertain the truth, then the jury has the right to infer that the defendant had no criminal intent, and was therefore not guilty of the crime.[63]

16-6-20 Bigamy

(a) A person commits the offense of bigamy when he, being married and knowing that his lawful spouse is living, marries another person or carries on a bigamous cohabitation with another person.

(b) It shall be an affirmative defense that the prior spouse has been continually absent for a period of seven years during which time the accused did not know the prior spouse to be alive, or that the accused reasonably believed he was eligible to remarry.

16-6-21 Marrying a bigamist

(a) An unmarried man or woman commits the offense of marrying a bigamist when he marries a person whom he knows to be the wife or husband of another.

(b) It shall be an affirmative defense that the prior spouse of the bigamist has been continually absent for a period of seven years during which time the accused did not know the prior spouse of the bigamist to be alive, or that the accused reasonably believed the bigamist was eligible to remarry.

5. State Statutes: Incest

Incest statutes typically prohibit the marriage of or sexual relations between persons who are related within certain degrees, established by statute. Statutes differ as to the degree of the relationship; however, they are fairly consistent in holding that marriage or sexual relations between father and daughter, mother and son, brother and sister, uncle and niece, and aunt and nephew, are prohibited. Some statutes include first cousins but, under other statutes, prohibition of marriage between first cousins does not make their marriage or cohabitation incest.[64]

As there is a moral difference between the marriage or sexual intercourse of persons related by consanguinity and persons related only by affinity, many statutes distinguish these two. In one case, the court held that a statutory prohibition expressly relating to degrees of consanguinity (relation by blood) will not, by implication, extend to degrees of affinity (relation by marriage).[65] However, other states have statutes that expressly extend to the relationship by affinity. Under these statutes, sexual intercourse between a stepfather and a stepdaughter, a stepmother and a stepson, or a brother-in-law and sister-in-law is prohibited.[66] As a general rule, affinity ceases on the divorce or death of the blood relative through whom the relationship was created. Therefore, in the absence of a statutory provision, after such a divorce or death, it is not incest for a man to marry or have intercourse with his former wife's daughter or sister.[67]

Legal News

When Woody Allen began a relationship with Soon-Yi, the adopted daughter of Mia Farrow, individuals wondered why he wasn't prosecuted for incest. Mia Farrow and Woody Allen had a long-term relationship and he had served as a father figure to the girl since she was seven. The affair came to light when Mia Farrow saw in Allen's apartment pictures of Soon-Yi posing naked. The two lived next to each other in their own apartments but had been together as a couple for 20 years and had a child together and had adopted another child together. Regardless of the morality of the relationship between Soon Yi and Woody Allen, it wasn't illegal. Woody Allen was not the legal father of Soon Yi, and as indicated, relations between a stepfather and a stepdaughter are not defined as incest in many states. Supposedly the affair started after she was no longer legally a child so other laws were not broken. Farrow accused Allen of molesting their younger child but the states of New York and Connecticut never charged him, although, in their custody dispute, he had limited custodial rights with the younger children. Woody Allen and Soon-Yi married in 1997 and they have adopted two daughters.

Source: M. Meade (2000). *The Unruly Life of Woody Allen*. New York, NY: Scribner; D. Frankel (1997). "I Now Pronounce You Father and Wife." Retrieved 9/21/2006 from www.eonline.com/news/items/0,1,2286,00.html.

In the commentary following § 13A-13-3 of the Alabama Code, the reasons for the offense are enumerated. These include:

> (a) The law against incest may represent a reinforcement by civil sanctions of a religious tenet.

(b) A second justification lies in the science of genetics. There is a secular utility in a prohibition against such inbreeding as would result in defective offspring by reason of the higher probability of unfavorable, recessive genes combining in the children of parents within certain blood relationships.

(c) A sociological and psychological justification is that the prohibition of incest tends to promote solidarity of the family by preventing sex rivalries and jealousies within the family unit.

(d) The utility of forbidding abuse by heads of households, especially male, of their authority and financial power over younger children, especially female.[68]

The elements of the crime of incest are: marriage or sexual intercourse; between persons within the degree of relationship proscribed by statute, with knowledge of the existence of the relationship (under some statutes).

As to the third element above, some statutes make the parties guilty even if the knowledge of the relationship is not present; therefore, in these states, knowledge is not an element of the offense. In one case, the justices reasoned that knowledge of the relationship on the part of both parties to the incestuous act is not essential to a conviction of the one who had such knowledge.[69] Most current statutes require knowledge as an element of the crime; however, a few still do not specifically require this level of *mens rea*. An example of a state statute that requires knowledge of the relationship is that of Alabama, which provides:[70]

(a) A person commits incest if he marries or engages in sexual intercourse with a person he knows to be, either legitimately or illegitimately:

    (1) His ancestor or descendant by blood or adoption; or
    (2) His brother or sister of the whole or half-blood or by adoption; or
    (3) His stepchild or stepparent, while the marriage creating the relationship exists; or
    (4) His aunt, uncle, nephew or niece of the whole or half-blood.

(b) A person shall not be convicted of incest or of an attempt to commit incest upon the uncorroborated testimony of the person with whom the offense is alleged to have been committed.

(c) Incest is a Class C felony.

The Georgia statute also requires knowledge, and includes stepchildren.

§ 16-6-22 Incest[71]

(a) A person commits the offense of incest when he engages in sexual intercourse with a person to whom he knows he is related, either by blood or by marriage as follows:

> Father and daughter or stepdaughter;
> Mother and son or stepson;
> Brother and sister of the whole blood or of the half blood;
> Grandparent and grandchild;
> Aunt and nephew; or
> Uncle and niece.
>
> A person convicted of the crime of incest shall be punished by imprisonment of not less than one nor more than 20 years.

The Georgia statute was challenged as violating the United States Constitution in the case of *Benton v. State*.[72] In this case, the defendant was convicted of incest along with other crimes. The 16-year-old stepdaughter of the defendant had testified at the trial that the defendant had repeatedly had forcible intercourse with her. The defendant, on appeal, asserted that the Georgia statute, which criminalizes sexual intercourse between a father and stepdaughter, unconstitutionally infringes on the right of privacy, because it bars intercourse with a non-blood-related consenting adult. The reviewing court found that the statute was not arbitrarily drawn in light of the government interest. Classification on the basis of stepparent and stepchild bears a rational relationship to the government interest in protecting children and family unity. Although the Georgia statute does not specifically require corroboration, a Georgia court has determined that testimony of the female accomplice must be corroborated in order to warrant conviction.[73]

In interpreting the Florida statute, the court held that the incest statute applies to half-siblings, i.e., those who have only one parent in common.[74] In addition, a Connecticut court confirmed that the statute prohibiting sexual intercourse between individuals of certain degrees of kinship encompassed adopted as well as blood relatives and that an adopted child became the legal child of the parents and should be treated as if the child were the biological child of the parents.[75]

D. Summary

Bigamy and polygamy have been criminal offenses in the United States since the formation of the union and continue to be punishable under the statutes of the states. Although the statutes are consistent in providing that a previous marriage and a contract for a subsequent marriage are elements, they may differ in regard to the *mens rea* and in specifying the defenses. The statutes also differ in establishing the criminal liability of the other party to the bigamous marriage and in grading the offenses as misdemeanors or felonies. It is therefore necessary that the statutes of the respective states, as well as the decisions interpreting those statutes, be carefully researched.

Incest was not a crime under the common law but has always been a statutory crime in this country. In general, statutes prohibit marriage or sexual intercourse between relatives related by consanguinity or affinity. Most statutes require knowledge of the relationship, but some do not specify any level of *mens rea*. In general, consent or lack of consent is not an element to the crime of incest. The statutes specify what degree of relationship is prohibited and this varies from state to state.

Bigamy

(A/R) Marriage, while previous marriage is still legally binding

(M/R) Knowing (although in some states it may be strict liability)

Polygamy

(A/R) Marriage, to more than one person, at the same time

(M/R) Knowing

Incest

(A/R) Sexual intercourse or marriage, between two persons related by proscribed degrees of consanguinity or affinity

(M/R) Knowledge (of the relationship) (in most jurisdictions)

---

§ 10.6   Other Offenses within the Family

Generally, criminal law does not intrude upon the privacy of the family unit. However, as we saw in the last section, there are certain private behaviors that have been determined to be against the interests of the state and can be punished. In addition to those already discussed, certain behaviors regarding the care of children can also be punished, such as not caring for children or not paying child support if one is ordered to do so by the court. We will take a brief look at some of these family-related crimes in this section.

A. *Common Law*

Modern statutes have more comprehensive laws regarding the care and support of children than did the common law. Prior to the last two centuries, the head of the household had the right to discipline his children and his wife as he saw fit, including the use of corporal punishment. Laws protecting children from physical discipline or poor working conditions did not exist at all until the nineteenth century. Of course, serious injury or death was penalized, but corporal punishment of children was not considered a matter for the criminal law until the twentieth century. The Society for the Prevention of Cruelty to Children was created in 1875 when it was discovered that although laws existed that punished individuals for beating their animals, no such laws existed to protect children. Early statutes were created to identify and punish injury to a child and, eventually, statutes also penalized abandoning children and even behaviors that put children in dangerous or unhealthy circumstances, whether or not the child was actually injured.

The concept of *parens patriae* means basically that the state will take the place of the parent when the parent is unable or unwilling to perform caregiver functions. This concept, if not part of the common law, emerged very early in the criminal codes of this country and was the basis for the creation of family courts or juvenile courts.

B. Model Penal Code

The Model Penal Code's Article 230 is titled "Offenses against the Family" and includes bigamy, polygamy, incest, and other family-related crimes. Other sections describe crimes of neglect and abandonment.

> Section 230.4. Endangering Welfare of Children.
>
> A parent, guardian, or other person supervising the welfare of a child under 18 commits a misdemeanor if he knowingly endangers the child's welfare by violating a duty of care, protection or support.
>
> Section 230.5. Persistent Non-Support.
>
> A person commits a misdemeanor if he persistently fails to provide support which he can provide and which he knows he is legally obliged to provide to a spouse, child or other dependent.

C. State Statutes

Family courts rather than criminal courts are the more likely avenue when there is an allegation of child abuse. Child abuse includes physical abuse, sexual abuse, emotional abuse, and neglect. Most child abuse falls under the category of neglect, which includes not providing adequate sustenance, supervision, or care. Generally, intervention is designed to assist parents to be better caregivers. However, if there is physical or sexual abuse or a lack of willingness to meet basic standards, then criminal prosecution is an option. States generally group family-related crimes under a section titled Family Offense, Abuse of Children, or Offenses Against the Family. For instance, in the Florida statutes, Chapter 827 is titled Abuse of Children and has the following sections:

- Abuse, aggravated abuse, and neglect of a child
- Newborn infants
- Contributing to the delinquency or dependency of a child
- Nonsupport of dependents
- Sexual performance by a child
- Misuse of child support money[76]

1. Non-Support of Dependents (and Abandonment)

All states and the Model Penal Code have laws that prohibit individuals from not taking care of dependents.[77] or abandoning them. First, there must be a duty to another (either by relationship, law, or contract). Then there must be a knowing and/or intentional omission, i.e., not feeding a child or leaving them alone with no food or proper supervision. Ohio's non-support statute provides:

(A) No person shall abandon, or fail to provide adequate support to:

    (1) the person's spouse, as required by law;

    (2) the person's child who is under age eighteen, or mentally or physically handicapped child who is under age twenty-one;

    (3) the person's aged or infirm parent or adoptive parent, who from lack of ability and means is unable to provide adequately for his or her own support;

(B) No person shall abandon, or fail to provide support as established by a court order to, another person whom, by court order or decree, the person is legally obligated to support.[78]

The Ohio Code also includes a duty to care for aged and infirm parents. This is unusual because most states do not specify such a duty. There is an affirmative defense to the charge if the actor is unable to provide adequate support, or if the parent abandoned or failed to support the accused as required by law, while the accused was under the age of 18 or was mentally or physically handicapped and under age 21.

Even though it is illegal to neglect or abandon your child, all states have passed a Baby Moses or "safe haven" statute (or defense to the abandonment statute) that allows a parent to abandon an infant at a fire station, hospital, or other designated location. These statutes are designed to prevent parents from leaving the infant in locations that would be dangerous to their health or, worse, killing the infant because they did not want the baby. In July 2008, the state of Nebraska was the last state to pass such a law but no age limit was specified in the statute and children as old as 18 were left at hospitals. In four months several dozen children and teenagers were abandoned to the state, causing consternation among officials who did not realize the legal loophole until parents began using the statute. While public commentary viewed the parents as uncaring, irresponsible, or evil for abandoning their older children, others and the parents themselves pointed out that the children left had severe mental problems and parents were unable to care for them. In some cases, the older children were dangerous and the parents were afraid of them. The state legislature did not solve the problem of parents who could not care for their children growing up with mental and behavioral problems, but they did change the safe haven law so that, after November 2008, only infants up to 30 days could be left legally at the designated locations.[79]

California's non-support law identifies the crime as a misdemeanor and requires a *mens rea* of willfulness. It allows a defense for those who withhold medical care from their child when their religious beliefs prescribe prayer rather than standardized medical treatment. Whether or not a parent has custody is less relevant than a legal determination of parental responsibility.

270. If a parent of a minor child willfully omits, without lawful excuse, to furnish necessary clothing, food, shelter or medical attendance, or other remedial care for his or her child, he or she is guilty of a misdemeanor punishable by a fine not exceeding two thousand dollars ($2,000), or by imprisonment in the county jail not exceeding one year, or by both such fine and imprisonment. If a court of competent jurisdiction has made a final adjudication in either a civil or a criminal action that a person is the parent of a minor child and the person has notice of such adjudication and he or she then willfully omits, without lawful excuse, to furnish necessary clothing, food, shelter, medical attendance or other remedial care for his or her child, this conduct is punishable by imprisonment in the county jail not exceeding one year or in a state prison for a determinate term of one year and one day, or by a fine not exceeding two thousand dollars ($2,000), or by both such fine and imprisonment. This statute shall not be construed so as to relieve such parent from the criminal liability defined herein for such omission merely because the other parent of such child is legally entitled to the custody of such child nor because the other parent of such child or any other person or organization voluntarily or involuntarily furnishes such necessary food, clothing, shelter or medical attendance or other remedial care for such child or undertakes to do so.

Proof of abandonment or desertion of a child by such parent, or the omission by such parent to furnish necessary food, clothing, shelter or medical attendance or other remedial care for his or her child is prima facie evidence that such abandonment or desertion or omission to furnish necessary food, clothing, shelter or medical attendance or other remedial care is willful and without lawful excuse.

The court, in determining the ability of the parent to support his or her child, shall consider all income, including social insurance benefits and gifts.

The provisions of this section are applicable whether the parents of such child are or were ever married or divorced, and regardless of any decree made in any divorce action relative to alimony or to the support of the child. A child conceived but not yet born is to be deemed an existing person insofar as this section is concerned.

The husband of a woman who bears a child as a result of artificial insemination shall be considered the father of that child for the purpose of this section, if he consented in writing to the artificial insemination.

If a parent provides a minor with treatment by spiritual means through prayer alone in accordance with the tenets and practices of a recognized church or religious denomination, by a duly accredited practitioner thereof, such treatment shall constitute "other remedial care", as used in this section.

2. Endangering the Welfare of a Minor

Many states have a criminal statute that covers what is considered reckless endangerment of a child. For instance, Kentucky's statute for endangering the welfare of a minor provides:

> (1) a parent, guardian or other person legally charged with the care or custody of a minor is guilty of endangering the welfare of a minor when he fails or refuses to exercise reasonable diligence in the control of such child to prevent him from becoming a neglected dependent or delinquent child.[80]

These statutes typically do not require a *mens rea* of intent but do require knowing or recklessness, rather than simple negligence. They cover a wide variety of behavior including, but not limited to, allowing the child to drive, drink, be present when drug use is occurring, be present in sexually charged situations, and so on.

The Texas Criminal Code places abandonment and endangering the child in the same statute. Because of public concern, those who expose their children to methamphetamine are specifically identified in this statute. Note that the last paragraph is an example of a safe haven law that allows abandonment when the parent leaves the child at a safe location.

> Sec. 22.041. ABANDONING OR ENDANGERING CHILD.
>
> (a) In this section, "abandon" means to leave a child in any place without providing reasonable and necessary care for the child, under circumstances under which no reasonable, similarly situated adult would leave a child of that age and ability.
>
> (b) A person commits an offense if, having custody, care, or control of a child younger than 15 years, he intentionally abandons the child in any place under circumstances that expose the child to an unreasonable risk of harm.
>
> (c) A person commits an offense if he intentionally, knowingly, recklessly, or with criminal negligence, by act or omission, engages in conduct that places a child younger than 15 years in imminent danger of death, bodily injury, or physical or mental impairment.
>
> (c-1) For purposes of Subsection (c), it is presumed that a person engaged in conduct that places a child in imminent danger of death, bodily injury, or physical or mental impairment if:
>
>> (1) the person manufactured, possessed, or in any way introduced into the body of any person the controlled substance methamphetamine in the presence of the child;
>>
>> (2) the person's conduct related to the proximity or accessibility of the controlled substance methamphetamine to the child and an analysis of a specimen of the child's blood, urine, or other

> bodily substance indicates the presence of methamphetamine in the child's body; or
>
> (3) the person injected, ingested, inhaled, or otherwise introduced a controlled substance listed in Penalty Group 1, Section 481.102, Health and Safety Code, into the human body when the person was not in lawful possession of the substance as defined by Section 481.002(24) of that code. [. . .]
>
> (h) It is an exception to the application of this section that the actor voluntarily delivered the child to a designated emergency infant care provider under Section 262.302, Family Code.

New York also has a statute that defines endangering children as a crime. It does not specify any particular behaviors; therefore, what might be considered endangerment is based on a reasonable person concept. Generally, if the parent or guardian was negligent, authorities may first attempt to use the resources of the family court. If necessary, the state has the authority to remove the children until such time as the parent proves that they are capable of supervising and caring for the child more appropriately. However, if the behavior is extreme or the parent is non-compliant, a criminal charge of endangerment is possible.

> Section 260.10 Endangering the welfare of a child
>
> A person is guilty of endangering the welfare of a child when:
>
> 1. He knowingly acts in a manner likely to be injurious to the physical, mental or moral welfare of a child less than seventeen years old or directs or authorizes such child to engage in an occupation involving a substantial risk of danger to his life or health; or
> 2. Being a parent, guardian or other person legally charged with the care or custody of a child less than eighteen years old, he fails or refuses to exercise reasonable diligence in the control of such child to prevent him from becoming an "abused child," a "neglected child," a "juvenile delinquent" or a "person in need of supervision," as those terms are defined in articles ten, three and seven of the family court act.
>
> Endangering the welfare of a child is a class A misdemeanor.

3. Injury to a Child

Physical injury to a child is assault, but many states take special note when the victim of assault is a child or one's own child or dependent. The Texas Penal Code places injury to a child in the chapter on assaultive offenses. Note that this statute is written broadly enough that it also could include behaviors that would, in other states, be prosecuted as endangerment. The statute provides a defense to those who are acting under religious beliefs and those who, by omission, fail to protect the child from the acts of another if they are also a victim.

Sec. 22.04. INJURY TO A CHILD, ELDERLY INDIVIDUAL, OR DISABLED INDIVIDUAL.

(a) A person commits an offense if he intentionally, knowingly, recklessly, or with criminal negligence, by act or intentionally, knowingly, or recklessly by omission, causes to a child, elderly individual, or disabled individual:

    (1) serious bodily injury;
    (2) serious mental deficiency, impairment, or injury; or
    (3) bodily injury. [. . .]
    [. . . sections b-j omitted]

(k) It is a defense to prosecution under this section that the act or omission consisted of:

    (1) reasonable medical care occurring under the direction of or by a licensed physician; or
    (2) emergency medical care administered in good faith and with reasonable care by a person not licensed in the healing arts.

(l) It is an affirmative defense to prosecution under this section:

    (1) that the act or omission was based on treatment in accordance with the tenets and practices of a recognized religious method of healing with a generally accepted record of efficacy;
    (2) for a person charged with an act of omission causing to a child, elderly individual, or disabled individual a condition described by Subsection (a)(1), (2), or (3) that:

        (A) there is no evidence that, on the date prior to the offense charged, the defendant was aware of an incident of injury to the child, elderly individual, or disabled individual and failed to report the incident; and
        (B) the person:

            (i) was a victim of family violence, as that term is defined by Section 71.004, Family Code, committed by a person who is also charged with an offense against the child, elderly individual, or disabled individual under this section or any other section of this title;
            (ii) did not cause a condition described by Subsection (a)(1), (2), or (3); and
            (iii) did not reasonably believe at the time of the omission that an effort to prevent the person also charged with an offense against the child, elderly individual, or disabled individual from committing the offense would have an effect; or

    (3) that:

        (A) the actor was not more than three years older than the victim at the time of the offense; and
        (B) the victim was a child at the time of the offense.

Injuries inflicted upon a child, by intent or recklessness, are considered more serious than when the victim is an adult. While some states have chosen to provide special penalties based on the age of the victim, others have created special statutes for injuries to children. In either case, the result is typically a more serious punishment. Behaviors that involve neglect, abandonment, or place the child in a situation that is dangerous to their health, emotional development, or morals are also subject to punishment.

§ 10.7   Abortion

A.   Common Law

Abortion was not a crime under the common law. In fact, the fetus had virtually no legal protection because it was not defined as a person apart from the mother. However, early statutes in this country did criminalize the intentional death of a fetus. As early as 1821, the first state law dealing directly with abortion was enacted by the Connecticut legislature. By 1868, at least 36 laws enacted by state or territorial legislatures limited abortion.[81]

Abortion is the expulsion of the fetus at so early a period of uterogestation that it has not acquired the power of sustaining an independent life. Generally, the term "abortion" does not include the use of an intrauterine device (IUD), the so-called "morning after" pill (estrogen pregnancy prophylaxis), or birth control pills; rather, these are more commonly considered forms of birth control or contraception. The Revised Uniform Abortion Act defines "abortion" as the termination of human pregnancy with an intention other than to produce a live birth or to remove a dead embryo or fetus.

In 1973 (the year of *Roe v. Wade*)[82] at least 36 states had laws limiting abortions. According to these statutes, purposely and unjustifiably terminating the pregnancy of another other than by a birth was a crime. For example, a Kansas statute provided that "whoever with intent to produce a miscarriage of any pregnant woman or of any woman, unlawfully administers, or causes to be given to her any drug or noxious substance whatever, or unlawfully uses any instrument or means whatever, with such intent, shall be guilty of the offense."[83]

The elements of the crime of abortion in the majority of the states prior to *Roe v. Wade* were:

- An intent to produce a miscarriage;
- Unlawful administration of drugs or noxious substances or using an instrument; and
- A resulting miscarriage.

In 1973, the Supreme Court decided *Roe v. Wade*.[84] In this case a woman challenged the Texas law that made it a crime to procure an abortion as defined therein or to attempt an abortion except on medical advice for the purpose of saving the life of the mother. That Supreme Court held that the Texas Criminal Abortion Statute was unconstitutional. While agreeing that the state had an interest in regulating abortions, the majority concluded that the right of personal privacy includes the right of a pregnant female to make the decision whether to terminate her pregnancy. The Court went on to explain, however, that a woman's right to terminate a pregnancy was not absolute.

The majority of the U.S. Supreme Court found that the state had a "compelling interest" that overcame the woman's privacy rights at a certain point in the pregnancy. Prior to approximately the end of the first trimester, the abortion decision and its effectuation must be left to the woman and attending physician. However, following the approximate end of the first trimester, the state may regulate abortion procedures in ways *reasonably related* to maternal health. After "viability" (the stage at which point the fetus might survive outside the womb), the state may regulate and even forbid abortion except where necessary for preservation of the life or health of the mother.

Subsequent to this decision, a number of state statutes have been passed and challenged. These subsequent decisions will be discussed in a following section.

B. Model Penal Code

The Model Penal Code is very complex and is patterned after the *Roe v. Wade* decision. Subsection (1) prohibits the unjustified termination of the pregnancy of another. This requires an actual termination of the pregnancy. Subsection (2) defines what constitutes justifiable abortion and exceptions. Subsection (3) requires that two physicians certify in advance their belief as to the circumstances justifying the abortion, but violation of this requirement would not itself make the abortion unlawful. Subsection (4) deals with the self-abortion late in pregnancy. Subsection (5) contains a provision relating to one who represents that he is performing an abortion although he may know or believe that the woman is not pregnant, and Subsection (6) deals with the distribution of anything specifically designed to terminate a pregnancy or held out by the actor as useful for that purpose. Subsection (7) is designed to make it clear that the use of contraception devices or drugs to prevent pregnancy do not come within the ambit of the offense.

§ 230.3 Abortion[85]

(1) Unjustified Abortion. A person who purposely and unjustifiably terminates the pregnancy of another otherwise than by a live birth commits a felony of the third degree or, where the pregnancy has continued beyond the twenty-sixth week, a felony of the second degree.

(2) Justifiable Abortion. A licensed physician is justified in terminating a pregnancy if he believes there is substantial risk that continuance of the

pregnancy would gravely impair the physical or mental health of the mother or that the child would be born with grave physical or mental defect, or that the pregnancy resulted from rape, incest, or other felonious intercourse. All illicit intercourse with a girl below the age of 16 shall be deemed felonious for purposes of this Subsection. Justifiable abortions shall be performed only in a licensed hospital except in case of emergency when hospital facilities are unavailable. [Additional exceptions from the requirement of hospitalization may be incorporated here to take account of situations in sparsely settled areas where hospitals are not generally accessible.]

(3) Physicians' Certificates; Presumption from Non-Compliance. No abortion shall be performed unless two physicians, one of whom may be the person performing the abortion, shall have certified in writing the circumstances which they believe to justify the abortion. Such certificate shall be submitted before the abortion to the hospital where it is to be performed and, in the case of abortion following felonious intercourse, to the prosecuting attorney or the police. Failure to comply with any of the requirements of this Subsection gives rise to a presumption that the abortion was unjustified.

(4) Self-Abortion. A woman whose pregnancy has continued beyond the twenty-sixth week commits a felony of the third degree if she purposely terminates her own pregnancy otherwise than by a live birth, or if she uses instruments, drugs or violence upon herself for that purpose. Except as justified under Subsection (2), a person who induces or knowingly aids a woman to use instruments, drugs or violence upon herself for the purpose of terminating her pregnancy otherwise than by a live birth commits a felony of the third degree whether or not the pregnancy has continued beyond the twenty-sixth week.

(5) Pretended Abortion. A person commits a felony of the third degree if, representing that it is his purpose to perform an abortion, he does an act adapted to cause abortion in a pregnant woman although the woman is in fact not pregnant, or the actor does not believe she is. A person charged with unjustified abortion under Subsection (1) or an attempt to commit that offense may be convicted thereof upon proof of conduct prohibited by this Subsection.

(6) Distribution of Abortifacients. A person who sells, offers to sell, possesses with intent to sell, advertises, or displays for sale anything specially designed to terminate a pregnancy, or held out by the actor as useful for that purpose, commits a misdemeanor, unless:

(a) the sale, offer or display is to a physician or druggist or to an intermediary in a chain of distribution to physicians or druggists; or

(b) the sale is made upon prescription or order of a physician; or

(c) the possession is with intent to sell as authorized in paragraphs (a) and (b); or

> (d) the advertising is addressed to persons named in paragraph (a) and confined to trade or professional channels not likely to reach the general public.
>
> (7) **Section Inapplicable to Prevention of Pregnancy.** Nothing in this Section shall be deemed applicable to the prescription, administration or distribution of drugs or other substances for avoiding pregnancy, whether by preventing implantation of a fertilized ovum or by any other method that operates before, at, or immediately after fertilization.

C. State Statutes, Codes, and Cases

When the decision in the case of *Roe v. Wade* was announced, many state abortion statutes became invalid. Subsequently, state legislatures responded with a variety of new abortion regulations. Many of these were also challenged as violating the woman's right to privacy. The most important case decisions are described below.

1. *Thornburgh v. American College of Obstetricians and Gynecologists*

In 1982, Pennsylvania enacted the Abortion Control Act, which regulated the information a woman was given before obtaining an abortion, the procedure a physician followed when performing a late-term abortion, and the data that was reported to public authorities. This statute was challenged in the case of *Thornburgh v. American College of Obstetricians and Gynecologists*.[86] In this case, an action was brought challenging the constitutionality of the statute and seeking declaratory and injunctive relief. By the time the case reached the U.S. Supreme Court, the dispute centered on three sections. One section listed a set of facts that was to be recited to every woman who sought an abortion. Another section prohibited doctors from performing an abortion after the fetus was viable, except when the procedure was necessary to preserve the mother's health. The law further provided that when a physician decided that such a late abortion was necessary, two duties were imposed upon the physician: first, the physician must try to remove the fetus alive, unless the attempt "would significantly increase the risk to the mother," and second, the physician must call a colleague into the room to take exclusive control and care for the aborted fetus.

The U.S. Supreme Court, after considering the jurisdiction question, decided that the requirement that the woman be advised that medical assistance may be available, and that the father is responsible for financial assistance in supporting the child, was unconstitutional. Also, the requirement that the physician inform the woman of the detrimental physical and psychological effects and of all the particular medical risks was also unconstitutional. The reporting requirements of the statute did not meet the constitutional requirements, nor did the provisions governing the degree of care for post-viability abortions. Finally, the provisions requiring the presence of a second physician, by failing to provide a medical emergency exception for the situation in which the mother's health is endangered by delay in the second physician's arrival, was unconstitutional. The Court, after specifically reaffirming *Roe v. Wade*, made this comment:

> The states are not free under the guise of protecting maternal health or potential life, to intimidate women into continuing pregnancies. Appellants claim that the statutory provisions before us today further legitimate compelling interests of the Commonwealth. Close analysis of these provisions, however, shows that they wholly subordinate constitutional privacy interests and concerns with maternal health in an effort to deter a woman from making a decision that, with her physician, is hers to make.

The *Thornburgh* decision, which reasserted the fundamental right of women to choose abortion, was a 5-to-4 decision.

2. *Webster v. Reproductive Services*

In the 1988 case of *Doe v. Smith*, the U.S. Supreme Court again upheld the mother's constitutional right to abortion.[87] In this case, the Court decided that the natural father's interest in an unborn fetus, although legitimate and apparently sincere, did not outweigh the mother's constitutionally protected right to abortion. However, it was the *Webster v. Reproductive Services* case in 1989 that garnered greater attention.[88] The case concerned a challenge to a Missouri abortion statute. The preamble to the Missouri statute declared that human life began at conception and included the following provisions:

- It prohibited public employees from performing or assisting abortions not necessary to save a pregnant woman's life;

- It prohibited the use of public funds for counseling a woman to have an abortion or the use of public facilities for performing abortions, even if no public funds are involved; and

- It required doctors, who believe a woman requesting an abortion may be at least 20 weeks pregnant, to perform tests to determine whether the fetus is viable, or capable of surviving outside the womb.

While five justices upheld the state requirements, the majority took three different approaches and the dissenting justices filed two separate opinions. Writing for the plurality (Justices Kennedy, White, and Rehnquist), Justice Rehnquist found that the provision requiring doctors to determine fetal viability only required a physician to perform such tests as are necessary in accordance with the exercise of the physician's professional judgment. These judges rejected *Roe's* rigid trimester framework.

Justice O'Connor agreed that the Missouri law was constitutional, in that requiring tests to ascertain fetal viability was consistent with the state's interest in potential human life, but refused to reexamine the trimester framework set forth in *Roe*. Justice Scalia also recognized the constitutionality of the law, but criticized the plurality opinion for refusing to repudiate *Roe* outright.

The dissenting justices would have reaffirmed the *Roe* trimester framework and declared the Missouri law unconstitutional. They objected to the statute's preamble ("the life of each human begins at conception" and "unborn children have protectable interests in life, health, and well-being"). However, the majority did not find this passage objectionable, arguing that it did not, by its terms, regulate abortions or any other aspect of medical practice. The majority opinion in *Webster* upheld Missouri's regulations on abortion, including the provision that prohibited any public funds to be used for abortions.

3. *Planned Parenthood v. Casey*

As anticipated, these cases did not settle the arguments relating to the constitutionality of state abortion statutes. In 1992, the U.S. Supreme Court considered the constitutionality of the Pennsylvania abortion statute in *Planned Parenthood v. Casey*.[89] At issue were five provisions of the Pennsylvania Abortion Control Act as amended in 1988 and 1989.[90] The Act requires that a woman seeking an abortion notify her husband prior to the abortion procedure, and that she be provided with certain information at least 24 hours before the abortion is performed. For a minor to obtain an abortion, the Act requires the informed consent of one of the minor's parents, but provides for a judicial bypass option if the minor does not wish to or cannot obtain a parent's consent. Another provision of the Act requires that, unless certain exceptions apply, a married woman seeking an abortion must sign a statement indicating that she has notified her husband about the intended abortion. The Act exempts compliance with some of these requirements in the event of a "medical emergency" that is defined in the Act. In addition to these provisions regulating the performance of abortions, the Act imposes certain recording requirements on facilities that provide abortion services.

As in previous cases, the members of the U.S. Supreme Court could find little ground for agreement. The majority refused to overturn *Roe v. Wade*. Three justices held that:

1. the doctrine of *stare decisis* requires reaffirmance of *Roe v. Wade's* essential holding recognizing a woman's right to choose an abortion before fetal viability;

2. the **undue burden test**, rather than the trimester framework, should be used in evaluating abortion restrictions before viability;

3. the medical emergency definition in the Pennsylvania statute was sufficiently broad in that it did not impose an undue burden;

4. the informed consent requirements, the 24-hour waiting period, parental consent provision, and reporting and record-keeping requirements of the Pennsylvania statute did not impose an undue burden; and

5. the spousal notification provision imposed an undue burden and was invalid.

The lack of agreement among the justices is evidenced by the fact that Justice Stevens filed an opinion concurring in part and dissenting in part; Justice Blackmun filed an opinion consenting in part, concurring in the judgment in part, and dissenting in part; Chief Justice Rehnquist filed an opinion concurring in the judgment in part and dissenting in the part in which Justices White, Scalia, and Thomas joined; and Justice Scalia filed an opinion concurring in the judgment in part and dissenting in part, in which Justices Rehnquist, White, and Thomas joined.

4. *Schenck v. Pro-Choice Network of Western New York*[91]

In the 1997 case of *Schenck v. Pro-Choice Network of Western New York*, the United States Supreme Court was presented with the question of whether an injunction that places restrictions on demonstrations outside an abortion clinic violates the First Amendment. The court stated that provisions imposing a "fixed buffer zone" limitation would be upheld, but that the provisions imposing "floating buffer zone" limitations violate the First Amendment. The Supreme Court reasoned that the governmental interests in ensuring public safety and order, promoting free flow of traffic on streets and sidewalks, protecting property rights, and protecting a woman's freedom to seek pregnancy-related services, in combination, were significant enough to justify an appropriately tailored preliminary injunction to secure unimpeded physical access to the clinics.

5. *Stenberg v. Carhart*[92] *and Gonzales v. Carhart*[93]

CASE: *Gonzales v. Carhart*, 550 U.S. 124 (2007)

What is the difference between intact birth abortion and the type of procedure that the Court said was the medical alternative?

What were the issues raised in these appeals?

What was the holding of the Supreme Court and the rationale as to why this was not an undue burden on the woman's right to abortion?

In 2000, the Court considered Nebraska's partial birth abortion law, which prohibited all second trimester abortions where the fetus is extracted from the uterus through the birth canal. Nebraska's law banned all such abortions without any definition as to whether such procedures were pre- or post-viability. The law also made no exceptions for such abortions to save the life or preserve the health of the mother.

The Supreme Court struck down the law, holding that it did not meet the undue burden test because it made no allowances for medical emergencies. The case decision hinted that a partial birth abortion ban that allowed for exceptions might be considered non-violative of the undue burden test. In *Gonzales v. Carhart*,[94] the Supreme Court heard an appeal regarding the federal Partial Birth Abortion Ban,[95] signed by President Bush in 2003. Both the Eighth and Ninth Circuits had overturned the federal Act, ruling that it was unconstitutional under the reasoning of *Stenberg v. Carhart*. The Supreme Court evaluated the arguments that the Act was vague and did not give physicians due notice as to whether their actions would be criminal; was overbroad in that it included behaviors that might have been inadvertent; and, that it posed an undue burden on the woman's right to abortion in that it did not provide for an exception for the woman's health (only life). The Court disagreed with these arguments and upheld the federal Act in a 5 to 4 decision. The dissent, led by Justice Ginsburg, and joined by Justices Breyer, Souter, and Stevens, argued that the decision was contrary to Stenberg and prior decisions that enforced a bright-line test between pre-viability and post-viability procedures. They argued that the decision was a chipping away of the precedent of *Roe v. Wade*.

6. Other Cases Concerning Abortion

A Utah statute that permitted abortions after 20 weeks gestational age in only three narrow circumstances was challenged in *Jane L. v. Bangerter*. The federal court held that this statute violated due process under *Planned Parenthood v. Casey*, because it placed an undue burden on the right to choose the abortion of a nonviable fetus. The court stated that this statute had both the

---

Legal News

One of President Bush's last acts as President was to pass an executive order that allowed individuals who worked for health care facilities that receive federal funds to refuse to perform acts that violate their faith or convictions. One of President Obama's first acts as President was to begin the process of rescinding this order. The executive order allowed workers at more than 500,000 hospitals and medical facilities who receive federal funding to refuse to provide patient care when they disagree with it. The rule is largely believed to target prescriptions for the "morning after pill," a drug that prevents a fertilized egg from being implanted in the uterus and parallels similar laws being passed or considered in a number of states. Arkansas, South Dakota, Mississippi, and Georgia already have such laws. Opponents are encouraging Congress and state legislatures to sponsor bills that would require hospitals and pharmacies to provide the drug when prescribed by a doctor. Some states have opposing bills under consideration. Individual pharmacists argue that they have a right to conduct their business according to their conscience without a law interfering in their decision. The laws may become moot if the Food and Drug Administration allows the drug to be sold over-the-counter as is being proposed.

Source: Meckler, L. (2008). "Bush Era Abortion Rule Faces Possible Reversal." *Washington Post*, December 17, 2008. Accessed 1/5/2009 from http://online.wsj.com/article/SB122947155578512197.html and Lengell, S. (2009). "Obama May Overturn Abortion Rule." *Washington Times*. Accessed 3/9/2009 from https://www3.washingtontimes.com/news/2009/feb/28/obama-may-overturn-abortion-rule/.

impermissible purpose and impermissible effect of placing an insurmountable obstacle in the path of a woman seeking non-therapeutic abortion of a nonviable fetus after 20 weeks.[96]

After considering the provisions of a Montana abortion statute, a federal appeals court ruled that:

Where a minor can show that (1) she is sufficiently mature to make her own decision whether to have an abortion or (2) abortion is in her best interests, the state law must allow her to obtain that abortion without obtaining parental consent.[97] Similarly, a federal court in Arizona agreed that the state may impose a parental consent requirement for minors seeking abortions, but must provide an anonymous and expeditious alternative.[98]

In a Missouri case, a federal circuit court declared that any constitutional right of clinics to provide abortion services is derived directly from the woman's constitutional right to choose abortion, and legislation affecting physicians and clinics that perform abortions will be found unconstitutional if it imposes an *undue burden* on women seeking abortions. The court reiterated that a statute that affects the right to abortion is an undue burden if it has the purpose or effect of placing a substantial obstacle in the path of a woman seeking an abortion.[99]

An Alabama court held that the trial court was correct in granting a minor's request for a waiver of parental consent to have an abortion when the trial judge conducted an adversarial hearing and gave both a *guardian ad litem* appointed for the minor and a *guardian ad litem* appointed for the fetus an opportunity to present evidence and to argue their respective positions.[100]

Answering a question that had come up in several courts, a West Virginia court concluded that an unwed biological father's right to establish and maintain a parental relationship with his child does not foreclose an unwed biological mother's right to terminate her pregnancy.[101]

An Illinois court stated that the mother's right to abort a fetus that had not yet become viable is essentially absolute. In this case the court held that the constitutional right to have an abortion without interference by the man who impregnated her precludes recognition of any constitutional right of the man to interfere.[102]

A federal district court held that a provision of a state's abortion statute requiring that abortions performed following the twelfth week of pregnancy be performed in a hospital was an undue burden and an unnecessary infringement upon a woman's constitutional right to abortion.[103]

While *Roe v. Wade* has essentially been upheld, the Supreme Court has allowed the states additional latitude in laws that regulate abortions. Specifically, the court accepted that the following did not impose an "undue burden" on a woman's right to privacy:

- parental notification (with alternative for mature minors)
- prohibition of any public funds to pay for an abortion
- informed consent requirements
- 24-hour waiting period
- ban on "intact birth" abortions unless life of mother was at stake

With the recent changes in the Supreme Court, it is to be expected that there will be continued challenges to the *Roe v. Wade* opinion that a woman's privacy right overcomes any rights of the fetus during the first trimester. The two most recent appointees to the Supreme Court, Chief Justice Roberts and Justice Alito, are presumed to be conservatives who may favor overturning *Roe*. In fact, South Dakota passed a statute in March of 2006 that criminalizes all abortions and this may eventually create the challenge that will force the court to once again revisit *Roe v. Wade*.

D. Summary

Abortion was not a crime under the common law, but very early statutes existed that criminalized intentional injury or death to a fetus. In 1973 the Supreme Court declared unconstitutional a Texas statute that prohibited abortions. That decision has been challenged many times since then but each time the majority opinion of the Supreme Court has upheld the essential holding that a woman's right to privacy is greater than the state's interest in protecting the fetus by restricting and/or prohibiting abortions, at least in the first trimester. At this point, the test is whether a state regulation or prohibition constitutes an "undue burden" on a woman's right to privacy.

§ 10.8 Summary

Some acts, such as murder, burglary, arson, and theft are so obviously wrong that punishment is provided in practically all societies. There are other acts where there is no consensus regarding punishment. Within this category are offenses designated as offenses against the public health, safety, and morals, or offenses against morality and decency.

Until recently, most states had statutes that prohibited adultery and fornication. Today, adultery and fornication statutes are largely anachronistic. The elements of adultery are voluntary sexual intercourse between parties not lawfully married to each other, with at least one of the parties being married to another person. Fornication is voluntary sexual intercourse between unmarried persons.

Soliciting prostitution is defined as offering (or requesting) sexual acts for money. Also, aiding and abetting prostitution, associating with prostitutes, and keeping and operating a place of prostitution are punishable under the statutes. The modern trend is to place less emphasis on prosecuting the prostitute, but to more aggressively enforce the laws relating to promoting prostitution.

Practically all states have laws that prohibit distributing obscene materials, but defining what is obscene is sometimes difficult. In order to comply with U.S. Supreme Court decisions, obscenity is very carefully defined in such statutes. The current definition of obscenity, provided by the Supreme Court, is called the *"Miller* test." Child pornography is the target of much stricter sanctions. For instance, while laws typically do not punish mere possession of obscenity involving adult actors, the mere possession of child pornography is a crime.

Bigamy, polygamy and incest were not crimes at common law, but were considered offenses in ecclesiastical tribunals. These later became specific crimes and were included in the early statutes of the states. The traditional legal definition of bigamy is willfully and knowingly contracting a second marriage when the contracting party knows that the first marriage still exists. Polygamy is a similar offense and the actus reus for polygamy also involves multiple coterminous marriages. Incest is defined as intermarriage, or sexual relations without marriage, between a man and a woman related to each other within any of the prohibited degrees of consanguinity or affinity.

There are other acts that fall within an offenses against the family category. Most, if not all, of these were not crimes under common law. Parents have a duty to provide support for their children. This means providing food, shelter, and medical care. Today, it may mean paying child support that is ordered by the court. A parent cannot abandon a child, unless their act falls within the exceptions described in safe haven laws. A parent or caregiver is committing a crime when they abuse a child, either physically, sexually, emotionally, or through neglect. Caregivers also are subject to punishment when they expose a child to dangerous or unhealthy conditions. These statutes could potentially cover a wide range of parental behaviors, but the general tendency of states is to work through family or juvenile courts if the caregivers' actions stem from inability to care for the child appropriately or through ignorance.

The term *abortion* does not necessarily imply a criminal act, because some abortions are permitted by law. The United States Supreme Court has rendered a series of decisions regarding abortion-related statutes. In the case of *Roe v. Wade*, the Supreme Court recognized a woman's right to choose an abortion before fetal viability. Following that case, a series of other cases established guidelines that must be followed by the states in enacting and enforcing statutes relating to abortions. Other courts have held that any statute that affects the right to abortion is an undue burden if it has as its purpose or effect the placing of a substantial obstacle in the path of a woman seeking an abortion.

Crimes relating to morality and decency differ from state to state, and definitions of various terms are often technical, thus it is essential to study the specific statutes, as well as cases interpreting the statutes, to understand the law of any particular state.

Review Questions

1. What were the traditional elements of the offense of adultery? In some states, it was essential that one party be married. Which party were some early statutes directed toward and why?

2. How is *fornication* distinguished from *adultery*? How does the penalty for these offenses differ in various states?

3. What Supreme Court case casts doubt on the constitutionality of any statute that seeks to criminalize sex between consenting adults? Explain.

4. What is the likely result when statutes criminalizing the sale of vibrators or other sex aids are challenged? How many states still have such laws?

5. Is the term *prostitution* synonymous with the offense of prostitution? Define *prostitution*.

6. Do the prostitution statutes encompass acts between two males?

7. In the case of *Miller v. California*, the U.S. Supreme Court established some guidelines relating to obscenity. What are these guidelines?

8. How are child pornography statutes different (what behavior do they encompass that obscenity involving adults does not)? Does an offender have to "know" the actor is a child?

9. Is it illegal to create computer-generated children in sexual poses or activities? Explain.

10. Define the terms *bigamy* and *polygamy*. Enumerate the elements of the offense of bigamy. What are the defenses?

11. Define *incest*. Is a state statute that criminalizes sexual intercourse between a father and stepdaughter constitutional? Do all states have such a statute?

12. When can a parent legally abandon a baby? Can they abandon older children?

13. What is a defense for a parent who does not provide medical care for a sick child?

14. What type of acts would fall under endangerment statutes?

15. What is the general definition of *abortion*? What did the case of *Roe v. Wade* hold?

16. Discuss the issue and holding in *Thornburgh v. American College of Obstetricians*. Under what circumstances, according to these cases, may the state regulate abortions?

17. What were the issue and holding in *Planned Parenthood v. Casey*?

18. What were the issue and holding in *Gonzales v. Carhart*?

19. What are the state laws or prohibitions currently in place that have not been ruled as "undue burdens" on women's rights to privacy?

Notes

[1] 4 BLACKSTONE, COMMENTARIES 65 (1776-1779).

[2] United States v. Clapox, 35 F. 575 (D. Or. 1888).

[3] People v. Stokes, 71 Cal. 263, 12 P. 71 (1886).

[4] MILLER, HANDBOOK ON CRIMINAL LAW § 136 (1934).

[5] Lyman v. People, 198 Ill. 544, 64 N.E. 974 (1902).

[6] MODEL PENAL CODE § 213.6 (1985).

[7] For example: 720 ILL. COMP. STAT. 5/11-7 (1996) 5/17/8 (2002).

[8] MISS. CODE ANN. § 97-29-1 (2002).

[9] Brown v. State, 8 So. 257 (Miss. 1890). *See also* Spike v. State, 98 Miss. 483, 54 So. 1 (1911). Reliable Consultants, Inc. v. Earle, No. 06-51067, Fifth Circuit Court of Appeals, March 10, 2008.

[10] *See*, for instance, Commonwealth v. Libby, 358 Mass. 617, 26 N.E.2d 641 (1971). *See also* Sanders v. Alford, 607 So. 2d 1214 (Miss. 1992). MASS. ANN. LAWS ch. 272, §§ 14, 18 (Michie/Law. Co-op. 1999). Section 14, as included here, is the redefined crime of adultery in gender-neutral terms. Formerly, this section prescribed a penalty for an unmarried man who had sexual intercourse with a married woman, but no similar penalty for an unmarried woman who had sexual intercourse with a married man. According to a 1981 court decision, prosecution by law enforcement officials for violation of this section is essentially nonexistent. Fort v. Fort, 12 Mass. App. 411, 425 N.E.2d 754 (1981).

[11] Phyllis Coleman, *Who's Been Sleeping in My Bed? You and Me, and the State Makes Three*, 24 IND. L. REV. 399 (1991).

[12] Lawrence et al. v. Texas, 539 U.S. 558 (2003).

[13] Williams v. Attorney General of Alabama, 378 F.3d 1232 (11th Cir. 2004).

[14] Leonard Pitts, *Deep in the Heart of Texas They're Nuts*, CHICAGO TRIBUNE, Feb. 17, 2004, at 19.

[15] Griswold v. Connecticut, 381 U.S. 479 (1965).

[16] Hatcher v. Dallas, 133 S.W. 914 (Tex. 1911); Ex parte Cannon, 94 Tex. Crim. 243, 250 S.W. 429 (1923).

[17] Commonwealth v. A Juvenile, 6 Mass. App. 194, 374 N.E.2d 335 (1978).

[18] State v. Gardner, 174 Iowa 748, 156 N.W. 747 (1916).

[19] State v. Phillips, 26 N.D. 206, 144 N.W. 94 (1913).

[20] Commonwealth v. Stingel, 146 Pa. 359, 40 A.2d 140 (1944).

[21] MODEL PENAL CODE § 251.2 (1985).

[22] CONN. GEN. STAT. §§ 53a-82-53a-89 (1999).

[23] Steinbach v. State, 979 S.W.2d 836 (Tex. 1998).

[24] People v. Medina, 685 N.Y.S.2d 599 (1999).

[25]   State v. Allen, 37 Conn. Supp. 506, 424 A.2d 651 (1980). *See also* State v. Savio, 924 P.2d 491 (Ariz. 1996), which held that the statute was not unconstitutional vague or overbroad.

[26]   People v. Hill, 776 N.E.2d 828 (Ill. 2002).

[27]   State v. Kittilstad, 603 N.W.2d 732 (Wis. 1999).

[28]   Roth v. United States, 354 U.S. 476, 77 S. Ct. 1304, 1 L. Ed. 2d 1498 (1957). *See also* Kanovitz & Kanovitz, Constitutional Law § 2.6 (10th ed. 2006).

[29]   Model Penal Code § 251.4 (1985).

[30]   *See* Model Penal Code § 251.4 (1985), for comments on obscenity.

[31]   Miller v. California, 413 U.S. 15, 93 S. Ct. 2607, 37 L. Ed. 2d 419 (1973).

[32]   Brockett v. Spokane Arcades, Inc., 472 U.S. 491, 105 S. Ct. 2794, 86 L. Ed. 2d 394 (1985).

[33]   Midtown Palace, Inc., v. City of Omaha, 193 Neb. 785, 225 N.W.2d 56 (1975).

[34]   Ward v. Illinois, 431 U.S. 767, 97 S. Ct. 2085, 52 L. Ed. 2d 738 (1977).

[35]   People v. Ridens, 59 Ill. 2d 362, 321 N.E.2d 264 (1974).

[36]   Blum v. State, 417 S.W.2d 66 (Tex. 1967).

[37]   *See,* for instance, Louisiana's statute. Byers v. Edmondson, 826 So. 2d 551 (La. 2002).

[38]   720 Ill. Comp. Stat. § 5/11-20 (Smith-Hurd 2002). *See also* ch. 720 § 5/11-20.1 "Child Pornography."

[39]   People v. Page Books, 601 N.E.2d 273 (Ill. Ct. App. 1992).

[40]   People v. Sclafani, 166 Ill. App. 3d 605, 520 N.E.2d 409 (1988).

[41]   Cal. Penal Code § 311.2 (West 2003).

[42]   *Id*. at § 311 (West 2003).

[43]   People v. Wiener, 91 Cal. App. 3d 238, 154 Cal. Rptr. 110 (1979)

[44]   Castillo v. State, 79 S.W.2d 817 (Tex. 2002).

[45]   State v. Haltom, 653 N.W.2d 232 (Neb. 2002).

[46]   Stanley v. Georgia, 394 U.S. 557 (1969).

[47]   United States v. Orito, 413 U.S. 139 (1973).

[48]   Osborne v. Ohio, 495 U.S. 103 (1990).

[49]   United States v. Romm, 455 F.3d 990 (9th Cir. 2006) (it is possession).

[50]   Ashcroft v. Free Speech Coalition, 535 U.S. 234 (2002).

[51]   *See,* for instance: State v. Sellers, 140 S.C. 66, 134 S.E. 873 (1926); Barber v. State, 50 Md. 161 (1878). 10 C.J.S. *Bigamy* § 2 (1983).

[52]   State v. Martinez, 43 Idaho 180, 250 P. 239 (1926).

[53]   *See,* for instance, these early cases: Commonwealth v. Ashey, 248 Mass. 259, 142 N.E. 788 (1924); Signs v. State, 35 Okla. Crim. 340, 250 P. 938 (1926); State v. Hurd, 101 Iowa 391, 70 N.W. 613 (1897).

[54]   Model Penal Code § 230.1 (1985).

[55]   Model Penal Code § 230.2 (1985).

[56]   Long v. State, 192 Ind. 524, 137 N.E. 49 (1922).

[57]   Bethany v. State, 91 Tex. Crim. 59, 237 S.W. 262 (1922). *See also* State v. Crosby, 420 P.2d 431 (Mont. 1966).

[58]   Adams v. State, 95 Tex. Crim. 542, 252 S.W. 537 (1923).

[59]   White v. State, 157 Tenn. 446, 9 S.W.2d 702 (1928).

[60]   State v. Hughes, 58 Iowa 165, 11 N.W. 706 (1882).

[61]   ALA. CODE § 13A-13-1 (2002).

[62]   GA. CODE ANN. §§ 16-6-20, 16-6-21 (1999).

[63]   Rogers v. State, 139 Ga. App. 656, 229 S.E.2d 132 (1976).

[64]   *See* these cases as examples: Henley v. State, 489 S.W.2d 53 (Tenn. 1972); Sizemore v. Commonwealth, 210 Ky. 637, 276 S.W. 524 (1925); State v. Couvillion, 117 La. 935, 42 So. 431 (1906).

[66]   Maxey v. Commonwealth, 225 Ky. 663, 9 S.W.2d 1001 (1928).

[66]   42 C.J.S. *Incest* § 3 (1983).

[67]   Wilson v. State, 100 Tenn. 596, 46 S.W. 451 (1898).

[68]   ALA. CODE § 13A-13-3 (1999).

[69]   Morgan v. State, 11 Ala. 289 (1847).

[70]   ALA. CODE § 13A-13-3 (1999).

[71]   GA. CODE ANN. § 16-6-22 (1999).

[72]   Benton v. State, 461 S.E.2d 202 (Ga. 1995).

[73]   Andrews v. State, 144 Ga. App. 243, 240 S.E.2d 744 (1977).

[74]   Carnes v. State, 725 So. 2d 417 (Fla. 1999).

[75]   State v. George, 785 A.2d 573 (Conn. 2001)

[76]   FLORIDA STATUTES, 2008. Title XLVI. Crimes. Chapter 827. Abuse of Children.

[77]   MODEL PENAL CODE § 230.5 (1985).

[78]   OHIO REV. CODE ANN. § 2919.21 (Anderson 2002).

[79]   Associated Press (2008). "Eighteen-Year-Old Abandoned." WIBW-TV.com, November 10, 2008. Accessed 1/2/2008 from www.wibw.com/home/headlines/34205614.html.

[80]   KY. REV. STAT. ANN. § 530.060 (Baldwin 1999). MODEL PENAL CODE § 230.4 (1985), providing the penalty for endangering the welfare of child.

[81]   Roe v. Wade, 410 U.S. 113, 93 S. Ct. 705, 35 L. Ed. 2d 147 (1973).

[82]   *Id.*

[83]   State v. Miller, 90 Kan. 230, 133 P. 878 (1913).

[84]   Roe v. Wade, 410 U.S. 113, 93 S. Ct. 705, 35 L. Ed. 2d 147 (1973).

[85]   MODEL PENAL CODE § 230.3 (1985).

[86]   476 U.S. 747, 106 S. Ct. 2169, 90 L. Ed. 2d 779 (1986).

[87]   Doe v. Smith, 486 U.S. 1308, 108 S. Ct. 2136, 100 L. Ed. 2d 909 (1988).

[88]   Webster v. Reproductive Health Services, 492 U.S. 490, 109 S. Ct. 3040, 106 L. Ed. 2d 410 (1989).

[89]   Planned Parenthood v. Casey, 505 U.S. 833, 112 S. Ct. 2791, 120 L. Ed 2d 674 (1992).

[90]   18 PA. CONS. STAT. §§ 3203-3220 (1990).

[91]   Schenck v. Pro-Choice Network of Western New York, 519 U.S. 357, 117 S. Ct. 855, 137 L. Ed. 2d 1 (1997)

[92]   Stenberg v. Carhart, 530 U.S. 914 (2000).

[93] Gonzales v. Carhart, 550 U.S. 124 (2007).

[94] 550 U.S. 124 (2007)

[95] 18 U.S.C. § 1531

[96] Jane L. v. Bangerter, 102 F.3d 1112 (10th Cir. 1996).

[97] Wicklund v. Salvagni, 93 F.3d 567 (9th Cir. 1996).

[98] Planned Parenthood of Southern Arizona v. Neely, 942 F. Supp. 1578 (D. Ariz. 1996).

[99] Planned Parenthood of Mid-Missouri and Eastern Kansas, Inc., v. Dempsey, 167 F.3d 458 (8th Cir. 1999).

[100] In re Anonymous 720 So. 2d 497 (Ala. 1998).

[101] Kessel v. Leavitt, 511 S.E.2d 720 (W. Va. 1998), *cert. denied*, 525 U.S. 1142, 119 S. Ct. 1035, 143 L. Ed. 2d 43 (1998)

[102] Coe v. County of Cook, 162 F.3d 491 (7th Cir. 1998).

[103] Minnesota/South Dakota v. Janklow, 216 F. Supp. 2d 983 (D.S.D. 2002).

Offenses Against
Public Peace   11

Chapter Outline

Cases

Loitering and vagrancy: *Papachristou et al. v. City of Jacksonville*,
    405 U.S. 156 (1972)
Stop and identify statutes: *Hiibel v. Sixth Judicial District of Nevada,*
    542 U.S. 177 (2004)

§ 11.1   Introduction

In discussing the offenses against public peace, it is important to note that the U.S. Constitution, as interpreted by the courts, limits state power to enact or enforce legislation that prohibit the free exercise of individual behaviors, such as movement or speech. For example, disorderly conduct statutes have, in many instances, been declared unconstitutional as either too vague or as infringing on First Amendment rights. The balance is to have criminal laws that prohibit behavior that is dangerous and/or offensive to the majority, while allowing the greatest degree of freedom for the individual. Sometimes this balance is difficult to achieve.

In this chapter, the offenses of riot, disorderly conduct, vagrancy and loitering, and obstructing a highway or public place are discussed. Crimes of drunkenness and drug use/possession/sale can be considered crimes against public morals as well as public peace and are considered in this chapter. Finally, *state* laws prohibiting eavesdropping and wiretapping and terrorism are discussed in this chapter, although the discussion of federal laws considering these behaviors is offered in more detail in Chapter 14.

§ 11.2   Riot and Related Offenses

In riot and riot-related offenses, the number of participants must be greater than one to constitute a crime. Group behavior is potentially more dangerous to the public peace and poses special problems for the police. In most instances, at least three or more persons must be involved if the offense is to be classified as a riot. The three crimes of unlawful assembly, rout, and riot represent the traditionally recognized steps in violent mob action.

1. Unlawful Assembly

An **unlawful assembly** consists of: (1) the coming together of three or more persons with a common purpose; (2) either to commit a crime by open force; or (3) to carry out their common purpose, lawful or unlawful, in such a manner as to cause persons of reasonable firmness and courage to apprehend a breach of the peace.[1]

In defining the term "unlawful assembly" and distinguishing this from the crimes of rout and riot, a West Virginia court made this comment:

> To constitute "unlawful assembly" there must be a gathering of three or more persons, to the disturbance of the public peace, with the intention of cooperating in the forcible and violent execution of some unlawful enterprise. If they take steps toward the performance of their purpose, it becomes a "rout"; and if they put their design to actual execution, it is a "riot."[2]

2. Rout

A **rout** is an unlawful assembly that has moved toward the execution of the common purpose of the persons assembled. When an unlawful assembly moves toward the accomplishment of the unlawful purpose, but no acts of violence or disorder have occurred, a rout has been committed.

3. Riot

A **riot** is either an actual beginning of the execution of an unlawful common purpose, or the execution of an unlawful purpose by an assembly that was lawful when its members first assembled; in each case, force and violence are used to engender terror.

A. *Common Law*

At common law, a "riot" was:

> [a] tumultuous disturbance of the peace by three persons or more, assembling together of their own authority, with an intent mutually to assist one

another against any who shall oppose them in execution of some enterprise of a private nature and afterward actually executing the same in a violent and turbulent manner, to the terror of the people, whether the act intended was, of itself, lawful or unlawful.[3]

In *Feinstein v. City of New York,* the court, referring to English common law, explained that a "riot" has been said to consist of the following elements:

- a number of persons, three at least;

- a common purpose;

- execution or inception of the common purpose;

- an intent to help one another by force if necessary against any person who may oppose them in the execution of their common purpose; and

- force or violence not merely used in demolishing, but displayed in such a manner as to alarm at least one person of reasonable firmness and courage.[4]

1. Inciting to Riot

"**Inciting to riot**" occurs when a person incites or encourages other persons to create or engage in a riot, as the term has been defined. In the case of *Kasper v. State*, the Supreme Court of Tennessee in 1959 affirmed that inciting to riot is a common law offense.[5]

"Inciting to riot" is a separate, distinct offense from participating in a riot. Therefore, one may incite a riot and not participate in it, or one may be involved in a riot without having incited it. However, the offense of inciting to riot may become merged with the more serious crime of riot if the actor participates during the inciting stage as well as in the execution phase of carrying out the unlawful purpose.[6]

B. Model Penal Code

The Model Penal Code does not carry forward the crimes of rout and unlawful assembly. Subsection (1) of § 250.1 punishes for riot one who, under specific circumstances, participates with two or more persons in a course of disorderly conduct; thus, the Model Code includes the requirement that three persons be involved.

§ 250.1 Riot; Failure to Disperse[7]

(1) Riot. A person is guilty of riot, a felony of the third degree, if he participates with [two] or more others in a course of disorderly conduct:

   (a) with purpose to commit or facilitate the commission of a felony or misdemeanor;

> (b) with purpose to prevent or coerce official action; or
>
> (c) when the actor or any other participant to the knowledge of the actor uses or plans to use a firearm or other deadly weapon.
>
> (2) Failure of Disorderly Persons to Disperse Upon Official Order. Where [three] or more persons are participating in a course of disorderly conduct likely to cause substantial harm or serious inconvenience, annoyance or alarm, a peace officer or other public servant engaged in executing or enforcing the law may order the participants and others in the immediate vicinity to disperse. A person who refuses or knowingly fails to obey such an order commits a misdemeanor.

The subsections spell out the circumstances under which participants may be guilty of riot. Paragraph (b) of subsection (1) applies to disorderly conduct committed with the purpose of preventing or coercing official action. Paragraph (c) covers disorderly conduct without regard to the purpose of the participation, but places the basis of liability on the actor or other participant who uses or plans to use a firearm or other deadly weapon.

C. State Statutes, Codes, and Cases

Some states' statutes and codes follow the wording of the Model Penal Code. Some specify five, rather than three, as the number of participants required to complete the crime. The range of participants required to constitute a riot ranges from two to 10 in state statutes.[8] The wording also varies from state to state. For example, the New York statutes prohibit "violent and tumultuous conduct" by which the actor "intentionally or recklessly causes or creates a grave risk of causing public alarm."[9] In a prosecution for causing a riot at a federal penitentiary, a federal court defined "riot" as a "tumultuous disturbance of the peace by three persons or more, assembling together of their own authority, with an intent mutually to assist each other against any who shall oppose them, in the execution of some unlawful enterprise of a private nature and afterward actually executing the same in a violent and turbulent manner."[10]

The section of the Model Code that applies to "disorderly conduct with the purpose of preventing or coercing official action" is not common to most state statutes. Some state statutes reach the same result by including the words "substantially obstructs law enforcement or other government function." An example is the Kentucky statute, which provides:

> KY. REV. STAT. ANN. § 525.010[11]
>
> Riot means a public disturbance involving an assemblage of five (5) or more persons which by tumultuous and violent conduct creates grave danger of damage or injury to property or persons or substantially obstructs law enforcement or other government functions.

According to that statute, a person is guilty of riot in the first degree when: (a) he knowingly participates in a riot; and (b) in the course of and as a result of such a riot a person other than one of the participants suffers physical injury or substantial property damage occurs.

State statutes also cover inciting a riot. The Ohio statute includes three violations under the general heading of "Inciting, Riot, and Related Offenses." Section 2917.01 makes it an offense to incite to violence, § 2917.02 relates to aggravated riot, and § 2917.03 defines a violation titled "riot." The section of the statute that defines the offense of "riot" provides that:

§ 2917.03[12]

(A) No person shall participate with four or more others in a course of disorderly conduct in violation of § 2917.11 of the Revised Code.

　(1) With purpose to commit or facilitate the commission of a misdemeanor other than disorderly conduct.

　(2) With purpose to intimidate a public official or employee into taking or refraining from official action, or with purpose to hinder, impede, or obstruct a function of government.

　(3) With purpose to hinder, impede, or obstruct the orderly process of administration or instruction at an educational institution, or to interfere with or obstruct lawful activities carried on at such institutions.

(B) No person shall participate with four or more others with purpose to do an act with unlawful force or violence, even though such act might otherwise be lawful.

(C) Whoever violates this section is guilty of riot, a misdemeanor of the first degree.

D. Summary

Riot has been a crime since common law, along with related crimes such as inciting to riot. Basically, what is necessary is at least three people who undertake either unlawful action or lawful action done in an unlawful manner (for instance, a peaceful protest that turns violent). Some states add the provision that the participants may be obstructing the orderly process of government or similar language.

Riot	
(A/R)	Three or more persons, undertake a common action, that is unlawful or lawful but done in an unlawful manner, that is violent and tumultuous, and that obstructs orderly government
(M/R)	General intent

§ 11.3 Disorderly Conduct

"**Disorderly conduct**" statutes cover a broad range of behavior. Starting in the 1970s, many state statutes were found to be unconstitutionally vague or overbroad. Today most states have attempted to comply with the requirements of the U.S. Supreme Court and structure their new statutes after the Model Penal Code. The main difference between old and new statutes is that the statutes now specify more clearly what behaviors are punishable and do not punish "free speech." Disorderly conduct is usually a misdemeanor.

A. Common Law

At common law, there was no offense known as "disorderly conduct," although misconduct that was of such a nature as to constitute a public nuisance was indictable.[13]

B. Model Penal Code

Section 250.2 limits disorderly conduct to specifically designated acts likely to create a public nuisance. An effort was made in drafting the proposed statute to keep within the limitations imposed by the U.S. Supreme Court. The act requires a level of culpability providing that the actor must not only engage in the proscribed conduct, but must do so with the purpose of causing public inconvenience, annoyance or alarm, or recklessly creating a risk thereof. As the Model Code limits the definition of the word "public," police officers would not be authorized to intrude into the home to control private misbehavior simply because such misbehavior may be offensive to others in the home. Instead, the offense is limited to persons who act purposely or recklessly with respect to public annoyance or alarm.

§ 250.2 Disorderly Conduct[14]

(1) Offense Defined. A person is guilty of disorderly conduct if, with purpose to cause public inconvenience, annoyance or alarm, or recklessly creating a risk thereof, he:

(a) engages in fighting or threatening, or in violent or tumultuous behavior; or

(b) makes unreasonable noise or offensively coarse utterance, gesture or display, or addresses abusive language to any person present; or

(c) creates a hazardous or physically offensive condition by any act which serves no legitimate purpose of the actor.

> "Public" means affecting or likely to affect persons in a place to which the public or a substantial group has access; among the places included are highways, transport facilities, schools, prisons, apartment houses, places of business or amusement, or any neighborhood.
>
> (2) Grading. An offense under this Section is a petty misdemeanor if the actor's purpose is to cause substantial harm or serious inconvenience, or if he persists in disorderly conduct after reasonable warning or request to desist. Otherwise disorderly conduct is a violation.

C. State Statutes, Codes, and Cases

The most common constitutional challenge to various state disorderly conduct statutes was that they were vague—for instance, statutes that defined disorderly conduct as ". . . anything that is disorderly, either by words or unbecoming conduct" was declared unconstitutional as being too vague.[15] In 1983, the U.S. Supreme Court struck down this California disorderly conduct statute:

> Every person . . . is guilty of disorderly conduct, a misdemeanor . . . who loiters or wanders upon the streets or from place to place without apparent business and who refuses to identify himself and to account for his presence when requested by any police officer to do so, if the surrounding circumstances are such to indicate to a reasonable man that the public safety demands such identification.[16]

The U.S. Supreme Court found that the statute violated the due process clause, because it vested virtually complete discretion in the hands of the police to determine whether the statute had been violated. Other disorderly conduct, vagrancy, and loitering statutes have undergone extensive change in order to enable them to withstand constitutional scrutiny. While statutes that define disorderly conduct fairly narrowly as those acts that "endanger the morals, safety, or health of the community" have been upheld; statutes that defined as a crime those acts that tended to "annoy, disturb, interfere with or obstruct, or are offensive to others" have been declared unconstitutionally overbroad and vague.[17]

Not every threatening or insulting word constitutes disorderly conduct. In order for conduct to rise to the level of disorderly conduct, such conduct must be a breach of the peace. Fighting is the most common example of disorderly conduct. If one party is the victim of a threat or battery by another, the appropriate charge is assault; however, when two parties mutually engage in fighting, the more appropriate charge is disorderly conduct. In effect, you do not have the right to consent to a fight unless it is in a licensed sport such as boxing. Public fighting is considered a breach of the peace.

Legal News

Fight clubs have emerged all across the country since the 1999 movie *Fight Club* first glorified the phenomenon. Authorities are especially alarmed at the rise of fight clubs among teens, who organize by word of mouth and texting, and then meet in alleyways or empty lots for bare-knuckle fighting, with participants some-times numbering in the hundreds. Video recordings of these fights appear on the Internet or are sold for profit. Similar clubs have emerged among young men, often white collar, who evidently have the same "no talking" rule as the teen clubs. The rule is necessary because the clubs are illegal. Various laws are broken by all the parties involved. Promoters can be charged with conspiracy, promoting a fighting sport without a license, and accessory. Participants can be charged with disorderly conduct, criminal mischief, assault, and, if there are more serious inju-ries or death, aggravated assault, involuntary manslaughter, or depraved heart murder. Even spectators can be charged with accessory to the crimes. Because of the secretive nature of the fighting, and because there is no general consensus among the public (or even enforcers of the law) that these activities should be illegal, there is little chance that the clubs will disappear anytime soon.

Source: McCarthy, M. (2006). "Illegal, Violent Teen Fight Clubs Face Police Crackdown." USA Today, July 31, 2006. Accessed 1/7/2008 from http://www.azcentral.com/families/articles/0731gns-teenfights31-ON.html.

Other acts, such as peaceful protests, may or may not be considered suf-ficient to justify a disorderly conduct conviction. In the activism of the civil rights era of the 1960s and 1970s, state statutes were used to punish protest-ers but this, in turn, led to constitutional scrutiny of the state's statute. Some representative cases are described below:

- (1971—Florida) Defendant went on stage during a performance, took over the microphone, and used obscene language toward the audience. Court upheld conviction for disorderly conduct despite the fact that the defendant's purpose was not "to create or encourage a disturbance," but to avert one.[18]

- (1973—Wisconsin) Defendant was arrested at an induction center for dis-orderly conduct even though there was no proven conduct that "tended to cause or provoke a disturbance." The court overturned the conviction.[19]

- (1962—Connecticut) Defendants staged a sit-in demonstration in the waiting room of a real estate firm sharing office space with lawyers and remaining there in protest against certain features of the local housing ordinances. Convictions were upheld.[20]

Generally, the use of disorderly conduct statutes to prohibit public fighting has met with little resistance from the courts; however, when used against pub-lic utterances, gestures, or displays, court holdings are inconsistent. In general, our freedom of speech is protected; however, there are certain types of speech that are not protected; including obscene speech and "fighting words."

- (1993—Indiana) Defendant noisily protested the arrest of someone in an alley on New Year's Eve, which caused the neighbors to come out and look. Court overturned conviction as unconstitutionally impinging on free speech.[21]

- (1994—Indiana) Defendant argued with her ex-boyfriend and his companions in a loud, screaming voice. Conviction was upheld.[22]

- (1989—Ohio) Defendant made insulting remarks to a police officer, including the assertion to the officer that he was "probably on the take." Court upheld conviction.[23]

- (1999—Massachusetts) Defendant refused a police officer's repeated requests to move her car, which was double-parked behind a school bus, while she waited for her six-year-old son to leave elementary school. Court overturned her conviction, stating that her actions served her legitimate interest in picking up her child from school.[24]

In *State v. Semple*, the 1989 Ohio case cited above, the court held that the repeated insults were sufficiently provocative to constitute "fighting words," falling within the prohibition of R.C. § 2917.11(A)(2). A dissenting judge in the *Semple* opinion disagreed, stating that he did not find that the words were: (1) likely to inflict injury by their utterance, or (2) likely to provoke the average person to an immediate retaliatory breach of peace as required by U.S. Supreme Court decisions. In the next year, a similar case resulted in a different finding from the same court and the language of the dissent in *Semple* became the majority opinion.

- (1990—Ohio) Defendant yelled at a police officer "just because you've got a f____ badge you think you can f___ with people," and continued by stating "f___ you and your gun, money talks so I'll walk." Conviction was overturned and the Ohio reviewing court warned that speech must, by its very utterance, be likely to "inflict injury or provoke the average person to an immediate retaliatory breach of the peace" in order to constitute disorderly conduct.[25]

- (2002—Ohio) Defendant refused to get back into his car after a law enforcement officers' drug search found nothing, and the defendant continued to loudly question the police as to why he had been stopped. Conviction was overturned because there was no testimony of complaints about the defendant's noise level, none of the officers testified that they were inconvenienced, and patrons at a nearby restaurant did not impede traffic, but rather parked their cars to watch the scene unfold.[26]

- (1992—Indiana) Defendant cursed loudly and shouted epithets at the investigating police officer. He told the officer "to get the f___ away," that the investigation was "bull____," and the officer was "a lying motherf____." Court held these were "fighting words" and stated that: "They skirt the depth of degradation despite the fact that they may be tolerated or in common usage by certain elements of our society."[27]

■ (1990—Nebraska) Defendant called a police officer an "a__hole" at the end of a narcotics investigation. Court overturned conviction because insult did not constitute "fighting words."[28]

■ (1999—Florida) Defendant engaged in a loud, belligerent, accusatory tirade targeting a police officer thereby exciting a gathering crowd to such a level that the second police officer developed safety concerns. Conviction was upheld.[29]

The review of case decisions indicates no consistency in what behaviors will be considered sufficient to uphold a conviction of disorderly conduct. Also, disorderly conduct statutes vary from state to state. Some are more inclusive and address various forms of misbehavior, while others serve as a catch-all for misconduct that is not dealt with more specifically under other statutes. Some statutes are very specific in their statement of the conduct that is prohibited. An example is the Ohio statute, which provides:

OHIO REV. CODE ANN. § 2917.11[30]

(A) No person shall recklessly cause inconvenience, annoyance, or alarm to another, by doing any of the following:

(1) Engaging in fighting, in threatening harm to persons or property, or in violent or turbulent behavior;

(2) Making unreasonable noise or offensively coarse utterance, gesture, or display, or communicating unwarranted and grossly abusive language to any person;

(3) Insulting, taunting, or challenging another, under circumstances in which such conduct is likely to provoke a violent response;

(4) Hindering or preventing the movement of persons on a public street, road, highway, or right-of-way, or to, from, within, or upon public or private property, so as to interfere with the rights of others and by any act which serves no lawful and reasonable purpose of the offender;

(5) Creating a condition which is physically offensive to persons or which presents a risk of physical harm to persons or property, by any act which serves no lawful and reasonable purpose of the offender.

The disorderly conduct statute in Texas covers the behaviors above and a range of other behaviors that might be defined as separate crimes in other jurisdictions. For instance, the disorderly conduct statute includes the prohibited behaviors of: displaying or discharging firearms (firearms violations), exposing one's anus or genitals in public (public indecency), and looking in others' windows for lewd and unlawful purposes (voyeurism).[31]

D. Summary

Disorderly conduct did not exist under common law. Early statutes were found to be unconstitutionally broad or vague and so have been rewritten to more specifically enumerate actions that can constitute disorderly conduct. Such actions typically fall into the categories of: fighting; threatening or tumultuous behavior; unreasonable noise or obscene utterance or display; "fighting words;" or actions that create a hazardous or physically offensive condition. Obscenity or speech that can be punished has been listed as: the lewd and obscene, the profane, the libelous, and the insulting or "fighting" words—those that by their very utterance inflict injury or tend to incite an immediate breach of the peace.[32]

Disorderly Conduct

(A/R)　Fighting, offensive language (either obscenity or fighting words), or other hazardous or dangerous actions—all must tend to incite an immediate breach of the peace.

(M/R)　Intent, Knowing or Reckless

---

§ 11.4　Vagrancy and Loitering

Many, if not most, of the early laws relating to **vagrancy** and **loitering** have been declared unconstitutional. Similar to the disorderly conduct statutes, state legislatures have been forced to draft statutes that are more narrowly worded so as to protect the constitutional rights of individuals. Vagrancy historically referred to the status of being homeless, penniless, and on the street or simply being an unsavory character. Loitering typically was defined as being someplace in public without purpose. The two overlap and so will be discussed together in this section.

A. Common Law

At common law, a person was deemed a "vagrant" who went from place to place without visible means of support, was idle and, although able to work for his maintenance, refused to do so and lived without labor or on the charity of others.[33] Another definition of a "vagrant" was: "One who strolls from place to place, an idle wanderer, specifically, one who has no settled habitation, a vagabond."[34]

Early statutes in this country continued the common law definition of vagrancy and basically criminalized being a "street person" with no visible means of support. In *Papachristou v. City of Jacksonville,* the Supreme Court ruled on a city ordinance that defined vagrants as including rogues or vagabonds, dissolute persons who beg, common gamblers, jugglers, or those who engaged in unlawful games or play, com-

> **CASE: *Papachristou et al v. City of Jacksonville,* 405 U.S. 156 (1972)**
>
> What was the holding of the case?
>
> What constitutional rights were violated by this ordinance?
>
> How could cities reform their ordinances and statutes to avoid being unconstitutional?

mon drunkards, common night walkers, thieves, pilferers, or pickpockets, traders in stolen property, lewd, wanton, and lascivious persons, and keepers of gambling places, among other descriptions.[35] The Supreme Court held that that such an ordinance did not give a person of ordinary intelligence fair notice that his conduct was criminal and it also allowed for arbitrary enforcement, thereby violating the due process clause.

B. Model Penal Code

Recognizing that statutes that were too broad violated the due process clause of the Fourteenth Amendment and, in some instances, First Amendment protections, recent legislation is more definite and contains more limiting language. Note that the "status" of being a vagrant can never be penalized, so modern statutes must identify specific behaviors that are against the public interest. The Model Penal Code is an example.

---

§ 250.6 Loitering or Prowling[36]

A person commits a violation if he loiters or prowls in a place, at a time, or in a manner not usual for law-abiding individuals under circumstances that warrant alarm for the safety of persons or property in the vicinity. Among the circumstances which may be considered in determining whether such alarm is warranted is the fact that the actor takes flight upon appearance of a peace officer, refuses to identify himself, or manifestly endeavors to conceal himself or any object. Unless flight by the actor or other circumstance makes it impracticable, a peace officer shall prior to any arrest for an offense under this Section afford the actor an opportunity to dispel any alarm which would otherwise be warranted, by requesting him to identify himself and explain his presence and conduct. No person shall be convicted of an offense under this Section if the peace officer did not comply with the preceding sentence, or if it appears at trial that the explanation given by the actor was true and, if believed by the peace officer at the time, would have dispelled the alarm.

Under this code, the actor must loiter or prowl in a place, at a time, or in a manner not usual for law-abiding individuals and under circumstances that warrant alarm for the safety of persons or property in the vicinity. Section 250.6 differs from prior legislation in that it is narrowly designed to reach only "alarming" loitering. According to the commentary, typical situations covered would be:

- a known professional pickpocket who is seen loitering in a crowded railroad station;

- a person not recognized as a local resident is seen lurking in the doorway and furtively looking up and down the street to see if he is being watched;

- an unknown man is seen standing for some time in a dark alley where he has no apparent business.

Obviously, there is still some vagueness in the wording of the statute because the terms used lack specific definition. However, there are some protective provisions in the statute, especially the last sentence, which requires the police officer to evaluate any innocent explanation for the suspicious behavior.

C. State Statutes, Codes, and Cases

While some states have enacted provisions patterned closely after the Model Penal Code, others have enacted loitering statutes that are even more specific. An example of such a statute is that enacted by the Kentucky legislature and provides:

§ 525.090—Loitering[37]

(1) A person is guilty of loitering when he:

(a) Loiters or remains in a public place for the purpose of gambling with cards, dice or other gambling paraphernalia, except that the provisions of this Section shall not apply if the person is participating in an activity defined by KRS 238.505; or

(b) Loiters or remains in a public place for the purpose of unlawfully using a controlled substance; or

(c) Loiters or remains in or about a school, college or university building or grounds, not having any reason or relationship involving custody of or responsibility for a pupil or student or any other specific legitimate reason for being there and not having written permission from anyone authorized to grant the same; or

(d) Loiters or remains in any transportation facility, unless specifically authorized to do so, for the purpose of soliciting or engaging in any business, trade or commercial transactions involving the sale of merchandise or services.

(2) Loitering is a violation.

This statute preserves the traditional objectives of apprehending those who are about to commit specific crimes or whose activities are offensive to the public-at-large while limiting possible abuse of broad police authority by setting forth specific standards for determining what conduct is prohibited.

Referring to a Florida statute, which is similar to the Model Penal Code, a Florida judge cautioned that the loitering and prowling statute is not directed at mere idling.[38] The court explained that in order to prove a charge of loitering and prowling, the state must prove: (1) that the defendant loitered or prowled in a place, at a time, or in a manner not usual for law-abiding individuals, and (2) the loitering and prowling were under circumstances that warranted a justifiable and reasonable alarm or immediate concern for the safety of persons or property in the vicinity. After stating the requirements, the court held that the behavior of the defendant and other juveniles in walking back and forth in front of a strip mall about eight times over a period of 40 minutes was not sufficiently alarming to raise an immediate concern for the safety of persons or property in the vicinity, and thus was insufficient to support a conviction for loitering and prowling. In a second Florida case, the court added that in order to prove that the accused was loitering and prowling in a manner not usual for law-abiding citizens, as required to support a conviction for loitering and prowling, the state must prove more than a vaguely suspicious presence.[39]

1. Failure to Identify Statutes

A more recent issue in this area is whether a state can make it a crime to refuse to identify oneself to law enforcement. This was the question asked in *Hiibel v. Sixth Judicial District of Nevada*.[40] Recall that states need to specifically identify the types of behaviors that form the basis for a loitering offense and, generally, such behavior has to be inconsistent with law-abiding behavior. One of the elements that might lead to a charge of loitering is the failure to identify oneself and the nature of one's business. Some states, however, have created separate **"failure to identify statutes."** In the Nevada case, the crime occurs when a police officer, with reasonable suspicion that a crime has been or is about to be committed, requests a person's identity and they refuse to give it. Mr. Hiibel believed that the Constitution gave him the right to refuse to answer. He was wrong. Other states, like Texas, require that police officers have probable cause to arrest before citizens are required to give their identity.[41]

> **CASE:** *Hiibel v. Sixth Judicial District of Nevada,*
> **542 U.S. 177 (2004)**
>
> What were the issue and holding of the case?
>
> Which constitutional rights were offered as the source for the right to refuse to identify oneself to police?

D. Summary

The common law crime of vagrancy basically criminalized poverty. Such statutes, when carried forward into modern times, carried the potential for arbitrary and capricious enforcement. The Supreme Court struck down Jacksonville's vagrancy ordinance as violative of the Fourteenth Amendment and, by doing so, invalidated any similar statutes across the country. Subsequently, loitering statutes were also struck down as being impermissibly vague unless they specified a type of action that was not "mere idling," but was consistent with unlawful behavior and raised a reasonable suspicion that criminal action was imminent. The latest category of such laws is failure to identify statutes. The Supreme Court has upheld such statutes as long as the police officer has at least reasonable suspicion to stop and detain for investigation although other states require that the officer have probable cause to believe that a crime was committed or is about to be committed.

Loitering

(A/R)   Loitering or prowling; in a way not consistent with law-abiding behavior, that creates a reasonable alarm or concern that crime was imminent

(M/R)   Intentional, Knowing

---

§ 11.5   Drunkenness

While *being* a "drunk" cannot be a crime; being drunk in public can be. These statutes are justified under the police power of the state. According to one court, this power relates to the the right of the state to care for the health, morals, and welfare of the people.[42] Statutes and ordinances have withstood constitutional challenges as long as they clearly identified behavior that was against the public good.

A. *Common Law*

Drunkenness was not an offense under the common law of England, but was punishable in the ecclesiastical courts.[43] Under early state statutes, a person could be punished for being under the influence of intoxicants in a private or public place, or sometimes the penalty applied only if the person appeared in an intoxicated condition in public.

In the case of *Powell v. Texas*, discussed in Chapter 1, a self-confessed alcoholic was convicted of being drunk in a public place.[44] On appeal, he contended that he was compelled to drink, and once drunk, would lose control over his behavior and that it was cruel and unusual punishment to impose criminal sanctions on him for appearing drunk in a public place. He relied on the reasoning in the case of *Robinson v. California*, which held that an individual could not be branded a criminal or subjected to penal sanctions, no matter how slight, simply because he occupied the status or condition of being a "known drug addict."[45]

The U.S. Supreme Court rejected the defendant's argument, explaining that although the state of Texas could not punish him for the status of being an alcoholic, the *Robinson* decision did not establish a constitutional doctrine of diminished criminal responsibility for addicts and others similarly affected. Penalizing a person for appearing in public while intoxicated does not violate the U.S. Constitution because it punishes an act, not a status.

According to the court in the *Powell* case, being an alcoholic is no defense to the crime of public intoxication. It follows, then, that being drunk cannot be used as a defense to any crime. In general, drunkenness or even being an alcoholic can not be used as a defense, although extreme intoxication may reduce a defendant's *mens rea* from specific intent to general intent or recklessness.

B. Model Penal Code

The Model Penal Code provides a penalty for appearing in public under the influence not only of alcohol, but also of narcotics or other drugs. It also requires that the influence be to the degree that the person charged may endanger himself or other persons or property, or annoy persons in his vicinity. The Model Code differs from some traditional statutes in that it provides a punishment for public drunkenness but not private drunkenness.

§ 250.5 Public Drunkenness; Drug Incapacitation[46]

A person is guilty of an offense if he appears in any public place manifestly under the influence of alcohol, narcotics or other drug, not therapeutically administered, to the degree that he may endanger himself or other persons or property, or annoy persons in his vicinity. An offense under this Section constitutes a petty misdemeanor if the actor has been convicted hereunder twice before within a period of one year. Otherwise the offense constitutes a violation.

C. State Statutes, Codes, and Cases

Some states subsequently enacted provisions that follow the Model Penal Code, while others have broader coverage. When the law applies only if the person is intoxicated in a public place, the prosecution must prove that the person did, in fact, appear in a public place while under the influence. According to one case, a public place does not mean a place devoted solely to the use of the public, but means a place that is in point of fact public, as distinguished from private; a place that is visited by many persons and usually accessible to the neighboring public. This includes not only public roads and streets, but various other places such as schools and places of worship.[47]

Some statutes punish intoxication in private, often with conditions attached. For example, in Ohio, a person may be punished for being intoxicated in a public place or in the presence of two or more persons. He may also be punished if he engages in conduct or creates a condition that presents a risk of harm to himself or the personal property of another.[48] As a part of the disorderly conduct section, the Ohio statute provides:

OHIO REV. CODE ANN. § 2917.11

(B) No person, while voluntarily intoxicated, shall do either of the following:

    (1) In a public place or in the presence of two or more persons, engage in conduct likely to be offensive or to cause inconvenience, annoyance, or alarm to persons of ordinary sensibilities, which conduct the offender, if he were not intoxicated, should know is likely to have such effect on others;

    (2) Engage in conduct or create a condition which presents a risk of physical harm to himself or another, or to the property of another.

Under the provisions of this statute, the prosecution must introduce evidence to show: voluntary intoxication, plus either being in a public place or, if in a private place, that the conduct is likely to be offensive. In the alternative, the prosecution may prove: voluntary intoxication, plus the person engaged in conduct or created a condition that presents a risk of physical harm to himself or another or to the property of another.

In interpreting the Ohio statute regarding voluntary intoxication, an appeals court decided that a trial court could find that the defendant was voluntarily intoxicated based on a combination of direct and circumstantial evidence. The facts indicated that a police officer testified that he smelled the odor of alcohol on the defendant's person and that the defendant was loud and "used a lot of slurring of his speech." This evidence, combined with evidence that the defendant was very antagonistic, used profanity, and was offensive, was sufficient to support a conviction under the statute.[49]

The Florida statute requires that the defendant be in a public place.

> FLA. STAT. ANN. § 856.011 (2003).[50]
>
> No person in the state shall be intoxicated and endanger the safety of another person or property, and no person in the state shall be intoxicated or drink any alcoholic beverage in a public place or in or upon any public conveyance and cause a public disturbance.

In interpreting this statute, the court held that the defendant's front porch was not a "public place" within the meaning of the statute, which prohibits intoxication or drinking of alcoholic beverages in a public place.[51] Note that if the person is intoxicated in a private place, public intoxication cannot be charged but the person may be convicted of other offenses, such as assault or disorderly conduct.

Legal News

In the spring of 2006, the Texas Alcoholic Beverage Commission operated a campaign of arresting public drunks. Undercover agents went into bars in Austin, Dallas, and the major cities of Texas and arrested people who "appeared drunk." The practice was not met with a great deal of enthusiasm on the part of the general public. One columnist quipped, "that's the reason why people go into bars." Spokespersons for the agency defended the action, arguing that bars were public places and that the campaign was designed to prevent drunk-driving incidents; however, evidently some of the arrests occurred in hotel bars and were of individuals who had rooms for the night and planned to drive nothing but the elevator. When state officials begin to receive feedback that some business conferences were being canceled and moved to other states because of a fear that their conference participants would be arrested, there was an announcement that TABC officers would be "retrained" to apply the law in a more tourist-friendly fashion.

Source: Retrieved 7/1/2006 from www.msnbc.msn.com/id/11965237/ and www.msnbc.msn.com/id/1230886.

1. Driving While Intoxicated/Driving Under the Influence

In some states, these terms are used for the same crime, in other states, they are two different crimes with "driving under the influence" a lesser crime than "driving while intoxicated." In all states, the definitions of "intoxication" and "influence" are set by statute and this element can be proven by Breathalyzer tests or by officer testimony.

Individuals have the right to refuse a Breathalyzer test, but state laws typically will respond to such a refusal with a mandatory confiscation of one's license. The legal rationale for such laws are that driving is a privilege and one's license creates an implied consent to submit to Breathalyzer tests or other tests in order to continue to receive the benefits of a driver's license.[52]

One issue that has been litigated in DWI or DUI prosecutions is the meaning of "in control" of the automobile. Individuals who have been found on the side of the road in the passenger seat have been convicted of DWI; as have individuals who are sitting in their car in their driveway. Even when the key is not anywhere to be found, an individual may be convicted because courts have defined "in control" broadly.[53]

D. *Summary*

There was no common law crime of public drunkenness, but the behavior was punished in the ecclesiastical courts in early England. Early statutes in this country made it a crime punishable in the criminal court system. Alcoholism cannot be used as a defense for public intoxication, nor can drunkenness be used as a defense for any crime (although it may reduce the *mens rea* of the individual if he or she is so incoherent as to not be able to form specific intent). DUI/DWI statutes punish those who are "in control" of a motor vehicle while intoxicated.

Public Drunkenness/Intoxication

(A/R) Voluntary alcoholic intoxication (sometimes includes drugs), in a public place (sometime private with other conditions, i.e., offensive behavior); sometimes offensive behavior is required even in a public place

(M/R) Intentional, reckless (*mens rea* goes to decision to drink)

---

§ 11.6 Drug Laws

Alcohol and drug crimes share some similarities, but also major differences. It is against the law to appear in public or operate a motor vehicle when one is intoxicated by alcohol or drug use; however, it is usually not against the law to merely possess alcohol (unless one is a minor). On the other hand, it is a crime to even possess certain types of drugs. Drug laws share certain characteristics with laws against gambling and prostitution in that certain segments of the population who engage in no other types of crimes and do not consider themselves "criminal," routinely violate such laws.

We will explore federal drug laws more thoroughly in Chapter 14, but it is impossible to discuss state drug laws without reference to the federal government's role. Beginning in 1970 with the Comprehensive Drug Abuse Prevention and Control Act, statutes were enacted by Congress to identify and control substances that are extremely harmful when used improperly. The Uniform Controlled Substances Act defines a large number of drugs and categorizes them by level of risk and seriousness. Most states have adopted the provisions of the Uniform Controlled Substances Act.[54] The Act was designed to supplant the Uniform Narcotic Drug Act and the Model State Abuse Control Act, relating to depressant, stimulant, and hallucinogenic drugs, promulgated in 1966. The Act was drafted to achieve uniformity among laws of the several states and those of the federal government, and to complement federal narcotics and dangerous drug legislation. In fact, there is probably more uniformity in drug laws than in most other criminal law areas.

A. Common Law

There were no drug laws under the common law.

B. Model Penal Code

The Model Penal Code does not have any provisions for drug possession or possession with intent to sell. Drug intoxication is included with public drunkenness.

C. State Statutes, Codes, and Cases

A state, under its police power, may regulate the administration, sale, prescription, possession, and use of narcotic drugs.[55] Courts have consistently held that it is a legitimate use of police power to regulate all aspects of drug use and possession. Statutes have been upheld, for instance, in the following areas:

- Possession of paraphernalia adapted for the use of narcotic drugs and classification of marijuana as a narcotic.[56]

- Growing, possession, and use of marijuana (with some exceptions).[57]

- Being under the influence of narcotic drugs.[58]

- Inhaling glue with the intent to become intoxicated.[59]

- The use of marijuana in a private place.[60]

- ■ The sale or purchase of drugs within 1,000 feet of a school.[61]

- ■ The use of marijuana as a sacrament for a religious ceremony.[62]

However, there have been a few cases in which statutes have been struck down.

- ■ Members of a native American church may use peyote as a religious sacrament.[63]

- ■ A city ordinance that punished individuals from visiting "any building or place" if they knew that drugs were used, sold or kept there was unconstitutionally broad.[64]

1. Uniform Controlled Substances Act

The Uniform Controlled Substances Act was promulgated by the National Conference of Commissioners on Uniform State Laws to create a coordinated and codified system of drug control, similar to that utilized at the federal level. The Act sets out prohibited activities in detail, but vests the authority to administer the Act in an agency to be established by the state legislature. Because the Act authorizes the agency or person who administers it to implement, enforce, and regulate the provisions of the Act, this authority is often vested in a high-ranking state official or a committee. For example, the authority could be vested in the Office of the Attorney General, a department of health, a division of public safety, or other agency within the state responsible for regulating and enforcing the drug laws. The intent is to create reasonable flexibility within the Uniform Act so that as new substances are discovered or found to have an abuse potential, they can quickly be brought under control without constant resort to the legislature.

To make the Uniform Act consistent with the federal law, the Uniform Act follows the federal controlled substances law and lists all of the **controlled substances** in five schedules that are identical to the federal law.

In categorizing the substances, eight criteria were followed:

- ■ the actual or relative potential for abuse

- ■ scientific evidence of pharmacological effects

- ■ the state of current scientific knowledge regarding the substance

- ■ its history and pattern of abuse

- ■ the scope, duration, and significance of abuse

- ■ what, if any, risks there are to the public health

- ■ its psychic or psychological dependence liability

- ■ whether the substance is an immediate precursor of a substance already controlled

The Uniform Controlled Substances Act deals with the manufacture and distribution of controlled substances. Much of the Act defines terms:

- "Controlled substance" means a drug, substance, or immediate precursor included in Schedules I through V of Article II.

- "Narcotic drug" means any of the following, however manufactured:
  - opium, opium derivative, and any derivative of either, including any salts, isomers, and salts of isomers of them that are theoretically possible within the specific chemical designation, but not isoquinoline alkaloids of opium;
  - synthetic opiate and any derivative of synthetic opiate, including any isomers, esters, ethers, salts, and salts of isomers, esters, and ethers of them that are theoretically possible within the specific chemical designation;
  - poppy straw and concentrate of poppy straw;
  - coca leaves, except coca leaves and extracts of coca leaves from which cocaine, ecgonine, and derivatives of ecgonine or their salts have been removed;
  - cocaine, or any salt, isomer, or salt of isomer of cocaine;
  - cocaine base;
  - ecgonine, or any derivative, salt, isomer, or salt isomer of ecgonine; and
  - compound, mixture, or preparation containing any quantity of a substance listed in this paragraph.

- **"Deliver,"** unless the context otherwise requires, means to transfer a substance, actually or constructively, from one person to another, whether or not there is an agency relationship.

- "Person" means an individual, corporation, business trust, estate, trust, partnership, association, joint venture, government, or governmental subdivision or agency, or any other legal or commercial entity.

All controlled substances are categorized in Schedules I, II, III, IV, or V. Under the Uniform Controlled Substances Act, the schedules are identical with the federal law; however, this does not prevent a state from adding or removing substances from the schedule or from reclassifying the substances from one schedule to another. Also, as new substances are discovered or found to have abuse potential, they can quickly be brought under control without resort to the legislature. The purpose of the classification is to create a coordinated codified system of drug control regulation and to establish criteria for prescribing specific fines or sentences. The Controlled Substances Act does not itself designate specific fines or sentences, but leaves this up to the discretion of the individual states.

The guidelines for determining the category into which any controlled substance should be included are as follows:

- Schedule I
  - has a high potential for abuse;
  - has no currently accepted medical use in the United States; and
  - lacks accepted safety for use under medical supervision.

- Schedule II
  - the substance has high potential for abuse;
  - the substance has currently accepted medical use in treatment in the United States, or currently accepted medical use with severe restrictions; and
  - the abuse of the substance may lead to severe psychic or physical dependence.

- Schedule III
  - the substance has a potential for abuse less than the substances listed in Schedules I and II;
  - the substance has currently accepted medical use in treatment in the United States; and
  - abuse of the substance may lead to moderate or low physical dependence or high psychological dependence.

- Schedule IV
  - the substance has a low potential for abuse relative to substances in Schedule III;
  - the substance has currently accepted medical use in treatment in the United States; and
  - abuse of the substance may lead to limited physical dependence or psychological dependence relative to the substances in Schedule III.

- Schedule V
  - the substance has low potential for abuse relative to the controlled substances included in Schedule IV;
  - the substance has currently accepted medical use in treatment in the United States; and
  - abuse of the substance may lead to limited physical dependence or psychological dependence liability relative to the controlled substances listed in Schedule IV.

Remember that controlled substances include not only "street drugs," but also pharmaceuticals that may be legal when properly prescribed and dispensed. States are free to follow or modify the suggested provisions. All states have laws that prohibit the possession, possession with intent to distribute (or traffic in), and use of controlled substances. Other statutes may also exist.

2. Drug Crimes

a. Possession of a Controlled Substance Except as Authorized

As stated above, states have the ability to punish mere possession of controlled substances such as cocaine, heroin, and marijuana. Possession statutes are comprised of two basic elements: knowledge and possession. Because knowledge is an element of the offense of possession of a controlled substance, the state has the burden of proving that a defendant's possession was knowing.[65]

The other element of the crime is possession. In many situations, the controlled substance is in the presence of, but not on the person of the defendant; or may even be at another location. Courts recognize **"constructive possession,"** which means that the defendant has custody or dominion over the substance, even if he does not have it on his person.[66] Of course, this begs the question as to what is "custody" or **"dominion."** The court holdings below further refine the definition of possession.

- "Possession" or "control" within the meaning of the drug statutes means either actual physical possession with knowledge of the same or constructive possession if the accused knows of the presence of the item on or about his premises and has the ability to maintain control over it.[67]

- Possession entails (1) the accused exercised care, control, and management over the contraband, and (2) the accused knew the matter possessed was contraband.[68]

- The state must prove that the defendant exercised actual care, custody, control, or management over the contraband and he or she knew the matter possessed to be contraband.[69]

- The defendant knew of the character of the substance and its presence and exercised dominion and control over it.[70]

In some situations, the defendant is in the presence of drugs with other people, purports that they were not his drugs, or argues that he did not know they were there. The case decisions in these areas are not uniform.

- Defendant's presence as a passenger in the bed of a pickup truck in which other persons were transporting cocaine was insufficient to show that the defendant actually or constructively possessed cocaine, for purposes of trafficking.[71]

- Defendant who was found sitting on a bedroom floor, talking on the telephone, in front of a closet containing cocaine, did not have constructive possession of cocaine absent a showing that the defendant was more than a mere visitor in the house or that she could otherwise exercise dominion or control over the drug.[72]

- Defendant's mere presence at a social club where narcotics were found did not establish sufficient dominion and control by the defendant over the premises to charge him with constructive possession of 312 vials of cocaine concealed in the door of the premises.[73]

- Defendant and two other men were found seated within arm's reach of each other and cocaine along with mirror and razor blades. Other drug-related accessories were found throughout the room. The conviction was affirmed despite defendant arguing lack of possession.[74]

- Defendant was found with 53 grams of pure cocaine under the seat of a car he borrowed from a friend. The suspect denied ownership of both the car and the cocaine and denied having knowledge of the cocaine. Court upheld conviction finding that evidence was sufficient to find knowledge and constructive possession.[75]

- Defendant was a visitor in an apartment that was subject to a search warrant. Court overturned conviction, holding that the state did not prove constructive possession, specifically, statements or conduct of the accused, or other facts or circumstances that tend to show that the accused was aware of both the presence and of the character of the drugs.[76]

In order for a state to prove possession, it must show knowledge of the presence of the drug, and either physical or constructive possession. The defendant does not have to hold the drug to "possess" it; however, the state must prove custody, dominion, and control over the drug. Most states also specify the amount of drug necessary to constitute a violation. Generally, there must be at least a "measurable" amount of the drug, but drug residue, when found on drug paraphernalia, has been sufficient to uphold a conviction of possession.[77] If the amount reaches a certain limit, then there is a *prima facie* case for not just possession, but, instead, "possession with intent to distribute."

Possession with intent to deliver is a more serious crime, with more serious penalties associated with it. The state must prove both elements—possession and intent to distribute. However, intent may be proven by the mere quantity of the drug. If a drug is found in quantities that exceed "personal use," then the defendant may be convicted of the more serious crime.[78] If the defendant is successful in delivering the drug or is found after transporting a drug in preparation for delivery, the offense is trafficking.

b. Trafficking in a Controlled Substance Except as Authorized

Trafficking involves a *mens rea* of knowing (that it is a controlled substance) and specific intent to deliver. The *actus reus* is some type of delivery or transfer of a controlled substance, A Louisiana court explained that, in order to obtain a conviction for distribution of cocaine, the state must show: (1) delivery or physical transfer; (2) guilty knowledge of the controlled dangerous substance at the time of the transfer; and (3) the exact identity of the controlled dangerous substance.[79]

The state may rely on evidence of constructive possession of cocaine to establish the element of transportation for the offense of trafficking in cocaine by transportation. Either proof of actual or constructive possession of cocaine is necessary to establish the element of transportation.[80]

Legal News

Tracey Ward was convicted of delivery of a controlled substance. In her case the substance was cocaine and the person she delivered it to was her unborn baby. She is one of many women who have been prosecuted under existing drug laws for using drugs while pregnant. In some states, the prosecutor's legal theory is that in the moment after birth (to ensure the definition of legal "person"), but before the umbilical cord is cut, the woman is "delivering" cocaine to her child. In Texas and other states, new statutes have been written to punish delivering drugs to a fetus, although such statutes have exceptions to cover doctors who prescribe drugs for legitimate medical purposes. The proof of delivery is in the tests that determine whether the newborn has any drugs in his or her system. In Ward's case, she pled guilty, thus averting a legal challenge of Texas's law.

Source: Betsy Blaney, "Mom Guilty of Giving Drugs to Fetus," *Austin American-Statesman*, September 8, 2004, at B6.

---

c. *Dispensing, Prescribing, Distributing, or Administering a Controlled Substance Except as Authorized*

The Uniform Controlled Substances Act and state statutes require persons who engage in, or intend to engage in, the manufacture, distribution, or dispensing of controlled substances to be registered by the state. The purpose of this part of the Act or statute is to allow the state to know who is responsible for a substance and who is dealing in the substances. This also gives those investigating violations specific authority to prosecute when the controlled substance laws have been violated. Statutes requiring pharmacists and practitioners to register, maintain records, and only prescribe, administer, and dispense controlled substances as provided in the Act have generally been held to be constitutional and are not so vague as to deny due process.[81]

A Mississippi decision indicated that "distribution" of drugs does not necessarily involve a sale. Delivery of drugs to third persons, whether or not accomplished in exchange for money or other consideration, is an act of distribution for which the law will punish the deliverer.[82] In defining a "constructive delivery," a Texas court reasoned that a "constructive delivery" occurs when a seller transfers a controlled substance, either belonging to him or under his control, by some other person or means, at the direction of the seller. An "actual delivery" consists of transferring real possession and control of a controlled substance from one person to another person.[83]

d. Other Crimes

States also have other statutes concerning drug use and distribution, including:

- "Obtaining or attempting to obtain a controlled substance by fraud, deceit, misrepresentation or subterfuge,"

- "Possessing, manufacturing, selling, dispensing, prescribing, distributing or administering any counterfeit substance."

- Certain advertising of controlled substances.

3. Seizure and Forfeiture of Controlled Substances, Vehicles, and Drug Paraphernalia

To further discourage the manufacture, possession, or traffic in controlled substances, many states have enacted statutes that authorize seizure and forfeiture of not only controlled substances, but any vessel, vehicle, aircraft, or drug paraphernalia that has been used in or was bought with the proceeds of drug trafficking. Under the Controlled Substance Forfeiture Act, the state must simply show a "nexus" between the seized property and the unlawful activity by a preponderance of evidence. Once the state has sustained its burden, the burden shifts to the property owner to disprove the state's case or establish a statutory defense.[84]

Historically, because the asset forfeiture action was a separate civil, rather than criminal, judicial proceeding, an individual could be acquitted of the underlying criminal offense, or not even arrested at all, and still be required to forfeit property used to facilitate the offense. The judicial challenges to what was perceived by some to be unfair met with mixed results in the state courts and the lower federal courts. The viability of asset forfeiture in drug cases was eventually addressed by the U.S. Supreme Court in three cases decided over the period 1989 through 1994. The holdings had consequences for any expansion of forfeiture laws in the states.

- In *United States v. Halper*, the Court held that a civil sanction that could not be characterized as remedial may constitute "punishment" under the double jeopardy clause.[85]

- In *Austin v. United States*, the Court held that the "civil" distinction of forfeiture did not exempt it from Eighth Amendment scrutiny against "excessive fines." This decision limited the use of asset forfeiture when a defendant was subjected to heavy fines as part of the criminal proceedings.[86]

- In *Department of Revenue of Montana v. Kurth Ranch*, the Court held that the double jeopardy clause barred the state of Montana from imposing a civil tax for illegal drug possession on a defendant convicted and punished for the same offense in a separate criminal proceeding.[87]

After 1994, the validity of the federal asset forfeiture statutes was questionable and the federal circuits, following the lead of the U.S. Supreme Court, all but closed the door on the practice. In 1996, the U.S. Supreme Court revisited the issue of the relationship between the federal asset forfeiture statutes and the double jeopardy clause of the U.S. Constitution in *United States v. Usery.* The Court expressly rejected the previously employed "balancing" test (the harm suffered by the government is compared to the forfeiture imposed) in favor of the following test:

1. Whether Congress intended the statutory scheme at issue to be criminal or civil, and

2. Whether the scheme is so punitive either in purpose or effect as to negate the intent of Congress to establish a civil asset forfeiture process.

Applying this new test, the Court concluded that asset forfeiture in drug cases did not violate the double jeopardy clause in that it was not an additional penalty for the commission of a criminal act, but, rather, a separate civil action, remedial in nature and expressly sanctioned by Congress.[88] Because *Austin v. United States* was not expressly overruled, legal scholars remain perplexed—the federal asset forfeiture statutes apparently do not violate the double jeopardy clause, but, where the forfeiture is too disproportionate to the offense, such statutes may violate the excessive fines clause.

4. Challenges to Marijuana Laws

The most contentious area of drug law has been in the regulation and punishment of marijuana use. Opponents argue that marijuana should not be a Schedule I drug and that it should not have the same severe penalties as other drugs. First, challenges based on individuals' rights to privacy over personal decisions have been raised. These challenges, although meeting some degree of success in lower state courts, are consistently rejected by appellate courts.[89] The second challenge is a medical necessity defense. This argument is that marijuana is the best medical alternative for those who are seriously ill and experiencing pain and nausea. Several states have passed medical marijuana laws that allow the drug to be prescribed and used for legitimate medical purposes. The Supreme Court, however, has upheld the right of the federal government to enforce federal drug laws even if they directly contradict state law.[90] The challenge that federal drug laws, based on the Commerce clause, did not reach marijuana that was grown and consumed entirely within one state was also rejected by the Supreme Court in *Gonzales v. Raich.*[91] As more states pass medical marijuana laws, it may be that the Supreme Court will see fit to reexamine their position on the issue.

D. Summary

As one might expect, the provisions of the acts prohibiting activities related to controlled substances have been challenged many times in both federal and state courts. Due to careful preparation, the laws have been upheld as not violating the due process clauses of the Constitution; nor do the acts generally violate the right of privacy.

The Uniform Controlled Substances Act sets out prohibited activities in detail and vests the authority to administer the act in an agency to be established by the state legislature. To make the Act consistent with federal law, the Uniform Act follows the federal Controlled Substances Act and lists all of the controlled substances in five schedules that are identical to the federal law but does not prevent the state from making changes. The Act includes guidelines for determining the category into which the controlled substance generally will be included.

The Uniform Controlled Substances Act and state statutes require persons who engage in, or intend to engage in, the manufacture, distribution, or dispensing of controlled substances to be registered by the state, among other things. These acts make it unlawful for any person to manufacture, deliver, or possess, with intent to manufacture or deliver, a controlled substance and allow for the law to provide penalties determined by the classification of the substance.

Possession

(A/R) Actual or constructive possession

(M/R) Knowing

Possession with Intent to Deliver

(A/R) Actual or constructive possession; with circumstances indicating intent is to deliver (i.e., quantity)

(M/R) Knowing (goes to possession); specific intent (goes to deliver/distribute)

Trafficking

(A/R) Actual or constructive possession; transfer or delivery (does not have to be for money)

(M/R) Knowing (goes to possession); general intent (goes to delivering)

---

§ 11.7 Wiretapping and Eavesdropping

A. Common Law

Eavesdropping was a common law crime, the essence of which consisted of listening under walls, windows, or eaves in order to vex or annoy another by spreading slanderous rumors against him.[92] An eavesdropper was that unsavory character who snooped under the eaves to satisfy his interest in gossip. From this practice, the term *eavesdropping* developed. Modern technology has provided increasingly efficient tools to listen to the conversations of others, and legislative bodies have attempted to draft legislation to control such activity.

The early eavesdropper listened by the naked ear under the eaves of houses or windows, or beyond their walls, seeking out private discourse. Technology has provided better vehicles for eavesdropping. Even with the advent of the telegraph, surreptitious interception of messages began. The telephone brought on a new and modern eavesdropping method known as **wiretapping**. As early as 1862, California found it necessary to prohibit the practice of eavesdropping by statute, and Illinois outlawed wiretapping by legislation in 1895. In 1905, California extended its telegraphic interception prohibition to the telephone. Most of the existing laws relating to wiretapping and eavesdropping result from decisions and legislation of the last four decades.[93] The most far-reaching legislation is federal and was enacted by Congress in 1968. Federal wiretapping laws will be addressed in Chapter 14.

A related issue to wiretapping and eavesdropping is invasion of privacy and the various ways that offenders can victimize unsuspecting individuals. Today, the use of camera phones and other devices have outstripped some states' ability to regulate such invasions of privacy. While some new statutes have been written to cover those who use camera phones in public bathrooms or locker rooms, other states adapt existing statutes to cover such behavior, such as voyeurism statutes, invasion of privacy statutes, or laws that prohibit secret video recordings.

Legal News

Examples of the use of camera phones indicate that it is a crime deterrent as well as a crime tool. Some individuals have been arrested for using a camera phone to take pictures of women's underwear, and others have taken surreptitious photos using camera phones in health clubs and gyms. On the other hand, camera phones have also been used to snap pictures of assailants, crimes in progress, and license plates, and have led to arrests.

Source: D. Ng (2006). "Smile! You're on My Cell Phone." Legalzoom.com. Retrieved 9/21/2006, www.legalzoom.com/articles/article_content/article11121.html.

B. Model Penal Code

The Model Penal Code prohibits unlawful eavesdropping or surveillance. Subsection (1) of §250.12 deals with unauthorized eavesdropping or surveillance in a private place and defines that term.

§ 250.12 Violation of Privacy[94]

(1) Unlawful Eavesdropping or Surveillance. A person commits a misdemeanor if, except as authorized by law, he:

  (a) trespasses on property with purpose to subject anyone to eavesdropping or other surveillance in a private place; or

  (b) installs in any private place, without the consent of the person or persons entitled to privacy there, any device for observing, photographing, recording, amplifying or broadcasting sounds or events in such place, or uses any such unauthorized installation; or

  (c) installs or uses outside a private place any device for hearing, recording, amplifying or broadcasting sounds originating in such place which would not ordinarily be audible or comprehensible outside, without the consent of the person or persons entitled to privacy there.

"Private place" means a place where one may reasonably expect to be safe from casual or hostile intrusion or surveillance, but does not include a place to which the public or a substantial group thereof has access.

(2) Other Breach of Privacy of Messages. A person commits a misdemeanor if, except as authorized by law, he:

  (a) intercepts without the consent of the sender or receiver a message by telephone, telegraph, letter or other means of communicating privately; but this paragraph does not extend to:
    (i) overhearing of messages through a regularly installed instrument on a telephone party line or on an extension, or
    (ii) interception by the telephone company or subscriber incident to enforcement of regulations limiting use of the facilities or incident to other normal operation and use; or

  (b) divulges without the consent of the sender or receiver the existence or contents of any such message if the actor knows that the message was illegally intercepted, or if he learned of the message in the course of employment with an agency engaged in transmitting it.

Following some of the provisions of the federal code, both paragraphs (a) and (b) exempt from liability the surveillance of a private place with the consent of "the person or persons entitled to privacy." Subsection (2) provides a penalty for other interceptions of messages and for disclosure of unlawfully intercepted messages. This contains exceptions similar to those of the federal statute.

C. State Statutes, Codes, and Cases

Most states and the District of Columbia all have their own laws governing the use of interception devices.[95] The United States Code, which defines the federal crimes related to interception of wire, electronic, and oral communications, does not preempt all state crimes for similar behavior. A state may impose greater restrictions than the federal statute. However, a state cannot authorize conduct that is prohibited by federal law.[96]

Many state statutes are modeled on the federal statutes; others follow the general provisions of the Model Penal Code. Many state statutes concerning the interception of communications apply only to communications that are private, or with respect to which there exists a reasonable expectation of privacy. An example of the latter is the Florida statute. It provides in part:

> 934.03—Interception and disclosure of wire, oral, or electronic communications prohibited[97]
>
> (1) Except as otherwise specifically provided in this chapter, any person who:
>   (a) Intentionally intercepts, endeavors to intercept, or procures any other person to intercept or endeavor to intercept any wire, oral, or electronic communication;
>   (b) Intentionally uses, endeavors to use, or procures any other person to use or endeavor to use any electronic, mechanical, or other device to intercept any oral communication when:
>   1. Such device is affixed to, or otherwise transmits a signal through, a wire, cable, or other like connection used in wire communication; or
>   2. Such device transmits communication by radio or interferes with the transmission of such communication;
>   (c) Intentionally discloses, or endeavors to disclose, to any other person the contents of any wire, oral, or electronic communication, knowing or having reason to know that the information was obtained through the interception of a wire, oral, or electronic communication in violation of this subsection; or
>   (d) Intentionally uses, or endeavors to use, the contents of any wire, oral, or electronic communication, knowing or having reason to know that the information was obtained through the interception of a wire, oral, or electronic communication in violation of this subsection; shall be punished as provided in subsection (4).

"Oral communication," as defined in the Florida statute, means any oral communication uttered by a person exhibiting an expectation that such communication is not subject to interception under circumstances justifying such exception and means any public oral communication uttered at a public meeting or any electronic communication.

A Florida court held that factors considered in determining whether the intercepted communication qualifies as "oral communication" protected under the security of communications statutes include the location in which the conversation or communications occurs, the manner in which the communication is made, and the type of communication. Thus, conversations that occur inside enclosed or secluded areas are more likely to be protected.[98]

A federal court commented that the Alabama statute prohibiting electronic eavesdropping is violated if there is: (1) a willful interception, (2) of an oral communication uttered by a person exhibiting an expectation that the communication would be private, and (3) a communication made under circumstances justifying an expectation of privacy.[99]

States generally follow the federal law in making some wiretapping and eavesdropping acceptable. State statutes may allow wiretapping when at least one party consents, and always allow wiretapping by law enforcement with appropriate judicial authority. The cases below represent some of the issues.

- A New Jersey court held that an unauthorized wiretap by law enforcement officers is a constitutional violation; however, consensual interceptions do not represent the same intrusions into constitutionally protected privacy.[100]

- A North Carolina court held that the Electronic Surveillance Act prohibits nonconsensual recordings by one spouse of the other even within their family home.[101]

- A Pennsylvania court found that the police department violated the disclosure provisions of the Wiretap Act when it disclosed intercepted telephone conversations between a police officer and his estranged wife to an advocate that had been assigned to represent the police department at a disciplinary hearing, because the Wiretap Act only authorized disclosure to investigative or law enforcement officers.[102]

Some state statutes are more restrictive than the federal statute and provide criminal penalties not provided by federal law. For example, federal law allows interception of communications if one party consents. Under Massachusetts law, the warrantless interception of an oral or wire communication is prohibited absent consent by all parties, except in two statutory circumstances.[103]

Legal News

A mother who, using a speakerphone, eavesdropped on her 14-year-old daughter's conversation with her boyfriend was guilty of the state's eavesdropping law. According to the Washington court, the law contained no parental exemption that at least one of the parties must know they are being monitored. The issue arose not because the mother was prosecuted, but, rather, because the boyfriend was in jail on an armed robbery charge and the mother heard and testified regarding incriminating statements made by him to her daughter. The conviction for armed robbery was overturned because of the mother's illegal action. The mother was not prosecuted.

Source: Retrieved 12/15/2004 from http://seattletimes.newsource.com/cgi-bin?PrintStory.pl?document_id=2002115125&zsection.

D. Summary

The federal government cannot usurp entirely the state's power to criminalize wiretapping. Although the states may pass their own laws regarding wiretapping, they cannot make any act legal that the federal criminal code has defined as illegal; on the other hand, they can make their statute more restrictive than the federal law and declare some acts criminal that the federal statute does not. Usually the same act may be criminal under either the state criminal code or the federal wiretapping statute, which will be discussed in Chapter 14. Some states and the Model Penal Code have included surveillance and video recording under wiretapping prohibitions when it is done without the consent or knowledge of the subjects. Other states cover these invasions of privacy under other statutes, such as voyeurism, invasion of privacy, or even disorderly conduct.

Eavesdropping/Wiretapping

(A/R)　Interception; of an oral communication; of one who has reasonable expectation of privacy in those circumstances (in some states, if at least one party consents it is lawful)

(M/R)　Willful/Intentional

---

§ 11.8　State Counter-Terrorism Laws

Following the terrorist attacks of September 11, 2001, many state legislatures recognized the necessity of enacting state legislation to make it less difficult to prevent terrorist attacks and to apprehend terrorists. These are called **counter-terrorism laws**.

A. Common Law

There was no common law crime of terrorism.

B. Model Penal Code

The Model Penal Code does not have a provision for terrorism.

C. State Statutes, Codes, and Cases

One of the first states to pass terrorism-specific legislation was New York. The New York penal law provides penalties for those who:

- provide material support for terrorism;

- engage in terroristic threats;

- engage in terrorism; and

- render assistance to a terrorist

Article 490 of the New York Penal Law on Terrorism[104] provides:

§ 490.05 Definitions

As used in this article, the following terms shall mean and include:

1. "Act of terrorism":
   (a) for purposes of this article means an act or acts constituting a specified offense as defined in subdivision three of this section for which a person may be convicted in the criminal courts of this state pursuant to article twenty of the criminal procedure law, or an act or acts constituting an offense in any other jurisdiction within or outside the territorial boundaries of the United States which contains all of the essential elements of a specified offense, that is intended to:
      (i) intimidate or coerce a civilian population;
      (ii) influence the policy of a unit of government by intimidation or coercion; or
      (iii) affect the conduct of a unit of government by murder, assassination or kidnapping; or

   (b) for purposes of subparagraph (xiii) of paragraph (a) of subdivision one of section 125.27 of this chapter means activities that involve a violent act or acts dangerous to human life that are in violation of the criminal laws of this state and are intended to:
      (i) intimidate or coerce a civilian population;
      (ii) influence the policy of a unit of government by intimidation or coercion; or
      (iii) affect the conduct of a unit of government by murder, assassination or kidnapping

2. "Material support or resources" means currency or other financial securities, financial services, lodging, training, safehouses, false documentation or identification, communications equipment, facilities, weapons, lethal substances, explosives, personnel, transportation, and other physical assets, except medicine or religious materials.

3. "Specified offense" for purposes of this article means a class A felony offense other than an offense as defined in article two hundred twenty, a violent felony offense as defined in section 70.02, manslaughter in the second degree as defined in section 125.15, criminal tampering in the first degree as defined in section 145.20 of this chapter, and includes an attempt or conspiracy to commit any such offenses.

4. "Renders criminal assistance" for purposes of sections 490.30 and 490.35 of this article shall have the same meaning as in section 205.50 of this chapter.

§ 490.10 Soliciting or providing support for an act of terrorism in the second degree

A person commits soliciting or providing support for an act of terrorism in the second degree when, with intent that material support or resources will be used, in whole or in part, to plan, prepare, carry out or aid in either an act of terrorism or the concealment of, or an escape from, an act of terrorism, he or she raises, solicits, collects or provides material support or resources.

Soliciting or providing support for an act of terrorism in the second degree is a class D felony.

§ 490.15 Soliciting or providing support for an act of terrorism in the first degree

A person commits soliciting or providing support for an act of terrorism in the first degree when he or she commits the crime of soliciting or providing support for an act of terrorism in the second degree and the total value of material support or resources exceeds one thousand dollars.

Soliciting or providing support for an act of terrorism in the first degree is a class C felony.

§ 490.20 Making a terroristic threat
1. A person is guilty of making a terroristic threat when with intent to intimidate or coerce a civilian population, influence the policy of a unit of government by intimidation or coercion, or affect the conduct of a unit of government by murder, assassination or kidnapping, he or she threatens to commit or cause to be committed a specified offense and thereby causes a reasonable expectation or fear of the imminent commission of such offense.
2. It shall be no defense to a prosecution pursuant to this section that the defendant did not have the intent or capability of committing the specified offense or that the threat was not made to a person who was a subject thereof.

Making a terroristic threat is a class D felony.

§ 490.25 Crime of terrorism
1. A person is guilty of terrorism when, with intent to intimidate or coerce a civilian population, influence the policy of a unit of government by intimidation or coercion, or affect the conduct of a unit of government by murder, assassination or kidnapping, he or she commits a specified offense.
2. Sentencing.
    (a) When a person is convicted of a crime of terrorism pursuant to this section, and the specified offense is a class B, C, D or E felony offense, the crime of terrorism shall be deemed a violent felony offense.

(b) When a person is convicted of a crime of terrorism pursuant to this section, and the specified offense is a class C, D or E felony offense, the crime of terrorism shall be deemed to be one category higher than the specified offense the defendant committed, or one category higher than the offense level applicable to the defendant's conviction for an attempt or conspiracy to commit the offense, whichever is applicable.

(c) When a person is convicted of a crime of terrorism pursuant to this section, and the specified offense is a class B felony offense, the crime of terrorism shall be deemed a class A-I felony offense and the sentence imposed upon conviction of such offense shall be in accordance with section 70.00 of this chapter.

(d) Notwithstanding any other provision of law, when a person is convicted of a crime of terrorism pursuant to this section, and the specified offense is a class A-I felony offense, the sentence upon conviction of such offense shall be life imprisonment without parole; provided, however, that nothing herein shall preclude or prevent a sentence of death when the specified offense is murder in the first degree as defined in section 125.27 of this chapter.

§ 490.30 Hindering prosecution of terrorism in the second degree

A person is guilty of hindering prosecution of terrorism in the second degree when he or she renders criminal assistance to a person who has committed an act of terrorism, knowing or believing that such person engaged in conduct constituting an act of terrorism.

Hindering prosecution of terrorism in the second degree is a class C felony.

§ 490.35 Hindering prosecution of terrorism in the first degree

A person is guilty of hindering prosecution of terrorism in the first degree when he or she renders criminal assistance to a person who has committed an act of terrorism that resulted in the death of a person other than one of the participants, knowing or believing that such person engaged in conduct constituting an act of terrorism.

Hindering prosecution of terrorism in the first degree is a class B felony.

In 2001 and 2002, the California legislature modified existing laws and added new counterterrorism statutes to the California penal code. These included:

§ 11418 Weapons of mass destruction; possession, transfer, use, etc.; penalties

§ 11418.1 False or facsimile weapons of mass destruction; transfer, delivery, placement, possession, etc.; penalties

§ 11418.5 Threats to use weapon of mass destruction; penalties

§ 11419 Possession of restricted biological agents; penalties; exceptions

We will deal with the Patriot Act and federal counter-terrorism laws in Chapter 14. In general, federal laws are used to prosecute individuals for terroristic acts. However, states may and have passed their own laws.

D. Summary

Of course, the federal terrorism laws, such as the Patriot Act, are more often considered as the source for defining and prosecuting terrorism as a crime. However, it should be noted that states also may pass statutes criminalizing activities associated with terrorism. Not all states have such laws but those that do basically concentrate on weapons of mass destruction and threats to the general population.

11.9   Other Offenses Against the Public Peace

In addition to the crimes described above, state statutes and the Model Penal Code have identified a variety of other activities as crimes. These offenses "against the public peace" all have in common the aspect of victimization of the general public, at least indirectly. Also, constitutional protections, such as freedom of speech and due process, require that the statutes be written very narrowly and specify targeted behaviors rather than vague categories of undesirable behavior or people.

A. Obstructing a Highway or Public Passage

In order to make it possible for citizens to carry on everyday business and to avoid undue interference, statutes have been written and enforced that regulate the use of highways and other public passages. Although the statutes and ordinances regulating the use of streets and buildings have been upheld, these must comply with the safeguards of the U.S. Constitution, especially First Amendment safeguards. However, the First Amendment does not protect all speech, as the following cases indicate.

- Municipal ordinances that prohibit door-to-door sale solicitations are constitutional.[105]

- Municipalities can regulate the time, place, and manner of using public streets for the purpose of holding outdoor parades, speeches, or mass assemblies.[106]

- Municipalities can enforce greater restrictions on public gatherings around hospital districts, jail yards, fire stations, and court facilities that can be more closely protected than other public facilities.[107]

However, any restrictions that unduly limit free speech and assembly—for example, an ordinance that permits an enforcement decision to be based on consideration of the message or speech content—will be struck down as unconstitutional.[108] Recent ordinances and statutes have attempted to balance the right of the public to use streets and highways for purposes of presenting ideas and the right of the public to use the streets and highways for travel.[109]

The Model Penal Code offers a statute that covers both unlawful assemblies and individual obstructions on public thoroughfares.

---

§ 250.7 Obstructing Highways and Other Public Passages[110]

(1) A person, who, having no legal privilege to do so, purposely or recklessly obstructs any highway or other public passage, whether alone or with others, commits a violation, or, in case he persists after warning by a law officer, a petty misdemeanor. "Obstructs" means renders impassable without unreasonable inconvenience or hazard. No person shall be deemed guilty of recklessly obstructing in violation of this Subsection solely because of a gathering of persons to hear him speak or otherwise communicate, or solely because of being a member of such a gathering.

(2) A person in a gathering commits a violation if he refuses to obey a reasonable official request or order to move:
    (a) to prevent obstruction of a highway or other public passage; or
    (b) to maintain public safety by dispersing those gathered in dangerous proximity to a fire or other hazard.

An order to move, addressed to a person whose speech or other lawful behavior attracts an obstructing audience, shall not be deemed reasonable if the obstruction can be readily remedied by police control of the size or location of the gathering.

The Model Penal Code, like other codes, has taken into consideration the possibility of constitutional challenge. Therefore, the phrase "having no legal privilege to do so" is included. Also, the language exempts from liability persons who have obtained permits or secured official permits to block off the streets. According to the comments following the statement, the result is to give the widest possible scope to picketing, protests, and other lawful assembly consistent with the need to protect reasonable public access to highways and other public passages.

Subsection (2) proscribes refusal to obey a reasonable official in order to prevent obstruction of a public passage or to disperse persons gathered in dangerous proximity to a fire or other hazard. The term "reasonable" is included so as to limit the authority of the police officer to order a person to move if the situation can be handled without stopping the speaker.

Some recently enacted codes and statutes include the provisions of the Model Penal Code. Some statutes describe the prohibited conduct more specifically. Arkansas, for example, defines obstruction as "rendering impassable."[111] In some states, the offense is made a part of the disorderly conduct statute. For example, the Ohio statute[112] provides:

> (A) No person shall recklessly cause inconvenience, annoyance, or alarm to another, by doing any of the following: . . .
>
>   (4) Hindering or preventing the movement of persons on a public street, road, highway, or right-of-way, or to, from, within, or upon public or private property, so as to interfere with the rights of others and by any act which serves no lawful and reasonable purpose of the offender.

Although the statute does not specifically exempt from liability a speaker or listener who is legally expressing ideas, it does exempt those who have a "lawful and reasonable purpose."

B. Harassment and Stalking

Although harassment targets individual victims rather than the general population as the other crimes in this chapter, it is included here because it shares similar constitutional issues. Harassment statutes and stalking statutes cover minor assaultive conduct in which the intent is to annoy or alarm a specific individual. They have been challenged as unconstitutional in that they infringe upon an individual's freedom of speech and movement. Harassment may involve driving up and down the street in front of someone's house, standing on the sidewalk, telephoning repeatedly, showing up at the victim's place of work, and so on. These behaviors are activities that are protected as freedoms up to a point, but the question is when can they become criminal? Statutes must be carefully drawn to avoid impinging on constitutional rights. An example of a harassment statute is that of New Jersey. It provides:

> 2C:33—4. Harassment
>
> Except as provided in subsection e., a person commits a petty disorderly persons offense if, with purpose to harass another, he:
>
> a.   Makes, or causes to be made, a communication or communications anonymously or at extreme inconvenient hours, or in offensively coarse language, or any other manner likely to cause annoyance or alarm;
> b.   Subjects another to striking, kicking, shoving, or other offensive touching, or threatens to do so; or
> c.   Engages in any other course of alarming conduct or of repeatedly committed acts with purpose to alarm or seriously annoy such other person.
>
> A communication under subsection a. may be deemed to have been made either at the place where it originated or at the place where it was received.

> e.   A person commits a crime of the fourth degree if in committing an offense under this section, he was serving a term of imprisonment or was on parole or probation as the result of a conviction of any indictable offense under the laws of this State, any other state or the United States.[113]

The New Jersey courts, as well as federal courts, have considered the validity and meaning of the statute. Some of the court holdings in harassment appeals are presented below.

- A federal court opined that, under the statute, a person must be permitted to communicate ill-will, hatred, or bias to others, but is prohibited from acting upon such sentiments in a harassing manner.[114]

- A defendant's acts of sending a ripped-up copy of a child support order by regular and certified mail to the estranged wife was not likely to cause "annoyance" within the meaning of the harassment statute.[115]

- The fact that a defendant that positioned himself in a location where his wife could see him as she exited her house, despite an injunction prohibiting him from "having contact with" his wife, was sufficient to establish that the defendant engaged in a course of alarming conduct as required to support a harassment conviction.[116]

The Model Penal Code provides the following provision for harassment.

---

§ 250.4 Harassment[117]

A Person commits a petty misdemeanor if, with purpose to harass another, he:

(1) makes a telephone call without purpose of legitimate communication; or

(2) insults, taunts or challenges another in a manner likely to provoke violent or disorderly response; or

(3) makes repeated communications anonymously or at extremely inconvenient hours, or in offensively coarse language; or

(4) subjects another to an offensive touching; or

(5) engages in any other course of alarming conduct serving no legitimate purpose of the actor.

Most states have responded to the problem of harassing behaviors by creating stand-alone statutes or incorporating harassing behavior into existing statutes such as disorderly conduct or assault. Stalking statutes are similar to harassment statutes and were created in the 1990s after the problem of stalking was publicized by the tragic Rebecca Shaeffer case in 1989. The next year California passed the country's first anti-stalking law. Stalking statutes cover much of the same behavior as harassment statutes: lying in wait, pursue or follow, trespass, intimidate, vandalize, harass, display a weapon, and so on. The California stalking statute also defines certain Internet activity as illegal when the offender relays a credible threat that can be given through an "electronic communication device" or the threat is implied through a pattern of conduct or a "combination of verbal, written, or electronically communicated statements." Florida also has passed a cyberstalking statute.[118] The challenge of all such statutes is to be specific enough to withstand constitutional challenge. Also, of course, a victim may obtain a civil order of protection and any violation of that order would result in a contempt of court citation that may be civil or criminal, depending on the state's laws.

Legal News

Harassment and "**anti-stalking laws**" were in the forefront of public concern after Rebecca Shaeffer was killed on the front step of her home in 1989. The young actress, a star in the television series *My Sister Sam* was the target of an obsessive fan who stabbed her to death when she was perceived to have spurned him. In 1990 California passed its anti-stalking law. Today, only Arizona and Maine have no such laws. The activities such laws prohibit include: approach, pursue, follow, trespass, lay in wait, intimidate, contact, and restrain. The National Institute of Justice defined stalking as a code of conduct that causes a reasonable person to fear bodily injury or death for him- or herself or members of his or her family.

Source: National Institute of Justice, U.S. Dept. of Justice. *Project to Develop a Model Anti-Stalking Code for States.* 1993, p. 43.

C. Desecration of Venerated Objects

Statutes that prohibit desecration of public monuments or objects, places of worship or burial, the national or state flags, or any other patriotic or religious symbol are present in most states. These statutes are aimed at special kinds of public or quasi-public property damages that result in an affront to members of the public. The statutes are aimed more at the protection of public sensibilities than the impairment of property interests.

The Model Penal Code also presents a statute that prohibits this type of behavior.

---

§ 250.9 Desecration of Venerated Objects

A person commits a misdemeanor if he purposely desecrates any public monument or structure, or place of worship or burial, or if he purposely desecrates the national flag or any other object of veneration by the public or a substantial segment thereof in any public place. "Desecrate" means defacing, damaging, polluting or otherwise physically mistreating in a way that the actor knows will outrage the sensibilities of persons likely to observe or discover his actions.

The problem with such statutes, however, is that the destruction may be "speech." In cases where the destruction can be defined as a valid exercise of one's speech (i.e., burning the flag to protest the war in Iraq) and does not break any other laws (i.e., destruction of someone else's property or public property), then the Supreme Court has ruled that such statutes unconstitutionally infringe on First Amendment rights. In *Texas v. Johnson*,[119] a case discussed in Chapter 1, the Texas statute that criminalized flag burning was challenged and the Supreme Court invalidated the statute, ruling that such activity was protected speech. Congress is currently considering an amendment to the Constitution that would bar any destruction of the American flag. Proponents argue that it is important to the country to have such an amendment and there is a harm that must be prohibited in such activity. Opponents argue that many who have no intent to denigrate the flag might also be in violation of any such law if they use the flag in clothing, wrap themselves up in it during sports games, or use it for room decoration. Free speech advocates argue that if the flag stands for anything, it stands for free speech; therefore, it would be ironic to punish those who wanted to use it to express their views.

D. Other

The Model Penal Code, and many states, also provide statutes for Cruelty to Animals, Violation of Privacy, Disrupting Meetings and Processions, and False Public Alarms. These behaviors are defined as criminal under the state's police power. The purpose of all such statutes is to deter behavior that outrages or offends the feelings of substantial groups of the population. Because the various state statutes contain other offenses against the public order, they must be researched by those who are involved in the criminal justice process in order to have a thorough knowledge of the charges that are available.

§ 11.10 Summary

In order to protect the public peace, laws defining offenses, some of which are minor in character, have been enacted. These offenses are often characterized as offenses against the public peace or offenses against public order. Generally, in order to convict a person for rioting, the prosecution must prove three or more persons: (1) intentionally undertake a common action; (2) that is unlawful or lawful but done in an unlawful manner; (3) that is violent and tumultuous, and (4) that obstructs orderly government. Related to riot is inciting to riot. This occurs when one incites, or encourages, other persons to create or engage in a riot as defined.

A crime that is common to all jurisdictions is disorderly conduct. What constitutes disorderly conduct depends on the terms of the statute or ordinance; however, it may be said that words and acts that tend to disturb the peace and endanger the morals, safety, or health of the community are punishable as disorderly conduct under most statutes.

Vagrancy at common law was defined as the wandering or going about from place to place by an idle person who has no lawful visible means of support and who exists on charity and does not work for a living, although able to do so. Many of the vagrancy and loitering statutes were declared unconstitutional because they were considered too vague. Modern loitering statutes are more specific and are drafted to make the person accused of the crime aware of what specific conduct is prohibited.

Although drunkenness was not a crime at common law, most state statutes now prohibit the appearance in any public place of a person who is manifestly under the influence of alcohol, drugs, or narcotics, if he is to the degree that he may endanger himself or other persons or property or annoy persons in his vicinity.

Drug interdiction and enforcement is a shared activity by both federal and state law enforcement. State laws all follow the Uniform Controlled Substances Act in their categorization of drugs, but enforcement provisions vary from state to state and between the federal government and states. Generally, the crimes associated with controlled substances include possession, possession with intent to deliver, and trafficking; however, there are many more, including those that penalize possession or delivery of counterfeit substances, and obtaining prescriptions under false pretenses.

Although the federal government generally enforces violations of federal laws against interception of wire or oral communications, states have also experimented with laws prohibiting eavesdropping, possession of eavesdropping devices, tampering with private communications, or divulging illegally obtained information.

States have also passed terrorism laws, especially after the terrorist attacks of September 11, 2001. Terrorism-specific state laws provide, among other things, penalties for those who provide material support for terrorism, engage in terroristic threats, engage in terrorism, or render criminal assistance to a terrorist.

In order to make it possible for citizens to carry on their everyday business and to avoid undue interference, statutes that regulate the use of highways and other passages have been written and enforced. These statutes have been challenged as being unconstitutional, but when written in accordance with constitutional guidelines, they have been upheld as a proper exercise of the police power of the state. Other offenses against the public peace include harassment (and anti-stalking laws), disrupting meetings, desecration of venerated objects, and cruelty to animals.

Review Questions

1. Define the three crimes that represent the traditional steps in violent mob action. Distinguish between *rout* and *riot*.

2. Explain the difference between *riot* and *inciting to riot*. In the Model Penal Code and some of the more recently enacted state statutes regarding riots, a certain number of persons must be involved as participants to constitute the crime. What is the range of the critical numbers in the various codes?

3. Some offenses against the public peace, such as disorderly conduct, have been declared unconstitutional by the U.S. Supreme Court. What are the two grounds for challenging the constitutionality of these statutory offenses?

4. What is "disorderly conduct" as defined by the Model Penal Code? Provide examples.

5. What are the most common prohibited acts under state disorderly conduct statutes?

6. What speech is protected by the First Amendment? What speech is not protected? Does making insulting remarks to a police officer constitute disorderly conduct? Give some examples of cases in which state courts have found that certain acts constitute disorderly conduct.

7. What crimes might participants, promoters, and spectators of "fight clubs" be charged with?

8. Many of the early laws relating to vagrancy and loitering were declared unconstitutional. What was the reasoning of the Supreme Court in finding that many of these statutes violated the Constitution?

9. In the Model Penal Code definition of loitering or prowling and in most state statutes, the manner of loitering or prowling is specified. What manner of loitering or prowling is prohibited?

10. What are "stop-and-identify" statutes? What was the Supreme Court's holding regarding the constitutionality of such statutes when they require a police officer to have reasonable suspicion that a crime has been or is about to be committed?

11. Discuss the holding of *Powell v. Texas*.

12. Is public drunkenness a violation of the law in most jurisdictions? Was it a crime under common law? Explain what is meant by public drunkenness. What factors may be taken into consideration in determining whether the statute is violated?

13. Under DWI laws, what does "in control" of the car mean? Give examples.

14. Explain the differences between the five schedules (categories) of drugs described in the Uniform Controlled Substances Act.

15. What are the issues in prosecuting possession crimes? (Define possession and the *mens rea* required). What is the difference between possession and possession with intent to deliver? What is the difference between possession with intent to deliver and trafficking?

16. What are some other crimes associated with drugs? What are state and federal forfeiture laws? What have been some challenges to such laws?

17. What was the common law crime akin to wiretapping? Describe state wiretapping statutes and what behaviors they prohibit.

18. What is the definition of "act of terrorism" in the New York statute? Can states have their own anti-terrorism laws after the USA PATRIOT Act?

19. Does the state have the authority to enact legislation prohibiting the obstruction of highways and other public passages? What are the limitations, if any?

20. Define *harassment* as used in state statutes. List some acts that are considered harassment. Describe the crime of desecration of venerated objects and what are the potential constitutional challenges to such laws?

Notes

[1] Heard v. Rizzo, 281 F. Supp. 720 (D. Pa. 1968).

[2] State v. Woolridge, 129 W. Va. 448, 40 S.E.2d 899 (1946).

[3] Schoolcraft v. State, 84 Okla. Crim. 20, 178 P.2d 641 (1947).

[4] Feinstein v. City of New York, 283 N.Y.S. 335 (1935).

[5] Kasper v. State, 206 Tenn. 434, 326 S.W.2d 664 (1959).

[6] Commonwealth v. Apriceno, 131 Pa. Super. 158, 198 A. 515 (1938).

[7] MODEL PENAL CODE § 250.1 (1985).

[8] MODEL PENAL CODE § 250.1 (1985) comments section.

[9] N.Y. PENAL LAW § 240.06 (McKinney 1992).

[10] United States v. Evans, 542 F.2d 805 (10th Cir. 1976).

[11] KY. REV. STAT. ANN. § 525.010 (Baldwin 1999).

[12] OHIO REV. CODE ANN. § 2917.01, § 2917.02, and § 2917.03 (2002). *See* In re Jesse S., 717 N.E.2d 1143 (Ohio 1998), which held that the offense of aggravated riot requires participation by five persons and an assault by one person in concern with three others is insufficient to support a conviction.

[13] 27 C.J.S. *Disorderly Conduct* § 1(1) (1995); In re Garafone, 193 A.2d 398 (N.J. 1963).

[14] MODEL PENAL CODE § 250.2 (1985).

[15] Thompson v. Louisville, 362 U.S. 199, 80 S. Ct. 624, 4 L. Ed. 2d 654 (1960); Griffin v. Smith, 184 Ga. 871, 193 S.E. 777 (1937); State v. Koetting, 616 S.W.2d 822 (Mo. 1981).

[16] Kolander v. Lawson, 461 U.S. 352, 103 S. Ct. 1855, 75 L. Ed. 2d 903 (1983).

[17] 27 C.J.S. *Disorderly Conduct* § 1(2) (1995). Steeley v. Ennis, 45 N.Y.S.2d 446 (1943).

[18] City of Miami v. Powers, 247 So. 2d 497 (Fla. 1971).

[19] State v. Werstein, 60 Wis. 2d 668, 211 N.W.2d 437 (1973).

[20] State v. Petty, 24 Conn. Supp. 337, 190 A.2d 502 (1962).

[21] Price v. State, 622 N.E.2d 954 (Ind. 1993).

[22] Stites v. State, 627 N.E.2d 1343 (Ind. 1994).

[23] State v. Semple, 568 N.E.2d 750 (Ohio Ct. App. 1989).

[24] Commonwealth v. Zettel, 46 Mass. App. 471, 706 N.E.2d 1158 (1999).

[25] State v. Hampton, 583 N.E.2d 400 (Ohio Ct. App. 1990).

[26] State v. Smith, 779 N.E.2d 776 (Ohio 2002).

[27] Robinson v. State, 588 N.E.2d 533 (Ind. Ct. App. 1992).

[28] Buffkins v. City of Omaha, 922 F.2d 465 (8th Cir. 1990), *cert. denied*, 502 U.S. 898, 112 S. Ct. 273, 116 L. Ed. 2d 225 (1991).

[29] Marsh v. State, 724 So. 2d 666 (Fla. 1999).

[30] OHIO REV. CODE ANN. § 2917.11 (Anderson 1999).

[31] TEX. PENAL CODE § 42.01 Disorderly Conduct.

[32] Robinson v. State, 588 N.E.2d 533 (Ind. Ct. App. 1992).

[33] People v. Banwer, 22 N.Y.S.2d 566 (1940).

[34] Nearing v. Illinois Central R.R. Co., 383 Ill. 366, 50 N.E.2d 497 (1943).

[35] Papachristou et al. v. City of Jacksonville, 405 U.S. 156, 92 S. Ct. 839, 31 L. Ed. 2d 110.

[36] MODEL PENAL CODE § 250.6 (1985).

[37] KY. REV. STAT. ANN. § 525.090 (Baldwin 2002).

[38] E.C. v. State, 724 So. 2d 1243 (Fla. 1999). *See also* Gonzalez v. State, 828 So. 2d 496 (Fla. 2002), in which the court reiterated that the offense of loitering and prowling requires proof that: (1) the defendant loitered or prowled at a place, at a time, or in a manner not usual for law-abiding individuals, and (2) such loitering and prowling were under circumstances that warranted a justifiable and reasonable alarm or immediate concern for the safety of persons or property

[39] J.S.B. v. State, 729 So. 2d 456 (Fla. 1999).

[40] 542 U.S. 177 (2004).

[41] TEX. PENAL CODE, § 38.02 Failure to Identify.

[42] Eberle v. Michigan, 232 U.S. 700, 34 S. Ct. 464, 58 L. Ed. 803 (1914).

[43] 2 STEPHEN, HISTORY OF THE CRIMINAL LAW IN ENGLAND 410 (1883).

[44] Powell v. Texas, 392 U.S. 514, 88 S. Ct. 2145, 20 L. Ed. 2d 1254 (1968).

[45] Robinson v. California, 370 U.S. 660, 82 S. Ct. 1417, 8 L. Ed. 2d 758 (1962).

[46] MODEL PENAL CODE § 250.5 (1985).

[47] State v. Moriarty, 74 Ind. 103 (1881); Thompson v. State, 153 Miss. 593, 121 So. 275 (1929); January v. State, 66 Tex Crim. 302, 146 S.W. 555 (1912).

[48] OHIO REV. CODE ANN. § 2917.11 (Anderson 2002). *See also* FLA. STAT. ANN. § 856.011 (West 2002) and S.C. CODE ANN. § 16-17-530 (Law. Co-op. 2002).

[49] State v. Butler, 578 N.E.2d 485 (Ohio 1989).

[50] FLA. STAT. ANN. § 856.011 (2003).

[51]   Royster v. State, 643 So. 2d 61 (Fla. 1994). *See also* Jernigan v. State, 566 So. 2d 39 (Fla. 1990) for an interpretation of the Florida statute. *See* § 856.015 of the Florida statute (Open House Party), which provides a penalty if an adult knowingly allows the possession or use of an alcoholic beverage or drug by a minor.

[52]   Felgate v. Arkansas, 63 Ark. App. 76, 974 S.W.2d 479 (Ark. App. 1998); State v. Widmaier, 157 N.J. 475, 724 A.2d 214 (1999).

[53]   Gallagher v. Commonwealth, 205 Va. 666, 139 S.W.2d 37 (1964).

[54]   *See* appendix for list of states.

[55]   Robinson v. California, 370 U.S. 660, 82 S. Ct. 1417, 8 L. Ed. 2d 758 (1962); State v. Martin, 192 La. 704, 189 So. 109 (1939).

[56]   Manson v. State, 166 Tex Crim. 514, 316 S.W.2d 414 (1958); People v. Sinclair, 387 Mich. 91, 194 N.W.2d 878 (1972).

[57]   People v. Fillhart, 403 N.Y.S.2d 642 (1978). Maisler v. State, 425 So. 2d 107 (Fla. 1982).

[58]   State v. Brown, 103 Ariz. 289, 440 P.2d 909 (1968).

[59]   People v. Orozco, 266 Cal. App. 507, 72 Cal. Rptr. 452 (1968).

[60]   Borras v. State, 229 So. 2d 244 (Fla. 1970), *cert. denied*, 400 U.S. 808, 91 S. Ct. 70, 27 L. Ed. 2d 37 (1970).

[61]   State v. Burch, 545 So. 2d 279 (Fla. Dist. Ct. App. 1989). *See also* State v. Crawford, 727 So. 2d 589 (La. 1998), which defined the meaning of "within 1,000 feet."

[62]   State v. Venet, 797 P.2d 1055 (Or. 1990).

[63]   After the Supreme Court held that it was not a First Amendment violation to punish a Native American for using peyote in a religious ceremony in Employment Division v. Smith, 494 U.S. 872 (1990), Congress passed the Act to Amend the American Indian Religious Freedom Act (Public Law 103-344; 108 Stat. 3125) October 6, 1994, that prohibits states from criminalizing peyote use in *bona fide* religious ceremonies.

[64]   State v. Mercherson, 488 N.W.2d 707 (Minn. Ct. App. 1989).

[65]   Jackson v. State, 832 So. 2d 773 (Fla. 2002). *See also* Knight v. State, 91 S.W.3d 418 (Tex. 2002).

[66]   State v. Brider, 386 So. 2d 818 (Fla. 1980).

[67]   Ellis v. State, 346 So. 2d 1044 (Fla. 1977). *See also* State v. Spruell, 788 P.2d 21 (Wash. 1990), which held that "actual possession" of drugs occurs when drugs are in the actual physical possession of the defendant, while "constructive possession" requires that the defendant have dominion and control over the drugs. *See also* Lawson v. State, 666 So. 2d 193 (Fla. 1995).

[68]   Abshure v. State, 87 S.W.3d 822 (Ark. 2002).

[69]   Grant v. State, 989 S.W.2d 428 (Tex. 1999).

[70]   State v. Mahon, 53 Conn. App. 231, 729 A.2d 242 (1999).

[71]   Harris v. State, 501 So. 2d 735 (Fla. 1987).

[72]   Brooks v. State, 501 So. 2d 176 (Fla. 1987).

[73]   People v. Roveter, 549 N.Y. Supp. 2d 488 (1989)

[74]   Brown v. Commonwealth, 364 S.E.2d 773 (Va. 1988).

[75]   Reed v. State, 367 S.E.2d 809 (Ga. 1988).

[76]   Wynn v. Commonwealth of Virginia, 362 S.E.2d 193 (Va. 1987).

[77]   Jones v. State, 589 So. 2d 1001 (Fla. Dist. Ct. App. 1991).

[78]   People v. Carrasquilla, 522 N.E.2d 139 (Ill. App. Ct. 1988); State v. Lassere, 683 So. 2d 922 (La. 1996); Kostelec v. State, 656 A.2d 1222 (Md. Ct. App. 1996); State v. Spencer, 683 So. 2d 1326 (La. 1996).

79   State v. McKinney, 728 So. 2d 1009 (La. 1999).

80   State v. Boyd, 572 S.E.2d 192 (N.C. 2002).

81   Cohn v. Department of Professional Regulation, 477 So. 2d 1039 (Fla. 1985).

82   Martin v. State, 726 So. 2d 1210 (Miss. 1998).

83   Marable v. State, 990 S.W.2d 421 (Tex. 1999).

84   Commonwealth v. McJett, 811 A.2d 104 (Pa. 2002).

85   United States v. Halper, 409 U.S. 435, 109 S. Ct. 1892, 104 L. Ed. 2d 487 (1989).

86   Austin v. United States, 509 U.S. 602, 113 S. Ct. 2801, 125 L. Ed. 2d 488 (1993).

87   Department of Revenue of Montana v. Kurth Ranch, 511 U.S. 767, 114 S. Ct. 1937, 128 L. Ed. 2d 767 (1994).

88   United States v. Usery, 518 U.S. 267, 116 S. Ct. 2135, 135 L. Ed. 2d 549 (1996).

89   People v. Sinclair, 387 Mich. 91, 194 N.W.2d 878 (1972).

90   United States v. Oakland Cannabis Buyer's Cooperative, 532 U.S. 483 (2001).

91   545 U.S. 1 (2004).

92   4 BLACKSTONE, COMMENTARIES 168.

93   Berger v. New York, 388 U.S. 41, 87 S. Ct. 1873, 18 L. Ed. 2d 1040 (1967).

94   MODEL PENAL CODE § 250.12 (1985).

95   Report of the Director of the Administrative Office of the United States Courts, Applications for Orders Authorizing or Approving the Interception of Wire, Oral, or Electronic Communications (1998).

96   86 C.J.S. *Telecommunications* § 243.

97   FLA. STAT. ANN. § 934.03 (1999).

98   Stevenson v. State, 667 So. 2d 410 (Fla. 1996).

99   Ages Group, L.P. v. Raytheon Aircraft Co., Inc., 22 F. Supp. 2d 1310 (N.D. Ala. 1998), interpreting Alabama Code § 13(a)-11-31.

100   State v. Toth, 804 A.2d 565 (N.J. 2002).

101   Kroh v. Kroh, 567 S.E.2d 760 (N.C. 2002).

102   Dance v. Com. Pennsylvania State Police, 726 A.2d 4 (Pa. 1999).

103   United States v. Sutherland, 929 F.2d 765 (1st Cir. 1991).

104   N.Y. PENAL LAW 490.05-490.35 (McKinney 2002).

105   Breard v. Alexandria, 341 U.S. 622, 71 S. Ct. 920, 95 L. Ed. 1233 (1951).

106   Cox v. New Hampshire, 312 U.S. 569, 61 S. Ct. 762, 85 L. Ed. 1049 (1941).

107   Adderley v. Florida, 385 U.S. 39, 87 S. Ct. 242, 17 L. Ed. 2d 149 (1967), *reh'g denied*, 385 U.S. 1020, 87 S. Ct. 698, 17 L. Ed. 2d 559 (1967).

108   Cox v. Louisiana, 379 U.S. 536, 85 S. Ct. 453, 13 L. Ed. 2d 471 (1965).

109   For a more thorough discussion, *see* KANOVITZ & KANOVITZ, CONSTITUTIONAL LAW § 2.5 (10th ed. 2006).

110   MODEL PENAL CODE § 250.7 (1985).

111   ARK. STAT. ANN. § 5-71-214 (1999).

112   OHIO REV. CODE ANN. § 2917.11 (Anderson 2002).

113   N.J. STAT. ANN. 2C:33—4 (2002).

[114] New Jersey v. Bazin, 913 F. Supp. 106 (D.N.J. 1995).

[115] State v. B.H., 676 A.2d 565 (N.J. Super. 1996).

[116] State v. J.T., 638 A.2d 1166 (N.J. Super. 1996).

[117] Model Penal Code § 250.4 Harassment.

[118] Cal. Crim. Code § 646.9; Fla. Stat. § 784.048 (2003).

[119] Texas v. Johnson, 491 U.S. 397 (1989).

Offenses Against Justice Administration 12

Chapter Outline

Cases

Obstruction: *Polk v. Virginia*, 358 S.E.2d 770 (Va. Ct. App. 1987)
Interference with arrest: *Houston v. Hill*, 482 U.S. 451 (1987)
Escape: *Medford v. Texas*, 990 S.W.2d 799 (Tex. Ct. App. 1999)

§ 12.1 Introduction

Some of the common law crimes that developed over the years, primarily through judicial action to protect the public have disappeared, while new offenses have been added as new or larger agencies have been created. For example, the common law crime of barratry, designed to prevent stirring up of strife and litigation, is no longer in existence for practical purposes.[1] While these common law crimes have disappeared, others have been added. An example of a modern statute enacted to ensure that evidence is properly protected for trial is "tampering with or fabricating physical evidence." Both state and federal legislative bodies have enacted legislation to supplement traditional sanctions against those who seek to subvert the justice process.

In this chapter, the well-known offenses relating to justice administration, such as perjury and bribery, are defined and explained. In addition, statutes including obstruction of justice, escape, resisting and evading arrest, and other offenses that affect the administration of justice are discussed.

§ 12.2   Perjury and Related Offenses

A. *Common Law*

The necessity of guaranteeing the integrity of a sworn statement in a judicial proceeding was recognized at common law. However, common law **perjury** was limited to the false oath *in a judicial proceeding*. As the practice of requiring sworn statements in other matters developed, the offense of perjury, whether by that name or some other title such as "false swearing," was extended to cover judicial or quasi-judicial proceedings as to some matter material to the issue or point in question.

Although in common parlance the terms "**false swearing**" and "perjury" are used interchangeably, in a strict legal sense there is a difference between them. At common law, false swearing is a separate and indictable offense, and is distinct from perjury in that the false oath in perjury must be made in a judicial proceeding, whereas in false swearing the act need not be made in such a proceeding.[2]

At common law, the offense of perjury was defined as a willful assertion as to a matter of fact, opinion, belief, or knowledge made by a witness in a judicial proceeding as a part of his evidence, either upon oath or in any form allowed by law to be substituted for an oath, whether in open court, in an affidavit, or otherwise, such assertion being known to such witness to be false, and being intended by him to mislead the court, jury, or person holding the proceedings. "Perjury" at common law was:

- the willful,
- giving of false testimony,
- on a material point,
- in a judicial proceeding,
- by a person to whom a lawful oath had been administered.[3]

An essential element is that the defendant must have acted with criminal intent—he must have believed that what he swore to was false and he must have had intent to deceive.[4]

B. *Model Penal Code*

The Model Penal Code includes definitions of the terms statement and **materiality**. The definition of materiality does not differ substantially from prior law and refers to the idea that the statement must relate to the issue at law.

---

§ 241.1 Perjury[5]

(1) Offense Defined. A person is guilty of perjury, a felony of the third degree, if in any official proceeding he makes a false statement under oath or equivalent affirmation, or swears or affirms the truth of a statement previously made, when the statement is material and he does not believe it to be true.

(2) Materiality. Falsification is material, regardless of the admissibility of the statement under rules of evidence, if it could have affected the course or outcome of the proceeding. It is no defense that the declarant mistakenly believed the falsification to be immaterial. Whether a falsification is material in a given factual situation is a question of law.

(3) Irregularities No Defense. It is not a defense to prosecution under this Section that the oath or affirmation was administered or taken in an irregular manner or that the declarant was not competent to make the statement. A document purporting to be made upon oath or affirmation at any time when the actor presents it as being so verified shall be deemed to have been duly sworn or affirmed.

(4) Retraction. No person shall be guilty of an offense under this Section if he retracted the falsification in the course of the proceeding in which it was made before it became manifest that the falsification was or would be exposed and before the falsification substantially affected the proceeding.

(5) Inconsistent Statements. Where the defendant made inconsistent statements under oath or equivalent affirmation, both having been made within the period of the statute of limitations, the prosecution may proceed by setting forth the inconsistent statements in a single count alleging in the alternative that one or the other was false and not believed by the defendant. In such case it shall not be necessary for the prosecution to prove which statement was false but only that one or the other was false and not believed by the defendant to be true.

(6) Corroboration. No person shall be convicted of an offense under this Section where proof of falsity rests solely upon contradiction by testimony of a single person other than the defendant.

To make the offense and definitions more clear, the Model Code also has subsections relating to retraction, inconsistent statements, and corroboration. While subornation of perjury is not specifically spelled out in the Model Code as an offense, in the comments following the statement of the provision, a comment is included explaining that this is covered under § 2.06(3)(a) of the Model Code, which provides that a person is the accomplice of another in the commission of an offense if he or she solicits the other person to commit it;

therefore, under the MPC, even though no statute defines subornation of perjury as an offense, the offender would be guilty of accomplice to perjury.

In addition to the crime of perjury, the Model Penal Code includes a separate offense titled false swearing. A perjured statement that is not material to the judicial proceeding is a violation of the false swearing section of the Code. A second section deals with falsifications that do not occur in an official proceeding, but are intended to mislead a public official in the performance of his official function. Both of these are graded as misdemeanors.

C. State Statutes, Codes, and Cases

A number of states have adopted the Model Penal Code in substance. In addition, some states list the specific types of proceedings to which perjury sanctions may be applied. An example of a state code that does not follow the Model Code is that of New York, where there are three degrees of perjury:

§ 210.05 Perjury in the third degree[6]

A person is guilty of perjury in the third degree when he swears falsely. Perjury in the third degree is a Class A misdemeanor.

§ 210.10 Perjury in the second degree

A person is guilty of perjury in the second degree when he swears falsely and when his false statement is
(a) made in a subscribed written instrument for which an oath is required by law, and
(b) made with intent to mislead a public servant in the performance of his official functions and
(c) material to the action, proceeding or matter involved.
Perjury in the second degree is a Class E felony.

§ 210.15 Perjury in the first degree

A person is guilty of perjury in the first degree when he swears falsely and when his false statement
(a) consists of testimony, and
(b) is material to the action, proceeding or matter in which it is made.
Perjury in the first degree is a Class D felony.

In the New York statute, perjury is the most serious level of the crime and false swearing is the least serious. Note that materiality is not an element of perjury in the third degree; however, a court ruled that a prosecutor must have some good faith purpose behind questions he puts to a grand jury witness, beyond setting the stage for perjury prosecution.[7]

Another issue that comes up in perjury appeals is whether the question was sufficiently precise to warrant finding the answer false. A court admonished that before a person may be convicted of perjury "the burden is on the questioner to pin the witness down to the specific object of the questioner's inquiry."[8]

Each of the elements of perjury must be proven beyond a reasonable doubt. In order for conviction, the state must prove the defendant:

1. Made an Intentional False Statement

In a Washington case, the court cautioned that opinions and legal conclusions are not subject to perjury convictions and that, for purposes of perjury, a false statement must relate to facts and must also be susceptible to proof as to its truth or falsity.[9]

2. That Was Material

Courts also emphasize that materiality is an essential element of the crime of perjury in the first degree and that the false statement, to be material, must reflect on a matter under consideration during the action or proceeding in which it is made.[10]

The materiality issue arose in a New Jersey case when a police officer was convicted of perjury after falsely stating that he saw the person he arrested strike another person with a shovel. The reviewing court upheld the conviction, finding that the evidence suggested the fact that the officer did not see the person strike another person with a shovel but that the supposed shovel-wielder struck the other person with her hand. The fact that the police officer merely exaggerated was a sufficient material falsehood to sustain the perjury charge.[11]

3. In a Judicial Proceeding under Oath

As noted above, perjury often is limited to false testimony in a judicial proceeding while making false statements in other venues is either a lesser degree of perjury or is defined as false swearing.

4. For the Purpose of Misleading the Court

The *mens rea* for perjury is specific intent; that is, the defendant must intend to make the false statement *and* intend the statement to mislead the court.

5. Other Issues

Some state statutes include a corroboration or "two witness" rule. A California court reiterated that the corroboration requirement in the perjury statute assumes that the defendant has made a statement under oath, and the issue for resolution is the veracity of that statement.[12]

6. False Swearing

In some states, a separate crime of false swearing is included in the statute. Generally, these statutes use somewhat the same language that is used in perjury statutes, but do not require that the false statements be made in a judicial proceeding, may not require materiality (as is required in perjury), and, in some instances, do not require intent to mislead. Where the statute includes the crime of false swearing, it is usually a lower degree offense.[13]

7. Subornation of Perjury

Subornation of perjury is the procuring of one person by another to commit the crime of perjury. This crime has two essential elements: one person must have willfully procured another to commit perjury, and the second person must have, in fact, committed the offense. If the person does not actually commit perjury, then the proper charge would be solicitation or attempted subornation.

Although the crimes of perjury and subornation of perjury may be closely related in point of time and conduct, the offenses are not the same—each having elements not common to the other. One court explained that there are sufficient inherent differences between the two to warrant the law-making power in separating the act into its component parts, making the subornation a new and independent offense, punishable with greater or less severity than that inflicted on the perjurer.[14]

D. Summary

While common law restricted the definition of perjury to only false statements under oath in a judicial proceeding, modern statutes have expanded the definition of perjury or created "false swearing" to cover other forms of false statements made under oath or after swearing to the truthfulness of the statement.

Perjury	
(A/R)	False statement (testimony), under oath, about a material element, in a judicial proceeding
(M/R)	Specific intent
False swearing	
(A/R)	False statement (writing), after swearing
(M/R)	General intent (to lie)
Subornation of perjury	
(A/R)	Entice, encourage, reward another to commit perjury and perjury did occur
(M/R)	Specific intent

§ 12.3 Bribery and Related Offenses

Although history reveals that among the Romans the giving of rewards and emoluments to public officers, especially judicial officers, was tolerated, later civilizations recognized the danger of the effect of corrupt private influences upon official action. Some early cases indicate that only the bribe-taker, for example, the judge, and not the bribe-giver, could be found guilty of an offense.[15]

As a public official in the service of the people, the primary duty is to protect and further their interest and the official should not be permitted to profit through the performance of his or her public functions. To prohibit this, the offense of bribery as it relates to public officials—executive, legislative, or judicial—was created. Note that this offense is different from the commercial bribery offense described in an earlier chapter because this crime can only be committed by public officials or agents. The essence of the offense is the prostitution of a public trust, the betrayal of public interest, or the debauchment of the public conscience.[16]

A. Common Law

Blackstone defined **bribery** as the receiving by a judge or other officer connected with the administration of justice, of "any undue reward to influence his behavior in his office."[17] Court decisions and early statutes defined the offense more broadly, including the offering, giving, receiving, or soliciting anything of value with the intent to influence the recipient's action as a public official, whether executive, legislative, or judicial.[18] Early common law only identified as criminal the public official who accepted the bribe; however, later opinions included both the receiver and the person who offers the bribe as criminal.[19]

The common law elements of bribery were: (1) receiving or soliciting (and later, offering or giving); (2) a thing of value; (3) with intent to influence the recipient's action; and (4) the recipient is a public official.

B. Model Penal Code

The Model Penal Code follows the more recent statutory provisions in reaching both the person who offers, gives, or agrees to give a bribe in an official or political matter and the public servant or other covered individual who solicits, accepts, or agrees to accept a bribe. It applies to full-time government employees, plus consultants to government, bribery of voters and political party officials, and bribery of anyone who exercises official discretion in a judicial or administrative proceeding. This section is very broad in its scope and uses terminology that is less likely to cause problems in interpretation.

§ 240.1 Bribery in Official and Political Matters[20]

A person is guilty of bribery, a felony of the third degree, if he offers, confers or agrees to confer upon another, or solicits, accepts or agrees to accept from another:

(1) any pecuniary benefit as consideration for the recipient's decision, opinion, recommendation, vote or other exercise of discretion as a public servant, party official or voter; or

(2) any benefit as consideration for the recipient's decision, vote, recommendation or other exercise of official discretion in a judicial or administrative proceeding; or

(3) any benefit as consideration for a violation of a known legal duty as public servant or party official.

It is no defense to prosecution under this section that a person whom the actor sought to influence was not qualified to act in the desired way whether because he had not yet assumed office, or lacked jurisdiction, or for any other reason.

C. State Statutes, Codes, and Cases

Many recently enacted state bribery statutes include most of the language of the Model Penal Code. Some, however, require specific intent. Others can be interpreted to require that the benefit be offered, or solicited upon an agreement or understanding that a specific official act will be influenced. This language indicates that an actual agreement must exist rather than simply the intent to influence.

An example of a state statute that is somewhat different from the Model Code is that of New York. It provides:

§ 200.04 Bribery in the first degree[21]

A person is guilty of bribery in the first degree when he confers, or offers or agrees to confer, any benefit upon a public servant upon an agreement or understanding that such public servant's vote, opinion, judgment, action, decision or exercise of discretion as a public servant will thereby be influenced in the investigation, arrest, detention, prosecution, or incarceration of any person for the commission or alleged commission of a Class A felony defined in article two hundred twenty of the penal law or an attempt to commit any such Class A felony.
Bribery in the first degree is a Class B felony.

A New York court has held that the legislative intent in using the words "as a public servant" in this section was to shield from corruption only the actions of a public servant that are related to or within the scope of his functions as a public servant.[22]

Legal News

In December 2008 the country was stunned when Governor Rod Blagojevich and his chief of staff were arrested by the FBI on federal charges of bribery and criminal conspiracy. Allegedly, he solicited bribes in return for the Senate seat vacated by President-elect Barack Obama. The investigation also revealed evidence that Blagojevich may also have solicited bribes in return for government contracts in large road construction projects. Although the investigation and probably charges are federal, Illinois law also addresses bribery by goverment officials. In the Illinois Criminal Code (720 ILCS 5 § 33-1), bribery is defined as someone who offers or solicits something of value for the performance of a public function.

> (e) He solicits, receives, retains, or agrees to accept any property or personal advantage pursuant to an understanding that he shall improperly influence or attempt to influence the performance of any act related to the employment or function of any public officer, public employee, juror or witness.

In Blagojevich's case, it appears he was soliciting campaign funds, a job for a relative, or a seat on a board or an ambassadorship for himself, in return for naming someone to the Senate seat. Even the non-monetary items could be considered "things of value." He is potentially subject to prosecution under both federal and state statutes.

Source: Long, R. and R. Pearson (2009). "Impeached Governor Blagojevich Removed from Office." *Chicago Tribune*, January 30, 2009. Accessed 3/9/2009 from http://www. chicagotribune.com/news/local/chi-blagojevich-impeachment-removal,0,5791846.story.

Bribery statutes are often categorized into sections that relate to bribery in specific situations and degrees of bribe receiving. For example, the New York statute includes, in addition to bribery in the first degree, bribery in the second degree, bribery in the third degree, bribe receiving in the third degree, bribe receiving in the second degree, and bribe receiving in the first degree.[23] The specific charge of bribery is determined by the wording of the statute and the activity of the accused. For example, a police officer was charged with a violation of § 200.10, bribe receiving in the third degree, which provides that:

> A public servant is guilty of bribe receiving when he solicits, accepts or agrees to accept any benefit from another person upon an agreement or understanding that his vote, opinion, judgment, action or exercise of discretion as a public servant will thereby be influenced.

In this case, the court held that evidence was sufficient to support the police officer's conviction for bribe receiving when the officer was compensated for the introduction of a narcotics dealer to another narcotics officer who was supposed to give protection to the drug dealer. As it turned out, the other officer was assigned to the police Internal Affairs Division and made tape-recordings of the transaction.[24]

In interpreting the Alabama bribery statute, an Alabama court advised that the critical inquiry in determining whether a defendant violated the bribery statute that prohibited the soliciting or accepting "something of value" is whether he or she did so knowingly and willfully.[25] And an Indiana appeals court noted that specific and explicit *quid pro quo* is an essential element of proof under the bribery statute.[26]

The Texas Penal Code bribery statute was considered in the case of *Rodriguez v. State.*[27] In this comprehensive decision the court stated that the essential premise of the bribery statute is that the conferring of a benefit upon a public servant and as consideration for a violation of one of his duties is an offense. Bribery focuses upon the mental state of the actor, and requires an agreement between the official and another party that some official performance will be influenced by the bribe.[28]

1. Offering, Giving, Receiving, or Soliciting

The crime is committed by one who gives a bribe as well as by one who receives it. It is also committed by one who offers a bribe or offers to accept it. One who conveys an offer to bribe, from a third person, is himself guilty, though the money is to be paid by the third person.

2. Thing of Value

Almost anything may serve as a bribe as long as it is of sufficient value in the eyes of the person bribed to influence his official conduct. It is not necessary that the thing have a value at the time it is offered or promised.[29] However, a vague offer to turn state's evidence, without anything further, was insufficient to constitute a "benefit" under the New York bribery statute.[30]

3. With Intent to Influence Public Duties

Criminal intent is a necessary element. The intent must be to corruptly influence an official in the discharge of his or her duty; and/or the intent to receive (by a public official) in return for being influenced. While the public official does not have to vote or make a favorable decision in order for the crime to be complete; these events may be used as evidence of the *mens rea* required in order for the acceptance of something of value to constitute bribery.

4. Of Public Official

Although at one time the term *public official* was more limited, the modern tendency is to include any public officer, agent, servant, or employee. As an example, the federal law covers any "officer or employee or person acting for or on behalf of the United States, or any department or agency thereof, in any official function."[31] *Public official* includes police officers, sheriffs, and deputy sheriffs under most state statutes.[32]

5. Conflict-of-Interest Statutes

To make it possible to prosecute persons who have committed acts that are similar to bribery but do not have all of the elements of bribery, legislative bodies have enacted related statutes. An example is the Pennsylvania statute, which provides:

> No person shall offer or give to a public official, public employee . . . anything of monetary value, including a gift, loan, political contribution, reward, or promise of future employment based on the offeror's or donor's understanding that the vote, official action, or judgment of the public official or public employee . . . would be influenced thereby.[33]

In the case of *Commonwealth v. Heistand,* the defendant was charged with bribery, commercial bribery, and conflict of interest (403[b]). The facts indicate that the defendant's roofing company had a contract with the school district and that the defendant had an "understanding" with the facilities manager that the defendant's payment of the manager's country club membership dues would influence the manager's judgment. In fact, the defendant's company was awarded a contract after the offer was made and a second contract after the dues were paid. The defendant was convicted only of the conflict of interest charge and appealed. The reviewing court affirmed the judgment, explaining that the conflict of interest statute has a different purpose than the bribery statute. The conflict of interest statute was enacted to avoid even the appearance of impropriety by public officials.[34]

D. Summary

Because the statutes vary from state to state, it is necessary to examine the respective statutes to determine the elements that must be proved and the correct statute to use in drafting the charge. In general, bribery can be committed by a person who offers or gives as well as the person who accepts or solicits. The receiver must be a public official but that term is broadly defined. The most crucial element of bribery is the *mens rea* element—there must be proof that the thing of value was given or accepted in return for a specific act related to the public official's performance of public duties. If this element cannot be proven, it may be that a conflict of interest crime has been committed (if it exists in that jurisdiction). The crime of conflict of interest punishes the mere giving or taking of items of value that may influence a public official's judgment and there is no requirement to prove an agreement regarding a specific act of the public servant in return for compensation. The following offers general elements that may be part of any particular state's penal code.

Bribery

(A/R)   Offer, give, solicit, receive, a thing of value, to (or by) a public official, to influence, performance of public duties

(M/R)   Intent to influence (or intent to receive in return for being influenced)

Conflict of Interest

(A/R)   Offer, give, solicit, receive; a thing of value; to (or by) a public official; that is against statutory limits

(M/R)   General intent; knowing

---

§ 12.4   Obstructing Justice

The courts recognized early that some laws were necessary to protect the integrity of the criminal justice process. Courts and legislative bodies have also recognized the difficulty in framing legislation that would accomplish the purpose of protecting the criminal justice process, yet preserve the rights of individuals.[35]

A.   Common Law

At common law, offenses were created first by court decision and later by statutes that provided misdemeanor penalties for misdeeds that tended to distort or impede the administration of law. Although the definitions relating to the offense of "**obstruction of justice**" differ, there is a common theme running through these definitions. Some early definitions will assist in understanding the purpose of the offense.

- To "obstruct justice" is to interpose obstacles or impediments, or to hinder, impede, or in any manner interrupt or prevent the administration of justice.[36]

- The phrase "obstructing justice" means impeding or obstructing those who seek justice in a court, or those who have duties or powers of administering justice therein.[37]

- The state has the inherent power to punish for obstruction of justice if it is found that a person acted in such a way as to play on human frailty and to defect and to deter the court from performing its duty.[38]

B.   Model Penal Code

The purpose of the Model Code was to make it possible to punish those who did not come within the technical definitions of bribery, threat, perjury, or escape, but did perform acts with the intent to subvert the justice process.

---

§ 242.1 Obstructing Administration of Law or Other Government Function[39]

A person commits a misdemeanor if he purposely obstructs, impairs or perverts the administration of law or other governmental function by force, violence, physical interference or obstacle, breach of official duty, or any other unlawful act, except that this Section does not apply to flight by a person charged with crime, refusal to submit to arrest, failure to perform a legal duty other than an official duty, or any other means of avoiding compliance with law without affirmative interference with governmental functions.

According to the comments following the proposed section of the Model Code, the drafters felt that it was desirable to include a residual misdemeanor offense but also recognized the necessity of not making the provision too broad in its coverage.

The offense punishes anyone who "obstructs, impairs, or perverts the administration of law, or other governmental function." It is not limited to the administration of justice, but applies to any other governmental function. In order to bring an offender within the statutory prohibition, the prosecution must show first that the person purposely obstructed or perverted the administration of law or other governmental function. The prosecution must also introduce evidence to prove that force, violence, physical interference or obstacle, breach of official duty, or other unlawful act was involved in obstructing the administration of law.

C. State Statutes, Codes, and Cases

In states where the statutes have been revised, many have followed the recommendation of the Model Penal Code and consolidated obstruction of government functions into one offense. Some use other terminology, such as "willful" obstruction. Others do not require any specific means of obstruction. Some cases in which courts have upheld obstruction convictions are:

- Conspiracy to induce or aid one who may be required as a witness in a pending proceeding to leave the jurisdiction, in order to escape service of a subpoena or to evade such service, constituted obstruction of justice.[40]

- An attorney general's persuading a municipal judge to dispose of various criminal cases without the consent and knowledge of the district attorney[41]

- A defendant's statement that he would kill the deputy sheriff when the threats were knowingly made in an attempt to intimidate or impede the testimony of the sheriff.[42]

Depending on whether separate statutes exist in a particular jurisdiction, obstruction charges may apply to those who hide or destroy evidence, lie on official reports, threaten jurors or prosecutors, delay or subvert the course of an official investigation, hide an offender and/or help the offender escape, or lie to investigating officers in such a way that it seriously hampers the investigation. However, "mere disagreement" or remonstrance with a police officer cannot constitute "obstruction of justice" unless the disagreement is so violent that it amounts to attempts to deter an officer from performing an arrest or official duty.[43]

An example of a code that differs somewhat from the Model Penal Code is that of Ohio. It provides:

OHIO REV. CODE ANN. § 2921.31[44]
(A) No person, without privilege to do so and with purpose to prevent, obstruct, or delay the performance by a public official of any authorized act within the public official's capacity, shall do any act which hampers or impedes a public official in the performance of his lawful duties.

This statute consolidates a large number of separate sections that were included in the former law. Under this section, the means used to commit the offense are unimportant, so long as it is done without privilege and with the purpose of preventing, obstructing, or delaying an official act, and actually has its intended effect. According to an Ohio court's interpretation of the statute, there must be some substantial stoppage of the officer's progress before one can say that he or she was hampered or impeded.

In *State v. Stephens*, several police officers observed a vehicle belonging to a person whose name was Hannah, for whom they had several outstanding traffic warrants, parked in front of the defendant's house. The officers walked up to the house and asked if they could speak to Hannah. The defendant told the officers she did not know Hannah and had never seen him before. One of the officers had previously seen the defendant in Hannah's company and knew that she did know him. Another officer looked through a window and observed Hannah hiding in the basement. The officers entered the house and arrested Hannah. The defendant was tried and convicted of hampering a public official in the performance of his duties, in violation of the Ohio statute.

On appeal, the conviction was reversed, the court holding that the statute, which prohibits "any act which hampers or impedes a public official in the performance of his lawful duties," did not encompass the defendant's conduct. The court indicated that the defendant's words in no way interrupted the officers' progress toward their objective and even though the defendant lied, the act did not in fact hamper or impede the officials.[45] It is entirely possible, however, that another court might have upheld this conviction.

Examples of acts that have been found to violate the obstruction statute in Ohio are:

- removing a chalk mark from the tire of a vehicle placed there by a police officer in furtherance of enforcing a parking time limitation.[46]

- blocking the police entrance to a residence to impede or delay a police officer in the performance of his duty.[47]

However, a driver refusing to show a driver's license to a police officer upon request was not "obstruction of justice.[48] The elements of obstruction will vary from state to state, but, in general, they include:

1. Intentionally

The intent element of obstructing official business can be inferred, but it must be specific intent. That is, the prosecution must prove that the defendant intended to do the act that impeded, prevented, obstructed or delayed the justice process *and* that he intended that the consequence of his action would be the obstruction of the justice process.[49]

2. Impede, Prevent, Obstruct, Delay

In a Florida case, the court cautioned that the police did not have probable cause to arrest the defendant for obstruction of justice arising out of the defendant's yelling the street term "ninety-nine," which means that police were in the area, while undercover officers were attempting the arrest of drug dealers, when the defendant was not the target of the drug bust and the officer was unaware if the actual target was caught.[50] However, a Washington court held that flight from officers when the officers have grounds for a *Terry* stop and a refusal to halt at their order may constitute obstruction of a public servant.[51]

CASE: *Polk v. Virginia*, 358 S.E.2d 770 (Va. App. 1987)

What was the holding in the case?

What specific acts constituted obstruction?

How do you differentiate the typical, to-be-expected, disgruntled exhortations of arrestees from those that constitute obstruction?

Case decisions indicate that arguing with or not cooperating with police is not obstruction, but blocking or subverting their investigation by running, lying, or threatening them or others might be. Hiding or destroying evidence might be prosecuted under an obstruction statute unless the state has a specific statute that covers that type of behavior. The *actus reus* of obstruction is broad and can cover a range of different types of behaviors. In *Polk v. Virginia*, the Virginia court upheld a conviction for obstruction based on threats made to the arresting officer.[52]

3. A Public Official from Performing an Official Duty in the Administration of Justice

Most of the cases described above concern private individuals and their interactions with police officers. It should be noted that other public officials may be the target of the obstruction, such as prosecutors, attorneys general, and the like. Also, personnel within the criminal justice system may be subject to prosecution on charges of obstructing justice for failure to disclose evidence or to pursue an investigation. In these cases, the public official is, in effect, obstructing himself from furthering the interests of justice. In *State v. Petty*, a sheriff's nondisclosure of evidence and failure to pursue an arson investigation against the daughter of a personal friend and political associate was properly the subject of prosecution on charges of obstructing justice. The argument that he was merely exercising his discretion as a law enforcement officer did not immunize the sheriff, when a jury could find that the discretion yielded to an ulterior criminal purpose.[53]

4. Other Issues

While the state has the authority to pass laws to protect the integrity of the judicial system, such laws cannot be enforced if they violate the First Amendment. The First Amendment comprehends as "free speech" critical and challenging remarks directed at police when performing their duties unless the remarks are shown likely to produce a "clear and present danger of a serious substantive evil that rises far above public inconvenience, annoyance, or unrest." In *Houston v. Hill*, a municipal ordinance made it unlawful to "oppose, molest, abuse, or interrupt any policeman in the execution of his duty"; however, the ordinance was challenged on First Amendment grounds and overturned.[54] This particular ordinance is very similar to an obstruction statute, and similarly, obstruction statutes cannot be enforced in such a way as to violate free speech when the actor is merely disagreeing with a police officer but not physically obstructing him or her from performing his or her duties, nor causing an imminent public disturbance or inciting a riot.

> **CASE: *Houston v. Hill*, 482 U.S. 451, 107 S. Ct. 2502, 96 L. Ed. 2d 398 (1987)**
>
> What was the holding of the case?
>
> What exactly did Mr. Hill do?
>
> What was the wording of the ordinance?
>
> Why was it struck down as unconstitutional?
>
> What language of an alternative ordinance might have been successfully defended?

D. Summary

The obstruction of justice charge is a catchall that can cover a multitude of behaviors, including interfering with an arrest, hiding evidence, or malfeasance of office on the part of a justice official. The most important point to note is that the statute or application of a statute cannot trample on constitutional rights of expression, nor can it be too vague and allow justice officials unbridled discretion. Further, specific intent must be proven.

Obstruction of Justice
(A/R)　Impede, prevent, delay, obstruct; justice official; from performing official functions in the administration of justice
(M/R)　Specific intent (intend to do the act, and intend that it obstruct justice)

§ 12.5   Escape

The offenses of escape, resisting arrest, and evading arrest are all related. Furthermore, at common law, **escape** was distinguished from a **prison break** and the offense of **rescue**. Prison break was defined as the breaking and going out of a place of confinement by one who is lawfully imprisoned. The crime was not committed unless there was an actual breaking or force was used. If there was no force, then the crime was not a prison break. Rescue was defined as the forcible delivery of a prisoner from lawful custody by one who knows that he is in custody. Rescue, at common law, could be a felony or misdemeanor, according to the crime with which the prisoner was charged.[55]

A. Common Law

Escape, at common law, was broadly defined as the voluntary departure of a person, without force, from the lawful custody of an officer or from any place where he is lawfully confined.[56] The person cannot escape unless he or she has actually been arrested; neither can an escape occur when the preceding arrest was defeated by successful resistance. However, one who has been taken into custody of the law by arrest or surrender and remains in legal custody and then departs unlawfully is guilty of escape.[57]

The fact that the escape occurs as a result of the negligence of a jailer in leaving a door open is not a defense.[58] Furthermore, the crime of escape included the situation in which an officer voluntarily allows a prisoner to escape. Under this law, the officer could be held criminally liable if he unlawfully permitted the prisoner to escape.[59]

An escape was not justified or excused even if a prisoner was wrongfully held in custody and could have been released if the proper legal steps were taken.[60] However, there is no escape if there was no custody. (The proper charge in this case might be evading arrest.)

The elements of common law escape are: the person must be in legal custody, and departure from the area of confinement. No intent is required other than the intent to go beyond permitted limits. Proof that the defendant was in legal custody and voluntarily departed therefrom without having been released is sufficient for a conviction in the absence of some satisfactory explanation.[61]

B. Model Penal Code

The Model Penal Code is written in clear language and includes failure to return following leave from a correctional institution granted for a specific purpose (for instance, a furlough or work-release). Also, official detention is clearly defined to include arrest and detention for law enforcement purposes.

The Model Code, in subsection 2 of §242.6, provides a penalty for a public official who permits or facilitates the escape. This is similar to provisions that existed at early common law. The punishment assigned to the offense of escape takes into consideration the crime charged and the force used in making the escape.

---

§ 242.6 Escape[62]

(1) Escape. A person commits an offense if he unlawfully removes himself from official detention or fails to return to official detention following temporary leave granted for a specific purpose or limited period. "Official detention" means arrest, detention in any facility for custody of persons under charge or conviction of crime or alleged or found to be delinquent, detention for extradition or deportation, or any other detention for law enforcement purposes; but "official detention" does not include supervision of probation or parole, or constraint incidental to release on bail.

(2) Permitting or Facilitating Escape. A public servant concerned in detention commits an offense if he knowingly or recklessly permits an escape. Any person who knowingly causes or facilitates an escape commits an offense.

(3) Effect of Legal Irregularity in Detention. Irregularity in bringing about or maintaining detention, or lack of jurisdiction of the committing or detaining authority, shall not be a defense to prosecution under this Section if the escape is from a prison or other custodial facility or from detention pursuant to commitment by official proceedings. In the case of other detentions, irregularity or lack of jurisdiction shall be a defense only if:

    (a) the escape involved no substantial risk of harm to the person or property of anyone other than the detainee; or
    (b) the detaining authority did not act in good faith under color of law.

(4) Grading of Offenses. An offense under this Section is a felony of the third degree where:

    (a) the actor was under arrest for or detained on a charge of felony or following conviction of crime; or
    (b) the actor employs force, threat, deadly weapon or other dangerous instrumentality to effect the escape; or
    (c) a public servant concerned in detention of persons convicted of crime purposely facilitates or permits an escape from a detention facility.

Otherwise an offense under this section is a misdemeanor.

C. State Statutes, Codes, and Cases

Statutes and codes in the various states differ in wording and in establishing penalties. Some states recognize a single grade of escape with no aggravating or mitigating factors, while other states include distinct grading levels depending upon the use of force, the severity of the escapee's original crime, and the escapee's status; that is, whether he has been convicted or merely detained on suspicion. For instance, in Kentucky, three degrees of escape are defined:

§ 520.020 Escape in the First Degree[63]

(1) A person is guilty of escape in the first degree when he escapes from custody or a detention facility by the use of force or threat of force against another person.
(2) Escape in the first degree is a Class C felony.

§ 520.030 Escape in the Second Degree

(1) A person is guilty of escape in the second degree when he escapes from a detention facility or, being charged with or convicted of a felony, he escapes from custody.
(2) Escape in the second degree is a Class D felony.

§ 520.040 Escape in the Third Degree

(1) A person is guilty of escape in the third degree when he escapes from custody.
(2) Escape in the third degree is a Class B misdemeanor.

In the Kentucky statute, the degrees of "escape" are based on the type of custody and whether force was used. "**Custody**" means restraint by a public servant pursuant to a lawful arrest, detention, or an order of a court for law enforcement purposes, but does not include supervision of probation or parole or constraint incidental to release on bail.[64]

According to the Kentucky Court of Appeals, a defendant may be charged under the statute with escape in the second degree, a felony, despite the fact that he had been in jail and charged with misdemeanors rather than a felony. The court explained that the penalty imposed is most severe on those who effect an escape by force or threat of force.[65]

The Florida statute provides that any prisoner, confined in any prison, jail, private correctional facility, road camp, or other penal institution, whether operated by the state, a county, or a municipality, or operated under a contract with the state, a county, or a municipality, working upon the public roads, or being transported to or from a place of confinement who escapes or attempts to escape from such confinement commits a felony of the second degree, punishable as provided in § 775.082, § 775.083, or § 775.084.[66]

In Florida, the crime of escape consists of two elements: The act of leaving custody coupled with the intent to avoid lawful confinement. In *Watford v. State*, the court reasoned that when a state has established the right to custody and a conscious and intentional act of leaving, the offense is *prima facie* established. In some cases, prisoners have used the defense of necessity when charged with escape. They have argued that they needed to escape to avoid being seriously injured or killed by other inmates. While necessity would be a possible defense, the defendant must show that there were reasonable grounds to believe that the escapee is faced with real and imminent danger and the escapee must go immediately to a justice official upon escape to report the threat.[67]

While state statutes vary in their definitions and grading of escape; in general, the elements can be described as follows:

1. Voluntary Departure

Obviously, the defendant must "depart" to the extent that they are no longer in custody. If they are found hiding in the airshaft of a prison facility, the proper charge would be "attempted escape" rather than escape because they have not yet effected the departure. On the other hand, once out of custody, there is no distance requirement; so a defendant who leaves police custody after arrest may be recaptured immediately and still be charged with escape. For instance, in one case a court held that conviction for escape was proper where the defendant voluntarily departed from the city jail while in police custody and handcuffed.[68]

2. From "Custody" (Includes Detention Facilities and Failure to Return from Authorized Leave)

Custody may be jail, police custody, or any type of correctional facility. Unauthorized departure from a halfway house can be escape if the departure was willful and intentional.[69] Sometimes the statute specifically requires custody in a detention facility (rather than police custody). A Michigan court, in discussing the elements of escape in that state, held that the jail escape statute requires a showing that: (1) the defendant was lawfully imprisoned in a jail or other place of confinement while awaiting legal proceedings or transfer to prison, and (2) the defendant broke or attempted to break out of the jail or place of confinement, regardless of whether the escape was actually made.[70]

A Texas appeals court stated that the elements of escape are that a person: (1) escapes; (2) from custody; (3) after having been arrested for, charged with, or convicted of an offense.[71]

3. With Intent to Not Return to Custody

With the increased use of alternative procedures designed to reduce costs and address jail overcrowding, new questions are reaching the courts. For example, is a person guilty of escape if that person leaves a privately operated "detention facility" without authority? And is a person "in custody" when released prior to trial on the condition that he or she wear an electronic monitoring device at all times?

A Kentucky appeals court agreed that a person in a privately operated "detention facility" could be guilty of escape.[72] In another case, the court held that a defendant whose probation is revoked in his or her presence after a probation revocation hearing and is informed by the judge that he or she is in custody and is to remain until a law enforcement officer can take him or her to jail, is in lawful custody for the purpose of the statute governing aggravated escape from custody.[73]

In another case, an Arizona appeals court made it clear that a defendant who was released prior to trial on felony charges on condition that he wear an electronic monitoring device and remain in his home was in "custody" so that removal of the device and unauthorized departure from his home and from the state constituted escape.[74]

> **CASE: *Medford v. State*, 990 S.W.2d 799 (Tex. Ct. App. 1999)**
>
> What was the holding of the case?
>
> How exactly would you describe Medford's status?
>
> At what point would the charge of escape be appropriate in this situation?
>
> What would have been the appropriate charge for Medford?
>
> Must officers say "you are under arrest" in order for custody to commence?

D. Summary

An escape must begin with custody. If there is no custody, there can be no escape. However, once custody is established, then voluntary departure can constitute an escape, even if the person is not in jail or prison. Inmates of halfway houses and work-release facilities commit the crime of escape when they do not return at the expected time. Individuals in police "custody" may be charged with escape, but not if they are merely being detained for investigative purposes.

Escape
(A/R) Voluntary departure, from custody, with intent not to return
(M/R) Knowing (one is in custody), intent (not to return)

§ 12.6 Resisting Arrest

While a person who is not in custody cannot commit the crime of escape, someone who actively resists being put in custody might be charged with the crime of resisting arrest. Some statutes dealing with the general offense of obstructing justice include the act of **resisting arrest**. Other statutes deal specifically with the offense of resisting arrest.

A. Common Law

At common law, if the arrest was legal and there was resistance, the offense of resisting arrest was complete. What amounted to resistance depended on the facts of the situation. There are numerous examples of cases in which the court found that resistance occurred. The use of any weapon such as a club, pistol, or revolver is undoubtedly sufficient to constitute the resistance prohibited. However, resisting arrest does not require an attempt to cause serious bodily injury to the police officer. It is sufficient to prove that the defendant created a substantial risk of bodily injury or that the defendant put up resistance requiring the police officer to use substantial force to overcome it.[75]

In distinguishing between escape and resisting arrest, it has been held that "escape from custody" implies unlawfully freeing oneself from a completed apprehension while "resisting apprehension" means active opposition to attempts to place one in lawful custody.[76]

At common law, resisting arrest was an offense; however, an individual had a right to use reasonable resistance to prevent being arrested illegally.[77] If an officer did not disclose his authority and the accused did not know that he was an officer, the accused had the right to resist with whatever force was necessary.[78] However, that is generally not the case today.

B. Model Penal Code

Section 242.2 of the Model Penal Code is concerned with resistance to arrest where there is a substantial risk of bodily injury to a public servant or anyone else, or when means are employed that justify or require substantial force to overcome the resistance. Exempted from liability is one who non-violently refuses to submit to arrest and such minor forms of resistance as running from a police officer or trying to shake free from his or her grasp.

---

§ 242.2 Resisting Arrest or Other Law Enforcement[79]

A person commits a misdemeanor if, for the purpose of preventing a public servant from effecting a lawful arrest or discharging any other duty, the person creates a substantial risk of bodily injury to the public servant or anyone else, or employs means justifying or requiring substantial force to overcome the resistance.

Under the Model Penal Code, resisting arrest is a misdemeanor regardless of the charge against the person who resists arrest. In the commentary following the provision, it is explained that continued resistance to the arresting officer after the arrest has been made may constitute an attempt to escape in violation of § 242.6. Therefore, if the arrest is for a felony, escape from custody may be punished as a felony.

Unlike some statutes prior to the Model Penal Code and drafted since the Model Code, the Model Code does not provide a penalty for a person who resists arrest if the arrest is unlawful, unless one of the other provisions of the Model Code is violated.

C. State Statutes, Codes, and Cases

In drafting legislation, the states have differed, especially regarding resistance to an unlawful arrest. Some have been persuaded by the argument that the officer should be protected even if the arrest is unlawful and that the remedy for the person who is unlawfully arrested is a civil action against the officer.

An Ohio statute states: "No person, recklessly or by force, shall resist or interfere with a lawful arrest of the person or another."[80] Under the Ohio statute, lawful arrest is an element of the offense of resisting arrest. Where articulable suspicion, but not probable cause, to arrest exists, fleeing from a request for a *Terry*-type stop, while not condoned, does not constitute resisting arrest.[81] In Ohio, a judge held that the prosecution need not prove the guilt of the arrested defendant beyond a reasonable doubt in determining whether the arrest was lawful; however, for the arrest to be a "lawful arrest" as used in the resisting arrest ordinance, there must be probable cause or reasonable grounds for the arrest.[82] Another Ohio court stated the law succinctly, holding that under Ohio law, where there is no arrest, a criminal resisting arrest charge cannot be sustained. Applying this rule, an Ohio court determined that the defendant's heckling a professional baseball player did not provide a reasonable police officer with a basis to believe that it constituted a criminal offense, as was required to convict the defendant of resisting arrest.[83]

A Florida court, discussing the resisting arrest statute of that state, held that, in order to support a conviction for resisting arrest, the state must show that: (1) the officer was engaged in the lawful execution of a legal duty, and (2) the action of the defendant constituted obstruction or resistance of that lawful duty.[84] In a second Florida case, the court determined that state law allows one who is illegally being arrested to resist that arrest without violence.[85] Using similar language, Pennsylvania courts have held that a valid charge of resisting arrest requires an underlying lawful arrest, which, in turn, requires the arresting officer to possess probable cause.[86]

On the other hand, other states do not allow the defense. An Indiana court has noted that, at common law, an individual had the right to use reasonable resistance to avoid an illegal arrest, but that rule no longer exists. That court advised that today a citizen may seek his or her remedy for a police officer's wrongful arrest by bringing a civil suit, while the common law right tends to promote violence. Thus, the court held, the defendant had no right to resist arrest.[87] In the case cited, the defendant was convicted of interfering with a police officer after a dispute developed when the officers ordered a tow truck to remove the defendant's vehicle from the street. The defendant contended upon appeal that he had a legal right to remove his own vehicle because, although it displayed the wrong kind of license plate, it was not otherwise illegally parked and should not have been treated as an abandoned vehicle. The court agreed that the officer had no right to have the car removed. However, the defendant had no right to resist being arrested; therefore, the conviction for resisting arrest was proper. The trend today is for states to refuse to allow individuals to resist unlawful arrests because there are other alternatives to respond, such as civil suits.[88]

When police use excessive force in effecting an arrest, some states allow the citizen to defend themselves against the arrest (since the illegal use of force turns it into an unlawful arrest). This right includes the use of deadly force if the individual felt their life was in danger. The right stems from the common law right of self defense.[89] Of course, for the person to benefit from this defense, there must be a finding that the use of force by police was excessive. The elements of resisting arrest, generally are as follows.

1. Resisting (Creating Risk of Bodily Injury and/or Requiring Substantial Force to Overcome)

According to one court in Texas, an arrestee can be convicted of forcefully resisting an arrest without ever successfully making physical contact with the person making the arrest. Applying this rule, the court held that "kicking at" an officer during arrest constitutes a use of force required under the penal code for the offense of resisting arrest.[90]

2. A (Lawful) Arrest

As indicated by the discussion above, in some states, the underlying arrest must be lawful in order to support a resisting arrest charge. In other states, for public policy reasons, the common law defense that allowed resisting an unlawful arrest has been rejected. Because the states differ in regard to the elements, it is essential that each officer be aware of the specific wording of the state statute and the decisions interpreting that statute.

D. Summary

While some states may cover resisting arrest in a general obstruction of justice statute, others have a separate statute that defines and penalizes resisting arrest. These statutes generally exempt nonviolent means of resistance, but punish those who create a substantial risk of harm by fighting with the police officer or otherwise creating a situation in which the police officer must use substantial force to overcome the resistance. While some states identify the lawfulness of the arrest as an element of the crime, others do not.

Resisting Arrest

(A/R)   Resisting, a (lawful) arrest

(M/R)   Knowing (one is being placed under arrest), Intentional (resistance)

---

§ 12.7   Evading Arrest

Evading is the third and least serious crime in the three related crimes of escape, resisting, and evading. Not all states have a specific statute for evading arrest.

A. Common Law

No record of this crime seems to exist under the common law.

B. Model Penal Code

The Model Penal Code has a section titled "Hindering Apprehension or Prosecution" that defines as criminal those who assist another to escape or avoid capture by law enforcement; however, there is no section of "Evading Arrest." Furthermore, because the "Resisting Arrest" section described in the previous paragraphs requires a substantial risk of bodily injury or means that require the public servant to use substantial force to overcome the resistance, that section does not cover behaviors that do not involve force, such as simply running. On the other hand, if, in evading, the offender created a situation that might cause substantial injury (such as a high-speed chase), it is possible that the crime would be "resisting," not evading.

C. State Statutes, Codes, and Cases

Not all states have a separate evading arrest statute. In some states, the behavior is covered under a section of the resisting statute; in others, it might be covered under a general obstruction of justice statute. However, some states distinguish evasion and resisting. In a case in which the court distinguished between resisting arrest and avoiding arrest, a court stated that resisting arrest is a crime committed against a person; a defendant must use or threaten to use physical force or any other means that creates a substantial risk of causing physical injury to the peace officer or another to violate the statute, whereas if a defendant prevented arrest without using or threatening to use physical force or other means creating a substantial risk of physical injury, he "avoids" arrest.[91]

D. Summary

While evading arrest is not a separate crime in many states, it has been distinguished from resisting arrest.

Evading Arrest

(A/R) Avoiding or fleeing, from arrest, without violence

(M/R) Knowing (that arrest is attempted), Intentional (flight)

---

§ 12.8 Other Offenses Against Justice Administration

All state statutes include other provisions that relate to conduct that impairs or obstructs governmental operations or public administration. The primary purpose is to preserve smooth and efficient administration of the government and to protect those who are charged with the responsibility of enforcing the laws and ordinances. Because these vary from state to state, it is obviously necessary that state statutes, and in some instances local ordinances, be studied to determine what conduct is prohibited and what elements must be proved in order to obtain a conviction when a person is charged with a violation of the ordinance or statute. Some of the offenses that are found in various state statutes are discussed here. It should be noted, however, that this list is not exhaustive.

A. Failure to Aid a Law Enforcement Officer

Many early statutes required persons to come to the aid of a law enforcement officer when asked to do so. In fact, at common law it was a criminal offense for any person to willfully disregard the summons of the sheriff to render assistance in apprehending a felon. Every citizen was bound to assist a known public officer in making an arrest when called upon to do so.[92] Some state statutes punished the failure to obey the call of an officer to assist in making an arrest.[93] An example of a modern statute that restates the requirement that persons come to the aid of officers is that of Ohio. It provides:

> Ohio Rev. Code Ann. § 2921.23[94]
>
> (A) No person shall negligently fail or refuse to aid a law enforcement officer, when called upon for assistance in preventing or halting the commission of an offense, or in apprehending or detaining an offender, when such aid can be given without a substantial risk of physical harm to the person giving it.

This requires that a person aid the officer in apprehending an offender even though the offender has not been formally charged. It excuses the failure to render aid on the ground that there is a strong possibility that the person called upon may be hurt in the process.

B. False Reports to Law Enforcement Authorities

There is some evidence to the effect that giving false reports to police or other law enforcement agencies was punishable at common law. In the case of *People v. Stephens,* an Illinois court held that one who falsely reports a crime is guilty of disorderly conduct.[95]

After several attempts to draft legislation that provided a penalty for giving false reports, many states now have statutes that accomplish the desired result. An example is that of Florida, which provides:

> § 837.05. False reports to law enforcement authorities[96]
>
> (1) Except as provided in subsection (2), whoever knowingly gives false information to any law enforcement officer concerning the alleged commission of any crime, commits a misdemeanor of the first degree, punishable as provided in s. 775.082 or s. 775.083.
>
> (2) Whoever knowingly gives false information to a law enforcement officer, concerning the alleged commission of a capital felony, commits a felony of the third degree, punishable as provided in s. 775.082, s. 775.083, or s. 775.084.

States that have similar statutes are Alaska, Georgia, California, and Maryland.

Under the Kentucky statute, a person is guilty of falsely reporting an incident when he or she knowingly causes a false alarm of fire or other emergency to be transmitted.[97] Also, under this section, a person is guilty if he or she knowingly reports false information to a law enforcement agency with the intent to implicate another or initiates a report of an alleged occurrence of a fire or other emergency under circumstances likely to cause inconvenience or alarm, when he or she knows that the information reported, conveyed, or circulated is false. The major thrust of this statute is to deter those who impede investigations by furnishing fictitious leads. Such statutes are considered necessary in many jurisdictions to aid law enforcement personnel and to avoid inconvenience to members of the public as well as government agents.

C. *Tampering with Witnesses*

Most state statutes provide penalties for tampering with those who are to testify in trials. In some states, this is dealt with in provisions relating to obstruction of justice. This crime is closely related to bribery and subornation of perjury, both of which could be charged if the circumstances warrant.

The Model Penal Code provision relating to tampering with witnesses includes tampering with informants. It provides:

---

§ 241.6 Tampering With Witnesses and Informants; Retaliation Against Them[98]

(1) Tampering. A person commits an offense if, believing that an official proceeding or investigation is pending or about to be instituted, he attempts to induce or otherwise cause a witness or informant to:

    (a) testify or inform falsely; or
    (b) withhold any testimony, information, document or thing; or
    (c) elude legal process summoning him to testify or supply evidence; or
    (d) absent himself from any proceeding or investigation to which he has been legally summoned.

The offense is a felony of the third degree if the actor employs force, deception, threat or offer of pecuniary benefit. Otherwise it is a misdemeanor.

(2) Retaliation Against Witness or Informant. A person commits a misdemeanor if he harms another by any unlawful act in retaliation for anything lawfully done in the capacity of witness or informant.

(3) Witness or Informant Taking Bribe. A person commits a felony of the third degree if he solicits, accepts or agrees to accept any benefit in consideration of his doing any of the things specified in clauses (a) to (d) of Subsection (1).

This provision defines three different offenses, each of which protects against some threat to the veracity and cooperation of witnesses and informants. Subsection (1) provides that a person commits an offense if he or she attempts to induce another to testify or inform falsely or otherwise subvert the process of criminal law. Subsection (2) condemns retaliation against a witness or informant. Subsection (3) imposes a felony penalty for solicitation, acceptance, or agreement to accept any benefit in consideration of doing any of the acts enumerated in the first 10 subsections.

Many of the recently revised statutes and codes have specific provisions relating to tampering with witnesses. Some are more restrictive and some less restrictive. These, of course, must be studied in detail before any charges are made.

D. Tampering with Evidence

In order to ensure that evidence is preserved for presentation in court, many states have enacted legislation that prohibits tampering with evidence or fabricating physical evidence. The provisions of the statutes apply to those who attempt to impair the integrity or availability of evidence in an official proceeding or investigation, or one who purposely fabricates evidence in order to mislead the investigator. The suggested legislation as prepared by the drafters of the Model Penal Code provides:

§ 241.7 Tampering with or Fabricating Physical Evidence[99]

A person commits a misdemeanor if, believing that an official proceeding or investigation is pending or about to be instituted, he:

(1) alters, destroys, conceals or removes any record, document or thing with purpose to impair its verity or availability in such proceeding or investigation; or

(2) makes, presents or uses any record, document or thing knowing it to be false and with purpose to mislead a public servant who is or may be engaged in such proceeding or investigation.

The Model Penal Code punishes one who alters, destroys, conceals, or removes evidence and reaches those who "make, present, or use any record, document or thing knowing it to be false with the purpose to mislead" those engaged in investigating crimes.

Some states that have similar legislation are Connecticut, Indiana, Maine, Missouri, Montana, New Hampshire, New Jersey, Ohio, Pennsylvania, Utah, Massachusetts, and Vermont. Other states have provisions that require that the accused intend to have the evidence "introduced" in the official proceeding.

The Ohio statute provides:

Ohio Rev. Code Ann. § 2921.12[100]

(A) No person, knowing that an official proceeding or investigation is in progress, or is about to be or likely to be instituted, shall do any of the following:

(1) Alter, destroy, conceal, or remove any record, document, or thing, with purpose to impair its value or availability as evidence in such proceeding or investigation;

(2) Make, present, or use any record, document, or thing, knowing it to be false and with purpose to mislead a public official who is or may be engaged in such proceeding or investigation, or with purpose to corrupt the outcome of any such proceeding or investigation.

A police officer filing a report with knowledge that its contents are inaccurate because of knowing omissions and with knowledge that the report will be relied upon in a likely investigation, may be in violation of this Ohio statute.[101]

Interpreting a Kentucky statute, a reviewing court agreed with the lower court opinion that evidence that an officer saw the defendant place a plastic bag containing a white powdery substance on the kitchen counter, and that this item of potential evidence disappeared from the counter after the defendant became aware of the presence of the officer and closed the front door, and before officers were granted entry through the back door, was sufficient to support a conviction of tampering with evidence.[102]

E. Other Offenses

Statutes of the various states include other offenses that relate to public justice and administration. Some include such offenses as:

- compounding a crime

- impersonating a public servant

- hindering apprehension or prosecution

- bail jumping

- criminal contempt

Even when a state does not have a specific statute, the activity can usually be prosecuted under a broader statute, such as obstruction of justice.

§ 12.9   Summary

As government functions developed, the need to protect them from willful interference became apparent. Legislation has been enacted to protect government agencies from interference by those outside the government and to protect the public from individuals who might take advantage of the authority granted as a result of government employment.

It was recognized early that the integrity of a sworn statement must be guaranteed to ensure the truth of statements made in judicial or quasi-judicial proceedings. To this end, the offense of perjury was created. Perjury is generally defined as the willful and corrupt false swearing or affirming after an oath has been lawfully administered in the cause of judicial or quasi-judicial proceedings as to some matter material to the issue or point in question. Subornation of perjury is the procuring of one person by another to commit the crime of perjury.

A second universally recognized offense that relates to the integrity of government administration is bribery. Bribery is defined as the offering, giving, receiving, or soliciting of anything of value with intent to influence the recipient's action as a public official. The elements of bribery are: (1) offering, giving, receiving or soliciting; (2) a thing of value; (3) intent to influence the recipient's action; and (4) the recipient is a public official.

Early courts and legislative bodies added a crime titled obstruction of justice. Generally, these statutes and cases prohibit interference with a witness, harboring criminals, influencing a jury, suppression or destruction of evidence, and other related acts.

Escape has been broadly defined as the voluntary departure of a person without force from the lawful custody of an officer or from any place where he is lawfully confined. The elements of escape are: the person is in legal custody and voluntary departure from the area of confinement. Related to escape is the offense of resisting arrest and, in some jurisdictions, evading arrest. At common law, if the arrest was legal and there was resistance, the offense of resisting arrest was complete. What amounted to resistance depended upon the facts of the situation. Under the Model Penal Code, resisting arrest is a violation when there is a substantial risk of bodily injury to a public servant or anyone else. At common law and in many states, an individual has the right to reasonable resistance to avoid an illegal arrest. That law has been changed in other states, which hold that the defendant has no right to resist an arrest, even if the arrest is illegal. The reasoning is that the common law rule tends to provoke violence and that the person wrongfully arrested has recourse by bringing a civil suit.

Other offenses against public justice and administration include failure to aid a law enforcement officer, making false reports to enforcement authorities, tampering with witnesses, and tampering with evidence. Because the state statutes differ regarding offenses against justice administration, individual state statutes should be reviewed by criminal justice personnel to determine the elements that constitute an offense in any specific state.

Review Questions

1. What are the essential elements of the offense of perjury? Explain the specific intent mens rea of perjury.

2. Distinguish between perjury and subornation of perjury. How is false swearing different from perjury?

3. According to the common law definition of bribery, who may commit the crime? How are statutes different today?

4. Is intent an element of the offense of bribery? Explain.

5. Generally, bribery statutes apply only to public officials. What is the definition of public official as used in the contemporary statutes?

6. How does a conflict of interest statute differ from a bribery statute?

7. What are the elements of obstructing justice statutes? Under the MPC, what acts would not be sufficient to support an obstruction of justice charge?

8. Can threats to police officers, such as: "I am going to get you," "I am going to get even," "I am going to kill him," and "I have got five friends to help me take care of him" be sufficient to support an obstruction of justice charge?

9. What are other examples of behaviors or actions that might form the actus reus of obstruction of justice?

10. What is a common challenge to the enforcement of obstruction or interfering in arrest charges? Distinguish what can and cannot be the subject of criminal prosecution.

11. Distinguish between common law escape and prison break crimes.

12. Under the Model Penal Code section relating to escape, the offense is a misdemeanor unless one of three conditions exists, in which case it is a felony. Name the three aggravating circumstances.

13. According to most state statutes, must a person be in legal custody before he or she can be convicted of escape? Define custody.

14. How does the offense of resisting arrest differ from the offense of escape? What is the common law definition of resisting arrest?

15. What is the difference between resisting arrest and avoiding/evading arrest?

16. When a person is prosecuted for resisting arrest, may the arrestee raise the unlawfulness of the arrest as a defense? Explain. Do the state laws agree on this defense? Give some examples.

17. What might a person who is the target of a police investigatory stop and runs away and/or struggles with the police officer be charged with?

18. Describe the crimes of "failure to aid a law enforcement officer" and "false reporting."

19. Describe the crimes of "tampering with witnesses" and "tampering with evidence." If a state does not have these statutes, what would the person be charged with?

20. List and describe at least three other crimes that are mentioned in the last section of this chapter.

Notes

1   Common barratry is the offense of frequently inciting and stirring up suits and quarrels. Commonwealth v. Davis, 28 Mass. (11 Pick.) 432 (1831).

2   Martin v. Miller, 4 Mo. 39 (1835); State v. Dallagiovanna, 69 Wash. 84, 124 P. 209 (1912).

3   *See* Wharton, Criminal Law 1780-1781 (12th ed. 1932); Gatewood v. State, 15 Md. App. 314, 290 A.2d 551 (1972); Bazarte v. State, 117 So. 2d 227 (Fla. 1959).

4   State v. Laurelli, 187 F. Supp. 30 (D. Pa. 1960).

5   Model Penal Code § 241.1 (1985).

6   N.Y. Penal Law §§ 210.05-210.15 (McKinney 2003).

7   People v. Pomerantz, 407 N.Y.S.2d 723, 63 A.2d 457 (1978).

8   People v. Siggia and Partridge, 588 N.Y.S.2d 518 (1990).

9   In re Disciplinary Proceeding Against Huddleston, 137 Wash. 2d 560, 974 P.2d 325 (1999).

10   People v. Stanard, 42 N.Y.2d 74, 365 N.E.2d 857, 369 N.Y.S.2d 825, *cert. denied*, 434 U.S. 986, 98 S. Ct. 615, 54 L. Ed. 2d 481 (1977). *See also* State v. Anderson, 603 A.2d 928 (N.J. 1992); People v. Evans, 704 N.Y.S.2d 418 (2000). *See also* Luna v. Massachusetts, 224 F. Supp. 2d 302 (D. Mass. 2000), which held that under Massachusetts law materiality is one of the elements of the crime of perjury, and each element must be proven beyond a reasonable doubt.

11   People v. Brown, 616 N.Y.S.2d 592 (1994).

12   People v. Trotter, 83 Cal. Rptr. 2d 753 (1999).

13   State v. Kowalczyk, 66 A.2d 175 (N.J. 1949); Plummer v. State, 84 S.E.2d 202 (Ga. 1954).

14   Stone v. State, 118 Ga. 705, 45 S.E. 630 (1903) (a defendant who induced his wife to make a false affidavit was guilty of subornation of perjury); Thomas v. State, 231 S.W. 200 (1921).

15   Perkins and Boyce, Criminal Law (3d ed. 1982).

16   Ex parte Winters, 10 Okla. Crim. 592, 140 P. 164 (1914).

17   4 Blackstone, Commentaries 139 (1898).

18   Honaker v. Board of Education, 42 W. Va. 170, 24 S.E. 544 (1896); Rudolph v. State, 128 Wis. 122, 107 N.W. 466 (1906).

19   People v. Northey, 77 Cal. 618, 19 P. 865 (1888); United States v. Forsythe, 429 F. Supp. 715 (D. Pa. 1977); State v. Smith, 252 La. 636, 212 So. 2d 410 (1968); United States v. Sisk, 476 F. Supp. 1061 (D. Tenn. 1979); People v. Ginsberg, 80 Misc. 2d 921, 364 N.Y.S.2d 260 (1974).

20   Model Penal Code § 240.1 (1985).

21   N.Y. Penal Law § 200.04 (McKinney 1999). *See also* §§ 200.10, 200.11, and 200.12.

22   People v. Herskowitz, 80 Misc. 2d 693, 364 N.Y.S.2d 350 (1975), *aff'd*, 41 N.Y.2d 1094, 364 N.E.2d 1127, 396 N.Y.2d 356 (1977).

23   Respectively, §§ 200-03, 200-00, 200-10, 200-11 and 200-12.

24   People v. Logan, 535 N.Y.S.2d 411 (1988).

25   Dill v. State, 723 So. 2d 787 (Ala. 1998).

26   Wurster v. State, 708 N.E.2d 587 (Ind. 1999).

27   Tex. Penal Code Ann. § 36.02(A)(1) (Vernon 2001).

28   Rodriguez v. State, 90 S.W.3d 340 (Tex. 2001).

[29]   People v. Hockberg, 62 A.D.2d 239, 404 N.Y.S.2d 161 (1978).

[30]   People v. Cavan, 84 Misc. 2d 510, 376 N.Y.S.2d 65 (1975).

[31]   18 U.S.C. § 201.

[32]   Usry v. State, 90 Ga. App. 644, 83 S.E.2d 843 (1954).

[33]   65 Pa. Cons. Stat. § 1103 (2002).

[34]   Commonwealth v. Heistand, 685 A.2d 1026 (Pa. Super. 1996).

[35]   58 Am. Jur. 2d *Obstructing Justice* § 1 (1989).

[36]   Baker v. State, 122 Ga. App. 587, 178 S.E.2d 278 (1970).

[37]   Shackelford v. Commonwealth, 185 Ky. 51, 214 S.W. 788 (1919).

[38]   State v. Sagumaker, 200 Ind. 623, 157 N.E. 769 (1927).

[39]   Model Penal Code § 242.1 (1985).

[40]   People v. Hefberd, 162 N.Y.S. 80 (1916).

[41]   People v. Martin, 185 Cal. Rptr. 556 (1982).

[42]   Polk v. Commonwealth, 4 Va. App. 590, 358 S.E.2d 770 (1987).

[43]   McCook v. State, 145 Ga. App. 3, 243 S.E.2d 289 (1978).

[44]   Ohio Rev. Code Ann. § 2921.31 (Anderson 2002).

[45]   State v. Stephens, 57 Ohio App. 2d 229, 387 N.E.2d 252 (1978).

[46]   Sandusky v. DeTidio, 555 N.E.2d 680 (Ohio 1988).

[47]   State v. Pitts, 509 N.E.2d 1284 (Ohio 1986).

[48]   State v. McCrone, 580 N.E.2d 468 (Ohio 1989).

[49]   State v. Puterbaugh, 755 N.E.2d 359 (Ohio 2001).

[50]   State v. Dennis, 684 So. 2d 848 (Fla. 1996).

[51]   State v. Mendez, 137 Wash. 2d 208, 970 P.2d 722 (1999).

[52]   Polk v. Virginia, 358 S.E.2d 770 (1987

[53]   State v. Petty, 5th District Court of App. Ohio 7-26-88.

[54]   Houston v. Hill, 482 U.S. 451, 107 S. Ct. 2502, 96 L. Ed. 2d 398 (1987).

[55]   State v. King, 114 Iowa 413, 87 N.W. 282 (1901). *See also* Duckworth v. Boyer, 125 So. 2d 844 (Fla. 1960).

[56]   United States v. Zimmerman, 71 F. Supp. 534 (D. Pa. 1947).

[57]   Whithead v. Keyes, 85 Mass. (3 Allen) 495 (1862).

[58]   State v. Hoffman, 30 Wash. 2d 475, 191 P.2d 865 (1948).

[59]   Houpt v. State, 100 Ark. 409, 140 S.W. 294 (1911).

[60]   People v. Hinze, 97 Cal. App. 2d 1, 217 P.2d 35 (1950).

[61]   Wiggins v. State, 194 Ind. 118, 141 N.E. 56 (1923).

[62]   Model Penal Code § 242.6 (1985).

[63]   Ky. Rev. Stat. Ann. §§ 520.020, 520.030, 520.040 (Baldwin 1999).

[64]   Ky. Rev. Stat. Ann. § 520.010 (Baldwin 1999).

[65]   Commonwealth v. Johnson, 615 S.W.2d 1 (Ky. 1981).

[66]   FLA. STAT. ANN. § 944.40 (2003). *See also* Harboring or Aiding an Escapee, § 944.46; Aiding of Escape by Prisoners, § 843.09 *et seq.*

[67]   Watford v. State, 353 So. 2d 1263 (Fla. Ct. App. 1978).

[68]   State v. Brown, 29 Wash. App. 770, 630 P.2d 1378 (1981).

[69]   State v. Brown, 8 Wash. App. 639, 509 P.2d 77 (1973).

[70]   People v. Fox, 232 Mich. App. 531, 591 N.W.2d 384 (1998).

[71]   Medford v. State, 990 S.W.2d 799 (Tex. Ct. App. 1999).

[72]   Phipps v. Commonwealth, 933 S.W.2d 825 (Ky. 1996).

[73]   United States v. Briggs, 48 P.3d 686 (Kan. 2002).

[74]   State v. Williams, 925 P.2d 1073 (Ariz. 1996).

[75]   Commonwealth v. Williams, 344 Pa. Super. 108, 496 A.2d 31 (1985).

[76]   United States v. Chavez, 6 Mil. Jus. 615 (1936).

[77]   Fields v. State, 384 N.E.2d 1127 (Ind. Ct. App. 1979).

[78]   Presley v. State, 75 Fla. 434, 78 So. 532 (1918).

[79]   MODEL PENAL CODE § 242.2 (1985).

[80]   OHIO REV. CODE ANN. § 2921.33 (Anderson 2003).

[81]   State v. Raines, 124 Ohio App. 3d 430, 706 N.E.2d 414 (1997).

[82]   State v. Maynard, 693 N.E.2d 603 (Ohio Ct. App. 1996).

[83]   Hummel v. City of Carlisle, W.L. 31465378 (S.D. Ohio 2002); Cleveland v. Swiecicki, 775 N.E.2d 899 (Ohio 2002).

[84]   Jay v. State, 731 So. 2d 774 (Fla. 1999).

[85]   Williams v. State, 727 So. 2d 1050 (Fla. 1999).

[86]   Commonwealth v. Hock, 728 A.2d 943 (Pa. 1999) *and see* Commonwealth v. Maxon, 798 A.2d 761 (Pa. 2002). *See also* Vaughn v. State, 983 S.W.2d 860 (Tex. 1998).

[87]   Fields v. State, 384 N.E.2d 1127 (Ind. Ct. App. 1979).

[88]   *See* CAL. PEN. CODE §834a (West 1985); State v. Valentine, 935 P.2d 1294 (Wash. 1997).

[89]   People v. White, 161 Cal. Rptr. 541 (Ct. App. 1980); Commonwealth v. French, 611 A.2d 175 (Pa. 1992).

[90]   Haliburton v. State, 80 S.W.3d 309 (Tex. 2002).

[91]   State v. Sorkhabi, 46 P.3d 1071 (Ariz. 2002).

[92]   Grau v. Forge, 183 Ky. 521, 209 S.W. 369 (1919); Firestone v. Rice, 71 Mich. 377, 38 N.W. 885 (1888).

[93]   Babington v. Yellow Taxi Corp., 250 N.Y. 14, 164 N.E. 726 (1928); 4 AM. JUR. *Arrest* § 129 (1936).

[94]   OHIO REV. CODE ANN. § 2921.23 (Anderson 2003).

[95]   40 Ill. App. 3d 303, 352 N.E.2d 352 (1976).

[96]   FLA. STAT. ANN. § 837.05 (West 2003).

[97]   KY. REV. STAT. ANN. § 519.040 (Baldwin 2002).

[98] MODEL PENAL CODE § 241.6 (1985).

[99] MODEL PENAL CODE § 241.7 (1985).

[100] OHIO REV. CODE ANN. § 2921.12 (Anderson 2003).

[101] State v. McNeeley, 548 N.E.2d 961 (Ohio 1988).

[102] Burdell v. Commonwealth, 990 S.W.2d 628 (Ky. 1999).

United States Criminal Code: Offenses Against Persons and Property

13

Chapter Outline

Cases

Defining crimes: *United States v. Fowler,* 879 F. Supp. 575
     (E.D. Va. 1995)
Factual/legal impossibility: *Helder v. United States*, 2006 U.S. App.
     LEXIS 15995 (6/26/2006)
Federal carjacking: *United States v. Cobb*, 144 F.3d 319 (4th Cir. 1998)
Extortion: *United States v. Jackson*, 986 F. Supp. 829 (S.D.N.Y. 1997)

§ 13.1.1 Introduction

In the last three chapters of this text, we will introduce some aspects of federal criminal law. Section numbers are keyed to the same discussions in Chapters 1 through 12 (i.e., this section refers to the similar discussion in Chapter 1; Section 1.1). This discussion is not meant to be an exhaustive treatment of the federal code and only highlights, using certain laws, how the federal laws are similar to or different from state statutes.

Federal crimes are enacted by Congress and defined in the United States Code. Common law is not the origin of federal law; federal laws are purely statutory. This means that courts, when interpreting federal laws, must decide what Congress intended by the passage of the law.

§ 13.1.2 Definitions of Crime—Source of Law

As stated above, the source of federal law is Congress. Recall that while the Constitution gives the states broad police powers, the federal government's powers are strictly enumerated in Article I, Section 8 of the Constitution. Federal criminal laws must be associated with one of these specifically enumerated powers. Some crimes, such as treason and smuggling, are clearly granted by the federal government's power and duty to protect our borders. These crimes, which are clearly federal in nature, have no counterpart in state criminal laws.

Other crimes, however, are not directly related to federal powers but are derived from them. For instance, the federal government has the power to regulate interstate and foreign commerce. The **commerce clause** has been interpreted broadly to allow the federal government to pass the Civil Rights Act of 1964 (and its progeny), prohibiting discrimination on the basis of race, sex, or membership in other protected classes by businesses that participate in interstate commerce. The commerce clause is also the source for the federal government's power to pass federal criminal statutes covering kidnapping (when the victim is transported across state lines or the federal mail is used in the crime). Furthermore, most of the regulatory crimes discussed in Chapter 15 that criminalize activities of corporations in the areas of health and safety and securities transactions are derived from the power of the commerce clause. In other areas, federal laws have been created that, historically, were addressed solely by the states' police power. Proponents of the "federalization" of criminal law argue that federal law enforcement and prosecutors have the jurisdiction and resources necessary to combat crime that is increasingly national and even international in scope. Opponents of the proliferation of federal laws argue that the federal government is usurping state authority in deciding what should and what should not be criminal.

Federal crimes can be found in the **United States Code**. Most federal crimes can be found in Title 18, although they also can be found in Title 42. Many complain that the United States Code is not organized in any logical way as are the Model Penal Code and most state penal codes; rather, the U.S. Code has crimes listed alphabetically. Efforts to modernize have been unsuccessful.

Federal crimes are prosecuted by U.S. District Attorneys in U.S. District Courts. There are 94 District Courts in the United States. These **District Courts** are organized into 12 circuits. Appeals from District Courts are heard in U.S. Courts of Appeal. There are 13 Courts of Appeal (one for each circuit and one special federal circuit). Appeals from a Court of Appeal may be heard by the Supreme Court.

Although the Supreme Court is the law of the land and governs all federal courts as well as state courts, lower-level federal courts have more limited jurisdiction. Thus, a holding from a District Court has only persuasive authority over other Districts. The same is true of **Courts of Appeals**. In fact, one of the reasons that the Supreme Court accepts a case is when there is disagreement among the Circuit Courts.

§ 13.1.6   Constitutional Challenges

While the federal government has the power to define federal crimes, the Constitution protects us against laws that abridge our freedoms. For instance, no federal law can be vague, punish behavior after the fact (ex post facto), or infringe on freedom of expression, association, or religion. We have already discussed these protections in Chapter 1.6, but it should be emphasized that the original intent of the framers was to put these protections in place against unfair federal laws. Their application to state statutes came later, with the interpretation of the due process clause of the Fourteenth Amendment as protecting state citizens against state violations that offend "fundamental liberties." The most common constitutional challenges are:

> **CASE: *United States v. Fowler*, 879 F. Supp. 575 (E.D. Va. 1995)**
>
> What was the holding of the case?
>
> What source did the government identify for their right to pass drug laws?

- Vagueness and overbreadth

- Ex post facto

- Infringements upon First Amendment rights of expression, association, religion

In *United States v. Fowler*, the challenge was basically that the federal government had no jurisdiction to pass drug laws, which are the province of the police power of the state. Not surprisingly, Fowler was not successful in his challenge.[1]

§ 13.2.1   Principles of Criminal Liability

In Chapter 2, the elements of criminal liability were discussed. Similar rules of law apply regarding liability for federal crimes. In order to find culpability, the federal prosecutor must prove both the *actus reus* and *mens rea* of the crime. Recall that federal criminal law is purely statutory so the elements of the crime and principles of criminal liability must be defined statutorily.

§ 13.2.2   Parties

Recall from Chapter 2.2 that modern law has, for the most part, abolished the common law designations of party liability. The federal code also abolishes the distinction between principals and accessories. Similar to the Model Penal Code and many state statutes, under federal law, anyone who commits an offense or "aids, abets, counsels, commands, induces or procures its commission" is punished as a principal.[2] In interpreting this provision of the federal code, a federal circuit court explained that, in order to sustain a conviction for aiding and abetting under the statute, the government must show that the underlying offense has occurred. The government must also demonstrate that the defendant associated with the criminal venture, purposely participated in the criminal venture, and sought by his or her actions to make the venture succeed. The court further noted that to participate in the criminal activity means that the defendant acted in some affirmative manner designed to aid the venture.[3]

In a case decided by the Seventh Circuit Court of Appeals, the court added that the aiding and abetting standard has two prongs—association and participation. To prove association, the state must show that the defendant shared the principal's criminal intent. To show participation, there must be evidence that the defendant engaged in some affirmative conduct or overt act, designed to aid in the success of the venture. To prove this affirmative conduct or overt act, "a high level of activity need not be shown, although mere 'presence' and guilt by association are insufficient."[4]

A. Accessory After the Fact

Federal law is similar to the Model Penal Code and many state statutes in that it recognizes accessory after the fact as a separate crime. The federal statute that provides a penalty for one convicted of the offense of accessory after the fact states that:

18 U.S.C. § 3

Whoever, knowing that an offense against the United States had been committed, receives, relieves, comforts or assists the offender in order to hinder or prevent his apprehension, trial or punishment, is an accessory after the fact.[5]

To establish a violation of the accessory after the fact statute, the government is required to prove that the defendant, knowing that the offender has committed an offense, gave him or her comfort or assistance for purposes of hindering or preventing the offender's apprehension, trial, or punishment.[6] A federal circuit court declared that a defendant who is accused of being an accessory after the fact must be shown to have had actual knowledge of each element of the underlying offense.[7]

§ 13.2.3; 13.2.4; 13.2.5   Elements of a Crime

Federal crimes, as state crimes, consist of a criminal act, the requisite state of mind, causation, and concurrence. The general principles that govern *actus reus* (and omission) and *mens rea* discussed in Chapter 2 apply to federal law.

§ 13.2.6   Causation

Federal courts and some state courts apply the "but for" test when considering the causation element of the criminal offense. To prove this element, the government must show that, *but for* the defendant's conduct, the harm would not have occurred. To rebut this argument, the defendant introduces evidence to show that the harm would have occurred in any event, regardless of the defendant's conduct. In *United States v. Pitt-Des Moines, Inc.*,[8] the court held that, in order to prove that the defendant's conduct was the illegal cause, that is, the proximate cause, of a harm, so as to prove the causation element of the criminal offense, the government must prove that the harm was *foreseeable* and the *natural* result of the conduct. The court continued by stating that where the "but for" relationship exists between the defendant's conduct and a harm, the defendant may yet escape criminal liability for the offense containing the causation element if the harmful result is so remote or accidental in its manner of occurrence as to make it unjust to hold the defendant liable for it. In effect, this is proximate cause—the defendant's actions must be the "but for" cause but the eventual result must not be so unforeseeable or unnatural that it cuts off the causal chain.

§ 13.3.1   Capacity and Defenses

As in state courts, federal defendants may argue that they might have committed the acts that were alleged, but that they had either an excuse or justification for their actions.

§ 13.3.2   Infancy

Title 18, Chapter 4032 of the United States Code, titled "Juvenile Delinquency," defines the procedure for disposing of juvenile cases in federal court. A **juvenile** is defined as a person who has not attained his or her eighteenth birthday. It is a policy of the federal government to surrender jurisdiction in juvenile cases to the appropriate legal authorities of the state. In fact, Title 18 § 5032 specifically provides that the proceedings shall not be in a United States Court unless the Attorney General certifies through the appropriate District Court of the United States that:

- the juvenile court or other appropriate court of the state does not have jurisdiction or refuses to assume jurisdiction over said juvenile with respect to such alleged act of juvenile delinquency,

- the State does not have available programs and services adequate for the needs of the juveniles, or

- the offense charged is a crime of violence that is a felony or offense described in specific Sections of the federal law under Title 21, and there is a substantial federal interest in the case or the offense to warrant the exercise of federal jurisdiction.

If the juvenile is not surrendered to state authorities, the case is processed as provided in Chapter 4032 of Title 18 of the U.S. Code. If the juvenile is alleged to have committed an act after his or her sixteenth birthday that, if committed by an adult, would be a felony offense that involves actual or threatened force against another, then the case may be directed to the appropriate District Court of the United States for criminal prosecution.

The purpose of this chapter of the U.S. Code is to remove juveniles from the adult criminal justice system and be helpful and rehabilitative, rather than punitive, and to reduce to some extent the stigma of criminal conviction.[9] In determining that the court did not abuse its discretion in ordering a 17-year-old defendant to be prosecuted as an adult, one court commented that:

> considering the heinous nature of the offense, the defendant's history of resistance to counseling efforts and defiance of authority and the slight prospects of rehabilitation before age 21, when, if proceeded against as a juvenile, defendant would be released, rehabilitated or not," there was no abuse of discretion.[10]

§ 13.3.3   Mental Impairment

Recall from Chapter 3 that many states have reevaluated the insanity defense and some have created the "guilty but insane" conviction instead of the "not guilty by reason of insanity" finding. Federal law has also changed in this regard. Following the jury's verdict of "not guilty by reason of insanity" in the John Hinckley Jr. case,[11] both the House and Senate received proposals to modify or completely abolish the insanity defense. In July 1982, the full Senate Judiciary Committee conducted hearings on proposed legislation. In 1986, Congress passed the "Insanity Defense Reform Act of 1986."[12] The federal law states:

> 18 U.S.C. § 17
>
> (a) Affirmative Defense. It is an affirmative defense to a prosecution under any Federal statute that, at the time of the commission of the acts constituting the offense, the defendant, as result of a severe mental disease or defect, was unable to appreciate the nature and quality or the wrongfulness of his acts. Mental disease or defect does not otherwise constitute a defense.
>
> (b) Burden of Proof. The defendant has the burden of proving the defense of insanity by clear and convincing evidence.[13]

One of the key factors in this federal law is that it shifts the burden of the insanity defense to the defendant. The defendant must demonstrate by clear and convincing evidence that his "severe mental disease or defect" caused him to not appreciate the nature and quality of his wrongful acts. The provisions of the Insanity Defense Reform Act, requiring a defendant to prove insanity by clear and convincing evidence, were challenged as being unconstitutional. However, in two 1986 federal cases, the courts considering the questions agreed that the provisions of the act that shifted the affirmative defense of insanity to the defendant do not violate the due process clause.[14]

A. Competency to Stand Trial

Title 18 U.S. Code § 4241 sets forth the procedures for establishing the mental capacity of the defendant to stand trial. This section provides that at any time after the commencement of a prosecution for an offense and prior to the sentencing of the defendant, the defendant or the attorney for the government may file a motion for a hearing to determine the mental competency of the defendant. The court shall grant the motion, or shall order such a hearing on its own motion, if there is reasonable cause to believe that the defendant may presently be suffering from a mental disease or defect, rendering him mentally incompetent to the extent that he is unable to understand the nature and the consequences of the proceedings against him or to assist properly in his defense. The preponderance of the evidence test is applied in determining whether the defendant is suffering from a mental disease or defect.[15]

§ 13.3.4   Duress or Compulsion

In the 1992 case of *United States v. Johnson*, the U.S. Court of Appeals for the Ninth Circuit stated that the federal criminal law had incorporated the defense of duress and that it had three elements:

- an immediate threat of death or serious bodily injury,
- a well-grounded fear that the threat will be carried out, and
- no reasonable opportunity to escape the threatened harm.[16]

The female defendants in the *Johnson* case were convicted of a variety of drug offenses. The testimony presented at the trial left no doubt that they were involved; however, they argued that their experience with the drug "kingpin" was one of severe physical abuse and that he and his associates threatened them and their family members if they did not continue to participate. The dominant issue on the appeals of the defendants was the duress defense as it interacts with sentencing. In a complicated decision, the court enumerated some general findings before making decisions on the cases; among these were:

- In some circumstances, gender is a factor to be considered in making an exculpatory judgment as to whether the defense of duress applies.

- In determining whether the fear was "well-grounded," the defense of duress permits the fact-finder to take into account the objective situation in which the defendant was allegedly subjected to duress.

- Fear that would be irrational in one set of circumstances may be well-grounded if the experience of the defendant with those applying the threat is such that the defendant can reasonably anticipate being harmed on failure to comply.

- The defendant in this case was not entitled to an instruction on duress in the trial on charges of distribution of drugs, where the defendant made no showing that she could not have escaped the violent drug "lord" far earlier than she finally did.

In this case, the convictions were affirmed but the sentences were vacated and remanded. The court decided that the defendants were entitled to raise the claim of incomplete duress for purposes of sentencing.

As discussed in Chapter 3, in order to present the defense of duress, the defendant must establish an immediate threat of death or serious bodily injury. A federal court explained that there must be a well-grounded fear that the threat will be carried out, and lack of a reasonable opportunity to escape the threatened harm. Fear alone is not enough to establish a prima facie case of duress.[17]

§ 13.3.5   Necessity

In applying the "necessity" rule, a federal court indicated that to invoke the necessity defense, the defendants must show that they were faced with a choice of evils and chose the lesser evil; that they acted to prevent imminent harm; that they reasonably anticipated a direct causal relationship between their conduct and the conduct to be averted, and they had no legal alternatives to violating the law.[18]

§ 13.3.6   Self-Defense

In the case of *United States v. Branch*, the court declared that self-defense and defense of another are affirmative defenses to both murder and voluntary manslaughter, but warned that these defenses must accommodate a citizen's duty to accede to lawful government power and special protection due to federal officers who are discharging their official duties.[19] Agreeing that the evidence did not support the defendant's requested self-defense instruction on the charge of voluntary manslaughter of the Federal Bureau of Alcohol, Tobacco, and Firearms agents, the court noted that a reasonable juror could not doubt that the defendants knew that their targets were federal agents, and the defendants responded to the agents' lawful force with a deadly barrage of gunfire. When a person is identified as a law enforcement officer and uses reasonable force in the performance of his or her law enforcement duties, the use of force to resist an officer is not justified and self-defense does not apply.[20]

Under the federal code, a defendant is entitled to a jury instruction on the theory of self-defense, provided that there is a foundation in evidence, even though the evidence may be weak, insufficient, inconsistent, or of doubtful credibility.[21]

§ 13.3.7   Entrapment

In a case decided in 1992, the U.S. Supreme Court established entrapment principles that not only must be followed in federal courts and by federal law enforcement personnel, but influence investigative procedures practiced by state agencies as well. In *Jacobson v. United States*, two federal government agencies, after finding Jacobson's name on a bookstore mailing list, sent mail to him through five fictitious organizations and bogus pen pals to explore his willingness to break the law.[22] Many of those agencies represented that they were funded to protect and promote sexual freedom and freedom of choice and that they promoted lobbying efforts through catalog sales. After two and one-half years on the government mailing list with periodic solicitations, he finally answered a letter that described concern about child pornography as hysterical nonsense and decried international censorship, and then received a catalog and ordered a magazine depicting young boys engaged in sexual activities. He was arrested after a controlled delivery of a photocopy of the magazine, but a search of his house revealed no material other than those sent by the government and the Bare Boys magazines.

The defendant was convicted in a United States District Court of receiving child pornography and he appealed. The Court of Appeals reversed, but on rehearing affirmed the conviction and certiorari was granted by the U.S. Supreme Court. On the entrapment claim, the jury had been instructed that if he "did not have any intent or disposition to commit the crime charged and was induced or persuaded by law enforcement officers or their agents to commit the crime," then he was entrapped. The majority of the U.S. Supreme Court, in a five-to-four decision, reversed the decision of the lower court and held that "it is our view that the Government did not prove that this predisposition was independent and not the product of the attention that the government had directed at the petitioner since January, 1985."

In explaining their decision, the majority noted that "the Government may not play on the weaknesses of a innocent party and beguile him into committing crimes which he otherwise would not have attempted." Law enforcement officials go too far when they "implant in the mind of an innocent person the disposition to commit the alleged offense and induce its commission in order that they may prosecute."

Following the *Jacobson* decision, the entrapment issue became a popular defense strategy. However, the courts have been reluctant to find that law enforcement officials have "gone too far." The defendant must make a prima facie case that the government's conduct created a substantial risk that the offense would be committed by a person who had no predisposition before the government's involvement.[23]

The justices of the Sixth Circuit Court of Appeals stated the entrapment rule very succinctly—to prove entrapment, the defendant must show that: (1) the government induced him to commit a crime, and (2) he lacked the predisposition to engage in criminal activity.[24] The Ninth Circuit Court elaborated, stating that for a defendant to prove the defense of entrapment, he must point to undisputed evidence making it patently clear that an otherwise innocent person was induced to commit the illegal act by trickery, persuasion, or fraud of a government agent. The Court continued by explaining that the mere suggestion to commit a crime does not amount to inducement for purposes of the entrapment defense, even if the suggestion is made by a friend.[25]

Some federal courts have used such terms as "**entrapment by estoppel**" and "sentencing entrapment" when discussing the entrapment defense. Entrapment by estoppel requires the defendant to establish: (1) that a government official told him the act was legal; (2) that he relied on the advice; (3) that the reliance was reasonable; and (4) that, given the reliance, the prosecution would be unfair.[26] "Sentencing entrapment" occurs when government agents convince offenders who are predisposed only to dealing in small quantities of drugs to deal in higher quantities for the purpose of increasing the resulting sentence of the entrapped defendant.[27]

§ 13.4.1   Preparatory Activity Offenses

The federal code follows the Model Penal Code and state statutes in ascribing criminal liability to acts that do not culminate in the completed crime.

§ 13.4.2   Attempt

The U.S. Code makes it a federal offense to attempt to commit specific acts. For instance, the United States Code includes penalties for attempt to commit murder or manslaughter, attempt to kill foreign officials, and attempt to escape.[28] Under Title 18 § 351 of the U.S. Code, it is a federal offense to kill or attempt to kill or kidnap any individual who is a member of Congress, a member of the Supreme Court, a member of the President's Cabinet, or other designated ranking official. Title 18 § 1751 makes it a crime punishable by imprisonment for any term of years or for life if a person is convicted of attempting to kill or kidnap the President of the United States, President-Elect, Vice President, Vice President-Elect, or members of the President's staff.

The federal statute most often used to prosecute an attempt to kill an officer or employee of the United States is Title 18 § 1114. This section—Protection of Officers and Employees of the United States—makes it possible to prosecute an offender who attempts to kill any officer or employee of the United States or of any branch of the United States government, while that officer or employee is engaged in or on account of the performance of his or her official duties. To obtain a conviction under § 1114 for attempting to kill an officer or an employee of the United States, the government is required to show that:

- the defendant engaged in conduct with the intent of killing the officer or employee,

- the defendant engaged in conduct constituting a substantial step toward the attempted killing, and

- the attempted killing took place while the officer or employee was engaged in or on account of the performance of his or her official duties.[29]

Whether a federal officer is engaged in the performance of his or her official duties depends on whether the federal officer is acting within the scope of what he or she is employed to do, or is engaging in a purely personal activity.[30] For purposes of the statute, Bureau of Alcohol, Tobacco, and Firearms agents and Bureau of Indian Affairs officers are "federal officers." However, an employee of a private company that contracts with the U.S. Postal Service to transport mail is not considered a federal employee.[31]

In federal court, to prove attempt, the government must establish an intent to commit the substantive offense and a substantial step toward its commission that is more than preparation but less than the last act necessary to commit the crime itself.[32] As one court explained, under the two-part test to determine whether a defendant is guilty of an attempted crime, the defendant must first have been acting with the kind of culpability otherwise required for the commission of the crime that he is charged with attempting, and then the defendant must have engaged in conduct that constitutes a substantial step toward the commission of the crime.[33]

A. Factual and Legal Impossibility

Recall that factual impossibility is usually not a defense to any attempt charge. Legal impossibility can be a defense, but it is difficult to distinguish legal impossibility (when the act contemplated is not against the law) from hybrid legal impossibility (when the act contemplated is against the law but the act actually engaged in by the offender is not). In federal law, factual impossibility is not a defense to a charge of attempted murder. In *United States v. Carothers*, the court answered the question concerning impossibility as a defense, stating that factual impossibility is not a defense to a charge of attempted sexual exploitation of a minor.[34] In recent cases, appellants have also argued that it is legal impossibility when the "minor" solicited in Internet chat rooms is actually an undercover officer. Whether it is defined as factual or legal impossibility, offenders who solicit sex from victims they believe to be minors but are actually police officers have no defense to an attempt conviction that the act they attempted was impossible to complete, according to federal court holdings. The defense of legal impossibility has also been used by individuals who thought they were smuggling controlled substances into the country, but the substance turned out to be something else. In these cases, the federal drug statutes specifically deny the use of legal impossibility as a defense. The defendant will be convicted of attempt if the prosecutor can show the other elements of the offense.

> **CASE: *United States v. Helder*, 2006 U.S. App. LEXIS 15995**
>
> What was the holding of this case?
>
> Is this a case of factual or legal impossibility? The "minor" solicited in an Internet chat room is really an adult police officer.

§ 13.4.3   Criminal Solicitation

The section of the federal statute that deals with solicitation to commit a crime of violence provides:

> 18 U.S.C. § 373
>
> (a) Whoever, with intent that another person engage in conduct constituting a felony that has as an element the use, attempted use, or threatened use of physical force against property or against another in violation of the laws of the United States, and under circumstances strongly corroborative of that intent, solicits, commands, induces or otherwise endeavors to persuade such other person to engage in such conduct, shall be imprisoned not more than one-half the maximum term of imprisonment or fined not more than one-half of the maximum fine prescribed for the punishment of the crime solicited, or both: or if the crime solicited is punishable by life imprisonment or death, shall be imprisoned for not more than twenty years.
>
> (b) It is an affirmative defense to a prosecution under this section that, under circumstances manifesting a voluntary and complete renunciation of his criminal intent, the defendant prevented the commission of the crime solicited. A renunciation is not "voluntary and complete" if it is motivated in whole or in part by a decision to postpone the commission of the crime until another time or to substitute another victim or another but similar objective. If the defendant raises the affirmative defense at trial, the defendant has the burden of proving the defense by a preponderance of the evidence.
>
> (c) It is not a defense to a prosecution under this section that the person solicited could not be convicted of the crime because he lacked the state of mind required for its commission, because he was incompetent or irresponsible, or because he is immune from prosecution or is not subject to prosecution.[35]

This provision not only spells out the elements of criminal solicitation and affixes the penalty, but it also includes a provision relating to the defense. According to this statute, renunciation is a defense if the defendant prevented the commission of the crime solicited, but the renunciation must be voluntary and complete. It also provides that the defendant has the burden of proving the affirmative defense by a preponderance of the evidence.

A federal court summarized the elements that must be proved in order to obtain a conviction under this statute. The court said that the elements of the offense of soliciting a crime of violence are: (1) the defendant intended that another commit a violent felony; (2) the circumstances were strongly corroborative of that intent; and (3) the defendant actually solicited, commanded, induced, or otherwise endeavored to persuade another person to commit the violent felony.[36]

In order to convict a person of violating this statute, the prosecution must prove that the solicitation was to commit a federal offense; the fact that the individual uses interstate channels (i.e., mail or telephone) to solicit is insufficient to give rise to federal solicitation unless the crime solicited is a federal offense.[37] However, it is only necessary that the jury find that the solicitation was to commit a federal offense; it is not necessary that a federal offense actually resulted from the solicitation.[38]

In the case of *United States v. McNeill*, the evidence indicated that the defendant, who had been a federal prisoner at the time the alleged offense occurred, sent typewritten letters to a person outside the prison asking that the recipient of the letter physically harm the defendant's brother-in-law and kill the defendant's probation officer. The court found that this, plus other corroborative evidence, was sufficient to sustain a conviction for criminal solicitation under the federal law.[39]

To support a conviction, evidence must show that the defendant clearly intended that another person commit a violent felony. Therefore, when an FBI agent, posing as a hit man, was asked to act as a bill collector, rather than to kill or injure the proposed victim, the evidence was insufficient to support the defendant's conviction. In this case, the defendant was surprised when the agent later appeared and told the defendant that he had kidnapped the victim and retrieved the goods on his own initiative. The defendant had not suggested any violence and never acquiesced in the agent's actions.[40]

§ 13.4.4   Conspiracy

The U.S. Code includes a separate chapter relating to the offense of conspiracy. Section 371 of Title 18 defines the offense of conspiracy and establishes the penalty for violation.

> 18 U.S.C. 371
>
> If two or more persons conspire either to commit any offense against the United States, or to defraud the United States or any agency thereof in any manner or for any purpose and one or more such persons do any act to effect the object of the conspiracy, each shall be fined under this title or imprisoned not more than five years or both.
>
> If, however, the offense, the commission of which is the object of the conspiracy, is a misdemeanor only, the punishment for such conspiracy shall not exceed the maximum punishment provided for each misdemeanor.[41]

One of the purposes of this statute is to make this preparatory crime easier to prosecute. The protection of society from the dangers of the concerted criminal activity of more than one person justifies making criminal conspiracy a federal violation.[42]

Legal News

In December 2008, five Muslim immigrants were convicted of conspiracy to kill American military personnel. The men, who all lived in the Philadelphia area, belonged to a loosely organized group that was infiltrated by a government agents. Although they were acquitted of attempted murder because their planning did not reach the substantial steps necessary for federal attempt, it was found that they had met the elements of conspiracy because they had conducted surveillance at several military installations before deciding on Fort Dix. Prosecutors admitted they were probably months away from an attack. Defense attorneys said there was no conspiracy, that it was all "just talk," and that the group was influenced by the two government informants. The evidence consisted largely of the informants' testimony, along with hundreds of hours of secretly recorded conversations.

Source: Mulvihill, G. (2008). "Jury: 5 Plotted to Kill Troops." Austin American-Statesman, December 23, 2008:A1, A12.

A federal court of appeals, in a case in which the defendant was charged with a violation of Title 18 § 371 of the federal statute, summarized that to prove conspiracy the government must prove beyond a reasonable doubt that two or more people agreed to pursue an unlawful objective together, that the defendant voluntarily agreed to join the conspiracy, and that one of the members of the conspiracy performed an overt act to further the objectives of the conspiracy.[43] That same court in a previous case had held that it was not necessary to prove the elements of the crime by direct evidence, but the elements may be inferred from circumstantial evidence.[44] Another court held that each element of conspiracy may be inferred from circumstantial evidence and the agreement may be inferred from concert of action.[45]

In order to convict a person for a violation of the conspiracy statute, the prosecution must establish that:

- two or more persons;

- conspired or combined together in an agreement;

- to accomplish an unlawful purpose;

- each had knowledge of the identity of the offense that the defendants allegedly conspired to commit, and

- where at least one conspirator committed an overt act in furtherance of the conspiracy.[46]

A federal court, in discussing the elements to be proved, commented that in a conspiracy case, the government must prove that there was an agreement among the defendants to achieve some illegal purpose and that each defendant knowingly contributed efforts in furtherance of the conspiracy.[47] However, it is only necessary that one of the conspirators commit the overt act in furtherance of the agreement if the other defendants knew of the conspiracy and voluntarily participated in it.[48]

In a decision made by the Tenth Circuit Court of Appeals, that court found that the defendant's conviction for conspiracy was supported by the co-conspirator's testimony that the defendant, who was in a position of authority and was in charge of the embezzlement scheme, decided when and how the co-conspirator would cash checks drawn from the account and how the proceeds would be divided.[49]

While generally an overt act is an essential element of the crime of conspiracy and must be alleged in the information, under the Narcotics Conspiracy Statute, the government need not prove any overt acts in furtherance of the conspiracy.[50] This means that the government must simply have evidence of an agreement or understanding to prove a violation of this statute.

A. Racketeer Influenced and Corrupt Organizations Statute (RICO)

In addition to the general conspiracy statute, conspiracy provisions are included in other federal statutes. For example, the Racketeer Influenced and Corrupt Organizations statute (**RICO**) makes it a federal offense to use or invest income derived from a pattern of racketeering activity to acquire an enterprise engaged in or affecting interstate commerce, to acquire an interest in such enterprise through a pattern of racketeering activity, to conduct the affairs of an enterprise through a pattern of racketeering activity, or to conspire to commit any of these violations.[51] The statute requires two or more of the predicate crimes (murder, kidnapping, arson, extortion, robbery, gambling, obstruction of justice, mail and wire fraud, securities fraud, bribery, sports bribery, counterfeiting, embezzlement, prostitution, bankruptcy fraud and drug violations) within 10 years. Most states also have their own RICO statutes that punish similar activities.

This statute, with the conspiracy clause, has resulted in the conviction of those engaged in organized racketeering activities that involve kidnapping, gambling, robbery, bribery, and extortion, as well as authorizing the prosecution of officials who operate on a local level. As an example, the sheriff of Bryan County, Oklahoma, was convicted of violating this federal statute when it was found that he used his position as sheriff to extort payoffs from club operators and others in return for selective enforcement of liquor, gambling, and other laws. Evidence introduced at the trial indicated that the sheriff and a "bag man" conspired to collect payoffs after agreeing not to harass a club operator for failure to close at the required time and for directing a deputy to terminate his investigation of gambling conducted at the club.[52]

Legal News

In United States v. Gotti, the head of the Gambino crime family was charged with racketeering, murder, conspiracy, and a long list of other crimes. Gotti received several life sentences for RICO violations and other crimes. He died in prison in 2002.

Source: United States v. Gotti, 171 F.R.D. 19 (E.D.N.Y. 1997).

Although the RICO statute was originally conceived as a means of prosecuting organized crime figures in federal court, it has been used extensively in various types of conspiracies. For example, a court found that a RICO enterprise existed when a lawyer, a lieutenant in the Cook County Sheriff's Department, and the Chief of Police of Willow Springs, Illinois, entered into an agreement in which the police officers would refer persons arrested, ticketed, or investigated by the Willow Springs Police Department to the lawyer for legal assistance. In addition to this scheme, the three members of this conspiracy were accused of having the attorney's wife killed after she was discovered having an affair, and agreed to conceal all of their actions relating to the wife's murder indefinitely.[53] The reviewing court agreed with the trial court that the jury had abundant evidence to find that the defendants had conspired to commit two or more criminal acts that constitute "racketeering activity" within the meaning of the RICO statute.

The RICO statute has also been used against those who engage in organized harassment or damage to abortion clinics or commit other crimes against those who run the clinics or use their services. However, the Supreme Court has held that the use of this statute in this type of case is improper.[54] We will discuss this case again in the next chapter.

§ 13.5.1   Offenses Against Persons

Not all federal crimes have corresponding state crimes and vice versa. However, in many instances, there are parallel state and federal crimes. Remember that the federal government must find a source for every federal crime in one of its enumerated powers. Thus, homicide, in order to be a federal crime, must victimize a federal official or occur within some federal jurisdiction. There must be a nexus between the crime and a federal power.

§ 13.5.2   Homicide

The federal code retains the common law definition of murder and divides murder into first and second degrees. The felony-murder concept is retained, but the person charged may be found guilty of murder in the first degree only if the felony is, in fact, committed, and the crime perpetrated is one designated in the statute.[55] It is noted that the crimes that are designated are the most serious felony crimes and most were felonies at early common law.

The United States Code defines murder as the unlawful killing of a human being with malice aforethought. Murder in the first degree includes murders that involve "poison, lying in wait, or any other kind of willful, deliberate, malicious, and premeditated killing; or committed in the perpetration of, or attempt to perpetrate, any arson, escape, murder, kidnapping, treason, espionage, sabotage, aggravated sexual abuse or sexual abuse, burglary, or robbery; or perpetrated from a premeditated design unlawfully and maliciously to effect the death of any human being other than him who is killed." All others are murders in the second degree.[56]

A. Definition of "Person"

In determining the meaning of "human being," a federal court decided that the defendant's infliction of injuries to the fetus who was born alive but died as a result of such injuries was within the federal statutory definition of murder.[57] The more current issue is whether the death of a fetus that is killed while in the womb can be considered a crime or whether the common law rule that the fetus must be born alive to be considered a person is applied to federal law.

In 2004, the Laci and Conner Law was passed, amending the United States Code and adding § 1841 "Protection of unborn children."

18 U.S.C. § 1841

(a)(1) Whoever engages in conduct that violates any of the provisions of law listed in subsection (b) and thereby causes the death of, or bodily injury (as defined in section 1365 [18 USCS § 1365]} to, a child, who is in utero at the time the conduct takes place, is guilty of a separate offense under this section.

(2)(A) Except as otherwise provided in this paragraph, the punishment for that separate offense is the same as the punishment provided under Federal law for that conduct had that injury or death occurred to the unborn child's mother.

   (B) An offense under this section does not require proof that—
       (i) the person engaging in the conduct had knowledge or should have had knowledge that he victim of the underlying offense was pregnant; or
       (ii) the defendant intended to cause the death of, or bodily injury to, the unborn child. . . .

The statute goes on to say that if the offender intended to kill the child, then the crime is to be prosecuted as a murder of a person; however, there are also three exceptions:

■ any act done with the consent of the woman to effect a legal abortion;

■ any act done by a medical person to save the life or for the health of the mother;

■ any act committed by the woman herself with respect to her unborn child.

B. Malice Aforethought

One of murder's essential elements is malice aforethought. This is the element that distinguishes manslaughter from murder. The federal courts generally follow the common law concept of malice aforethought. As one federal court explained, common law malice includes three distinct mental states, any one of which is sufficient to prove murder: (1) intent to kill, (2) intent to do serious bodily harm, and (3) "depraved heart."[58]

Although deliberation and premeditation involve prior design to commit murder, no particular period is necessary for such deliberation and premeditation. Premeditation need exist only for a moment before the actual slaying and may be inferred from the brutality of the killing, the number of blows inflicted, physical disparity between the defendant and the victim, and the defendant's efforts to conceal the crime or to avoid detection.[59] The jury, according to one court, is generally allowed to infer premeditation from the fact that the defendant brought a deadly weapon to the scene of the murder.[60]

§ 13.5.4; § 13.5.5   Manslaughter

The U.S. Code defines manslaughter as the unlawful killing of a human being without malice and distinguishes between voluntary and involuntary manslaughter. Voluntary manslaughter is the unlawful killing of a human being without malice upon sudden quarrel or heat of passion.[61]

In explaining this provision of the U.S. Code, a federal court noted that manslaughter occupies the middle ground between excusable, or justifiable, homicide on the one hand, and murder on the other.[62] Another court pointed out that the crime of manslaughter is, in some sense, "irrational" by definition, in that it arises out of a person's passions, but provocations to reduce murder to manslaughter must be such as would arouse reasonable and ordinary persons to kill someone.[63]

Under the federal statute, manslaughter is distinguished from murder by the absence of malice, one of murder's essential elements.[64] Commenting upon the terminology "sudden quarrel or heat of passion" as used in the statute, the majority in the case of *United States v. Paul* stated that if a defendant killed with the mental state required for murder, but the killing occurred in the "heat of passion" caused by adequate provocation, then the defendant is guilty of voluntary manslaughter.[65]

The U.S. Code's definition of *involuntary* manslaughter is similar to the traditional definition. It defines it as the unlawful killing that occurs in the commission of an unlawful act not amounting to a felony, or in the commission of a lawful act done in an unlawful manner or without due caution or circumspection.[66] The elements necessary to prove involuntary manslaughter under the federal code are:

- That the defendant inflicted injuries upon the deceased from which the deceased died;

- That the defendant acted with wanton and reckless disregard for human life;

- That the defendant was at the time committing an unlawful act not amounting to a felony;

- That the defendant knew that his conduct was a threat to the lives of others or had knowledge of circumstances that could have enabled him to reasonably foresee peril to which his act might subject others;

- That it occurred within the special maritime or territorial jurisdiction of the United States.[67]

In interpreting this provision of the federal statute, federal courts have held that manslaughter may result from an accidental or unintentional act and that neither intent nor malice are factors in involuntary manslaughter. As to the degree of negligence, a federal judge explained that a charge of manslaughter by negligence is not made out by proof of simple negligence that would constitute civil liability, but must amount to gross negligence, to be determined on consideration of all the facts of a particular case, and the gross negligence must be shown beyond a reasonable doubt.[68]

§ 13.5.7   Assault and Battery

The three primary federal laws relating to assault are: Title 18 § 111, "Assaulting, resisting, or impeding certain officers or employees"; Title 18 § 112, "Assaulting certain foreign diplomatic and other official personnel"; and Title 18 § 113, "Assaults within maritime and territorial jurisdiction." The federal law relating to assault that is most often enforced is Title 18 § 111. It provides:

> 18 U.S.C. § 111. Assaulting, resisting, or impeding certain officers or employees
>
> (a) In general—Whoever—
>   (1) forcibly assaults, resists, opposes, impedes, intimidates, or interferes with any person designated in section 1114 of this title while engaged in or on account of the performance of official duties; or
>   (2) forcibly assaults or intimidates any person who formerly served as a person designated in section 1114 on account of the performance of official duties during such person's term of service, shall, where the acts in violation of this section constitute only simple assault, be fined under this title or imprisoned not more than one year, or both, and in all other cases, be fined under this title or imprisoned not more than three years, or both.
>
> (b) Enhanced penalty—Whoever, in the commission of any acts described in subsection (a), uses a deadly or dangerous weapon (including a weapon intended to cause death or danger but that fails to do so by reason of a defective component) or inflicts bodily injury, shall be fined under this title or imprisoned not more than ten years, or both.

While no intent to injure a federal officer is required, the prosecution must prove beyond a reasonable doubt that at the time of the assault the victim was engaged in the performance of his or her official duties or was attacked on account of these duties.[69] Federal courts have held the statute covers those who attack a federal officer *because* of the officer's activities (even if not during their performance) and may be violated by a minimal physical contact, or even by threats without physical contact.[70]

As stated in the case of *United States v. Lopez*, the purpose is to provide a federal offense, triable in a federal forum, by which to punish attacks upon federal officers, which is a matter central to the efficiency of federal law enforcement activities.[71] The *Lopez* case also makes it clear that, in determining whether the officers are acting in the performance of their "official duties," the decision is a legal question to be determined by federal courts.

The federal law relating to assault encompasses both assault and battery as defined under the common law. Therefore, physical contact is not necessary. However, the threat of force must be a present one and there must be an ability to inflict harm, not merely interfere with the performance of duty.[72] According to the interpretation by the federal courts, it is not necessary that the assailant be aware that his victim is a federal officer; all that the section requires is an intent to assault, not an intent to assault a federal officer.[73]

§ 13.5.8   Kidnapping

In 1931, Congress and the public became concerned about mounting incidents of professional kidnapping and the apparent inability of state and local authorities to cope with the interstate aspects of the problem. In response to this, bills were introduced in both houses of Congress forbidding the transportation in interstate or foreign commerce of any person kidnapped and held for ransom or reward. Several months after the kidnapping of the Lindbergh baby in March 1932, Congress enacted the first Federal Kidnapping Act, which became known as the "**Lindbergh Law**."[74] This law has since been modified by Congress and interpreted by the courts. The present federal kidnapping statute provides:

18 U.S.C. § 1201. Kidnapping[75]

(a) Whoever unlawfully seizes, confines, inveigles, decoys, kidnaps, abducts, or carries away and holds for ransom or reward or otherwise any person, except in the case of a minor by the parent thereof, when—

   (1) the person is willfully transported in interstate or foreign commerce, regardless of whether the person was alive when transported across a State boundary if the person was alive when the transportation began;

   (2) any such act against the person is done within the special maritime and territorial jurisdiction of the United States;

   (3) any such act against the person is done within the special aircraft jurisdiction of the United States as defined in section 46501 of title 49;

   (4) the person is a foreign official, an internationally protected person, or an official guest as those terms are defined in section 1116(b) of this title; or

(5) the person is among those officers and employees described in section 1114 of this title and any such act against the person is done while the person is engaged in, or on account of, the performance of official duties. . .

shall be punished by imprisonment for any term of years or for life and, if the death of any person results, shall be punished by death or life imprisonment.

(b) With respect to subsection (a)(1), above, the failure to release the victim within twenty-four hours after he shall have been unlawfully seized, confined, inveigled, decoyed, kidnapped, abducted, or carried away shall create a rebuttable presumption that such person has been transported in interstate or foreign commerce. Notwithstanding the preceding sentence, the fact that the presumption under this section has not yet taken effect does not preclude a Federal investigation of a possible violation of this section before the 24-hour period has ended.

(c) If two or more persons conspire to violate this section and one or more of such persons do any overt act to effect the object of the conspiracy, each shall be punished by imprisonment for any term of years or for life.

(d) Whoever attempts to violate subsection (a) shall be punished by imprisonment for not more than twenty years.

(e) If the victim of an offense under subsection (a) is an internationally protected person outside the United States, the United States may exercise jurisdiction over the offense if (1) the victim is a representative, officer, employee, or agent of the United States, (2) an offender is a national of the United States, or (3) an offender is afterwards found in the United States. As used in this subsection, the United States includes all areas under the jurisdiction of the United States including any of the places within the provisions of sections 5 and 7 of this title and section 46501(2) of title 49. For purposes of this subsection, the term "national of the United States" has the meaning prescribed in section 101(a)(22) of the Immigration and Nationality Act (8 U.S.C. 1101(a)(22)).

(f) In the course of enforcement of subsection (a)(4) and any other sections prohibiting a conspiracy or attempt to violate subsection (a)(4), the Attorney General may request assistance from any Federal, state, or local agency, including the Army, Navy, and Air Force, any statute, rule, or regulation to the contrary notwithstanding . . .

A defendant may not be found guilty of kidnapping under the federal statute unless the prosecution can establish transportation in interstate commerce of an unconsenting person who was held for ransom or reward.[76] A federal court explained that the Federal Kidnapping Act was not intended to confer rights on the victims of kidnapping, but rather was enacted to assist the states in enforcement of state kidnapping laws by making it impossible for kidnappers to avoid apprehension merely by moving their victims across state lines.[77] To obtain a conviction for kidnapping, the government must prove four elements:

- transportation in interstate or foreign commerce;

- of an unconsenting person who is;

- held for ransom, reward, or otherwise; and

- acts knowingly and willfully.[78]

In proving that the transportation is in interstate commerce, the prosecution need only show that the victim was taken across any state line, even for a short time.[79] A case decided in 2000 concerned the requirement that the person be willfully transported in interstate commerce. The district court dismissed the charge where the victim, acting because of false pretenses initiated by the defendant, transported himself across state lines, without accompaniment by the alleged perpetrator. The question before the court of appeals was whether the "transportation element" could be met if the defendant did not accompany the victim over state lines but arranged for the victim to cross state lines under false pretenses to discuss a purported job interview. After discussing the provisions of the Federal Kidnapping Act, the appeals court reversed the district court's decision and held that the fact that the defendant willfully caused unaccompanied travel over state lines was sufficient to confer jurisdiction. Referring to previous cases, the court noted that nothing in the policy behind the passage of the Act justifies "rewarding the kidnapper simply because he is ingenious enough to conceal his true motives from his victim."[80]

The phrase "holds for ransom or reward *or otherwise*" was challenged as being unconstitutionally void for vagueness. The court, however, held that the defendant was guilty of kidnapping, because the statute gave fair notice to the defendant that he acted illegally in forcing a woman to ride in an automobile with him, inasmuch as he was motivated by his self-interest in convincing her to remain in a relationship with him, and thus the statute was not unconstitutionally void for vagueness.[81] In another case, the "holds for ransom or reward or otherwise" element was satisfied when the victim was taken away from her home for purposes of silencing her as a potential witness. This came within the "or otherwise" provision of the section, which required that the kidnapping be "for ransom or reward or otherwise."[82]

§ 13.5.10   Hate Crimes

Recognizing that almost all states have enacted hate/bias legislation, is it necessary that Congress pass legislation that would make such crimes federal offenses? If Congress determines that such crimes are a necessary addition, does Congress have the power to enact this legislation? The major arguments against such legislation are that such legislation punishes thoughts, and, as such, violates First Amendment protections and that the behavior is already punished under existing statutes.

Today there is no federal hate crime statute *per se* even though the Hate Crimes Statistics Act of 1990 (and its subsequent amendments), mandate the collection of hate crime statistics. There are sections in the U.S. Code that can be used to prosecute those who commit crimes against an individual or group based on their race, religion, nationality, or ethnicity. The sections include 18 U.S.C. §241 (Conspiracy Against Rights); 18 U.S.C. §245 (Interference with Federally Protected Activities); and, 18 U.S.C. §247 (Damage to Religious Property, Obstruction in Free Exercise of Religious Beliefs).

§ 13.6.1   Offenses Against Persons—Sex Offenses

There must be a nexus between any federal crime and a federal power. The nexus for sex offenses is typically the commerce clause by transporting the victim across state lines or using the mail or wire transmissions. The other possible nexus is that the offense occurred within federal maritime or other territorial jurisdiction.

§ 13.6.2   Rape and 13.6.4 Sexual Abuse

The federal sexual abuse statute includes the *actus reus* of common law rape and modern sexual assault. It defines sexual assault similarly to state statutes, and the application is limited to offenses that occur within federal jurisdiction.

18 U.S.C. § 2241 Aggravated Sexual Abuse[83]

(a) By force or threat. Whoever, in the special maritime and territorial jurisdiction of the United States or in a Federal prison, knowingly causes another person to engage in a sexual act—
    (1) by using force against that other person; or
    (2) by threatening or placing that other person in fear that any person will be subjected to death, serious bodily injury, or kidnapping;

or attempts to do so, shall be fined under this title, imprisoned for any term of years or life, or both.

(b) By other means. Whoever, in the special maritime and territorial jurisdiction of the United States or in a Federal prison, knowingly—

    (1) renders another person unconscious and thereby engages in a sexual act with that other person; or
    (2) administers to another person by force or threat of force, or without the knowledge or permission of that person, a drug, intoxicant, or other similar substance and thereby—

      (A) substantially impairs the ability of that other person to appraise or control conduct; and

      (B) engages in a sexual act with that other person;

or attempts to do so, shall be fined under this title, imprisoned for any term of years or life, or both.

(c) **With children.**—Whoever crosses a State line with intent to engage in a sexual act with a person who has not attained the age of 12 years, or in the special maritime and territorial jurisdiction of the United States or in a Federal prison, knowingly engages in a sexual act with another person who has not attained the age of 12 years, or knowingly engages in a sexual act under the circumstances described in subsections (a) and (b) with another person who has attained the age of 12 years but has not attained the age of 16 years (and is at least 4 years younger than the person so engaging), or attempts to do so, shall be fined under this title, imprisoned for any term of years or life, or both. If the defendant has previously been convicted of another Federal offense under this subsection, or of a State offense that would have been an offense under either such provision had the offense occurred in a Federal prison, unless the death penalty is imposed, the defendant shall be sentenced to life in prison.

(d) **State of mind proof requirement.**—In a prosecution under subsection (c) of this section, the Government need not prove that the defendant knew that the other person engaging in the sexual act had not attained the age of 12 years.

If a rape occurs in a federal prison, it will be prosecuted under federal law. In a prosecution under this statute, a federal court found that the disparity in power between a jail warden and an inmate, combined with physical restraint, is sufficient to satisfy the force requirement of the statute proscribing aggravated sexual abuse within the special maritime or territorial jurisdiction of the United States.[84]

In addition to the aggravated sexual abuse statute, the federal code includes the description of a "sexual abuse" crime with lesser penalties. It provides:

18 U.S.C. § 2242 Sexual Abuse[85]

Whoever, in the special maritime and territorial jurisdiction of the United States or in a Federal prison, knowingly—

(1) causes another person to engage in a sexual act by threatening or placing that other person in fear (other than by threatening or placing that other person in fear that any person will be subjected to death, serious bodily injury or kidnapping); or

(2) engages in a sexual act with another person if that other person is—
    (A) incapable of appraising the nature of the conduct; or
    (B) physically incapable of declining participation in, or communicating unwillingness to engage in, that sexual act; or attempts to do so, shall be fined under this title, imprisoned not more than 20 years, or both.

These statutes apply if the acts occur within the special maritime and territorial jurisdiction of the United States or in a federal prison. If the acts do occur in the exclusive jurisdiction of the United States, as defined, the trial is held in federal court. In some instances concurrent jurisdiction exists and both the federal government and the state involved have jurisdiction; in this case, the defendant may be tried in either federal or state court.

Two sections of the United States Code prohibit the interstate transportation of individuals for the purpose of engaging in prostitution or any other sexual activity that is a crime (18 U.S.C. §2421); or the enticing, encouraging, or otherwise fraudulently persuading an individual to cross state lines for criminal sexual activity (18 U.S.C. § 2422)[86] This provision has been used when an offender transports the victim across state lines and then sexually assaults them because sexual assault falls under the residual category of sexual activity. In a 1985 case, a federal court of appeals agreed that transporting a female for the purpose of committing rape was within the purview of 18 U.S.C. §§ 2421 and 2422.[87]

§ 13.6.3   Sodomy

There is no general federal code provision relating to sodomy, although the Uniform Code of Military Justice (UCMJ) contains a punitive article making oral sex illegal for members of the armed forces.[88]

§ 13.6.7   Other Sex-Related Offenses Against the Person

In addition to Sections 2241 and 2242, there are several other provisions of the United States Code that relate to sexual offenses that occur within the maritime or territorial jurisdiction of the federal government. Section 2243 ("Sexual abuse of a minor or ward") makes it a crime to knowingly engage in a sexual act with another person who has attained the age of 12 but has not attained the age of 16, or knowingly engages in a sexual act with another person who is in official detention and under the custody, supervisory, or disciplinary authority of the person so engaging. Section 2244 ("Abusive sexual contact") makes it a crime for a person to knowingly engage in or cause sexual conduct with or by another person, if to do so would violate § 2241 of Title 18, or knowingly engages in sexual conduct with another person without that other person's permission. Section 2244 includes a provision that if the sexual contact is with an individual who has not attained the age of 12 years, the maximum term of imprisonment that may be imposed for the offense shall be twice that otherwise provided in the section.

Finding that child exploitation has become a multimillion dollar industry infiltrated by elements of organized crime, Congress in 1986 added the federal offense of "Sexual exploitation of children."[89] This comprehensive statute makes it possible for federal agents to work in concert with state agents in apprehending and prosecuting child exploiters. It was held to be constitutional by a federal district court in Pennsylvania in 1987.[90]

§ 13.7.1   Offenses Against Property— Destruction and Intrusion Offenses

As with all federal crimes, there must be a nexus between one of the federal powers and the crime. In property cases, it is typically because the crime involves a federal building or property.

§ 13.7.2   Arson

Title 18 § 81 of the U.S. Code provides a penalty for those who commit arson within the special maritime and territorial jurisdiction of the United States. This section provides:

> 18 U.S.C. § 81[91]
>
> Whoever, within the special maritime and territorial jurisdiction of the United States, willfully and maliciously sets fire to or burns any building, structure or vessel, any machinery or building materials or supplies, military or naval stores, munitions of war, or any structural aids or appliances for navigation or shipping, or attempts or conspires to do such an act, shall be imprisoned for not more than 25 years, fined the greater of the fine under this title or the cost of repairing or replacing any property that is damaged or destroyed, or both. If the building be a dwelling or if the life of any person be placed in jeopardy, he shall be fined under this title or imprisoned for any term of years or for life, or both.

This statute punishes arson when it is committed within the maritime and territorial jurisdiction of the United States. A federal court determined that the criminal intent necessary to satisfy the "willful and malicious" elements of the arson statute includes not only acts done with the intent of burning the buildings, but acts done with the knowledge that the burning of the building was practically certain to result.[92]

A different arson statute utilizes the commerce clause power of the federal government and assumes jurisdiction of arson when it is directed to targets that are involved in interstate or foreign commerce or in an activity affecting interstate commerce. The statute provides:

18 U.S.C. § 844[93]

(i) Whoever maliciously damages or destroys, or attempts to damage or
     destroy, by means of fire or an explosive, any building, vehicle, or other
     real or personal property used in interstate or foreign commerce or in
     any activity affecting interstate or foreign commerce, shall be impris-
     oned for not less than 5 years and not more than 20 years, fined under
     this title, or both; and if personal injury results to any person, including
     any public safety officer performing duties as a direct or proximate
     result of conduct prohibited by this subsection, shall be imprisoned for
     not less than 7 years and not more than 40 years, fined under this title,
     or both; and if death results to any person, including any public safety
     officer performing duties as a direct or proximate result of conduct
     prohibited by this subsection, shall also be subject to imprisonment for
     any term of years, or to the death penalty or to life imprisonment.

This statute, which gives broad authority to federal agencies, has been
challenged as overbroad and outside the federal government's power. However, the courts have been consistent in upholding the constitutionality of
the statute. As one court pointed out, the federal arson statute falls within
permissible regulation under Congress's commerce power, in that it protects
property that is used in either interstate or foreign commerce or in any activity
affecting interstate or foreign commerce.[94]

Under the statute, the government must establish that the damaged or
destroyed property was used in interstate commerce or in an activity that
affected interstate or foreign commerce. The phrase, "any activity affecting
interstate or foreign commerce," has been interpreted exceedingly broadly.
For example, a restaurant that the defendant burned down for purposes of col-
lecting insurance proceeds had a "substantial effect on interstate commerce,"
thus supporting the conviction under the federal arson statute, because the
restaurant purchased meat and poultry from an out-of-state supplier on a
regular basis, and the insurer's headquarters were out-of-state.[95]

In another case, a commercial establishment, which received supplies of
natural gas via interstate commerce, satisfied the interstate commerce element.[96] A federal court found no difficulty in determining that the interstate
commerce requirement was satisfied when the case involved the arson of a
building that was located in Iowa, owned by a Kansas resident, and served by
natural gas arriving from out-of-state.[97] Further defining the scope of the federal arson statute, a federal circuit court indicated that in resolving whether a
sufficient interstate commerce nexus exists, as required to support a conviction
for arson of a building used in an activity affecting interstate commerce, the
proper inquiry is into the function of the building itself, and then a determination of whether that function affects interstate commerce.[98]

A review of the federal cases indicates that there is still some conflict as
to the definition of interstate commerce as used in the statute. In one case,

the court held that property occupied and used by its owner, not for any commercial venture, but as a private residence, was not "properly used in interstate or foreign commerce or in any activity affecting interstate or foreign commerce" within the meaning of the federal arson statute. The fact that the residence received natural gas, a mortgage, and an insurance policy that had crossed state lines did not bring it within the statute.[99] However, a victim's home (firebombed by the defendant), which contained a home office of the victim's family-owned construction business, was used in an activity that "substantially affected" interstate commerce, as required to establish a violation of the federal arson statute. The office was the primary location for the business, business records and supplies were stored at the home, employee payments were written and picked up there, and the business vehicles were occasionally parked there overnight.[100]

§ 13.7.3   Malicious Mischief

To protect property of the United States as well as property within the special maritime and territorial jurisdiction of the United States, federal legislation has been enacted. It provides:

18 U.S.C. § 1361. Government property or contracts[101]

Whoever willfully injures or commits any depredation against any property of the United States, or of any department or agency thereof, or any property which has been or is being manufactured or constructed for the United States, or any department or agency thereof, or attempts to commit any of the foregoing offenses, shall be punished as follows:

If the damage or attempted damage to such property exceeds the sum of $1,000, by a fine under this title or imprisonment for not more than ten years, or both; if the damage or attempted damage to such property does not exceed the sum of $1,000, by a fine under this title or by imprisonment for not more than one year, or both.

This section of the federal code requires proof that the act was done willfully. A federal court decided that a defendant's conviction under this statute was not prejudiced by the court's refusal to give "specific intent" instructions, when the court defined "willfully" as used in the criminal statutes and when evidence was sufficient to support a conviction under the "willful" standard.[102] In addition, the prosecution must show ownership of the property as defined in the statute. The fact that the Navy exercised dominion and control over planes and that they had been subject to practical usage of the government was sufficient to establish a "property right" for purposes of the statute.[103] Furthermore, the government must prove the damage amount element to convict a defendant.[104]

The second malicious mischief statute provides:

18 U.S.C. § 1363 Buildings or property within special maritime and territorial jurisdiction[105]

Whoever, within the special maritime and territorial jurisdiction of the United States, willfully and maliciously destroys or injures or attempts to destroy or injure any structure, conveyance, or other real or personal property, shall be fined under this title or imprisoned not more than five years, or both, and if the building be a dwelling, or the life of any person be placed in jeopardy, shall be fined under this title or imprisoned not more than twenty years, or both.

In addition to introducing evidence to show that the acts occurred within the special maritime and territorial jurisdiction of the United States as defined in Title 18 U.S.C. § 7, the government must prove willful and malicious destruction or injury, or attempts to destroy or injure a structure, conveyance, or other real or personal property, as defined by statute or case law. As the statute indicates, if one is convicted of violating this statute, the penalty is as defined under the title or imprisonment of not more than five years, or both. However, if the building is a dwelling or if the life of any person is placed in jeopardy, the person convicted shall be fined as provided in the statute or imprisoned for not more than 20 years, or both.[106]

§ 13.7.4   Criminal Trespass

Because trespass is generally a personal property crime, there is no general trespass law in the U.S. Code. Instead, there are a variety of specific statutes directed to types of trespass, either prohibiting trespass on certain federal property, trespass to perform certain prohibited acts, or both. For instance, in Chapter 91 (Public Land), Section 183, the crime of "trespass on national forest lands" is defined. In Chapter 97 (Railroads), Section 1991, the crime of "Entering a train to commit a crime" is defined. The U.S. Code also has a statute directed toward trespass on military installations:

18 U.S.C. § 1382 Entering Military, Naval, or Coast Guard Property[107]

Whoever, within the jurisdiction of the United States, goes upon any military, naval, or Coast Guard reservation, post, fort, arsenal, yard, station, or installation, for any purpose prohibited by law or lawful regulation; or

Whoever reenters or is found within any such reservation, post, fort, arsenal, yard, station, or installation, after having been removed therefrom or ordered not to reenter by any officer or person in command or charge thereof—

Shall be fined under this title or imprisoned not more than six months, or both.

A federal court decided that this statute was not unconstitutional under the First Amendment when applied to defendants who were protesting against the military in light of the traditional need of the military to retain control over the scope and extent of public activity on military bases.[108] However, the government must prove beyond a reasonable doubt that the area where the defendant was arrested constituted part of a military reservation for purposes of this statute.[109]

§ 13.7.6   Burglary

Chapter 103 of the United States Code includes the federal offenses relating to robbery and burglary. This chapter defines the crimes that have general application, such as bank robbery, as well as crimes that apply within the special maritime and territorial jurisdiction of the United States. There are some federal crimes that have elements similar to those that make up the common law offense of burglary. For example, the federal code relating to breaking into a federal post office provides:

> 18 U.S.C. § 2115
>
> Whoever forcibly breaks into or attempts to break into any post office, or any building used in whole or in part as a post office, with intent to commit in such post office, or building or part thereof, so used, any larceny or other deprivation, shall be fined under this title or imprisoned not more than 5 years, or both.[110]

In the case of *United States v. Gibson*, the Circuit Court, in discussing the elements of this offense, indicated that an offense is established when the government shows forcible entry into some part of the building and an intent to commit larceny in a part of the building used as a post office.[111] As in the case of a common law burglary offense, if the prosecution indicates in the indictment that there is a breaking, then there must be substantial evidence to show affirmatively and beyond a reasonable doubt that there was, in fact, a breaking of a building in which a post office is located.[112]

A second federal crime, which includes some of the elements of common law burglary, provides a penalty for breaking into railway or steamboat post offices.[113] Section 2117 of the United States Code makes it a crime to break the seal or lock of any railroad car, vessel, aircraft, mortar truck, wagon, or other vehicle or any pipeline system containing interstate or foreign shipments, of freight or express or other property, or entering any such vehicle or pipeline system with the intent in either case to commit larceny. Violators of this section may be fined as provided in the U.S. Code or imprisoned not more than 10 years, or both. An unusual provision of this statute makes it clear that a judgment of conviction or acquittal on the merits under the laws of any state shall be a bar to prosecution under this section for the same act or acts.

A more recently enacted federal statute deals with robberies and burglaries involving controlled substances. Section 2118 of the U.S. Code provides for a fine or imprisonment, or both, if one is found guilty of entering or attempting to enter, without authority, business premises or property of a person registered with the Drug Enforcement Administration, with intent to steal any material or a compound containing any quantity of a controlled substance.[114] The part of the Controlled Substance Registration Protection Act making it illegal to enter business premises of the registrant with intent to steal controlled substances was challenged as unconstitutional. The federal court decided, however, that the authority granted to the federal government to enact this statute did not exceed the scope of Congress's power under the commerce clause of the Constitution.[115] A federal reviewing court determined that a drugstore was a "person registered with the Drug Enforcement Administration" for purposes of the federal statute prohibiting burglaries involving controlled substances.[116] Thus, burglary of a drugstore might be prosecuted as a federal crime rather than as a state crime.

§ 13.8.1 Theft Offenses

The U.S. Code provision relating to larceny includes the common law elements of larceny plus the requirement that the offense be committed within the special maritime and territorial jurisdiction of the United States.[117]

> 18 U.S.C. § 661. Within special maritime and territorial jurisdiction
>
> Whoever, within the special maritime and territorial jurisdiction of the United States, takes and carries away, with intent to steal or purloin, any personal property of another shall be punished as follows:
>
> If the property taken is of a value exceeding $1,000, or is taken from the person of another, by a fine under this title, or imprisonment for not more than five years, or both; in all other cases, by a fine under this title or by imprisonment not more than one year, or both.[118]

In interpreting the provisions of the federal statute, the federal courts have indicated that the purpose of the law is to broaden the common law crime of larceny.[119] Examples of thefts that come within the purview of this provision include stealing from an officer's club on a U.S. Army post in Virginia, and taking and carrying away with intent to steal a coat and purse belonging to another at a Veterans Administration Hospital.[120]

In addition to the law relating to thefts on government property, federal law provides penalties for theft from interstate commerce, and thefts from organizations, governments, or agencies annually receiving in excess of $10,000 in federal assistance.[121]

Legal News

In December 2008, a computer technician who worked for the Naval Research Laboratory in southwest Washington D.C. was convicted of federal theft after officials discovered he was responsible for perhaps the largest computer theft crime in federal history. Over the course of 10 years, the man carried so many pieces of computer equipment from the facility he worked in that he built a 2,775 square foot warehouse to store it in. It cost the government $150,000 just to inventory the vast store of keyboards, floppy disks, hard drives, cables, and devices that he had stored. He sold some of the stolen items on Ebay and used others to install and repair computers in a side business, but the sheer volume of the items indicated an obsessive-compulsive disorder, according to his lawyer. Officials were especially concerned that many of the stolen items, including floppy disks, held sensitive data.

Source: Wilber, D. (2008). "Navy Lab Thief Gets 18 Months in Prison." Washington Post, December 23, 2008:B01.

§ 13.8.3   Robbery

Chapter 103 of the U.S. Code relates to both robbery and burglary. Some sections apply throughout the United States, while others relate to crimes committed within the special maritime or territorial jurisdiction of the United States. Many of the common law elements of robbery are carried over into the federal offense of bank robbery. They include taking, by force and violence or by intimidation, from the person or presence of another, any personal property or money or other things of value. However, the larceny portion of 18 U.S.C. § 2113(a), defining bank robbery and incidental crimes, does not require the common law elements of taking and carrying away.[122]

Title 18 § 2112 makes it a federal crime for one person to rob another of any kind of personal property belonging to the United States.[123] Anyone found guilty of violating this statute shall be imprisoned for not more than 15 years. To be found guilty under this statute, possession or use of a deadly weapon is not required; all that is required is that the prosecution establish that the taking was by force, or threat of force, and the property taken was personal property belonging to the United States.[124]

In addition to providing a penalty for stealing or robbing another of personal property of the United States, the U.S. Code provides a penalty for bank robbery.[125] This very comprehensive bank robbery statute was added to make it possible for federal investigators to assist in protecting the assets of banks, credit unions, and savings and loan associations. It provides in part:

> 18 U.S.C. § 2113
>
> (a) Whoever, by force and violence, or by intimidation, takes, or attempts to take, from the person or presence of another, or obtains or attempts to obtain by extortion, any property or money or any other thing of value belonging to, or in the care, custody, control, management, or possession of, any bank, credit union, or any savings and loan association, shall be fined under this title or imprisoned not more than 20 years, or both.

A federal court considering the constitutionality of this federal statute held that the federal bank robbery statute has the necessary nexus to interstate commerce because the statute's coverage is limited to banks that are members of the Federal Reserve System or insured by the Federal Deposit Insurance Corporation (FDIC).[126] The court explained that those financial institutions are instrumentalities and channels of interstate commerce, and regulation of those institutions is within the Congress's commerce clause power.

To prove the offense of bank robbery, the government must show that:

- an individual or individuals;

- used force and violence or intimidation;

- to take or attempt to take;

- from the person or presence of another;

- money, property, or anything of value;

- belonging to or in the care, custody, control, management, or possession;

- of a bank, credit union, or savings and loan institution.[127]

"Force and violence," within the meaning of this bank robbery statute, includes robbery of a bank teller at gunpoint.[128] "Intimidation," as used in the bank robbery statute, includes the threat of force, even though the threat is a bluff.[129] The intimidation element of the bank robbery statute is satisfied even if the defendant did not intend intimidation. A defendant was charged with the robbery of a bank in Spring Lake, North Carolina. The facts indicate that the defendant reached over a bank teller counter "as if trying to grab" the teller, vaulted over the counter, and took money from the money drawer. The defendant argued that the government failed to prove that he intended to intimidate the teller,[130] but his actions were sufficient to sustain the conviction of robbery

An additional section of the statute also includes a penalty for entering or attempting to enter a bank, credit union, or savings and loan association with the intent to commit any felony affecting one of the financial institutions. If, in committing or attempting to commit robbery as defined, the perpetrator puts in jeopardy the life of any person by the use of a dangerous weapon or device, the penalty is a fine as provided under this title or imprisonment for not more than 25 years, or both.[131]

In interpreting the term "enter" as used in this statute, one federal case held that entry into the night depository located within the walls of the bank is an "entry" into a bank for purposes of this statute, which prohibits entry with intent to commit a felony.[132] Also, the removal of unprocessed deposits from the bank's night depository is a felony that "affects" a bank within the meaning of the statute prohibiting entry into a bank with intent to commit a felony affecting the bank.[133]

This statute does not apply unless the bank is a member of the Federal Reserve System, is organized or operated under the laws of the United States, or is a bank whose deposits are insured by the Federal Deposit Insurance Corporation (FDIC). This wording and the limitations that refer to the savings and loan associations and credit unions are necessary to avoid a successful constitutional challenge.[134]

Recognizing the increase in motor vehicle theft with its growing threat to human life and to the economic well-being of the nation, Congress enacted the "Anti-Car Theft Act" (the carjacking statute). The act provides:[135]

> 18 U.S.C. § 2119
>
> Whoever, with the intent to cause death or serious bodily harm, takes a motor vehicle that has been transported, shipped, or received in interstate or foreign commerce from the person or presence of another by force or violence or by intimidation, or attempts to do so, shall—
>
> (1) be fined under this title or imprisoned not more than 15 years, or both,
>
> (2) if serious bodily injury (as defined in § 1365 of this title, including any conduct that, if the conduct occurred in the special maritime and territorial jurisdiction of the United States, would violate § 2241 or § 2242 of this title) results, be fined under this title or imprisoned not more than 25 years, or both, and
>
> (3) if death results, be fined under this title or imprisoned for any number of years up to life, or both, or sentenced to death.

Following the passage of the act, several courts found no problems with its constitutionality. In a 1998 case, a federal court held that the federal carjacking statute, under which the defendant was prosecuted, contained an express jurisdictional element, in that it applied only to a forcible taking of motor vehicles that had moved in interstate commerce, and the statute thus satisfied the minimal nexus required for the statute to be a valid exercise of Congress's commerce clause power.[136]

The statute, as amended, requires a specific intent element. The amendment to the carjacking statute, requiring that the defendant act with intent to cause death or serious bodily harm, converted carjacking from

CASE: *United States v. Cobb*, 144 F.3d 319 (4th Cir. 1998)

What was the holding of the case?

Is it possible for a carjacking to not fall under the federal statute?

a general intent to a specific intent offense, thus requiring the government to prove the mental element above and beyond the special mental state required with respect to taking a vehicle.[137] As the statute and the cases reveal, there can be a conviction if the government proves forcible taking of motor vehicles that have moved in interstate commerce. The wording of the statute gives broad authority to federal agencies in carjacking cases. However, if the government fails to prove that the victim's car had ever been in interstate commerce, the defendant will be entitled to have the carjacking charge dismissed.[138]

In addition to these federal crimes, the federal code includes a penalty for robberies committed within the special maritime and territorial jurisdiction of the United States.[139] This statute provides:

> **18 U.S.C. § 2111**
>
> Whoever, within the special maritime and territorial jurisdiction of the United States, by force and violence, or by intimidation, takes from the person or presence of another anything of value, shall be imprisoned not more than 15 years.

As in other "special maritime and territorial jurisdiction" statutes, this only applies when the crime takes place within the territory defined. In the District of Columbia, robbery retains its common law elements.[140] To support a robbery conviction, the government must prove that there was:

- a felonious taking;

- accompanied by asportation (or carrying away); of

- personal property of value;

- from the person of another in his or her presence;

- against his or her will;

- by violence or by putting in fear;

- animo furandi (the intention to steal).

§ 13.8.4   Embezzlement

The federal statute combines embezzlement and theft and provides:

> **18 U.S.C. § 641**
>
> Whoever embezzles, steals, purloins, or knowingly converts to his own use or the use of another, or without authority, sells, conveys, or disposes of any record, voucher, money, or thing of value of the United States or of any department or agency thereof, or any property made or being made under contract for the United States or any department or agency thereof; or

> Whoever receives, conceals, or retains the same with intent to convert it to his own use or gain, knowing it to have been embezzled, stolen, purloined, or converted—
>
> Shall be fined not more than $10,000 or imprisoned not more than ten years, or both; but if the value of such property does not exceed the sum of $1,000, he shall be fined not more than $1,000 or imprisoned not more than one year, or both.[141]

Making it clear that the statute was to be broadly interpreted, a federal court explained that the statute prohibiting conversion of a "thing of value" of the federal government encompasses a prohibition on conversion of intangible property; Congress intended to enact a broad prohibition against misappropriation of anything belonging to the national government, unrestrained by fine and technical distinctions of common law.[142] Several decisions have been rendered to clarify the meaning of "thing of value of the United States." One federal court held that funds advanced to fuel subcontractors by the Small Business Administration were "property of the United States," within the meaning of the embezzlement statute.[143] In another case, the fact that the marijuana that a customs officer was accused of taking was an illegal substance, and the fact that the government had paid for its destruction did not preclude the marijuana from being a "thing of value" within the statute.[144] However, if the property involved in the dispute does not belong to the United States, then no violation of the statute that deals with embezzlement, stealing, purloining, or knowingly converting property of the United States is possible.[145]

The federal statute also includes an offense of "theft, embezzlement, or misapplication by a bank officer or employee."[146] This provides a penalty where an employee of a federal bank or a bank that is a member of the Federal Reserve System embezzles, abstracts, purloins, or willfully misapplies any of the monies, funds, or credits of such bank. The four essential elements of the offense are:

- the accused was an officer or director of the bank,
- the bank was connected in some way with a national bank or a federally insured bank,
- the accused willfully misapplied the funds of the bank, and
- the accused acted with intent to defraud the bank.[147]

Title 18 § 666 of the federal statute is titled "Theft or bribery concerning programs receiving federal funds."[148] Under this statute, a person may be convicted of embezzlement if the organization from which the property is embezzled is a government or agency that receives in any one-year period benefits in excess of $10,000 under a federal program involving a grant, contract, subsidy, loan, guarantee, insurance, or other form of federal assistance.

In the case of *United States v. Suarez,* the defendant was convicted under this statute of converting police evidence and victim restitution money to his own benefit.[149] Suarez had been charged with taking property, consisting of evidence and restitution payments from the Dearborn Police Department, an organization receiving federal funds for the DARE Program. On appeal, the defendant argued, among other things, that the agency from which he had stolen had an insufficient connection with the federal government to fit within the language of the statute. In reply, the reviewing court held that the conversion conviction did not require a minimal nexus between the alleged criminal activity and the requisite federal funding received by the city police department. The court continued by stating that under 18 U.S.C. § 666 the defendant need not be shown to have actually stolen any of the federal funds given to the "federal recipient" or even that his malfeasance affected these federal funds. The defendant's conviction was affirmed.

§ 13.8.5   Obtaining Property by False Pretenses

Title 18 § 1341 of the U.S. Code is titled "Frauds and Swindles."[150] The purpose of this statute is to protect the integrity of the mails by making it a crime to use them to implement fraudulent schemes of any kind, including the use of the mails to implement fraudulent schemes directed at a state agency.[151]

Any offender who uses the U.S. mail, Internet, or wire transmissions to commit fraud could be subject to federal prosecution in addition to state prosecution. In the fall of 2008, Bernard Madoff was exposed as perpetrating one of the largest frauds, if not the largest, in history with a "Ponzi scheme" that pays off early investors with the money of later investors. Victims who enter Ponzi schemes early believe that the investment is legitimate because they are getting the returns they were promised; however, the whole fraud comes apart when the offender is forced to pay out more than is coming in. Madoff is being charged with violations of the Securities Exchange Commission rather than fraud. We will discuss the case again in Chapter 15.

The mail and wire fraud statutes make it illegal to use the mails or any interstate electronic communication network to perpetrate a fraudulent scheme.[152] These statutes may be invoked in any case in which there is criminal activity that involves even peripheral use of the postal system or telephone communications. The original federal mail fraud statute was enacted in 1872 and has undergone many changes since that time. The original statute only applied to illegal uses of the U.S. Postal Service; however, in September 1994, this statute was amended to include private interstate delivery services, such as Federal Express and United Parcel Service, as well as the U.S. Postal Service.

To prove **mail fraud** under § 1341, the government must show:

1. a scheme to defraud;

2. committed within intent to defraud; and

3. use of the United States mail or private interstate commercial carrier to further the fraudulent scheme.[153] Court decisions have indicated that the government is not required to prove that the scheme to defraud was successful. The government need only prove that a scheme existed in which the use of the mails was reasonably foreseeable and that an actual mailing occurred in furtherance of the scheme.[154]

In enacting the **wire fraud** statute, Congress relied upon the commerce clause; therefore, the wire fraud statute, unlike the mail fraud statute, requires that the communication cross state lines. However, the mail fraud statute and the wire fraud statute share the same language in relevant parts and accordingly the court applies the same analysis to both sets of offenses.[155]

Some examples of frauds that have been prosecuted under these statutes are:

- fraudulent insurance claims[156]

- law partners who worked with a doctor to defraud an insurance company[157]

- use of the mails to file a fraudulent burglary claim[158]

- a police officer who aided and abetted a fraud by skewing an arson investigation[159]

- fraudulent investment schemes[160]

- misrepresentations in the sale of used automobiles[161]

- owners of video gambling devices who lied about their ownership to obtain a state license[162]

In interpreting and explaining the mail fraud statute, the justices of the Seventh Circuit Court of Appeals decided that to convict for mail fraud, the government is not required to prove that the scheme to defraud was successful, but need only prove that a scheme existed in which the use of the mails was reasonably foreseeable and that the actual mailing occurred in furtherance of that scheme.[163] After discussing the elements that must be proved, a federal court reasoned that the federal mail fraud statute requires proof of a knowing and willful scheme or artifice to defraud another of property or money and a subsequent mailing to execute the purpose of the scheme. To satisfy the "use of mails" element of mail fraud, the government must prove that the mails were used for the specific purpose of executing a fraudulent scheme even if the use of the mails was not an essential element of the scheme. It is sufficient that the mailing be incident to an essential part of the scheme.[164]

§ 13.8.6 Extortion

Title 18 of the U.S. Code contains seven sections dealing with extortion and threats.[165] The section that most closely resembles the traditional extortion law is § 873, titled "Blackmail." It provides:

> 18 U.S.C. § 873
>
> Whoever, under a threat of informing, or as a consideration for not informing, against any violation of any law of the United States, demands or receives any money or other valuable thing, shall be fined under this title or imprisoned not more than one year, or both.

The essential elements of this crime are coercion and unlawful consideration.[166] Title 18 § 872 of the federal statute applies to extortion by officers

CASE: *United States v. Jackson*, 986 F. Supp. 829 (1997)

What was the holding of the case?

Can an illegitimate child ever seek compensation from the biological father by threatening action without it being considered extortion?

and employees of the United States.[167] Under this section, an officer or employee of the United States or any department or agency thereof, or representing himself to him or assuming to act as such, under color or pretense of his office or employment, who commits or attempts an act of extortion may be fined or imprisoned as provided in the statute, or both.

Recall from Chapter 8 that Autumn Jackson and her crime partners were charged with violations of 18 U.S.C. § 875 titled "Interstate Communications as well as violations of the New York statute against extortion.[168] This provision punishes those who use interstate communications in ransom demands or threats, but also has a section that punishes extortion threats.

18 U.S.C. § 875 Interstate Communications

. . . (d) Whoever, with intent to extort from any person, firm, association, or corporation, any money or other thing of value, transmits in interstate or foreign commerce any communication containing any threat to injure the property or reputation of the addressee or of another or the reputation of a deceased person or any threat to accuse the addressee or any other person of a crime, shall be fined under this title or imprisoned not more than two years, or both.

18 U.S.C. § 1951 is titled "Interference with Commerce by Threats or Violence:

(a) Whoever in any way or degree obstructs, delays, or affects commerce or the movement of any article or commodity in commerce, by robbery or extortion or attempts or conspires so to do, or commits or threatens physical violence to any person or property in furtherance of a plan or purpose to do anything in violation of this section shall be fined under this title or imprisoned not more than twenty years or both.

(b) As used in this section— . . .
  (2) The term "extortion" means the obtaining of property from another, with his consent, induced by wrongful use of actual or threatened force, violence, or fear, or under color of official right.

Note that some of the statutes described above are based on the federal government's power via jurisdiction, i.e., that the targets or offenders are federal officials, while others are based on the commerce clause, i.e., that the offenders use the mail or telephone in their threats.

§ 13.8.7   Receiving Stolen Property

Title 18 § 2312 makes it a crime for a person to transport a stolen vehicle in interstate commerce.[169] This section provides:

18 U.S.C. § 2312

Whoever transports in interstate or foreign commerce a motor vehicle or aircraft, knowing the same has been stolen, shall be fined under this title or imprisoned not more than five years, or both.

To be convicted of transporting stolen vehicles in interstate commerce, the government must prove that there was a stolen vehicle, that the defendant knew that it was stolen, and the defendant transported the vehicle in interstate commerce.[170] It is not necessary to show that the defendant operated the vehicle, only that the defendant knew it was stolen and facilitated the interstate journey.[171]

The federal law relating to transportation of motor vehicles in interstate commerce was first enacted in 1919 to make it possible for federal officers to assist in reducing the number of auto thefts. The constitutionality of this section was challenged on "void for vagueness" grounds on several occasions, but was found to be valid.[172] In order to convict a person of transporting stolen vehicles in interstate commerce, the government must prove that the vehicle was, in fact, stolen, and that the defendant transported the vehicle in interstate commerce.[173]

The federal statute that deals with receiving stolen property when the crime is committed within the special maritime and territorial jurisdiction of the United States is Title 18 § 662.[174] This section provides:

> **18 U.S.C. § 662**
>
> Whoever, within the special maritime and territorial jurisdiction of the United States, buys, receives, or conceals any money, goods, bank notes, or other things which may be the subject of larceny, which has been feloniously taken, stolen, or embezzled from any other person, knowing the same to have been so taken, stolen, or embezzled, shall be fined not more than $1,000 or imprisoned not more than 3 years, or both; but if the amount or value of the thing so taken, stolen, or embezzled does not exceed $100, he shall be fined not more than $1,000 or imprisoned not more than one year, or both.

After discussing the question of jurisdiction to try a person for receiving stolen property within the special jurisdiction of the United States, a court of appeals agreed that receipt or concealment of the stolen property within the confines of a military reservation was a violation of this section.[175] As in state receiving cases, in order to convict a person for the crime of receiving stolen property, the government must prove:

- that the property was stolen by some person other than the defendant;

- that the defendant received the property and converted it to his own use;

- that the defendant knew that the property that he or she received had been stolen.

A second federal statute specifies a penalty in which a person receives, conceals, stores, barters, or sells vehicles that have been moved in interstate commerce, if that person knew that the vehicle was stolen. This section provides:

> **18 U.S.C. § 2313**
>
> (a) Whoever receives, possesses, conceals, stores, barters, sells, or disposes of any motor vehicle or aircraft, which has crossed a State or United States boundary after being stolen, knowing the same to have been stolen, shall be fined under this title or imprisoned not more than ten years, or both.
>
> (b) For purposes of this section, the term "State" includes a State of the United States, the District of Columbia, and any commonwealth, territory, or possession of the United States.[176]

To convict one of a violation of this section, which proscribes receiving or concealing stolen automobiles, the government must demonstrate that:

- the motor vehicle or aircraft involved was stolen;

- the defendant knew that the motor vehicle or aircraft had been stolen;

- the defendant possessed, concealed, stored, received, bartered, sold, or disposed of the motor vehicle; and

- the vehicle involved was moved in interstate traffic at the time of the defendant's activities.[177]

§ 13.9.1   Forgery

Although Title 18 of the federal code does not include a provision relating to the general crime of forgery, numerous sections include penalties for forgery of specific documents. Title 18 § 495[178] provides that:

> **18 U.S.C. § 495**
>
> Whoever falsely makes, alters, forges, or counterfeits any deed, power of attorney, order, certificate, receipt contract or other writing for the purpose of obtaining or receiving, or of enabling any other person, either directly or indirectly, to obtain or receive from the United States or any officers or agents thereof, any sum of money; or
>
> Whoever utters or publishes as true any such false, forged, altered, or counterfeited writing, with intent to defraud the United States, knowing the same to be false, altered, forged, or counterfeited; or
>
> Whoever transmits to, or presents at any office or officer of the United States, any such writing in support of, or in relation to, any account or claim, with intent to defraud the United States, knowing the same to be false, altered, forged, or counterfeited—
>
> Shall be fined under this title or imprisoned not more than ten years, or both.

In interpreting this code section, the U.S. Supreme Court explained that in the absence of anything to the contrary, it is fair to assume that Congress, in using the word "forgery" in this section, which was adopted in 1823 and which remained in substantially the same form, used that word in its common law sense.[179]

After examining the provisions of Title 18 § 495 and other provisions of the federal code, the Court of Appeals for the Ninth Circuit reasoned that the forger of a treasury check endorsement may be prosecuted under the statutes penalizing those who falsely make, alter, forge, or counterfeit "other writings" with the intent of defrauding the United States (Title 18 § 495) or under the statute providing specific penalties for forgery of treasury checks (Title 18 § 493).[180] A defendant who qualifies for a prosecution under one section could be prosecuted under the other. The federal code provision relating to the federal crime of forgery also applies when the document is offered as genuine when known to be false.

§ 13.9.5   False Advertising

There is no specific provision in the United States Code designated as "deceptive business practices or false advertising." There is, however, a code provision titled "Fair Packaging and Labeling."[181] Title 18 § 893 prohibits financing extortionate extension of credit and § 894 punishes collection of extensions of credit by extortionate means.[182]

§ 13.9.7   Computer Fraud

All federal computer crimes will be discussed in Chapter 15.

§ 13.10 Summary

Not all sections from the chapters discussing state crimes have parallels in this chapter. It is important to understand that federal crimes are defined statutorily in the U.S. Code, they are prosecuted by federal prosecutors, and they are tried in federal courts. Offenders serve time, if convicted and sentenced to prison, in the Federal Bureau of Prisons. In order for the legislature to pass a law creating a crime, it must not violate any of the constitutional rights discussed in Chapter 1 and this chapter. Further, it must have some nexus to federal powers. Most typically, acts that are federal crimes have some connection to interstate commerce or they are committed within the maritime or territorial jurisdiction of the United States.

Review Questions

1. What are the sources for federal criminal laws? Explain the federal court system.

2. What is the source for federal drug laws?

3. Explain the constitutional challenges that are used against federal laws.

4. Explain the federal law's rules of party liability.

5. Explain how the Insanity Defense Reform Act of 1986 changed the federal law regarding prosecution of those who alleged insanity.

6. Explain the elements necessary to use the duress claim against a federal prosecution.

7. What were the issue and holding in *Jacobsen v. United States*? What test of entrapment does the federal government use?

8. Explain how the federal code defines *attempt*. Is there a general attempt statute or not? Explain factual and legal impossibility under federal law.

9. Explain the RICO conspiracy provisions; how are they different from Section 371 of Title 18?

10. What is the Laci and Conner law? What types of homicide are recognized in federal law?

11. The federal law relating to assault that is most often enforced is Title 18 §111. What are the provisions of this federal statute? How have the courts defined "while engaged in the performance of official duties"?

12. Explain the nexus between kidnapping and federal power. Explain the nexus between the rape statute and federal power. Explain what, if any, federal laws address hate crimes.

13. What two sources of power are used for federal arson statutes? Explain. Does the U.S. Code have a general trespass statute? Explain.

14. The federal code section titled "Stolen Property" deals with the transportation and sale of stolen vehicles, securities, and other personal property. What must the government prove in order to convict a person of transporting a stolen vehicle in interstate commerce? How is this different from the carjacking statutes?

15. In addition to state laws regarding robbery, the federal code includes descriptions of robbery offenses. What elements must be proved in order to convict a person of bank robbery under the federal law? What element is required for federal violations that is not required for state violations?

16. The federal statute includes an offense titled "Theft, Embezzlement or Misappropriation by a Bank Officer or Employee." What are the elements of this offense? What other ways might embezzlement become a federal crime?

17. When does a fraud become a federal offense?

18. Discuss the federal crime that Autumn Jackson was charged with. Why wasn't she charged in state court?

19. Discuss the crime of "Interference with Commerce by Threats or Violence."

20. What are the elements of the federal forgery statute described in the text?

Notes

[1]   879 F. Supp. 575 (1995).

[2]   18 U.S.C. § 2.

[3]   United States v. Stewart, 145 F.3d 273 (5th Cir. 1998). *See also* United States v. Hodge, 211 F.3d 74 (3d Cir. 2000), which held that the defendant can be convicted of aiding and abetting a principal in the commission of a crime even if the principal was either acquitted or not charged.

[4]   United States v. Sewell, 159 F.3d 275 (7th Cir. 1998).

[5]   18 U.S.C. § 3.

[6]   United States v. Triplett, 922 F.2d 1174 (5th Cir. 1991).

[7]   United States v. Graves, 143 F.3d 1185 (9th Cir. 1998).

[8]   United States v. Pitt-Des Moines, Inc., 970 F. Supp. 1359 (N.D. Ill. 1997).

[9]   United States v. Frasquillo-Zomosa, 626 F.2d 99 (9th Cir. 1980), *cert. denied*, 449 U.S. 987, 101 S. Ct. 405, 66 L. Ed. 2d 249 (1980); United States v. Hill, 538 F.2d 1072 (4th Cir. 1976). *See also* United States v. Angelo, 88 F.2d 856 (10th Cir. 1996).

[10]   United States v. A.W.J., 804 F.2d 492 (8th Cir. 1986).

[11]   John W. Hinckley, Jr. was charged with the attempted assassination of Ronald Reagan, then President of the United States, assault on a federal officer (a United States Secret Service agent), and the use of a firearm in the commission of a federal offense. He was found not guilty by reason of insanity and committed to the custody of St. Elizabeth's Hospital.

[12]   18 U.S.C. § 4241 *et seq.*

[13]   18 U.S.C. § 17.

[14]   United States v. Freeman, 804 F.2d 1574 (11th Cir. 1986); United States v. Amos, 803 F.2d 419 (8th Cir. 1986).

[15]   United States v. Young, 199 F.2d 697 (S.D. Ohio 2001).

[16]   United States v. Johnson, 956 F.2d 894 (9th Cir. 1992).

[17]   United States v. Moreno, 102 F.3d 994 (9th Cir. 1996). *See also* United States v. Caban, 173 F.3d 89 (1999).

[18]   United States v. Schoon, 955 F.2d 1238 (9th Cir. 1991).

[19]   United States v. Branch, 91 F.3d 699 (5th Cir. 1996).

[20]   United States v. Jennings, 855 F. Supp. 1427 (N.D. Pa. 1994).

[21]   United States v. Sanchez-Lima, 161 F.3d 545 (9th Cir. 1998).

[22]   Jacobson v. United States, 503 U.S. 540, 112 S. Ct. 1535, 118 L. Ed. 2d 174 (1992).

[23]   United States v. Bradfield, 103 F.3d 1207 (5th Cir. 1997). *See also* United States v. Edmonds, 103 F.3d 822 (9th Cir. 1997).

[24]   United States v. Cope, 312 F.3d 757 (6th Cir. 2002).

[25]   United States v. Mendoza-Prado, 314 F.3d 1099 (9th Cir. 2002). *See also* Matteo v. Superintendent, SCI Albion, 171 F.3d 877 (3d Cir. 1999).

[26]   United States v. Ellis, 168 F.3d 558 (1st Cir. 1999).

[27]   United States v. Hunt, 171 F.3d 1192 (8th Cir. 1999).

28   18 U.S.C. § 1113; 18 U.S.C. § 1116; 18 U.S.C. § 751.

29   United States v. Saunders, 166 F.3d 907 (7th Cir. 1999).

30   United States v. Clemons, 32 F.3d 1504 (11th Cir. 1994).

31   United States v. Alvarez, 755 F.2d 830 (11th Cir. 1995); United States v. Oakie, 12 F.3d 1436 (8th Cir. 1993); United States v. Kirkland, 12 F.3d 199 (11th Cir. 1994).

32   United States v. LiCausi, 167 F.3d 36 (1st Cir. 1999).

33   United States v. Crow, 164 F.3d 229 (5th Cir. 1999).

34   United States v. Carothers, 121 F.3d 659 (11th Cir. 1997).

35   18 U.S.C. § 373.

36   United States v. Johnson, 225 F. Supp. 2d 1022 (N.D. Iowa 2002).

37   United States v. Korav, 393 F.2d 212 (9th Cir. 1989).

38   United States v. Razo-Leora, 961 F.2d 1140 (5th Cir. 1992).

39   United States v. McNeill, 387 F.2d 448 (3d Cir. 1989).

40   United States v. Rahman, 34 F.3d 1331 (7th Cir. 1994).

41   18 U.S.C. § 371. *See also* 18 U.S.C. § 372 Conspiracy to Impede or Injure an Officer.

42   United States v. Kohne, 347 F. Supp. 1178 (D. Pa. 1972); United States v. Feola, 420 U.S. 671, 95 S. Ct. 1255, 43 L. Ed. 2d 541 (1975).

43   United States v. Parekh, 926 F.2d 402 (5th Cir. 1991).

44   United States v. Schmick, 904 F.2d 936 (5th Cir. 1990).

45   United States v. Virgen-Moreno, 265 F.3d 276 (5th Cir. 2001).

46   United States v. Rahseparian, 231 F.3d 1267 (10th Cir. 2000).

47   United States v. Maza, 93 F.3d 1390 (8th Cir. 1996). *See also* United States v. Branch, 91 F.3d 699 (5th Cir. 1996). *See also* United States v. Overholt, 307 F.2d 1231 (10th Cir. 2002).

48   United States v. Jobe, 90 F.3d 920 (5th Cir. 1996). *See also* United States v. Wilson, 103 F.3d 1402 (8th Cir. 1997).

49   United States v. Stoner, 98 F.3d 527 (10th Cir. 1996).

50   United States v. Partela, 167 F.3d 687 (1st Cir. 1999); United States v. Jackson, 167 F.3d 1280 (9th Cir. 1999). *See also* United States v. Dumes, 313 F.3d 372 (7th Cir. 2002), which held that to prove conspiracy to possess and distribute cocaine, no overt act need be charged or proven and guilt may be inferred from circumstances and conduct of the parties.

51   Racketeer Influenced and Corrupt Organizations Act, 18 U.S.C. § 1961.

52   United States v. Hampton, 786 F.2d 977 (10th Cir. 1986).

53   United States v. Masters, 924 F.2d 1362 (7th Cir. 1991).

54   Scheidler v. N.O.W., 164 L. Ed. 2d 10 (2006).

55   United States v. Chischilly, 30 F.3d 1144 (9th Cir. 1994).

56   18 U.S.C. § 1111 (1999).

57   United States v. Spencer, 839 F.2d 1341 (9th Cir. 1988), *cert. denied*, 487 U.S. 1238, 108 S. Ct. 2708, 101 L. Ed. 2d 939 (1988).

58   United States v. Quintero, 21 F.3d 885 (9th Cir. 1994); United States v. Livoti, 22 F. Supp. 2d 235 (S.D.N.Y. 1998).

[59] Pruett v. Thompson, 771 F. Supp. 1428 (E.D. Va. 1991).

[60] United States v. Blue Thunder, 604 F.2d 550 (8th Cir.), *cert. denied*, 444 U.S. 902, 100 S. Ct. 215, 62 L. Ed. 2d 139 (1979).

[61] 18 U.S.C. § 1112.

[62] United States v. Hart, 162 F. 192 (N.D. Fla. 1908).

[63] United States v. Collins, 690 F.2d 431, *cert. denied*, 460 U.S. 1046, 103 S. Ct. 1447, 75 L. Ed. 2d 801 (1982).

[64] United States v. Quintero, 21 F.3d 885 (9th Cir. 1994).

[65] United States v. Paul, 37 F.3d 496 (9th Cir. 1994).

[66] 18 U.S.C. § 1112 Manslaughter (Involuntary).

[67] United States v. Sasnett, 925 F.2d 392 (11th Cir. 1991).

[68] Thomas v. United States, 419 F.2d 1203 (D.C. Cir. 1969); United States v. Pardee, 368 F.2d 368 (4th Cir. 1966).

[69] United States v. Sanchez, 914 F.2d 1355 (9th Cir.), *cert. denied*, 111 S. Ct. 1626, 113 L. Ed. 2d 723 (1990).

[70] United States v. Hernandez, 921 F.2d 1569 (11th Cir. 1991).

[71] United States v. Lopez, 710 F.2d 1071 (5th Cir. 1983).

[72] United States v. Bamberger, 452 F.2d 696 (2d Cir.), *cert. denied*, 405 U.S. 1043, 92 S. Ct. 1326, 31 L. Ed. 2d 585 (1971).

[73] United States v. Feola, 420 U.S. 671, 95 S. Ct. 1255, 43 L. Ed. 2d 541 (1975).

[74] United States v. Jackson, 390 U.S. 570, 88 S. Ct. 1209, 20 L. Ed. 2d 138 (1968).

[75] 18 U.S.C. § 1201 as amended in 1971, 1976, 1977, 1978, and 1984.

[76] United States v. Crosby, 713 F.2d 1066 (5th Cir. 1983), *cert. denied*, 464 U.S. 1001 (1983).

[77] Giano v. Martino, 673 F. Supp. 92 (E.D.N.Y. 1987).

[78] United States v. Osborne, 68 F.3d 94 (5th Cir. 1995).

[79] Hall v. United States, 410 F.2d 653 (4th Cir. 1969), *cert. denied*, 396 U.S. 970, 90 S. Ct. 455, 24 L. Ed. 2d 436 (1969).

[80] United States v. Wills, 234 F.3d 174 (4th Cir. 2000).

[81] United States v. Walker, 137 F.3d 1217 (10th Cir. 1998).

[82] United States v. Satterfield, 743 F.2d 827 (11th Cir. 1984), *cert. denied*, 471 U.S. 1117, 105 S. Ct. 2363, 86 L. Ed. 2d 262 (1984).

[83] 18 U.S.C. § 2421.

[84] United States v. Lucas, 157 F.3d 998 (1998).

[85] 18 U.S.C. 2242 Sexual Abuse (1999).

[86] 18 U.S.C. §2421; 2422 (1999).

[87] United States v. Mitchell, 778 F.2d 1271 (7th Cir. 1985).

[88] UCMJ, Article 125 (18 U.S.C. § 925).

[89] 18 U.S.C. § 2251 Sexual Abuse of Children (1999).

[90] United States v. Fenton, 654 F. Supp. 379 (E.D. Pa. 1987). *See also* United States v. Buculei, 262 F.3d 322 (4th Cir. 2001).

[91]   18 U.S.C. 81 (1999).

[92]   United States v. M.W., 890 F.2d 239 (10th Cir. 1989); United States v. Dreamer, 88 F.3d 655 (8th Cir. 1996).

[93]   18 U.S.C. § 844(i). *See also* Title 18 U.S.C. § 1861.

[94]   United States v. Chowdbury, 118 F.3d 742 (11th Cir. 1997). *See also* United States v. Dascenzo, 152 F.3d 1300 (11th Cir. 1998).

[95]   United States v. Latouf, 182 F.3d 820 (6th Cir. 1997).

[96]   United States v. Disanto, 86 F.3d 1238 (1st Cir. 1996).

[97]   United States v. Ryan, 23 F. Supp. 2d 1044 (S.D. Iowa 1998).

[98]   United States v. Tush, 287 F.3d 1294 (10th Cir. 2002).

[99]   Jones v. United States, 529 U.S. 848, 120 S. Ct. 1904, 146 L. Ed. 2d 902 (2000).

[100] United States v. Jimenez, 256 F.3d 330 (5th Cir. 2001).

[101] 18 U.S.C. § 1361 (1999).

[102] United States v. Mills, 835 F.2d 1262 (8th Cir. 1987); *see also* United States v. Seaman, 18 F.3d 649 (9th Cir. 1994).

[103] United States v. Erodhead, 714 F. Supp. 593 (D. Mass. 1989).

[104] United States v. Seaman, 18 F.3d 649 (9th Cir. 1994).

[105] 18 U.S.C. § 1363.

[106] For other federal crimes relating to malicious mischief, *see* 18 U.S.C. § 1362, relating to damage to communication lines, stations, or systems, and 18 U.S.C. § 1366, relating to destruction of an energy facility.

[107] 18 U.S.C. § 1382.

[108] United States v. Corrigan, 114 F.3d 763 (11th Cir. 1998).

[109] United States v. Zukowsky, 967 F. Supp. 269 (S.D. Ohio 1997).

[110] 18 U.S.C. § 2115.

[111] United States v. Gibson, 444 F.2d 275 (5th Cir. 1971).

[112] Smith v. United States, 413 F.2d 1121 (5th Cir. 1969).

[113] 18 U.S.C. § 2116; *see* U.S. Code Annotated for the wording of this offense and the cases that interpret the provisions of the statute.

[114] 18 U.S.C. § 2118 (b).

[115] United States v. Workman, 990 F. Supp. 473 (S.D. W. Va. 1998).

[116] United States v. Martin, 866 F.2d 972 (8th Cir. 1989).

[117] *See* 49 U.S.C. § 1472 for references concerning federal violations in which the action occurs aboard an aircraft in flight, and 49 U.S.C. § 1151 for provisions relating to larceny committed in Indian territory. In *United States v. Pemberton*, 904 F.2d 515 (9th Cir. 1990), the court discusses the process used in determining the value of property for purposes of this statute.

[118] 18 U.S.C. § 661.

[119] United States v. Henry, 447 F.2d 283 (3d Cir. 1971).

[120] Clark v. United States, 267 F.2d 99 (4th Cir. 1959); England v. United States, 174 F.2d 466 (5th Cir. 1949).

[121] Title 18 U.S.C. § 666; United States v. Phillips, 17 F. Supp. 2d 1016 (M.D. La. 1998).

[122]   United States v. Urrutia, 897 F.2d 430 (9th Cir. 1990).

[123]   18 U.S.C. § 2112.

[124]   United States v. Torres, 809 F.2d 429 (7th Cir. 1987).

[125]   18 U.S.C. § 2113.

[126]   United States v. Harris, 108 F.3d 1107 (9th Cir. 1997). *See also* United States v. Watts, 256 F.3d 630 (7th Cir. 2001).

[127]   United States v. Rasco, 123 F.3d 222 (5th Cir. 1997).

[128]   United States v. Daily, 846 F.2d 707 (11th Cir. 1988).

[129]   United States v. Jones, 732 F.2d 624 (7th Cir. 1991). *See also* United States v. Smith, 131 F.3d 185 (7th Cir. 1997).

[130]   United States v. Woodrup, 86 F.3d 359 (4th Cir. 1996). *See also* United States v. Credit, 95 F.3d 362 (5th Cir. 1996).

[131]   18 U.S.C. § 2113(d). *See* other provisions of this statute for definitions of terms. *See also* United States v. McCall, which held that for purposes of this statute, "dangerous weapon or device is not synonymous with firearms and may include a toy gun." 85 F.3d 1193 (6th Cir. 1996).

[132]   United States v. Hanson, 751 F. Supp. 177 (D. Or. 1990).

[133]   United States v. Biajos, 292 F.3d 1068 (9th Cir. 2002).

[134]   United States v. Mays, 822 F.2d 793 (8th Cir. 1987). This case also considers the admissibility of evidence of other crimes. *See also* United States v. Alexander, 48 F.3d 1477 (9th Cir. 1995).

[135]   18 U.S.C. § 2119.

[136]   United States v. Cobb, 144 F.3d 319 (4th Cir. 1998). *See also* United States v. Romero, 122 F.3d 1334 (10th Cir. 1997), which held that Congress did not exceed its power under the Commerce Clause in enacting the federal carjacking statute.

[137]   United States v. Randolph, 93 F.3d 656 (9th Cir. 1996).

[138]   United States v. Gamble, 939 F. Supp. 569 (E.D. Mich. 1996).

[139]   18 U.S.C. § 2111.

[140]   Lattimore v. United States, 684 A.2d 357 (D.C. App. 1996).

[141]   18 U.S.C. § 641. *See* United States v. Schneider, 14 F.3d 876 (7th Cir. 1994) for a discussion of the "meaning of the statute."

[142]   United States v. Collins, 56 F.3d 1416 (D.C. Cir. 1995); *cert. denied*, 516 U.S. 1060, 116 S. Ct. 737, 133 L. Ed. 2d 687 (1995).

[143]   United States v. Lanier, 920 F.2d 887 (11th Cir. 1991).

[144]   United States v. Gordon, 638 F.2d 886 (5th Cir. 1981).

[145]   American Computer Trust Leasing v. Jack Farrell Implement Co., 763 F. Supp. 1473 (D. Minn. 1991).

[146]   18 U.S.C. § 656.

[147]   United States v. Tidwell, 559 F.2d 1215 (5th Cir. 1977), *cert. denied*, 435 U.S. 492, 98 S. Ct. 1520, 55 L. Ed. 2d 538 (1978). *See also* Thompson v. State, 223 Ga. App. 792, 505 S.E.2d 535 (1998).

[148]   18 U.S.C. § 666.

[149]   United States v. Suarez, 263 F.3d 468 (6th Cir. 2001).

[150]   18 U.S.C. § 1341; *see also* 18 U.S.C. § 1342 "Fictitious Name and Address," 18 U.S.C. § 1343 "Fraud by Wire, Radio or Television," and 18 U.S.C. § 2314.

[151]   United States v. Rendini, 738 F.2d 530 (1st Cir. 1984).

[152]   18 U.S.C. §§ 1341-1343.

[153]   United States v. Sawyer, 85 F.3d 713 (1st Cir 1996), in which the court held that in order to prove mail and wire fraud, the government must prove beyond a reasonable doubt: (1) the defendant's knowing and willing participation in a scheme or artifice to defraud with the specific intent to defraud, and (2) use of the mails or interstate wire communications in furtherance of the scheme.

[154]   United States v. Coppel, 24 F.3d 535 (3d Cir. 1994). *See also* United States v. Pierce, 224 F.3d 158 (2d Cir. 2000), which held that intent to defraud does not hinge on whether or not the appellees were successful.

[155]   United States v. Lemire, 720 F.2d 1334 (D.C. Cir. 1983), *cert. denied*, 467 U.S. 1226, 104 S. Ct. 2679, 81 L. Ed. 2d 874 (1984).

[156]   United States v. Cavalier, 17 F.3d 90 (5th Cir. 1994). United States v. Martin, 195 F.3d 961 (7th Cir. 1999).

[157]   United States v. Console, 13 F.3d 641 (3d Cir. 1993).

[158]   United States v. Noland, 960 F.2d 1384 (8th Cir. 1992).

[159]   United States v. Figueroa, 832 F.2d 691 (1st Cir. 1987).

[160]   United States v. Richards, 204 F.3d 177 (5th Cir. 2000).

[161]   United States v. Brown, 186 F.3d 661 (5th Cir. 1999).

[162]   Cleveland v. United States, 531 U.S. 12 (2000).

[163]   United States v. Brisco, 65 F.3d 576 (7th Cir. 1995).

[164]   United States v. Moore, 3 F.3d 169 (5th Cir. 1994); United States v. Hollis, 971 F.2d 1441 (10th Cir. 1992), *cert. denied*, 507 U.S. 985, 113 S. Ct. 1580, 123 L. Ed. 2d 148 (1992). *See also* United States v. Altman, 48 F.3d 96 (2d Cir. 1995).

[165]   18 U.S.C. § 871, Threats against the president and successors to the presidency; 18 U.S.C. § 872, Extortion by officers or employees of the United States; 18 U.S.C. § 873, Blackmail; 18 U.S.C. § 874, Kickbacks from public works employees; 18 U.S.C. § 875, Interstate communications; 18 U.S.C. § 876, Mailing threatening communications; and 18 U.S.C. § 877, Mailing threatening communications from foreign countries.

[166]   United States v. Smith, 228 F. Supp. 345 (E.D. La. 1964).

[167]   Title 18 U.S.C. § 872.

[168]   United States v. Jackson, 986 F. Supp. 829 (1997).

[169]   18 U.S.C. § 2312.

[170]   United States v. Spoone, 741 F.2d 680 (4th Cir.), *cert. denied*, 469 U.S. 1162, 105 S. Ct. 917, 83 L. Ed. 2d 929 (1984).

[171]   United States v. Spudic, 795 F.2d 1334 (7th Cir. 1986).

[172]   United States v. Baker, 429 F.2d 1344 (7th Cir. 1970).

[173]   United States v. Spoone, 741 F.2d 680 (4th Cir.), *cert. denied*, 469 U.S. 1162, 105 S. Ct. 917, 83 L. Ed. 2d 929 (1984). See also United States v. Henry, 861 F. Supp. 1190 (S.D.N.Y. 1994), which indicated that the temporary taking of a motor vehicle can violate the statute.

[174]   18 U.S.C. § 662.

[175]   United States v. Townsend, 474 F.2d 209 (5th Cir. 1973).

[176]   18 U.S.C. § 2313.

[177] United States v. Thomas, 676 F.2d 239 (7th Cir.), *cert. denied*, 449 U.S. 1091, 101 S. Ct. 887, 66 L. Ed. 2d 820 (1980). Other federal statutes dealing with the transportation, receipt, or sale of stolen property are 18 U.S.C. § 2314 (Transportation of Stolen Goods, Securities, Monies, Fraudulent State Tax Stamps, Articles Used in Counterfeiting); 18 U.S.C. § 2315 (Sale or Receipt of Stolen Goods, Securities, Monies, or Fraudulent State Tax Stamps); 18 U.S.C. § 2316 (Transportation of Livestock); 18 U.S.C. § 2317 (Sale or Receipt of Livestock).

[178] Other federal statutes are Title 18 § 473, Bonds and obligations of certain lending agencies; Title 18 § 485, Falsely making, forging or counterfeiting coins; Title 18 § 472, Forgery of obligations or securities of the United States; and Title 18 § 494, which relates to falsely making, altering, or forging contractor's bonds, bids, and public records.

[179] Gilbert v. United States, 370 U.S. 650, 82 S. Ct. 1399, 8 L. Ed. 2d 750 (1962). *See also* United States v. Chenault, 844 F.2d 1124 (5th Cir. 1988).

[180] United States v. LeCoe, 936 F.2d 398 (9th Cir. 1991).

[181] Title 15 § 1451 *et seq.* and Title 18 § 922. Also Title 18 § 892 of the Code, which includes a penalty provision for making extortionate extensions of credit.

[182] Chapter 18, §§ 892, 893, and 894.

United States Criminal Code: Offenses Against: Morality and Decency; Public Peace; Justice Administration   14

Chapter Outline

Cases

Virtual child pornography: *Ashcroft v. Free Speech Coalition*, 535 U.S. 234 (2002)

Marijuana and medical necessity: *Gonzales v. Raich*, 545 U.S. 1, 125 S. Ct. 2195 (2005)

Assisted suicide and federal drug laws: *Gonzales v. Oregon*, 126 S. Ct. 904, 163 L. Ed. 2d 748 (2006)

§ 14.1   Introduction

In this chapter we continue to examine the United State Code for crimes that parallel state crimes. As with all the crimes in the preceding chapter, federal crimes in the areas of morality, offenses against public peace, and offenses against justice administration must have a nexus to some federal power.

§ 14.10.1   Offenses Against Morality

Recall that Chapter 10 dealt with a range of behaviors that were determined to offend public morality to the extent that they were defined as criminal, including various forms of sexual activity, pornography, and abortion. Because police power lies in the state, it is largely up to the states to legislate against these activities. However, there are some federal laws that parallel state laws and punish offenses that occur under federal maritime or territorial jurisdiction or cover activities that affect interstate commerce.

§ 14.10.2; 14.10.3   Adultery and Fornication

Although Title 18 of the federal code contains no provision that directly prohibits adultery or fornication, Title 18 § 2421 includes a penalty for one who knowingly transports an individual in interstate or foreign commerce with intent that such individual engage in "any sexual activity for which any person can be charged with a criminal offense." This applies to adultery if adultery is a crime under the state law.[1]

§ 14.10.4 Prostitution

Title 18 § 2421 was designated "White Slave Traffic" and has now been retitled "Transportation for Illegal Sexual Activity and Related Crimes." This Act, relating to the transportation in interstate or foreign commerce of any woman or girl for the purpose of prostitution or debauchery, etc., was originally passed in 1910. The code was amended in 1948, 1978, and 1986. The 1986 version is as follows:

> 18 U.S.C. § 2421—Transportation generally
>
> Whoever knowingly transports any individual in interstate or foreign commerce, or any Territory or Possession of the United States, with intent that such individual engage in prostitution, or in any sexual activity for which any person can be charged with criminal offense, or attempts to do so, shall be fined under this title or imprisoned not more than 10 years, or both.[2]

The amended act, unlike previous versions, does not restrict application to females, although the initial law, when originally passed, was "to curb white slave traffic in interstate commerce and to eliminate traffic in women by procurers who forced victims to lead a life of debauchery."[3] In order to constitute an offense under § 2421, the prosecution must prove, among other elements, that the defendant knowingly transported an individual in interstate or foreign commerce or attempted to do so. Also, the prosecution must necessarily prove that the defendant transported such individual with intent for that person to engage in prostitution or other sexual activity for which a person can be charged with a criminal offense.[4]

Legal News

Eliot Spitzer resigned his position as governor of the state of New York when a federal investigation of a prostitution ring exposed his patronage of the club. Mark Brener, the alleged owner, ran the "Emperor's V.I.P. Club," a call girl ring where patrons paid thousands of dollars for the company of young women. Brener was charged with money laundering and conspiracy to violate federal prostitution laws. This was a federal prosecution because the phone was used to set up assignations and, in some instances, patrons like Spitzer sent cash payments through the U.S. mail. Furthermore, in at least one instance, at Spitzer's request, a woman was sent to him from New York to Washington, D.C. for a sexual assignation.

Source: Rashbaum, W. (2008). www.nytimes.com. Accessed 1/2/2009 from http://www.nytimes.com/2008/06/10/nyregion/10spitzer.html?fta=y.

After examining the "purpose" element of the statute, the justices of the Second Circuit concluded that prostitution or any criminal sexual activity needs to be *one of the* dominant purposes, but need not be *the* dominant purpose of travel in order to convict.[5]

A second federal statute proscribes knowingly persuading, inducing, enticing, or coercing an individual to travel in interstate or foreign commerce to engage in prostitution or other sexual activities prohibited by law. This section provides:

> 18 U.S.C. § 2422—Coercion and enticement
>
> (a) Whoever knowingly persuades, induces, entices, or coerces any individual to travel in interstate or foreign commerce, or in any Territory or Possession of the United States, to engage in prostitution, or in any sexual activity for which any person can be charged with a criminal offense, or attempts to do so, shall be fined under this title or imprisoned not more than 10 years, or both.
>
> (b) Whoever, using the mail or any facility or means of interstate or foreign commerce, or within the special maritime and territorial jurisdiction of the United States knowingly persuades, induces, entices, or coerces any individual who has not attained the age of 18 years, to engage in prostitution or any sexual activity for which any person can be charged with a criminal offense, or attempts to do so, shall be fined under this title, imprisoned not more than 15 years, or both.[6]

Finding that this section of the statute is not unconstitutional, a federal court reasoned that the criminal statute that prohibits using the means of interstate commerce to persuade a minor to engage in a sexual act did not violate the First Amendment. Although the method of persuasion usually involves some form of speech, this statute did not attempt to regulate the content of the speech, but merely criminalized the conduct that incidentally involved speech.[7]

It is not **double jeopardy** to convict a defendant under both Sections 2421 and 2422, because these are separate and distinct offenses.[8] Also, it is not improper to convict one defendant of two violations for the single act of transporting a minor female and an adult woman across the state line for purposes of prostitution.[9]

Title 18 § 2423 relates to transportation of minors with the intent that the minor engage in prostitution. The penalty for violating this provision is "not more than fifteen years" while the penalty under § 2421 is 10 years. The statute provides:

> 18 U.S.C. § 2423 Transportation of Minors[10]
>
> (a) Transportation with intent to engage in criminal sexual activity. A person who knowingly transports any individual under the age of 18 years in interstate or foreign commerce, or in any Territory or Possession of the United States, with intent that the individual engage in prostitution, or in any sexual activity for which any person can be charged with a criminal offense, or attempts to do so shall be fined under this title or imprisoned not more than fifteen years, or both.

In the case of *United States v. Scisum*, the defendant appealed his conviction, arguing that the definition of "intent" was too vague.[11] The reviewing court held that the word "intent" was of common enough usage to be clear to a reasonable lay juror. The court advised, however, that the government must prove that the defendant formed intent before the defendant transported the person across state lines.

Ignorance of the victim's age provides no defense. In *United States v. Taylor*, the court indicated that if a person knowingly transports a person for the purposes of prostitution or another sex offense, the transporter assumes the risk that the victim is a minor, regardless of what the victim says or how the victim appears.[12] In another case, prohibiting transporting a minor in interstate commerce with intent that the minor engage in illegal sexual activity did not require a determination that the defendant intended to have illegal sex with the minor when he initially transported her from her state of origin, but rather that the defendant intended such illegal acts before the conclusion of his interstate journey.[13]

In addition to these statutes, Title 18 § 1384 authorizes the secretaries of the Army, Navy, and Air Force to designate areas within a reasonable distance of any military or naval camp, station, or post, where prostitution and other related offenses shall be prohibited, and provides a fine or imprisonment for failure to comply with such directive.[14]

§ 14.10.5   Obscenity

Chapter 71 of the United States Code ("**Obscenity**") comprehensively lists and defines offenses dealing with obscenity and related issues. These statutes have been so expanded and amended that there is little that is not covered. The statutes, as written and broadly interpreted, give the federal government broad authority to investigate and prosecute crimes that are related to obscenity. The offenses described in Chapter 71 are:

- Section 1460—Possession with intent to sell, and sale of, obscene matter on federal property.
- Section 1461—Mailing obscene or crime-inciting matter.
- Section 1462—Importation or transportation of obscene matters.
- Section 1463—Mailing indecent matter on wrappers or envelopes.
- Section 1464 Broadcasting obscene language
- Section 1465—Transportation of obscene matters for sale or distribution.
- Section 1466—Engaging in the business of selling or transferring obscene matter.
- 1466A - Obscene visual representations of the sexual abuse of children
- Section 1467—Criminal forfeiture.

- Section 1468—Distributing obscene material by cable or subscription television.

- Section 1470—Transfer of obscene materials to minors.

- Section 2252A—Certain activities relating to material involving the sexual exploitation of minors

Section 1460 applies only where the possession or sale occurs in the special maritime and territorial jurisdiction of the United States. The other sections have more universal coverage. Title 18 § 1461 of the federal statute is the provision most often used in prosecuting at the federal level. This section mandates a fine or imprisonment for not more than five years, or both, if the defendant is convicted of using the mail to distribute obscene, lewd, lascivious, indecent, filthy, or vile articles, matter, things, devices, or substances and other materials as defined in the statute.

In interpreting this provision of the U.S. Code, federal courts follow the Supreme Court definition of "obscene" as approved in the case of *Miller v. California*,[15] discussed in Chapter 10. Recall that in that case, obscenity was defined by answering the following questions: (1) Does the material appeal to prurient interests? (2) Does it depict "hard-core" sexual acts previously defined by state law in a patently offensive way? and (3) Does it lack serious literary, artistic, political, scientific, or other value?

The Eleventh Circuit Court of Appeals decided that § 1461, which prohibits knowingly using the mail for obscene materials, applies to persons who order obscene materials through the mail, even if they are for personal use. In the case of *United States v. Schein*, the defendant was convicted of mailing obscene materials. The defendant appealed, claiming that similar material had been shown at an exhibit funded by the government's National Endowment for the Arts, and that his tapes promoted sexual safety. The reviewing court rejected the defendant's arguments. Citing other cases, the court held that:

- Obscene material is not protected by the First Amendment.

- The fact that the photographs of urolagnic pornography were shown at exhibits funded by the National Endowment for the Arts did not establish that videotapes containing graphic depictions of urination, masturbation, and oral and anal sex among homosexual males were not obscene.

- Merely promoting safe sex does not bring the material within the exception noted in part (c) of the *Miller* case.

- Mere availability of similar material means nothing more than other persons are engaged in similar activity.[16]

Title 18 § 1462 provides a penalty of a fine or five years' imprisonment, or both, for the first offense, and a fine and 10 years' imprisonment for the second offense if the defendant is convicted of importation or transportation of obscene matters as defined in the statute.

Title 18 § 1463 prohibits the mailing of indecent matters on wrappers or envelopes, and § 1464 provides a penalty for one who utters any obscene, indecent, or profane language by means of radio communications. Section 1465 makes it a crime punishable by a fine or five years' imprisonment, or both, to knowingly transport, travel in, or use a facility, or means of interstate or foreign commerce or an interactive computer service in or affecting such commerce, for the purpose of sale or distribution of any obscene, lewd, lascivious, or filthy book, pamphlet, picture, film, paper, letter, writing, print, silhouette, drawing, figure, image, cast, phonograph recording, electrical transcription, or other article capable of producing sound or any matter of indecent or immoral character.

In the case of *United States v. Thomas*, the federal court made it clear that this statute, as amended, applies to computer-generated images moved from the defendants' computer bulletin board in one state to a personal computer in another state.[17]

Section 1466 makes it a crime to engage in the business of selling or transferring obscene matters. Violators shall be punished by imprisonment of not more than five years or by a fine or both. To further discourage related violations, § 1467 provides for forfeiture of obscene material as well as property, real or personal, used or intended to be used to commit or to promote the commission of such offenses. In 1988, the offense of "Distributing obscene material by cable or subscription television" was added. Section 1468 provides in part that:

> 18 U.S.C. § 1468
>
> [W]hoever knowingly utters any obscene language or distributes any obscene matter by means of cable television or subscription service on television, shall be punished by imprisonment for not more than two years or by fine in accordance with this title, or both.[18]

Another federal statute, 18 U.S.C. § 2252, titled "Certain activities relating to material involving the sexual exploitation of minors," has resulted in **"child pornography"** cases being investigated by federal officers and more cases being tried in federal court. This statute[19] provides:

> 18 U.S.C. § 2252
>
> (a) Any person who—
>
>   (1) knowingly transports or ships in interstate or foreign commerce by any means including by computer or mails, any visual depiction, if—
>   (A) the producing of such visual depiction involves the use of a minor engaging in sexually explicit conduct; and
>   (B) such visual depiction is of such conduct;
>
>   (2) knowingly receives, or distributes, any visual depiction that has been mailed, or has been shipped or transported in interstate or foreign commerce, or which contains materials which have been mailed or so shipped or transported, by any means including by computer, or knowingly reproduces any visual depiction for distribution in interstate or foreign commerce or through the mails, if—

   (A) in the special maritime and territorial jurisdiction of the United States, or on any land or building owned by, leased to, or otherwise used by or under the control of the Government of the United States, or in the Indian country as defined in § 1151 of this title, knowingly sells or possesses with intent to sell any visual depiction; or

   (B) knowingly sells or possesses with intent to sell any visual depiction that has been mailed, or has been shipped or transported in interstate or foreign commerce, or which was produced using materials which have been mailed or so shipped or transported, by any means, including by computer, if—

      (i) the producing of such visual depiction involves the use of a minor engaging in sexually explicit conduct; and

      (ii) such visual depiction is of such conduct; or

(3) either—

   (A) in the special maritime and territorial jurisdiction of the United States, or on any land or building owned by, leased to or otherwise used by or under the control of the Government of the United States, or in the Indian country as defined in § 1151 of this title, knowingly possesses 1 or more books, magazines, periodicals, films, video tapes, or other matter which contain any visual depiction; or

   (B) knowingly possesses 1 or more books, magazines, periodicals, films, video tapes, or other matter which contain any visual depiction that has been mailed, or has been shipped or transported in interstate or foreign commerce, or which was produced using materials which have been mailed or so shipped or transported, by any means including computer, if—

      (i) the producing of such visual depiction involves the use of a minor engaging in sexually explicit conduct; and

      (ii) such visual depiction is of such conduct; shall be punished as provided in subsection (b) of this section. . .

This statute has been challenged on several constitutional grounds. The federal courts have rejected the argument that the federal government has no power under the commerce clause to punish purely private use of obscene materials. The courts have found that, the government had made a sufficient showing that a defendant's possession of pornography has a sufficiently substantial effect on interstate commerce to show a nexus between the federal pornography statute and a defendant's conduct.[20] The statute has also been challenged as being in violation of the First Amendment and overbroad; however, federal courts held that the conviction for possession of child pornography that has been transported in interstate commerce met constitutional standards.[21] Note that this statute covers material that would not necessarily be viewed as obscene if all the performers were adult, the fact that one or more are children is what makes the material illegal.

In *United States v. X-Citement Video*,[22] the Supreme Court dealt with the question of whether the offender had to *know* the performer was a minor, or whether the verb "know" related to knowingly transport, receive, or distribute.

The Supreme Court held that "knowing" refers to the knowledge that one of the performers in the material was underage. However, in *United States v. Davis*, a court held that age is a matter on which everyone has an opinion so it is therefore particularly appropriate for a lay witness to express an opinion on the subject.[23]

In the case of *United States v. Hersh*, the circuit court held that a conviction for receipt and possession of child pornography was supported by evidence that the defendant knowingly received and possessed computer files containing images, that the images were received via the Internet, and the images portrayed real minors engaged in sexually explicit conduct, and that the defendant was aware of such.[24] The act requires the introduction of evidence that shows that the visual depiction involves the use of a minor engaging in sexually explicit conduct, and such visual depiction is of such conduct.

One of the newest areas of contention is the legality of pornography that utilizes computer-generated images of children. United States Code § 2252A covers the receipt or transmission of pornography via the Internet that uses computer-generated images of children. The argument presented is that because there are no children harmed by the production of such pornography, it is impermissibly overbroad to apply the statute to such activity. The opposing argument is that the statute not only was created to protect children, but also societal morals; in addition, children may be shown such pornography to reduce their inhibitions against sexual behavior.

CASE: *Ashcroft v. Free Speech Coalition*, 535 U.S. 234 (2002)

What was the holding of the case?

What was the argument for applying the statute to computer images?

What is the purpose of child pornography statutes?

One federal court dealt with the issue in *United States v. Fox* and held that it was not unconstitutional to apply the child pornography definition to computer-generated images.[25] Then in *Ashcroft v. Free Speech Coalition*,[26] the Supreme Court ruled on the question and concluded that the provision violated First Amendment freedoms because it was overbroad and not closely related to the purpose of the statute, which was to protect children.

§ 14.10.6   Bigamy

Title 18 of the U.S. Code contains no specific provision concerning bigamy.

§ 14.10.7   Incest

Title 18 of the U.S. Code contains no specific provision concerning the offense of incest except in reference to offenses committed within Indian territory.[27] This section provides that the offense of incest shall be defined and punished in accordance with the laws of the state in which such offense was committed and as are in force at the time of such offense.

§ 14.10.8   Abortion

The laws restricting and/or criminalizing abortions are state laws, therefore most of the important cases in this area have already been covered in Chapter 10. If the federal legislature ever passes a law that criminalizes abortion across the nation by making it a federal crime, it would have to find the power to do so in the commerce clause. This is unlikely. Therefore, the federal crimes relating to abortion are incidental to the act itself.

The Freedom of Access to Clinic Entrances Act was passed to protect individuals from demonstrators at abortion clinics and family planning centers. It includes a criminal as well as a civil penalty section. This Act[28] provides:

18 U.S.C. § 248

(a) Prohibited activities.—Whoever—

(1) by force or threat or by physical obstruction, intentionally injures, intimidates or interferes with or attempts to injure, intimidate or interfere with any person because that person is or has been, or in order to intimidate such person or any other person or any class of persons from, obtaining or providing reproductive health services;

(2) by force or threat of force or by physical obstruction, intentionally injures, intimidates or interferes with or attempts to injure, intimidate or interfere with any person lawfully exercising or seeking to exercise the First Amendment right of religious freedom at a place of religious freedom at a place of religious worship; or

(3) intentionally damages or destroys the property of a facility, or attempts to do so, because such facility provides reproductive health services, or intentionally damages or destroys the property of a place of religious worship.

Shall be subject to the penalties provided in subsection (b) and the civil remedies provided in subsection (c), except that a parent or legal guardian of a minor shall not be subject to any penalties or civil remedies under this section for such activities insofar as they are directed exclusively at that minor . . .

A federal court decided that the Freedom of Access to Clinic Entrances Act is not unconstitutionally vague in violation of due process.[29] The justices of the Eighth Circuit Court of Appeals agreed that parking rental trucks at the entrances of abortion clinics could constitute a "threat of force" in violation of the Freedom of Access to Clinic Entrances Act. The court noted that the clinic staff did, in fact, perceive the trucks as a threat of force, and there was testimony that the defendant sought, by his actions, to frighten clinic patients and staff.[30]

In *Scheidler v. National Organization for Women, Inc.*[31] an organization that supports the legal availability of abortion and two facilities that perform abortions filed a class action alleging that petitioners, individuals, and organizations that oppose legal abortion violated the Racketeer Influenced and

Corrupt Organizations Act (RICO) by engaging in a nationwide conspiracy to shut down abortion clinics through "a pattern of racketeering activity" that included acts of extortion in violation of the Hobbs Act.

The District Court agreed with the respondents and awarded damages, and entered a permanent nationwide injunction against the petitioners. The Court of Appeals upheld the issuance of the injunction. The United States Supreme Court reversed the decision of the District Court and held that, because the acts of physical violence were not in pursuit of pecuniary gain, there was no underlying felony that could constitute the necessary racketeering required for RICO.[32] The Court of Appeals, upon remand, ordered the case to go back to the District Court to determine whether any other acts committed by the abortion protesters, unrelated to extortion, might be considered violations of the Hobbs Act. Upon appeal back to the Supreme Court, the majority ruled that no acts of abortion protesters were properly prosecuted under the RICO statute.

Other federal statutes that relate to abortion are 18 U.S.C. § 1461, which prohibits the mailing of articles or things designed, adapted, or intended to produce abortion and 18 U.S.C. § 1462, which prohibits bringing into the United States any drug, medicine, article, or thing designed, adapted, or intended to produce abortion.[33]

§ 14.11.1   Offenses Against Public Peace

Various laws that prohibit activities that could be described as offending the public peace were described in Chapter 11. In the next several sections, similar federal laws are described.

§ 14.11.2   Riot and Related Offenses

The U.S. Code in Title 18 § 2101 prescribes penalties for one who travels in interstate commerce to incite a riot.[34] It states in part that:

18 U.S.C. § 2101

(a) Whoever travels in interstate or foreign commerce or uses any facility of interstate or foreign commerce, including, but not limited to, the mail, telegraph, telephone, radio, or television, with intent:
   (1) to incite a riot; or
   (2) to organize, promote, encourage, participate in, or carry on a riot; or
   (3) to commit any act of violence in furtherance of a riot; or
   (4) to aid or abet any person in inciting or participating in or carrying on a riot or committing any act of violence in furtherance of the riot; and who either, during the course of any such travel or use there-

> after, performs or attempts to perform any other overt act for any
> purpose specified in subparagraphs (1), (2), (3) or (4)—
>
> shall be fined under this title or imprisoned for not more than 5 years, or both.

This statute goes on to provide that a judgment of conviction or acquittal on the merits of the laws of any state shall be a bar to any prosecution hereunder for the same act or acts. Title 18 § 2102 defines the term "riot." To assure that the First Amendment provisions are not violated, the definition of the term "to incite a riot" includes a statement that this shall not be deemed to mean the mere oral or written advocacy of ideas or expression of belief, not involving advocacy of any act or acts of violence or assertion of the rightness of, or the right to commit any such act or acts. The federal riot act has been upheld as not in violation of the U.S. Constitution.[35]

In interpreting the provisions of Title 18 §§ 2101 and 2102, a federal circuit court considered two issues: (1) Are interstate telephone calls to summon others to participate in a riot proscribed by the federal anti-riot act? and (2) What amounts to a "riot" for the purposes of the Act?[36] The court decided that when the defendant made an international call to summon Oneida Indians to New York and evidence of the defendant's subsequent actions demonstrated that he sought to cause an intratribal controversy, the evidence permitted a finding of "interstate commerce" as proscribed by the Act. The court also agreed that an attack by 25 people on a gas station, the break-in of a bingo hall, and an assault on two people who wanted to investigate the disturbance fit the definition of "riot" for purposes of the anti-riot act.

§ 14.11.3   Disorderly Conduct

Title 18 § 1752 provides a fine or imprisonment not exceeding six months, or both, if any person is found guilty of entering or remaining in any building or grounds designated by the Secretary of the Treasury as a temporary residence of the president or other persons protected by the Secret Service in violation of regulations.[37] This section also makes it unlawful for any person or persons with intent to impede or disrupt the orderly conduct of government business or official functions, to engage in disorderly or disruptive conduct in, or within such proximity to any building or grounds designated as a temporary residence for the president or other person protected by the Secret Service.[38]

In addition, Title 40 § 101 of the U.S. Code provides a penalty of not more than $500 or imprisonment for not more than six months, or both, if any person is guilty of disorderly and unlawful conduct in and about public buildings and public grounds belonging to the United States within the District of Columbia.[39]

§ 14.11.4 Vagrancy and Loitering

Title 18 of the U.S. Code contains no criminal statute relating to vagrancy or loitering.

§ 14.11.5 Drunkenness

The U.S. Code has no specific provision relating to drunkenness or intoxication but does have a section regulating transportation of intoxicating liquor into any state, territory, or district for sale in that state, territory, or district where the state laws prohibit the sale of intoxicating liquor.[40]

The purpose of this section is to simplify enforcement by federal agents. It was designed to provide federal protection to "dry" states against violators who sought to bring alcohol into the state.[41]

§ 14.11.6 Drug Laws

Prior to 1970, there were numerous separate federal drug control statutes on the books, each of which was aimed at a particular set of drug problems. Some of these acts relied upon the taxing power of Congress, while others relied upon the authority granted to Congress under the interstate commerce clause of the Constitution. The Narcotics Manufacturing Act of 1960, which set up a licensing system for narcotic drug manufacturers, relied upon the commerce power rather than the power to tax. In 1965, amendments to the Food, Drug and Cosmetic Act, dealing with dangerous drugs, were found to be within the power of Congress to regulate interstate commerce.[42]

The Comprehensive Drug Abuse Prevention and Control Act of 1970 created for the first time an all-encompassing scheme covering both narcotics and dangerous drugs. The provisions of this section, authorizing the Secretary of Health, Education, and Welfare to make scientific evaluations and recommendations regarding the classification of a drug, were challenged but held to be constitutional.[43] The constitutional authorization for the 1970 Act was based entirely on the commerce clause, the taxing power no longer being relied upon.

In 1984, 1986, 1988, and again in 1990, federal legislation was drafted to make it less difficult to prosecute violators and to increase the penalties. In 1986, Congress enacted a very comprehensive law titled the Anti-Drug Abuse Act of 1986. In addition to creating new offenses, the main thrust of the act was to increase the penalties for drug offenders. Also, legislation was enacted that authorized the Department of Defense to assist in enforcing the drug laws. Over objections raised by the Secretary of Defense and military officials, both houses of Congress passed bills broadening the role of the military in the drug war. Federal law enforcement officers, as well as state and local enforcement officers, are given specific powers of enforcement by the federal statute.[44]

Also, in 1986, the Congress of the United States added subtitle (H), "Money Laundering Control Act of 1986." This created a new offense for laundering the monetary instruments, with a separate penalty if a person is convicted of laundering money knowing that the property involved in the financial transaction represents the proceeds of some form of unlawful activity.[45]

The Anti-Drug Abuse Act of 1988 further strengthened the authority of enforcement agents to continue the war on drugs. In addition to increasing penalties for personal use of drugs, the Act included the death penalty for those convicted of drug-related killings. A new provision added a federal penalty for endangering human life while illegally manufacturing drugs and provides a mandatory life term for three-time felony drug offenders.[46]

Recall that in *United States v. Fowler*, presented as a case for chapter 13, a federal court, after reviewing previous cases, affirmed the authority of federal courts to prosecute, convict, or sentence a defendant for a crime involving the wholly intrastate possession of a controlled substance.[47] In this case, the defendant pled guilty to one count of possession of cocaine base, but later filed a motion to vacate or set aside the conviction, complaining that the United States "has no territorial jurisdiction over non-federally owned areas inside the jurisdictional boundaries of the states within the American Union." The court rejected the defendant's argument, reiterating that "the commerce clause empowers Congress to regulate broad classes of activities which are found to have a substantial impact on interstate commerce." The court continued by stating that "Congress possesses the power to regulate wholly intrastate activities which have an effect upon interstate commerce."[48]

A. *Uniform Schedule of Controlled Substances*

Title 21 § 812 of the U.S. Code establishes five schedules of **controlled substances**, known as Schedules I, II, II, IV and V. Such schedules are the same as those previously described in Chapter 11.[49] The criteria for determining which drug was to be placed in each schedule are set out in the statute and are similar to the criteria used in establishing the schedules for the respective states.

In 1982, a federal appeals court dealt with a challenge to the classification of marijuana as a Schedule I drug. In this case, the court found that the defendant did not meet his heavy burden of proving the irrationality of a Schedule I classification of marijuana in light of the ongoing dispute as to physical and psychological effects of marijuana, its potential for abuse, and whether it had any medical value.[50]

Schedule of Drugs: Controlled Substances Act of 1970

Schedule I	
no established medical usage cannot be used safely, great potential for abuse	heroin, LSD, mescaline, peyote, Quaaludes, psilocybin, marijuana hashish, etc.
Schedule II	
high potential for abuse, currently accepted medical use	opium, morphine, codeine, cocaine PCP, Ritalin, Preludin, etc.
Schedule III	
some potential for abuse, accepted medical use, potential for psychological addiction	anabolic steroids, cold medicines & pain relievers containing codeine
Schedule IV	
low potential for abuse, medical uses	valium, librium, equanil, stimulants
Schedule VI	
prescription drugs with low potential for abuse	cough and other medicines with low levels of opium, morphine or codeine

The challenges to categorizing marijuana as a Schedule I drug continued. In 2001, the Supreme Court considered a case from California. In 1996, California voters passed the Compassionate Use Act of 1996, which allowed for the medical use of marijuana as a necessity exception to state possession, use, and trafficking laws. The U.S. Attorney General issued a policy announcement that the state of California could not usurp the federal government's right to enforce federal laws against marijuana and the case arose as a challenge to such enforcement. In *United States v. Oakland Cannabis Buyers' Cooperative*,[51] the Court ruled that the state of California could not create an exception to the federal drug law that placed marijuana in **Schedule I**. This case is interesting because it is also a question of **state rights** and many conservatives who are in favor of drug laws, nevertheless, were dismayed when the Supreme Court did not protect the state's police power to create and enforce laws that, arguably, did not implicate federal interests. In *Gonzales v. Raich*,[52] another challenge was heard against the federal drug law, with California petitioners arguing that the power of the federal government through the commerce clause did not reach the intrastate manufacture or delivery of marijuana. They lost again and the Supreme Court upheld the Attorney General's argument that federal drug laws override any state statute that recognizes a medical necessity for marijuana.

CASE: *Gonzales v. Raich*, 545 U.S. 1, 125 S. Ct. 2195 (2005)

What was the holding in the case?

Why is marijuana categorized as a Schedule I drug?

What evidence exists that it is medically "necessary"?

What evidence exists that intrastate manufacture and delivery will affect national prices?

Interestingly, in the most recent case concerning the enforcement of federal drug laws, the Supreme Court upheld states' rights. In *Gonzales v. Oregon*,[53] the Supreme Court dealt with Oregon's Death with Dignity Act, which allowed doctors to prescribe lethal doses of certain drugs to patients who had six months or less to live. Attorney General Ashcroft announced that, despite the state statute, such behavior violated federal law because it was not a medically accepted use of the controlled substance, and that any doctors who did prescribe controlled substances in the manner described would be prosecuted. In the case, which was actually brought by Ashcroft's successor, Attorney General Gonzales, the Supreme Court held that such an interpretation of the law exceeded the Attorney General's authority.

> **CASE: *Gonzales v. Oregon*, 126 S. Ct. 904, 163 L. Ed. 2d 748 (2006)**
>
> What was the holding of the case?
>
> Whose power is it to decide whether it is a medically accepted use of a drug to aid suicide?
>
> Why is it o.k. for Oregon voters to allow drugs to be used to aid suicide, but California voters can't decide it is acceptable to allow the medical use of marijuana to ease pain?

B. Possession

Title 21 § 844 of the U.S. Code as amended in 1986 provides in part:

> **21 U.S.C. § 844**
>
> (a) It shall be unlawful for any person knowingly or intentionally to possess a controlled substance unless such substance was obtained directly, or pursuant to a valid prescription order, from a practitioner while acting in the course of his professional practice, or except as otherwise authorized by this subchapter or subchapter II of this chapter.

The statute continues with sentencing provisions and a scheme that distinguishes those with prior convictions from first-time offenders under either state or federal drug laws. Another section includes a definition of drug or narcotic offense as "any offense which proscribes the possession, distribution, manufacture, cultivation, sale, transfer or the attempt or conspiracy to possess, distribute, manufacture, cultivate, sell or transfer any substance the possession of which is prohibited under this subchapter."[54]

To convict a person under this provision, the investigator must obtain information to show that the suspect:

- knowingly or intentionally,
- possessed,
- a controlled substance.

1. Knowing/Intentional

In considering the knowledge or intent element, a federal court held that "irrespective of what the defendant's intentions were regarding the ultimate disposition of heroin he claimed to have found while performing his duties as a janitor in prison, the defendant's knowledge of the illicit nature of the substance and purposeful possession of the substance was in violation of the heroin possession statute."[55]

2. Possession

One does not have to have *actual* possession of the controlled substance to violate this section. A person having an association with those having physical control of the drugs so as to enable him to assure their production, without difficulty, to a customer as a matter of course, may be held to have constructive possession.[56]

Section 844(a) provides a civil penalty for possession of small amounts of certain controlled substances. According to this section, if the controlled substance is possessed for personal use in small amounts, the possessor shall be subject to a civil penalty in an amount not to exceed $10,000 for each violation. This section authorizes the Attorney General to compromise, modify, or remit, with or without conditions, any civil penalty imposed under this section. It also provides that the civil penalty under this section may not be assessed on an individual on more than two separate occasions.

3. A Controlled Substance

Obviously, the clear meaning of what constitutes a controlled substance is exhaustively provided in the Schedule of Controlled Substances.

C. The Manufacture, Distribution, and Dispensing of Controlled Substances (Intent to Distribute)

Title 21 § 841 of the U.S. Code provides in part:

21 U.S.C. § 841

(a) Except as authorized by this subchapter, it shall be unlawful for any person knowingly or intentionally—

    (1) to manufacture, distribute, dispense or possess with intent to manufacture, distribute or dispense a controlled substance; or

    (2) to create, distribute, dispense or possess with intent to distribute or dispense, a counterfeit substance.[57]

In investigating and prosecuting violations of this section, each element must be proved beyond a reasonable doubt. In one case, the court enumerated three elements that must be proven by the government in order to sustain a conviction for possession of heroin with intent to distribute:

- knowing,

- possession,

- with intent to distribute (in this case heroin)..

1. Knowing

The Fourth Circuit Court of Appeals declared that a defendant's knowledge and intent are clearly elements that the prosecution must establish in order to prove a conspiracy to violate this section, but knowledge may be proven by extrinsic evidence.[58]

Knowledge refers to knowledge that one possesses a controlled substance; it is not necessary to know the particular controlled substance; therefore, a person can be convicted of importation of heroin and possession with intent to distribute even though he believed he was carrying cocaine rather than heroin.[59]

In a case prosecuted under 18 U.S.C. § 841, the court decided that a defendant charged with importing or possessing a drug is not required to know the type and the amount of the drug; rather, the defendant can be convicted if he believes he has some controlled substance in his possession, and the *mens rea* attaches to the possession of a controlled substance, not the type or quantity.[60] The Seventh Circuit Court agreed, holding that the offense of possession with intent to distribute illegally controlled substances requires only that the defendant knowingly possess a controlled substance with the intent to distribute it; the drug type is not an element.[61]

2. Possession

In a 1999 case, the justices of the Tenth Circuit Court of Appeals summarized the requirements necessary to convict a person of violating § 841(a). In this case, the court held that a conviction for possession of cocaine with intent to distribute requires that the defendant: (1) possessed a controlled substance; (2) knew he possessed a controlled substance; and (3) intended to distribute the controlled substance.[62] The court continued by affirming that "constructive possession" satisfies the first element and that the defendant has constructive possession of drugs when the defendant knowingly has ownership, dominion, or control over the narcotics and the premises where the narcotics were found. The second and third elements were not contested.

In proving the possession element, a federal court decided that the prosecution must show that the defendant had ultimate control over the drugs; it need not have been literally in hand or on the premises that he occupied but he must have a right to possess them. But mere association with those who possess drugs is not enough to justify a conviction.[63]

3. Intent to Distribute

The Seventh Circuit Court of Appeals held that a charge of possession of cocaine with intent to distribute requires proof that the defendant acted with the specific intent to commit the underlying offense. The prosecution also must prove that the defendant took a substantial step toward carrying out the intent.[64] In the case of *United States v. Vergara,* the court added that the elements may be proved by circumstantial as well as direct evidence, and possession may be shown if the heroin was possessed jointly among several defendants.[65]

As is true of other offenses, the "intent" element is often difficult to prove. The introduction of several facts sometimes makes a stronger case. For example, a conviction for possession with intent to distribute cocaine base was supported by showing that an informant told police that the defendant was dealing crack cocaine out of his home, the informant made a controlled drug buy, and 3.8 grams of crack cocaine were recovered during a search of the defendant's home.[66]

D. Other Federal Drug-Related Offenses

Section 859 includes a separate provision prohibiting distribution of a controlled substance to a person less than 21 years of age. This section mandates a greater penalty for those who violate this section, with a provision that a term of imprisonment under this subsection shall not be less than one year. Section 860 makes it a separate violation for one to distribute or manufacture a controlled substance in, on, or within 1,000 feet of the real property comprising a public or private elementary, vocational, or secondary school or a public or private college, junior college, or university.[67] Section 861 makes it unlawful for any person at least 18 years of age to knowingly and intentionally "employ, hire, use, persuade, induce, entice or coerce" anyone under 18 to violate the provisions of the law.

Title 18 § 2118 imposes a penalty on anyone who takes or attempts to take from the person or presence of another by force or violence or by intimidation any material or compound containing any quantity of a controlled substance belonging to or in the care, custody, control, or possession of a person registered with the Drug Enforcement Administration.

In Chapter 21 (Drug Abuse, Prevention, and Control) of the U.S. Code, Section 846 defines Attempt and Conspiracy as they relate to drug offenses.

In this conspiracy offense, no overt act is necessary; a simple agreement to commit a federal drug offense is sufficient to prove guilt and the parties are subject to the same penalties as if the crime was completed. Section 848 is titled Continuing Criminal Enterprise and is similar to the RICO statute, except that it is directed specifically to someone who commits drug offenses as part of a continuing criminal enterprise. An offender may be charged with the underlying crimes, i.e., possession with intent to distribute, and Statute 848 (CCE).

E.   Federal Forfeiture Statutes

Federal statutes provide for the **forfeiture** of property used to facilitate drug-related offenses and for the forfeiture of proceeds from drug transactions.[68] In 1996, the U.S. Supreme Court revisited the issue of the relationship between the federal asset forfeiture statutes and the double jeopardy clause of the U.S. Constitution. The Court expressly rejected the previously employed "balancing" test (the harm suffered by the government is compared to the forfeiture imposed) in favor of the following test: (1) Whether Congress intended the statutory scheme at issue to be criminal or civil, and (2) Whether the scheme is so punitive either in purpose or effect as to negate the intent of Congress to establish a civil asset forfeiture process. Applying this new test, the Court concluded that asset forfeiture in drug cases did not violate the double jeopardy clause in that it was not an additional penalty for the commission of a criminal act, but rather a separate civil action, remedial in nature and expressly sanctioned by Congress.[69]

Austin v. United States,[70] discussed in Chapter 11, was a ruling in which the Supreme Court held that a federal forfeiture was not outside the spectrum of Eighth Amendment protection, so that if it was deemed disproportional or excessive to the crime committed, the forfeiture action of the government could be overturned. Because *Austin* was not expressly overruled, legal scholars remain perplexed—the federal asset forfeiture statutes apparently do not violate the double jeopardy clause; but, where the forfeiture is too disproportionate to the offense, such statutes may violate the excessive fines clause.

§ 14.11.7   Wiretapping and Eavesdropping

In 1929 and again in 1931, Congress introduced legislation designed to protect against interception of telephone communications by the use of wiretaps. However, it was not until 1934, when Congress passed the Federal Communications Act, that **wiretapping** was made illegal.[71] This act included the following provision:

> 18 U.S.C. § 2510
>
> No person not being authorized by the sender shall intercept any communication or divulge or publish the existence, contents, substance, purport, effect, or meaning of such intercepted communication to any person.

The amended provisions of the United States Code comprehensively regulate eavesdropping and the interception of communications. Title 18 §§ 2510 through 2522 contain provisions that prohibit intentional interception or attempts to intercept any wire or electronic communication and includes criminal penalties for violations of the statutes and detailed provisions for exceptions. Title 18 U.S. Code § 2511 prohibits the interception and disclosure of wire, oral, or electronic communications and includes criminal as well as civil penalties. This section also has provisions for exceptions with detailed requirements for each exception. Subsection 2(c) of the statute provides that it shall not be unlawful for a person acting under color of law to intercept a wire, oral, or electronic communication where such person is a party to the communication or one of the parties to the communication has given prior consent to such interception. Subsection (2)(d) provides that it shall not be unlawful under this chapter for a person not acting under color of law to intercept a wire, oral, or electronic communication where such person is a party to the communication or where one of the parties to the communication has given prior consent to such interception unless such communication is intercepted for the purpose of committing any criminal or tortious act in violation of the Constitution or laws of the United States or of any state.

Legal News

In December 2008, a Hollywood private eye (Anthony Pellicano) was sentenced to 15 years in prison for violating federal wiretapping laws. Evidently he utilized wiretapping in his investigations of the rich and famous. He was known as the "P.I. of the stars" and did work for a long list of celebrities and business people. Some of his work involved spying on reporters who were doing stories on his clients. Charges included 78 counts of wiretapping and related crimes.

Source: Associated Press (2008). "Private Eye Gets 15 Year Term." Austin American-Statesman, December 16, 2008:A2.

The consent provisions of the statutes have been interpreted in several court cases. In a federal court case, the court held that the consent is not voluntary when it is coerced by either explicit or implied means, or by an implied threat of covert force.[72] The courts have also interpreted the consent provisions to include implied consent. In a New York federal court, the judges decided that the defendant had no reasonable expectation of privacy that warranted the suppression of tapes of telephone calls he made from pay telephones in the jail cell, where the sign in the jail booking room implied that some telephone calls, other than those to attorneys, were subject to interception and would be recorded.[73] The statute provides an exception that allows wiretapping and eavesdropping when a court order is properly obtained.

Although the statute does not apply to eavesdropping with the unaided ear, listening to a conversation at a distance with a highly sensitive amplifying device does violate the law.[74]

While state agents must comply with both the federal minimum standards and any additional restrictions imposed by their state, federal agents need only follow federal regulations.[75]

Legal News

In 2006, a controversy arose after it was revealed that federal officers had been using wiretaps without a warrant. A Presidential Order signed in 2002 allowed the National Security Agency to monitor international telephone calls and international e-mail messages of thousands of people inside the United States without warrants. The concern expressed by opponents of the practice is that the National Security Agency has traditionally been involved in investigations external to the borders of the U.S. and that any domestic wiretapping requires a warrant from the Foreign Intelligence Surveillance Court. The 1978 law that created the court has been interpreted to bar all domestic wiretapping, even for national security, unless it is sanctioned by a warrant, and the secret court was created to grant such warrants. The administration's position is that Congress authorized the President to take any and all steps required to combat terrorism in the wake of September 11, 2001. Others' opinion is that the federal wiretapping without a warrant violates federal laws. A federal court dismissed a challenge to the practice by the ACLU in 2007, concluding that the ACLU had no standing to bring the case. Congress passed the "Protect America Act" in 2007, which legalized warrantless wiretapping for national security.

Source: ACLU v. NSA, No. 06-20951/2140. U.S. District Court (E.D. Michigan). Decided July 6, 2007.

In addition to the civil penalties, the Act provides a criminal penalty for those who violate the statute. One provision of the Act states that except as provided in paragraph (b) of subsection 2511(4) or in subsection (5), whoever violates subsection (1) shall be fined or imprisoned not more than five years, or both.[76] The penalty section of the Act continues with a detailed discussion of exceptions and modifications of penalties.

The courts continue to receive requests to interpret certain words of the statutes such as "intentionally intercepts" and the terms "use" or "disclosure." According to a federal court in Texas, criminal violation of the federal wiretap statute only requires proof of general intent, not specific intent to violate the law.[77] An individual who acted consciously, as opposed to accidentally, in taping a cordless telephone conversation of his neighbor, intentionally intercepted electronic communications in violation of the Electronic Communications Privacy Act.[78]

§ 14.11.8   Terrorism

In the aftermath of the terrorist attacks on September 11, 2001, Congress enacted comprehensive legislation to vest those involved in the criminal justice system with the authority to combat terrorism. Prior to the attacks, few were aware that counterterrorism laws were in effect. Recognizing that additional legislation was required to combat terrorism, Congress enacted comprehensive legislation that made it possible for those involved in the criminal justice process to more effectively investigate and prosecute violators.

A. USA Patriot Act

In October 2001, the 107th Congress enacted Public Law 107-56, which is titled "Uniting and Strengthening America by Providing Appropriate Tools Required to Intercept and Obstruct Terrorism Act." This Act is known as the USA **Patriot Act** of 2001. This lengthy act amends existing statutes concerning terrorism and adds additional provisions to the law. The numerous sections of the Act are included under 10 titles:

> Title I—ENHANCING DOMESTIC SECURITY AGAINST TERRORISM
>
> Title II—ENHANCED SURVEILLANCE PROCEDURES
>
> Title III—INTERNATIONAL MONEY LAUNDERING ABATEMENT AND ANTITERRORIST FINANCING ACT OF 2001
>
> Title IV—PROTECTING THE BORDER
>
> Title V—REMOVING OBSTACLES TO INVESTIGATING TERRORISM
>
> Title VI—PROVIDING FOR VICTIMS OF TERRORISM, PUBLIC SAFETY OFFICERS, AND THEIR FAMILIES
>
> Title VII—INCREASED INFORMATION SHARING FOR CRITICAL INFRASTRUCTURE PROTECTION
>
> Title VIII—STRENGTHENING THE CRIMINAL LAWS AGAINST TERRORISM
>
> Title IX—IMPROVED INTELLIGENCE
>
> Title X—MISCELLANEOUS

Most of the remaining discussion in this section regards the provisions of Title VIII of the Patriot Act: "Strengthening the Criminal Laws against Terrorism." Prior to the passing of the Patriot Act, Chapter 113B, titled "Terrorism," was included in the United States Code. It included criminal penalties for a series of acts relating to terrorism. Among these were:

18 U.S.C. § 2332(a) Use of Weapons of Mass Destruction

18 U.S.C. § 2332(b) Acts of Terrorism Transcending National Boundaries

18 U.S.C § 2332(d) Financial Transactions

18 U.S.C. § 2339(A) Providing Material to Terrorists

18 U.S.C. § 2339(B) Providing Material Support or Resources to Designated Foreign Terrorist Organizations

B. Definitions

Title 18 U.S.C. § 2331, as it existed prior to the Patriot Act, defined international terrorism as activities that "involve violent acts or acts dangerous to human life that are a violation of the criminal laws of the United States or of any State, or that would be a criminal violation if committed within the jurisdiction of the United States or of any State" and that appear to be intended to do one or more of the following:

(i)   to intimidate or coerce a civilian population;

(ii)   to influence the policy of a government by intimidation or coercion; or

(iii) to affect the conduct of a government by assassination or kidnapping; and

      (C)   occur primarily outside the territorial jurisdiction of the United States, or transcend national boundaries in terms of the means by which they are accomplished, the persons they appear intended to intimidate or coerce, or the locale in which their perpetrators operate or seek asylum;

Recognizing the limitations of these definitions, § 2331 of Title 18 was amended to include "by mass destruction, assassination or kidnapping" as one of the acts that constitutes terrorism. Also "domestic terrorism" was included and defined as those acts "dangerous to human life that are a violation of the criminal laws of United States or of any State and that appear to be intended to do one of the following:

(i)   to intimidate or coerce a civilian population;

(ii)   to influence the policy of a government by intimidation or coercion; or

(iii) to affect the policy of a government by mass destruction, assassination, or kidnapping; and

      (C)   occur primarily within the territorial jurisdiction of the United States."

Title 18 U.S.C. 2332a is titled "Use of Certain Weapons of Mass Destruction." This section provides:

(a) an offense against a national of the United States or within the United States. A person who, without lawful authority, uses, threatens, or attempts or conspires to use, a weapon of mass destruction, other than a chemical weapon as that term is defined in § 3229(f), including any biological agent, toxin, or vector.

  (1) against a national of the United States while such national is outside the United States;
  (2) against any person within the United States, and the results of which use after interstate or foreign commerce, or, in the case of a threat, attempt, or conspiracy, would have affected interstate or foreign commerce; or
  (3) against any property that is owned, leased or used by the United States or by any department or agency of the United States, whether the property is within or outside the United States;

shall be imprisoned for any term of years or for life, and if death results, shall be punished by death or imprisoned for any term of years or for life.

Section 2332b is titled "Acts of Terrorism Transcending National Boundaries." This section provides that whoever, involving transcending national boundaries and in circumstances described in the Act:

(A) kills, kidnaps, maims, commits an assault resulting in serious bodily injury, or assaults with a dangerous weapon any person within the United States; or

(B) creates a substantial risk of serious bodily injury to any other person by destroying or damaging any structure, conveyance, or other real or personal property within the United States or by attempting or conspiring to destroy or damage any structure, conveyance, or other real or personal property within the United States;

(C) in violation of the laws of any state, or the United States, shall be punished as provided in the Act.

This section was amended by the Patriot Act to increase the violations included in the term "federal crime of terrorism" as used in the Act. John Phillip Walker Lindh was charged under this Act with conspiracy to murder nationals of the United States, including American military personnel and other government employees serving in Afghanistan following the September 11, 2001, terrorist attacks, in violation of 18 U.S.C. § 2332b. He was not convicted of violating the statute but was found guilty of other offenses.[79]

Title 18 U.S.C. § 2339, "Harboring or Concealing Terrorists" imposes a fine as provided in the Act or imprisonment for not more than 10 years or both if a person is convicted of harboring or concealing any person who he knows or has reasonable grounds to believe has committed, or is about the commit, an offense of any of the acts included in the statute.

Title 18 U.S.C. § 2339A, "Providing Material Support to Terrorists" provides that whoever, within the United States, provides material support or resources or conceals or disguises the nature, location, source, or ownership of material support or resources, knowing or intending that they are to be used in preparation for carrying out a violation of the sections indicated, or in preparation for, or in carrying out, the concealment or escape from the commission of such violations, shall be fined under this title, imprisoned not more than 10 years, or both. This section was amended by the Patriot Act by striking out "within the United States" and by adding sections of the law covered by the Act. The effect of deleting "within the United States" makes the provisions enforceable when the acts described occur outside the United States.

Title 18 U.S.C. § 2339B, "Providing Material Support or Resources to Designated Foreign Terrorist Organizations" was amended in part by the Patriot Act to read:

> (a) prohibited activities
>   (1) unlawful conduct—whoever, within the United States, or subject to the jurisdiction of the United States, knowingly provides material support or resources to a foreign terrorist organization, or attempts or conspires to do so, shall be fined under this title or imprisoned not more than fifteen years, or both, and, if the death of any person results, shall be imprisoned for any term of years or for life.

The existing chapter on terrorism was amended by the Patriot Act to include an offense designated "Terrorist attacks and other acts of violence against mass transportation systems."[80] This comprehensive law provides penalties where one wrecks, derails, sets fire to, or disables a mass transportation vehicle or ferry. The Act also prohibits using biological weapons, impairing operations of mass transportation systems, interfering with employees, or using dangerous weapons with intent to cause injury to employees or passengers.

The following is a list of additional terrorism-related statutes that grant jurisdiction to investigative agencies:

> TITLE 18 U.S.C. § 831—PROHIBITED TRANSACTION INVOLVING NUCLEAR MATERIALS
>
> TITLE 18 U.S.C. § 842(p)—TEACHING, DEMONSTRATING, OR DISTRIBUTION OF INFORMATION RELATIVE TO EXPLOSIVES, DESTRUCTIVE DEVICES AND WEAPONS OF MASS DESTRUCTION
>
> TITLE 18 U.S.C. §§ 921-930—UNLAWFUL ACTIVITIES RELATING TO FIREARMS
>
> TITLE 18 U.S.C. § 1203—ACTS FOR THE PREVENTION AND PUNISHMENT OF THE CRIME OF HOSTAGE TAKING
>
> TITLE 18 U.S.C. § 1344—BANK FRAUD

TITLE 18 U.S.C. §§ 1541-1546—CRIMES BASED UPON IMPROPER ACQUISITION OR MISUSES OF PASSPORT, VISA, OR ENTRY DOCUMENTS

TITLE 18 U.S.C. § 1956—MONEY LAUNDERING AS IT RELATES TO TERRORISM OFFENSES

TITLE 18 U.S.C. § 1960—PROHIBITION OF ILLEGAL MONEY TRANSMITTING BUSINESS

The specific criminal laws against terrorism are included in Title VIII of the Patriot Act. Other provisions of interest to criminal justice personnel are Title II and Title V. Title II, "Enhanced Surveillance Procedures," among other things, authorizes law enforcement agencies to share investigative information. Title V, "Removing Obstacles to Investigating Terrorism," makes it less difficult to identify and locate terrorists and terrorist organizations and to acquire information to convict those who commit terrorist acts.

Legal News

On March 7, 2006, Congress approved the renewal of the Patriot Act. Three provisions of the Act will be reviewed in four years, the other provisions of the Act have been made permanent. The bill created a "National Security Division" in the Department of Justice. It continued the "roving wiretap" provision of the Patriot Act, as well as the power of federal officials to access library, business, and medical records without a court order.

Source: Retrieved 7/4/06 from www.cnn.com/2006/POLITICS/03/07/patriot.act/

§ 14.11.9   Other Offenses Against the Public Peace

In Chapter 11, one of the other offenses against public peace described was harassment and stalking. The federal government has also responded to this issue with the National Stalker and Domestic Violence Reduction Act.[81] In the United States Code, the federal stalking law is 18 U.S.C. § 2261A, which makes it a crime to cross state lines with the intent to injure or harass another and 18 U.S.C. § 2262, which makes it a crime to cross state lines to violate a protective order.

§ 14.12.1   Offenses Against Justice Administration

Recall that the offenses in Chapter 12 concerned crimes that were directed to the obstruction or manipulation of the justice process or the administration of government. The state criminal laws prohibit such actions against state justice and administration while federal laws prohibit the same types of activities when directed toward the federal government or federal court system.

§ 14.12.2   Perjury and Related Offenses

Chapter 79 of Title 18 of the U.S. Code defines three perjury-related offenses: perjury, subornation of perjury, and false declaration before a grand jury or court. The crime of perjury is defined as:

> 18 U.S.C. § 1621
>
> Whoever—
>
> (1) having taken an oath before a competent tribunal, officer, or person, in any case in which a law of the United States authorizes an oath to be administered, that he will testify, declare, depose, or certify truly, or that any written testimony, declaration, deposition, certificate by him subscribed, is true, willfully and contrary to such oaths states or subscribes any material matter which he does not believe to be true; or
> (2) in any declaration, certificate, verification, or statement under a penalty of perjury as permitted under Section 1746 of Title 28, U.S. Code, willfully subscribes as true any material matter which he does not believe to be true;
>
> is guilty of perjury and shall, except as otherwise expressly provided by law, be fined under this title or imprisoned not more than five years or both.[82]

This section applies whether the statement or subscription is made within or outside the United States. This federal statute contains provisions that are similar to state statutes and has been found to meet constitutional standards.[83] The essential elements to prove a violation of this section are:

- taking an oath in a case in which a law of the United States authorizes the oath to be administered,

- to testify willfully and contrary to such oath,

- making a false statement,

- as to a material fact, and

- which the defendant did not believe to be true.

The justices of the Eighth Circuit explained that a witness commits perjury when he or she testifies falsely under oath about a material matter, with a willful intent to deceive the factfinder.[84]

The Court of Appeals for the Ninth Circuit believed that § 1621 of the federal statute was violated by a police officer who gave false deposition testimony in a civil rights case. In this case, the police officer testified that officers who took sick leave were actually sick when in fact they were not sick. This false testimony, according to the court, would have a "tendency to influence" the jury's decision whether the department's disciplinary action for a violation of the sick leave policy was imposed for harassment and retaliation.[85]

A. Subornation of Perjury

Section 1622 of the federal statute provides:

> 18 U.S.C. § 1622
>
> Whoever procures another to commit any perjury is guilty of subornation of perjury, and shall be fined under this title or imprisoned not more than five years, or both.[86]

A federal court, in interpreting the subornation provision, found that in order to constitute the offense of subornation of perjury, the offense of perjury must actually *have been committed* by another.[87] This is different than some state laws that do not require the perjury to occur before finding that the subornation has been committed. Another federal court indicated that this statute was correctly applied when an attorney was charged with subornation of perjury of a witness in violation of this section. A prosecutor who procures false testimony is also subject to a penalty under the subornation of perjury statute.[88] A federal court also found that an attorney suborned perjury of a witness in violation of 18 U.S.C. § 1622 by not advising the witness, after hearing the witness propose testimony and knowing it to be false, against testifying in that manner.[89]

B. False Swearing

In addition to the perjury statute, the United States Code criminalizes false statements under 18 U.S.C. § 1001, which states:

> 18 U.S.C. § 1001
>
> (a) Except as otherwise provided in this section, whoever, in any matter within the jurisdiction of the executive, legislative, or judicial branch of the government of the United States, knowingly and willfully—
>
> (1) Falsifies, conceals, or covers up by any trick, scheme, or device a material fact;
> (2) Makes any materially false, fictitious, or fraudulent statement or representation; or
> (3) Makes or uses any false writing or document knowing the same to contain any materially false, fictitious, or fraudulent statement or entry.

§ 14.12.3   Bribery and Related Offenses

Chapter 11 of Title 18 of the U.S. Code is titled "Bribery, Graft and Conflicts of Interest." It includes ethical standards of conduct for government employees and laws relating to:

- "bribery of public officials and witnesses,"
- "bribery in sporting contests,"
- "acceptance or solicitation to obtain appointment of public office,"
- "acceptance of loan or gratuity by bank examiner."

A. Gratuities

Section 201(c)(1)(A) sets forth the elements of an illegal **gratuity** offense applicable to the gratuity giver, and § 201(c)(1)(B) sets forth the elements applicable to a gratuity recipient. To prove an illegal gratuity offense, the government must demonstrate: (1) a thing of value; (2) was given, offered, or promised to (or demanded, sought, received, or accepted by); (3) a public official; and (4) "for or because of any official act performed or to be performed by such public official."[90] "Public official" is defined as a person who has been selected to be a public official and includes any of the following:

> Members of Congress, Delegate, or Resident Commissioner, either before or after such official has qualified or an officer or employee or person acting for or on behalf of the United States, or any department, agency or branch of Government thereof, including the District of Columbia, in any official function, under or by authority of any such department, agency, or branch of government, or a juror; any person who has been nominated or appointed to be a public official, or has been officially informed that such person will be so nominated or appointed.[91]

B. Bribery

Section 201 states the following as the definition of bribery:

18 U.S.C. § 201

(b) Whoever—

    (1) directly or indirectly, corruptly gives, offers or promises anything of value to any public official or person who has been selected to be a public official, or offers or promises any public official or any person who has been selected to be a public official to give anything of value to any other person or entity, with intent—

    (A) to influence any official act; or

(B) to influence such public official or person who has been selected to be a public official to commit or aid in committing, or collude in or allow, any fraud, or make opportunity for the commission of any fraud, on the United States; or

(C) to induce such public official or such person who has been selected to be a public official to do or omit to do any act in violation of the lawful duty of such official or person;

(2) being a public official or person selected to be a public official, directly or indirectly, corruptly demands, seeks, receives, accepts, or agrees to receive or accept anything of value personally or for any other person or entity, in return for:

(A) being influenced in the performance of any official act;

(B) being influenced to commit or aid in committing, or to collude in, or allow, any fraud, or make opportunity for the commission of any fraud, on the United States; or

(C) being induced to do or omit to do any act in violation of the official duty of such official or person;

(3) directly or indirectly, corruptly gives, offers, or promises anything of value to any person, or offers to promise such person to give anything of value to any other person or entity, with intent to influence the testimony under oath or affirmation of such first-mentioned person as a witness upon a trial, hearing, or other proceeding, before any court, any committee of either House or both Houses of Congress, or any agency, commission, or officer authorized by the laws of the United States to hear evidence or take testimony, or with intent to influence such person to absent himself therefrom;

(4) directly or indirectly, corruptly demands, seeks, receives, accepts, or agrees to receive or accept anything of value personally or for any other person or entity in return for being influenced in testimony under oath or affirmation as a witness upon any such trial, hearing, or other proceeding, or in return for absenting himself therefrom:

shall be fined not more than three times the monetary equivalent of the thing of value, or imprisoned for not more than fifteen years, or both, and may be disqualified from holding any office of honor, trust, or profit under the United States.

(c) Whoever—

(1) otherwise than as provided by law for the proper discharge of official duty—

(A) directly or indirectly gives, offers, or promises anything of value to any public official, former public official, or person selected to be a public official, for or because of any official act performed or to be performed by such public official, former public official, or person selected to be a public official; or

    (B) being a public official, former public official, or person selected to be a public official, otherwise than as provided by law for the proper discharge of official duty, directly or indirectly demands, seeks, receives, accepts, or agrees to receive or accept anything of value personally for or because of any official act performed or to be performed by such official or person;

(2) directly or indirectly, gives, offers or promises anything of value to any person, for or because of the testimony under oath or affirmation given or to be given by such person as a witness upon a trial, hearing, or other proceeding, before any court, any committee of either House or both Houses of Congress, or any agency, commission, or officer authorized by the laws of the United States to hear evidence or take testimony, or for or because of such person's absence therefrom;

(3) directly or indirectly demands, seeks, receives, accepts, or agrees to receive or accept anything of value personally for or because of the testimony under oath or affirmation given or to be given by such person as a witness upon any such trial, hearing, or other proceeding, or for or because of such person's absence therefrom;

shall be fined under this title or imprisoned for not more than two years, or both.

(d) Paragraphs (3) and (4) of subsection (b) and paragraphs (2) and (3) of subsection (c) shall not be construed to prohibit the payment or receipt of witness fees provided by law, or the payment by the party upon whose behalf a witness is called and receipt by a witness, of the reasonable cost of travel and subsistence incurred and the reasonable value of time lost in attendance at any such trial, hearing, or proceeding, or in the case of expert witnesses, a reasonable fee for time spent in the preparation of such opinion and in appearing and testifying.

(e) The offenses and penalties prescribed in this section are separate from and in addition to those prescribed in sections 1503, 1504 and 1505 of this Title.

1. Public Official

The definition of public official is fairly broad under the federal bribery statute and includes state and county officials as well. A deputy sheriff was "a public official" within the meaning of the federal bribery statute, although he was a county employee receiving no federal funds and the federal prisoners he supervised were not segregated from the state inmates.[92] In another case, a juror was considered to be a federal official for the purposes of the bribery statute.[93]

2. Official Acts

Official acts are also defined fairly broadly. The most typical acts involve decisions or votes by the public official, but can include other activities as well. A congressman engaged in "official acts," within the meaning of the federal bribery statute, when he wrote letters on behalf of a party who had paid for his vacations, using his congressional stationery, to urge federal and city officials to take action favorable to the party.[94]

3. Thing of Value

"A thing of value" within the meaning of the statute is to be broadly construed to encompass intangible benefits, as long as the jury is instructed that they must determine whether the donee placed any value on the intangible gifts.[95] As an example, a defendant agricultural cooperative provided a federal official with "a thing of value" by providing for transportation and expenses of a former Secretary of Agriculture's girlfriend, so that she could be with him in Greece when he presented a speech before an agricultural group.[96] The court advised that companionship, as well as money, can be "a thing of value" to an official. Also, as used in the statute, "anything of value" covered the alleged intangible benefit of receiving favors from police in the form of an officer ignoring certain state offenses committed by the briber.[97]

Legal News

Unfortunately, there is no shortage of bribery cases involving public officials. Randall "Duke" Cunningham, a long-term congressman from California, was one of the most powerful men in recent years to be convicted of federal bribery charges. Evidence indicated that he received benefits totaling hundreds of thousands of dollars, mostly from defense contractors. In his position as chair of the defense appropriations committee, he was able to influence the awarding of defense contracts to his benefactors. Cunningham received a prison sentence in 2005 for his crimes and is currently in a federal prison. The most recent case was Ted Stevens of Alaska. His charges were not bribery, however, but a different charge of failing to report gifts. Evidence indicates that he accepted house renovations that were worth more than 100,000 and other gifts without reporting them on financial disclosure forms. In the 2008 election, the fact that he had been convicted did not convince him to resign from the Senate; however, voters elected his opponent, averting the need for Senate sanctions.

Sources: cnn.com. "Congressman Resigns after Bribery Plea." Accessed 3/9/2009 from http://www.cnn.com/2005/POLITICS/11/28/cunningham/index.html?iref=newssearch. Demer, L., R. Mauer, and E. Bolstad (2008). "Alaska Sen. Stevens Indicted; "I'm Innocent." *Anchorage Daily News*, July 30. Accessed 3/9/2009 from http://www.adn.com/news/politics/fbi/stevens/story/478349.html.

In *United States v. Frega*, the accused was an attorney who was prosecuted under the RICO statute as well as mail fraud and bribery. He evidently paid the equivalent of more than $100,000 to three California Superior Court judges over a 12-year period in the form of cars, car repairs, health club memberships, and at least one queen-size bed. What he received in return was favorable treatment when he had a case before the judge.[98] He argued that the gifts were given in the nature of friendship and goodwill and were not bribes. The appellate court upheld his conviction.

4. Other Applications

In interpreting Section 201(b)(4), a reviewing court ruled that an unabash-edly expressed willingness of a witness to tailor her testimony to the highest bidder was sufficient to show that the defendant acted "corruptly" within the meaning of the statute.[99]

The federal statute is very comprehensive and applies to those who receive or accept anything of value. It also applies not only to proceedings before any court, but also to proceedings before committees of either House of Congress or any agency, commission, or officer authorized by the laws of the United States to hear evidence, or give testimony. Cases interpreting the provisions of the statute have held that these provisions are neither uncon-stitutionally vague nor overbroad.[100]

Several federal courts have considered the application of the federal bribery statute where payments are made to confidential informants by law enforcement agencies. In the case of *United States v. Levenite*, a federal circuit court agreed that payment to a confidential FBI informant in a large-scale methamphetamine trafficking conspiracy who testified at criminal proceeding did not violate the statute prohibiting bribery of public officials and witnesses, because the government was explicitly authorized to pay witnesses fees as authorized by law.[101] Courts have held that the antigratuity statute, which criminalizes giving or promising anything of value in exchange for witness testimony, does not apply to the United States or to any assistant United States attorney acting within his or her official capacity.[102]

Although the bribery statutes have been interpreted broadly, a conviction will not stand if the defendant can show entrapment. For example, when a taxpayer offered a bribe only after an IRS agent's persistent solicitations and reminders as to the substantial amount of tax liability, the bribery charge was dismissed.[103]

§ 14.12.4   Obstructing Justice

Chapter 73 of Title 18 of the U.S. Code has 14 sections relating to the obstruction of justice. Obstruction of justice is governed principally by 18 U.S.C. §§ 1501 through 1818, which forbid the obstruction of justice and protect the integrity of proceedings before the federal judiciary and other governmental bodies.[104]

A. § 1503

The section that is employed most frequently is § 1503, which provides:

18 U.S.C. § 1503. Influencing or injuring officer or juror (generally)

(a) Whoever corruptly, or by threats or force, or by any threatening letter or communication, endeavors to influence, intimidate, or impede any grand or petit juror, or officer in or of any court of the United States, or officer who may be serving at any examination or other proceeding before any United States magistrate judge or other committing magistrate, in the discharge of his duty, or injures any such grand or petit juror in his person or property on account of any verdict or indictment assented to by him, or on account of his being or having been such juror, or injures any such officer, magistrate judge, or other committing magistrate in his person or property on account of the performance of his official duties, or corruptly or by threats or force, or by any threatening letter or communication, influences, obstructs, or impedes, or endeavors to influence, obstruct, or impede, the due administration of justice, shall be punished as provided in subsection (b). If the offense under this section occurs in connection with a trial of a criminal case, and the act in violation of this section involves the threat of physical force or physical force, the maximum term of imprisonment which may be imposed for the offense shall be the higher of that otherwise provided by law or the maximum term that could have been imposed for any offense charged in such case.

(b) the punishment for an offense under this section is—

(1) in the case of a killing, the punishment provided in sections 1111 and 1112;

(2) in the case of an attempted killing, or a case in which the offense was committed against a petit juror and in which a class A or B felony was charged, imprisonment for not more than 20 years, a fine under this title, or both; and

(3) in any other case, imprisonment for not more than 10 years, a fine under this title, or both.

18 U.S.C. § 1503 governs any obstruction of justice affecting jurors, officers of the court, and judges. The elements of a § 1503 offense are:

- a nexus with a pending federal judicial proceeding;

- that the defendant knew of or had notice about the proceeding; and

- that the defendant acted corruptly with intent to obstruct or interfere with the proceedings or due administration of justice.[105]

While the government need not prove that the defendant had the specific purpose of obstructing justice, it must establish that the defendant's conduct possessed, at least in part, a corrupt motive.[106] One need not succeed in obstructing justice to be convicted of a violation of § 1503.[107] This section was challenged as being unconstitutionally vague, but the courts that have heard arguments agree that the statute does not suffer from unconstitutional vagueness.[108]

Defendants have been successfully prosecuted for knowingly, willfully, and corruptly:

- attempting to impede the administration of justice in a matter under investigation by intentionally destroying documents[109]

- giving false testimony to a grand jury concerning a third person's presence at a meeting[110]

- corruptly influencing a grand jury witness to refuse to testify[111]

To show the offense of endeavoring to influence a juror in the discharge of his or her duty, the government must prove: (1) that a judicial proceeding was pending; (2) that the defendant had knowledge of the judicial proceeding; and (3) that the defendant acted corruptly with the specific intent to influence, obstruct, or impede that proceeding and its due administration of justice.[112]

Legal News

On March 30, 2006, it was reported that a former federal prosecutor and investigator were indicted on charges of conspiracy, obstruction of justice, and making false statements in connection with a 2003 terrorism prosecution. Allegedly, the prosecutor did not turn over dozens of pieces of evidence to the defense that it was entitled to have and made false statements in another case. The prosecutor has filed a civil whistleblower suit against the government and alleges that the charges are retaliation. It is extremely rare for prosecutors to be prosecuted for obstruction.

Source: "Official, Ex-Prosecutor of Terror Trial Indicted." *Austin American-Statesman*, March 30, 2006, at A14.

B. Other Crimes

Title 18 § 1512 of the U.S. Code includes penalties for tampering with a witness, victim, or informant. That section includes the following provisions:

18 U.S.C. § 1572

(2) Whoever uses physical force or the threat of physical force against any person, or attempts to do so, with intent to—

(A) influence, delay, or prevent the testimony of any person in an official proceeding;

(B) cause or induce any person to—
    (i) withhold testimony, or withhold a record, document, or other object, from an official proceeding;
    (ii) alter, destroy, mutilate, or conceal an object with intent to impair the integrity or availability of the object for use in an official proceeding;
    (iii) evade legal process summoning that person to appear as a witness, or to produce a record, document, or other object, in an official proceeding; or
    (iv) be absent from an official proceeding to which that person has been summoned by legal process; or

(C) hinder, delay, or prevent the communication to a law enforcement officer or judge of the United States of information relating to the commission or possible commission of a Federal offense or a violation of conditions of probation, supervised release, parole, or release pending judicial proceedings; shall be punished as provided in paragraph (3).[113]

14.12.5   Escape

Chapter 35 of Title 18 of the U.S. Code includes a provision relating to the escape of prisoners in the custody of an institutional officer, a second provision making it a crime to rescue a person who has been lawfully arrested, and a third provision making it possible to punish an officer who voluntarily allows a prisoner to escape.[114]

Title 18 § 751 of the United States Code (Prisoners in Custody of Institution or Officer) provides:

18 U.S.C. § 751. Prisoners in custody of institution or officer

(a) Whoever escapes or attempts to escape from the custody of the Attorney General or his authorized representative, or from any institution or facility in which he is confined by direction of the Attorney General, or from any custody under or by virtue of any process issued under the laws of the United States by any court, judge or magistrate judge, or from the custody of an officer or employee of the United States pursuant to lawful arrest, shall, if the custody or confinement is by virtue of an arrest on a charge of felony, or conviction of any offense, be fined under this title or imprisoned not more than five years, or both; or if the custody or confinement is for extradition, or for exclusion or expulsion proceedings under the immigration laws, or by virtue of an arrest or charge of or for a misdemeanor, and prior to conviction, be fined under this title or imprisoned no more than one year, or both.

The elements of the offense of escape from custody are:

- the defendant is held in a statutory type of custody,

- for a felony violation,

- leaving without authorization.[115]

To prove a violation of the statute prohibiting escape from federal custody, the government must show that an escapee knew his action would result in his leaving physical confinement without permission.[116]

In the case of *United States v. Novak*, the defendant left a work detail and was charged with escape in violation of this statute. At the trial, the parties agreed that Novak escaped from nonsecure custody on December 8, 2000, and returned voluntarily at approximately 2:30 P.M. on December 12, 2000. The time of the escape became important in determining whether the defendant was entitled to a "seven-level" downward adjustment for returning to custody voluntarily within 96 hours of his escape.[117] The court decided that escape begins when the defendant departs from local custody with the intent to evade detention, even if no one saw him wander from his work detail, rather than from the time his absence was reported.

Title 18 § 752 of the U.S. Code makes it a crime to instigate or assist an escape.[118] Under this provision, whoever rescues or attempts to rescue, or instigates, aids, or assists the escape, or attempt to escape, of any person arrested under a warrant or other process issued under any law of the United States, shall be punished. In a prosecution for aiding and assisting the escape of a federal prisoner under this section, evidence that the defendant knew the prisoner's departure from prison was unauthorized was sufficient to sustain a conviction.[119]

Section 755 of Title 18 makes it a crime for an officer to permit an escape:[120]

18 U.S.C. § 755

Whoever, having in his custody any prisoner by virtue of process issued under the laws of the United States by any court, judge, or magistrate judge, voluntarily suffers such prisoner to escape, shall be fined under this title or imprisoned not more than five years, or both; or if he negligently suffers such person to escape, he shall be fined under this title or imprisoned not more than one year, or both.

As the wording indicates, this section applies only if the person accused has custody of a prisoner and either voluntarily allows the prisoner to escape or negligently permits the prisoner to escape.

§ 14.12.6   Resisting Arrest

Title 18 § 111 makes resisting arrest a felony punishable by a fine or imprisonment of not more than eight years, or both, if a person is convicted of forcibly assaulting, resisting, opposing, impeding, or intimidating an officer in the performance of his or her official duties. If deadly force or a dangerous weapon is used, the imprisonment may be increased to 20 years.[121]

A federal court of appeals found that this section gives a person of ordinary intelligence fair notice of what conduct is proscribed and is not unconstitutionally vague, indefinite, or ambiguous.[122]

The provision prohibiting assault against a federal officer was enacted to protect federal officers and federal functions and to provide a federal forum in which to try the alleged offender. As is the law in many states, federal officers engaged in good faith and colorable performance of their duties may not be forcibly resisted even if the person resisting is correct that the resisted action should not have been taken. The statute requires the arrestee to submit peaceably and seek legal redress thereafter. When a person is identified as a law enforcement officer, and uses reasonable force in the performance of his or her law enforcement duties, the use of force to resist that officer is not justified and self-defense does not apply.[123] The federal law making it a felony to resist arrest or intimidate an officer in the performance of his or her official duties may be violated by minimal physical contact, or even by threats, without physical contact.[124]

§ 14.13 Summary

In this chapter, a wide range of federal crimes have been described. In general, federal powers to define crimes in the area of morals, public peace, and justice administration must be constrained by the limits of federal power. The federal government must have some justification to pass such laws in either the commerce clause or some other enumerated federal power.

In Chapter 10, state laws in the area of pubic morals were discussed. Similar federal laws also exist. Laws relating to prostitution require interstate transportation in order to bring the offense into federal jurisdiction. The federal government has been active in prosecuting child pornography; however, recent decisions of the Supreme Court indicate that the law punishing the use of "virtual children" when they are portrayed engaging in sex acts or posing for sexual gratification violates the Constitution.

In Chapter 11 we explored "Offenses Against the Public Peace," which included riot, disorderly conduct, drunkenness, drugs, and terrorism. The "federalization" of drug laws has dramatically changed the prosecution of drug offenders in this country from largely a state and local activity to one shared almost equally between federal law enforcement and state law enforcement. The source of the federal power to pass drug laws is the commerce clause. While we discussed state counter-terrorism laws in Chapter 11, obviously the most well-known of such laws is "The Patriot Act," which identifies powers and defines crimes based either on the federal government's right to defend borders or the commerce clause.

In Chapter 12 "Offenses Against Public Order and Administration" were described and, in this chapter, the federal versions of such laws were explored. In general, perjury, bribery, obstruction of justice, and tampering with witnesses are similar crimes when done in state or federal venues.

Review Questions

1. When can the federal government pass laws that restrict personal decisions of who to have sex with, or whether or not to use drugs in one's own home?

2. Is there any federal law that might punish adultery?

3. What are the federal statutes related to prostitution? By what authority can the federal government create such laws?

4. Explain the law regarding the defense of mistake of age as it applies to the federal law criminalizing transportation of minors across state lines for the purpose of prostitution.

5. Explain the *Miller* test for the definition of pornography. List and describe some of the many federal laws concerning obscenity.

6. In *United States v. X-Citement Video*, the issue was whether the defendant had to "know" the child was underage to be guilty of the federal crime. Explain the court's holding.

7. Describe the coverage of 18 U.S.C. § 2252. How is this different from obscenity statutes with adult participants? Describe the holdings of the Supreme Court cases dealing with obscenity.

8. Does the U.S. Code have an abortion statute? Explain. Describe the issue and holding of *Scheidler v. National Organization for Women*.

9. What elements are required to be found guilty of the federal crime of *riot*? What behaviors might violate federal disorderly conduct laws? Are there federal vagrancy laws? Are there federal public drunkenness laws?

10. Under what authority does the federal government enact laws regulating the use of drugs? Are such laws constitutional? Under what constitutional provisions are they challenged?

11. What is the Uniform Controlled Substances Act? What is the purpose of the Act? What controlled substances are likely to be included in Schedule I? What are the characteristics of Schedule I drugs?

12. What are the definitions of *controlled substance*, *delivery*, and *possession*, as used in the federal statutes?

13. Does the federal drug offender need to know what specific type of controlled substance he is in possession of in order to be guilty of the federal offense? Does he need to be in actual possession? How are the drug conspiracy statute and the general conspiracy statute different?

14. Federal statutes that provide for forfeiture of property used to facilitate drug-related offenses and for the forfeiture of proceeds from drug transactions have been challenged, and suggestions for changes to these laws have been made. Have the courts held that these forfeiture statutes violate the double jeopardy clause of the U.S. Constitution? Explain.

15. Describe the federal wiretapping statute.

16. Explain the provisions of the USA PATRIOT Act in Title VIII that relate to criminal laws.

17. Does the U.S. Code have an anti-stalking statute? What is the nexus to federal powers?

18. Describe the three federal perjury-related crimes.

19. Distinguish among bribery, gratuities, and conflict of interest under the federal law. What is the definition of "other public officials" for purposes of this Act? Is payment to a confidential informant a violation of the federal statute prohibiting bribery of public officials and witnesses?

20. Describe the scope of behavior covered by the federal obstruction of justice statute. What are the elements of the federal escape statute? What are the elements of resisting arrest?

Notes

[1]   18 U.S.C. § 2421.

[2]   18 U.S.C. § 2421.

[3]   United States v. Wheeler, 444 F.2d 385 (10th Cir. 1971).

[4]   United States v. Jones, 909 F.2d 533 (D.C. Cir. 1990).

[5]   United States v. Miller, 148 F.3d 207 (2d Cir. 1998); United States v. Kennedy, 442 F.2d 444 (10th Cir. 1971).

[6]   18 U.S.C. § 2422. Section 2423 has similar provisions relating to transportation of minors in interstate or foreign commerce. The maximum term under this statute is 15 years.

[7]   United States v. Kufrovich, 997 F. Supp. 246 (D. Conn. 1997).

[8]   United States v. Taitano, 442 F.2d 467 (9th Cir.), cert. denied, 404 U.S. 852, 92 S. Ct. 92, 30 L. Ed. 2d 92 (1971).

[9] United States v. Parr, 741 F.2d 878 (5th Cir. 1984). See also United States v. Rashkovski, 301 F.3d 1133 (9th Cir. 2002), for cases relating to transporting Russian women to the United States in violation of this section.

[10] 18 U.S.C. § 2423.

[11] United States v. Scisum, 32 F.3d 1479 (10th Cir. 1994). See also United States v. Footman, 33 F. Supp. 2d 60 (D. Mass. 1988).

[12] United States v. Taylor, 239 F.3d 994 (9th Cir. 2001).

[13] United States v. Cole, 262 F.3d 704 (8th Cir. 2001).

[14] 18 U.S.C. § 1384.

[15] 413 U.S. 15 (1983)

[16] United States v. Schein, 31 F.3d 135 (3d Cir. 1994).

[17] United States v. Thomas, 74 F.3d 701 (6th Cir. 1996). See also Digest of Decisions included in the United States Code.

[18] See Title 18 U.S.C. § 2252 of the federal code, which provides a penalty for activities relating to material involving the sexual exploitation of minors. This statute is also discussed in Jacobson v. United States, 503 U.S. 540, 112 S. Ct. 1535, 118 L. Ed. 2d 174 (1992).

[19] 18 U.S.C. § 2252.

[20] United States v. Harden, 45 Fed. Appx. 237 (4th Cir. 2002). See also United States v. Tucker, 150 F. Supp. 2d 1263 (C.D. Utah 2001), which held that the Child Pornography Prevention Act was passed pursuant to Congress's Commerce Power, and the Act is intended to prevent the traffic in and consumption of child pornography.

[21] United States v. Maxwell, 49 F.3d 410 (4th Cir. 2002).

[22] 513 U.S. 64 (1994).

[23] United States v. Davis, 41 F.3d 566 (3d Cir. 2002).

[24] United States v. Hersh, 297 F.3d 1233 (11th Cir. 2002).

[25] United States v. Fox, 248 F.3d 394 (5th Cir. 2001).

[26] 535 U.S. 234 (2002)

[27] 18 U.S.C. § 1153.

[28] 18 U.S.C. § 248.

[29] United States v. Balint, 201 F.3d 928 (7th Cir. 2000).

[30] United States v. Hart, 212 F.3d 1067 (8th Cir. 2000).

[31] Scheidler v. N.O.W., Inc., 126 S. Ct. 1264 (2006).

[32] Scheidler v. N.O.W., Inc., 537 U.S. 393 (2003).

[33] 18 U.S.C. § 1461 and 18 U.S.C. § 1462.

[34] 18 U.S.C. § 2101.

[35] United States v. Dellinger, 472 F.2d 340 (7th Cir.), cert. denied, 410 U.S. 970, 93 S. Ct. 1443, 35 L. Ed. 2d 706 (1972).

[36] United States v. Markiewiez, 978 F.2d 786 (2d Cir.), cert. denied, 506 U.S. 1086 (1992).

[37] 18 U.S.C. § 1752.

[38] See 18 U.S.C. § 1752(f) for a definition of "other persons protected by the Secret Service."

[39] 40 U.S.C. § 101.

[40]   18 U.S.C. § 1262. See also 18 U.S.C. § 1263-1264.

[41]   United States v. Williams, 184 F.2d 663 (10th Cir. 1950).

[42]   United States v. Walsh, 331 U.S. 432, 67 S. Ct. 1283, 91 L. Ed. 1585 (1947).

[43]   United States v. Pastor, 557 F.2d 930 (2d Cir. 1977); United States v. Davis, 564 F.2d 840 (9th Cir. 1977). See also United States v. Wacker, 72 F.3d 1953 (10th Cir. 1995).

[44]   21 U.S.C. § 878.

[45]   Subtitle (H), § 1351, Anti-Drug Abuse Act of 1986, Pub. L. No. 99-570.

[46]   Anti-Drug Abuse Act of 1988, §§ 6301 and 6452, 134 Cong. Rec. H 11155, Oct. 21, 1988.

[47]   United States v. Fowler, 879 F. Supp. 575 (E.D. Va. 1995).

[48]   See also United States v. Davis, 561 F.2d 1014 (D.C. Cir. 1977) and United States v. Bramble, 894 F. Supp. 1394 (D. Haw. 1995).

[49]   See 21 U.S.C. § 812 as amended for a list of the drugs in each of the five schedules.

[50]   United States v. Fogarty, 692 F.2d 542 (8th Cir. 1982), cert. denied, 460 U.S. 1040, 103 S. Ct. 1434, 75 L. Ed. 2d 792 (1982). See also United States v. Green, 892 F.2d 453 (6th Cir. 1989), which held that classification of marijuana as a Schedule I controlled substance is not arbitrary or capricious or a violation of due process.

[51]   532 U.S. 483, 121 S. Ct. 1711, 149 L. Ed. 2d 722 (2001).

[52]   545 U.S. 1, 125 S. Ct. 2195 (2005).

[53]   126 S. Ct. 904, 163 L. Ed.2d 748 (2006).

[54]   18 U.S.C. § 844.

[55]   United States v. Halloway, 744 F.2d 527 (6th Cir. 1984).

[56]   United States v. White, 660 F.2d 1178 (7th Cir. 1981).

[57]   21 U.S.C. § 841.

[58]   United States v. Mark, 943 F.2d 444 (4th Cir. 1991).

[59]   United States v. Samad, 754 F.2d 1091 (4th Cir. 1984); United States v. Kairouz, 751 F.2d 467 (1st Cir. 1985).

[60]   United States v. Sanchez-Hernandez, 53 F.3d 842 (9th Cir. 2002).

[61]   United States v. Martinez, 301 F.3d 860 (7th Cir. 2003).

[62]   United States v. Dozal, 173 F.3d 787 (10th Cir. 1999). See also United States v. Randall, 171 F.3d 195 (4th Cir. 1999).

[63]   United States v. Manzella, 791 F.2d 1263 (7th Cir. 1986).

[64]   United States v. Cea, 914 F.2d 881 (7th Cir. 1990).

[65]   United States v. Vergara, 687 F.2d 57 (5th Cir. 1981).

[66]   United States v. Hawkins, 102 F.3d 973 (8th Cir. 1996). See also United States v. Payne, 102 F.3d 289 (7th Cir. 1996).

[67]   The Ninth Circuit Court of Appeals noted that providing an enhanced penalty for dispensing a controlled substance within 1,000 feet of a school did not violate the commerce clause of the Constitution. United States v. Ekinci, 101 F.3d 838 (2d Cir. 1996).

[68]   21 U.S.C. § 881(a). See statute for exceptions.

[69]   United States v. Usery, 518 U.S. 267, 116 S. Ct. 2135, 135 L. Ed. 2d 549 (1996).

[70]   Austin v. United States, 509 U.S. 602, 113 S. Ct. 2801, 125 L. Ed. 2d 488 (1993).

71   18 U.S.C. § 2510 et seq.

72   United States v. Antoon, 933 F.2d 200 (3d Cir. 1991).

73   United States v. Friedman, 300 F.3d 111 (2d Cir. 2002).

74   Malpas v. State, 16 Md. App. 69, 695 A.2d 588 (1997).

75   United States v. Pratt, 913 F.2d 983 (1st Cir. 1990), *cert. denied*, 408 U.S. 1028, 111 S. Ct. 681, 112 L. Ed. 2d 673 (1990).

76   18 U.S. Code § 2511 (4)(a).

77   Peavy v. Harmon, 37 F. Supp. 2d 495 (N.D. Tex. 1999).

78   Goodspeed v. Harman, 39 F. Supp. 2d 787 (N.D. Tex. 1999).

79   United States v. Lindh, 227 F. Supp. 2d 565 (E.D. Va. 2002).

80   18 U.S.C. 1993.

81   28 U.S.C. 534 *et seq.* and 42 U.S.C. 14031 *et seq.*

82   18 U.S.C. § 1621

83   United States v. Masters, 484 F.2d 1251 (10th Cir. 1973).

84   United States v. Molina, 172 F.3d 1048 (8th Cir. 1999). See also United States v. Quarrell, 310 F.3d 664 (10th Cir. 2002).

85   United States v. Clark, 918 F.2d 843 (9th Cir. 1990).

86   18 U.S.C. § 1622.

87   United States v. Silverman, 745 F.2d 1386 (11th Cir. 1984).

88   United States v. Singleton, 165 F.3d 1297 (10th Cir. 1999).

89   Tedesco v. Mishkin, 629 F. Supp. 1474 (S.D.N.Y. 1986).

90   18 U.S.C. §201(c)(1)(A).

91   18 U.S.C. § 201.

92   United States v. Velazquez, 847 F.2d 140 (4th Cir. 1988). See also Acquah v. State, 686 A.2d 690 (Md. 1996).

93   United States v. Snell, 152 F.3d 345 (5th Cir. 1998).

94   United States v. Biaggi, 853 F.2d 89 (2d Cir.), *cert. denied*, 489 U.S. 1052, 109 S. Ct. 1312, 103 L. Ed. 2d 581 (1988).

95   United States v. Williams, 7 F. Supp. 2d 40 (D.D.C. 1998).

96   United States v. Sun Diamond Growers of California, 941 F. Supp. 1262 (D.D.C. 1996).

97   United States v. McCormick, 31 F. Supp. 2d 176 (D. Mass. 1998).

98   United States v. Frega, 179 F.3d 793 (9th Cir. 1999).

99   United States v. Donathan, 65 F.3d 537 (6th Cir. 1995).

100 United States v. Brewster, 506 F.2d 62 (D.C. Cir. 1974). See also United States v. McDade, 827 F. Supp. 1153 (E.D. Pa. 1993).

101 United States v. Levenite, 277 F.3d 454 (4th Cir. 2002). See also United States v. Harris, 198 F.3d 957 (8th Cir. 1999).

102 United States v. Stephenson, 183 F.3d 110 (2d Cir. 1999), *cert. denied*, 528 U.S. 1013, 120 S. Ct. 517, 145 L. Ed. 2d 400 (1999). See also United States v. Hartmon, 194 F.3d 390 (8th Cir. 1999).

103 United States v. Sandoval, 20 F.3d 134 (5th Cir. 1994).

[104]   18 U.S.C. §§ 1501-1515.

[105]   State of West Virginia v. Moore, 897 F. Supp. 276 (S.D. W. Va. 1995).

[106]   United States v. Brenson, 104 F.3d 1267 (11th Cir. 1997).

[107]   United States v. Fleming, 215 F.3d 930 (9th Cir. 2000).

[108]   United States v. Mitchell, 397 F. Supp. 166 (D.D.C.), *cert. denied*, 431 U.S. 733, 97 S. Ct. 2641, 53 L. Ed. 2d 250 (1974); United States v. Jeter, 775 F.2d 670 (6th Cir. 1985).

[109]   United States v. McKnight, 799 F.2d 443 (8th Cir. 1986).

[110]   United States v. Langella, 776 F.2d 1078 (2d Cir. 1985), *cert. denied*, 106 S. Ct. 1207, 89 L. Ed. 2d 320 (1985).

[111]   United States v. Arnold, 773 F.2d 823 (7th Cir. 1985). For other examples, see United States v. Silverman, 745 F.2d 1386 (11th Cir. 1984).

[112]   United States v. DeLaRoss, 171 F.3d 215 (5th Cir. 1999).

[113]   18 U.S.C. § 1512. See also United States v. Tyler, 281 F.3d 84 (3d Cir. 2002), which held that the statute complied with the due process requirements.

[114]   18 U.S.C. §§ 751, 752, and 755.

[115]   United States v. Evans, 886 F. Supp. 800 (D. Kan. 1995).

[116]   United States v. Hambrick, 299 F.3d 911 (8th Cir. 2002).

[117]   United States v. Novak, 284 F.3d 986 (9th Cir. 2002).

[118]   18 U.S.C. § 752.

[119]   United States v. Nordstrom, 730 F.2d 556 (8th Cir. 1984).

[120]   18 U.S.C. § 755.

[121]   18 U.S.C. § 111.

[122]   United States v. Linn, 438 F.2d 456 (10th Cir. 1971).

[123]   United States v. Lopez, 710 F.2d 1071 (5th Cir. 1983); United States v. Cunningham, 509 F.2d 961 (D.C. Cir. 1973); United States v. Jennings, 855 F. Supp. 1427 (M.D. Pa. 1994).

[124]   United States v. Hernandez, 921 F.2d 1569 (11th Cir. 1991).

Corporate and Computer Crime

15

Chapter Outline

Cases

State law/federal regulations: *People v. Hegedus*, 443 N.W.2d 127
    (Mich. 1989)
Cyberstalking: *United States v. Bowker*, 372 F.3d 365 (6th Cir. 2004).

> *Key Terms and Concepts*
>
> anti-structuring laws   insider trading
> antitrust laws   money laundering
> churning   Occupational Safety and Health Act
> corporate crime   *respondeat superior*
> environmental crime   RICO
> Fair Labor Standards Act   white-collar crime

§ 15.1 Introduction

While the last two chapters have covered federal crimes that are roughly parallel to those found in state criminal codes and the common law, this chapter explores federal crimes that are more unique to federal jurisdiction and enforcement. The federal government is more effective than state law enforcement in the investigation and enforcement of crimes that cross state borders and/or are international in scope. These types of crimes are largely white collar and may be quite complicated. Federal law enforcement agencies now give greater priority to crimes that have these characteristics.

According to the Federal Register, the FBI has jurisdiction to investigate violations in such areas as copyright matters, mail fraud, passport and visa matters, fraud against the government, bankruptcy fraud, jury panel investigations, election laws, antitrust violations, perjury, interception of communications, consumer credit protection act violations, and environmental crimes.[1]

The Supreme Court has agreed that Congress can delegate to a federal agency the power to make regulations that have the force of law.[2] Thus the Federal Aviation Administration can use criminal sanctions to enforce its regulations, as can the Securities and Exchange Commission and other federal agencies.

A. Corporate Culpability

As federal and state agencies increase their investigative focus on **white-collar crime** and as many of the federal laws target corporations as well as individuals, the courts have found it necessary to review the laws concerning **corporate crime**. Corporate criminal liability existed well before the coining of the term white-collar crime. At common law, corporations could not be held liable for criminal acts.[3] However, with the recognition by state legislatures and the courts that the imposition of corporate criminal liability is an essential part of the regulatory process, a body of law pertaining to corporate criminal liability soon developed. Without corporate liability, many crimes would be punished insufficiently because the size and structure of many corporations makes it impossible to adequately allocate responsibility to individuals. When state and federal statutes making corporations criminally liable are upheld, corporations, as well as officers and agents of the corporations, are made defendants in a number of cases.[4]

The current law of corporate criminal liability developed as a series of reactions to problems that courts historically encountered in assigning criminal blame to corporations.[5] The most fundamental hurdle for courts to overcome was the idea of holding fictional entities culpable in a legal system based on individual moral accountability. Courts gradually applied aspects of the criminal law, including sentencing, to the abstract nature of the corporation.

The Model Penal Code, discussed in earlier chapters of this book, includes a section defining the liability of corporations.[6] This comprehensive section indicates the circumstances under which a corporation may be held criminally liable, provides principles for the interpretation of statutes defining offenses for which a corporation may be liable, and deals with problems relating to the individual criminal liability of the directors, officers, and servants of corporations. In a jurisdiction following the Model Penal Code, a corporation may be criminally liable for its agent's acts when the illegal acts are codified or where "the commission of the offense was authorized, requested, commanded, performed or recklessly tolerated by the board of directors or by a high managerial agent acting on behalf of the corporation within the scope of his office or employment."

In the case of *First Federal Savings Bank of Hegewisch v. United States*, the court held that, in general, a corporation can only act through its agents, and "when they are clothed with authority to act for it, the corporation is responsible for their acts."[7] This does not mean, however, that every action an employee takes is automatically imputed to the corporation. If the employee is acting outside his or her actual or apparent authority, for example, the corporation is generally not liable for the action.

Sentencing for corporations changed in 1991 with the inclusion of organizational sentencing in the United States Sentencing Guidelines. These guidelines were an effort by the United States Sentencing Commission to establish sound and consistent sentencing policies for corporate crime. Under the guidelines, the court determines the initial fine by calculating a "base fine" level. A court can then adjust the fine up or down based on the corporation's "culpability score."[8]

Many states have also adopted specific statutory language defining liability for criminal acts committed by "high managerial agents." In some states, the corporation may be liable for an employee's action even if the corporation's directors, officers, or other high managerial agents did not specifically approve of the employee's behavior, while in other states only the individual agents are culpable.[9] Whether the state or federal agencies utilize *respondeat superior* theory for imposing criminal liability, or state and federal statutes, empirical studies demonstrate that corporations have been and will continue to be held criminally liable for acts of their agents, especially acts that are prohibited by the white-collar crime statutes.

Title 18, § 3551 of the United State Code provides that:

> U.S.C. § 3551
>
> Organizations—An organization found guilty of an offense shall be sentenced in accordance with the provisions of § 3553 to—
>
> (1) a term of probation as authorized by subchapter B; or (2) a fine as authorized by subsection (C).
>
> A sentence to pay a fine may be imposed in addition to probation. A sanction authorized by Section 3554, 3555, or 3556 may be imposed in addition to the sentence required by this subsection.

Although the guidelines are applicable to all "organizations," they were designed with corporations in mind, and it is on corporations that they are expected to have the greatest impact. The guidelines define "organization" to include "corporations, partnerships, associations, joint stock companies, unions, trusts, pension funds, unincorporated organizations, governments and political subdivisions thereof, and nonprofit organizations.[10]

Organizations convicted of federal felony and class A misdemeanor offenses are sentenced under the organizational guidelines. The guidelines operate under four general principles:

- the corporation must remedy any harm caused by its offense;

- a corporation run primarily for criminal purposes should receive fines high enough to divest the business of all of its assets;

- businesses run for other than criminal purposes should be fined according to the seriousness of their offenses and the culpability of the corporation

- the corporation shall be subject to probation if it will ensure that a company complies with sanctions or if it reduces the likelihood of future violations by the corporation.[11]

§ 15.2   Money Laundering

Money laundering is the process by which one conceals the existence, illegal source, or illegal application of income, and disguises that income to make it appear legitimate. Laundering criminally derived proceeds has become a lucrative, sophisticated business in the United States and is an indispensable element of organized crime's activities. Without the ability to move and hide its enormous wealth through laundering techniques, large-scale criminal activities could operate at only a small fraction of current levels, and with far less flexibility.[12]

The federal government has attacked money laundering in different ways, beginning indirectly by imposing statutory reporting requirements. The Bank Secrecy Act made failure to report certain transactions a crime, although large cash transactions were not themselves illegal. Statutory loopholes and mixed judicial interpretations of the statute led to the Money Laundering Control Act of 1986 (MLCA).[13]

The money laundering offenses in MLCA are twofold. First, § 1956 prohibits an individual's involvement in a financial transaction when the individual knows that the property involved in the transaction represents the proceeds of specified unlawful activities. The individual must engage in the transaction with either the intent to promote the carrying on of a specified unlawful activity, or with the knowledge that the purpose of the transaction is either to avoid a reporting requirement or to conceal the nature, location, source, ownership, or control of the specified unlawful activity proceeds.

Section 1957 prohibits an individual from engaging or attempting to engage in a monetary transaction involving property valued at more than $10,000 when the individual knows that the property is derived from specific unlawful activities. A monetary transaction is defined in the statute as a "deposit, withdrawal, transfer, or exchange, in or affecting interstate or foreign commerce or funds . . . by, through, or to a financial institution."

There are four elements that must be established in order to obtain a conviction under 18 U.S.C. §§ 1956-1957. These elements are:

- knowledge,
- the existence of a specified unlawful activity,
- a financial transaction, and
- intent.[14]

The justices of the Tenth Circuit Court of Appeals noted that under the statute that prohibits engaging in monetary transactions with criminally derived property, the requirement that the monetary transaction in question be "in or affecting interstate or foreign commerce" is both jurisdictional and an essential element of the defense.[15] In discussing the elements required to prove a violation of § 1957, a federal court determined that the particular motive or cause that led the defendant to attempt transfer of the funds from one bank account to another was not material and thus did not preclude conviction on a charge of engaging in monetary transactions derived from unlawful activity.[16] In interpreting the money laundering statute, the courts have consistently held that the statute is not unconstitutionally vague.[17]

Another statute that makes it more difficult to hide illegally acquired funds is the **anti-structuring law**.[18] Federal law requires banks and other financial institutions to file reports with the Secretary of the Treasury whenever they are involved in a cash transaction that exceeds $10,000. It is illegal to "structure" transactions—that is, to break up a single transaction above the reporting threshold into two or more separate transactions for the purpose of evading the financial institution's reporting requirements. A person who willfully violates this anti-structuring provision is subject to criminal penalties.[19]

To establish that a defendant willfully violated the anti-structuring law, the government must prove that the defendant acted with knowledge that the conduct was unlawful. In the case of *Ratzlaf v. United States*, the defendant ran up a debt of $160,000 playing blackjack at a Reno, Nevada, casino. The casino gave the defendant one week to pay. On the due date, the defendant returned to the casino with $100,000 in cash. After the casino official advised the defendant that all transactions involving more than $10,000 in cash must be reported to the state and federal authorities, the casino placed a limousine at the defendant's disposal and assigned an employee to accompany him to banks in the vicinity. The defendant purchased cashier's checks, each for less than $10,000 and each from a different bank. The defendant was charged with "structuring transactions" to evade the bank's obligation to report cash transactions exceeding $10,000, violating 31 U.S.C. §§ 5322 and 5324. The trial judge instructed the jury that the government had to prove the defendant's knowledge of the bank's reporting obligations and its attempt to evade the obligation, but did not have to prove that the defendant knew the structuring was unlawful. The defendant was convicted, fined, and sentenced to prison. On appeal, the defendant maintained that he could not be convicted because this was not a "willful violation." The U.S. Supreme Court agreed with the defendant that the government had an obligation to prove that the defendant knew that the structuring was unlawful and reversed the conviction. The court noted that the "willfulness" requirement of the statute mandates both "knowledge of the reporting requirement" and a "specific intent to commit the crime."[20]

Congress responded to the perceived interaction of money laundering and terrorism by passing the Uniting and Strengthening America by Providing Appropriate Tools Required to Intercept and Obstruct Terrorism (USA Patriot Act), the Act of 2001. In this Act, the Secretary of the Treasury is given broad discretion and power to require banks and financial institutions in the United States to play a significant role in the process of uncovering money laundering. Part of the Act requires banks to take reasonable action to discover the identity of foreign account owners and the source of their funds. The Act also provides that the president should direct the Secretary of State, the Attorney General, and/or the Secretary of the Treasury to negotiate with the appropriate state officials and financial institutions of foreign nations to provide for cooperative enforcement efforts and better mechanisms for information sharing.[21]

§ 15.3   Environmental Crimes (EPA)

The U.S. Environmental Protection Agency (EPA) has a range of enforcement tools available—administrative, civil, and criminal to combat **environmental crime**.

Prosecution for acts that affect the environment received little attention until recently. However, as governments have become more concerned with the protection of the quality of water, land, and air, regulations and laws have increased. While laws containing overlapping civil, criminal, and administrative penalty provisions have originated in both the federal and state legislatures, the federal government has taken the lead in controlling acts relating to the environment. In fact, in the last 40 years, environmental laws have increased in number, length, and complexity. In the paragraphs that follow, some of the prohibited acts that are most likely to come to the attention of law enforcement and criminal justice personnel are briefly discussed.

A.   The Clean Air Act (CAA)[22]

The Clean Air Act (CAA) imposes penalties on those who knowingly violate federal or state regulations designed to achieve ambient air quality standards established by the U.S. Environmental Protection Agency (EPA). In justifying the passage of this legislation, Congress determined that federal legislation was necessary as violations crossed boundary lines and often extended to two or more states, and that federal financial assistance and leadership is essential for the development of cooperative federal, state, and local programs to prevent and control air pollution. The CCA mandates that the Environmental Protection Agency prescribe national air quality standards, although states are free to adopt more stringent protection. Each state then is required to adopt an implementation plan of its own for that state. If a state implementation plan is approved by the EPA, its requirements become federal law and are fully enforceable in federal court.[23] A CAA violation occurs when a source emits pollution in excess of levels established by regulation.

Criminal sanctions apply to any person who:

- violates the CAA by making false statements,
- fails to report as required,
- tampers with EPA monitoring devices, or
- fails to pay fees owed to the United States.

Criminal sanctions may be imposed on both the organizations and the individuals responsible for the actions of an organization. According to the penalty provisions, a knowing violation of any emission standard under the

CAA, a knowing failure to pay fees assessed, or a knowing violation of any reporting or monitoring requirement is punishable by criminal fines, up to five years in prison, or both.[24]

B. *Safe Drinking Water Act (SDWA)*[25]

The Safe Drinking Water Act (SDWA) was designed to regulate levels of harmful contaminants in public water systems and the underground injection of contaminants into ground water that supplies public drinking water. Under the provisions of the Act, the EPA is required to establish national primary drinking water regulations, and discharges must obtain permits for underground injection of contaminants. The Act also regulates the amount of lead found in drinking water coolers, and penalizes tampering with public water systems. The Act requires the EPA to establish minimum standards to prevent the contamination of underground water resources. Failure to comply with the standards could lead to civil penalties as well as criminal penalties.[26]

As with some other environmental crime provisions, states may secure primary enforcement authority for the regulation of underground water sources if the EPA approves the state's underground injection control program. Failure of the state to comply with this program makes it possible for the EPA to revoke the state's authority.[27]

C. *Clean Water Act (CWA)*[28]

The Clean Water Act (CWA) was enacted to restore and maintain the chemical, physical, and biological integrity of the nation's waters by minimizing the effects of water pollution. The Clean Water Act is also referred to as the Federal Water Pollution Control Act. Under the terms of the Act, federal, state, and local authorities are authorized to establish programs that prohibit or regulate the discharge of pollutants into the water of the United States. In administering and enforcing the Clean Water Act, the Environmental Protection Agency and the Army Corps of Engineers share responsibility. The Corps has the nondiscretionary duty to regulate discharge of dredged or fill material by issuing permits after applying guidelines established by the EPA and has the authority to enforce permit violations. The EPA holds the ultimate responsibility for wetlands protection, has authority to seek penalties for unpermitted discharges of pollutants into United States waters and, after consulting with Corps of Engineers, can block or overrule the Corps decision to issue permits.[29]

Under various sections of the statute, government agencies may establish effluent limitations and water quality standards, impose discharge reporting and monitoring requirements, mandate the cleanup of oil and other hazardous substances, prohibit unpermitted dredging or filling and the discharge of sewage sludge, and set up permit programs regulating discharge of pollutants and the dredging and filling of wetlands.[30]

In interpreting the Act, a federal court held that the Clean Water Act is entitled to a broad construction to implement its objective of protecting human health, welfare, and environment.

Criminal penalties may be assessed against any "person" who fails to comply with the statutory requirements of the Clean Water Act. The Act established four levels of criminal penalties, depending on whether a violation was negligent, knowing, involved knowing endangerment, or involved knowing falsification of information or tampering with monitoring equipment.[31]

The "knowledge" element of the offense reached the Circuit Court when it was asked to determine whether the government must prove that the defendant had knowledge of the law he was accused of violating, as well as knowledge of the underlying conduct that resulted in the charge. In the case of *United States v. Sinskey*, the defendants were charged with a number of Clean Water Act violations. Specifically, they were charged with participating in a "flow game"—discharging low levels of wastewater when performing monitoring tests, then discharging exceedingly high levels of ammonia and nitrogen-rich wastewater at other times. They would also submit only the best monitoring reports.

At the trial, the jury was instructed that, in order to find a knowing violation, the proof had to show that the defendant was aware of the nature of the acts, performed them intentionally, and did not act or fail to act through ignorance, mistake, or accident. The instructions further advised the jury that the government was not required to prove that the defendant knew the acts violated the permit or the Clean Water Act. On appeal, the defendant argued that the government must prove that he knew his conduct violated the permit or the Clean Water Act. The circuit court disagreed with the defendant, holding that the government is only required to prove knowledge of the underlying conduct, not knowledge of the law.[32]

D. Toxic Substance Control Act (TSCA)[33]

To further the protection of the environment, Congress enacted the Toxic Substance Control Act (TSCA). The purpose of the Act is to prevent toxic substances in commerce from presenting an "unreasonable risk of injury to health or the environment," and to stem the tide of chemical substances and mixtures considered "imminent hazards." The Act also requires private industries that manufacture toxic substances to generate data with respect to the effects of the toxic chemicals.

Under the provisions of the Act, the EPA is authorized to regulate testing, pre-manufacturing clearance, manufacturing, and distribution of toxic substances. However, the Act also provides that enforcement agencies should not "impede unduly or create unnecessary economic barriers to technological innovation." In a federal case, the court made it clear that the Environmental Protection Agency must articulate an "understandable basis" to support action with respect to each substance or application of substance banned. The court stated that the EPA must make findings of unreasonable risk based upon this assessment and must balance the probability that harm will occur from activities against the effects of the proposed regulatory action on availability to society of benefits of the banned substance.[34]

Section 15(b) authorizes criminal penalties against a "person who knowingly and willfully violates TSCA." The Act provides the criminal sanctions in addition to or in lieu of any civil or administrative penalties.

E. *Resource Conservation and Recovery Act (RCRA)*[35]

The Resource Conservation and Recovery Act (RCRA) establishes a detailed scheme for federal regulation of all wastes, including hazardous wastes. It sets standards that govern the generation, treatment, storage, transportation, and disposal of hazardous wastes. According to Section 6902 of the Act, the objectives are to promote the protection of health and the environment and to conserve valuable material and energy resources by training and establishing practices as enumerated in the act.

Like most of the other laws establishing standards and penalties relating to the environment, this Act was promulgated by Congress pursuant to the Commerce Clause of the Constitution. In the case of *United States v. Rogers*, the court explained that the nexus between commercial activity and generation of solid waste was well documented, and Congress could rationally conclude that the activity affected interstate commerce.[36]

The Act provides criminal penalties for persons who knowingly treat, store, or dispose of hazardous waste without a permit, or transport hazardous waste to a facility lacking a permit. A "solid waste" is a "hazardous waste" if the EPA has listed it as such, or if the waste exhibits any of these four characteristics: ignitability, corrosivity, reactivity, or toxicity. The EPA has listed more than 700 solid wastes as hazardous, and the universe of wastes covered by the four characteristics is large and expanding.[37]

Some of the penalties imposed for violation of the Act are quite severe. Knowingly transporting hazardous waste to a nonpermitted facility or knowingly treating, storing, or disposing of hazardous waste without a permit are subject to penalties of up to five years imprisonment and fines of $50,000 per day. Even more severe penalties result if the violators are concurrently convicted of knowingly placing another person in imminent danger of death or serious bodily injury. In these cases, individuals may be fined up to $250,000, imprisoned for up to 15 years, or both, while organizations may face fines up to $1,000,000.[38]

F. Other Crimes

Other environment-related federal statutes include the Rivers and Harbors Act of 1899, the Comprehensive Environmental Response, Compensation and Liability Act (Superfund), which mandates the cleanup of hazardous substances at contaminated sites and imposes criminal penalties on those who violated it, and the Federal Insecticide, Fungicide and Rodenticide Act, which regulates the manufacture, registration, transportation, and sale of toxic pesticides.[39]

§ 15.4   Antitrust and Securities Violations (SEC)

The Sherman Act of 1890 was enacted to prevent sabotage of the free enterprise system. The central purpose of **antitrust laws** is to prevent any acts that take away the freedom of purchasers to buy in the open market and to maintain freedom of competition.[40]

The criminal provision of the present Sherman Act provides for criminal sanctions against any person "who shall make any contract or engage in any combination or conspiracy" in restraint of interstate commerce. This part of the Act provides:

> 15 U.S.C. § 1
>
> Every contract, combination in the form of trust or otherwise, or conspiracy, in restraint of trade or commerce among the several states, or with foreign nations, is declared to be illegal. Every person who shall make any contract or engage in any combination or conspiracy hereby declared to be illegal shall be deemed guilty of a felony, and, on conviction thereof, shall be punished by fine of $10,000,000, if a corporation, or, if any person, $350,000, or by imprisonment not exceeding three years, or by both said punishments, in the discretion of the court.[41]

To prove a criminal violation, the government must establish four elements:

- two or more entities formed a combination or a conspiracy;
- the combination or conspiracy produces, or potentially produces, an unreasonable restraint of trade or commerce;
- the restrained trade or commerce is interstate in nature;
- general intent.[42]

According to interpretations by the federal courts, Congress did not intend the text of Sections 1 to 7 of the Antitrust Act to delineate the full meaning of their application in concrete situations; rather, Congress expected courts to give shape to their broad mandate by drawing on common law tradition.[43]

Congress drafted this legislation initially and modified the law over a period of years to give the federal government much more authority in the area of antitrust matters. According to one court's interpretation, the comprehensive language of this section shows that Congress intended to utilize its commerce clause power to the fullest extent and that this section should apply to every person who agrees or conspires to restrain or monopolize commercial intercourse among the states.[44]

The "conspiracy" element can be satisfied if there is "a combination or some form of concerted action between two legally distinct economic entities." The courts have made it clear that the government's success in demonstrating an interstate commerce nexus is both a critical jurisdictional fact and an element of the substantive offense under the act.[45] In discussing the intent requirement, a reviewing court commented that the defendants can be convicted of participation in price-fixing conspiracies without any demonstration of specific intent to violate antitrust laws.[46]

Over the years there have been several other laws passed by Congress to bolster the ability of the federal government to protect free trade, including the Robinson-Patman Act, the Clayton Act, and the Federal Trade Commission Act. Some of the activities that are addressed by federal laws include:

- artificially lowering the price of goods or services to force out competitors

- mergers to eliminate competition

- exclusive dealing arrangements (i.e., a manufacturer forces its distributors to not carry competing products)

- unfair or deceptive advertising

- price fixing (competitors agree to keep prices similar)

- market allocation agreements (between competitors)

- boycotts of traders

- "tying arrangements" (forcing buyers to buy a second product if they want to buy the first product)

- monopolies

A. State Antitrust Laws

Most states have statutes similar to the Sherman Act, but they are not uniform. States can enforce antitrust laws in two ways: by prosecution for violations of state antitrust laws or by suing as plaintiffs in federal court under the federal law. The Illinois Act, similar to some other states' provisions, is more detailed and leaves less interpretation to the court than the federal Antitrust Law. A federal court determined that the Illinois Antitrust Act is not preempted by federal antitrust law, but if two antitrust regimes differ, federal antitrust law may preempt state antitrust law.[47] One court, in explaining the preemption principle, noted that federal law can preempt state law in three ways: first, Congress may expressly declare that state law is preempted; second, state law is preempted if Congress intends the federal government to occupy the field exclusively; third, federal law preempts state law if the two actually conflict.[48]

Legal News

One of the most famous monopoly cases was when federal prosecutors, joined by more than a dozen states, brought a case against Bill Gates' Microsoft corporation for its practices in bundling Internet Explorer browser software with the Windows operating system, in effect closing the door for other competitors, such as Netscape Navigator. Microsoft also was alleged to have engaged in restrictive licensing agreements that required hardware manufacturers to load Windows and Internet Explorer together. Microsoft was found to have engaged in a monopoly that violated parts of the Sherman Act; however, on appeal, the ruling was overturned and after years of wrangling, Microsoft and the government reached a settlement agreement in 2001 and in 2004 the settlement was approved by the Court of Appeals.

Source: Associated Press (September 7, 2006). "Judge OKs New Microsoft Antitrust Deadline." Retrieved 9/21/2006, http://news.zdnet.com/2100-3513_22-6113275.html.

B. Securities Exchange Violations

Securities are legal documents that represent shares of ownership or debt; for instance, stocks, bonds, notes, options, and so on. The Securities Act of 1933 and the Securities and Exchange Act of 1934 required that publicly traded securities be registered and the trading of such stock be regulated, including the requirement to provide accurate information to purchasers. The Securities and Exchange Commission (SEC) is the federal agency that regulates securities trading. A number of crimes can be committed in relation to securities trading, including fraud and insider trading.

1. Securities Fraud

We have previously described the federal mail and wire fraud statute. A securities fraud shares some of the same elements but is specifically related to frauds perpetrated in the buying or selling of securities. An offender violates the law when he or she:

- Makes a material false statement or omission
- Knowingly, with intent to defraud

- That causes another party damages

- If it is an omission, the party had a duty to disclose the information.

This would involve, for instance, a company presenting false audits that made the company appear to be more profitable than it was for the purpose of selling shares, or a broker who does not disclose negative aspects of a purchase to his or her clients in order to get them to invest. The Ponzi scheme perpetrated by Bernie Madoff also falls into this category of securities fraud. He purported that investing in his hedge fund would earn investors, on average, 10 to 12 percent returns, and investors did receive those returns, even when the market declined. However, rather than investing in stock, he used later investors' money to pay dividends to early investors, thus encouraging more and more people to give him money. When the stock market crashed in the fall of 2008, so many of Madoff's investors wanted to cash out that his whole scheme fell apart because he did not have enough assets to give investors their money. The fraud is estimated at more than $50 billion and is probably the largest Ponzi scheme in history. Some of his investors were charities who were forced into bankruptcy, and at least one investor committed suicide. Madoff was charged with civil violations and one criminal count of securities fraud in the criminal complaint filed against him in December 2008:

> 1. From at least in or about December 2008 through the present, in the southern District of New York and elsewhere, BERNARD L. MADOFF, the defendant, unlawfully, willfully, and knowingly, by the use of the means and instrumentalities of interstate commerce and of the mails, directly and indirectly, in connection with the purchase and sale of securities, would and did use and employ manipulative and deceptive devices and contrivances in violation of Title 17, Code of Federal Regulations, Section 240.10b-5, by (a) employing devices, schemes, and artifices to defraud; (b) making untrue statements of material facts and omitting to state material facts necessary in order to make the statements made, in the light of the circumstances under which they were made, not misleading, and 9c) engaging in acts, practices, and courses of business which operated and would operate as a fraud and deceit upon persons, to wit, MADOFF deceived investors by operating a securities business in which he traded and lost investor money, and then paid certain investors purported returns on investment with the principal received from other, different investors, which resulted in losses of approximately billions of dollars . . . .[49]

2. Insider Trading

Perhaps the most frequent type of securities violation is **insider trading**. This is when someone who owns more than 10 percent of the stock in a publicly traded company buys or sells their shares. This is not illegal unless the person does so based on insider information not available to the general public. Congress enacted the Insider Trading Sanctions Act of 1984, which increased penalties for this offense.

The most famous insider trading case in recent years was Martha Stewart's conviction in 2002. She sold her shares of ImClone stock days before negative information about the company caused the shares to plummet in value. She reached a plea agreement by confessing to perjury for lying to officials about her actions and paid a fine for the insider trading violation.

3. Sarbanes-Oxley Act of 2002

The Sarbanes-Oxley Act created new federal offenses in the area of securities violations. The new laws were passed after the Enron collapse and other major businesses such as WorldCom went bankrupt suddenly, with investors losing billions of dollars. The laws are directed toward individuals who destroy documents when they are under investigation for securities fraud or insider trading. It also requires that the chief officers of corporations certify that financial statements comply with SEC regulations, increases the penalties for fraud and conspiracy, and has a provision to protect whistle-blowers in a corporation when such people expose illegal acts such as fraud or other financial improprieties.

One of the most important changes this Act has made to the enforcement of securities frauds is that the *mens rea* has been changed from *intentional* to *knowing*. This is in response to the Enron CFOs and executives, and auditing companies like Arthur Anderson, who knew the financial reports were not accurate but did nothing to prevent unsuspecting stockholders from continuing to trade in company stock. Now, such individuals are responsible for certifying the accuracy of financial statements, and whether they intentionally defraud investors or just know that a fraud is being perpetrated, they are guilty of securities fraud.

4. Other Crimes

There are other crimes that are investigated and prosecuted by the SEC. For instance, **churning** is a term used to describe when brokers buy and sell stock for clients solely to increase their own brokerage fees rather than for the benefit of the client. This violation of their fiduciary duty can be prosecuted when the government proves that the trading was excessive and the broker showed intent to defraud or exhibited a willful and reckless disregard for the investor's interests.

§ 15.5   Occupational Safety and Health (OSHA)[50]

In December 1970, Congress enacted the **Occupational Safety and Health Act** (OSHA). Congress had determined that legislation was necessary due to the trend of increasing employee deaths and injuries in the late 1960s. The stated purpose of Congress was to exercise its powers to regulate commerce among the states to assure, as far as possible, every working man and woman in the nation safe and healthful working conditions and to preserve human resources.[51]

OSHA includes a general duty clause that requires employers to furnish their employees with a working environment free from recognized hazards. In addition, the statute requires employers to comply with specific occupational safety and health rules promulgated by the Secretary of Labor. The Act provides for both civil and criminal penalties. Criminal prosecutions have been initiated either when an employer's willful violation of a standard, rule, order, or regulation causes the death of an employee, or when an employer makes a false representation regarding compliance with the Act.

Discussing the "willful violation," a federal court noted that whether a violation was willful depends on whether it resulted from the conscious disregard of the regulation.[52] Another court held that willfulness in a criminal case may be proved by showing deliberate indifference to the fact or the law or by showing awareness of significant risk coupled with steps to avoid additional information, but in either case what must be proved beyond a reasonable doubt is actual rather than constructive knowledge.[53] In light of its broad remedial purpose, the Occupational Safety and Health Act (OSHA) and its accompanying regulations should be liberally construed so as to afford the broadest possible protection to workers.[54]

A. State Laws

The enactment of federal statutes left unanswered the question of to what extent OSHA preempted state criminal sanctions. Although states are preempted by OSHA from regulating workplace safety, the application of certain state criminal sanctions against employers is not preempted. For example, in a Texas case, the court held that applying state criminal laws to workplace conduct was not preempted by OSHA because it does not interfere with the goals of the Act.[55] Making clear that the federal government would have primary jurisdiction in these cases, the U.S. Supreme Court noted that the design of the Occupational Safety and Health Act shows that Congress intended to subject employers and employees to only one set of regulations, be it federal or state, and that the only way that a state may regulate occupational and health issues that are regulated by OSHA is pursuant to an OSHA-approved state plan that displaces the federal standards.[56]

In the case of *People v. Hegedus*, an employee's supervisor was charged with involuntary manslaughter. These charges arose as a result of the death of an employee who died of carbon monoxide intoxication while working in a company-owned van. The prosecution contended that the poor condition of the van's undercarriage and exhaust system allowed exhaust fumes to leak inside the van, causing the employee's death. The defendant contended that if he were subject to any criminal liability for his acts or omissions in causing the victim's death, it was under the criminal provisions of OSHA, not under any state criminal law such as the manslaughter statute under which he was charged.

The Michigan Supreme Court, in discussing the preemption issue, noted that generally, the existence of federal laws or regulations in a particular area can preempt state action in the same field where preemption is either express, implied, or the result of a conflict between state and federal law, but the extent to which federal law actually preempts state authority is a question of congressional intent and concluded that, in the case of OSHA violations, the state was not pre-empted from pursuing criminal sanctions.[57] Where Congress has not completely displaced a state regulation in a specific area, state law is nullified only to the extent that it actually conflicts with federal law.[58]

B. *Fair Labor Standards Act*[59]

The **Fair Labor Standards Act** (FLSA) of 1938 prohibits an employer from failing to pay minimum wages or overtime compensation to an employee, failing to keep individual work records for each employee, discriminating on the basis of sex by paying different wages for equal work, or using oppressive child labor.[60]

To constitute an offense punishable by criminal sanctions under the FLSA, an employee must show that: (1) the employer, (2) willfully, (3) violated the Act's provisions. A person who violates any of the provisions of § 215 of the FLSA shall, on conviction, be subject to a fine of not more than $10,000 or imprisonment of not more than six months, or both.[61]

After some conflicting decisions concerning the application of FLSA to state and local agencies, it was determined that the Fair Labor Standards Act contains clear statements of congressional intent to abrogate state sovereign immunity, based on FLSA provisions defining "employer" to include a public agency, defining "individual employed by a public agency," as including one employed by a state, and providing for actions against a public agency in any federal or state court of competent jurisdiction.[62]

C. *Minimum Wage Provisions*

This section of the Fair Labor Standards Act provides that every employer shall pay to each of his employees who in any workweek is engaged in commerce or in the production of goods for commerce, or is employed in an enterprise engaged in commerce, or in the production of goods for commerce, wages as established by the Act.[63]

The FLSA has special overtime provisions to address the unique employment conditions of domestic servants, hospital workers, firefighters, police officers, and transportation workers. In interpreting the provision of the act that makes certain exceptions for firefighters and police officers, a federal court held that the practice of "averaging" firefighters' straight-time and over-time wages over a biweekly pay period does not violate the FLSA.[64] Another court applied similar reasoning in deciding that the Fair Labor Standards Act did not require firefighters to be paid extra for hours during a pay period in excess of the 95 hours for which they were paid and the 106-hour threshold at which overtime pay comes into effect, because the pay received per hour, based on 106 hours, exceeded the minimum wage.[65]

To constitute an offense punishable by criminal sanctions, an employee must show that:

- the employer-employee relationship existed, and
- the employer willfully violated the Act's provisions.

The criminal penalties for a violation are outlined in § 216 of the statute. One provision is "any person who willfully violates any provisions of § 215 of the FLSA shall upon conviction thereof be subject to a fine of not more than $10,000 or to imprisonment of not more than six months, or both. The Secretary of Labor is assigned the responsibility of enforcing this provision of the Act. To carry out this responsibility, a special Wage and Hour Division was created in the Labor Department to allow the Administrator and the Secretary to make periodic investigations and reports in order to keep the law up-to-date and to detect violations.[66]

D. Equal Pay Provisions

The Fair Labor Standards Act prohibits discrimination on the basis of sex.[67] These statutes provide in part that:

> 29 U.S.C. § 206(d)
>
> No employer having employees subject to any provisions of this section shall discriminate, within any establishment at which such employees are employed, between employees on the basis of sex by paying wages to employees in such establishment at a rate of less than the rate at which he pays wages to employees of the opposite sex in such establishment for equal work on jobs the performance of which requires equal skill, effort, and responsibility, and which are performed under similar working conditions.

In the case of *Tidwell v. Fort Howard Corp.*, the court explained that the underlying rationale of the Equal Pay Act is that individuals who are doing equal work should be paid equal wages, regardless of their sex.[68] Interpreting this statute, a federal court determined that a female employee established a *prima facie* case under the Act that she was paid less than the male employees, even though they performed substantially equal work under similar working conditions, although the designation of the positions had different names.[69] However, another federal court found that a female employee occupied a position and performed functions that were not substantially equal to those of better paid male co-workers, because the tasks and functions the employee performed were dissimilar in level of experience required and level of complexity in performing the required functions.[70]

E. Maximum Hour Standards

In addition to the minimum wage provision and the provision prohibiting discrimination on the basis of sex by paying different wages for equal work, the FLSA includes a provision concerning maximum hours.[71]

One section of the act provides that:

> 29 U.S.C. § 207
>
> Except if otherwise provided in this section, no employer shall employ any of his employees who in any workweek is engaged in commerce or in a production of goods for commerce, or is employed in an enterprise engaged in commerce or the production of goods for commerce, for a workweek longer than 40 hours unless such employee receives compensation for his employment in excess of the hours above specified at a rate of not less than one or one-half times the regular rate at which he is employed.

The section of the Fair Labor Standards Act that deals with maximum hours has exceptions and conditions.[72] For example, employees in defined hospitals in certain conditions are exempt, employees in fire protection activities and law enforcement activities are exempt if they meet the specific provisions stated in the Act, and certain employees receiving remedial education are exempt. Although the statutes contain exceptions to the overtime requirements of the Fair Labor Standards Act, these are to be narrowly construed against the employer asserting them, and the employer carries the burden by proving by clear and affirmative evidence that it is entitled to exemption.[73]

A federal court agreed that Arizona's decision to cease counting leave time as hours worked for purposes of computing firefighters' overtime did not violate the FLSA, because Arizona's action was not undertaken in response to the extension of FLSA to state employees or as an invasion of FLSA overtime requirements.[74]

F. "Whistle-Blower" Protection

The FLSA also makes it unlawful for an employer to discharge or discriminate against an employee due to the employee's filing of an FLSA complaint.[75] This provision has become known as the "whistle-blower" statute. According to a circuit court, the purpose of this statute is not merely to vindicate the rights of the complaining party, but to foster an environment in which employees are unfettered in their decision to voice grievances without fear of economic retaliation or reprisal.[76]

§ 15.6   Food and Drug Violations (FDA)

The FDA is the federal agency that protects consumers from unsafe or adulterated food or drugs and investigates violations of the Food, Drug, and Cosmetic Act (FDCA). The crimes that are addressed by the FDA include: manufacturing, introducing, delivering or receiving adulterated or misbranded food, drugs, or cosmetics into interstate commerce; and, refusal to permit FDA food inspections. Violators may have civil or criminal penalties assessed against them. Violations are misdemeanors unless there is a showing of specific intent and/or prior violations, in which case the offense is a felony.

Legal News

In 2007 there was a major scandal involving pet food imported from China that was adulterated with melamine. The pet food was eventually traced as the cause of death for a large number of dogs and cats. Evidently the wheat gluten used to make the pet food was laced with melamine, a little-known compound that had the effect of indicating higher amounts of protein than what was actually present in the wheat gluten. The manufacturer used melamine to tamper with the nutritional content tests. Melamine created crystals and inflammation in the urinary tracts of the affected pets and, in many cases, urinary blockage led to renal failure and death.

In 2008, melamine was again in the news when China admitted that large supplies of infant formula and other milk-based products were adulterated with melamine. Again, the intent evidently was to bolster the product's protein levels (or, more accurately, apparent protein levels), and again, the result was death. Chinese infants died after ingesting the melamine-laced milk. In infants, the effect was the same as with the pets described above—melamine created urinary blockages and renal failure. There may be more melamine-laced products in China and other countries that bought the same milk powder used in the formula. The FDA in the U.S. and its European counterpart have now published safe levels of melamine in food products and are scrutinizing all products imported from China for the substance.

Source: "Melamine-Contamination Event, China, 2008." *A World Health Organization Report.* Accessed 1/10/2009 from http://www.who.int/foodsafety/fs_management/infosan_events/en/print.html.

An adulterated food refers to one that has ingredients that are poisonous, unsanitary, or contaminated. In *United States v. Park*,[77] the president of a national food chain was held liable for violations when it was proven that food was stored in a warehouse that allowed rodents to reach the food and rodent droppings were found in the food. The company president argued that lower-level employees, not he, were responsible for storage decisions or the lack of cleanup. The Supreme Court held that when a defendant, by his position, has either the responsibility or authority to prevent or correct a violation and does not do so, he will be held strictly liable. In early 2009, it was discovered that one company's peanut products, infected with salmonella, were distributed throughout the country. The products have been linked to several deaths. Warehouses owned by the company were determined to be unsanitary and it was discovered that the inspector did not check to see if appropriate health certificates were issued. It is too soon to say, at the time this book goes to press, whether any company officials will be prosecuted.[78]

§ 15.7 Computer Crimes (Cybercrimes)

As discussed in Chapter 9, the use of computers in crime has necessitated a response by legislators and law enforcement. Computers can be the object of crime (theft), the subject (vandalism and hacking), or the instrument (child pornography, fraud). The first federal legislation became law in October 1984, when President Ronald Reagan signed into law the Counterfeit Access Device and Computer Fraud and Abuse Act of 1984. This was part of the Comprehensive Crime Control Act of 1984. The Department of Justice (DOJ) broadly defines computer crime as "any violation of criminal law that involves knowledge of computer technology for their perpetration, investigation, or prosecution."[79]

A. Computer Pornography

Computer-based child pornography and obscenity has been previously discussed in Chapter 13. The use of computers in the distribution of obscenity and child pornography has made enforcement of criminal laws extremely difficult because the product might be made internationally and distributed instantaneously across the world. One of the targets of federal laws is the person who distributes child pornography (discussed previously), but also anyone who exposes children to pornography is subject to federal laws, as the following section indicates.

This section makes it a crime to expose minors to materials commercially distributed by means of World Wide Web that are harmful to minors.

18 U.S.C. § 231

(a) Requirement to restrict access.

    (1) Prohibited conduct. Whoever knowingly and with knowledge of the character of the material, in interstate or foreign commerce

by means of the World Wide Web, makes any communication for commercial purposes that is available to any minor and that includes any material that is harmful to minors shall be fined not more than $50,000, imprisoned not ore than 6 months, or both.

(2) Intentional violations. In addition to the penalties under paragraph (1), whoever intentionally violates such paragraph shall be subject to a fine of not more than $50,000 for each violation. For purposes of the paragraph, each day of violation shall constitute a separate violation.

B. Computer Fraud and Hacking

Title 18 § 1030 of the U.S. Code protects against various crimes involving "protected" computers. Protected computers include those used in interstate commerce or communications. Subsection 1030(a) lists the seven specific acts of computer-related crime that the NIIPA prohibits.

- Subsection 1030(a)(1) makes it a crime to access computer files without authorization or in excess of authorization, and subsequently to transmit classified government action.

- Subsection 1030(a)(2) prohibits obtaining, without access or in excess of authorized access, information from financial institutions, the United States government, or private sector computers that are used in interstate commerce.

- Subsection 1030(a)(3) proscribes intentionally accessing a United States department or agency nonpublic computer without authorization. If the government or a government agency does not use the computer exclusively, the illegal access must affect the government's use in order to violate this law.

- Subsection 1030(a)(4) prohibits accessing a protected computer, without or beyond authorization, with the intent to defraud and obtain something of value. There is an exception if the defendant only obtained computer time with a value less than $5,000 per year.

- Subsection 1030(a)(5), which addresses computer hacking, has sustained the most substantial modifications following passage of the USA Patriot Act of 2001. In response to concerns about malicious computer cracking and computer terrorism, the USA Patriot Act reduced the *mens rea* required in order to commit the crime and now anyone who is reckless or negligent in their actions and that causes damage can be guilty of this federal crime. Furthermore, those who have authorization but intentionally cause damage may also be guilty of the crime.[80]

- Section 1030(a)(6) prohibits one with intent to defraud from trafficking in passwords that would either permit unauthorized access to a government computer or affect interstate or foreign commerce.

- Finally, § 1030(a)(7) makes it illegal to transmit in interstate or foreign commerce any threat to cause damage to a protected computer with intent to extort something of value.

Whereas the 1996 Act's definition of "damage" contained certain minimum requirements, the USA Patriot Act amends the 1996 Act's definition of "damage," so that now § 1030(a)(5)(A) can be violated by "any impairment to the integrity or availability of data, a program, a system, or information." The effect of the amendments to § 1030(a)(5) has been to prohibit and punish crimes under this section that cause minimal damage and to increase the punishment for crimes causing significant damage.

In interpreting United States Code § 1030, a federal court of appeals decided that the computer fraud statute did not require the government to prove that the defendant intentionally damaged the computer files, but only that the defendant intentionally accessed the computer without authorization.[81] In this case, the defendant, a former bank employee, returned to her former work site and used a key that she kept and an old password to log onto the bank's mainframe. As a result, the bank's files were severely damaged. The defendant was convicted of violating the computer fraud statute. The court enumerated the elements that must be proved, stating that in order to have violated the statute, a defendant must have: (1) accessed, (2) a federal interest computer, (3) without authorization, (4) have altered, damaged, or destroyed information, (5) resulting in the loss to one or more others, and (6) of at least $1,000. In deciding this case, the court made reference to *United States v. Morris* in discussing the "intentionally" standard, and decided that the "intentionally" standard applies only to the "accesses" phase of § 1030(a)(5)(A), and not to the "damages" phase.[82]

In the case of *United States v. Middleton*, the defendant was convicted of intentionally causing damage to a protected computer in violation of 18 U.S. Code § 1030. The defendant worked as the personal computer administrator for an Internet service provider. Dissatisfied with his job, the defendant quit, then began to write threatening e-mails to his former employer. In addition to other violations, the defendant accessed the account of a sales representative and created two new accounts. He also changed all of the administrative passwords, altered the computer's registry, deleted the entire billing system, and deleted two internal databases. The defendant moved to dismiss the indictment, arguing that the corporation was not an "individual" within the meaning of the statute. The court disagreed, holding that the statute is broad enough to include corporations as well as natural persons and that the statute criminalizes computer crime that damages natural persons and corporations alike.[83]

C. Other Crimes

The use of technology, especially computers, will continue to challenge law enforcement and require additional laws. Congress enacted the Family Entertainment and Copyright Act of 2005, which makes it a felony to use a computer to upload unreleased movies, games, or software, even if the use is purely personal. Laws related to spam, spoofing, and phishing either have

Legal News

One of the most novel applications of the Computer Fraud and Abuse Act was the prosecution of Lori Drew, who was accused of cyber-bullying in 2008. In this case, two teenage girls were feuding and Drew, the mother of one of the girls, helped her daughter set up a MySpace account in the name of "Josh," a supposed 16-year-old boy. "Josh" made contact with the other teen girl and developed an online relationship with her and then rejected her and told her "the world would be better off without you." The victim, evidently already experiencing problems of depression, committed suicide. Drew was charged with felony and misdemeanor counts of computer hacking because she violated the terms of service of MySpace by creating the fictitious Josh. The trial resulted in the jury acquitting her of the felony counts (which required intent to harm), but convicted her of the misdemeanor counts (which did not require intent to harm). The fact that the emails went from Missouri through MySpace servers in California brought it into federal jurisdiction. The judge has not yet (as of January 2009) ruled on the defense motion for a directed verdict of acquittal and sentencing is due in April. If the judge does not set aside the jury verdict and acquit Drew, the case will no doubt go to the Ninth Circuit on appeal. Opponents of the prosecutor's use of the computer hacking law say that any verdict of guilty will freeze First Amendment rights of all who use the Internet for social contacts or agree to terms of service agreements on a wide range of Web sites because few read the terms of service and, as some argue: "everybody lies on the Internet."

Source: Zetter, K. (2008). "Can Lori Drew Verdict Survive the 9th Circuit?" Wired.BlogNetwork. Accessed 1/14/2008 from http://blog.wired.com/27bstroke6/2008/12/can-lori-drew-v.html.

been passed or are being considered. The prevalence of identity theft connected with the Internet has led to passage of the Fair and Accurate Credit Transactions Act (FACTA), which allows consumers one free credit report per year and the ability to freeze their credit so that identity thieves cannot obtain credit. The case of Lori Drew highlighted in the news box above and other examples of cyberstalking have prompted Congress to address the crime. Cyberstalking is arguably a difficult offense to prosecute because of the anonymity of the device and because stalking on the Internet encompasses a wide range of behaviors that do not fall into the category of traditional threats. For instance, victims (primarily women) have had stalkers pester them with hundreds of e-mail messages a day despite attempts to block them, have had their name and address posted in chat rooms with an apparent invitation to strangers to come and rape them, have had their credit ruined, have had threatening and insulting letters sent to others signed with their names and addresses, have had their name and address posted with the message that they are a prostitute and so on.

CASE: *United States v. Bowker*, 372 F.3d 365 (2004)

What was Bowker charged with?

What was his argument as to the wording of the statutes he was charged under?

What were the (excerpted) issues and holding of the case?

The Interstate Communications Act[84] prohibits the transmission of any interstate communication that makes a threat to another person; however, this law does not reach activities that do not fall clearly into a threat category. The Federal Telephone Harassment Statute,[85] passed in 1934, makes it a crime to use the telephone to anonymously and knowingly annoy, abuse, threaten, or harass a person. In 2006, Congress added a provision to the Violence Against Women and Department of Justice Reauthorization Act that attempted to respond to cyberstalking. Section 113—"Preventing Cyberstalking"—changed the telecommunications act to include e-mail messages:

Whoever . . . utilizes any device or software that can be used to originate telecommunications or other types of communications that are transmitted, in whole or in part, by the Internet . . . without disclosing his identity and with intent to annoy, abuse, threaten, or harass any person . . . who receives the communication . . . shall be fined under title 18 or imprisoned not more than two years, or both.[86]

Critics of the law argued that it was unconstitutional because the term "annoy" was vague and overbroad, but thus far= federal courts have upheld the use in telephone harassment cases. Critics on the other side argue that the law is not comprehensive in that it does not cover cases in which the harasser is not anonymous and only applies to direct communications, not situations in which the harasser uses the Internet to enlist third parties to instill fear (i.e., posting a message that purports to be from the victim inviting rape).

The other law that can be used to address cyberstalking is the Federal Interstate Stalking Punishment and Prevention Act (footnote: 18 U.S.C. § 2261A). We have discussed this law previously. Recall that the harasser must travel interstate or use interstate communication to fall under federal jurisdiction. A 2000 amendment to the law changed the definition of interstate travel to include e-mail messages or other communications that were interstate (bringing cyberstalking into the province of the law if messages traveled interstate). In 2006, in the same Violence Against Women Act described above, an amendment to the Interstate Stalking law was passed that prohibited the use of "any interactive computer service" to cause "substantial emotional distress."[87] This is a broader law that includes activities that do not constitute a direct threat to the victim.[88]

§ 15.8 Summary

The increased number of interstate violations and the complex nature of corporate crime has resulted in an expansion in the investigation of corporate crimes by federal agents. As the investigative focus on corporate crime has increased, federal laws concerning corporate criminality have received additional attention. American jurisprudence utilizes two general standards for imposing criminal liability on corporations: (1) traditional respondeat superior liability and (2) statutes specifically making corporations liable.

Money laundering is the process by which one conceals the existence, illegal source, or illegal applications of income, and disguises that income to make it appear legitimate. To make it possible to attack the money-laundering business, statutes have been enacted to require financial agencies to report certain transactions and to prohibit an individual's involvement in a financial transaction when the individual knows that the property involved in the transaction represents the proceeds of specified unlawful activities.

Enforcement of environmental crime statutes has received considerable attention by both federal and state personnel. Some of the many statutes are those relating to the Clean Air Act, the Safe Drinking Water Act, the Toxic Substance Control Act, and the Resource Conservation and Recovery Act. These acts include enforcement policies and establish the elements that must be proved in order to obtain convictions.

The central policy of the antitrust laws is against agreements that take away the freedom of purchasers to buy in the open market and to maintain, in the public interest, freedom of competition. The federal antitrust legislation provides for criminal sanctions against any person who makes any contract or engages in any combination or conspiracy in restraint of interstate commerce. The Securities and Exchange Commission regulates the stock market and investigates securities fraud, insider trading, and other crimes related to the buying, trading, and selling of securities.

The purpose of the Occupational Safety and Health Act (OSHA) is to assure, as far as possible, every working man and woman safe and healthful working conditions and to preserve human resources. The Act requires employers to furnish employees with a working environment free from recognized hazards, and requires employers to comply with specific safety and health rules. The Fair Labor Standards Act (FLSA) prohibits an employer from failing to pay minimum wages or overtime compensation to an employee, failing to keep individual work records for each employee, discrimination on the basis of sex by paying different wages for equal work, or using oppressive child labor. The FLSA also makes it unlawful for an employer to discharge or discriminate against an employee due to the employee's filing of an FLSA complaint.

The Food and Drug Administration polices the purity of products purchased and used by the American public. Those who adulterate or misbrand products can face both civil and criminal sanctions.

Cyberbullying is only one of the many computer crimes that are investigated and prosecuted by the federal government. Computers can be either the object or target of crime or the vehicle by which crimes are committed. Various federal laws have been passed to combat hacking and other computer crimes. Cyberstalking is a relatively new area of crime and laws are only now being developed to address this offense. It should be remembered that state statutes are enforceable and states may adopt more stringent protection than that authorized by federal laws. In some states, federal, state, and local enforcement personnel work as a task force in enforcing state and federal laws.

Review Questions

1. Why have federal agencies taken the lead in enforcing white-collar and corporate violations? Were corporations criminally liable under common law? When is a corporation liable for the acts of its agents?

2. What is the definition of money laundering? Why was it necessary to make money laundering a crime? What elements must be proved in order to obtain a conviction under the federal money laundering statute?

3. What are anti-structuring laws? How does the Patriot Act extend the importance of the Money Laundering Act?

4. Briefly summarize the provisions of the Clean Air Act, the Safe Drinking Water Act, the Clean Water Act and the Toxic Substance Control Act. Must the government prove the defendant had knowledge of the provisions of the Clean Water Act?

5. When was the first antitrust legislation enacted? What elements must be proved in order to obtain a conviction under the Federal Antitrust Act? What are the types of activities that constitute a violation of this law? Do states have antitrust acts?

6. What are securities? What are the types of crimes investigated and prosecuted by the SEC? What is "churning"? What is insider trading?

7. Explain a Ponzi scheme. What crimes are committed in such a scheme?

8. How did the Saxes-Oxley Act change the mens rea requirement for securities fraud?

9. In 1970, Congress enacted the first Occupational Safety and Health Act (OSHA). Under what provision of the Constitution does Congress have the authority to enact such legislation?

10. What general and specific duties does OSHA place on employers? By enacting OSHA, did Congress intend to prohibit states from enforcing laws relating to worker health and safety?

11. What is the Fair Labor Standards Act? What elements must be proven in order to constitute a violation of the minimum wage provisions? What are the provisions of the Equal Pay statute?

12. How does the "whistle-blower" provision in the Fair Labor Standards Act protect employees? Does the FLSA apply to state agencies?

13. What is the Department of Justice definition of "computer crime?"

14. In addition to distributing child pornography through the internet, what are other crimes related to computer child pornography?

15. Does the federal computer fraud statute (18 U.S. Code § 1030) require that the government prove the defendant intentionally damaged the computer files?

16. In the case of *United States v. Middleton*, what was included in the statute's term damage to the victim by computer hacking? How does the U.S. Patriot Act change that definition?

17. What behavior has become criminal through the passage of the Family Entertainment and Copyright Act of 2005? Explain.

18. What has Congress done to combat the growing problem of identity theft? Explain.

19. What is cyberstalking? What federal laws can be used to address this offense?

20. What are some other federal laws that were not covered in this textbook?

Notes

[1] Federal Register, Vol. 55 No. 227, November 1990.

[2] United States v. Grimaud, 220 U.S. 506 (1911).

[3] LaFave & Scott, Criminal Law 2d Ed. § 3:10 (1986).

[4] New York Central and Hudson River Railroad v. United States, 212 U.S. 481 (1909).

[5] *See* 39 Amer. Crim. Law Rev. 327 (2002) for a comprehensive discussion of corporate criminal liability.

[6] Model Penal Code § 2.07 (1985).

[7] First Federal Savings Bank of Hegewisch v. United States, 52 Fed. Cl. 774 (2002).

[8] *See* United States Sentencing Guidelines Manual § 8 (1998).

[9] *See* Byrne v. Nezhat, 261 F.3d 1075 (11th Cir. 2001), which held that while the Georgia law prohibits a corporation qua from being held to answer for a crime, this is not to say that a corporation may disregard the law with impunity, and if a crime has been committed, the agents for the corporation who are responsible are subject to prosecution.

[10] Jennifer Moore, *Corporate Culpability Under the Federal Sentencing Guidelines*, 34 Ariz. Law Rev. 745 (1992).

[11] Annie Geraghty, *Corporate Criminal Liability*, 39 Crim. Law Rev. 338 (2002).

[12] *Money Laundering*, 39 Am. Crim. L. Rev. 839 (2002).

[13] 18 U.S.C. §§ 1956-1957 (1988).

[14] For a discussion of the provisions of the Money Laundering Control Act, see 33 Am. Crim. L. Rev. 881 (1996). *Let the Seller Beware: Money Laundering Merchants and 18 U.S.C. §§ 1956-1957*, B.C. L. Rev. Vol. XXXIII (July 1992).

[15] United States v. Allen, 129 F.3d 1159 (10th Cir. 1997).

[16] United States v. Norman, 143 F.3d 375 (8th Cir. 1998).

[17] United States v. Jackson, 988 F.2d 757 (7th Cir. 1993). *See also* United States v. Antzoulatos, 962 F.2d 720 (7th Cir. 1992), *cert. denied*, 506 U.S. 919, 113 S. Ct. 331, 121 L. Ed. 2d 250 (1992).

18   31 U.S.C. § 5313.

19   31 U.S.C. § 5322.

20   Ratzlaf v. United States, 510 U.S. 135, 114 S. Ct. 655, 126 L. Ed. 2d 615 (1994).

21   *Money Laundering*, 39 AMER. CRIM. LAW REV. 839, 861 (2002).

22   42 U.S.C. §§ 7401-7671 (1994).

23   Her Majesty, The Queen v. City of Detroit, 874 F.2d 332 (6th Cir. 1989). *See also* Whitman v. A.M.Trucking Assn., 531 U.S. 457 (2002).

24   39 AMER. CRIM. LAW REV. 457 (2002).

25   42 U.S.C. §§ 300f - 300j 26 (1994).

26   *Environmental Crimes*, 33 AM. CRIM. L. REV. 607, 648 (1996).

27   42 U.S.C. § 300h (1994).

28   33 U.S.C. §§ 1251-1387 (1994).

29   Orange Environment Inc. v. County of Orange, 811 F. Supp. 926 (S.D.N.Y. 1993).

30   United States v. Holland, 874 F.2d 1470 (11th Cir. 1985).

31   United States v. Aluminum Co. of America, 824 F. Supp. 640 (E.D. Tex. 1993). *See also* United States v. Overholt, 307 F.3d 1231 (10th Cir. 2002).

32   United States v. Sinskey, 119 F.3d 712 (8th Cir. 1997).

33   15 U.S.C. §§ 2601-2692 (1994).

34   Corrosion Proof Fittings v. EPA, 947 F.2d 1201 (5th Cir. 1991).

35   42 U.S.C. §§ 6901-6992k (1994).

36   United States v. Rogers, 685 F. Supp. 201 (D. Minn. 1987).

37   *Environmental Crimes*, 33 AM. CRIM. L. REV. 607, 623 (1996); 39 CRIM. L. REV. 439 (2002).

38   42 U.S.C. § 6928(d).

39   33 U.S.C. § 407 (1997); 42 U.S.C. §§ 9601-9675; 7 U.S.C. § 136 (1994).

40   COLEMAN, THE CRIMINAL ELITE 2 (1989).

41   15 U.S.C. § 1.

42   *See* 39 AM. CRIM. L. REV. 225 (2002).

43   National Society of Professional Engineers v. United States, 435 U.S. 67, 98 S. Ct. 1355, 55 L. Ed. 2d 637 (1978).

44   Tondas v. Amateur Hockey Assn. of U.S., 438 F. Supp. 310 (W.D.N.Y. 1977).

45   Primetime 24 Joint Venture v. Nat'l Broad Co., Inc., 219 F.3d 92 (2d Cir. 2000); United States v. Romer, 148 F.3d 359 (4th Cir. 1998).

46   United States v. Nippon Paper Company, 109 F.3d 1 (1st Cir. 1997), *cert. denied*, 522 U.S. 1044, 118 S. Ct. 685, 139 L. Ed. 2d 632 (1999).

47   740 ILL. COMP. STAT. 5/7 1996; Illinois ex rel. Borris v. Panhandle Eastern Pipeline Co., 935 F.2d 1469 (7th Cir.), *reh'g denied, cert. denied*, 502 U.S. 1094, 112 S. Ct. 1169, 117 L. Ed. 2d 415 (1991). *See also* Storer Cable Communications v. City of Montgomery, Alabama, 806 F. Supp. 1518 (N.D. Ala. 1992), in which the court held that state laws that proscribe conduct permitted by the Sherman Act are not preempted.

48   Totemoff v. State, 905 P.2d 954 (Alaska 1995).

[49]   United States v. Madoff. Complaint. Violation of 15 U.S.C. § 78j(b), 78ff; 17 C.F.R. Sec. 240.10b-5. Filed in Southern District of New York, Magistrate Douglas Eaton.

[50]   29 U.S.C. §§ 651-678.

[51]   33 AM. CRIM. L. REV. 575 (1996).

[52]   Caterpillar, Inc. v. Herman, 154 F.3d 400 (7th Cir. 1998).

[53]   United States v. Ledish Malting Co., 135 F.3d 484 (7th Cir. 1998).

[54]   E. & R. Erectors, Inc. v. Secretary of Labor, 107 F.3d 157 (3d Cir. 1997)

[55]   Consol v. State, 806 S.W.2d 553 (Tex. Crim. 1991).

[56]   Gade v. National Solid Waste Management Association, 505 U.S. 88, 112 S. Ct. 2374, 120 L. Ed. 2d 73 (1992).

[57]   People v. Hegedus, 443 N.W.2d 127 (Mich. 1989).

[58]   Hillsborough Co. v. Automated Medical Labs, Inc., 471 U.S. 707, 105 S. Ct. 2371, 85 L. Ed. 2d 714 (1985).

[59]   29 U.S.C. §§ 201-219.

[60]   29 U.S.C. §§ 206, 207, 211, 212, and 215.

[61]   29 U.S.C. § 216(a).

[62]   Abril v. Commonwealth of Virginia, 145 F.3d 182 (4th Cir. 1998).

[63]   29 U.S.C. § 206.

[64]   29 U.S.C. § 207. Mullins v. Howard County, 730 F. Supp. 667 (D. Md. 1990).

[65]   Carter v. City of Charleston, South Carolina, 995 F. Supp. 620 (D.S.C. 1997). *See also* Holzapfel v. Town of Newburgh, 145 F.3d 516 (2d Cir. 1998), in which the court stated that the trial judge was responsible for determining as a matter of law whether a police officer's activities could potentially constitute work in an action for overtime compensation for off-duty activities performed by a police dog handler.

[66]   Fagot v. Flintkote, 305 F. Supp. 407 (E.D. La. 1969).

[67]   29 U.S.C. § 206(d).

[68]   Tidwell v. Fort Howard Corp., 756 F. Supp. 1487 (E.D. Okla. 1991).

[69]   Tomka v. Seiler Corp., 66 F.3d 1295 (2d Cir. 1995).

[70]   Sprague v. Thorn Americas, Inc., 129 F.3d 1355 (10th Cir 1997).

[71]   29 U.S.C. § 207.

[72]   29 U.S.C. § 207 through 219.

[73]   Carter v. City of Charleston, South Carolina, 995 F. Supp. 622 (D.S.C. 1997). *See also* Jerzak v. City of South Bend, 996 F. Supp. 840 (N.D. Ind. 1998), in which the court agreed that the city and police department had sufficiently proved that they had complied with the act.

[74]   Drollinger v. Arizona, 962 F.2d 956 (9th Cir. 1992).

[75]   29 U.S.C. § 215(a).

[76]   Saffels v. Rice, 40 F.3d 1546 (8th Cir. 1994).

[77]   United States v. Park, 421 U.S. 658 (1975)

[78]   U.S. Food and Drug Administration (2009). "Peanut Product Recalls: Salmonella Typhimurium." Available at: http://www.fda.gov/oc/opacom/hottopics/salmonellatyph.html#update. Accessed 3/11/2009.

[79]   National Institute of Justice, COMPUTER CRIME: CRIMINAL JUSTICE RESOURCE MANUAL (1989).

[80]   1030(a)(5)(A)(ii)–reckless and 1030(a)(5)(A)(iii)–negligent ; Subsection 1030(a)(5)(A)(i).

[81]   United States v. Sablan, 92 F.3d 865 (9th Cir. 1996).

[82]   United States v. Morris, 928 F.2d 504 (2d Cir. 1991), *cert. denied*, 502 U.S. 817, 112 S. Ct. 72, 116
       L. Ed. 2d 46 (1991).

[83]   United States v. Middleton, 231 F.3d 1207 (9th Cir. 2000).

[84]   18 U.S.C. § 875(c).

[85]   47 U.S.C. § 223.

[86]   Violence Against Women and Dept. of Justice Reauthorization Act of 2005. PUB. L. NO. 109-162,
       Tit. 1 & 113 (codified as amended in 47 U.S.C. § 223.]

[87]   Violence Against Women and Dept. of Justice Reauthorization Act of 2005. PUB. L. NO. 109-162.

[88]   Goodno, N. (2007). *Cyberstalking: A New Crime: Evaluating the Effectiveness of Current State and
       Federal Laws*. MO. L. REV. 72: 125-238.

Part II
Judicial Decisions

Part II: Table of Cases

Cases Related to Chapter 15
Corporate and Computer Crimes

Cases Relating to Chapter 1

Defining Crime

City of Chicago

v.

Jesus Morales

Supreme Court of the United States
527 U.S. 41 (1999)

Justice Stevens announced the judgment of the Court and delivered the opinion of the Court with respect to Parts I, II, and V, and an opinion with respect to Parts II, IV, and VI, in which Justice Souter and Justice Ginsburg join.

In 1992, the Chicago City Council enacted the Gang Congregation Ordinance, which prohibits "criminal street gang members" from "loitering" with one another or with other persons in any public place. The question presented is whether the Supreme Court of Illinois correctly held that the ordinance violates the Due Process Clause of the Fourteenth Amendment to the Federal Constitution.

I.

Before the ordinance was adopted, the city council's Committee on Police and Fire conducted hearings to explore the problems created by the city's street gangs, and more particularly, the consequences of public loitering by gang members. Witnesses included residents of the neighborhoods where gang members are most active, as well as some of the aldermen who represent those areas. Based on that evidence, the council made a series of findings that are included in the text of the ordinance and explain the reasons for its enactment. . . .

The council found that a continuing increase in criminal street gang activity was largely responsible for the city's rising murder rate, as well as an escalation of violent and drug related crimes. It noted that in many neighborhoods throughout the city, "the burgeoning presence of street gang members in public places has intimidated many law abiding citizens.". . . . Furthermore, the council stated that gang members "establish control over identifiable areas . . . by loitering in those areas and intimidating others from entering those areas; and . . . members of criminal street gangs avoid arrest by committing no offense punishable under existing laws when they know the police are present. . . .". . . . It further found that "loitering in public places by criminal street gang members creates a justifiable fear for the safety of persons and property in the area" and that "aggressive action is necessary to preserve the city's streets and other public places so that the public may use such places without fear." Moreover, the council concluded that the city "has an interest in discouraging all persons from loitering in public places with criminal gang members.". . . .

The ordinance creates a criminal offense punishable by a fine of up to $500, imprisonment for not more than six months, and a requirement to perform up to 120 hours of community service. Commission of the offense involves four predicates. First, the police officer must reasonably believe that at least one of the two or more persons present in a "public place" is a "criminal street gang member." Second, the persons must be "loitering," which the ordinance defines as "remaining in any one place with no apparent purpose." Third, the officer must then order "all" of the persons to disperse and remove themselves "from the area." Fourth, a person must disobey the officer's order. If any person, whether a gang member or not, disobeys the officer's order, that person is guilty of violating the ordinance. . . .

Two months after the ordinance was adopted, the Chicago Police Department promulgated General Order 92-4 to provide guidelines to govern its enforcement. That order purported to establish limitations on the enforcement discretion of police officers "to ensure that the anti-gang loitering ordinance is not enforced in an arbitrary or discriminatory way." . . . The limitations confine the authority to arrest gang members who violate the ordinance to sworn "members of the Gang Crime Section" and certain other designated officers, and establish detailed criteria for defining street gangs and membership in such gangs. . . . In addition, the order directs district commanders to "designate areas in which the presence of gang members has a demonstrable effect on the activities of law abiding persons in the surrounding community," and provides that the ordinance "will be enforced only within the designated areas." . . . The city, however, does not release the locations of these "designated areas" to the public.

II.

During the three years of its enforcement, the police issued over 89,000 dispersal orders and arrested over 42,000 people for violating the ordinance. In the ensuing enforcement proceedings, two trial judges upheld the constitutionality of the ordinance, but eleven others ruled that it was invalid. In respondent Youkhana's case, the trial judge held that the "ordinance fails to notify individuals what conduct is prohibited, and it encourages arbitrary and capricious enforcement by police."

[case history ending in Illinois Supreme Court ruling omitted]

The Illinois Supreme Court . . . held "that the gang loitering ordinance violates due process of law in that it is impermissibly vague on its face and an arbitrary restriction on personal liberties.". . . .The court did not reach the contentions that the ordinance "cre-

ates a status offense, permits arrests without probable cause or is overbroad.". . . .

In support of its vagueness holding, the court pointed out that the definition of "loitering" in the ordinance drew no distinction between innocent conduct and conduct calculated to cause harm. "Moreover, the definition of 'loiter' provided by the ordinance does not assist in clearly articulating the proscriptions of the ordinance." . . . Furthermore, it concluded that the ordinance was "not reasonably susceptible to a limiting construction which would affirm its validity."

We granted certiorari, . . . and now affirm. Like the Illinois Supreme Court, we conclude that the ordinance enacted by the city of Chicago is unconstitutionally vague.

III.

The basic factual predicate for the city's ordinance is not in dispute. As the city argues in its brief, "the very presence of a large collection of obviously brazen, insistent, and lawless gang members and hangers-on on the public ways intimidates residents, who become afraid even to leave their homes and go about their business. That, in turn, imperils community residents' sense of safety and security, detracts from property values, and can ultimately destabilize entire neighborhoods." The findings in the ordinance explain that it was motivated by these concerns. We have no doubt that a law that directly prohibited such intimidating conduct would be constitutional, but this ordinance broadly covers a significant amount of additional activity. Uncertainty about the scope of that additional coverage provides the basis for respondents' claim that the ordinance is too vague.

We are confronted at the outset with the city's claim that it was improper for the state courts to conclude that the ordinance is invalid on its face. The city correctly points out that imprecise laws can be attacked on their face under two different doctrines. First, the overbreadth doctrine permits the facial invalidation of laws that inhibit the exercise of First Amendment rights if the impermissible applications of the law are substantial when "judged in relation to the statute's plainly legitimate sweep." . . . Second, even if an enactment does not reach a substantial amount of constitutionally protected conduct, it may be impermissibly vague because it fails to establish standards for the police and public that are sufficient to guard against the arbitrary deprivation of liberty interests. . . .

While we, like the Illinois courts, conclude that the ordinance is invalid on its face, we do not rely on the overbreadth doctrine. We agree with the city's submission that the law does not have a sufficiently substantial impact on conduct protected by the First Amendment to render it unconstitutional. The ordinance does not prohibit speech. Because the term "loiter" is defined as remaining in one place "with no apparent purpose," it is also clear that it does not prohibit any form of conduct that is apparently intended to convey a message. By its terms, the ordinance is inapplicable to assemblies that are designed to demonstrate a group's support of, or opposition to, a particular point of view. . . .Its impact on the social contact between gang members and others does not impair the First Amendment "right of association" that our cases have recognized. . . .

On the other hand, as the United States recognizes, the freedom to loiter for innocent purposes is part of the "liberty" protected by the Due Process Clause of the Fourteenth Amendment. We have expressly identified this "right to remove from one place to another according to inclination" as "an attribute of personal liberty" protected by the Constitution. . . . Indeed, it is apparent that an individual's decision to remain in a public place of his choice is as much a part of his liberty as the freedom of movement inside frontiers that is "a part of our heritage". . . , or the right to move "to whatsoever place one's own inclination may direct" identified in Blackstone's Commentaries. . . .

There is no need, however, to decide whether the impact of the Chicago ordinance on constitutionally protected liberty alone would suffice to support a facial challenge under the overbreadth doctrine. . . .For it is clear that the vagueness of this enactment makes a facial challenge appropriate. This is not an ordinance that "simply regulates business behavior and contains a scienter requirement." . . . It is a criminal law that contains no *mens rea* requirement, . . . , and infringes

on constitutionally protected rights,. . . . When vagueness permeates the text of such a law, it is subject to facial attack.

Vagueness may invalidate a criminal law for either of two independent reasons. First, it may fail to provide the kind of notice that will enable ordinary people to understand what conduct it prohibits; second, it may authorize and even encourage arbitrary and discriminatory enforcement. . . . Accordingly, we first consider whether the ordinance provides fair notice to the citizen and then discuss its potential for arbitrary enforcement.

IV.

"It is established that a law fails to meet the requirements of the Due Process Clause if it is so vague and standardless that it leaves the public uncertain as to the conduct it prohibits. . . .". . . . The Illinois Supreme Court recognized that the term "loiter" may have a common and accepted meaning, . . . , but the definition of that term in this ordinance — "to remain in any one place with no apparent purpose" — does not. It is difficult to imagine how any citizen of the city of Chicago standing in a public place with a group of people would know if he or she had an "apparent purpose." If she were talking to another person, would she have an apparent purpose? If she were frequently checking her watch and looking expectantly down the street, would she have an apparent purpose?

Since the city cannot conceivably have meant to criminalize each instance a citizen stands in public with a gang member, the vagueness that dooms this ordinance is not the product of uncertainty about the normal meaning of "loitering," but rather about what loitering is covered by the ordinance and what is not. The Illinois Supreme Court emphasized the law's failure to distinguish between innocent conduct and conduct threatening harm. Its decision followed the precedent set by a number of state courts that have upheld ordinances that criminalize loitering combined with some other overt act or evidence of criminal intent. However, state courts have uniformly invalidated laws that do not join the term "loitering" with a second specific element of the crime.

The city's principal response to this concern about adequate notice is that loiterers are not subject to sanction until after they have failed to comply with an officer's order to disperse. "Whatever problem is created by a law that criminalizes conduct people normally believe to be innocent is solved when persons receive actual notice from a police order of what they are expected to do." We find this response unpersuasive for at least two reasons.

First, the purpose of the fair notice requirement is to enable the ordinary citizen to conform his or her conduct to the law. "No one may be required at peril of life, liberty or property to speculate as to the meaning of penal statutes.". . . . Although it is true that a loiterer is not subject to criminal sanctions unless he or she disobeys a dispersal order, the loitering is the conduct that the ordinance is designed to prohibit. If the loitering is in fact harmless and innocent, the dispersal order itself is an unjustified impairment of liberty. If the police are able to decide arbitrarily which members of the public they will order to disperse, then the Chicago ordinance becomes indistinguishable from the law we held invalid in *Shuttlesworth* v. *Birmingham,* . . . Because an officer may issue an order only after prohibited conduct has already occurred, it cannot provide the kind of advance notice that will protect the putative loiterer from being ordered to disperse. Such an order cannot retroactively give adequate warning of the boundary between the permissible and the impermissible applications of the law.

Second, the terms of the dispersal order compound the inadequacy of the notice afforded by the ordinance. It provides that the officer "shall order all such persons to disperse and remove themselves from the area.". . . . This vague phrasing raises a host of questions. After such an order issues, how long must the loiterers remain apart? How far must they move? If each loiterer walks around the block and they meet again at the same location, are they subject to arrest or merely to being ordered to disperse again? As we do here, we have found vagueness in a criminal statute exacerbated by the use of the standards of "neighborhood" and "locality.". . . . We remarked in *Connally* that "both terms are elastic and, dependent upon circumstances, may be equally satisfied by areas measured by rods or by miles.". . . .

Lack of clarity in the description of the loiterer's duty to obey a dispersal order might not render the ordinance unconstitutionally vague if the definition of the forbidden conduct were clear, but it does buttress our conclusion that the entire ordinance fails to give the ordinary citizen adequate notice of what is forbidden and what is permitted. The Constitution does not permit a legislature to "set a net large enough to catch all possible offenders, and leave it to the courts to step inside and say who could be rightfully detained, and who should be set at large.". . . . This ordinance is therefore vague "not in the sense that it requires a person to conform his conduct to an imprecise but comprehensible normative standard, but rather in the sense that no standard of conduct is specified at all.". . . .

V.

The broad sweep of the ordinance also violates " 'the requirement that a legislature establish minimal guidelines to govern law enforcement.' ". . . . There are no such guidelines in the ordinance. In any public place in the city of Chicago, persons who stand or sit in the company of a gang member may be ordered to disperse unless their purpose is apparent. The mandatory language in the enactment directs the police to issue an order without first making any inquiry about their possible purposes. It matters not whether the reason that a gang member and his father, for example, might loiter near Wrigley Field is to rob an unsuspecting fan or just to get a glimpse of Sammy Sosa leaving the ballpark; in either event, if their purpose is not apparent to a nearby police officer, she may — indeed, she "shall" — order them to disperse.

Recognizing that the ordinance does reach a substantial amount of innocent conduct, we turn, then, to its language to determine if it "necessarily entrusts lawmaking to the moment-to-moment judgment of the policeman on his beat.". . . . As we discussed in the context of fair notice, . . . , the principal source of the vast discretion conferred on the police in this case is the definition of loitering as "to remain in any one place with no apparent purpose."

As the Illinois Supreme Court interprets that definition, it "provides absolute discretion to police officers to determine what activities constitute loitering." . . . We have no authority to construe the language of a state statute more narrowly than the construction given by that State's highest court. "The power to determine the meaning of a statute carries with it the power to prescribe its extent and limitations as well as the method by which they shall be determined." . . .

Nevertheless, the city disputes the Illinois Supreme Court's interpretation, arguing that the text of the ordinance limits the officer's discretion in three ways. First, it does not permit the officer to issue a dispersal order to anyone who is moving along or who has an apparent purpose. Second, it does not permit an arrest if individuals obey a dispersal order. Third, no order can issue unless the officer reasonably believes that one of the loiterers is a member of a criminal street gang.

Even putting to one side our duty to defer to a state court's construction of the scope of a local enactment, we find each of these limitations insufficient. That the ordinance does not apply to people who are moving — that is, to activity that would not constitute loitering under any possible definition of the term — does not even address the question of how much discretion the police enjoy in deciding which stationary persons to disperse under the ordinance. Similarly, that the ordinance does not permit an arrest until after a dispersal order has been disobeyed does not provide any guidance to the officer deciding whether such an order should issue. The "no apparent purpose" standard for making that decision is inherently subjective because its application depends on whether some purpose is "apparent" to the officer on the scene.

Presumably an officer would have discretion to treat some purposes — perhaps a purpose to engage in idle conversation or simply to enjoy a cool breeze on a warm evening — as too frivolous to be apparent if he suspected a different ulterior motive. Moreover, an officer conscious of the city council's reasons for enacting the ordinance might well ignore its text and issue a dispersal order, even though an illicit purpose is actually apparent.

It is true, as the city argues, that the requirement that the officer reasonably believes that a group of loiterers contains a gang member does place a limit on the authority to order dispersal. That limitation would no doubt be sufficient if the ordinance only applied to loitering that had an apparently harmful purpose or effect, or possibly if it only applied to loitering by persons reasonably believed to be criminal gang members. But this ordinance, for reasons that are not explained in the findings of the city council, requires no harmful purpose and applies to non-gang members as well as suspected gang members. It applies to everyone in the city who may remain in one place with one suspected gang member as long as their purpose is not apparent to an officer observing them. Friends, relatives, teachers, counselors, or even total strangers might unwittingly engage in forbidden loitering if they happen to engage in idle conversation with a gang member.

Ironically, the definition of loitering in the Chicago ordinance not only extends its scope to encompass harmless conduct, but also has the perverse consequence of excluding from its coverage much of the intimidating conduct that motivated its enactment. As the city council's findings demonstrate, the most harmful gang loitering is motivated either by an apparent purpose to publicize the gang's dominance of certain territory, thereby intimidating nonmembers, or by an equally apparent purpose to conceal ongoing commerce in illegal drugs. As the Illinois Supreme Court has not placed any limiting construction on the language in the ordinance, we must assume that the ordinance means what it says and that it has no application to loiterers whose purpose is apparent. The relative importance of its application to harmless loitering is magnified by its inapplicability to loitering that has an obviously threatening or illicit purpose.

Finally, in its opinion striking down the ordinance, the Illinois Supreme Court refused to accept the general order issued by the police department as a sufficient limitation on the "vast amount of discretion" granted to the police in its enforcement. . . . That the police have adopted internal rules limiting their enforcement to certain designated areas in the city would not provide a defense to a loiterer who might be arrested elsewhere. Nor could a person who knowingly loitered with a well-known gang member anywhere in the city safely assume that they would not be ordered to disperse no matter how innocent and harmless their loitering might be.

VI.

In our judgment, the Illinois Supreme Court correctly concluded that the ordinance does not provide sufficiently specific limits on the enforcement discretion of the police "to meet constitutional standards for definiteness and clarity.". . . . We recognize the serious and difficult problems testified to by the citizens of Chicago that led to the enactment of this ordinance. "We are mindful that the preservation of liberty depends in part on the maintenance of social order.". . . . However, in this instance the city has enacted an ordinance that affords too much discretion to the police and too little notice to citizens who wish to use the public streets.

Footnotes and citations omitted. Concurring and dissenting opinions omitted.

Texas
v.
Johnson

Supreme Court of the United States
491 U.S. 397 (1989)

Justice Brennan, J., delivered the opinion of the Court, in which Marshall, Blackmun, Scalia, and Kennedy, JJ., joined. Kennedy, J., filed a concurring opinion. Rehnquist, C. J., filed a dissenting opinion, in which White and O'Connor, JJ., joined. Stevens, J., filed a dissenting opinion, . . .

After publicly burning an American flag as a means of political protest, Gregory Lee Johnson was convicted of desecrating a flag in violation of Texas law. This case presents the question whether his conviction is consistent with the First Amendment. We hold that it is not.

I.

While the Republican National Convention was taking place in Dallas in 1984, respondent Johnson participated in a political demonstration dubbed the "Republican War Chest Tour." As explained in literature distributed by the demonstrators and in speeches made by them, the purpose of this event was to protest the policies of the Reagan administration and of certain Dallas-based corporations. The demonstrators marched through the Dallas streets, chanting political slogans and stopping at several corporate locations to stage "die-ins" intended to dramatize the consequences of nuclear war. On several occasions they spray-painted the walls of buildings and overturned potted plants, but Johnson himself took no part in such activities. He did, however, accept an American flag handed to him by a fellow protestor who had taken it from a flagpole outside one of the targeted buildings.

The demonstration ended in front of Dallas City Hall, where Johnson unfurled the American flag, doused it with kerosene, and set it on fire. While the flag burned, the protestors chanted: "America, the red, white, and blue, we spit on you." After the demonstrators dispersed, a witness to the flag burning collected the flag's remains and buried them in his backyard. No one was physically injured or threatened with injury, though several witnesses testified that they had been seriously offended by the flag burning.

Of the approximately 100 demonstrators, Johnson alone was charged with a crime. The only criminal offense with which he was charged was the desecration of a venerated object in violation of Tex. Penal Code Ann. § 42.09(a)(3) (1989). After a trial, he was convicted, sentenced to one year in prison, and fined $2,000. The Court of Appeals for the Fifth District of Texas at Dallas affirmed Johnson's conviction, . . . , but the Texas Court of Criminal Appeals reversed, . . . holding that the State could not, consistent with the First Amendment, punish Johnson for burning the flag in these circumstances.

The Court of Criminal Appeals began by recognizing that Johnson's conduct was symbolic speech protected by the First Amendment: "Given the context of an organized demonstration, speeches, slogans, and the distribution of literature, anyone who observed appellant's act would have understood the message that appellant intended to convey. The act for which appellant was convicted was clearly 'speech' contemplated by the First Amendment." . . . To justify Johnson's conviction for engaging in symbolic speech, the State asserted two interests: preserving the flag as a symbol of national unity and preventing breaches of the peace. The Court of Criminal Appeals held that neither interest supported his conviction.

Acknowledging that this Court had not yet decided whether the Government may criminally sanction flag desecration in order to preserve the flag's symbolic value, the Texas court nevertheless concluded that our decision in *West Virginia Board of Education* v. *Barnette*, . . . (1943), suggested that furthering this interest by curtailing speech was impermissible. "Recognizing that the right to differ is the centerpiece of our First Amendment freedoms," the court explained, "a government cannot mandate by fiat a feeling of unity in its citizens. Therefore, that very same government cannot carve out a symbol of unity and prescribe a set of approved messages to be associated with that symbol when it cannot mandate the status or feeling the symbol purports to represent.". . . . Noting that the State had not shown that the flag was in "grave and immediate danger," . . . , of being stripped of its symbolic value, the Texas court also decided that the flag's special status was not endangered by Johnson's conduct. . . .

As to the State's goal of preventing breaches of the peace, the court concluded that the flag-desecration statute was not drawn narrowly enough to encompass only those flag burnings that were likely to result in a serious disturbance of the peace. And in fact, the court emphasized, the flag burning in this particular case did not threaten such a reaction. " 'Serious offense' occurred," the court admitted, "but there was no breach of peace nor does the record reflect that the situation was potentially explosive. One cannot equate 'serious offense' with incitement to breach the peace.". . . . The court also stressed that another Texas statute, Tex. Penal Code Ann. § 42.01 (1989), prohibited

breaches of the peace. Citing *Boos* v. *Barry*, . . . (1988), the court decided that § 42.01 demonstrated Texas' ability to prevent disturbances of the peace without punishing this flag desecration.

Because it reversed Johnson's conviction on the ground that § 42.09 was unconstitutional as applied to him, the state court did not address Johnson's argument that the statute was, on its face, unconstitutionally vague and overbroad. We granted certiorari, . . . and now affirm.

II.

Johnson was convicted of flag desecration for burning the flag rather than for uttering insulting words. This fact somewhat complicates our consideration of his conviction under the First Amendment. We must first determine whether Johnson's burning of the flag constituted expressive conduct, permitting him to invoke the First Amendment in challenging his conviction. . . . If his conduct was expressive, we next decide whether the State's regulation is related to the suppression of free expression. . . . If the State's regulation is not related to expression, then the less stringent standard we announced in *United States* v. *O'Brien* for regulations of noncommunicative conduct controls. . . . If it is, then we are outside of *O'Brien*'s test, and we must ask whether this interest justifies Johnson's conviction under a more demanding standard. . . . A third possibility is that the State's asserted interest is simply not implicated on these facts, and in that event the interest drops out of the picture.

The First Amendment literally forbids the abridgment only of "speech," but we have long recognized that its protection does not end at the spoken or written word. While we have rejected "the view that an apparently limitless variety of conduct can be labeled 'speech' whenever the person engaging in the conduct intends thereby to express an idea," . . . , we have acknowledged that conduct may be "sufficiently imbued with elements of communication to fall within the scope of the First and Fourteenth Amendments," . . .

In deciding whether particular conduct possesses sufficient communicative elements to bring the First Amendment into play, we have asked whether "[a]n intent to convey a particularized message was present, and [whether] the likelihood was great that the message would be understood by those who viewed it.". . . . Hence, we have recognized the expressive nature of students' wearing of black armbands to protest American military involvement in Vietnam, . . . ; of a sit-in by blacks in a "whites only" area to protest segregation, . . . ; of the wearing of American military uniforms in a dramatic presentation criticizing American involvement in Vietnam, . . .

Especially pertinent to this case are our decisions recognizing the communicative nature of conduct relating to flags. Attaching a peace sign to the flag, . . . ; refusing to salute the flag, . . . ; and displaying a red flag, . . . , we have held, all may find shelter under the First Amendment. . . . That we have had little difficulty identifying an expressive element in conduct relating to flags should not be surprising. The very purpose of a national flag is to serve as a symbol of our country; it is, one might say, "the one visible manifestation of two hundred years of nationhood." . . . Thus, we have observed:

"[T]he flag salute is a form of utterance. Symbolism is a primitive but effective way of communicating ideas. The use of an emblem or flag to symbolize some system, idea, institution, or personality, is a short cut from mind to mind. Causes and nations, political parties, lodges and ecclesiastical groups seek to knit the loyalty of their followings to a flag or banner, a color or design." . . .

Pregnant with expressive content, the flag as readily signifies this Nation as does the combination of letters found in "America."

We have not automatically concluded, however, that any action taken with respect to our flag is expressive. Instead, in characterizing such action for First Amendment purposes, we have considered the context in which it occurred. In *Spence*, for example, we emphasized that Spence's taping of a peace sign to his flag was "roughly simultaneous with and concededly triggered by the Cambodian incursion and the Kent State tragedy.". . . . The State of Washington had conceded, in fact, that Spence's conduct was

a form of communication, and we stated that "the State's concession is inevitable on this record.". . . .

The State of Texas conceded for purposes of its oral argument in this case that Johnson's conduct was expressive conduct, . . . and this concession seems to us as prudent as was Washington's in *Spence*. Johnson burned an American flag as part — indeed, as the culmination — of a political demonstration that coincided with the convening of the Republican Party and its renomination of Ronald Reagan for President. The expressive, overtly political nature of this conduct was both intentional and overwhelmingly apparent. At his trial, Johnson explained his reasons for burning the flag as follows: "The American Flag was burned as Ronald Reagan was being renominated as President. And a more powerful statement of symbolic speech, whether you agree with it or not, couldn't have been made at that time.["]. . . . In these circumstances, Johnson's burning of the flag was conduct "sufficiently imbued with elements of communication," . . . to implicate the First Amendment.

III.

The government generally has a freer hand in restricting expressive conduct than it has in restricting the written or spoken word. . . . It may not, however, proscribe particular conduct *because* it has expressive elements. "[W]hat might be termed the more generalized guarantee of freedom of expression makes the communicative nature of conduct an inadequate *basis* for singling out that conduct for proscription. A law *directed at* the communicative nature of conduct must, like a law directed at speech itself, be justified by the substantial showing of need that the First Amendment requires.". . . . It is, in short, not simply the verbal or nonverbal nature of the expression, but the governmental interest at stake, that helps to determine whether a restriction on that expression is valid.

Thus, although we have recognized that where "'speech' and 'nonspeech' elements are combined in the same course of conduct, a sufficiently important governmental interest in regulating the nonspeech element can justify incidental limitations on First Amendment freedoms," . . . , we have limited the applicability of *O'Brien*'s relatively lenient standard to those cases in which "the governmental interest is unrelated to the suppression of free expression.". . . . In stating, moreover, that *O'Brien*'s test "in the last analysis is little, if any, different from the standard applied to time, place, or manner restrictions," . . . , we have highlighted the requirement that the governmental interest in question be unconnected to expression in order to come under *O'Brien*'s less demanding rule.

In order to decide whether *O'Brien*'s test applies here, therefore, we must decide whether Texas has asserted an interest in support of Johnson's conviction that is unrelated to the suppression of expression. If we find that an interest asserted by the State is simply not implicated on the facts before us, we need not ask whether *O'Brien*'s test applies. . . . The State offers two separate interests to justify this conviction: preventing breaches of the peace and preserving the flag as a symbol of nationhood and national unity. We hold that the first interest is not implicated on this record and that the second is related to the suppression of expression.

A.

Texas claims that its interest in preventing breaches of the peace justifies Johnson's conviction for flag desecration. However, no disturbance of the peace actually occurred or threatened to occur because of Johnson's burning of the flag. Although the State stresses the disruptive behavior of the protestors during their march toward City Hall, . . . , it admits that "no actual breach of the peace occurred at the time of the flagburning or in response to the flagburning.". . . . The State's emphasis on the protestors' disorderly actions prior to arriving at City Hall is not only somewhat surprising given that no charges were brought on the basis of this conduct, but it also fails to show that a disturbance of the peace was a likely reaction to *Johnson's* conduct. The only evidence offered by the State at trial to show the reaction to Johnson's actions was the testimony of several persons who had been seriously offended by the flag burning. . . .

The State's position, therefore, amounts to a claim that an audience that takes serious

offense at particular expression is necessarily likely to disturb the peace and that the expression may be prohibited on this basis. Our precedents do not countenance such a presumption. On the contrary, they recognize that a principal "function of free speech under our system of government is to invite dispute. It may indeed best serve its high purpose when it induces a condition of unrest, creates dissatisfaction with conditions as they are, or even stirs people to anger." . . . It would be odd indeed to conclude *both* that "if it is the speaker's opinion that gives offense, that consequence is a reason for according it constitutional protection," . . . , *and* that the government may ban the expression of certain disagreeable ideas on the unsupported presumption that their very disagreeableness will provoke violence.

Thus, we have not permitted the government to assume that every expression of a provocative idea will incite a riot, but have instead required careful consideration of the actual circumstances surrounding such expression, asking whether the expression "is directed to inciting or producing imminent lawless action and is likely to incite or produce such action." . . . To accept Texas' arguments that it need only demonstrate "the potential for a breach of the peace," . . . and that every flag burning necessarily possesses that potential, would be to eviscerate our holding in *Brandenburg*. This we decline to do.

Nor does Johnson's expressive conduct fall within that small class of "fighting words" that are "likely to provoke the average person to retaliation, and thereby cause a breach of the peace." . . . No reasonable onlooker would have regarded Johnson's generalized expression of dissatisfaction with the policies of the Federal Government as a direct personal insult or an invitation to exchange fisticuffs. . . .

We thus conclude that the State's interest in maintaining order is not implicated on these facts. The State need not worry that our holding will disable it from preserving the peace. We do not suggest that the First Amendment forbids a State to prevent "imminent lawless action.". . . . And, in fact, Texas already has a statute specifically prohibiting breaches of the peace, Tex. Penal Code Ann. § 42.01 (1989), which tends to confirm that Texas need not punish this flag desecration in order to keep the peace. . . .

B.

The State also asserts an interest in preserving the flag as a symbol of nationhood and national unity. In *Spence*, we acknowledged that the government's interest in preserving the flag's special symbolic value "is directly related to expression in the context of activity" such as affixing a peace symbol to a flag. . . . We are equally persuaded that this interest is related to expression in the case of Johnson's burning of the flag. The State, apparently, is concerned that such conduct will lead people to believe either that the flag does not stand for nationhood and national unity, but instead reflects other, less positive concepts, or that the concepts reflected in the flag do not in fact exist, that is, that we do not enjoy unity as a Nation. These concerns blossom only when a person's treatment of the flag communicates some message, and thus are related "to the suppression of free expression" within the meaning of *O'Brien*. We are thus outside of *O'Brien*'s test altogether.

IV.

It remains to consider whether the State's interest in preserving the flag as a symbol of nationhood and national unity justifies Johnson's conviction.

As in *Spence*, "[w]e are confronted with a case of prosecution for the expression of an idea through activity," and "[a]ccordingly, we must examine with particular care the interests advanced by [petitioner] to support its prosecution.". . . . Johnson was not, we add, prosecuted for the expression of just any idea; he was prosecuted for his expression of dissatisfaction with the policies of this country, expression situated at the core of our First Amendment values. . . .

Moreover, Johnson was prosecuted because he knew that his politically charged expression would cause "serious offense." If he had burned the flag as a means of disposing of it because it was dirty or torn, he would not have been convicted of flag desecration under this Texas law: federal law designates

burning as the preferred means of disposing of a flag "when it is in such condition that it is no longer a fitting emblem for display," . . . and Texas has no quarrel with this means of disposal. . . . The Texas law is thus not aimed at protecting the physical integrity of the flag in all circumstances, but is designed instead to protect it only against impairments that would cause serious offense to others. Texas concedes as much: "Section 42.09(b) reaches only those severe acts of physical abuse of the flag carried out in a way likely to be offensive. The statute mandates intentional or knowing abuse, that is, the kind of mistreatment that is not innocent, but rather is intentionally designed to seriously offend other individuals." . . .

Whether Johnson's treatment of the flag violated Texas law thus depended on the likely communicative impact of his expressive conduct. Our decision in *Boos* v. *Barry*, . . . tells us that this restriction on Johnson's expression is content based. In *Boos*, we considered the constitutionality of a law prohibiting "the display of any sign within 500 feet of a foreign embassy if that sign tends to bring that foreign government into 'public odium' or 'public disrepute.'". . . . Rejecting the argument that the law was content neutral because it was justified by "our international law obligation to shield diplomats from speech that offends their dignity," . . . , we held that "[t]he emotive impact of speech on its audience is not a 'secondary effect' " unrelated to the content of the expression itself. . . .

According to the principles announced in *Boos*, Johnson's political expression was restricted because of the content of the message he conveyed. We must therefore subject the State's asserted interest in preserving the special symbolic character of the flag to "the most exacting scrutiny." . . .

Texas argues that its interest in preserving the flag as a symbol of nationhood and national unity survives this close analysis. Quoting extensively from the writings of this Court chronicling the flag's historic and symbolic role in our society, the State emphasizes the " 'special place' " reserved for the flag in our Nation. . . .The State's argument is not that it has an interest simply in maintaining the flag as a symbol of *something*, no matter what it symbolizes; indeed, if that were the State's position, it would be difficult to see how that interest is endangered by highly symbolic conduct such as Johnson's. Rather, the State's claim is that it has an interest in preserving the flag as a symbol of *nationhood* and *national unity*, a symbol with a determinate range of meanings. . . .According to Texas, if one physically treats the flag in a way that would tend to cast doubt on either the idea that nationhood and national unity are the flag's referents or that national unity actually exists, the message conveyed thereby is a harmful one and therefore may be prohibited.

If there is a bedrock principle underlying the First Amendment, it is that the government may not prohibit the expression of an idea simply because society finds the idea itself offensive or disagreeable. . . .

We have not recognized an exception to this principle even where our flag has been involved. In *Street* v. *New York*, . . . (1969), we held that a State may not criminally punish a person for uttering words critical of the flag. Rejecting the argument that the conviction could be sustained on the ground that Street had "failed to show the respect for our national symbol which may properly be demanded of every citizen," we concluded that "the constitutionally guaranteed 'freedom to be intellectually . . . diverse or even contrary,' and the 'right to differ as to things that touch the heart of the existing order,' encompass the freedom to express publicly one's opinions about our flag, including those opinions which are defiant or contemptuous.". . . . Nor may the government, we have held, compel conduct that would evince respect for the flag. "To sustain the compulsory flag salute we are required to say that a Bill of Rights which guards the individual's right to speak his own mind, left it open to public authorities to compel him to utter what is not in his mind.". . . .

In holding in *Barnette* that the Constitution did not leave this course open to the government, Justice Jackson described one of our society's defining principles in words deserving of their frequent repetition: "If there is any fixed star in our constitutional constellation, it is that no official, high or petty, can prescribe what shall be orthodox

in politics, nationalism, religion, or other matters of opinion or force citizens to confess by word or act their faith therein." . . . In *Spence*, we held that the same interest asserted by Texas here was insufficient to support a criminal conviction under a flag-misuse statute for the taping of a peace sign to an American flag. "Given the protected character of [Spence's] expression and in light of the fact that no interest the State may have in preserving the physical integrity of a privately owned flag was significantly impaired on these facts," we held, "the conviction must be invalidated." . . .

In short, nothing in our precedents suggests that a State may foster its own view of the flag by prohibiting expressive conduct relating to it. To bring its argument outside our precedents, Texas attempts to convince us that even if its interest in preserving the flag's symbolic role does not allow it to prohibit words or some expressive conduct critical of the flag, it does permit it to forbid the outright destruction of the flag. The State's argument cannot depend here on the distinction between written or spoken words and nonverbal conduct. That distinction, we have shown, is of no moment where the nonverbal conduct is expressive, as it is here, and where the regulation of that conduct is related to expression, as it is here. . . .In addition, both *Barnette* and *Spence* involved expressive conduct, not only verbal communication, and both found that conduct protected.

Texas' focus on the precise nature of Johnson's expression, moreover, misses the point of our prior decisions: their enduring lesson, that the government may not prohibit expression simply because it disagrees with its message, is not dependent on the particular mode in which one chooses to express an idea. If we were to hold that a State may forbid flag burning wherever it is likely to endanger the flag's symbolic role, but allow it wherever burning a flag promotes that role — as where, for example, a person ceremoniously burns a dirty flag — we would be saying that when it comes to impairing the flag's physical integrity, the flag itself may be used a symbol — as a substitute for the written or spoken word or a "short cut from mind to mind" — only in one direction. We would be permitting a State to "prescribe what shall be orthodox" by saying that one may burn the flag to convey one's attitude toward it and its referents only if one does not endanger the flag's representation of nationhood and national unity.

We never before have held that the Government may ensure that a symbol be used to express only one view of that symbol or its referents. Indeed, in *Schacht* v. *United States*, we invalidated a federal statute permitting an actor portraying a member of one of our Armed Forces to "'wear the uniform of that armed force if the portrayal does not tend to discredit that armed force.'" . . . This proviso, we held, "which leaves Americans free to praise the war in Vietnam but can send persons like Schacht to prison for opposing it, cannot survive in a country which has the First Amendment." . . .

We perceive no basis on which to hold that the principle underlying our decision in *Schacht* does not apply to this case. To conclude that the government may permit designated symbols to be used to communicate only a limited set of messages would be to enter territory having no discernible or defensible boundaries. Could the government, on this theory, prohibit the burning of state flags? Of copies of the Presidential seal? Of the Constitution? In evaluating these choices under the First Amendment, how would we decide which symbols were sufficiently special to warrant this unique status? To do so, we would be forced to consult our own political preferences, and impose them on the citizenry, in the very way that the First Amendment forbids us to do. . . .

There is, moreover, no indication — either in the text of the Constitution or in our cases interpreting it — that a separate juridical category exists for the American flag alone. Indeed, we would not be surprised to learn that the persons who framed our Constitution and wrote the Amendment that we now construe were not known for their reverence for the Union Jack. The First Amendment does not guarantee that other concepts virtually sacred to our Nation as a whole — such as the principle that discrimination on the basis of race is odious and destructive — will go unquestioned in the market-place of ideas. . . . We decline, therefore, to create for the flag an exception to the joust of principles protected by the First Amendment.

It is not the State's ends, but its means, to which we object. It cannot be gainsaid that there is a special place reserved for the flag in this Nation, and thus we do not doubt that the government has a legitimate interest in making efforts to "preserv[e] the national flag as an unalloyed symbol of our country." . . . We reject the suggestion, urged at oral argument by counsel for Johnson, that the government lacks "any state interest whatsoever" in regulating the manner in which the flag may be displayed. . . . Congress has, for example, enacted precatory regulations describing the proper treatment of the flag, see 36 U. S. C. §§ 173-177, and we cast no doubt on the legitimacy of its interest in making such recommendations. To say that the government has an interest in encouraging proper treatment of the flag, however, is not to say that it may criminally punish a person for burning a flag as a means of political protest. "National unity as an end which officials may foster by persuasion and example is not in question. The problem is whether under our Constitution compulsion as here employed is a permissible means for its achievement." . . .

We are fortified in today's conclusion by our conviction that forbidding criminal punishment for conduct such as Johnson's will not endanger the special role played by our flag or the feelings it inspires. To paraphrase Justice Holmes, we submit that nobody can suppose that this one gesture of an unknown man will change our Nation's attitude towards its flag. . . . Indeed, Texas' argument that the burning of an American flag "'is an act having a high likelihood to cause a breach of the peace,'" . . . and its statute's implicit assumption that physical mistreatment of the flag will lead to "serious offense," tend to confirm that the flag's special role is not in danger; if it were, no one would riot or take offense because a flag had been burned.

We are tempted to say, in fact, that the flag's deservedly cherished place in our community will be strengthened, not weakened, by our holding today. Our decision is a reaffirmation of the principles of freedom and inclusiveness that the flag best reflects, and of the conviction that our toleration of criticism such as Johnson's is a sign and source of our strength. Indeed, one of the proudest images of our flag, the one immortalized in our own national anthem, is of the bombardment it survived at Fort McHenry. It is the Nation's resilience, not its rigidity, that Texas sees reflected in the flag — and it is that resilience that we reassert today.

The way to preserve the flag's special role is not to punish those who feel differently about these matters. It is to persuade them that they are wrong. "To courageous, self-reliant men, with confidence in the power of free and fearless reasoning applied through the processes of popular government, no danger flowing from speech can be deemed clear and present, unless the incidence of the evil apprehended is so imminent that it may befall before there is opportunity for full discussion. If there be time to expose through discussion the falsehood and fallacies, to avert the evil by the processes of education, the remedy to be applied is more speech, not enforced silence." . . . And, precisely because it is our flag that is involved, one's response to the flag burner may exploit the uniquely persuasive power of the flag itself. We can imagine no more appropriate response to burning a flag than waving one's own, no better way to counter a flag burner's message than by saluting the flag that burns, no surer means of preserving the dignity even of the flag that burned than by — as one witness here did — according its remains a respectful burial. We do not consecrate the flag by punishing its desecration, for in doing so we dilute the freedom that this cherished emblem represents.

V.

Johnson was convicted for engaging in expressive conduct. The State's interest in preventing breaches of the peace does not support his conviction because Johnson's conduct did not threaten to disturb the peace. Nor does the State's interest in preserving the flag as a symbol of nationhood and national unity justify his criminal conviction for engaging in political expression. The judgment of the Texas Court of Criminal Appeals is therefore

Affirmed.

Footnotes and citations omitted. Concurring and dissenting opinions omitted.

**In re Winship
Supreme Court of the United States
397 U.S. 358 (1970)**

Mr. Justice Brennan delivered the opinion of the Court.

Constitutional questions decided by this Court concerning the juvenile process have centered on the adjudicatory stage at "which a determination is made as to whether a juvenile is a 'delinquent' as a result of alleged misconduct on his part, with the consequence that he may be committed to a state institution.". . . . *Gault* decided that, although the Fourteenth Amendment does not require that the hearing at this stage conform with all the requirements of a criminal trial or even of the usual administrative proceeding, the Due Process Clause does require application during the adjudicatory hearing of "the essentials of due process and fair treatment.". . . . This case presents the single, narrow question whether proof beyond a reasonable doubt is among the "essentials of due process and fair treatment" required during the adjudicatory stage when a juvenile is charged with an act which would constitute a crime if committed by an adult.

Section 712 of the New York Family Court Act defines a juvenile delinquent as "a person over seven and less than sixteen years of age who does any act which, if done by an adult, would constitute a crime." During a 1967 adjudicatory hearing, conducted pursuant to § 742 of the Act, a judge in New York Family Court found that appellant, then a 12-year-old boy, had entered a locker and stolen $112 from a woman's pocketbook. The petition which charged appellant with delinquency alleged that his act, "if done by an adult, would constitute the crime or crimes of larceny." The judge acknowledged that the proof might not establish guilt beyond a reasonable doubt, but rejected appellant's contention that such proof was required by the Fourteenth Amendment. The judge relied instead on § 744(b) of the New York Family Court Act which provides that "any determination at the conclusion of [an adjudicatory] hearing that a [juvenile] did an act or acts must be based on a preponderance of the evidence." During a subsequent dispositional hearing, appellant was ordered placed in a training school for an initial period of 18 months, subject to annual extensions of his commitment until his 18th birthday — six years in appellant's case. The Appellate Division of the New York Supreme Court, First Judicial Department, affirmed without opinion, . . . The New York Court of Appeals then affirmed by a four-to-three vote, expressly sustaining the constitutionality of § 744(b),. . . . We noted probable jurisdiction, . . . We reverse.

I.

The requirement that guilt of a criminal charge be established by proof beyond a reasonable doubt dates at least from our early years as a Nation. The "demand for a higher degree of persuasion in criminal cases was recurrently expressed from ancient times, [though] its crystallization into the formula 'beyond a reasonable doubt' seems to have occurred as late as 1798. It is now accepted in common law jurisdictions as the measure of persuasion by which the prosecution must convince the trier of all the essential elements of guilt.". . . . Although virtually unanimous adherence to the reasonable-doubt standard in common-law jurisdictions may not conclusively establish it as a requirement of due process, such adherence does "reflect a profound judgment about the way in which law should be enforced and justice administered." . . .

Expressions in many opinions of this Court indicate that it has long been assumed that proof of a criminal charge beyond a reasonable doubt is constitutionally required. . . .

. . . Mr. Justice Frankfurter stated that "it is the duty of the Government to establish . . . guilt beyond a reasonable doubt. This notion — basic in our law and rightly one of the boasts of a free society — is a requirement and a safeguard of due process of law in the historic, procedural content of 'due process.'" . . .

In a similar vein, the Court said in *Brinegar v. United States*, . . . , that "guilt in a criminal case must be proved beyond a reasonable doubt and by evidence confined to that which long experience in the common-law tradition, to some extent embodied in the Constitution, has crystallized into rules of evidence consistent with that standard. These rules are historically grounded rights of our system, developed to safeguard men from dubious and unjust convictions, with resulting forfeitures of life, liberty and property." . . ., the requirement is implicit in "constitutions . . . [which] recognize the fundamental principles that are deemed essential for the protection of life and liberty." In *Davis* a murder conviction was reversed because the trial judge instructed the jury that it was their duty to convict when the evidence was equally balanced regarding the sanity of the accused. This Court said: "On the contrary, he is entitled to an acquittal of the specific crime charged if upon all the evidence there is reasonable doubt whether he was capable in law of committing crime. . . . No man should be deprived of his life under the forms of law unless the jurors who try him are able, upon their consciences, to say that the evidence before them . . . is sufficient to show beyond a reasonable doubt the existence of every fact necessary to constitute the crime charged." . . .

The reasonable-doubt standard plays a vital role in the American scheme of criminal procedure. It is a prime instrument for reducing the risk of convictions resting on factual error. The standard provides concrete substance for the presumption of innocence — that bedrock "axiomatic and elementary" principle whose "enforcement lies at the foundation of the administration of our criminal law.". . . . As the dissenters in the New York Court of Appeals observed, and we agree, "a person accused of a crime . . . would be at a severe disadvantage, a disadvantage amounting to a lack of fundamental fairness, if he could be adjudged guilty and imprisoned for years on the strength of the same evidence as would suffice in a civil case." . . .

The requirement of proof beyond a reasonable doubt has this vital role in our criminal procedure for cogent reasons. The accused during a criminal prosecution has at stake interests of immense importance, both because of the possibility that he may lose his liberty upon conviction and because of the certainty that he would be stigmatized by the conviction. Accordingly, a society that values the good name and freedom of every individual should not condemn a man for commission of a crime when there is reasonable doubt about his guilt. As we said in *Speiser v. Randall*, . . . : "There is always in litigation a margin of error, representing error in factfinding, which both parties must take into account. . . .

(continued discussion of due process omitted)

Moreover, use of the reasonable-doubt standard is indispensable to command the respect and confidence of the community in applications of the criminal law. It is critical that the moral force of the criminal law not be diluted by a standard of proof that leaves people in doubt whether innocent men are being condemned. It is also important in our free society that every individual going about his ordinary affairs have confidence that his government cannot adjudge him guilty of a criminal offense without convincing a proper factfinder of his guilt with utmost certainty.

Lest there remain any doubt about the constitutional stature of the reasonable-doubt standard, we explicitly hold that the Due Process Clause protects the accused against conviction except upon proof beyond a reasonable doubt of every fact necessary to constitute the crime with which he is charged.

II.

We turn to the question whether juveniles, like adults, are constitutionally entitled to proof beyond a reasonable doubt when they are charged with violation of a criminal law. The same considerations that demand extreme caution in factfinding to protect the innocent adult apply as well to the innocent child. We do not find convincing the contrary arguments of the New York Court of Appeals. *Gault* rendered untenable much of the reasoning relied upon by that court to sustain the constitutionality of § 744(b).

The Court of Appeals indicated that a delinquency adjudication "is not a 'conviction' (§ 781); that it affects no right or privilege, including the right to hold public office or to obtain a license (§ 782); and a cloak of protective confidentiality is thrown around all the proceedings (§§ 783-784)." . . . The court said further: "The delinquency status is not made a crime; and the proceedings are not criminal. There is, hence, no deprivation of due process in the statutory provision [challenged by appellant] . . .". . . .

In effect the Court of Appeals distinguished the proceedings in question here from a criminal prosecution by use of what *Gault* called the " 'civil' label-of-convenience which has been attached to juvenile proceedings." . . . But *Gault* expressly rejected that distinction as a reason for holding the Due Process Clause inapplicable to a juvenile proceeding. . . . The Court of Appeals also attempted to justify the preponderance standard on the related ground that juvenile proceedings are designed "not to punish, but to save the child.". . . . Again, however, *Gault* expressly rejected this justification. . . . We made clear in that decision that civil labels and good intentions do not themselves obviate the need for criminal due process safeguards in juvenile courts, for "[a] proceeding where the issue is whether the child will be found to be 'delinquent' and subjected to the loss of his liberty for years is comparable in seriousness to a felony prosecution.". . . .

Nor do we perceive any merit in the argument that to afford juveniles the protection of proof beyond a reasonable doubt would risk destruction of beneficial aspects of the juvenile process. Use of the reasonable-doubt standard during the adjudicatory hearing will not disturb New York's policies that a finding that a child has violated a criminal law does not constitute a criminal conviction, that such a finding does not deprive the child of his civil rights, and that juvenile proceedings are confidential. Nor will there be any effect on the informality, flexibility, or speed of the hearing at which the factfinding takes place. And the opportunity during the post-adjudicatory or dispositional hearing for a wide-ranging review of the child's social history and for his individualized treatment will remain unimpaired. Similarly, there will be no effect on the procedures distinctive to juvenile proceedings that are employed prior to the adjudicatory hearing.

The Court of Appeals observed that "a child's best interest is not necessarily, or even probably, promoted if he wins in the particular inquiry which may bring him to the juvenile court.". . . . It is true, of course, that the juvenile may be engaging in a general course of conduct inimical to his welfare that calls for judicial intervention. But that intervention cannot take the form of subjecting the child to the stigma of a finding that he violated a criminal law and to the possibility of institutional confinement on proof insufficient to convict him were he an adult.

The more comprehensive and effective the procedures used to prevent public disclosure of the finding, the less the danger of stigma. As we indicated in *Gault,* however, often the "claim of secrecy . . . is more rhetoric than reality." . . .

III.

In sum, the constitutional safeguard of proof beyond a reasonable doubt is as much required during the adjudicatory stage of a delinquency proceeding as are those constitutional safeguards applied in *Gault* — notice of charges, right to counsel, the rights of confrontation and examination, and the privilege against self-incrimination. We therefore hold, in agreement with Chief Judge Fuld in dissent in the Court of Appeals, "that, where a 12-year-old child is charged with an act of stealing which renders him liable to confinement for as long as six years, then, as a matter of due process . . . the case against him must be proved beyond a reasonable doubt." . . .

Reversed.

Footnotes and citations omitted. Concurring and dissenting opinions omitted.

Cases Relating to Chapter 2

Principles of Criminal Liability

Raymond Lee Sutton

v.

Commonwealth of Virginia;

Virginia Gray Sutton

v.

Commonwealth of Virginia

Supreme Court of Virginia
228 Va. 654 (1985)

Cochran, J., delivered the opinion of the Court.

In a joint trial, the trial court, sitting without a jury, convicted Raymond Lee Sutton and Virginia Gray Sutton, his wife, of the rape of Virginia's 15-year-old niece on July 23, 1982. Virginia was convicted as a principal in the second degree. The court sentenced each to confinement in the penitentiary for 30 years. In separate appeals, consolidated for argument, each contends that the evidence is not sufficient to sustain the conviction.

The prosecutrix, Beverly, complained to the authorities in February of 1983. Raymond gave a signed statement admitting that he and Beverly had a sexual relationship after she came to live with him and his wife in 1982 and that he had sexual intercourse with Beverly more than once. The statement was introduced in evidence as an exhibit at trial. We will review the evidence, of course, in the light most favorable to the Commonwealth.

Beverly lived with her parents in North Carolina until they were divorced when she was seven. For the next five years she lived with her mother in Fayetteville. When she was ten, she was raped by a male friend of her mother. She began to drink alcoholic beverages and use drugs. Her mother, no longer able to control her, sent Beverly to live with her father in another location in North Carolina when she was twelve. Describing life with her father as "horrible," Beverly said that he beat her "all the time." Beverly, who has had a hearing problem throughout her life, wears a hearing aid and reads lips.

While she was growing up, Beverly often saw her mother's sister, Virginia, and Virginia's husband, Raymond. Beverly corresponded with Virginia during the period 1979-1981 when the Suttons were living in Germany. Raymond, age 44, was an Army sergeant with 12 years of service at the time of trial. The Suttons were aware of Beverly's use of alcohol and drugs; they knew that her father beat her. Beverly testified that she had not used drugs for four years before the trial, except for the use of marijuana on one occasion.

Beverly visited the Suttons for two weeks in December of 1981. During this visit, Virginia told her that before the Suttons went to Germany, Raymond had sexual intercourse with Beverly's sister who was then living with them. Virginia further stated that it would be good for Beverly to have sexual intercourse with Raymond. Virginia, believing that Beverly thought that all men would beat her because her father did so, suggested that she could overcome her fear by going to bed with Raymond. On each of the two occasions that Virginia brought up the subject, Beverly rejected the suggestion.

About two or three in the morning on Christmas Day, 1981, Raymond and Beverly returned home in his van from his landlady's residence. Parking in the driveway, Raymond began kissing and fondling Beverly and even "got [her] down" on the floor of the vehicle. Beverly begged Raymond to leave her alone, and he finally released her. Beverly said she was scared at the time and was also afraid to tell her father what had happened. The next day Raymond informed Virginia of the incident; Virginia advised Beverly that she should have submitted to Raymond, that it would have helped her.

During the December visit, the Suttons talked to Beverly about getting her away from her father because of his mistreatment of her. In May, after her father had administered another beating, Beverly called the Suttons to report the intolerable situation. In July, after the school session was over, the Suttons brought Beverly from her father's home in North Carolina to theirs in Newport News. For a week, her older sister also stayed with the Suttons. After her sister left, Raymond tried to get Beverly to go to bed with him. When she refused, he became angry. Subsequently, Raymond and Beverly agreed that, in order to get school clothes and anything she needed, she would have sexual intercourse with him. Her choice was to agree or to return to her father, who would beat her. She did not know where her mother was at that time.

The Suttons and Beverly spent a July weekend in North Carolina. Upon their return on July 18, Raymond again attempted to have sexual intercourse with Beverly; she "begged and begged" until he abandoned the effort. Raymond again became angry. The next day, Virginia charged Beverly with thinking she was "too good to go to bed with" her uncle and warned that if she were not "any better than that," Virginia would take her back to North Carolina. Virginia said that it was Beverly's fault that Raymond was "hurting."

Beverly had observed violence in the Suttons' home. She saw Virginia and Raymond hit each other during arguments. She once saw Raymond strike his stepson in the face, causing him to bleed. Beverly believed the Suttons when they said that since they had custody of her, they could punish her for anything she did of which they disapproved.

On July 22, the Suttons took Beverly to get birth control pills for which the Suttons paid. The next night, Beverly went to bed early. Raymond came into her bedroom, waked her, began to talk, and fondled her breasts and vaginal area. She repeatedly begged him to leave her alone, but he would not do so. His voice rose as he became angry. She was frightened when he began to fondle her again. She testified, "I was so scared, I didn't push him away, and I didn't say anything except to please stop." She was afraid that either the Suttons would send her back to North Carolina or Raymond might become so angry that he would beat her. She could not fight him off, she was too scared to move. Raymond forced himself on her. She thought he was "mad" at her and was afraid that he would hit her, so they had sexual intercourse. Their earlier agreement to have sexual relations "never crossed" her mind. She recorded in her diary that she and Raymond "made love" on July 23.

After this first incident, Raymond and Beverly had sexual intercourse a number of times. Beverly said she was afraid not to comply. Virginia expressed the desire to see her husband have intercourse with her niece; accordingly, on two occasions, all three were in the same bed when the act occurred.

Several months later, Raymond asked Beverly to try to get her friend Teresa to go to bed with him. Beverly then revealed to Teresa and Beth, another friend, what had transpired between Raymond and herself. Teresa testified that Beverly was upset, that she said she had been abused but was afraid to tell anyone about it. With the encouragement of Teresa, Teresa's mother, and Beth, Beverly went to the school guidance counselor and to the police and made a full report.

Raymond, testifying in his own behalf, acknowledged that he and his wife believed Beverly when she told them that her father beat her and she was afraid of him. When Raymond first asked Beverly to have sexual relations with him in July she refused. He asked her again "to see whether she had changed her mind." Raymond, conceding that he wanted to have sex with her, said he agreed that he would make sure she would not have to return to her father if she submitted. He admitted that he first had sexual intercourse with her on July 23. Raymond denied ever threatening, assaulting, coercing, or intimidating Beverly. He admitted that he gave her the money to buy birth control pills. He also admitted that he had discussed with Virginia more than once his desire to have sex with Beverly and that on two occasions Virginia was on the bed with him when he was having sexual intercourse with Beverly.

1. Raymond Lee Sutton

Prior to its amendment in 1981, Code § 18.2-61 (Repl. Vol. 1975) provided punishment for any person who shall "carnally know a female of thirteen years of age or more against her will, by force."

Code § 18.2-61 (Repl. Vol. 1982), as amended (Acts 1981, c. 397), provides in pertinent part as follows:

If any person has sexual intercourse with a female or causes a female to engage in sexual intercourse with any person and such act is accomplished (i) against her will, by force, threat or intimidation . . . , he or she shall, in the discretion of the court or jury, be punished with confinement in the penitentiary for life or for any term not less than five years.

In substituting the words "sexual intercourse" for "carnally know" the General Assembly made no change in meaning. . . . But the definition of rape was significantly enlarged. Under the statute prior to amendment, it was necessary to prove sexual intercourse against the victim's will "by force.". . . . Under the amended statute it is sufficient to prove sexual intercourse against the victim's will "by force, threat or intimidation."

(some discussion is omitted)

The evidence shows that an atmosphere of fear was developed and maintained by the Suttons to intimidate this 15-year-old physically handicapped girl and that her fear of bodily harm was reasonable. We hold that the evidence is sufficient to affirm Raymond's conviction of rape.

2. Virginia Gray Sutton

Virginia Sutton was convicted of rape as a principal in the second degree. Principals in the second degree and accessories before the fact may be indicted, tried, convicted, and punished as principals in the first degree. . . . To sustain Virginia's conviction

as a principal in the second degree, it must be established that the offense was committed by Raymond as principal in the first degree. . . . But the fact that she is incapable of committing the offense as a principal in the first degree does not absolve her of criminal liability for aiding and abetting Raymond in commission of the offense. . . .

To establish Virginia as a principal in the second degree, the Commonwealth was required to prove that she was present, either actually or constructively, when the rape was committed. . . . Presence alone, however, is not sufficient to make Virginia a principal in the second degree. It must also be established that she procured, encouraged, countenanced, or approved Raymond's commission of the crime; she must have shared his criminal intent or have committed some overt act in furtherance of the offense. . . . Virginia Sutton's actions meet these requirements for a principal in the second degree to rape as that crime is now defined by Code § 18.2-61.

The trial judge found, from undisputed evidence, that Virginia solicited Beverly to have sexual intercourse with Raymond. The judge also found that both Virginia and Raymond knew that Beverly was afraid to go back to her father. By preying on that fear, Virginia applied relentless pressure on Beverly to submit to Raymond. Shortly before July 23, Virginia reproached Beverly for refusing to submit to Raymond and threatened to return her to her father if she maintained the attitude that she was "too good to go to bed with [her] uncle." On July 22, Virginia and Raymond took Beverly to get birth control pills and paid for the purchase. When Raymond and Beverly had intercourse the following night, Beverly testified, she was afraid that Virginia would send her back to North Carolina.

During the rape, Virginia was not physically present but was in bed in another room. Nevertheless, her malevolent, intimidating influence on her niece was present and continued unabated. This evidence is sufficient to establish Virginia's constructive presence during the commission of the crime. Long ago, this Court said in Dull's Case, . . . of constructive presence:

the presence need not be a strict, actual, immediate presence, such a presence as would make [the defendant] an eye or ear witness of what passes, but may be a constructive presence. So that if several persons set out together . . . upon one common design, be it murder or other felony, or for any other purpose unlawful in itself, and each takes the part assigned him; . . . they are all, provided the fact be committed, in the eyes of the law, present at it . . . "

In this case, Virginia and Raymond discussed Raymond's desire to have intercourse with Beverly and Beverly's resistance. They embarked on a common purpose of inducing Beverly by intimidation to submit to Raymond's advances. Virginia's part in the scheme was to so overcome Beverly with the prospect of returning to North Carolina and a life of physical abuse that she would no longer refuse Raymond's demands. By her reprimands of Beverly and her warning about the consequences of continued resistance, Virginia executed her part in the crime and helped ensure the success of their common enterprise.

The evidence also adequately establishes that Virginia shared Raymond's criminal intent and committed overt acts in furtherance of the crime. She and Raymond were determined to have Beverly submit. They knew her fear of her father and could have intended no less than to coerce her submission by their threat to return her to him. Virginia contends that she did no more than encourage Beverly to consent, but the very nature of the inducements she used contradicts this argument. She did more than urge consent when, by stating the alternative, she placed Beverly in the untenable position of submitting against her will or risking physical injury at her father's hand. Coerced submission is not consent, and Virginia's purpose was to achieve such submission. Her motive, showing the depths of her depravity, is revealed in her determination to see her husband and her niece engage in sexual intercourse so that she could help Beverly improve her technique.

Nor can Virginia argue that statements she made several days prior to the rape incident were too removed to constitute intimidation during the crime. The threat of being sent home was an ongoing force in a series of repeated confrontations with Raymond. The warning was not limited to one specific

encounter but was intended to, and in fact did, induce submission to a continuing sexual relationship. As such it was sufficiently close to the events of July 23 to instill fear in Beverly and induce her submission. Because she procured, encouraged, countenanced, and approved Raymond's having sexual intercourse with Beverly against her will by intimidation, the trial court properly found her guilty of rape as a principal in the second degree.

Accordingly, we will affirm both convictions.

Footnotes and citations omitted. Concurring and dissenting opinions omitted.

Powell
v.
Texas

Supreme Court of the United States
392 U.S. 514 (1968)

Mr. Justice Marshall announced the judgment of the Court and delivered an opinion in which The Chief Justice, Mr. Justice Black, and Mr. Justice Harlan join.

In late December 1966, appellant was arrested and charged with being found in a state of intoxication in a public place, in violation of Texas Penal Code, Art. 477 (1952), which reads as follows:

"Whoever shall get drunk or be found in a state of intoxication in any public place, or at any private house except his own, shall be fined not exceeding one hundred dollars."

Appellant was tried in the Corporation Court of Austin, Texas, found guilty, and fined $20. He appealed to the County Court at Law No. 1 of Travis County, Texas, where a trial *de novo* was held. His counsel urged that appellant was "afflicted with the disease of chronic alcoholism," that "his appearance in public [while drunk was] . . . not of his own volition," and therefore that to punish him criminally for that conduct would be cruel and unusual, in violation of the Eighth and Fourteenth Amendments to the United States Constitution.

The trial judge in the county court, sitting without a jury, made certain findings of fact,

..., but ruled as a matter of law that chronic alcoholism was not a defense to the charge. He found appellant guilty, and fined him $50. There being no further right to appeal within the Texas judicial system, appellant appealed to this Court; we noted probable jurisdiction. . . .

I.

The principal testimony was that of Dr. David Wade, a Fellow of the American Medical Association, duly certificated in psychiatry. His testimony consumed a total of 17 pages in the trial transcript. Five of those pages were taken up with a recitation of Dr. Wade's qualifications. In the next 12 pages Dr. Wade was examined by appellant's counsel, cross-examined by the State, and re-examined by the defense, and those 12 pages contain virtually all the material developed at trial which is relevant to the constitutional issue we face here. Dr. Wade sketched the outlines of the "disease" concept of alcoholism; noted that there is no generally accepted definition of "alcoholism"; alluded to the ongoing debate within the medical profession over whether alcohol is actually physically "addicting" or merely psychologically "habituating"; and concluded that in either case a "chronic alcoholic" is an "involuntary drinker," who is "powerless not to drink," and who "loses his self-control over his drinking." He testified that he had examined appellant, and that appellant is a "chronic alcoholic," who "by the time he has reached [the state of intoxication] . . . is not able to control his behavior, and [who] . . . has reached this point because he has an uncontrollable compulsion to drink." Dr. Wade also responded in the negative to the question whether appellant has "the willpower to resist the constant excessive consumption of alcohol." He added that in his opinion jailing appellant without medical attention would operate neither to rehabilitate him nor to lessen his desire for alcohol.

On cross-examination, Dr. Wade admitted that when appellant was sober he knew the difference between right and wrong, and he responded affirmatively to the question whether appellant's act of taking the first drink in any given instance when he was sober was a "voluntary exercise of his will." Qualifying his answer, Dr. Wade stated that "these individuals have a compulsion, and this compulsion, while not completely overpowering, is a very strong influence, an exceedingly strong influence, and this compulsion coupled with the firm belief in their mind that they are going to be able to handle it from now on causes their judgment to be somewhat clouded."

Appellant testified concerning the history of his drinking problem. He reviewed his many arrests for drunkenness; testified that he was unable to stop drinking; stated that when he was intoxicated he had no control over his actions and could not remember them later, but that he did not become violent; and admitted that he did not remember his arrest on the occasion for which he was being tried.. . . . .

. . . In the first place, the record in this case is utterly inadequate to permit the sort of informed and responsible adjudication which alone can support the announcement of an important and wide-ranging new constitutional principle. We know very little about the circumstances surrounding the drinking bout which resulted in this conviction, or about Leroy Powell's drinking problem, or indeed about alcoholism itself. The trial hardly reflects the sharp legal and evidentiary clash between fully prepared adversary litigants which is traditionally expected in major constitutional cases. The State put on only one witness, the arresting officer. The defense put on three — a policeman who testified to appellant's long history of arrests for public drunkenness, the psychiatrist, and appellant himself.

Furthermore, the inescapable fact is that there is no agreement among members of the medical profession about what it means to say that "alcoholism" is a "disease." One of the principal works in this field states that the major difficulty in articulating a "disease concept of alcoholism" is that "alcoholism has too many definitions and disease has practically none." This same author concludes that *"a disease is what the medical profession recognizes as such."* In other words, there is widespread agreement today that "alcoholism" is a "disease," for the simple reason that the medical profession has concluded that it should attempt to treat those who have drinking problems. There the agreement stops. Debate rages within the medical profession as to whether "alcoholism" is a separate "disease" in any meaningful biochemical, physiological or psychological sense, or whether it represents one peculiar manifestation in some individuals of underlying psychiatric disorders.

Nor is there any substantial consensus as to the "manifestations of alcoholism." E. M. Jellinek, one of the outstanding authorities on the subject, identifies five different types of alcoholics which predominate in the United States, and these types display a broad range of different and occasionally inconsistent symptoms. Moreover, wholly distinct types, relatively rare in this country, predominate in nations with different cultural attitudes regarding the consumption of alcohol. Even if we limit our consideration to the range of alcoholic symptoms more typically found in this country, there is substantial disagreement as to the manifestations of the "disease" called "alcoholism." Jellinek, for example, considers that only two of his five alcoholic types can truly be said to be suffering from "alcoholism" as a "disease," because only these two types attain what he believes to be the requisite degree of physiological dependence on alcohol. He applies the label "gamma alcoholism" to "that species of alcoholism in which (1) acquired increased tissue tolerance to alcohol, (2) adaptive cell metabolism . . ., (3) withdrawal symptoms and 'craving,' i.e., physical dependence, and (4) loss of control are involved." A "delta" alcoholic, on the other hand, "shows the first three characteristics of gamma alcoholism as well as a less marked form of the fourth characteristic — that is, instead of loss of control there is inability to abstain." Other authorities approach the problems of classification in an entirely different manner and, taking account of the large role which psycho-social factors seem to play in "problem drinking," define the "disease" in terms of the earliest identifiable manifestations of any sort of abnormality in drinking patterns.

(Further discussion of cultural elements of drinking omitted)

. . . . It is one thing to say that if a man is deprived of alcohol his hands will begin to shake, he will suffer agonizing pains and ultimately he will have hallucinations; it is quite another to say that a man has a "compulsion" to take a drink, but that he also retains a certain amount of "free will" with which to resist. It is simply impossible, in the present state of our knowledge, to ascribe a useful meaning to the latter statement. This definitional confusion reflects, of course, not merely the undeveloped state of the psychiatric art but also the conceptual difficulties inevitably attendant upon the importation of scientific and medical models into a legal system generally predicated upon a different set of assumptions.

(Some discussion omitted)

. . . . The picture of the penniless drunk propelled aimlessly and endlessly through the law's "revolving door" of arrest, incarceration, release and re-arrest is not a pretty one. But before we condemn the present practice across-the-board, perhaps we ought to be able to point to some clear promise of a better world for these unfortunate people. Unfortunately, no such promise has yet been forthcoming. If, in addition to the absence of a coherent approach to the problem of treatment, we consider the almost complete absence of facilities and manpower for the implementation of a rehabilitation program, it is difficult to say in the present context that the criminal process is utterly lacking in social value. This Court has never held that anything in the Constitution requires that penal sanctions be designed solely to achieve therapeutic or rehabilitative effects, and it can hardly be said with assurance that incarceration serves such purposes any better for the general run of criminals than it does for public drunks.

Ignorance likewise impedes our assessment of the deterrent effect of criminal sanctions for public drunkenness. The fact that a high percentage of American alcoholics conceal their drinking problems, not merely by avoiding public displays of intoxication but also by shunning all forms of treatment, is indicative that some powerful deterrent operates to inhibit the public revelation of the existence of alcoholism. Quite probably this deterrent effect can be largely attributed to the harsh moral attitude which our society has traditionally taken toward intoxication and the shame which we have associated with alcoholism. Criminal conviction represents the degrading public revelation of what Anglo-American society has long condemned as a moral defect, and the existence of criminal sanctions may serve to reinforce this cultural taboo, just as we presume it serves to reinforce other, stronger feelings against murder, rape, theft, and other forms of antisocial conduct.

(Some discussion omitted)

. . . .Appellant claims that his conviction on the facts of this case would violate the Cruel and Unusual Punishment Clause of the Eighth Amendment as applied to the States through the Fourteenth Amendment. The primary purpose of that clause has always been considered, and properly so, to be directed at the method or kind of punishment imposed for the violation of criminal statutes; the nature of the conduct made criminal is ordinarily relevant only to the fitness of the punishment imposed. . . .

Appellant, however, seeks to come within the application of the Cruel and Unusual Punishment Clause announced in *Robinson* v. *California,* . . . (1962), which involved a state statute making it a crime to "be addicted to the use of narcotics." This Court held there that "a state law which imprisons a person thus afflicted [with narcotic addiction] as a criminal, even though he has never touched any narcotic drug within the State or been guilty of any irregular behavior there, inflicts a cruel and unusual punishment. . . ." . . .

On its face the present case does not fall within that holding, since appellant was convicted, not for being a chronic alcoholic, but for being in public while drunk on a particular occasion. The State of Texas thus has not sought to punish a mere status, as California did in *Robinson;* nor has it attempted to regulate appellant's behavior in the privacy of his own home. Rather, it has imposed upon appellant a criminal sanction for public behavior which may create substantial health and safety hazards, both for appellant and for members of the general public, and which offends the moral and esthetic sensibilities of a large segment of the community. This seems a far cry from convicting one for being an addict, being a chronic alcoholic, being "mentally ill, or a leper. . . ." . . .

Robinson so viewed brings this Court but a very small way into the substantive crimi-

nal law. And unless *Robinson* is so viewed it is difficult to see any limiting principle that would serve to prevent this Court from becoming, under the aegis of the Cruel and Unusual Punishment Clause, the ultimate arbiter of the standards of criminal responsibility, in diverse areas of the criminal law, throughout the country.

It is suggested in dissent that *Robinson* stands for the "simple" but "subtle" principle that "[criminal] penalties may not be inflicted upon a person for being in a condition he is powerless to change.". . . . In that view, appellant's "condition" of public intoxication was "occasioned by a compulsion symptomatic of the disease" of chronic alcoholism, and thus, apparently, his behavior lacked the critical element of *mens rea.* Whatever may be the merits of such a doctrine of criminal responsibility, it surely cannot be said to follow from *Robinson.* The entire thrust of *Robinson*'s interpretation of the Cruel and Unusual Punishment Clause is that criminal penalties may be inflicted only if the accused has committed some act, has engaged in some behavior, which society has an interest in preventing, or perhaps in historical common law terms, has committed some *actus reus.* It thus does not deal with the question of whether certain conduct cannot constitutionally be punished because it is, in some sense, "involuntary" or "occasioned by a compulsion."

Likewise, as the dissent acknowledges, there is a substantial definitional distinction between a "status," as in *Robinson,* and a "condition," which is said to be involved in this case. Whatever may be the merits of an attempt to distinguish between behavior and a condition, it is perfectly clear that the crucial element in this case, so far as the dissent is concerned, is whether or not appellant can legally be held responsible for his appearance in public in a state of intoxication. The only relevance of *Robinson* to this issue is that because the Court interpreted the statute there involved as making a "status" criminal, it was able to suggest that the statute would cover even a situation in which addiction had been acquired involuntarily. . . . That this factor was not determinative in the case is shown by the fact that there was no indication of how Robinson himself had become an addict.

Ultimately, then, the most troubling aspects of this case, were *Robinson* to be extended to meet it, would be the scope and content of what could only be a constitutional doctrine of criminal responsibility. In dissent it is urged that the decision could be limited to conduct which is "a characteristic and involuntary part of the pattern of the disease as it afflicts" the particular individual, and that "[it] is not foreseeable" that it would be applied "in the case of offenses such as driving a car while intoxicated, assault, theft, or robbery." . . . That is limitation by fiat. In the first place, nothing in the logic of the dissent would limit its application to chronic alcoholics. If Leroy Powell cannot be convicted of public intoxication, it is difficult to see how a State can convict an individual for murder, if that individual, while exhibiting normal behavior in all other respects, suffers from a "compulsion" to kill, which is an "exceedingly strong influence," but "not completely overpowering." Even if we limit our consideration to chronic alcoholics, it would seem impossible to confine the principle within the arbitrary bounds which the dissent seems to envision.

It is not difficult to imagine a case involving psychiatric testimony to the effect that an individual suffers from some aggressive neurosis which he is able to control when sober; that very little alcohol suffices to remove the inhibitions which normally contain these aggressions, with the result that the individual engages in assaultive behavior without becoming actually intoxicated; and that the individual suffers from a very strong desire to drink, which is an "exceedingly strong influence" but "not completely overpowering." Without being untrue to the rationale of this case, should the principles advanced in dissent be accepted here, the Court could not avoid holding such an individual constitutionally unaccountable for his assaultive behavior.

Traditional common-law concepts of personal accountability and essential considerations of federalism lead us to disagree with appellant. We are unable to conclude, on the state of this record or on the current state of medical knowledge, that chronic alcoholics in general, and Leroy Powell in particular, suffer from such an irresistible compulsion to drink and to get drunk in public that they are utterly unable to control their performance of either or both of these acts and thus cannot be deterred at all from public intoxication. And in any event this Court has never articulated a general constitutional doctrine of *mens rea*.

We cannot cast aside the centuries-long evolution of the collection of interlocking and overlapping concepts which the common law has utilized to assess the moral accountability of an individual for his antisocial deeds. The doctrines of *actus reus, mens rea*, insanity, mistake, justification, and duress have historically provided the tools for a constantly shifting adjustment of the tension between the evolving aims of the criminal law and changing religious, moral, philosophical, and medical views of the nature of man. This process of adjustment has always been thought to be the province of the States.

Nothing could be less fruitful than for this Court to be impelled into defining some sort of insanity test in constitutional terms. Yet, that task would seem to follow inexorably from an extension of *Robinson* to this case. If a person in the "condition" of being a chronic alcoholic cannot be criminally punished as a constitutional matter for being drunk in public, it would seem to follow that a person who contends that, in terms of one test, "his unlawful act was the product of mental disease or mental defect," . . . , would state an issue of constitutional dimension with regard to his criminal responsibility had he been tried under some different and perhaps lesser standard, *e.g.,* the right-wrong test of *M'Naghten's Case*. The experimentation of one jurisdiction in that field alone indicates the magnitude of the problem. . . .But formulating a constitutional rule would reduce, if not eliminate, that fruitful experimentation, and freeze the developing productive dialogue between law and psychiatry into a rigid constitutional mold. It is simply not yet the time to write into the Constitution formulas cast in terms whose meaning, let alone relevance, is not yet clear either to doctors or to lawyers.

Affirmed.

Footnotes and citations omitted. Concurring and dissenting opinions omitted.

Cases Relating to Chapter 3

Capacity and Defenses

Clark

v.

Arizona

548 U.S. 735 (2006)

Justice Souter delivered the opinion of the Court.

The case presents two questions: whether due process prohibits Arizona's use of an insanity test stated solely in terms of the capacity to tell whether an act charged as a crime was right or wrong; and whether Arizona violates due process in restricting consideration of defense evidence of mental illness and incapacity to its bearing on a claim of insanity, thus eliminating its significance directly on the issue of the mental element of the crime charged (known in legal shorthand as the *mens rea*, or guilty mind). We hold that there is no violation of due process in either instance.

. . . In the early hours of June 21, 2000, Officer Jeffrey Moritz of the Flagstaff Police responded in uniform to complaints that a pickup truck with loud music blaring was circling a residential block. When he located the truck, the officer turned on the emergency lights and siren of his marked patrol car, which prompted petitioner Eric Clark, the truck's driver (then 17), to pull over. Officer Moritz got out of the patrol car and told Clark to stay where he was. Less than a minute later, Clark shot the officer, who died soon after but not before calling the police dispatcher for help. Clark ran away on foot but was arrested later that day with gunpowder residue on his hands; the gun that killed the officer was found nearby, stuffed into a knit cap.

Clark was charged with first-degree murder under Ariz. Rev. Stat. Ann. §13-1105(A)(3) (West Supp. 2005) for intentionally or knowingly killing a law enforcement officer in the line of duty. In March 2001, Clark was found incompetent to stand trial and was committed to a state hospital for treatment, but two years later the same trial court found his competence restored and ordered him to be tried. Clark waived his right to a jury, and the case was heard by the court.

At trial, Clark did not contest the shooting and death, but relied on his undisputed paranoid schizophrenia at the time of the incident in denying that he had the specific intent to shoot a law enforcement officer or knowledge that he was doing so, as required by the statute. Accordingly, the prosecutor offered circumstantial evidence that Clark knew Officer Moritz was a law enforcement officer. The evidence showed that the officer was in uniform at the time, that he caught up with Clark in a marked police car with emergency lights and siren going, and that Clark acknowledged the symbols of police authority and stopped. The testimony for the prosecution indicated that Clark had intentionally lured an officer to the scene to kill him, having told some people a few weeks before the incident that he wanted to shoot police officers. At the close of the State's evidence, the trial court denied Clark's motion for judgment of acquittal for failure to prove intent to kill a law enforcement officer or knowledge that Officer Moritz was a law enforcement officer.

In presenting the defense case, Clark claimed mental illness, which he sought to introduce for two purposes. First, he raised the affirmative defense of insanity, putting the burden on himself to prove by clear and convincing evidence, §13-502(C) (West 2001), that "at the time of the commission of the criminal act [he] was afflicted with a mental disease or defect of such severity that [he] did not know the criminal act was wrong," §13-502(A). Second, he aimed to rebut the prosecution's evidence of the requisite *mens rea*, that he had acted intentionally or knowingly to kill a law enforcement officer. ....

The trial court ruled that Clark could not rely on evidence bearing on insanity to dispute the *mens rea*. The court cited *State v. Mott*, . . . (1997), which "refused to allow psychiatric testimony to negate specific intent," . . ., and held that "Arizona does not allow evidence of a defendant's mental disorder short of insanity . . . to negate the *mens rea* element of a crime,"

As to his insanity, then, Clark presented testimony from classmates, school officials, and his family describing his increasingly bizarre behavior over the year before the shooting. . . . A psychiatrist testified that Clark was suffering from paranoid schizophrenia with delusions about "aliens" when he killed Officer Moritz, and he concluded that Clark was incapable of luring the officer or understanding right from wrong and that he was thus insane at the time of the killing. In rebuttal, a psychiatrist for the State gave his opinion that Clark's paranoid schizophrenia did not keep him from appreciating the wrongfulness of his conduct, as shown by his actions before and after the shooting (such as circling the residential block with music blaring as if to lure the police to intervene, evading the police after the shooting, and hiding the gun).

... The judge then issued a special verdict of first-degree murder, expressly finding that Clark shot and caused the death of Officer Moritz beyond a reasonable doubt and that Clark had not shown that he was insane at the time. The judge noted that though Clark was indisputably afflicted with paranoid schizophrenia at the time of the shooting, the mental illness "did not . . . distort his perception of reality so severely that he did not know his actions were wrong." . . .

Clark moved to vacate the judgment and sentence, arguing, among other things, that

Arizona's insanity test and its *Mott* rule each violate due process. As to the insanity standard, Clark claimed (as he had argued earlier) that the Arizona Legislature had impermissibly narrowed its standard in 1993 when it eliminated the first part of the two-part insanity test announced in *M'Naghten's Case*, . . . The court denied the motion.

The Court of Appeals of Arizona affirmed Clark's conviction, treating the conclusion on sanity as supported by enough evidence to withstand review for abuse of discretion, and holding the State's insanity scheme consistent with due process. . . . As to the latter, the Court of Appeals reasoned that there is no constitutional requirement to recognize an insanity defense at all, the bounds of which are left to the State's discretion. Beyond that, the appellate court followed *Mott*, reading it as barring the trial court's consideration of evidence of Clark's mental illness and capacity directly on the element of *mens rea*. The Supreme Court of Arizona denied further review.

We granted certiorari to decide whether due process prohibits Arizona from thus narrowing its insanity test or from excluding evidence of mental illness and incapacity due to mental illness to rebut evidence of the requisite criminal intent. . . . We now affirm.

…When the Arizona Legislature first codified an insanity rule, it adopted the full *M'Naghten* statement. . . . In 1993, the legislature dropped the cognitive incapacity part, leaving only moral incapacity as the nub of the stated definition. . . . Under current Arizona law, a defendant will not be adjudged insane unless he demonstrates that "at the time of the commission of the criminal act [he] was afflicted with a mental disease or defect of such severity that [he] did not know the criminal act was wrong," . . .

…Even a cursory examination of the traditional Anglo-American approaches to insanity reveals significant differences among them, with four traditional strains variously combined to yield a diversity of American standards. The main variants are the cognitive incapacity, the moral incapacity, the volitional incapacity, and the product-of-mental-illness tests. The first two emanate from the alternatives stated in the *M'Naghten* rule. The volitional incapacity or irresistible-impulse test, which surfaced over two centuries ago (first in England, then in this country), asks whether a person was so lacking in volition due to a mental defect or illness that he could not have controlled his actions. And the product-of-mental-illness test was used as early as 1870, and simply asks whether a person's action was a product of a mental disease or defect. Seventeen States and the Federal Government have adopted a recognizable version of the *M'Naghten* test with both its cognitive incapacity and moral incapacity components. One State has adopted only *M'Naghten*'s cognitive incapacity test, and 10 (including Arizona) have adopted the moral incapacity test alone. Fourteen jurisdictions, inspired by the Model Penal Code, have in place an amalgam of the volitional incapacity test and some variant of the moral incapacity test, satisfaction of either (generally by showing a defendant's substantial lack of capacity) being enough to excuse. Three States combine a full *M'Naghten* test with a volitional incapacity formula. And New Hampshire alone stands by the product-of-mental-illness test. The alternatives are multiplied further by variations in the prescribed insanity verdict: a significant number of these jurisdictions supplement the traditional "not guilty by reason of insanity" verdict with an alternative of "guilty but mentally ill." Finally, four States have no affirmative insanity defense, though one provides for a "guilty and mentally ill" verdict. These four, like a number of others that recognize an affirmative insanity defense, allow consideration of evidence of mental illness directly on the element of *mens rea* defining the offense.

With this varied background, it is clear that no particular formulation has evolved into a baseline for due process, and that the insanity rule, like the conceptualization of criminal offenses, is substantially open to state choice. . . . There being such fodder for reasonable debate about what the cognate legal and medical tests should be, due process imposes no single canonical formulation of legal insanity.

. . . Nor does Arizona's abbreviation of the *M'Naghten* statement raise a proper claim that some constitutional minimum has been shortchanged. Clark's argument of course assumes that Arizona's former statement of the *M'Naghten* rule, with its express alternative of cognitive incapacity, was constitutionally adequate (as we agree). That being so, the abbreviated rule is no less so, for cognitive incapacity is relevant under that statement, just as it was under the more extended formulation, and evidence going to cognitive incapacity has the same significance under the short form as it had under the long.

Though Clark is correct that the application of the moral incapacity test (telling right from wrong) does not necessarily require evaluation of a defendant's cognitive capacity to appreciate the nature and quality of the acts charged against him, . . . his argument fails to recognize that cognitive incapacity is itself enough to demonstrate moral incapacity. . . . In practical terms, if a defendant did not know what he was doing when he acted, he could not have known that he was performing the wrongful act charged as a crime. . . .

We are satisfied that neither in theory nor in practice did Arizona's 1993 abridgment of the insanity formulation deprive Clark of due process.

. . . Clark's second claim of a due process violation challenges the rule adopted by the Supreme Court of Arizona in *State v. Mott*, . . . This case ruled on the admissibility of testimony from a psychologist offered to show that the defendant suffered from battered women's syndrome and therefore lacked the capacity to form the *mens rea* of the crime charged against her. . . . The state court held that testimony of a professional psychologist or psychiatrist about a defendant's mental incapacity owing to mental disease or defect was admissible, and could be considered, only for its bearing on an insanity defense; such evidence could not be considered on the element of *mens rea*, that is, what the State must show about a defendant's mental state (such as intent or understanding) when he performed the act charged against him. . . .

Understanding Clark's claim requires attention to the categories of evidence with a potential bearing on *mens rea*. First, there is "observation evidence" in the everyday sense, testimony from those who observed what Clark did and heard what he said; this category would also include testimony that an expert witness might give about Clark's tendency to think in a certain way and his behavioral characteristics. ...

Second, there is "mental-disease evidence" in the form of opinion testimony that Clark suffered from a mental disease with features described by the witness. As was true here, this evidence characteristically but not always comes from professional psychologists or psychiatrists who testify as expert witnesses and base their opinions in part on examination of a defendant, usually conducted after the events in question. ...

Third, there is evidence we will refer to as "capacity evidence" about a defendant's capacity for cognition and moral judgment (and ultimately also his capacity to form *mens rea*). This, too, is opinion evidence. Here, as it usually does, this testimony came from the same experts and concentrated on those specific details of the mental condition that make the difference between sanity and insanity under the Arizona definition. ...

...It is clear that *Mott* itself imposed no restriction on considering evidence of the first sort, the observation evidence. We read the *Mott* restriction to apply, rather, to evidence addressing the two issues in testimony that characteristically comes only from psychologists or psychiatrists qualified to give opinions as expert witnesses: mental-disease evidence (whether at the time of the crime a defendant suffered from a mental disease or defect, such as schizophrenia) and capacity evidence (whether the disease or defect left him incapable of performing or experiencing a mental process defined as necessary for sanity such as appreciating the nature and quality of his act and knowing that it was wrong).

Mott was careful to distinguish this kind of opinion evidence from observation evidence generally and even from observation evidence that an expert witness might offer, such as descriptions of a defendant's tendency to think in a certain way or his behavioral characteristics; the Arizona court made it clear that this sort of testimony was perfectly admissible to rebut the prosecution's evidence of *mens rea*, . . . Thus, only opinion testimony going to mental defect or disease, and its effect on the cognitive or moral capacities on which sanity depends under the Arizona rule, is restricted....*[The majority

then held that Clark did not argue that the trial court erroneously applied the Mott rule by disregarding observational evidence, but, rather, objected to the Mott rule itself.]*

In sum, the trial court's ruling, with its uncertain edges, may have restricted observation evidence admissible on *mens rea* to the insanity defense alone, but we cannot be sure. But because a due process challenge to such a restriction of observation evidence was, by our measure, neither pressed nor passed upon in the Arizona Court of Appeals, we do not consider it. . . . What we do know, and now consider, is Clark's claim that Mott denied due process because it *"preclude[d] Eric from contending that . . . factual inferences"* of the "mental states which were necessary elements of the crime charged" *"should not be drawn"* because the behavior was explainable, instead, as a manifestation of his chronic paranoid schizophrenia." . . . We consider the claim, as Clark otherwise puts it, that "Arizona's prohibition of 'diminished capacity' evidence by criminal defendants violates" due process . . .

...The first presumption is that a defendant is innocent unless and until the government proves beyond a reasonable doubt each element of the offense charged. . . . Before the last century, the *mens rea* required to be proven for particular offenses was often described in general terms like "malice," . . ., but the modern tendency has been toward more specific descriptions, as shown in the Arizona statute defining the murder charged against Clark: the State had to prove that in acting to kill the victim, Clark intended to kill a law enforcement officer on duty or knew that the victim was such an officer on duty. . . . As applied to *mens rea* (and every other element), the force of the presumption of innocence is measured by the force of the showing needed to overcome it, which is proof beyond a reasonable doubt that a defendant's state of mind was in fact what the charge states. . . .

...The presumption of sanity is equally universal in some variety or other, being (at least) a presumption that a defendant has the capacity to form the *mens rea* necessary for a verdict of guilt and the consequent criminal responsibility. . . . The force of this presumption, like the presumption of innocence, is measured by the quantum of evidence necessary to overcome it; unlike the presumption of innocence, however, the force of the presumption of sanity varies across the many state and federal jurisdictions, and prior law has recognized considerable leeway on the part of the legislative branch in defining the presumption's strength through the kind of evidence and degree of persuasiveness necessary to overcome it, ...

There are two points where the sanity or capacity presumption may be placed in issue. First, a State may allow a defendant to introduce (and a factfinder to consider) evidence of mental disease or incapacity for the bearing it can have on the government's burden to show *mens rea*. . . . If it is shown that a defendant with mental disease thinks all blond people are robots, he could not have intended to kill a person when he shot a man with blond hair, even though he seemed to act like a man shooting another man. In jurisdictions that allow mental-disease and capacity evidence to be considered on par with any other relevant evidence when deciding whether the prosecution has proven *mens rea* beyond a reasonable doubt, the evidence of mental disease or incapacity need only support what the factfinder regards as a reasonable doubt about the capacity to form (or the actual formation of) the *mens rea*, in order to require acquittal of the charge. . . .

The second point where the force of the presumption of sanity may be tested is in the consideration of a defense of insanity raised by a defendant. Insanity rules like *M'Naghten* . . . are attempts to define, or at least to indicate, the kinds of mental differences that overcome the presumption of sanity or capacity and therefore excuse a defendant from customary criminal responsibility, . . . even if the prosecution has otherwise overcome the presumption of innocence by convincing the factfinder of all the elements charged beyond a reasonable doubt. The burden that must be carried by a defendant who raises the insanity issue, again, defines the strength of the sanity presumption. A State may provide, for example, that whenever the defendant raises a claim of insanity by some quantum of credible evidence, the presumption disappears and the government must prove sanity to a specified degree of

certainty (whether beyond reasonable doubt or something less). . . . Or a jurisdiction may place the burden of persuasion on a defendant to prove insanity as the applicable law defines it, whether by a preponderance of the evidence or to some more convincing degree, . . . In any case, the defendant's burden defines the presumption of sanity, whether that burden be to burst a bubble or to show something more.

. . . As Clark recognizes, however, the right to introduce relevant evidence can be curtailed if there is a good reason for doing that. "While the Constitution . . . prohibits the exclusion of defense evidence under rules that serve no legitimate purpose or that are disproportionate to the ends that they are asserted to promote, well-established rules of evidence permit trial judges to exclude evidence if its probative value is outweighed by certain other factors such as unfair prejudice, confusion of the issues, or potential to mislead the jury." . . . And if evidence may be kept out entirely, its consideration may be subject to limitation, which Arizona claims the power to impose here. State law says that evidence of mental disease and incapacity may be introduced and considered, and if sufficiently forceful to satisfy the defendant's burden of proof under the insanity rule it will displace the presumption of sanity and excuse from criminal responsibility. But mental-disease and capacity evidence may be considered only for its bearing on the insanity defense, and it will avail a defendant only if it is persuasive enough to satisfy the defendant's burden as defined by the terms of that defense. The mental-disease and capacity evidence is thus being channeled or restricted to one issue and given effect only if the defendant carries the burden to convince the factfinder of insanity; the evidence is not being excluded entirely, and the question is whether reasons for requiring it to be channeled and restricted are good enough to satisfy the standard of fundamental fairness that due process requires. We think they are. . . .

To begin with, the diagnosis may mask vigorous debate within the profession about the very contours of the mental disease itself. . . . Next, there is the potential of mental-disease evidence to mislead jurors (when they are the factfinders) through the power of this kind of evidence to suggest that a defendant suffering from a recognized mental disease lacks cognitive, moral, volitional, or other capacity, when that may not be a sound conclusion at all. . . .There are, finally, particular risks inherent in the opinions of the experts who supplement the mental-disease classifications with opinions on incapacity: on whether the mental disease rendered a particular defendant incapable of the cognition necessary for moral judgment or *mens rea* or otherwise incapable of understanding the wrongfulness of the conduct charged. Unlike observational evidence bearing on *mens rea*, capacity evidence consists of judgment, and judgment fraught with multiple perils: a defendant's state of mind at the crucial moment can be elusive no matter how conscientious the enquiry, and the law's categories that set the terms of the capacity judgment are not the categories of psychology that govern the expert's professional thinking. . . .In sum, these empirical and conceptual problems add up to a real risk that an expert's judgment in giving capacity evidence will come with an apparent authority that psychologists and psychiatrists do not claim to have. We think that this risk, like the difficulty in assessing the significance of mental-disease evidence, supports the State's decision to channel such expert testimony to consideration on the insanity defense, on which the party seeking the benefit of this evidence has the burden of persuasion.

It bears repeating that not every State will find it worthwhile to make the judgment Arizona has made, and the choices the States do make about dealing with the risks posed by mental-disease and capacity evidence will reflect their varying assessments about the presumption of sanity as expressed in choices of insanity rules. The point here simply is that Arizona has sensible reasons to assign the risks as it has done by channeling the evidence . . .

Arizona's rule serves to preserve the State's chosen standard for recognizing insanity as a defense and to avoid confusion and misunderstanding on the part of jurors. For these reasons, there is no violation of due process under *Chambers* and its progeny, and no cause to claim that channeling evidence on mental disease and capacity offends any " 'principle of justice so rooted in the traditions and conscience of our people as to be ranked as fundamental,' " . . .

The judgment of the Court of Appeals of Arizona is, accordingly, affirmed.

Dissenting opinions deleted. Footnotes deleted.

Montana
v.
James Allen Egelhoff

Supreme Court of the United States
518 U.S. 37 (1996)

Justice Scalia announced the judgment of the Court and delivered an opinion, in which The Chief Justice, Justice Kennedy, and Justice Thomas join.

We consider in this case whether the Due Process Clause is violated by Montana Code Annotated § 45-2-203, which provides, in relevant part, that voluntary intoxication "may not be taken into consideration in determining the existence of a mental state which is an element of [a criminal] offense."

I.

In July 1992, while camping out in the Yaak region of northwestern Montana to pick mushrooms, respondent made friends with Roberta Pavola and John Christenson, who were doing the same. On Sunday, July 12, the three sold the mushrooms they had collected and spent the rest of the day and evening drinking, in bars and at a private party in Troy, Montana. Some time after 9 p.m., they left the party in Christenson's 1974 Ford Galaxy station wagon. The drinking binge apparently continued, as respondent was seen buying beer at 9:20 p.m. and recalled "sitting on a hill or a bank passing a bottle of Black Velvet back and forth" with Christenson. . . .

At about midnight that night, officers of the Lincoln County, Montana, sheriff's department, responding to reports of a possible drunk driver, discovered Christenson's station wagon stuck in a ditch along U.S. Highway 2. In the front seat were Pavola and Christenson, each dead from a single gunshot to the head. In the rear of the car lay respondent, alive and yelling obscenities. His blood-alcohol content measured .36 percent over one hour later. On the floor of the car, near the brake pedal, lay respondent's .38 caliber handgun, with four loaded rounds and two empty casings; respondent had gunshot residue on his hands.

Respondent was charged with two counts of deliberate homicide, a crime defined by Montana law as "purposely" or "knowingly" causing the death of another human being. . . . A portion of the jury charge, uncontested here, instructed that "[a] person acts purposely when it is his conscious object to engage in conduct of that nature or to cause such a result," and that "[a] person acts knowingly when he is aware of his conduct or when he is aware under the circumstances his conduct constitutes a crime; or, when he is aware there exists the high probability that his conduct will cause a specific result." . . .

Respondent's defense at trial was that an unidentified fourth person must have committed the murders; his own extreme intoxication, he claimed, had rendered him physically incapable of committing the murders, and accounted for his inability to recall the events of the night of July 12. Although respondent was allowed to make this use of the evidence that he was intoxicated, the jury was instructed, pursuant to Mont. Code Ann. § 45-2-203 (1995), that it could not consider respondent's "intoxicated condition . . . in determining the existence of a mental state which is an element of the offense." . . . The jury found respondent guilty on both counts, and the court sentenced him to 84 years' imprisonment.

The Supreme Court of Montana reversed. It reasoned (1) that respondent "had a due process right to present and have considered by the jury all relevant evidence to rebut the State's evidence on all elements of the offense charged," . . . , and (2) that evidence of respondent's voluntary intoxication was "clearly . . . relevant to the issue of whether [respondent] acted knowingly and purposely," . . . . Because § 45-2-203 prevented the jury from considering that evidence with regard to that issue, the court concluded that the State had been "relieved of part of its burden to prove beyond

a reasonable doubt every fact necessary to constitute the crime charged," . . . , and that respondent had therefore been denied due process. We granted certiorari. . . .

II.

The cornerstone of the Montana Supreme Court's judgment was the proposition that the Due Process Clause guarantees a defendant the right to present and have considered by the jury *all relevant evidence* to rebut the State's evidence on all elements of the offense charged." . . . (emphasis added). Respondent does not defend this categorical rule; he acknowledges that the right to present relevant evidence "has not been viewed as absolute.". . . . That is a wise concession, since the proposition that the Due Process Clause guarantees the right to introduce all relevant evidence is simply indefensible. As we have said: "The accused does not have an unfettered right to offer [evidence] that is incompetent, privileged, or otherwise inadmissible under standard rules of evidence." . . . Relevant evidence may, for example, be excluded on account of a defendant's failure to comply with procedural requirements. . . . And any number of familiar and unquestionably constitutional evidentiary rules also authorize the exclusion of relevant evidence. For example, Federal (and Montana) Rule of Evidence 403 provides: "*Although relevant*, evidence may be excluded if its probative value is substantially outweighed by the danger of unfair prejudice, confusion of the issues, or misleading the jury, or by considerations of undue delay, waste of time, or needless presentation of cumulative evidence" (emphasis added). Hearsay rules, . . ., similarly prohibit the introduction of testimony which, though unquestionably relevant, is deemed insufficiently reliable. Of course, to say that the right to introduce relevant evidence is not absolute is not to say that the Due Process Clause places *no* limits upon restriction of that right. But it is to say that the defendant asserting such a limit must sustain the usual heavy burden that a due process claim entails:

"Preventing and dealing with crime is much more the business of the States than it is of the Federal Government, and

... we should not lightly construe the Constitution so as to intrude upon the administration of justice by the individual States. Among other things, it is normally 'within the power of the State to regulate procedures under which its laws are carried out,' ... and its decision in this regard is not subject to proscription under the Due Process Clause unless 'it offends some principle of justice so rooted in the traditions and conscience of our people as to be ranked as fundamental.' " ...

... Respondent's task, then, is to establish that a defendant's right to have a jury consider evidence of his voluntary intoxication in determining whether he possesses the requisite mental state is a "fundamental principle of justice."

Our primary guide in determining whether the principle in question is fundamental is, of course, historical practice. . . . Here that gives respondent little support. By the laws of England, wrote Hale, the intoxicated defendant "shall have no privilege by this voluntary contracted madness, but shall have the same judgment as if he were in his right senses.". . . . According to Blackstone and Coke, the law's condemnation of those suffering from *dementia affectata* was harsher still: Blackstone, citing Coke, explained that the law viewed intoxication "as an aggravation of the offence, rather than as an excuse for any criminal misbehaviour.". . . . This stern rejection of inebriation as a defense became a fixture of early American law as well. The American editors of the 1847 edition of Hale wrote:

"Drunkenness, it was said in an early case, can never be received as a ground to excuse or palliate an offence: this is not merely the opinion of a speculative philosopher, the argument of counsel, or the *obiter dictum* of a single judge, but it is a sound and long established maxim of judicial policy, from which perhaps a single dissenting voice cannot be found. But if no other authority could be adduced, the uniform decisions of our own Courts from the first establishment of the government, would constitute it now a part of the common law of the land." ...

(Similar quotes from other sources omitted)

The historical record does not leave room for the view that the common law's rejection of intoxication as an "excuse" or "justification" for crime would nonetheless permit the defendant to show that intoxication prevented the requisite *mens rea*. Hale, Coke, and Blackstone were familiar, to say the least, with the concept of *mens rea*, and acknowledged that drunkenness "deprive[s] men of the use of reason," ... It is inconceivable that they did not realize that an offender's drunkenness might impair his ability to form the requisite intent; and inconceivable that their failure to note this massive exception from the general rule of disregard of intoxication was an oversight. Hale's statement that a drunken offender shall have the same judgment "as if he were in his right senses" must be understood as precluding a defendant from arguing that, because of his intoxication, he could not have possessed the *mens rea* required to commit the crime. And the same must be said of the exemplar of the common-law rule cited by both Hale and Blackstone, ... : "If a person that is drunk kills another, this shall be Felony, and he shall be hanged for it, and yet he did it through Ignorance, for when he was drunk he had *no Understanding* nor Memory; but inasmuch as that Ignorance was occasioned by his own Act and Folly, and he might have avoided it, he shall not be privileged thereby" (emphasis added). ...

Against this extensive evidence of a lengthy common-law tradition decidedly against him, the best argument available to respondent is the one made by his *amicus* and conceded by the State: Over the course of the 19th century, courts carved out an exception to the common law's traditional across-the-board condemnation of the drunken offender, allowing a jury to consider a defendant's intoxication when assessing whether he possessed the mental state needed to commit the crime charged, where the crime was one requiring a "specific intent." The emergence of this new rule is often traced to an 1819 English case, in which Justice Holroyd is reported to have held that "though voluntary drunkenness cannot excuse from the commission of crime, yet where, as on a charge of murder, the material question is, whether an act was premeditated or done only with sudden heat and impulse, the fact of the party being intoxicated [is] a circumstance proper to be taken into consideration." . . . This exception was "slow to take root," however, . . . even in England. Indeed, in the 1835 case of *King* v. *Carroll*, . . . Justice Park claimed that Holroyd had "retracted his opinion" in *Grindley*, and said "there is no doubt that that case is not law." In this country, as late as 1858 the Missouri Supreme Court could speak as categorically as this:

> "To look for deliberation and forethought in a man maddened by intoxication is vain, for drunkenness has deprived him of the deliberating faculties to a greater or less extent; and if this deprivation is to relieve him of all responsibility or to diminish it, the great majority of crimes committed will go unpunished. This however is not the doctrine of the common law; and to its maxims, based as they obviously are upon true wisdom and sound policy, we must adhere." . . .

And as late as 1878, the Vermont Supreme Court upheld the giving of the following instruction at a murder trial:

> "'The voluntary intoxication of one who without provocation commits a homicide, although amounting to a frenzy, that is, although the intoxication amounts to a frenzy, does not excuse him from the same construction of his conduct, and the same legal inferences upon the question of premeditation and intent, as affecting the grade of his crime, which are applicable to a person entirely sober.'" . . .

. . . Eventually, however, the new view won out, and by the end of the 19th century, in most American jurisdictions, intoxication could be considered in determining whether a defendant was capable of forming the specific intent necessary to commit the crime charged. . . .

On the basis of this historical record, respondent's *amicus* argues that "the old common-law rule . . . was no longer deeply rooted at the time the Fourteenth Amendment was ratified." . . . That conclusion is questionable, but we need not pursue the point, since the argument of *amicus* mistakes the nature of our inquiry. It is not the State which bears the burden of demonstrating that its rule is "deeply rooted," but rather respondent who must show that the principle of procedure *violated* by the rule (and allegedly

required by due process) is "'so rooted in the traditions and conscience of our people as to be ranked as fundamental.'" . . . Thus, even assuming that when the Fourteenth Amendment was adopted the rule Montana now defends was no longer generally applied, this only cuts off what might be called an *a fortiori* argument in favor of the State. The burden remains upon respondent to show that the "new common-law" rule — that intoxication may be considered on the question of intent — was so deeply rooted at the time of the Fourteenth Amendment (or perhaps has become so deeply rooted since) as to be a fundamental principle which that Amendment enshrined.

That showing has not been made. Instead of the uniform and continuing acceptance we would expect for a rule that enjoys "fundamental principle" status, we find that fully one-fifth of the States either never adopted the "new common-law" rule at issue here or have recently abandoned it. . . .

It is not surprising that many States have held fast to or resurrected the common-law rule prohibiting consideration of voluntary intoxication in the determination of *mens rea*, because that rule has considerable justification — which alone casts doubt upon the proposition that the opposite rule is a "fundamental principle." A large number of crimes, especially violent crimes, are committed by intoxicated offenders; modern studies put the numbers as high as half of all homicides, for example. . . . Disallowing consideration of voluntary intoxication has the effect of increasing the punishment for all unlawful acts committed in that state, and thereby deters drunkenness or irresponsible behavior while drunk.

The rule also serves as a specific deterrent, ensuring that those who prove incapable of controlling violent impulses while voluntarily intoxicated go to prison. And finally, the rule comports with and implements society's moral perception that one who has voluntarily impaired his own faculties should be responsible for the consequences. . . .

There is, in modern times, even more justification for laws such as § 45-2-203 than there used to be. Some recent studies suggest that the connection between drunkenness and crime is as much cultural as pharmacological — that is, that drunks are violent not simply because alcohol makes them that way, but because they are behaving in accord with their learned belief that drunks are violent. . . . This not only adds additional support to the traditional view that an intoxicated criminal is not deserving of exoneration, but it suggests that juries — who possess the same learned belief as the intoxicated offender — will be too quick to accept the claim that the defendant was biologically incapable of forming the requisite *mens rea.* Treating the matter as one of excluding misleading evidence therefore makes some sense.

In sum, not every widespread experiment with a procedural rule favorable to criminal defendants establishes a fundamental principle of justice. Although the rule allowing a jury to consider evidence of a defendant's voluntary intoxication where relevant to *mens rea* has gained considerable acceptance, it is of too recent vintage, and has not received sufficiently uniform and permanent allegiance, to qualify as fundamental, especially since it displaces a lengthy common law tradition which remains supported by valid justifications today.

III.

The Supreme Court of Montana's conclusion that Mont. Code Ann. § 45-2-203 (1995) violates the Due Process Clause purported to rest on two lines of our jurisprudence. First, it derived its view that the Due Process Clause requires the admission of all relevant evidence from the statement in *Chambers* v. *Mississippi*, . . . , that "the right of an accused in a criminal trial to due process is, in essence, the right to a fair opportunity to defend against the State's accusations." Respondent relies heavily on this statement, which he terms "the *Chambers* principle," . . .

We held in *Chambers* that "the exclusion of [certain] critical evidence, coupled with the State's refusal to permit [petitioner] to cross-examine McDonald, denied him a trial in accord with traditional and fundamental standards of due process." . . . We continued, however:

"In reaching this judgment, we establish no new principles of constitutional law.

Nor does our holding signal any diminution in the respect traditionally accorded to the States in the establishment and implementation of their own criminal trial rules and procedures. Rather, we hold quite simply that *under the facts and circumstances of this case* the rulings of the trial court deprived Chambers of a fair trial." . . . (emphasis added).

(Further discussion of Chambers and other cases omitted)

The second line of our cases invoked by the Montana Supreme Court's opinion requires even less discussion. *In re Winship*, . . . (1970), announced the proposition that the Due Process Clause requires proof beyond a reasonable doubt of every fact necessary to constitute the charged crime, and *Sandstrom* v. *Montana*, . . . (1979), established a corollary, that a jury instruction which shifts to the defendant the burden of proof on a requisite element of mental state violates due process. These decisions simply are not implicated here because, as the Montana court itself recognized, "the burden is not shifted" under § 45-2-203. . . . The trial judge instructed the jury that "the State of Montana has the burden of proving the guilt of the Defendant beyond a reasonable doubt," . . . , and that "[a] person commits the offense of deliberate homicide if he purposely or knowingly causes the death of another human being. . . . Thus, failure by the State to produce evidence of respondent's mental state would have resulted in an acquittal. That acquittal did not occur was presumably attributable to the fact, noted by the Supreme Court of Montana, that the State introduced considerable evidence from which the jury might have concluded that respondent acted "purposely" or "knowingly.". . . . For example, respondent himself testified that, several hours before the murders, he had given his handgun to Pavola and asked her to put it in the glove compartment of Christenson's car. . . .That he had to retrieve the gun from the glove compartment before he used it was strong evidence that it was his "conscious object" to commit the charged crimes; as was the execution-style manner in which a single shot was fired into the head of each victim.

Recognizing that *Sandstrom* is not directly on point, the Supreme Court of Montana described § 45-2-203 as a burden-*reducing*, rather than burden-shifting, statute. . . . This obviously was not meant to suggest that the statute formally reduced the burden of proof to clear and convincing, or to a mere preponderance; there is utterly no basis for that, neither in the text of the law nor in the jury instruction that was given. What the court evidently meant is that, by excluding a significant line of evidence that might refute *mens rea*, the statute made it easier for the State to meet the requirement of proving *mens rea* beyond a reasonable doubt — reduced the burden in the sense of making the burden easier to bear. But *any* evidentiary rule can have that effect. "Reducing" the State's burden in this manner is not unconstitutional, unless the rule of evidence itself violates a fundamental principle of fairness (which, as discussed, this one does not). We have "rejected the view that anything in the Due Process Clause bars States from making changes in their criminal law that have the effect of making it easier for the prosecution to obtain convictions." . . .

Finally, we may comment upon the Montana Supreme Court's citation of the following passage in *Martin* v. *Ohio*, . . . (1987), a case upholding a state law that placed on the defendant the burden of proving self-defense by a preponderance of the evidence:

"It would be quite different if the jury had been instructed that self-defense evidence could not be considered in determining whether there was a reasonable doubt about the State's case, *i. e.*, that self-defense evidence must be put aside for all purposes unless it satisfied the preponderance standard. Such an instruction would relieve the State of its burden and plainly run afoul of *[In re] Winship*'s mandate. The instructions in this case . . . are adequate to convey to the jury that all of the evidence, including the evidence going to self-defense, must be considered in deciding whether there was a reasonable doubt about the sufficiency of the State's proof of the elements of the crime." . . .

This passage can be explained in various ways — *e. g.*, as an assertion that the right to have a jury consider self-defense evidence (unlike the right to have a jury consider evidence of voluntary intoxication) is fundamental, a proposition that the historical record may support. But the only explanation needed for present purposes is the one given in *Kokkonen* v. *Guardian Life Ins. Co.*, . . . (1994): "It is to the holdings of our cases, rather than their dicta, that we must attend." If the *Martin* dictum means that the Due Process Clause requires all relevant evidence bearing on the elements of a crime to be admissible, the decisions we have discussed show it to be incorrect.

(Continued discussion of these issues omitted)

"The doctrines of *actus reus, mens rea*, insanity, mistake, justification, and duress have historically provided the tools for a constantly shifting adjustment of the tension between the evolving aims of the criminal law and changing religious, moral, philosophical, and medical views of the nature of man. This process of adjustment has always been thought to be the province of the States." . . . The people of Montana have decided to resurrect the rule of an earlier era, disallowing consideration of voluntary intoxication when a defendant's state of mind is at issue. Nothing in the Due Process Clause prevents them from doing so, and the judgment of the Supreme Court of Montana to the contrary must be reversed.

It is so ordered.

Footnotes and citations omitted. Concurring and dissenting opinions omitted.

Keith Jacobson

v.

United States

Supreme Court of the United States
503 U.S. 540 (1992)

Justice White delivered the opinion of the Court.

On September 24, 1987, petitioner Keith Jacobson was indicted for violating a provision of the Child Protection Act of 1984 (Act), . . . which criminalizes the knowing receipt through the mails of a "visual depiction [that] involves the use of a minor engaging in sexually explicit conduct. . . ." . . . .

Petitioner defended on the ground that the Government entrapped him into committing the crime through a series of communications from undercover agents that spanned the 26 months preceding his arrest. Petitioner was found guilty after a jury trial. The Court of Appeals affirmed his conviction, holding that the Government had carried its burden of proving beyond reasonable doubt that petitioner was predisposed to break the law and hence was not entrapped.

Because the Government overstepped the line between setting a trap for the "unwary innocent" and the "unwary criminal," . . . , and as a matter of law failed to establish that petitioner was independently predisposed to commit the crime for which he was arrested, we reverse the Court of Appeals' judgment affirming his conviction.

I.

In February 1984, petitioner, a 56-year-old veteran-turned-farmer who supported his elderly father in Nebraska, ordered two magazines and a brochure from a California adult bookstore. The magazines, entitled Bare Boys I and Bare Boys II, contained photographs of nude preteen and teenage boys. The contents of the magazines startled petitioner, who testified that he had expected to receive photographs of "young men 18 years or older.". . . .

The young men depicted in the magazines were not engaged in sexual activity, and petitioner's receipt of the magazines was legal under both federal and Nebraska law. Within three months, the law with respect to child pornography changed; Congress passed the Act illegalizing the receipt through the mails of sexually explicit depictions of children. In the very month that the new provision became law, postal inspectors found petitioner's name on the mailing list of the California bookstore that had mailed him Bare Boys I and II. There followed over the next 2 1/2 years repeated efforts by two Government agencies, through five fictitious organizations and a bogus pen pal, to explore petitioner's willingness to break the new law by ordering sexually explicit photographs of children through the mail.

The Government began its efforts in January 1985 when a postal inspector sent peti-

tioner a letter supposedly from the American Hedonist Society, which in fact was a fictitious organization. The letter included a membership application and stated the Society's doctrine: that members had the "right to read what we desire, the right to discuss similar interests with those who share our philosophy, and finally that we have the right to seek pleasure without restrictions being placed on us by outdated puritan morality.". . . . Petitioner enrolled in the organization and returned a sexual attitude questionnaire that asked him to rank on a scale of one to four his enjoyment of various sexual materials, with one being "really enjoy," two being "enjoy," three being "somewhat enjoy," and four being " do not enjoy." Petitioner ranked the entry "preteen sex" as a two, but indicated that he was opposed to pedophilia. . . .

For a time, the Government left petitioner alone. But then a new "prohibited mailing specialist" in the Postal Service found petitioner's name in a file, Tr. 328-331, and in May 1986, petitioner received a solicitation from a second fictitious consumer research company, "Midlands Data Research," seeking a response from those who "believe in the joys of sex and the complete awareness of those lusty and youthful lads and lasses of the neophite [sic] age.". . . . The letter never explained whether "neophite" referred to minors or young adults. Petitioner responded: "Please feel free to send me more information, I am interested in teenage sexuality. Please keep my name confidential.". . . .

Petitioner then heard from yet another Government creation, "Heartland Institute for a New Tomorrow" (HINT), which proclaimed that it was "an organization founded to protect and promote sexual freedom and freedom of choice. We believe that arbitrarily imposed legislative sanctions restricting *your* sexual freedom should be rescinded through the legislative process.". . . . The letter also enclosed a second survey. Petitioner indicated that his interest in "preteen sex-homosexual" material was above average, but not high. In response to another question, petitioner wrote: "Not only sexual expression but freedom of the press is under attack. We must be ever vigilant to counter attack right wing fundamentalists who are determined to curtail our freedoms." . . .

HINT replied, portraying itself as a lobbying organization seeking to repeal "all statutes which regulate sexual activities, except those laws which deal with violent behavior, such as rape. HINT is also lobbying to eliminate any legal definition of 'the age of consent.'". . . . These lobbying efforts were to be funded by sales from a catalog to be published in the future "offering the sale of various items which we believe you will find to be both interesting and stimulating.". . . . HINT also provided computer matching of group members with similar survey responses; and, although petitioner was supplied with a list of potential "pen pals," he did not initiate any correspondence.

Nevertheless, the Government's "prohibited mailing specialist" began writing to petitioner, using the pseudonym "Carl Long." The letters employed a tactic known as "mirroring," which the inspector described as "reflecting whatever the interests are of the person we are writing to.". . . . Petitioner responded at first, indicating that his interest was primarily in "male-male items.". . . . Inspector "Long" wrote back:

"My interests too are primarily male-male items. Are you satisfied with the type of VCR tapes available? Personally, I like the amateur stuff better if its [sic] well produced as it can get more kinky and also seems more real. I think the actors enjoy it more.". . .

Petitioner responded:

"As far as my likes are concerned, I like good looking young guys (in their late teens and early 20's) doing their thing together.". . .

Petitioner's letters to "Long" made no reference to child pornography. After writing two letters, petitioner discontinued the correspondence.

By March 1987, 34 months had passed since the Government obtained petitioner's name from the mailing list of the California bookstore, and 26 months had passed since the Postal Service had commenced its mailings to petitioner. Although petitioner had responded to surveys and letters, the Government had no evidence that petitioner had ever intentionally possessed or been exposed to child pornography. The Postal Service had not checked petitioner's mail to determine whether he was receiving questionable mailings from persons — other than the Government — involved in the child pornography industry. . . .

At this point, a second Government agency, the Customs Service, included petitioner in its own child pornography sting, "Operation Borderline," after receiving his name on lists submitted by the Postal Service. . . . Using the name of a fictitious Canadian company called "Produit Outaouais," the Customs Service mailed petitioner a brochure advertising photographs of young boys engaging in sex. . . . Petitioner placed an order that was never filled. . . .

The Postal Service also continued its efforts in the Jacobson case, writing to petitioner as the "Far Eastern Trading Company Ltd." The letter began:

"As many of you know, much hysterical nonsense has appeared in the American media concerning 'pornography' and what must be done to stop it from coming across your borders. This brief letter does not allow us to give much comments; however, why is your government spending millions of dollars to exercise international censorship while tons of drugs, which makes yours the world's most crime ridden country are passed through easily.". . . .

The letter went on to say:

"We have devised a method of getting these to you without prying eyes of U. S. Customs seizing your mail. . . . After consultations with American solicitors, we have been advised that once we have posted our material through your system, it cannot be opened for any inspection without authorization of a judge.". . . .

The letter invited petitioner to send for more information. It also asked petitioner to sign an affirmation that he was "not a law enforcement officer or agent of the U. S. Government acting in an undercover capacity for the purpose of entrapping Far Eastern Trading Company, its agents or customers." Petitioner responded. . . . A catalog was sent, . . . , and petitioner ordered Boys Who Love Boys, . . . , a pornographic magazine depicting young boys engaged in various sexual activities. Petitioner was arrested after a controlled delivery of a photocopy of the magazine.

When petitioner was asked at trial why he placed such an order, he explained that the

Government had succeeded in piquing his curiosity:

"Well, the statement was made of all the trouble and the hysteria over pornography and I wanted to see what the material was. It didn't describe the — I didn't know for sure what kind of sexual action they were referring to in the Canadian letter."....

In petitioner's home, the Government found the Bare Boys magazines and materials that the Government had sent to him in the course of its protracted investigation, but no other materials that would indicate that petitioner collected, or was actively interested in, child pornography.

Petitioner was indicted for violating 18 U. S. C. § 2252(a) (2)(A). The trial court instructed the jury on the petitioner's entrapment defense, n1 petitioner was convicted, and a divided Court of Appeals for the Eighth Circuit, sitting *en banc*, affirmed, concluding that "Jacobson was not entrapped as a matter of law.".... We granted certiorari....

II.

There can be no dispute about the evils of child pornography or the difficulties that laws and law enforcement have encountered in eliminating it.... Likewise, there can be no dispute that the Government may use undercover agents to enforce the law. "It is well settled that the fact that officers or employees of the Government merely afford opportunities or facilities for the commission of the offense does not defeat the prosecution. Artifice and stratagem may be employed to catch those engaged in criminal enterprises." ...

In their zeal to enforce the law, however, Government agents may not originate a criminal design, implant in an innocent person's mind the disposition to commit a criminal act, and then induce commission of the crime so that the Government may prosecute.... Where the Government has induced an individual to break the law and the defense of entrapment is at issue, as it was in this case, the prosecution must prove beyond reasonable doubt that the defendant was disposed to commit the criminal act prior to first being approached by Government agents....

Thus, an agent deployed to stop the traffic in illegal drugs may offer the opportunity to

buy or sell drugs and, if the offer is accepted, make an arrest on the spot or later. In such a typical case, or in a more elaborate "sting" operation involving government-sponsored fencing where the defendant is simply provided with the opportunity to commit a crime, the entrapment defense is of little use because the ready commission of the criminal act amply demonstrates the defendant's predisposition.... Had the agents in this case simply offered petitioner the opportunity to order child pornography through the mails, and petitioner — who must be presumed to know the law — had promptly availed himself of this criminal opportunity, it is unlikely that his entrapment defense would have warranted a jury instruction....

But that is not what happened here. By the time petitioner finally placed his order, he had already been the target of 26 months of repeated mailings and communications from Government agents and fictitious organizations. Therefore, although he had become predisposed to break the law by May 1987, it is our view that the Government did not prove that this predisposition was independent and not the product of the attention that the Government had directed at petitioner since January 1985....

The prosecution's evidence of predisposition falls into two categories: evidence developed prior to the Postal Service's mail campaign, and that developed during the course of the investigation. The sole piece of preinvestigation evidence is petitioner's 1984 order and receipt of the Bare Boys magazines. But this is scant if any proof of petitioner's predisposition to commit an illegal act, the criminal character of which a defendant is presumed to know. It may indicate a predisposition to view sexually oriented photographs that are responsive to his sexual tastes; but evidence that merely indicates a generic inclination to act within a broad range, not all of which is criminal, is of little probative value in establishing predisposition.

Furthermore, petitioner was acting within the law at the time he received these magazines. Receipt through the mails of sexually explicit depictions of children for noncommercial use did not become illegal under federal law until May 1984, and Nebraska had no law that forbade petitioner's possession of such material until 1988. . . .Evidence of predisposition to do what once was lawful is not, by itself, sufficient to show predisposition to do what is now illegal, for there is a common understanding that most people obey the law even when they disapprove of it. This obedience may reflect a generalized respect for legality or the fear of prosecution, but for whatever reason, the law's prohibitions are matters of consequence.

Hence, the fact that petitioner legally ordered and received the Bare Boys magazines does little to further the Government's burden of proving that petitioner was predisposed to commit a criminal act. This is particularly true given petitioner's unchallenged testimony that he did not know until they arrived that the magazines would depict minors.

The prosecution's evidence gathered during the investigation also fails to carry the Government's burden. Petitioner's responses to the many communications prior to the ultimate criminal act were at most indicative of certain personal inclinations, including a predisposition to view photographs of preteen sex and a willingness to promote a given agenda by supporting lobbying organizations. Even so, petitioner's responses hardly support an inference that he would commit the crime of receiving child pornography through the mails. Furthermore, a person's inclinations and "fantasies . . . are his own and beyond the reach of government. . . ."

. . . On the other hand, the strong arguable inference is that, by waving the banner of individual rights and disparaging the legitimacy and constitutionality of efforts to restrict the availability of sexually explicit materials, the Government not only excited petitioner's interest in sexually explicit materials banned by law but also exerted substantial pressure on petitioner to obtain and read such material as part of a fight against censorship and the infringement of individual rights. For instance, HINT described itself as "an organization founded to protect and promote sexual freedom and freedom of choice" and stated that "the most appropriate means to accomplish [its] objectives is to promote honest dialogue among concerned individuals and to continue its lobbying efforts with State Legislators." . . . These lobbying efforts were to be financed through catalog

sales. Mailings from the equally fictitious American Hedonist Society, . . . and the correspondence from the nonexistent Carl Long, . . . endorsed these themes.

Similarly, the two solicitations in the spring of 1987 raised the spectre of censorship while suggesting that petitioner ought to be allowed to do what he had been solicited to do. The mailing from the Customs Service referred to "the worldwide ban and intense enforcement on this type of material," observed that "what was legal and commonplace is now an 'underground' and secretive service," and emphasized that "this environment forces us to take extreme measures" to ensure delivery. . . . The Postal Service solicitation described the concern about child pornography as "hysterical nonsense," decried "international censorship," and assured petitioner, based on consultation with "American solicitors," that an order that had been posted could not be opened for inspection without authorization of a judge. . . . It further asked petitioner to affirm that he was not a Government agent attempting to entrap the mail order company or its customers. . . . In these particulars, both Government solicitations suggested that receiving this material was something that petitioner ought to be allowed to do.

Petitioner's ready response to these solicitations cannot be enough to establish beyond reasonable doubt that he was predisposed, prior to the Government acts intended to create predisposition, to commit the crime of receiving child pornography through the mails. . . . The evidence that petitioner was ready and willing to commit the offense came only after the Government had devoted 2 1/2 years to convincing him that he had or should have the right to engage in the very behavior proscribed by law. Rational jurors could not say beyond a reasonable doubt that petitioner possessed the requisite predisposition prior to the Government's investigation and that it existed independent of the Government's many and varied approaches to petitioner. As was explained in *Sherman*, where entrapment was found as a matter of law, "the Government [may not] play on the weaknesses of an innocent party and beguile him into committing crimes which he otherwise would not have attempted." . . .

Law enforcement officials go too far when they "implant in the mind of an innocent person the *disposition* to commit the alleged offense and induce its commission in order that they may prosecute.". . . . Like the *Sorrells* Court, we are "unable to conclude that it was the intention of the Congress in enacting this statute that its processes of detection and enforcement should be abused by the instigation by government officials of an act on the part of persons otherwise innocent in order to lure them to its commission and to punish them.". . . . When the Government's quest for convictions leads to the apprehension of an otherwise law-abiding citizen who, if left to his own devices, likely would have never run afoul of the law, the courts should intervene.

Because we conclude that this is such a case and that the prosecution failed, as a matter of law, to adduce evidence to support the jury verdict that petitioner was predisposed, independent of the Government's acts and beyond a reasonable doubt, to violate the law by receiving child pornography through the mails, we reverse the Court of Appeals' judgment affirming the conviction of Keith Jacobson.

It is so ordered.

[Footnotes and citations omitted. Concurring and dissenting opinions omitted.]

Cases Relating to Chapter 4

Preparatory Activity Offenses

**Commonwealth of Pennsylvania,
Appellee**

v.

Samuel Henley, Appellant

**Supreme Court of Pennsylvania
504 Pa. 408, 474 A.2d 1115 (1984)**

PAPADAKOS, Justice.

This is the appeal of Samuel Henley (Appellant) from the en banc Opinion and Order of the Superior Court, Commonwealth v. Henley, ___ Pa. Superior Ct. ___, 459 A.2d 365 (1983), which reversed a Philadelphia Common Pleas Order sustaining Appellant's demurrer to the evidence charging him with attempting to receive stolen property.

The facts are not in dispute and can be easily summarized. Appellant is the owner of the Henley Brothers Jewelry Store located at 740 Samson Street in the City of Philadelphia. On December 22, 1980, an informant, wired with a tape recording device, was given five (5) specially coated chains by the police, and sent to Appellant's jewelry store. The informant entered the store and offered to sell the five (5) gold chains to Appellant. He represented to Appellant that the chains were stolen. Appellant, believing them to be stolen, purchased the chains for $30.00, took possession of them, and expressed a willingness to buy more stolen goods in the future. This conversation was recorded. The informant then left the store, met with the detective who had accompanied him, played the tape recording, and turned over the $30.00.

The detective then entered the store and arrested Appellant, charging him with the crime of theft by receiving stolen goods and receiving stolen property as a business.

. . . These charges were later amended to attempted theft by unlawful taking or disposition, . . . and he was tried on this charge at a non-jury trial on November 18, 1981.

At the conclusion of the Commonwealth's case, Appellant demurred to the evidence, arguing that the chains were not stolen property because they were in police custody, and that, therefore, he could not be found guilty of an attempt to receive stolen property which was not stolen. The trial court found this defense of legal impossibility persuasive and granted the demurrer.

The Commonwealth appealed to the Superior Court, which reversed and remanded for trial, concluding that the defense of legal impossibility had been abolished in Pennsylvania. Because this issue was one of first impression, we granted allocatur.

Impossibility defenses were usually classified as either legal or factual in nature. "Factual impossibility denotes conduct where the objective is proscribed by the criminal law but a circumstance unknown to the actor prevents him from bringing it about. The classic example is the thief who picks an empty pocket." . . . Legal impossibility was said to occur where the intended acts would not amount to a crime even if completed. A frequently cited case standing for this proposition is *People v. Jaffe*, . . . The *Jaffe* Court held that where an element of the completed crime required the goods be stolen, the fact that the goods were not stolen was a defense to the completed act. Consequently, an attempt to do an act which would not be criminal if completed could not itself be criminal regardless of the actor's intent....

Factual impossibility has never been recognized as a defense to an attempt charge by any American Court, . . . and this Court specifically rejected factual impossibility as a defense to an attempt charge. . . .

Legal impossibility had been recognized in many jurisdictions as a defense to attempt charges, and this Court cited the *Jaffe* case approvingly . . ., indicating that the defense of legal impossibility was available as a defense to attempt charges in this Commonwealth.

The reasoning in the *Jaffe* line of cases has come under considerable criticism in the last twenty-five years, and in response to the criticism the defense has been uniformly rejected by the highest courts of most states where the issue has been raised. Additionally, many states have passed legislation which specifically abrogated the defense. The suggested abrogation of the impossibility defense through legislation was first introduced to most state legislatures via the Model Penal Code. . . .

Our Legislature was keenly aware of the necessity to consolidate, amend, and revise the penal laws of the Commonwealth, and as early as 1963 began preparing legislation for a new crimes code. *[Discussion of legislative action in preparing new Criminal Attempt statute which Court provides:]*

SECTION 901 CRIMINAL ATTEMPT

(a) Definition of attempt--a person commits an attempt when, with intent to commit a specific crime, he does any act which constitutes a substantial step toward commission of that crime.

(b) Impossibility--it shall not be a defense to a charge of attempt that because of a misapprehension of the circumstances it would have been impossible for the accused to commit the crime attempted. . . .

Because of variance in the language of the Model Penal Code and our Crimes Code, appellant argues that the Legislature intended to reject the provision of the Model Penal Code and to retain the legal impossibility defense to inchoate crimes. We disagree. The mere fact that our Legislature improved upon the language in its Criminal Attempt Section over that found in the Model Penal Code cannot by itself support the conclusion that the Legislature intended to reject the provisions

of the Model Penal Code and thus, to retain the legal impossibility defense.

Our Crimes Code is clear in defining the two (2) elements of the offense of attempt by providing: (1) that the actor intend to commit an offense; and (2) that the actor take a substantial step toward completion of the offense. The Code then specifically provides that impossibility is not a defense if the completed offense could have occurred had the circumstances been as the accused apprehended them to be. Read as a whole, the provisions of Section 901(a) and (b) of our Crimes Code parallel the provisions of the Model Penal Code and other states' crimes codes (which are all based on the provisions of the Model Penal Code) in their intent if not in their terminology.

Those sections have all been interpreted as eliminating the defense of legal impossibility because of statutory language to the effect that impossibility (factual or legal) is not a defense if the completed offense could have occurred had the circumstances been as the accused believed them to be. Our Code's provisions are strikingly similar except that our statute speaks to the accused's misapprehension.

The choice in terminology between "beliefs" and "misapprehensions," however, is of no consequence since both terms would require the actor mentally or intellectually to perceive, comprehend, or accept a reality, phenomenon, or set of occurrences without regard to actual extrinsic circumstances. The use of either term then is interchangeable, and the Legislature could just as easily have used words referring to the actor's "beliefs" instead of his "apprehensions" or "misapprehensions" of the circumstances. . . .

We are thoroughly aware of the unsound basis for the legal impossibility defense and we hasten to add that the application of either of the impossibility defenses "is so fraught with intricacies and artificial distinctions that the defense has little value as an analytical method for reaching substantial justice." . . .

The effort to compartmentalize factual patterns into these judicially created categories of factual or legal impossibilities is but an illusory test leading to contradictory and sometimes absurd results, because courts are left to evaluate an actor's beliefs or apprehensions in the light of the actual facts. Our statute abandons this out-dated approach with its former distinctions of legal and factual impossibilities and instead evaluates the actor's conduct according to his mental frame of reference alone.

Thus, if one forms intent to commit a substantive crime, then proceeds to perform all the acts necessary to commit the crime, and it is shown that completion of the substantive crime is impossible, the actor can still be culpable of attempt to commit the substantive crime. A defense based on the old legal or factual impossibility argument clearly is no longer available. Under the new Code, an intent to commit an act which is not characterized as a crime by the laws of the subject jurisdiction can not be the basis of a criminal charge and conviction even though the actor believes or misapprehends the intended act to be proscribed by the criminal laws. An example of this is where a fisherman believes he is committing an offense in fishing on a certain lake without a license when a fishing license is, in fact, not required in the subject jurisdiction. Since the conduct here would be perfectly legal, the actor could not be held accountable for any attempted crime. In all other cases, the actor should be held responsible for his conduct. Our reading of Section 901(b) would do just that.

Since the defense of legal impossibility has been abrogated, it was not available to Appellant and the demurrer was improperly granted. This matter must, therefore, be remanded to the Court of Common Pleas for trial.

The Order of the Superior Court is affirmed.

Anthony Thomas Bolden,
Appellant
v.
Supreme Court of Nevada

124 P.3d 191; 2005 Nev. LEXIS 103;
121 Nev. Adv. Rep. 86

December 15, 2005, Decided

OPINION

Appellant Anthony Thomas Bolden and four other masked men broke into Silvia Rascon's apartment and committed a number of crimes against the occupants. A jury convicted Bolden of burglary while in possession of a deadly weapon, home invasion while in possession of a deadly weapon, first-degree kidnapping with use of a deadly weapon, second-degree kidnapping with use of a deadly weapon, two counts of robbery with use of a deadly weapon, and conspiracy to commit robbery and/or kidnapping. In this appeal, Bolden alleges that the district court committed error during jury selection under *Batson v. Kentucky* and that the State failed to present sufficient evidence to support the jury's verdicts with respect to all the charged offenses, failed to prove that the kidnapping charges were not incidental to the robbery charges, and failed to present sufficient evidence in support of the deadly weapon enhancements.

Although we reject Bolden's specific contentions, in resolving his sufficiency of the evidence challenge, we have found it necessary to determine whether the jury could have properly based its verdicts for the specific intent crimes of burglary and kidnapping on the State's theory of vicarious coconspirator liability. We conclude that the jury was not properly instructed on this theory of vicarious coconspirator liability and that the error cannot be held harmless under the circumstances of this case. Therefore, we reverse Bolden's conviction with respect to the counts concerning the specific intent crimes of burglary and first- and second-degree kidnapping, and we remand this matter for further proceedings consistent with this opinion. We affirm Bolden's conviction of the remaining counts.

FACTS

On December 7, 2002, at approximately 2 a.m., Bolden and four other masked men kicked in the door of Silvia Rascon's apartment. Rascon, her three children and a friend were present. The men apparently broke into the apartment looking for drugs and money. With the aid of knives, box cutters or other sharp objects, one or more of the men separately moved Rascon and her oldest daughter from room to room for the purposes of locating items to steal and sexually molesting the daughter. Police arrived and apprehended all of the intruders, three of whom had exited the residence in possession of property stolen from Rascon and her family. Police found Bolden inside the apartment, hiding under a bedroom mattress. Ironically, these men were misinformed concerning the presence of either drugs or considerable financial lucre.

The State charged Bolden and his compatriots with burglary, home invasion, first-degree kidnapping of Rascon, second-degree kidnapping of Rascon's daughter, robbery of Rascon, robbery of Rascon's son, and conspiracy to commit robbery and/or kidnapping. All of the charges, save the conspiracy count, were accompanied by deadly weapon enhancements. This timely appeal followed. . . .

Bolden contends that the State failed to present sufficient evidence to convict him on any of the charges. In short, he claims that the entire body of proof against him established no more than his mere presence during the events in question. In this, the district court instructed the jury that "mere presence" of the defendant, or his "knowledge that a crime is being committed," is insufficient to establish guilt without proof that the defendant was "a participant and not merely a knowing spectator."

More specifically, Bolden asserts that the State failed to prove his participation in a conspiracy; failed to prove the intent elements of the home invasion, robbery, burglary, first-degree kidnapping and second-degree kidnapping charges; failed to prove that the kidnapping charges were not incidental to the robbery charges; and failed to present sufficient evidence in support of the deadly weapon enhancements.

The relevant inquiry in reviewing the sufficiency of the evidence supporting a jury's verdict is "'whether, after viewing the evidence in the light most favorable to the prosecution, any rational trier of fact could have found the essential elements of the crime beyond a reasonable doubt.'" Moreover, "circumstantial evidence alone may support a conviction." In resolving Bolden's contentions, we have reviewed the evidence supporting the jury's findings of guilt with respect to each of the charged offenses. Additionally, with respect to the nonconspir-

acy offenses, we have reviewed the evidence supporting the jury's verdicts under the three separate theories of guilt alleged by the State for those offenses.

Conspiracy to commit robbery and/or kidnapping

The State alleged that Bolden and the other defendants met with each other and willfully, unlawfully, and feloniously conspired and agreed to commit robbery and/or kidnapping. Additionally, the State alleged that in furtherance of the conspiracy the defendants in fact committed the crimes of robbery and kidnapping. Nevada law defines a conspiracy as "an agreement between two or more persons for an unlawful purpose." "A person who knowingly does any act to further the object of a conspiracy, or otherwise participates therein, is criminally liable as a conspirator . . . ." "Evidence of a coordinated series of acts furthering the underlying offense is sufficient to infer the existence of an agreement and support a conspiracy conviction." "However, absent an agreement to cooperate in achieving the purpose of a conspiracy, mere knowledge of, acquiescence in, or approval of that purpose does not make one a party to conspiracy."

Here, the evidence presented at trial established that Bolden and his cohorts forcibly entered the Rascon apartment armed with switchblades, box cutters or other sharp objects and robbed the occupants. Some of the men moved two of the victims around in the residence for purposes that were both incidental and not incidental to the robberies themselves. The State presented overwhelming circumstantial and direct evidence that Bolden participated in the joint enterprise to acquire drugs and money; that he entered into an agreement to rob the Rascon family; that he was not merely a spectator in the Rascon apartment, as he claims; and that when the police arrived, Bolden was found hiding under a mattress. To the extent that Bolden contends that the evidence fails to support his participation in the conspiracy, his contention is without merit. The State presented more than sufficient evidence to support Bolden's conviction for conspiracy to commit robbery and/or kidnapping.

The burglary, home invasion, robbery, and kidnapping charges

With respect to the burglary, home invasion, robbery and kidnapping charges, the State alleged three alternative theories of criminal liability: (1) that Bolden directly committed the offenses, (2) that he aided and abetted his cohorts, or (3) that he was vicariously responsible for all of the acts of his cohorts done in aid of the conspiracy. When alternate theories of criminal liability are presented to a jury and all of the theories are legally valid, a general verdict can be affirmed even if sufficient evidence supports only one of the theories. When any one of the alleged theories is legally erroneous, however, reversal of a general verdict is required--except under the very narrowly defined circumstances discussed below--regardless of the legal and factual sufficiency of the other theories. Accordingly, we turn to an analysis of the legal and evidentiary support for each of the State's theories of liability.

Aiding and abetting and direct participation

Bolden contends that the jury convicted him primarily upon an aiding and abetting theory. A person aids and abets the commission of a crime if he aids, promotes, encourages or instigates, by act or advice, the commission of such crime with the intention that the crime be committed. Relying upon our decision in *Sharma v. State*, Bolden argues that the State failed to prove that he specifically intended to aid and abet the crimes committed at the Rascon residence.

In *Sharma*, we held,

> In order for a person to be held accountable for the specific intent crime of another under an aiding or abetting theory of principal liability, the aider or abettor must have knowingly aided the other person with the intent that the other person commit the charged crime.

Bolden's reliance on *Sharma* is misplaced for several reasons. First, robbery and home invasion are not specific intent crimes. Second, the State proceeded on two additional alternate theories of criminal liability, direct participation as a principal and perpetration of the offenses in furtherance of a conspiracy. Third, the State presented sufficient evidence for the jury to convict Bolden under all of its theories of culpability. Fourth, per *Sharma*, the district court correctly instructed the jury concerning the State's aiding and abetting theory:

> All persons concerned in the commission of a crime who either directly and actively commit the act constituting the offense or who knowingly and with criminal intent aid and abet in its commission or, whether present or not, who advise and encourage its commission, with the intent that the crime be committed, are regarded by the law as principals in the crime thus committed and are equally guilty thereof.

As noted above, Bolden was one of five masked men who entered a private residence by force, committed the robberies, and moved two of the victims around in the residence. The State provided ample circumstantial evidence of direct participation in, and the specific intent to aid and abet, all of the nonconspiracy crimes committed that morning. Bolden was not, as he now reasons, "merely present" or a "mere spectator." We therefore conclude that substantial evidence supports the State's direct participation and aiding and abetting theories of home invasion, burglary, robbery and kidnapping.

Coconspirator liability

Our conclusion that there is sufficient evidentiary and legal support for Bolden's conviction of the charged crimes as a principal and as an aider and abettor does not end our inquiry. Bolden's sufficiency argument, coupled with his reliance on this court's holding in *Sharma*, calls into question the legal viability of the State's remaining theory of vicarious coconspirator liability. As noted above, if any one of the theories of criminal liability alleged by the State is legally erroneous, reversal of a verdict that fails to specify the precise theory upon which the verdict is based is generally required regardless of the legal and factual sufficiency of the other theories. Despite our conclusion that Bolden's conviction of the nonconspiracy crimes is legally and factually sufficient under the State's theories of principal and aiding and abetting liability, we must now determine whether there is a valid legal and factual basis supporting Bolden's conviction of the nonconspiracy crimes under the State's theory of vicarious coconspirator liability.

In this respect, the district court gave the following instruction:

Each member of a criminal conspiracy is liable for each act and bound by each declaration of every other member of the conspiracy if the act or the declaration is in furtherance of the object of the conspiracy.

The act of one conspirator pursuant to or in furtherance of the common design of the conspiracy is the act of all conspirators. Every conspirator is legally responsible for an act of a co-conspirator that follows as one of the probable and natural consequences of the object of the conspiracy even if that was not intended as part of the original plan and even if he was not present at the time of commission of such act. . . .

In *Garner v. State*, this court approved the above-quoted "probable and natural consequences" doctrine, which exposes conspirators to criminal liability for any act so long as the act was committed in furtherance of the conspiracy as a natural or probable consequence of the unlawful agreement. However, *Garner* restricted the doctrine considerably by holding that "this rule does not constitute a per se basis for holding an accomplice to one crime liable for a related crime by the principal simply because the related crime was foreseeable." To do so, we concluded, "would be 'to base criminal liability only on a showing of negligence rather than criminal intent.'" Consequently, *Garner* concluded that if "the relationship between the defendant's acts and the charged crime is too attenuated, the State must provide 'some showing of specific intent to aid in, or specific knowledge of, the crime charged.'" *Garner*, however, did not discuss vicarious coconspirator and accomplice liability as discrete concepts.

As previously noted, in *Sharma v. State,* this court overruled *Garner* to the extent that a defendant could be held accountable for the specific intent crime of another, under an aiding or abetting theory of liability, without proof that he specifically intended to aid the other in the commission of the charged crime. We stated,

[The natural and probable consequences] doctrine has been harshly criticized by most commentators . . . as both incongru-

ous and unjust because it imposes accomplice liability solely upon proof of foreseeability or negligence when typically a higher degree of mens rea is required of the principal. It permits criminal liability to be predicated upon negligence even when the crime involved requires a different state of mind. Having reevaluated the wisdom of the doctrine, we have concluded that its general application in Nevada to specific intent crimes is unsound precisely for that reason: it permits conviction without proof that the accused possessed the state of mind required by the statutory definition of the crime. . . . As the Supreme Court of New Mexico observed in rejecting the doctrine for similar reasons, the doctrine thus allows a defendant to be convicted for crimes the defendant may have been able to foresee but never intended. . . . Because the natural and probable consequences doctrine permits a defendant to be convicted of a specific intent crime where he or she did not possess the statutory intent required for the offense, we hereby disavow and abandon the doctrine. It is not only inconsistent with more fundamental principles of our system of criminal law, but is also inconsistent with those Nevada statutes that require proof of a specific intent to commit the crime alleged.. . . .Accordingly, we . . . hold that in order for a person to be held accountable for the specific intent crime of another under an aiding or abetting theory of principal liability, the aider or abettor must have knowingly aided the other person with the intent that the other person commit the charged crime.

Thus, *Sharma* addressed the natural and probable consequences doctrine only with respect to a theory alleging that a defendant could be held criminally liable for the specific intent crime of another under an aiding and abetting theory of principal liability. The question left unanswered in *Garner* and *Sharma*, but presented in this case, is whether a theory of vicarious coconspirator liability based upon the natural and probable consequences doctrine is a legally viable theory in this state.

Nearly 60 years ago in *Pinkerton v. United States*, the United States Supreme Court defined coconspirator liability in terms of reasonable foreseeability and reaffirmed the concept that a conspiracy and the completion of the substantive offense are two distinct criminal acts. The Court concluded,

> . . . If [the overt act] can be supplied by the act of one conspirator, we fail to see why the same or other acts in furtherance of the conspiracy are likewise not attributable to the others for the purpose of holding them responsible for the substantive offense.

A different case would arise if the substantive offense committed by one of the conspirators was not in fact done in furtherance of the conspiracy, did not fall within the scope of the unlawful project, or was merely a part of the ramifications of the plan which could not be reasonably foreseen as a necessary or natural consequence of the unlawful agreement.

. . . The Nevada Legislature has not adopted the *Pinkerton* rule, but a number of states have addressed the issue by judicial decision. Several states have embraced the rule and permit defendants to be held liable for the criminal acts of a coconspirator so long as the crime was foreseeable and committed in furtherance of the conspiracy. Nonetheless, the *Pinkerton* rule has garnered significant disfavor. Concerns respecting the ramifications of the rule arose shortly after the opinion issued:

> In the final analysis the *Pinkerton* decision extends the wide limits of the conspiracy doctrine to the breaking-point and opens the door to possible new abuses by over-zealous public prosecutors. While membership in a conspiracy may well be evidence for the jury's consideration in holding others than the direct actor guilty, it should not be sufficient, in the absence of some further showing of knowledge, acquiescence, aid or assistance, to convict one conspirator for another's criminal act.

. . . The drafters of the Model Penal Code have similarly rejected the *Pinkerton* view, commenting that the "law would lose all sense of just proportion" if by virtue of his crime of conspiracy a defendant was "held accountable for thousands of additional offenses of which he was completely unaware and which he did not influence at all."

The Washington Supreme Court has rejected *Pinkerton* as an inaccurate reflection of state law. A Washington criminal statute provides liability for criminal conspiracy but is silent respecting vicarious liability for coconspirators. The Washington court concluded that vicarious liability of coconspirators, if any, must be based on a state accomplice liability statute, which requires knowledge of the crime charged. Therefore, the court held that liability based on foreseeability alone is incompatible with its state law.

The Arizona Supreme Court has also rejected the *Pinkerton* rule, holding that conspiratorial liability does not extend to separate criminal acts of coconspirators when a particular coconspirator is not an accomplice or principal to those crimes, even though he may be guilty of conspiracy. That court noted that its holding "simply prevents a conspirator, who is not also an accomplice, from being held liable for a potentially limitless number of criminal acts which, though later determined to be 'foreseeable,' are at the time of their commission totally beyond the conspirator's knowledge and control." . . .

The natural and probable consequences doctrine under Nevada law

Nevada case law addressing the principles of conspiracy is limited to the following concepts. As we noted above, a conspiracy is generally defined as "an agreement between two or more persons for an unlawful purpose." "A person who knowingly does any act to further the object of a conspiracy, or otherwise participates therein, is criminally liable as a conspirator . . . ." "Evidence of a coordinated series of acts furthering the underlying offense is sufficient to infer the existence of an agreement and support a conspiracy conviction." "However, absent an agreement to cooperate in achieving the purpose of a conspiracy, mere knowledge of, acquiescence in, or approval of that purpose does not make one a party to conspiracy."

We have never expressly adopted the *Pinkerton* rule and our discussion of coconspirator liability has been limited. . . . In *McKinney v. Sheriff*, McKinney challenged the sufficiency of the evidence supporting an indictment for murder, which was committed during the course of a robbery. McKinney argued that he was unaware of and did not participate in the murder and thus there was no probable cause to support the murder charge. In rejecting his claim, this court stated that the fact that McKinney's cohorts deviated from their agreed-upon plan by committing the murder did not absolve McKinney of liability. "Where the purpose of the conspiracy is to commit a dangerous felony, each member runs the risk of having the venture end in homicide . . . . Hence each is guilty of murder if one of them commits homicide in the perpetration . . . of an agreed-upon robbery. . . ."

. . . [O]ur overarching concern in *Sharma* centered on the fact that the natural and probable consequences doctrine regarding accomplice liability permits a defendant to be convicted of a specific intent crime where he or she did not possess the statutory intent required for the offense. We are of the view that vicarious coconspirator liability for the specific intent crimes of another, based on the natural and probable consequences doctrine, presents the same problem addressed in *Sharma*, and we conclude that *Sharma's* rationale applies with equal force under the circumstances of the instant case. To convict Bolden of burglary and kidnapping, the State was required to prove under Nevada law that he had the specific intent to commit those offenses. Holding otherwise would allow the State to sidestep the statutory specific intent required to prove those offenses.

The overriding factor in our decision to reject the natural and probable consequences doctrine for coconspirator liability respecting specific intent crimes is the absence of a statutory basis for it. Our statutes lack a comprehensive statutory definition or explanation of coconspirator liability. Nevada distinguishes parties as principals or accessories and by statute outlines the criminal liability of both. NRS 195.010 classifies parties as principals and accessories. NRS 195.020 defines criminal liability as a principal:

> Every person concerned in the commission of a felony, gross misdemeanor or misdemeanor, whether he directly commits the act constituting the offense, or aids or abets in its commission, and whether present or absent; and every person who, directly or indirectly, counsels, encourages, hires, commands, induces or otherwise procures another to commit a felony, gross misdemeanor or misdemeanor is a principal, and shall be proceeded

against and punished as such. The fact that the person aided, abetted, counseled, encouraged, hired, commanded, induced or procured, could not or did not entertain a criminal intent shall not be a defense to any person aiding, abetting, counseling, encouraging, hiring, commanding, inducing or procuring him.

Additionally, NRS 199.480 sets forth the penalties for conspiracy offenses. These statutes are silent respecting the parameters of coconspirator vicarious liability. . . .

In the absence of statutory authority providing otherwise, we conclude that a defendant may not be held criminally liable for the specific intent crime committed by a coconspirator simply because that crime was a natural and probable consequence of the object of the conspiracy. To prove a specific intent crime, the State must show that the defendant actually possessed the requisite statutory intent.

Although we refuse to adopt the natural and probable consequences doctrine in general, our decision is limited to vicarious coconspirator liability based on that doctrine for specific intent crimes only. The mental state required to commit a general intent crime does not raise the same concern as that necessary to commit a specific intent crime. General intent is "the intent to do that which the law prohibits. It is not necessary for the prosecution to prove that the defendant intended the precise harm or the precise result which eventuated." On the other hand, specific intent is "the intent to accomplish the precise act which the law prohibits." To hold a defendant criminally liable for a specific intent crime, Nevada requires proof that he possessed the state of mind required by the statutory definition of the crime. Although we affirm Bolden's conviction for the general intent crimes of home invasion and robbery, we conclude that in future prosecutions, vicarious coconspirator liability may be properly imposed for general intent crimes only when the crime in question was a "reasonably foreseeable consequence" of the object of the conspiracy. We caution the State that this court will not hesitate to revisit the doctrine's applicability to general intent crimes if it appears that the theory of liability is alleged for crimes too far removed and attenuated from the object of the conspiracy.

We conclude that the district court understandably but erroneously instructed the jury that Bolden could be found guilty of the specific intent crimes of burglary and first- and second-degree kidnapping as long as the commission of those offenses was a natural and probable consequence of the conspiracy, and even if Bolden never intended the commission of those crimes. We further conclude, however, that the error is applicable only with respect to Bolden's conviction of the specific intent crimes of burglary and kidnapping and does not require reversal of his conviction of the general intent crimes of home invasion and robbery. . . .

[Other points of error deleted.]

CONCLUSION

Although sufficient evidence supports Bolden's convictions for the specific intent offenses of burglary and kidnapping under the State's alternative theories of direct participation and aiding and abetting liability, we must reverse these convictions because under the particular facts of this case, the jury's general verdict precludes us from concluding with absolute certainty that the jury did not find Bolden guilty of these offenses based on the State's alleged theory of coconspirator liability. We affirm Bolden's remaining convictions. Accordingly, we affirm Bolden's conviction in part, reverse it in part, and remand this matter for further proceedings consistent with this opinion.

[Footnotes deleted.]

Cases Relating to Chapter 5

Offenses Against Persons— Excluding Sex Offenses

State of Tennessee

v.

James Clark Thornton

Supreme Court of Tennessee
730 S.W.2d 309 (1987)

Opinion by Judge William J. Harbison.

Appellant was convicted of murder in the first degree as a result of shooting his wife's paramour in the home of appellant and his wife on May 3, 1983. Appellant found his wife and the victim, Mark McConkey, engaged in sexual relations in the front bedroom of appellant's home. He fired a single shot which struck McConkey in the left hip. The victim died sixteen days later as a result of a massive infection resulting from the bullet wound. Before the night in question appellant had never been acquainted with McConkey or had any previous contact with him.

Appellant and his wife had been married just under four years, and their three-year-old son was in the home in an upstairs bedroom when the shooting occurred in a downstairs bedroom. Appellant and his wife had been separated for about six weeks, but no divorce action had been filed and appellant had been making a serious effort toward reconciliation with his wife.

Under these undisputed facts, in our opinion, the case does not warrant a conviction of homicide greater than that of voluntary manslaughter. The charges accordingly will be reduced to that offense, and the cause will be remanded to the trial court for sentencing and disposition on that basis.

In several previous decisions from this Court and in the almost unanimous course of judicial authority from other states, the encountering by a spouse of the situation which occurred here has been held, as a matter of law, to constitute sufficient provocation to reduce a charge of homicide from one of the degrees of murder to manslaughter absent actual malice, such as a previous grudge, revenge, or the like. Every case, of course, must be decided upon its own facts, but the facts in the present case were entirely undisputed. Appellant's wife testified at the trial and admitted her unfaithfulness to her husband and simply sought to excuse it upon the view that she was separated from him, and that she had told him earlier on the evening of the homicide that she had met someone else and planned to "date" him. In fact she had met McConkey on the evening of Saturday, April 30, 1983, and had had intimate sexual relations with him on that night and on each of the succeeding three nights, including the night of May 3 just before appellant burst into the bedroom and found both of them nude and in bed together.

The previous Tennessee cases, in chronological order, are *Toler v. State*, . . . (1924); *Davis v. State*, . . . (1930); *Drye v. State*, . . . (1944); *Whitsett v. State*, . . . (1957). . . .

A. The Factual Background

As previously stated, there is almost no dispute as to the material facts in this case. Appellant, James Clark Thornton, III, was thirty-one years of age at the time of the trial of this case in June 1984. His wife, Lavinia, was twenty-seven years of age; they had been married on May 19, 1979, and at the time of the homicide had one child, a son about three years of age. Appellant was a second-year law student at Memphis State University, having previously received his undergraduate degree from the University of Tennessee at Chattanooga. His wife had not completed her undergraduate work when the parties married, but at the time of the homicide she was taking some additional class work toward her undergraduate degree. The victim, Mark McConkey, was twenty-five years of age, single, and a third-year student at the University of Tennessee Medical School in Memphis.

As stated, appellant had never met McConkey and did not even know his name. Mrs. Thornton had met him four days before the homicide and had engaged in sexual relations with him in the home belonging to her and appellant every night since that time, including the night of the homicide. She testified that she thought that when she told her husband that she might want to "date" someone else, that this, in modern society, indicated that she intended to have sexual relations. In that manner she sought to mitigate her infidelity and misconduct toward a husband who had never been unfaithful to her insofar as disclosed by the record.

The marriage of the parties was in some difficulty, apparently as a result of dissatisfaction of Mrs. Thornton. She had advised her husband in March 1983 that she wanted to be separated from him for a time, and he had voluntarily taken an apartment about two miles away from their home. He visited the home almost daily, however, and there has been no suggestion that he was ever guilty of violence, physical misconduct or mistreatment toward his wife or son. He was particularly devoted to the child, and frequently kept the child with him at his apartment on weekends or in the evenings.

Appellant had graduated from a public high school in Chattanooga, after having taken his first three years of high school at a private institution, Baylor. During his junior year at Baylor it was discovered that he had developed a severe case of scoliosis, or curvature of the spine, and he had undergone surgery to correct that condition. He

was disabled to the point that he received a vocational rehabilitation grant which enabled him to attend undergraduate school at the University of Tennessee at Chattanooga. He was slightly built, being only five feet six inches in height and weighing about 125 to 130 pounds. McConkey was an athlete, a former basketball and football player in high school. He was five feet nine inches in height and weighed about 183 pounds.

Mrs. Thornton testified that she told McConkey when she first met him that she was married but separated from her husband. She had consulted an attorney and had signed a divorce petition, but the same apparently had not been filed on the date of the homicide.

Appellant, according to uncontradicted testimony, was deeply disturbed over the separation of the parties. He had sought assistance from a marriage counselor, and had persuaded his wife to go with him to the marriage counselor on several occasions. They had a joint meeting scheduled with the counselor on May 4, the day after the homicide. Appellant testified that the parties had agreed to a separation of six months, and both he and the marriage counselor testified that the parties had agreed that they would not have sexual relations with each other or with anyone else during that period. Mrs. Thornton denied making that agreement, but she did admit meeting with the marriage counselor on several occasions.

Mrs. Thornton was from a very wealthy family and had a generous trust fund which enabled the parties to live on a much more elaborate scale than most graduate students. Appellant, however, had also inherited some property through his family. This had been sold at a profit, and all of his assets had been invested in the home which the parties had purchased in Memphis, together with substantial additions from Mrs. Thornton. It was suggested by the State throughout the trial that appellant was insincere in his concern for the marriage, and that his principal concern was for his financial security.

The record indicates that as early as May 1, two days before the homicide, Mrs. Thornton had stated to her husband that she did not think that the parties would ever be reconciled. On the evening of May 3, appellant picked her and their child up at their home, and the three went to dinner. Again on that occasion Mrs. Thornton reiterated that she thought that the marriage was over, and on this occasion she told appellant that she planned to date someone else whom she had met. Appellant was concerned over the situation, but on a previous occasion his wife had told him that she had had sexual relations with another student, and this had proved to be false.

He returned his wife and child to their home at about 7:30 p.m. and then went to his apartment to study for a final examination in the law school. He called two close friends of the parties, however, and discussed his marital situation with them. Both of them verified that he was very concerned about the situation, but both told him that they believed that his wife was serious about going through with a divorce. One of them advised him that his wife apparently did not believe his feelings about a reconciliation were sincere.

Acting on that suggestion, appellant returned to the home of the parties in his automobile, stating that he wanted to try once more to convince his wife that he was indeed sincere. When he arrived at the home he saw an automobile parked in the driveway. He did not recognize the car as being one belonging to any of his wife's friends. Accordingly he parked around the corner and walked back to the house. Observing from the rear of the house, he saw his wife and McConkey in the kitchen with the child. He observed as Mrs. Thornton washed some laundry for McConkey and as they were eating dinner. Thereafter they sat and read. They drank wine and smoked some marijuana, and appellant saw them kissing.

He decided to go home to get his camera, but before doing so he let the air out of one of the tires on McConkey's car. He went to his apartment, and obtained his camera and an old pistol which had belonged to his father. He visited a convenience store in an attempt to find film for the camera, and finally obtained some at a drugstore. He then returned to the marital residence, arriving at about 9:30 p.m. He testified that he intended to take pictures for the purpose of showing them to the marriage counselor on the next day and possibly also for use in evidence if divorce proceedings did ensue.

Appellant spent more than an hour in the backyard of his home observing his wife and McConkey in the den and kitchen. Thereafter they left the den area, but appellant remained behind the house, thinking that McConkey was about to leave. When he went around the house, however, he found that McConkey's car was still in the driveway and saw the drapes in the front guest bedroom downstairs had been closed. He listened near the window and heard unmistakable sounds of sexual intercourse. He then burst through the front door and into the bedroom where he found the nude couple and attempted to take some pictures. At that point he testified that he thought McConkey was attempting to attack him. In all events he drew his pistol and fired a single shot, striking McConkey in the left hip. Appellant did not harm either his wife or child, although Mrs. Thornton said that he did make some threats against her. He went upstairs and brought down the little boy, who had been awakened and who was crying. He assisted in giving directions to enable an ambulance to bring aid to McConkey, and he remained at the house until the police arrived.

Appellant testified that he simply lost control and "exploded" when he found his wife in bed with the victim. He testified that he had armed himself because McConkey was much larger than he, and he felt that he needed protection if there was trouble when he returned to the residence with the camera.

Appellant testified that he did not intend to kill McConkey, but simply to shoot him in order to disable him and also because of his outrage at the situation which he had found. The single shot was not aimed at a vital organ, but the victim ultimately died because of the spread of a massive infection from the wound.

The marriage counselor who had been seeing appellant and his wife examined appellant on a number of occasions after the shooting. When McConkey died sixteen days later, appellant attempted to take his own life. The psychologist, Dr. Hunsacker, testified that appellant was under severe emotional pressure at the time of shooting to the point that he believed appellant had a brief period of temporary insanity and was not legally responsible for his actions. An expert on behalf of the State testified to the contrary with respect to the issue of temporary insanity, but she testified that appellant was undoubtedly under severe emotional stress on the evening in question both before and at the time of the shooting.

Appellant attempted to interpose alternative defenses of self-defense and insanity. The jury rejected both of these defenses, and we agree with the Court of Criminal Appeals that this was entirely within their province. We further agree with the Court of Criminal Appeals that the State is entitled to the strongest legitimate view of the evidence on appeal. . . .

There are, however, legal principles with respect to the sufficiency of provocation to reduce charges of homicide from murder to manslaughter, and, in our opinion, these principles are controlling here.

B. The Legal Issues

The attorneys who represented appellant at trial and in the Court of Criminal Appeals, as well as in the original application for review in this Court, assigned twelve issues as error. The lead attorney for appellant, however, died after review was granted in this Court, and counsel arguing the case orally conceded that only one real issue was presented in this case; that is, whether the homicide was a degree of murder or voluntary manslaughter. With the issue of insanity, or legal responsibility, having been resolved against appellant, we agree with that assertion. The record does not support a finding of justifiable homicide from self defense, and there was ample testimony from which the jury could reject a defense of insanity or lack of mental capacity.

Nevertheless, as previously stated, it has long been a well-settled legal principle that the commission of unlawful sexual intercourse with a female relative is an act obviously calculated to arouse ungovernable passion, and that the killing of the seducer or adulterer under the influence or in the heat of that passion constitutes voluntary manslaughter, and not murder, in the absence of evidence of actual malice.

One of the leading cases in this jurisdiction is *Toler v. State*, . . . (1924). There the defendant learned during a noon hour that on a previous occasion the victim had seduced his teenage daughter and had attempted to molest his nine-year-old daughter. The defendant immediately armed himself, walked a quarter of a mile to a field in which the unarmed victim was working, and shot him several times, killing him instantly.

There, as here, the jury rejected a theory of self-defense. It returned a verdict of murder in the second degree. Reversing and remanding for a new trial, this Court said:

"We are, however, of the opinion that the facts did not warrant a verdict of murder in the second degree. It is undisputed that within less than an hour before he killed the deceased defendant had been informed of the outrage by the deceased of his young daughter. He was convinced of its truth, and, in all probability, it was true. This greatly shocked him and greatly aroused his passion, as it was calculated to do. Defendant, no doubt, from the time he was informed of this assault upon his young daughter until the shooting was done, was greatly agitated and was not capable of cool and deliberate thinking and reasoning, and killed the deceased while in this state of mind; in fact, we think the record fairly shows that this was the state of the defendant's mind at the time he did the shooting. He says that he was greatly shocked and so bothered that he did not know what to do. At any rate his mental stress must have been great, and in view of the fact that less than an hour had elapsed between the time he received information of the assault by deceased upon his daughter and the shooting, there was hardly time for his passion to subside or cool. There could therefore have been neither malice, express or implied, in the killing of deceased under such circumstances." . . .

The Court further stated:

"It is not necessary to reduce killing to manslaughter that the passion should be so great as to render the defendant incapable of deliberation or premeditation. If the circumstances be such as are calculated to produce such excitement and passion as would obscure the reason of an ordinary man and induce him, under such excitement and passion, to strike the blow that causes the death of the deceased, this will reduce the killing to manslaughter. . . .

"We think the facts of the instant case meet this test, and that defendant was improperly convicted of murder in the second degree." . . .

The Court pointed out that if there had been sufficient time for the passion or emotion of the defendant to cool before the shooting, then a verdict of murder might be sustained. It found no such time in that case, nor, in our opinion, was there any such showing in the present case.

[Discussion of other cases omitted]

In *Whitsett v. State*, . . . (1957), a verdict of murder in the second degree was reduced by this Court, as a matter of law, to voluntary manslaughter. There the defendant had learned of infidelity by his wife and within an hour he shot to death her paramour after an automobile chase in which he pursued the victim's vehicle for a considerable distance.

The Court said:

"It is properly conceded by the Attorney General, . . . that if the defendant had not had any suspicions or information as to his wife's infidelity prior to the morning of the conversation with young Mills, and had then killed McPhearson within the time in which he did kill him after receiving that information, the unlawful homicide would not have arisen to a degree higher than that of voluntary manslaughter." . . .

It was insisted by the State that the defendant had known for some time of the misconduct between his wife and McPhearson, and that therefore there had been ample time for the cooling of passion. It appeared, however, that the defendant had received additional information on the morning of the homicide.

The Court said:

"No repetition of the facts established by this record need be had in support of the necessary conclusion that at the moment defendant pursued and killed McPhearson he was laboring under an adequately aroused passion so great as to obscure his reason. Under these circumstances 'the killing will be reduced to manslaughter,' . . . , provided the passion has not had time to cool.

"The intense and adequately provoked passion under which he was laboring at this moment was produced by the additional information just furnished him by Mills. There is no other explanation for it in the light of his previous conduct for eight months prior to receiving this information, and strongly supports his testimony that when he unexpectedly saw McPhearson just before he killed him 'all of this stuff this boy told me that morning came back to me and him riding around with his wife and both of them looked happy and my home tore all to pieces, I don't know what happened, I lost control of myself . . .' " . . .

The facts of the present case are far stronger than any of the foregoing. Appellant actually discovered his wife *in flagrante delicto* with a man who was a total stranger to him, and at a time when appellant was trying to save his marriage and was deeply concerned about both his wife and his young child. He did not fire a shot or in any way harm the victim until he actually discovered the victim and his wife engaged in sexual intercourse in appellant's own home. In our opinion the passions of any reasonable person would have been inflamed and intensely aroused by this sort of discovery, given the factual background of this case. Even though he was not legally insane so as to relieve him of all criminal responsibility for the tragic death which occurred, in our opinion this was a classic case of voluntary manslaughter and no more.

We are of the opinion that the necessary elements of malice and premeditation were not demonstrated in this case and that the appellant acted under legally sufficient provocation. The conviction of murder in the first degree is set aside, and the cause will be remanded to the trial court for sentencing of the defendant for voluntary manslaughter and for such other disposition as may be appropriate in view of the time already served by the appellant. Costs of the appeal are taxed to the State. All other costs will be fixed by the trial court.

Brock, C.J., Fones, J., and Greer, Sp. J., concur; Drowota, J., files separate Opinion, concurring in part and dissenting in part.

Footnotes and Citations omitted. Concurring opinions omitted.

Opinion Concurring in part and dissenting in part: Justice Frank F. Drowata, III:

While I concur with the result of the majority opinion insofar as the evidence in this case will not sustain the jury's finding that Defendant, James C. Thornton, III, is guilty of murder in the first degree, I must respectfully dissent from the holding of the majority that the conviction should be reduced to voluntary manslaughter. Because the evidence clearly establishes that Defendant acted with sufficient malice, the killing constitutes murder in the second degree.

[Discussion of facts of case omitted]

Aside from the use of a firearm, which in itself permits an inference of malice, . . . , Defendant threatened the victim immediately before the weapon discharged, striking the victim precisely where Defendant threatened to shoot. Defendant intentionally aimed the weapon at the victim to avoid a fatal wound, but this inadequate precaution was insufficient to prevent the foreseeable consequence of death from a serious wound at close range with a large caliber weapon. . . . In *Ferguson v. State*, . . . (Tenn. 1975), the use of a firearm coupled with threatening statements supported the finding of malice to sustain a conviction for second degree murder. Other evidence of malice exists in this record as well, but these two facts are sufficient to negate the majority's conclusions that no malice exists and that Defendant is guilty of voluntary manslaughter.

Furthermore, assuming that Defendant was provoked to act when he heard the sounds of sexual relations emanating from the guest room and was provoked to such an extent that he was able to break through the locked front doors, he did not fire immediately upon entering the bedroom but instead attempted to take photographs and then threatened the victim before the gun discharged. These actions preceding the shooting do not indicate that Defendant's reason had been so overcome by passion and excitement to make him incapable of malice. . . . For a killing to be considered voluntary manslaughter, absence of malice as well as sufficient provocation are among the required elements of the offense. Any killing that is not first degree murder but cannot constitute a lesser offense of manslaughter is second degree murder. . . . Defendant acted in passion and without any previously formed design to kill, but he didn't act without malice at the time of the shooting. The reasoning of the Court in *Drye v. State*. . . , is applicable here:

"If the killing is done in passion, the offense is not murder in the first degree; if in passion adequately provoked and acted on before the passion has cooled, it is voluntary manslaughter; and, if in passion in fact, although the provocation be insufficient to reduce the offense to manslaughter, it will nevertheless be murder in the second degree only." . . .

Similarly, as in this case, if a killing is provoked but committed *with malice*, it will constitute second degree murder because not every element of voluntary manslaughter is shown but every element of second degree murder is shown on the facts. Consequently, I would reduce the conviction to second degree murder.

Wisconsin
v.
Todd Mitchell

Supreme Court of the United States
508 U.S. 476 (1993)

Chief Justice Rehnquist delivered the opinion of the Court.

Respondent Todd Mitchell's sentence for aggravated battery was enhanced because he intentionally selected his victim on account of the victim's race. The question presented in this case is whether this penalty enhancement is prohibited by the First and Fourteenth Amendments. We hold that it is not.

On the evening of October 7, 1989, a group of young black men and boys, including Mitchell, gathered at an apartment complex in Kenosha, Wisconsin. Several members of the group discussed a scene from the motion picture "Mississippi Burning," in which a white man beat a young black boy who was praying.

The group moved outside and Mitchell asked them: "'Do you all feel hyped up to move on some white people?'" . . . Shortly thereafter, a young white boy approached the group on the opposite side of the street where they were standing. As the boy walked by, Mitchell said: "'You all want to fuck somebody up? There goes a white boy; go get him.'" . . . Mitchell counted to three and pointed in the boy's direction. The group ran toward the boy, beat him severely, and stole his tennis shoes. The boy was rendered unconscious and remained in a coma for four days.

After a jury trial in the Circuit Court for Kenosha County, Mitchell was convicted of aggravated battery. . . .That offense ordinarily carries a maximum sentence of two years' imprisonment. §§ 940.19(1m) and 939.50(3)(e). But because the jury found that Mitchell had intentionally selected his victim because of the boy's race, the maximum sentence for Mitchell's offense was increased to seven years under § 939.645. That provision enhances the maximum penalty for an offense whenever the defendant "intentionally selects the person against whom the crime . . . is committed . . . because of the race, religion, color, disability, sexual orientation, national origin or ancestry of that person. . . . The Circuit Court sentenced Mitchell to four years' imprisonment for the aggravated battery.

Mitchell unsuccessfully sought postconviction relief in the Circuit Court. Then he appealed his conviction and sentence, challenging the constitutionality of Wisconsin's penalty-enhancement provision on First Amendment grounds. The Wisconsin Court of Appeals rejected Mitchell's challenge, . . . but the Wisconsin Supreme Court reversed. The Supreme Court held that the statute "violates the First Amendment directly by punishing what the legislature has deemed to be offensive thought.". . . It rejected the State's contention "that the statute punishes only the 'conduct' of intentional selection of a victim.". . . According to the court, "the statute punishes the 'because of' aspect of the defendant's selection, the *reason* the defendant selected the victim, the *motive* behind the selection.". . . And under *R. A. V.* v. *St. Paul*, . . . (1992), "the Wisconsin legislature cannot criminalize bigoted thought with which it disagrees." . . .

The Supreme Court also held that the penalty-enhancement statute was unconstitutionally overbroad. It reasoned that, in order to prove that a defendant intentionally selected his victim because of the victim's protected status, the State would often have to introduce evidence of the defendant's prior speech, such as racial epithets he may have uttered before the commission of the offense. This evidentiary use of protected speech, the court thought, would have a "chilling effect" on those who feared the possibility of prosecution for offenses subject to penalty enhancement. . . . Finally, the court distinguished antidiscrimination laws, which have long been held constitutional, on the ground that the Wisconsin statute punishes the "subjective mental process" of selecting a victim because of his protected status, whereas antidiscrimination laws prohibit "objective acts of discrimination." . . .

We granted certiorari because of the importance of the question presented and the existence of a conflict of authority among state high courts on the constitutionality of statutes similar to Wisconsin's penalty-enhancement provision, . . . We reverse.

Mitchell argues that we are bound by the Wisconsin Supreme Court's conclusion that the statute punishes bigoted thought and not conduct. There is no doubt that we are bound by a state court's construction of a state statute. . . .In *Terminiello*, for example, the Illinois courts had defined the term "'breach of the peace,'" in a city ordinance prohibiting disorderly conduct, to include "'stirs the public to anger . . . or creates a disturbance.'". . . . We held this construction to be binding on us. But here the Wisconsin Supreme Court did not, strictly speaking, construe the Wisconsin statute in the sense of defining the meaning of a particular statutory word or phrase. Rather, it merely characterized the "practical effect" of the statute for First Amendment purposes. . . .This assessment does not bind us. Once any ambiguities as to the meaning of the statute are resolved, we may form our own judgment as to its operative effect.

The State argues that the statute does not punish bigoted thought, as the Supreme Court of Wisconsin said, but instead punishes only conduct. While this argument is literally correct, it does not dispose of Mitchell's First Amendment challenge. To be sure, our cases reject the "view that an apparently limitless variety of conduct can be labeled 'speech' whenever the person engaging in the conduct intends thereby to express an idea." . . . Thus, a physical assault is not by any stretch of the imagination expressive conduct protected by the First Amendment. . . .

But the fact remains that under the Wisconsin statute the same criminal conduct may be more heavily punished if the victim is selected because of his race or other protected status than if no such motive obtained. Thus, although the statute punishes criminal conduct, it enhances the maximum penalty for conduct motivated by a discriminatory point of view more severely than the same conduct engaged in for some other reason or for no reason at all. Because the only reason for the enhancement is the defendant's discriminatory motive for selecting his victim, Mitchell argues (and the Wisconsin Supreme Court held) that the statute violates the First Amendment by punishing offenders' bigoted beliefs.

Traditionally, sentencing judges have considered a wide variety of factors in addition to evidence bearing on guilt in determining what sentence to impose on a convicted defendant. . . .The defendant's motive for committing the offense is one important factor. . . .Thus, in many States the commission of a murder, or other capital offense, for pecuniary gain is a separate aggravating circumstance under the capital sentencing statute. . . .

But it is equally true that a defendant's abstract beliefs, however obnoxious to most people, may not be taken into consideration by a sentencing judge. . . . In *Dawson*, the State introduced evidence at a capital sentencing hearing that the defendant was a member of a white supremacist prison gang. Because "the evidence proved nothing more than [the defendant's] abstract beliefs," we held that its admission violated the defendant's First Amendment rights. . . . In so holding, however, we emphasized that "the Constitution does not erect a *per se* barrier to the admission of evidence concerning one's beliefs and associations at sentencing simply because those beliefs and associations are protected by the First Amendment." . . .

Thus, in *Barclay* v. *Florida*, . . . (1983) (plurality opinion), we allowed the sentencing judge to take into account the defendant's racial animus towards his victim. The evidence in that case showed that the defendant's membership in the Black Liberation Army and desire to provoke a "race war" were related to the murder of a white man for which he was convicted. . . .Because "the elements of racial hatred in [the] murder" were relevant to several aggravating factors, we held that the trial judge permissibly took this evidence into account in sentencing the defendant to death. . . .

Mitchell suggests that *Dawson* and *Barclay* are inapposite because they did not involve application of a penalty-enhancement provision. But in *Barclay* we held that it was permissible for the sentencing court to consider the defendant's racial animus in determining whether he should be sentenced to death, surely the most severe "enhancement" of all. And the fact that the Wisconsin Legislature has decided, as a general matter, that bias-motivated offenses warrant greater maximum penalties across the board does not alter the result here. For the primary responsibility for fixing criminal penalties lies with the legislature. . . .

Mitchell argues that the Wisconsin penalty-enhancement statute is invalid because it punishes the defendant's discriminatory motive, or reason, for acting. But motive plays the same role under the Wisconsin statute as it does under federal and state antidiscrimination laws, which we have previously upheld against constitutional challenge. . . .Title VII of the Civil Rights Act of 1964, for example, makes it unlawful for an employer to discriminate against an employee "*because of* such individual's race, color, religion, sex, or national origin." . . . In *Hishon*, we rejected the argument that Title VII infringed employers' First Amendment rights. And more recently, in *R. A. V.* v. *St. Paul*, . . . we cited Title VII (as well as 18 U.S.C. § 242 and 42 U.S.C. §§ 1981 and 1982) as an example of a permissible content-neutral regulation of conduct.

Nothing in our decision last Term in *R. A. V.* compels a different result here. That case involved a First Amendment challenge to a municipal ordinance prohibiting the use of "'fighting words' that insult, or provoke violence, 'on the basis of race, color, creed, religion or gender.'" . . . Because the ordinance only proscribed a class of "fighting words" deemed particularly offensive by the city — *i.e.*, those "that contain . . . messages of 'bias-motivated' hatred," . . . — we held that it violated the rule against content-based discrimination. . . . But whereas the ordinance struck down in *R. A. V.* was explicitly directed at expression (*i.e.*, "speech" or "messages"), . . . , the statute in this case is aimed at conduct unprotected by the First Amendment.

Moreover, the Wisconsin statute singles out for enhancement bias-inspired conduct because this conduct is thought to inflict greater individual and societal harm. For example, according to the State and its *amici*, bias-motivated crimes are more likely to provoke retaliatory crimes, inflict distinct emotional harms on their victims, and incite community unrest. . . . The State's desire to redress these perceived harms provides an adequate explanation for its penalty-enhancement provision over and above mere disagreement with offenders' beliefs or biases. As Blackstone said long ago, "it is but reasonable that among crimes of different natures those should be most severely punished, which are the most destructive of the public safety and happiness." . . .

Finally, there remains to be considered Mitchell's argument that the Wisconsin statute is unconstitutionally overbroad because of its "chilling effect" on free speech. Mitchell argues (and the Wisconsin Supreme Court agreed) that the statute is "overbroad" because evidence of the defendant's prior speech or associations may be used to prove that the defendant intentionally selected his victim on account of the victim's protected status. Consequently, the argument goes, the statute impermissibly chills free expression with respect to such matters by those concerned about the possibility of enhanced sentences if they should in the future commit a criminal offense covered by the statute. We find no merit in this contention.

The sort of chill envisioned here is far more attenuated and unlikely than that contemplated in traditional "over-breadth" cases. We must conjure up a vision of a Wisconsin citizen suppressing his unpopular bigoted opinions for fear that if he later commits an offense covered by the statute, these opinions will be offered at trial to establish that he selected his victim on account of the victim's protected status, thus qualifying him for penalty enhancement. To stay within the realm of rationality, we must surely put to one side minor misdemeanor offenses covered by the statute, such as negligent operation of a motor vehicle . . . for it is difficult, if not impossible, to conceive of a situation where such offenses would be racially motivated. We are left, then, with the prospect of a citizen suppressing his bigoted beliefs for fear that evidence of such beliefs will be introduced against him at trial if he commits a more serious offense against person or property. This is simply too speculative a hypothesis to support Mitchell's overbreadth claim.

The First Amendment, moreover, does not prohibit the evidentiary use of speech to establish the elements of a crime or to prove motive or intent. Evidence of a defendant's previous declarations or statements is commonly admitted in criminal trials subject to evidentiary rules dealing with relevancy, reliability, and the like. Nearly half a century ago, in *Haupt* v. *United States*, . . . (1947), we rejected a contention similar to that advanced by Mitchell here. Haupt was tried for the offense of treason, which, as defined by the Constitution . . . , may depend very much on proof of motive. To prove that the acts in question were committed out of "adherence to the enemy " rather than "parental solicitude," . . . , the Government introduced evidence of conversations that had taken place long prior to the indictment, some of which consisted of statements showing Haupt's sympathy with Germany and Hitler and hostility towards the United States. We rejected Haupt's argument that this evidence was improperly admitted. While "such testimony is to be scrutinized with care to be certain the statements are not expressions of mere lawful and permissible difference of opinion with our own government or quite proper appreciation of the land of birth," we held that "these statements . . . clearly were admissible on the question of intent and adherence to the enemy.". . . .

For the foregoing reasons, we hold that Mitchell's First Amendment rights were not violated by the application of the Wisconsin penalty-enhancement provision in sentencing him. The judgment of the Supreme Court of Wisconsin is therefore reversed, and the case is remanded for further proceedings not inconsistent with this opinion.

It is so ordered.

Footnotes and citations omitted. Concurring opinions were omitted. There were no dissenting opinions.

Cases Relating to Chapter 6

Offenses Against Persons—Sex Related

The People of the State of New York

v.

Mario Liberta

Court of Appeals of New York
64 N.Y.2d 152 (1984)

Judge Wachtler delivered the opinion of the court.

The defendant, while living apart from his wife pursuant to a Family Court order, forcibly raped and sodomized her in the presence of their 2½ year old son. Under the New York Penal Law a married man ordinarily cannot be prosecuted for raping or sodomizing his wife. The defendant, however, though married at the time of the incident, is treated as an unmarried man under the Penal Law because of the Family Court order. On this appeal, he contends that because of the exemption for married men, the statutes for rape in the first degree . . . and sodomy in the first degree . . . , violate the equal protection clause of the Federal Constitution. . . . The defendant also contends that the rape statute violates equal protection because only men, and not women, can be prosecuted under it.

I.

Defendant Mario Liberta and Denise Liberta were married in 1978. Shortly after the birth of their son, in October of that year, Mario began to beat Denise. In early 1980 Denise brought a proceeding in the Family Court in Erie County seeking protection from the defendant. On April 30, 1980 a temporary order of protection was issued to her by the Family Court. Under this order, the defendant was to move out and remain away from the family home, and stay away from Denise. The order provided that the defendant could visit with his son once each weekend.

On the weekend of March 21, 1981, Mario, who was then living in a motel, did not visit his son. On Tuesday, March 24, 1981 he called Denise to ask if he could visit his son on that day. Denise would not allow the defendant to come to her house, but she did agree to allow him to pick up their son and her and take them both back to his motel after being assured that a friend of his would be with them at all times. The defendant and his friend picked up Denise and their son and the four of them drove to defendant's motel.

When they arrived at the motel the friend left. As soon as only Mario, Denise, and their son were alone in the motel room, Mario attacked Denise, threatened to kill her, and forced her to perform fellatio on him and to engage in sexual intercourse with him. The son was in the room during the entire episode, and the defendant forced Denise to tell their son to watch what the defendant was doing to her.

The defendant allowed Denise and their son to leave shortly after the incident. Denise, after going to her parents' home, went to a hospital to be treated for scratches on her neck and bruises on her head and back, all inflicted by her husband. She also went to the police station, and on the next day she swore out a felony complaint against the defendant. On July 15, 1981 the defendant was indicted for rape in the first degree and sodomy in the first degree.

II.

Section 130.35 of the Penal Law provides in relevant part that "A male is guilty of rape in the first degree when he engages in sexual intercourse with a female . . . by forcible compulsion." "Female," for purposes of the rape statute, is defined as "any female person who is not married to the actor". . . . Section 130.50 of the Penal Law provides in relevant part that "a person is guilty of sodomy in the first degree when he engages in deviate sexual intercourse with another person . . . by forcible compulsion." "Deviate sexual intercourse" is defined as "sexual conduct between persons not married to each other consisting of contact between the penis and the anus, the mouth and penis, or the mouth and the vulva". . . . Thus, due to the "not married" language in the definitions of "female" and "deviate sexual intercourse," there is a "marital exemption" for both forcible rape and forcible sodomy. The marital exemption itself, however, has certain exceptions. For purposes of the rape and sodomy statutes, a husband and wife are considered to be "not married" if at the time of the sexual assault they "are living apart . . . pursuant to a valid and effective: (i) order issued by a court of competent jurisdiction which by its terms or in its effect requires such living apart, or (ii) decree or judgment of separation, or (iii) written agreement of separation". . . .

Defendant moved to dismiss the indictment, asserting that because he and Denise were still married at the time of the incident he came within the "marital exemption" to both rape and sodomy. The People opposed the motion, contending that the temporary order of protection required Mario and Denise to live apart, and they in fact were living apart, and thus were "not married" for purposes of the statutes. The trial court granted the defendant's motion and dismissed the indictment, concluding that the temporary order of protection did not require Mario and Denise to live apart from each other, but instead required only that he remain away from her, and that therefore the "marital exemption" applied.

On appeal by the People, the Appellate Division reversed the trial court, reinstated the indictment, and remanded the case for trial. The Appellate Division held that a Family Court order of protection is within the scope of "[an] order . . . which by its terms or in its effect requires such living apart" even though it is directed only at a husband, and thus found that Mario and Denise were "not married" for purposes of the statute at the time of the incident.

The defendant was then convicted of rape in the first degree and sodomy in the first degree and the conviction was affirmed by the Appellate Division. Defendant asserts on this appeal that the temporary order of protection is not the type of order which enables a court to treat him and Denise as "not married" and that thus he is within the marital exemption. Defendant next asserts, assuming that because of the Family Court order he is treated just as any unmarried male would be, that he cannot be convicted of either rape in the first degree or sodomy in the first degree because both statutes are unconstitutional. Specifically, he contends that both statutes violate equal protection because they burden some, but not all males (all but those within the "marital exemption"), and that the rape statute also violates equal protection for burdening only men, and not women. The lower courts rejected the defendant's constitutional arguments, finding that neither statute violated the equal protection clause in the Fourteenth Amendment. Although we affirm the conviction of the defendant, we do not agree with the constitutional analysis of the lower courts and instead conclude that the marital and gender exemptions must be read out of the statutes prohibiting forcible rape and sodomy.

III.

We first address the defendant's argument that, despite the order of protection, he was within the "marital exemption" to rape and sodomy and thus could not be prosecuted for either crime. Until 1978, the marital exemption applied as long as the marriage still legally existed. In 1978, the Legislature expanded the definition of "not married" to include those cases where the husband and wife were living apart pursuant to either a court order "which by its terms or in its effect requires such living apart" or a decree, judgment, or written agreement of separation. . . . We agree with the Appellate Division that the order of protection in the present case falls squarely within the first of these situations.

The legislative memorandum submitted with the original version of the 1978 amendment, after referring to the situations brought within the scope of "not married," stated: "In each of the alternatives set forth in this bill, there must be documentary evidence of a settled and mutual intention to dissolve the marital relationship, or a court determination that the spouses should, for the well-being of one or both, live apart". . . . Although the language of the amendment was subsequently changed to the form in which it was enacted, this legislative memorandum was submitted with the final version of the bill. In addition to this clear statement of legislative intent, the plain language of the statute indicates that an order of protection is within the meaning of an order "which by its terms or in its effect requires [the spouses to live] apart." This language would be virtually meaningless if it did not encompass an order of protection, as the statute separately provides for the other obvious situation where a court order would require spouses to live apart, i.e., where there is a decree or judgment of separation.

Accordingly, the defendant was properly found to have been statutorily "not married" to Denise at the time of the rape.

IV.

The defendant's constitutional challenges to the rape and sodomy statutes are premised on his being considered "not married" to Denise and are the same challenges as could be made by any unmarried male convicted under these statutes. The defendant's claim is that both statutes violate equal protection because they are underinclusive classifications which burden him, but not others similarly situated. . . . A litigant has standing to raise this claim even though he does not contend that under no circumstances could the burden of the statute be imposed upon him . . . This rule of standing applies as well to a defendant in a criminal prosecution who, while conceding that it is within the power of a State to make criminal the behavior cov-

ered by a statute, asserts that the statute he is prosecuted under violates equal protection because it burdens him but not others. . . . Thus, defendant's constitutional claims are properly before this court.

A. The Marital Exemption

As noted above, under the Penal Law a married man ordinarily cannot be convicted of forcibly raping or sodomizing his wife. This is the so-called marital exemption for rape. . . . Although a marital exemption was not explicit in earlier rape statutes . . . , an 1852 treatise stated that a man could not be guilty of raping his wife. . . . The assumption, even before the marital exemption was codified, that a man could not be guilty of raping his wife, is traceable to a statement made by the 17th century English jurist Lord Hale, who wrote: "[The] husband cannot be guilty of a rape committed by himself upon his lawful wife, for by their mutual matrimonial consent and contract the wife hath given up herself in this kind unto her husband, which she cannot retract". . . . Although Hale cited no authority for his statement it was relied on by State Legislatures which enacted rape statutes with a marital exemption and by courts which established a common-law exemption for husbands.

The first American case to recognize the marital exemption was decided in 1857 by the Supreme Judicial Court of Massachusetts, which stated in dictum that it would always be a defense to rape to show marriage to the victim. . . . Decisions to the same effect by other courts followed, usually with no rationale or authority cited other than Hale's implied consent view. In New York, a 1922 decision noted the marital exemption in the Penal Law and stated that it existed "on account of the matrimonial consent which [the wife] has given, and which she cannot retract", . . .

Presently, over 40 States still retain some form of marital exemption for rape. While the marital exemption is subject to an equal protection challenge, because it classifies unmarried men differently than married men, the equal protection clause does not prohibit a State from making classifications, provided the statute does not arbitrarily burden a particular group of individuals. . . . Where a statute draws a distinction based upon marital status, the classification must be reasonable and must be based upon "some ground of difference that rationally explains the different treatment". . . .

We find that there is no rational basis for distinguishing between marital rape and non-marital rape. The various rationales which have been asserted in defense of the exemption are either based upon archaic notions about the consent and property rights incident to marriage or are simply unable to withstand even the slightest scrutiny. We therefore declare the marital exemption for rape in the New York statute to be unconstitutional.

Lord Hale's notion of an irrevocable implied consent by a married woman to sexual intercourse has been cited most frequently in support of the marital exemption. . . . Any argument based on a supposed consent, however, is untenable. Rape is not simply a sexual act to which one party does not consent. Rather, it is a degrading, violent act which violates the bodily integrity of the victim and frequently causes severe, long-lasting physical and psychic harm. . . . To ever imply consent to such an act is irrational and absurd. Other than in the context of rape statutes, marriage has never been viewed as giving a husband the right to coerced intercourse on demand. . . . Certainly, then, a marriage license should not be viewed as a license for a husband to forcibly rape his wife with impunity. A married woman has the same right to control her own body as does an unmarried woman. . . . If a husband feels "aggrieved" by his wife's refusal to engage in sexual intercourse, he should seek relief in the courts governing domestic relations, not in "violent or forceful self-help". . . .

The other traditional justifications for the marital exemption were the common-law doctrines that a woman was the property of her husband and that the legal existence of the woman was "incorporated and consolidated into that of the husband". . . . Both these doctrines, of course, have long been rejected in this State. Indeed, "[nowhere] in the common-law world — [or] in any modern society — is a woman regarded as chattel or demeaned by denial of a separate legal identity and the dignity associated with recognition as a whole human being". . . .

Because the traditional justifications for the marital exemption no longer have any validity, other arguments have been advanced in its defense. The first of these recent rationales, which is stressed by the People in this case, is that the marital exemption protects against governmental intrusion into marital privacy and promotes reconciliation of the spouses, and thus that elimination of the exemption would be disruptive to marriages. While protecting marital privacy and encouraging reconciliation are legitimate State interests, there is no rational relation between allowing a husband to forcibly rape his wife and these interests. The marital exemption simply does not further marital privacy because this right of privacy protects consensual acts, not violent sexual assaults. . . . Just as a husband cannot invoke a right of marital privacy to escape liability for beating his wife, he cannot justifiably rape his wife under the guise of a right to privacy.

Similarly, it is not tenable to argue that elimination of the marital exemption would disrupt marriages because it would discourage reconciliation. Clearly, it is the violent act of rape and not the subsequent attempt of the wife to seek protection through the criminal justice system which "disrupts" a marriage. . . . Moreover, if the marriage has already reached the point where intercourse is accomplished by violent assault it is doubtful that there is anything left to reconcile. . . . This, of course, is particularly true if the wife is willing to bring criminal charges against her husband which could result in a lengthy jail sentence.

Another rationale sometimes advanced in support of the marital exemption is that marital rape would be a difficult crime to prove. A related argument is that allowing such prosecutions could lead to fabricated complaints by "vindictive" wives. The difficulty of proof argument is based on the problem of showing lack of consent. Proving lack of consent, however, is often the most difficult part of any rape prosecution, particularly where the rapist and the victim had a prior relationship. . . . Similarly, the possibility that married women will fabricate complaints would seem to be no greater than the possibility of unmarried women doing so. . . . The criminal justice system, with all of its built-in safeguards, is presumed to be capable of handling any false complaints. Indeed, if the possibility of fabricated complaints were a basis for not criminalizing behavior which would otherwise be sanctioned, virtually all crimes other than homicides would go unpunished.

The final argument in defense of the marital exemption is that marital rape is not as serious an offense as other rape and is thus adequately dealt with by the possibility of prosecution under criminal statutes, such as assault statutes, which provide for less severe punishment. The fact that rape statutes exist, however, is a recognition that the harm caused by a forcible rape is different, and more severe, than the harm caused by an ordinary assault. . . . Under the Penal Law, assault is generally a misdemeanor unless either the victim suffers "serious physical injury" or a deadly weapon or dangerous instrument is used. . . . Thus, if the defendant had been living with Denise at the time he forcibly raped and sodomized her he probably could not have been charged with a felony, let alone a felony with punishment equal to that for rape in the first degree.

Moreover, there is no evidence to support the argument that marital rape has less severe consequences than other rape. On the contrary, numerous studies have shown that marital rape is frequently quite violent and generally has more severe, traumatic effects on the victim than other rape . . .

Among the recent decisions in this country addressing the marital exemption, only one court has concluded that there is a rational basis for it. . . . We agree with the other courts which have analyzed the exemption, which have been unable to find any present justification for it. . . . Justice Holmes wrote: "It is revolting to have no better reason for a rule of law than that so it was laid down in the time of Henry IV. It is still more revolting if the grounds upon which it was laid down have vanished long since, and the rule simply persists from blind imitation of the past". . . . This statement is an apt characterization of the marital exemption; it lacks a rational basis, and therefore violates the equal protection clauses of both the Federal and State Constitutions . . .

B. The Exemption for Females

Under the Penal Law only males can be convicted of rape in the first degree. Insofar as the rape statute applies to acts of "sexual intercourse," which, as defined in the Penal Law . . .) can only occur between a male and a female, it is true that a female cannot physically rape a female and that therefore there is no denial of equal protection when punishing only males for forcibly engaging in sexual intercourse with females. The equal protection issue, however, stems from the fact that the statute applies to males who forcibly rape females but does not apply to females who forcibly rape males.

Rape statutes historically applied only to conduct by males against females, largely because the purpose behind the proscriptions was to protect the chastity of women and thus their property value to their fathers or husbands. . . . New York's rape statute has always protected only females, and has thus applied only to males. . . .

Presently New York is one of only 10 jurisdictions that does not have a gender-neutral statute for forcible rape.

A statute which treats males and females differently violates equal protection unless the classification is substantially related to the achievement of an important governmental objective. . . . This test applies whether the statute discriminates against males or against females. . . . The People bear the burden of showing both the existence of an important objective and the substantial relationship between the discrimination in the statute and that objective. . . . This burden is not met in the present case, and therefore the gender exemption also renders the statute unconstitutional.

The first argument advanced by the People in support of the exemption for females is that because only females can become pregnant the State may constitutionally differentiate between forcible rapes of females and forcible rapes of males. This court and the United States Supreme Court have upheld statutes which subject males to criminal liability for engaging in sexual intercourse with underage females without the converse being true. . . . The rationale behind these decisions was that the primary purpose of such "statutory rape" laws is to protect against the harm caused by teenage pregnancies, there being no need to provide the same protection to young males. . . .

There is no evidence, however, that preventing pregnancies is a primary purpose of the statute prohibiting forcible rape, nor does such a purpose seem likely. . . . Rather, the very fact that the statute proscribes "forcible compulsion" shows that its overriding purpose is to protect a woman from an unwanted, forcible, and often violent sexual intrusion into her body. . . . Thus, due to the different purposes behind forcible rape laws and "statutory" (consensual) rape laws, the cases upholding the gender discrimination in the latter are not decisive with respect to the former, and the People cannot meet their burden here by simply stating that only females can become pregnant.

The People also claim that the discrimination is justified because a female rape victim "faces the probability of medical, sociological, and psychological problems unique to her gender." This same argument, when advanced in support of the discrimination in the statutory rape laws, was rejected by this court in *People v. Whidden* . . . , and it is no more convincing in the present case. "[An] 'archaic and overbroad generalization' . . . which is evidently grounded in long-standing stereotypical notions of the differences between the sexes, simply cannot serve as a legitimate rationale for a penal provision that is addressed only to adult males". . . .

Finally, the People suggest that a gender-neutral law for forcible rape is unnecessary, and that therefore the present law is constitutional, because a woman either cannot actually rape a man or such attacks, if possible, are extremely rare. Although the "physiologically impossible" argument has been accepted by several courts . . . , it is simply wrong. The argument is premised on the notion that a man cannot engage in sexual intercourse unless he is sexually aroused, and if he is aroused then he is consenting to intercourse. "Sexual intercourse" however, "occurs upon any penetration, however slight" . . . ; this degree of contact can be achieved without a male being aroused and thus without his consent.

As to the "infrequency" argument, while forcible sexual assaults by females upon males are undoubtedly less common than those by males upon females this numerical disparity cannot by itself make the gender discrimination constitutional. Women may well be responsible for a far lower number of all serious crimes than are men, but such a disparity would not make it permissible for the State to punish only men who commit, for example, robbery. . . .

To meet their burden of showing that a gender-based law is substantially related to an important governmental objective the People must set forth an "exceedingly persuasive justification" for the classification . . . , which requires, among other things, a showing that the gender-based law serves the governmental objective better than would a gender-neutral law. . . . The fact that the act of a female forcibly raping a male may be a difficult or rare occurrence does not mean that the gender exemption satisfies the constitutional test. A gender-neutral law would indisputably better serve, even if only marginally, the objective of deterring and punishing forcible sexual assaults. The only persons "benefitted" by the gender exemption are females who forcibly rape males. As the Supreme Court has stated, "[a] gender-based classification which, as compared to a gender-neutral one, generates additional benefits only for those it has no reason to prefer cannot survive equal protection scrutiny". . . .

Accordingly, we find that section 130.35 of the Penal Law violates equal protection because it exempts females from criminal liability for forcible rape.

V.

Having found that the statutes for rape in the first degree and sodomy in the first degree are unconstitutionally underinclusive, the remaining issue is the appropriate remedy for these equal protection violations. When a statute is constitutionally defective because of underinclusion, a court may either strike the statute, and thus make it applicable to nobody, or extend the coverage of the statute to those formerly excluded. . . . Accordingly, the unconstitutionality of one part of a criminal statute does not necessarily render the entire statute void. . . .

This court's task is to discern what course the Legislature would have chosen to follow if it had foreseen our conclusions as to underinclusiveness.... As Judge Cardozo wrote over 50 years ago, "The question is in every case whether the Legislature, if partial invalidity had been foreseen, would have wished the statute to be enforced with the invalid part exscinded, or rejected altogether".... These principles of severance apply as well where elimination of an invalid exemption will impose burdens on those not formerly burdened by the statute....

The question then is whether the Legislature would prefer to have statutes which cover forcible rape and sodomy, with no exemption for married men who rape or sodomize their wives and no exception made for females who rape males, or instead to have no statutes proscribing forcible rape and sodomy. In any case where a court must decide whether to sever an exemption or instead declare an entire statute a nullity it must look at the importance of the statute, the significance of the exemption within the over-all statutory scheme, and the effects of striking down the statute.... Forcible sexual assaults have historically been treated as serious crimes and certainly remain so today.... Statutes prohibiting such behavior are of the utmost importance, and to declare such statutes a nullity would have a disastrous effect on the public interest and safety. The inevitable conclusion is that the Legislature would prefer to eliminate the exemptions and thereby preserve the statutes.

Accordingly we choose the remedy of striking the marital exemption from sections 130.35 and 130.50 of the Penal Law and the gender exemption from section 130.35 of the Penal Law, so that it is now the law of this State that any person who engages in sexual intercourse or deviate sexual intercourse with any other person by forcible compulsion is guilty of either rape in the first degree or sodomy in the first degree. Because the statutes under which the defendant was convicted are not being struck down, his conviction is affirmed.

Though our decision does not "create a crime," it does, of course, enlarge the scope of two criminal statutes. We recognize that a court should be reluctant to expand criminal

statutes, due to the danger of usurping the role of the Legislature, but in this case overriding policy concerns dictate our following such a course in light of the catastrophic effect that striking down the statutes and thus creating a hiatus would have... Courts in other States have in numerous cases applied these same principles in eliminating an unconstitutional exception from a criminal statute and thereby enlarging the scope of the statute. The decision most similar factually to the present one comes from the Alaska Supreme Court in *Plas v. State*.... That court addressed an equal protection challenge by a female prostitute to a statute which criminalized prostitution, and defined it as a female offering her body for sexual intercourse for hire. The court agreed with the defendant that the statute violated equal protection because it covered only females, but chose to remedy this underinclusion by striking the definition, thereby expanding the statute to cover any person who engaged in prostitution, and affirmed her conviction.

The defendant cannot claim that our decision to retain the rape and sodomy statutes, and thereby affirm his conviction, denies him due process of the law. The due process clause of the Fourteenth Amendment requires that an accused have had fair warning at the time of his conduct that such conduct was made criminal by the State.... Defendant did not come within any of the exemptions which we have stricken, and thus his conduct was covered by the statutes as they existed at the time of his attack on Denise.

Neither can it be said that by the affirmance of his conviction the defendant is deprived of a constitutionally protected right to equal protection. The remedy chosen by our opinion is to extend the coverage of the provisions for forcible rape and sodomy to all those to whom these provisions can constitutionally be applied. While this remedy does treat the defendant differently than, for example, a married man who, while living with his wife, raped her prior to this decision, the distinction is rational inasmuch as it is justified by the limitations imposed on our remedy by the notice requirements of the due process clause (US Const, 14th Amdt), and the prohibition against ex post facto laws (US Const, art I, § 10). Thus, for purposes of choosing the proper remedy, the defendant is simply not similarly situated to those persons who were not within the scope of the statutes as they existed prior to our decision.

To reverse the defendant's conviction would mean that all those persons now awaiting trial for forcible rape or sodomy would be entitled to dismissal of the indictment. Indeed if we were to reverse no person arrested for forcible rape or sodomy prior to the date of this decision could be prosecuted for that offense, and every person already convicted of forcible rape or sodomy who raised the equal protection challenge would be entitled to have the conviction vacated. As the equal protection clause does not require us to reach such a result, we decline to do so.

Accordingly, the order of the Appellate Division should be affirmed.

[Footnotes and citations omitted. Concurring and dissenting opinions omitted.]

John Geddes Lawrence and Tyron Garner
v.
Texas

Court of Appeals of Texas
539 U.S. 558 (2003)

Justice Kennedy delivered the opinion of the Court.

Liberty protects the person from unwarranted government intrusions into a dwelling or other private places. In our tradition the State is not omnipresent in the home. And there are other spheres of our lives and existence, outside the home, where the State should not be a dominant presence. Freedom extends beyond spatial bounds. Liberty presumes an autonomy of self that includes freedom of thought, belief, expression, and certain intimate conduct. The instant case involves liberty of the person both in its spatial and more transcendent dimensions.

I

The question before the Court is the validity of a Texas statute making it a crime for two persons of the same sex to engage in certain intimate sexual conduct.

In Houston, Texas, officers of the Harris County Police Department were dispatched to a private residence in response to a reported weapons disturbance. They entered an apartment where one of the petitioners, John Geddes Lawrence resided. The right of the police to enter does not seem to have been questioned. The officers observed Lawrence and another man, Tyron Garner, engaging in a sexual act. The two petitioners were arrested, held in custody over night, and charged and convicted before a Justice of the Peace.

The complaints described their crime as "deviate sexual intercourse, namely anal sex, with a member of the same sex (man)."... The applicable state law is Tex. Penal Code Ann. § 21.06(a) (2003). It provides: "A person commits an offense if he engages in deviate sexual intercourse with another individual of the same sex." The statute defines "deviate sexual intercourse" as follows:

> "(A) any contact between any part of the genitals of one person and the mouth or anus of another person; or
>
> "(B) the penetration of the genitals or the anus of another person with an object." § 21.01(1).

The petitioners exercised their right to a trial *de novo* in Harris County Criminal Court. They challenged the statute as a violation of the Equal Protection Clause of the Fourteenth Amendment and of a like provision of the Texas Constitution. Tex. Const., Art. 1, § 3a. Those contentions were rejected. The petitioners, having entered a plea of *nolo contendere*, were each fined $200 and assessed court costs of $141.25....

The Court of Appeals for the Texas Fourteenth District considered the petitioners' federal constitutional arguments under both the Equal Protection and Due Process Clauses of the Fourteenth Amendment. After hearing the case *en banc* the court, in a divided opinion, rejected the constitutional arguments and affirmed the convictions.... The majority opinion indicates that the Court of Appeals considered our decision in *Bowers* v. *Hardwick*, ... (1986), to be controlling on the federal due process aspect of the case. *Bowers* then being authoritative, this was proper.

We granted certiorari, . . . to consider three questions:

"1. Whether Petitioners' criminal convictions under the Texas "Homosexual Conduct" law — which criminalizes sexual intimacy by same-sex couples, but not identical behavior by different-sex couples — violate the Fourteenth Amendment guarantee of equal protection of laws?

"2. Whether Petitioners' criminal convictions for adult consensual sexual intimacy in the home violate their vital interests in liberty and privacy protected by the Due Process Clause of the Fourteenth Amendment?

"3. Whether *Bowers* v. *Hardwick*, . . . , should be overruled?" . . .

The petitioners were adults at the time of the alleged offense. Their conduct was in private and consensual.

II

We conclude the case should be resolved by determining whether the petitioners were free as adults to engage in the private conduct in the exercise of their liberty under the Due Process Clause of the Fourteenth Amendment to the Constitution. For this inquiry we deem it necessary to reconsider the Court's holding in *Bowers*.

There are broad statements of the substantive reach of liberty under the Due Process Clause in earlier cases, including *Pierce* v. *Society of Sisters*, . . . (1925), and *Meyer* v. *Nebraska*, . . . (1923); but the most pertinent beginning point is our decision in *Griswold* v. *Connecticut*, . . . (1965).

In *Griswold* the Court invalidated a state law prohibiting the use of drugs or devices of contraception and counseling or aiding and abetting the use of contraceptives. The Court described the protected interest as a right to privacy and placed emphasis on the marriage relation and the protected space of the marital bedroom. . . .

After *Griswold* it was established that the right to make certain decisions regarding sexual conduct extends beyond the marital relationship. In *Eisenstadt* v. *Baird*, . . . (1972), the Court invalidated a law prohibiting the distribution of contraceptives to unmarried persons. The case was decided under the Equal Protection Clause, . . . ; but with respect to unmarried persons, the Court went on to state the fundamental proposition that the law impaired the exercise of their personal rights. . . . It quoted from the statement of the Court of Appeals finding the law to be in conflict with fundamental human rights, and it followed with this statement of its own:

"It is true that in *Griswold* the right of privacy in question inhered in the marital relationship. . . . If the right of privacy means anything, it is the right of the *individual*, married or single, to be free from unwarranted governmental intrusion into matters so fundamentally affecting a person as the decision whether to bear or beget a child." . . .

The opinions in *Griswold* and *Eisenstadt* were part of the background for the decision in *Roe* v. *Wade*, . . . (1973). As is well known, the case involved a challenge to the Texas law prohibiting abortions, but the laws of other States were affected as well. Although the Court held the woman's rights were not absolute, her right to elect an abortion did have real and substantial protection as an exercise of her liberty under the Due Process Clause. The Court cited cases that protect spatial freedom and cases that go well beyond it. *Roe* recognized the right of a woman to make certain fundamental decisions affecting her destiny and confirmed once more that the protection of liberty under the Due Process Clause has a substantive dimension of fundamental significance in defining the rights of the person.

In *Carey* v. *Population Services Int'l*, . . . (1977), the Court confronted a New York law forbidding sale or distribution of contraceptive devices to persons under 16 years of age. Although there was no single opinion for the Court, the law was invalidated. Both *Eisenstadt* and *Carey*, as well as the holding and rationale in *Roe*, confirmed that the reasoning of *Griswold* could not be confined to the protection of rights of married adults. This was the state of the law with respect to some of the most relevant cases when the Court considered *Bowers* v *Hardwick*.

The facts in *Bowers* had some similarities to the instant case. A police officer, whose right to enter seems not to have been in question, observed Hardwick, in his own bedroom, engaging in intimate sexual conduct with another adult male. The conduct was in violation of a Georgia statute making it a criminal offense to engage in sodomy. One difference between the two cases is that the Georgia statute prohibited the conduct whether or not the participants were of the same sex, while the Texas statute, as we have seen, applies only to participants of the same sex. Hardwick was not prosecuted, but he brought an action in federal court to declare the state statute invalid. He alleged he was a practicing homosexual and that the criminal prohibition violated rights guaranteed to him by the Constitution. The Court, in an opinion by Justice White, sustained the Georgia law. Chief Justice Burger and Justice Powell joined the opinion of the Court and filed separate, concurring opinions. Four Justices dissented. . . .

The Court began its substantive discussion in *Bowers* as follows: "The issue presented is whether the Federal Constitution confers a fundamental right upon homosexuals to engage in sodomy and hence invalidates the laws of the many States that still make such conduct illegal and have done so for a very long time.". . . . That statement, we now conclude, discloses the Court's own failure to appreciate the extent of the liberty at stake. To say that the issue in *Bowers* was simply the right to engage in certain sexual conduct demeans the claim the individual put forward, just as it would demean a married couple were it to be said marriage is simply about the right to have sexual intercourse. The laws involved in *Bowers* and here are, to be sure, statutes that purport to do no more than prohibit a particular sexual act. Their penalties and purposes, though, have more far-reaching consequences, touching upon the most private human conduct, sexual behavior, and in the most private of places, the home. The statutes do seek to control a personal relationship that, whether or not entitled to formal recognition in the law, is within the liberty of persons to choose without being punished as criminals.

This, as a general rule, should counsel against attempts by the State, or a court, to define the meaning of the relationship or to set its boundaries absent injury to a person or abuse of an institution the law protects. It suffices for us to acknowledge that adults may choose to enter upon this relationship in the confines of their homes and their own private lives and still retain their dignity as free persons. When sexuality finds overt expression in intimate conduct with another person, the conduct can be but one element in a personal bond that is more enduring. The liberty protected by the Constitution allows homosexual persons the right to make this choice.

Having misapprehended the claim of liberty there presented to it, and thus stating the claim to be whether there is a fundamental right to engage in consensual sodomy, the *Bowers* Court said: "Proscriptions against that conduct have ancient roots.". . . . In academic writings, and in many of the scholarly *amicus* briefs filed to assist the Court in this case, there are fundamental criticisms of the historical premises relied upon by the majority and concurring opinions in *Bowers*. . . . We need not enter this debate in the attempt to reach a definitive historical judgment, but the following considerations counsel against adopting the definitive conclusions upon which *Bowers* placed such reliance.

At the outset it should be noted that there is no longstanding history in this country of laws directed at homosexual conduct as a distinct matter. Beginning in colonial times there were prohibitions of sodomy derived from the English criminal laws passed in the first instance by the Reformation Parliament of 1533. The English prohibition was understood to include relations between men and women as well as relations between men and men. . . . Nineteenth-century commentators similarly read American sodomy, buggery, and crime-against-nature statutes as criminalizing certain relations between men and women and between men and men. . . . The absence of legal prohibitions focusing on homosexual conduct may be explained in part by noting that according to some scholars the concept of the homosexual as a distinct category of person did not emerge until the late 19th century. . . . Thus early American sodomy laws were not directed at homosexuals as such but instead sought to prohibit nonprocreative sexual activity more generally. This does not suggest approval of homosexual conduct. It does tend to show that this particular form of conduct was not thought of as a separate category from like conduct between heterosexual persons.

Laws prohibiting sodomy do not seem to have been enforced against consenting adults acting in private. A substantial number of sodomy prosecutions and convictions for which there are surviving records were for predatory acts against those who could not or did not consent, as in the case of a minor or the victim of an assault. As to these, one purpose for the prohibitions was to ensure there would be no lack of coverage if a predator committed a sexual assault that did not constitute rape as defined by the criminal law. Thus the model sodomy indictments presented in a 19th-century treatise, . . . addressed the predatory acts of an adult man against a minor girl or minor boy. Instead of targeting relations between consenting adults in private, 19th-century sodomy prosecutions typically involved relations between men and minor girls or minor boys, relations between adults involving force, relations between adults implicating disparity in status, or relations between men and animals.

To the extent that there were any prosecutions for the acts in question, 19th-century evidence rules imposed a burden that would make a conviction more difficult to obtain even taking into account the problems always inherent in prosecuting consensual acts committed in private. Under then-prevailing standards, a man could not be convicted of sodomy based upon testimony of a consenting partner, because the partner was considered an accomplice. A partner's testimony, however, was admissible if he or she had not consented to the act or was a minor, and therefore incapable of consent. . . . The rule may explain in part the infrequency of these prosecutions. In all events that infrequency makes it difficult to say that society approved of a rigorous and systematic punishment of the consensual acts committed in private and by adults. The longstanding criminal prohibition of homosexual sodomy upon which the *Bowers* decision placed such reliance is as consistent with a general condemnation of nonprocreative sex as it is with an established tradition of prosecuting acts because of their homosexual character.

The policy of punishing consenting adults for private acts was not much discussed in the early legal literature. We can infer that one reason for this was the very private nature of the conduct. Despite the absence of prosecutions, there may have been periods in which there was public criticism of homosexuals as such and an insistence that the criminal laws be enforced to discourage their practices. But far from possessing "ancient roots," . . . , American laws targeting same-sex couples did not develop until the last third of the 20th century. The reported decisions concerning the prosecution of consensual, homosexual sodomy between adults for the years 1880-1995 are not always clear in the details, but a significant number involved conduct in a public place. . . .

It was not until the 1970's that any State singled out same-sex relations for criminal prosecution, and only nine States have done so. . . .Over the course of the last decades, States with same-sex prohibitions have moved toward abolishing them. . . .

In summary, the historical grounds relied upon in *Bowers* are more complex than the majority opinion and the concurring opinion by Chief Justice Burger indicate. Their historical premises are not without doubt and, at the very least, are overstated.

It must be acknowledged, of course, that the Court in *Bowers* was making the broader point that for centuries there have been powerful voices to condemn homosexual conduct as immoral. The condemnation has been shaped by religious beliefs, conceptions of right and acceptable behavior, and respect for the traditional family. For many persons these are not trivial concerns but profound and deep convictions accepted as ethical and moral principles to which they aspire and which thus determine the course of their lives. These considerations do not answer the question before us, however. The issue is whether the majority may use the power of the State to enforce these views on the whole society through operation of the criminal law. "Our obligation is to define the liberty of all, not to mandate our own moral code." . . .

Chief Justice Burger joined the opinion for the Court in *Bowers* and further explained his views as follows: "Decisions of individuals relating to homosexual conduct have been subject to state intervention throughout the history of Western civilization. Condemnation of those practices is firmly rooted in Judeo-Christian moral and ethical standards." ... As with Justice White's assumptions about history, scholarship casts some doubt on the sweeping nature of the statement by Chief Justice Burger as it pertains to private homosexual conduct between consenting adults. . . . In all events we think that our laws and traditions in the past half century are of most relevance here. These references show an emerging awareness that liberty gives substantial protection to adult persons in deciding how to conduct their private lives in matters pertaining to sex. . . .

This emerging recognition should have been apparent when *Bowers* was decided. In 1955 the American Law Institute promulgated the Model Penal Code and made clear that it did not recommend or provide for "criminal penalties for consensual sexual relations conducted in private.". . . . It justified its decision on three grounds: (1) The prohibitions undermined respect for the law by penalizing conduct many people engaged in; (2) the statutes regulated private conduct not harmful to others; and (3) the laws were arbitrarily enforced and thus invited the danger of blackmail. . . . In 1961 Illinois changed its laws to conform to the Model Penal Code. Other States soon followed. . . .

In *Bowers* the Court referred to the fact that before 1961 all 50 States had outlawed sodomy, and that at the time of the Court's decision 24 States and the District of Columbia had sodomy laws. . . .Justice Powell pointed out that these prohibitions often were being ignored, however. Georgia, for instance, had not sought to enforce its law for decades. . . .

The sweeping references by Chief Justice Burger to the history of Western civilization and to Judeo-Christian moral and ethical standards did not take account of other authorities pointing in an opposite direction. A committee advising the British Parliament recommended in 1957 repeal of laws punishing homosexual conduct. . . .Parliament enacted the substance of those recommendations 10 years later. . . .

Of even more importance, almost five years before *Bowers* was decided the European Court of Human Rights considered a case with parallels to *Bowers* and to today's case. An adult male resident in Northern Ireland alleged he was a practicing homosexual who desired to engage in consensual homosexual conduct. The laws of Northern Ireland forbade him that right. He alleged that he had been questioned, his home had been searched, and he feared criminal prosecution. The court held that the laws proscribing the conduct were invalid under the European Convention on Human Rights. . . . Authoritative in all countries that are members of the Council of Europe (21 nations then, 45 nations now), the decision is at odds with the premise in *Bowers* that the claim put forward was insubstantial in our Western civilization.

In our own constitutional system the deficiencies in *Bowers* became even more apparent in the years following its announcement. The 25 States with laws prohibiting the relevant conduct referenced in the *Bowers* decision are reduced now to 13, of which 4 enforce their laws only against homosexual conduct. In those States where sodomy is still proscribed, whether for same-sex or heterosexual conduct, there is a pattern of nonenforcement with respect to consenting adults acting in private. The State of Texas admitted in 1994 that as of that date it had not prosecuted anyone under those circumstances. . . .

Two principal cases decided after *Bowers* cast its holding into even more doubt. In *Planned Parenthood of Southeastern Pa.* v. *Casey,* . . . (1992), the Court reaffirmed the substantive force of the liberty protected by the Due Process Clause. The *Casey* decision again confirmed that our laws and tradition afford constitutional protection to personal decisions relating to marriage, procreation, contraception, family relationships, child rearing, and education. . . . In explaining the respect the Constitution demands for the autonomy of the person in making these choices, we stated as follows:

"These matters, involving the most intimate and personal choices a person may make in a lifetime, choices central to personal dignity and autonomy, are central to the liberty protected by the Fourteenth Amendment. At the heart of liberty is the right to define one's own concept of existence, of meaning, of the universe, and of the mystery of human life. Beliefs about these matters could not define the attributes of personhood were they formed under compulsion of the State." . . .

Persons in a homosexual relationship may seek autonomy for these purposes, just as heterosexual persons do. The decision in *Bowers* would deny them this right.

The second post-*Bowers* case of principal relevance is *Romer* v. *Evans*, . . . (1996). There the Court struck down class-based legislation directed at homosexuals as a violation of the Equal Protection Clause. *Romer* invalidated an amendment to Colorado's constitution which named as a solitary class persons who were homosexuals, lesbians, or bisexual either by "orientation, conduct, practices or relationships," . . . , and deprived them of protection under state antidiscrimination laws. We concluded that the provision was "born of animosity toward the class of persons affected" and further that it had no rational relation to a legitimate governmental purpose. . . .

As an alternative argument in this case, counsel for the petitioners and some *amici* contend that *Romer* provides the basis for declaring the Texas statute invalid under the Equal Protection Clause. That is a tenable argument, but we conclude the instant case requires us to address whether *Bowers* itself has continuing validity. Were we to hold the statute invalid under the Equal Protection Clause some might question whether a prohibition would be valid if drawn differently, say, to prohibit the conduct both between same-sex and different-sex participants.

Equality of treatment and the due process right to demand respect for conduct protected by the substantive guarantee of liberty are linked in important respects, and a decision on the latter point advances both interests. If protected conduct is made criminal and the law which does so remains unexamined for its substantive validity, its stigma might remain even if it were not enforceable as drawn for equal protection reasons. When homosexual conduct is made criminal by the law of the State, that declaration in and of itself is an invitation to subject homosexual persons to discrimination both in the public and in the private spheres. The central holding of *Bowers* has been brought in question by this case, and it should be addressed. Its continuance as precedent demeans the lives of homosexual persons.

The stigma this criminal statute imposes, moreover, is not trivial. The offense, to be sure, is but a class C misdemeanor, a minor offense in the Texas legal system. Still, it remains a criminal offense with all that imports for the dignity of the persons charged. The petitioners will bear on their record the history of their criminal convictions. Just this Term we rejected various challenges to state laws requiring the registration of sex offenders. . . . We are advised that if Texas convicted an adult for private, consensual homosexual conduct under the statute here in question the convicted person would come within the registration laws of at least four States were he or she to be subject to their jurisdiction. . . . This underscores the consequential nature of the punishment and the state-sponsored condemnation attendant to the criminal prohibition. Furthermore, the Texas criminal conviction carries with it the other collateral consequences always following a conviction, such as notations on job application forms, to mention but one example.

The foundations of *Bowers* have sustained serious erosion from our recent decisions in *Casey* and *Romer*. When our precedent has been thus weakened, criticism from other sources is of greater significance. In the United States criticism of *Bowers* has been substantial and continuing, disapproving of its reasoning in all respects, not just as to its historical assumptions. . . . The courts of five different States have declined to follow it in interpreting provisions in their own state constitutions parallel to the Due Process Clause of the Fourteenth Amendment, . . .

To the extent *Bowers* relied on values we share with a wider civilization, it should be noted that the reasoning and holding in *Bowers* have been rejected elsewhere. The European Court of Human Rights has followed not *Bowers* but its own decision in *Dudgeon* v *United Kingdom*. . . . Other nations, too, have taken action consistent with an affirmation of the protected right of homosexual adults to engage in intimate, consensual conduct. . . . The right the petitioners seek in this case has been accepted as an integral part of human freedom in many other countries. There has been no showing that in this country the governmental interest in circumscribing personal choice is somehow more legitimate or urgent.

The doctrine of *stare decisis* is essential to the respect accorded to the judgments of the Court and to the stability of the law. It is not, however, an inexorable command. . . . In *Casey* we noted that when a Court is asked to overrule a precedent recognizing a constitutional liberty interest, individual or societal reliance on the existence of that liberty cautions with particular strength against reversing course. . . . The holding in *Bowers*, however, has not induced detrimental reliance comparable to some instances where recognized individual rights are involved. Indeed, there has been no individual or societal reliance on *Bowers* of the sort that could counsel against overturning its holding once there are compelling reasons to do so. *Bowers* itself causes uncertainty, for the precedents before and after its issuance contradict its central holding.

The rationale of *Bowers* does not withstand careful analysis. In his dissenting opinion in *Bowers* Justice Stevens came to these conclusions:

"Our prior cases make two propositions abundantly clear. First, the fact that the governing majority in a State has traditionally viewed a particular practice as immoral is not a sufficient reason for upholding a law prohibiting the practice; neither history nor tradition could save a law prohibiting miscegenation from constitutional attack. Second, individual decisions by married persons, concerning the intimacies of their physical relationship, even when not intended to produce offspring, are a form of "liberty" protected by the Due Process Clause of the Fourteenth Amendment. Moreover, this protection extends to intimate choices by unmarried as well as married persons." . . .

Justice Stevens' analysis, in our view, should have been controlling in *Bowers* and should control here.

Bowers was not correct when it was decided, and it is not correct today. It ought not to remain binding precedent. *Bowers* v. *Hardwick* should be and now is overruled.

The present case does not involve minors. It does not involve persons who might be injured or coerced or who are situated in relationships where consent might not easily be refused. It does not involve public conduct or prostitution. It does not involve whether the government must give formal recognition to any relationship that homosexual persons seek to enter. The case does involve two adults who, with full and mutual consent from each other, engaged in sexual practices common to a homosexual lifestyle. The petitioners are entitled to respect for their private lives. The State cannot demean their existence or control their destiny by making their private sexual conduct a crime. Their right to liberty under the Due Process Clause gives them the full right to engage in their conduct without intervention of the government. "It is a promise of the Constitution that there is a realm of personal liberty which the government may not enter." . . . . The Texas statute furthers no legitimate state interest which can justify its intrusion into the personal and private life of the individual.

Had those who drew and ratified the Due Process Clauses of the Fifth Amendment or the Fourteenth Amendment known the components of liberty in its manifold possibilities, they might have been more specific. They did not presume to have this insight. They knew times can blind us to certain truths and later generations can see that laws once thought necessary and proper in fact serve only to oppress. As the Constitution endures, persons in every generation can invoke its principles in their own search for greater freedom.

The judgment of the Court of Appeals for the Texas Fourteenth District is reversed, and the case is remanded for further proceedings not inconsistent with this opinion.

It is so ordered.

Footnotes and citations omitted. Concurring and dissenting omitted.

Cases Relating to Chapter 7

Offenses Against Property—
Destruction and Intrusion Offenses

People of the State of Michigan

v.

Juma Reeves, Auneray Barber, and Ronald Williams

Supreme Court of Michigan
448 Mich. 1 (1995)

MALLET, Justice

This is a statutory construction case involving the interpretation of the word "arson" in the first degree (felony) murder statute, M.C.L. § 750.316; M.S.A. § 28.548. Defendant Juma Reeves, and codefendants, Ronald Williams and Auneray Barber, were charged, *inter alia*, with felony murder, with the underlying felony being the burning of other real property, M.C.L. § 750.73; M.S.A. § 28.268. Thirty-sixth District Court Judge Thomas A. Van Tiem, Sr., bound over all three defendants for trial on, *inter alia*, felony murder and burning other real property charges. Detroit Recorder's Court Judge Daphne Means Curtis reduced the felony murder charge to involuntary manslaughter, . . . , finding that the word "arson" in the felony murder statute does not include the burning of property other than a dwelling house. The trial was stayed to allow the prosecutor's interlocutory appeal to the Court of Appeals.

The Court of Appeals construed the word "arson" in accordance with the common-law definition, "at common-law, 'arson' referred only to the 'burning of another's house or dwelling house' and appurtenances." . . . We granted the prosecution's application for leave to appeal to determine whether the word "arson" in the felony murder statute includes the burning of other real property. We conclude that the construction of the word "arson" in the felony murder statute refers to the common-law crime of arson, that is, the malicious and voluntary or wilful burning of a dwelling house of another.

Facts

During the preliminary examination, the confessions of each of the defendants was read into the record. Each defendant admitted participation in setting the fire at 8340 Kenney, a dilapidated abandoned house in Detroit.

Defendants admitted that they retrieved a mattress from the backyard at 8340 Kenney, carried it inside, doused the mattress and other furnishings located in the house with charcoal lighter fluid, and threw a lighted match on the mattress. The Detroit Fire Department was summoned to extinguish the blaze. Despite the fire department's efforts the resulting fire consumed the structure.

Before the fire, the old-fashioned brick coat siding had been removed from the foundation to the eaves, exposing the wooden frame. The foundation was weakened by the removal of the bricks. The fire burned through the floor joists and wood structure of the house, eventually causing it to collapse on a fire fighter trainee, killing him.

Although the defendants initially fled from the scene, they returned moments later to watch the flames spread from 8340 Kenney to 8334 Kenney. Both the homes were completely consumed by the fire, but not before spreading to 8328 Kenney, an occupied dwelling. The roof and second floor dormer of the occupied dwelling were charred.

The prosecution argues that the Legislature defined the crime of arson in 1927 PA 38. The 1927 enactment expanded the common-law definition of arson to include any unlawful burning. The Legislature amended the statutory language in 1929, but retained the use of the word "arson.". . . .

The prosecution avers that *People v. Clemons* . . . (1990), clarified the modern statutory definition of the crime of arson. The *Clemons* Court determined that "the Legislature intended that the word 'arson' apply to M.C.L. § 750.73; M.S.A. § 28.268, burning of real property," stating that "[t]his statute was derived from 1929 CL 16935 which was specifically designated as the crime of arson."

Defendants respond that the statutory history of the arson and burning statute does not indicate an expansion of arson beyond the burning of a habitable structure. Defendants contend that a careful review of the statutory history of the arson and the burning statute compels the conclusion that the Legislature, when it enacted the Penal Code in 1931, did not intend all types of unlawful burning to constitute arson. Defendants argue that the Legislature was careful to delete the key language on which the prosecution relies. . . .

The Court of Appeals declined to follow *Clemons*, stating that *People v. Foster*, . . . (1981), is indistinguishable from the present case and is better reasoned than Clemons. We agree.

I.

The Court of Appeals has previously considered the issue whether the word "arson" included the burning of other real property in *Foster* and *Clemons*, reaching inconsistent conclusions. Both the prosecution and the defendants in the present case attempt to resolve the conflict by arguments based on an analysis of the history of the arson and burning statute.

In *Foster*, the defendant and a codefendant were charged with felony murder and burning a dwelling house or its contents after setting fire to a vacant house. A rookie fire fighter was killed while inside the building. The defendant was convicted of manslaughter.

The Court of Appeals reversed the defendant's conviction in *Foster*, . . . , noting that the structure was merely a shell of a house and was not a dwelling. The Court concluded that the structure must be habitable to qualify as a dwelling house under the burning dwelling house statute. Before the fire, the radiators, hot water heater, and toilet were removed. The windows were broken, and the door was kicked in. The utilities had been disconnected. Also, the building was infested with rats. Under these conditions, the house was not a dwelling house; therefore, there was no arson to serve as the predicate offense for felony murder. The Court of Appeals panel implicitly determined that the word "arson" in the felony murder statute referred to the burning of a dwelling house and not the burning of other real property.

In *Clemons*, the defendant was charged with three counts of felony murder and one count of burning real property. He pleaded guilty of three counts of second-degree murder, . . . , and one count of burning real property. The defendant claimed that his plea bargain was illusory because the burning of real property cannot serve as the predicate offense for felony murder. Relying exclusively on 1929 CL 16935, and without mentioning subsequent statutory revisions or the *Foster* decision, the Court of Appeals concluded that the meaning of "arson" within the felony murder statute included the burning of other real property.

In the present case, the prosecution argues that in 1927, the Legislature broadened the common-law definition of arson to include the burning of other real property. The defendants respond that when the Legislature enacted the Penal Code in 1931, it did not intend to include in the definition of arson the burning of real property other than a dwelling house. The Penal Code of 1931, defendants argue, did not clearly expand or alter the common-law definition of arson.

II.

In interpreting penal statutes, courts cannot expand the scope of the statutory prohibition. . . . The court's construction of the statutory language must further the legislative intent and purpose. . . .

(Some discussion omitted)

To ascertain the meaning of the word "arson" referred to in the felony murder statute, we must examine the history of the felony murder statute in relation to the arson and burning statute to determine what constitutes the crime of arson. After defining the crime of arson, we construe the language of the felony murder statute to further the goals and facilitate the intent of the Legislature. . . .

III.

As early as 1827, the laws of Michigan reflected a distinction between the common-law definition of arson and the burning of other real property. The definitions were set forth in separate sections of the 1827 statute. The 1827 statute codified the common-law definition of arson. The relevant portions of that act provide:

> That if any person willingly and maliciously, shall burn or cause to be burned, or aid, counsel, procure, or consent to the burning of the dwelling house of another, or, . . . belonging or adjoining thereto, or any other building, by means whereof a dwelling house shall be burnt, then and in every such case, the person so offending, shall . . . be punished . . .

The 1827 statute also contained prohibitions of other types of burnings. Specifically, § 22 prohibited burning public buildings, mills and out houses. Section 23 prohibited setting fire to public buildings, mills and out houses. However, these other burnings were not defined as arson.

The Revised Statutes of 1838 eliminated the word "arson" from the statutory language, providing in relevant part:

> Every person who shall wilfully and maliciously burn, in the night time, the dwelling-house of another, or shall, in the night time, wilfully and maliciously set fire to any other building, owned by himself or another, by burning whereof, such dwelling-house shall be burnt in the night time, shall be punished . . . ; but if the defendant shall prove . . . , that at the time of committing the offence, there was no person lawfully in the dwelling-house so

burnt, the punishment, instead of imprisonment for life, may be imprisonment in the state prison for any term of years. . . .

The laws proscribing the burning of a dwelling house, burning of other real property, and burning of personal property remained relatively unchanged until 1927.

The Revised Statutes of 1838 contain eight statutory provisions pertaining to unauthorized burnings (§§ 1-8). Section 2 required life (or a term of years) imprisonment for burning a dwelling house during the day time. Sections 3-6 and 8 proscribed the burning of other real and personal property.

The 1827 statute contained a felony murder provision that included arson, but did not include the burning of other real property as one of the predicate felonies. In 1871, the Legislature clarified its intention that the word "any" in the felony murder statute modified the word "arson." Specifically, 1871 CL 7510 provides:

> All murder which shall be perpetrated by means of poison, or lying in wait, or any other kind of willful, deliberate, and premeditated killing, or which shall be committed in the perpetration, or attempt to perpetrate, any arson, rape, robbery, or burglary, shall be deemed murder of the first degree. . . . [Emphasis added.]

In 1927, the word "arson" appeared, for the first time since 1827, in the statute that proscribed the burning of property. The preamble to the statute stated:

> An Act to define and punish the crime of arson, and to repeal sections, one, two, three, four, five, six, seven, eight and nine of chapter [154] of the revised statutes of [1846], being [§§ 15,281 to 15,286]. [1927 PA 38]

In the 1927 statute, arson was essentially defined to include any unlawful burning of a dwelling house, other real property and personal property.

In 1929, the Legislature revised the arson statute to eliminate the word "arson" as a specifically defined provision. The 1929 statute retained the definition of arson of a dwelling house as set forth in the 1927 statute, identifying the 1929 provision in its catchline as "[w]ilful or malicious burning of property; dwelling or building within curtilage; penalty."

[Further discussion of intervening statutes omitted]

The arson and burning statute has remained relatively unchanged since the 1931 enactment. The statute in the present case is virtually identical to the 1931 arson and burning statute. Specifically, the statutes at issue provide:

Any person who willfully or maliciously burns any dwelling house, either occupied or unoccupied, or the contents thereof, whether owned by himself or another, or any building within the curtilage of such dwelling house, or the contents thereof, shall be guilty of a felony, punishable by imprisonment in the state prison not more than 20 years....

Murder which is perpetrated by means of poison, lying in wait, or other wilful, deliberate, and premeditated killing, or which is committed in the perpetration, or attempt to perpetrate arson, ... is murder of the first degree......

IV.

In interpreting penal statutes, this Court "require[s] clarity and explicitness in the defining of the crime and the classification of acts which may constitute it"; however, we will not usurp the Legislature's role by expanding the scope of the proscribed conduct....

The history of the felony murder statute reveals that the Legislature always considered as an aggravating circumstance conduct described as arson. In 1827, the Legislature expressly included the crime of arson as one of the predicate felonies for felony murder. All of the predicate felonies listed in that and subsequent felony murder statutes were crimes against persons. It was clearly the intent of the Legislature to prevent the endangering of human lives. Thus, a construction of the present statute that would include a meaning of arson encompassing a crime against property would be inconsistent with the history of the felony murder offense and the legislative intent.

The most recent statutory definition of arson was presented in the 1927 statute. In that statute, the common-law definition of arson was enlarged to include other real property and personal property. This was the trend of the day.... The Legislature eliminated the 1927 definition of arson in its 1929 enactment. The 1929 statutory references to the crime of arson were expressly repealed by the 1931 statute.

In 1931, the Legislature decided not to define the word "arson" and removed it from the provisions governing the burning proscriptions. In the absence of a clear and explicit definition of the criminal offense, we construe the statutory crime by resorting to the common-law definition of the criminal offense....

In 1931, the common-law offense of arson differed from the burning offenses described in the 1931 statutory provisions. In the former, the proscribed conduct included the burning of a dwelling house of another. However, the statutory provisions included the burning of any building, other real property, or personal property, whether owned by the actor or someone else. Since the Legislature is presumed to know that the courts will apply the common-law meaning to words in the statute having a common-law definition and crimes not clearly or explicitly defined, this Court infers from the circumstances that the Legislature intended to include only the common-law definition of arson in the 1931 felony murder statute....

The arson and burning statute in the present case is virtually identical to the 1931 arson and burning statute. Similarly, the felony murder statute in the present case includes arson as a predicate offense without clearly and explicitly defining the criminal offense. Therefore, we conclude that the legislative intent would be furthered by ascribing the same construction of the word "arson" referred to in the 1931 felony murder statute to the word "arson" appearing in the current felony murder statute, that is, the burning of the dwelling house of another.

V.

In the present case, the defendants set fire to a dilapidated abandoned house. Our task is to determine whether the house was a dwelling house so that the burning of it would constitute the crime of arson. In our pursuit, we find guidance in cases from this and foreign jurisdictions.

This Court first considered "whether the building that was set on fire was a dwelling house within the meaning of the statute" in *People v. Losinger*, (1951). In *Losinger*, the defendant pleaded guilty of burning the dwelling house of another. On appeal, the defendant claimed that the cabin burned did not constitute a dwelling house. The owner of the cabin testified that the cabin was sufficiently sound and equipped for immediate occupancy. More particularly, the cabin owner testified:

> [The cabin] had an air-tight wooden floor built over a cement foundation. . . . [It] contained 3 beds . . . with bedding, curtains on the windows and between the beds. It contained some furniture, a kerosene cooking stove, cooking utensils, groceries and canned milk in the cupboards, some personal possessions, clothing, a heating stove and fuel and all equipment necessary so that occupants could move in and immediately have the facilities of a furnished dwelling house.

The owner had regularly dwelt in and occupied the cabin, but not on a daily basis. The *Losinger* Court, noting that "the crime of burning a dwelling house was an offense against a habitation and not against fee title," held that the building burned was a dwelling house. . . . The Court accepted the following as the definition of dwelling house:

> "The term 'dwelling house' has a broader meaning than a house that is actually occupied as such. It means any house intended to be occupied as a residence, and would include any such residence, even though not occupied by the complaining witness at the time of the burning." . . .

The arson and burning statute considered by the *Losinger* Court was virtually identical to the statute at issue in the present case.

The definition of a dwelling house set forth in *Losinger* is consistent with the intent of the Legislature. In 1931, the Legislature deleted the definition of the crime of arson and removed references to the crime from the arson and burning statutory provisions. However, the crime of arson continued to be a predicate offense for the crime of felony murder. Like *Fillman v. State*, . . . (Del., 1969), this Court infers from the circumstances that the Legislature intended to include only the common-law definitions of the crime of arson and the term of art "dwelling house." . . . Therefore, this Court reaffirms the *Losinger* Court's definition of a dwelling house.

In *Fillman*, . . . , the Delaware Supreme Court was also called upon to determine whether the structure burned was a dwelling house. The court concluded that, at common law, the structure burned would not constitute a dwelling house. The court stated:

> At common law . . . [w]here a building, although formerly used as a dwelling, has been abandoned for such purpose, has been unoccupied for a prolonged period of time, and has become unfit for habitation, it is deemed to have lost its character as a dwelling house and is not subject as such to common law arson. . . .

The court concluded that the common-law definition of dwelling house applied because its statute did not define the "word of art." . . .

These cases establish the distinction between unoccupied and abandoned. If a dwelling is simply unoccupied at the time it is burned, common-law arson has been committed. If a dwelling house is unoccupied and dilapidated to the extent that it is deemed abandoned, then the structure is no longer considered a dwelling house and common-law arson has not been perpetuated.

At common law a house was required to be in a condition that could be dwelt in. Under the circumstances of this case, we conclude that the house was not in such a condition and that the owner had abandoned any intent to inhabit the house in the future.

As so aptly stated by the panel in *Foster*, . . . :

> While some poor wayfarer on the urban landscape might have decided that the building in dispute provided shelter and was therefore habitable, this fact cannot be seized upon to justify a conclusion that the building was indeed a "dwelling house." Were we to accept this reasoning in finding the structure a "dwelling house," our expansive construction would eliminate the special character of the arson statute. For those in our society who live a marginal existence on the streets, any abandoned building might be viewed as a habitable shelter.

We are neither willing nor empowered to expand the scope of the crime of arson or the definition of dwelling house beyond the legislative intent. The Legislature intended that the crime of arson and the definition of dwelling house be defined as at common law. The *Clemons* Court improperly expanded the scope of the crime of arson. Therefore, we overrule the decision in that case.

The *Foster* decision is consistent with the history of the arson and burning statute and reflects the legislative intent. The Court of Appeals panel in the present case was free to follow *Foster* because *Clemons* was decided before November 1, 1990, the effective date of Administrative Order No. 1990-6,. . . . We hold that the house burned in the present case was not a dwelling house. Therefore, the defendants could not be charged with arson.

VI.

In the present case, the defendants were charged with, *inter alia*, felony murder with the underlying felony being the burning of other real property. The felony murder statute at issue includes the crime of arson as a predicate offense.

A review of the history of the felony murder statute and the crime of arson reveals the legislative intent to retain the common-law definition of arson for purposes of construing the felony murder statute. The common-law definition of arson referred only to the burning of another's dwelling house and appurtenances. At common law, the structure burned must be a habitable dwelling. The house at issue in the present case was not a dwelling house. Because the prosecution charged the defendants with felony murder with the predicate felony being the burning of other real property, the trial court properly determined that the felony murder charge was improperly lodged. Similarly, the Court of Appeals properly construed the word "arson" in accordance with its common-law definition.

We remand this case for trial on the remaining counts.

[Footnotes and citations omitted. Concurring and dissenting opinions omitted.]

The People, Plaintiff and Respondent

v.

Edmond James Ramos,
Defendant and Appellant

No. B098452.

Court of Appeal of California, Second
Appellant District, Division One
52 Cal. App. 4th 300;
60 Cal. Rptr. 2d 523; 1997

January 27, 1997, Decided

VOGEL (Miriam A.), J.

Is a dead man "temporarily absent" from his house? Since we doubt that he will ever return, we think not. We therefore reduce Edmond James Ramos's conviction of first degree burglary to second degree burglary and remand for resentencing.

FACTS

On November 23, 1994, Virgil Wagner died at home from natural causes. His daughter-in-law, Marilyn Ball, was notified of his death, and when she went to Wagner's house two days later, she found that a microwave and a VCR were missing. Although Ball locked the house when she left, there were at least two more unauthorized entries into the house and other items were taken. When the police investigated, they found Ramos's fingerprints inside Wagner's house. When he was arrested, Ramos told the police that he went to Wagner's house on November 23, knocked on the front door and, when no one answered, walked around to the back of the house. Since it appeared that no one was home, Ramos decided to go in and take something he could sell to obtain money to buy drugs. Ramos broke a window, entered the house, walked by Wagner's bedroom, looked in and saw a body on the bed. The body did not move, so Wagner entered the bedroom to get a closer look. When he saw Wagner's stiff body and his face "turned to the left with the eyes open," Ramos ran out the door, grabbing the VCR on his way.

Ramos was charged with five counts of first degree burglary. At trial, the People presented evidence of the November 23 entry plus others occurring before and after Wagner's death. During argument, the prosecutor conceded the later entries were second degree burglaries but argued that the November 23 entry was a first degree burglary because the house was "occupied" until Wagner's remains were removed. The jury convicted Ramos of three counts, finding the November 23 entry was a first degree burglary and two other entries (after Wagner's death) were second degree burglaries. Ramos appeals.

DISCUSSION

(1) Ramos contends the evidence is insufficient to support his first degree burglary conviction because it shows that Wagner was dead at the time Ramos entered his house on November 23. We agree.

To prove first degree burglary of an inhabited dwelling, the People must present evidence that the house is "currently being used for dwelling purposes, whether occupied or not." What this means is that a dwelling is inhabited if the occupant is absent but intends to return and to use the house as a dwelling. . . . To put it plainly, a dead body is not using a house for a "dwelling" and there is no way to say that a dead man is going to return or that he has an "intent" of any kind. It follows that, at the time of Ramos's entry on November 23, the house was not occupied within the meaning of section.

We reject as metaphysical sophistry the Attorney General's suggestion that the house was inhabited because Wagner "went to sleep, fully intending to remain in his house." By the time Ramos got there, Wagner was dead and, to the best of our knowledge, unable to entertain any intent of any kind. The house was no longer occupied. . . . "a house left unoccupied by its occupant's death is not an 'occupied' dwelling"; . . . the inhabitant's death renders a dwelling uninhabited "since someone must 'live' in a dwelling for it to be 'inhabited' . . .

It follows that Ramos's first degree burglary conviction must be reduced to second degree burglary.

DISPOSITION

The judgment is modified by reducing Ramos's conviction of first degree burglary to second degree burglary and, as modified, is affirmed and remanded to the trial court for resentencing, with directions to not impose the two 5-year enhancements pursuant to section 667, subdivision (a), to reconsider Ramos's presentence conduct credits, to exercise the discretion granted . . .and, after resentencing, to issue a corrected abstract of judgment.

[Footnotes and concurrences deleted.]

Cases Relating to Chapter 8

Offenses Involving Theft

Gerald Lattimore, William Lattimore, and James Hunt

v.

United States

**District of Columbia Court of Appeals
684 A.2d 357 (1996)**

Newman, Senior Judge:

Gerald Lattimore was convicted, after a jury trial, of armed robbery and possession of a fire-arm during a crime of violence. William Lattimore and James Hunt were convicted by the same jury of armed robbery. On this appeal, they argue there was insufficient evidence to prove the elements of armed robbery and urge reversal. We affirm.

I.

On June 11, 1993, at approximately 9:55 P.M., Genaro Villegas and his sister-in-law, Alipia Sanchez, left the Rhode Island Avenue Metro station headed for his home. As they were walking by the bus area, four men accosted them. Gerald Lattimore struck Villegas, pointed a revolver into his side and demanded money. Hunt held Villegas while William Lattimore patted him down and fully searched him. William Lattimore pulled a wallet from Villegas' pocket, opened it, looked inside, and threw it back. Villegas opened the wallet and gave William Lattimore his payroll check of $431. William Lattimore took the check, looked at it, and threw it back at Villegas.

Angered that their victim had no money, Gerald Lattimore struck Villegas across the face and on the side of his face with the handle of his gun while Hunt continued to restrain him and William Lattimore further searched him. During the entire confrontation, a fourth suspect restrained Sanchez and prevented her from seeking help. This suspect was never apprehended.

Because of a recent string of robberies, Metro Transit Officer Paul Ludwig was stationed at the back of the parking lot, approximately sixty yards from the bus area. When he observed the confrontation between the bandits and the victims, Ludwig called for backup and rode his mountain bike to the scene. When Ludwig announced himself, the bandits turned and ran. Ludwig apprehended James Hunt approximately four yards from the scene. William Lattimore was apprehended on Bryant Street, approximately two and a half blocks from the scene and approximately three minutes after the robbery. Out of breath, William immediately remarked he was not the one with the gun. Gerald Lattimore was arrested a few minutes later further down on Bryant Street. No weapon was ever recovered.

At trial, Sanchez and Officer Ludwig each positively identified all three appellants as Villegas' assailants. Villegas, who suffered multiple injuries requiring stitches and a four-day hospitalization, testified as to the confrontation but could not identify any of the individual appellants or describe any distinguishing characteristics.

II.

Appellants do not dispute the facts, but argue that they are legally insufficient to sustain their respective armed robbery convictions. Rather, they contend that the government failed to prove some of the elements of armed robbery, namely "taking," "asportation" or "carrying away," and "intent to steal." .... Specifically, they allege that, because none of Villegas' property was in fact taken from the scene of the incident, nor possessed by appellants for a significant period of time, the evidence is only sufficient to support an attempted robbery charge or assault with intent to commit robbery. . . . We disagree.

To determine whether evidence is sufficient to sustain a conviction, we view the evidence in the light most favorable to the government, giving due deference to "the jury's prerogative to weigh the evidence, determine witnesses' credibility, and draw reasonable inferences from the evidence presented." .... The evidence need not compel a finding of guilt or negate every possible inference of innocence. . . . Thus, if a trier of fact could find the essential elements of the crime beyond a reasonable doubt, we must affirm the convictions. . . . Conversely, we must reverse "if 'there is no evidence upon which a reasonable mind might fairly conclude guilt beyond a reasonable doubt.'" . . .

In the District of Columbia, robbery retains its common law elements. . . . Thus the government must prove larceny and assault. . . . To support a robbery conviction, the government must prove that there was "(1) a felonious taking, (2) accompanied by an asportation [or carrying away], of (3) personal property of value, (4) from the person of another or in his presence, (5) against his will, (6) by violence or by putting him in fear, (7) *animo furandi* [the intention to steal]." . . . Additionally, to prove armed robbery, the government must establish that, at the time of the offense, the defendant was armed with a firearm. . . .

Because robbery is comprised of larceny and assault, . . . , we examine what constitutes a "taking" and "asportation" of property in larceny. It is not disputed that an assault against Villegas took place; therefore, if the evidence supports a taking, asportation, and the requisite intent, the evidence will sufficiently support appellants' armed robbery convictions.

An individual has committed larceny if that person "without right took and carried away property of another with the intent to permanently deprive the rightful owner thereof.". . . . It does not matter that the person possessed the property for only a brief amount of time or that the person was apprehended before removing the goods from the owner's premises. . . .

In the present case the fact that the Lattimores and Hunt never kept any of Villegas' property does not purge their original taking and asportation of his property. . . . During the confrontation appellants acquired at gunpoint Villegas' wallet and paycheck valued at $431. Both items were clearly within their complete and exclusive control as they had the opportunity to keep (or permanently remove from Villegas' person) the wallet and check if they so chose. Their complete and exclusive control is demonstrated as they physically held the items in their hands while restraining and threatening to shoot Villegas. Moreover, they retained their control over Villegas (and any of his property) by pistol-whipping Villegas after finding nothing of value on him. It is irrelevant whether they personally took the wallet and check out of his pocket or whether Villegas handed them both items for a jury could properly find that Villegas was reacting to their threats and demands for money.

An individual may hold onto the property for only a brief amount of time and still commit a larceny. . . . Here it does not matter that the appellants might have held the check and the wallet for only a brief amount of time before throwing both back at Villegas. A jury could properly find that they took the items with the intention of permanently depriving Villegas of his property. The fact that the property did not meet their needs or that they did not depart from the crime scene with any property does not absolve them of their original taking and asportation. In fact, "the slightest moving of an object from its original location may constitute an asportation." . . .

Because the government established that there was a taking and asportation in conjunction with proof of the appellants' intent to take Villegas' property, the government has sufficiently proven the crime of larceny. Combined with the assault in this case, the government also has established the elements of robbery. . . . Finally, because at the time of the robbery appellants were armed with a firearm, there is sufficient evidence to support their armed robbery convictions,. . . .

Affirmed.

Footnotes and citations omitted. Concurring and dissenting opinions omitted.

State of Ohio, Plaintiff-Appellee

v.

Robert Cunningham,
Defendant-Appellant

Appellate Case No. 08-CA-09

Court of Appeals of Ohio,
Second Appellate District, Clark County
2008 Ohio 5164;
2008 Ohio App. LEXIS 4354

October 3, 2008, Rendered

OPINION

BROGAN, J.

A jury found Robert Cunningham guilty of child enticement, extortion, coercion, and menacing by stalking, and he was sentenced to prison. In this appeal, he directly challenges only his child enticement and extortion convictions. He contends that the child enticement statute under which he was convicted is unconstitutional, that there is insufficient evidence to support a finding of extortion, and that the prosecutor committed misconduct during closing arguments. We recently held unconstitutional the child enticement statute used to convict him, so we will vacate that conviction. But the remainder of the trial court's judgment will be affirmed.

H.D., a twelve-year old girl, was the victim of Robert Cunningham's crimes for the second time in as many years. In 2005, he was convicted of gross sexual imposition for sexually assaulting her and another young girl. He was classified as a sexually-oriented offender and received probation. He was ordered not to have any contact with his two victims or unsupervised contact with other minors. In May 2007, his probation ended early based in part on his probation officer's

belief that he had consistently obeyed the rules of his probation.

Some time in 2006, H.D. received an envelope in the mail. She thought that it was from her grandmother because her return address sticker was on it. Upon opening it, however, she quickly discovered that Cunningham had written the letter inside. More disguised letters followed, some with money, most telling her how much he longed to see her again. Some of these letters she hid away in a dresser drawer; others she threw out. Cunningham admonished her in several letters not to tell anyone that he was writing to her. For a time, she didn't.

One day, in May 2007, H.D. was walking home from school, as she usually did, with her cousin. They suddenly heard a voice behind them. "H.D.," they heard someone call. Turning around, they were surprised to see Cunningham driving along behind them. He pulled along side them and stopped. They walked up to his car and he talked to H.D. for several minutes. She encountered him this way several more times. Sometimes, he gave her money. Once, he asked her to come to his house, and he wanted her to bring a friend. Many times he asked her to get in his car so that he could drive her home, but H.D. never did. He would also instruct her, "don't tell your grandma or anybody that you saw me or I saw you."

H.D. soon discovered that he also wanted her to do something. Every time he talked to her he demanded that she tell everyone that her testimony that had helped convict him two years earlier was a lie. She refused so he threatened her. He passed her notes that he had written. "When you're done reading it, give it back to me," he would tell her. He wrote the notes, as he later admitted to police, as threats to pressure her into recanting. When he was arrested, police found in his wallet several notes, which he had not yet shown H.D., many of which contained threats, spelled out in X-rated language, that if she did not tell people that she had lied, he would expose her past sexual activity to her parents. He also threatened to expose this when she resisted talking to him. He held up an envelope for her to see and threatened that if she would not see him, he would use it to send a letter to her parents. Although

H.D. did not know what the letter said, based on the notes that she had read and what she knew that he knew she felt fairly certain what it was that he was threatening to expose. Cunningham was successful in making her afraid. Her step-mother, Sarah, noticed a change come over H.D. when confronted with issues dealing with him. She was just not herself. She "gets upset, very nervous, sort of shameful," Sarah noticed. "[S]he just kind of coils back into herself."

The last time H.D. encountered him before he was arrested was while she walked home from school with a group of friends. As they neared one of their houses, Cunningham pulled along side them and began trying to talk to H.D. When Katie (the mother of the friend whose house they were near) stepped outside her house, she saw the group placing themselves between H.D. and Cunningham's car. Thinking that they were fighting, she marched up to the group in time to hear Cunningham say to H.D., "It's okay, honey. You can get in." Grasping the situation, she quickly grabbed a panicked and scared looking H.D. and brought her into her home. H.D.'s step-mother, Sarah, soon received a phone call from a distressed-sounding Katie. Sarah arrived to find her step-daughter visibly upset. Once they were home, Sarah and H.D. talked about what had happened. Eventually, she showed Sarah the hidden letters from Cunningham. The following day Sarah called the police, and Cunningham was eventually arrested.

The grand jury indicted him on charges of child enticement with a specification of a prior offense, extortion, coercion, and menacing by stalking with two specifications--a prior offense and a minor victim. A one-day jury trial was held in December 2007. All of the available letters and notes that Cunningham had written were shown—many read—to the jury. Despite Cunningham's objections, the trial judge admitted each into evidence. The following day closing arguments were made by both sides. While reminding the jury of the evidence against Cunningham, the prosecutor read, a second time, portions of a particularly graphic note. Later that same day, the jury returned from its deliberations and delivered its verdict: guilty, guilty, guilty, guilty.

The trial court sentenced Cunningham to seven and one-half years in prison--one year for child enticement, eighteen months for menacing by stalking, and five years for extortion. Cunningham now appeals his child enticement and extortion convictions based on four alleged errors.

. . . For his second assignment of error, Cunningham contends that the jury improperly found him guilty of extortion because the State failed to present legally-sufficient evidence for each essential element. 'Sufficiency' is a term of meaning that legal standard which is applied to determine . . . whether the evidence is legally sufficient to support the jury verdict as a matter of law." . . .That is, tautology-free, "whether [a] rational finder of fact, viewing the evidence in a light most favorable to the state, could have found the essential elements of [extortion] proven beyond a reasonable doubt." . . . We will marshal the evidence that the State presented to determine whether it is sufficient to support the essential elements.

The pertinent portion of the extortion statute, the portion used to find Cunningham guilty, reads: "No person, with purpose to obtain any valuable thing or valuable benefit or to induce another to do an unlawful act, shall do any of the following: . . . Expose or threaten to expose any matter tending to subject any person to hatred, contempt, or ridicule, or to damage any person's personal or business repute, or to impair any person's credit." Cunningham contests the sufficiency of the State's evidence for three essential elements. He contends that there is insufficient evidence to prove, first, that he sought to obtain a "valuable thing or valuable benefit"; second, that he sought an "unlawful act"; and third, that he threatened to expose a "matter tending to subject any person to hatred, contempt, or ridicule, or to damage any person's personal . . . repute.". . .

. . . Cunningham does not challenge the State's evidence per se but raises a question of law: how the phrase "valuable thing or valuable benefit" ought to be construed. He asserts that it must be construed to mean that the State must prove a "valuable thing or valuable benefit" that is tangible. If it were construed to include intangibles, he argues, nothing would distinguish extortion from the separate statutory offense of coercion as the elements and evidence would be the same for both. In his case, he points out, he was found guilty of extortion for trying to pressure H.D., using threats, into saying that she lied. He was also found guilty of coercion for trying to coerce her, using threats, to say that she lied. In short, he was found guilty of two offenses based on the same conduct (threatening H.D.) that sought the same intangible thing (her recantation).

The question raised, then, is one of statutory meaning, which is the court's job to determine. Our duty is to give effect to the Legislature's intended meaning. ...

The meaning of "valuable thing and valuable benefit" is clear and unambiguous. Common usage of the words "thing" and "benefit" includes reference to intangibles. . . . Moreover, prior cases have found intangibles encompassed by the meaning of "thing" and "benefit." . . .

Moreover, even when viewed in the context of the criminal code, "thing" and "benefit" retain their common meanings. Cunningham's assertion that this interpretation results in identical offenses is wrong, and is based on a misreading of his cited authorities. Far from supporting his conclusion they actually support ours. He primarily relies on the Model Penal Code and the U.S. Supreme Court's use of it . . . The correct reading of these [cases], however, reveals that neither the Code nor *Scheidler* restricts "property" to tangible property. On the contrary, *Scheidler* expressly rejected the notion. Indeed, the Court did not exclude the possibility under the Hobbs Act "that liability might be based on obtaining something as intangible as another's right to exercise exclusive control over the use of a party's business assets."

. . . Said the Court, citing the Model Code, while coercion and extortion certainly overlap to the extent that extortion necessarily involves the use of coercive conduct to obtain property, there has been and continues to be a recognized difference between these two crimes." The recognized difference to which *Scheidler* refers is extortion's requirement that one "obtains [the] property of another."

Similarly, under Ohio law, while coercive conduct is necessary for extortion, it is not sufficient. Although the same coercive conduct

can underlie both offenses, the purpose and effect of the conduct differs. The language of these two offenses bears this out. On the one hand, coercion requires proof of a "purpose to coerce another into taking or refraining from action concerning which the other person has a legal freedom of choice." The effect is to deprive another of the freedom to act. Extortion, on the other hand, requires proof of a "purpose to obtain any valuable thing or valuable benefit or to induce another to do an unlawful act." The effect of extortion is to coerce another in order to obtain something to which the extorter has no right. The important distinction, then, is extortion's additional evidentiary requirement of an intent to obtain something. It matters not that the thing sought is intangible.

Cunningham sought to obtain an intangible "valuable benefit" from H.D. Despite his assertions to the contrary, we are unconvinced that he was seeking to obtain her recantation for its own sake. Rather, we think that he wanted to obtain the valuable benefits that her recantation would bring--benefits such as the ability to deny that he had committed a crime, which would help restore his reputation and permit him to challenge his conviction. That he sought these benefits, and not simply the recantation, is a permissible inference that a reasonable juror could, and most likely would, draw from the evidence.

A rational juror, then, viewing the evidence offered in support of this element in the light most favorable to the State, and drawing all reasonable inferences, could find that Cunningham threatened H.D. into recanting because he wanted to obtain the "valuable benefits" that the recantation would bring. Therefore, we find that the evidence in support of this element is legally sufficient.

. . . Cunningham next asserts that the evidence is not sufficient to find that he made threats to induce another to do an "unlawful act." It would not be unlawful, he argues, for H.D. to recant. To prove extortion, the State needed to show the alleged extorter threatened another with the purpose either to obtain a valuable thing or benefit, or alternatively, to induce another to do an "unlawful act." Because "valuable benefit" and "unlawful act" are disjunctive, the evidence need show only one. We just determined that there is sufficient evidence to find that Cunningham threatened H.D. because he wanted to obtain "valuable benefits." As a result, we do not have to determine also whether recanting would be an "unlawful act."

. . . Finally, Cunningham asserts that there is insufficient evidence that the "matter" that he threatened to expose would tend to subject H.D. to "hatred, contempt, or ridicule, or to damage" her reputation. Here, he does challenge the State's evidence directly. He argues that the State presented no evidence that the envelope with which he threatened H.D. contained tell of such a matter. Therefore, he concludes, without knowing what was inside, the jury could not have properly concluded that it concerned a matter that could be characterized in the way required by the extortion statute.

Although Cunningham raises only an issue of fact, we begin with an issue of law, namely, the meaning of "matter." Again, we need not engage the rules of statutory construction because the meaning of "matter" is clear and unambiguous. Turning to the dictionary for guidance on common usage, we find the word "matter" pertinently defined as a "subject of concern, feeling, or action." . . . A matter, then, refers to a vaguely specified concern. Cunningham admitted to police that he had written the notes intending to pressure H.D. into recanting. All of the available notes that he had written were admitted into evidence and were before the jury. The common subject that links them

together is H.D.'s sexual relationships. We suspect that few would disagree that a young girl would be concerned to prevent others from knowing this information. Further, it is not hard to accept the notion that exposure of this subject could subject a young girl to the opprobrium of others and consequent damage to her reputation. Cunningham must have thought so; otherwise, how would his threats create the fear in her that he needed to force her to recant?

Cunningham's argument that H.D. did not know the precise content of the envelope is unavailing because the exact language is immaterial. Regardless of the exact words used, a reasonable juror could find that the matter that he threatened to expose was one that would tend to damage her reputation. Therefore, there is sufficient evidence to meet this element.

The purpose behind Cunningham's threats was broader than just to coerce a particular course of action. He also used fear in an attempt to get something to which he was not entitled. We hold that when viewing the evidence in the light most favorable to the State, and drawing all reasonable inferences, a reasonable juror could find evidence to support each of the contested elements of the crime of extortion. Accordingly, we overrule Cunningham's second assignment of error. . . .

[Other issues are omitted].

[Footnotes omitted.]

Cases Relating to Chapter 9

Forgery and Other Fraud Offenses

The State of New Mexico
v.
Bradley Wasson

Court of Appeals of New Mexico
125 N.M. 656 (1998)

ARMIJO, Judge.

The State appeals the district court's order dismissing three counts of forgery arising from allegations that Defendant signed his brother's name to a set of traffic citations issued by a sheriff's deputy. Because we determine that these allegations fall within the forgery statute, NMSA 1978, Section 30-16-10(A) (1963), we reverse the district court's order and remand for further proceedings consistent with this opinion.

I. BACKGROUND

On February 28, 1997, a San Juan County sheriff's deputy stopped a vehicle driven by Defendant. According to the sheriff's deputy, Defendant identified himself as "Ryan Wasson" and said his birth date was September 14, 1978. After determining that there was no driver's license corresponding to the name and date of birth given by Defendant, the sheriff's deputy issued three traffic citations for failure to stop at a stop sign, no insurance, and no driver's license. Defendant allegedly signed the name "Ryan Wasson" to all three traffic citations. The sheriff's deputy later ascertained that "Ryan Wasson" is Defendant's brother.

On March 27, 1997, the State filed a criminal information alleging that Defendant committed three counts of forgery by mak-

ing false signatures on the traffic citations. Defendant waived the preliminary examination on March 13, 1997, and responded with a motion to dismiss all the forgery charges on June 12, 1997. Defendant's motion asserted that his alleged conduct did not constitute the crime of forgery or, in the alternative, that his alleged conduct could be prosecuted only under the statute making it a petty misdemeanor to conceal one's identity. . . .

On June 23, 1997, the district court granted Defendant's motion to dismiss based on its conclusion that Defendant destroyed the legal efficacy of the traffic citations by signing his brother's name on them. Without any legal efficacy, the district court reasoned, the citations could not evince any intent to injure or defraud Defendant's brother. This appeal followed.

II. DISCUSSION

A. Standard of Review

For purposes of this appeal, we assume the truth of the factual allegations in the State's pleadings. . . . Defendant's motion to dismiss does not attempt to contradict these allegations, . . . , and thus it presents a purely legal issue of whether forgery charges can be predicated on Defendant's alleged conduct, . . .

Whether forgery charges can be predicated on Defendant's alleged conduct is a question of statutory interpretation to which we afford *de novo* review. . . . "The language of penal statutes should be given a reasonable or common sense construction consonant with the objects of the legislation, and the evils sought to be overcome should be given special attention." . . . .

B. Legal Efficacy of Uniform Traffic Citations

We first address the district court's conclusion that forgery charges could not be predicated on the traffic citations because Defendant destroyed their legal efficacy by signing his brother's name on them. The forgery statute provides, in relevant part, that "forgery consists of . . . falsely making or altering any signature to, or any part of, any writing purporting to have any legal efficacy with intent to injure or defraud." . . . . Interpreting the forgery statute, this Court has defined the element of "legal efficacy" in terms of " 'an instrument which upon its face could be made the foundation of liability' and 'an instrument good and valid for the purpose for which it was created.' The writing must be such that, if genuine, it would apparently operate to the legal prejudice of another." . . .

Although forgeries often involve documents relied upon to establish financial obligations and entitlements in the conduct of private business, . . . , they also may involve "any document required by law to be filed or recorded or necessary or convenient to the discharge of a public official's duties." . . .

Uniform traffic citations are relied upon in the discharge of a law enforcement officer's duties. When an arrested person does not contest the violations with which he or she is charged, the uniform traffic citation functions as an agreement to pay a penalty assessment. . . . When the arrested person declines to accept a penalty assessment notice, the uniform traffic citation functions as a complaint which provides the arrested person with notice to appear in court. . . . Moreover, uniform traffic citations may have legal efficacy because, "in order to secure his release, the arrested person must give his written promise to appear in court or to pay the penalty assessment prescribed.". . . . Even when the arrested person does not assume a financial obligation by agreeing to pay the penalty assessment, uniform traffic citations provide the foundation for liability because "it is a misdemeanor for any person to violate his written promise to appear in court, given to an officer upon issuance of a uniform traffic citation, regardless of the disposition of the charge for which the citation was issued." . . . For these reasons, other states have analogized a traffic citation to an appearance bond. . . .

Based on these authorities, we conclude that the forgery statute includes uniform traffic citations among the types of writings which may purport to have legal efficacy. The district court's concern that Defendant's false signatures may have destroyed the legal efficacy of the traffic citations at issue here does not alter this conclusion because the statute plainly is not limited to writings which actually have legal efficacy. Rather, the statute applies to any writing which purports to have legal efficacy, . . . , and the crime of forgery is complete as soon as the false signature is made on such a writing with the requisite intent, ... Here the allegations are sufficient to show that the traffic citations purported to have legal efficacy because Defendant allegedly made the signatures to appear as if they were valid acknowledgements that he agreed to pay a penalty assessment or appear in court to answer the charges. . . . Thus, it was error to dismiss the information based on a lack of purported legal efficacy.

C. Intent to Injure or Defraud

We next address the trial court's ruling that Defendant's conduct did not provide a basis for charging him with forgery because he had no intent to injure or defraud his brother, Ryan Wasson. The forgery statute does not require that the forger intend to injure or defraud a particular person. . . . In addition, there is no requirement that the person whom the forger intends to defraud or injure be the same person whose name is forged. . . . Hence, the inquiry is not limited to whether Defendant intended to injure or defraud his brother.

Moreover, a forgery conviction does not depend on whether Defendant actually succeeded in defrauding or injuring someone. The forgery is complete when the forger makes the false signature with the requisite intent, regardless of whether its falsity is detected before the forger absconds with the fruits of the crime or shifts liability to another person. . . . Thus, the forgery charges against Defendant are not precluded by the allegation that the arresting officer detected the falsity of the signatures before any further effort was made to hold Defendant or his brother liable for a penalty assessment or a failure to appear.

The current procedural posture of this case presents an additional obstacle to Defendant's contention that he lacked the requisite intent to sustain a forgery conviction. A defendant's knowledge or intent generally presents a question of fact for a jury to decide. . . . Further, since a defendant's intent is rarely subject to direct proof, it may be proven by circumstantial evidence. . . . Thus, in the context of a pretrial motion that simply tests the legal sufficiency of the criminal information and assumes the State's factual allegations to be true, we must limit our inquiry to the purely legal question of whether Defendant's false signatures on the traffic citations were capable of evincing an intent to injure or defraud anyone under the facts and circumstances alleged by the State. . . .

In answering this question, we need not speculate about what injury might befall the person whose name Defendant falsely signed on the traffic citations because we determine that such false signatures are sufficiently capable of evincing an intent to injure or defraud the arresting officer and the court in which the traffic citations are filed. The signatures on the traffic citations were to serve as Defendant's promise that he would pay the penalty assessments or appear in court. . . . The arresting officer was required to secure such a promise as a condition of Defendant's immediate release. . . .

However, making false signatures on the citations would render Defendant's promises meaningless, thus allowing him to obtain his release without actually agreeing to pay a penalty assessment or appear in court. . . . Under these circumstances, making a false signature could give rise to a reasonable inference that Defendant intended "to obtain the release, without incarceration, of someone not entitled to release.". . . . For the purposes of the forgery statute, such a fraudulent intent to obtain an individual's release from custody is essentially the same as the fraudulent intent involved in other cases where people forge documents in order to obtain something that is not rightfully theirs. . . . In addition, Defen-

dant's false signatures on the traffic citations may evince an intent to injure or defraud law enforcement officers or the courts by "concealing the true identity of the perpetrator of the alleged crime," . . . , " 'temporarily hiding from the authorities his prior criminal history[, and] hampering his identification by the police in future investigations.' "

. . . We determine that the forgery statute encompasses the above-described types of fraudulent intent. Thus, it was error to dismiss the information based on a lack of intent to injure or defraud. . . .

III. CONCLUSION

For the foregoing reasons, we reverse the district court's order of dismissal and remand for further proceedings consistent with this opinion.

IT IS SO ORDERED.

[Footnotes and citations omitted. Concurring and dissenting opinions deleted.]

The State of Washington,
Respondent
v.
Steven Edward Leyda,
Petitioner

No. 75866-2

Supreme Court of Washington
157 Wn.2d 335; 138 P.3d 610;
2006 Wash. LEXIS 594

May 24, 2005, Argued
July 20, 2006, Filed.

OPINION

Steven Leyda was convicted of four counts of second degree identity theft, one count of second degree theft, two counts of third degree theft, and one count of second degree possession of stolen property. The Court of Appeals affirmed all eight convictions. On appeal here, Leyda claims that his multiple second degree identity theft convictions under RCW 9.35.020 violate constitutional prohibitions against double jeopardy because he committed only one offense when he unlawfully obtained another person's credit card and subsequently used it four times. He contends, additionally, that the charging document was constitutionally deficient because it did not include an essential element of second degree identity theft and third degree theft--namely, the value of the items unlawfully obtained.

We agree with the Court of Appeals that value is not an essential element of either second degree identity theft or third degree theft. We determine, however, that the Court of Appeals employed the wrong unit of prosecution when it held that each use of a victim's means of identification or financial information constitutes a separate punishable act under RCW 9.35.020. We conclude that the unit of prosecution for identity theft is any one act of either knowingly "obtain[ing], possess[ing], us[ing], or transfer[ring] a means of identification or financial information of another person . . . with the intent to commit, or to aid or abet, any crime." . . . Applying this unit of prosecution to the facts of this case, we hold that Leyda's single course of proscribed criminal conduct should not have been divided into multiple offenses by the State and that doing so violated double jeopardy principles. Thus, we reverse three of the four second degree identity theft convictions and remand for resentencing. We, however, affirm both third degree theft convictions . . .

On October 21, 2002, Leyda and his girl friend, Nikkoleen Cooley, visited the Bon Marche store at the SeaTac Mall. At that time, Leyda had in his possession a Bon Marche credit card belonging to Cynthia Austin. Leyda gave Austin's card to Cooley, who used it at the store to purchase several items. Austin testified at trial that she was not acquainted with Leyda and had not given him or Cooley permission to use her credit card.

Five days after their October 21, 2002, visit to the SeaTac Bon Marche, Leyda and Cooley returned to that store. Using Austin's card, Cooley purchased a watch at the jewelry department. A few minutes later, Leyda and Cooley jointly used Austin's card to purchase items in another department of the Bon Marche.

On November 2, Leyda and Cooley again returned to the SeaTac Bon Marche. On this occasion, Cooley presented Austin's credit card to a cashier who, suspecting that the card was stolen, called the Bon Marche's Loss Prevention Department to verify the card's use. The cashier also asked Cooley for her address, Social Security number, and identification. Cooley responded that she needed to go to a car to get identification. Leyda and Cooley then exited the store with Austin's card.

While the cashier was questioning Cooley, a loss prevention employee at the Bon Marche telephoned Cynthia Austin. Austin informed the employee that she had not provided her credit card to anyone. Although the loss prevention employee subsequently tried to stop Cooley and Leyda from entering their car, Leyda was able to drive away. As Leyda did so, he threw Austin's credit card out the window. Federal Way police officers stopped the car a short time later and arrested Leyda and Cooley.

Leyda was charged in King County Superior Court with a separate count of identity theft for each of the four uses or attempted uses of Austin's credit card. He was charged, additionally, with two counts of third degree theft and one count of second degree theft based upon the three purchases that were made with Austin's card. Only the second degree theft charge specified the value of the property unlawfully obtained. Leyda was also charged with possession of stolen property based upon his possession of Austin's credit card. Cooley pleaded guilty to possession of stolen property in the third degree, a gross misdemeanor. Leyda went to trial, and a jury found him guilty on all counts. The Court of Appeals affirmed all of Leyda's convictions. . . .Leyda then petitioned this court for direct review and we granted his petition . . .

Leyda challenges his four identity theft convictions here, arguing that the unit of prosecution was the act of obtaining the identity information rather than its subsequent use. Leyda also challenges his second degree identity theft and third degree theft convictions on a separate ground, contending that the charging document was constitutionally deficient because it did not list the value of the items unlawfully obtained.

… Leyda claims that the information violated both the federal and Washington State

Constitutions because it did not include all essential elements of the charges of second degree identity theft and third degree theft. . . . Specifically, he argues that the value of the goods, services, credit, etc., obtained through the theft is an essential element of the crimes and, therefore, should have been set forth in the information. The Court of Appeals rejected this argument, holding that the reference to value in each of the challenged statutory provisions establishes "a ceiling above which the offense is elevated to a higher degree, not a floor that must exist to support the charge or conviction."

We recently addressed this issue . . ., we held that value is not an essential element of third degree theft, reasoning that value is only an essential element of the first and second degree theft statutes because these charging statutes explicitly state a "minimum value threshold." . . .

Turning to the challenges made to the identity theft charges, we hold that value is not an essential element of second degree identity theft and need not be alleged in the charging document. An "essential element is one whose specification is necessary to establish the very illegality of the behavior." . . . [W]e conclude that value cannot be an essential element of second degree identity theft given that the statute provides that the crime occurs even "when no credit, money, goods, services, or anything of value is obtained." By its very terms, the statute obviates value as an element of the crime of second degree identity theft and, thus, specification of the value is not necessary to establish the illegality of the behavior. However, similar to the higher degree theft statutes, value is an essential element that needs to be included when charging first degree identity theft because the statute provides a minimum value threshold of $1,500. Because Leyda was charged with second, not first, degree identity theft, we hold that the challenged charging information is not constitutionally infirm.

Leyda's principal claim is that he should have been convicted of only one count of second degree identity theft. Specifically, he asserts that the Court of Appeals misidentified the applicable unit of prosecution and that his multiple convictions under RCW 9.35.020 violate double jeopardy by punishing him multiple times for the same offense. This is an issue of first impression.

The double jeopardy provisions of the United States and Washington State Constitutions preclude convicting a defendant more than once under the same criminal statute if only one "unit" of the crime has been committed. . . . Thus, when a defendant is convicted of multiple violations of a single statute, the double jeopardy question focuses on what the legislature intended as the punishable act under the statute, i.e., what is the unit of prosecution. That question may be answered by examining the plain language of the relevant statute; however, we conclude that the legislature has failed to specifically define the unit of prosecution in the statute or if its intent in that regard is not clear, we must resolve the ambiguity in favor of the criminal defendant, thus preventing the State from turning a single transaction or course of conduct into multiple offenses.

The identity theft statute provides, in pertinent part, as follows:

(1) No person may knowingly obtain, possess, use, or transfer a means of identification or financial information of another person, living or dead, with the intent to commit, or to aid or abet, any crime.

(2)(a) Violation of this section when the accused or an accomplice uses the victim's means of identification or financial information and obtains an aggregate total of credit, money, goods, services, or anything else of value in excess of one thousand five hundred dollars in value shall constitute identity theft in the first degree. Identity theft in the first degree is a class B felony.

(b) Violation of this section when the accused or an accomplice uses the victim's means of identification or financial information and obtains an aggregate total of credit, money, goods, services, or anything else of value that is less than one thousand five hundred dollars in value, or when no credit, money, goods, services, or anything of value is obtained shall constitute identity theft in the second degree. Identity theft in the second degree is a class C felony.

Former RCW 9.35.020(1)-(2).

Leyda contends that the language of this statute and its legislative history reveal that the legislature intended that the unit of prosecution is each piece of another person's financial information or identification that is unlawfully obtained, not the number of uses or attempted uses to which the single piece of unlawfully obtained information or identification is put. Leyda reads the statute; as creating a continuing offense encompassing multiple uses of one individual's appropriated means of identification or financial information into a single unit of crime.

The State responds that because RCW 9.35.020 prohibits "use" of another's identification or information, it is apparent that the legislature intended that each use of the stolen identification or financial information "qualifies" as a unit of prosecution. The State reads the legislative history as revealing that when the legislature enacted the statute, it was primarily concerned with the harm caused by the use of the victim's stolen identity. It argues, therefore, that the legislature's intent was and is to make each discrete use of another's means of identification or financial information a unit of prosecution.

The Court of Appeals agreed with the State. In doing so, it relied heavily on policy arguments to support its conclusion that "[t]he plain language of RCW 9.35.020 indicates the legislature intended to penalize the use of stolen information." As a result, the Court of Appeals held that the identity theft unit of prosecution is each separate use of the victim's means of identification or financial information with intent to commit a crime.

Although we disagree with both the Court of Appeals and the dissent that RCW 9.35.020, on its face, unambiguously states what is the unit of prosecution and, consequently, resort to principles of statutory construction to determine the legislature's intent, we believe that neither the State's nor Leyda's position entirely reflects what the legislature intended as to the punishable act under the statute. For reasons we set forth hereafter, we conclude that the language of RCW 9.35.020 and its legislative history indicate that the legislature intended that the prosecution unit be any one act of either knowingly "obtain[ing], possess[ing],

us[ing], or transfer[ring]" a single piece of another's identification or financial information with the requisite unlawful intent. Former RCW 9.35.020(1) . . . Thus, once the accused has engaged in any one of the statutorily proscribed acts against a particular victim, and thereby committed the crime of identity theft, the unit of prosecution includes any subsequent proscribed conduct, such as using the victim's information to purchase goods after first unlawfully obtaining such information. . . .

. . . Contrary to the conclusion reached by the Court of Appeals, our reading of RCW 9.35.020 convinces us that the actual use of another's single means of identification or financial information may be an element of the offense of identity theft, but not always. The language of the statute reveals that the legislature intended to establish an offense which has two elements--first, the accused must have engaged in a proscribed act involving another's means of identity or financial information and, second, the accused must have done so with the intent to commit, or to aid or abet, a crime. ... As indicated by the use of the word "or," the proscribed acts are disjunctive. Thus, under the statute's express language, "use" is a way to commit identity theft, but it is not the only way. An individual also commits identity theft when he has either possessed, obtained, used, or transferred a means of another's identification or information with the requisite intent.

This is not to suggest that the statute does not allow an accused to be charged with multiple counts of identity theft. Under RCW 9.35.020(1), identity theft is a crime committed against each person whose identity has been stolen. Therefore, there would not be a constitutional violation if the State charged an accused with a different count each time he uses, possesses, transfers, or obtains a separate individual's means of identification or financial information. Thus, Leyda could have been properly charged with multiple counts of identity theft if he had obtained/ used, etc., the stolen credit cards of two or more persons. But, that is not the factual scenario here, the record showing that Leyda obtained, possessed, etc., a single credit card of one other individual, Ms. Austin. Thus, the State improperly charged him with multiple thefts of Austin's identity, who, common sense suggests, has only one identity that can be unlawfully appropriated.

...Under former RCW 9.35.020(2)(a) and (b), an offender who actually uses another's single piece of identification or financial information multiple times is subject to only one unit of prosecution, with the degree of the crime determined by the "aggregate" economic value of what he obtained while using the information or identification. . . .However, even if the offender does not use the stolen means of identification or information to obtain anything of value or if nothing of value is obtained by the use, the defendant has still committed the crime of identity theft due to an act of obtaining, possessing, or transferring another's identification or information.

... The legislative history of the identity theft statute supports our determination as well. As enacted, RCW 9.35.020(1) proscribed both the use and / or transfer of the unlawfully obtained information, indicating the legislature was concerned with more than just the misuse of the stolen identity. . . . Furthermore, as demonstrated by the findings it set forth, in enacting RCW 9.35.020, the legislature intended to criminalize the act by which another's identity is misappropriated, not the act(s) of using another's identity after stolen. It is, in our view, difficult to reconcile the stated focus on the act of improperly obtaining another's identity with the Court of Appeals' and the dissent's authoritative pronouncements that the legislature's clear intent was to penalize each use of the identity once obtained.

The initial statutory construct indicates that the legislature sought, by enacting RCW 9.35.020, to discourage individuals from stealing another person's identity in the first instance by defining identity theft as an improper acquisition of personal information. The legislature was primarily concerned about, and thereby sought to criminalize, the harm done to the victim by the actual theft of his or her identity, not the use of the identity after the initial theft as the State asserts. A subsequent change to the statute bears out that view of the statute at hand.

In 2001, the legislature amended the identity theft statute by dividing the crime into two degrees. . . .This legislative determination to bifurcate further supports the conclusion that the legislature intended that the punishable conduct encompass more than the act(s) of actually using the stolen identity. Recognizing that repeated misuse of the victim's identity, once stolen, results in ever increasing harm to the victim, RCW 9.35.020(2), as amended, elevates the degree and classification of the offense based on a sliding scale of aggregate economic damages. The more the accused uses the stolen identification or information, the more severe the offense charged (increasing from a class C to a class B felony), and the more severe the sentence imposed.

... Applying what the legislature intended as the proper unit of prosecution to the facts of this case shows that Leyda was wrongly charged with and convicted of four counts of identity theft. Under RCW 9.35.020(1), Leyda committed the crime of identity theft the moment he "obtained" a means of financial information (i.e., the Bon Marche credit card) of Cynthia Austin with the intent to commit, or to aid or abet, the crime of theft. He did not violate the statute each of the four times the stolen card was subsequently presented to make a purchase. Under former RCW 9.35.020(2), the prosecutor was required to determine whether Leyda used the stolen means of financial information and to determine the aggregate total of value obtained by use of that information. In this case, Leyda used the card and the aggregate total of goods obtained by the use was less than $ 1,500. Under RCW 9.35.020(2)(b), Leyda's single course of illegal conduct amounted to one count of second degree identity theft. He should have been charged and convicted accordingly. . . .

[Footnotes deleted.]

[Concurring and dissenting opinions omitted.]

Cases Relating to Chapter 10

Offenses Involving Morality and Decency

Miller

v.

California

Supreme Court of the United States
413 U.S. 15, (1973)

Mr. Chief Justice Burger delivered the opinion of the Court.

This is one of a group of "obscenity-pornography" cases being reviewed by the Court in a re-examination of standards enunciated in earlier cases involving what Mr. Justice Harlan called "the intractable obscenity problem." . . .

Appellant conducted a mass mailing campaign to advertise the sale of illustrated books, euphemistically called "adult" material. After a jury trial, he was convicted of violating California Penal Code § 311.2 (a), a misdemeanor, by knowingly distributing obscene matter, and the Appellate Department, Superior Court of California, County of Orange, summarily affirmed the judgment without opinion. Appellant's conviction was specifically based on his conduct in causing five unsolicited advertising brochures to be sent through the mail in an envelope addressed to a restaurant in Newport Beach, California. The envelope was opened by the manager of the restaurant and his mother. They had not requested the brochures; they complained to the police.

The brochures advertise four books entitled "Intercourse," "Man-Woman," "Sex Orgies Illustrated," and "An Illustrated History of Pornography," and a film entitled "Marital Intercourse." While the brochures contain some descriptive printed material, primar-

ily they consist of pictures and drawings very explicitly depicting men and women in groups of two or more engaging in a variety of sexual activities, with genitals often prominently displayed.

I.

This case involves the application of a State's criminal obscenity statute to a situation in which sexually explicit materials have been thrust by aggressive sales action upon unwilling recipients who had in no way indicated any desire to receive such materials. This Court has recognized that the States have a legitimate interest in prohibiting dissemination or exhibition of obscene material when the mode of dissemination carries with it a significant danger of offending the sensibilities of unwilling recipients or of exposure to juveniles. . . . It is in this context that we are called on to define the standards which must be used to identify obscene material that a State may regulate without infringing on the First Amendment as applicable to the States through the Fourteenth Amendment.

The dissent of Mr. Justice Brennan reviews the background of the obscenity problem, but since the Court now undertakes to formulate standards more concrete than those in the past, it is useful for us to focus on two of the landmark cases in the somewhat tortured history of the Court's obscenity decisions. In *Roth* v. *United States*, . . . (1957), the Court sustained a conviction under a federal statute punishing the mailing of "obscene, lewd, lascivious or filthy . . ." materials. The key to that holding was the Court's rejection of the claim that obscene materials were protected by the First Amendment. Five Justices joined in the opinion stating:

"All ideas having even the slightest redeeming social importance — unorthodox ideas, controversial ideas, even ideas hateful to the prevailing climate of opinion — have the full protection of the [First Amendment] guaranties, unless excludable because they encroach upon the limited area of more important interests. But implicit in the history of the First Amendment is the rejection of obscenity as utterly without redeeming social importance. . . . This is the same judgment expressed by this Court in *Chaplinsky* v. *New Hampshire*, . . .:

" '. . . There are certain well-defined and narrowly limited classes of speech, the prevention and punishment of which have never been thought to raise any Constitutional problem. *These include the lewd and obscene . . . . It has been well observed that such utterances are no essential part of any exposition of ideas, and are of such slight social value as a step to truth that any benefit that may be derived from them is clearly outweighed by the social interest in order and morality. . . .* ' [Emphasis by Court in *Roth* opinion.]

"We hold that obscenity is not within the area of constitutionally protected speech or press." . . .

Nine years later, in *Memoirs* v. *Massachusetts*, . . . (1966), the Court veered sharply away from the *Roth* concept and, with only three Justices in the plurality opinion, articulated a new test of obscenity. The plurality held that under the *Roth* definition

"as elaborated in subsequent cases, three elements must coalesce: it must be established that (a) the dominant theme of the material taken as a whole appeals to a prurient interest in sex; (b) the material is patently offensive because it affronts contemporary community standards relating to the description or representation of sexual matters; and (c) the material is utterly without redeeming social value." . . . .

The sharpness of the break with *Roth*, represented by the third element of the *Memoirs* test and emphasized by Mr. Justice White's dissent, . . ., was further underscored when the *Memoirs* plurality went on to state:

"The Supreme Judicial Court erred in holding that a book need not be 'unquali-

fiedly worthless before it can be deemed obscene.' A book cannot be proscribed unless it is found to be *utterly* without redeeming social value." . . .

While *Roth* presumed "obscenity" to be "utterly without redeeming social importance," *Memoirs* required that to prove obscenity it must be affirmatively established that the material is "*utterly* without redeeming social value." Thus, even as they repeated the words of *Roth*, the *Memoirs* plurality produced a drastically altered test that called on the prosecution to prove a negative, *i.e.*, that the material was "*utterly* without redeeming social value" — a burden virtually impossible to discharge under our criminal standards of proof. Such considerations caused Mr. Justice Harlan to wonder if the "*utterly* without redeeming social value" test had any meaning at all . . .

Apart from the initial formulation in the *Roth* case, no majority of the Court has at any given time been able to agree on a standard to determine what constitutes obscene, pornographic material subject to regulation under the States' police power. . . . We have seen "a variety of views among the members of the Court unmatched in any other course of constitutional adjudication." . . .This is not remarkable, for in the area of freedom of speech and press the courts must always remain sensitive to any infringement on genuinely serious literary, artistic, political, or scientific expression. This is an area in which there are few eternal verities.

The case we now review was tried on the theory that the California Penal Code § 311 approximately incorporates the three-stage *Memoirs* test, ... But now the *Memoirs* test has been abandoned as unworkable by its author, and no Member of the Court today supports the *Memoirs* formulation.

II.

This much has been categorically settled by the Court, that obscene material is unprotected by the First Amendment. . . . We acknowledge, however, the inherent dangers of undertaking to regulate any form of expression. State statutes designed to regulate obscene materials must be carefully limited. . . . As a result, we now confine the permissible scope of such regulation to works which depict or describe sexual conduct. That conduct must be specifically defined by the applicable state law, as written or authoritatively construed. A state offense must also be limited to works which, taken as a whole, appeal to the prurient interest in sex, which portray sexual conduct in a patently offensive way, and which, taken as a whole, do not have serious literary, artistic, political, or scientific value.

The basic guidelines for the trier of fact must be: (a) whether "the average person, applying contemporary community standards" would find that the work, taken as a whole, appeals to the prurient interest, . . .; (b) whether the work depicts or describes, in a patently offensive way, sexual conduct specifically defined by the applicable state law; and (c) whether the work, taken as a whole, lacks serious literary, artistic, political, or scientific value. We do not adopt as a constitutional standard the "*utterly* without redeeming social value" test of *Memoirs* v. *Massachusetts*, . . .; that concept has never commanded the adherence of more than three Justices at one time. . . . If a state law that regulates obscene material is thus limited, as written or construed, the First Amendment values applicable to the States through the Fourteenth Amendment are adequately protected by the ultimate power of appellate courts to conduct an independent review of constitutional claims when necessary. . . .

We emphasize that it is not our function to propose regulatory schemes for the States. That must await their concrete legislative efforts. It is possible, however, to give a few plain examples of what a state statute could define for regulation under part (b) of the standard announced in this opinion, . . .:

  (a) Patently offensive representations or descriptions of ultimate sexual acts, normal or perverted, actual or simulated.

  (b) Patently offensive representations or descriptions of masturbation, excretory functions, and lewd exhibition of the genitals.

Sex and nudity may not be exploited without limit by films or pictures exhibited or sold in places of public accommodation any more than live sex and nudity can be exhibited or sold without limit in such public places.

At a minimum, prurient, patently offensive depiction or description of sexual conduct must have serious literary, artistic, political, or scientific value to merit First Amendment protection. . . . For example, medical books for the education of physicians and related personnel necessarily use graphic illustrations and descriptions of human anatomy. In resolving the inevitably sensitive questions of fact and law, we must continue to rely on the jury system, accompanied by the safeguards that judges, rules of evidence, presumption of innocence, and other protective features provide, as we do with rape, murder, and a host of other offenses against society and its individual members.

Mr. Justice Brennan, author of the opinions of the Court, or the plurality opinions, in *Roth* v. *United States*. . .; *Jacobellis* v. *Ohio*. . .; *Ginzburg* v. *United States*, . . ., *Mishkin* v. *New York*, . . .; and *Memoirs* v. *Massachusetts*, . . ., has abandoned his former position and now maintains that no formulation of this Court, the Congress, or the States can adequately distinguish obscene material unprotected by the First Amendment from protected expression, ... Paradoxically, Mr. Justice Brennan indicates that suppression of unprotected obscene material is permissible to avoid exposure to unconsenting adults, as in this case, and to juveniles, although he gives no indication of how the division between protected and nonprotected materials may be drawn with greater precision for these purposes than for regulation of commercial exposure to consenting adults only. Nor does he indicate where in the Constitution he finds the authority to distinguish between a willing "adult" one month past the state law age of majority and a willing "juvenile" one month younger.

Under the holdings announced today, no one will be subject to prosecution for the sale or exposure of obscene materials unless these materials depict or describe patently offensive "hard core" sexual conduct specifically defined by the regulating state law, as written or construed. We are satisfied that these specific prerequisites will provide fair notice to a dealer in such materials that his public and commercial activities may bring prosecution. . . . If the inability to define regulated materials with ultimate, god-like precision altogether removes the power of the States or the Congress to regulate, then "hard core" pornography may be exposed without limit to the juvenile, the passerby, and the consenting adult alike, as, indeed, Mr. Justice Douglas contends. . . . In this belief, however, Mr. Justice Douglas now stands alone.

Mr. Justice Brennan also emphasizes "institutional stress" in justification of his change of view. Noting that "the number of obscenity cases on our docket gives ample testimony to the burden that has been placed upon this Court," he quite rightly remarks that the examination of contested materials "is hardly a source of edification to the members of this Court." . . . He also notes, and we agree, that "uncertainty of the standards creates a continuing source of tension between state and federal courts . . . . " "The problem is . . . that one cannot say with certainty that material is obscene until at least five members of this Court, applying inevitably obscure standards, have pronounced it so." . . . .

It is certainly true that the absence, since *Roth*, of a single majority view of this Court as to proper standards for testing obscenity has placed a strain on both state and federal courts. But today, for the first time since *Roth* was decided in 1957, a majority of this Court has agreed on concrete guidelines to isolate "hard core" pornography from expression protected by the First Amendment. Now we may abandon the casual practice of *Redrup* v. *New York*, . . . (1967), and attempt to provide positive guidance to federal and state courts alike.

This may not be an easy road, free from difficulty. But no amount of "fatigue" should lead us to adopt a convenient "institutional" rationale — an absolutist, "anything goes" view of the First Amendment — because it will lighten our burdens. "Such an abnegation of judicial supervision in this field would be inconsistent with our duty to uphold the constitutional guarantees." . . . . Nor should we remedy "tension between state and federal courts" by arbitrarily depriving the States of a power reserved to them under the Constitution, a power which they have enjoyed and exercised continuously from before the adoption of the First Amendment to this day. . . . "Our duty admits of no 'substitute for facing up to the tough individual prob-

lems of constitutional judgment involved in every obscenity case.' . . .

III.

Under a National Constitution, fundamental First Amendment limitations on the powers of the States do not vary from community to community, but this does not mean that there are, or should or can be, fixed, uniform national standards of precisely what appeals to the "prurient interest" or is "patently offensive." These are essentially questions of fact, and our Nation is simply too big and too diverse for this Court to reasonably expect that such standards could be articulated for all 50 States in a single formulation, even assuming the prerequisite consensus exists. When triers of fact are asked to decide whether "the average person, applying contemporary community standards" would consider certain materials "prurient," it would be unrealistic to require that the answer be based on some abstract formulation. The adversary system, with lay jurors as the usual ultimate factfinders in criminal prosecutions, has historically permitted triers of fact to draw on the standards of their community, guided always by limiting instructions on the law. To require a State to structure obscenity proceedings around evidence of a *national* "community standard" would be an exercise in futility.

As noted before, this case was tried on the theory that the California obscenity statute sought to incorporate the tripartite test of *Memoirs*. This, a "national" standard of First Amendment protection enumerated by a plurality of this Court, was correctly regarded at the time of trial as limiting state prosecution under the controlling case law. The jury, however, was explicitly instructed that, in determining whether the "dominant theme of the material as a whole . . . appeals to the prurient interest" and in determining whether the material "goes substantially beyond customary limits of candor and affronts contemporary community standards of decency," it was to apply "contemporary community standards of the State of California."

During the trial, both the prosecution and the defense assumed that the relevant "community standards" in making the factual determination of obscenity were those of the

State of California, not some hypothetical standard of the entire United States of America. Defense counsel at trial never objected to the testimony of the State's expert on community standards or to the instructions of the trial judge on "statewide" standards. On appeal to the Appellate Department, Superior Court of California, County of Orange, appellant for the first time contended that application of state, rather than national, standards violated the First and Fourteenth Amendments.

We conclude that neither the State's alleged failure to offer evidence of "national standards," nor the trial court's charge that the jury consider state community standards, were constitutional errors. Nothing in the First Amendment requires that a jury must consider hypothetical and unascertainable "national standards" when attempting to determine whether certain materials are obscene as a matter of fact. Mr. Chief Justice Warren pointedly commented in his dissent in *Jacobellis* v. *Ohio,* . . .:

> "It is my belief that when the Court said in *Roth* that obscenity is to be defined by reference to 'community standards,' it meant community standards — not a national standard, as is sometimes argued. I believe that there is no provable 'national standard' . . . . At all events, this Court has not been able to enunciate one, and it would be unreasonable to expect local courts to divine one."

It is neither realistic nor constitutionally sound to read the First Amendment as requiring that the people of Maine or Mississippi accept public depiction of conduct found tolerable in Las Vegas, or New York City. . . . People in different States vary in their tastes and attitudes, and this diversity is not to be strangled by the absolutism of imposed uniformity. As the Court made clear in *Mishkin* v. *New York*, . . ., the primary concern with requiring a jury to apply the standard of "the average person, applying contemporary community standards" is to be certain that, so far as material is not aimed at a deviant group, it will be judged by its impact on an average person, rather than a particularly susceptible or sensitive person — or indeed a totally insensitive one. . . . We hold that the requirement that the jury evaluate the materials with

reference to "contemporary standards of the State of California" serves this protective purpose and is constitutionally adequate.

IV.

The dissenting Justices sound the alarm of repression. But, in our view, to equate the free and robust exchange of ideas and political debate with commercial exploitation of obscene material demeans the grand conception of the First Amendment and its high purposes in the historic struggle for freedom. It is a "misuse of the great guarantees of free speech and free press . . . . " . . . . The First Amendment protects works which, taken as a whole, have serious literary, artistic, political, or scientific value, regardless of whether the government or a majority of the people approve of the ideas these works represent. "The protection given speech and press was fashioned to assure unfettered interchange of *ideas* for the bringing about of political and social changes desired by the people," . . . . But the public portrayal of hard-core sexual conduct for its own sake, and for the ensuing commercial gain, is a different matter.

There is no evidence, empirical or historical, that the stern 19th century American censorship of public distribution and display of material relating to sex, . . ., in any way limited or affected expression of serious literary, artistic, political, or scientific ideas. On the contrary, it is beyond any question that the era following Thomas Jefferson to Theodore Roosevelt was an "extraordinarily vigorous period," not just in economics and politics, but in *belles lettres* and in "the outlying fields of social and political philosophies." We do not see the harsh hand of censorship of ideas — good or bad, sound or unsound — and "repression" of political liberty lurking in every state regulation of commercial exploitation of human interest in sex.

Mr. Justice Brennan finds "it is hard to see how state-ordered regimentation of our minds can ever be forestalled." . . .These doleful anticipations assume that courts cannot distinguish commerce in ideas, protected by the First Amendment, from commercial exploitation of obscene material. Moreover, state regulation of hard-core pornography so as to make it unavailable to nonadults, a regulation which Mr. Justice Brennan finds constitutionally permissible, has all the elements of "censorship" for adults; indeed even more rigid enforcement techniques may be called for with such dichotomy of regulation. . . . One can concede that the "sexual revolution" of recent years may have had useful byproducts in striking layers of prudery from a subject long irrationally kept from needed ventilation. But it does not follow that no regulation of patently offensive "hard core" materials is needed or permissible; civilized people do not allow unregulated access to heroin because it is a derivative of medicinal morphine.

In sum, we (a) reaffirm the *Roth* holding that obscene material is not protected by the First Amendment; (b) hold that such material can be regulated by the States, subject to the specific safeguards enunciated above, without a showing that the material is "*utterly* without redeeming social value"; and (c) hold that obscenity is to be determined by applying "contemporary community standards," . . . not "national standards." The judgment of the Appellate Department of the Superior Court, Orange County, California, is vacated and the case remanded to that court for further proceedings not inconsistent with the First Amendment standards established by this opinion. . . .

Vacated and remanded.

[Footnotes and citations omitted. Concurring and dissenting opinions omitted.]

Alberto R. Gonzales, Attorney General, Petitioner
v.
Leroy Carhart, et al. Alberto R. Gonzales, Attorney General, Petitioner
v.
Planned Parenthood Federation of America, Inc., et al.

550 U.S. 124; 127 S. Ct. 1610 (2007)

Justice Kennedy delivered the opinion of the Court.

These cases require us to consider the validity of the Partial-Birth Abortion Ban Act of 2003 (Act), 18 U.S.C. § 1531 (2000 ed., Supp. IV), a federal statute regulating abortion procedures. In recitations preceding its operative provisions the Act refers to the Court's opinion in *Stenberg v. Carhart*, 530 U.S. 914, 120 S. Ct. 2597, 147 L. Ed. 2d 743 (2000), which also addressed the subject of abortion procedures used in the later stages of pregnancy. Compared to the state statute at issue in *Stenberg*, the Act is more specific concerning the instances to which it applies and in this respect more precise in its coverage. We conclude the Act should be sustained against the objections lodged by the broad, facial attack brought against it.

In No. 05-380 (Carhart) respondents are LeRoy Carhart, William G. Fitzhugh, William H. Knorr, and Jill L. Vibhakar, doctors who perform second-trimester abortions. These doctors filed their complaint against the Attorney General of the United States in the United States District Court for the District of Nebraska. They challenged the constitutionality of the Act and sought a permanent injunction against its enforcement. *Carhart v. Ashcroft*, 331 F. Supp. 2d 805 (2004). In 2004, after a 2-week trial, the District Court granted a permanent injunction that prohibited the Attorney General from enforcing the Act in all cases but those in which there was no dispute the fetus was viable . . . The Court of Appeals for the Eighth Circuit affirmed. . . . We granted certiorari.

In No. 05-1382 (Planned Parenthood) respondents are Planned Parenthood Federation of America, Inc., Planned Parenthood Golden Gate, and the City and County of San Francisco. The Planned Parenthood entities sought to enjoin enforcement of the Act in a suit filed in the United States District Court for the Northern District of California. . . . The City and County of San Francisco intervened as a plaintiff. In 2004, the District Court held a trial spanning a period just short of three weeks, and it, too, enjoined the Attorney General from enforcing the Act. . . . The Court of Appeals for the Ninth Circuit affirmed. . . . We granted certiorari.

The Act proscribes a particular manner of ending fetal life, so it is necessary here, as it was in , to discuss abortion procedures in some detail. Three United States District Courts heard extensive evidence describing the procedures. In addition to the two courts involved in the instant cases the District

Court for the Southern District of New York also considered the constitutionality of the Act. It found the Act unconstitutional, . . ., and the Court of Appeals for the Second Circuit affirmed, . . . The three District Courts relied on similar medical evidence; indeed, much of the evidence submitted to the Carhart court previously had been submitted to the other two courts. . . . We refer to the District Courts' exhaustive opinions in our own discussion of abortion procedures.

Abortion methods vary depending to some extent on the preferences of the physician and, of course, on the term of the pregnancy and the resulting stage of the unborn child's development. Between 85 and 90 percent of the approximately 1.3 million abortions performed each year in the United States take place in the first three months of pregnancy, which is to say in the first trimester. . . . The most common first-trimester abortion method is vacuum aspiration (otherwise known as suction curettage) in which the physician vacuums out the embryonic tissue. Early in this trimester an alternative is to use medication, such as mifepristone (commonly known as RU-486), to terminate the pregnancy. . . . The Act does not regulate these procedures.

Of the remaining abortions that take place each year, most occur in the second trimester. The surgical procedure referred to as "dilation and evacuation" or "D&E" is the usual abortion method in this trimester. . . . Although individual techniques for performing D&E differ, the general steps are the same.

A doctor must first dilate the cervix at least to the extent needed to insert surgical instruments into the uterus and to maneuver them to evacuate the fetus. . . . The steps taken to cause dilation differ by physician and gestational age of the fetus. . . . A doctor often begins the dilation process by inserting osmotic dilators, such as laminaria (sticks of seaweed), into the cervix. The dilators can be used in combination with drugs, such as misoprostol, that increase dilation. The resulting amount of dilation is not uniform, and a doctor does not know in advance how an individual patient will respond. In general the longer dilators remain in the cervix, the more it will dilate. Yet the length of time doctors employ osmotic dilators varies. Some may keep dilators in the cervix for two days, while others use dilators for a day or less. . . .

After sufficient dilation the surgical operation can commence. The woman is placed under general anesthesia or conscious sedation. The doctor, often guided by ultrasound, inserts grasping forceps through the woman's cervix and into the uterus to grab the fetus. The doctor grips a fetal part with the forceps and pulls it back through the cervix and vagina, continuing to pull even after meeting resistance from the cervix. The friction causes the fetus to tear apart. For example, a leg might be ripped off the fetus as it is pulled through the cervix and out of the woman. The process of evacuating the fetus piece by piece continues until it has been completely removed. A doctor may make 10 to 15 passes with the forceps to evacuate the fetus in its entirety, though sometimes removal is completed with fewer passes. Once the fetus has been evacuated, the placenta and any remaining fetal material are suctioned or scraped out of the uterus. The doctor examines the different parts to ensure the entire fetal body has been removed. ....

Some doctors, especially later in the second trimester, may kill the fetus a day or two before performing the surgical evacuation. They inject digoxin or potassium chloride into the fetus, the umbilical cord, or the amniotic fluid. Fetal demise may cause contractions and make greater dilation possible. Once dead, moreover, the fetus' body will soften, and its removal will be easier. Other doctors refrain from injecting chemical agents, believing it adds risk with little or no medical benefit. ...

The abortion procedure that was the impetus for the numerous bans on "partial-birth abortion," including the Act, is a variation of this standard D&E. . . . The medical community has not reached unanimity on the appropriate name for this D&E variation. It has been referred to as "intact D&E," "dilation and extraction" (D&X), and "intact D&X." . . . For discussion purposes this D&E variation will be referred to as intact D&E. The main difference between the two procedures is that in intact D&E a doctor extracts the fetus intact or largely intact with only a few passes. There are no comprehensive statistics indicating what percentage of all D&Es are performed in this manner.

Intact D&E, like regular D&E, begins with dilation of the cervix. Sufficient dilation is essential for the procedure. To achieve intact extraction some doctors thus may attempt to dilate the cervix to a greater degree. This approach has been called "serial" dilation. . . . Doctors who attempt at the outset to perform intact D&E may dilate for two full days or use up to 25 osmotic dilators. . . .

In an intact D&E procedure the doctor extracts the fetus in a way conducive to pulling out its entire body, instead of ripping it apart. . . .

Intact D&E gained public notoriety when, in 1992, Dr. Martin Haskell gave a presentation describing his method of performing the operation. . . . In the usual intact D&E the fetus' head lodges in the cervix, and dilation is insufficient to allow it to pass. . . . Haskell explained the next step as follows:

"'At this point, the right-handed surgeon slides the fingers of the left [hand] along the back of the fetus and "hooks" the shoulders of the fetus with the index and ring fingers (palm down).

"'While maintaining this tension, lifting the cervix and applying traction to the shoulders with the fingers of the left hand, the surgeon takes a pair of blunt curved Metzenbaum scissors in the right hand. He carefully advances the tip, curved down, along the spine and under his middle finger until he feels it contact the base of the skull under the tip of his middle finger.

"'[T]he surgeon then forces the scissors into the base of the skull or into the foramen magnum. Having safely entered the skull, he spreads the scissors to enlarge the opening.

"'The surgeon removes the scissors and introduces a suction catheter into this hole and evacuates the skull contents. With the catheter still in place, he applies traction to the fetus, removing it completely from the patient.'" . . .

This is an abortion doctor's clinical description. Here is another description from a nurse who witnessed the same method performed on a 26 1/2-week fetus and who testified before the Senate Judiciary Committee:

"'Dr. Haskell went in with forceps and grabbed the baby's legs and pulled them down into the birth canal. Then he delivered the baby's body and the arms—everything but the head. The doctor kept the head right inside the uterus. . . .

"'The baby's little fingers were clasping and unclasping, and his little feet were kicking. Then the doctor stuck the scissors in the back of his head, and the baby's arms jerked out, like a startle reaction, like a flinch, like a baby does when he thinks he is going to fall.

"'The doctor opened up the scissors, stuck a high-powered suction tube into the opening, and sucked the baby's brains out. Now the baby went completely limp. . . .

"'He cut the umbilical cord and delivered the placenta. He threw the baby in a pan, along with the placenta and the instruments he had just used.'" . . .

Dr. Haskell's approach is not the only method of killing the fetus once its head lodges in the cervix, and "the process has evolved" since his presentation . . . Another doctor, for example, squeezes the skull after it has been pierced "so that enough brain tissue exudes to allow the head to pass through." . . . Still other physicians reach into the cervix with their forceps and crush the fetus' skull. . . . Others continue to pull the fetus out of the woman until it disarticulates at the neck, in effect decapitating it. These doctors then grasp the head with forceps, crush it, and remove it. . . .

Some doctors performing an intact D&E attempt to remove the fetus without collapsing the skull. . . . Yet one doctor would not allow delivery of a live fetus younger than 24 weeks because "the objective of [his] procedure is to perform an abortion," not a birth. . . . The doctor thus answered in the affirmative when asked whether he would "hold the fetus' head on the internal side of the [cervix] in order to collapse the skull" and kill the fetus before it is born. . . . Another doctor testified he crushes a fetus' skull not only to reduce its size but also to ensure the fetus is dead before it is removed. For the staff to have to deal with a fetus that has "some viability to it, some movement of limbs," according to this doctor, "[is] always a difficult situation." . . .

D&E and intact D&E are not the only second-trimester abortion methods. Doctors also may abort a fetus through medical induction. The doctor medicates the woman to induce labor, and contractions occur to deliver the fetus. Induction, which unlike D&E should occur in a hospital, can last as little as 6 hours but can take longer than 48. It accounts for about 5 percent of second-trimester abortions before 20 weeks of gestation and 15 percent of those after 20 weeks. Doctors turn to two other methods of second-trimester abortion, hysterotomy and hysterectomy, only in emergency situations because they carry increased risk of complications. In a hysterotomy, as in a cesarean section, the doctor removes the fetus by making an incision through the abdomen and uterine wall to gain access to the uterine cavity. A hysterectomy requires the removal of the entire uterus. These two procedures represent about .07% of second-trimester abortions. . . .

After Dr. Haskell's procedure received public attention, with ensuing and increasing public concern, bans on "'partial birth abortion'" proliferated. By the time of the decision, about 30 States had enacted bans designed to prohibit the procedure. . . . In 1996, Congress also acted to ban partial-birth abortion. President Clinton vetoed the congressional legislation, and the Senate failed to override the veto. Congress approved another bill banning the procedure in 1997, but President Clinton again vetoed it. In 2003, after this Court's decision in , Congress passed the Act at issue here. . . . On November 5, 2003, President Bush signed the Act into law. It was to take effect the following day. . . .

The Act responded to in two ways. First, Congress made factual findings. Congress determined that this Court in "was required to accept the very questionable findings issued by the district court judge," . . ., but that Congress was "not bound to accept the same factual findings," Congress found, among other things, that "[a] moral, medical, and ethical consensus exists that the practice of performing a partial-birth abortion . . . is a gruesome and inhumane procedure that is never medically necessary and should be prohibited."

Second, and more relevant here, the Act's language differs from that of the Nebraska statute struck down in . . . . The operative provisions of the Act provide in relevant part:

"(a) Any physician who, in or affecting interstate or foreign commerce, knowingly performs a partial-birth abortion and

thereby kills a human fetus shall be fined under this title or imprisoned not more than 2 years, or both. This subsection does not apply to a partial-birth abortion that is necessary to save the life of a mother whose life is endangered by a physical disorder, physical illness, or physical injury, including a life-endangering physical condition caused by or arising from the pregnancy itself. This subsection takes effect 1 day after the enactment.

"(b) As used in this section—

"(1) the term 'partial-birth abortion' means an abortion in which the person performing the abortion—

"(A) deliberately and intentionally vaginally delivers a living fetus until, in the case of a head-first presentation, the entire fetal head is outside the body of the mother, or, in the case of breech presentation, any part of the fetal trunk past the navel is outside the body of the mother, for the purpose of performing an overt act that the person knows will kill the partially delivered living fetus; and

"(B) performs the overt act, other than completion of delivery, that kills the partially delivered living fetus; and

"(2) the term 'physician' means a doctor of medicine or osteopathy legally authorized to practice medicine and surgery by the State in which the doctor performs such activity, or any other individual legally authorized by the State to perform abortions: Provided, however, That any individual who is not a physician or not otherwise legally authorized by the State to perform abortions, but who nevertheless directly performs a partial-birth abortion, shall be subject to the provisions of this section.

. . .

"(d)(1) A defendant accused of an offense under this section may seek a hearing before the State Medical Board on whether the physician's conduct was necessary to save the life of the mother whose life was endangered by a physical disorder, physical illness, or physical injury, including a life-endangering physical condition caused by or arising from the pregnancy itself.

"(2) The findings on that issue are admissible on that issue at the trial of the defendant. Upon a motion of the defendant, the court shall delay the beginning of the trial for not more than 30 days to permit such a hearing to take place.

"(e) A woman upon whom a partial-birth abortion is performed may not be prosecuted under this section, for a conspiracy to violate this section, or for an offense under section 2, 3, or 4 of this title based on a violation of this section." . . .

The Act also includes a provision authorizing civil actions that is not of relevance here. . . .

The District Court in Carhart concluded the Act was unconstitutional for two reasons. First, it determined the Act was unconstitutional because it lacked an exception allowing the procedure where necessary for the health of the mother. Second, the District Court found the Act deficient because it covered not merely intact D&E but also certain other D&Es.

The Court of Appeals for the Eighth Circuit addressed only the lack of a health exception. The court began its analysis with what it saw as the appropriate question--"whether 'substantial medical authority' supports the medical necessity of the banned procedure." . . . This was the proper framework, according to the Court of Appeals, because "when a lack of consensus exists in the medical community, the Constitution requires legislatures to err on the side of protecting women's health by including a health exception." The court rejected the Attorney General's attempt to demonstrate changed evidentiary circumstances since and considered itself bound by *Stenberg's* conclusion that a health exception was required. . . . It invalidated the Act.

The District Court in Planned Parenthood concluded the Act was unconstitutional "because it (1) pose[d] an undue burden on a woman's ability to choose a second trimester abortion; (2) [was] unconstitutionally vague; and (3) require[d] a health exception as set forth by . . . *Stenberg.*"

The Court of Appeals for the Ninth Circuit agreed. Like the Court of Appeals for the Eighth Circuit, it concluded the absence of a health exception rendered the Act unconstitutional. The court interpreted *Stenberg*

to require a health exception unless "there is consensus in the medical community that the banned procedure is never medically necessary to preserve the health of women." Even after applying a deferential standard of review to Congress' factual findings, the Court of Appeals determined "substantial disagreement exists in the medical community regarding whether" the procedures prohibited by the Act are ever necessary to preserve a woman's health.

The Court of Appeals concluded further that the Act placed an undue burden on a woman's ability to obtain a second-trimester abortion. The court found the textual differences between the Act and the Nebraska statute struck down in *Stenberg* insufficient to distinguish D&E and intact D&E. As a result, according to the Court of Appeals, the Act imposed an undue burden because it prohibited D&E.

Finally, the Court of Appeals found the Act void for vagueness. Abortion doctors testified they were uncertain which procedures the Act made criminal. The court thus concluded the Act did not offer physicians clear warning of its regulatory reach. Resting on its understanding of the remedial framework established by this . . ., the Court of Appeals held the Act was unconstitutional on its face and should be permanently enjoined.

II

. . . Whatever one's views concerning the *Casey* joint opinion, it is evident a premise central to its conclusion—that the government has a legitimate and substantial interest in preserving and promoting fetal life—would be repudiated were the Court now to affirm the judgments of the Courts of Appeals.

Casey involved a challenge to *Roe v. Wade*, 410 U.S. 113, 93 S. Ct. 705, 35 L. Ed. 2d 147 (1973). . . .

To implement its holding, *Casey* rejected both *Roe's* rigid trimester framework and the interpretation of *Roe* that considered all previability regulations of abortion unwarranted. . . . On this point *Casey* overruled the holdings in two cases because they undervalued the State's interest in potential life. . . .

We assume the following principles for the purposes of this opinion. Before viability, a State "may not prohibit any woman from making the ultimate decision to terminate her pregnancy." It also may not impose upon this right an undue burden, which exists if a regulation's "purpose or effect is to place a substantial obstacle in the path of a woman seeking an abortion before the fetus attains viability." On the other hand, "[r]egulations which do no more than create a structural mechanism by which the State, or the parent or guardian of a minor, may express profound respect for the life of the unborn are permitted, if they are not a substantial obstacle to the woman's exercise of the right to choose." *Casey*, in short, struck a balance. The balance was central to its holding. We now apply its standard to the cases at bar.

III

We begin with a determination of the Act's operation and effect. A straightforward reading of the Act's text demonstrates its purpose and the scope of its provisions: It regulates and proscribes, with exceptions or qualifications to be discussed, performing the intact D&E procedure.

Respondents agree the Act encompasses intact D&E, but they contend its additional reach is both unclear and excessive. Respondents assert that, at the least, the Act is void for vagueness because its scope is indefinite. In the alternative, respondents argue the Act's text proscribes all D&Es. Because D&E is the most common second-trimester abortion method, respondents suggest the Act imposes an undue burden. In this litigation the Attorney General does not dispute that the Act would impose an undue burden if it covered standard D&E.

We conclude that the Act is not void for vagueness, does not impose an undue burden from any overbreadth, and is not invalid on its face.

A

The Act punishes "knowingly perform[ing]" a "partial-birth abortion." It defines the unlawful abortion in explicit terms.

First, the person performing the abortion must "vaginally delive[r] a living fetus." The Act does not restrict an abortion procedure involving the delivery of an expired fetus. The Act, furthermore, is inapplicable to abortions that do not involve vaginal delivery (for instance, hysterotomy or hysterectomy). The Act does apply both previability and postviability because, by common understanding and scientific terminology, a fetus is a living organism while within the womb, whether or not it is viable outside the womb. We do not understand this point to be contested by the parties.

Second, the Act's definition of partial-birth abortion requires the fetus to be delivered "until, in the case of a head-first presentation, the entire fetal head is outside the body of the mother, or, in the case of breech presentation, any part of the fetal trunk past the navel is outside the body of the mother." The Attorney General concedes, and we agree, that if an abortion procedure does not involve the delivery of a living fetus to one of these "anatomical 'land-marks' "—where, depending on the presentation, either the fetal head or the fetal trunk past the navel is outside the body of the mother—the prohibitions of the Act do not apply.

Third, to fall within the Act, a doctor must perform an "overt act, other than completion of delivery, that kills the partially delivered living fetus." For purposes of criminal liability, the overt act causing the fetus' death must be separate from delivery. And the overt act must occur after the delivery to an anatomical landmark. This is because the Act proscribes killing "the partially delivered" fetus, which, when read in context, refers to a fetus that has been delivered to an anatomical landmark.

Fourth, the Act contains scienter requirements concerning all the actions involved in the prohibited abortion. To begin with, the physician must have "deliberately and intentionally" delivered the fetus to one of the Act's anatomical landmarks. If a living fetus is delivered past the critical point by accident or inadvertence, the Act is inapplicable. In addition, the fetus must have been delivered "for the purpose of performing an overt act that the [doctor] knows will kill [it]." If either intent is absent, no crime has occurred. This follows from the general principle that where scienter is required no crime is committed absent the requisite state of mind. . . .

B

Respondents contend the language described above is indeterminate, and they thus argue the Act is unconstitutionally vague on its face. As generally stated, the void-for-vagueness doctrine requires that a penal statute define the criminal offense with sufficient definiteness that ordinary people can understand what conduct is prohibited and in a manner that does not encourage arbitrary and discriminatory enforcement." . . . The Act satisfies both requirements.

The Act provides doctors "of ordinary intelligence a reasonable opportunity to know what is prohibited." . . . Indeed, it sets forth "relatively clear guidelines as to prohibited conduct" and provides "objective criteria" to evaluate whether a doctor has performed a prohibited procedure. . . . Unlike the statutory language in *Stenberg* that prohibited the delivery of a "'substantial portion'" of the fetus—where a doctor might question how much of the fetus is a substantial portion— the Act defines the line between potentially criminal conduct on the one hand and lawful abortion on the other. . . . Doctors performing D&E will know that if they do not deliver a living fetus to an anatomical landmark they will not face criminal liability.

This conclusion is buttressed by the intent that must be proved to impose liability. The Court has made clear that scienter requirements alleviate vagueness concerns. . . . The Act requires the doctor deliberately to have delivered the fetus to an anatomical landmark. Because a doctor performing a D&E will not face criminal liability if he or she delivers a fetus beyond the prohibited point by mistake, the Act cannot be described as "a trap for those who act in good faith . . .

Respondents likewise have failed to show that the Act should be invalidated on its face because it encourages arbitrary or discriminatory enforcement. Just as the Act's anatomical landmarks provide doctors with objective standards, they also "establish minimal guidelines to govern law enforcement." The scienter requirements narrow the scope of the Act's prohibition and limit prosecutorial discretion. It cannot be said that the Act "vests virtually complete discretion in the hands of [law enforcement] to determine whether the [doctor] has satisfied [its provisions]." . . . Respondents' arguments concerning arbitrary enforcement, furthermore, are somewhat speculative. This is a preenforcement challenge, where "no evidence has been, or could be, introduced to indicate whether the [Act] has been enforced in a discriminatory manner or with the aim of inhibiting [constitutionally protected conduct]." . . . The Act is not vague.

C

We next determine whether the Act imposes an undue burden, as a facial matter, because its restrictions on second-trimester abortions are too broad. A review of the statutory text discloses the limits of its reach. The Act prohibits intact D&E; and, notwithstanding respondents' arguments, it does not prohibit the D&E procedure in which the fetus is removed in parts.

1

The Act prohibits a doctor from intentionally performing an intact D&E. The dual prohibitions of the Act, both of which are necessary for criminal liability, correspond with the steps generally undertaken during this type of procedure. First, a doctor delivers the fetus until its head lodges in the cervix, which is usually past the anatomical landmark for a breech presentation. This step satisfies the overt-act requirement because it kills the fetus and is distinct from delivery. . . . The Act's intent requirements, however, limit its reach to those physicians who carry out the intact D&E after intending to undertake both steps at the outset.

The Act excludes most D&Es in which the fetus is removed in pieces, not intact. If the doctor intends to remove the fetus in parts from the outset, the doctor will not have the requisite intent to incur criminal liability. A doctor performing a standard D&E procedure can often "tak[e] about 10-15 'passes' through the uterus to remove the entire fetus." . . . Removing the fetus in this manner does not violate the Act because the doctor will not have delivered the living fetus to one of the anatomical landmarks or committed an additional overt act that kills the fetus after partial delivery.

A comparison of the Act with the Nebraska statute struck down in *Stenberg* confirms this point. The statute in *Stenberg* prohibited "'deliberately and intentionally delivering into the vagina a living unborn child, or a substantial portion thereof, for the purpose of performing a procedure that the person performing such procedure knows will kill the unborn child and does kill the unborn child.'" . . . The Court concluded that this statute encompassed D&E because "D&E will often involve a physician pulling a 'substantial portion' of a still living fetus, say, an arm or leg, into the vagina prior to the death of the fetus." . . . The Court also rejected the limiting interpretation urged by Nebraska's Attorney General that the statute's reference to a "procedure" that "'kill[s] the unborn child'" was to a distinct procedure, not to the abortion procedure as a whole.

Congress, it is apparent, responded to these concerns because the Act departs in material ways from the statute in *Stenberg*. It adopts the phrase "delivers a living fetus," instead of "'delivering . . . a living unborn child, or a substantial portion thereof,'" . . . The Act's language, unlike the statute in *Stenberg*, expresses the usual meaning of "deliver" when used in connection with "fetus," namely, extraction of an entire fetus rather than removal of fetal pieces. . . .The Act thus displaces the interpretation of "delivering" dictated by the Nebraska statute's reference to a "substantial portion" of the fetus. . . . In interpreting statutory texts courts use the ordinary meaning of terms unless context requires a different result. . . . Here, unlike in *Stenberg*, the language does not require a departure from the ordinary meaning. D&E does not involve the delivery of a fetus because it requires the removal of fetal parts that are ripped from the fetus as they are pulled through the cervix.

The identification of specific anatomical landmarks to which the fetus must be partially delivered also differentiates the Act from the statute at issue in *Stenberg*. The Court in *Stenberg* interpreted "'substantial portion'" of the fetus to include an arm or a leg. The Act's anatomical landmarks, by contrast, clarify that the removal of a small portion of the fetus is not prohibited. The landmarks also require the fetus to be delivered so that it is partially "outside the body of the mother." To come within the ambit of the Nebraska statute, on the other hand, a substantial portion of the fetus only had to be delivered into the vagina; no part of the fetus had to be outside the body of the mother before a doctor could face criminal sanctions.

By adding an overt-act requirement Congress sought further to meet the Court's objections to the state statute considered in *Stenberg*. . . . The Act makes the distinction the Nebraska statute failed to draw (but the Nebraska Attorney General advanced) by differentiating between the overall partial-abortion and the distinct overt act that kills the fetus. The fatal overt act must occur after delivery to an anatomical landmark, and it must be something "other than [the] completion of delivery." This distinction matters because, unlike intact D&E, standard D&E does not involve a delivery followed by a fatal act.

The canon of constitutional avoidance, finally, extinguishes any lingering doubt as to whether the Act covers the prototypical D&E procedure. "'[T]he elementary rule is that every reasonable construction must be resorted to, in order to save a statute from unconstitutionality.'" . . . It is true this longstanding maxim of statutory interpretation has, in the past, fallen by the wayside when the Court confronted a statute regulating abortion. The Court at times employed an antagonistic "'canon of construction under which in cases involving abortion, a permissible reading of a statute [was] to be avoided at all costs.'"

. . . *Casey* put this novel statutory approach to rest. . . . *Stenberg* need not be interpreted to have revived it. We read that decision instead to stand for the uncontroversial proposition that the canon of constitutional avoidance does not apply if a statute is not "genuinely susceptible to two constructions." . . . In *Stenberg* the Court found the statute covered D&E. Here, by contrast, interpreting the Act so that it does not prohibit standard D&E is the most reasonable reading and understanding of its terms.

2

Contrary arguments by respondents are unavailing. . . . [Argument that doctors may mistakenly violate law omitted. Court says scienter requirement prevents doctors who perform intact D&E unintentionally from being prosecuted.]

IV

Under the principles accepted as controlling here, the Act, as we have interpreted it, would be unconstitutional "if its purpose or effect is to place a substantial obstacle in the path of a woman seeking an abortion before the fetus attains viability." The abortions affected by the Act's regulations take place both previability and postviability; so the quoted language and the undue burden analysis it relies upon are applicable. The question is whether the Act, measured by its text in this facial attack imposes a substantial obstacle to late-term, but previability, abortions. The Act does not on its face impose a substantial obstacle, and we reject this further facial challenge to its validity.

A

The Act's purposes are set forth in recitals preceding its operative provisions. A description of the prohibited abortion procedure demonstrates the rationale for the congressional enactment. The Act proscribes a method of abortion in which a fetus is killed just inches before completion of the birth process. Congress stated as follows: "Implicitly approving such a brutal and inhumane procedure by choosing not to prohibit it will further coarsen society to the humanity of not only newborns, but all vulnerable and innocent human life, making it increasingly difficult to protect such life." The Act expresses respect for the dignity of human life.

Congress was concerned, furthermore, with the effects on the medical community and on its reputation caused by the practice of partial-birth abortion. The findings in the Act explain:

> "Partial-birth abortion . . . confuses the medical, legal, and ethical duties of physicians to preserve and promote life, as the physician acts directly against the physical life of a child, whom he or she had just delivered, all but the head, out of the womb, in order to end that life."

. . .

The government may use its voice and its regulatory authority to show its profound respect for the life within the woman. A central premise of the opinion was that the Court's precedents after *Roe* had "undervalue[d] the State's interest in potential life." The plurality opinion indicated "[t]he fact that a law which serves a valid purpose, one not designed to strike at the right itself, has the incidental effect of making it more difficult or more expensive to procure an abortion cannot be enough to invalidate it." This was not an idle assertion. The three premises of *Casey* must coexist. The third premise, that the State, from the inception of the pregnancy, maintains its own regulatory interest in protecting the life of the fetus that may become a child, cannot be set at naught by interpreting *Casey's* requirement of a health exception so it becomes tantamount to allowing a doctor to choose the abortion method he or she might prefer. Where it has a rational basis to act, and it does not impose an undue burden, the State may use its regulatory power to bar certain procedures and substitute others, all in furtherance of its legitimate interests in regulating the medical profession in order to promote respect for life, including life of the unborn.

The Act's ban on abortions that involve partial delivery of a living fetus furthers the Government's objectives. No one would dispute that, for many, D&E is a procedure itself laden with the power to devalue human life. Congress could nonetheless conclude that the type of abortion proscribed by the Act requires specific regulation because it implicates additional ethical and moral concerns that justify a special prohibition. Congress determined that the abortion methods it proscribed had a "disturbing similarity to the killing of a newborn infant," and thus it was concerned with "draw[ing] a bright line that clearly distinguishes abortion and infanticide," The Court has in the past confirmed the validity of drawing boundaries to prevent certain practices that extinguish life and are close to actions that are condemned. . . .

It is objected that the standard D&E is in some respects as brutal, if not more, than the intact D&E, so that the legislation accomplishes little. What we have already said, however, shows ample justification for the regulation. Partial-birth abortion, as defined by the Act, differs from a standard D&E because the former occurs when the fetus is partially outside the mother to the point of one of the Act's anatomical landmarks. It was reasonable for Congress to think that partial-birth abortion, more than standard D&E, "undermines the public's perception of the appropriate role of a physician during the delivery process, and perverts a process during which life is brought into the world." There would be a flaw in this Court's logic, and an irony in its jurisprudence, were we first to conclude a ban on both D&E and intact D&E was overbroad and then to say it is irrational to ban only intact D&E because that does not proscribe both procedures. In sum, we reject the contention that the congressional purpose of the Act was "to place a substantial obstacle in the path of a woman seeking an abortion."

B

The Act's furtherance of legitimate government interests bears upon, but does not resolve, the next question: whether the Act has the effect of imposing an unconstitutional burden on the abortion right because it does not allow use of the barred procedure where "'necessary, in appropriate medical judgment, for the preservation of the . . . health of the mother.'" . . . The prohibition in the Act would be unconstitutional, under precedents we here assume to be controlling, if it "subject[ed] [women] to significant health risks." . . . In *Ayotte* the parties agreed a health exception to the challenged parental-involvement statute was necessary "to avert serious and often irreversible damage to . . . Here, by contrast, whether the Act creates significant health risks for women has been a contested question. The evidence presented in the trial courts and before Congress demonstrates both sides have medical support for their position.

Respondents presented evidence that intact D&E may be the safest method of abortion, for reasons similar to those adduced in *Stenberg*. Abortion doctors testified, for example, that intact D&E decreases the risk of cervical laceration or uterine perforation because it requires fewer passes into the uterus with surgical instruments and does not require the removal of bony fragments of the dismembered fetus, fragments that may be sharp. Respondents also presented evidence that intact D&E was safer both because it reduces the risks that fetal parts will remain in the uterus and because it takes less time to complete. Respondents, in addition, proffered evidence that intact D&E was safer for women with certain medical conditions or women with fetuses that had certain anomalies. . . .

These contentions were contradicted by other doctors who testified in the District Courts and before Congress. They concluded that the alleged health advantages were based on speculation without scientific studies to support them. They considered D&E always to be a safe alternative. . . .

There is documented medical disagreement whether the Act's prohibition would ever impose significant health risks on women. . . . The three District Courts that considered the Act's constitutionality appeared to be in some disagreement on this central factual question. The District Court for the District of Nebraska concluded "the banned procedure is, sometimes, the safest abortion procedure to preserve the health of women." The District Court for the Northern District of California reached a similar conclusion. . . . The District Court for the Southern District of New York was more skeptical of the purported health benefits of intact D&E. It found the Attorney General's "expert witnesses reasonably and effectively refuted [the plaintiffs'] proffered bases for the opinion that [intact D&E] has safety advantages over other second-trimester abortion procedures." . . . In addition it did "not believe that many of [the plaintiffs'] purported reasons for why [intact D&E] is medically necessary [were] credible; rather [it found them to be] theoretical or false." The court nonetheless invalidated the Act because it determined "a significant body of medical opinion . . . holds that D & E has safety advantages over induction and that [intact D&E] has some safety advantages (however hypothetical and unsubstantiated by scientific evidence) over D & E for some women in some circumstances.

The question becomes whether the Act can stand when this medical uncertainty persists.

The Court's precedents instruct that the Act can survive this facial attack. The Court has given state and federal legislatures wide discretion to pass legislation in areas where there is medical and scientific uncertainty. . . .

This traditional rule is consistent with *Casey*, which confirms the State's interest in promoting respect for human life at all stages in the pregnancy. Physicians are not entitled to ignore regulations that direct them to use reasonable alternative procedures. The law need not give abortion doctors unfettered choice in the course of their medical practice, nor should it elevate their status above other physicians in the medical community. In *Casey* the controlling opinion held an informed-consent requirement in the abortion context was "no different from a requirement that a doctor give certain specific information about any medical procedure." The opinion stated "the doctor-patient relation here is entitled to the same solicitude it receives in other contexts." . . .

Medical uncertainty does not foreclose the exercise of legislative power in the abortion context any more than it does in other contexts. The medical uncertainty over whether the Act's prohibition creates significant health risks provides a sufficient basis to conclude in this facial attack that the Act does not impose an undue burden.

The conclusion that the Act does not impose an undue burden is supported by other considerations. Alternatives are available to the prohibited procedure. As we have noted, the Act does not proscribe D&E. One District Court found D&E to have extremely low rates of medical complications. Another indicated D&E was "generally the safest method of abortion during the second trimester." . . . In addition the Act's prohibition only applies to the delivery of "a living fetus." If the intact D&E procedure is truly necessary in some circumstances, it appears likely an injection that kills the fetus is an alternative under the Act that allows the doctor to perform the procedure.

The instant cases, then, are different from *Planned Parenthood of Central Mo. v. Danforth*, 428 U.S. 52, 77-79, 96 S. Ct. 2831, 49 L. Ed. 2d 788 (1976), in which the Court invalidated a ban on saline amniocentesis, the then-dominant second-trimester abor-

tion method. The Court found the ban in *Danforth* to be "an unreasonable or arbitrary regulation designed to inhibit, and having the effect of inhibiting, the vast majority of abortions after the first 12 weeks." Here the Act allows, among other means, a commonly used and generally accepted method, so it does not construct a substantial obstacle to the abortion right.

In reaching the conclusion the Act does not require a health exception we reject certain arguments made by the parties on both sides of these cases. On the one hand, the Attorney General urges us to uphold the Act on the basis of the congressional findings alone. Although we review congressional factfinding under a deferential standard, we do not in the circumstances here place dispositive weight on Congress' findings. The Court retains an independent constitutional duty to review factual findings where constitutional rights are at stake. . . .

As respondents have noted, and the District Courts recognized, some recitations in the Act are factually incorrect. . . . Whether or not accurate at the time, some of the important findings have been superseded. Two examples suffice. Congress determined no medical schools provide instruction on the prohibited procedure. The testimony in the District Courts, however, demonstrated intact D&E is taught at medical schools. . . . Congress also found there existed a medical consensus that the prohibited procedure is never medically necessary. The evidence presented in the District Courts contradicts that conclusion . . . .Uncritical deference to Congress' factual findings in these cases is inappropriate.

On the other hand, relying on the Court's opinion in *Stenberg*, respondents contend that an abortion regulation must contain a health exception "if 'substantial medical authority supports the proposition that banning a particular procedure could endanger women's health.'" . . . As illustrated by respondents' arguments and the decisions of the Courts of Appeals, *Stenberg* has been interpreted to leave no margin of error for legislatures to act in the face of medical uncertainty. . . .

A zero tolerance policy would strike down legitimate abortion regulations, like the present one, if some part of the medical community were disinclined to follow the proscription. This is too exacting a standard to impose on the legislative power, exercised in this instance under the Commerce Clause, to regulate the medical profession. Considerations of marginal safety, including the balance of risks, are within the legislative competence when the regulation is rational and in pursuit of legitimate ends. When standard medical options are available, mere convenience does not suffice to displace them; and if some procedures have different risks than others, it does not follow that the State is altogether barred from imposing reasonable regulations. The Act is not invalid on its face where there is uncertainty over whether the barred procedure is ever necessary to preserve a woman's health, given the availability of other abortion procedures that are considered to be safe alternatives.

V

The considerations we have discussed support our further determination that these facial attacks should not have been entertained in the first instance. In these circumstances the proper means to consider exceptions is by as-applied challenge. The Government has acknowledged that preenforcement, as-applied challenges to the Act can be maintained. This is the proper manner to protect the health of the woman if it can be shown that in discrete and well-defined instances a particular condition has or is likely to occur in which the procedure prohibited by the Act must be used. In an as-applied challenge the nature of the medical risk can be better quantified and balanced than in a facial attack.

The latitude given facial challenges in the First Amendment context is inapplicable here. Broad challenges of this type impose "a heavy burden" upon the parties maintaining the suit. What that burden consists of in the specific context of abortion statutes has been a subject of some question. . . . We need not resolve that debate.

As the previous sections of this opinion explain, respondents have not demonstrated that the Act would be unconstitutional in a large fraction of relevant cases. We note that the statute here applies to all instances in which the doctor proposes to use the prohibited procedure, not merely those in which the woman suffers from medical complications. It is neither our obligation nor within our traditional institutional role to resolve questions of constitutionality with respect to each potential situation that might develop. "[I]t would indeed be undesirable for this Court to consider every conceivable situation which might possibly arise in the application of complex and comprehensive legislation." For this reason, "[a]s-applied challenges are the basic building blocks of constitutional adjudication." . . .

The Act is open to a proper as-applied challenge in a discrete case. . . .No as-applied challenge need be brought if the prohibition in the Act threatens a woman's life because the Act already contains a life exception.

* * *

Respondents have not demonstrated that the Act, as a facial matter, is void for vagueness, or that it imposes an undue burden on a woman's right to abortion based on its overbreadth or lack of a health exception. For these reasons the judgments of the Courts of Appeals for the Eighth and Ninth Circuits are reversed.

It is so ordered.

[Footnotes omitted.]

[Concurring and dissenting opinions omitted.]

Cases Relating to Chapter 11

Offenses Against Public Peace

Papachristou et al.

v.

City of Jacksonville

**Supreme Court of the United States
405 U.S. 156 (1972)**

Mr. Justice Douglas delivered the opinion of the Court.

This case involves eight defendants who were convicted in a Florida municipal court of violating a Jacksonville, Florida, vagrancy ordinance. Their convictions were affirmed by the Florida Circuit Court in a consolidated appeal, and their petition for certiorari was denied by the District Court of Appeal on the authority of *Johnson* v. *State*, . . .The case is here on a petition for certiorari, which we granted. . . . For reasons which will appear, we reverse.

At issue are five consolidated cases. Margaret Papachristou, Betty Calloway, Eugene Eddie Melton, and Leonard Johnson were all arrested early on a Sunday morning, and charged with vagrancy — "prowling by auto."

Jimmy Lee Smith and Milton Henry were charged with vagrancy — "vagabonds."

Henry Edward Heath and a codefendant were arrested for vagrancy — "loitering" and "common thief."

Thomas Owen Campbell was charged with vagrancy — "common thief."

Hugh Brown was charged with vagrancy — "disorderly loitering on street" and "disorderly conduct — resisting arrest with violence."

The facts are stipulated. Papachristou and Calloway are white females. Melton and Johnson are black males. Papachristou was enrolled in a job-training program sponsored by the State Employment Service at Florida Junior College in Jacksonville. Calloway was a typing and shorthand teacher at a state mental institution located near Jacksonville. She was the owner of the automobile in which the four defendants were arrested. Melton was a Vietnam war veteran who had been released from the Navy after nine months in a veterans' hospital. On the date of his arrest he was a part-time computer helper while attending college as a full-time student in Jacksonville. Johnson was a tow-motor operator in a grocery chain warehouse and was a lifelong resident of Jacksonville.

At the time of their arrest the four of them were riding in Calloway's car on the main thoroughfare in Jacksonville. They had left a restaurant owned by Johnson's uncle where they had eaten and were on their way to a nightclub. The arresting officers denied that the racial mixture in the car played any part in the decision to make the arrest. The arrest, they said, was made because the defendants had stopped near a used-car lot which had been broken into several times. There was, however, no evidence of any breaking and entering on the night in question.

Of these four charged with "prowling by auto" none had been previously arrested except Papachristou who had once been convicted of a municipal offense.

Jimmy Lee Smith and Milton Henry (who is not a petitioner) were arrested between 9 and 10 a. m. on a weekday in downtown Jacksonville, while waiting for a friend who was to lend them a car so they could apply for a job at a produce company. Smith was a part-time produce worker and part-time organizer for a Negro political group. He had a common-law wife and three children supported by him and his wife. He had been arrested several times but convicted only once. Smith's companion, Henry, was an 18-year-old high school student with no previous record of arrest.

This morning it was cold, and Smith had no jacket, so they went briefly into a dry cleaning shop to wait, but left when requested to do so. They thereafter walked back and forth two or three times over a two-block stretch looking for their friend. The store owners, who apparently were wary of Smith and his companion, summoned two police officers who searched the men and found neither had a weapon. But they were arrested because the officers said they had no identification and because the officers did not believe their story.

Heath and a codefendant were arrested for "loitering" and for "common thief." Both were residents of Jacksonville, Heath having lived there all his life and being employed at an automobile body shop. Heath had previously been arrested but his codefendant had no arrest record. Heath and his companion were arrested when they drove up to a residence shared by Heath's girl friend and some other girls. Some police officers were already there in the process of arresting another man. When Heath and his companion started backing out of the driveway, the officers signaled to them to stop and asked them to get out of the car, which they did. Thereupon they and the automobile were searched. Although no contraband or incriminating evidence was found, they were both arrested, Heath being charged with being a "common thief" because he was reputed to be a thief. The codefendant was charged with "loitering" because he was standing in the driveway, an act which the officers admitted was done only at their command.

Campbell was arrested as he reached his home very early one morning and was charged with "common thief." He was stopped by officers because he was traveling at a high rate of speed, yet no speeding charge was placed against him.

Brown was arrested when he was observed leaving a downtown Jacksonville hotel by a police officer seated in a cruiser. The police testified he was reputed to be a thief, narcotics pusher, and generally opprobrious

character. The officer called Brown over to the car, intending at that time to arrest him unless he had a good explanation for being on the street. Brown walked over to the police cruiser, as commanded, and the officer began to search him, apparently preparatory to placing him in the car. In the process of the search he came on two small packets which were later found to contain heroin. When the officer touched the pocket where the packets were, Brown began to resist. He was charged with "disorderly loitering on street" and "disorderly conduct — resisting arrest with violence." While he was also charged with a narcotics violation, that charge was *nolled*.

Jacksonville's ordinance and Florida's statute were "derived from early English law," . . ., and employ "archaic language" in their definitions of vagrants. . . . The history is an oftentold tale. The breakup of feudal estates in England led to labor shortages which in turn resulted in the Statutes of Laborers, designed to stabilize the labor force by prohibiting increases in wages and prohibiting the movement of workers from their home areas in search of improved conditions. Later vagrancy laws became criminal aspects of the poor laws. The series of laws passed in England on the subject became increasingly severe. But "the theory of the Elizabethan poor laws no longer fits the facts," . . . . The conditions which spawned these laws may be gone, but the archaic classifications remain.

This ordinance is void for vagueness, both in the sense that it "fails to give a person of ordinary intelligence fair notice that his contemplated conduct is forbidden by the statute," . . ., and because it encourages arbitrary and erratic arrests and convictions. . . .

Living under a rule of law entails various suppositions, one of which is that "[all persons] are entitled to be informed as to what the State commands or forbids." . . .

Lanzetta is one of a well-recognized group of cases insisting that the law give fair notice of the offending conduct. . . . In the field of regulatory statutes governing business activities, where the acts limited are in a narrow category, greater leeway is allowed. . . .

The poor among us, the minorities, the average householder are not in business and not alerted to the regulatory schemes of vagrancy laws; and we assume they would have no understanding of their meaning and impact if they read them. Nor are they protected from being caught in the vagrancy net by the necessity of having a specific intent to commit an unlawful act. . . .

The Jacksonville ordinance makes criminal activities which by modern standards are normally innocent. "Nightwalking" is one. Florida construes the ordinance not to make criminal one night's wandering, . . . We know, however, from experience that sleepless people often walk at night, perhaps hopeful that sleep-inducing relaxation will result.

Luis Munoz-Marin, former Governor of Puerto Rico, commented once that "loafing" was a national virtue in his Commonwealth and that it should be encouraged. It is, however, a crime in Jacksonville.

"Persons able to work but habitually living upon the earnings of their wives or minor children" — like habitually living "without visible means of support" — might implicate unemployed pillars of the community who have married rich wives.

"Persons able to work but habitually living upon the earnings of their wives or minor children" may also embrace unemployed people out of the labor market, by reason of a recession or disemployed by reason of technological or so-called structural displacements.

Persons "wandering or strolling" from place to place have been extolled by Walt Whitman and Vachel Lindsay. The qualification "without any lawful purpose or object" may be a trap for innocent acts. Persons "neglecting all lawful business and habitually spending their time by frequenting . . . places where alcoholic beverages are sold or served" would literally embrace many members of golf clubs and city clubs.

Walkers and strollers and wanderers may be going to or coming from a burglary. Loafers or loiterers may be "casing" a place for a holdup. Letting one's wife support him is an intra-family matter, and normally of no concern to the police. Yet it may, of course, be the setting for numerous crimes.

The difficulty is that these activities are historically part of the amenities of life as we have known them. They are not mentioned in the Constitution or in the Bill of Rights. These unwritten amenities have been in part responsible for giving our people the feeling of independence and self-confidence,

the feeling of creativity. These amenities have dignified the right of dissent and have honored the right to be nonconformists and the right to defy submissiveness. They have encouraged lives of high spirits rather than hushed, suffocating silence.

They are embedded in Walt Whitman's writings, especially in his "Song of the Open Road." They are reflected, too, in the spirit of Vachel Lindsay's "I Want to Go Wandering," and by Henry D. Thoreau.

This aspect of the vagrancy ordinance before us is suggested by what this Court said in 1876 about a broad criminal statute enacted by Congress: "It would certainly be dangerous if the legislature could set a net large enough to catch all possible offenders, and leave it to the courts to step inside and say who could be rightfully detained, and who should be set at large." . . .

While that was a federal case, the due process implications are equally applicable to the States and to this vagrancy ordinance. Here the net cast is large, not to give the courts the power to pick and choose but to increase the arsenal of the police. In *Winters* v. *New York*, . . ., the Court struck down a New York statute that made criminal the distribution of a magazine made up principally of items of criminal deeds of bloodshed or lust so massed as to become vehicles for inciting violent and depraved crimes against the person. The infirmity the Court found was vagueness — the absence of "ascertainable standards of guilt" . . . in the sensitive First Amendment area. Mr. Justice Frankfurter dissented. But concerned as he, and many others, had been over the vagrancy laws, he added:

"Only a word needs to be said regarding *Lanzetta* v. *New Jersey*, ... The case involved a New Jersey statute of the type that seek to control 'vagrancy.' These statutes are in a class by themselves, in view of the familiar abuses to which they are put. . . . Definiteness is designedly avoided so as to allow the net to be cast at large, to enable men to be caught who are vaguely undesirable in the eyes of police and prosecution, although not chargeable with any particular offense. In short, these 'vagrancy statutes' and laws against 'gangs' are not fenced in by the text of the statute or by the subject matter so as to give notice of conduct to be avoided." . . .

Where the list of crimes is so all-inclusive and generalized as the one in this ordinance, those convicted may be punished for no more than vindicating affronts to police authority:

"The common ground which brings such a motley assortment of human troubles before the magistrates in vagrancy-type proceedings is the procedural laxity which permits 'conviction' for almost any kind of conduct and the existence of the House of Correction as an easy and convenient dumping-ground for problems that appear to have no other immediate solution." . . .

Another aspect of the ordinance's vagueness appears when we focus, not on the lack of notice given a potential offender, but on the effect of the unfettered discretion it places in the hands of the Jacksonville police. Caleb Foote, an early student of this subject, has called the vagrancy-type law as offering "punishment by analogy." . . . Such crimes, though long common in Russia, are not compatible with our constitutional system. We allow our police to make arrests only on "probable cause," a Fourth and Fourteenth Amendment standard applicable to the States as well as to the Federal Government. Arresting a person on suspicion, like arresting a person for investigation, is foreign to our system, even when the arrest is for past criminality. Future criminality, however, is the common justification for the presence of vagrancy statutes. . . . Florida has, indeed, construed her vagrancy statute "as necessary regulations," *inter alia*, "to deter vagabondage and prevent crimes." . . .

A direction by a legislature to the police to arrest all "suspicious" persons would not pass constitutional muster. A vagrancy prosecution may be merely the cloak for a conviction which could not be obtained on the real but undisclosed grounds for the arrest. . . . But as Chief Justice Hewart said in *Frederick Dean*, . . . (1924):

"It would be in the highest degree unfortunate if in any part of the country those who are responsible for setting in motion the criminal law should entertain, connive at or coquette with the idea that in a case where there is not enough evidence to charge the prisoner with an attempt to commit a crime, the prosecution may, nevertheless, on such insufficient evidence, succeed in obtaining and upholding a conviction under the Vagrancy Act, 1824."

Those generally implicated by the imprecise terms of the ordinance — poor people, nonconformists, dissenters, idlers — may be required to comport themselves according to the lifestyle deemed appropriate by the Jacksonville police and the courts. Where, as here, there are no standards governing the exercise of the discretion granted by the ordinance, the scheme permits and encourages an arbitrary and discriminatory enforcement of the law. It furnishes a convenient tool for "harsh and discriminatory enforcement by local prosecuting officials, against particular groups deemed to merit their displeasure." . . . It results in a regime in which the poor and the unpopular are permitted to "stand on a public sidewalk . . . only at the whim of any police officer." . . . . Under this ordinance,

"If some carefree type of fellow is satisfied to work just so much, and no more, as will pay for one square meal, some wine, and a flophouse daily, but a court thinks this kind of living subhuman, the fellow can be forced to raise his sights or go to jail as a vagrant." . . .

A presumption that people who might walk or loaf or loiter or stroll or frequent houses where liquor is sold, or who are supported by their wives or who look suspicious to the police are to become future criminals is too precarious for a rule of law. The implicit presumption in these generalized vagrancy standards — that crime is being nipped in the bud — is too extravagant to deserve extended treatment. Of course, vagrancy statutes are useful to the police. Of course, they are nets making easy the roundup of so-called undesirables. But the rule of law implies equality and justice in its application. Vagrancy laws of the Jacksonville type teach that the scales of justice are so tipped that even-handed administration of the law is not possible. The rule of law, evenly applied to minorities as well as majorities, to the poor as well as the rich, is the great mucilage that holds society together.

The Jacksonville ordinance cannot be squared with our constitutional standards and is plainly unconstitutional.

Reversed.

[Footnotes and citations omitted. Concurring and dissenting opinions omitted.]

Larry D. Hiibel

v.

**Sixth Judicial District Court of Nevada,
Humboldt County**

**Supreme Court of the United States
542 U.S. 177 (2004)**

Justice Kennedy delivered the opinion of the Court.

The petitioner was arrested and convicted for refusing to identify himself during a stop allowed by *Terry* v. *Ohio,* ... (1968). He challenges his conviction under the Fourth and Fifth Amendments to the United States Constitution, applicable to the States through the Fourteenth Amendment.

I.

The sheriff's department in Humboldt County, Nevada, received an afternoon telephone call reporting an assault. The caller reported seeing a man assault a woman in a red and silver GMC truck on Grass Valley Road. Deputy Sheriff Lee Dove was dispatched to investigate. When the officer arrived at the scene, he found the truck parked on the side of the road. A man was standing by the truck, and a young woman was sitting inside it. The officer observed skid marks in the gravel behind the vehicle, leading him to believe it had come to a sudden stop.

The officer approached the man and explained that he was investigating a report of a fight. The man appeared to be intoxicated. The officer asked him if he had "any identification on [him]," which we understand as a request to produce a driver's license or some other form of written identification. The man refused and asked why the officer wanted to see identification. The officer responded that he was conducting an investigation and needed to see some identification. The unidentified man became agitated and insisted he had done nothing wrong. The officer explained that he wanted to find out who the man was and what he was doing there. After continued refusals to comply with the officer's request for identification, the man began to taunt the officer by placing his hands behind his back and telling the officer to arrest him and take

him to jail. This routine kept up for several minutes: the officer asked for identification 11 times and was refused each time. After warning the man that he would be arrested if he continued to refuse to comply, the officer placed him under arrest.

We now know that the man arrested on Grass Valley Road is Larry Dudley Hiibel. Hiibel was charged with "willfully resist[ing], delay[ing], or obstruct[ing] a public officer in discharging or attempting to discharge any legal duty of his office" in violation of Nev. Rev. Stat. (NRS) § 199.280 (2003). The government reasoned that Hiibel had obstructed the officer in carrying out his duties under § 171.123, a Nevada statute that defines the legal rights and duties of a police officer in the context of an investigative stop. Section 171.123 provides in relevant part:

> "1. Any peace officer may detain any person whom the officer encounters under circumstances which reasonably indicate that the person has committed, is committing or is about to commit a crime.

> . . . . .

> "3. The officer may detain the person pursuant to this section only to ascertain his identity and the suspicious circumstances surrounding his presence abroad. Any person so detained shall identify himself, but may not be compelled to answer any other inquiry of any peace officer."

Hiibel was tried in the Justice Court of Union Township. The court agreed that Hiibel's refusal to identify himself as required by § 171.123 "obstructed and delayed Dove as a public officer in attempting to discharge his duty" in violation of § 199.280. . . . Hiibel was convicted and fined $250. The Sixth Judicial District Court affirmed, rejecting Hiibel's argument that the application of § 171.123 to his case violated the Fourth and Fifth Amendments. On review the Supreme Court of Nevada rejected the Fourth Amendment challenge in a divided opinion. . . . Hiibel petitioned for rehearing, seeking explicit resolution of his Fifth Amendment challenge. The petition was denied without opinion. We granted certiorari, . . .

II.

NRS § 171.123(3) is an enactment some-times referred to as a "stop and identify" statute. . . .

Stop and identify statutes often combine elements of traditional vagrancy laws with provisions intended to regulate police behav-ior in the course of investigatory stops. The statutes vary from State to State, but all permit an officer to ask or require a suspect to disclose his identity. A few States model their statutes on the Uniform Arrest Act, a model code that permits an officer to stop a person reasonably suspected of commit-ting a crime and "demand of him his name, address, business abroad and whither he is going." . . . . Other statutes are based on the text proposed by the American Law Institute as part of the Institute's Model Penal Code. . . . The provision, originally designated § 250.12, provides that a person who is loitering "under circumstances which justify suspicion that he may be engaged or about to engage in crime commits a violation if he refuses the request of a peace officer that he identify himself and give a reasonably credible account of the lawfulness of his con-duct and purposes." § 250.12 . . . . In some States, a suspect's refusal to identify himself is a misdemeanor offense or civil violation; in others, it is a factor to be considered in whether the suspect has violated loitering laws. In other States, a suspect may decline to identify himself without penalty.

Stop and identify statutes have their roots in early English vagrancy laws that required suspected vagrants to face arrest unless they gave "a good Account of themselves," . . ., a power that itself reflected common-law rights of private persons to "arrest any sus-picious night-walker, and detain him till he give a good account of himself . . . . ". In recent decades, the Court has found constitu-tional infirmity in traditional vagrancy laws. In Papachristou v. Jacksonville, . . . (1972), the Court held that a traditional vagrancy law was void for vagueness. Its broad scope and imprecise terms denied proper notice to potential offenders and permitted police officers to exercise unfettered discretion in the enforcement of the law. . . .

The Court has recognized similar consti-tutional limitations on the scope and opera-tion of stop and identify statutes. In Brown v. Texas, . . . (1979), the Court invalidated a conviction for violating a Texas stop and identify statute on Fourth Amendment grounds. The Court ruled that the initial stop was not based on specific, objective facts establishing reasonable suspicion to believe the suspect was involved in criminal activ-ity. . . . Absent that factual basis for detain-ing the defendant, the Court held, the risk of "arbitrary and abusive police practices" was too great and the stop was impermis-sible. . . . Four Terms later, the Court invali-dated a modified stop and identify statute on vagueness grounds. . . . The California law in Kolender required a suspect to give an officer " 'credible and reliable' " identifica-tion when asked to identify himself. . . . The Court held that the statute was void because it provided no standard for determining what a suspect must do to comply with it, resulting in " 'virtually unrestrained power to arrest and charge persons with a violation.' " . . .

The present case begins where our prior cases left off. Here there is no question that the initial stop was based on reasonable suspicion, satisfying the Fourth Amendment requirements noted in Brown Further, the peti-tioner has not alleged that the statute is uncon-stitutionally vague, as in Kolender. Here the Nevada statute is narrower and more precise. The statute in Kolender had been interpreted to require a suspect to give the officer "cred-ible and reliable" identification. In contrast, the Nevada Supreme Court has interpreted NRS § 171.123(3) to require only that a sus-pect disclose his name. . . . As we understand it, the statute does not require a suspect to give the officer a driver's license or any other doc-ument. Provided that the suspect either states his name or communicates it to the officer by other means — a choice, we assume, that the suspect may make — the statute is satisfied and no violation occurs. . . .

III.

Hiibel argues that his conviction cannot stand because the officer's conduct violated his Fourth Amendment rights. We disagree.

Asking questions is an essential part of police investigations. In the ordinary course a police officer is free to ask a person for identification without implicating the Fourth

Amendment. "[I]nterrogation relating to one's identity or a request for identification by the police does not, by itself, constitute a Fourth Amendment seizure." . . . . Beginning with *Terry* v. *Ohio*, . . . (1968), the Court has recognized that a law enforcement officer's reasonable suspicion that a person may be involved in criminal activity permits the officer to stop the person for a brief time and take additional steps to investigate further. . . . To ensure that the resulting seizure is constitutionally reasonable, a *Terry* stop must be limited. The officer's action must be " 'justified at its inception, and . . . reasonably related in scope to the circumstances which justified the interference in the first place.' " . . . . For example, the seizure cannot continue for an excessive period of time, . . . or resemble a traditional arrest, ...

Our decisions make clear that questions concerning a suspect's identity are a routine and accepted part of many *Terry* stops. . . .

Obtaining a suspect's name in the course of a *Terry* stop serves important government interests. Knowledge of identity may inform an officer that a suspect is wanted for another offense, or has a record of violence or mental disorder. On the other hand, knowing identity may help clear a suspect and allow the police to concentrate their efforts elsewhere. Identity may prove particularly important in cases such as this, where the police are investigating what appears to be a domestic assault. Officers called to investigate domestic disputes need to know whom they are dealing with in order to assess the situation, the threat to their own safety, and possible danger to the potential victim.

Although it is well established that an officer may ask a suspect to identify himself in the course of a *Terry* stop, it has been an open question whether the suspect can be arrested and prosecuted for refusal to answer. . . . Petitioner draws our attention to statements in prior opinions that, according to him, answer the question in his favor. In *Terry*, Justice White stated in a concurring opinion that a person detained in an investigative stop can be questioned but is "not obliged to answer, answers may not be compelled, and refusal to answer furnishes no basis for an arrest." . . . . The Court cited this opinion in dicta in *Berkemer* v. *McCarty*, . . . (1984), a decision holding that a routine traffic stop is

not a custodial stop requiring the protections of *Miranda* v. *Arizona*, . . . (1966). In the course of explaining why *Terry* stops have not been subject to *Miranda*, the Court suggested reasons why *Terry* stops have a "non-threatening character," among them the fact that a suspect detained during a *Terry* stop "is not obliged to respond" to questions. . . . According to petitioner, these statements establish a right to refuse to answer questions during a *Terry* stop.

We do not read these statements as controlling. The passages recognize that the Fourth Amendment does not impose obligations on the citizen but instead provides rights against the government. As a result, the Fourth Amendment itself cannot require a suspect to answer questions. This case concerns a different issue, however. Here, the source of the legal obligation arises from Nevada state law, not the Fourth Amendment. Further, the statutory obligation does not go beyond answering an officer's request to disclose a name. . . . As a result, we cannot view the dicta in *Berkemer* or Justice White's concurrence in *Terry* as answering the question whether a State can compel a suspect to disclose his name during a *Terry* stop.

The principles of *Terry* permit a State to require a suspect to disclose his name in the course of a *Terry* stop. The reasonableness of a seizure under the Fourth Amendment is determined "by balancing its intrusion on the individual's Fourth Amendment interests against its promotion of legitimate government interests." . . . . The Nevada statute satisfies that standard. The request for identity has an immediate relation to the purpose, rationale, and practical demands of a *Terry* stop. The threat of criminal sanction helps ensure that the request for identity does not become a legal nullity. On the other hand, the Nevada statute does not alter the nature of the stop itself: it does not change its duration, . . ., or its location, ... A state law requiring a suspect to disclose his name in the course of a valid *Terry* stop is consistent with Fourth Amendment prohibitions against unreasonable searches and seizures.

Petitioner argues that the Nevada statute circumvents the probable cause requirement, in effect allowing an officer to arrest a person for being suspicious. According to petitioner, this creates a risk of arbitrary police conduct that the Fourth Amendment does not permit. . . . These are familiar concerns; they were central to the opinion in *Papachristou,* and also to the decisions limiting the operation of stop and identify statutes in *Kolender* and *Brown.* Petitioner's concerns are met by the requirement that a *Terry* stop must be justified at its inception and "reasonably related in scope to the circumstances which justified" the initial stop. . . . Under these principles, an officer may not arrest a suspect for failure to identify himself if the request for identification is not reasonably related to the circumstances justifying the stop. The Court noted a similar limitation in *Hayes*, where it suggested that *Terry* may permit an officer to determine a suspect's identity by compelling the suspect to submit to fingerprinting only if there is "a reasonable basis for believing that fingerprinting will establish or negate the suspect's connection with that crime." . . . . It is clear in this case that the request for identification was "reasonably related in scope to the circumstances which justified" the stop. . . . The officer's request was a commonsense inquiry, not an effort to obtain an arrest for failure to identify after a *Terry* stop yielded insufficient evidence. The stop, the request, and the State's requirement of a response did not contravene the guarantees of the Fourth Amendment.

IV.

Petitioner further contends that his conviction violates the Fifth Amendment's prohibition on compelled self-incrimination. The Fifth Amendment states that "[n]o person . . . shall be compelled in any criminal case to be a witness against himself." To qualify for the Fifth Amendment privilege, a communication must be testimonial, incriminating, and compelled. . . .

Respondents urge us to hold that the statements NRS § 171.123(3) requires are nontestimonial, and so outside the Clause's scope. We decline to resolve the case on that basis. "[T]o be testimonial, an accused's communication must itself, explicitly or implicitly, relate a factual assertion or disclose information." . . . . Stating one's name may qualify as an assertion of fact relating to identity. Production of identity documents might meet

the definition as well. As we noted in *Hubbell*, acts of production may yield testimony establishing "the existence, authenticity, and custody of items [the police seek]." . . . . Even if these required actions are testimonial, however, petitioner's challenge must fail because in this case disclosure of his name presented no reasonable danger of incrimination.

The Fifth Amendment prohibits only compelled testimony that is incriminating. . . . A claim of Fifth Amendment privilege must establish

> "'reasonable ground to apprehend danger to the witness from his being compelled to answer. . . . [T]he danger to be apprehended must be real and appreciable, with reference to the ordinary operation of law in the ordinary course of things, — not a danger of an imaginary and unsubstantial character, having reference to some extraordinary and barely possible contingency, so improbable that no reasonable man would suffer it to influence his conduct.'" . . .

As we stated in *Kastigar* v. *United States,* . . . (1972), the Fifth Amendment privilege against compulsory self-incrimination "protects against any disclosures that the witness reasonably believes could be used in a criminal prosecution or could lead to other evidence that might be so used." Suspects who have been granted immunity from prosecution may, therefore, be compelled to answer; with the threat of prosecution removed, there can be no reasonable belief that the evidence will be used against them. . . .

In this case petitioner's refusal to disclose his name was not based on any articulated real and appreciable fear that his name would be used to incriminate him, or that it "would furnish a link in the chain of evidence needed to prosecute" him. . . . As best we can tell, petitioner refused to identify himself only because he thought his name was none of the officer's business. Even today, petitioner does not explain how the disclosure of his name could have been used against him in a criminal case. While we recognize petitioner's strong belief that he should not have to disclose his identity, the Fifth Amendment does not override the Nevada Legislature's judgment to the contrary absent a reasonable belief that the disclosure would tend to incriminate him.

The narrow scope of the disclosure requirement is also important. One's identity is, by definition, unique; yet it is, in another sense, a universal characteristic. Answering a request to disclose a name is likely to be so insignificant in the scheme of things as to be incriminating only in unusual circumstances. . . . In every criminal case, it is known and must be known who has been arrested and who is being tried. . . . Even witnesses who plan to invoke the Fifth Amendment privilege answer when their names are called to take the stand. Still, a case may arise where there is a substantial allegation that furnishing identity at the time of a stop would have given the police a link in the chain of evidence needed to convict the individual of a separate offense. In that case, the court can then consider whether the privilege applies, and, if the Fifth Amendment has been violated, what remedy must follow. We need not resolve those questions here.

The judgment of the Nevada Supreme Court is affirmed.

[Footnotes and citations omitted. Concurring and dissenting opinions omitted.]

Cases Relating to Chapter 12

Offenses Against Justice Administration

Ottie Bernard Polk

v.

Commonwealth of Virginia

Court of Appeals of Virginia
4 Va. App. 590 (1987)

Keenan, Judge

Ottie B. Polk was convicted in a bench trial of obstructing justice by threats or force in violation of Code § 18.2-460(A). He was sentenced to six months in jail, with five months suspended, and fined $100. On appeal, Polk argues that: (1) the evidence was insufficient to support his conviction because words alone will not support a conviction under Code § 18.2-460(A), and because there was no evidence of his criminal intent; and (2) he was entitled to use reasonable force to resist arrest, under the authority of *United States v. Moore*, . . . (E.D. Va. 1971). We affirm Polk's conviction, finding that his verbal threat to kill was sufficient to constitute an obstruction of justice under Code § 18.2-460(A), that there was sufficient evidence of his criminal intent, and that Moore is inapplicable because it did not interpret Code § 18.2-460(A), and unlike the facts presented here, it dealt with an apparently illegal arrest.

I.

At trial, the evidence showed that Polk was stopped pursuant to a license "checking detail" operated by the Lancaster County Sheriff's Department and the Virginia State Police. Deputy Sheriff Martin Shirilla effected the stop. Upon realizing that he had stopped Polk about one year earlier concerning "some discrepancy about his driving status," Shirilla radioed to his dispatcher to confirm the status of Polk's license. The dispatcher informed Shirilla that Polk's license was suspended, and that there was an outstanding bench warrant for Polk's arrest on a charge of failing to appear in court. Based on this information, Shirilla arrested Polk.

Shirilla testified that, at the time of the arrest, Polk threatened to sue him for false arrest and further stated: "If I lose, I'll get you some other way." Polk was handcuffed, placed in Shirilla's vehicle, and transported to the Lancaster County Sheriff's office where Shirilla served him with the failure to appear warrant. Shirilla testified that while they were awaiting the arrival of a magistrate, Polk continually repeated statements such as "I'm going to get you," and "I'm going to get even." Shirilla testified that he then read Polk his Miranda warnings and asked him: "Are you talking civil suit or are you looking for a piece of my ass?" According to Shirilla, Polk only responded: "I'm going to get you."

When the magistrate arrived, Shirilla left the booking room to talk to him. Deputy Casto, who had assisted Shirilla in Polk's arrest, remained with Polk in the booking room. Casto testified that after Shirilla left the room, Polk stated that he was going to kill him. Casto concluded that Polk was referring to Shirilla. When Shirilla returned, Casto apparently related this threat to Shirilla. Shirilla testified that based on his conversation with Casto, he obtained a warrant charging Polk with obstruction of justice.

According to Shirilla, a final threat occurred after Polk had been charged with the obstruction offense. The threat occurred when Polk was issued jail clothing and was being taken to the shower. Shirilla testified that at that time he heard Polk say: "I've got five friends to help me take care of him."

During the entire sequence of these events, neither Shirilla nor Casto observed Polk make any physically threatening gestures or possess any weapons. On cross-examination, Shirilla acknowledged that, except for the verbal exchanges, the arrest proceeded in a normal fashion.

It was later learned that Polk's license was not, in fact, suspended at the time of his arrest, and the failure to appear charge had already been disposed of. Polk testified in his own behalf. He denied having threatened to kill Shirilla, although he admitted saying that he would sue him. Polk specifically denied making a comment about having five friends who would "get" Shirilla. Polk testified that he did not even have five friends. No other witnesses were called by the defense.

In finding the defendant guilty, the court stated:

> There's no question in the mind of this court about the extent of his threats and the language that he used and I feel that he is guilty in violating the law, in violating the statute of obstructing an officer in the discharge of his duties, and . . . so find him guilty.

II.

Polk first challenges the sufficiency of the evidence. He contends that the Commonwealth failed to prove: (1) that his words alone constituted an attempt to intimidate or impede within the meaning of Code § 18.2-460(A); and (2) that he actually intended to intimidate or impede Shirilla.

(1-2) Initially, we reject Polk's argument that words alone cannot constitute a violation under Code § 18.2-460(A) without evidence that they caused fear or apprehension in the recipient, or delay in the legal process. The plain language of Code § 18.2-460(A) provides that threats constitute a violation of the statute when they are knowingly made in an attempt to intimidate or impede law enforcement officers who are performing their duties. Thus, it is the threats made by

the offender, coupled with his intent, that constitute the offense. The resulting effect of the offender's threats, such as fear, apprehension, or delay, is not an element of the crime defined in Code § 18.2-460. By the express terms of the statute, it is immaterial whether the officer is placed in fear or apprehension. The offense is complete when the attempt to intimidate is made. Where a statute contains language which has a definite and precise meaning, and is expressed in clear and concise terms which manifest the intent, courts must adopt that plain meaning. . . . We, therefore, conclude that Polk's statement that he would kill Shirilla was a threat as contemplated by the statute.

(3) We disagree with Polk's contention that the Supreme Court's decision in *Jones v. Commonwealth*, . . . (1925), cited with approval in *Love v. Commonwealth*, . . . (1971), is contrary to our interpretation of Code § 18.2-460(A). Polk directs our attention to the following language in Jones:

> To constitute obstruction of an officer in the performance of his duty, it is not necessary that there be an actual or technical assault upon the officer, but there must be acts clearly indicating an intention on the part of the accused to prevent the officer from performing his duty, as to "obstruct" ordinarily implies opposition or resistance by direct action and forcible or threatened means. It means to obstruct the officer himself not merely to oppose or impede the process with which the officer is armed.

. . . In *Jones*, the accused was charged with violating former Code § 55-C, what was known as the Mapp Prohibition Law . . . . That statute provided:

> Any person who shall hinder or obstruct any officer of this state charged with the duty of inspecting baggage for ardent spirits . . . shall be deemed guilty of a misdemeanor.

This statute required actual hindrance or obstruction of the officer. The definition of "obstruction" cited above included the requirement of opposition or resistance by direct action. In contrast, Code § 18.2-460(A) provides that an attempt to intimidate or impede by threats, in itself, constitutes a substantive offense. Since *Jones* involved a statute requiring actual "obstruction," it is not applicable here. Code § 18.2-460(A), in contrast, is violated when, by threats or force, one attempts to intimidate or impede a law enforcement officer.

We also disagree with Polk's contention that the Supreme Court's holding in Love is contrary to our interpretation of Code § 18.2-460(A). In Love, the Supreme Court did not address whether words alone could constitute an attempt to intimidate or impede. In that case, the accused confronted police officers with a shotgun when they attempted to serve an arrest warrant on him. In finding that the accused had clearly attempted to impede and obstruct an orderly arrest, the court was not required to resolve whether words alone can constitute a violation of the statute.

Polk also argues that since he was under arrest and in custody when he made his threat to kill Shirilla, he could not have performed a direct ineffectual act toward the commission of the offense, and therefore, no attempted crime was completed. This argument, however, confuses an attempt to commit a substantive offense with the substantive offense defined in Code § 18.2-460(A). As defined in that section, threats knowingly made in an attempt to intimidate or impede constitute the offense. There is no overt act requirement, as such, contained in the statute.

(4) We turn now to consider Polk's claim that there was insufficient evidence of his criminal intent. Specifically, he argues that the evidence does not show that he actually intended to intimidate or impede Deputy Shirilla. In reviewing this claim, we examine the evidence presented in the light most favorable to the Commonwealth, and accord to the evidence all reasonable inferences fairly deducible therefrom. . . .

Intent is the purpose formed in a person's mind which may be shown by his statements or conduct. . . . We find that the trier of fact was entitled to conclude that Polk threatened to kill Shirilla, . . ., and that this threat made by Polk to Shirilla demonstrated his intent to intimidate Shirilla from completion of the post-arrest processing. For this reason, we hold that the evidence presented was sufficient to establish Polk's criminal intent.

III.

Finally, Polk argues that he was entitled to use reasonable force to resist arrest. In support of his argument, he relies exclusively on United States v. Moore, . . . (E.D. Va. 1971). In Moore, the accused grabbed the arm of an officer who was in the process of arresting her husband for simple assault. The court held that she was not criminally liable for this conduct, and emphasized that the arrest appeared unlawful to the wife because she did not know the difference between an "arrest" and an "apprehension" under the Uniform Code of Military Justice. . . . In Moore, the court also emphasized the fact that unnecessary force was used in effecting the husband's arrest. . . .

We believe that the Moore decision is inapplicable to the case at bar. First, although Polk argues that he was entitled to use reasonable force to resist arrest, he does not contest that he was lawfully arrested based upon the information given Shirilla by his dispatcher. Instead, he contends that since, contrary to the information received by Shirilla, his license was not suspended and there was no pending failure to appear charge, he was entitled to offer reasonable resistance. We disagree. An individual is not entitled to resist a lawful arrest. . . . Further, Polk does not argue, and the record does not show, any use of unnecessary or unreasonable force by the officers making the arrest. Therefore, we reject Polk's argument that he was entitled to use reasonable force under the authority of Moore.

In summary, we find that words alone may constitute an offense under Code § 18.2-460(A) when the words are threats knowingly made in an attempt to intimidate or impede law enforcement officers who are performing their duties; that the evidence was sufficient to demonstrate Polk's criminal intent; and that Polk cannot avoid criminal liability for his actions under the authority of Moore. Accordingly, we affirm his conviction.

Affirmed.

[Footnotes and citations omitted. Concurring and dissenting opinions omitted.]

City of Houston, Texas

v.

Hill

Supreme Court of the United States
482 U.S. 451 (1987)

Justice Brennan delivered the opinion of
the Court.

This case presents the question whether a
municipal ordinance that makes it unlawful
to interrupt a police officer in the performance of his or her duties is unconstitutionally overbroad under the First Amendment.

I.

Appellee Raymond Wayne Hill is a lifelong resident of Houston, Texas. At the time
this lawsuit began, he worked as a paralegal
and as executive director of the Houston
Human Rights League. A member of the
board of the Gay Political Caucus, which he
helped found in 1975, Hill was also affiliated
with a Houston radio station, and had carried
city and county press passes since 1975. He
lived in Montrose, a "diverse and eclectic
neighborhood" that is the center of gay
political and social life in Houston. . . .

The incident that sparked this lawsuit
occurred in the Montrose area on February
14, 1982. Hill observed a friend, Charles Hill,
intentionally stopping traffic on a busy street,
evidently to enable a vehicle to enter traffic.
Two Houston police officers, one of whom
was named Kelley, approached Charles and
began speaking with him. According to
the District Court, "shortly thereafter" Hill
began shouting at the officers "in an admitted attempt to divert Kelley's attention from
Charles Hill." . . .Hill first shouted: "Why
don't you pick on somebody your own size?"
After Officer Kelley responded: "Are you
interrupting me in my official capacity as a
Houston police officer?" Hill then shouted:
"Yes, why don't you pick on somebody my
size?" . . .Hill was arrested under Houston
Code of Ordinances, § 34-11(a), for "wil-
fully or intentionally interrupt[ing] a city
policeman . . . by verbal challenge during
an investigation." . . .Charles Hill was not
arrested. Hill was then acquitted after a non-
jury trial in Municipal Court.

Code of Ordinances, City of Houston,
Texas, § 34-11(a) (1984), reads:

"Sec. 34-11. Assaulting or interfering
with policemen. "(a) It shall be unlawful
for any person to assault, strike or in any
manner oppose, molest, abuse or interrupt
any policeman in the execution of his
duty, or any person summoned to aid in
making an arrest."

Following his acquittal in the Charles Hill
incident, Hill brought the suit in the Federal
District Court for the Southern District of
Texas, seeking (1) a declaratory judgment
that § 34-11(a) was unconstitutional both
on its face and as it had been applied to
him, (2) a permanent injunction against any
attempt to enforce the ordinance, (3) an order
expunging the records of his arrests under the
ordinance, and (4) damages and attorney's
fees under 42 U. S. C. §§ 1983 and 1988.

At trial, Hill introduced records provided
by the city regarding both the frequency with
which arrests had been made for violation of
the ordinance and the type of conduct with
which those arrested had been charged. He
also introduced evidence and testimony concerning the arrests of several reporters under
the ordinance. Finally, Hill introduced evidence regarding his own experience with the
ordinance, under which he has been arrested
four times since 1975, but never convicted.

The District Court held that Hill's evidence did not demonstrate that the ordinance
had been unconstitutionally applied. The
court also rejected Hill's contention that the
ordinance was unconstitutionally vague or
overbroad on its face. The ordinance was not
vague, the court stated, because:

"the wording of the ordinance is sufficiently definite to put a person of reasonable intelligence on fair notice of what
actions are forbidden. In particular, the
Court finds that the use of words such as
'interrupt' are sufficiently clear by virtue
of their commonly-understood, everyday
definitions. Interrupt commonly means
to cause one to cease, such as stopping
someone in the middle of something. The
Plaintiff, for example, clearly 'interrupted'
the police officers regarding the Charles
Hill incident." . . .

The court also held that the statute was not
overboard because "the ordinance does not,

at least facially, proscribe speech or conduct which is protected by the First Amendment."
. . . .

A panel of the Court of Appeals reversed. . . . The city's suggestion for rehearing *en banc* was granted, and the Court of Appeals, by a vote of 8-7, upheld the judgment of the panel. . . . The Court of Appeals agreed with the District Court's conclusion that the ordinance was not vague, and that it "plainly encompasse[d] mere verbal as well as physical conduct." . . . . Applying the standard established in *Broadrick* v. *Oklahoma*, . . . (1973), however, the Court of Appeals concluded that the ordinance was substantially overbroad. It found that "[a] significant range of protected speech and expression is punishable and might be deterred by the literal wording of the statute." . . . .

The Court of Appeals also reviewed the evidence of the unconstitutional application of the ordinance which Hill had introduced at trial. The court did not disturb the District Court's ruling that the statute had not been unconstitutionally applied to Hill or to the reporters. It did conclude, however, that other evidence not mentioned by the District Court revealed "a realistic danger of, and a substantial potential for, the unconstitutional application of the ordinance." . . . . This evidence showed that the ordinance "is officially regarded as penalizing the mere interruption of a policeman while in the line of duty," . . ., and has been employed to make arrests for, *inter alia*, "arguing," "talking," "interfering," "failing to remain quiet," "refusing to remain silent," "verbal abuse," "cursing," "verbally yelling," and "talking loudly, walking through scene." . . .

The city appealed, claiming that the Court of Appeals erred in holding the ordinance facially overboard and in not abstaining until the ordinance had been construed by the state courts. We noted probable jurisdiction, . . .and now affirm.

II.

The elements of First Amendment overbreadth analysis are familiar. Only a statute that is substantially overbroad may be invalidated on its face. . . . Criminal statutes must be scrutinized with particular care, . . .; those that make unlawful a substantial amount of constitutionally protected conduct may be held facially invalid even if they also have legitimate application. . . .

The city's principal argument is that the ordinance does not inhibit the exposition of ideas, and that it bans "core criminal conduct" not protected by the First Amendment. . . . In its view, the application of the ordinance to Hill illustrates that the police employ it only to prohibit such conduct, and not "as a subterfuge to control or dissuade free expression." . . . Since the ordinance is "content-neutral," and since there is no evidence that the city has applied the ordinance to chill particular speakers or ideas, the city concludes that the ordinance is not substantially overbroad.

We disagree with the city's characterization for several reasons. First, the enforceable portion of the ordinance deals not with core criminal conduct, but with speech. As the city has conceded, the language in the ordinance making it unlawful for any person to "assault" or "strike" a police officer is preempted by the Texas Penal Code. . . . The city explains, . . ., that "any species of physical assault on a police officer is encompassed within the provisions [§§ 22.01, 22.02] of the Texas Penal Code," and under § 1.08 of the Code, "[no] governmental subdivision or agency may enact or enforce a law that makes any conduct covered by this code an offense subject to a criminal penalty." . . . . Accordingly, the enforceable portion of the ordinance makes it "unlawful for any person to . . . in any manner oppose, molest, abuse or interrupt any policeman in the execution of his duty," and thereby prohibits verbal interruptions of police officers.

Second, contrary to the city's contention, the First Amendment protects a significant amount of verbal criticism and challenge directed at police officers. "Speech is often provocative and challenging. . . . [But it] is nevertheless protected against censorship or punishment, unless shown likely to produce a clear and present danger of a serious substantive evil that rises far above public inconvenience, annoyance, or unrest." . . .In *Lewis* v. *City of New Orleans*, . . . (1974), for example, the appellant was found to have yelled obscenities and threats at an officer

who had asked appellant's husband to produce his driver's license. Appellant was
convicted under a municipal ordinance that
made it a crime " 'for any person wantonly
to curse or revile or to use obscene or opprobrious language toward or with reference to
any member of the city police while in the
actual performance of his duty.' " .... We
vacated the conviction and invalidated the
ordinance as facially overbroad. Critical to
our decision was the fact that the ordinance
"punishe[d] only spoken words" and was not
limited in scope to fighting words that " 'by
their very utterance inflict injury or tend to
incite an immediate breach of the peace.' "
...Moreover, in a concurring opinion in
Lewis, Justice Powell suggested that even
the "fighting words" exception recognized in
Chaplinsky v. *New Hampshire*, ... (1942),
might require a narrower application in cases
involving words addressed to a police officer, because "a properly trained officer may
reasonably be expected to 'exercise a higher
degree of restraint' than the average citizen,
and thus be less likely to respond belliger-
ently to 'fighting words.' " ...

The Houston ordinance is much more
sweeping than the municipal ordinance
struck down in *Lewis*. It is not limited to
fighting words nor even to obscene or opprobrious language, but prohibits speech that "in
any manner ... interrupt[s]" an officer. The
Constitution does not allow such speech to
be made a crime. The freedom of individuals
verbally to oppose or challenge police action
without thereby risking arrest is one of the
principal characteristics by which we distinguish a free nation from a police state.

The city argues, however, that even if
the ordinance encompasses some protected
speech, its sweeping nature is both inevitable
and essential to maintain public order. The
city recalls this Court's observation in *Smith*
v. *Goguen*, ... (1974):

> "There are areas of human conduct
> where, by the nature of the problems
> presented, legislatures simply cannot
> establish standards with great precision.
> Control of the broad range of disorderly
> conduct that may inhibit a policeman
> in the performance of his official duties
> may be one such area requiring as it does

an on-the-spot assessment of the need to
keep order."

The city further suggests that its ordinance
is comparable to the disorderly conduct
statute upheld against a facial challenge in
Colten v. *Kentucky*, ... (1972).

This Houston ordinance, however, is not
narrowly tailored to prohibit only disorderly conduct or fighting words, and in no
way resembles the law upheld in *Colten*.
Although we appreciate the difficulties of
drafting precise laws, we have repeatedly
invalidated laws that provide the police with
unfettered discretion to arrest individuals for
words or conduct that annoy or offend them.
As the Court observed over a century ago, "it
would certainly be dangerous if the legislature could set a net large enough to catch all
possible offenders, and leave it to the courts
to step inside and say who could be rightfully
detained, and who should be set at large."
United States v. *Reese*, ... (1876).

*[Further discussion of similar cases
omitted.]*

Houston's ordinance criminalizes a substantial amount of constitutionally protected
speech, and accords the police unconstitutional discretion in enforcement. The ordinance's plain language is admittedly violated
scores of times daily, ..., yet only some individuals — those chosen by the police in their
unguided discretion — are arrested. Far from
providing the "breathing space" that "First
Amendment freedoms need ... to survive,"
..., the ordinance is susceptible of regular application to protected expression. We
conclude that the ordinance is substantially
overbroad, and that the Court of Appeals did
not err in holding it facially invalid.

III.

The city has also urged us not to reach the
merits of Hill's constitutional challenge, but
rather to abstain for reasons related to those
underlying our decision in *Railroad Comm'n*
v. *Pullman Co.*, ... (1941). In its view, there
are certain limiting constructions readily
available to the state courts that would eliminate the ordinance's overbreadth.

*[Discussion of state's request for court to
consider "abstention" and allow a limited
construction of the statute omitted.]*

IV.

Today's decision reflects the constitutional requirement that, in the face of verbal challenges to police action, officers and municipalities must respond with restraint. We are mindful that the preservation of liberty depends in part upon the maintenance of social order. . . . But the First Amendment recognizes, wisely we think, that a certain amount of expressive disorder not only is inevitable in a society committed to individual freedom, but must itself be protected if that freedom would survive. We therefore affirm the judgment of the Court of Appeals.

It is so ordered.

[Footnotes and citations omitted. Concurring and dissenting opinions deleted.]

Billy Doyle Medford
v.
The State of Texas

Court of Appeals of Texas
990 S.W.2d 799 (1999)

Opinion by Judge Dea Ann Smith.

Appellant Billy Doyle Medford appeals from the trial court's denial of his motion to suppress evidence and his subsequent conviction for the offenses of felony escape and possession of cocaine in an amount less than one gram. . . . The jury found that appellant had five prior felony convictions as alleged in the enhancement paragraphs of the indictment. Pursuant to the habitual felony offender statute, the jury assessed punishment for the cocaine possession at 20 years' imprisonment and life imprisonment for the escape conviction. The trial court ordered the sentences to run concurrently. In this appeal, Medford claims that the trial court erred in denying his motion to suppress evidence and by submitting to the jury improper definitions of "custody" and "under arrest" in the escape charge; he also challenges the sufficiency of the evidence to support his escape conviction. We will affirm in part and reverse and render in part the trial-court judgment.

[Discussion concerning all issues other than escape conviction omitted.]

Legal Sufficiency of the Evidence

In his fourth point of error, appellant challenges the legal sufficiency of evidence to convict him of escape. In conducting a legal sufficiency review, we determine whether, after viewing the evidence in the light most favorable to the verdict, any rational trier of fact could have found the essential elements of the crime beyond a reasonable doubt. . . . The elements of escape are that a person (1) escape (2) from custody (3) after having been arrested for, charged with or convicted of an offense. . . .

Appellant argues that the evidence adduced at trial did not legally establish that he escaped from custody while he was under arrest for an offense.

"Escape" is statutorily defined for purposes of chapter 38 of the Penal Code as "unauthorized departure from custody," and "custody" is defined as "under arrest by a peace officer or under restraint by a public servant pursuant to an order of a court." . . . Thus, in order to sustain appellant's conviction, we must find that Medford had been placed under restraint or taken into custody at the time he fled from officers Price and Baladez.

The State argues that actual, physical restraint is not a prerequisite to a showing of custody, citing *Harrell v. State*, . . . (Tex. Crim. App. 1987). The State also posits that an "oral pronouncement of arrest by a police officer to a suspect, with or without any evidence of physical restraint, is sufficient to establish the element of custody, if a reasonable person in the suspect's position would have believed he was not free to leave." For this proposition, the State relies on *Morris v. State*, . . . (*Tex. Crim. App.* 1987) and *Gilbert v. State*, . . . (Tex. App. — Fort Worth 1990, . . .). For reasons we will discuss, we believe that neither proposition is a valid statement of the law as applied to this case.

The issue in *Harrell* was whether a prisoner transferred to a hospital out of medical necessity retained the legal status of arrestee for purposes of determining whether he was in "custody" under section 38.06(a). Before entering the hospital, Harrell was told that he was still under arrest and in custody, and that if he ran away from the hospital he would be treated as if he had escaped from jail. Harrell ignored that admonition and drove to Florida with another patient and a local woman. . . .

The Court of Criminal Appeals upheld Harrell's conviction for escape. The court stated: "We now hold that actual, physical 'hands-on' restraint is not a prerequisite to a showing of custody in the context of the offense of escape. Rather, it is important to look at the legal status of the individual at the time of the escape." . . . .

Examining Harrell's legal status, the court held that Harrell remained under arrest while at the hospital. . . . Because Harrell was still "in custody" regardless of his physical location, it held that the court of appeals had erred in focusing on the fact that Harrell was not under any kind of physical restraint while at the hospital. . . .

As the Harrell court recognized, the issue of what constitutes an initial arrest was not before the court in that case. . . . However, that is precisely the issue in the present case: whether a person who has been stopped for questioning and who then flees prior to being handcuffed has escaped from "custody" under section 38.06(a). Because Harrell only instructs that physical restraint is not a necessary prerequisite to continuing custody after an arrest and conviction, that rule is inapplicable to the present case.

We next examine the proposition that a person is under arrest or in custody for the purpose of escape if a reasonable person in the position of the arrestee would have believed that he was not free to leave. In *Morris*, the defendant was appealing his conviction for theft; he had not been charged with escape. The court of appeals found that, after being arrested but before being searched, the appellant committed the felony offense of escape by running from the police officer who arrested him. . . . The intermediate court concluded that since Morris's escape in the presence of the police officer provided probable cause for the second arrest, the evidence seized subsequent thereto was properly admitted. . . .

A divided Court of Criminal Appeals affirmed. The three-judge plurality looked to *United States v. Mendenhall*, . . . (1980),

which held that a person has been "seized" within the meaning of the Fourth Amendment only if, in view of all the circumstances surrounding the incident, a reasonable person would have believed that he was not free to leave. . . . The plurality then applied the Mendenhall test for "seizure" to the issue of whether a person is "in custody" for purposes of committing the offense of escape. . . . However, as the dissent observed:

> When we treat an offense based on a statutorily defined element of "custody," resort to decisions construing the meaning of "seizure" in the Fourth Amendment is not likely to solve the problem. . . . Whether a person was "seized" is merely a threshold inquiry in determining a claim that an intrusion upon his liberty or privacy occurred without particularized and objective justification required in the circumstances to render the "seizure" reasonable. Therefore, a "seizure" for purposes of the Fourth Amendment does not necessarily equate with "custody" within the meaning of [the escape statute]. So, federal decisions relied on by the majority do not dictate our construction of a state statute in which the critical component is "custody," not "seizure.". . . .

Two courts of appeals have cited *Morris* and used the *Mendenhall* test to determine that an appellant committed the offense of escape. . . . However, a majority of the Court of Criminal Appeals has never embraced the view advanced by the *Morris* plurality. This Court has discussed *Morris* and questioned the soundness of equating seizure for Fourth Amendment purposes with the statutory definition of "arrest" in the context of escape or resisting arrest. . . . We have also held that the term "custody" in the escape context clearly implies a degree of physical limitation, restraint, or control. . . .

Common sense does not support the idea that a person is "in custody," in the context of the offense of escape, when a reasonable person would not feel free to leave. As appellant's counsel urged at oral argument, a reasonable person might not feel free to leave if a police officer telephoned him at home and instructed him to remain there. Adopting the State's definition of "custody" would lead to the conclusion that a person in that situation would commit the offense of escape simply by departing his home. This result is not compelled either by the statutory definition of "custody" or by controlling case law.

We also find *Morris* distinguishable on its facts. In *Morris*, the detention took place in the controlled space of a probation officer's office; the appellant sat in a chair and was questioned by the arresting officer after being told he was under arrest. Morris decided to flee only after discussing the impact of his arrest on his probation. The arresting officer did not handcuff Morris because he did not have handcuffs with him and presumably he did not feel the need to subdue Morris any further when Morris was sitting in a chair in the probation office, surrounded by the police officer and the probation officer. The factual circumstances of Morris are similar to those in Harrell because in both cases, the appellant had been placed under arrest and was in a situation in which enough control was being exerted over him that further physical restraint was not believed to be necessary. In the present case, however, custody had not clearly been established when Medford fled, since Officer Price was unsuccessful in his attempt to handcuff Medford immediately after a Terry encounter that took place on a public street.

For these reasons, we believe that *Gilbert v. State*, . . . (Tex. App. — Fort Worth 1990, ...) was wrongly decided. In *Gilbert*, the appellant and a young female passenger were observed in a parked car by police officers Solomon and Riddle in an area in which vehicles were prohibited. Both officers ordered the driver to stop after the car began to pull away. As Officer Solomon approached the vehicle, he saw the female passenger pulling up her panties and blue jeans; she exclaimed to Solomon, "he made me do it" and told the officer that she was eleven years old. Officer Solomon then directed Gilbert to stand by the car, where he was ordered into a spread-eagle position, searched, and advised that he was under arrest. However, Gilbert refused to be handcuffed and fled into a nearby park. . . .

The Fort Worth Court of Appeals upheld Gilbert's conviction for escape. . . . The court adopted the Morris plurality's rule that a person is under arrest or in custody for purposes of the escape statute if a reasonable person in the defendant's position would

have believed that they were not free to leave. . . . The Gilbert court also repeated the statement from Harrell that "actual, physical 'hands-on' restraint is not a prerequisite to a showing of custody in the context of the offense of escape." . . . . Because a reasonable person in Gilbert's position at the time Officer Solomon was attempting to handcuff him would not have believed that he was free to leave, the court reasoned, Gilbert was in custody and sufficient evidence existed to support his conviction for escape. . . .

Extending the Gilbert court's reasoning, Gilbert would have apparently been in "custody" at the moment the police officers approached his car and advised him to stop — even if they only shouted the warning across a parking lot — since a reasonable person in that situation would presumably not feel free to leave. However, this is precisely the type of situation contemplated by the offense of evading arrest. . . . We decline to expand *Harrell* beyond its facts or follow the *Morris* plurality in borrowing Fourth Amendment case law to define "custody" in the context of escape.

We believe that a better analysis is found in *Snabb v. State*, . . . (Tex. App. — Corpus Christi 1984, . . .). In *Snabb*, an airport security officer saw the defendant, whom he knew to be intoxicated, attempting to drive out of the parking lot. After pursuing Snabb on foot, the officer and his partner succeeded in stopping her. The officer told Snabb that she was under arrest and ordered her to gather her possessions, lock her car, and come with him. Snabb refused to cooperate and ran away in disregard of his command to stop, but was quickly apprehended. Based on this evidence, Snabb was convicted of escaping from the officer's custody following arrest. . . .

The court of appeals reversed, noting that "the offense of escape occurs after having been arrested, not before the arrest is complete. . . . The court cited to *Smith v. State*, . . . (Tex. Crim. App. 1949), which held:

> An arrest of a person carries with it an element of detention, custody or control of the accused. The mere fact that an officer makes the statement to an accused that he is under arrest does not complete the arrest. There must be custody or detention and submission to such arrest.

. . . . Applying this standard, the court found that Snabb had not been arrested when she fled. While she apparently committed the offense of evading arrest, she had not been charged with that crime. Because the evidence was insufficient to show that Snabb had escaped from an arrest or from custody, the court ordered her acquittal. . . .

Two resisting arrest cases are also helpful to our determination of whether Medford was arrested or in custody when he fled. In *White v. State*, . . . (Tex. Crim. App. 1980), the arresting officer had drawn his pistol, placed the defendant in a spread-eagle position against a horse trailer, and was preparing to handcuff him when White turned around and kicked the officer in the groin. . . . The court affirmed White's conviction for resisting arrest and noted that the arrest was taking place at the time of the appellant's action. . . . The facts of *Schrader v. State*, . . . (Tex. App. — Austin 1988, . . .) are similar. In that case, two peace officers were preparing to arrest Schrader in a restaurant parking lot for public intoxication after ejecting him from the restaurant. Schrader accompanied one officer to a point near the restaurant while the other officer called to determine if there were any outstanding warrants for Schrader's arrest. After learning that there was an outstanding arrest warrant, the officer informed Schrader that he was under arrest and attempted to handcuff him. Schrader resisted by hitting, kicking, and biting one of the officers in a brief struggle. . . .

On appeal, Schrader argued that his assault on the officers while they were attempting to handcuff him could not constitute resisting arrest because his arrest was complete when he submitted to their authority in the parking lot. Instead, he claimed, the assault was an attempt to escape from custody. . . . This Court rejected Schrader's attempt to define the phrase "effecting an arrest" using Fourth Amendment standards. First, we noted the different purposes behind the Fourth Amendment and the resisting arrest statute: the former was designed to protect citizens' privacy interests, while the latter was enacted to protect police officers attempting to carry out their duties. See id. While agreeing that Schrader's arrest was "complete" with his detention in the parking lot, for some purpos-

es of the law, we held that the officers were still effecting his arrest when he assaulted them at the point near the restaurant. . . .

At Medford's trial, there was some dispute about whether Officer Price had made contact with appellant's arm when he attempted to handcuff him. Officer Price testified at the suppression hearing that his right arm was free when he reached for the handcuffs with his left hand; he described Medford as being "within touching distance" at the moment Medford fled. However, at trial he testified that his left hand was on Medford's left arm as he reached for his handcuffs. Price further testified that as he grabbed Medford's left wrist in an attempt to secure him, Medford "went down and lunged and ran south . . ."

This account of an actual touching or grabbing differs from that given by Officer Baladez, who testified both at the suppression hearing and at trial that Medford started to put his hands to his side (free of any touching) when he fled, lunging between Baladez and the police car.

Viewing this evidence in the light most favorable to the verdict, as we must, we must accept as true Officer Price's testimony that he was touching Medford's wrist or arm just before Medford fled. However, we cannot say that the State carried its burden of establishing that Medford had been placed under restraint or taken into custody; by his own account, Officer Price attempted to gain physical control of Medford but was unsuccessful. While Medford apparently committed the offense of evading arrest, . . ., the State elected not to charge him with that offense. By its pleading charging Medford with escape, the State assumed the burden of proving a completed arrest. Because the evidence viewed in a light most favorable to the prosecution shows that Officer Price never succeeded in securing custody and control of appellant, the State did not satisfy that burden. We find the evidence of escape legally insufficient and sustain appellant's fourth point of error.

[Discussion of other points of error omitted.]

[Footnotes and citations omitted. Concurring and dissenting opinions omitted.]

Cases Relating to Chapter 13

U.S. Criminal Code: Offenses Against Persons and Property

REBECCA BEACH SMITH, District Judge.

I. Procedural History

On September 21, 1993, Sean Ryan Fowler pled guilty to one count of possession of cocaine base under 21 U.S.C. § 844. On December 2, 1993, the Court sentenced him, in accordance with Federal Sentencing Guidelines, to eighty-seven months to be followed by a period of two years supervised release. Defendant Fowler did not appeal his sentence. On December 29, 1994, Defendant Fowler filed a motion to vacate, set aside, or correct his conviction under 28 U.S.C. § 2255. Specifically, in support of his section 2255 motion, Defendant Fowler alleges that the federal government lacked jurisdiction to prosecute, convict, or sentence him for possession of cocaine base. The Government responded to Defendant Fowler's section 2255 motion on January 25, 1994.

II. Standard of Review

Defendant proceeds under 28 U.S.C. § 2255, which provides, "A prisoner in custody under sentence of a court established by Act of Congress claiming the right to be released upon the ground . . . that the court was without jurisdiction to impose such sentence . . . may move the court which imposed the sentence to vacate, set aside or correct the sentence." In deciding a section 2255 motion, the court need not hold a hearing if "the motion and the files and records of the case conclusively show that the prisoner is entitled to no relief. . . . ". Further, if the motion is brought before the sentencing judge, the judge may rely on recollections of previous events to dismiss the motion. . . . Accordingly, this Court finds no hearing necessary and addresses Defendant's section 2255 motion.

III. Analysis

Defendant Fowler complains that the United States had no jurisdiction to prosecute, convict, or sentence him for possession of cocaine base. Specifically, Defendant claims that the United States "has no territorial jurisdiction over non-federally owned areas inside the jurisdiction boundaries of the States within the American Union." A liberal reading of Defendant's *pro se* complaint indicates that Defendant has really contested the federal district court's jurisdiction over a crime involving the wholly intrastate possession of cocaine base.

The Fourth Circuit has held that, "the statutory definition and proscription of transactions of 'controlled substances,' . . ., entirely within a state is altogether constitutional." . . .*Atkinson* involved a challenge to the constitutionality of the Comprehensive Drug

Abuse Prevention and Control Act of 1970 (the "Act") based on the fact that the wholly intrastate possession of heroin, a controlled substance, did not affect interstate commerce. . . . The Fourth Circuit stated, "Congressional findings on which the [Act] rested disclosed that intrastate possession, distribution and sale of drugs such as heroin directly and injuriously effected the introduction of them into other States to the injury of the public health and welfare. . . .

Defendant Fowler's case differs slightly from *Atkinson* because Fowler's conviction involved cocaine base instead of heroin and because Fowler's conviction involved the mere possession of a controlled substance rather than the possession of a controlled substance with the intent to distribute. The Court examines whether these distinctions prevent if from applying the holding in *Atkinson* to Fowler's case.

Specifically, Defendant Fowler pled guilty to possession of cocaine base under 21 U.S.C. § 844. The Fourth Circuit has not made a specific finding as to whether the intrastate possession of cocaine base invokes the Commerce Clause, Const. Art. I, § 8, cl. 3. However, such a specific finding that cocaine base affects interstate commerce is not required for the federal government to assert jurisdiction over Plaintiff's claim. . . . In *Davis*, the District of Columbia Circuit ruled that "the Commerce Clause empowers Congress to regulate broad classes of activities which are found to have a substantial impact on interstate commerce." . . . Therefore, the fact that *Atkinson* involved another controlled substance does not prevent this Court from applying the *Atkinson* holding to the case at bar. . . .

This Court also addresses whether the possession of a controlled substance unaccompanied by the intent to distribute implicates the Commerce Clause. . . . Congress possesses the power to regulate wholly intrastate activities which have an effect upon interstate commerce, . . .Congress has also explicitly declared that the intrastate possession of a controlled substance, in this case, cocaine base, affects interstate commerce. . . . These Congressional findings allow the Court to extend the Fourth Circuit's ruling in *Atkinson* to the facts of Defendant's case. . . .

IV. Conclusion

Because of the possession of cocaine base affects interstate commerce, the Court had jurisdiction to prosecute, convict, and sentence Defendant. Fourth Circuit precedent, as stated in *United States v. Atkinson*, compels this Court to reach that conclusion. . . . Consequently, the Court DENIES Defendant's section 2255 motion.

Discussion of procedural issues omitted.

IT IS SO ORDERED.

[Footnotes and citations omitted. Concurring and dissenting opinions omitted.]

United States of America
v.
Jan P. Helder

United States Court of Appeals for the Eighth Circuit
2006 U.S. App LEXIS 15995 (2006)

Smith, Circuit Judge.

Jan P. Helder, Jr. was charged with using a facility of interstate commerce, the Internet, to attempt to entice a minor to engage in illegal sexual activity, in violation of 18 U.S.C. § 2422(b). The district court granted Helder's motion for judgment of acquittal. The government appeals, arguing that the district court erred by granting Helder's motion for judgment of acquittal because § 2422(b) does not require the intended victim to be an actual minor. We reverse.

I. Background

Helder, a 41-year-old male, entered an Internet Yahoo! chat room under the screen name "trialkc" while at his law office. An undercover officer, Detective Mark Stephens of the CyberCrimes Unit of the Platte County, Missouri, Sheriff's Department, using the screen name "lisa_mo_13" ("lisa"), entered a chat room labeled "Missouri 1." Within ten minutes of entering the chat room, "lisa" was instant messaged by "trialkc." "Trialkc" asked "lisa" if she was "near [K]ansas [C]ity." When "lisa" answered in the affirmative, "trialkc" asked "lisa" how old she was, and "lisa" responded that she was 14 years old. "Trialkc" told "lisa" to watch out for "dirty ole men." When "lisa" said that most of the men in the chat room were cool, "trialkc" opined that was because of a "sting" that was occurring.

"Trialkc" continued to chat with "lisa," eventually asking her about her looks, her clothing, her bra size, her sexual experience, and when her mother was home. "Lisa" told "trialkc" that she had previously engaged in sexual activity with an older man whom she met online and with whom she "did it" over Christmas break while her mom was at work. "Trialkc" asked "lisa" if she was "looking for another experience" to which "lisa" responded that she was "thinking it would be cool." "Trialkc" obtained "lisa's" address and indicated that he would meet her at her apartment complex in 20 minutes. After the chat ended, Detective Stephens accessed "trialkc's" Yahoo! Profile to learn his identity. While the profile was not complete, it did contain a picture of a male wearing a blue shirt in an office setting.

Detective Stephens and a colleague went to the undercover apartment to wait for "trialkc" to arrive. Detective Stephens observed a white BMW drive in the south entrance of the apartment complex parking lot that "lisa" had identified during the chat. As the vehicle drove past, Detective Stephens identified the driver as "trialkc" from the Yahoo! profile photograph. Detective Stephens observed the driver's shirt and noticed it looked like the shirt worn by "trialkc" in the profile photograph. After spotting the detectives, the driver sped away before he could be confronted.

By checking Yahoo! records, Stephens traced the Internet protocol address of "trialkc" to computers owned by the Kansas City Firm of Steve Helder Siegel, LLC. Jan Helder was listed as the "Tech Administrator." Detective Stephens matched the driver's license photograph of Helder and the photograph of "trialkc" depicted in the Yahoo! profile.

Detective Stephens, with the assistance of the FBI, obtained and executed a federal search warrant for Helder's law office computer. Helder was not present when the search warrant was executed at his office. Detective Stephens and Special Agent Brian Stone later interviewed Helder at his home. During the interview, Helder admitted that what he did was wrong. He said he would never do it again. He said he believed it was an online sting that was close to entrapment. He said he just traveled to the meeting place "out of curiosity" to see if there were television cameras. He admitted using Yahoo! to chat with the apparent minor. He admitted removing his photograph from his profile following his trip to the apartment. He said he never intended to have sex with a minor. A computer forensic analysis of Helder's desktop computer revealed that he had used MapQuest.com to search for "lisa's address and had accessed her Yahoo! profile.

Federal authorities charged Helder with violating 18 U.S.C. § 2422(b). Helder pleaded not guilty, and the matter proceeded to trial. At the conclusion of the government's evidence presentation, Helder moved for judgment of acquittal, arguing that the government's case failed for "legal impossibility" because § 2422(b) requires that the targeted victim be an actual minor. The district court denied Helder's motion, but it encouraged Helder to renew the motion at the close of the case. Helder chose not to produce any evidence and renewed his motion for judgment of acquittal. After taking the motion under advisement, the district court submitted the case to the jury.

The jury found Helder guilty of violating § 2422(b). After discharging the jury, the district court set aside the jury's guilty verdict and then granted Helder's motion for judgment of acquittal at the close of all the evidence. The district court held that the plain reading of the statute requires the government to prove that the individual involved in the communication was under the age of 18.

II. Discussion

The government's sole argument is that 18 U.S.C. § 2422(b) does not require that the intended victim be an actual minor and that the district court therefore erred when it granted Helder's motion for judgment of acquittal. The government asserts Helder violated the Act because he believed he was communicating with a minor and thus made an attempt to entice a minor into engaging in unlawful sexual activity. We review *de novo* the district court's grant or denial of a motion for judgment of acquittal. . . .

Section 2422(b) provides:

Whoever, using the mail or any facility or means of interstate or foreign commerce, or within the special maritime and territorial jurisdiction of the United States knowingly persuades, induces, entices, or coerces any individual who has not attained the age of 18 years, to engage in prostitution or any sexual activity for which any person can be charged with a criminal offense, or attempts to do so, shall be fined under this title and imprisoned not less than 5 years and not more than 30 years. . . .

Our circuit has not previously decided whether an attempt to entice a minor to engage in illegal sexual activity requires that the intended victim be an actual minor. However, prior similar cases do offer some guidance.

First, we have upheld attempt convictions under 18 U.S.C. § 2422(b) where the enticed "minor" was actually an undercover police officer. . . .

Second, under plain error review, we rejected a defendant's argument that the evidence was insufficient to convict him of attempting to entice a minor because an undercover officer actually posed as the minor. . . . The defendant in *Blazek* based his argument on the district court's decision in this case. . . . We noted that "[t]he decision in *Helder* is inconsistent with, and did not cite, our decision in *United States v. Patten*, that upheld an attempt conviction under 18 U.S.C. § 2422(b) in which the enticed 'minor' was an undercover police officer." . . . Furthermore, we stated that while "this issue was not raised or discussed in *Patten*, it was raised and squarely rejected in" three other circuits. . . . In holding that "the law at the time of trial was *not* settled in this circuit" as to whether a conviction for attempting to entice a minor to engage in sexual activity requires the targeted victim to be an actual minor, we stated that "even if this court should ultimately affirm the district court's decision in *Helder*, thereby

creating a conflict with at least three other circuits, the error is not plain at this time. Therefore, the evidence was sufficient to convict [the defendant] of attempted enticement of a minor." . . .

Also, in *Blazek*, the appellant argued that the district court erred when it increased his offense level and criminal history category under U.S.S.G. § 4B1.5(a). The appellant asserted that because the enhancement only applies to sex crimes involving "minors," and the undercover officer was, under the application notes to the Guidelines, a "minor victim," not a "minor," the enhancement should not apply. . . . We rejected the defendant's argument, stating, "As explained in Part I of this opinion, this court in *Patten* and at least three other circuits have upheld convictions for attempted enticement under 18 U.S.C. § 2422(b) even though the intended victim was in fact an undercover police officer, because the defendant believed the victim to be a minor." . . . .

We also find the reasoning of other circuits that have addressed this issue persuasive. First, the Fifth Circuit rejected a defendant's argument that it was legally impossible for him to attempt to entice a minor to engage in unlawful sexual activity because the alleged "minor" was actually an undercover FBI agent. . . . The court viewed the case as one of factual impossibility "because the defendant unquestionably intended to engage in the conduct proscribed by law but failed to only because of the circumstances unknown to him." . . . (explaining that factual impossibility is not a defense to the crime if the defendant could have committed the crime had the attendant circumstances been as the actor believed them to be, while legal impossibility is where the defendant's actions, even if carried out, do not constitute a crime). In addition, the court identified two elements that the government must prove in criminal attempt cases:

[F]irst, [the government must prove] that the defendant acted with the kind of culpability otherwise required for the commission of the underlying substantive offense, and, second, that the defendant had engaged in conduct which constitutes a substantial step toward the commission of the crime. The substantial step must be conduct which strongly corroborates the firmness of defendant's criminal attempt.

. . . The court held that the evidence showed that the defendant "intended to engage in sexual acts with a 14-year-old girl and that he took substantial steps toward committing the crime" because the defendant's scheme, "if fully carried out as he 'desired' or 'planned,' was not to engage in sexual relations with an adult FBI officer," but to entice a minor female. . . .

Second, the Eleventh Circuit held that existence of an actual minor victim is not required to convict a defendant of attempting to persuade a minor to engage in criminal activity under § 2422(b). . . . The court first found that the plain language of § 2422(b) criminalizes the attempt conduct because the statute states that a person can be charged with the criminal offense if he "attempts to" knowingly persuade, induce, entice, or coerce a minor to engage in unlawful sexual activity. . . . Thus, "the fact that [the defendant's] crime has not ripened into a completed offense is no obstacle to an attempt conviction. [The defendant's] belief that a minor was involved is sufficient to sustain an attempt conviction under 18 U.S.C. § 2422(b)." . . .

Third, the Ninth Circuit also "joined [its] sister circuits in concluding that 'an actual minor victim is not required for an attempt conviction under 18 U.S.C. § 2422(b).'" . . . Looking to the plain language of the statute, the court identified four elements of criminal liability:

[A] person must "knowingly" (1) actually or attempt to (2) persuade, induce, entice, or coerce (3) a person under 18 years of age (4) to engage in sexual activity that would constitute a criminal offense. Following [the] canons of statutory interpretation, it is apparent that the term "knowingly" refers both to the verbs — "persuades, induces, entices, or coerces" — as well as to the object — "a person who has not achieved the age of 18 years."

. . . The *mens rea* requirement of "knowledge" refers to the defendant's subjective intent — "it is what is in the mind of the defendant." . . . . Therefore, the court concluded that a jury could "reasonably infer that [the defendant] knowingly sought

sexual activity, and knowingly sought it with a minor. That he was mistaken in his knowledge is irrelevant." . . . .

The court also found that attempted enticement of a minor is "no different than an attempted solicitation of prostitution, where the criminal conduct is the knowing effort to solicit an individual for prostitution." . . . . Just because the alleged prostitute turns out to be an undercover police officer "does not vitiate" the defendant's criminal conduct. . . .

Finally, the Tenth Circuit rejected a defendant's impossibility defense to his conviction under § 2422(b) where the "minor" was actually the fictitious persona of an undercover law enforcement agent. . . . The court held that "factual impossibility is generally not a defense to criminal attempt because success is not an essential element of attempt crimes." . . . . The court "agreed with [its] sister circuits that this general rule applies to the case at bar — that is, it is not a defense to an offense involving enticement and exploitation of minors that the defendant falsely believed a minor to be involved." . . .

Based on our sister circuits' thorough analysis of the plain meaning of the statute, as well as our holdings in *Patten, Naiden, Dickson*, and *Blazek*, we hold that an actual minor victim is not required for an attempt conviction under § 2422(b).

III. Conclusion

Accordingly, we reverse the order of the district court granting Helder's motion for judgment of acquittal and remand the case to the district court for sentencing.

[Footnotes and citations omitted. Concurring and dissenting opinions omitted.]

United States of America

v.

William Nathaniel Cobb

**United States Court of Appeals
for the Fourth Circuit
144 F.3D 319 (1998)**

Wilkinson, Chief Judge:

William Nathaniel Cobb was convicted of carjacking, 18 U.S.C. § 2119, use of a firearm during a crime of violence, 18 U.S.C. § 924(c), and bank fraud, 18 U.S.C. § 1344. Cobb appeals the district court's denial of his motion to dismiss the carjacking and firearm counts. He argues that the federal carjacking statute, which also defined the crime of violence for his firearm conviction, exceeds Congress' authority under the Commerce Clause. Because we find the carjacking statute to lie within the bounds of Congress' commerce power, we affirm the judgment of the district court.

I.

On the morning of October 6, 1995, Amanda Yezerski departed Charleston, South Carolina in her Mercury Cougar for Savannah, Georgia. Along the way she stopped in Summerville, South Carolina to retrieve cash from an automatic teller machine (ATM) and to fill her car with gas. While pumping gas at a service station, Yezerski saw the defendant loitering in the area. Once she finished at the pump, Yezerski walked around to the driver's side of her car and again noticed Cobb through her peripheral vision. Before she was able to shut her door and drive away, Cobb cornered Yezerski against her car. Yezerski observed that Cobb was carrying a tote bag with a gun partially protruding from it. He demanded her car and told her not to scream. Yezerski did scream, however, and Cobb pulled her from the car and squeezed past her into the driver's seat himself. When she reached into the car in an attempt to retrieve her keys, Cobb started the car. He then proceeded to pull Yezerski's body partially into the car, such that her legs were left dangling out the open door. Cobb then exited the gas station and drove across a multilane highway into a store parking lot,

where he pushed Yezerski from the car and drove away. At the point Yezerski began screaming at the gas station, another woman who had stopped there became aware of the carjacking in progress. That woman, Tuesday Crosby, jumped into her truck and pursued the carjacker. When Cobb exited the store parking lot after pushing Yezerski from the car, Crosby followed him onto the interstate. She ended her pursuit, however, when Cobb extended his arm out the car window and pointed a gun in Crosby's direction. Cobb then moved into the emergency lane and sped off.

Cobb escaped with both Yezerski's Mercury Cougar and purse, which held her cash, debit card, ATM card, and checkbook. Evidence showed that Cobb used Yezerski's debit card to purchase clothing, that he and another woman successfully forged one of Yezerski's checks, and that Cobb made at least five unsuccessful attempts to withdraw money using the stolen ATM card.

Cobb was eventually arrested and indicted by a grand jury on one count of carjacking, 18 U.S.C. § 2119, one count of use of a firearm during that carjacking, 18 U.S.C. § 924(c), and five counts of bank fraud, 18 U.S.C. § 1344. Cobb moved to dismiss the first two counts of the indictment, arguing that the federal carjacking statute was an unconstitutional exercise of Congress' power under the Commerce Clause. The district court denied Cobb's motion and a trial was held in May 1996. The jury found Cobb guilty on all counts of the indictment. The district court sentenced Cobb to a total imprisonment term of 248 months. Cobb now appeals the district court's denial of his motion to dismiss.

II.

At the time Cobb committed the acts charged in the indictment, the federal carjacking statute provided:

Whoever, with the intent to cause death or serious bodily harm takes a motor vehicle that has been transported, shipped, or received in interstate or foreign commerce from the person or presence of another by force and violence or by intimidation, or attempts to do so, shall —

(1) be fined under this title or imprisoned not more than 15 years, or both,

(2) if serious bodily injury (as defined in section 1365 of this title) results, be fined under this title or imprisoned not more than 25 years, or both, and

(3) if death results, be fined under this title or imprisoned for any number of years up to life, or both, or sentenced to death.

... Arguing against the weight of all seven circuits that have considered the question, ..., Cobb challenges Congress' authority to enact this criminal statute. He contends that, in light of the Supreme Court's decision in *United States v. Lopez*, ...(1995), section 2119 is beyond the reach of Congress' commerce power and therefore unconstitutional.

Cobb's challenge is without merit. The Lopez Court's articulation of the scope of Congress' commerce power is by now familiar. The Court recognized Congress' authority to (1) "regulate the use of the channels of interstate commerce;" (2) "regulate and protect the instrumentalities of interstate commerce, or persons or things in interstate commerce;" and (3) regulate "those activities that substantially affect interstate commerce." ... When determining whether the Gun-Free School Zones Act of 1990 fit within the third category, the Court found that 18 U.S.C. § 922(q) lacked a "jurisdictional element which would ensure, through case-by-case inquiry, that the firearm possession in question affects interstate commerce." .... Because section 2119 does contain just such a jurisdictional element, and because the statute falls within Congress' power to regulate the instrumentalities of interstate commerce, we reject Cobb's constitutional challenge.

A.

The *Lopez* Court acknowledged that Congress could include a jurisdictional element in criminal statutes to ensure that each instance of criminalized conduct also has "an explicit connection with or effect on interstate commerce." .... The Court cited its prior interpretation of the former felon-in-possession statute in *United States v. Bass*, ...(1971), as an example of such a jurisdictional requirement. In *Bass*, the Court suggested that the government could satisfactorily prove a nexus with interstate commerce by demonstrating "that the firearm received has previously traveled in interstate commerce." .... The Court confirmed that this reading was correct in *Scarborough v. United States*, ...(1977), holding that the government need only prove "that the firearm have been, at some time, in interstate commerce." ....

In *United States v. Wells*, ... (4th Cir. 1996), we rejected a Lopez challenge to 18 U.S.C. § 922(g), which criminalizes the shipment, transport, possession, or receipt of a firearm by a specific class of persons. Section 922(g) permits the government to prove a commerce nexus by showing that the defendant received a firearm "which has been shipped or transported in interstate or foreign commerce." .... We turned aside the constitutional challenge, holding that the jurisdictional element both distinguished the case from *Lopez* and satisfied the requirements of the Commerce Clause. ...

The federal carjacking statute also contains an express jurisdictional element. Section 2119 applies only to the forcible taking of motor vehicles that have been "transported, shipped, or received in interstate or foreign commerce." Thus, in Cobb's case the government was forced to prove — and did prove — that Yezerski's Mercury Cougar was manufactured in Ohio and shipped in interstate commerce to South Carolina. Like our decision in Wells, therefore, we find that section 2119's jurisdictional element "distinguishes *Lopez* and satisfies the minimal nexus required for the Commerce Clause." .... Additionally, we note that our holding is in accord with the decisions of four other circuits that have similarly relied on section 2119's jurisdictional element in finding the statute a valid exercise of Congress' authority under the Commerce Clause. ...

B.

Section 2119 is also a valid exercise of Congress' power to regulate an instrumentality of interstate commerce — cars. In *Lopez*, the Court confirmed that Congress can protect such instrumentalities, "even though the threat may come only from intra-state activities." . . . . The Court has also held that interstate roads, . . ., and toll roads and drawbridges connecting interstate roads, . . ., are instrumentalities of interstate commerce because they are essential to the carriage of persons and goods moving in interstate commerce. As the Third Circuit has observed, "Instrumentalities differ from other objects that affect interstate commerce because they are used as a means of transporting goods and people across state lines. Trains and planes are inherently mobile; highways and bridges, though static, are critical to the movement of automobiles." Bishop, ...

Undoubtedly, if planes and trains qualify as instrumentalities of interstate commerce, so too do automobiles. The fact that not every car, train, or plane trip has an interstate destination has never been thought to remove these means of transport from the category of an instrumentality of commerce. Cars, like trains and aircraft, are both inherently mobile and indispensable to the interstate movement of persons and goods. We therefore hold that section 2119 is a valid exercise of Congress' power to regulate and protect an instrumentality of interstate commerce. In this respect, our conclusion is in accord with the decisions of four other circuits. . . .

III.

For the foregoing reasons, we affirm the judgment of the district court.

[Footnotes and citations omitted. Concurring and dissenting opinions omitted.]

**United States of America
v.
Autumn Jackson, Jose Medina, and
Boris Sabas**

**United States District Court
986 F. Supp. 829 (1997)**

Barbara S. Jones, United States District Judge:

Pending is a motion by defendant Autumn Jackson, in which co-defendant Yosi Medina joins, to dismiss the Superseding Indictment

pursuant to Federal Rule of Criminal Procedure 12(b)(2). Specifically, Jackson argues that 18 U.S.C. § 875(d) ("§ 875(d)") and § 155.05.2(e)(v) of the New York Penal Law ("§ 155.05") are unconstitutionally overbroad and vague on their face and as applied in this case. For the reasons set forth below, the Court denies the motion.

BACKGROUND

On February 27, 1997, the Grand Jury returned a superseding indictment charging Jackson, Medina, and co-defendant Boris Sabas, a/k/a "Boris Shmulevich," in three counts.

Count One charged that from late 1996 until January 18, 1997, in violation of 18 U.S.C. § 371, the defendants and others conspired to (1) transmit in interstate commerce communications threatening to injure the reputation of the actor Bill Cosby with the intent to extort money from him, in violation of 18 U.S.C. § 875(d), and (2) travel in and use interstate commerce facilities with the intent to carry on extortion in violation of 18 U.S.C. § 875(d) and § 155.05 of the New York Penal Law, in violation of the Travel Act, 18 U.S.C. § 1952(a)(3).

Count Two charged that, from late 1996 to January 18, 1997, the defendants transmitted in interstate commerce communications containing threats to injure the reputation of Bill Cosby with the intent to extort money from him, in violation of 18 U.S.C. § 875(d).

Count Three charged that the defendants violated the Travel Act by using facilities and traveling in interstate commerce with the intent to carry on extortion in violation of 18 U.S.C. § 875(d) and Section 155.05 of the New York Penal Law.

During a thirteen day trial that began July 7, 1997 and concluded July 25, 1997, the Government introduced evidence in the form of testimony, tape-recorded conversations, and documents. This proof established that from late 1996 to January 18, 1997, the defendants engaged in a campaign to threaten to publicize in tabloid newspapers that Jackson was Cosby's daughter out-of-wedlock and that he was mistreating her if Cosby did not pay Jackson millions of dollars. The Government established that the defendants conveyed this threat to Cosby through his attorneys, his television network CBS, and his sponsors, including Eastman Kodak Company. The campaign culminated with Jackson's January 16, 1997 demand to Cosby's attorney that if Cosby did not pay her $40 million, she would take her damaging story to The Globe. This threat was accompanied by an unsigned copy of a contract between Jackson, Medina and The Globe for the sale of Jackson's story about Cosby.

On July 25, 1997, the jury found Jackson and Medina guilty of all three counts of the Superseding Indictment and found Sabas guilty of Counts One and Three.

DISCUSSION

I. Overbreadth

Jackson asserts both a facial and an as applied overbreadth challenge to §§ 875(d) and 155.05.

A. Facial Overbreadth

As an initial matter, only a statute that is substantially overbroad may be invalidated on its face. Accordingly, in addressing a facial overbreadth challenge, a court's first task is to ascertain whether the enactment reaches a substantial amount of constitutionally protected conduct. . . . An act's overbreadth "must not only be real, but substantial as well, judged in relation to the statute's plainly legitimate sweep.". . . . The overbreadth doctrine is "strong medicine," and should be used "sparingly and only as a last resort.". . . .

Jackson argues that §§ 875(d) and 155.05, on their face and as interpreted by this Court, sweep constitutionally protected speech — "non-violent communications uttered in a good-faith effort to resolve legitimate financial disputes or accomplish legitimate political, social or economic goals" . . . — within their ambit. Her claim is incorrect, as the statutes do not cover such protected speech.

First, it is well settled that the punishment of certain threats does not offend the First Amendment. In this connection, courts have upheld similar statutes in the face of overbreadth challenges by narrowly interpreting the term "threats." Consistent with the First Amendment, Congress can proscribe threats

that, according to their language and context, convey a gravity of purpose and likelihood of execution that render them beyond the pale of constitutional protection.. . . .A "true threat" — which "on its face and in the circumstances in which it is made is so unequivocal, unconditional, immediate and specific as to the person threatened, as to convey a gravity of purpose and imminent prospect of execution" — may be punished because it, itself, affronts the important social interests of "justice" and "equal rights under the law." . . .

Accordingly, this Court has interpreted the "threats" punishable by §§ 875(d) and 155.05 as only those that are unequivocal, unconditional, and specific. For example, in this case the jury was instructed that:

a threat is an avowed present determination to injure, at once or in the future. The mere hope, desire, or wish to injure someone's reputation is insufficient to constitute a threat. In order to find that the defendant you are considering threatened to injure Bill Cosby's reputation, you must find that a reasonable person would have understood the defendant's statement as a serious expression of intent, determination, or purpose to injure the reputation of another person.

To determine whether or not the defendant you are considering threatened to injure Bill Cosby's reputation, you should consider the circumstances under which the statement was made, including the kind of statement made, the place where it was made, to whom it was made, how it was spoken, whether it was said plainly and unconditionally or in jest, and its context with respect to surrounding conversation. You may also consider the language the defendant used and the reaction of the person to whom the communication was addressed. . . .

Second, the "threats" prohibited by §§ 875(d) and 155.05 are not expressions of ideas or advocacy that typically implicate the First Amendment. Rather, § 875(d) is confined to (1) threats to injure the reputation of another, that are (2) made with the intent to extort money or things of value. Similarly, § 155.05 prohibits (1) threats to expose a secret tending to subject some person to hatred, contempt or ridicule, that are

(2) made with intent to deprive another of property. This limited scope takes the statutes "out of the realm of social or political conflict where threats to engage in behavior that may be unlawful may nevertheless be part of the marketplace of ideas, broadly conceived to embrace the rough competition that is so much the staple of social or political discourse." . . .

Jackson also argues that only threats to perform independently unlawful actions, such as kidnapping or physical injury, can be constitutionally proscribed. This argument is wrong. Courts have rejected constitutional challenges to statutes similar to § 875(d) that proscribe threats to injure reputation as a means of obtaining money or property. . . .

The cases cited by Jackson in her Reply Memorandum, in which state courts have struck down various state coercion statutes, do not dictate a different result. Although in *State v. Robertson*, . . . (Or. 1982), the court sustained an overbreadth challenge to Oregon's coercion statute, it did so because the statute impermissibly extended the principal of extortion to cover threats made in a public setting designed to inform and perhaps involve others in the issues posed by the demand. Robertson, . . . Further, the Robertson court confirmed that extortion statutes are, and historically have been, constitutionally valid because they punish threats made to obtain property for "selfish gain" or personal benefit from a victim in a private, bilateral transaction akin to robbery. . . .

Similarly, the criminal extortion statutes struck down in *Whimbush v. People*, . . . (Colo. 1994), and *State v. Weinstein*, . . . (Ariz. 1995) and the coercion statute invalidated in *City of Seattle v. Ivan*, . . . (Wash. 1993) failed to require an intent to extort money or thing of value. In fact, the statutes in *Robertson* and *Ivan* had no express intent element at all.

Jackson also complains that § 875(d) fails to define the requisite "intent to extort money or thing of value" and that the Court interpreted that intent element too broadly. The facial validity of statutes providing no greater specification or definition of intent, however, has been often upheld. . . .

With respect to the Court's interpretation of the intent element, the Court first notes

that while § 875(d) may criminalize extortionate threats to injure reputation that are common, their frequency does not necessarily render them constitutionally protected or legal. Moreover, the Court narrowly defined "intent to extort money or thing of value" by instructing the jury that "to extort means to obtain money or a thing of value from another by use of threats to reputation." . . .

Jackson further argues that the Court's refusal to graft a "specific intent" requirement onto § 875(d) (i.e. a requirement that the statute requires a "guilty mind") and to allow for a "claim of right" defense under it renders the statute unconstitutionally overbroad. While Jackson may disagree with the Court's rulings on statutory interpretation, she fails to explain how these rulings affect or even implicate her First Amendment argument. Moreover, with respect to a specific intent element, the Court notes that it instructed the jury that Count One (conspiracy to violate §§ 875(d) and the Travel Act) required the Government to prove beyond a reasonable doubt that the defendants acted with bad purpose to disobey or disregard the law. . . . Similarly, the Court instructed the jury that Count Three required a finding that the defendants knew that the activity they intended to facilitate was illegal. . . .

Finally, the hypothetical situations that Jackson poses do not indicate that the statutes could be used to punish a substantial amount of constitutionally protected conduct. Several of the scenarios do not contain specific, unconditional, immediate threats or threats to injure another's reputation. In others, the postulated speakers do not necessarily have the requisite "intent to extort money or thing of customer value." In this connection, the store owner who threatens to report a non-paying to a credit reporting agency, the homeowner who threatens to report a poorly performing contractor to the Better Business Bureau, and the accident victim who threatens litigation are not engaging in "self-help." Rather, they are turning to neutral governmental or quasi-governmental intermediaries who then independently review the speaker's claim. Also, as the Government correctly points out, in these hypothetical situations the potential injury to reputation is incidental to the threat of raising the claim.

Accordingly, Jackson's facial overbreadth challenge to the statutes fails.

B. As Applied Challenge

Not surprisingly, Jackson's papers are silent with respect to the application of §§ 875(d) and 155.05 to her own speech in this case. Here, the Superseding Indictment charged and the jury rationally found beyond a reasonable doubt that Jackson and her co-conspirators communicated a "true threat" to Cosby, by faxing an unsigned contract from The Globe to print Jackson's life story along with a demand for $40 million. This was precisely the kind of private transaction, motivated purely by selfish gain, that extortion statutes have always validly punished.

Accordingly, the statutes were constitutionally applied to Jackson and her co-conspirators.

II. Void for Vagueness

The void for vagueness doctrine requires that a penal statute define the criminal offense with sufficient definiteness such that ordinary people can understand what conduct is prohibited and in a manner that does not encourage arbitrary and discriminatory enforcement. . . .

Jackson now claims that §§ 875(d) and 155.05 are unconstitutionally vague. Specifically, she argues that the statutes are impermissibly vague because (1) the statutes fail to provide or to refer to definitions for "extortion" or "intent to extort," and (2) the Court "left it up to the jury to use their 'common sense' to decide what 'extortion' means." . . .

Jackson's first argument is simply wrong. "Extortion" does have a meaning, far wider than the original common law concept, that courts have repeatedly sanctioned when interpreting statutes involving extortion. . . .

Moreover, the language of § 875(d) clearly defines the nature of the intent element: in making threats to injure another's reputation, the defendant must have acted with the intent of extorting money or a thing of value.

As for her second argument, Jackson misunderstands the Court's instructions to the jury. When instructing the jury on the ele-

ments under § 875(d), the Court charged that:

the final element that the Government must prove beyond a reasonable doubt is that the defendant you are considering acted with the intent to extort money or a thing of value from Bill Cosby. You should use your common sense to determine whether the defendant you are considering had the requisite intent to extort.
. . . As is plainly clear, the Court simply preserved for the jury its most basic task — the determination of intent. In fact, the Court further explained to the jury that "to extort means to obtain money or a thing of value from another by use of threats to reputation." . . .

Further, the scienter requirement — "intent to extort money or thing of value" — helps to ensure adequate notice of the proscribed conduct. . . .

Finally, law enforcers are sufficiently guided by the fact that the statutes apply only to threats to injure reputation, and only when such threats are made with the intent to extort money or a thing of value. Additionally, as stated above, the Hobbs Act and common law provide definitions of "extortion" to guide law enforcement.

The Court also notes that this is not a case where the challenged statutes contain absolutely no standard of conduct or have no core. Rather, the statutes apply to threats to injure reputation made with the intent to extort money or things of value. . . . Moreover, even if the outer boundaries of the statutes are imprecise, any such uncertainty has little relevance here, where Jackson's conduct falls squarely within the "hard core" of the statutes' proscriptions. . . .

Accordingly, the Court finds that §§ 875(d) and § 155.05 are not unconstitutionally vague, either facially or as applied.

CONCLUSION

For the reasons set forth above, the defendant's motion is denied.

So ordered.

Footnotes and citations omitted. Concurring and dissenting opinions omitted.

Cases Relating to Chapter 14

U.S. Criminal Code: Offenses Against: Morals and Decency; Public Peace; Justice Administration

John D. Ashcroft,
Attorney General, et al.

v.

The Free Speech Coalition, et al.

Supreme Court of the United States
535 U.S. 234 (2002)

Justice Kennedy delivered the opinion of the Court.

We consider in this case whether the Child Pornography Prevention Act of 1996 (CPPA), 18 U.S.C. § 2251 *et seq.,* abridges the freedom of speech. The CPPA extends the federal prohibition against child pornography to sexually explicit images that appear to depict minors but were produced without using any real children. The statute prohibits, in specific circumstances, possessing or distributing these images, which may be created by using adults who look like minors or by using computer imaging. The new technology, according to Congress, makes it possible to create realistic images of children who do not exist. . . .

By prohibiting child pornography that does not depict an actual child, the statute goes beyond *New York* v. *Ferber,* . . . (1982), which distinguished child pornography from other sexually explicit speech because of the State's interest in protecting the children exploited by the production process. . . . As a general rule, pornography can be banned only if obscene, but under *Ferber,* pornography showing minors can be proscribed whether or not the images are obscene under the definition set forth in *Miller* v. *California,* . . .

(1973). *Ferber* recognized that "the *Miller* standard, like all general definitions of what may be banned as obscene, does not reflect the State's particular and more compelling interest in prosecuting those who promote the sexual exploitation of children." . . . .

While we have not had occasion to consider the question, we may assume that the apparent age of persons engaged in sexual conduct is relevant to whether a depiction offends community standards. Pictures of young children engaged in certain acts might be obscene where similar depictions of adults, or perhaps even older adolescents, would not. The CPPA, however, is not directed at speech that is obscene; Congress has proscribed those materials through a separate statute. . . . Like the law in *Ferber,* the CPPA seeks to reach beyond obscenity, and it makes no attempt to conform to the *Miller* standard. For instance, the statute would reach visual depictions, such as movies, even if they have redeeming social value.

The principal question to be resolved, then, is whether the CPPA is constitutional where it proscribes a significant universe of speech that is neither obscene under *Miller* nor child pornography under *Ferber.*

I.

Before 1996, Congress defined child pornography as the type of depictions at issue in *Ferber,* images made using actual minors. . . . The CPPA retains that prohibition at 18 U.S.C. § 2256(8)(A) and adds three other prohibited categories of speech, of which the first, § 2256(8)(B), and the third, § 2256(8)(D), are at issue in this case. Section 2256(8)(B) prohibits "any visual depiction, including any photograph, film, video, picture, or computer or computer-generated image or picture" that "is, or appears to be, of a minor engaging in sexually explicit conduct." The prohibition on "any visual depiction" does not depend at all on how the image is produced. The section captures a range of depictions, sometimes called "virtual child pornography," which include computer-generated images, as well as images produced by more traditional means. For instance, the literal terms of the statute embrace a Renaissance painting depicting a scene from classical mythology, a "picture" that "appears to be, of a minor engaging in sexually explicit conduct." The statute also prohibits Hollywood movies, filmed without any child actors, if a jury believes an actor "appears to be" a minor engaging in "actual or simulated . . . sexual intercourse." . . . .

These images do not involve, let alone harm, any children in the production process; but Congress decided the materials threaten children in other, less direct, ways. Pedophiles might use the materials to encourage children to participate in sexual activity. "[A] child who is reluctant to engage in sexual activity with an adult, or to pose for sexually explicit photographs, can sometimes be convinced by viewing depictions of other children 'having fun' participating in such activity." . . . . Furthermore, pedophiles might "whet their own sexual appetites" with the pornographic images, "thereby increasing the creation and distribution of child pornography and the sexual abuse and exploitation of actual children." . . . Under these rationales, harm flows from the content of the images, not from the means of their production. In addition, Congress identified another problem created by computer-generated images: Their existence can make it harder to prosecute pornographers who do use real minors. . . . As imaging technology improves, Congress found, it becomes more difficult to prove that a particular picture was produced using actual children. To ensure that defendants possessing child pornography using real minors cannot evade prosecution, Congress extended the ban to virtual child pornography.

Section 2256(8)(C) prohibits a more common and lower tech means of creating virtual images, known as computer morphing. Rather than creating original images, pornographers can alter innocent pictures of real children so that the children appear to be engaged in sexual activity. Although morphed images may fall within the definition of virtual child pornography, they implicate the interests of real children and are in that sense closer to the images in *Ferber*. Respondents do not challenge this provision, and we do not consider it.

Respondents do challenge § 2256(8)(D). Like the text of the "appears to be" provision, the sweep of this provision is quite broad. Section 2256(8)(D) defines child pornography to include any sexually explicit image that was "advertised, promoted, presented, described, or distributed in such a manner that conveys the impression" it depicts "a minor engaging in sexually explicit conduct." One Committee Report identified the provision as directed at sexually explicit images pandered as child pornography. . . . The statute is not so limited in its reach, however, as it punishes even those possessors who took no part in pandering. Once a work has been described as child pornography, the taint remains on the speech in the hands of subsequent possessors, making possession unlawful even though the content otherwise would not be objectionable.

Fearing that the CPPA threatened the activities of its members, respondent Free Speech Coalition and others challenged the statute in the United States District Court for the Northern District of California. The Coalition, a California trade association for the adult-entertainment industry, alleged that its members did not use minors in their sexually explicit works, but they believed some of these materials might fall within the CPPA's expanded definition of child pornography. The other respondents are Bold Type, Inc., the publisher of a book advocating the nudist lifestyle; Jim Gingerich, a painter of nudes; and Ron Raffaelli, a photographer specializing in erotic images. Respondents alleged that the "appears to be" and "conveys the impression" provisions are overbroad and vague, chilling them from producing works protected by the First Amendment. The District Court disagreed and granted summary judgment to the Government. The court dismissed the overbreadth claim because it was "highly unlikely" that any "adaptations of sexual works like 'Romeo and Juliet,' will be treated as 'criminal contraband.'" . . .

The Court of Appeals for the Ninth Circuit reversed. . . . The court reasoned that the Government could not prohibit speech because of its tendency to persuade viewers to commit illegal acts. The court held the CPPA to be substantially overbroad because it bans materials that are neither obscene nor produced by the exploitation of real children as in *New York* v. *Ferber*, . . . (1982). Judge Ferguson dissented on the ground that virtual images, like obscenity and real child pornography, should be treated as a category of speech unprotected by the First Amendment. . . . The Court of Appeals voted to deny the petition for rehearing *en banc*, over the dissent of three judges. . . .

While the Ninth Circuit found the CPPA invalid on its face, four other Courts of Appeals have sustained it. . . .

II.

The First Amendment commands, "Congress shall make no law . . . abridging the freedom of speech." The government may violate this mandate in many ways, . . . but a law imposing criminal penalties on protected speech is a stark example of speech suppression. The CPPA's penalties are indeed severe. A first offender may be imprisoned for 15 years. . . . A repeat offender faces a prison sentence of not less than 5 years and not more than 30 years in prison. . . . While even minor punishments can chill protected speech, . . . this case provides a textbook example of why we permit facial challenges to statutes that burden expression. With these severe penalties in force, few legitimate movie producers or book publishers, or few other speakers in any capacity, would risk distributing images in or near the uncertain reach of this law. The Constitution gives significant protection from overbroad laws that chill speech within the First Amendment's vast and privileged sphere. Under this principle, the CPPA is unconstitutional on its face if it prohibits a substantial amount of protected expression. . . .

The sexual abuse of a child is a most serious crime and an act repugnant to the moral instincts of a decent people. In its legislative findings, Congress recognized that there are subcultures of persons who harbor illicit desires for children and commit criminal acts to gratify the impulses. . . . Congress also found that surrounding the serious offenders are those who flirt with these impulses and trade pictures and written accounts of sexual activity with young children.

Congress may pass valid laws to protect children from abuse, and it has. . . . The prospect of crime, however, by itself does not justify laws suppressing protected speech. . . . It is also well established that speech may not be prohibited because it concerns subjects offending our sensibilities. . . .

As a general principle, the First Amendment bars the government from dictating what we see or read or speak or hear. The freedom of speech has its limits; it does not embrace certain categories of speech, including defamation, incitement, obscenity, and pornography produced with real children. . . . While these categories may be prohibited without violating the First Amendment, none of them includes the speech prohibited by the CPPA. In his dissent from the opinion of the Court of Appeals, Judge Ferguson recognized this to be the law and proposed that virtual child pornography should be regarded as an additional category of unprotected speech. . . . It would be necessary for us to take this step to uphold the statute.

As we have noted, the CPPA is much more than a supplement to the existing federal prohibition on obscenity. Under *Miller* v. *California*, . . . (1973), the Government must prove that the work, taken as a whole, appeals to the prurient interest, is patently offensive in light of community standards, and lacks serious literary, artistic, political, or scientific value. . . . The CPPA, however, extends to images that appear to depict a minor engaging in sexually explicit activity without regard to the *Miller* requirements. The materials need not appeal to the prurient interest. Any depiction of sexually explicit activity, no matter how it is presented, is proscribed. The CPPA applies to a picture in a psychology manual, as well as a movie depicting the horrors of sexual abuse. It is not necessary, moreover, that the image be patently offensive. Pictures of what appear to be 17-year-olds engaging in sexually explicit activity do not in every case contravene community standards.

The CPPA prohibits speech despite its serious literary, artistic, political, or scientific value. The statute proscribes the visual depiction of an idea — that of teenagers engaging in sexual activity — that is a fact of modern society and has been a theme in art and literature throughout the ages. Under the CPPA, images are prohibited so long as the persons appear to be under 18 years of age.... This is higher than the legal age for marriage in many States, as well as the age at which persons may consent to sexual relations.... It is, of course, undeniable that some youths engage in sexual activity before the legal age, either on their own inclination or because they are victims of sexual abuse.

Both themes — teenage sexual activity and the sexual abuse of children — have inspired countless literary works. William Shakespeare created the most famous pair of teenage lovers, one of whom is just 13 years of age.... In the drama, Shakespeare portrays the relationship as something splendid and innocent, but not juvenile. The work has inspired no less than 40 motion pictures, some of which suggest that the teenagers consummated their relationship.... Shakespeare may not have written sexually explicit scenes for the Elizabethan audience, but were modern directors to adopt a less conventional approach, that fact alone would not compel the conclusion that the work was obscene.

Contemporary movies pursue similar themes. Last year's Academy Awards featured the movie, Traffic, which was nominated for Best Picture.... The film portrays a teenager, identified as a 16-year-old, who becomes addicted to drugs. The viewer sees the degradation of her addiction, which in the end leads her to a filthy room to trade sex for drugs. The year before, American Beauty won the Academy Award for Best Picture.... In the course of the movie, a teenage girl engages in sexual relations with her teenage boyfriend, and another yields herself to the gratification of a middle-aged man. The film also contains a scene where, although the movie audience understands the act is not taking place, one character believes he is watching a teenage boy performing a sexual act on an older man.

Our society, like other cultures, has empathy and enduring fascination with the lives and destinies of the young. Art and literature express the vital interest we all have in the formative years we ourselves once knew, when wounds can be so grievous, disappointment so profound, and mistaken choices so tragic, but when moral acts and self-fulfillment are still in reach. Whether or not the films we mention violate the CPPA, they explore themes within the wide sweep of the statute's prohibitions. If these films, or hundreds of others of lesser note that explore those subjects, contain a single graphic depiction of sexual activity within the statutory definition, the possessor of the film would be subject to severe punishment without inquiry into the work's redeeming value. This is inconsistent with an essential First Amendment rule: The artistic merit of a work does not depend on the presence of a single explicit scene.... Under *Miller*, the First Amendment requires that redeeming value be judged by considering the work as a whole. Where the scene is part of the narrative, the work itself does not for this reason become obscene, even though the scene in isolation might be offensive.... For this reason, and the others we have noted, the CPPA cannot be read to prohibit obscenity, because it lacks the required link between its prohibitions and the affront to community standards prohibited by the definition of obscenity.

The Government seeks to address this deficiency by arguing that speech prohibited by the CPPA is virtually indistinguishable from child pornography, which may be banned without regard to whether it depicts works of value.... Where the images are themselves the product of child sexual abuse, *Ferber* recognized that the State had an interest in stamping it out without regard to any judgment about its content.... The production of the work, not its content, was the target of the statute. The fact that a work contained serious literary, artistic, or other value did not excuse the harm it caused to its child participants. It was simply "unrealistic to equate a community's toleration for sexually oriented materials with the permissible scope of legislation aimed at protecting children from sexual exploitation." ...

Ferber upheld a prohibition on the distribution and sale of child pornography, as well as its production, because these acts were "intrinsically related" to the sexual abuse of children in two ways. . . . First, as a permanent record of a child's abuse, the continued circulation itself would harm the child who had participated. Like a defamatory statement, each new publication of the speech would cause new injury to the child's reputation and emotional well-being. . . . Second, because the traffic in child pornography was an economic motive for its production, the State had an interest in closing the distribution network. "The most expeditious if not the only practical method of law enforcement may be to dry up the market for this material by imposing severe criminal penalties on persons selling, advertising, or otherwise promoting the product." . . . . Under either rationale, the speech had what the Court in effect held was a proximate link to the crime from which it came.

Later, in *Osborne* v. *Ohio*, . . . (1990), the Court ruled that these same interests justified a ban on the possession of pornography produced by using children. "Given the importance of the State's interest in protecting the victims of child pornography," the State was justified in "attempting to stamp out this vice at all levels in the distribution chain." . . . . *Osborne* also noted the State's interest in preventing child pornography from being used as an aid in the solicitation of minors. . . . The Court, however, anchored its holding in the concern for the participants, those whom it called the "victims of child pornography." . . . . It did not suggest that, absent this concern, other governmental interests would suffice. . . .

In contrast to the speech in *Ferber*, speech that itself is the record of sexual abuse, the CPPA prohibits speech that records no crime and creates no victims by its production. Virtual child pornography is not "intrinsically related" to the sexual abuse of children, as were the materials in *Ferber*. . . . While the Government asserts that the images can lead to actual instances of child abuse, see *infra*, at 13-16, the causal link is contingent and indirect. The harm does not necessarily follow from the speech, but depends upon some unquantified potential for subsequent criminal acts.

The Government says these indirect harms are sufficient because, as *Ferber* acknowledged, child pornography rarely can be valuable speech. . . . This argument, however, suffers from two flaws. First, *Ferber*'s judgment about child pornography was based upon how it was made, not on what it communicated. The case reaffirmed that where the speech is neither obscene nor the product of sexual abuse, it does not fall outside the protection of the First Amendment. . . .

The second flaw in the Government's position is that *Ferber* did not hold that child pornography is by definition without value. On the contrary, the Court recognized some works in this category might have significant value, . . ., but relied on virtual images — the very images prohibited by the CPPA — as an alternative and permissible means of expression: "If it were necessary for literary or artistic value, a person over the statutory age who perhaps looked younger could be utilized. Simulation outside of the prohibition of the statute could provide another alternative." . . . . *Ferber*, then, not only referred to the distinction between actual and virtual child pornography, it relied on it as a reason supporting its holding. *Ferber* provides no support for a statute that eliminates the distinction and makes the alternative mode criminal as well.

III.

The CPPA, for reasons we have explored, is inconsistent with *Miller* and finds no support in *Ferber*. The Government seeks to justify its prohibitions in other ways. It argues that the CPPA is necessary because pedophiles may use virtual child pornography to seduce children. There are many things innocent in themselves, however, such as cartoons, video games, and candy, that might be used for immoral purposes, yet we would not expect those to be prohibited because they can be misused. The Government, of course, may punish adults who provide unsuitable materials to children, . . ., and it may enforce criminal penalties for unlawful solicitation. The precedents establish, however, that speech within the rights of adults to hear may not be silenced completely in an attempt to shield children from it. . . . In *Butler* v. *Michigan*,

. . . (1957), the Court invalidated a statute prohibiting distribution of an indecent publication because of its tendency to "incite minors to violent or depraved or immoral acts." A unanimous Court agreed upon the important First Amendment principle that the State could not "reduce the adult population . . . to reading only what is fit for children." . . . . We have reaffirmed this holding. . . .

Here, the Government wants to keep speech from children not to protect them from its content but to protect them from those who would commit other crimes. The principle, however, remains the same: The Government cannot ban speech fit for adults simply because it may fall into the hands of children. The evil in question depends upon the actor's unlawful conduct, conduct defined as criminal quite apart from any link to the speech in question. This establishes that the speech ban is not narrowly drawn. The objective is to prohibit illegal conduct, but this restriction goes well beyond that interest by restricting the speech available to law-abiding adults.

The Government submits further that virtual child pornography whets the appetites of pedophiles and encourages them to engage in illegal conduct. This rationale cannot sustain the provision in question. The mere tendency of speech to encourage unlawful acts is not a sufficient reason for banning it. The government "cannot constitutionally premise legislation on the desirability of controlling a person's private thoughts." . . . First Amendment freedoms are most in danger when the government seeks to control thought or to justify its laws for that impermissible end. The right to think is the beginning of freedom, and speech must be protected from the government because speech is the beginning of thought.

To preserve these freedoms, and to protect speech for its own sake, the Court's First Amendment cases draw vital distinctions between words and deeds, between ideas and conduct. . . . The government may not prohibit speech because it increases the chance an unlawful act will be committed "at some indefinite future time." . . . . The government may suppress speech for advocating the use of force or a violation of law only if "such advocacy is directed to inciting or producing

imminent lawless action and is likely to incite or produce such action." . . . . There is here no attempt, incitement, solicitation, or conspiracy. The Government has shown no more than a remote connection between speech that might encourage thoughts or impulses and any resulting child abuse. Without a significantly stronger, more direct connection, the Government may not prohibit speech on the ground that it may encourage pedophiles to engage in illegal conduct.

The Government next argues that its objective of eliminating the market for pornography produced using real children necessitates a prohibition on virtual images as well. Virtual images, the Government contends, are indistinguishable from real ones; they are part of the same market and are often exchanged. In this way, it is said, virtual images promote the trafficking in works produced through the exploitation of real children. The hypothesis is somewhat implausible. If virtual images were identical to illegal child pornography, the illegal images would be driven from the market by the indistinguishable substitutes. Few pornographers would risk prosecution by abusing real children if fictional, computerized images would suffice.

In the case of the material covered by *Ferber*, the creation of the speech is itself the crime of child abuse; the prohibition deters the crime by removing the profit motive. . . . Even where there is an underlying crime, however, the Court has not allowed the suppression of speech in all cases. . . . We need not consider where to strike the balance in this case, because here, there is no underlying crime at all. Even if the Government's market deterrence theory were persuasive in some contexts, it would not justify this statute.

Finally, the Government says that the possibility of producing images by using computer imaging makes it very difficult for it to prosecute those who produce pornography by using real children. Experts, we are told, may have difficulty in saying whether the pictures were made by using real children or by using computer imaging. The necessary solution, the argument runs, is to prohibit both kinds of images. The argument, in essence, is that protected speech may be banned as a means to ban unprotected speech. This analysis turns the First Amendment upside down.

The Government may not suppress lawful speech as the means to suppress unlawful speech. Protected speech does not become unprotected merely because it resembles the latter. The Constitution requires the reverse. "The possible harm to society in permitting some unprotected speech to go unpunished is outweighed by the possibility that protected speech of others may be muted . . . . " . . . . The overbreadth doctrine prohibits the Government from banning unprotected speech if a substantial amount of protected speech is prohibited or chilled in the process.

To avoid the force of this objection, the Government would have us read the CPPA not as a measure suppressing speech but as a law shifting the burden to the accused to prove the speech is lawful. In this connection, the Government relies on an affirmative defense under the statute, which allows a defendant to avoid conviction for nonpossession offenses by showing that the materials were produced using only adults and were not otherwise distributed in a manner conveying the impression that they depicted real children. . . .

The Government raises serious constitutional difficulties by seeking to impose on the defendant the burden of proving his speech is not unlawful. An affirmative defense applies only after prosecution has begun, and the speaker must himself prove, on pain of a felony conviction, that his conduct falls within the affirmative defense. In cases under the CPPA, the evidentiary burden is not trivial. Where the defendant is not the producer of the work, he may have no way of establishing the identity, or even the existence, of the actors. If the evidentiary issue is a serious problem for the Government, as it asserts, it will be at least as difficult for the innocent possessor. The statute, moreover, applies to work created before 1996, and the producers themselves may not have preserved the records necessary to meet the burden of proof. Failure to establish the defense can lead to a felony conviction.

We need not decide, however, whether the Government could impose this burden on a speaker. Even if an affirmative defense can save a statute from First Amendment challenge, here the defense is incomplete and insufficient, even on its own terms. It allows persons to be convicted in some instances where they can prove children were not exploited in the production. A defendant charged with possessing, as opposed to distributing, proscribed works may not defend on the ground that the film depicts only adult actors. . . . So while the affirmative defense may protect a movie producer from prosecution for the act of distribution, that same producer, and all other persons in the subsequent distribution chain, could be liable for possessing the prohibited work. Furthermore, the affirmative defense provides no protection to persons who produce speech by using computer imaging, or through other means that do not involve the use of adult actors who appear to be minors. . . . In these cases, the defendant can demonstrate no children were harmed in producing the images, yet the affirmative defense would not bar the prosecution. For this reason, the affirmative defense cannot save the statute, for it leaves unprotected a substantial amount of speech not tied to the Government's interest in distinguishing images produced using real children from virtual ones.

In sum, § 2256(8)(B) covers materials beyond the categories recognized in *Ferber* and *Miller*, and the reasons the Government offers in support of limiting the freedom of speech have no justification in our precedents or in the law of the First Amendment. The provision abridges the freedom to engage in a substantial amount of lawful speech. For this reason, it is overbroad and unconstitutional.

IV.

[Discussion of another issue is omitted.]

V.

For the reasons we have set forth, the prohibitions of §§ 2256(8)(B) and 2256(8)(D) are overbroad and unconstitutional. Having reached this conclusion, we need not address respondents' further contention that the provisions are unconstitutional because of vague statutory language.

The judgment of the Court of Appeals is affirmed.

Footnotes and citations omitted. Concurring and dissenting opinions omitted.

**Alberto R. Gonzales,
Attorney General, et al.**

v.

Angel McClary Raich et al.

**Supreme Court of the United States
545 U.S. 1 (2005)**

Justice Stevens delivered the opinion of the Court.

California is one of at least nine States that authorize the use of marijuana for medicinal purposes. The question presented in this case is whether the power vested in Congress by Article I, § 8, of the Constitution "[t]o make all Laws which shall be necessary and proper for carrying into Execution" its authority to "regulate Commerce with foreign Nations, and among the several States" includes the power to prohibit the local cultivation and use of marijuana in compliance with California law.

I.

California has been a pioneer in the regulation of marijuana. In 1913, California was one of the first States to prohibit the sale and possession of marijuana, and at the end of the century, California became the first State to authorize limited use of the drug for medicinal purposes. In 1996, California voters passed Proposition 215, now codified as the Compassionate Use Act of 1996. The proposition was designed to ensure that "seriously ill" residents of the State have access to marijuana for medical purposes, and to encourage Federal and State Governments to take steps towards ensuring the safe and affordable distribution of the drug to patients in need. The Act creates an exemption from criminal prosecution for physicians, as well as for patients and primary caregivers who possess or cultivate marijuana for medicinal purposes with the recommendation or approval of a physician. A "primary caregiver" is a person who has consistently assumed responsibility for the housing, health, or safety of the patient.

Respondents Angel Raich and Diane Monson are California residents who suffer from a variety of serious medical conditions and have sought to avail themselves of medical marijuana pursuant to the terms of the Compassionate Use Act. They are being treated by licensed, board-certified family practitioners, who have concluded, after prescribing a host of conventional medicines to treat respondents' conditions and to alleviate their associated symptoms, that marijuana is the only drug available that provides effective treatment. Both women have been using marijuana as a medication for several years pursuant to their doctors' recommendation, and both rely heavily on cannabis to function on a daily basis. Indeed, Raich's physician believes that forgoing cannabis treatments would certainly cause Raich excruciating pain and could very well prove fatal.

Respondent Monson cultivates her own marijuana, and ingests the drug in a variety of ways including smoking and using a vaporizer. Respondent Raich, by contrast, is unable to cultivate her own, and thus relies on two caregivers, litigating as "John Does," to provide her with locally grown marijuana at no charge. These caregivers also process the cannabis into hashish or keif, and Raich herself processes some of the marijuana into oils, balms, and foods for consumption.

On August 15, 2002, county deputy sheriffs and agents from the federal Drug Enforcement Administration (DEA) came to Monson's home. After a thorough investigation, the county officials concluded that her use of marijuana was entirely lawful as a matter of California law. Nevertheless, after a 3-hour standoff, the federal agents seized and destroyed all six of her cannabis plants.

Respondents thereafter brought this action against the Attorney General of the United States and the head of the DEA seeking injunctive and declaratory relief prohibiting the enforcement of the federal Controlled Substances Act (CSA), 84 Stat. 1242, 21 U.S.C. § 801 *et seq.*, to the extent it prevents them from possessing, obtaining, or manufacturing cannabis for their personal medical use. In their complaint and supporting affidavits, Raich and Monson described the severity of their afflictions, their repeatedly futile attempts to obtain relief with conventional medications, and the opinions of their doctors concerning their need to use marijuana. Respondents claimed that enforcing the CSA against them would violate the Commerce Clause, the Due Process Clause of the Fifth

Amendment, the Ninth and Tenth Amendments of the Constitution, and the doctrine of medical necessity.

The District Court denied respondents' motion for a preliminary injunction.... Although the court found that the federal enforcement interests "wane[d]" when compared to the harm that California residents would suffer if denied access to medically necessary marijuana, it concluded that respondents could not demonstrate a likelihood of success on the merits of their legal claims. . . .

A divided panel of the Court of Appeals for the Ninth Circuit reversed and ordered the District Court to enter a preliminary injunction. . . . The court found that respondents had "demonstrated a strong likelihood of success on their claim that, as applied to them, the CSA is an unconstitutional exercise of Congress' Commerce Clause authority." . . . . The Court of Appeals distinguished prior Circuit cases upholding the CSA in the face of Commerce Clause challenges by focusing on what it deemed to be the "*separate and distinct class of activities*" at issue in this case: "the intrastate, noncommercial cultivation and possession of cannabis for personal medical purposes as recommended by a patient's physician pursuant to valid California state law." . . . . The court found the latter class of activities "different in kind from drug trafficking" because interposing a physician's recommendation raises different health and safety concerns, and because "this limited use is clearly distinct from the broader illicit drug market — as well as any broader commercial market for medicinal marijuana — insofar as the medicinal marijuana at issue in this case is not intended for, nor does it enter, the stream of commerce." . . . .

The majority placed heavy reliance on our decisions in *United States* v. *Lopez,* . . . (1995), and *United States* v. *Morrison,* . . . (2000), as interpreted by recent Circuit precedent, to hold that this separate class of purely local activities was beyond the reach of federal power. In contrast, the dissenting judge concluded that the CSA, as applied to respondents, was clearly valid under *Lopez* and *Morrison;* moreover, he thought it "simply impossible to distinguish the relevant conduct surrounding the cultivation and use of the marijuana crop at issue in this case

from the cultivation and use of the wheat crop that affected interstate commerce in *Wickard* v. *Filburn.*" . . . .

The obvious importance of the case prompted our grant of certiorari. . . . The case is made difficult by respondents' strong arguments that they will suffer irreparable harm because, despite a congressional finding to the contrary, marijuana does have valid therapeutic purposes. The question before us, however, is not whether it is wise to enforce the statute in these circumstances; rather, it is whether Congress' power to regulate interstate markets for medicinal substances encompasses the portions of those markets that are supplied with drugs produced and consumed locally. Well-settled law controls our answer. The CSA is a valid exercise of federal power, even as applied to the troubling facts of this case. We accordingly vacate the judgment of the Court of Appeals.

II.

Shortly after taking office in 1969, President Nixon declared a national "war on drugs." As the first campaign of that war, Congress set out to enact legislation that would consolidate various drug laws on the books into a comprehensive statute, provide meaningful regulation over legitimate sources of drugs to prevent diversion into illegal channels, and strengthen law enforcement tools against the traffic in illicit drugs. That effort culminated in the passage of the Comprehensive Drug Abuse Prevention and Control Act of 1970, 84 Stat. 1236.

This was not, however, Congress' first attempt to regulate the national market in drugs. Rather, as early as 1906 Congress enacted federal legislation imposing labeling regulations on medications and prohibiting the manufacture or shipment of any adulterated or misbranded drug traveling in interstate commerce. Aside from these labeling restrictions, most domestic drug regulations prior to 1970 generally came in the guise of revenue laws, with the Department of the Treasury serving as the Federal Government's primary enforcer. For example, the primary drug control law, before being repealed by the passage of the CSA, was the Harrison Narcotics Act of 1914, . . .

(repealed 1970). The Harrison Act sought to exert control over the possession and sale of narcotics, specifically cocaine and opiates, by requiring producers, distributors, and purchasers to register with the Federal Government, by assessing taxes against parties so registered, and by regulating the issuance of prescriptions.

Marijuana itself was not significantly regulated by the Federal Government until 1937 when accounts of marijuana's addictive qualities and physiological effects, paired with dissatisfaction with enforcement efforts at state and local levels, prompted Congress to pass the Marihuana Tax Act, . . . (repealed 1970). Like the Harrison Act, the Marihuana Tax Act did not outlaw the possession or sale of marijuana outright. Rather, it imposed registration and reporting requirements for all individuals importing, producing, selling, or dealing in marijuana, and required the payment of annual taxes in addition to transfer taxes whenever the drug changed hands. Moreover, doctors wishing to prescribe marijuana for medical purposes were required to comply with rather burdensome administrative requirements. Noncompliance exposed traffickers to severe federal penalties, whereas compliance would often subject them to prosecution under state law. Thus, while the Marihuana Tax Act did not declare the drug illegal *per se*, the onerous administrative requirements, the prohibitively expensive taxes, and the risks attendant on compliance practically curtailed the marijuana trade.

Then in 1970, after declaration of the national "war on drugs," federal drug policy underwent a significant transformation. A number of noteworthy events precipitated this policy shift. First, in *Leary* v. *United States,* . . . (1969), this Court held certain provisions of the Marihuana Tax Act and other narcotics legislation unconstitutional. Second, at the end of his term, President Johnson fundamentally reorganized the federal drug control agencies. The Bureau of Narcotics, then housed in the Department of Treasury, merged with the Bureau of Drug Abuse Control, then housed in the Department of Health, Education, and Welfare (HEW), to create the Bureau of Narcotics and Dangerous Drugs, currently housed in the Department of Justice. Finally, prompted

by a perceived need to consolidate the growing number of piecemeal drug laws and to enhance federal drug enforcement powers, Congress enacted the Comprehensive Drug Abuse Prevention and Control Act.

Title II of that Act, the CSA, repealed most of the earlier antidrug laws in favor of a comprehensive regime to combat the international and interstate traffic in illicit drugs. The main objectives of the CSA were to conquer drug abuse and to control the legitimate and illegitimate traffic in controlled substances. Congress was particularly concerned with the need to prevent the diversion of drugs from legitimate to illicit channels.

To effectuate these goals, Congress devised a closed regulatory system making it unlawful to manufacture, distribute, dispense, or possess any controlled substance except in a manner authorized by the CSA. . . . The CSA categorizes all controlled substances into five schedules. . . . The drugs are grouped together based on their accepted medical uses, the potential for abuse, and their psychological and physical effects on the body. . . . Each schedule is associated with a distinct set of controls regarding the manufacture, distribution, and use of the substances listed therein. . . . The CSA and its implementing regulations set forth strict requirements regarding registration, labeling and packaging, production quotas, drug security, and recordkeeping. . . .

In enacting the CSA, Congress classified marijuana as a Schedule I drug. . . . This preliminary classification was based, in part, on the recommendation of the Assistant Secretary of HEW "that marihuana be retained within schedule I at least until the completion of certain studies now underway." Schedule I drugs are categorized as such because of their high potential for abuse, lack of any accepted medical use, and absence of any accepted safety for use in medically supervised treatment. . . . These three factors, in varying gradations, are also used to categorize drugs in the other four schedules. For example, Schedule II substances also have a high potential for abuse which may lead to severe psychological or physical dependence, but unlike Schedule I drugs, they have a currently accepted medical use. . . . By classifying marijuana as a Schedule I drug, as opposed to listing it on a lesser schedule, the manufacture, distribution, or possession of marijuana became a criminal offense, with the sole exception being use of the drug as part of a Food and Drug Administration pre-approved research study. . . .

The CSA provides for the periodic updating of schedules and delegates authority to the Attorney General, after consultation with the Secretary of Health and Human Services, to add, remove, or transfer substances to, from, or between schedules. . . . Despite considerable efforts to reschedule marijuana, it remains a Schedule I drug.

III.

Respondents in this case do not dispute that passage of the CSA, as part of the Comprehensive Drug Abuse Prevention and Control Act, was well within Congress' commerce power. . . . Nor do they contend that any provision or section of the CSA amounts to an unconstitutional exercise of congressional authority. Rather, respondents' challenge is actually quite limited; they argue that the CSA's categorical prohibition of the manufacture and possession of marijuana as applied to the intrastate manufacture and possession of marijuana for medical purposes pursuant to California law exceeds Congress' authority under the Commerce Clause.

In assessing the validity of congressional regulation, none of our Commerce Clause cases can be viewed in isolation. As charted in considerable detail in *United States* v. *Lopez*, our understanding of the reach of the Commerce Clause, as well as Congress' assertion of authority thereunder, has evolved over time. The Commerce Clause emerged as the Framers' response to the central problem giving rise to the Constitution itself: the absence of any federal commerce power under the Articles of Confederation. For the first century of our history, the primary use of the Clause was to preclude the kind of discriminatory state legislation that had once been permissible. Then, in response to rapid industrial development and an increasingly interdependent national economy, Congress "ushered in a new era of federal regulation under the commerce power," beginning with

the enactment of the Interstate Commerce Act in 1887, . . ., and the Sherman Antitrust Act in 1890, ...

Cases decided during that "new era," which now spans more than a century, have identified three general categories of regulation in which Congress is authorized to engage under its commerce power. First, Congress can regulate the channels of interstate commerce. . . . Second, Congress has authority to regulate and protect the instrumentalities of interstate commerce, and persons or things in interstate commerce. . . . Third, Congress has the power to regulate activities that substantially affect interstate commerce. . . . Only the third category is implicated in the case at hand.

Our case law firmly establishes Congress' power to regulate purely local activities that are part of an economic "class of activities" that have a substantial effect on interstate commerce. . . . As we stated in *Wickard*, "even if appellee's activity be local and though it may not be regarded as commerce, it may still, whatever its nature, be reached by Congress if it exerts a substantial economic effect on interstate commerce." . . . . We have never required Congress to legislate with scientific exactitude. When Congress decides that the " 'total incidence' " of a practice poses a threat to a national market, it may regulate the entire class. . . . In this vein, we have reiterated that when " 'a general regulatory statute bears a substantial relation to commerce, the *de minimis* character of individual instances arising under that statute is of no consequence.' " . . .

Our decision in *Wickard*, . . ., is of particular relevance. In *Wickard*, we upheld the application of regulations promulgated under the Agricultural Adjustment Act of 1938, . . ., which were designed to control the volume of wheat moving in interstate and foreign commerce in order to avoid surpluses and consequent abnormally low prices. The regulations established an allotment of 11.1 acres for Filburn's 1941 wheat crop, but he sowed 23 acres, intending to use the excess by consuming it on his own farm. Filburn argued that even though we had sustained Congress' power to regulate the production of goods for commerce, that power did not authorize "federal regulation [of] production not intended in any part for commerce but wholly for consumption on the farm." . . . Justice Jackson's opinion for a unanimous Court rejected this submission. He wrote:

"The effect of the statute before us is to restrict the amount which may be produced for market and the extent as well to which one may forestall resort to the market by producing to meet his own needs. That appellee's own contribution to the demand for wheat may be trivial by itself is not enough to remove him from the scope of federal regulation where, as here, his contribution, taken together with that of many others similarly situated, is far from trivial." . . .

Wickard thus establishes that Congress can regulate purely intrastate activity that is not itself "commercial," in that it is not produced for sale, if it concludes that failure to regulate that class of activity would undercut the regulation of the interstate market in that commodity.

The similarities between this case and *Wickard* are striking. Like the farmer in *Wickard*, respondents are cultivating, for home consumption, a fungible commodity for which there is an established, albeit illegal, interstate market. Just as the Agricultural Adjustment Act was designed "to control the volume [of wheat] moving in interstate and foreign commerce in order to avoid surpluses . . ." and consequently control the market price, . . . a primary purpose of the CSA is to control the supply and demand of controlled substances in both lawful and unlawful drug markets. . . . In *Wickard*, we had no difficulty concluding that Congress had a rational basis for believing that, when viewed in the aggregate, leaving home-consumed wheat outside the regulatory scheme would have a substantial influence on price and market conditions. Here too, Congress had a rational basis for concluding that leaving home-consumed marijuana outside federal control would similarly affect price and market conditions.

More concretely, one concern prompting inclusion of wheat grown for home consumption in the 1938 Act was that rising market prices could draw such wheat into the interstate market, resulting in lower market prices. . . . The parallel concern making it appropriate to include marijuana grown for home consumption in the CSA is the likelihood that the high demand in the interstate market will draw such marijuana into that market. While the diversion of homegrown wheat tended to frustrate the federal interest in stabilizing prices by regulating the volume of commercial transactions in the interstate market, the diversion of homegrown marijuana tends to frustrate the federal interest in eliminating commercial transactions in the interstate market in their entirety. In both cases, the regulation is squarely within Congress' commerce power because production of the commodity meant for home consumption, be it wheat or marijuana, has a substantial effect on supply and demand in the national market for that commodity.

Nonetheless, respondents suggest that *Wickard* differs from this case in three respects: (1) the Agricultural Adjustment Act, unlike the CSA, exempted small farming operations; (2) *Wickard* involved a "quintessential economic activity" — a commercial farm — whereas respondents do not sell marijuana; and (3) the *Wickard* record made it clear that the aggregate production of wheat for use on farms had a significant impact on market prices. Those differences, though factually accurate, do not diminish the precedential force of this Court's reasoning.

The fact that Wickard's own impact on the market was "trivial by itself" was not a sufficient reason for removing him from the scope of federal regulation . . . . That the Secretary of Agriculture elected to exempt even smaller farms from regulation does not speak to his power to regulate all those whose aggregated production was significant, nor did that fact play any role in the Court's analysis. Moreover, even though Wickard was indeed a commercial farmer, the activity he was engaged in — the cultivation of wheat for home consumption — was not treated by the Court as part of his commercial farming operation. And while it is true that the record in the *Wickard* case itself established the causal connection between the production for local use and the national market, we have before us findings by Congress to the same effect.

Findings in the introductory sections of the CSA explain why Congress deemed it appropriate to encompass local activities within the scope of the CSA.... The submissions of the parties and the numerous *amici* all seem to agree that the national, and international, market for marijuana has dimensions that are fully comparable to those defining the class of activities regulated by the Secretary pursuant to the 1938 statute. Respondents nonetheless insist that the CSA cannot be constitutionally applied to their activities because Congress did not make a specific finding that the intrastate cultivation and possession of marijuana for medical purposes based on the recommendation of a physician would substantially affect the larger interstate marijuana market. Be that as it may, we have never required Congress to make particularized findings in order to legislate, ... While congressional findings are certainly helpful in reviewing the substance of a congressional statutory scheme, particularly when the connection to commerce is not self-evident, and while we will consider congressional findings in our analysis when they are available, the absence of particularized findings does not call into question Congress' authority to legislate.

In assessing the scope of Congress' authority under the Commerce Clause, we stress that the task before us is a modest one. We need not determine whether respondents' activities, taken in the aggregate, substantially affect interstate commerce in fact, but only whether a "rational basis" exists for so concluding.... Given the enforcement difficulties that attend distinguishing between marijuana cultivated locally and marijuana grown elsewhere, ..., and concerns about diversion into illicit channels, we have no difficulty concluding that Congress had a rational basis for believing that failure to regulate the intrastate manufacture and possession of marijuana would leave a gaping hole in the CSA. Thus, as in *Wickard*, when it enacted comprehensive legislation to regulate the interstate market in a fungible commodity, Congress was acting well within its authority to "make all Laws which shall be necessary and proper" to "regulate Commerce ... among the several States." .... That the regulation ensnares some purely intrastate activity is of no moment. As we have done many times before, we refuse to excise individual components of that larger scheme.

IV.

To support their contrary submission, respondents rely heavily on two of our more recent Commerce Clause cases. In their myopic focus, they overlook the larger context of modern-era Commerce Clause jurisprudence preserved by those cases. Moreover, even in the narrow prism of respondents' creation, they read those cases far too broadly.

Those two cases, of course, are *Lopez*, ... 4, and *Morrison*, ... As an initial matter, the statutory challenges at issue in those cases were markedly different from the challenge respondents pursue in the case at hand. Here, respondents ask us to excise individual applications of a concededly valid statutory scheme. In contrast, in both *Lopez* and *Morrison*, the parties asserted that a particular statute or provision fell outside Congress' commerce power in its entirety. This distinction is pivotal for we have often reiterated that "[w]here the class of activities is regulated and that class is within the reach of federal power, the courts have no power 'to excise, as trivial, individual instances' of the class." ...

At issue in *Lopez*, ..., was the validity of the Gun-Free School Zones Act of 1990, which was a brief, single-subject statute making it a crime for an individual to possess a gun in a school zone.... The Act did not regulate any economic activity and did not contain any requirement that the possession of a gun have any connection to past interstate activity or a predictable impact on future commercial activity. Distinguishing our earlier cases holding that comprehensive regulatory statutes may be validly applied to local conduct that does not, when viewed in isolation, have a significant impact on interstate commerce, we held the statute invalid. We explained:

"Section 922(q) is a criminal statute that by its terms has nothing to do with 'commerce' or any sort of economic enterprise, however broadly one might define those terms. Section 922(q) is not an essential part of a larger regulation of economic activity, in which the regulatory scheme could be undercut unless the intrastate activity were regulated. It cannot, therefore, be sustained under our cases upholding regulations of activities that arise out of or are connected with a commercial transaction, which viewed in the aggregate, substantially affects interstate commerce." . . . .

The statutory scheme that the Government is defending in this litigation is at the opposite end of the regulatory spectrum. As explained above, the CSA, enacted in 1970 as part of the Comprehensive Drug Abuse Prevention and Control Act, . . ., was a lengthy and detailed statute creating a comprehensive framework for regulating the production, distribution, and possession of five classes of "controlled substances." Most of those substances — those listed in Schedules II through V — "have a useful and legitimate medical purpose and are necessary to maintain the health and general welfare of the American people." . . . . The regulatory scheme is designed to foster the beneficial use of those medications, to prevent their misuse, and to prohibit entirely the possession or use of substances listed in Schedule I, except as a part of a strictly controlled research project.

While the statute provided for the periodic updating of the five schedules, Congress itself made the initial classifications. It identified 42 opiates, 22 opium derivatives, and 17 hallucinogenic substances as Schedule I drugs. . . . Marijuana was listed as the 10th item in the third subcategory. That classification, unlike the discrete prohibition established by the Gun-Free School Zones Act of 1990, was merely one of many "essential part[s] of a larger regulation of economic activity, in which the regulatory scheme could be undercut unless the intrastate activity were regulated." . . . Our opinion in *Lopez* casts no doubt on the validity of such a program.

Nor does this Court's holding in *Morrison*, ... The Violence Against Women Act of 1994, . . ., created a federal civil remedy for the victims of gender-motivated crimes of violence. . . . The remedy was enforceable in both state and federal courts, and generally depended on proof of the violation of a state law. Despite congressional findings that such crimes had an adverse impact on interstate commerce, we held the statute unconstitutional because, like the statute in *Lopez*, it did not regulate economic activity. We concluded that "the noneconomic, criminal nature of the conduct at issue was central

to our decision" in *Lopez*, and that our prior cases had identified a clear pattern of analysis: " 'Where economic activity substantially affects interstate commerce, legislation regulating that activity will be sustained.' " . . .

Unlike those at issue in *Lopez* and *Morrison*, the activities regulated by the CSA are quintessentially economic. "Economics" refers to "the production, distribution, and consumption of commodities." . . . . The CSA is a statute that regulates the production, distribution, and consumption of commodities for which there is an established, and lucrative, interstate market. Prohibiting the intrastate possession or manufacture of an article of commerce is a rational (and commonly utilized) means of regulating commerce in that product. Such prohibitions include specific decisions requiring that a drug be withdrawn from the market as a result of the failure to comply with regulatory requirements as well as decisions excluding Schedule I drugs entirely from the market. Because the CSA is a statute that directly regulates economic, commercial activity, our opinion in *Morrison* casts no doubt on its constitutionality.

The Court of Appeals was able to conclude otherwise only by isolating a "separate and distinct" class of activities that it held to be beyond the reach of federal power, defined as "the intrastate, noncommercial cultivation, possession and use of marijuana for personal medical purposes on the advice of a physician and in accordance with state law." . . . . The court characterized this class as "different in kind from drug trafficking." . . . . The differences between the members of a class so defined and the principal traffickers in Schedule I substances might be sufficient to justify a policy decision exempting the narrower class from the coverage of the CSA. The question, however, is whether Congress' contrary policy judgment, *i.e.*, its decision to include this narrower "class of activities" within the larger regulatory scheme, was constitutionally deficient. We have no difficulty concluding that Congress acted rationally in determining that none of the characteristics making up the purported class, whether viewed individually or in the aggregate, compelled an exemption from the CSA; rather, the subdivided class of activities defined by the Court of Appeals was an essential part of the larger regulatory scheme.

First, the fact that marijuana is used "for personal medical purposes on the advice of a physician" cannot itself serve as a distinguishing factor. . . . The CSA designates marijuana as contraband for *any* purpose; in fact, by characterizing marijuana as a Schedule I drug, Congress expressly found that the drug has no acceptable medical uses. Moreover, the CSA is a comprehensive regulatory regime specifically designed to regulate which controlled substances can be utilized for medicinal purposes, and in what manner. Indeed, most of the substances classified in the CSA "have a useful and legitimate medical purpose." . . . . Thus, even if respondents are correct that marijuana does have accepted medical uses and thus should be redesignated as a lesser schedule drug, the CSA would still impose controls beyond what is required by California law. The CSA requires manufacturers, physicians, pharmacies, and other handlers of controlled substances to comply with statutory and regulatory provisions mandating registration with the DEA, compliance with specific production quotas, security controls to guard against diversion, recordkeeping and reporting obligations, and prescription requirements. . . . Furthermore, the dispensing of new drugs, even when doctors approve their use, must await federal approval. . . . Accordingly, the mere fact that marijuana — like virtually every other controlled substance regulated by the CSA — is used for medicinal purposes cannot possibly serve to distinguish it from the core activities regulated by the CSA.

Nor can it serve as an "objective marke[r]" or "objective facto[r]" to arbitrarily narrow the relevant class as the dissenters suggest, ... More fundamentally, if, as the principal dissent contends, the personal cultivation, possession, and use of marijuana for medicinal purposes is beyond the " 'outer limits' of Congress' Commerce Clause authority," . . ., it must also be true that such personal use of marijuana (or any other homegrown drug) for recreational purposes is also beyond those " 'outer limits,' " whether or not a State elects to authorize or even regulate such use.

Justice Thomas' separate dissent suffers from the same sweeping implications. That

is, the dissenters' rationale logically extends to place *any* federal regulation (including quality, prescription, or quantity controls) of *any* locally cultivated and possessed controlled substance for *any* purpose beyond the " 'outer limits' " of Congress' Commerce Clause authority. One need not have a degree in economics to understand why a nationwide exemption for the vast quantity of marijuana (or other drugs) locally cultivated for personal use (which presumably would include use by friends, neighbors, and family members) may have a substantial impact on the interstate market for this extraordinarily popular substance. The congressional judgment that an exemption for such a significant segment of the total market would undermine the orderly enforcement of the entire regulatory scheme is entitled to a strong presumption of validity. Indeed, that judgment is not only rational, but "visible to the naked eye," . . ., under any commonsense appraisal of the probable consequences of such an open-ended exemption.

Second, limiting the activity to marijuana possession and cultivation "in accordance with state law" cannot serve to place respondents' activities beyond congressional reach. The Supremacy Clause unambiguously provides that if there is any conflict between federal and state law, federal law shall prevail. It is beyond peradventure that federal power over commerce is " 'superior to that of the States to provide for the welfare or necessities of their inhabitants,' " however legitimate or dire those necessities may be. . . . Just as state acquiescence to federal regulation cannot expand the bounds of the Commerce Clause, . . ., so too state action cannot circumscribe Congress' plenary commerce power. . . .

Respondents acknowledge this proposition, but nonetheless contend that their activities were not "an essential part of a larger regulatory scheme" because they had been "isolated by the State of California, and [are] policed by the State of California," and thus remain "entirely separated from the market." . . . . The dissenters fall prey to similar reasoning. . . . The notion that California law has surgically excised a discrete activity that is hermetically sealed off from the larger interstate marijuana market is a dubious proposition, and, more importantly, one that Congress could have rationally rejected.

Indeed, that the California exemptions will have a significant impact on both the supply and demand sides of the market for marijuana is not just "plausible" as the principal dissent concedes, . . ., it is readily apparent. The exemption for physicians provides them with an economic incentive to grant their patients permission to use the drug. In contrast to most prescriptions for legal drugs, which limit the dosage and duration of the usage, under California law the doctor's permission to recommend marijuana use is open-ended. The authority to grant permission whenever the doctor determines that a patient is afflicted with "any other illness for which marijuana provides relief," . . ., is broad enough to allow even the most scrupulous doctor to conclude that some recreational uses would be therapeutic. And our cases have taught us that there are some unscrupulous physicians who overprescribe when it is sufficiently profitable to do so.

The exemption for cultivation by patients and caregivers can only increase the supply of marijuana in the California market. The likelihood that all such production will promptly terminate when patients recover or will precisely match the patients' medical needs during their convalescence seems remote; whereas the danger that excesses will satisfy some of the admittedly enormous demand for recreational use seems obvious. Moreover, that the national and international narcotics trade has thrived in the face of vigorous criminal enforcement efforts suggests that no small number of unscrupulous people will make use of the California exemptions to serve their commercial ends whenever it is feasible to do so. Taking into account the fact that California is only one of at least nine States to have authorized the medical use of marijuana, a fact Justice O'Connor's dissent conveniently disregards in arguing that the demonstrated effect on commerce while admittedly "plausible" is ultimately "unsubstantiated," . . ., Congress could have rationally concluded that the aggregate impact on the national market of all the transactions exempted from federal supervision is unquestionably substantial.

So, from the "separate and distinct" class of activities identified by the Court of Appeals (and adopted by the dissenters), we are left with "the intrastate, noncommercial cultivation, possession and use of marijuana." . . . . Thus the case for the exemption comes down to the claim that a locally cultivated product that is used domestically rather than sold on the open market is not subject to federal regulation. Given the findings in the CSA and the undisputed magnitude of the commercial market for marijuana, our decisions in *Wickard* v. *Filburn* and the later cases endorsing its reasoning foreclose that claim.

V.

Respondents also raise a substantive due process claim and seek to avail themselves of the medical necessity defense. These theories of relief were set forth in their complaint but were not reached by the Court of Appeals. We therefore do not address the question whether judicial relief is available to respondents on these alternative bases. We do note, however, the presence of another avenue of relief. As the Solicitor General confirmed during oral argument, the statute authorizes procedures for the reclassification of Schedule I drugs. But perhaps even more important than these legal avenues is the democratic process, in which the voices of voters allied with these respondents may one day be heard in the halls of Congress. Under the present state of the law, however, the judgment of the Court of Appeals must be vacated. The case is remanded for further proceedings consistent with this opinion.

It is so ordered.

[Footnotes and citations omitted. Concurring and dissenting opinions omitted.]

**Alberto R. Gonzales, Attorney General,
et al.**

v.

Oregon, et al.

**Supreme Court of the United States
126 S. Ct. 904 (2006)**

Justice Kennedy delivered the opinion of the Court.

The question before us is whether the Controlled Substances Act allows the United States Attorney General to prohibit doctors from prescribing regulated drugs for use in physician-assisted suicide, notwithstanding a state law permitting the procedure. As the Court has observed, "Americans are engaged in an earnest and profound debate about the morality, legality, and practicality of physician-assisted suicide." . . . The dispute before us is in part a product of this political and moral debate, but its resolution requires an inquiry familiar to the courts: interpreting a federal statute to determine whether Executive action is authorized by, or otherwise consistent with, the enactment.

In 1994, Oregon became the first State to legalize assisted suicide when voters approved a ballot measure enacting the Oregon Death With Dignity Act (ODWDA). . . . ODWDA, which survived a 1997 ballot measure seeking its repeal, exempts from civil or criminal liability state-licensed physicians who, in compliance with the specific safeguards in ODWDA, dispense or prescribe a lethal dose of drugs upon the request of a terminally ill patient.

The drugs Oregon physicians prescribe under ODWDA are regulated under a federal statute, the Controlled Substances Act (CSA or Act). . . . The CSA allows these particular drugs to be available only by a written prescription from a registered physician. In the ordinary course the same drugs are prescribed in smaller doses for pain alleviation.

A November 9, 2001 Interpretive Rule issued by the Attorney General addresses the implementation and enforcement of the CSA with respect to ODWDA. It determines that using controlled substances to assist suicide is not a legitimate medical practice and that dispensing or prescribing them for

this purpose is unlawful under the CSA. The Interpretive Rule's validity under the CSA is the issue before us.

I.

A.

We turn first to the text and structure of the CSA. Enacted in 1970 with the main objectives of combating drug abuse and controlling the legitimate and illegitimate traffic in controlled substances, the CSA creates a comprehensive, closed regulatory regime criminalizing the unauthorized manufacture, distribution, dispensing, and possession of substances classified in any of the Act's five schedules. . . . The Act places substances in one of five schedules based on their potential for abuse or dependence, their accepted medical use, and their accepted safety for use under medical supervision. Schedule I contains the most severe restrictions on access and use, and Schedule V the least. . . . Congress classified a host of substances when it enacted the CSA, but the statute permits the Attorney General to add, remove, or reschedule substances. He may do so, however, only after making particular findings, and on scientific and medical matters he is required to accept the findings of the Secretary of Health and Human Services (Secretary). These proceedings must be on the record after an opportunity for comment. . . .

The present dispute involves controlled substances listed in Schedule II, substances generally available only pursuant to a written, nonrefillable prescription by a physician. . . . A 1971 regulation promulgated by the Attorney General requires that every prescription for a controlled substance "be issued for a legitimate medical purpose by an individual practitioner acting in the usual course of his professional practice." . . .

To prevent diversion of controlled substances with medical uses, the CSA regulates the activity of physicians. To issue lawful prescriptions of Schedule II drugs, physicians must "obtain from the Attorney General a registration issued in accordance with the rules and regulations promulgated by him." . . . . The Attorney General may deny, suspend, or revoke this registration if, as relevant here, the physician's registration would be "inconsistent with the public interest." . . . . When deciding whether a practitioner's registration is in the public interest, the Attorney General "shall" consider:

"(1) The recommendation of the appropriate State licensing board or professional disciplinary authority.

"(2) The applicant's experience in dispensing, or conducting research with respect to controlled substances.

"(3) The applicant's conviction record under Federal or State laws relating to the manufacture, distribution, or dispensing of controlled substances.

"(4) Compliance with applicable State, Federal, or local laws relating to controlled substances.

"(5) Such other conduct which may threaten the public health and safety." § 823(f).

The CSA explicitly contemplates a role for the States in regulating controlled substances, as evidenced by its pre-emption provision.

"No provision of this subchapter shall be construed as indicating an intent on the part of the Congress to occupy the field in which that provision operates . . . to the exclusion of any State law on the same subject matter which would otherwise be within the authority of the State, unless there is a positive conflict between that provision . . . and that State law so that the two cannot consistently stand together." . . . .

B.

Oregon voters enacted ODWDA in 1994. For Oregon residents to be eligible to request a prescription under ODWDA, they must receive a diagnosis from their attending physician that they have an incurable and irreversible disease that, within reasonable medical judgment, will cause death within six months. . . . Attending physicians must also determine whether a patient has made a voluntary request, ensure a patient's choice is informed, and refer patients to counseling if they might be suffering from a psychological disorder or depression causing impaired judg-

ment. . . . A second "consulting" physician must examine the patient and the medical record and confirm the attending physician's conclusions. . . . Oregon physicians may dispense or issue a prescription for the requested drug, but may not administer it. . . .

The reviewing physicians must keep detailed medical records of the process leading to the final prescription, . . ., records that Oregon's Department of Human Services reviews. . . . Physicians who dispense medication pursuant to ODWDA must also be registered with both the State's Board of Medical Examiners and the federal Drug Enforcement Administration (DEA). . . . In 2004, 37 patients ended their lives by ingesting a lethal dose of medication prescribed under ODWDA. . . .

C.

In 1997, Members of Congress concerned about ODWDA invited the DEA to prosecute or revoke the CSA registration of Oregon physicians who assist suicide. They contended that hastening a patient's death is not legitimate medical practice, so prescribing controlled substances for that purpose violates the CSA. . . . The letter received an initial, favorable response from the director of the DEA, . . ., but Attorney General Reno considered the matter and concluded that the DEA could not take the proposed action because the CSA did not authorize it to "displace the states as the primary regulators of the medical profession, or to override a state's determination as to what constitutes legitimate medical practice," . . . . Legislation was then introduced to grant the explicit authority Attorney General Reno found lacking; but it failed to pass. . . .

In 2001, John Ashcroft was appointed Attorney General. Perhaps because Mr. Ashcroft had supported efforts to curtail assisted suicide while serving as a Senator, . . ., Oregon Attorney General Hardy Myers wrote him to request a meeting with Department of Justice officials should the Department decide to revisit the application of the CSA to assisted suicide. . . . Attorney General Myers received a reply letter from one of Attorney General Ashcroft's advisers writing on his behalf, which stated

"I am aware of no pending legislation in Congress that would prompt a review of the Department's interpretation of the CSA as it relates to physician-assisted suicide. Should such a review be commenced in the future, we would be happy to include your views in that review." . . . .

On November 9, 2001, without consulting Oregon or apparently anyone outside his Department, the Attorney General issued an Interpretive Rule announcing his intent to restrict the use of controlled substances for physician-assisted suicide. Incorporating the legal analysis of a memorandum he had solicited from his Office of Legal Counsel, the Attorney General ruled

"assisting suicide is not a 'legitimate medical purpose' within the meaning of 21 CFR 1306.04 (2001), and that prescribing, dispensing, or administering federally controlled substances to assist suicide violates the Controlled Substances Act. Such conduct by a physician registered to dispense controlled substances may 'render his registration . . . inconsistent with the public interest' and therefore subject to possible suspension or revocation under 21 U.S.C. 824(a)(4). The Attorney General's conclusion applies regardless of whether state law authorizes or permits such conduct by practitioners or others and regardless of the condition of the person whose suicide is assisted." . . .

There is little dispute that the Interpretive Rule would substantially disrupt the ODWDA regime. Respondents contend, and petitioners do not dispute, that every prescription filled under ODWDA has specified drugs classified under Schedule II. A physician cannot prescribe the substances without DEA registration, and revocation or suspension of the registration would be a severe restriction on medical practice. Dispensing controlled substances without a valid prescription, furthermore, is a federal crime. . . .

In response the State of Oregon, joined by a physician, a pharmacist, and some terminally ill patients, all from Oregon, challenged the Interpretive Rule in federal court. The United States District Court for the District of Oregon entered a permanent injunction against the Interpretive Rule's enforcement.

A divided panel of the Court of Appeals for the Ninth Circuit granted the petitions for review and held the Interpretive Rule invalid. . . . It reasoned that, by making a medical procedure authorized under Oregon law a federal offense, the Interpretive Rule altered the "'usual constitutional balance between the States and the Federal Government'" "without the requisite clear statement that the CSA authorized such action. . . . The Court of Appeals held in the alternative that the Interpretive Rule could not be squared with the plain language of the CSA, which targets only conventional drug abuse and excludes the Attorney General from decisions on medical policy. . . .

We granted the Government's petition for certiorari. . . .

II.

Executive actors often must interpret the enactments Congress has charged them with enforcing and implementing. The parties before us are in sharp disagreement both as to the degree of deference we must accord the Interpretive Rule's substantive conclusions and whether the Rule is authorized by the statutory text at all. Although balancing the necessary respect for an agency's knowledge, expertise, and constitutional office with the courts' role as interpreter of laws can be a delicate matter, familiar principles guide us. An administrative rule may receive substantial deference if it interprets the issuing agency's own ambiguous regulation. . . . An interpretation of an ambiguous statute may also receive substantial deference. . . . Deference in accordance with Chevron, however, is warranted only "when it appears that Congress delegated authority to the agency generally to make rules carrying the force of law, and that the agency interpretation claiming deference was promulgated in the exercise of that authority." . . . . Otherwise, the interpretation is "entitled to respect" only to the extent it has the "power to persuade." . . .

A.

The Government first argues that the Interpretive Rule is an elaboration of one of the Attorney General's own regulations, . . ., which requires all prescriptions be issued "for a legitimate medical purpose by an individual practitioner acting in the usual course of his professional practice." As such, the Government says, the Interpretive Rule is entitled to considerable deference in accordance with Auer.

In our view Auer and the standard of deference it accords to an agency are inapplicable here. Auer involved a disputed interpretation of the Fair Labor Standards Act of 1938 as applied to a class of law enforcement officers. Under regulations promulgated by the Secretary of Labor, an exemption from overtime pay depended, in part, on whether the employees met the "salary basis" test. . . . In this Court the Secretary of Labor filed an amicus brief explaining why, in his view, the regulations gave exempt status to the officers. . . . We gave weight to that interpretation, holding that because the applicable test was "a creature of the Secretary's own regulations, his interpretation of it is, under our jurisprudence, controlling unless plainly erroneous or inconsistent with the regulation. " . . .

In Auer, the underlying regulations gave specificity to a statutory scheme the Secretary was charged with enforcing and reflected the considerable experience and expertise the Department of Labor had acquired over time with respect to the complexities of the Fair Labor Standards Act. Here, on the other hand, the underlying regulation does little more than restate the terms of the statute itself. The language the Interpretive Rule addresses comes from Congress, not the Attorney General, and the near-equivalence of the statute and regulation belies the Government's argument for Auer deference.

The Government does not suggest that its interpretation turns on any difference between the statutory and regulatory language. The CSA allows prescription of drugs only if they have a "currently accepted medical use," . . . requires a "medical purpose" for dispensing the least controlled substances of those on the schedules, . . . and, in its reporting provision, defines a "valid prescription" as one "issued for a legitimate medical purpose," . . . Similarly, physicians are considered to be acting as practitioners under the statute if they dispense controlled substances "in the course of professional practice." . . . .

The regulation uses the terms "legitimate medical purpose" and "the course of professional practice," . . ., but this just repeats two statutory phrases and attempts to summarize the others. It gives little or no instruction on a central issue in this case: Who decides whether a particular activity is in "the course of professional practice" or done for a "legitimate medical purpose"? Since the regulation gives no indication how to decide this issue, the Attorney General's effort to decide it now cannot be considered an interpretation of the regulation. Simply put, the existence of a parroting regulation does not change the fact that the question here is not the meaning of the regulation but the meaning of the statute. An agency does not acquire special authority to interpret its own words when, instead of using its expertise and experience to formulate a regulation, it has elected merely to paraphrase the statutory language.

Furthermore, as explained below, if there is statutory authority to issue the Interpretive Rule it comes from the 1984 amendments to the CSA that gave the Attorney General authority to register and deregister physicians based on the public interest. The regulation was enacted before those amendments, so the Interpretive Rule cannot be justified as indicative of some intent the Attorney General had in 1971. That the current interpretation runs counter to the "intent at the time of the regulation's promulgation," is an additional reason why Auer deference is unwarranted. . . . Deference under Auer being inappropriate, we turn to the question whether the Interpretive Rule, on its own terms, is a permissible interpretation of the CSA.

B.

Just as the Interpretive Rule receives no deference under Auer, neither does it receive deference under Chevron. If a statute is ambiguous, judicial review of administrative rulemaking often demands Chevron deference; and the rule is judged accordingly. All would agree, we should think, that the statutory phrase "legitimate medical purpose" is a generality, susceptible to more precise definition and open to varying constructions, and thus ambiguous in the relevant sense. Chevron deference, however, is not accorded

PART II: CASES RELATING TO CHAPTER 14
ALBERTO GONZALES, ATTORNEY GENERAL V. OREGON ET AL.

809

merely because the statute is ambiguous and an administrative official is involved. To begin with, the rule must be promulgated pursuant to authority Congress has delegated to the official. . . .

The Attorney General has rulemaking power to fulfill his duties under the CSA. The specific respects in which he is authorized to make rules, however, instruct us that he is not authorized to make a rule declaring illegitimate a medical standard for care and treatment of patients that is specifically authorized under state law.

The starting point for this inquiry is, of course, the language of the delegation provision itself. In many cases authority is clear because the statute gives an agency broad power to enforce all provisions of the statute. . . . The CSA does not grant the Attorney General this broad authority to promulgate rules.

The CSA gives the Attorney General limited powers, to be exercised in specific ways. His rulemaking authority under the CSA is described in two provisions: (1) "The Attorney General is authorized to promulgate rules and regulations and to charge reasonable fees relating to the registration and control of the manufacture, distribution, and dispensing of controlled substances and to listed chemicals," . . . and (2) "The Attorney General may promulgate and enforce any rules, regulations, and procedures which he may deem necessary and appropriate for the efficient execution of his functions under this subchapter," . . . . As is evident from these sections, Congress did not delegate to the Attorney General authority to carry out or effect all provisions of the CSA. Rather, he can promulgate rules relating only to "registration" and "control," and "for the efficient execution of his functions" under the statute.

Turning first to the Attorney General's authority to make regulations for the "control" of drugs, this delegation cannot sustain the Interpretive Rule's attempt to define standards of medical practice. Control is a term of art in the CSA. "As used in this subchapter," § 802 — the subchapter that includes § 821 —

"The term 'control' means to add a drug or other substance, or immediate precursor, to a schedule under part B of this subchapter, whether by transfer from another schedule or otherwise." . . .

To exercise his scheduling power, the Attorney General must follow a detailed set of procedures, including requesting a scientific and medical evaluation from the Secretary. . . . The statute is also specific as to the manner in which the Attorney General must exercise this authority: "Rules of the Attorney General under this subsection [regarding scheduling] shall be made on the record after opportunity for a hearing pursuant to the rulemaking procedures prescribed by . . . 21 U.S.C. § 811(a). The Interpretive Rule now under consideration does not concern the scheduling of substances and was not issued after the required procedures for rules regarding scheduling, so it cannot fall under the Attorney General's "control" authority.

Even if "control" in § 821 were understood to signify something other than its statutory definition, it would not support the Interpretive Rule. The statutory references to "control" outside the scheduling context make clear that the Attorney General can establish controls "against diversion," . . ., but do not give him authority to define diversion based on his view of legitimate medical practice. As explained below, the CSA's express limitations on the Attorney General's authority, and other indications from the statutory scheme, belie any notion that the Attorney General has been granted this implicit authority. Indeed, if "control" were given the expansive meaning required to sustain the Interpretive Rule, it would transform the carefully described limits on the Attorney General's authority over registration and scheduling into mere suggestions.

We turn, next, to the registration provisions of the CSA. Before 1984, the Attorney General was required to register any physician who was authorized by his State. The Attorney General could only deregister a physician who falsified his application, was convicted of a felony relating to controlled substances, or had his state license or registration revoked. . . . The CSA was amended in 1984 to allow the Attorney General to deny registration to an applicant "if he determines that the issuance of such registration would be inconsistent with the public interest." . . . . Registration may also be revoked or suspended by the Attorney General on the same grounds. . . . In determining consistency with the public interest, the Attorney General must, as discussed above, consider five factors, including: the State's recommendation; compliance with state, federal, and local laws regarding controlled substances; and public health and safety. . . .

The Interpretive Rule cannot be justified under this part of the statute. It does not undertake the five-factor analysis and concerns much more than registration. Nor does the Interpretive Rule on its face purport to be an application of the registration provision in § 823(f). It is, instead, an interpretation of the substantive federal law requirements . . . for a valid prescription. It begins by announcing that assisting suicide is not a "legitimate medical purpose" under § 1306.04, and that dispensing controlled substances to assist a suicide violates the CSA. . . . Violation is a criminal offense, and often a felony, under 21 U.S.C. § 841 . . . . The Interpretive Rule thus purports to declare that using controlled substances for physician-assisted suicide is a crime, an authority that goes well beyond the Attorney General's statutory power to register or deregister.

The Attorney General's deregistration power, of course, may carry implications for criminal enforcement because if a physician dispenses a controlled substance after he is deregistered, he violates § 841. The Interpretive Rule works in the opposite direction, however: it declares certain conduct criminal, placing in jeopardy the registration of any physician who engages in that conduct. To the extent the Interpretive Rule concerns registration, it simply states the obvious because one of the five factors the Attorney General must consider in deciding the "public interest" is "compliance with applicable State, Federal, or local laws relating to controlled substances." . . . . The problem with the design of the Interpretive Rule is that it cannot, and does not, explain why the Attorney General has the authority to decide what constitutes an underlying violation of the CSA in the first place. The explanation the Government seems to advance is that the Attorney General's authority to decide whether a physician's actions are inconsistent with the "public interest" provides the basis for the Interpretive Rule.

By this logic, however, the Attorney General claims extraordinary authority. If the Attorney General's argument were correct, his power to deregister necessarily would include the greater power to criminalize even the actions of registered physicians, whenever they engage in conduct he deems illegitimate. This power to criminalize — unlike his power over registration, which must be exercised only after considering five express statutory factors — would be unrestrained. It would be anomalous for Congress to have so painstakingly described the Attorney General's limited authority to deregister a single physician or schedule a single drug, but to have given him, just by implication, authority to declare an entire class of activity outside "the course of professional practice," and therefore a criminal violation of the CSA. . . .

Sutton v. United Air Lines, Inc., . . . (1999), is instructive. The statute at issue was the Americans with Disabilities Act of 1990 (ADA), which, like the CSA, divides interpretive authority among various Executive actors. The Court relied on "the terms and structure of the ADA" to decide that neither the Equal Employment Opportunity Commission, nor any other agency had authority to define "disability" in the ADA. . . .

[Discussion of case concerning ADA omitted.]

The same principle controls here. It is not enough that the terms "public interest," "public health and safety," and "Federal law" are used in the part of the statute over which the Attorney General has authority. The statutory terms "public interest" and "public health" do not call on the Attorney General, or any other Executive official, to make an independent assessment of the meaning of federal law. The Attorney General did not base the Interpretive Rule on an application of the five-factor test generally, or the "public health and safety" factor specifically. Even if he had, it is doubtful the Attorney General could cite the "public interest" or "public health" to deregister a physician simply because he deemed a controversial practice permitted by state law to have an illegitimate medical purpose.

As for the federal law factor, though it does require the Attorney General to decide "compliance" with the law, it does not suggest that he may decide what the law says. Were it otherwise, the Attorney General could authoritatively interpret "State" and "local laws," which are also included in 21 U.S.C. § 823(f), despite the obvious constitutional problems in his doing so. Just as he must evaluate compliance with federal law in deciding about registration, the Attorney General must as surely evaluate compliance with federal law in deciding whether to prosecute; but this does not entitle him to *Chevron* deference. . . .

The limits on the Attorney General's authority to define medical standards for the care and treatment of patients bear also on the proper interpretation of § 871(b). This section allows the Attorney General to best determine how to execute "his functions." It is quite a different matter, however, to say that the Attorney General can define the substantive standards of medical practice as part of his authority. To find a delegation of this extent in § 871 would put that part of the statute in considerable tension with the narrowly defined delegation concerning control and registration. It would go, moreover, against the plain language of the text to treat a delegation for the "execution" of his functions as a further delegation to define other functions well beyond the statute's specific grants of authority. When Congress chooses to delegate a power of this extent, it does so not by referring back to the administrator's functions but by giving authority over the provisions of the statute he is to interpret. . . .

The authority desired by the Government is inconsistent with the design of the statute in other fundamental respects. The Attorney General does not have the sole delegated authority under the CSA. He must instead share it with, and in some respects defer to, the Secretary, whose functions are likewise delineated and confined by the statute.

[Further discussion of the Attorney General and Secretary's powers omitted.]

In a similar vein the 1970 Act's regulation of medical practice with respect to drug rehabilitation gives the Attorney General a limited role; for it is the Secretary who, after consultation with the Attorney General and national medical groups, "determines the appropriate methods of professional practice in the medical treatment of . . . narcotic addiction." . . .

Post enactment congressional commentary on the CSA's regulation of medical

practice is also at odds with the Attorney General's claimed authority to determine appropriate medical standards. In 1978, in preparation for ratification of the Convention on Psychotropic Substances, Feb. 21, 1971. . ., Congress decided it would implement the United States' compliance through "the framework of the procedures and criteria for classification of substances provided in the" CSA. . . . It did so to ensure that "nothing in the Convention will interfere with ethical medical practice in this country as determined by [the Secretary] on the basis of a consensus of the views of the American medical and scientific community." . . .

The structure of the CSA, then, conveys unwillingness to cede medical judgments to an Executive official who lacks medical expertise. In interpreting statutes that divide authority, the Court has recognized: "Because historical familiarity and policymaking expertise account in the first instance for the presumption that Congress delegates interpretive lawmaking power to the agency rather than to the reviewing court, we presume here that Congress intended to invest interpretive power in the administrative actor in the best position to develop these attributes." . . . This presumption works against a conclusion that the Attorney General has authority to make quintessentially medical judgments.

The Government contends the Attorney General's decision here is a legal, not a medical, one. This generality, however, does not suffice. The Attorney General's Interpretive Rule, and the Office of Legal Counsel memo it incorporates, place extensive reliance on medical judgments and the views of the medical community in concluding that assisted suicide is not a "legitimate medical purpose." . . . . This confirms that the authority claimed by the Attorney General is both beyond his expertise and incongruous with the statutory purposes and design.

The idea that Congress gave the Attorney General such broad and unusual authority through an implicit delegation in the CSA's registration provision is not sustainable. "Congress, we have held, does not alter the fundamental details of a regulatory scheme in vague terms or ancillary provisions — it does not, one might say, hide elephants in mouseholes." . . .

The importance of the issue of physician-assisted suicide, which has been the subject of an "earnest and profound debate" across the country, . . ., makes the oblique form of the claimed delegation all the more suspect. Under the Government's theory, moreover, the medical judgments the Attorney General could make are not limited to physician-assisted suicide. Were this argument accepted, he could decide whether any particular drug may be used for any particular purpose, or indeed whether a physician who administers any controversial treatment could be deregistered. This would occur, under the Government's view, despite the statute's express limitation of the Attorney General's authority to registration and control, with attendant restrictions on each of those functions, and despite the statutory purposes to combat drug abuse and prevent illicit drug trafficking.

We need not decide whether *Chevron* deference would be warranted for an interpretation issued by the Attorney General concerning matters closer to his role under the CSA, namely preventing doctors from engaging in illicit drug trafficking. In light of the foregoing, however, the CSA does not give the Attorney General authority to issue the Interpretive Rule as a statement with the force of law.

If, in the course of exercising his authority, the Attorney General uses his analysis in the Interpretive Rule only for guidance in deciding when to prosecute or deregister, then the question remains whether his substantive interpretation is correct. Since the Interpretive Rule was not promulgated pursuant to the Attorney General's authority, its interpretation of "legitimate medical purpose" does not receive *Chevron* deference. Instead, it receives deference only in accordance with *Skidmore*. "The weight of such a judgment in a particular case will depend upon the thoroughness evident in its consideration, the validity of its reasoning, its consistency with earlier and later pronouncements, and all those factors which give it power to persuade, if lacking power to control." . . . . The deference here is tempered by the Attorney General's lack of expertise in this area and the apparent absence of any consultation with anyone outside the Department of Jus-

tice who might aid in a reasoned judgment. In any event, under *Skidmore*, we follow an agency's rule only to the extent it is persuasive, . . . and for the reasons given and for further reasons set out below, we do not find the Attorney General's opinion persuasive.

III.

As we have noted before, the CSA "repealed most of the earlier antidrug laws in favor of a comprehensive regime to combat the international and interstate traffic in illicit drugs." . . . . In doing so, Congress sought to "conquer drug abuse and to control the legitimate and illegitimate traffic in controlled substances." . . . It comes as little surprise, then, that we have not considered the extent to which the CSA regulates medical practice beyond prohibiting a doctor from acting as a drug " 'pusher' " instead of a physician. . . . In *Moore*, we addressed a situation in which a doctor "sold drugs, not for legitimate purposes, but primarily for the profits to be derived therefrom." . . . . There the defendant, who had engaged in large-scale overprescribing of methadone, "conceded in his brief that he did not observe generally accepted medical practices." . . . And in *United States v. Oakland Cannabis Buyers' Cooperative*, . . . (2001), Congress' express determination that marijuana had no accepted medical use foreclosed any argument about statutory coverage of drugs available by a doctor's prescription.

In deciding whether the CSA can be read as prohibiting physician-assisted suicide, we look to the statute's text and design. The statute and our case law amply support the conclusion that Congress regulates medical practice insofar as it bars doctors from using their prescription-writing powers as a means to engage in illicit drug dealing and trafficking as conventionally understood. Beyond this, however, the statute manifests no intent to regulate the practice of medicine generally. The silence is understandable given the structure and limitations of federalism, which allow the States " 'great latitude under their police powers to legislate as to the protection of the lives, limbs, health, comfort, and quiet of all persons.' " . . . .

The structure and operation of the CSA presume and rely upon a functioning medical profession regulated under the States' police powers. The Attorney General can register a physician to dispense controlled substances "if the applicant is authorized to dispense . . . controlled substances under the laws of the State in which he practices." . . . . When considering whether to revoke a physician's registration, the Attorney General looks not just to violations of federal drug laws; but he "shall" also consider "the recommendation of the appropriate state licensing board or professional disciplinary authority" and the registrant's compliance with state and local drug laws. . . . The very definition of a "practitioner" eligible to prescribe includes physicians "licensed, registered, or otherwise permitted, by the United States or the jurisdiction in which he practices" to dispense controlled substances. . . . Further cautioning against the conclusion that the CSA effectively displaces the States' general regulation of medical practice is the Act's pre-emption provision, which indicates that, absent a positive conflict, none of the Act's provisions should be "construed as indicating an intent on the part of the Congress to occupy the field in which that provision operates . . . to the exclusion of any State law on the same subject matter which would otherwise be within the authority of the State." . . . .

Oregon's regime is an example of the state regulation of medical practice that the CSA presupposes. Rather than simply decriminalizing assisted suicide, ODWDA limits its exercise to the attending physicians of terminally ill patients, physicians who must be licensed by Oregon's Board of Medical Examiners. . . . The statute gives attending physicians a central role, requiring them to provide prognoses and prescriptions, give information about palliative alternatives and counseling, and ensure patients are competent and acting voluntarily. . . . Any eligible patient must also get a second opinion from another registered physician, . . ., and the statute's safeguards require physicians to keep and submit to inspection detailed records of their actions, ...

Even though regulation of health and safety is "primarily, and historically, a matter of local concern," . . ., there is no question

that the Federal Government can set uniform national standards in these areas. . . . In connection to the CSA, however, we find only one area in which Congress set general, uniform standards of medical practice. Title I of the Comprehensive Drug Abuse Prevention and Control Act of 1970, of which the CSA was Title II, provides that

"[The Secretary], after consultation with the Attorney General and with national organizations representative of persons with knowledge and experience in the treatment of narcotic addicts, shall determine the appropriate methods of professional practice in the medical treatment of the narcotic addiction of various classes of narcotic addicts, and shall report thereon from time to time to the Congress." . . . .

This provision strengthens the understanding of the CSA as a statute combating recreational drug abuse, and also indicates that when Congress wants to regulate medical practice in the given scheme, it does so by explicit language in the statute.

In the face of the CSA's silence on the practice of medicine generally and its recognition of state regulation of the medical profession it is difficult to defend the Attorney General's declaration that the statute impliedly criminalizes physician-assisted suicide. This difficulty is compounded by the CSA's consistent delegation of medical judgments to the Secretary and its otherwise careful allocation of powers for enforcing the limited objects of the CSA. . . . The Government's attempt to meet this challenge rests, for the most part, on the CSA's requirement that every Schedule II drug be dispensed pursuant to a "written prescription of a practitioner." . . . . A prescription, the Government argues, necessarily implies that the substance is being made available to a patient for a legitimate medical purpose. The statute, in this view, requires an anterior judgment about the term "medical" or "medicine." The Government contends ordinary usage of these words ineluctably refers to a healing or curative art, which by these terms cannot embrace the intentional hastening of a patient's death. It also points to the teachings of Hippocrates, the positions of prominent medical organizations, the Federal Government, and the judgment of the 49 States that have not legalized physician-assisted suicide as further support for the proposition that the practice is not legitimate medicine. . . .

On its own, this understanding of medicine's boundaries is at least reasonable. The primary problem with the Government's argument, however, is its assumption that the CSA impliedly authorizes an Executive officer to bar a use simply because it may be inconsistent with one reasonable understanding of medical practice. Viewed alone, the prescription requirement may support such an understanding, but statutes "should not be read as a series of unrelated and isolated provisions." . . . . The CSA's substantive provisions and their arrangement undermine this assertion of an expansive federal authority to regulate medicine.

The statutory criteria for deciding what substances are controlled, determinations which are central to the Act, consistently connect the undefined term "drug abuse" with addiction or abnormal effects on the nervous system. When the Attorney General schedules drugs, he must consider a substance's psychic or physiological dependence liability. . . . To classify a substance in Schedules II through V, the Attorney General must find abuse of the drug leads to psychological or physical dependence. . . . Indeed, the differentiation of Schedules II through V turns in large part on a substance's habit-forming potential: The more addictive a substance, the stricter the controls. . . . When Congress wanted to extend the CSA's regulation to substances not obviously habit forming or psychotropic, moreover, it relied not on Executive ingenuity, but rather on specific legislation. . . .

The statutory scheme with which the CSA is intertwined further confirms a more limited understanding of the prescription requirement. When the Secretary considers FDA approval of a substance with "stimulant, depressant, or hallucinogenic effect," he must forward the information to the Attorney General for possible scheduling. Shedding light on Congress' understanding of drug abuse, this requirement appears under the heading "Abuse potential." . . .Similarly, when Congress prepared to implement the Convention on Psychotropic Substances, it did so through the CSA. . . .

The Interpretive Rule rests on a reading of the prescription requirement that is persuasive only to the extent one scrutinizes the provision without the illumination of the rest of the statute. . . . Viewed in its context, the prescription requirement is better understood as a provision that ensures patients use controlled substances under the supervision of a doctor so as to prevent addiction and recreational abuse. As a corollary, the provision also bars doctors from peddling to patients who crave the drugs for those prohibited uses. . . . To read prescriptions for assisted suicide as constituting "drug abuse" under the CSA is discordant with the phrase's consistent use throughout the statute, not to mention its ordinary meaning.

The Government's interpretation of the prescription requirement also fails under the objection that the Attorney General is an unlikely recipient of such broad authority, given the Secretary's primacy in shaping medical policy under the CSA, and the statute's otherwise careful allocation of decisionmaking powers. Just as the conventions of expression indicate that Congress is unlikely to alter a statute's obvious scope and division of authority through muffled hints, the background principles of our federal system also belie the notion that Congress would use such an obscure grant of authority to regulate areas traditionally supervised by the States' police power. It is unnecessary even to consider the application of clear statement requirements, . . ., or presumptions against pre-emption, . . .to reach this commonsense conclusion. For all these reasons, we conclude the CSA's prescription requirement does not authorize the Attorney General to bar dispensing controlled substances for assisted suicide in the face of a state medical regime permitting such conduct.

IV.

The Government, in the end, maintains that the prescription requirement delegates to a single Executive officer the power to effect a radical shift of authority from the States to the Federal Government to define general standards of medical practice in every locality. The text and structure of the CSA show that Congress did not have this far-reaching intent to alter the federal-state balance and the congressional role in maintaining it.

The judgment of the Court of Appeals is

Affirmed.

[Footnotes and citations omitted. Concurring and dissenting opinions omitted.]

Cases Relating to Chapter 15

Corporate and Computer Crimes

People of the State of Michigan

v.

Patrick Hegedus

Supreme Court of Michigan
432 Mich. 598 (1989)

Boyle, Justice.

We consider in this case whether the criminal sanctions for certain violations of health and safety standards set forth in the Occupational Safety and Health Act preclude the state from prosecuting the defendant for involuntary manslaughter. We hold that the statute does not preempt state action in this case, even though the victim's death occurred "in the workplace" and was allegedly caused by conduct that violated OSHA standards. Congress did not intend to preclude the enforcement by this state of its criminal laws simply because the alleged criminal activity occurred in the employment setting.

I. Facts and Proceedings

The defendant, Patrick Hegedus, was charged with involuntary manslaughter, . . ., and conspiracy to violate the Michigan Occupational Safety and Health Act, ... The charges arose out of the January 18, 1985, death of William Hatherill, an employee of Jackson Enterprises, a company for which defendant Hegedus worked as a supervisor. Mr. Hatherill died of carbon monoxide intoxication while working in a company-owned van. The prosecution contends that the poor condition of the van's undercarriage and exhaust system allowed exhaust fumes to leak inside the van, causing Hatherill's death.

After a preliminary examination, the defendant was bound over on the charge of involuntary manslaughter. Defendant's subsequent motion to quash the information on the manslaughter charge and reverse the binding over was granted by the circuit court, substantially on the basis that the defendant either had no duty to inspect the van or no duty or ability to take it out of service. The prosecution appealed as of right.

After receiving the parties' initial briefs, the Court of Appeals ordered supplemental briefs addressing the issue whether criminal prosecutions based on conditions in the workplace are preempted by either MI-OSHA or OSHA. The Court of Appeals ultimately affirmed the trial court's quashing of the information, finding that criminal prosecution was preempted by OSHA. . . . This Court granted leave to appeal. . . .

II. OSHA

OSHA's stated "purpose and policy" is "to assure so far as possible every working man and woman in the Nation safe and healthful working conditions and to preserve our human resources." . . . . To that end, the act gives the Secretary of Labor broad authority and responsibility to establish specific health and safety standards for "businesses affecting interstate commerce." . . . . The act also imposes upon every employer a general duty to "furnish to each of his employees employment and a place of employment which are free from recognized hazards that are causing or are likely to cause death or serious physical harm to his employees." . . .

OSHA is primarily regulatory in nature, designed to prevent workplace deaths and injuries before they occur. Thus, its emphasis is on the promulgation of health and safety standards and enforcement and review procedures, rather than the assessment of penalties for injuries already suffered. As the United States Supreme Court stated in *Whirlpool v. Marshall*, . . . (1980), "the legislation's remedial orientation is prophylactic in nature."

The act does contain, however, both civil and criminal penalties that can be assessed against employers who violate either specific, promulgated standards or the general-duty clause of § 5(a)(1). For example, OSHA provides for civil penalties of up to $1000 for "serious" violations of either the general-duty clause or specific standards. Up to $10,000 may be assessed for "willful" or repeated violations.

OSHA also provides for criminal sanctions under certain circumstances. Section 17(f) makes the unauthorized advance notification of an OSHA inspection a crime punishable by a fine of not more than $1000 or by imprisonment for not more than six months, or both. Section 17(g) makes knowingly filing false statements with the Occupational Safety and Health Review Commission (OSHRC) a crime punishable by a fine of up to $10,000 or by imprisonment for up to six months, or both.

The relevant section in this case is § 17(e), which provides criminal sanctions for a "willful" violation of a specific standard that results in the death of an employee. Section 17(e) states:

> Any employer who willfully violates any standard, rule, or order promulgated pursuant to section 655 of this title, or of any regulations prescribed pursuant to this chapter, and that violation caused death to any employee, shall, upon conviction, be punished by a fine of not more than $10,000 or by imprisonment for not more than six months, or by both; except that if the conviction is for a violation committed after a first conviction of such person, punishment shall be by a fine of not more than $20,000 or by imprisonment for not more than one year, or by both.

The defendant contends that if he is subject to any criminal liability for his acts or omissions in causing the victim's death, it is under this section of OSHA, not under any state criminal law such as the manslaughter statute under which he was charged. . . . The defendant argues that both the legislative history of OSHA and its comprehensive scope indicate that Congress intended to fully occupy the entire field of worker health and safety, and that to the extent that the state criminal sanctions sought to be applied in this case differ from or conflict with those found in OSHA, they are inapplicable as a result of the Supremacy Clause of the United States Constitution.

III. OSHA Preemption

A.

Generally, the existence of federal laws or regulations in a particular area can preempt state action in the same field where preemption is either express, implied, or the result of a conflict between state and federal law. In each of these situations, the extent to which federal law actually preempts state authority is a question of congressional intent. . . . In addition, "[w]here, as here, the field which Congress is said to have pre-empted has been traditionally occupied by the States . . . 'we start with the assumption that the historic police powers of the States were not to be superseded by the Federal Act unless that was the clear and manifest purpose of Congress.' . . .

B. Express Preemption

The defendant does not argue that OSHA expressly preempts the application of state criminal laws to conduct in the workplace. The Court of Appeals, however, apparently found such express preemption by virtue of § 18 of the act. Section 18 provides in relevant part:

> (a) Assertion of State standards in absence of applicable Federal standards.

> Nothing in this chapter shall prevent any State agency or court from asserting jurisdiction under State law over any occupational safety or health issue with respect to which no standard is in effect under section 655 of this title.

> (b) Submission of State plan for development and enforcement of State

standards to preempt applicable Federal standards.

Any State which, at any time, desires to assume responsibility for development and enforcement therein of occupational safety and health standards relating to any occupational safety or health issue with respect to which a Federal standard has been promulgated under section 655 of this title shall submit a State plan for the development of such standards and their enforcement.

The Court of Appeals properly interpreted this language to mean that a state may assert jurisdiction over an occupational safety and health issue "only if there is no federal standard in effect . . . or the state has submitted its own enforcement plan to the United States Secretary of Labor for approval pursuant to [§ 18(b)]." . . . However, the Court of Appeals then improperly concluded that the prosecution of the defendant in this case in fact amounted to an assertion of jurisdiction over just such an issue.

The Court of Appeals reasoned that since OSHA does contain standards regulating the existence and allowable proportions of carbon monoxide in the workplace, the state may not exert jurisdiction over "this issue" except through an approved state plan. . . . Observing that this case was not prosecuted under the state's approved plan (MIOSHA), but rather on "general criminal charges," the Court concluded that such prosecution was an improper attempt not only to circumvent the penalties prescribed in MIOSHA, but also to assert jurisdiction over a federally covered occupational safety and health issue through means other than an approved plan.

The Court of Appeals misreads § 18. Section 18(a) has the clear effect of actually preserving state jurisdiction over safety and health issues with respect to which no federal standard exists, while the language of § 18(b) is expressly limited to the development and enforcement of state standards relating to such issues, and thus does not affect the enforcement of a state's general criminal laws.

The term "occupational safety and health standard" is defined as "a standard which requires conditions, or the adoption or use of one or more practices, means, methods, operations, or processes, reasonably necessary to provide safe or healthful employment and places of employment." . . . . The manslaughter statute under which the defendant was charged in this case is not a "standard" in the sense intended by the act. It does not require particular conditions, or mandate the use of prescribed practices or means, etc., in order to ensure the existence of a safe and healthful work environment. As one commentator explained, "[s]tandards are . . . ex ante, prophylactic measures prescribing or proscribing specific practices. In contrast, general state criminal laws . . . are ex post, reactive measures, focusing on conduct after an injury has occurred." For the same reasons, § 17(c) itself cannot be called a "standard." It is a penalty provision. It does not literally prescribe or proscribe conduct.

The Court of Appeals characterized the prosecution of the defendant under the state's general criminal laws as an attempt to "assert jurisdiction over a federally covered occupational safety and health issue other than through an approved state plan." . . . . To allow such action, it concluded, would "emasculate" the requirement of § 18 that the state act through an approved plan. It thus appears that what the Court really was concerned with is the state's apparent ability to accomplish the same purpose or end to which safety and health standards are created — regulation of workplace conduct — without having to go through the process of approval the act requires. It therefore in effect concluded that Congress intended § 18(b) to preempt all state laws to the extent that they regulate workplace safety and health. We disagree.

In *People v. Chicago Magnet Wire Corp.*, . . . (1987), the Illinois Court of Appeals similarly concluded that the state was precluded from enforcing its criminal laws as to "conduct related to working conditions now regulated by OSHA." On appeal, the Illinois Supreme Court rejected this implicit regulation analysis and in reversing the intermediate court stated:

We cannot accept the defendants' contention that it must be concluded that Congress intended to preempt the enforcement of State criminal laws in regard to conduct of employers in the workplace because the State criminal laws implicitly enforce occupational health and safety standards. . . .

It is true that the knowledge that general criminal sanctions, such as prosecution for manslaughter, are available in sufficiently egregious situations is likely to affect and employer's actions in the workplace. It is also likely that the fear of a criminal conviction would cause an employer to adhere more closely to promulgated OSHA standards to ensure that no such situation results. However, as myriad overlapping areas of state and federal law demonstrate, it can only rarely be said that the enforcement of state laws is precluded simply because it tends of necessity to affect the regulated conduct. We agree with the Illinois Supreme Court that in this context the preemption question cannot be resolved with reference to the possible incidental effects of state action. Rather, it is the purpose of the state action that governs the express preemption inquiry.

In *Environmental Encapsulating Corp. v. New York City*, . . . (CA 2, 1988), the United States Court of Appeals for the Second Circuit considered the claim that the city's program for training and certification of workers who handle asbestos, administered through its Department of Environmental Protections, was preempted by OSHA. In rejecting the claim that § 18 expressly preempted the city's program, the court in *Environmental Encapsulating* first observed that the program had a "dual" purpose, both to protect public health and to safeguard employee health and safety. . . . It then went on to consider the effect of § 18 on state or local regulations "which have a legitimate purpose apart from one promoting occupational health and safety, but which also — even if incidentally — in fact promote occupational health and safety." . . . . The court ultimately concluded that OSHA does not preempt such regulations:

> Thus, we hold that in order to avoid preemption the City must demonstrate only that for each of the DEP requirements there is a legitimate and substantial purpose apart from protecting asbestos workers. If this is demonstrated, the particular requirement is not a state 'occupational safety and health standard' preempted by § 18. . . .

The "legitimate and substantial purpose" test of *Environmental Encapsulating* recognizes both the intention of Congress to establish a "federal floor for safety in the workplace," . . ., and the interest of the states in retaining their historic police powers.

We similarly conclude that there is a "legitimate and substantial purpose" on the part of this state, apart from regulating occupational health and safety, in enforcing its criminal laws even though the conduct occurred in the workplace. While deterrence, and thus to some extent regulation, is one aim of general criminal laws, so too is punishment — clearly not one of OSHA's primary goals. A more important purpose, however, is the protection of employees as members of the general public. While OSHA is concerned with protecting employees as "workers" from specific safety and health hazards connected with their occupations, the state is concerned with protecting the employees as "citizens" from criminal conduct. Whether that conduct occurs in public or in private, in the home or in the workplace, the state's interest in preventing it, and punishing it, is indeed both legitimate and substantial.

We thus cannot agree with the Court of Appeals that § 18 of the act, the focus of which is the administrative regulation of workplace health and safety through specific, promulgated standards, was clearly intended to deprive citizens, merely by virtue of their status as employees, of the historic protection of this state's criminal laws.

In addition to the limited relevance of § 18 to the question before us, we note the inclusion of a "saving clause" within the act to guard against undue restrictions upon state action in this area. Section 4(b)(4) of the act states:

> Nothing in this chapter shall be construed to supersede or in any manner affect any workmen's compensation law or to enlarge or diminish or affect in any other manner the common law or statutory rights, duties, or liabilities of employers and employees under any law with respect to injuries, diseases, or death of employees arising out of, or in the course of, employment.

The Court of Appeals interpreted this provision as reflecting a congressional intent to "leave undisturbed private rights and liabilities of employers and employees such as those found in the Worker's Disability Compensation Act or the Civil Rights Act." . . . . It should be strictly construed, the

Court argued, to preserve only other laws regulating relations between employers and employees, which criminal laws are not primarily designed to do.

There is some merit to the argument that § 4(b)(4) was never intended by Congress specifically to save criminal law from preemption. As one author points out, there is no indication in either the act itself or its legislative history that Congress ever contemplated the effect that criminal laws might have on OSHA enforcement. . . .

However, it is also true that § 4(b)(4) arguably includes criminal laws among those specifically not "superseded." It states that the act should not be read to supersede or affect either any workers' compensation law or the "common law or statutory rights, duties, or liabilities of employers . . . under any law with respect to injuries, diseases, or death of employees arising out of, or in the course of, employment." The manslaughter law under which the state seeks to impose "statutory liability" upon the defendant for the death of an employee arguably qualifies as "any law" under the above language. As written, the section does not appear to be in any way qualified, other than by the "arising out of, or in the course of, employment" language, which also apparently is met here.

When the broad language of § 4(b)(4), evidencing a general congressional intent to leave existing state common-law rules and statutes intact so far as possible, is considered along with the general presumption against preemption discussed above, the conclusion that the § 18 jurisdictional requirements are to be read narrowly to preempt only unauthorized workplace standards, not the state's criminal laws, is inescapable.

C. Implied Preemption

The Court in *Hillsborough Co. v. Automated Medical Labs, Inc.*, . . . (1985), narrowed the application of implied preemption theory to two distinct situations. First, "Congress' intent to pre-empt all state law in a particular area may be inferred where the scheme of federal regulation is sufficiently comprehensive to make reasonable the inference that Congress 'left no room' for supplementary state regulation. . . . Preemption also

may be inferred if the field sought to be preempted "is one in which 'the federal interest is so dominant that the federal system will be assumed to preclude enforcement of state laws on the same subject.' . . .

It cannot seriously be contended, with respect to this second theory of implied preemption, that the federal interest in workplace health and safety outweighs the state's interests in this situation. Against that federal interest must be balanced not only the state's own — and in fact predominant — historical interest in the regulation of health and safety matters, . . .

The defendant, however, does not argue the dominancy of the federal interest in this case. He argues instead that the comprehensiveness of the federal act evidences an intent on the part of Congress to "occupy the field" of workplace safety and health that would be undermined by allowing the application of state criminal laws in cases such as this. He contends that Congress has created a comprehensive regulatory scheme that is "unquestionably a clear, thorough set of guideposts for employers and employees" that leaves no room for state involvement, and that, in any event, the act's statutory scheme sets specific "standards" for criminal liability in this area, thus evidencing Congress' intent to occupy entirely at least that portion of the safety and health field.

There is no merit to the argument that we may infer from OSHA's broad scope a congressional intent to occupy the entire field of safety and health regulation or to exclude the stakes therefrom. The act itself clearly belies that conclusion, since, as discussed above, it preserves in § 18(a) the states' jurisdiction over issues for which there is no existing federal standard, and allows states in § 18(b), albeit with OSHA approval, to formulate their own standards for workplace safety and health. The act thus contemplates an active role by the states in all areas of regulation. Indeed, it actually encourages states "to assume the fullest responsibility for the administration and enforcement of their occupational safety and health laws. . . . "

. . . The sheer length of the act, in our view, merely reflects the complexity of the subject matter. When considered in the context of that subject matter, the act's apparent comprehensiveness is not surprising. As the United States Supreme Court stated in *New York Dep't of Social Services v. Dublino*, ... (1973). "The subjects of modern social and regulatory legislation often by their very nature require intricate and complex responses from Congress, but without Congress necessarily intending its enactment as the exclusive means of meeting the problem. ... "

Despite its length and thoroughness, OSHA is far from complete. The incompleteness of OSHA's provisions for criminal penalties is but one example of the incompleteness of the act as a whole, and serves to answer the defendant's second argument, that the inclusion of such sanctions within the act evidences Congress' intent to preempt at least that portion of the occupational safety and health field. The act itself contains only a few very minor criminal sanctions that can hardly be said to compose a comprehensive and exclusive scheme. Under § 17(e), a wilful violation of a specific OSHA standard that results in an employee's death is punishable by only up to six months' imprisonment. A similar violation that "only" seriously injures an employee carries no criminal penalties at all. A violation of the general-duty clause of § 5(a), even if it results in death, also carries no criminal penalty. Thus, as the Illinois Supreme Court concluded in Chicago Magnet Wire, supra:

> [I]t seems clear that providing for appropriate criminal sanctions in cases of egregious conduct causing serious or fatal injuries to employees was not considered. Under these circumstances, it is totally unreasonable to conclude that Congress intended that OSHA's penalties would be the only sanctions available for wrongful conduct which threatens or results in serious physical injury or death to workers. ...

Rather, as one author has concluded, "[t]he interpretation most consistent with the Act's goals is that Congress did not intend to preclude state penalties but rather [intended] to allow states to supplement OSHA penalties with their own sanctions." ...

D. Conflict Preemption

Preemption of state action lastly may be found if a conflict exists between the state and federal laws. Such a conflict arises "when 'compliance with both federal and state regulations is a physical impossibility,' ..., or when state law 'stands as an obstacle to the accomplishment and execution of the full purposes and objectives of Congress,' ...."

This case does not involve conflicting sets of regulations in the same area, making compliance with both a physical impossibility, as might happen, for example, when compliance with federal regulations necessarily violates state regulations. The defendant argues only that criminal prosecutions other than under OSHA for conduct in the workplace "stand[] as an obstacle to the accomplishment and execution" of that act's purposes. ... The defendant argues in particular that allowing criminal prosecutions other than under OSHA would frustrate the goal of uniformity of sanctions for violations of the act. According to the defendant, the fact that states may already incorporate different criminal sanctions, with federal approval, into their own occupational safety and health legislation is burden enough on employers. To allow the states to also apply their own criminal laws, which obviously vary from state to state, to workplace conduct, would completely defeat the prospect of uniformity.

We are unpersuaded by this argument, since we are not convinced that uniformity of sanctions — or even of regulations, for that matter — was a significant concern of Congress when it adopted OSHA. In our view, "[t]he statute's purpose was to assure minimum — but not necessarily uniform — occupational health and safety standards." .... The fact that states are encouraged in the first section of the act to develop their own occupational safety and health standards, subject only to the condition in § 18(c)(2) that they be "at least as effective" as the federal standards, indicates that Congress was not primarily concerned with uniformity, but rather intended the federal act to provide a kind of "floor" of protection to employees. As the Court of Appeals for the Third Circuit stated in *United Steelworkers of America v. Auchter*, ..., "[r]eduction of burdens posed by multiple state laws does not appear to have been a significant congressional concern; rather, Congress favored a uniform federal law so that those states providing vigorous protection would not be disadvantaged by those that did not." The application of this state's criminal laws to conduct in the workplace does not in our view present an obstacle to the accomplishment of OSHA's stated goal of assuring employees "safe and healthful working conditions."

E.

The result we reach today is compelled by the Supremacy Clause preemption analysis that has been established by the United States Supreme Court. Common sense likewise dictates this result. Consider the hypothetical example in which an explosion occurs in a factory as a result of hazardous conditions amounting not only to a violation of a specific OSHA standard but also to criminal negligence. It could not seriously be contended in this situation that the prosecution under state criminal laws (such as a manslaughter statute) of the employer for the resulting deaths of his employees is preempted by OSHA's provision in § 17(e) of six months imprisonment for such a violation, while as to the deaths of any visitors, passersby, or members of the surrounding community, the state's ability to prosecute the employer as it sees fit is unaffected.

To take the hypothetical example one step further, suppose the employer actually intended to cause the deaths of his employees. Surely it could not be contended that, since the employer's act involved "conduct related to working conditions," . . ., the state is precluded from charging the employer with murder, having instead to settle for a six-month prison term for a wilful violation of an OSHA standard. The difference between this hypothetical example and the case at bar is at most one of degree or of levels of criminal intent.

We do not believe that the inclusion by Congress of a few truly minor criminal sanctions within OSHA for "willful" violations of its standards, and only for those violations which actually result in death, evidences an intent to subordinate the traditional police powers of this state to the limited authority of the federal government to such an extent that the state is unable to enforce its laws against serious criminal conduct directed against its citizens.

The mere fact that such conduct takes place in an employment setting, where there is a limited federal interest in protecting the safety and health of employees, is not sufficient to remove from the state its traditional authority and responsibility to protect the welfare of its citizens.

IV. Conclusion

Our decision on the preemption question addressed by the Court of Appeals does not resolve this case, however. The prosecution's appeal in that Court initially concerned the circuit court's decision to quash the information against the defendant and dismiss the manslaughter charge. The Court of Appeals raised the preemption issue *sua sponte*, requesting supplemental briefs from the parties. Since the Court of Appeals found that the prosecution was preempted by OSHA, it failed to reach the question whether the magistrate abused his discretion in binding over the defendant on the involuntary manslaughter charge for the reasons stated by the circuit judge. We therefore remand this case to the Court of Appeals for consideration of that issue.

The defendant in this case is charged with manslaughter, not simply with a "willful" violation of an OSHA standard. While his conduct, if proved, might also satisfy the elements of that "crime," the state has chosen, in a valid exercise of its police powers, to pursue this matter under its own criminal laws. We cannot construe OSHA, the stated purpose of which is "to assure so far as possible . . . safe and healthful working conditions and to preserve our human resources," as a grant of immunity to employers who are responsible for the deaths or serious injuries of their employees. We therefore reverse the decision of the Court of Appeals and remand the case to that Court for consideration of those issues raised on appeal that it failed to consider.

[Footnotes and citations omitted. Concurring and dissenting opinions omitted.]

United States of America

v.

Erik Bowker

United States Court of Appeals for the Sixth Circuit

372 F.3d 365; 2004 U.S. App. LEXIS 11536; 2004 FED App. 0178P (6th Cir.)

June 11, 2004, Decided
June 11, 2004, Filed

OPINION

CLAY, Circuit Judge.

Defendant-Appellant Erik S. Bowker appeals his convictions and sentence for one count of interstate stalking, in violation of 18 U.S.C. § 2261A(1); one count of cyberstalking, in violation of 18 U.S.C. § 2261A(2); one count of theft of mail, in violation of 18 U.S.C. § 1708; and one count of telephone harassment, in violation of 47 U.S.C. § 223(a)(1)(C). Bowker also appeals the district court's failure to rule on his motion to return seized property and the district court's enhancement of his sentence based on extreme psychological harm to the victim. For the reasons that follow, we AFFIRM Bowker's convictions and sentence, but REMAND to the district court for a ruling on Bowker's motion to return seized property. . . .

On August 28, 2001, United States Magistrate Judge George J. Limbert signed a criminal complaint charging Erik. S. Bowker ("Bowker") with one count of telephone harassment in violation of 47 U.S.C. § 223(a)(1)(C). Bowker was arrested on August 29, 2001. On September 7, 2001, the magistrate judge held a preliminary examination and detention hearing for Bowker. The magistrate judge determined that probable cause for Bowker's arrest had been established, and he ordered Bowker detained. . . .

Bowker's jury trial commenced on June 3, 2002. On June 6, 2002, the jury returned verdicts of guilty against Bowker on all counts. On September 5, 2002, the government moved for an upward departure from the sentencing guidelines based on the victim's extreme psychological harm. On September 10, 2002, the district court sentenced Bowker to 96 months'

incarceration, three years of supervised release, and a $ 400 special assessment. In assessing the term of incarceration, the district court granted the government's motion for an upward departure. . . .

In March, 2000, Tina Knight began working as a part-time general assignment reporter at WKBN Television in Youngstown, Ohio. WKBN has a general email account for most employees, and in June, 2000, WKBN received a number of emails relating to Knight. The emails were sent from several different email addresses and purported to be from an individual variously identified as "User x," Eric Neubauer, Karen Walters, and "BB." Several of the emails attached photographs with verbal captions. One caption referred to Knight being shot with a pellet gun, and another email said, "Thanks for my daily Tina Knight fix. Thanks for helping me get my nuts off," and another said "More Tina Knight, that is what I want and need." After receiving approximately nine of these types of email, WKBN's news director took them to the station's general manager. They then contacted Special Agent Deane Hassman of the FBI. Soon thereafter, Knight was shown the emails, and she was stunned and frightened.

FBI Agent Hassman began investigating the Tina Knight emails in July, 2000. Hassman was concerned about Knight's personal safety based on the content of the emails. One of the emails that concerned Hassman stated, "I'm not the type of obsessed viewer that hides in the bushes near your home to watch you come home from work, but we shall see. That may actually be fun." Another disturbing email stated, in part, "Dear Ms. Knight. Now I'm really pissed that you were looking even cuter than normally. You fucked up a little bit and here I am watching on this black and white thrift store TV. Cute, cute, cute. I bet you were a Ho at Ohio University in Athens, doing chicks and everything. Wow."

On July 25, 2000, Hassman sent emails to the various email addresses on the correspondence pertaining to Knight. Hassman asked the sender of the emails to contact him so that he could determine the sender's intent. Within 24 to 48 hours, Hassman received a telephone call from an individual who identified himself as Erik Bowker. Hassman wanted to set up a meeting with Bowker so Hassman could positively identify the sender of the emails and also ask him to cease and desist contacting Knight. They arranged to meet at the public library in Youngstown, but Bowker never showed.

A few weeks later, Knight began receiving hand-written notes at WKBN, the majority of which were signed by "Doug Wagner." By September, the letters were arriving at the station almost every couple of days. One of the letters included the phrase, "All this week I will be playing the role of Doug Wagner." A letter dated August 9, 2000 was signed "Chad Felton"; stated, "I think you are a super babe"; and included a necklace. The return addresses on the letters were one of two P.O. Boxes registered to Erik Bowker or his mother.

Knight left her employment at WKBN in November, 2000 to take a position at WOWK CBS13 in Charleston, West Virginia. WKBN did not inform the general public of Knight's new location.

In late December, 2000, Knight's parents, who reside in Medina, Ohio, received a card and a handwritten note at their home. The card purported to be from "Kathryn Harris." The letter read, "Dear Tina Knight: I am Kathryn Harris today. I didn't want your parents asking you a lot of questions, nor did I want to attract a lot of attention to you. My letters to you are all online at yahoo.com in a standard mail account. It is all explained there so please check in and read what I have written. . . . The E-mail address is tinahatesme@ yahoo.com." Agent Hassman visited the email address to check if any letters had been sent to the email address mentioned in the letter. Hassman discovered that an email had been sent December 25, 2000. At the end of the email, the name "Doug Wagner" was typed. The email read, in part, "I told you I would not contact you by mail anymore but I am sorry, I am in agony. I'm thinking about you all the time. You really are my dream girl. . . . I am blinded with affection for you. I did not ask for this. Nope, it's all your fault. . . . Please don't cat dance on my emotions by failing to respond to me at all."

In February, 2001, Bowker filed a lawsuit against Knight in the Mahoning County Common Pleas Court. Knight's social securi-

ty number was stated in the complaint, which was served at Knight's home address in West Virginia. Bowker's lawsuit accused Knight of stalking him. Agent Hassman attended a status conference for the lawsuit on March 16, 2001, so that he could make face-to-face contact with Bowker. After meeting Bowker at the hearing and confirming that Bowker had been sending the unsolicited correspondence to Knight, Hassman told Bowker that the correspondence was unwelcome and might be a violation of federal law. Hassman advised Bowker that if the conduct continued, it might result in his arrest. Bowker responded that he had a First Amendment right to engage in that type of conduct. Nevertheless, during the meeting, Bowker wrote and signed a note stating, "I understand that Tina M. Knight wishes all further contact with her or any family member to stop and I agree to do so, pursuant to conversation with Deane Hassman, special agent, Federal Bureau of Investigation . . ." Bowker also agreed to voluntarily dismiss his lawsuit against Knight.

Despite Bowker's March, 16, 2001 agreement to cease and desist from any further contact with Knight, on that very same day, Bowker mailed a letter to Knight. Bowker also continued to attempt telephone contact with Knight. Between January 26 and August 29, 2001, Bowker made 146 telephone calls from his cell phone to WOWK CBS 13, where Knight worked. Bowker also made 16 calls to Knight's personal residential telephone in West Virginia between August 11 and 28, 2001. Knight's number was unlisted and unpublished. According to telephone records, each of the 16 calls placed to Knight's home were preceded by *67, which enables a caller to block identification of his telephone number on the recipient's caller identification display. Bowker also called Knight's co-worker and a neighbor.

As the telephone calls to Knight's television station persisted through the summer of 2001, Agent Hassman believed it was important to capture Bowker's voice on tape, so Hassman provided Knight with a recording device at the television station. On June 12, 2001, Knight recorded a 45 minute telephone call from Bowker who, at one point, identified himself as "Mike." During the conversation, Bowker referred to Knight's neighbors, her family members and her social security number. He also indicated he might be watching Knight with his binoculars. Knight provided the tape to the FBI and never spoke to Bowker again on the telephone.

On July 16, 2001, Knight received a letter at the television station. In the letter, Bowker referred to Knight's parents and stated several times, "You do not hang up on me." The letter also crassly referred to Knight's car, threatened to file a mechanic's lien on her car and her co-worker's car, accused Knight and her colleague of being "fuck-ups, assholes and seriously emotional and mentally unbalanced," and contained numerous sexual references. The letter stated that Bowker would be contacting Knight's neighbors, pointed out that Knight had not registered her car in West Virginia, and concluded with the words, "So bye-by, fuck you, you are an asshole and a sociopath and an embarrassment to mothers everywhere sir. . . . Adios, Eric . . . Smooch, Smooch."

On August 10, 2001, Knight received a certified letter mailed to her residence in West Virginia. Accompanying the letter were numerous photographs of Bowker at various locations in West Virginia, Knight's home state. The letter stated, in part, "Send me an E-Mail address. It keeps me long distance, you know what I mean." Knight forwarded the letter and the photographs to the FBI. Bowker's credit card statement later revealed purchases from a Kmart and a Kroger near Knight's place of employment and residence in West Virginia between June 12 and July 30, 2001.

In August 2001, Bowker left a series of messages on Knight's answering machine asking that Knight or Knight's friend call him back, which did not occur. Among other things, Bowker stated:

I don't even know why I'm nice to you ever at all, you and your fucked-up friend should not even be working in the media. You know you gotta mother-fucking realize there's like 50 percent men in this country and you better mother-fucking learn that you're going to have to deal with us sometime. . . .

Well, it looks like nobody is going to answer me if Tina Knight is okay, so

I'm gonna take the 1:00 a.m. bus out of Columbus, Ohio and come down there and see for myself. Okay, I'll be there about 6:00 a.m. Bye.

Knight testified that these messages made her afraid to leave the house everyday, and she feared that Bowker might try to rape her. She gave the answering machine recordings to the FBI.

Bowker was arrested on August 29, 2001 at a self-storage facility in Youngstown where he kept some of his possessions. Among other things recovered from the storage facility, Bowker's car and other locations, were a police scanner set to the frequency of the Youngstown Police Department, a paper with scanner frequencies from the Dunbar, West Virginia Police Department, letters bearing the name "Chad Felton, " a credit report for Tina Knight, Knight's birth certificate, a map of Dunbar, West Virginia, Greyhound bus schedules with West Virginia routes, and photos taken by Bowker during a West Virginia trip on July 11, 2001, which included pictures of Knight's place of work, her car and CBS news trucks. The FBI also discovered that Bowker had in his possession a Discover Card credit card bill addressed to Tina Knight in West Virginia. Knight never received that statement in the mail. . . .

Bowker argues that the magistrate judge erroneously found that there was probable cause to issue a warrant for his arrest premised on an alleged violation of 47 U.S.C. § 223(a)(1)(C), which prohibits telephone harassment. He further argues that trial court committed the same error when it denied Bowker's motion to suppress evidence obtained through the arrest warrant. We reject Bowker's arguments for the reasons stated below.

. . . The Court defers to findings of probable cause made by a magistrate, and will not set aside such findings unless they were arbitrarily made. When reviewing a district court's denial of a motion to suppress, the Court reviews the district court's findings of fact for clear error and its conclusions of law de novo.

At the preliminary hearing, the government brought a one-count criminal complaint against Bowker for the crime of telephone harassment, in violation of 47 U.S.C. §

223(a)(1)(C). That section provides for a fine, imprisonment, or both for anyone, who in interstate or foreign communications:

> makes a telephone call or utilizes a tele-communications device, whether or not conversation or communication ensues, without disclosing his identity and with intent to annoy, abuse, threaten, or harass any person at the called number or who receives the communications.

Incorporated into the criminal complaint was the affidavit of FBI Agent Deane Hassman, who alleged that Bowker had made numerous telephone calls to Tina Knight in which Bowker did not identify himself, including a conversation with Knight on June 12, 2001, and messages left on Knight's answering machine on August 17-19 and 25-26, 2001. Agent Hassman's affidavit also provided extensive background details on Bowker's campaign of harassment against Knight via emails, letters and telephone calls.

Bowker concedes that the magistrate judge could have found probable cause on the elements of using the telephone with the intent to annoy, abuse, threaten or harass. He argues, however, that the magistrate had no basis to find the element of failing to disclose identity during the telephone calls because Knight, the recipient of those calls, allegedly recognized his voice, making it unnecessary for him to state his name. . . . Bowker points to the fact that during the June 12, 2001 telephone conversation with Knight, she referred to Bowker as "Eric" [sic].

Bowker's argument is flawed in several respects. His argument does not address the numerous occasions when Bowker called Knight and no conversation ensued and no messages were left or her answering machine. The evidence before the magistrate showed that Bowker used a caller identification blocking feature to place these calls, thereby concealing his identity. Since the telephone harassment law prohibits calls made with the intent to harass or annoy "whether or not conversation or communication ensues," there was probable cause to find that Bowker had concealed his identity in those instances. Knight's alleged ability to identify Bowker's voice was irrelevant. . . .

Even assuming that Knight was able to identify Bowker's voice, the magistrate judge

properly found probable cause to believe that Bowker had not disclosed his identity during the June 12, 2001 conversation in which he mis-identified himself as "Mike" and in August, 2001, when he left messages on Knight's answering machine without providing any name at all. On its face, the telephone harassment statute makes it illegal to place a call, with the intent to annoy, abuse threaten or harass, whenever the caller fails to identify himself. Since Bowker concedes that the magistrate judge could have found probable cause that he had the requisite intent, it was Bowker's provision of a false name and/or his failure to identify himself - not an erroneous judicial determination about the victim's recognition of his voice - that led to the issuance of his arrest warrant.

. . .

[Argument concerning failure to suppress evidence deleted.]

Bowker argues that the district court erred in failing to dismiss Counts 1 (interstate stalking), 2 (cyberstalking) and 4 (telephone harassment) of the indictment on the ground that the indictment inadequately alleged the elements of the offenses charged, and on the ground that the statutes that the indictment alleged he violated are unconstitutionally vague and overbroad. We review the denial of a motion to dismiss de novo. For the reasons that follow, we affirm the decision of the district court.

Under the Notice Clause of the Sixth Amendment, a criminal defendant has the right "to be informed of the nature and cause of the accusation" against him. . . . "To be legally sufficient, the indictment must assert facts which in law constitute an offense; and which, if proved, would establish prima facie the defendant's commission of that crime." . . .

Count 1 (interstate stalking), Count 2 (cyberstalking) and Count 4 (telephone harassment) track the language of the relevant statutes. Count 1 alleges that, between July 10 and July 30, 2001, Bowker knowingly and intentionally traveled across the Ohio state line with the intent to injure, harass, and intimidate Tina Knight, and as a result of such travel placed Knight in reasonable fear of death or serious bodily injury, in violation of 18 U.S.C. § 2261A(1). Count 2 alleges that between December 25, 2000 and August 18, 2001 Bowker, located in Ohio, knowingly and repeatedly used the internet to engage in a course of conduct that intentionally placed Knight, then located in West Virginia, in reasonable fear of death or serious bodily injury, in violation of 18 U.S.C. § 2261A(2). Count 4 alleges that between June 12, 2001, and August 27, 2001, Bowker, located in Ohio, knowingly made telephone calls, whether or not conversation or communication ensued, without disclosing his identity and with the intent to annoy, abuse, threaten and harass Knight, in violation of 47 U.S.C. § 223(a)(1)(C). Because the indictment stated all of the statutory elements of the offenses, and because the relevant statutes state the elements unambiguously, the district court properly denied Bowker's motion to dismiss Counts 1, 2 and 4 of the indictment. The indictment's reference to the specific dates and locations of the offenses, as well as the means used to carry them out (travel, internet, telephone), provided Bowker fair notice of the conduct with which he was being charged.

. . . Bowker argues that the indictment was defective because it does not charge him with making direct threats against Knight and therefore should have contained a statement of facts and circumstances surrounding the alleged indirect threats he made against her, such as an explanation of the parties' relationship. ...

. . . All of the statutory elements of the prohibited conduct were properly alleged, including the intent to cause a reasonable fear of death or serious bodily harm. And unlike the parties involved in Landham, whose custody battle was highly relevant to the charged conduct, Bowker's relationship with Knight had no relevant bearing on the alleged illegality of his conduct. We therefore reject Bowker's challenge to the sufficiency of the indictment. . . .

According to the Supreme Court, imprecise laws can be attacked on their face under two different doctrines - overbreadth and vagueness. The "overbreadth doctrine is a limited exception to the traditional standing rule that a person to whom a statute may constitu-

tionally be applied may not challenge that statute on the basis that it may conceivably be applied in an unconstitutional manner to others not before the court." However, "overbreadth scrutiny diminishes as the behavior regulated by the statute moves from pure speech toward harmful, unprotected conduct." "'Particularly where conduct and not merely speech is involved, we believe that the overbreadth of a statute must not only be real, but substantial as well, judged in relation to the statute's plainly legitimate sweep.'"

Bowker has provided absolutely no argument as to how 18 U.S.C. § 2261A, which prohibits interstate stalking and cyberstalking, is facially overbroad, merely asserting that the statute "reaches large amounts of protected speech and conduct" and "potentially targets political or religious speech." We fail to see how a law that prohibits interstate travel with the intent to kill, injure, harass or intimidate has a substantial sweep of constitutionally protected conduct. The same is true with respect to the prohibition of intentionally using the internet in a course of conduct that places a person in reasonable fear of death or seriously bodily injury. It is difficult to imagine what constitutionally-protected political or religious speech would fall under these statutory prohibitions. Most, if not all, of these laws' legal applications are to conduct that is not protected by the First Amendment. Thus, Bowker has failed to demonstrate how 18 U.S.C. § 2261A is substantially overbroad.

We also reject Bowker's argument as to the purported overbreadth of the telephone harassment statute. Bowker relies on the Supreme Court's decision in *Coates v. City of Cincinnati* . . . which involved a city ordinance that made it a criminal offense for three or more persons to assemble on a sidewalk and to be "annoying" to passersby. The Court struck down the ordinance, reasoning that it was "unconstitutionally broad because it authorizes the punishment of constitutionally protected conduct."

Coates is distinguishable. First, the focus of the telephone harassment statute is not simply annoying telephonic communications. It also prohibits abusive, threatening or harassing communications. Thus, the thrust of the statute is to prohibit communications intended to instill fear in the victim, not to provoke a discussion about political issues of the day. Second, the telephone harassment statute operates in a distinctly different realm of communication than the ordinance in *Coates*, which governed the manner in which individuals could assemble and communicate in the open on public property. . . .

We acknowledge that the telephone harassment statute, if interpreted to its semantic limits, may have unconstitutional applications. For example, if Bowker had been charged with placing anonymous telephone calls to a public official with the intent to annoy him or her about a political issue, the telephone harassment statute might have been unconstitutional as applied to him. . . . But Bowker was not so charged. His calls were predominately, if not exclusively, for the purpose of invading his victim's privacy and communicating express and implied threats of bodily harm. This type of speech is not constitutionally protected. . . .

Even if an enactment does not reach a substantial amount of constitutionally protected conduct, it may be impermissibly vague because it fails to establish standards for the police and public that are sufficient to guard against the arbitrary deprivation of liberty interests." Vagueness may invalidate a criminal statute if it either (1) fails "to provide the kind of notice that will enable ordinary people to understand what conduct it prohibits" or (2) authorizes or encourages "arbitrary and discriminatory enforcement." "It is established that a law fails to meet the requirements of the Due Process Clause if it is so vague and standardless that it leaves the public uncertain as to the conduct it prohibits." . . .

The stalking and telephone harassment statutes charged in Bowker's indictment provide sufficient notice of their respective prohibitions because citizens need not guess what terms such as "harass" and "intimidate" mean. This Court's decision in *Staley v. Jones* . . ., is instructive. That case involved a habeas corpus review of a conviction for stalking under a Michigan law that defines stalking as "a willful course of conduct involving repeated or continuing harassment of another individual that would cause a reasonable person to feel terrorized, fright-

ened, intimidated, threatened, harassed, or molested and that actually causes the victim to feel terrorized, frightened, intimidated, threatened, harassed, or molested." Michigan law defines "harassment" as "conduct directed toward a victim that includes, but is not limited to, repeated or continuing unconsented contact that would cause a reasonable individual to suffer emotional distress and that actually causes the victim to suffer emotional distress." Expressly excluded from the definition of "harassment" is "constitutionally protected activity or conduct that serves a legitimate purpose." This Court rejected the petitioner's vagueness challenge to the Michigan statute, reasoning as follows:

A person of reasonable intelligence would not need to guess at the meaning of the stalking statutes, nor would his interpretation of the statutory language differ with regard to the statutes' application, in part because the definitions of crucial words and phrases that are provided in the statutes are clear and would be understandable to a reasonable person reading the statute. . . . Also, the meaning of the words used to describe the conduct can be ascertained fairly by reference to judicial decisions, common law, dictionaries, and the words themselves because they possess a common and generally accepted meaning. We therefore conclude that the statutes are not void for vagueness on the basis of inadequate notice.

The Michigan prohibition against willful harassment that causes a reasonable person to feel fear is almost indistinguishable from the federal anti-stalking statute, which prohibits intentional harassment that causes a reasonable fear of death or serious bodily injury. In fact, the federal statute arguably is less vague because it circumscribes the type of fear a victim must feel, namely a fear of death or serious bodily injury, whereas the Michigan law does not.

Bowker attempts to distinguish the Michigan statute by pointing to the fact that Michigan law defines the word "harassment," whereas federal law does not. The harassment definition under Michigan law, however, contains nothing not already reflected in the federal statute's general prohibition. The Michigan definition of harassment requires conduct directed toward a victim, but this requirement is implicitly reflected in the federal statute's requirement that a perpetrator intend to harass a victim. Michigan's harassment definition also requires that the conduct cause a reasonable individual to suffer emotional distress, but the federal statute requires conduct that causes a fear of death or serious bodily injury. There simply is no principled basis to distinguish the language of the federal statute from the Michigan statute which this Court upheld in *Staley*.

We also reject Bowker's argument that the stalking and telephone harassment statutes' failure to define words like "harass" and "intimidate" render them void for vagueness. As noted by the Court in *Staley*, the meaning of these words "can be ascertained fairly by reference to judicial decisions, common law, dictionaries, and the words themselves because they possess a common and generally accepted meaning." Indeed, the Michigan anti-stalking statute, which the *Staley* Court upheld, does not appear to define the word "intimidate," a word that Bowker claims is too vague in the federal law. For this reason as well, we reject Bowker's vagueness challenge to the federal law. . . .

We further reject Bowker's argument that the federal stalking and telephone harassment statutes authorize or encourage arbitrary or discriminatory enforcement. Although the statutes provide no guidelines on terms like harass and intimidate, the meanings of these terms "can be ascertained fairly by reference to judicial decisions, common law, dictionaries, and the words themselves because they possess a common and generally accepted meaning." Thus, Bowker has not demonstrated that these statutes fail to provide "sufficiently specific limits on the enforcement discretion of the police to meet constitutional standards for definiteness and clarity."

Only Bowker's vagueness challenge to part of the telephone harassment statute, merits further discussion. As noted above, that statute prohibits using a telephone, without disclosing identity, with the intent to annoy, abuse, threaten, or harass any person at the number called. Bowker argues that the term "annoy" is unconstitutionally vague, relying on the Supreme Court's decision in *Coates* . . .

We agree that the word "annoy," standing alone and devoid of context and definition, may pose vagueness concerns. But that is not the case with the telephone harassment statute. The statute reads "annoy, abuse, threaten, or harass." The Supreme Court has observed that canons of construction ordinarily suggest that terms connected by a disjunctive be given separate meanings, unless the context dictates otherwise." Here, the statutory language must be read in the context of Congressional intent to protect innocent individuals from fear, abuse or annoyance at the hands of persons who employ the telephone, not to communicate, but for other unjustifiable motives. This context suggests that the words annoy, abuse, threaten or harass should be read together to be given similar meanings. Any vagueness associated with the word "annoy" is mitigated by the fact that the meanings of "threaten" and "harass" can easily be ascertained and have generally accepted meanings.

Even assuming, arguendo, that Bowker's vagueness argument theoretically has merit, he cannot rely on it to invalidate the indictment or his conviction for telephone harassment, because the statute clearly applies to the conduct he allegedly committed. . . .

Here, Bowker engaged in an anonymous campaign of threatening and harassing conduct directed toward Knight through use of the telephone (as well as the mails and the computer) that clearly fell within the statute's prohibition. This type of conduct lies at the core of what the telephone harassment statute was designed to prohibit. FBI Agent Hassman specifically warned Bowker that he might be arrested if he persisted in his course of telephone harassment, but Bowker ignored that warning. Moreover, the fact that Bowker engaged in this campaign with an intent to threaten or harass mitigates any concern that he may have been punished for merely having a communication over the telephone. . . . The appellant cannot claim confusion about the conduct proscribed where, as here, the statute precisely specifies that the actor must intend to perform acts of harassment in order to be culpable. Thus, Bowker vagueness challenge fails. The district court did not err in denying his motion to dismiss Counts 1, 2 and 4 of the indictment.

. . .

[Remaining arguments deleted.]

B. Interstate Stalking Count

Count 1 of the indictment charges Bowker with interstate stalking, in violation of 18 U.S.C. § 2261A(1). The government was required to prove:

(1) that the defendant traveled in interstate or foreign commerce;

(2) with the intent to kill, injure, harass, or intimidate another person; and

(3) in the course of, or as a result of, such travel places that person in reasonable fear of the death of, or serious bodily injury to, that person, a member of the immediate family of that person, or the spouse or intimate partner of that person.

Bowker argues that the government did not prove, pursuant to the interstate stalking count, that the "result of" Bowker's travel from Ohio to West Virginia in July, 2001, was to put Knight in reasonable fear of her life or bodily injury, because Knight did not learn of Bowker's travels until August 2001, after he had completed his travel. This argument is specious. Knight learned of Bowker's travel to West Virginia because he sent her numerous photographs informing her that he had been in the state the preceding month. Accompanying the photographs was the statement, "Take the photos out to read the backs of them. Send me an E-mail address. It keeps me long distance, you know what I mean." The clear implication of this statement was that Bowker would continue to communicate with Knight, unless she provided him with her email address. The jury was entitled to infer that this statement, combined with the photographs of Bowker at various locations in West Virginia, was intended to intimidate Knight by showing her that Bowker had traveled to her state and would do so in the future. The statute did not require the government to show that Bowker actually intended to harass or intimidate Knight during his travels, only that the result of the travel was a reasonable apprehension of fear in the victim. Since Knight testified that she was afraid that Bowker might rape her, and her fear seemed reasonable, the government proved all of the elements of the interstate stalking count.

C. Cyberstalking Count

Count 2 of the indictment charges Bowker with cyberstalking, in violation of 18 U.S.C. § 2261A(2). The government was required to prove:

(1) Bowker intentionally used the mail or any facility of interstate or foreign commerce;

(2) Bowker engaged in a course of conduct with the intent to place Knight in reasonable fear of death of, or serious bodily injury to, herself, her spouse or intimate partner, or a member of her immediate family; and

(3) Bowker's course of conduct actually placed Knight in reasonable fear of death of, or serious bodily injury to, herself.

The evidence shows that Bowker's intended to instill in Knight a fear of death or serious bodily harm through use of the mails and other facilities of interstate commerce, required elements of the cyberstalking count. During a June 12, 2001 telephone conversation with Knight, Bowker told her: You don't know where I'm at. I might be in your house in Dunbar, West Virginia]; you don't know that. . . . I know all of your neighbors. . . . And I have access to all that information, just like anybody else does who knows where to find it. I have an enormous amount of things about you that I'm not going to disclose unless I have to. I'm not going to tell anybody about it except if you lie to me. I might not say anything to you at the time, but that might come back, you know. . . . I know the names of all your relatives and where they live. . . . I know your brothers' wives['] names, their ages, their Social Security numbers and their birth dates … and their property values. . . . Maybe I live on 20th street in Dunbar. . . . Maybe I watch you with binoculars all the time and maybe I don't." A July 16, 2001 letter that Bowker sent to Knight at the television station had both sexual and threatening connotations. . . .

In August 2001, Bowker left a series of messages on Knight's answering machine asking that Knight or Knight's friend call him back, which did not occur. These messages contained statements that Knight reasonably could perceive to be threats to her personal safety. . . . Since Knight testified that these intentionally intimidating, threatening and harassing interstate communications made her afraid to leave the house every day and that Bowker might try to rape her, the government proved all of the elements of the cyberstalking count.

D. Telephone Harassment Count

Count 4 of the indictment charged Bowker with telephone harassment, in violation of 47 U.S.C. § 223(a)(1)(C). The government had to prove that:

(1) Bowker made interstate telephone calls to Knight;

(2) Bowker did not disclose his identity in the telephone calls; and

(3) in the telephone calls, whether or not conversation or communication ensued, Bowker intended to annoy, abuse, threaten, or harass Knight or any person at the called number.

Bowker's primary argument against his conviction for telephone harassment is that Knight allegedly was aware of Bowker's identity when she received his calls. The statute, however, does not preclude criminal responsibility merely because the recipient may suspect, or have a very good idea of, the caller's identity. Rather, assuming that Bowker called Knight with the requisite intent to annoy, abuse, threaten, or harass, the only issue is whether Bowker disclosed his identity in those calls. It is clear that in all of the at-issue telephone calls, Bowker never affirmatively identified himself as Erik Bowker. In fact, he denied being Bowker during a conversation with Knight on June 12, 2001, and instead stated that his name was Mike. Thus, a straightforward application of the telephone harassment statute shows that the jury reasonably found the non-disclosure element to be satisfied.

. . .

[Motion for a New Trial argument deleted.]

[Upward Departure for Extreme Psychological Harm to the Victim deleted.]

[Other arguments deleted.]

Conclusion

For all the foregoing reasons, we AFFIRM Defendant Bowker's convictions and sentence. This case shall be REMANDED for the district court to conduct a hearing and to rule on Bowker's motion to return seized property.

[Footnotes and citations deleted.]

Glossary

abandonment: a defense to a criminal charge stating that the person voluntarily abandoned his or her proposed plan of crime before actual commission of the crime; if he or she does so voluntarily, he or she cannot be guilty of attempt.

abortion: a miscarriage or premature expulsion of the fetus.

accessory after the fact: a person who, knowing a felony to have been committed by another, receives, relieves, comforts or assists the felon, in order to enable him to escape from punishment, or the like.

accessory before the fact: one who orders, counsels, encourages, or otherwise aids and abets another to commit a felony and who is not present at the commission of the offense.

actus reus: evil act; a deed, an act, an offense, or an omission of conduct; the wrongful act that renders one criminally liable if combined with *mens rea*.

adultery: the voluntary sexual intercourse of a married person with someone other than his or her spouse.

affirmative defense: in pleading, matter constituting a defense; new matter that, assuming the complaint to be true, constitutes a defense to it; defendant has burden to put forward evidence reaching preponderance

alibi: a defense that the offender was in a different place at the time the offense was committed.

anti-structuring laws: federal laws that prohibit breaking up deposits into amounts smaller than $10,000 to avoid reporting requirements.

antitrust: various federal and state statutes intended to protect trade and commerce from unlawful restraints and monopolies.

arson: the crime of purposely setting fire to a house or other building.

asportation: the removal of things from one place to another; the carrying away of goods; one of the circumstances requisite to constitute the offense of larceny.

assault: attempting to cause or purposely, knowingly, or recklessly causing bodily injury to another, or negligently causing bodily injury to another with a deadly weapon, or attempting by physical menace to put another in fear of imminent serious bodily injury; also called simple assault.

assisted suicide: purposely aiding or soliciting another to commit suicide.

attempt: an intent to commit a crime, combined with an act that falls short of accomplishment of the thing intended.

battered woman defense: a defense that victims of battering suffer a type of posttraumatic stress syndrome that causes them to do extreme acts; also described as a type of duress, as a type of self-defense, and as a type of temporary insanity.

battery: an unlawful touching, beating, wounding, or laying hold, however trifling, of another's person or clothes without his or her consent.

bigamy: the offense of having two husbands or two wives at the same time.

Bill of Rights: first ten amendments to the U.S. Constitution.

breaking and entering: term used to describe unlawful entry; must be without consent and breach a threshold, i.e., closed door or window.

bribery: the offense of giving or receiving a gift or reward intended to influence a person in the exercise of a judicial, public, or fiduciary duty.

burden of proof: In the law of evidence, the necessity or duty of affirmatively proving a fact or facts in dispute on an issue raised between the parties in a cause. The obligation of a party to establish by evidence a requisite degree of belief concerning a fact in the mnd of the trier of fact or the court.

burglary: breaking and entering by night into a dwelling house with the intent to commit a felony inside.

burning: some consuming of the material of a house (It must be present to constitute the traditional crime of arson.)

caption: old common law term for "capture" or the idea of taking

carjacking: armed robbery with the specific target of robbery being the automobile of the victim

carnal knowledge: coitus; copulation; the act of a man having sexual bodily connection with a woman or child

child pornography: depictions of sexual activity involving children

"cheats": a group of common law crimes that were misdemeanors and involved crimes against the consumer.

Churning: a violation of a broker's fiduciary duty to their client when they advise the client to buy and sell stock solely to increase their own brokerage fees rather than for the benefit of the client.

commerce clause: provision of the U.S. Constitution that gives Congress exclusive powers over interstate commerce.

commercial bribery: the offense of giving or receiving a gift intended to influence a person in the exercise of his or her fiduciary responsibility

common law: accumulation of early English case law (except for those cases from equity and ecclesiastical courts); origin of American laws

computer-related crimes: categorized into three categories (1) the "object" of a crime. This category primarily refers to the theft of computer hardware or software. (2) the "subject" of a crime. The computer is a subject of the attack and the site of the damage caused. (3) the "instrument" used to commit the traditional crimes in a more complex manner. These traditional crimes include identity theft, child pornography, copyright infringement, and mail and wire fraud.

concurrence: a meeting or coming together; agreement or union in action; meeting of minds; union in design; consent.

conspiracy: an unlawful combination or agreement between two or more persons to carry into effect a purpose hurtful to some individual, or class, or the public at large.

constructive possession: possession that stems from dominion or control rather than physical possession.

controlled substance: various drugs or other substances classified into Schedules I, II, III, IV, and V of the Uniform Schedule of Controlled Substances.

conversion: an unauthorized assumption and exercise of the right of ownership over goods or personal chattels belonging to another, to the alteration of their condition or the exclusion of the owner's rights.

corporate crime: crimes committed by corporations either through traditional *respondeat superior* principles, or statutes that specifically make corporations liable for criminal acts.

counter-terrorism laws: the Patriot Act and other federal and state statutes that address acts of terrorists and their accomplices.

courts of appeal: intermediate courts; they hear appeals from trial courts.

crime: a flexible term for violations of law that are punished by the state or nation because of their effect on the public.

criminal facilitation: imposing liability for providing aid to someone, knowing that he or she has committed or is about to commit an offense.

criminal law: law for the purpose of preventing harm to society; it (a) declares what conduct is criminal, and (b) prescribes the punishment to be imposed for such conduct.

criminal mischief: a species of wilful and malicious injury to property made punishable by statutes in most jurisdictions.

criminal omission: liability rests upon the failure to act when there is a duty.

criminal simulation: forgery in which the subject of the offense is not a writing, but an object

curtilage: the inclosed space of ground and buildings immediately surrounding a dwellinghouse.

custody: having the care and control of a thing or person; or dominion over the object.

deliver: to transfer care, custody, or dominion over something to a second party.

depraved heart murder: not intentional murder, but second-degree murder that stems from performing an act that had an almost virtual certainty of causing injury.

deviate sexual intercourse: a general term that can encompass sodomy as well as fellatio and cunnilingus.

disorderly conduct: conduct with purpose to cause public inconvenience, annoyance or alarm, or recklessly creating a risk thereof: (a) engaging in fighting or threatening, or in violent or tumultuous behavior; (b) making unreasonable noise or offensively coarse utterance, gesture, or display, or addressing abusive language to a person present; or (c) creating a hazardous or physically offensive condition by an act that serves no legitimate purpose of the actor. Model Penal Code § 250.2(1).

district courts: federal trial courts.

dominion: perfect control in right of ownership; both title and possession.

double jeopardy: common law and constitutional (Fifth Amendment) prohibition against a second prosecution after a first trial for the same offense.

drunkenness: the condition of a person whose mind is affected by the use of alcoholic beverages; intoxication; inebriation.

due process: the procedural protections designed to protect against governmental error in the deprivation of life, liberty, or property.

duress: compulsion; coercion.

***Durham* Rule:** test applied in some states for the defense of insanity; under this test, an accused is not responsible for an unlawful act if the act was the product of mental disease or defect.

dwelling: the house or other structure in which a person or persons live; a residence; abode; habitation; the apartment or building, or group of buildings, occupied by a family as a place of residence.

eavesdropping: listening under walls, windows, or eaves in order to seek out private discourse.

embezzlement: conversion to his or her own use, by an agent or employee, of money or property received by him or her for and on behalf of his or her employer.

entrapment: a defense that law enforcement officers enticed persons to commit a crime who had no pre-existing disposition to do so.

entrapment by estoppel: a defense that the offender was enticed to commit a crime with the promise that there would be no prosecution.

environmental crime: illegal acts that affect the quality of water, land, and air.

escape: the voluntary departure of a prisoner from custody before he is released by lawful authority.

evading: (arrest), physically avoiding arrest without necessarily having physical contact with a police officer (as in resisting); some states require that the offender place an officer in danger in order to find culpability for evading

excusable homicide: the killing of a human being, either by misadventure or in self-defense.

ex post facto: made after the occurrence; every law that makes criminal an act that was innocent when done, or that inflicts a greater punishment than the law annexed to the crime when committed.

extortion: obtaining money or other things of value by threats or coercion.

extraneous intervening factors: outside factors that cause the abandonment of the final execution of a crime (the presence of these factors would negate the possibility of using abandonment as a defense).

factual impossibility: does not constitute a defense. When a defendant attempts to commit an act that is illegal and does everything to commit the crime, but fails in his effort to commit the actual crime.

Fair Labor Standards Act: an act to provide for the establishment of fair labor standards in employment in and affecting interstate commerce. 29 U.S.C. § 201 *et seq.*

false advertising: the publication of a false or misleading statement or representation concerning merchandise, with the intent to sell, barter, or exchange, with the intent to deceive or mislead.

false pretenses: a false representation of a material present or past fact that causes the victim to pass title to his property to the wrongdoer, who (a) knows his representation to be false and (b) intends thereby to defraud the victim.

false swearing: a person who makes a false statement under oath or equivalent affirmation, or swears or affirms the truth of such a statement previously made, when he does not believe the statement to be true in an official proceeding; or to a public servant in performing his official function.

felony: a serious crime punishable by death or imprisonment in the state penitentiary, usually for more than one year.

felony-murder rule: rule that any death that occurs in the perpetration of an inherently dangerous felony could be prosecuted as murder.

feticide: destruction of the fetus; the act by which criminal abortion is produced.

fiduciary relationship: a legal, social, domestic, or personal relationship where one party is duty-bound to act in the best interests of the other party.

forfeiture: the loss of some right or property as a penalty for some illegal act.

forgery: the false making or altering of an instrument that purports on its face to be good and valid for the purposes for which it was created.

fornication: a flexible term, often defined by various state statutes as sexual intercourse by an unmarried person.

general intent: is present when one consciously chooses to do a prohibited act.

good Samaritan laws: laws that require one who sees a person in imminent and serious peril to effect a rescue, provided the attempt does not endanger oneself.

gratuity: something acquired without bargain or inducement by virtue of position or power rather than individual effort.

hate crime: certain specified (illegal) acts, i.e., murder, assault, vandalism, kidnapping to specific victims that are members of protected groups.

homicide: committing an act that results in the death of a human being; usually defined by various state statutes.

identity theft: when an offender uses a victim's name, Social Security number, and other personal identifiers to obtain goods, services, credit, and currency.

importuning: solicitation of sexual activity.

incest: carnal knowledge of persons so related to each other that their marriage is prohibited by law, e.g., of brother and sister, father and daughter, uncle and niece.

inchoate: imperfect; partial; unfinished; begun, but not completed.

inciting to riot: occurs when one incites or encourages other persons to create or engage in a riot.

incompetency: lack of ability, capacity, or fitness to discharge the required duty.

infancy: at common law, a child under the age of seven; legal effect is that there is no criminal culpability; typically set by statute.

insanity: the term is a legal term rather than a medical one, and indicates a condition that renders the affected person incapable of rational thought; thereby removing criminal culpability.

insider trading: buying or selling stock based on information regarding the company that is obtained as an "insider" or from an insider of the company and not available to the general public.

involuntary manslaughter: the unlawful and unintentional killing of a human being, directly and proximately resulting from the commission of an unlawful act.

irresistible impulse rule: an insanity defense holding that notwithstanding that one accused of committing a crime may have been able to comprehend the nature and consequences of his or her act, and to know that it was wrong, he or she may be excused if he or she was forced to its exertion by an impulse that he or she was powerless to control in consequence of an actual disease of the mind.

joyriding: the temporary use of another person's automobile without permission.

justifiable homicide: may be committed intentionally, but without any evil design, and under such circumstances of necessity or duty as to render the act legal and not criminal.

juvenile: a person who has not attained his or her eighteenth birthday.

kidnapping: the forcible abduction or carrying away of a person from his or her domicile, parents, or legal protector through force or coercion with evil intent (statutes may define differently).

knowingly: in the Model Penal Code, knowledge is the second level of *mens rea* and refers to the guilty mind that knows what they are doing is wrong but may not necessarily intend the final result.

larceny: the unlawful taking and carrying away of personal property, without permission, and with the intent to deprive the rightful owner of the same.

legal impossibility: defense of "legal impossibility" may be established only where a defendant's actions, if fully performed, would not constitute a crime.

lewdness (indecent exposure): at common law, intentionally and indecently and offensively exposing the sex organs in the presence of another in an offensive manner.

Lindbergh law: federal law that punishes kidnapping for ransom or reward when the victim is transported from one state to another or to a foreign county (failure to release the victim within 24 hours creates a rebuttable presumption that such person has been transported in interstate or foreign commerce).

loitering: wandering or remaining in a place, at a time, or in a manner not usual for law-abiding individuals under circumstances that warrant alarm for the safety of persons or property in the vicinity.

mail fraud: statutes that make it illegal to use the mails to perpetrate a fraudulent scheme.

mala in se: acts that are wrong in and of themselves, whether prohibited by human laws or not, as distinguished from *mala prohibita.*

mala prohibita: acts that are prohibited by human laws, but not necessarily *mala in se*, or wrong in themselves.

malice aforethought: a predetermination to commit an act without legal justification or excuse.

malicious mischief (criminal mischief): the intentional and unlawful injury to or destruction of the property of another with the malicious intent to injure the owner.

Marital exemption: common law and some states defined a marital exemption that stated that a married man could not rape his wife; many states have excluded this exemption from new rape statutes.

materiality: having legal import.

mayhem: at common law, the deprivation of a member of the body proper for the defense in a fight, e.g., an arm, leg, eye, or other appendage.

mens rea: criminal intent; evil intent; guilty intent.

"*Miller* test": test from the case of *Miller v. California* to determine whether something is obscene.

misdemeanor: any crime or offense not amounting to a felony and not an ordinance or regulation.

M'Naghten **Rule**: test applied in some states for the defense of insanity; states that the proper standard or test for criminal responsibility is whether the accused was laboring under such a defect of reason, from disease of the mind, as to not know the nature and quality of the act he was doing or, if he did know it, he did not know that what he was doing was wrong.

money laundering: the process by which a person conceals the existence, illegal source, or illegal application of income, and disguises that income to make it appear legitimate.

murder: the willful killing of a human being with malice aforethought, either express or implied.

necessity: pressing need, overruling power, compulsion, or irresistible force; a defense (sometimes called the lesser of two evils defense) that allows an offender to claim that he or she avoided a greater evil by committing a crime.

negligence: undertaking actions that cause an unreasonable amount of risk when one should have known of the risk.

negligent homicide: the criminal offense committed by one whose negligence is the direct and proximate cause of another's death.

obscenity: conduct that is objectionable or offensive to accepted standards of decency and that tends to corrupt the public morals by its indecency and lewdness.

obstructing a highway: crime of obstructing a public thoroughfare with no authorization

obstructing justice: the offense of intentionally hindering or obstructing the arrest, conviction, and punishment of accused persons, including all proper and necessary proceedings for administering justice.

Occupational Safety and Health Act: an act to assure safe and healthful working conditions by authorizing enforcement of standards.

overt act: an element of attempt, a concrete act.

paternalistic laws: refers to the type of authority exercised by parents over their children and are those laws that punish behaviors that typically only have the capacity to injure oneself.

Patriot Act: an act passed by Congress after September 11, 2001, that expanded law enforcement investigative powers and strengthened laws against terroristic actions and those actions that might assist or contribute to terrorism.

perjury: a false statement under oath or affirmation, willfully made in regard to a material matter of fact.

phishing: form of false representation using a computer; offender sends computer messages to unknowing victims that look as though sent by actual businesses and ask for account or financial information, then uses such information to perpetrate fraud or other crimes.

Pinkerton rule: co-conspirators are culpable for all foreseeable acts in furtherance of the conspiracy that are committed by any one of the co-conspirators.

police power: the Tenth Amendment to the U.S. Constitution confers upon the individual states the power to enact laws for the comfort, safety, morals, health, and prosperity of their citizens.

polygamy: plurality of wives or husbands.

premeditated: designed or intended, idea formed to commit a crime or do an act before it is done.

principal in the first degree: one who, with the requisite mental state, engages in the act or omission concurring with the mental state, which causes the criminal result.

principal in the second degree: one who aids, counsels, commands, or encourages the principal in the first degree in the commission of the offense.

prison break: the common law offense of one who, being lawfully in custody, escapes from the place where he is confined, by the employment of force and violence.

procedural criminal law: that which prescribes method of enforcing rights or obtaining redress for their invasion; machinery for carrying on procedural aspects of civil or criminal action.

prostitution: engaging in sexual activity for hire.

provocation: the act of inciting another to do a particular deed because of aroused rage, resentment, or fury in the latter against the former.

proximate cause: any original event that, in natural and unbroken sequence, produces a particular foreseeable result, without which the result would not have occurred.

prurient interest: a shameful or morbid interest in nudity, sex, or excretion.

puffery: refers to exaggerations or statements unlikely to deceive ordinary persons in the group addressed.

purposely: descriptive of an act of the will, of an act by intention, or of an act by design.

racketeering: an organized conspiracy to commit the crimes of extortion or coercion, or attempts to commit extortion or coercion.

rape: the act of having sexual intercourse with a woman by force and against her will.

rape shield statutes: statutes that restrict testimony about a rape victim's prior sexual behavior (or sexual history) to that genuinely relevant to the defense.

real property: land, and generally whatever is erected or growing upon or affixed to land.

receiving stolen property: purposely receiving, retaining, or disposing of movable property of another, knowing that it has been stolen, or believing that it probably has been stolen, unless the property is received, retained, or disposed with purpose to restore it to the owner. Model Penal Code § 223.6.

recklessly: carelessly, heedlessly, indifferently; a state of mind that disregards the possibility or probability of injurious consequences, or altogether, foreseeing such consequences, continues in spite of them.

renunciation: the act by which a person abandons a right acquired without transferring it to another.

rescue: act of saving or freeing.

resisting arrest: using physical force to resist being brought into custody by a law enforcement officer.

respondeat superior: this maxim means that a master is liable in certain cases for the wrongful acts of his servant, and a principal for those of his agent.

RICO: Racketeer Influenced and Corrupt Organizations Act. Addresses organized racketeering activity; punishes those separately for having a pattern of criminal activity in concert with others.

riot: a tumultuous disturbance of the peace by three or more persons assembled of their own authority and with intent to obstruct or upset governmental officials.

robbery: theft from a person, accompanied by violence or threats putting the person in fear.

rout: common law offense between unlawful assembly and riot; typically means when more than three persons have come together and committed at least one overt act against the public peace.

Schedule I drugs: drugs defined by the Uniform Schedule of Controlled Substances as drugs with no redeeming social value, little medical application, and high risk of addiction (i.e., heroin, cocaine, marijuana)

seduction: the offense of a man deceitfully inducing a woman to have unlawful sexual intercourse with him.

self-defense: a defnese that the action charged as a crime was for the protection of one's person and property from injury.

sexual abuse/sexual assault: occurs when one person touches another or subjects another person to sexual contact without the other's consent.

sexual contact: touching the sexual or intimate parts of another person for the purpose of gratifying the sexual desire of either party.

sexual misconduct: in some states, sexual intercourse between a defendant under age 18 and a victim under age 16.

sexual predator laws: identify the types of crimes that lead to a sexual predator designation, and then may specify certain enhanced punishments, treatment, or, more controversially, sexual predator registration.

social contract: in political philosophy, a term applied to the theory of the origin of society associated chiefly with the names of Hobbes, Locke, and Rousseau, though it can be traced back to the Greek **Sophists.** Rousseau held that in the pre-social state man was unwarlike and timid. Laws resulted from the combination of men who agreed, for mutual protection, to surrender individual freedom of action. Government must therefore rest on the consent of the governed.

sodomy: carnal copulation between two human beings, or between man and animal, contrary to nature.

solicitation: the offense of asking or enticing another to engage in illegal conduct for hire.

solicitation of prostitution: requesting, offering sex for hire.

specific intent: intent to commit the *actus reus* and intent to cause the result (i.e., to violate the law).

states' rights: rights not conferred on the federal government or forbidden to the States according to the Tenth Amendment to the U.S. Constitution.

statute of limitations: various periods of time, fixed by different state and federal statutes, within which a lawsuit must be commenced, and after the expiration of which the claimant will be forever barred from the right to bring the action.

statutory law: law created by, or depending upon, a statute, as distinguished from equitable or common law rules.

statutory rape: sexual intercourse with a female under the age of consent.

stop-and-identify statutes: statutes that require a citizen to identify him- or herself if asked by a law enforcement officer.

strict liability: culpability that occurs without *mens rea;* in strict liability crimes, the state need not prove any level of *mens rea* on the part of the offender.

subornation of perjury: the offense of procuring another to take such a false oath as would constitute perjury in the principal.

substantial step: conduct that is strongly corroborative of the firmness of the defendant's criminal intent.

substantive criminal law: that part of law which creates, defines, and regulates rights.

superseding intervening factor: an act of a third person or other force, which by its intervention cuts off the culpability of the actor.

theft by deception: another term for fraud; a taking through the use of deception.

theft of services: purposely obtaining labor, professional service, transportation, telephone, or other public service, by deception or threat, or by false token or other means to avoid payment

trafficking: selling a controlled substance.

transferred intent: doctrine holding that if the defendant shoots or strikes at A, intending to wound or kill him, and unforeseeably hits B instead, he is guilty of the originally intended crime.

trespass: criminal trespass is entering or surreptitiously remaining in a building or occupied structure, or separately secured or occupied portion thereof, knowing that he or she is not licensed or privileged to do so. Model Penal Code § 221.2(1).

"undue burden test": current test to apply to statutes that seek to curtail or place guidelines on the use of abortion; if the state law "unduly burdens" the woman's ability to choose, then it would be ruled unconstitutional.

United States Code: the code of federal laws.

unlawful assembly: a gathering of three or more persons with the intent of committing a crime with force. Often defined by various state statutes.

utmost resistance standard: required that a woman expend the greatest effort of which she was capable to foil a rapist, otherwise the sexual contact was not without consent; abandoned by modern courts.

uttering: to put or send (as a forged check) into circulation; to publish or put forth; to offer.

vagrancy: at common law, going from place to place without visible means of support, being idle, refusing to work, living without labor, and relying on the charity of others.

vandalism: willful and malicious acts committed with the intent to damage or destroy property of another.

vicarious liability: substituted or indirect responsibility, e.g., the responsibility of an employer for the torts committed by his employee within the scope of employment.

voluntary manslaughter: manslaughter committed voluntarily upon a sudden heat of the passions; as if, upon a sudden quarrel, two persons fight, and one of them kills the other.

voyeurism: committing trespass or otherwise surreptitiously invading the privacy of another, to spy or eavesdrop on another, for the purpose of sexually arousing or gratifying oneself.

Wharton rule: in crimes that require at least two people (bigamy, adultery, incest), a conspiracy charge cannot be based solely on the agreement of only the two people necessarily involved in the crime.

white-collar crime: differs from traditional crimes and includes insider trading, antitrust conspiracy, restraint of trade, embezzlement, mail and wire fraud, money laundering, securities fraud, tax fraud, tax evasion, environmental crime, and employment-related crimes.

wire fraud: statutes making it illegal to use any interstate electronic communication network to perpetrate a fraudulent scheme.

wiretapping: intercepting a communication by making a connection with a telephone line. Usually defined by various statutes.

year-and-a-day-rule: if death did not take place within a year and a day of the time of receiving the wound, the law draws the conclusion that it was not the cause of death; and neither the court nor jury can draw a contrary one.

Table of Cases

Index